MACROECONOMICS

TWELFTH EDITION

MACROECONOMICS

Roger A. Arnold

California State University
San Marcos

CENGAGE
Learning®

Australia • Brazil • Japan • Korea • Mexico • Singapore • Spain • United Kingdom • United States

Macroeconomics, 12e
Roger A. Arnold

Vice President, General Manager, Social Science & Qualitative Business: Erin Joyner

Product Director: Mike Worls

Product Manager: Michael Parthenakis

Content Developer: Daniel Noguera

Product Assistant: Mary Umbarger

Sr. Marketing Manager: John Carey

Sr. Content Project Manager: Colleen A. Farmer

Media Developer: Anita Verma

Manufacturing Planner: Kevin Kluck

Production Service: MPS Limited

Sr. Art Director: Michelle Kunkler

Internal and Cover Designer: Mike Stratton/ Stratton Design

Cover Image: © iurii/Shutterstock.com

Intellectual Property

Analyst: Jen Nonemacher

Project Manager: Sarah Shainwald

For product information and technology assistance, contact us at **Cengage Learning Customer & Sales Support, 1-800-354-9706**

For permission to use material from this text or product, submit all requests online at **www.cengage.com/permissions**
Further permissions questions can be emailed to **permissionrequest@cengage.com**

Unless otherwise noted, all items © Cengage Learning.

Library of Congress Control Number: 2014954394

ISBN: 978-1-285-73831-4

Cengage Learning
20 Channel Center Street
Boston, MA 02210
USA

Cengage Learning is a leading provider of customized learning solutions with office locations around the globe, including Singapore, the United Kingdom, Australia, Mexico, Brazil, and Japan. Locate your local office at: **www.cengage.com/global**

Cengage Learning products are represented in Canada by Nelson Education, Ltd.

To learn more about Cengage Learning Solutions, visit **www.cengage.com**

Purchase any of our products at your local college store or at our preferred online store **www.cengagebrain.com**

Printed in the United States of America
Print Number: 01   Print Year: 2014

To Sheila, Daniel, and David

BRIEF CONTENTS

AN INTRODUCTION TO ECONOMICS

Part 1   **Economics: The Science of Scarcity**

Chapter 1   What Economics Is About   1
Appendix A   Working with Diagrams   29
Appendix B   Should You Major in Economics?   38
Chapter 2   Production Possibilities Frontier Framework   47
Chapter 3   Supply and Demand: Theory   65
Chapter 4   Prices: Free, Controlled, and Relative   103
Chapter 5   Supply, Demand, and Price: Applications   123

MACROECONOMICS

Part 2   **Macroeconomics Fundamentals**

Chapter 6   Macroeconomic Measurements, Part I: Prices and Unemployment   147
Chapter 7   Macroeconomic Measurements, Part II: GDP and Real GDP   166

Part 3   **Macroeconomic Stability, Instability, and Fiscal Policy**

Chapter 8   Aggregate Demand and Aggregate Supply   190
Chapter 9   Classical Macroeconomics and the Self-Regulating Economy   225
Chapter 10   Keynesian Macroeconomics and Economic Instability: A Critique of the Self-Regulating Economy   249
Chapter 11   Fiscal Policy and the Federal Budget   281

Part 4   **Money, the Economy, and Monetary Policy**

Chapter 12   Money, Banking, and the Financial System   309
Chapter 13   The Federal Reserve System   329
Appendix C   The Market for Reserves (or the Federal Funds Market)   349
Chapter 14   Money and the Economy   353
Chapter 15   Monetary Policy   382
Appendix D   Bond Prices and the Interest Rate   407

Part 5   **Expectations and Growth**

Chapter 16   Expectations Theory and the Economy   410

Chapter 17   Economic Growth: Resources, Technology, Ideas, and Institutions   437

Part 6   **The Financial Crisis of 2007–2009**

Chapter 18   The Financial Crisis of 2007–2009   456

Part 7   **Government and the Economy**

Chapter 19   Debates in Macroeconomics over the Role and Effects of Government   484

Part 8   **Market Failure, Public Choice, and Special-Interest-Group Politics**

Chapter 20   Public Choice and Special-Interest Group Politics   501

Part 9   **Economics Theory-Building and Everyday Life**

Chapter 21   Building Theories to Explain Everyday Life: From Observations to Questions to Theories to Predictions   522

THE GLOBAL ECONOMY

Part 10   **International Economics and Globalization**

Chapter 22   International Trade   547
Chapter 23   International Finance   567
Chapter 24   Globalization and International Impacts on the Economy   585

WEB CHAPTERS

Chapter 25:   The Economic Case For and Against Government: Five Topics Considered   615
Chapter 26   Stocks, Bonds, Futures, and Options   636
Chapter 27   Agriculture: Problems, Policies, and Unintended Effects   656

Self-Test Appendix   615
Glossary   635
Index   645

CONTENTS

AN INTRODUCTION TO ECONOMICS

Part 1 Economics: The Science of Scarcity

ECONOMICS 24/7

Rationing Spots at Yale 6

Scarcity and Friendship 9

When Is It Too Costly to Attend College? 11

Is It Possible to Be Too Healthy and to Study Too Much? 14

Can Incentives Make You Smarter? 17

When Are People the Most Likely to "Lose" Library Books? The Case of Alchian and Allen's *University Economics* 22

Office Hours

"I Don't Believe That Every Time a Person Does Something, He Compares the Marginal Benefits and Costs" 24

CHAPTER 1: WHAT ECONOMICS IS ABOUT 1

Your Life, 2016–2026 1

A Definition of Economics 2
Goods and Bads 2   Resources 2   Scarcity and a Definition of Economics 3
The Counterintuitive in Economics 3

Key Concepts in Economics 5
Opportunity Cost 5   Opportunity Cost and Behavior 7   Benefits and
Costs 7   Decisions Made at the Margin 10   Efficiency 12   Economics Is About
Incentives 13   Unintended Effects 15   Exchange 16

The Market and Government 18

***Ceteris Paribus* and Theory 19**
Ceteris Paribus Thinking 19   What Is a Theory? 20

Economic Categories 23
Positive Economics and Normative Economics 23 Microeconomics and
Macroeconomics 23

Chapter Summary 25

Key Terms and Concepts 26

Video Questions and Problems 27

Questions and Problems 27

Working with Numbers and Graphs 28

APPENDIX A: WORKING WITH DIAGRAMS 29

Slope of a Line 30

The Slope of a Line Is Constant 31

Slope of a Curve 31

The 45-degree Line 32

Pie Charts 33

Bar Graphs 33

Line Graphs 35

Appendix Summary 36

Key Terms and Concepts 37

Questions and Problems 37

APPENDIX B: SHOULD YOU MAJOR IN ECONOMICS? 38

Five Myths about Economics and Being an Economics Major 39
What Awaits You as an Economics Major? 42
What Do Economists Do? 44
Places to Find More Information 45
Concluding Remarks 46

CHAPTER 2: PRODUCTION POSSIBILITIES FRONTIER FRAMEWORK 47

The Production Possibilities Frontier 47
The Straight-Line PPF: Constant Opportunity Costs 47   The Bowed-Outward
(Concave-Downward) PPF: Increasing Opportunity Costs 48   Law of Increasing
Opportunity Costs 50   Economic Concepts in a Production Possibilities Frontier
Framework 51

Specialization and Trade Can Move Us Beyond Our PPF 56
A Simple Two-Person PPF Model 56   On or Beyond the PPF? 57

Chapter Summary 62
Key Terms and Concepts 62
Video Questions and Problems 62
Questions and Problems 63
Working with Numbers and Graphs 63

CHAPTER 3: SUPPLY AND DEMAND: THEORY 65

What Is Demand? 65
The Law of Demand 66   Four Ways to Represent the Law of Demand 66   Why Does
Quantity Demanded Go Down as Price Goes Up? 67   Individual Demand Curve and
Market Demand Curve 69   A Change in Quantity Demanded Versus a Change in
Demand 70   What Factors Cause the Demand Curve to Shift? 73   Movement Factors
and Shift Factors 76

Supply 77
The Law of Supply 78   Why Most Supply Curves Are Upward Sloping 79
Changes in Supply Mean Shifts in Supply Curves 79   What Factors Cause the Supply
Curve to Shift? 79   A Change in Supply Versus a Change in Quantity Supplied 82

The Market: Putting Supply and Demand Together 83
Supply and Demand at Work at an Auction 83   The Language of Supply and Demand:
A Few Important Terms 84   Moving to Equilibrium: What Happens to Price When
There Is a Surplus or a Shortage? 84   Speed of Moving to Equilibrium 85   Moving
to Equilibrium: Maximum and Minimum Prices 86   The Connection Between
Equilibrium and Predictions 87   Equilibrium in Terms of Consumers' and Producers'
Surplus 88   What Can Change Equilibrium Price and Quantity? 91   Epilogue:
Who Feeds Cleveland? 94

Chapter Summary 99
Key Terms and Concepts 99

ECONOMICS 24/7

Where Was Sherlock Holmes
on His Production Possibilities
Frontier? 51

Studying and Your PPF 55

Politics and the PPF 59

Why Do People Specialize and
Trade? 60

Office Hours

"What Purpose Does the PPF
Serve?" 61

ECONOMICS 24/7

Weight Loss, the Price of Food,
and the Law of Demand 68

What Do the Following Have
in Common? Losing One's
Temper, Arriving to Class Late,
and Buying the Textbook for a
Class 69

Kindles and the Law of
Demand 74

Why a Dowry? 89

Are You Buying More Than You
Want to Buy? 93

"Sorry, But This Flight Has Been
Overbooked" 95

Office Hours

"I Thought Prices Equaled Costs
Plus 10 Percent" 98

Video Questions and Problems 100

Questions and Problems 100

Working with Numbers and Graphs 101

CHAPTER 4: PRICES: FREE, CONTROLLED, AND RELATIVE 103

Price 103

Price as a Rationing Device 103   Price as a Transmitter of Information 104

Price Controls 105

Price Ceiling 105   Price Floor: Definition and Effects 111

Two Prices: Absolute and Relative 116

Absolute (Money) Price and Relative Price 116   Taxes on Specific Goods and Relative Price Changes 117

Chapter Summary 121

Key Terms and Concepts 121

Video Questions and Problems 121

Questions and Problems 121

Working with Numbers and Graphs 122

CHAPTER 5: SUPPLY, DEMAND, AND PRICE: APPLICATIONS 123

Application 1: Tickets to *The Big Bang Theory* 123

Application 2: Easier-to-obtain Loans and Higher Housing Prices 125

Application 3: The Price of an Aisle Seat 126

Application 4: What Will Happen to the Price of Marijuana if the Purchase and Sale of Marijuana Are Legalized? 127

Application 5: Speculators, Price Variability, and Patterns 128

Application 6: Why Is Medical Care So Expensive? 129

Application 7: Why Do Colleges Use GPAs, ACTs, and SATs for Purposes of Admission? 132

Application 8: Supply and Demand on a Freeway 134

Application 9: Are Renters Better Off? 136

Application 10: Do You Pay for Good Weather? 137

Application 11: College Superathletes 139

Application 12: 10 a.m. Classes in College 140

Application 13: Salsa, Chips, and Beer 142

Chapter Summary 144

Video Questions and Problems 145

Questions and Problems 145

Working with Numbers and Graphs 146

A Price Ceiling in the Kidney Market 108

1973 and 1979 110

What Does Price Have to Do with Being Late to Class? 115

Obesity and a Soda Tax 118

Relative Prices and Having Children 119

Office ✺ Hours

"I Thought Price Ceilings Were Good for Consumers" 120

Office ✺ Hours

"Doesn't High Demand Mean High Quantity Demanded?" 143

MACROECONOMICS

Part 2   Macroeconomics Fundamentals

ECONOMICS24/7

The Beatles at Shea
Stadium 152

When Is a Penny a
Quarter? 155

Does Culture Affect
Unemployment? 158

Who Should Be Considered
Unemployed? 159

Office Hours

"Is There More Than One
Reason the Unemployment Rate
Will Fall?" 162

ECONOMICS24/7

Gross Family Product 169

No One Utters the Actual
Number 170

Money and Happiness 170

1820 178

Office Hours

"Why Do We Use the
Expenditure Approach to
Measure Production?" 185

CHAPTER 6: MACROECONOMIC MEASUREMENTS, PART I: PRICES AND UNEMPLOYMENT 147

Measuring the Price Level 147
Using the CPI to Compute the Price Level 147   Inflation and the CPI 149
GDP Implicit Price Deflator 150   Converting Dollars from One Year to Another 151

Measuring Unemployment 153
Who Are the Unemployed? 153   The Unemployment Rate and the
Employment Rate 154   Common Misconceptions about the Unemployment
and Employment Rates 154   Reasons for Unemployment 155   Discouraged
Workers 156   Types of Unemployment 156   The Natural Unemployment Rate and
Full Employment 157   Cyclical Unemployment 160

Chapter Summary 164

Key Terms and Concepts 164

Video Questions and Problems 164

Questions and Problems 165

Working with Numbers and Graphs 165

CHAPTER 7: MACROECONOMIC MEASUREMENTS, PART II: GDP AND REAL GDP 166

Gross Domestic Product 166
Calculating GDP 166   Final Goods and Intermediate Goods 167   What
GDP Omits 167   GDP Is Not Adjusted for Bads Generated
in the Production of Goods 168   Per-Capita GDP 169

The Expenditure Approach to Computing GDP for a Real-World Economy 172
Using the Expenditure Approach to Compute GDP 174   Common Misconceptions
about Increases in GDP 175

The Income Approach to Computing GDP for a Real-World Economy 176
Computing National Income 176   From National Income to GDP: Making Some
Adjustments 178   Other National Income Accounting Measurements 180   Net
Domestic Product 180   Personal Income 180   Disposable Income 181

Real GDP 181
Why We Need Real GDP 181   Computing Real GDP 181   The General Equation
for Real GDP 182   What Does It Mean if Real GDP Is Higher in One Year Than in
Another? 182   The Economy in 1950 and in 2012 183   Real GDP, Economic Growth,
and Business Cycles 183

Chapter Summary 186

Key Terms and Concepts 187

Video Questions and Problems 188

Questions and Problems 188

Working with Numbers and Graphs 188

Part 3   Macroeconomic Stability, Instability, and Fiscal Policy

ECONOMICS 24/7

When Would You Want to Be Paid in a Currency Other Than U.S. Dollars? 204

Can There Be More Than One Possible Cause? 213

Your First Job After College May Depend on the *AD* and *SRAS* Curves 217

Reality Can Be Messy, and Correct Predictions Can Be Difficult to Make 219

Office Hours

"What Purpose Does the *AD–AS* Framework Serve?" 220

ECONOMICS 24/7

Is Saving the Same as "Not Spending"? 229

Unpaid Internships 239

If the Economy Is Removing Itself from a Recessionary Gap, Where Is the Declining Price Level? 244

CHAPTER 8: AGGREGATE DEMAND AND AGGREGATE SUPPLY 190

A Way to View the Economy 190

Aggregate Demand 191
Why Does the Aggregate Demand Curve Slope Downward? 192   An Important Word on the Three Effects 193   A Change in Quantity Demanded of Real GDP Versus a Change in Aggregate Demand 195   Changes in Aggregate Demand: Shifts in the *AD* Curve 196   How Spending Components Affect Aggregate Demand 196   Why Is There More Total Spending? 197   Factors That Can Change *C, I, G,* and *NX* (*EX – IM*) and Therefore Can Change *AD* (Shift the *AD* Curve) 198   Can a Change in the Money Supply Change Aggregate Demand? 203   If Consumption Rises, Does Some Other Spending Component Have to Decline? 204

Short-Run Aggregate Supply 206
Short-Run Aggregate Supply Curve: What It Is and Why It Is Upward Sloping 206   What Puts the "Short Run" in the *SRAS* Curve? 208   Changes in Short-Run Aggregate Supply: Shifts in the *SRAS* Curve 208   Something More to Come: Peoples' Expectations 209

Putting *AD* and *SRAS* Together: Short-Run Equilibrium 210
How Short-Run Equilibrium in the Economy Is Achieved 210   Thinking in Terms of Short-Run Equilibrium Changes in the Economy 211   An Important Exhibit 215

Long-Run Aggregate Supply 216
Going from the Short Run to the Long Run 216   Short-Run Equilibrium, Long-Run Equilibrium, and Disequilibrium 218

Chapter Summary 221

Key Terms and Concepts 222

Video Questions and Problems 222

Questions and Problems 222

Working with Numbers and Graphs 223

CHAPTER 9: CLASSICAL MACROECONOMICS AND THE SELF-REGULATING ECONOMY 225

The Classical View 225
Classical Economists and Say's Law 225   Classical Economists and Interest Rate Flexibility 226   Classical Economists on Prices and Wages: Both Are Flexible 228

Three States of the Economy 230
Real GDP and Natural Real GDP: Three Possibilities 230   The Labor Market and the Three States of the Economy 232   Common Misconceptions About the Unemployment Rate and the Natural Unemployment Rate 233

The Self-Regulating Economy 236
What Happens If a Self-Regulating Economy Is in a Recessionary Gap? 236   What Happens If the Economy Is in an Inflationary Gap? 237   The Self-Regulating Economy: A Recap 238   Policy Implication of Believing That the Economy Is Self-Regulating 240   Changes in a Self-Regulating Economy: Short Run and Long Run 240   A Recap of Classical Macroeconomics and a Self-Regulating Economy 242   Business-Cycle Macroeconomics and Economic-Growth Macroeconomics 242

Office Hours

"Do Economists Really Know What the Natural Unemployment Rate Equals?" 245

ECONOMICS 24/7

The Financial and Economic Crisis of 2007–2009: Can a Housing Bust Lead to an Imploding Economy? 254

Was Keynes a Revolutionary in Economics? 257

The Economics of Spring Break 263

Office Hours

"Does a Lot Depend on Whether Wages Are Flexible or Inflexible?" 277

ECONOMICS 24/7

Two Cab Drivers on New Year's Eve, or Turning Equal into Unequal 285

Do Voting Rules Matter to Taxing and Spending? 288

Unemployment Compensation Benefits, Searching for Work, and the Unemployment Rate 296

Chapter Summary 246

Key Terms and Concepts 247

Video Questions and Problems 247

Questions and Problems 247

Working with Numbers and Graphs 248

CHAPTER 10: KEYNESIAN MACROECONOMICS AND ECONOMIC INSTABILITY: A CRITIQUE OF THE SELF-REGULATING ECONOMY 249

Questioning the Classical Position and the Self-Regulating Economy 249
    Keynes's Criticism of Say's Law in a Money Economy 250   Keynes on Wage Rates 251   Different Markets, Different Rates of Adjustment 252   Keynes on Prices 255   Is It a Question of the Time It Takes for Wages and Prices to Adjust? 255

The Simple Keynesian Model 258
    Assumptions 258   The Consumption Function 259   Consumption and Saving 260   The Multiplier 261   The Multiplier and Reality 262

The Simple Keynesian Model in the *AD–AS* Framework 264
    Shifts in the Aggregate Demand Curve 264   The Keynesian Aggregate Supply Curve 265   The Economy in a Recessionary Gap 266   Government's Role in the Economy 267   The Theme of the Simple Keynesian Model 267

The Simple Keynesian Model in the *TE–TP* Framework 268
    Deriving a Total Expenditures (*TE*) Curve 269   Where the Consumption Curve and the Total Expenditures Curve Cut the Vertical Axis: More on Exhibit 11 269   What Will Shift the *TE* Curve? 271   Comparing Total Expenditures (*TE*) and Total Production (*TP*) 271   Moving from Disequilibrium to Equilibrium 272   The Economy in a Recessionary Gap and the Role of Government 274   Equilibrium in the Economy 275   The Theme of the Simple Keynesian Model 275

Chapter Summary 278

Key Terms and Concepts 278

Video Questions and Problems 279

Questions and Problems 279

Working with Numbers and Graphs 280

CHAPTER 11: FISCAL POLICY AND THE FEDERAL BUDGET 281

The Federal Budget 281
    Government Expenditures 281   Government Tax Revenues 282   Social Security, Medicare, and Medicaid in the Future 282   Budget Projections 283   Budget Deficit, Surplus, or Balance 284   An Interesting Fact: Taxing Millionaires and the Budget Deficit 286   Structural and Cyclical Deficits 286   The Public Debt 286   Valued-Added Tax 287   Tax Deductions vs Subsidies 290

Fiscal Policy 291
    Some Relevant Fiscal Policy Terms 291   Two Important Notes 291

Demand-Side Fiscal Policy 291
    Shifting the Aggregate Demand Curve 291   Fiscal Policy: Keynesian Perspective (Economy Is Not Self-Regulating) 292   Crowding Out: Questioning Expansionary Fiscal Policy 293   Lags and Fiscal Policy 297   Crowding Out, Lags, and the Effectiveness of Fiscal Policy 298   Democracy in Deficit 298

Office Hours

"Is There a Looming Fiscal Crisis?" 305

Supply-Side Fiscal Policy 301
Marginal Tax Rates and Aggregate Supply 301   The Laffer Curve: Tax Rates and Tax Revenues 302   Fiscal Policy and Expectations 304

Chapter Summary 306

Key Terms and Concepts 306

Video Questions and Problems 307

Questions and Problems 307

Working with Numbers and Graphs 308

Part 4   Money, The Economy, and Monetary Policy

ECONOMICS 24/7

English and Money 312

Bitcoins 315

eBay and Match.com 317

Economics on the Yellow Brick Road 318

The FDIC and Intended and Unintended Effects 323

The Financial Crisis, Risky Loans, and Bank Insolvency 325

Office Hours

"I Thought Money Had to Be Backed by Gold to Have Value" 326

ECONOMICS 24/7

Inside an FOMC Meeting 331

Some History of the Fed 333

Flying in with the Money 343

CHAPTER 12: MONEY, BANKING, AND THE FINANCIAL SYSTEM 309

Money: What Is It and How Did It Come to Be? 309
Money: A Definition 309   Three Functions of Money 310   From a Barter Economy to a Money Economy: The Origins of Money 310   Money, Leisure, and Output 313

Defining the Money Supply 314
M1 314   Money Is More Than Currency 314   M2 314   Where Do Credit Cards Fit In? 316

How Banking Developed 317
The Early Bankers 317   The Bank's Reserves and More 319

The Financial System 320
Direct and Indirect Finance 320   Adverse Selection Problems and Moral Hazard Problems 321   A Thought Experiment: No Financial Intermediaries 322   The Bank's Balance Sheet 323   A Bank's Business: Turning Liabilities into Assets 324

Chapter Summary 326

Key Terms and Concepts 327

Video Questions and Problems 327

Questions and Problems 327

Working with Numbers and Graphs 328

CHAPTER 13: THE FEDERAL RESERVE SYSTEM 329

The Structure and Functions of the Federal Reserve System (the Fed) 329
The Structure of the Fed 329   Functions of the Fed 330   Common Misconceptions About the U.S. Treasury and the Fed 332

The Money Supply Expansion Process 334
A Quick Review of Reserves, Required Reserves, and Excess Reserves 334   The Money Supply Expansion Process 334   The Money Supply Contraction Process 337

Other Fed Tools and Recent Fed Actions 339
The Required Reserve Ratio 339   The Discount Window and the Federal Funds Market 339   The Fed and the Federal Funds Rate Target 340   Dealing with a Financial Crisis 340   Quantitative Easing 341   What Is Free Banking? 343

Office Hours

"Can Something I Do End Up Changing the Money Supply?" 345

ECONOMICS24/7

The California Gold Rush, or Really Expensive Apples 357

Grade Inflation: It's All Relative 367

Hyperinflation 371

Office Hours

"What Is the Current Expected Inflation Rate?" 378

ECONOMICS24/7

The Fed Can't Always Be Sure That Banks Will Lend 392

Who Gets the Money First, and What Happens to Relative Prices? 396

Things May Not Always Go the Way the Fed Wants 397

Chapter Summary 346
Key Terms and Concepts 347
Video Questions and Problems 347
Questions and Problems 347
Working with Numbers and Graphs 348

APPENDIX C: THE MARKET FOR RESERVES (OR THE FEDERAL FUNDS MARKET) 349

The Demand for Reserves 349
The Supply of Reserves 350
Two Different Supply Curves for Reserves 350
The Corridor and Changing the Federal Funds Rate 352

CHAPTER 14: MONEY AND THE ECONOMY 353

Money and the Price Level 353
The Equation of Exchange 353   From the Equation of Exchange to the Simple Quantity Theory of Money 355   The Simple Quantity Theory of Money in an *AD–AS* Framework 356   Dropping the Assumptions that *V* and *Q* Are Constant 358
Monetarism 359
The Four Monetarist Positions 359   Monetarism and *AD–AS* 360   The Monetarist View of the Economy 362
Inflation 363
One-Shot Inflation 363   Continued Inflation 366   Can You Get Rid of Inflation with Price Controls? 370
Money and Interest Rates 372
Which Economic Variables Does a Change in the Money Supply Affect? 372   The Money Supply, the Loanable Funds Market, and Interest Rates 373   What Happens to the Interest Rate as the Money Supply Changes? 376   The Nominal and Real Interest Rates 377
Chapter Summary 379
Key Terms and Concepts 379
Video Questions and Problems 380
Questions and Problems 380
Working with Numbers and Graphs 381

CHAPTER 15: MONETARY POLICY 382

Transmission Mechanisms 382
The Money Market in the Keynesian Transmission Mechanism 382   The Keynesian Transmission Mechanism: Indirect 384   The Keynesian Mechanism May Get Blocked 385   The Monetarist Transmission Mechanism: Direct 388
Monetary Policy and the Problem of Inflationary and Recessionary Gaps 389
A Different View of the Economy: Patterns of Sustainable Specialization and Trade (PSST) 391

"Does Monetary Policy Always Have the Same Effects?" 403

Monetary Policy and the Activist–Nonactivist Debate 393
The Case for Activist (or Discretionary) Monetary Policy 394   The Case for Nonactivist (or Rules-Based) Monetary Policy 394

Nonactivist Monetary Proposals 397
The Constant-Money-Growth-Rate Rule 398   The Predetermined-Money-Growth-Rate Rule 398   The Fed and the Taylor Rule 399   Inflation Targeting 399   Nominal GDP Targeting 400   A Gold Standard as Monetary Policy and the Value of the Dollar 400

Chapter Summary 404

Key Terms and Concepts 404

Video Questions and Problems 405

Questions and Problems 405

Working with Numbers and Graphs 406

APPENDIX D: BOND PRICES AND THE INTEREST RATE 407

Appendix Summary 409

Questions and Problems 409

Part 5　Expectations and Growth

ECONOMICS 24/7

Bubbles and Expectations 420

Rational Expectations in the College Classroom 421

Deficits, Money, Expectations, and Unintended Effects 428

The Money Supply, an Increase in Productivity, and What You Think 429

Office Hours

"Does New Classical Theory Call the Effects of Fiscal and Monetary Policy into Question?" 433

ECONOMICS 24/7

Thinking in Terms of Production Functions and Equations 443

Growth and Morality 444

Economic Freedom and Growth Rates 450

Religious Beliefs and Economic Growth 451

CHAPTER 16: EXPECTATIONS THEORY AND THE ECONOMY 410

Phillips Curve Analysis 410
The Phillips Curve 410   Samuelson and Solow: The Americanization of the Phillips Curve 411

The Controversy Begins: Are There Really Two Phillips Curves? 412
Things Aren't Always as We Think They Are 412   Friedman and the Natural Rate Theory 412   How Do People Form Their Expectations? 416

Rational Expectations and New Classical Theory 417
Rational Expectations 417   Do People Really Anticipate Policy? 417   Price-Level Expectations and the *SRAS* Curve 418   Expected and Actual Price Levels 422   New Classical Economics and Four Different Cases 422   Comparing Exhibits 9 and 10 427

New Keynesians and Rational Expectations 430

Looking at Things from the Supply Side: Real Business Cycle Theorists 431

Chapter Summary 434

Key Terms and Concepts 435

Video Questions and Problems 435

Questions and Problems 435

Working with Numbers and Graphs 436

CHAPTER 17: ECONOMIC GROWTH: RESOURCES, TECHNOLOGY, IDEAS, AND INSTITUTIONS 437

A Few Basics About Economic Growth 437
Do Economic Growth Rates Matter? 437

A Production Function and Economic Growth 439
The Graphical Representation of the Production Function 440   From the Production Function to the *LRAS* Curve 440   Emphasis on Labor 441   Emphasis on Capital 446   Emphasis on Other Resources: Natural Resources and Human

Office ☀ Hours

"What Is the Difference Between Business Cycle Macroeconomics and Economic Growth Macroeconomics?" 453

Capital 446   Emphasis on the Technology Coefficient and Ideas 447   Discovery and Ideas 447   Expanding Our Horizons 448   Institutions Matter 448

Chapter Summary 454

Key Terms and Concepts 454

Video Questions and Problems 454

Questions and Problems 455

Working with Numbers and Graphs 455

Part 6   The Financial Crisis of 2007–2009

CHAPTER 18: THE FINANCIAL CRISIS OF 2007–2009 456

The TED Spread 470

Too Big to Fail 471

The Financial Crisis and Hyman Minsky: Model an Economy with a Wall Street 476

The Financial and Real Sectors of the Economy 456

The Financial Crisis as a Balance Sheet Problem 457
    Which Assets Were Risky? 458   Three Questions 459

The Fed, Interest Rates, and Housing Prices 460
    The Global Savings Glut and Low Interest Rates 461   Our Story So Far 462

The Taylor Rule and Interest Rates 463
    Alan Greenspan Responds 464   Rising House Prices, Delinquency Rates, and Foreclosures 465

The Politics of Housing 466
    The Community Reinvestment Act 467

Fannie Mae and Freddie Mac 467

The Role of Leverage and Regulatory Capital Arbitrage 468
    Leverage 468   Regulatory Capital Arbitrage 469   Where We Are So Far 474   House Prices Decline 474   Domino Effects 475   How the Real Sector Affects the Financial Sector 475   The Government Response 475   The Great Recession 477

Office ☀ Hours

"Do Economists and the Public Always Understand the Causes of Financial Crises?" 480

Chapter Summary 481

Key Terms and Concepts 482

Video Questions and Problems 482

Questions and Problems 483

Working with Numbers and Graphs 483

Part 7   Government and the Economy

CHAPTER 19: DEBATES IN MACROECONOMICS OVER THE ROLE AND EFFECTS OF GOVERNMENT 484

ECONOMICS 24/7

If It Sounds Reasonable, Is It Right? If It Sounds Unreasonable, Is It Wrong? 487

Macroeconomics and Government: The Debate 484

Tax Cuts, Tax Revenue, and Budget Deficits 485

The Economy: Self-Regulating or Not? 486

More Government Spending or a Cut in Taxes: Which Gives a Bigger Bang for the Buck? 488

More Government Spending or a Cut in Taxes: The Size and
Scope of Government 488

The Degree of Crowding Out 489

The Politics of Government Spending 490

Monetary Policy: Rules Versus Discretion 491

Bailouts 492

Demand-Side and Supply-Side Views of the Economy and Government Tools for
Changing Real GDP 493

Chapter Summary 497

Key Terms and Concepts 498

Video Questions and Problems 498

Questions and Problems 498

Working with Numbers and Graphs 499

Office **Hours**

"What Kinds of Debates Do
Macroeconomists Have?" 496

Part 8   Market Failure, Public Choice, and Special-Interest-Group Politics

ECONOMICS24/7

A Simple-Majority Voting Rule:
The Case of the Statue in the
Public Square 504

Economic Illiteracy and
Democracy 507

Inheritance, Heirs, and Why
the Firstborn Became King or
Queen 516

Office **Hours**

"Doesn't Public Choice Paint
a Bleak Picture of Politics and
Government?" 518

**CHAPTER 20: PUBLIC CHOICE AND SPECIAL-INTEREST GROUP
POLITICS 501**

Public Choice Theory 501

The Political Market 502
    Moving Toward the Middle: The Median Voter Model 502   What Does the Theory
    Predict? 503

Voters and Rational Ignorance 505
    The Costs and Benefits of Voting 505   Rational Ignorance 506

More About Voting 508
    Example 1: Voting for a Nonexcludable Public Good 509   Example 2: Voting and
    Efficiency 509

Special-Interest Groups 511
    Information and Lobbying 511   Congressional Districts as Special-Interest
    Groups 511   Public-Interest Talk, Special-Interest Legislation 512   Rent
    Seeking 512   Bringing About Transfers 513   Information, Rational Ignorance, and
    Seeking Transfers 514

Constitutional Economics 517

Chapter Summary 519

Key Terms and Concepts 520

Video Questions and Problems 520

Questions and Problems 520

Working with Numbers and Graphs 521

Part 9   Economics Theory-Building and Everyday Life

CHAPTER 21: BUILDING THEORIES TO EXPLAIN EVERYDAY LIFE: FROM OBSERVATIONS TO QUESTIONS TO THEORIES TO PREDICTIONS 522

A Different Kind of Chapter 522

The Process 523

Observation/Thought 1: The Birthrates in Various Countries Are Different 524
The Question 524   The Theory 524   The Predictions 524   A Detour: The Issue of Falsifiability (Refutability) 524

Observation/Thought 2: The Ethical Code of People Who Live in a Small Town Is Different From That of People Who Live in a Large City 525
The Question 526   The Theory 526   The Predictions 526

Observation/Thought 3: The Closer the Dollar Tuition the Student Pays Is to the Equilibrium Tuition, the More on Time and Responsive University Instructors Will Be for Office Hours 528
The Question 528   The Theory 528   The Predictions 530

Observation/Thought 4: Criminals Are Not Rational 530
The Question 530   The Theory 530   The Predictions 531   A Detour: Does Evidence Prove a Theory Correct? 532   Another Detour: After You Have One Theory That Explains and Predicts, Search for Another 532   A Final Detour: Why Prediction Is So Important, or Why Good-Sounding Stories Are Not Enough 534

Observation/Thought 5: More Students Wear Baseball Caps in Class on Exam Days Than on Other Days 535
The Question 535   The Theory 535   The Predictions 535

Observation/Thought 6: Houses in "Good" School Districts Are Often More Expensive Than Comparable Houses in "Bad" School Districts 537
The Question 537   The Theory 537   The Predictions 538

Observation/Thought 7: Are People Better Off With or Without Health Care Vouchers? 539
The Question 539   The Theory 539   The Predictions 539

Observation/Thought 8: People Who Give to Others Often Complain That They End Up Giving Too Much 540
The Question 540   The Theory 540   The Predictions 543

Chapter Summary 544

Video Questions and Problems 546

Questions and Problems 546

Working with Numbers and Graphs 546

ECONOMICS 24/7

Can Social Media Affect Whom a Person Dates? 527

Talking on a Cell Phone in Public 536

Office Hours

"Can Anyone Build a Theory?" 544

THE GLOBAL ECONOMY

Part 10   International Economics and Globlization

ECONOMICS 24/7

Dividing the Work 551

Offshore Outsourcing, or Offshoring 559

Are Social Media Making the World Smaller? 561

CHAPTER 22: INTERNATIONAL TRADE 547

International Trade Theory 547
How Countries Know What to Trade 548   A Common Misconception about How Much We Can Consume 550   How Countries Know When They Have a Comparative Advantage 550

Office Hours

"Should We Impose Tariffs if
They Impose Tariffs?" 562

The U.S. Dollar as the Primary
Reserve Currency 573

Chinese Imports and the U.S.
Economy 575

Office Hours

"Why Is the Depreciation
of One Currency Tied to the
Appreciation of Another?" 581

ECONOMICS 24/7

Should You Leave a Tip? 587

Proper Business Etiquette
Around the World 592

Will Globalization Change the
Kind of Music We Hear? 597

How Hard Will It Be to Get into
Harvard in 2025? 603

Trade Restrictions 552
The Distributional Effects of International Trade 553   Consumers' and Producers'
Surpluses 553   The Benefits and Costs of Trade Restrictions 554   Why Nations
Sometimes Restrict Trade 558

Chapter Summary 564

Key Terms and Concepts 564

Video Questions and Problems 564

Questions and Problems 565

Working with Numbers and Graphs 565

CHAPTER 23: INTERNATIONAL FINANCE 567

The Foreign Exchange Market 567
The Demand for Goods 568   The Demand for, and Supply of, Currencies 568

Flexible Exchange Rates 569
The Equilibrium Exchange Rate 569   Changes in the Equilibrium Exchange
Rate 570   Factors That Affect the Equilibrium Exchange Rate 570

Fixed Exchange Rates 574
Fixed Exchange Rates and Overvalued or Undervalued Currency 574
What Is So Bad about an Overvalued Dollar? 576   Government Involvement in a Fixed
Exchange Rate System 577   Options Under a Fixed Exchange Rate System 577

Fixed Exchange Rates Versus Flexible Exchange Rates 579
Promoting International Trade 579   Optimal Currency Areas 579

Chapter Summary 582

Key Terms and Concepts 583

Video Questions and Problems 583

Questions and Problems 583

Working with Numbers and Graphs 584

CHAPTER 24: GLOBALIZATION AND INTERNATIONAL IMPACTS ON THE ECONOMY 585

What Is Globalization? 585
A Smaller World 585   A World Economy 586

Two Ways to See Globalization 587
No Barriers 588   A Union of States 588

Globalization Facts 588
International Trade 588   Globalization Indexes 589

The Movement Toward Globalization 591
The End of the Cold War 591   Advancing Technology 591   Policy Changes 593

Benefits and Costs of Globalization 594
The Benefits 594   The Costs 595

The Continuing Globalization Debate 597

Less Globalization or More: A Tug-of-War? 598
Less Globalization 598   More Globalization 599

International Factors and Aggregate Demand 600
Net Exports 600   The J-Curve 601

International Factors and Aggregate Supply 604
Foreign Input Prices 604   Why Foreign Input Prices Change 604

Factors That Affect Both Aggregate Demand and Aggregate Supply 605
The Exchange Rate 605   The Role That Interest Rates Play 606

Deficits: International Effects and Domestic Feedback 607
The Budget Deficit and Expansionary Fiscal Policy 607   The Budget Deficit and
Contractionary Fiscal Policy 608   The Effects of Monetary Policy 609

Chapter Summary 612

Key Terms and Concepts 613

Video Questions and Problems 613

Questions and Problems 613

Working with Numbers and Graphs 614

"Why Do Some People Favor
Globalization and Others
Don't?" 611

WEB CHAPTERS

CHAPTER 25: THE ECONOMIC CASE FOR AND AGAINST GOVERNMENT: FIVE TOPICS CONSIDERED 615

Economics and Government 615

The Economic Case For a Government Role 616
Government Can Remove Individuals from a Prisoner's Dilemma Setting 616
Externalities 621   Nonexcludable Public Goods 621   The Case for Smaller or Larger
Government 622

The Economic Case Against a Government Role 624
Unintended Effects of Government Actions 624   Government as a Transfer
Mechanism 626   Economic Growth Versus Transfers 628   Following the Leader in
Pushing for Transfers 630   Divisive Society: A Nonexcludable Public Bad 631

Chapter Summary 633

Key Terms and Concepts 633

Video Questions and Problems 634

Questions and problems 634

Working with Numbers and Graphs 634

CHAPTER 26: STOCKS, BONDS, FUTURES, AND OPTIONS 636

Financial Markets 636

Stocks 637
Where Are Stocks Bought and Sold? 637   The Dow Jones Industrial Average
(DJIA) 638   How the Stock Market Works 639   Why Do People Buy
Stock? 640   How to Buy and Sell Stock 640   Buying Stocks or Buying the
Market 642   How to Read the Stock Market Page 643

Bonds 645
The Components of a Bond 645   Bond Ratings 645   Bond Prices and Yields
(or Interest Rates) 645   Common Misconceptions about the Coupon Rate and
Yield (Interest Rate) 647   Types of Bonds 647   How to Read the Bond Market
Page 648   Risk and Return 649

ECONOMICS24/7

Culture as a Public Good 623

"I'm No Longer Sure What I
Think." 632

ECONOMICS24/7

Are Some Economists Poor
Investors? 641

$1.3 Quadrillion 646

What Do Private Equity Firms
Do? 651

"I Have Three Questions." 653

Futures and Options 650
  Futures 650   Options 652
Chapter Summary 654
Key Terms and Concepts 655
Video Questions and Problems 655
Questions and Problems 655
Working with Numbers and Graphs 655

CHAPTER 27: AGRICULTURE: PROBLEMS, POLICIES, AND UNINTENDED EFFECTS 656

The Politics of Agriculture 664

Agriculture: The Issues 656
  A Few Facts 656   Agriculture and Income Inelasticity 657   Agriculture and Price Inelasticity 658   Price Variability and Futures Contracts 659   Can Bad Weather Be Good for Farmers? 660
Agricultural Policies 660
  Price Supports 661   Restricting Supply 661   Target Prices and Deficiency Payments 662   Production Flexibility Contract Payments, (Fixed) Direct Payments, and Countercyclical Payments 663   Nonrecourse Commodity Loans 665

"Why Don't Farmers Agree to Cut Back Output?" 665

Chapter Summary 666
Key Terms and Concepts 667
Video Questions and Problems 667
Questions and problems 667
Working with Numbers and Graphs 667

Self-Test Appendix 615
Glossary 635
Index 645

Roger Arnold's **MACROECONOMICS** opens up the world of economic analysis. Substantive content, detailed diagrams, popular economic features, and innovative pedagogy are just the beginning. **MACROECONOMICS** continues to blaze the trail for constantly updated content and applications balanced with unequaled media and study assets, including the new Adaptive Test Prep app.

NEW! Only available in MindTap™, the new **Adaptive Practice Test App** helps students prepare for test success by allowing them to generate multiple practice tests across chapters. Once a practice test is complete, the student is presented with a personalized Study Plan featuring a series of highly targeted remediation resources, including "Teachable Moment" videos created by author Roger Arnold.

Adaptive Test Prep helps students more effectively gauge their understanding before taking an exam.

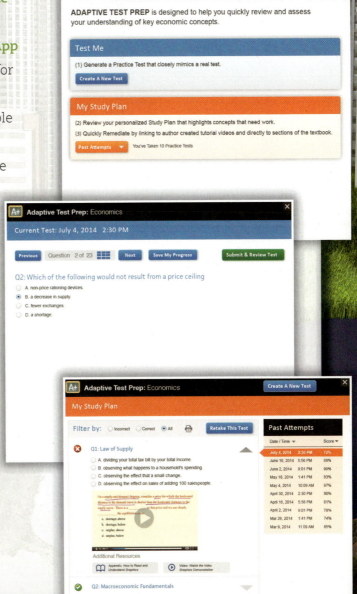

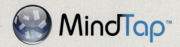

MindTap Economics 12th Edition is a personalized learning solution empowering students to analyze, apply, and improve their thinking. With MindTap™, students can measure their progress and improve outcomes. Using the unique Learning Path in MindTap™, students can follow prescribed steps that highlight valuable learning tools, such as readings, Video Office Hours, End-of-Chapter practice problems, the new Adaptive Test Prep App, new Progression Graphs in the eReader, ConceptClip videos, Aplia™, and much more.

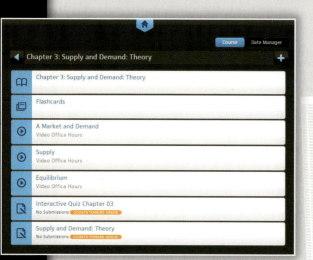

NEW! Progression Graphs.

Available in both MindTap and Aplia! Many economic graphs have been digitally enhanced in Arnold's eReader using our new Progression Graph technology. This feature allows students to work at their own pace in order to see a complex graph being built step-by-step. Progression Graphs decompose each graphical exhibit into several layers while still maintaining a rich, economic pedagogy.

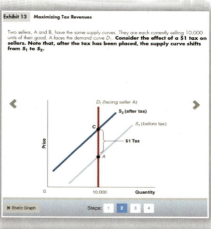

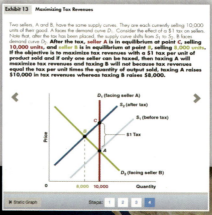

Aplia is the most successful and widely used homework solution in the Economics market, with over 1 billion answers entered. Online interactive problem sets, analyses, tutorials, experiments, and critical-thinking exercises give students hands-on application without adding to instructors' workload. Based on discovery learning, Aplia requires students to take an active role in the learning process—helping them improve their economic understanding and ability to relate to the economic concepts presented. Instructors can assign homework that is automatically graded and recorded.

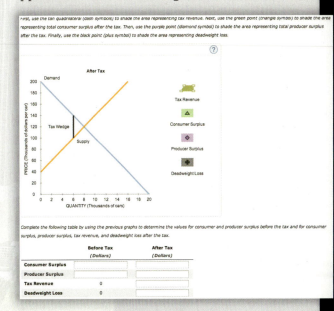

Embedded in the Aplia product for Arnold's 12th Edition is the fully interactive, media rich eReader. Combining the functionality you and your students are coming to expect from a modern eReader (text search, highlighting, note-taking) with our exclusive embedded media—Video Questions and Problems, Working with Diagrams, ConceptClips, and Video Office Hours, this robust reading experience is just a click away as students work through their Aplia problem sets.

Because cultivating an economic way of thinking requires building on a foundation of theory and its application to real-world examples, **MACROECONOMICS, 12e** continues to set the standard for thoroughly updated content. There are 40 new Economics 24/7 features including Where Was Sherlock Holmes on His Production Possibilities Frontier, The Beatles at Shea Stadium, Do Voting Rules Matter to Taxing and Spending, The Financial Crisis and Hyman Minsky, The Ultimatum Game and Facebook, YouTube, and Wikipedia, Social Media and Entrepreneurship, Can Social Media Affect Who a Person Dates?, Iceland Produces Its Constitution Through Crowdsourcing, and much more.

The 12th Edition also includes new coverage of unpaid internships, the economics of social media, democracies and deficits, a gold standard and monetary policy, quantitative easing, digital currency, and more.

ECONOMICS 24/7

Where Was Sherlock Holmes on His Production Possibilities Frontier?

Of Sherlock Holmes, it has been said that "his ignorance was as remarkable as his knowledge."[1] In fact, his companion, Dr. Watson, said, "Of contemporary literature, philosophy and politics he appeared to know next to nothing. . . . My surprise reached a climax, however, when I found incidentally that he was ignorant of the Copernican Theory and of the composition of the Solar System. That any civilized being in this nineteenth century should not be aware that the earth travelled round the sun appeared to be to me such an extraordinary fact that I could hardly realize it."[2]

Time & Life Pictures/Getty Images

When Dr. Watson expressed his surprise to Sherlock Holmes, Holmes told Watson that now that Watson had told him that the earth revolves around the sun, he would try his best to forget it. Holmes said, "You see, I consider that a man's brain originally is like a little empty attic, and you have to stock it with such furniture as you choose. A fool takes in all the lumber of every sort that he comes across, so that the knowledge which might be useful to him gets crowded out. . . . He will have nothing but the tools which may help him in doing his work. . . . Depend upon it there comes a time when for every addition of knowledge you forget something that you knew before."[3]

Holmes was interested in solving crimes, and he wanted his brain filled with only the things that would help him achieve his sole purpose.

If he learned something that was irrelevant to this task, then something that was relevant to the purpose at hand would be discarded. In other words, he was on his PPF and more of one thing necessarily meant less of something else.

Not only that, but Holmes wanted to stay at a particular point on his PPF. But which point? Well, let's deduce the answer together. Suppose that on the vertical axis there is "knowing more about things about the world, none of which is helpful in solving crime" and on the horizontal axis is "number of crimes solved." Now, if Holmes wants to solve as many crimes as possible, obviously he wants to be on his PPF at the point where it touches the horizontal axis. He wants to solve as many crimes as possible, given his resources (physical and mental). In other words, he wants to use all of his resources to do one thing and one thing only: solve crimes.

---

1. Sir Arthur Conan Doyle, "A Study in Scarlet," *The Adventures of Sherlock Holmes,* Modern Library paperback edition (New York: Random House, 2003), chapter 2.
2. Ibid.
3. Ibid.

IN APPRECIATION

Many colleagues have contributed to the success of this text over the last eleven editions. Their feedback continues to influence and enhance the text and ancillary package and I'm grateful for their efforts. Now into our 12th edition, space dictates that we can no longer list all of the names of all reviewers for each past edition; we are including here instructors who contributed to the development of the 12th edition, but continue to be grateful for the improvements suggested by all of the reviewers and contributors to this product over the years.

Randy Barcus
Embry Riddle Aero University - Daytona Beach, Daytona Beach, FL

Yosef Bonaparte
University of British Columbia, Kelowna, BC

Anthony Chan
Santa Monica College, Los Angeles, CA

Amy Chataginer
Mississippi Gulf Coast Community College, Biloxi, MS

Megan Cummins
Mt. San Jacinto College, Long Beach, CA

Ribhi Daoud
Sinclair Community College, Dayton, OH

Carol Decker
Tennessee Wesleyan College, Niota, TN

Brittany Dobill
John a Logan College, Carterville, IL

Tila Dorina
Embry Riddle Aero University - Daytona Beach, FL

Matthew Dudman
California State University - Maritime, Vallejo, CA

Harry Ellis
University of North Texas, Denton, TX

Susan Emens
Kent State University - Trumbull, Warren, OH

Fidel Ezeala-Harrison
Jackson State University, Jackson, MS

John Finley
Columbus State University, Columbus, GA

Lea Frances
Germanna Community College, Orange, VA

John Gaughan
Penn State University - Lehigh Valley, Center Valley, PA

Sherry Grosso
University of South Carolina, Sumter, SC

Travis Hayes
Dalton State College, Dalton, GA

Aubrey Haynes
Southwest Texas Jr College, Uvalde, TX

Dewey Heinsma
Mt. San Jacinto College, Yucaipa, CA

Tony Hunnicutt
College of the Ouachitas, Malvern, AR

Joe Hutlak
Union County College, Cranford, NJ

Andres Jauregui
Columbus State University, Columbus, GA

Deb Jones
Iowa Lakes Community College, Emmetsburg, IA

Barry Kotlove
Edmonds Community College, Lynnwood, WA

Katie Lotz
Lake Land College, Mattoon, IL

Brian Lynch
Lake Land College, Mattoon, IL

Michael Machiorlatti
Oklahoma City Community College, Oklahoma City, OK

Mehrdad Madresehee
Lycoming College, Williamsport, PA

Mike Mcgay
Wilmington University, Newark, DE

Shah Mehrabi
Montgomery College, Arlington, VA

José Mendez
John a Logan College, Carterville, IL

Elizabeth Moorhouse
Lycoming College, Williamsport, PA

Edward Murphy
Embry Riddle Aero University - Daytona Beach, Daytona Beach, FL

Charles Myrick
Oklahoma City Community College, Warr Acres, OK

Charles Newton
Houston Community College, Stafford, TX

Ogbonnaya Nwoha
Grambling State University, Ruston, LA

Charles Parker
Wayne State College, Wayne, NE

Van Pham
Salem State University, Salem, MA

John Pharr
Brookhaven College, Garland, TX

Germain Pichop
Oklahoma City Community College, Oklahoma City, OK

Craig Richardson
*Winston-Salem State University,
Winston-Salem,* NC

April Ruhmann
Southwest Texas Jr College, Uvalde, TX

Sara Saderion
Houston Community College, Houston, TX

Richard Sarkisian
*Camden County College,
Blackwood,* NJ

Daniel Saros
Valparaiso University, Valparaiso, IN

Anthony Sawyer
Paris Junior College, Paris, TX

Bill Schweizer
University of Mount Union, Alliance, OH

Matt Shekels
North Arkansas College, Harrison, AR

Kent Sickmeyer
Kaskaskia College, Centralia, IL

Donald Sparks
The Citadel, Charleston, SC

Boo Su
College of the Canyons, Santa Clarita, CA

Omari Swinton
Howard University, Upper Marlboro, MD

Krystal Thrailkill
*Rich Mountain Community College,
Mena,* AR

Kelly Whealan-George
*Embry-Riddle Aeronautical University,
South Riding,* VA

Beth Wilson
Humboldt State University, Arcata, CA

Davin Winger
*Oklahoma Panhandle State University,
Goodwell,* OK

Peter Wui
*University of Arkansas Pine Bluff,
Little Rock,* AR

Mustafa Younis
Jackson State University, Jackson, MS

Evaristo Zapata
Southwest Texas Jr College, Eagle Pass, TX

I would like to thank Peggy Crane of Southwestern College, who revised the Test Bank, and Jason Gurtovoy of California State University, Fullerton for creating the PowerPoint slides that accompany this text. I owe a debt of gratitude to all the fine and creative people I worked with at Cengage Learning. These persons include Erin Joyner, Editorial Director; Michael Worls, Product Director for Economics; Michael Parthenakis, Product Manager; Daniel Noguera, Content Developer; Colleen Farmer, Senior Content Project Manager; John Carey, Senior Marketing Manager; Anita Verma, Media Developer; Michelle Kunkler, Senior Art Director; and Kevin Kluck, Manufacturing Planner.

My deepest debt of gratitude goes to my wife, Sheila, and to my two sons, David, 23 years old, and Daniel, 26 years old. They continue to make all my days happy ones.

Roger A. Arnold

MACROECONOMICS

© Denise Lett/Shutterstock.com

INTRODUCTION

You are about to begin your study of economics. Before discussing particular topics in economics, we think it best to give you an overview of what economics is and of some of the key concepts. The key concepts can be compared to musical notes: Just as musical notes are repeated in any song (you hear the musical note G over and over again), so are the key concepts in economics repeated. Some of these concepts are scarcity, opportunity cost, efficiency, marginal decision making, incentives, and exchange.

1-1 YOUR LIFE, 2016–2026

What will your life be like during the years 2016–2026? What kind of work will you do after college? How much will you earn in that first job after college? Where will you be living and who will your friends be? How many friends will you have? Who might you marry? Will you buy a house in the next few years? If so, how much will you pay for the house? And, perhaps most importantly, will you be happy?

The specific answers to these questions and many more have to do with economics. For example, the salary you will earn has to do with the economic concept of *opportunity cost*. What you will do in your first job after college has to do with the *state of the economy* when you graduate. Whom you marry has to do with the *costs and benefits* connected to the people you date. The price you pay for a house has to do with the state of the *housing market*. How many friends you have has to do with the economic concept of *scarcity*. Whether you are happy will depend on such things as the *net benefits* you receive in various activities, the *utility* you gain by doing certain things, and more.

In this chapter we begin our study of economics. As you read the chapter (and those which follow), ask yourself how much of what you are reading is relevant to your life today and tomorrow. Ask: What does what I am reading have to do with *my* life? Our guess is that after answering this question a few dozen times, you will be convinced that economics explains much about your present and future.

1-2   A DEFINITION OF ECONOMICS

In this section, we discuss a few key economic concepts; then we incorporate knowledge of these concepts into a definition of economics.

1-2a   Goods and Bads

Economists talk about *goods* and *bads.* A **good** is anything that gives a person **utility**, or satisfaction. Here is a partial list of some goods: a computer, a car, a watch, a television set, friendship, and love. You will notice from our list that a good can be either tangible or intangible. A computer is a tangible good; friendship is an intangible good. Simply put, for something to be a good (whether tangible or intangible), it only has to give someone utility or satisfaction.

A **bad** is something that gives a person **disutility**, or dissatisfaction. If the flu gives you disutility or dissatisfaction, then it is a bad. If the constant nagging of an acquaintance is something that gives you disutility or dissatisfaction, then it is a bad.

People want goods, and they do not want bads. In fact, they will pay to get goods ("Here is $1,000 for the computer"), and they will pay to get rid of bads ("I'd be willing to pay you, doctor, if you can prescribe something that will shorten the time I have the flu").

Can something be a *good* for one person and a *bad* for another person? Smoking cigarettes gives some people utility; it gives others disutility. We conclude that smoking cigarettes can be a *good* for some people and a *bad* for others. This must be why the wife tells her husband, "If you want to smoke, you should do it outside." In other words, "Get those *bads* away from me."

1-2b   Resources

Goods do not just appear before us when we snap our fingers. It takes resources to produce goods. (Sometimes *resources* are referred to as *inputs* or *factors of production.*)

Generally, economists divide resources into four broad categories: *land, labor, capital,* and *entrepreneurship.*

- **Land** includes natural resources, such as minerals, forests, water, and unimproved land. For example, oil, wood, and animals fall into this category. (Sometimes economists refer to the category simply as *natural resources.*)

- **Labor** consists of the physical and mental talents that people contribute to the production process. For example, a person building a house is using his or her own labor.

- **Capital** consists of produced goods that can be used as inputs for further production. Factories, machinery, tools, computers, and buildings are examples of capital. One country might have more capital than another; that is, it has more factories, machinery, tools, and the like.

- **Entrepreneurship** refers to the talent that some people have for organizing the resources of land, labor, and capital to produce goods, seek new business opportunities, and develop new ways of doing things.

Good
Anything from which individuals receive utility or satisfaction.

Utility
The satisfaction one receives from a good.

Bad
Anything from which individuals receive disutility or dissatisfaction.

Disutility
The dissatisfaction one receives from a bad.

Land
All natural resources, such as minerals, forests, water, and unimproved land.

Labor
The work brought about by the physical and mental talents that people contribute to the production process.

Capital
Produced goods, such as factories, machinery, tools, computers, and buildings, that can be used as inputs for further production.

Entrepreneurship
The talent that some people have for organizing the resources of land, labor, and capital to produce goods, seek new business opportunities, and develop new ways of doing things.

1-2c Scarcity and a Definition of Economics

We are now ready to define a key concept in economics: *scarcity*. **Scarcity** is the condition in which our wants (for goods) are greater than the limited resources (land, labor, capital, and entrepreneurship) available to satisfy those wants. In other words, we want goods, but not enough resources are available to provide us with all the goods we want.

Look at it this way: Our wants (for goods) are infinite, but our resources (which we need to produce the goods) are finite. Scarcity is the result of our infinite wants hitting up against finite resources.

Many economists say that if scarcity didn't exist, neither would economics. In other words, if our wants weren't greater than the limited resources available to satisfy them, there would be no field of study called economics. This is similar to saying that if matter and motion didn't exist, neither would physics or that if living things didn't exist, neither would biology. For this reason, we define **economics** in this text as the science of scarcity. More completely, *economics is the science of how individuals and societies deal with the fact that wants are greater than the limited resources available to satisfy those wants.*

Scarcity
The condition in which our wants are greater than the limited resources available to satisfy those wants.

Economics
The science of scarcity; the science of how individuals and societies deal with the fact that wants are greater than the limited resources available to satisfy those wants.

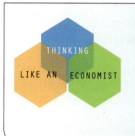

THINKING LIKE AN ECONOMIST

Scarcity Affects Everyone Everyone in the world—even a billionaire—has to face scarcity. Billionaires may be able to satisfy more of their wants for tangible goods (houses, cars) than most people, but they still may not have the resources to satisfy all their wants. Their wants might include more time with their children, more friendship, no disease in the world, peace on earth, and a hundred other things that they don't have the resources to "produce."

1-2d The Counterintuitive in Economics

As we said, scarcity is the condition in which our wants for goods and services are greater than the resources available to satisfy those wants. In other words, we want more than we can possibly have. If we stopped here—with only our definition of scarcity—we would leave thinking that we are doomed to a life of poverty—of not having enough. But that would leave the wrong impression. Scarcity can exist at the same time that wealth does. A society that faces scarcity can be a very wealthy society indeed—but there is no guarantee that it will be. Scarcity, a fact of life, can come with poverty or wealth.

To understand how scarcity can be consistent with either poverty or wealth, consider any country in the world today, either a rich one, like the United States, or a poor one, like Cuba. As measured by real output per capita, the United States is a rich country and Cuba is a poor country. Both countries, however, face scarcity. The people who live in both countries have infinite wants for goods and services and finite resources with which to produce those goods and services.

But if both countries face scarcity, then why is one of the countries rich and the other poor. If scarcity is all that matters, then why aren't both countries rich, or both countries poor? The answer is that the two countries do not function under the same economic and political systems. Stated differently, both the economic and political institutions in the two countries are different and it is the difference here that matters to poverty and wealth. To be more specific, consider how prices are determined in the two countries. In the United States, prices are determined largely by market forces. In Cuba, prices are determined largely by government edict.

Or consider the incentive to produce in the two countries. In the United States, people and firms can produce what they want to and not produce what they don't want to produce. In Cuba, these decisions are made largely by the government.

In the United States, profit and loss guide a whole host of economic choices; in Cuba, profit and loss are replaced with government officials who decide things like what gets produced, how much a worker gets paid, how much a seller can charge, and so on. In the United States, private property rights play a big role in determining how and what things get done; in Cuba, not so much.

The reason that Cuba is a poor country and the United States is a rich country isn't because Cuba faces scarcity and the United States does not—because, as we know, in both countries people must grapple with scarcity. Scarcity is a little like the sky: It exists everywhere, for everyone. The reason that Cuba is poor and the United States is rich is because of the different ways that the two countries deal with scarcity.

Economists often summarize by saying, "Institutions matter." What this means is that the economic and political institutions under which a country operates matter to the outcomes that the country faces. Or put it this way: Scarcity is a fact of life; it is how we deal with that fact of life that matters.

Thinking in Terms of Scarcity's Effects
Scarcity has effects. Here are three: (1) the need to make choices, (2) the need for a rationing device, and (3) competition.

Choices   People have to make choices because of scarcity. Because our unlimited wants are greater than our limited resources, some wants must go unsatisfied. We must choose which wants we will satisfy and which we will not. Jeremy asks, "Do I go to Hawaii, or do I pay off my car loan earlier?" Ellen asks, "Do I buy the new sweater or two new shirts?"

Rationing Device
A means for deciding who gets what of available resources and goods.

Need for a Rationing Device   A **rationing device** is a means of deciding who gets what of available resources and goods. Scarcity implies the need for a rationing device. If people have infinite wants for goods and if only limited resources are available to produce the goods, then a rationing device is needed to decide who gets the available quantity of goods. Dollar price is a rationing device. For example, 100 cars are on the lot, and everyone wants a new car. How do we decide who gets what quantity of the new cars? The answer is to use the rationing device called *dollar price*. The people who pay the dollar price for a new car end up with one.

Scarcity and Competition   Do you see competition in the world? Are people competing for jobs? Are states and cities competing for businesses? Are students competing for grades? The answer to all these questions is yes. The economist wants to know why this competition exists and what form it takes. First, the economist concludes, *competition exists because of scarcity*. If there were enough resources to satisfy all our seemingly unlimited wants, people would not have to compete for the available, but limited, resources.

Second, the economist sees that competition takes the form of people trying to get more of the rationing device. If dollar price is the rationing device, people compete to earn dollars. Look at your own case. You are a college student working for a degree. One reason (but perhaps not the only reason) you are attending college is to earn a higher income after graduation. But why do you want a higher income? You want it because it will allow you to satisfy more of your wants.

Suppose muscular strength (measured by lifting weights), instead of dollar price, were the rationing device. Then people with more muscular strength would receive more resources and goods than people with less muscular strength. In that case, people would compete for muscular strength. (Would they spend more time at the gym lifting weights?) The lesson is simple: *Whatever the rationing device is, people will compete for it.*

FINDING ECONOMICS

At the campus bookstore   To learn economics well, you must practice what you learn. One of the ways to practice economics is to find it in everyday life. Consider the following scene: You are in the campus bookstore buying a book for your computer science course, and you are handing over $85 to the cashier. Can you find the economics in this simple scene? Before you read on, think about it for a minute.

Let's work backward to find the economics. You are currently handing the cashier $85. We know that dollar price is a rationing device. But let's now ask ourselves why we would need a rationing device to get the book. The answer is scarcity. In other words, scarcity is casting its long shadow there in the bookstore as you buy a book. We have found one of the key economic concepts—scarcity—in the campus bookstore. (If you also said that a book is a good, then you have found even more economics in the bookstore. Can you find more than scarcity and a good?)

SELF-TEST

(Answers to Self-Test questions are in Answers to Self-Test Questions at the back of the book.)

1. True or false? Scarcity is the condition of finite resources. Explain your answer.

2. How does competition arise out of scarcity?

3. How does choice arise out of scarcity?

1-3 KEY CONCEPTS IN ECONOMICS

A number of key concepts in economics define the field. We discuss a few of these concepts next.

1-3a Opportunity Cost

So far, we have established that people must make choices because scarcity exists. In other words, because our seemingly unlimited wants push up against limited resources, some wants must go unsatisfied. We must therefore *choose* which wants we will satisfy and which we will not. The most highly valued opportunity or alternative forfeited when we make a choice is known as **opportunity cost**. Every time you make a choice, you incur an opportunity cost. For example, you have chosen to read this chapter. In making this choice, you denied yourself the benefits of doing something else. You could have watched television, written a text message to a friend, taken a nap, eaten a few slices of pizza, read a novel, shopped for a new computer, and so on. Whatever you *would have chosen* to do is the opportunity cost of your reading this chapter. For instance, if you would have watched television instead of reading this chapter—if that was your next best alternative—then the opportunity cost of reading the chapter is watching television.

Opportunity Cost
The most highly valued opportunity or alternative forfeited when a choice is made.

ECONOMICS 24/7

Rationing Spots at Yale

Each year, Yale University receives more applications for admission to the freshmen class than spots are available. In most years, for every 100 applications for admission that Yale receives, it can accept only seven applicants for admission. What Yale has to do, then, is ration its available admission spots.

How does it ration its available spots? One way is simply to use money as a rationing device. In other words, raise the dollar amount of attending Yale to a high enough level so that the number of spots equals the number of students willing and available to pay for admission. To illustrate, think of Yale as auctioning off spots in its freshman class. It calls out a price of $50,000 a year, and at this price more people wish to be admitted to Yale than there are spots available. Yale keeps on raising the price until the number of students who are willing and able to pay the tuition is equal to the number of available spots. Maybe this price is, say, $200,000.

As we know, Yale does not ration its available spots this way. In fact, it uses numerous rationing devices in an attempt to whittle down the number of applicants to the number of available spots. For example, it might use the rationing device of high school grades. Anyone with a GPA in high school of less than, say, 3.50 is not going to be admitted. If, after doing this, Yale still has too many applicants, it might then make use of the rationing device of standardized test scores. Anyone with an SAT score of under, say, 2100 is eliminated from the pool of applicants. If there are still too many applicants, then perhaps other rationing devices will be used, such as academic achievements, community service, degree of interest in attending Yale, and so on.

Yale might also decide that it wants to admit certain students over others, even if the two categories of students

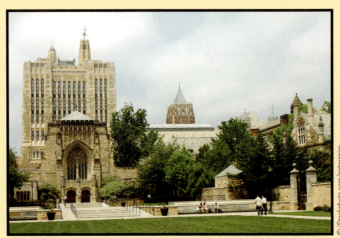

© iStockphoto.com/peterspiro

have the same academic credentials. For example, suppose Yale wants at least one student from each state in the country, and only 10 students from Wyoming have applied to go to Yale whereas 300 students from California have applied. Then Yale could very well use the rationing device of state diversity to decide in favor of the student from Wyoming instead of the applicant from California.

In the first week of April each year, Yale sends out many more rejection letters than acceptance letters. No doubt, some students who are rejected by Yale feel that some of the students who were accepted might not be as academically strong as they are. No doubt, the student with a 4.00 GPA and a perfect SAT score of 2400 feels that he might have been slighted by Yale when he learns that a student in his high school with a 3.86 GPA and SAT score of 2180 was chosen over him. What did the 3.86–2180 student have that he didn't have? What rationing device benchmark did the rejected student score lower on?

In life, you will often hear people arguing over what the rationing device for certain things should be. Should high school grades and standardized test scores be the only two rationing devices for college admission? What role should money play as a rationing device when a high school graduate applies to college? What role should ethnic or racial diversity, or state diversity, or income diversity play in the application process? Our point is a simple one: With scarcity comes the need for a rationing device. More people want a spot at Yale than there are spots available. Yale has to use one or more rationing devices to decide who will be accepted and who will be rejected.

There Is No Such Thing as a Free Lunch   Economists are fond of saying that *there is no such thing as a free lunch*. This catchy phrase expresses the idea that opportunity costs are incurred whenever choices are made. Perhaps this is an obvious point, but consider how often people mistakenly assume that there *is* a free lunch. For example, some parents think that education is free, because they do not pay tuition for their children to attend public elementary school. That's a misconception. "Free" implies no sacrifice and no opportunities forfeited, but an elementary school education requires resources that could be used for other things.

Consider the people who speak about free medical care, free housing, free bridges ("there's no charge to cross it"), and free parks. Again, free medical care, free housing, free bridges, and free parks are misconceptions. The resources that provide medical care, housing, bridges, and parks could have been used in other ways.

Zero Price Doesn't Mean Zero Cost A friend gives you a ticket to an upcoming concert for zero price (i.e., you pay nothing). Does it follow that zero price means zero cost? No. There is still an opportunity cost of attending the concert. Whatever you would be doing if you don't go to the concert is the opportunity cost of attending. To illustrate, if you don't attend the concert, you would hang out with friends. The value you place on hanging out with friends is the opportunity cost of your attending the concert.

1-3b Opportunity Cost and Behavior

Economists believe that a change in opportunity cost can change a person's behavior. For example, Ryan, who is a sophomore at college, attends classes Monday through Thursday of every week. Every time he chooses to go to class, he gives up the opportunity to do something else, such as earn $12 an hour working at a job. The opportunity cost of Ryan's spending an hour in class is $12.

Now let's raise the opportunity cost of attending class. On Tuesday, we offer Ryan $70 to skip his economics class. He knows that if he attends his economics class, he will forfeit $70. What will Ryan do? An economist would predict that as the opportunity cost of attending class increases relative to the benefits of attending, Ryan is less likely to go to class.

This is how economists think about behavior: *The higher the opportunity cost of doing something, the less likely it is that it will be done.* This is part of the economic way of thinking.

Look at Exhibit 1, which summarizes some of the things about scarcity, choice, and opportunity cost up to this point.

1-3c Benefits and Costs

If we could eliminate air pollution completely, should we do it? If your answer is yes, then you are probably focusing on the *benefits* of eliminating air pollution.

EXHIBIT 1

Scarcity and Related Concepts

Scarcity

→ Because of scarcity, a rationing device is needed. → Whatever the rationing device, people will compete for it. Scarcity and competition are linked.

→ Because of scarcity, people must make choices. → When choices are made, opportunity costs are incurred. → Changes in opportunity cost affect behavior.

FINDING ECONOMICS

In Being Late to Class John is often a few minutes late to his biology class. The class starts at 10 a.m., but John usually walks into the class at 10:03 a.m. The instructor has asked John to be on time, but John usually excuses his behavior by saying that the traffic getting to college was bad or that his alarm didn't go off at the right time or that something else happened to delay him.

One thing the instructor observes, though, is that John is never late when it comes to test day. He is usually in class a few minutes before the test begins. Where is the economics?

We would expect behavior to change as opportunity cost changes. When a test is being given in class, the opportunity cost of being late to class is higher than when a test is not being given and the instructor is simply lecturing. If John is late to class on test day, he then has fewer minutes to complete the test, and having less time can adversely affect his grade. In short, the higher the opportunity cost of being late to class, the less likely it is that John will be late.

For example, one benefit might be healthier individuals. Certainly, individuals who do not breathe polluted air have fewer lung disorders than people who do breathe polluted air.

But benefits rarely come without costs. The economist reminds us that, although eliminating pollution has its benefits, it has costs too. To illustrate, one way to eliminate all car pollution tomorrow is to pass a law stating that anyone caught driving a car will go to prison for 40 years. With such a law in place and enforced, very few people would drive cars and all car pollution would be a thing of the past. Presto! Cleaner air! However, many people would think that the cost of obtaining that cleaner air is too high. Someone might say, "I want cleaner air, but not if I have to completely give up driving my car. How will I get to work?"

What distinguishes the economist from the noneconomist is that the economist thinks in terms of *both* costs *and* benefits. Often, the noneconomist thinks in terms of one or the other. Studying has its benefits, but it has costs too. Coming to class has benefits,

ECONOMICS 24/7

Scarcity and Friendship

At first glance, scarcity and the number of friends you have probably seem unrelated. But friendship implies choice, and choice implies opportunity cost; thus, if a person incurs an opportunity cost when he or she makes a friend, the link between the number of friends a person has and scarcity is established.

But does a person incur an opportunity cost when he or she makes a friend? The answer is yes. First, you have to meet someone (could you be doing something else?), you have to talk to that person (could you be doing something else?), you may have to drive over to the person's house for a party (could you be doing something else?), you may have to invite the person over to your house for dinner (could you be doing something else?), and you have to be there for the person when he or she needs your help (could you be doing something else?). In short, making friends comes at a cost. (It comes with benefits too.)

Now, the higher the opportunity cost of making friends, the fewer friends you will have, all other things remaining constant. For example, the average five-year-old may say she has 10 friends and that she plays with each of them every week. The average 40-year-old may say he has four friends and that he talks to, or gets together with, maybe one or two every two weeks. Are adults less friendly than children, or do adults simply face higher opportunity costs of making friends than children do? We suggest that it is the latter. An adult who spent as much time a week making and keeping friends as a child does would have to forfeit the opportunity to work at a job and earn an income.

Pursuing the analysis, would there be any difference between the number of friends a person would have in a large city than in a small town? In large towns there are museums, plays, numerous restaurants, libraries, concerts, sports events, and, usually, better opportunities to earn a large income than exist in small towns. We conclude that the opportunity cost of making friends is higher in a large city than in a small town and that the "average" person will have fewer friends in a large city than in a small town. Perhaps this is why large cities are so often said to be cold and impersonal and small towns are said to be friendly.

© Rob Marmion/Shutterstock.com

but it has costs too. Getting up early each morning and exercising has its costs, but let's not forget that there are benefits too.

1-3d Decisions Made at the Margin

It is late at night, and you have already studied three hours for your biology test tomorrow. You look at the clock and wonder if you should study another hour. How would you summarize your thinking process? What question or questions do you ask yourself to decide whether to study another hour?

Perhaps without knowing it, you think in terms of the costs and benefits of further study. You probably realize that studying an additional hour has certain benefits (you may be able to raise your grade a few points), but it has costs too (you will get less sleep or have less time to watch television or talk on the phone with a friend). *That* you think in terms of costs and benefits, however, doesn't tell us *how* you think in terms of costs and benefits. For example, when deciding what to do, do you look at the total costs and total benefits of the proposed action, or do you look at something less than the total costs and benefits? According to economists, for most decisions, you think in terms of *additional,* or *marginal,* costs and benefits, not *total* costs and benefits. That's because most decisions deal with making a small, or additional, change.

To illustrate, suppose you just finished eating a hamburger and drinking a soda for lunch. You are still a little hungry and are considering whether to order another hamburger. An economist would say that, in deciding whether to order another hamburger, you compare the additional benefits of the second hamburger with its additional costs. In economics, the word *marginal* is a synonym for *additional.* So we say that you compare the **marginal benefits** (*MB*) of the (next) hamburger to its **marginal costs** (*MC*). If the marginal benefits are greater than the marginal costs, you obviously expect a net benefit to ordering the next hamburger, and therefore you order another. If, however, the marginal benefits are less than the marginal costs, you obviously expect a net cost to ordering the next hamburger, and therefore you do not order another. Logically, the situation is as follows:

Condition	Action
MB of next hamburger > MC of next hamburger	Buy next hamburger
MB of next hamburger < MC of next hamburger	Do not buy next hamburger

What you don't consider when making this decision are the *total* benefits and *total* costs of hamburgers. That's because the benefits and costs connected with the first hamburger (the one you have already eaten) are no longer relevant to the current decision. You are not deciding between eating two hamburgers or eating no hamburgers; your decision is whether to eat a second hamburger after you have already eaten one.

According to economists, when individuals make decisions by comparing marginal benefits with marginal costs, they are making **decisions at the margin**. The employee makes a decision at the margin in deciding whether to work two hours overtime; the economics professor makes a decision at the margin in deciding whether to put an additional question on the final exam.

Marginal Benefits
Additional benefits; the benefits connected with consuming an additional unit of a good or undertaking one more unit of an activity.

Marginal Costs
Additional costs; the costs connected with consuming an additional unit of a good or undertaking one more unit of an activity.

Decisions at the Margin
Decision making characterized by weighing the additional (marginal) benefits of a change against the additional (marginal) costs of a change with respect to current conditions.

ECONOMICS 24/7

When Is It Too Costly to Attend College?

Look around your class. Are there any big-name actors, sports stars, or comedians between the ages of 18 and 25 in your class? Probably not. The reason is that, for these people, the opportunity cost of attending college is much higher than it is for most 18-to-25-year-olds. Think of LeBron James, a basketball star, Chris Rock, a comedian, Johnny Depp, an actor, Will Smith, also an actor—these people and many more like them chose not to go to college. Why didn't they go to college? The fact is that they didn't go to college because it was too expensive for them to go to college. Not "too expensive" in the sense that the "tuition was too high," but expensive in terms of what they would have had to give up if they attended college—expensive in opportunity cost terms.

To understand this idea, think of what it's costing you to attend college. If you pay $3,000 tuition a semester for eight semesters, the full tuition amounts to $24,000. However, $24,000 is not the full cost of attending college, because if you were not a student, you could be earning income working at a job. For example, you could be working at a full-time job earning $32,000 annually. Certainly, this $32,000, or at least part of it if you are currently working part time, is forfeited because you are attending college. It is part of the total cost of your attending college.

The *tuition cost* may be the same for everyone who attends your college, but the *opportunity cost* is not. Some people have higher opportunity costs of attending college than others. It just so happens that Johnny Depp, LeBron James, Will Smith, and Chris Rock had extremely high opportunity costs of attending college. Each would have to give up hundreds of thousands of dollars if he were to attend college on a full-time basis.

Simply put, our story illustrates two related points we have made in this chapter. First, earlier we said that *the higher the opportunity cost of doing something, the less likely it will be done.* The opportunity cost of attending college is higher for some people than others, and that is why not everyone who can pay for college chooses to attend college.

Second, we said that economists believe that individuals think and act in terms of costs and benefits and that they undertake actions only if they expect the benefits to outweigh the costs. Thus, Johnny Depp, LeBron James, Will Smith, and Chris Rock saw certain benefits to attending college—just as you see certain benefits to attending college. But those benefits—although they may be the same for you and everyone else—are not enough to get everyone to attend college. That's because the benefits are not all that matters. The costs matter, too. In the case of Johnny Depp, LeBron James, Will Smith, and Chris Rock, the costs of attending college were much higher than the benefits, so they chose not to attend college. In your case, the benefits are higher than the costs, so you have decided to attend college.

© Domenic Gareri/Shutterstock.com

1-3e Efficiency

What is the right amount of time to study for a test? In economics, the *right amount* of anything is the *optimal* or *efficient* amount—the amount for which the marginal benefits equal the marginal costs. Stated differently, you have achieved **efficiency** when the marginal benefits equal the marginal costs.

Suppose you are studying for an economics test, and for the first hour of studying, the marginal benefits (*MB*) are greater than the marginal costs (*MC*):

MB studying first hour > MC studying first hour

Given this condition, you will certainly study for the first hour, because it is worth it: The additional benefits are greater than the additional costs, so there is a net benefit to studying.

Suppose, for the second hour of studying, the marginal benefits are still greater than the marginal costs:

MB studying second hour > MC studying second hour

Then you will study for the second hour, because the additional benefits are still greater than the additional costs. In other words, studying the second hour is worthwhile. In fact, you will continue to study as long as the marginal benefits are greater than the marginal costs. Exhibit 2 illustrates this discussion graphically.

The marginal benefit (*MB*) curve of studying is downward sloping because we have assumed that the benefits of studying for the first hour are greater than the benefits of studying for the second hour and so on. The marginal cost (*MC*) curve of studying is upward sloping because we have assumed that studying the second hour costs a person more (in terms of goods forfeited) than studying the first hour, studying the third hour costs more than studying the second, and so on. (If we assume that the additional costs of studying are constant over time, the *MC* curve is horizontal.)

Efficiency
Exists when marginal benefits equal marginal costs.

> **EXHIBIT 2**

Efficiency

MB = marginal benefits and *MC* = marginal costs. In the exhibit, the *MB* curve of studying is downward sloping and the *MC* curve of studying is upward sloping. As long as *MB* > *MC*, the person will study. The person stops studying when *MB* = *MC*. This point is where efficiency is achieved.

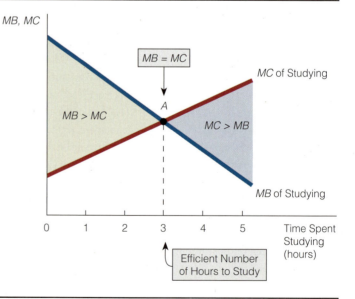

In the exhibit, the marginal benefits of studying equals the marginal costs of studying at three hours. So, three hours is the *efficient* length of time to study in this situation. At less than three hours, the marginal benefits of studying are greater than the marginal costs; thus, at all these hours, studying has net benefits. At more than three hours, the marginal costs of studying are greater than the marginal benefits, so studying beyond three hours is not worthwhile.

Maximizing Net Benefits   Take another look at Exhibit 2. Suppose you had stopped studying after the first hour (or, equivalently, after the 60th minute). Would you have given up anything? Yes, you would have given up the *net benefits* of studying longer. To illustrate, notice that between the first and the second hour, the marginal benefits (*MB*) curve lies above the marginal costs (*MC*) curve. This means that studying the second hour has net benefits. But if you hadn't studied that second hour—if you had stopped after the first hour—then you would have given up the opportunity to collect those net benefits. The same analysis holds for the third hour. We conclude that, by studying three hours (but not one minute longer), you have maximized net benefits. In short, efficiency, which is consistent with $MB = MC$, is also consistent with maximizing net benefits.

No $10 Bills on the Sidewalk An economist says that people try to maximize their net benefits. You ask for proof. The economist says, "You don't find any $10 bills on the sidewalk." What is the economist getting at by making this statement? Keep in mind that you don't find any $10 bills on the sidewalk because, if there were a $10 bill on the sidewalk, the first person to see it would pick it up; when you came along, it wouldn't be there. But why would the first person to find the $10 bill pick it up? The reason is that people don't pass by net benefits, and picking up the $10 bill comes with net benefits. The *benefits* of having an additional $10 are obvious; the *costs* of obtaining the additional $10 bill are simply what you give up during the time you are stooping down to pick it up. In short, the marginal benefits are likely to be greater than the marginal costs (giving us net benefits), and that is why the $10 bill is picked up. Saying that there are no $10 bills on the sidewalk is the same as saying that no one leaves net benefits on the sidewalk. In other words, people try to maximize net benefits.

1-3f Economics Is About Incentives

An **incentive** is something that encourages or motivates a person to undertake an action.

Often, what motivates a person to undertake an action is the belief that, by taking that action, she can make herself better off. For example, if we say that Jane has an incentive to study for the upcoming exam, we imply that, by studying, Jane can make herself better off, probably in terms of receiving a higher grade on the exam than if she didn't study.

Incentives are closely related to benefits and costs. Individuals have an incentive to undertake actions for which the benefits are greater than the costs or, stated differently, for which they expect to receive net benefits (benefits greater than costs).

Incentive
Something that encourages or motivates a person to undertake an action.

ECONOMICS 24/7

Is It Possible to Be Too Healthy and to Study Too Much?

There is a tendency to think that you can never get enough of some things. For example, someone might think that you can never get too healthy or that you can never study too much. But can you? Can you get too healthy? Can you study too much?

Consider the two tables that follow. The first looks at the marginal benefits and marginal costs of additional units of health, in dollar terms. The second looks at the marginal benefits and marginal costs of additional hours of studying (say, for an exam), in dollar terms.

Table 1

Units of Good Health	Marginal Benefits ($)	Marginal Costs ($)
1	10	3
2	9	4
3	8	7
4	7	9
5	6	10

Table 2

Hours of Studying	Marginal Benefits ($)	Marginal Costs ($)
1	9	2
2	8	3
3	7	4
4	6	5
5	5	8

Now let's tabulate the total benefits and total costs of good health and of studying? The total benefits of goods health is simply the sum of the various marginal benefits of the various units of good health. This is $40. The total cost of good health is $33. The total benefit of studying is $35 and the total cost is $22.

Now, if you simply compare the total benefits of good health with the total costs of good health, it would seem that you should try to achieve 5 units of good health. Obviously, it is worth it, right? The answer is no? That's because the fifth unit of good health comes with a greater cost than benefit. That is, the marginal cost of the fifth unit of good health is $10, whereas the marginal benefit of the fifth unit is only $6. Therefore, the person takes a "loss" on the fifth unit of good health. Can you get too much good health? Sure, 5 units of good health is too much. Of course, the same holds for the fourth unit, because, for that unit, the marginal costs of good health outweigh the marginal benefits. The "right amount" of good health is 3 units, because, for every unit from the first through the third, there is a "gain" to be had. For each of these units, the marginal benefit outweighs the marginal cost.

Applying the same logic to studying, we see that 5 hours of study is too much, because, at the fifth hour of study, the marginal costs are greater than the marginal benefits. The right amount of time to study is 4 hours. That doesn't mean, though, that you will get a higher grade on the exam studying 4 hours than 5. You could very well get a higher grade studying 5 hours instead of 4. What we mean when we say that studying 5 hours is too long for you to study is simply that, for that fifth hour, you incur greater additional costs than additional benefits. The "additional benefits" could be a higher grade (such as receiving an A instead of an A–). It's just that moving your grade from an A– to an A isn't worth it in terms of what you have to give up to get it. In other words, there could be additional benefits from studying more, but there are additional costs too, and for the fifth hour of study, the additional costs outweigh the additional benefits.

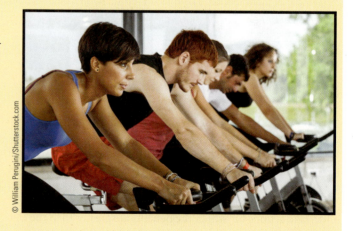

© William Perugini/Shutterstock.com

Economists are interested in what motivates behavior. Why does the person buy more of good X when its price falls? Why might a person work longer hours when income tax rates decline? Why might a person buy more of a particular good today if he expects the price of that good to go up next week? The general answer to many of these questions is that people do what they have an incentive to do. Economists then hunt for what the incentive is. For example, if a person buys more of good X when its price goes down, what specifically is the incentive? How, specifically, does the person make himself better off by buying a good when its price declines. Does he get more utility or satisfaction? Or how does a person make herself better off if she buys a good today that she expects will go up in price next week?

1-3g Unintended Effects

Economists think in terms of unintended effects. For example, Andrés, 16 years old, currently works after school at a grocery store. He earns $6.50 an hour.

Suppose the state legislature passes a law specifying that the minimum dollar wage a person can be paid to do a job is $9.50 an hour. The legislators' intention in passing the law is to help people like Andrés earn more income.

Will the $9.50-an-hour legislation have the intended effect? Perhaps not. The manager of the grocery store may not find it worthwhile to continue employing Andrés if she has to pay him $9.50 an hour. In other words, Andrés may have a job at $6.50 an hour but not at $9.50 an hour. If the law specifies that no one may earn less than $9.50 an hour and the manager of the grocery store decides to fire Andrés rather than pay that amount, then an unintended effect of the legislation is Andrés losing his job.

As another example, let's analyze mandatory seat-belt laws to see whether they have any unintended effects. States have laws that require drivers to wear seat belts. The intended effect is to reduce the number of car-related fatalities by making it more likely that drivers will survive accidents.

Could these laws have an unintended effect? Some economists think so. They look at accident fatalities in terms of this equation:

$$\text{Total number of fatalities} = \text{Number of accidents} \times \text{Fatalities per accident}$$

For example, if there are 200,000 accidents and 0.10 fatality per accident, the total number of fatalities is 20,000.

The objective of a mandatory seat-belt program is to reduce the total number of fatalities by reducing the number of fatalities per accident (the fatality rate). Many studies have found that wearing seat belts does just that. If you are in an accident, you have a better chance of not being killed if you are wearing a seat belt.

Let's assume that, with seat belts, there is 0.08, instead of 0.10, fatality per accident. If there are still 200,000 accidents, then the total number of fatalities falls from 20,000 to 16,000. Thus, as the following table shows, the total number of fatalities drops if the number of fatalities per accident is reduced and the number of accidents is constant:

Number of Accidents	Fatalities per Accident	Total Number of Fatalities
200,000	0.10	20,000
200,000	0.08	16,000

However, some economists wonder whether the number of accidents stays constant. Specifically, they suggest that seat belts may have an unintended effect: *The number of accidents may increase* because wearing seat belts may make drivers feel safer. Feeling safer may cause them to take chances that they wouldn't ordinarily take, such as driving faster or more aggressively, or concentrating less on their driving and more on the music on the radio. For example, if the number of accidents rises to 250,000, then the total number of fatalities is again 20,000:

Number of Accidents	Fatalities per Accident	Total Number of Fatalities
200,000	0.10	20,000
250,000	0.08	20,000

We conclude the following: If a mandatory seat-belt law reduces the number of fatalities per accident (the intended effect) but increases the number of accidents (an unintended effect), then the law may not, contrary to popular belief, reduce the total number of fatalities. In fact, some economics studies show just that.

What does all this mean for you? You may be safer if you know that this unintended effect exists and you adjust accordingly. To be specific, when you wear your seat belt, your chances of getting hurt in a car accident are less than if you don't wear your seat belt. But if this added sense of protection causes you to drive less carefully than you would otherwise, then you could unintentionally offset the measure of protection your seat belt provides. To reduce the probability of hurting yourself and others in a car accident, *the best policy is to wear a seat belt and to drive as carefully as you would if you weren't wearing a seat belt.* Knowing about the unintended effect of wearing your seat belt could save your life.

1-3h Exchange

Exchange, or **trade**, is the giving up of one thing for something else. Economics is sometimes called the "science of exchange" because so much that is discussed in economics has to do with exchange.

We start with a basic question: Why do people enter into exchanges? The answer is that they do so to make themselves better off. When a person voluntarily trades $100 for a jacket, she is saying, "I prefer to have the jacket instead of the $100." And, of course, when the seller of the jacket voluntarily sells the jacket for $100, he is saying, "I prefer to have the $100 instead of the jacket." In short, through trade or exchange, each person gives up something he values less for something he values more.

You can think of trade in terms of utility or satisfaction. Imagine a utility scale that goes from 1 to 10, with 10 being the highest utility you can achieve. Now, suppose you currently have $40 in your wallet and you are at 7 on the utility scale. A few minutes later, you are in a store looking at some new CDs. The price of each is $10, and you end up buying four CDs for $40.

After you traded your $40 for the four CDs, are you still at 7 on the utility scale? The likely answer is no. If you expected to have the same utility after the trade as you did before, you probably would not have traded your $40 for the four CDs. The only reason you entered into the trade is that you *expected* to be better off after the trade than you were before it. In other words, you thought that trading your $40 for the four CDs would move you up the utility scale from 7 to, say, 8.

ECONOMICS 24/7

Can Incentives Make You Smarter?

Most people seem to think themselves smarter when it comes to some things than other things. For example, a person may say that she is fairly smart when it comes to learning biology, but not so smart when it comes to learning mathematics. Another person might say that he is smart when it comes to fixing cars, but not so smart when it comes to learning languages.

Now ask yourself if incentives can affect how smart you are when it comes to any given subject: economics, mathematics, biology, history, and so on. Consider the experiment described next, and consider what you think the results of the experiment are likely to be.

An economics instructor teaches two classes of economics, A and B. In each class there are 45 students, and in each class the instructor gives the same eight quizzes. In class A, the instructor tells each student that, for every quiz on which the student receives a grade of 90 or higher, he or she will receive $100. In class B, the instructor offers no such incentive.

Now predict whether grades in the two classes will be the same or different? If different, in which class, A or B, are students likely to earn higher grades? Finally, ask yourself if you would study harder for a quiz given in class A or class B? If your answer to the last question is class A (in which there is a chance of earning $800 over eight quizzes), then it is very likely that your grades will be higher in class A than in class B. In fact, by studying harder and earning higher grades, you might even end up concluding that you are smarter when it comes to economics than you thought you were. It's very likely

© wavebreakmedia/Shutterstock.com

that the incentive encouraged or motivated you to study harder (and more), which then had the unintended effect of getting you to realize you were smarter than you initially thought.

Now suppose someone asks how smart you are when it comes to physics or mathematics. If you feel that these subjects are beyond you somehow, you might say, "I don't think I am that smart when it comes to physics or mathematics. I don't really understand a lot that is taught in those subjects." But perhaps the correct answer is, "I'm not sure how smart or not I am when it comes to physics or mathematics. A lot depends on the incentives that exist to learn physics and mathematics. Under certain incentives, I seem to be smarter than under other incentives."

SELF-TEST

1. Give an example to illustrate how a change in opportunity cost can affect behavior.

2. Studying has both costs and benefits. If you continue to study (say, for a test) for as long as the marginal benefits of studying are greater than the marginal costs, and you stop studying when the two are equal, will your action

be consistent with having maximized the net benefits of studying? Explain your answer.

3. You stay up an additional hour to study for a test. The intended effect is to raise your test grade. What might be an unintended effect of staying up another hour to study?

1-4 THE MARKET AND GOVERNMENT

In recent years, major economic problems and issues have plagued the United States, such as the following:

- Financial problems in the banking sector

- The economic effects of falling real estate prices

- Growing federal budget deficits

- Downgrading of the U.S. debt

- A fall in economic activity, as measured by the total output of goods and services produced in the country

- High unemployment

- The looming crisis in Social Security

- Health-care issues

- Issues related to climate change and the environment

- The proper role of monetary policy

- The proper role of government regulatory policy in the economy, and much more

When it comes to economic problems, the national debate usually proceeds along these lines:

- First, the problem is *identified* and *defined* or *described*.

- Second, individuals attempt to identify the *cause* of the problem.

- Third, individuals propose *solutions* to the problem.

This three-step process was evident in recent discussions of the U.S. financial crisis of 2007–2009 and in discussions of health care. After first *identifying* the financial crisis and describing it, individuals turned to identifying its *cause(s)* and proposing *solutions*.

In this process, there is little debate about identifying the problem. Most of the debate focuses on the cause(s) of the problem and the proposed solutions. With respect to both the cause and the solution, we often hear two words mentioned: the "market" and "government." For example, we might have the following claims:

- *Either:* The *market* (or capitalism) is the *cause* of the problem.

- *Or:* The *government* is the *cause* of the problem.

- *Either:* The *market* (or capitalism) is the solution to the problem.

- *Or:* The *government* is the solution to the problem.

The market-versus-government debate is an important one to know about, but it takes time to learn the particulars. Much of this book will help you learn those particulars, including the following ones:

- How a market system works.

- What markets are and are not capable of doing.

- How government operates.

- How government actions and policies can affect the market system.

At this point, you may be wondering why we don't simply tell you the "right" way to think. Your thinking might be, "Well, which is it? Did the market or government *cause* the problem? Is the market or government the *solution*?" If these are your questions, we sympathize with your frustration over not getting straight answers. We resist telling you the "right" answer for two reasons: First, not all economists agree on what the "right" answer is in a given case. Second, knowing the "right" answer without first understanding how markets and how governments work will leave you feeling unsatisfied because you will have little foundation on which to understand the answer. After all, no matter which "right" answer we give you now, you are going to want it explained, and this book is part of that explanation.

1-5 *CETERIS PARIBUS* AND THEORY

We cover two important topics in this section: (1) *ceteris paribus* and (2) theory.

1-5a *Ceteris Paribus* Thinking

Wilson has eaten regular ice cream for years, and for years his weight has been 170 pounds. One day, Wilson decides he wants to lose weight. With this objective in mind, he buys a new fat-free ice cream at the grocery store. The fat-free ice cream has half the calories of regular ice cream.

Wilson eats the fat-free ice cream for the next few months. He then weighs himself and finds that he has gained two pounds. Does this mean that fat-free ice cream causes people to gain weight and regular ice cream does not? The answer is no. Why, then, did Wilson gain weight when he substituted fat-free ice cream for regular ice cream? Perhaps Wilson ate three times as much fat-free ice cream as regular ice cream. Or perhaps during the time he was eating fat-free ice cream, he wasn't exercising, and during the time he was eating regular ice cream, he was exercising. In other words, a number of factors—such as eating more ice cream or exercising less—may have offset the weight loss that Wilson would have experienced had these other factors not changed.

Now, suppose you want to make the point that Wilson would have lost weight by substituting fat-free ice cream for regular ice cream had these other factors not changed. What would you say? A scientist would say, "If Wilson has been eating regular ice cream and his weight has stabilized at 170 pounds, then substituting fat-free ice cream for regular ice cream will lead to a decline in weight, *ceteris paribus*."

The term **ceteris paribus** means "all other things constant" or "nothing else changes." In our ice cream example, if nothing else changes—such as how much ice cream Wilson eats, how much exercise he gets, and so on—then switching to fat-free ice cream will result in weight loss. This expectation is based on the theory that a reduction in calorie consumption will result in weight loss and an increase in calorie consumption will result in weight gain.

Using the *ceteris paribus* assumption is important because, with it, we can clearly designate what we believe is the correct relationship between two variables. In the ice cream example, we can designate the correct relationship between calorie intake and weight gain.

Economists don't often talk about ice cream, but they will often make use of the *ceteris paribus* assumption. An economist might say, "If the price of a good decreases, the quantity of it consumed increases, *ceteris paribus*." For example, if the price of Pepsi-Cola decreases, people will buy more of it, assuming that nothing else changes.

Ceteris Paribus
A Latin term meaning "all other things constant" or "nothing else changes."

But some people ask, "Why would economists want to assume that when the price of Pepsi-Cola falls, nothing else changes? Don't other things change in the real world? Why make assumptions that we know are not true?"

Of course, economists do not specify *ceteris paribus* because they want to say something false about the world. They specify it because they want to clearly define what they believe to be the real-world relationship between two variables. Look at it this way: If you drop a ball off the roof of a house, it will fall to the ground, unless someone catches it. This statement is true, and probably everyone would willingly accept it as true. But here is another true statement: If you drop a ball off the roof of a house, it will fall to the ground, *ceteris paribus*. In fact, the two statements are identical in meaning. This is because adding the phrase "unless someone catches it" in the first sentence is the same as saying "*ceteris paribus*" in the second sentence. If one statement is acceptable to us, the other should be too.

1-5b What Is a Theory?

Almost everyone, including you, builds and tests theories or models on a regular basis. (In this text, the words *theory* and *model* are used interchangeably.) Perhaps you thought that only scientists and others with high-level mathematics at their fingertips built and tested theories. However, theory building and testing is not the domain of only the highly educated and mathematically proficient. Almost everyone builds and test theories.

People build theories any time they do not know the answer to a question. Someone asks, "Why is the crime rate higher in the United States than in Belgium?" Or, "Why did Aaron's girlfriend break up with him?" Or, "Why does Professor Avalos give easier final exams than Professor Shaw, even though they teach the same subject?" If you don't know the answer to a question, you are likely to build a theory so that you can provide an answer.

Theory

An abstract representation of the real world designed with the intent to better understand it.

Abstraction

The process (used in building a theory) of focusing on a limited number of variables to explain or predict an event.

What exactly is a theory? To an economist, a **theory** is an abstract representation of the world. In this context, **abstract** means that you omit certain variables or factors when you try to explain or understand something. For example, suppose you were to draw a map for a friend, showing him how to get from his house to yours. Would you draw a map that showed every single thing your friend would see on the trip, or would you simply draw the main roads and one or two landmarks? If you'd do the latter, you would be abstracting from reality; you would be omitting certain things.

You would abstract for two reasons. First, to get your friend from his house to yours, you don't need to include everything on your map. Simply noting main roads may be enough. Second, if you did note everything on your map, your friend might get confused. Giving too much detail could be as bad as giving too little.

When economists build a theory or model, they do the same thing you do in drawing a map. They abstract from reality; they leave out certain things. They focus on the major factors or variables that they believe will explain the phenomenon they are trying to understand.

Suppose a criminologist's objective is to explain why some people turn to crime. Before actually building the theory, he considers a number of variables that may explain why some people become criminals: (1) the ease of getting a gun, (2) child-rearing practices, (3) the neighborhood a person grew up in, (4) whether a person was abused as a child, (5) family education, (6) the type of friends a person has, (7) a person's IQ, (8) climate, and (9) a person's diet.

The criminologist may think that some of these variables greatly affect the chance that a person will become a criminal, some affect it only slightly, and others do not affect it at all. For example, a person's diet may have only a 0.0001 percent effect on the person becoming a criminal, whereas whether a person was abused as a child may have a 30 percent effect.

A theory emphasizes only the variables that the theorist believes are the main or critical ones that explain an activity or event. Thus, if the criminologist in our example thinks that parental child-rearing practices and family education are likely to explain much more about criminal behavior than the other variables are, then his (abstract) theory will focus on these two variables and ignore the others.

All theories are abstractions from reality. But it doesn't follow that (abstract) theories cannot explain reality. The objective in theory building is to ignore the variables that are essentially irrelevant to the case at hand, making it easier to isolate the important variables that the untrained observer would probably miss.

In the course of reading this text, you will come across numerous theories. Some of these theories are explained in words, and others are represented graphically. For example, Chapter 3 presents the theory of supply and demand. First, the parts of the theory are explained. Then the theory is represented graphically in terms of a supply curve and a demand curve.

What to Ask a Theorist

Physicists, chemists, and economists aren't the only persons who build and test theories. Historians, sociologists, anthropologists, and many others build and test theories. In fact, as suggested earlier in this section, almost everyone builds theories (although not everyone tests theories).

Anytime you listen to someone expound on a theory, you should always ask a key question: *"If your theory is correct, what do you predict we will see in the world?"* To illustrate, let's consider a very simple example. Suppose your history professor comes to class each day clean shaven and dressed in slacks, shirt, tie, and sports jacket. One day he comes to class unshaven and dressed in jeans and a somewhat wrinkled T-shirt. The difference in appearance is obvious. You turn to your friend who sits next to you in class and ask, "What do you think explains the difference in his appearance and dress?"

Notice that you have asked a question that does not have an obvious answer. Such questions are ripe for theory building. Your friend proposes an explanation. She says, "I think the professor forgot to set his alarm clock last night. He got up late this morning and didn't have time to shave or to dress the way he usually does. He just threw on the first clothes he found and rushed to class."

Your friend has advanced a theory of sorts. She has implicitly assumed that the professor wants to shave and dress in slacks, shirt, tie, and sports jacket but that some unusual event prevented him from doing so today.

Somehow, you don't think your friend's theory is correct. Instead, you think your history professor has decided to make a life change of some sort. He has decided to look more casual, to take life a little easier, to be less formal. You tell your friend what you think explains your professor's new behavior.

You, like your friend, have advanced a theory of sorts. Whose theory, if either, is correct? Now is the time for you to ask your friend, and your friend to ask you, *"If your theory is correct, what do you predict we will see in the world?"*

Your friend's answer should be, "If my theory is correct, then the next time the professor comes to class, he will be clean shaven and dressed in his old way—slacks, shirt, tie, and sports jacket." Your answer should be, "If *my* theory is correct, then the next time the professor comes to class, he will be unshaven and dressed as he is today—in jeans, T-shirt, and the like."

The question—If your theory is correct, what do you predict we will see in the world?—gives us a way to figure out who might be closer to the truth when people disagree. It minimizes talk and maximizes the chances of establishing who is correct and who is incorrect.

ECONOMICS 24/7

When Are People the Most Likely to "Lose" Library Books? The Case of Alchian and Allen's *University Economics*

Do all the theories that economists build and test have to be "big" theories—theories about prices, unemployment, interest rates, economic growth, and so on? Not at all. An economist can build a theory about almost anything, such as why some library books have a higher probability of not being returned than others.

Start with the obvious: Every day, individuals borrow books from public and college libraries, but not every book borrowed is returned. If a book is not returned, it is because either (1) the book borrower misplaced or lost the book, (2) the book borrower forgot to return the book, or (3) the book borrower decided to keep the book.

Does every book in a library (such as your college library) have an equal chance of not being returned? Most persons say no, because not every book has the same probability of being borrowed. Before a book is not returned, it has to be borrowed; so books with a higher probability of being borrowed have a higher probability of not being returned.

But why do some books have a higher probability of being borrowed? One answer is that people either want to read (for pleasure) or have to read (say, for a class) some books more than others. Books are also borrowed if the borrower intends to sell the borrowed book, a possibility that brings us to a well-known

economics text, *University Economics: Elements of Inquiry*, by Armen A. Alchian and William R. Allen.

University Economics was published in the mid-1960s to early 1970s. Economists often say that it is one of the best introductory economics books ever written. Although the book has been out of print for years, you can still buy a copy of it. On September 12, 2013, the book could be purchased on Amazon.com for $1,877.

What does the $1,877 price mean for the copies of *University Economics* that sit on library bookshelves in college and public libraries all over the country? It means that those copies have a high probability of being checked out of the libraries and never returned. In other words, they have a high probability of being checked out and "lost."

But don't the libraries charge borrowers for the books they lose and never return? Sure they do, and the price they charge will have much to do with whether the borrower "chooses" to lose the book in the first place. If the library charges the borrower the purchase price of the book instead of the replacement price, the borrower has a stronger incentive to lose the book. To illustrate, suppose the library purchased *University Economics* 10 years ago for $150. If it charges this price, the borrower is more likely to lose the book than if the library charges the price it has to pay to replace the book ($1,877). In short, library policies will influence how many copies of *University Economics* end up not being returned.

SELF-TEST

1. What is the purpose of building a theory?

2. How might a theory of the economy differ from a description of it?

3. Why is it important to test a theory? Why not simply accept a theory if it sounds right?

4. Your economics instructor says, "If the price of going to the movies goes down, people will go to the movies more often." A student in class says, "Not if the quality of the movies goes down." Who is right, the economics instructor or the student?

1-6 ECONOMIC CATEGORIES

Economics is sometimes broken down into different categories according to the type of questions asked. Four common economic categories are positive economics, normative economics, microeconomics, and macroeconomics.

1-6a Positive Economics and Normative Economics

Positive economics attempts to determine *what is*. **Normative economics** addresses *what should be*. Essentially, positive economics deals with cause–effect relationships that can be tested. Normative economics deals with value judgments and opinions that cannot be tested.

Many topics in economics can be discussed in both a positive and a normative framework. Consider a proposed cut in federal income taxes. An economist practicing positive economics would want to know the *effect* of a cut in income taxes. For example, she may want to know how a tax cut will affect the unemployment rate, economic growth, inflation, and so on. An economist practicing normative economics would address issues that directly or indirectly relate to whether the federal income tax *should* be cut. For example, he may say that federal income taxes should be cut because the income tax burden on many taxpayers is currently high.

This book deals mainly with positive economics. For the most part, we discuss the economic world as it is, not the way someone might think it should be. Keep in mind, too, that no matter what your normative objectives are, positive economics can shed some light on how they might be accomplished. For example, suppose you believe that absolute poverty should be eliminated and that the unemployment rate should be lowered. No doubt you have ideas as to how these goals can be accomplished. But will your ideas work? For example, will a greater redistribution of income eliminate absolute poverty? Will lowering taxes lower the unemployment rate? There is no guarantee that the means you think will bring about certain ends will do so. This is where sound positive economics can help us see what is. As someone once said, "It is not enough to want to do good; it is important also to know how to do good."

1-6b Microeconomics and Macroeconomics

It has been said that the tools of microeconomics are microscopes and the tools of macroeconomics are telescopes. Macroeconomics stands back from the trees to see the forest. Microeconomics gets up close and examines the tree itself—its bark, its limbs, and its roots. **Microeconomics** is the branch of economics that deals with human behavior and choices as they relate to relatively small units: an individual, a firm, an industry, a single market. **Macroeconomics** is the branch of economics that deals with human behavior and choices as they relate to an entire economy. In microeconomics, economists discuss a single price; in macroeconomics, they discuss the price level. Microeconomics deals with the demand for a particular good or service; macroeconomics deals with aggregate, or total, demand for goods and services. Microeconomics examines how a tax change affects a single firm's output; macroeconomics looks at how a tax change affects an entire economy's output.

Microeconomists and macroeconomists ask different types of questions. A microeconomist might be interested in answering such questions as the following:

- How does a market work?
- What level of output does a firm produce?
- What price does a firm charge for the good it produces?

Positive Economics
The study of "what is" in economics.

Normative Economics
The study of "what should be" in economics.

Microeconomics
The branch of economics that deals with human behavior and choices as they relate to relatively small units: an individual, a firm, an industry, a single market.

Macroeconomics
The branch of economics that deals with human behavior and choices as they relate to highly aggregate markets (e.g., the market for goods and services) or the entire economy.

- How does a consumer determine how much of a good to buy?
- Can government policy affect business behavior?
- Can government policy affect consumer behavior?

A macroeconomist, by contrast, might be interested in answering such questions as these:

- How does the economy work?
- Why is the unemployment rate sometimes high and sometimes low?
- What causes inflation?
- Why do some national economies grow faster than others?
- What might cause interest rates to be low one year and high the next?
- How do changes in the money supply affect the economy?
- How do changes in government spending and taxes affect the economy?

Office ✦ Hours

"I Don't Believe That Every Time a Person Does Something, He Compares the Marginal Benefits and Costs"

STUDENT:

In class yesterday, you said that individuals compare the marginal benefits (*MB*) of doing something (say, exercising) with the marginal costs (*MC*). If the marginal benefits are greater than the marginal costs, they exercise; if the marginal costs are greater than the marginal benefits, they don't. Here is what I am having a problem with: I don't believe that every time people do something, they compare the marginal benefits and costs. I think people do some things without thinking of benefits and costs; they do some things instinctively or because they have always done them.

INSTRUCTOR:

Can you give an example?

STUDENT:

I don't think of the benefits and costs of eating breakfast in the morning; I just eat breakfast. I don't think of the benefits and costs of doing my homework; I just do the homework before it is due. For me, many activities are automatic; I do them without thinking.

INSTRUCTOR:

It doesn't necessarily follow that you are not considering benefits and costs when you do something automatically. All you have to do is sense whether doing something comes with net benefits (benefits greater than costs) or net costs (costs greater than benefits). All you have to do is sense whether something is likely to make you better off or worse off. You eat breakfast in the morning because you have "decided" that it makes you better off. But making you better off is no different from saying that you receive net benefits from eating breakfast, which is no different from saying that the benefits of eating breakfast are greater than the costs. In other words, "better off" equals "net benefits" equals "benefits greater than costs."

STUDENT:

I see what you're saying. But then how would you explain the fact that Smith smokes cigarettes and Jones does not. If both Smith and Jones consider the benefits and costs of smoking cigarettes, then it seems that either both would have to smoke or both would have to not smoke. The fact that different people do different things tells me that not everyone is considering the costs and benefits of their actions. If everyone did, they would all do the same thing.

INSTRUCTOR:

I disagree. Not everyone sees the costs and benefits of the same thing the same way. Smith and Jones may not see the benefits or costs of smoking the same way. For Smith, the benefits of smoking may be high, but for Jones they may be low. It is no different from saying different people estimate the benefits of playing chess or eating a doughnut or riding a bicycle differently. The same holds for costs. Not everyone will estimate the costs of playing chess or eating a doughnut or riding a bicycle the same way. The costs of a person with diabetes eating a doughnut are much higher than the costs of a person without diabetes eating a doughnut.

STUDENT:

Let me see if I have this right. You are making two points. First, not everyone has the same benefits and costs of, say, running a mile.

Second, everyone who does run a mile believes that the benefits are greater than the costs, and everyone who does not run a mile believes that the costs are greater than the benefits.

INSTRUCTOR:

Yes, that's it. Everybody is trying to make himself better off (reap net benefits), but not everybody will do *X* because not everybody will be made better off by doing *X*.

Points to remember

1. If you undertake those actions for which you expect to receive net benefits, then you are "thinking" in terms of costs and benefits. Specifically, you expect the marginal benefits to be greater than the marginal costs.
2. The costs and benefits of doing any activity are not necessarily the same for everybody. Smith may expect higher benefits than Jones when it comes to doing *X*; Jones may expect higher costs than Smith when it comes to doing *X*.

CHAPTER SUMMARY

GOODS, BADS, AND RESOURCES

- A good is anything that gives a person utility or satisfaction.
- A bad is anything that gives a person disutility or dissatisfaction.
- Economists divide resources into four categories: land, labor, capital, and entrepreneurship.
- Land includes natural resources, such as minerals, forests, water, and unimproved land.
- Labor is brought about by the physical and mental talents that people contribute to the production process.
- Capital consists of produced goods, such as machinery, tools, computers, trucks, buildings, and factories, that can be used as inputs for further production.
- Entrepreneurship is the talent that some people have for organizing the resources of land, labor, and capital to produce goods, seek new business opportunities, and develop new ways of doing things.

SCARCITY

- Scarcity is the condition in which our wants are greater than the limited resources available to satisfy them.

- Scarcity implies choice. In a world of limited resources, we must choose which wants will be satisfied and which will go unsatisfied.
- Because of scarcity, there is a need for a rationing device. A rationing device is a means of deciding who gets what quantities of the available resources and goods.
- Scarcity implies competition. If resources were ample to satisfy all our seemingly unlimited wants, people would not have to compete for the available, but limited, resources.

OPPORTUNITY COST

- Every time a person makes a choice, he or she incurs an opportunity cost. Opportunity cost is the most highly valued opportunity or alternative forfeited when a choice is made. The higher the opportunity cost of doing something, the less likely it is that it will be done.

COSTS AND BENEFITS

- What distinguishes the economist from the noneconomist is that the economist thinks in terms of *both* costs and benefits. Asked what the benefits of taking a walk may be, an economist will also mention the related costs. Asked what the costs of studying are, an economist will also point out its benefits.

DECISIONS MADE AT THE MARGIN

• Marginal benefits and costs are not the same as total benefits and costs. When deciding whether to talk on the phone one more minute, an individual would not consider the total benefits and total costs of speaking on the phone. Instead, the person would compare only the marginal benefits (additional benefits) of talking on the phone one more minute with the marginal costs (additional costs) of talking on the phone one more minute.

INCENTIVES

• An incentive is something that encourages or motivates a person to undertake an action. Incentives are closely related to benefits and costs. Individuals have an incentive to undertake actions for which the benefits are greater than the costs or, stated differently, for which they expect to receive some net benefits (benefits greater than costs).

EFFICIENCY

• As long as the marginal benefits of an activity are greater than its marginal costs, a person gains by continuing to do the activity—whether the activity is studying, running, eating, or watching television. The net benefits of an activity are maximized when the marginal benefits of the activity equal its marginal costs. Efficiency exists at this point.

UNINTENDED EFFECTS

• Economists often think in terms of causes and effects. Effects may be either intended or unintended. Economists want to denote both types of effects when speaking of effects in general.

EXCHANGE

• Exchange, or trade, is the process of giving up one thing for something else. People enter into exchanges to make themselves better off.

CETERIS PARIBUS

• *Ceteris paribus* is a Latin term that means "all other things constant" or "nothing else changes." *Ceteris paribus* is used to designate what we believe is the correct relationship between two variables.

THE MARKET AND THE GOVERNMENT

• When it comes to economic problems and issues, we often see the following three-step process: (1) The problem is identified, and then it is defined or described. (2) The causes of the problem are identified. (3) Proposed solutions to the problem are put forth. With respect to both the cause(s) of the problem and the proposed solutions to the problem, we often hear individuals speaking about the market and the government. Opinions differ as to whether the market or the government is the cause of the problem. Similarly, opinions differ as to whether the market or the government is the solution to the problem. Much of this text will focus on the market-versus-government debate that lies beneath the surface of many economic problems and issues.

THEORY

• Economists build theories to explain and predict real-world events. Theories are necessarily abstractions from, as opposed to descriptions of, the real world.

• All theories abstract from reality; they focus on the critical variables that the theorist believes explain and predict the phenomenon in question.

ECONOMIC CATEGORIES

• Positive economics attempts to determine what is; normative economics addresses what should be.

• Microeconomics deals with human behavior and choices as they relate to relatively small units: an individual, a firm, an industry, a single market. Macroeconomics deals with human behavior and choices as they relate to an entire economy.

KEY TERMS AND CONCEPTS

Good	Entrepreneurship	Decisions at the Margin	Positive Economics
Utility	Scarcity	Efficiency	Normative Economics
Bad	Economics	Incentive	Microeconomics
Disutility	Rationing Device	Exchange (Trade)	Macroeconomics
Land	Opportunity Cost	*Ceteris Paribus*	
Labor	Marginal Benefits	Theory	
Capital	Marginal Costs	Abstract	

VIDEO QUESTIONS AND PROBLEMS

Video Questions and Problems are available on MindTap for Arnold 12e or by searching for Arnold on www.cengagebrain.com

1. There are 30 students in an economics class. Is the opportunity cost of attending the class the same for each of the 30 students? Why or why not.

2. Scarcity is the condition in which peoples' wants (for goods and services) are unlimited or infinite. Do you agree or disagree? Explain your answer.

3. Explain what it means to make a decision "at the margin."

4. Can a person exercise "too much"? Explain your answer

5. All theories are "abstractions" from reality. What does this mean?

QUESTIONS AND PROBLEMS

1. The United States is considered a rich country because Americans can choose from an abundance of goods and services. How can there be scarcity in a land of abundance?

2. Give two examples for each of the following: (a) an intangible good, (b) a tangible good, (c) a bad.

3. Give an example of something that is a good for one person and a bad for someone else.

4. What do economists mean when they say that "institutions matter"?

5. What is the difference between labor as a resource and entrepreneurship as a resource?

6. Can either scarcity or one of the effects of scarcity be found in a car dealership? Explain your answer.

7. Explain the link between scarcity and each of the following: (a) choice, (b) opportunity cost, (c) the need for a rationing device, (d) competition.

8. Is it possible for a person to incur an opportunity cost without spending any money? Explain.

9. Discuss the opportunity costs of attending college for four years. Is college more or less costly than you thought it was? Explain.

10. Explain the relationship between changes in opportunity cost and changes in behavior.

11. Smith says that we should eliminate all pollution in the world. Jones disagrees. Who is more likely to be an economist, Smith or Jones? Explain your answer.

12. A friend pays for your lunch. Is this an example of a free lunch? Why or why not?

13. A layperson says that a proposed government project simply costs too much and therefore shouldn't be undertaken. How might an economist's evaluation be different?

14. Economists say that individuals make decisions at the margin. What does this mean?

15. How would an economist define the efficient amount of time spent playing tennis?

16. Ivan stops studying before the point at which his marginal benefits of studying equals his marginal costs. Is Ivan forfeiting any net benefits? Explain your answer.

17. What does an economist mean if she says that there are no $10 bills on the sidewalk?

18. A change in X will lead to a change in Y. The predicted change is desirable, so we should change X. Do you agree or disagree? Explain.

19. Why do people enter into exchanges?

20. When two individuals enter into an exchange, you can be sure that one person benefits and the other person loses. Do you agree or disagree with this statement? Explain your answer.

21. What is the difference between positive economics and normative economics? Between microeconomics and macroeconomics?

22. Would there be a need for a rationing device if scarcity did not exist? Explain your answer.

23. Jackie's alarm clock buzzes. She reaches over to the small table next to her bed and turns it off. As she pulls the covers back up, Jackie thinks about her 8:30 American history class. Should she go to the class today or sleep a little longer? She worked late last night and really hasn't had enough sleep. Besides, she's fairly sure her professor will be discussing a subject she already knows well. Maybe it would be okay to miss class today. Is Jackie more likely

to miss some classes than she is to miss other classes? What determines which classes Jackie will attend and which classes she won't?

24. If you found $10 bills on the sidewalk regularly, we might conclude that individuals don't try to maximize net benefits. Do you agree or disagree with this statement. Explain your answer.

25. The person who smokes cigarettes cannot possibly be thinking in terms of costs and benefits because it has been proven that cigarette smoking increases one's chances of getting lung cancer. Do you agree or disagree with the part of the statement that reads "the person who smokes cigarettes cannot possibly be thinking in terms of costs and benefits"? Explain your answer.

26. Janice decides to go out on a date with Kyle instead of Robert. Do you think Janice is using some kind of rationing device to decide whom she dates? If so, what might that rationing device be?

27. A theory is an abstraction from reality. What does this statement mean?

WORKING WITH NUMBERS AND GRAPHS

1. Suppose the marginal costs of reading are constant and the marginal benefits of reading decline (over time). Initially, the marginal benefits of reading are greater than the marginal costs. Draw the marginal-benefit curve and marginal-cost curve of reading, and identify the efficient amount of reading. Next, explain why the efficient point is the point at which the net benefits of reading are maximized.

2. Using the diagram you drew in question 1, lower the marginal costs of reading and identify the new efficient amount of reading. Also, identify the additional net benefits derived as a result of the lower marginal cost of reading.

3. Jim could undertake activity X, but chooses not to. Draw how the marginal-benefit and marginal-cost curves look for activity X from Jim's perspective.

WORKING WITH DIAGRAMS

Most of the diagrams in this book represent the relationship between two variables. Economists compare two variables to see how a change in one variable affects the other.

Suppose our two variables of interest are *consumption* and *income*. We want to show how consumption changes as income changes. We collect the data shown in Table 1. Simply by looking at the data in the first two columns, we can see that, as income rises (column 1), consumption rises (column 2). If we wanted to show the relationship between income and consumption on a graph, we could place *income* on the horizontal axis, as in Exhibit 1, and *consumption* on the vertical axis. Point *A* represents income of $0 and consumption of $60, point *B* represents income of $100 and consumption of $120, and so on. If we draw a straight line through the points we have plotted, we have a picture of the relationship between income and consumption, based on the data we collected.

Notice that the line in Exhibit 1 slopes upward from left to right. As income rises, so does consumption. For example, as you move from point *A* to point *B*, income rises from $0 to $100 and consumption rises from $60 to $120. The line in Exhibit 1 also shows that, as income falls, so does consumption. For example, as you move from point *C* to point *B*, income falls from $200 to $100 and consumption falls from $180 to $120. When two variables—such as consumption and income—change in the same way, they are said to be **directly related**.

> **EXHIBIT 1**

A Two-Variable Diagram Representing a Direct Relationship

In this exhibit, we have plotted the data in Table 1 and then connected the points with a straight line. The data represent a direct relationship: as one variable (say, income) rises, the other variable (consumption) rises too.

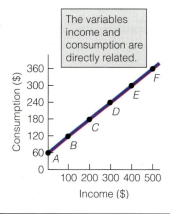

The variables income and consumption are directly related.

Table 1

(1) When Income Is:	(2) Consumption Is:	(3) Point
$0	$60	A
100	120	B
200	180	C
300	240	D
400	300	E
500	360	F

Directly Related
Two variables are directly related if they change in the same way.

Table 2

(1) When Price of CDs Is:	(2) Quantity Demanded of CDs Is:	(3) Point
$20	100	A
18	120	B
16	140	C
14	160	D
12	180	E

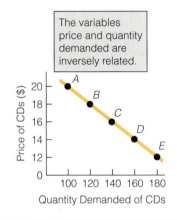

> **EXHIBIT 2**

A Two-Variable Diagram Representing an Inverse Relationship

In this exhibit, we have plotted the data in Table 2 and then connected the points with a straight line. The data represent an inverse relationship: As one variable (price) falls, the other variable (quantity demanded) rises.

The variables price and quantity demanded are inversely related.

Now let's take a look at the data in Table 2. Our two variables are the *price of compact discs (CDs)* and the *quantity demanded of CDs*. Just by looking at the data in the first two columns, we see that, as price falls (column 1), quantity demanded rises (column 2). Suppose we want to plot these data. We could place *price of CDs* on the vertical axis, as in Exhibit 2, and *quantity demanded of CDs* on the horizontal axis. Point *A* represents a price of $20 and a quantity demanded of 100, point *B* represents a price of $18 and a quantity demanded of 120, and so on. If we draw a straight line through the plotted points, we have a picture of the relationship between price and quantity demanded, based on the data in Table 2.

Notice:

- As price falls, quantity demanded rises. For example, as price falls from $20 to $18, quantity demanded rises from 100 to 120.

- As price rises, quantity demanded falls. For example, when price rises from $12 to $14, quantity demanded falls from 180 to 160.

When two variables—such as price and quantity demanded—change in opposite ways, they are said to be **inversely related**.

Inversely Related
Two variables are inversely related if they change in opposite ways.

Independent
Two variables are independent if, as one changes, the other remains constant.

Slope
The ratio of the change in the variable on the vertical axis to the change in the variable on the horizontal axis.

As you have seen so far, variables may be directly related (when one increases, the other also increases) or inversely related (when one increases, the other decreases). Variables can also be **independent** of each other: As one variable changes, the other does not.

In Exhibit 3(a), as the *X* variable rises, the *Y* variable remains the same (20). Obviously, the *X* and *Y* variables are independent of each other: As one changes, the other does not.

In Exhibit 3(b), as the *Y* variable rises, the *X* variable remains the same (30). Again, we conclude that the *X* and *Y* variables are independent of each other: As one changes, the other does not.

A-1 SLOPE OF A LINE

In addition to knowing *how* two variables are related, we also often need to know *how much* one variable changes as the other changes. To find out, we need only calculate the slope of the line. The **slope** is the ratio of the change in the variable on the vertical axis to the change

> **EXHIBIT 3**

Two Diagrams Representing Independence Between Two Variables

In (a) and (b), the variables X and Y are independent: As one changes, the other does not.

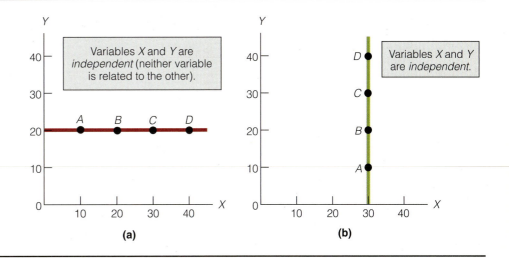

(a)   (b)

in the variable on the horizontal axis. For example, if Y is on the vertical axis and X is on the horizontal axis, the slope is equal to $\Delta Y/\Delta X$ (the symbol "Δ" means "change in"):

$$\text{Slope} = \frac{\Delta Y}{\Delta X}$$

Exhibit 4 shows four lines. In each case, the slope is calculated. After studying (a)–(d), see if you understand why the slopes are negative, positive, zero, and infinite, respectively.

A-2 THE SLOPE OF A LINE IS CONSTANT

Look again at the line in Exhibit 4(a). The slope between points A and B is computed to be -1. If we had computed the slope between points B and C or between points C and D, would it still be -1? Let's compute the slope between points B and C. Moving from point B to point C, we see that the change in Y is -10 and the change in X is $+10$. So the slope is -1, as it was between points A and B. Now let's compute the slope between points A and D. Moving from point A to point D, we see this time that the change in Y is -30 and the change in X is $+30$. So again, the slope is -1. Our conclusion is that the slope between any two points on a straight line is always the same as the slope between any other two points. To see this for yourself, compute the slope between points A and B and between points A and C, using the line in Exhibit 4(b).

A-3 SLOPE OF A CURVE

In addition to utilizing straight lines, economics graphs use *curves*. The slope of a curve is not constant throughout, as it is for a straight line. The slope of a curve varies from one point to another. Calculating the slope of a curve at a given point requires two steps, as illustrated

> **EXHIBIT 4**

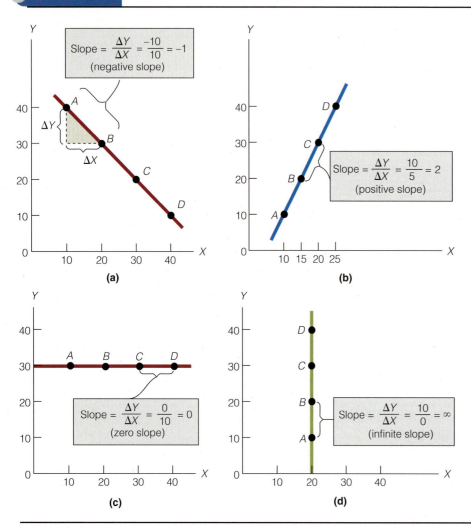

Calculating Slopes

The slope of a line is the ratio of the change in the variable on the vertical axis to the change in the variable on the horizontal axis. In (a)–(d), we have calculated the slope.

for point *A* in Exhibit 5. First, draw a line tangent to the curve at the point. (A tangent line is a line that just touches the curve but does not cross it.) Second, pick any two points on the tangent line and determine the slope. In Exhibit 5, the slope of the line between points *B* and *C* is 0.67. The slope of the curve at point *A* (and only at point *A*) is therefore 0.67.

A-4 THE 45-DEGREE LINE

Economists sometimes use a *45-degree line* to represent data. A 45-degree line is a straight line that bisects the right angle formed by the intersection of the vertical and horizontal axes. (See Exhibit 6.) As a result, the 45-degree line divides the space enclosed by the two axes into *two equal parts*, as shown in the exhibit by the shading in different colors. The major characteristic of the 45-degree line is that any point on it is equidistant from both the horizontal and vertical axes. For example, point *A* is exactly as far from the horizontal

> **EXHIBIT 5**

Calculating the Slope of a Curve at a Particular Point

The slope of the curve at point *A* is 0.67. The slope is calculated by drawing a line tangent to the curve at point *A* and then determining the slope of the line.

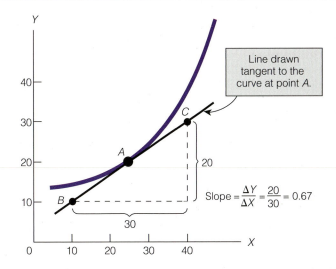

axis as it is from the vertical axis. Thus, point *A* represents as much *X* as it does *Y*. Specifically, in the exhibit, point *A* represents 20 units of *X* and 20 units of *Y*.

A-5 PIE CHARTS

Pie charts appear in numerous places throughout this text. A pie chart is a convenient way to represent the different parts of something such that, when the parts are added together, they equal the whole. Let's consider a typical 24-hour weekday for Charles Myers. On such a weekday, Charles spends 8 hours sleeping, 4 hours taking classes at the university, 4 hours working at his part-time job, 2 hours doing homework, 1 hour eating, 2 hours watching television, and 3 hours doing nothing in particular ("hanging around"). Exhibit 7 shows the breakdown, in pie chart form, of a typical weekday for Charles.

Pie charts send a quick visual message about rough percentage breakdowns and relative relationships. For example, Exhibit 7 clearly shows that Charles spends twice as much time working as doing homework.

A-6 BAR GRAPHS

The *bar graph* is another visual aid that economists use to convey relative relationships. Suppose we want to represent the gross domestic product for the United States in different years. The **gross domestic product (GDP)** is the value of the entire output produced annually within a country's borders. The bar graph in Exhibit 8 is a quick picture not only

> **EXHIBIT 6**

The 45-Degree Line

Any point on the 45-degree line is equidistant from each axis. For example, point *A* is the same distance from the vertical axis as it is from the horizontal axis.

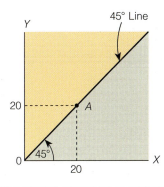

Gross Domestic Product (GDP)

The value of the entire output produced annually within a country's borders.

> EXHIBIT 7

A Pie Chart

The breakdown of activities for Charles Myers during a typical 24-hour weekday is represented in pie chart form.

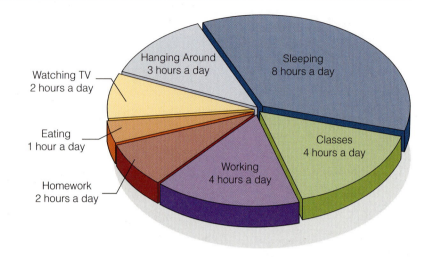

Hanging Around
3 hours a day

Sleeping
8 hours a day

Watching TV
2 hours a day

Classes
4 hours a day

Eating
1 hour a day

Working
4 hours a day

Homework
2 hours a day

> EXHIBIT 8

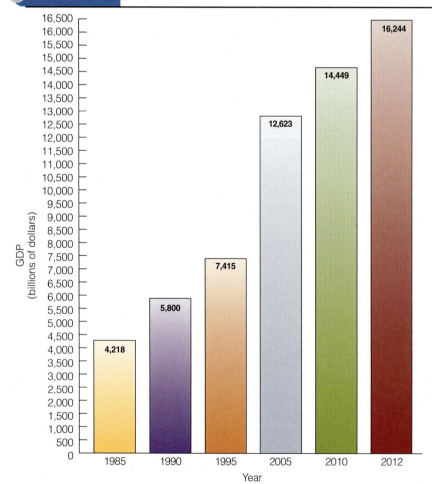

A Bar Graph

U.S. gross domestic product for different years is illustrated in bar graph form. Source: Bureau of Economic Analysis.

of the actual GDP for each year, but also of the relative relationships between the GDP numbers for different years. For example, the graph makes it easy to see that the GDP in 2005 was more than double what it was in 1990.

A-7   LINE GRAPHS

Sometimes information is best and most easily displayed in a *line graph*, which is particularly useful for illustrating changes in a variable over a given period. For example, suppose we want to illustrate the variations in average points per game for a college basketball team over a number of years. The line graph in Exhibit 9(a) shows that the basketball team was on a roller coaster during the years 2001–2014. Perhaps the visual message is that the team's performance has not been consistent from one year to the next.

Suppose we plot the same data again, except this time using a different measurement scale on the vertical axis. As you can see in Exhibit 9(b), the variation in the team's performance appears much less pronounced than in part (a). In fact, we could choose a scale that, if we were to plot the data, would give us something close to a straight line. The point is simple: Data plotted in a line graph may convey different messages, depending on the measurement scale used.

> **EXHIBIT 9**

The Two Line Graphs Plot the Same Data

In (a), we plotted the average number of points per game for a college basketball team in different years. The variation between the years is pronounced. In (b), we plotted the same data as in (a), but the variation in the performance of the team appears much less pronounced than in (a).

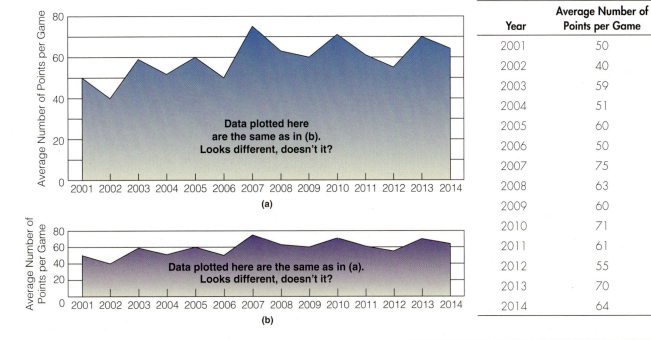

(a)

(b)

Year	Average Number of Points per Game
2001	50
2002	40
2003	59
2004	51
2005	60
2006	50
2007	75
2008	63
2009	60
2010	71
2011	61
2012	55
2013	70
2014	64

> EXHIBIT 10

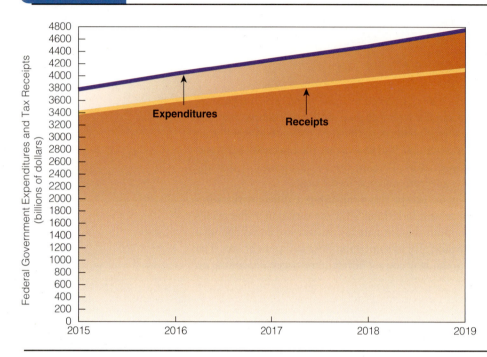

Projected Federal Government Expenditures and Projected Tax Receipts, 2015–2019

Projected federal government expenditures and projected tax receipts are shown in line graph form for the period 2015–2019.

Year	Expenditures	Receipts
2015	3,777	3,399
2016	4,038	3,606
2017	4,261	3,779
2018	4,485	3,943
2019	4,752	4,103

Source: *Congressional Budget Office.*

Sometimes economists show two line graphs on the same axes. Usually, the purpose is to draw attention to either (1) the *relationship* between two variables or (2) the *difference* between them. In Exhibit 10, the line graphs show the variation and trend in (1) projected federal government expenditures and (2) projected tax receipts for the years 2015–2019, drawing attention to the "gap" between the two over the years.

APPENDIX SUMMARY

- Two variables are directly related if one variable rises as the other rises.
- An upward-sloping line (from left to right) represents two variables that are directly related.
- Two variables are inversely related if one variable rises as the other falls.
- A downward-sloping line (from left to right) represents two variables that are inversely related.
- Two variables are independent if one variable rises as the other remains constant.
- The slope of a line is the ratio of the change in the variable on the vertical axis to the change in the variable on the horizontal axis. The slope of a straight line is the same between any two points on the line.

- To determine the slope of a curve at a point, draw a line tangent to the curve at the point and then determine the slope of the tangent line.
- Any point on a 45-degree line is equidistant from the two axes.
- A pie chart is a convenient way to represent the different parts of something such that, when the parts are added together, they equal the whole. Visually, a pie chart shows rough percentage breakdowns and relative relationships.
- A bar graph is a convenient way to represent relative relationships.
- Line graphs are particularly useful for illustrating changes in one or more variables over time.

KEY TERMS AND CONCEPTS

Directly Related
Inversely Related

Independent
Slope

Gross Domestic Product
(GDP)

QUESTIONS AND PROBLEMS

1. For each of the following, what type of relationship would you expect between the variables?
   a. Sales of hot dogs and sales of hot dog buns
   b. The price of winter coats and sales of winter coats
   c. The price of personal computers and the production of personal computers
   d. Sales of toothbrushes and sales of cat food
   e. The number of children in a family and the number of toys in a family

2. Represent the following data in bar graph form:

Year	U.S. Money Supply (billions of dollars)
2008	1,604
2009	1,695
2010	1,836
2011	2,160
2012	2,440

3. Plot the following data, and specify the type of relationship between the two variables (place "Price" on the vertical axis and "Quantity Demanded" on the horizontal axis):

Price of Apples ($)	Quantity Demanded of Apples
0.25	1,000
0.50	800
0.70	700
0.95	500
1.00	400
1.10	350

4. In Exhibit 4(a), determine the slope between points *C* and *D*.

5. In Exhibit 4(b), determine the slope between points *A* and *D*.

6. What is the special characteristic of a 45-degree line?

7. What is the slope of a 45-degree line?

8. When is a pie chart better than a bar graph for illustrating data?

9. Plot the following data, and specify the type of relationship between the two variables (place "Price" on the vertical axis and "Quantity Supplied" on the horizontal axis):

Price of Apples ($)	Quantity Supplied of Apples
0.25	350
0.50	400
0.70	500
0.95	700
1.00	800
1.10	1,000

B SHOULD YOU MAJOR IN ECONOMICS?

You are probably reading this textbook as part of your first college course in economics. You may be taking the course to satisfy a requirement in your major. Economics courses are sometimes required for students who plan to major in business, history, liberal studies, social science, or computer science.

Or you may be planning to major in economics. If you are like many college students, you may complain that not enough information is available about the various majors at your college or university. For example, students who major in business sometimes say that they are not quite certain what a business major is all about, but then they add that majoring in business is a safe bet. "After all," they assert, "you're pretty sure of getting a job if you have a business degree. That's not always the case with other degrees."

Many college students choose their majors on the basis of their high school courses. History majors, for example, might say that they decided to major in history because they "liked history in high school." Similarly, chemistry, biology, and math students say they chose their majors on the basis of their experiences in high school. If a student found both math and economics easy and interesting in high school, then she is likely to major in math or economics. Conversely, if a student had a hard time with chemistry in high school and found it boring, then he doesn't usually want to major in chemistry in college.

Students also often look to the dollars at the end of the college degree. A student may enjoy history and want to learn more of it in college, but she may tell herself that she will earn a higher starting salary after graduation if she majors in computer science or engineering. Thus, when choosing a major, students often consider (1) how much they enjoy studying a particular subject, (2) what they would like to see themselves doing in the future, and (3) what their income prospects are.

People may weight these three factors differently, but, regardless of the weighting, having more information is better than not having it, *ceteris paribus*. (We note "*ceteris paribus*" because having more information is not better if you have to pay more for it than it is worth. Who wants to pay $10 for information that provides only $1 in benefits? This appendix is therefore a low-cost way of providing you with more information about an economics major.)

We start by dispelling some of the misinformation about an economics major. Stated bluntly, some perceptions about an economics major and about a career in economics are just not true. For example, some people think that economics majors almost never study social relationships, but rather only such things as inflation, interest rates, and unemployment. Not true. Economics majors study some of the same things that sociologists, historians, psychologists, and political scientists study.

In addition to busting myths, the appendix also provides you with information about economics as a major: what courses you study, how many courses you are likely to have to take, and more.

Finally, we tell you something about a career in economics. If you have opted to become an economics major, the day will come when you have your degree in hand. What's next? What is your starting salary likely to be? What will you be doing? Are you going to be happy doing what economists do? (If you never thought economics was about happiness, you already have some misinformation about the field. Contrary to what most laypeople think, economics is not just about money. It is about happiness too.)

B-1 FIVE MYTHS ABOUT ECONOMICS AND BEING AN ECONOMICS MAJOR

Myth 1: Economics Is All Mathematics and Statistics. Some students choose not to major in economics because they think that economics is all mathematics and statistics. Math and statistics *are* used in economics, but certainly not overwhelmingly at the undergraduate degree level. Economics majors are usually required to take one statistics course and one math course (usually an introductory calculus course). Even students who say, "Math isn't my subject," are sometimes happy with the amount of math they need in economics. The fact is that, at the undergraduate level at many colleges and universities, economics is not a very math-intensive course of study. Economics uses many diagrams, but not a large amount of math.

A proviso: The amount of math in the economics curriculum varies across colleges and universities. Some economics departments do not require their students to learn much math or statistics; others do. The majority of economics departments do not require much math or statistics at the undergraduate level. The graduate level is a different story.

If you are thinking of pursuing economics at the graduate level, you should enroll in numerous mathematics and statistics courses as an undergraduate.

Myth 2: Economics Is Only About Inflation, Interest Rates, Unemployment, and Other Such Things. If you study economics at college and then go on to become a practicing economist, no doubt people will ask you certain questions when they learn your chosen profession. Here are some:

- Do you think the economy is going to pick up?
- Do you think the economy is going to slow down?
- What stocks would you recommend?
- Do you think interest rates are going to fall?
- Do you think interest rates are going to rise?
- What do you think about buying bonds right now? Is it a good idea?

People ask these kinds of questions because most believe that economists study only stocks, bonds, interest rates, inflation, unemployment, and so on. Although economists do study these topics, they are only a tiny part of what economists study. It is not hard to find many economists today, both inside and outside academia, who spend most of their time studying anything but inflation, unemployment, stocks, bonds, and the like.

In fact, much of what economists study may surprise you. Some economists use their economic tools and methods to study crime, marriage, divorce, sex, obesity, addiction, sports, voting behavior, bureaucracies, presidential elections, and much more. In short, today's economics is not your grandfather's economics. Many more topics are studied today in economics than were studied in years past.

Myth 3: People Become Economists Only If They Want to "Make Money." A while back we asked a few well-respected and well-known economists what got them interested in economics. Here is what some of them had to say:[1]

Gary Becker, the 1992 winner of the Nobel Prize in Economics, said,

> *I got interested in economics when I was an undergraduate in college. I came into college with a strong interest in mathematics and at the same time with a strong commitment to do something to help society. I learned in the first economics course I took that economics could deal rigorously, à la mathematics, with social problems. That stimulated me because, in economics, I saw that I could combine both the mathematics and my desire to do something to help society.*

Vernon Smith, the 2002 winner of the Nobel Prize in Economics, said,

> *My father's influence started me in science and engineering at Cal Tech, but my mother, who was active in socialist politics, probably accounts for the great interest I found in economics when I took my first introductory course.*

Alice Rivlin, an economist and former member of the Federal Reserve Board, said,

> *My interest in economics grew out of concern for improving public policy, both domestic and international. I was a teenager in the tremendously idealistic period after World War II when it seemed terribly important to get nations working together to solve the world's problems peacefully.*

Allan Meltzer, professor of political economy at Carnegie Mellon University and winner of the Irving Kristol award for contributions to public policy and social welfare, said,

> *Economics is a social science. At its best it is concerned with ways (1) to improve well-being by allowing individuals the freedom to achieve their personal aims or goals and (2) to harmonize their individual interests. I find working on such issues challenging, and progress is personally rewarding.*

Robert Solow, the 1987 winner of the Nobel Prize in Economics, said,

> *I grew up in the 1930s, and it was very hard not to be interested in economics. If you were a high school student in the 1930s, you were conscious of the fact that our economy was in deep trouble and no one knew what to do about it.*

Charles Plosser, president of the Federal Reserve Bank of Philadelphia and co-coiner of the term "real business cycle," said,

> *I was an engineer as an undergraduate with little knowledge of economics. I went to the University of Chicago Graduate School of Business to get an MBA and there became fascinated with economics. I was impressed with the seriousness with which economics was viewed as a way of organizing one's thoughts about the world to address interesting questions and problems.*

Walter Williams, professor of economics at George Mason University and winner of numerous fellowships and awards, said,

> *I was a major in sociology in 1963 and I concluded that it was not very rigorous. Over the summer I was reading a book by W. E. B. DuBois, Black Reconstruction, and somewhere in the book it said something along the lines that blacks could*

---

[1] See various interviews in Roger A. Arnold, *Economics*, 2nd ed. (St. Paul, MN: West Publishing Company, 1992).

not melt into the mainstream of American society until they understood economics, and that was something that got me interested in economics.

Murray Weidenbaum, professor of economics at Washington University of St. Louis and former chairman of the Council of Economic Advisors, said,

A specific professor got me interested in economics. He was very prescient: He correctly noted that while lawyers dominated the policy-making process up until the 1940s, in the future economics would be an important tool for developing public policy. And he was right.

Irma Adelman, professor of agricultural and resource economics at the University of California at Berkeley, said,

I hesitate to say because it sounds arrogant. My reason [for getting into economics] was that I wanted to benefit humanity. And my perception at the time was that economic problems were the most important problems that humanity has to face. That is what got me into economics and into economic development.

Lester Thurow, political economist and dean of the MIT Sloan School of Management, said,

[I got interested in economics because of] the belief—some would see it as naïve belief—that economics was a profession where it would be possible to help make the world better.

Myth 4: Economics Wasn't Very Interesting in High School, So It's Not Going to Be Very Interesting in College. A typical high school economics course emphasizes, and spends much time discussing, consumer economics. Students learn about credit cards, mortgage loans, budgets, buying insurance, renting an apartment, and other such things. These are important topics because not knowing their ins and outs can make your life much harder. Still, many students come away from high school thinking that economics is always and everywhere about consumer topics.

However, a high school economics course and a college economics course are usually as different as day and night. Simply leaf through this book and look at the variety of topics covered, compared with those you might have covered in high school economics. Go on to look at texts used in other economics courses—ranging from law and economics, to the history of economic thought, to international economics, to sports economics—and you will see what we mean.

Myth 5: An Economics Degree Is a Lot Like a Business Degree, But a Business Degree Is More Marketable. Although business and economics have some common topics, much that one learns in economics is not taught in business and much that one learns in business is not taught in economics. The area of intersection between business and economics is not large.

Still, many people think otherwise. Regarding business and economics as pretty much the same thing, they often choose to major in the subject that they believe has greater marketability—which they believe is business.

Well, consider the following:

1. A few years ago, *Business Week* magazine asked the chief executive officers of major companies what they thought was the best undergraduate degree. Their first choice was engineering. Their second was economics. Economics scored higher than business administration.

2. Often, the starting median salary and midcareer median salary are higher in economics than in other areas (even business-related areas). Table 1 lists the top 30 undergraduate college degrees by salary. Economics is ranked number 15.

	Table 1	
	Top 30 undergraduate degrees by salary	
Major	**Starting Median Pay**	**Midcareer Salary**
Petroleum Engineering	$98,000	$163,000
Aerospace Engineering	$62,500	$118,000
Actuarial Mathematics	$56,100	$112,000
Chemical Engineering	$67,500	$111,000
Nuclear Engineering	$66,800	$107,000
Electrical Engineering (EE)	$63,400	$106,000
Computer Engineering (CE)	$62,700	$105,000
Applied Mathematics	$50,800	$102,000
Computer Science (CS)	$58,400	$100,000
Statistics	$49,300	$99,500
Physics	$51,200	$99,100
Mechanical Engineering (ME)	$60,100	$98,400
Biomedical Engineering (BME)	$54,900	$98,200
Government	$42,000	$95,600
Economics	**$48,500**	**$94,900**
International Relations	$40,600	$93,000
Materials Science & Engineering	$60,100	$91,900
Industrial Engineering (IE)	$59,900	$91,200
Software Engineering	$59,100	$90,700
Environmental Engineering	$47,900	$89,700
Geology	$45,000	$89,400
Civil Engineering (CE)	$53,800	$88,800
Management Information Systems (MIS)	$51,600	$88,600
Biochemistry (BCH)	$43,200	$88,500
Chemistry	$44,700	$87,500
Electrical Engineering Technology (EET)	$58,400	$86,900
Information Systems (IS)	$50,900	$86,700
Construction Management	$49,500	$86,100
Mathematics	$48,500	$85,800
Finance	$47,700	$85,400

Source: *PayScale.com.*

B-2 WHAT AWAITS YOU AS AN ECONOMICS MAJOR?

If you become an economics major, what courses will you take? What are you going to study?

At the lower division level, economics majors must take courses in the principles of macroeconomics and the principles of microeconomics. They usually also take a statistics course and a math course (usually calculus).

At the upper division level, they must take intermediate microeconomics and intermediate macroeconomics, along with a certain number of electives. Some of the elective courses, among many others, are as follows:

- Money and banking
- Law and economics
- History of economic thought
- Behavioral economics
- Public finance
- Labor economics
- International economics
- Antitrust and regulation
- Health economics
- Economics of development
- Urban and regional economics
- Econometrics
- Mathematical economics
- Environmental economics
- Public choice
- Global managerial economics
- Economic approach to politics and sociology
- Sports economics

Most economics majors take between 12 and 15 economics courses.

One of the attractive things about studying economics is that you will acquire many of the skills employers value highly. First, you will have the quantitative skills that are important in many business and government positions. Second, you will acquire the writing skills necessary in almost all lines of work. Third, and perhaps most importantly, you will develop the thinking skills that almost all employers agree are critical to success.

A study published in the 1998 edition of the *Journal of Economic Education* ranked economics majors as having the highest average scores on the Law School Admission Test (LSAT). Also, consider the words of the Royal Economic Society:

> *One of the things that makes economics graduates so employable is that the subject teaches you to think in a careful and precise way. The fundamental economic issue is how society decides to allocate its resources: how the costs and benefits of a course of action can be evaluated and compared, and how appropriate choices can be made. A degree in economics gives a training in decision making principles, providing a skill applicable in a very wide range of careers.*

Keep in mind, too, that economics is one of the most popular majors at some of the most respected universities in the country. As of this writing, economics is the top major at Harvard, Princeton, Columbia, Stanford, the University of Pennsylvania, and the University of Chicago. It is the second most popular major at Brown, Yale, and the University of California at Berkeley. It is the third most popular major at Cornell and Dartmouth.

B-3　WHAT DO ECONOMISTS DO?

The employment of economists is expected to grow 6 percent from 2008 to 2018. According to the *Occupational Outlook Handbook*,

> *Employment growth [in economics] should be fastest in private industry, especially in management, scientific, and technical consulting services. Rising demand for economic analysis in virtually every industry should stem from the growing complexity of the global economy, the effects of competition on businesses, and increased reliance on quantitative methods for analyzing and forecasting business, sales, and other economic trends. Some corporations choose to hire economic consultants to fill these needs, rather than keeping an economist on staff. This practice should result in more economists being employed in consulting services.*

Today, economists work in many and varied fields. Here are some of the fields and some of the positions that economists hold in those fields:

Education

　College professor

　Researcher

　High school teacher

Journalism

　Researcher

　Industry analyst

　Economic analyst

Accounting

　Analyst

　Auditor

　Researcher

　Consultant

General Business

　Chief executive officer

　Business analyst

　Marketing analyst

　Business forecaster

　Competitive analyst

Government

　Researcher

　Analyst

　Speechwriter

　Forecaster

Financial Services

　Business journalist

　International analyst

Newsletter editor

Broker

Investment banker

Banking

Credit analyst

Loan officer

Investment analyst

Financial manager

Other

Business consultant

Independent forecaster

Freelance analyst

Think tank analyst

Entrepreneur

Economists do a myriad of things, including the following:

- In business, economists often analyze economic conditions, make forecasts, offer strategic-planning initiatives, collect and analyze data, predict exchange rate movements, and review regulatory policies, among other things.

- In government, economists collect and analyze data, analyze international economic situations, research monetary conditions, advise on policy, and do much more.

- As private consultants, economists work with accountants, business executives, government officials, educators, financial firms, labor unions, state and local governments, and others.

In May 2010, the median annual wage and salary earnings of economists were $89,450. The lowest 10 percent earned less than $48,250, and the top 10 percent earned more than $155,490.

In May 2010, the average annual salary for economists employed by the federal government was $106,840. Starting salaries were higher in selected geographical areas where the prevailing local pay was higher.

B-4 PLACES TO FIND MORE INFORMATION

If you are interested in a major and perhaps a career in economics, here are some places you can go to and people you can speak with to acquire more information:

- To learn about the economics curriculum, speak with the economics professors at your college or university. Ask them what courses you would have to take as an economics major and what elective courses are available. In addition, ask them why they chose to study economics: What is it about economics that interested them?

- For more information about salaries and what economists do, you may want to visit the *Occupational Outlook Handbook* website (http://www.bls.gov/oco/).

B-5 CONCLUDING REMARKS

Choosing a major is a big decision and therefore should not be made quickly and without much thought. This short appendix has provided you with some information about an economics major and a career in economics. Economics is not for everyone, but it may be right for you. A major in economics trains you in today's most marketable skills: good writing, quantitative analysis, and rigorous thinking. It is a major in which professors and students daily ask and answer some very interesting and relevant questions. It is a major that is highly regarded by employers. It may just be the right major for you. Give it some thought.

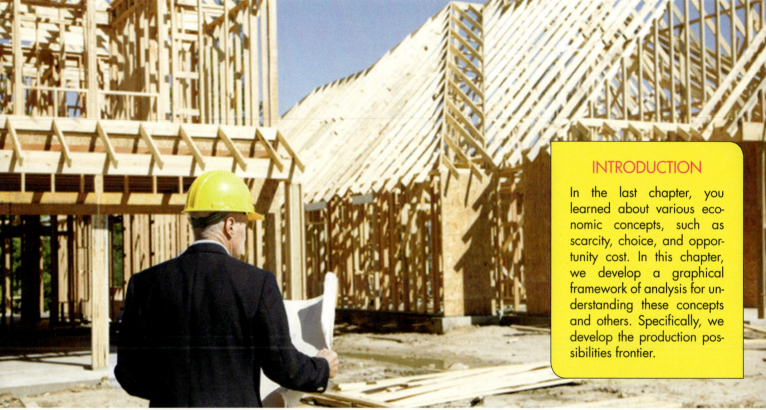

PRODUCTION POSSIBILITIES FRONTIER FRAMEWORK

© iStockphoto.com/Pamela Moore

INTRODUCTION

In the last chapter, you learned about various economic concepts, such as scarcity, choice, and opportunity cost. In this chapter, we develop a graphical framework of analysis for understanding these concepts and others. Specifically, we develop the production possibilities frontier.

2-1 THE PRODUCTION POSSIBILITIES FRONTIER

Think of yourself as being alone on an island. You can produce two goods and only two goods: coconuts and pineapples. Because your resources are limited, producing more of one good means producing less of the other. That type of thinking is the intuition behind the *production possibilities frontier*. Now keep that intuition in mind as we proceed.

2-1a The Straight-Line PPF: Constant Opportunity Costs

In Exhibit 1(a), we have identified five combinations of books and shirts that can be produced in an economy. For example, combination *A* is 4 books and 0 shirts, combination *B* is 3 books and 1 shirt, and so on. Next, we plotted these five combinations of books and shirts in Exhibit 1(b), with each combination representing a different point. For example, the combination of 4 books and 0 shirts is represented by point *A*. The line that connects points *A–E* is the production possibilities frontier. A **production possibilities frontier (PPF)** is the combination of two goods that can be produced in a certain span of time under the conditions of a given state of technology and fully employed resources.

Production Possibilities Frontier (PPF)

The possible combinations of two goods that can be produced during a certain span of time under the conditions of a given state of technology and fully employed resources.

Notice that the PPF is a straight line. This is because the opportunity cost of books and shirts (in our example) is constant:

Straight-line PPF = Constant opportunity costs

To illustrate what *constant opportunity costs* means, suppose the economy were to move from point *A* to point *B*. At point *A*, 4 books and 0 shirts are produced; at point *B*, 3 books and 1 shirt are produced:

- Point *A*: 4 books and 0 shirts
- Point *B*: 3 books and 1 shirt

What does the economy have to forfeit (in terms of books) to get 1 shirt? The answer is 1 book. We conclude that, in moving from point *A* to point *B*, the opportunity cost of 1 shirt is 1 book.

Now let's move from point *B* to point *C*. At point *B*, 3 books and 1 shirt are produced; at point *C*, 2 books and 2 shirts are produced:

- Point *B*: 3 books and 1 shirt
- Point *C*: 2 books and 2 shirts

So, how many books does the economy have to forfeit to get another shirt? The answer is 1 book. We conclude that, in moving from point *B* to *C*, the opportunity cost of 1 shirt is 1 book.

In fact, when we move from *C* to *D* or from *D* to *E*, we also notice that the opportunity cost of 1 shirt is 1 book. This is what we mean when we speak of constant opportunity costs: The opportunity cost of 1 shirt is *always* 1 book. And because opportunity costs are constant, the PPF in Exhibit 1(b) is a straight line. When opportunity costs are not constant, the PPF will not be a straight line, as you will see next.

2-1b The Bowed-Outward (Concave-Downward) PPF: Increasing Opportunity Costs

In Exhibit 2(a), we have identified five combinations of cell phones and coffee makers that can be produced in an economy. For example, combination *A* is 10 cell phones and 0 coffee makers, combination *B* is 9 cell phones and 1 coffee makers, and so on. We plotted these five combinations of cell phones and coffee makers in Exhibit 2(b), again with each combination representing a different

> **EXHIBIT 1**

Production Possibilities Frontier (Constant Opportunity Costs)

The economy can produce any of the five combinations of books and shirts in part (a). We have plotted these combinations in part (b). The PPF in part (b) is a straight line because the opportunity cost of producing either good is constant.

Combination	Books	Shirts	Point in Part (b)
A	4	0	A
B	3	1	B
C	2	2	C
D	1	3	D
E	0	4	E

(a)

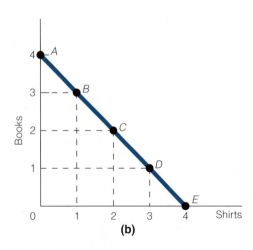

(b)

> **EXHIBIT 2**

Production Possibilities Frontier (Increasing Opportunity Costs)

The economy can produce any of the five combinations of cell phones and coffee makers in part (a). We have plotted these combinations in part (b). The PPF in part (b) is bowed outward because the opportunity cost of producing coffee makers increases as more coffee makers are produced.

Combination	Cell Phones	Coffee Makers	Point in Part (b)
A	10	0	A
B	9	1	B
C	7	2	C
D	4	3	D
E	0	4	E

(a)

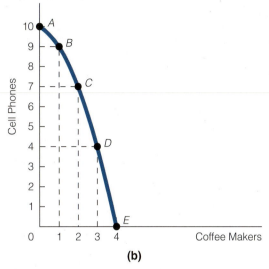

(b)

point. The curved line that connects points *A–E* is the PPF. In this case, the production possibilities frontier is bowed outward (concave downward) because the opportunity cost of coffee makers increases as more coffee makers are produced:

Bowed-outward PPF = Increasing opportunity costs

To illustrate, let's start at point *A*, where the economy is producing 10 cell phones and 0 coffee makers, and move to point *B*, where the economy is producing 9 cell phones and 1 coffee makers:

- Point *A*: 10 cell phones and 0 coffee makers
- Point *B*: 9 cell phones and 1 coffee makers

What is the opportunity cost of a coffee makers in moving from point *A* to point *B*? Stated differently, what does the economy have to forfeit (in terms of cell phones) to get 1 coffee makers? The answer is 1 cell phone.

Now let's move from point *B* to point *C*. At point *B*, the economy is producing 9 cell phones and 1 coffee makers; at point *C*, the economy is producing 7 cell phones and 2 coffee makers:

- Point *B*: 9 cell phones and 1 coffee makers
- Point *C*: 7 cell phones and 2 coffee makers

Now how many cell phones does the economy have to forfeit to get 1 additional coffee makers? The answer this time is 2 cell phones. We conclude that, in moving from point *A* to point *B*, the opportunity cost of 1 coffee makers was 1 cell phone, but that, in moving from point *B* to point *C*, the opportunity cost of 1 (additional) coffee makers is 2 cell phones. If we were to continue producing additional coffee makers, we would see that we would have to give up increasingly more cell phones. You can see this easily if you consider the economy moving from point *C* to point *D* (where the opportunity cost of producing an additional coffee makers is 3 cell phones) or moving from point to *D* to point *E* (where the opportunity cost of producing an additional coffee makers is 4 cell phones). We end with a question: Why is the PPF in Exhibit 2(b) bowed outward? The reason is the increasing opportunity costs of producing coffee makers.

2-1c Law of Increasing Opportunity Costs

We know that the shape of the PPF depends on whether opportunity costs (1) are constant or (2) increase as more of a good is produced. In Exhibit 1(b), the PPF is a straight line; in Exhibit 2(b), it is bowed outward (curved). In the real world, most PPFs are bowed outward. In other words, for most goods, the opportunity costs *increase* as more of the good is produced. This relationship is referred to as the **law of increasing opportunity costs**.

     The law of increasing opportunity costs holds for most goods because people have varying abilities. For example, some individuals are better suited to building houses than others are. When a construction company first starts building houses, it employs the people most skilled at doing so. The most skilled persons can build houses at lower opportunity costs than others can. But as the construction company builds more houses, it finds that it has already employed the most skilled builders; so it must employ those who are less skilled at building houses. The less skilled people build houses at higher opportunity costs: Whereas three skilled house builders could build a house in a month, as many as seven unskilled builders may be required to build one as fast. Exhibit 3 summarizes the points in this section.

Law of Increasing Opportunity Costs

As more of a good is produced, the opportunity costs of producing that good increase.

> **EXHIBIT 3**

A Summary Statement About Increasing Opportunity Costs and a Production Possibilities Frontier That Is Bowed Outward (Concave Downward)

Many of the points about increasing opportunity costs and a PPF that is bowed outward are summarized here.

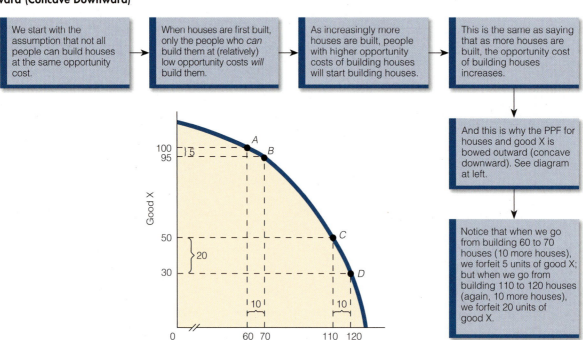

We start with the assumption that not all people can build houses at the same opportunity cost.

→ When houses are first built, only the people who *can* build them at (relatively) low opportunity costs *will* build them.

→ As increasingly more houses are built, people with higher opportunity costs of building houses will start building houses.

→ This is the same as saying that as more houses are built, the opportunity cost of building houses increases.

And this is why the PPF for houses and good X is bowed outward (concave downward). See diagram at left.

Notice that when we go from building 60 to 70 houses (10 more houses), we forfeit 5 units of good X; but when we go from building 110 to 120 houses (again, 10 more houses), we forfeit 20 units of good X.

ECONOMICS 24/7

Where Was Sherlock Holmes on His Production Possibilities Frontier?

Of Sherlock Holmes, it has been said that "his ignorance was as remarkable as his knowledge."[1] In fact, his companion, Dr. Watson, said, "Of contemporary literature, philosophy and politics he appeared to know next to nothing. . . . My surprise reached a climax, however, when I found incidentally that he was ignorant of the Copernican Theory and of the composition of the Solar System. That any civilized being in this nineteenth century should not be aware that the earth travelled round the sun appeared to be to me such an extraordinary fact that I could hardly realize it."[2]

When Dr. Watson expressed his surprise to Sherlock Holmes, Holmes told Watson that now that Watson had told him that the earth revolves around the sun, he would try his best to forget it. Holmes said, "You see, I consider that a man's brain originally is like a little empty attic, and you have to stock it with such furniture as you choose. A fool takes in all the lumber of every sort that he comes across, so that the knowledge which might be useful to him gets crowded out. . . . He will have nothing but the tools which may help him in doing his work. . . . Depend upon it there comes a time when for every addition of knowledge you forget something that you knew before."[3]

Holmes was interested in solving crimes, and he wanted his brain filled with only the things that would help him achieve his sole purpose.

Time & Life Pictures/Getty Images

If he learned something that was irrelevant to this task, then something that was relevant to the purpose at hand would be discarded. In other words, he was on his PPF and more of one thing necessarily meant less of something else.

Not only that, but Holmes wanted to stay at a particular point on his PPF. But which point? Well, let's deduce the answer together. Suppose that on the vertical axis there is "knowing more about things about the world, none of which is helpful in solving crime" and on the horizontal axis is "number of crimes solved." Now, if Holmes wants to solve as many crimes as possible, obviously he wants to be on his PPF at the point where it touches the horizontal axis. He wants to solve as many crimes as possible, given his resources (physical and mental). In other words, he wants to use all of his resources to do one thing and one thing only: solve crimes.

---

[1]. Sir Arthur Conan Doyle, "A Study in Scarlet," *The Adventures of Sherlock Holmes*, Modern Library paperback edition (New York: Random House, 2003), chapter 2.
[2]. Ibid.
[3]. Ibid.

2-1d Economic Concepts in a *Production Possibilities Frontier* Framework

The PPF framework is useful for illustrating and working with economic concepts. This section discusses seven economic concepts in terms of the PPF framework. (see Exhibit 4.)

Scarcity   Recall that scarcity is the condition in which the wants (for goods) are greater than the resources available to satisfy them. The finiteness of resources is graphically portrayed by the PPF in Exhibit 5. If the frontier could speak, it would tell us, "At this point in time, that's as far as you can go. You cannot go any farther. You are limited to choosing any combination of the two goods on the frontier or below it."

The PPF separates the production possibilities of an economy into two regions: (1) an attainable region, which consists of the points on the PPF itself and all points below it (this region includes points *A–F*), and (2) an unattainable region, which

> **EXHIBIT 4**

The PPF Economic Framework

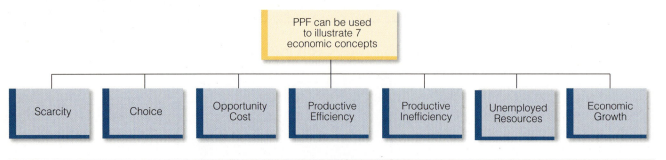

consists of the points above and beyond the PPF (such as point *G*). Recall that scarcity implies that some things are attainable and others are unattainable. Point *A* on the PPF is attainable, as is point *F*; point *G* is not.

Choice and opportunity cost are also shown in Exhibit 5. Note that, within the attainable region, individuals must choose the combination of the two goods they want to produce. Obviously, hundreds of combinations exist, but let's consider only two, represented by points *A* and *B*, respectively. Which of the two will individuals choose? They can't be at both points; they must make a choice.

Opportunity cost is illustrated as we move from one point to another on the PPF in Exhibit 5. Suppose we are at point *A* and choose to move to point *B*. At point *A*, we have 55,000 television sets and 5,000 cars; at point *B*, we have 50,000 television sets

> **EXHIBIT 5**

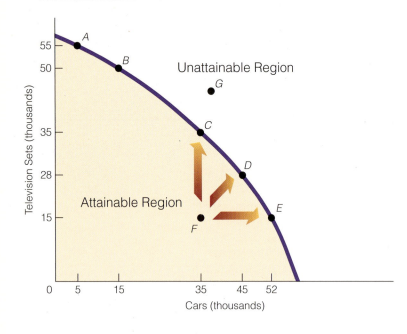

The PPF and Various Economic Concepts

The PPF can illustrate various economic concepts:
(1) Scarcity is illustrated by the frontier itself. Implicit in the concept of scarcity is the idea that we can have some things but not all things. The PPF separates an attainable region from an unattainable region.
(2) Choice is represented by our having to decide among the many attainable combinations of the two goods. For example, will we choose the combination of goods represented by point *A* or by point *B*?
(3) Opportunity cost is most easily seen as movement from one point to another, such as movement from point *A* to point *B*. More cars are available at point *B* than at point *A*, but fewer television sets are available. In short, the opportunity cost of more cars is fewer television sets.
(4) Productive efficiency is represented by the points *on* the PPF (such as *A–E*), while productive inefficiency is represented by any point *below* the PPF (such as *F*).
(5) Unemployment (in terms of resources being unemployed) exists at any productive-inefficient point (such as *F*), whereas resources are fully employed at any productive-efficient point (such as any point in the range *A–E*).

and 15,000 cars. What is the opportunity cost of a car? Because 10,000 *more* cars come at a cost of 5,000 *fewer* television sets, the opportunity cost of 1 car is 1/2 television set.

Productive Efficiency

Economists often say that an economy is **productive efficient** if it is producing the maximum output with the resources and technology that it has. In Exhibit 5, points *A*, *B*, *C*, *D*, and *E* are all productive-efficient points. Notice that all these points lie on the PPF. In other words, we are getting the most output from what we have of available resources and technology.

It follows that an economy is **productive inefficient** if it is producing less than the maximum output with the resources and technology that it has. In Exhibit 5, point *F* is a productive-inefficient point. It lies below the PPF; it is below the outer limit of what is possible. In other words, we can produce more goods with the available resources, or we can get more of one good without getting less of another.

To illustrate, suppose we move from inefficient point *F* to efficient point *C*. We produce more television sets and no fewer cars. What if we move from *F* to *D*? We produce more television sets and more cars. Finally, if we move from *F* to *E*, we produce more cars and no fewer television sets. Thus, moving from *F* can give us more of at least one good and no less of another good. In short, productive inefficiency implies that gains are possible in one area without losses in another.

Unemployed Resources

When the economy exhibits productive inefficiency, it is not producing the maximum output with the available resources and technology. One reason may be that the economy is not using all of its resources; that is, some of its resources are unemployed, as at point *F* in Exhibit 5.

When the economy exhibits productive efficiency, it is producing the maximum output with the available resources and technology. In other words, it is using all its resources to produce goods; its resources are fully employed, and none are unemployed. At the productive-efficient points *A*–*E* in Exhibit 5, no resources are unemployed.

Economic Growth

The term *economic growth* refers to the increased productive capabilities of an economy. Economic growth is illustrated by an outward shift in the PPF. Two major factors that produce economic growth are (1) an increase in the quantity of resources and (2) an advance in technology.

An increase in the quantity of resources (e.g., through a discovery of new resources) makes a greater quantity of output possible. In Exhibit 6, an increase in the quantity of resources makes it possible to produce both more military goods and more civilian goods. Thus, the PPF shifts outward from PPF_1 to PPF_2.

Technology refers to the body of skills and knowledge involved in the use of resources in production. An advance in technology commonly increases the ability to produce more output with a fixed quantity of resources or the ability to produce the same output with a smaller quantity of resources. For example, suppose an advance in technology allows the production of more of *both* military goods and civilian goods with the same quantity of resources. As a result, the PPF in Exhibit 6(a) shifts outward from PPF_1 to PPF_2. The outcome is the same as when the quantity of resources is increased.

If the advance in technology allows only more of *one good* (instead of both goods) to be produced with the same quantity of resources, then the PPF shifts outward, but not in the same way as shown in Exhibit 6(a). To illustrate, suppose an advance in technology allows only more civilian goods to be produced but not more military goods. Therefore, the maximum amount of military goods that can be produced does not change, but the maximum amount of civilian goods rises. This situation gives us the shift from PPF_1 to PPF_2 shown in Exhibit 6(b).

Productive Efficient
The condition in which the maximum output is produced with the given resources and technology.

Productive Inefficient
The condition in which less than the maximum output is produced with the given resources and technology. Productive inefficiency implies that more of one good can be produced without any less of another being produced.

Technology
The body of skills and knowledge involved in the use of resources in production. An advance in technology commonly increases the ability to produce more output with a fixed amount of resources or the ability to produce the same output with fewer resources.

> **EXHIBIT 6**

Economic Growth Within a PPF Framework

An increase in resources or an advance in technology (that can lead to more of both goods being produced) can increase the production capabilities of an economy, leading to economic growth and a shift outward in the PPF, as shown in part (a). If the advance in technology leads to the greater production of only one good (such as civilian goods in this exhibit), then the PPF shifts outward, as shown in (b).

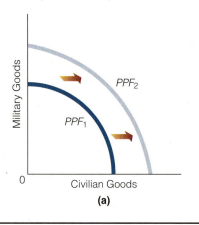

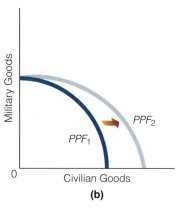

(a)   (b)

FINDING ECONOMICS

In an Attorney's Office Suppose an attorney is sitting in his office working. Where is the economics?

Let's first talk about farmers and a change in technology. During the twentieth century, many farmers left farming because it experienced major technological advances. Where farmers once farmed with minimal capital equipment, today they use computers, tractors, pesticides, cellular phones, and much more. In 1910, the United States had 32.1 million farmers; today, there are around 4.8 million farmers. Where did all the farmers go?

Because of technological advancements, fewer farmers were needed to produce food, so many of them left the farms for the cities, where they entered the manufacturing and service industries. In other words, people who were once farmers (or whose parents and grandparents were farmers) began to produce cars, airplanes, television sets, and computers. They became attorneys, accountants, and police officers.

What we learn from this is that a technological advancement in one sector of the economy can have ripple effects throughout the economy. We also learn that a technological advancement can affect the composition of employment.

SELF-TEST

(Answers to Self-Test questions are in Answers to Self-Test Questions at the back of the book.)

1. What does a straight-line PPF represent? What does a bowed-outward PPF represent?

2. What does the law of increasing costs have to do with a bowed-outward PPF?

3. A politician says, "If you elect me, we can get more of everything we want." Under what conditions is the politician telling the truth?

4. In an economy, only one combination of goods is productive efficient. True or false? Explain your answer.

ECONOMICS 24/7

Studying and Your PPF

You have your own PPF; you just may not know it. Suppose you are studying for two upcoming exams. You have only a total of six hours before you have to take the first exam, after which you will immediately proceed to take the second exam. Thus, time spent studying for the first exam (in economics) takes away from time that could be spent studying for the second exam (in math), and vice versa. Also, *time spent studying* is a resource in the production of a good grade: Less time spent studying for the economics exam and more time spent studying for the math exam means a higher grade in math and a lower grade in economics. For you, the situation may look as it does in Exhibit 7(a). We have identified four points (1–4) in the exhibit that correspond to the four combinations of two grades (one grade in economics and one grade in math).

Notice that each grade comes with a certain amount of time spent studying. This time is specified under the grade.

Given the resources you currently have (your labor and time), you can achieve any of the four combinations. For example, you can spend six hours studying for economics and get a *B* (point 1), but then you study math for zero hours and get an F in that course. Or you can spend four hours studying for economics and get a *C* (point 2), leaving you two hours to study for math, in which you get a *D*.

What do you need to get a higher grade in one course without getting a lower grade in the other course? You need more resources, which in this case is more time. If you have eight hours to study, your PPF shifts rightward, as in Exhibit 7(b). Now point 5 is possible (whereas it was not possible before you got more time). At point 5, you can get a *C* in economics and in math, an impossible combination of grades when you had less time (a PPF closer to the origin).

> **EXHIBIT 7**

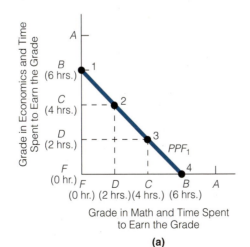

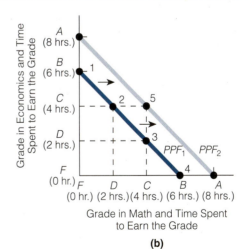

(a)

(b)

Grade in Math and Time Spent to Earn the Grade

2-2 SPECIALIZATION AND TRADE CAN MOVE US BEYOND OUR PPF

In this section, we explain how a country that specializes in the production of certain goods and then trades those goods to countries for other goods can make itself better off. In terms of its PPF, it can consume at a level *beyond* its PPF.

2-2a A Simple Two-Person PPF Model

Two individuals, Elizabeth and Brian, live near each other, and each engages in two activities: baking bread and growing apples. Let's suppose that, within a certain period, Elizabeth can produce 20 loaves of bread and no apples, or 10 loaves of bread and 10 apples, or no bread and 20 apples. (See Exhibit 8.) In other words, three points on Elizabeth's PPF correspond, respectively, to 20 loaves of bread and no apples, 10 loaves of bread and 10 apples, and no bread and 20 apples. As a consumer, Elizabeth likes to eat both bread and apples; so she decides to produce (and consume) 10 loaves of bread and 10 apples. This combination is represented by point *B* in Exhibit 8(a).

During the same period, Brian can produce 10 loaves of bread and no apples, or 5 loaves of bread and 15 apples, or no bread and 30 apples. In other words, these three combinations correspond, respectively, to three points on Brian's PPF. Brian, like Elizabeth, likes to eat both bread and apples; so he decides to produce and consume 5 loaves of bread and 15 apples. This combination is represented by point *F* in Exhibit 8(b).

Elizabeth thinks that both she and Brian may be better off if each specializes in producing only one of the two goods and trading it for the other. In other words, Elizabeth should produce either bread or apples but not both. Brian thinks that this may be a good idea but is not sure which good each person should specialize in producing.

An economist would advise each to produce the good that he or she can produce at a lower cost. In economics, a person who can produce a good at a lower cost than another person is said to have a **comparative advantage** in the production of the good.

Exhibit 8 shows that, for every 10 units of bread Elizabeth does not produce, she can produce 10 apples. In other words, the opportunity cost of producing 1 loaf of bread *(B)* is 1 apple *(A)*:

Comparative Advantage
The situation in which someone can produce a good at lower opportunity cost than someone else can.

Opportunity costs for Elizabeth: $1B = 1A$
$$1A = 1B$$

For every 5 loaves of bread that Brian does not produce, he can produce 15 apples. So, for every 1 loaf of bread he does not produce, he can produce 3 apples. Therefore, for every 1 apple he chooses to produce, he forfeits 1/3 loaf of bread:

Opportunity costs for Brian: $1B = 3A$
$$1A = 1/3B$$

Comparing opportunity costs, we see that Elizabeth can produce bread at a lower opportunity cost than Brian can. (Elizabeth forfeits 1 apple when she produces 1 loaf of bread, whereas Brian forfeits 3 apples for 1 loaf of bread.) By contrast, Brian can produce apples at a lower opportunity cost than Elizabeth can. We conclude that Elizabeth has a comparative advantage in the production of bread and Brian has a comparative advantage in the production of apples.

> **EXHIBIT 8**

Elizabeth's PPF, Brian's PPF

In (a) we show the combination of the two goods that Elizabeth can produce, first in terms of a table and then in terms of a PPF. Because Elizabeth wants to consume some of both goods, she chooses to produce the combination of the two goods represented by point B.

In (b) we show the combination of the two goods that Brian can produce, first in terms of a table and then in terms of a PPF. Because Brian wants to consume some of both goods, he chooses to produce the combination of the two goods represented by point F.

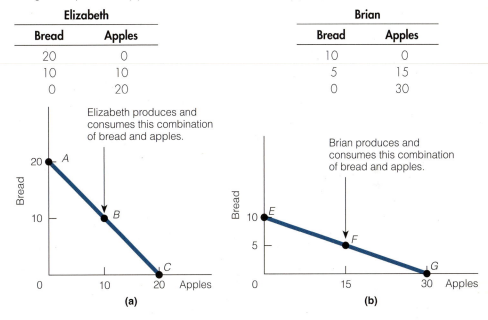

Elizabeth	
Bread	**Apples**
20	0
10	10
0	20

Brian	
Bread	**Apples**
10	0
5	15
0	30

Elizabeth produces and consumes this combination of bread and apples.

Brian produces and consumes this combination of bread and apples.

(a)

(b)

Suppose both individuals specialize in the production of the good in which they have a comparative advantage. Then Elizabeth produces only bread and makes 20 loaves. Brian produces only apples and grows 30 of them.

Now suppose that Elizabeth and Brian decide to trade 8 loaves of bread for 12 apples. In other words, Elizabeth produces 20 loaves of bread and then trades 8 of them for 12 apples. After the trade, Elizabeth consumes 12 loaves of bread and 12 apples. Compare this situation with what she consumed when she didn't specialize and didn't trade. In that situation, she consumed 10 loaves of bread and 10 apples. Clearly, Elizabeth is better off when she specializes and trades than when she does not.

But what about Brian? He produces 30 apples and trades 12 of them to Elizabeth for 8 loaves of bread. In other words, he consumes 8 loaves of bread and 18 apples. Compare this situation with what he consumed when he didn't specialize and didn't trade. In that situation, he consumed 5 loaves of bread and 15 apples. Thus, Brian is also better off when he specializes and trades than when he does not.

2-2b **On or Beyond the PPF?**

In Exhibit 9(a), we show the PPF for Elizabeth. When she was not specializing and not trading, she consumed the combination of bread and apples represented by point B (10 loaves of bread and 10 apples). When she did specialize and trade, her consumption of both goods increased, moving her to point D (12 loaves of bread and 12 apples). Here

> EXHIBIT 9

Consumption for Elizabeth and Brian With and Without Specialization and Trade

A comparison of the consumption of bread and apples before and after specialization and trade shows that both Elizabeth and Brian benefit from producing the good in which each has a comparative advantage and trading for the other good.

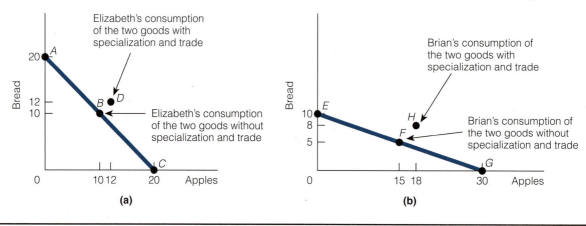

(a)   (b)

is the lesson learned: Through specialization and trade, Elizabeth's consumption moved beyond her PPF. It is easy to see the benefits of specialization and trade.

In Exhibit 9(b), we show the PPF for Brian. When he was not specializing and not trading, he consumed the combination of bread and apples represented by point *F* (5 loaves of bread and 15 apples). When he did specialize and trade, his consumption of both goods increased, moving him to point *H* (8 loaves of bread and 18 apples). Here is *this* lesson learned: Through specialization and trade, Brian's consumption moved beyond his PPF.

What holds for Elizabeth and Brian through specialization and trade holds for countries too. For example, if both Americans and Brazilians specialize in producing those goods for which they have a comparative advantage and then trade some of those goods for the other's goods, both Americans and Brazilians can consume more of both goods than if they don't specialize and don't trade.

FINDING ECONOMICS

At the Airport Suppose you wake up in the morning and drive to the airport. You have your bags checked curbside at the airport. You tip the person who checks your luggage. You then line up to go through security. Once on the plane, you hear the pilot telling you the flying time for today's flight. Later in the flight, the flight attendant brings you a soft drink and a snack. What you see at the airport and on board the plane is different people performing different tasks. The pilot is flying the plane, the customer service person at the check-in counter is receiving your luggage, and so on. Can you find the economics in this situation? Think about it for a minute before you read on.

What you see at the airport and on board the plane is specialization. The pilot isn't flying the plane and checking your luggage too. He is only flying the plane. The flight attendant isn't serving you food and checking you through security too. He is only serving you food. Why do people specialize? Largely, it's because individuals have found that they are better off specializing than not specializing. And usually what people specialize in is that activity in which they have a comparative advantage.

ECONOMICS 24/7

Politics and the PPF

Strictly speaking, the PPF is simply a curve that represents the combination of two goods that a country can produce under certain conditions (a given amount of resources and a certain technology). But the PPF is not only a curve; it is a framework of analysis. With it, we can often gain insights into what is happening in the real world. Specifically, the PPF, used as a framework of analysis, can give us some idea of what is behind political battles.

In Exhibit 10, we show the PPF for a country. We assume that the country's economy is currently located at point A, producing 30 units of good X and 35 units of good Y. Notice that the country is efficient in its production: It is located at a point *on* its PPF instead of below it.

Now let's suppose that there are two major political parties in this country: the X and Y parties. On the one hand, party X represents people who would like to move the country in the direction of producing more X. In other words, party X would prefer that the country locate at point B, instead of at point A, on the PPF.

On the other hand, party Y represents people who would like to move the country in the direction of producing more Y. Thus, party Y would prefer that the country locate at point C, instead of at point A, on the PPF.

Will political parties X and Y do battle? Will they be involved in a political tug-of-war, each trying to move the country in a different direction? Probably so.

Now consider what happens when the country falls below its PPF and moves to a point like D in the exhibit. Point D is representative of a country that has unemployed resources; it likely represents an economy in recession, producing far less than it could be producing. At point D, both parties are less content than they were at point A, for the simple reason that less of both goods is

being produced at point D than at point A. One thing we ought to observe, then, is that both political parties will want to move the country out of the recession. But might the ways they propose to move the country be different? Because political party Y prefers point C to point A, and political party X prefers point B to point A, might each party's proposal for "solving the recession" be geared toward its preferred point on the country's PPF? To illustrate, if each political party is proposing federal monies or tax cuts to stimulate output, might political party X's specific proposal be geared toward producing more of good X while political party Y's specific proposal is geared toward producing more of good Y?

> **EXHIBIT 10**

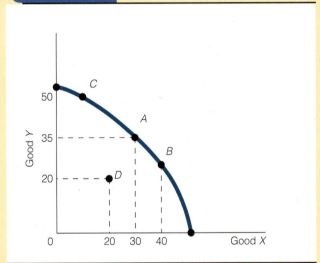

ECONOMICS 24/7

Why Do People Specialize and Trade?

We are born into a world that looks a certain way. For example, we are born into a world where people specialize in producing certain goods. Some people simply produce accounting services, other people simply produce attorney services, or chairs, or computers, and so on.

Having been born into a world where people specialize in the production of some good or service, we take that specialization for granted. That is just the way life is. But "that is just the way life is" because one person's comparative advantage is different from another person's comparative advantage. Usually, the people who have a comparative advantage in producing X produce X, and those who have a comparative advantage in producing Y produce Y.

But do you wonder what would happen if people didn't have different comparative advantages? Do you wonder what would happen if no one could produce a good or service at a lower opportunity cost than anyone else? In other words, do you wonder what would happen if there were no comparative advantages?

To illustrate, suppose there are two persons, A and B, and each can produce two goods, X and Y, in the following combinations:

Hill Street Studios/Blend Images/Alamy

Person A and Person B

Good X	Good Y
0	100
50	50
100	0

The opportunity cost of producing each good, for each person, is the same. The opportunity cost of producing 1X is 1Y, for each person. Neither individual has a comparative advantage in producing either good. There are no "comparative advantages" to be had. It follows that neither person has a reason to specialize in the production of one of the two goods and then trade it for the other good. To see this idea clearly, look at things from the perspective of each person. Suppose each person agreed to produce a different good. Person A chose to produce X and person B chose to produce Y. Person A produces 100 X and person B produces 100 Y. Then, each person trades 50 units of what she has produced to the other person. Each person ends up with 50X and 50Y, which is a combination of two goods that each person could have produced or consumed on her own. In other words, there is no benefit in specializing and trading: Specializing and trading doesn't give one anything more than one gets by not specializing and not trading. Given this state of affairs, we would expect to see less specialization and trade in a world where there are no comparative advantages than in a world where there are comparative advantages.

Why does the world you live in look the way it does? Why do people specialize and trade? Because people have comparative advantages: Some people can produce certain goods and services at a lower opportunity cost than others.

Office  Hours

"What Purpose Does the PPF Serve?"

STUDENT:

Economists seem to have many uses for the PPF. For example, they can talk about scarcity, choice, opportunity costs, and many other topics in terms of the PPF. Beyond this capability, however, what purpose does the PPF serve?

INSTRUCTOR:

One purpose is to ground us in reality. For example, the frontier (or boundary) of the PPF represents scarcity, which is a fact of life. In other words, the frontier of the PPF is essentially saying, "Here is scarcity. Work with it." One of the important effects of acknowledging this fact is that we come to understand what *is* and what *is not* possible. For example, if the economy is currently on the frontier of its PPF, producing 100 units of X and 200 units of Y, then getting more of X is possible, but not without getting less of Y. In other words, the frontier of the PPF grounds us in reality: More of one thing means less of something else.

STUDENT:

But isn't this something we already knew?

INSTRUCTOR:

We understand that more of X means less of Y once someone makes this point, but think of how often we might act as if we didn't know it. John thinks he can work more hours at his job and get a good grade on his upcoming chemistry test. Well, he might be able to get a good grade (say, a 90), but this possibility ignores how much higher the grade could have been (say, five points higher) if he hadn't worked more hours at his job. The frontier of the PPF reminds us that there are trade-offs in life. That is an important reality to be aware of. We ignore it at our own peril.

STUDENT:

I've also heard that the PPF can show us what is necessary before the so-called average person in a country can become richer? Is this true? And how much richer do we mean here?

INSTRUCTOR:

We are talking about becoming richer in terms of having more goods and services. It's possible for the average person to become richer through economic growth. In other words, the average person in society becomes richer if the PPF shifts rightward by more than the population grows. To illustrate, suppose that a 100-person economy is currently producing 100 units of X and 200 units of Y. The average person can then have 1 unit of X and 2 units of Y. Now suppose there is economic growth (shifting the PPF to the right) and the economy can produce more of both goods, X and Y. It produces 200 units of X and 400 units of Y. If the population has not changed (if it is still 100 people), then the average person can now have 2 units of X and 4 units of Y. The average person is richer in terms of both goods. If we change things and let the population grow from 100 persons to, say, 125 persons, it is still possible for the average person to have more through economic growth. With a population of 125 people, the average person now has 1.6 units of X and 3.2 units of good Y. In other words, as long as the productive capability of the economy grows by a greater percentage than the population, the average person can become richer (in terms of goods and services).

STUDENT:

Even if the economy is producing more of both goods (X and Y), the average person isn't necessarily better off in terms of goods and services, right? Can't all the extra output end up in the hands of only a few people instead of being evenly distributed across the entire population.

INSTRUCTOR:

That's correct. What we are assuming when we say that the average person can be better off is that, if we took the extra output and divided it evenly across the population, then the average person would be better off in terms of having more goods and services. By the way, this idea is exactly what economists mean when they say that the output (goods and services) per capita in a population has risen.

Points to remember

1. The PPF grounds us in reality. It tells us what is and what is not possible in terms of producing various combinations of goods and services.
2. The PPF tells us that when we have efficiency (i.e., when we are at a point on the frontier itself), more of one thing means less of

something else. In other words, the PPF tells us life has its trade-offs.
3. If the PPF shifts rightward and the population does not change, then output per capita rises.

CHAPTER SUMMARY

AN ECONOMY'S PRODUCTION POSSIBILITIES FRONTIER

• An economy's PPF represents the possible combinations of two goods that the economy can produce in a certain span of time under the conditions of a given state of technology and fully employed resources.

INCREASING AND CONSTANT OPPORTUNITY COSTS

• A straight-line PPF represents constant opportunity costs: Increased production of a good comes at a constant opportunity cost.
• A bowed-outward (concave-downward) PPF represents the law of increasing opportunity costs: Increased production of a good comes at an increasing opportunity cost.

THE PRODUCTION POSSIBILITIES FRONTIER AND VARIOUS ECONOMIC CONCEPTS

• The PPF can be used to illustrate various economic concepts. Scarcity is illustrated by the frontier itself. Choice is illustrated

by the fact that we have to find a point either on or below the frontier. In short, of the many attainable positions, one must be chosen. Opportunity cost is illustrated by a movement from one point to another on the PPF. Unemployed resources and productive inefficiency are illustrated by a point below the PPF. Productive efficiency and fully employed resources are illustrated by a point on the PPF. Economic growth is illustrated by a shift outward in the PPF.

SPECIALIZATION, TRADE, AND THE PPF

• Individuals can make themselves better off by specializing in the production of the good in which they have a comparative advantage and then trading some of that good for other goods. Someone who can produce the good at a lower opportunity cost than another person can has a comparative advantage in the production of the good.
• By specializing in the production of the good for which they have a comparative advantage and then trading it for other goods, people can move beyond their PPF.

KEY TERMS AND CONCEPTS

Production Possibilities Frontier (PPF)

Law of Increasing Opportunity Costs

Productive Efficiency
Productive Inefficiency

Technology
Comparative Advantage

VIDEO QUESTIONS AND PROBLEMS

Video Questions and Problems are available on MindTap for Arnold 12e or by searching for Arnold on www.cengagebrain.com

1. Explain how to derive a PPF.
2. What does a PPF that is bowed outward imply about the opportunity cost of production?

3. On the basis of the following data, identify which good each person has a comparative advantage in producing:
   a. Person A can produce the following three combinations of goods: (1) 10X and 0Y, (2) 5X and 5Y, (3) 0X and 10Y.

b. Person B can produce the following three combinations of goods: (1) 10X and 0Y, (2) 5X and 15Y, (3) 0X and 30Y.

4. Illustrate scarcity, opportunity cost, and economic growth within a PPF framework of analysis.

5. A country is currently experiencing a high unemployment rate. Represent the country diagrammatically within a PPF framework of analysis.

QUESTIONS AND PROBLEMS

1. Describe how each of the following would affect the U.S. PPF: (a) an increase in the number of illegal immigrants entering the country, (b) a war that takes place on U.S. soil, (c) the discovery of a new oil field, (d) a decrease in the unemployment rate, and (e) a law that requires individuals to enter lines of work for which they are not suited.

2. Explain how the following can be represented in a PPF framework: (a) the finiteness of resources implicit in the scarcity condition, (b) choice, (c) opportunity cost, (d) productive efficiency, and (e) unemployed resources.

3. What condition must hold for the PPF to be bowed outward (concave downward)? To be a straight line?

4. Give an example to illustrate each of the following: (a) constant opportunity costs and (b) increasing opportunity costs.

5. Why are most PPFs for goods bowed outward (concave downward)?

6. Within a PPF framework, explain each of the following: (a) a disagreement between a person who favors more domestic welfare spending and one who favors more national defense spending, (b) an increase in the population, and (c) a technological change that makes resources less specialized.

7. Explain how to derive a PPF. For instance, how is the extreme point on the vertical axis identified? How is the extreme point on the horizontal axis identified?

8. If the slope of the PPF is the same between any two points, what does this relationship imply about costs? Explain your answer.

9. Suppose a nation's PPF shifts inward as its population grows. What happens, on average, to the material standard of living of the people? Explain your answer.

10. Can a technological advancement in sector X of the economy affect the number of people who work in sector Y of the economy? Explain your answer.

11. Use the PPF framework to explain something in your everyday life that was not mentioned in the chapter.

12. What exactly allows individuals to consume more if they specialize and trade than if they don't?

WORKING WITH NUMBERS AND GRAPHS

1. Illustrate constant opportunity costs in a table similar to the one in Exhibit 1(a). Next, draw a PPF that is based on the data in the table.

2. Illustrate increasing opportunity costs (for one good) in a table similar to the one in Exhibit 2(a). Next, draw a PPF based on the data in the table.

3. Draw a PPF that represents the production possibilities for goods X and Y if there are constant opportunity costs. Next, represent an advance in technology that makes it possible to produce more of X but not more of Y. Finally, represent an advance in technology that makes it possible to produce more of Y but not more of X.

4. In the following figure, which graph depicts a technological breakthrough in the production of good X only?

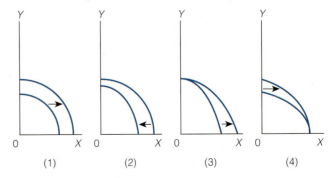

(1)   (2)   (3)   (4)

5. In the preceding figure, which graph depicts a change in the PPF that is a likely consequence of war?

6. If PPF_2 in the graph that follows is the relevant PPF, then which points are unattainable? Explain your answer.

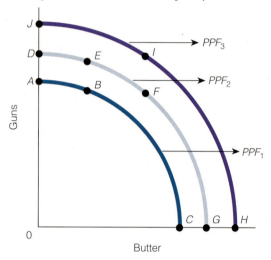

7. If PPF_1 in the preceding figure is the relevant PPF, then which point(s) represent productive efficiency? Explain your answer.

8. Tina can produce any of the following combinations of goods X and Y: (a) 100 X and 0 Y, (b) 50 X and 25 Y, and (c) 0 X and 50 Y. David can produce any of the following combinations of X and Y: (a) 50 X and 0 Y, (b) 25 X and 40 Y, and (c) 0 X and 80 Y. Who has the comparative advantage in the production of good X? Of good Y? Explain your answer.

9. Using the data in problem 8, prove that both Tina and David can be made better off through specialization and trade.

SUPPLY AND DEMAND: THEORY

©Tony Taylor Stock/Shutterstock.com

3-1 WHAT IS DEMAND?

The word **demand** has a precise meaning in economics. It refers to

1. the willingness and ability of buyers to purchase different quantities of a good

2. at different prices

3. during a specific period (per day, week, etc.).[1]

For example, we can express part of John's demand for magazines by saying that he is willing and able to buy 10 magazines a month at $4 per magazine and that he is willing and able to buy 15 magazines a month at $3 per magazine.

Remember this important point about demand: Unless both willingness and ability to buy are present, there is neither demand nor a buyer. For example, Josie may be willing to buy a computer but be unable to pay the price; Tanya may be able to buy a computer but be unwilling to do so. Neither Josie nor Tanya demands a computer, and neither is a buyer of a computer.

Market
Any place people come together to trade.

Demand
The willingness and ability of buyers to purchase different quantities of a good at different prices during a specific period.

---

[1]. Demand takes into account *services* as well as goods. A few examples of goods are shirts, books, and television sets. A few examples of services are dental care, medical care, and an economics lecture. To simplify the discussion, we refer only to goods.

3-1a **The Law of Demand**

Will people buy more units of a good at lower prices than at higher prices? For example, will people buy more shirts at $10 apiece than at $70 apiece? If your answer is yes, you instinctively understand the law of demand. The **law of demand** states that as the price of a good rises, the quantity demanded of the good falls, and that as the price of a good falls, the quantity demanded of the good rises, *ceteris paribus*. Simply put, the law of demand states that the price of a good and the quantity demanded of it are inversely related, *ceteris paribus*. That is,

$$P\uparrow Q_d\downarrow$$

$$P\downarrow Q_d\uparrow, \text{ ceteris paribus}$$

where P = price and Q_d = quantity demanded.

Quantity demanded is the number of units of a good that individuals are willing and able to buy at a particular price during a particular period. For example, suppose individuals are willing and able to buy 100 TV dinners per week at a price of $4 per dinner. Therefore, 100 units is the quantity demanded of TV dinners at $4 per dinner.

A warning: We know that the words "demand" and "quantity demanded" sound alike, but be aware that they do not describe the same thing. Demand is different from quantity demanded. Keep that in mind as you continue to read this chapter. For now, remind yourself that demand speaks to the willingness and ability of buyers to buy different quantities of a good at different prices. Quantity demanded speaks to the willingness and ability of buyers to buy a specific quantity (say, 100 units of a good) at a specific price (say, $10 per unit).

3-1b **Four Ways to Represent the Law of Demand**

Here are four ways to represent the law of demand:

- *In Words.* We can represent the law of demand in words; we have done so already. Earlier we said that as the price of a good rises, quantity demanded falls, and as price falls, quantity demanded rises, *ceteris paribus*. That was the statement (in words) of the law of demand.

- *In Symbols.* We can also represent the law of demand in symbols, as we have also already done. In symbols, the law of demand is

$$P\uparrow Q_d\downarrow$$

$$P\downarrow Q_d\uparrow, \text{ ceteris paribus}$$

- *In a Demand Schedule.* A **demand schedule** is the numerical representation of the law of demand. A demand schedule for good X is illustrated in Exhibit 1(a).

- *As a Demand Curve.* In Exhibit 1(b), the four price–quantity combinations in part (a) are plotted and the points connected, giving us a (downward-sloping) demand curve. A (downward-sloping) **demand curve** is the graphical representation of the inverse relationship between price and quantity demanded specified by the law of demand. In short, a demand curve is a picture of the law of demand.

Law of Demand

As the price of a good rises, the quantity demanded of the good falls, and as the price of a good falls, the quantity demanded of the good rises, *ceteris paribus*.

Demand Schedule

The numerical tabulation of the quantity demanded of a good at different prices. A demand schedule is the numerical representation of the law of demand.

Demand Curve

The graphical representation of the law of demand.

> **EXHIBIT 1**

Demand Schedule and Demand Curve

Part (a) shows a demand schedule for good X. Part (b) shows a demand curve, obtained by plotting the different price–quantity combinations in part (a) and connecting the points. On a demand curve, the price (in dollars) represents price per unit of the good. The quantity demanded, on the horizontal axis, is always relevant for a specific period (a week, a month, and so on).

Demand Schedule for Good X

Price (dollars)	Quantity Demanded	Point in Part (b)
4	10	A
3	20	B
2	30	C
1	40	D

(a)

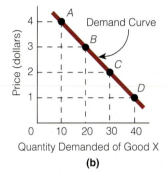

(b)

In a Visit Home to See Mom A friend tells you that she flies home to see her mother only once a year. You ask why. She says, "Because the price of the ticket to fly home is $1,100." She then adds, "If the price were, say, $600 instead of $1,100, I'd fly home twice a year instead of once." Can you find any economics in what she is telling you? If you listen closely to what she says, she has identified two points on her demand curve for air travel home: One point corresponds to $1,100 and buying one ticket home, and the other point corresponds to $600 and buying two tickets home.

3-1c Why Does Quantity Demanded Go Down as Price Goes Up?

The law of demand states that price and quantity demanded are inversely related. This much you know. But do you know *why* quantity demanded moves in the direction opposite that of price? We identify two reasons.

The first reason is that *people substitute lower priced goods for higher priced goods.* Often, many goods serve the same purpose. Many different goods will satisfy hunger, and many different drinks will satisfy thirst. For example, both orange juice and grapefruit juice will satisfy thirst. On Monday, the price of orange juice equals the price of grapefruit juice, but on Tuesday the price of orange juice rises. As a result, people will choose to buy less of the relatively higher priced orange juice and more of the relatively lower priced grapefruit juice. In other words, a rise in the price of orange juice will lead to a decrease in the quantity demanded of it.

The second reason for the inverse relationship between price and quantity demanded has to do with the **law of diminishing marginal utility**, which states that, over a given period, the marginal (or additional) utility or satisfaction gained by consuming equal successive units of a good will decline as the amount of the good consumed increases. For

Law of Diminishing Marginal Utility

Over a given period, the marginal (or additional) utility or satisfaction gained by consuming equal successive units of a good will decline as the amount consumed increases.

ECONOMICS 24/7

Weight Loss, the Price of Food, and the Law of Demand

Start with the law of demand, which states that price and quantity demanded are inversely related, *ceteris paribus*. Applied to food, the law of demand states that as the price of food rises, the quantity demanded of food declines.

Now consider some of the ads that you see on television and in magazines about losing weight. One company that widely advertises its dieting products and services to assist weight loss and management is WeightWatchers. Over the years, spokespersons for WeightWatchers have included celebrities Jennifer Hudson, Charles Barkley, Jessica Simpson, Lynn Redgrave, Sarah Ferguson, and others. Spokespersons appear in ads touting their weight loss due to their following the WeightWatchers weight-loss program. We have no doubt that if people consistently follow the WeightWatchers program they can lose weight. But they could probably do so with other weight-loss programs too, because most such programs offer some combination of lower calorie intake with exercise—both of which can lead to weight loss.

But what might matter more than the particular weight-loss program is the motivation one has to follow the program. The motivation that spokespersons have is that, if they don't lose weight and then keep the weight off, they no longer will be a spokesperson for the weight-loss company and consequently will forfeit a certain amount of income. It is the "potential loss of income" that makes the price of eating food higher (than it ordinarily is) for the spokespersons of the weight-loss program.

Let's put things in the context of spokesperson X for WeightWatchers. Before becoming a spokesperson for WeightWatchers, the person knows that there is a certain price he must pay for food. Given this price, the quantity demanded of food is, say, 3,500 calories of food per day.

But as a spokesperson for a weight-loss program, the individual knows that the price of eating food rises, for the reasons we just specified. Thus, the quantity demanded of food falls to, say, 2,000 calories a day. In the end, is it the specific weight-loss program or the "potential loss of income" that really takes off the weight for the spokesperson?

example, you may receive more utility, or satisfaction, from eating your first hamburger at lunch than from eating your second and, if you continue, more utility from your second hamburger than from your third.

What does marginal utility have to do with the law of demand? Economists state that, the more utility you receive from a unit of a good, the higher the price you are

ECONOMICS 24/7

What Do the Following Have in Common? Losing One's Temper, Arriving to Class Late, and Buying the Textbook for a Class

The answer is that they all abide by the law of demand.

The law of demand states that the price of a good and the quantity demanded of that good are inversely related, *ceteris paribus*. Applied to losing one's temper, this law means that a person is more likely to lose his or her temper with someone who charges a low price than a high price.

The price of something is what you have to give up to get it. Usually, we speak about price in monetary terms. But there are also nonmonetary prices. Consider a person's boss and the person's girlfriend. If a person loses his temper in front of his boss, he might end up "paying a high price" for that. In fact, he could lose his job or end up not getting that promotion. But if he loses his temper in front of his girlfriend, he isn't likely to pay as high a price. On the basis of the law of demand, then, we predict that people will lose their temper more often when the price of losing one's temper is low rather than high.

The same goes for arriving late to class. Very rarely are students late to class when they have to take an exam. That's because, if they are late on exam dates, they will end up with less time to complete the exam, and that can adversely affect their grade. In other words, the price of arriving late to class on exam

Doug Jones/Portland Press Herald/Getty Images

day is fairly high, compared with, say, arriving late to class on a non-exam day.

Lastly, will everyone buy the textbook for a given course? What we observe is that, the higher the price of a text is, the fewer the number of students who will buy the text and the greater the number of students who will try to find a substitute for the assigned text—such as an older edition of it.

willing to pay for it, and the less utility you receive from a unit of a good, the lower the price you are willing to pay for it. According to the law of diminishing marginal utility, individuals obtain less utility from additional units of a good. Therefore, they will buy larger quantities of a good only at lower prices, and their behavior reflects the law of demand.

3-1d Individual Demand Curve and Market Demand Curve

There is a difference between an individual demand curve and a market demand curve.

An individual demand curve represents the price–quantity combinations of a particular good for a *single buyer.* For example, an individual demand curve could show Jones's demand for CDs. By contrast, a market demand curve represents the price–quantity combinations of a good for *all buyers.* In this case, the demand curve would show all buyers' demand for CDs.

A market demand curve is derived by "adding up" individual demand curves, as shown in Exhibit 2. The demand schedules for Jones, Smith, and other buyers are shown in part (a).

> **EXHIBIT 2**

Deriving a Market Demand Schedule and a Market Demand Curve

Part (a) shows four demand schedules combined into one table. The market demand schedule is derived by adding the quantities demanded at each price. In (b), the data points from the demand schedule are plotted to show how a market demand curve is derived. Only two points on the market demand curve are noted.

		Quantity Demanded		
Price	Jones	Smith	Other Buyers	All Buyers
$15	1	2	20	23
14	2	3	45	50
13	3	4	70	77
12	4 +	5 +	100 =	109
11	5 +	6 +	130 =	141
10	6	7	160	173

(a)

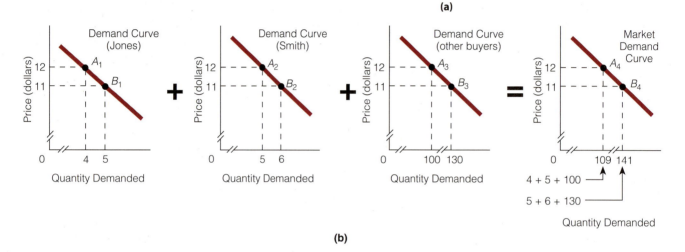

(b)

The market demand schedule is obtained by adding the quantities demanded at each price. For example, at $12, the quantities demanded are 4 units for Jones, 5 units for Smith, and 100 units for other buyers. Thus, a total of 109 units are demanded at $12. In part (b), the data points for the demand schedules are plotted and added to produce a market demand curve. The market demand curve could also be drawn directly from the market demand schedule.

3-1e A Change in Quantity Demanded Versus a Change in Demand

Economists often talk about (1) a change in quantity demanded and (2) a change in demand. As stated earlier, although the phrase "quantity demanded" may sound like "demand," the two are not the same. In short, a change in quantity demanded *is not* the same as a change in demand. (Read the last sentence at least two more times.) We use Exhibit 1 to illustrate the difference between a change in quantity demanded and a change in demand.

A Change in Quantity Demanded   Look at Exhibit 1. The horizontal axis is labeled "Quantity Demanded of Good X." Notice that quantity demanded is a *number*—such as 10, 20, 30, 40, and so on. More specifically, it is the number of units of a good that individuals are willing and able to buy at a particular price during some period. In Exhibit 1, if the price is $4, then the quantity demanded is 10 units of good X; if the price is $3, then the quantity demanded is 20 units of good X. In general,

*Quantity demanded = The number of units of a good that individuals
are willing and able to buy at a particular price*

Now, again looking at Exhibit 1, see if you can figure out what can change quantity demanded from 10 (which it is at point *A*) to 20 (which it is at point *B*). Or what has to change before quantity demanded will change. The answer is on the vertical axis of Exhibit 1. The only thing that can change the quantity demanded of a good is its price:

*Change in quantity demanded = A movement from one point to another point
on the same demand curve that is caused by
a change in the price of the good*

The price of a good is also called **own price**.

A Change in Demand   Look again at Exhibit 1, this time focusing on the demand curve. Demand is represented by the *entire* curve. When talking about a change in demand, an economist is actually talking about a change—or shift—in the entire demand curve:

Change in demand = Shift in demand curve

Demand can change in two ways: Demand can increase, and demand can decrease. Let's look first at an *increase* in demand. Suppose we have the following demand schedule:

Own Price

The price of a good. For example, if the price of oranges is $1, this is its own price.

Demand Schedule A

Price	Quantity Demanded
$20	500
$15	600
$10	700
$5	800

The demand curve for this demand schedule will look like the demand curve labeled D_A in Exhibit 3(a).

What does an increase in demand mean? It means that individuals are willing and able to buy more units of the good at each and every price. In other words, demand schedule *A* will change as follows:

Demand Schedule B (increase in demand)

Price	Quantity Demanded
$20	~~500~~ 600
$15	~~600~~ 700
$10	~~700~~ 800
$5	~~800~~ 900

Whereas individuals were willing and able to buy 500 units of the good at $20, now they are willing and able to buy 600 units of the good at $20; whereas individuals were willing and able to buy 600 units of the good at $15, now they are willing and able to buy 700 units of the good at $15; and so on.

> **EXHIBIT 3**

Shifts in the Demand Curve

In part (a), the demand curve shifts rightward from D_A to D_B. This shift represents an increase in demand. At each price, the quantity demanded is greater than it was before. For example, the quantity demanded at $20 increases from 500 units to 600 units. In part (b), the demand curve shifts leftward from D_A to D_C. This shift represents a decrease in demand. At each price, the quantity demanded is less. For example, the quantity demanded at $20 decreases from 500 units to 400 units.

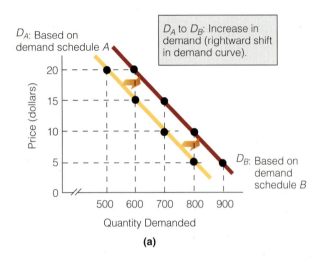

D_A: Based on demand schedule A

D_A to D_B: Increase in demand (rightward shift in demand curve).

D_B: Based on demand schedule B

(a)

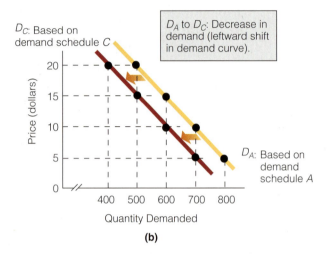

D_C: Based on demand schedule C

D_A to D_C: Decrease in demand (leftward shift in demand curve).

D_A: Based on demand schedule A

(b)

As shown in Exhibit 3(a), the demand curve that represents demand schedule B (D_B) lies to the right of the demand curve that represents demand schedule A (D_A). We conclude that *an increase in demand is represented by a rightward shift in the demand curve and means that individuals are willing and able to buy more of a good at each and every price:*

Increase in demand = Rightward shift in the demand curve

Now let's look at a decrease in demand. A decrease in demand means that individuals are willing and able to buy less of a good at each and every price. In this case, demand schedule A will change as follows:

Demand Schedule C (decrease in demand)

Price	Quantity Demanded
$20	~~500~~ 400
$15	~~600~~ 500
$10	~~700~~ 600
$5	~~800~~ 700

As shown in Exhibit 3(b), the demand curve that represents demand schedule C (D_C) obviously lies to the left of the demand curve that represents demand schedule A (D_A). We conclude that a *decrease in demand is represented by a leftward shift in the demand curve and means that individuals are willing and able to buy less of a good at each and every price:*

Decrease in demand = Leftward shift in the demand curve

3-1f What Factors Cause the Demand Curve to Shift?

We know what an increase in demand and a decrease in demand mean: An increase in demand means that consumers are willing and able to buy *more* of a good at every price. A decrease in demand means that consumers are willing and able to buy *less* of a good at every price. We also know that an increase in demand is graphically portrayed as a rightward shift in a demand curve and that a decrease in demand is graphically portrayed as a leftward shift in a demand curve.

But what factors or variables can increase or decrease demand? What factors or variables can shift demand curves? They are (1) income, (2) preferences, (3) prices of related goods, (4) the number of buyers, and (5) expectations of future prices.

Income   As a person's income changes (increases or decreases), that individual's demand for a particular good may rise, fall, or remain constant.

For example, suppose Jack's income rises and, as a consequence, his demand for CDs rises. Then, for Jack, CDs are a normal good. For a **normal good**, demand rises as income rises and demand falls as income falls:

X is a normal good: If income↑, then D_X↑ If income↓, then D_X↓

Now suppose Marie's income rises and, as a consequence, her demand for canned baked beans falls. Then, for Marie, canned baked beans are an inferior good. For an **inferior good**, demand falls as income rises and demand rises as income falls:

Y is an inferior good: If income↑, then D_Y↓ If income↓, then D_Y↑

Finally, suppose that, when George's income rises, his demand for toothpaste neither rises nor falls. Then, for George, toothpaste is neither a normal good nor an inferior good. Instead, it is a neutral good. For a **neutral good**, demand does not change as income rises or falls.

Preferences   People's preferences affect the amount of a good they are willing to buy at a particular price. A change in preferences in favor of a good shifts the demand curve rightward. A change in preferences away from the good shifts the demand curve leftward. For example, if people begin to favor Elmore Leonard novels to a greater degree than previously, the demand for his novels increases and the demand curve shifts rightward.

Prices of Related Goods   There are two types of related goods: substitutes and complements. Two goods are **substitutes** if they satisfy similar needs or desires. For many people, Coca-Cola and Pepsi-Cola are substitutes. If two goods are substitutes, then, as the price of one rises (falls), the demand for the other rises (falls). For instance, higher Coca-Cola prices will increase the demand for Pepsi-Cola as people substitute Pepsi for the higher priced

Normal Good
A good for which demand rises (falls) as income rises (falls).

Inferior Good
A good for which demand falls (rises) as income rises (falls).

Neutral Good
A good for which demand does not change as income rises or falls.

Substitutes
Two goods that satisfy similar needs or desires. If two goods are substitutes, the demand for one rises as the price of the other rises (or the demand for one falls as the price of the other falls).

ECONOMICS 24/7

Kindles and the Law of Demand

The law of demand holds that the price of a good and the quantity demanded of the good are inversely related. But does the law of demand hold for an individual when it comes to a good like an eReader, such as the Kindle? Will the individual buy more Kindles at $199 than at $299? Perhaps she will, if only to give some Kindles to friends.

But suppose that the person doesn't want to give away any Kindles as gifts. She wants only a Kindle for herself. How many more than one Kindle does she need? Probably none, because there is little use in buying two Kindles if one Kindle holds all the books she wants. In other words, instead of having a downward-sloping demand curve for Kindles, an individual's demand curve might look like the one in Exhibit 4(a). This curve says that the individual will buy one Kindle no matter what the price is between zero and $300. But if the price is above $300, she will not buy a Kindle, because the demand curve doesn't extend that high.

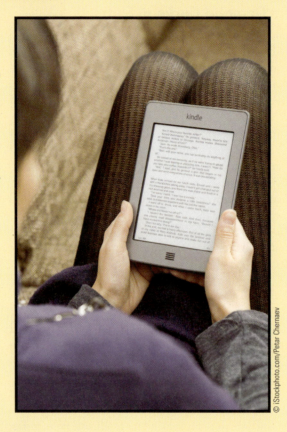

© iStockphoto.com/Petar Chernaev

Suppose no person has a downward-sloping demand curve. Is it still possible for the market demand curve to be downward sloping? The answer is yes. To understand why, consider another person's demand curve for a Kindle, shown in Exhibit 4(b). This demand curve says that the person is willing and able to buy one Kindle if the price is anywhere between zero and $200 but she won't buy a Kindle if the price is higher than $200.

If we horizontally sum the two demand curves in parts (a) and (b) to get the market demand curve, we see that, at a price of $300 one Kindle will be purchased, and at $200 two Kindles will be purchased. [See Exhibit 4(c).] Notice that summing in this manner gives us a downward-sloping demand curve: More Kindles are bought at a lower price than at a higher price.

> **EXHIBIT 4**

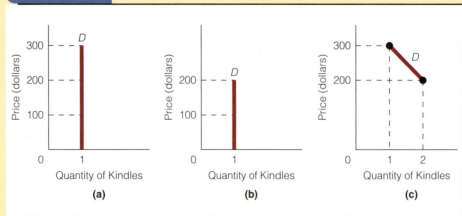

Coke. [See Exhibit 5(a).] Other examples of substitutes are coffee and tea, corn chips and potato chips, different brands of margarine, and foreign and domestic cars. Generalizing, we obtain

X and Y are substitutes: If $P_X\uparrow$, then $D_Y\uparrow$ If $P_X\downarrow$, then $D_Y\downarrow$

Two goods are **complements** if they are consumed jointly. For example, tennis rackets and tennis balls are used together to play tennis. If two goods are complements, then, as the price of one rises (falls), the demand for the other falls (rises). For example, higher tennis racket prices will decrease the demand for tennis balls, as Exhibit 5(b) shows. Other examples of complements are cars and tires, lightbulbs and lamps, and golf clubs and golf balls. Generalizing yields the following relationship:

X and Y are complements: If $P_X\uparrow$, then $D_Y\downarrow$ If $P_X\downarrow$, then $D_Y\uparrow$

Complements

Two goods that are used jointly in consumption. If two goods are complements, the demand for one rises as the price of the other falls (or the demand for one falls as the price of the other rises).

> **EXHIBIT 5**

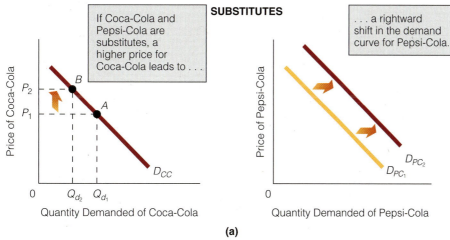

Substitutes and Complements

(a) Coca-Cola and Pepsi-Cola are substitutes: The price of one and the demand for the other are directly related. As the price of Coca-Cola rises, the demand for Pepsi-Cola increases. (b) Tennis rackets and tennis balls are complements: The price of one and the demand for the other are inversely related. As the price of tennis rackets rises, the demand for tennis balls decreases.

Number of Buyers   The demand for a good in a particular market area is related to the number of buyers in the area: more buyers means higher demand; fewer buyers means lower demand. The number of buyers may increase owing to a heightened birthrate, rising immigration, the migration of people from one region of the country to another, and so on. The number of buyers may decrease owing to an increased death rate, war, the migration of people from one region of the country to another, and so on.

Expectations of Future Price   Buyers who expect the price of a good to be higher next month may buy it now, thus increasing the current (or present) demand for the good. Buyers who expect the price of a good to be lower next month may wait until next month to buy it, thus decreasing the current (or present) demand for the good.

For example, suppose you are planning to buy a house. One day, you hear that house prices are expected to go down in a few months. Consequently, you decide to delay your purchase for a while. Alternatively, if you hear that prices are expected to rise in a few months, you might go ahead and make your purchase now.

3-1g Movement Factors and Shift Factors

Economists often distinguish between (1) factors that can bring about movement along curves and (2) factors that can shift curves.

The factors that cause movement along curves are sometimes called *movement* factors. In many economic diagrams, such as the demand curve in Exhibit 1, the movement factor (price) is on the vertical axis.

The factors that actually shift the curves are sometimes called *shift* factors. The shift factors for the demand curve are income, preferences, the price of related goods, and so on. Often, shift factors do not appear in the economic diagrams. For example, although in Exhibit 1 the movement factor—price—is on the vertical axis, the shift factors do not appear anywhere in the diagram. We just know what they are and that they can shift the demand curve.

When you see a curve in this book, first ask which factor will move us along the curve. In other words, what is the movement factor? Second, ask which factors will shift the curve. In other words, what are the shift factors? Exhibit 6 summarizes the shift factors that can change demand and the movement factors that can change quantity demanded.

Soft Drinks Go on Sale Karen buys more soft drinks when they go on sale. Two people interpret this action differently. John says that if Karen buys more soft drinks when they go on sale, then Karen's demand curve has shifted to the right. Laura says that if Karen buys more soft drinks when they go on sale, then Karen is simply moving down on her individual demand curve. "Karen's quantity demanded of soft drinks," says Laura, "has increased."

Who is right? Laura is. Saying that soft drinks went on sale is no more than saying that the price of soft drinks declined. As price declines, quantity demanded (not demand) increases.

> **EXHIBIT 6**

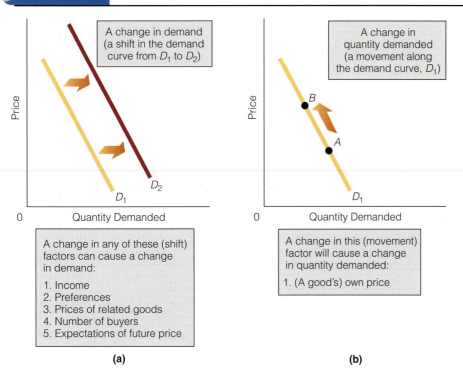

A change in demand (a shift in the demand curve from D_1 to D_2)

A change in quantity demanded (a movement along the demand curve, D_1)

A change in any of these (shift) factors can cause a change in demand:

1. Income
2. Preferences
3. Prices of related goods
4. Number of buyers
5. Expectations of future price

A change in this (movement) factor will cause a change in quantity demanded:

1. (A good's) own price

(a)

(b)

A Change in Demand Versus a Change in Quantity Demanded

(a) A change in demand refers to a shift in the demand curve. A change in demand can be brought about by a number of factors. (see the exhibit and the text.) (b) A change in quantity demanded refers to a movement along a given demand curve. A change in quantity demanded is brought about only by a change in (a good's) own price.

SELF-TEST

(Answers to Self-Test questions are in Answers to Self-Test Questions at the back of the book.)

1. As Sandi's income rises, her demand for popcorn rises. As Mark's income falls, his demand for prepaid telephone cards rises. What kinds of goods are popcorn for Sandi and telephone cards for Mark?

2. Why are demand curves downward sloping?

3. Give an example that illustrates how to derive a market demand curve.

4. What factors can change demand? What factors can change quantity demanded?

3-2 SUPPLY

Just as the word "demand" has a specific meaning in economics, so does the word "supply." **Supply** refers to

1. the willingness and ability of sellers to produce and offer to sell different quantities of a good

2. at different prices

3. during a specific period (per day, week, etc.).

Supply
The willingness and ability of sellers to produce and offer to sell different quantities of a good at different prices during a specific period.

> EXHIBIT 7

A Supply Curve

The upward-sloping supply curve is the graphical representation of the law of supply, which states that price and quantity supplied are directly related, *ceteris paribus*. On a supply curve, the price (in dollars) represents the price per unit of the good. The quantity supplied, on the horizontal axis, is always relevant for a specific period (a week, a month, and so on).

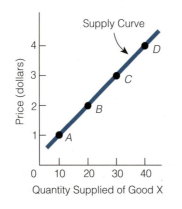

Law of Supply

As the price of a good rises, the quantity supplied of the good rises, and as the price of a good falls, the quantity supplied of the good falls, *ceteris paribus*.

(Upward-Sloping) Supply Curve

The graphical representation of the law of supply.

3-2a The Law of Supply

The **law of supply** states that as the price of a good rises, the quantity supplied of the good rises, and as the price of a good falls, the quantity supplied of the good falls, *ceteris paribus*. Simply put, the price of a good and the quantity supplied of the good are directly related, *ceteris paribus*. (The quantity supplied is the number of units that sellers are willing and able to produce and offer to sell at a particular price.) The **(upward-sloping) supply curve** is the graphical representation of the law of supply. (see Exhibit 7.) The law of supply can be summarized as

$$P \uparrow Q_s \uparrow$$

$$P \downarrow Q_s \downarrow, \text{ ceteris paribus}$$

where P = price and Q_s = quantity supplied.

The law of supply holds for the production of most goods. It does not hold when there is no time to produce more units of a good. For example, suppose a theater in Atlanta is sold out for tonight's play. Then, even if ticket prices increased from $30 to $40, the theater would have no additional seats and no time to produce more. The supply curve for theater seats is illustrated in Exhibit 8(a). It is fixed at the number of seats in the theater, 500.[2]

The law of supply also does not hold for goods that cannot be produced over any period. For example, the violin maker Antonio Stradivari died in 1737, so, because he

> EXHIBIT 8

Supply Curves When There Is No Time to Produce More or When No More Can Be Produced

The supply curve is not upward sloping when there is no time to produce additional units or when additional units cannot be produced. In those cases, the supply curve is vertical.

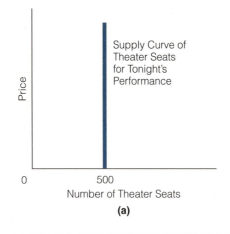

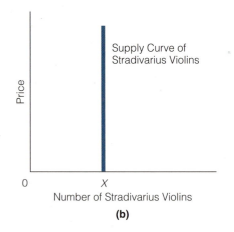

---

2. The vertical supply curve is said to be *perfectly inelastic*.

cannot produce any violins anymore, a rise in the price of Stradivarius violins does not affect the number of Stradivarius violins supplied, as Exhibit 8(b) illustrates.

3-2b Why Most Supply Curves Are Upward Sloping

Most supply curves are upward sloping. The fundamental reason for this behavior involves the *law of diminishing marginal returns*, discussed in a later chapter. Here, suffice it to say that an upward-sloping supply curve reflects the fact that, under certain conditions, a higher price is an incentive to producers to produce more of the good. The incentive comes in the form of higher profits. For example, suppose the price of good X rises, and nothing else (such as the per-unit costs of producing good X) changes. In that case, the producers of good X will earn higher profits per unit and are thus encouraged to increase the quantity of good X that they supply to the market.

Generally, though, producing more of a good does not come with constant per-unit costs. As we learned in Chapter 2, the law of increasing opportunity costs is usually at work. In other words, the increased production of a good comes at increased opportunity costs. An upward-sloping supply curve simply reflects the fact that costs rise when more units of a good are produced.

The Market Supply Curve An individual supply curve represents the price–quantity combinations for a single seller. The market supply curve represents the price–quantity combinations for all sellers of a particular good. Exhibit 9 shows how a market supply curve can be derived by adding individual supply curves. In part (a), a **supply schedule**, the numerical tabulation of the quantity supplied of a good at different prices is given for Brown, Alberts, and other suppliers. The market supply schedule is obtained by adding the quantities supplied at each price, *ceteris paribus*. For example, at $11, the quantities supplied are 2 units for Brown, 3 units for Alberts, and 98 units for the other suppliers. Thus, 103 units are supplied at $11. In part (b), the data points for the supply schedules are plotted and added to produce a market supply curve (which could also be drawn directly from the market supply schedule).

Supply Schedule
The numerical tabulation of the quantity supplied of a good at different prices. A supply schedule is the numerical representation of the law of supply.

3-2c Changes in Supply Mean Shifts in Supply Curves

Just as demand can change, so can supply. The supply of a good can rise or fall. An increase in the supply of a good means that suppliers are willing and able to produce, and offer to sell more of, the good at all prices. For example, suppose that in January sellers are willing and able to produce and offer for sale 600 shirts at $25 each and that in February they are willing and able to produce and sell 900 shirts at $25 each. Then an increase in supply shifts the entire supply curve to the right, as shown in Exhibit 10(a).

The supply of a good decreases if sellers are willing and able to produce and offer to sell less of the good at all prices. For example, suppose that in January sellers are willing and able to produce and offer for sale 600 shirts at $25 each and that in February they are willing and able to produce and sell only 300 shirts at $25 each. Then a decrease in supply shifts the entire supply curve to the left, as shown in Exhibit 10(b).

3-2d What Factors Cause the Supply Curve to Shift?

We know that the supply of any good can change, but what causes supply to change? What causes supply curves to shift? The factors that can change supply include (1) the prices of relevant resources, (2) technology, (3) the prices of related goods, (4) the number of sellers, (5) expectations of future price, (6) taxes and subsidies, and (7) government restrictions.

> **EXHIBIT 9**

Price	Quantity Supplied			
	Brown	**Alberts**	**Other Suppliers**	**All Suppliers**
$10	1	2	96	99
11	2 +	3 +	98 =	103
12	3 +	4 +	102 =	109
13	4	5	106	115
14	5	6	108	119
15	6	7	110	123

(a)

Deriving a Market Supply Schedule and a Market Supply Curve

Part (a) shows four supply schedules combined into one table. The market supply schedule is derived by adding the quantities supplied at each price. In (b), the data points from the supply schedules are plotted to show how a market supply curve is derived. Only two points on the market supply curve are noted.

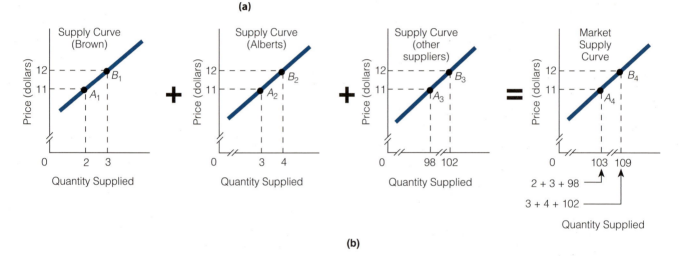

(b)

> **EXHIBIT 10**

Shifts in the Supply Curve

(a) The supply curve shifts rightward from S_1 to S_2. This shift represents an increase in the supply of shirts: At each price, the quantity supplied of shirts is greater. For example, the quantity supplied at $25 increases from 600 shirts to 900 shirts. (b) The supply curve shifts leftward from S_1 to S_2. This shift represents a decrease in the supply of shirts: At each price, the quantity supplied of shirts is less. For example, the quantity supplied at $25 decreases from 600 shirts to 300 shirts.

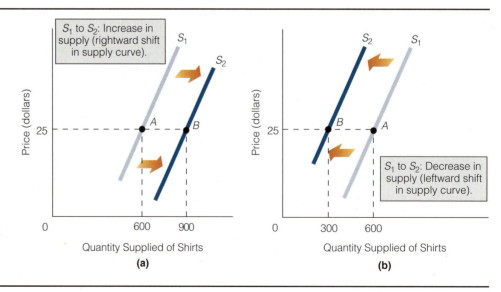

Prices of Relevant Resources

Resources are needed to produce goods. For example, wood is needed to produce doors. If the price of wood falls, producing doors becomes less costly. How will door producers respond? Will they produce more doors, the same number, or fewer? With lower costs and prices unchanged, the profit from producing and selling doors has increased; as a result, the (monetary) incentive to produce doors is increased. So door producers will produce and offer to sell more doors at each and every price. Thus, the supply of doors will increase, and the supply curve of doors will shift rightward. If the price of wood rises, producing doors becomes more costly. Consequently, the supply of doors will decrease, and the supply curve of doors will shift leftward.

Technology

In Chapter 2, technology was defined as the body of skills and knowledge involved in the use of resources in production. Also, an advance in technology was said to refer to the ability to produce more output with a fixed amount of resources, reducing per-unit production costs. To illustrate, suppose it takes $100 to produce 40 units of a good. Then the per-unit cost is $2.50. If an advance in technology makes it possible to produce 50 units at a cost of $100, then the per-unit cost falls to $2.00.

We expect that if the per-unit production costs of a good decline, then the quantity supplied of the good at each price will increase. Why? Lower per-unit costs increase profitability and therefore provide producers with an incentive to produce more. For example, if corn growers develop a way to grow more corn by using the same amount of water and other resources, then per-unit production costs will fall, profitability will increase, and growers will want to grow and sell more corn at each price. The supply curve of corn will shift rightward.

Prices of Other Goods

Think of a farmer who is producing wheat. Suddenly, the price of something he is not producing (say, corn) rises relative to the price of wheat. The farmer might then shift his farming away from wheat to corn. In other words, as the price of corn rises relative to wheat, the farmer switches from wheat production to corn production. We conclude that a change in the price of one good can lead to a change in the supply of another good.

Number of Sellers

If more sellers begin producing a good, perhaps because of high profits, the supply curve will shift rightward. If some sellers stop producing a good, perhaps because of losses, the supply curve will shift leftward.

Expectations of Future Price

If the price of a good is expected to be higher in the future, producers may hold back some of the product today (if possible—perishables cannot be held back). Then they will have more to sell at the higher future price. Therefore, the *current* supply curve will shift leftward. For example, if oil producers expect the price of oil to be higher next year, some may hold oil off the market this year to be able to sell it next year. Similarly, if they expect the price of oil to be lower next year, they might pump more oil this year than previously planned.

Taxes and Subsidies

Some taxes increase per-unit costs. Suppose a shoe manufacturer must pay a $2 tax per pair of shoes produced. This tax leads to a leftward shift in the supply curve, indicating that the manufacturer wants to produce and offer to sell fewer pairs of shoes at each price. If the tax is eliminated, the supply curve shifts rightward.

Subsidies have the opposite effect. Suppose the government subsidizes the production of corn by paying corn farmers $2 for every bushel of corn they produce. Then,

Subsidy
A monetary payment by government to a producer of a good or service.

because of the subsidy, the quantity supplied of corn is greater at each price and the supply curve of corn shifts rightward. The removal of the subsidy shifts the supply curve of corn leftward. A rough rule of thumb is that we get more of what we subsidize and less of what we tax.

Government Restrictions   Sometimes government acts to reduce supply. Consider a U.S. import quota—a quantitative restriction on foreign goods—on Japanese television sets. The quota reduces the supply of Japanese television sets in the United States. It thus shifts the supply curve leftward. The elimination of the import quota allows the supply of Japanese television sets in the United States to shift rightward.

Licensure has a similar effect. With licensure, individuals must meet certain requirements before they can legally carry out a task. For example, owner–operators of day-care centers must meet certain requirements before they are allowed to sell their services. No doubt this requirement reduces the number of day-care centers and shifts the supply curve of day-care centers leftward.

3-2e A Change in Supply Versus a Change in Quantity Supplied

A change in *supply* is not the same as a change in *quantity supplied*. A change in supply is a shift in the supply curve, as illustrated in Exhibit 11(a). For example, saying that the supply of oranges has increased is the same as saying that the

> **EXHIBIT 11**

A Change in Supply Versus a Change in Quantity Supplied

(a) A change in supply refers to a shift in the supply curve. A change in supply can be brought about by a number of factors. (See the exhibit and the text.) (b) A change in quantity supplied refers to a movement along a given supply curve. A change in quantity supplied is brought about only by a change in (a good's) own price.

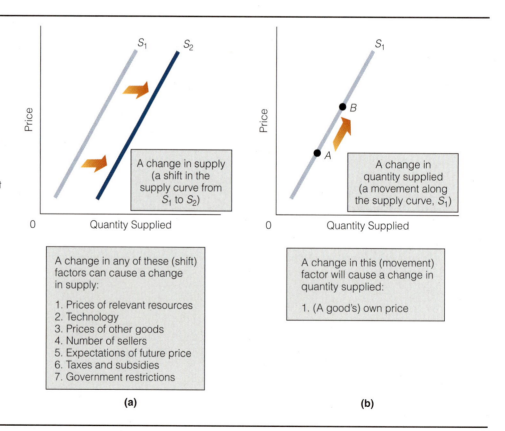

A change in supply (a shift in the supply curve from S_1 to S_2)

A change in quantity supplied (a movement along the supply curve, S_1)

A change in any of these (shift) factors can cause a change in supply:

1. Prices of relevant resources
2. Technology
3. Prices of other goods
4. Number of sellers
5. Expectations of future price
6. Taxes and subsidies
7. Government restrictions

A change in this (movement) factor will cause a change in quantity supplied:

1. (A good's) own price

(a)   (b)

supply curve for oranges has shifted rightward. The factors that can change supply (i.e., shift the supply curve) are prices of relevant resources, technology, prices of other goods, the number of sellers, expectations of future prices, taxes and subsidies, and government restrictions.

A change in quantity supplied refers to a movement along a supply curve, as in Exhibit 11(b). The only factor that can directly cause a change in the quantity supplied of a good is a change in the price of the good.

SELF-TEST

1. What would the supply curve for houses (in a given city) look like for a period of (a) the next 10 hours and (b) the next three months?

2. What happens to the supply curve if each of the following occurs?

   a. The number of sellers decreases.

   b. A per-unit tax is placed on the production of a good.

   c. The price of a relevant resource falls.

3. "If the price of apples rises, the supply of apples will rise." True or false? Explain your answer.

3-3 THE MARKET: PUTTING SUPPLY AND DEMAND TOGETHER

In this section, we put supply and demand together and discuss the market. The purpose of the discussion is to gain some understanding about how prices are determined.

3-3a Supply and Demand at Work at an Auction

In Exhibit 12, the supply curve of corn is vertical. It intersects the horizontal axis at 40,000 bushels; that is, the quantity supplied is 40,000 bushels. The demand curve for corn is downward sloping.

Now, suppose you are at a computerized auction where bushels of corn are bought and sold. At this auction, the auctioneer will adjust the corn price to sell all the corn offered for sale. Each potential buyer of corn is sitting in front of a computer and can immediately input the number of bushels he or she wants to buy. For example, if Nancy wants to buy 5,000 bushels of corn, she simply keys "5,000" into her computer. The total number of bushels that all potential buyers are willing and able to buy appears on the auctioneer's computer screen.

> **EXHIBIT 12**

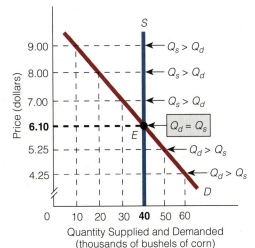

Supply and Demand at Work at an Auction

Let Q_d = quantity demanded and Q_s = quantity supplied. The auctioneer calls out different prices, and buyers record how much they are willing and able to buy. At prices of $9.00, $8.00, and $7.00, $Q_s > Q_d$. At prices of $4.25 and $5.25, $Q_d > Q_s$. At a price of $6.10, $Q_d = Q_s$.

The auction begins. Follow along in Exhibit 12 as it develops. The auctioneer announces the price on the computer screens:

- *$9.00!* The potential buyers think for a second and then register the numbers of bushels they are willing and able to buy at that price. On the auctioneer's screen, the total is 10,000 bushels, which is the quantity demanded of corn at $9.00. The auctioneer, realizing that 30,000 bushels of corn (40,000 – 10,000 = 30,000) will go unsold at this price, decides to lower the price per bushel.

- *$8.00!* The quantity demanded increases to 20,000 bushels, but still the quantity supplied of corn at this price is greater than the quantity demanded. The auctioneer tries again.

- *$7.00!* The quantity demanded increases to 30,000 bushels, but the quantity supplied at $7.00 is still greater than the quantity demanded. The auctioneer drops the price further.

- *$4.25!* At this price, the quantity demanded jumps to 60,000 bushels, but that is 20,000 bushels more than the quantity supplied. The auctioneer calls out a higher price.

- *$5.25!* The quantity demanded drops to 50,000 bushels, but buyers still want to buy more corn at this price than there is corn to be sold. The auctioneer calls out one more time.

- *$6.10!* At this price, the quantity demanded of corn is 40,000 bushels and the quantity supplied of corn is 40,000 bushels. The auction stops. Sold! The 40,000 bushels of corn are bought and sold at $6.10 per bushel.

3-3b The Language of Supply and Demand: A Few Important Terms

If the quantity supplied is greater than the quantity demanded, a **surplus**, or **excess supply**, exists. If the quantity demanded is greater than the quantity supplied, a **shortage**, or **excess demand**, exists. In Exhibit 12, a surplus exists at $9.00, $8.00, and $7.00. A shortage exists at $4.25 and $5.25. The price at which the quantity demanded equals the quantity supplied is the **equilibrium price**, or **market-clearing price**. In our example, $6.10 is the equilibrium price. The quantity that corresponds to the equilibrium price is the **equilibrium quantity**. In our example, it is 40,000 bushels of corn. Any price at which quantity demanded is not equal to quantity supplied is a **disequilibrium price**.

A market that exhibits either a surplus ($Q_s > Q_d$) or a shortage ($Q_d > Q_s$) is said to be in **disequilibrium**. A market in which the quantity demanded equals the quantity supplied ($Q_d = Q_s$) is said to be in **equilibrium** (point *E* in Exhibit 12).

3-3c Moving to Equilibrium: What Happens to Price When There Is a Surplus or a Shortage?

What did the auctioneer do when the price was $9.00 and there was a surplus of corn? He lowered the price. What did the auctioneer do when the price was $5.25 and there was a shortage of corn? He raised the price. The behavior of the auctioneer can be summarized in this way: If a surplus exists, lower the price; if a shortage exists, raise the price. That is how the auctioneer moved the corn market into equilibrium.

Not all markets have auctioneers. (When was the last time you saw an auctioneer in the grocery store?) But many markets act *as if* an auctioneer were calling out higher and lower prices until the equilibrium price is reached. In many real-world, auctioneerless markets, prices fall when there is a surplus and rise when there is a shortage. Why?

Surplus (Excess Supply)
A condition in which the quantity supplied is greater than the quantity demanded. Surpluses occur only at prices above the equilibrium price.

Shortage (Excess Demand)
A condition in which the quantity demanded is greater than the quantity supplied. Shortages occur only at prices below the equilibrium price.

Equilibrium Price (Market-Clearing Price)
The price at which the quantity demanded of a good equals the quantity supplied.

Equilibrium Quantity
The quantity that corresponds to the equilibrium price. The quantity at which the amount of the good that buyers are willing and able to buy equals the amount that sellers are willing and able to sell, and both equal the amount actually bought and sold.

Disequilibrium Price
A price other than the equilibrium price. A price at which the quantity demanded does not equal the quantity supplied.

Disequilibrium
A state of either surplus or shortage in a market.

Equilibrium
Equilibrium means "at rest." Equilibrium in a market is the price–quantity combination from which buyers or sellers do not tend to move away. Graphically, equilibrium is the intersection point of the supply and demand curves.

Why Does Price Fall When There Is a Surplus?   In Exhibit 13, there is a surplus at a price of $15: The quantity supplied (150 units) is greater than the quantity demanded (50 units). At $15, suppliers will not be able to sell all they had hoped to sell. As a result, their inventories will grow beyond the level they hold in preparation for changes in demand. Sellers will then want to reduce their inventories. Some will lower prices to do so, some will cut back on production, and others will do a little of both. As shown in the exhibit, price and output tend to fall until equilibrium is achieved.

Why Does Price Rise When There Is a Shortage   In Exhibit 13, there is a shortage at a price of $5: The quantity demanded (150 units) is greater than the quantity supplied (50 units). At $5, buyers will not be able to buy all they had hoped to buy. Some buyers will then bid up the price to get sellers to sell to them instead of to other buyers. Some sellers, seeing buyers clamor for the goods, will realize that they can raise the price of the goods they have for sale. Higher prices will also call forth added output. Thus, price and output tend to rise until equilibrium is achieved.

Exhibit 14 brings together much of what we have discussed about supply and demand.

3-3d Speed of Moving to Equilibrium

On April 30, 2014, at 9:01 a.m. (Eastern time), the price of a share of IBM stock was $194.38. A few minutes later, the price had risen to $195.11. Obviously, the stock market equilibrates quickly. If demand rises, then initially there is a shortage of the stock at the current equilibrium price. The price is then bid up, and there is no longer a shortage. All this happens in seconds.

Now consider a house offered for sale in any city in the United States. The sale price of a house may remain the same even though the house does not sell for months. For example, a person offers to sell her house for $400,000. One month passes, no sale; two months pass, no sale; three months pass, no sale; and so on. Ten months later, the house is still not sold and the price is still $400,000.

> **EXHIBIT 13**

Moving to Equilibrium

If there is a surplus, sellers' inventories rise above the level the sellers hold in preparation for changes in demand. Sellers will want to reduce their inventories. As a result, price and output fall until equilibrium is achieved. If there is a shortage, some buyers will bid up the price of a good to get sellers to sell to them instead of to other buyers. Some sellers will realize they can raise the price of the goods they have for sale. Higher prices will call forth added output. Price and output rise until equilibrium is achieved. (*Note:* Recall that price, on the vertical axis, is price per unit of the good, and quantity, on the horizontal axis, is for a specific period. In this text, we do not specify those qualifications on the axes themselves, but consider them to be understood.)

Price	Q_s	Q_d	Condition
$15	150	50	Surplus
10	100	100	Equilibrium
5	50	150	Shortage

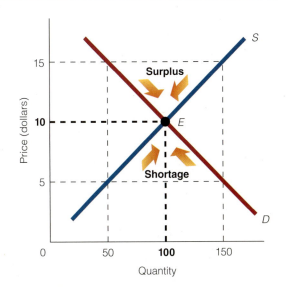

> EXHIBIT 14

A Summary Exhibit of a Market (Supply and Demand)

This exhibit ties together the topics discussed so far in the chapter. A market is composed of both supply and demand, as shown. Also shown are the factors that affect supply and demand and therefore indirectly affect the equilibrium price and quantity of a good.

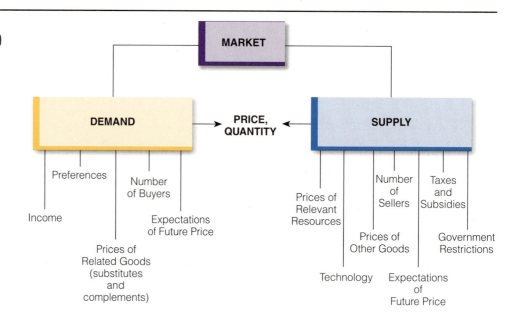

Is $400,000 the equilibrium price of the house? Obviously not. At the equilibrium price, there would be a buyer for the house and a seller of the house: The quantity demanded would equal the quantity supplied. At a price of $400,000, there is a seller but no buyer. The $400,000 price is above the equilibrium price. At $400,000, the housing market has a surplus; equilibrium has not been achieved.

Some people may be tempted to argue that supply and demand are at work in the stock market but not in the housing market. A better explanation, though, is that *not all markets equilibrate at the same speed.* Although the stock market may take only seconds to go from surplus or shortage to equilibrium, the housing market may take months to do so.

3-3e Moving to Equilibrium: Maximum and Minimum Prices

There is another way to demonstrate how a market moves to equilibrium. Exhibit 15 shows the market for good X. Look at the first unit of good X. What is the *maximum price buyers are willing to pay* for it? The answer is $70. Just follow the dotted line up from the first unit of the good to the demand curve. What is the *minimum price sellers need to receive before they are willing to sell* this unit of good X? It is $10. Follow the dotted line up from the first unit to the supply curve. Because the maximum buying price is greater than the minimum selling price, the first unit of good X will be exchanged.

What about the second unit? For the second unit, buyers are willing to pay a maximum price of $60 and sellers need to receive a minimum price of $20. Thus, the second unit of good X will be exchanged. In fact, exchange will occur as long as the maximum buying price is greater than the minimum selling price. The exhibit shows that a total of four units of good X will be exchanged. The fifth unit will not be exchanged, because the maximum buying price ($30) is less than the minimum selling price ($50).

> **EXHIBIT 15**

Moving to Equilibrium in Terms of Maximum and Minimum Prices

As long as the maximum buying price of a good is greater than the minimum selling price, an exchange will occur. This condition is met for units 1–4. The market converges on equilibrium through a process of mutually beneficial exchanges.

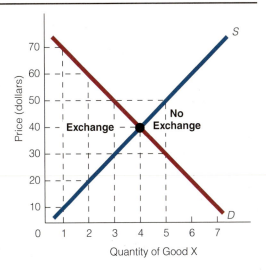

Units of Good X	Maximum Buying Price	Minimum Selling Price	Result
1st	$70	$10	Exchange
2nd	60	20	Exchange
3rd	50	30	Exchange
4th	40	40	Exchange
5th	30	50	No exchange

In this process, buyers and sellers trade money for goods as long as both benefit from the trade. The market converges on a quantity of 4 units of good X and a price of $40 per unit. This point is the equilibrium point. In other words, mutually beneficial trade drives the market to equilibrium.

3-3f The Connection Between Equilibrium and Predictions

In a market setting, both equilibrium and disequilibrium are real-world states. A market is in disequilibrium if there is either a shortage or a surplus in the market. In other words, if quantity demanded is not equal to quantity supplied, the market is in disequilibrium. In contrast, if quantity demanded equals quantity supplied, the market is in equilibrium.

Besides being real-world states, equilibrium and disequilibrium are mental constructs that economists use to think about things. As a mental construct, equilibrium represents a balance of forces from which there is no tendency to move. Disequilibrium represents an imbalance, from which there is a tendency to move. To illustrate, when a market is in disequilibrium, such as when quantity demanded is greater than quantity supplied, price will *move up*. When quantity supplied is greater than quantity demanded, price will *move down*. In other words, disequilibrium, as a mental construct, means that something is going to happen. What exists now won't continue to exist for long. The last page of the book has yet to be read.

Seen in this light, the concepts of equilibrium and disequilibrium are used by economists to "foreshadow" what is about to happen. Hence, both concepts are related to the predictions that economists make.

To see this relationship explicitly, consider again a market in disequilibrium: The quantity demanded of a good is greater than the quantity supplied. For the economist, this state of affairs is temporary. The market, currently in disequilibrium, will soon edge its way over to equilibrium. The economist, then, knows where the market is headed.

Knowing where it is headed—to equilibrium—he then makes a prediction that might sound something like this:

> *The market is currently in disequilibrium, with quantity demanded being greater than quantity supplied. A state of equilibrium exists when quantity demanded equals quantity supplied. So, disequilibrium will soon turn into equilibrium. (Notice here that the economist is making a prediction: Disequilibrium will turn into equilibrium.) It follows that things will soon change. How will they change, you ask? Well, quantity demanded will need to go down, and quantity supplied will need to rise, so that they equal each other. (Again, the economist is making a prediction of what is to come.) And how will this state of affairs come about? By price rising (again, another prediction).*

We conclude that the economist's concept of equilibrium is related to the economist's predictions. It is a two-step process:

1. *The economist compares "what is" with what exists in equilibrium. For example, the market shortage is compared with market equilibrium.*

2. *If "what is" is not what exists in equilibrium, then the economist predicts the path the market will take to get from "what is" to equilibrium. For example, price will rise until quantity demanded and quantity supplied are equal.*

In short, the economist uses the concepts of disequilibrium and equilibrium in much the same way that a person uses a map. We are at point X and we want to go to point Y. The shortest route is this way. The economist says, the market is in disequilibrium and soon it will be in equilibrium. Here is the "path" (I predict) that the market will follow to get from disequilibrium to equilibrium.

3-3g Equilibrium in Terms of Consumers' and Producers' Surplus

Consumers' Surplus (CS)
The difference between the maximum price a buyer is willing and able to pay for a good or service and the price actually paid. (CS = Maximum buying price − Price paid.)

Equilibrium can be viewed in terms of two important economic concepts: consumers' surplus and producers' (or sellers') surplus. **Consumers' surplus** is the difference between the maximum buying price and the price paid by the buyer:

$$Consumers'\ surplus = Maximum\ buying\ price - Price\ paid$$

For example, if the highest price you would pay to see a movie is $10 and you pay $7 to see it, then you have received a $3 consumers' surplus. Obviously, the more consumers' surplus that consumers receive, the better off they are. Wouldn't you have preferred to pay, say, $4 to see the movie instead of $7? If you had paid only $4, your consumers' surplus would have been $6 instead of $3.

Producers' (Sellers') Surplus (PS)
The difference between the price sellers receive for a good and the minimum or lowest price for which they would have sold the good. (PS = Price received − Minimum selling price.)

Producers' (or sellers') surplus is the difference between the price received by the producer or seller and the minimum selling price:

$$Producers'\ (sellers')\ surplus = Price\ received - Minimum\ selling\ price$$

Suppose the minimum price the owner of the movie theater would have accepted for admission is $5. But she sells admission for $7, not $5. Her producers' or sellers' surplus is therefore $2. A seller prefers a large producers' surplus to a small one. The theater owner would have preferred to sell admission to the movie for $8 instead of $7 because then she would have received a $3 producers' surplus.

Total Surplus (TS)
The sum of consumers' surplus and producers' surplus. (TS = CS + PS.)

Total surplus is the sum of consumers' surplus and producers' surplus:

$$Total\ surplus = Consumers'\ surplus + Producers'\ surplus$$

ECONOMICS 24/7

Why a Dowry?

Men and women generally accept the idea that monogamy is the ideal marriage practice. In other words, polygyny (the practice of one man being able to have more than one wife) is not the ideal marriage practice and therefore should be illegal. Some anthropologists and evolutionary biologists challenge orthodoxy by arguing that polygyny gives women greater choice. Here is how they structure their argument: Suppose there are 1,000 men and 1,000 women. Suppose each man and each woman is given a ranking between 1 and 1,000 for a variety of characteristics. The number-1 man is ranked higher than the number-2 man (and so on). Women are also so ranked.

Virginia Sherwood/NBC/NBCU Photo Bank/Getty Images

The woman marries the man with whom she shares the same ranking. Thus, the number-1 man is matched up with the number-1 woman, the number-2 man with the number-2 woman, and so on. Now, suppose the 404th-ranked woman (who is scheduled to marry the 404th-ranked man) prefers to be the second wife of the 40th-ranked man than the only wife of the 404th man. If polygyny is allowed, the 404th-ranked woman could marry the 40th-ranked man and share him with another wife. If polygyny is outlawed, she can't.

Now let's put that argument into economic terms. We know that a shortage exists if the quantity demanded of a good is greater than the quantity supplied. In the event that two women might want to marry the same man, the quantity supplied of the man is 1, but the quantity demanded (of him) is 2. This sounds like a shortage of the man, unless polygyny is permitted, because in that case the two women can be married to the same man.

But suppose polygyny is not permitted, even though the two women still want to be married to the same man. Now we have the problem of a shortage (of this particular man) that cannot be eliminated through the adoption of polygyny. What other way remains to eliminate the shortage? Normally, we think of money as eliminating a shortage, and this is exactly what might be the purpose of the dowry. A dowry is (usually) a transfer of assets from the bride's family to the groom's family before the marriage takes place. If two women want to be married to the same man but only one can be legally married to him, then the dowry may effectively take the place of polygyny in eliminating the shortage of the man. All other things being equal, the prospective bride's family that offers the better dowry to the groom's family ends up with the groom as their son-in-law. This outcome is consistent with the findings of anthropologists Steven J. C. Gaulin and James S. Boster, who have shown that the dowry is almost exclusively found in societies where monogamy has been imposed (and polygyny outlawed).

In Exhibit 16(a), consumers' surplus is represented by the shaded triangle. This triangle includes the area under the demand curve and above the equilibrium price. According to the definition, consumers' surplus is the highest price that buyers are willing to pay (the maximum buying price) minus the price they pay. For example, the window in part (a) shows that buyers are willing to pay as high as $7 for the 50th unit but they pay only $5. Thus, the consumers' surplus on the 50th unit of the good is $2.

> **EXHIBIT 16**

Consumers' and Producers' Surplus

(a) *Consumers' surplus.* As the shaded area indicates, the difference between the maximum, or highest, amount that buyers would be willing to pay for a good and the price that they actually pay is consumers' surplus. (b) *Producers' surplus.* As the shaded area indicates, the difference between the price that sellers receive for a good and the minimum or lowest price they would be willing to sell the good for is producers' surplus.

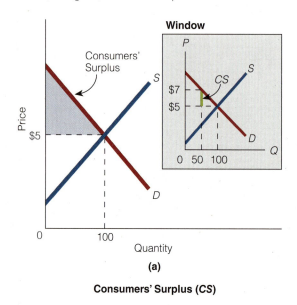

Consumers' Surplus (CS)

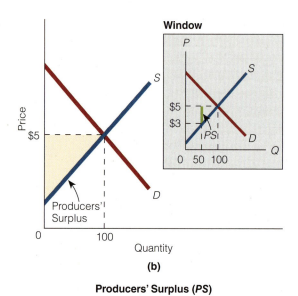

Producers' Surplus (PS)

If we add the consumers' surplus on each unit of the good between the first and the 100th unit, inclusive (the equilibrium quantity), we obtain the shaded consumers' surplus triangle.

In Exhibit 16(b), producers' surplus is also represented by a shaded triangle. This triangle includes the area above the supply curve and under the equilibrium price. Keep in mind the definition of producers' surplus: the price received by the seller minus the lowest price the seller would accept for the good. For example, the window in part (b) shows that sellers would have sold the 50th unit for as low as $3 but actually sold it for $5. Thus, the producers' surplus on the 50th unit of the good is $2. If we add the producers' surplus on each unit of the good between the first and the 100th unit, inclusive, we obtain the shaded producers' surplus triangle.

Now consider consumers' surplus and producers' surplus at the equilibrium quantity. Exhibit 17 shows that the consumers' surplus at equilibrium is equal to areas $A + B + C + D$ and the producers' surplus at equilibrium is equal to areas $E + F + G + H$. At any other exchangeable quantity, such as 25, 50, or 75 units, both consumers' surplus and producers' surplus are less. For example, at 25 units, consumers' surplus is equal to area A and producers' surplus is equal to area E. At 50 units, consumers' surplus is equal to areas $A + B$ and producers' surplus is equal to areas $E + F$.

Equilibrium has a special property: At equilibrium, both consumers' surplus and producers' surplus are maximized. In short, total surplus is maximized.

> **EXHIBIT 17**

Equilibrium, Consumers' Surplus, and Producers' Surplus

Consumers' surplus is greater at the equilibrium quantity (100 units) than at any other exchangeable quantity. Producers' surplus is greater at the equilibrium quantity than at any other exchangeable quantity. For example, consumers' surplus is areas $A + B + C$ at 75 units, but areas $A + B + C + D$ at 100 units. Producers' surplus is areas $E + F + G$ at 75 units, but areas $E + F + G + H$ at 100 units.

Quantity (units)	Consumers' Surplus	Producers' Surplus
25	A	E
50	$A + B$	$E + F$
75	$A + B + C$	$E + F + G$
100 (equilibrium)	$A + B + C + D$	$E + F + G + H$

(a)

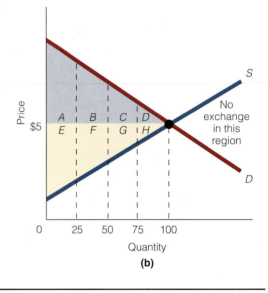

(b)

3-3h What Can Change Equilibrium Price and Quantity?

Equilibrium price and quantity are determined by supply and demand. Whenever demand changes, or supply changes, or both change, equilibrium price and quantity change. Exhibit 18 illustrates eight different cases where this scenario occurs. Cases (a)–(d) illustrate the four basic changes in supply and demand: either supply changes or demand changes. Cases (e)–(h) illustrate changes in both supply and demand.

- *Case (a):* Demand rises (the demand curve shifts rightward from D_1 to D_2), and supply is constant (the supply curve does not move). As a result of demand rising and supply remaining constant, the equilibrium price rises from P_1 to P_2 and the equilibrium quantity rises from 10 units to 12 units. Now, let's see if you can identify what has happened to quantity supplied (not supply) as price has risen from P_1 to P_2. (Remember, quantity supplied changes if *price* changes.) As price rises from P_1 to P_2, quantity supplied rises from 10 units to 12 units. We see this situation as a movement up the supply curve from point 1 to point 2, corresponding (on the horizontal axis) to a change from 10 units to 12 units.

- *Case (b):* Demand falls (the demand curve shifts leftward from D_1 to D_2), and supply is constant. As a result, the equilibrium price falls from P_1 to P_2 and the equilibrium quantity falls from 10 to 8 units. Now ask, has the quantity supplied (not supply) changed? Yes, it has. As a result of price falling from P_1 to P_2, we move down the supply curve from point 1 to point 2 and the quantity supplied falls from 10 units to 8 units.

> **EXHIBIT 18**

Equilibrium Price and Quantity Effects of Supply Curve Shifts and Demand Curve Shifts

The exhibit illustrates the effects on equilibrium price and quantity of a change in demand, a change in supply, and a change in both. Below each diagram, the condition leading to the effects is noted, using the following symbols: (1) a bar over a letter means *constant* (thus, $\bar{S}$ means that

supply is constant); (2) a downward-pointing arrow ($\downarrow$) indicates a fall; (3) an upward-pointing arrow ($\uparrow$) indicates a rise. A rise (fall) in demand is the same as a rightward (leftward) shift in the demand curve. A rise (fall) in supply is the same as a rightward (leftward) shift in the supply curve.

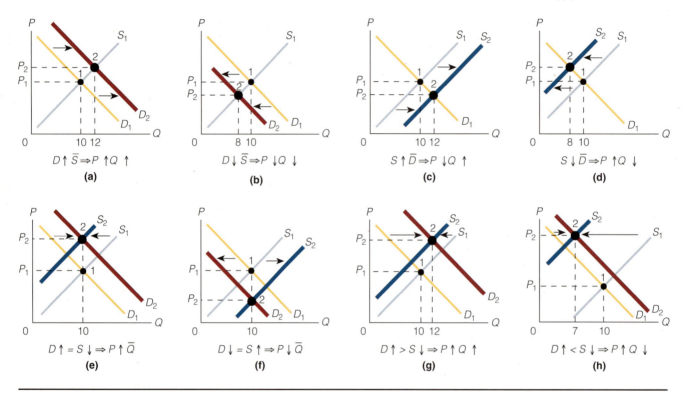

(a) $D \uparrow \bar{S} \Rightarrow P \uparrow Q \uparrow$

(b) $D \downarrow \bar{S} \Rightarrow P \downarrow Q \downarrow$

(c) $S \uparrow \bar{D} \Rightarrow P \downarrow Q \uparrow$

(d) $S \downarrow \bar{D} \Rightarrow P \uparrow Q \downarrow$

(e) $D \uparrow = S \downarrow \Rightarrow P \uparrow \bar{Q}$

(f) $D \downarrow = S \uparrow \Rightarrow P \downarrow \bar{Q}$

(g) $D \uparrow > S \downarrow \Rightarrow P \uparrow Q \uparrow$

(h) $D \uparrow < S \downarrow \Rightarrow P \uparrow Q \downarrow$

- *Case (c):* Supply rises (the supply curve shifts rightward from S_1 to S_2), and demand is constant. As a result, the equilibrium price falls from P_1 to P_2 and the equilibrium quantity rises from 10 units to 12 units. Now ask, has the quantity demanded (not demand) changed? Yes, it has. As a result of price falling from P_1 to P_2, we move down the demand curve from point 1 to point 2 and the quantity demanded rises from 10 units to 12 units.

- *Case (d):* Supply falls (the supply curve shifts leftward from S_1 to S_2), and demand is constant. As a result, the equilibrium price rises from P_1 to P_2 and the equilibrium quantity falls from 10 to 8 units. One last time: Has quantity demanded (not demand) changed? Yes, it has. As a result of price rising from P_1 to P_2, we move up the demand curve from point 1 to point 2, and quantity demanded falls from 10 units to 8 units.

- *Case (e):* Demand rises (the demand curve shifts from D_1 to D_2), and supply falls (the supply curve shifts leftward from S_1 to S_2) by an equal amount. As a result, the equilibrium price rises from P_1 to P_2 and the equilibrium quantity remains constant at 10 units.

ECONOMICS 24/7

Are You Buying More Than You Want to Buy?

ROBERTO SCHMIDT/AFP/Getty Images

Consumers' surplus is the difference between the maximum buying price and the price paid. For example, if you'd be willing to pay a maximum of $10 for good X, but you pay only $4 for the good, then your consumers' surplus is $6.

Now, suppose you receive $10 consumers surplus on the first unit of good X that you buy, $9 on the second unit of good X, $8 on the third unit, and so on. How many units of the good will you buy? The answer is that you will continue to buy additional units of the good as long as you receive positive consumers' surplus. You will receive positive consumers' surplus on items 1 through 10. You will not receive any consumers' surplus on the 11th unit, so you will stop buying at the 10th unit.

Now suppose that the seller of good X comes to you and says this: No longer will I allow you to buy individual units of good X. From now on, you must buy either 11 units or nothing at all. In other words, the seller of good X presents you with an "all-or-nothing" deal: Either buy all that he says you will buy (11), or buy nothing.

What would you do? The answer is, it depends on the negative consumers' surplus you would receive on the 11th unit? If things follow the path we have outlined—according to which, for each additional unit of the good you buy, you receive $1 less in consumers' surplus than you received for the previous unit purchased—then you will receive $1 in negative consumers' surplus on the 11th unit. So, will you buy the 11 units or zero units?

Think things through in this way: If you buy 11 units, you will receive positive consumers' surplus on units 1–10 and negative consumers' surplus on the 11th unit. Thus, on units 1–10, you will receive a total positive consumers' surplus of $55 ($10 on the first unit + $9 on the second unit + $8 on the third unit and so on) and you will receive a negative $1 in consumers' surplus on the 11th unit. Fifty-five dollars minus $1 leaves you with $54 in consumers' surplus if you buy all 11 units. Of course, if you don't buy all 11 units, but instead choose to buy zero units, you will receive zero dollars in consumers' surplus. So the choice is between buying 11 units and receiving $54 in consumers' surplus or buying zero units and receiving $0 in consumer's surplus. Better the $54 in consumers' surplus than the zero dollars.

Better to accept the "all" than the "nothing." Of course, it is still better to buy only 10 units of good X than 11 units, but 10 units was no longer a choice. It was 11 or nothing. The "all-or-nothing" deal ended up reducing your consumers' surplus (from $55 to $54).

Now think of two institutions that sometimes offer, or threaten to offer, all-or-nothing deals. One is private firms. A cable company could offer you 100 channels to choose from for, say, $2 a channel a month. If you want to purchase 10 channels, then purchase 10 channels; if you want to purchase 14 channels, then purchase 14 channels. But cable companies do not usually sell channels this way. Instead, they offer a number of all-or-nothing packages. Buy these 10 channels or buy nothing; buy these 50 channels or buy nothing. It could very well be that some of the channels a consumer buys offer either no or negative consumers' surplus, but still the overall package comes with positive consumers' surplus, albeit not quite as much as would be the case if channels were selected one by one.

Or consider the purchase of a cell phone or cell phone plan. Often, you choose a particular plan or a particular phone with a host of features. Your phone and plan may come with more features than you would buy if you purchased each feature separately. Still, both the plan and the phone may be worth it to you because, overall, you receive positive consumers' surplus, albeit once again not as much as you might have received had you been able to decide on each feature separately.

Now move from private firms to government. There may be some things you receive from government—roads, schools, national defense, etc.—for which you receive positive consumers' surplus. In other words, what you would have been willing to pay for each of these goods or services that you consume is more than what you pay in taxes. But then there might be some things you receive from government for which you receive negative consumers' surplus.

While government doesn't have to be an "all-or-nothing" deal—it is possible to cut some things out of government and keep other things—often elected government officials threaten to cut some of the things for which people receive a positive consumers' surplus if they aren't willing to pay (through taxes) for some of the things for which they might receive negative consumers' surplus. Here is a fictional, yet representative, scenario of how things might proceed at a local government public meeting:

Taxpayers:	We don't want to pay higher taxes.
City Council:	Then we will have to cut services.
Taxpayers:	Maybe that is the right thing to do, given these tight budgetary times.
City Council:	Well, then, we might have to cut police and fire protection.
Taxpayers:	But what about cutting all the waste in government? Why not start there? Or what about cutting your salaries or putting off some of your proposed projects?
City Council:	That might be very hard to do. We might need to start with police and fire protection.
Taxpayers:	Give us a few minutes to think.
City Council:	Take your time.

- *Case (f):* Demand falls (the demand curve shifts leftward from D_1 to D_2), and supply rises (the supply curve shifts rightward from S_1 to S_2) by an equal amount. As a result, the equilibrium price falls from P_1 to P_2 and the equilibrium quantity is constant at 10 units.

- *Case (g):* Demand rises (the demand curve shifts rightward from D_1 to D_2) by a greater amount than supply falls (the supply curve shifts leftward from S_1 to S_2). As a result, the equilibrium price rises from P_1 to P_2 and the equilibrium quantity rises from 10 units to 12 units.

- *Case (h):* Demand rises (the demand curve shifts rightward from D_1 to D_2) by a smaller amount than supply falls (the supply curve shifts leftward from S_1 to S_2). As a result, the equilibrium price rises from P_1 to P_2 and the equilibrium quantity falls from 10 units to 7 units.

3-3i Epilogue: Who Feeds Cleveland?

Here is a question to think about: Who feeds Cleveland? If you have a hard time answering the question, or even making sense of the question, then that is probably for one of two reasons. First, asking "who" feeds Cleveland is an odd question. No one person feeds Cleveland. We can't point to the president of the United States, or to the CEO of a

ECONOMICS 24/7

"Sorry, But This Flight Has Been Overbooked"

Airlines often overbook flights; that is, they accept more reservations than they have seats available on a flight. Airlines know that a certain (usually small) percentage of individuals with reservations will not show up. An empty seat means that the airline's cost per actual passenger on board is higher than it would be if the seat were occupied by a paying passenger. So airlines try to make sure to have few empty seats. One way to reduce the number of empty seats is to overbook.

In the past, when more people with reservations showed up for a flight than there were seats available, the airline simply "bumped" passengers. In other words, the airline would tell some passengers that they could not fly on that flight. Understandably, the bumped passengers were disappointed and angry.

One day while shaving, economist Julian Simon (1932–1998) came up with a better way to deal with overbooking. He argued that the airline should enter into a market transaction with the ticket holders who had reserved seats for an overbooked flight. Instead of bumping people randomly, an airline should ask passengers to sell their seats back to the airline. Passengers who absolutely had to get from one city to another would not sell their seats, but passengers who did not have to fly right away might be willing to sell their tickets for, say, first class on a later flight or some other compensation.

Simon wrote the executives of various airlines and outlined the details of his plan. He even told them that the first airline which enacted the plan would likely reap larger sales. The airline could, after all, guarantee its passengers that they would not get bumped. Most airline executives wrote back and told him that his idea was a reasonably good one but was unworkable.

Simon then contacted various economists and asked them to support his idea publicly. Some did; some didn't. For years, Simon pushed his idea with airline executives and government officials.

Then Alfred Kahn, an economist, was appointed chairman of the Civil Aeronautics Board. Simon contacted Kahn with his plan, and Kahn liked it. According to Simon, "Kahn announced something like the scheme in his first press conference. He also had the great persuasive skill to repackage it as a 'voluntary' bumping plan, and at the same time to increase the penalties that airlines must pay to involuntary bumpees, a nice carrot-and-stick combination."

The rest, as people say, is history. Simon's plan has been in operation since 1978. Simon wrote, "The volunteer system for handling airline oversales exemplifies how markets can improve life for all concerned parties. In case of an oversale, the airline agent proceeds from lowest bidder upwards until the required number of bumpees is achieved. Low bidders take the next flight, happy about it. All other passengers fly as scheduled, also happy. The airlines can overbook more, making them happy too."

large company, or to a specific farmer, and say, "He feeds Cleveland." That's why the "who feeds" question may initially draw a blank stare.

But more importantly, the question is hard to answer because we have been born into a world where food always has existed for people in Cleveland. We never hear of any stories of mass starvation in Cleveland. We never hear that the people in

Cleveland are hungry. We have just taken it for granted—and never really given it much thought—that people in Cleveland eat, just as people in New York, Los Angeles, or Topeka, Kansas, eat.

But still, the question nags at us. Obviously, there must be some reason that the people in Cleveland always seem to have food to eat. Who or what is it that makes this possible? Is there a government agency called the Department of Food that is located in Washington, D.C., that gives orders to people to send food to Cleveland? We know there isn't. Well, then, how does Cleveland get all the food that it consumes? Who or what does feed Cleveland?

The answer is "the market." The market feeds Cleveland. It also feeds every other city in the country. Here is how the market works: The people in Cleveland want to eat. They want to eat all kinds of things: steaks, potato chips, chicken, tomatoes, carrots, bananas, and bread. There are other people who produce these items. They produce these items for one single reason: because they want to sell them for money, which they can then use to buy themselves things they want.

The producers and sellers of these food items send these items to Cleveland. Some of these people even build stores and restaurants in Cleveland where this food can be purchased or eaten. The people who build these stores and restaurants in Cleveland do what they do for the same reason that the producers of the food items did what they did: because they want to sell what they have to sell for money, which they can then use to buy themselves things they want.

Now let's enter a grocery store in Cleveland. The manager of the store is walking down the snacks aisle when she notices that Oreo cookies are leaving the shelves more quickly than before. She thinks to herself that people must really want to buy Oreo cookies. So, she places an order for Oreo cookies that is larger than the order she placed last week. If the same thing is happening in other grocery stores—if Oreo cookies are flying off the shelves—then other managers are doing the same thing too: placing larger orders for Oreo cookies. The manufacturers of Oreo cookies end up producing more Oreo cookies and sending them out to grocery stores to be sold. If Oreo cookies have been flying off the shelves faster than ever because the demand for Oreo cookies has increased, Oreo cookies might go up in price.

The higher price of Oreo cookies might then prompt other cookie manufacturers to come out with a cookie that is similar to an Oreo cookie. After all, almost nothing is copied as often as success.

Now leave the grocery store and go to a restaurant. On the menu at the restaurant are numerous items. Some of those items sell better than other items. If an item sells well, the restaurant keeps the item on the menu. If an item sells poorly, it removes the item from the menu. For example, if, for some reason, peoples' preferences for food changes from Mexican cuisine to Italian cuisine, then the Mexican restaurants either convert to Italian restaurants or go out of business.

So we now know that "the market" feeds Cleveland, and we have some idea of exactly how it feeds Cleveland, namely, sellers of food get together with buyers of food and then trade their food for money. Also, as the demand for a food item changes, the producers or sellers of food respond in a way that the buyers of food want them to respond. When the buyers want more cookies, the suppliers of cookies give them more cookies; when the buyers want more Italian food and less Mexican food, the restaurateurs deliver.

Now, if "the market" were an invention, much the way a car or TV or personal computer were invented, we'd have to say that it is quite some invention. It would be a more significant invention than almost anything you can think of because "the market" does something as important as feed Cleveland. It is also "the thing" within which other inventions appear. If there were no market, would there be any reason to invent cars, computers, cell telephones, and so on?

So, if "the market" were an invention, it would be a most important invention, if not the most important invention of all time. But, alas, no one invented the market. The market is simply the very quiet and invisible manifestation of the actions of millions of people simply trying to make themselves better off.

The market—that "thing" that ends up feeding Cleveland, making more Oreo cookies, changing the menu when restaurant goers want a change in the menu, and so on—is a **spontaneous order**. It is something that emerged as an unintended effect of peoples' actions directed at trying to make themselves better off.

Spontaneous Order
The spontaneous and unintended emergence of order out of the self-interested actions of individuals; an unintended consequence of human action, with emphasis placed on the word "unintended."

SELF-TEST

1. When a person goes to the grocery store to buy food, there is no auctioneer calling out prices for bread, milk, and other items. Therefore, supply and demand cannot be operative. Do you agree or disagree? Explain your answer.

2. The price of a personal computer of a given quality is lower today than it was five years ago. Is this necessarily the result of a lower demand for computers? Explain your answer.

3. What is the effect on equilibrium price and quantity of the following?

   a. A decrease in demand that is greater than the increase in supply

   b. An increase in supply

   c. A decrease in supply that is greater than the increase in demand

   d. A decrease in demand

4. At equilibrium quantity, what is the relationship between the maximum buying price and the minimum selling price?

5. If the price paid for a certain item is $40 and the consumers' surplus is $4, then what is the maximum buying price for that item? If the minimum selling price is $30 and the producers' surplus is $4, then what is the price received by the seller?

Office  Hours

"I Thought Prices Equaled Costs Plus 10 Percent"

STUDENT:

My uncle produces and sells lamps. I asked him once how he determines the price he sells his lamps for. He said he takes his costs and adds 10 percent. In other words, if it cost him $200 to make a lamp, he sells it for a price of $220. If all sellers do the same thing, then prices aren't being determined by supply and demand, are they?

INSTRUCTOR:

Supply and demand could still be at work, even given what your uncle said. For example, the $220 could be the equilibrium price (determined by supply and demand) for the type of lamps your uncle is producing and selling. Look at it this way: If your uncle could sell the lamps for, say, $250 each, then he would have told you that he takes his cost (of $200) and adds on 25 percent ($50) to get "his price" of $250.

STUDENT:

Is the point that what looks like *cost plus 10 percent* to me could really be supply and demand?

INSTRUCTOR:

Yes, that's the point. But we can add something else to make the point stronger. Think of the housing market for a minute. Are the prices of houses determined by *cost plus 10 percent* or by supply and demand? Let's see if we can think through an example together. Suppose you buy a house for $400,000 in one year and then decide to sell it 10 years later. What price do you charge for the house? Do you charge the (market) equilibrium price for that house, or do you charge what

you paid for the house ($400,000) plus 10 percent ($40,000), for a total of $440,000?

STUDENT:

Oh, I think I see what you mean. You mean that if the equilibrium price for the house happened to be $650,000, I wouldn't charge only $440,000.

INSTRUCTOR:

Exactly. In other words, the price determined by supply and demand would take precedence over the cost-plus-10-percent price. Now, going back to your uncle, we see that he might have just thought that he was charging a price of cost plus 10 percent because the equilibrium price for the good he produced and sold happened to be 10 percent higher than his cost. But, as stated before, if that equilibrium price had been 25 percent higher, your uncle would have told you that his price was determined by his taking his costs and adding 25 percent. The equilibrium price was determining the percentage that your uncle said he added to costs; he didn't just pick a percentage out of thin air.

Points to remember

1. What looks like cost plus 10 percent (cost plus some markup) could instead be supply and demand at work.

2. Supply and demand are obviously determining prices at, say, an auction. A single good (say, a painting) is for sale, and numerous buyers bid on it. The bidding stops when only one buyer is left. At the price the last bidder bid, the quantity demanded (of the painting) equals the quantity supplied, and both equal 1. Even if you do not see supply and demand at work in nonauction settings, supply and demand are still at work determining prices.

CHAPTER SUMMARY

DEMAND

- The law of demand states that as the price of a good rises, the quantity demanded of it falls, and that as the price of a good falls, the quantity demanded of it rises, *ceteris paribus*. The law of demand holds that price and quantity demanded are inversely related.
- Quantity demanded is the total number of units of a good that buyers are willing and able to buy at a particular price.
- A (downward-sloping) demand curve is the graphical representation of the law of demand.
- Factors that can change demand and cause the demand curve to shift are income, preferences, the prices of related goods (substitutes and complements), the number of buyers, and expectations of future price.
- The only factor that can directly cause a change in the quantity demanded of a good is a change in the good's own price.

SUPPLY

- The law of supply states that as the price of a good rises, the quantity supplied of the good rises, and that as the price of a good falls, the quantity supplied of the good falls, *ceteris paribus*. The law of supply asserts that price and quantity supplied are directly related.
- The law of supply does not hold when there is no time to produce more units of a good during a given period or when goods cannot be produced at all over that period.
- An upward-sloping supply curve is the graphical representation of the law of supply. More generally, a supply curve (no matter how it slopes) represents the relationship between the price and quantity supplied.
- Factors that can change supply and cause the supply curve to shift are the prices of relevant resources, technology, the prices of other goods, expectations of future price, taxes and subsidies, and government restrictions.

- The only factor that can directly cause a change in the quantity supplied of a good is a change in the good's own price.

THE MARKET

- Demand and supply together establish the equilibrium price and equilibrium quantity.
- A surplus exists in a market if, at some price, the quantity supplied is greater than the quantity demanded. A shortage exists if, at some price, the quantity demanded is greater than the quantity supplied.
- Mutually beneficial trade between buyers and sellers drives the market to equilibrium.

CONSUMERS' SURPLUS, PRODUCERS' SURPLUS, AND TOTAL SURPLUS

- Consumers' surplus is the difference between the maximum buying price and the price paid by the buyer:

Consumers' surplus = Maximum buying price − Price paid

- Producers' (or sellers') surplus is the difference between the price the seller receives and the minimum selling price:

Producers' surplus = Price received − Minimum selling price

- The more consumers' surplus that buyers receive, the better off they are. The more producers' surplus that sellers receive, the better off they are. Total surplus is the sum of consumers' surplus and producers' surplus.
- Total surplus (the sum of consumers' surplus and producers' surplus) is maximized at equilibrium.

KEY TERMS AND CONCEPTS

Market	Inferior Good	Subsidy	Consumers' Surplus
Demand	Neutral Good	Surplus (Excess Supply)	Producers' (Sellers') Surplus
Law of Demand	Substitutes	Shortage (Excess Demand)	Total Surplus
Demand Schedule	Complements	Equilibrium Price (Market-	Spontaneous Order
Demand Curve	Supply	Clearing Price)	
Law of Diminishing	Law of Supply	Equilibrium Quantity	
Marginal Utility	Upward-Sloping Supply	Disequilibrium Price	
Own Price	Curve	Disequilibrium	
Normal Good	Supply Schedule	Equilibrium	

VIDEO QUESTIONS AND PROBLEMS

Video Questions and Problems are available on MindTap for Arnold 12e or by searching for Arnold on www.cengagebrain.com

1. Explain how to derive a market demand curve, and represent your explanation diagrammatically.

2. Does an increase in income always shift demand curves (for goods) to the right? Why or why not?

3. What is the difference between a change in demand and a change in quantity demanded? Between a change in supply and a change in quantity supplied?

4. If the supply of a good declines, what happens to consumers' surplus? Explain your answer and represent it diagrammatically.

5. Suppose demand increases more than supply increases. Represent diagrammatically what happens to equilibrium price and quantity.

6. Suppose both demand and supply rise but equilibrium price does not change. Why? Explain your answer and represent it diagrammatically.

QUESTIONS AND PROBLEMS

1. What is wrong with the following statement? Demand refers to the willingness of buyers to purchase different quantities of a good at different prices during a specific period.

2. What is the difference between *demand* and *quantity demanded*?

3. True or false? As the price of oranges rises, the demand for oranges falls, *ceteris paribus.* Explain your answer.

4. "The price of a bushel of wheat, which was $3.00 last month, is $3.70 today. The demand curve for wheat must have shifted rightward between last month and today." Discuss.

5. Some goods are bought largely because they have "snob appeal." For example, the residents of Beverly Hills gain prestige by buying expensive items. In fact, they won't buy some items unless they are expensive. The law of demand, which holds that people buy more at lower prices than higher prices, obviously doesn't hold for the residents of Beverly Hills. The following rules apply in Beverly Hills: high prices, buy; low prices, don't buy. Discuss.

6. "The price of T-shirts keeps rising and rising, and people keep buying more and more. T-shirts must have an upward-sloping demand curve." Identify the error.

7. With respect to each of the following changes, identify whether the demand curve will shift rightward or leftward:

   a. An increase in income (the good under consideration is a normal good)

   b. A rise in the price of a substitute good

   c. A fall in the price of a complementary good

   d. A fall in the number of buyers

8. What does a sale on shirts have to do with the law of demand (as applied to shirts)?

9. What is wrong with this statement: As the price of a good falls, the supply of that good falls, *ceteris paribus.*

10. In the previous chapter you learned about the law of increasing opportunity costs. What does this law have to do with an upward-sloping supply curve?

11. How might the price of corn affect the supply of wheat?

12. What is the difference between supply and quantity supplied?

13. Predict what happens to the equilibrium price of marijuana if it is legalized.

14. Compare the ratings for television shows with prices for goods. How are ratings like prices? How are ratings different from prices? (*Hint:* How does rising demand for a particular television show manifest itself?)

15. At equilibrium in a market, the maximum price that buyers would be willing to pay for the good is equal to the minimum price that sellers need to receive before they are willing to sell the good. Do you agree or disagree with this statement? Explain your answer.

16. Must consumers' surplus equal producers' surplus at the equilibrium price? Explain your answer.

17. Many movie theaters charge a lower admission price for the first show on weekday afternoons than they do for a weeknight or weekend show. Explain why.

18. A Dell computer is a substitute for an HP® computer. What happens to the demand for HP computers and the quantity demanded of Dell computers as the price of a Dell falls?

19. Describe how each of the following will affect the demand for personal computers:

   a. A rise in income (assuming that computers are a normal good)

   b. A lower expected price for computers

   c. Cheaper software

   d. Computers that are simpler to operate

20. Describe how each of the following will affect the supply of personal computers:

   a. A rise in wage rates

   b. An increase in the number of sellers of computers

   c. A tax placed on the production of computers

   d. A subsidy for the production of computers

21. Use the law of diminishing marginal utility to explain why demand curves slope downward.

22. Explain how the market moves to equilibrium in terms of shortages and surpluses and in terms of maximum buying prices and minimum selling prices.

23. Identify what happens to equilibrium price and quantity in each of the following cases:

   a. Demand rises and supply is constant.

   b. Demand falls and supply is constant.

   c. Supply rises and demand is constant.

   d. Supply falls and demand is constant.

   e. Demand rises by the same amount that supply falls.

   f. Demand falls by the same amount that supply rises.

   g. Demand falls less than supply rises.

   h. Demand rises more than supply rises.

   i. Demand rises less than supply rises.

   j. Demand falls more than supply falls.

   k. Demand falls less than supply falls.

24. Suppose the demand curve for a good is downward sloping and the supply curve is upward sloping. Now suppose demand rises. Will producers' surplus rise or fall? Explain your answers.

25. When speeding tickets were $100, usually 500 speeders were on the roads each month in a given city; when ticket prices were raised to $250, usually 215 speeders were on the roads in the city each month. Can you find any economics in this observation?

26. On most days, more people want to see the taping of *The Tonight Show Starring Jimmy Fallon* (in New York City) than there are seats in the taping studio. What might explain this shortage?

27. What does it mean to say that "the market" feeds Cleveland, Austin, Atlanta, or Indianapolis?

WORKING WITH NUMBERS AND GRAPHS

1. Suppose the price is $10, the quantity supplied is 50 units, and the quantity demanded is 100 units. For every $1 rise in price, the quantity supplied rises by 5 units and the quantity demanded falls by 5 units. What is the equilibrium price and quantity?

2. Using numbers, explain how a market demand curve is derived from two individual demand curves.

3. Draw a diagram that shows a larger increase in demand than the decrease in supply.

4. Draw a diagram that shows a smaller increase in supply than the increase in demand.

5. At equilibrium in the following figure, what area(s) represent consumers' surplus? producers' surplus?

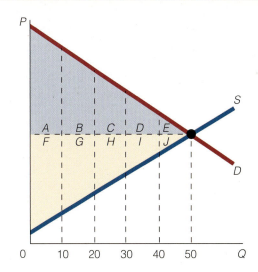

6. At what quantity in the preceding figure is the maximum buying price equal to the minimum selling price?

7. In the figure that follows, can the movement from point 1 to point 2 be explained by a combination of an increase in the price of a substitute and a decrease in the price of nonlabor resources? Explain your answer.

8. Suppose the demand curve is downward sloping, the supply curve is upward sloping, and the equilibrium quantity is 50 units. Show on a graph that the difference between the maximum buying price and minimum selling price is greater at 25 units than at 33 units.

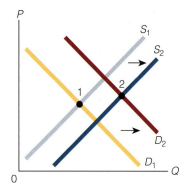

Enzo Baradel/age fotostock Spain, S.L. /Alamy

INTRODUCTION

In the last chapter, we discussed supply and demand. Mainly, we saw how supply and demand work together to determine prices. In this chapter we discuss prices at greater length. First, we discuss two of the key "jobs" that price performs: (1) rationing resources and goods and (2) transmitting information. Second, we discuss government controls that can be imposed on prices. Specifically, we discuss both price ceilings and price floors. Third, we discuss two types of price: absolute (or money) price and relative price.

4-1 PRICE

To most people, price is a number with a dollar sign in front of it, such as $10. But price is much more. Price performs two major jobs: It acts (1) as a rationing device and (2) as a transmitter of information.

4-1a Price as a Rationing Device

In Chapter 1 we said that wants (for goods) are unlimited and resources are limited, so scarcity exists. As a result of scarcity, a rationing device is needed to determine who gets what of the available limited resources and goods. (Because resources are limited, goods are also, given that the production of goods requires resources.) Price serves as that rationing device. It rations resources to the producers who pay the price for the resources. It rations goods to those buyers who pay the price for the goods. The process is as simple as this: Pay the price, and the resources or goods are yours. Don't pay the price, and they aren't.

Is dollar price a fair rationing device? Doesn't it discriminate against the poor? After all, the poor have fewer dollars than the rich, so the rich can get more of what they want than can the poor. True, dollar price does discriminate against the poor. But then, as economists know, every rationing device discriminates against someone. To illustrate, suppose for some reason that tomorrow dollar price could not be used as a rationing device. Some rationing device would still be necessary, because scarcity would still exist. How would we ration gas at the gasoline station, food in the grocery store, or tickets for the Super Bowl? Let's consider some alternatives to dollar price as a rationing device.

Suppose *first come, first served* is the rationing device. For example, suppose only 40,000 Super Bowl tickets are available. If you are one of the first 40,000 in line for a Super Bowl ticket, you get a ticket. If you are person number 40,001 in line, you don't. Such a method discriminates against those who can't get in line quickly enough. What about slow walkers or people with disabilities? What about people without cars who can't drive to where the tickets are distributed?

Or suppose *brute force* is the rationing device. For example, of the 40,000 Super Bowl tickets, you get one as long as you can take it away from someone else. Against whom does this rationing method discriminate? Obviously, it discriminates against the weak and nonaggressive.

Or suppose *beauty* is the rationing device. The more beautiful you are, the better your chances are of getting a Super Bowl ticket. Again, the rationing device discriminates against someone.

These and many other alternatives to dollar price could be used as rationing devices. However, each discriminates against someone, and none is clearly superior to dollar price.

In addition, if first come, first served, brute force, beauty, or another alternative to dollar price is the rationing device, what incentive would the producer of a good have to produce the good? With dollar price as a rationing device, a person produces computers and sells them for money. He then takes the money and buys what he wants. But if the rationing device were, say, brute force, he would not have an incentive to produce. Why produce anything when someone will end up taking it away from you? In short, in a world where dollar price isn't the rationing device, people are likely to produce much less than in a world where dollar price is the rationing device.

4-1b Price as a Transmitter of Information

Rationing isn't the only job that price performs. Price also *transmits information*. That may sound odd. Consider the following story: On Saturday, Noelle walks into a local grocery store and purchases a half gallon of orange juice for $2.50. On Sunday, unknown to her, a cold spell hits Florida and wipes out half the orange crop. The cold spell ends up shifting the supply curve of oranges leftward, which drives up the price of oranges. Because oranges are a resource in the production of orange juice, the supply curve of orange juice shifts leftward and the price of orange juice rises.

Noelle returns to the grocery store in a week. She notices that the half gallon of orange juice she bought last week for $2.50 has now risen to $3.50. Because Noelle has a downward-sloping demand curve for orange juice, she ends up buying less orange juice. She buys only a quart of orange juice instead of a half gallon.

What role did price play in Noelle's decision to cut back on the consumption of orange juice? It played a major role. If the price hadn't risen, Noelle probably wouldn't have reduced her purchases and consumption of orange juice. Noelle reacted to the price rise, but what the price rise was "saying"—if we had ears to hear it—is this: "The relative scarcity of a good has risen because of a cold spell in Florida. In other words, the gap between people's wants for orange juice and the amount of orange juice available to satisfy those wants has widened."

Now, we know that Noelle might not have "heard" price saying this. But if you understand economics, that is just what price *is* saying. In other words, price is a transmitter of information that often relates to the relative scarcity of a good. A market system, oddly enough, is powerful enough to have people respond in appropriate ways to the information that price is transmitting, even if the people do not fully hear or understand that information. In the case of Noelle, her cutting back on the consumption of orange juice conserves orange juice in the face of an act of nature that ended up making orange juice relatively scarcer.

Think of how this reaction is similar to what people who tell you to conserve water want. For example, in California in the summer of 2009, advertisements on television asked people to cut back on their consumption of water because water in the state was in short supply. The appropriate behavior to take was to cut back on the consumption of water, because it had become relatively scarcer. You were being civic minded if you did so. Well, movements in price can get you to be civic minded too. When the price of orange juice rises because of a cold spell in Florida, you might automatically cut back on your consumption, thus conserving on the consumption of a good that has become relatively scarcer.

SELF-TEST

(Answers to Self-Test questions are in Answers to Self-Test Questions at the back of the book.)

1. Why is there a need for a rationing device, whether it is price or something else?

2. If price is not the rationing device used, then individuals won't have as sharp an incentive to produce. Explain.

3. What kind of information does price often transmit?

4-2 PRICE CONTROLS

A rationing device—such as dollar price—is needed because scarcity exists. But price is not always allowed to be a rationing device. Sometimes price is controlled. There are two types of price controls: price ceilings and price floors. In the discussion of price controls, the word "price" is used in the generic sense. It refers to the price of an apple, for example, the price of labor (a wage), the price of credit (the interest rate), and so on.

4-2a Price Ceiling

Definition and Effects   A price ceiling is a government-mandated maximum price above which legal trades cannot be made. For example, suppose the government mandates that the maximum price at which good X can be bought and sold is $8. Therefore, $8 is a price ceiling. If $8 is below the equilibrium price of good X, as in Exhibit 1, any or all of the following effects may arise:[1] shortages, fewer exchanges, nonprice-rationing devices, buying and selling at prohibited prices, and tie-in sales.

---

[1] If the price ceiling is above the equilibrium price (say, $8 is the price ceiling and $4 is the equilibrium price), the ceiling has no effect. Usually, however, a price ceiling is below the equilibrium price.

> **EXHIBIT 1**

A Price Ceiling

The price ceiling is $8 and the equilibrium price is $12. At $12, quantity demanded = quantity supplied. At $8, quantity demanded > quantity supplied. (Recall that price, on the vertical axis, always represents price per unit. Quantity, on the horizontal axis, always holds for a specific period.)

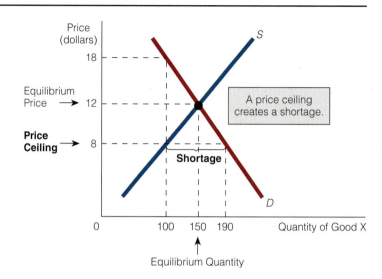

Shortages   At the $12 equilibrium price in Exhibit 1, the quantity demanded of good X (150) is equal to the quantity supplied (150). At the $8 price ceiling, a shortage exists: The quantity demanded (190) is greater than the quantity supplied (100). When a shortage exists, price and output tend to rise to equilibrium. But when a price ceiling exists, they cannot rise to equilibrium because it is unlawful to trade at the equilibrium price.

Fewer Exchanges   At the equilibrium price of $12 in Exhibit 1, 150 units of good X are bought and sold. At the price ceiling of $8, 100 units of good X are bought and sold. (Buyers would prefer to buy 190 units, but only 100 are supplied.) We conclude that price ceilings cause fewer exchanges to be made.

   Notice in Exhibit 1 that the demand curve is above the supply curve for all quantities less than 150 units. (At 150 units, the demand curve and the supply curve intersect and thus share the same point in the two-dimensional space.) Thus, the maximum buying price is greater than the minimum selling price for all units less than 150. In particular, the maximum buying price is greater than the minimum selling price for units 101 to 149. For example, buyers might be willing to pay $17 for the 110th unit, and sellers might be willing to sell the 110th unit for $10. But no unit after the 100th unit (not the 110th unit, not the 114th unit, not the 130th unit) will be produced and sold because of the price ceiling. In short, the price ceiling prevents mutually advantageous trades from being realized.

Nonprice-Rationing Devices   If the equilibrium price of $12 fully rations good X before the price ceiling is imposed, then a lower price of $8 only partly rations this good. In short, price ceilings prevent price from rising to the level sufficient to ration goods fully. But if price is responsible for only part of the rationing, what accounts for the rest?

   The answer is that some other (nonprice) rationing device, such as first come, first served. In Exhibit 1, 100 units of good X will be sold at $8, although buyers are willing to buy 190 units at this price. What happens? Possibly, good X will be sold on a first-come, first-served basis for $8 per unit. In other words, to buy good X, a person must not only pay $8 per unit but also be one of the first people in line.

Buying and Selling at a Prohibited Price   Buyers and sellers may regularly circumvent a price ceiling by making their exchanges under the table. For example, some buyers may offer some sellers more than $8 per unit for good X. No doubt, some sellers will accept the offers. But why would some buyers offer more than $8 per unit when they can buy good X for $8? Because not all buyers can buy the amount of good X they want at $8. As Exhibit 1 shows, there is a shortage. Buyers are willing to buy 190 units at $8, but sellers are willing to sell only 100 units. In short, 90 fewer units will be sold than buyers would like to buy. Some buyers will go unsatisfied. How, then, does any one buyer make it more likely that sellers will sell to him or her instead of to someone else? The answer is by offering to pay a higher price. However, because it is illegal to pay a higher price, the transaction must be made under the table.

Tie-In Sales   In Exhibit 1, the maximum price buyers would be willing and able to pay per unit for 100 units of good X is $18. (This is the price on the demand curve at a quantity of 100 units.) The maximum legal price, however, is $8. The difference between the two prices often prompts a **tie-in sale**, a sale whereby one good can be purchased only if another good is also purchased. For example, if Ralph's Gas Station sells gasoline to customers only if they buy a car wash, the two goods are linked in a tie-in sale.

Suppose that the sellers of good X in Exhibit 1 also sell good Y. Then they might offer to sell buyers good X at $8 only if the buyers agree to buy good Y at, say, $10. We choose $10 as the price for good Y because $10 is the difference between the maximum per-unit price buyers are willing and able to pay for 100 units of good X ($18) and the maximum legal price ($8).

In New York City and other communities with rent-control laws, tie-in sales sometimes result from rent ceilings on apartments. Occasionally, to rent an apartment, an individual must agree to buy the furniture in the apartment.

Buyers and Higher and Lower Prices

Do buyers prefer lower to higher prices? "Of course," you might say, "buyers prefer lower prices to higher prices. What buyer would want to pay a higher price for anything?" And yet, even though **price ceilings** are often lower than equilibrium prices, does it follow that buyers prefer price ceilings to equilibrium prices? Not necessarily. Price ceilings have effects that equilibrium prices do not: shortages, the use of first come, first served as a rationing device, tie-in sales, and so on. A buyer could prefer to pay a higher price (an equilibrium price) than pay a lower price and have to deal with the effects of a price ceiling. All we can say for certain is that buyers prefer lower prices to higher prices, *ceteris paribus*. As in many cases, the *ceteris paribus* condition makes all the difference.

Price Ceilings and False Information

Let's go back to the orange juice example in the first section of this chapter. In that example, a cold spell destroys part of the orange crop, leading to a higher price for oranges and orange juice. The market price of orange juice then rises from $2.50 to $3.50 a half gallon.

Now let's change things. Suppose that, instead of letting the new, lower supply of orange juice and demand for orange juice determine the market price of orange juice at $3.50 a half gallon, government imposes a price ceiling on orange juice at $2.50 a half gallon. Think about what the price ceiling does to prevent price from transmitting information.

Tie-in Sale
A sale whereby one good can be purchased only if another good is also purchased.

Price Ceiling
A government-mandated maximum price above which legal trades cannot be made.

ECONOMICS 24/7

A Price Ceiling in the Kidney Market

Just as some people want to buy houses, computers, and books, others want to buy kidneys. These people have kidney failure, and they will either die without a new kidney or have to endure years of costly and painful dialysis. This demand for kidneys is shown as D_K in Exhibit 2, and the supply of kidneys is shown as S_K.

Notice that, at a $0 price, the quantity supplied of kidneys is 350. These kidneys are from people who donate their kidneys to others, asking nothing in return. They may donate upon their death, or they may donate one of their two kidneys while living. We have drawn the supply curve as upward sloping because we assume that some people who today are unwilling to donate a kidney for $0 might be willing to do so for some positive dollar amount. Specifically, we assume that, as the price of a kidney rises, the quantity supplied of kidneys also will rise.

If there were a free market in kidneys, the price of a kidney would be P_1 in Exhibit 2. At this price, 1,000 kidneys would be purchased and sold; that is, 1,000 kidney transplants would occur.

Today, there is no free market in kidneys. Buying or selling kidneys is illegal at any dollar amount. In essence, then, there is a price ceiling in the kidney market, and the ceiling is set at $0. What is the effect of the ceiling?

If the demand curve for kidneys and the supply curve of kidneys intersected at $0, there would be neither a surplus nor a shortage of kidneys. But there is evidence that the demand and supply curves do not intersect at $0; they look more like the curves shown in Exhibit 2. In other words, there is a shortage of kidneys at $0: The quantity supplied of kidneys is 350, and the quantity demanded is 1,500.

> ## EXHIBIT 2

The Market for Kidneys

We have identified the demand for kidneys as D_K and the supply of kidneys as S_K. Given the demand for and supply of kidneys, the equilibrium price of a kidney is P_1. It does not follow, though, that simply because there is an equilibrium price, people will be allowed to trade at that price. Today, it is unlawful to buy and sell kidneys at

any positive price. In short, there is a price ceiling in the kidney market, and the ceiling is $0. At the price ceiling, there are at least four effects: a shortage of kidneys, a nonprice-rationing device for kidneys (first come, first served), fewer kidney transplants (than there would be at P_1), and illegal purchases and sales of kidneys.

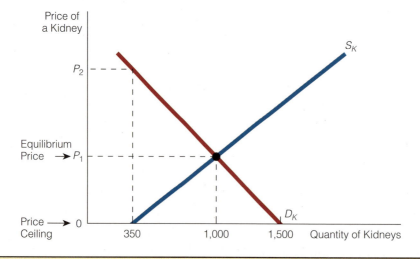

(Although these are not the actual numbers of kidneys demanded and supplied at $0, they are representative of the current situation in the kidney market.)

This chapter has described the possible effects of a price ceiling set below the equilibrium price: shortages, nonprice-rationing devices, fewer exchanges, tie-in sales, and buying and selling at prohibited prices (in other words, illegal trades). Are any of these effects actually occurring in the kidney market?

First, there is evidence of a shortage. In almost every country in the world, more people on national lists want a kidney than there are kidneys available. Some of these people die waiting for a transplant.

Second, as just intimated, the nonprice-rationing device used in the kidney market is (largely) first come, first served. A person who wants a kidney registers on a national waiting list. How long people wait is a function of how far down the list their names appear.

Third, there are fewer exchanges, so not everyone who needs a kidney gets one. With a price ceiling of $0, only 350 kidneys are supplied. All these kidneys are from people who freely donate their kidneys. If P_1 were permitted, some people who are unwilling to supply a kidney (at $0) would be willing to do so. In short, monetary payment would provide the incentive for some people to supply a kidney. At P_1, 1,000 kidneys are demanded and supplied, so more people would get kidney transplants when the price of a kidney is P_1 (1,000 people in all) than when the price of a kidney is $0 (350 people). More transplants, of course, means that fewer people die waiting for a kidney.

Fourth, kidneys are bought and sold at prohibited prices. People buy and sell kidneys today; they just do so illegally. People are reported to have paid between $25,000 and $200,000 for a kidney.

Some argue that a free market in kidneys would be wrong. Such a system would place the poor at a disadvantage. Think of it: A rich person who needed a kidney could buy one, but a poor person could not. The rich person would get a second chance at life, whereas the poor person would not. No one enjoys contemplating this stark reality.

But consider another stark reality. If it is unlawful to pay someone for a kidney, fewer kidneys will be forthcoming. In other words, the quantity supplied of kidneys is less at $0 than at, say, $20,000. Fewer kidneys supplied means fewer kidney transplants. And fewer kidney transplants means that more people will die from kidney failure.

Specifically, the price ceiling prevents the correct information about the increased relative scarcity of orange juice (due to the cold spell) from getting through to consumers. It's as if price is a radio signal and the price ceiling jams the signal. Because of the jammed price signal, consumers mistakenly believe that nothing has changed. As far as they are concerned, they can continue buying orange juice at the same rate of consumption they did earlier. But, of course, they can't: There are fewer oranges and less orange juice in the world. One way or another, some people are going to have to curtail their consumption of orange juice.

The lesson is simple: Price ceilings (that are below the equilibrium price) distort the flow of accurate information to buyers. Buyers get a false view of reality; they then base their buying behavior on incorrect information. Problems follow, and the unintended, unexpected, and undesirable effects of price ceilings soon occur.

THINKING LIKE AN ECONOMIST

Look for the Unintended Effects. Economists think in terms of unintended effects. For example, a price ceiling policy intended to lower prices for the poor may cause shortages, the use of nonprice rationing devices, illegal market transactions, and tie-in sales. When we consider both the price ceiling and its effects, whether the poor have been helped is not so clear. The economist knows that wanting to do good (for others) is not sufficient: Knowing how to do good is important too.

ECONOMICS 24/7

1973 and 1979

In 1973, there were gas lines in the United States. Drivers in their cars waited in long lines to buy gas. Sometimes they waited a couple of hours or more. In some states, a person couldn't buy gas on just any day of the week. Those who had a license plate number that ended with an odd number (such as TBN-347) could buy gas on odd-numbered days of the month, while those who had a license plate number that ended with an even number (such as BNR-874) could buy gas on even-numbered days of the month. In 1979, it was much the same: long lines of drivers waiting to buy gas.

In 1965 there were no long lines of drivers waiting to buy gas, nor was this the case in, say, 1987, 1995, or 2011. What was so different about 1973 and 1979? In those two years, the federal government imposed price ceilings on gasoline. The price ceilings made all the difference, because, as we have pointed out in this chapter, price ceilings lead to shortages and shortages lead to rationing devices other than only money price being used to ration goods. One common nonprice-rationing device is first come, first served, which leads to long lines.

As you might expect, sometimes those long lines produced certain problems, as when someone tried to cut in front of drivers waiting in line. In one case, an attendant at the gas station tried to prevent someone from cutting into line and was almost run over by the driver of the car. In many cases, fights broke out among drivers waiting in line.

McDonald's ran a television ad in 1979 based on gas lines. In fact, the ad was titled "Gas Line." The scene is a gas station with a long line of drivers in cars waiting to buy gas. One man says to another right behind him in line, "Excuse me, would you watch my place in line, I'm just going to run over to McDonald's." The second man responds, "Yeah," and then asks the first man if he could bring him back a Big Mac. On his way to McDonald's, other drivers in cars ask for a variety of McDonald's products: fries, a Coke, a strawberry shake, and so on. The last scene shows everyone eating their McDonald's products and having a good time but still waiting in the gas line. If you would like to see the actual ad, it can be found on YouTube at http://www.youtube.com/watch?v=tjXhwevOVAE.

AP Images

4-2b Price Floor: Definition and Effects

A **price floor** is a government-mandated minimum price below which legal trades cannot be made. For example, suppose the government mandates that the minimum price at which good X can be sold is $20. Then the $20 minimum is a price floor. (See Exhibit 3.)

Price Floor

A government-mandated minimum price below which legal trades cannot be made.

Effects of a Price Floor   If the price floor is above the equilibrium price, the following two effects arise:[2] surpluses and fewer exchanges.

Surpluses   At the $15 equilibrium price in Exhibit 3, the quantity demanded of good X (130) is equal to the quantity supplied (130). At the $20 price floor, a surplus exists.

The quantity supplied (180) is greater than the quantity demanded (90). Usually, a surplus is temporary. When a surplus exists, price and output tend to fall to equilibrium. But when a price floor exists, they cannot fall to equilibrium because it is unlawful to trade at the equilibrium price.

Fewer Exchanges   At the equilibrium price in Exhibit 3, 130 units of good X are bought and sold. At the price floor, 90 units are bought and sold. (Sellers want to sell 180 units, but buyers buy only 90.) Thus, price floors cause fewer exchanges to be made.

The Minimum Wage   If a price floor is a legislated minimum price below which trades cannot legally be made, then the *minimum wage* is a price floor—a government-mandated minimum price for labor. It affects the market for unskilled labor. In Exhibit 4, we assume that the minimum wage is W_M and the equilibrium wage is W_E. At the equilibrium wage, N_1 workers are employed. At the higher minimum wage, N_3 workers want to work but only N_2 actually do work. There is a surplus of workers equal to $N_3 - N_2$ in this unskilled

> **EXHIBIT 3**

A Price Floor

The price floor is $20 and the equilibrium price is $15. At $15, quantity demanded = quantity supplied. At $20, quantity supplied > quantity demanded.

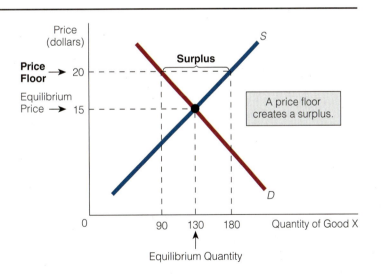

---

2. If the price floor is below the equilibrium price (say, $20 is the price floor and $25 is the equilibrium price), then the price floor has no effects. Usually, however, a price floor is above the equilibrium price.

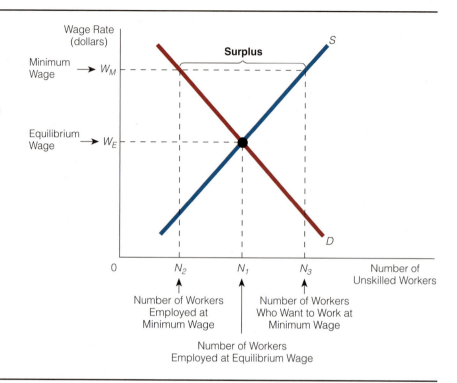

EXHIBIT 4

Effects of the Minimum Wage

At a minimum wage of W_M an hour, there is a surplus of workers and fewer workers are employed than would be employed at the equilibrium wage W_E.

labor market. In addition, fewer workers are working at the minimum wage (N_2) than at the equilibrium wage (N_1). Overall, the effects of the minimum wage are (1) a surplus of unskilled workers and (2) fewer workers employed.

Suppose two economists decide to test the theory that as the minimum wage rises some unskilled workers will lose their jobs. They look at the number of unskilled workers before and after the minimum wage is raised, and surprisingly they find that the number of unskilled workers is the same. Is this sufficient evidence to conclude that an increase in the minimum wage does not cause some workers to lose their jobs?

The answer to that question depends on whether the economists have adequately tested their theory. Instead of focusing on the number of people who lose their jobs, suppose they look at the number of people who keep their jobs but have their hours reduced as a result of the higher minimum wage. Let's look at an example. Suppose a local hardware store currently employs David and Francesca to work after school cleaning up and stocking shelves. The owner of the store pays each of them the minimum wage of, say, $7.25 an hour. Then the minimum wage is raised to $8.75 an hour. Will either David or Francesca lose their jobs as a result? Not necessarily. Instead, the owner of the store could reduce the number of hours he employs the two workers. For example, instead of having each of them work 20 hours a week, he might ask each to work only 14 hours a week.

Now let's consider our original question again: Has the higher minimum wage eliminated jobs? In a way, no. It has, however, reduced the number of hours a person works in a job. (Of course, if we define a job as including both a particular task and a certain number of hours taken to complete that task, then the minimum wage increase has eliminated

Direction Versus Magnitude In economics, some questions relate to direction and some to magnitude. For example, suppose someone asks, "If the demand for labor is downward sloping and the labor market is competitive, how will a minimum wage that is above the equilibrium wage affect employment?" This person is asking a question that relates to the direction of the change in employment. Usually, these types of questions can be answered by applying a theory. Applying the theory of demand, an economist might say, "At higher wages, the quantity demanded of labor, or the employment level, will be lower than at lower wages." The word "lower" speaks to the *directional change* in employment.

Now suppose someone asks, "How much will employment decline?" This question relates to *magnitude*. Usually, questions that deal with magnitude can be answered only through some kind of empirical (data collection and analysis) work. In other words, we would have to collect employment figures at the equilibrium wage and at the minimum wage and then find the difference.

"part" of the job.) This discussion argues for changing the label on the horizontal axis in Exhibit 4 from "Number of Unskilled Workers" to "Number of Unskilled Labor Hours."

Price Floors, Changes in Consumers' and Producers' Surplus, and Deadweight Losses

We now turn to a discussion of consumers' surplus, producers' surplus, and price floors in terms of a specific example: a price floor on an agricultural foodstuff.

Exhibit 5 shows the demand for and supply of an agricultural foodstuff (corn, wheat, soybeans, etc.). If the market is allowed to move to equilibrium, the equilibrium price will be P_1 and the equilibrium quantity will be Q_1. Consumers' surplus will equal the area under the demand curve and above the equilibrium price: areas 1 + 2 + 3. Producers' surplus will equal the area under the equilibrium price and above the supply curve: areas 4 + 5. Total surplus, of course, is the sum of consumers' surplus and producers' surplus: areas 1 + 2 + 3 + 4 +5.

Now, suppose that the suppliers of the foodstuff argue for (and receive) a price floor P_F. At this higher price, consumers do not buy as much as they once did. They now buy Q_2, whereas they used to buy Q_1. In addition, consumers' surplus is now only area 1, and producers' surplus is areas 2 + 4.

Obviously, consumers have been hurt by the increased (government-mandated) price P_F; specifically, they have lost consumers' surplus equal to areas 2 + 3.

How have suppliers fared? Whereas their producers' surplus was equal to areas 4 + 5 at P_1, it is now equal to areas 2 + 4. (Area 2, which used to be part of consumers' surplus, has been transferred to producers and is now part of producers' surplus.) Whether producers are better off depends on whether area 2 (what they gain from P_F) is larger than area 5 (what they lose from P_F). Visually, we can tell that area 2 is larger than area 5, so producers are better off.

What is the overall effect of the price floor? Have producers gained more than consumers have lost, or have consumers lost more than producers have gained? To answer this question, we note that consumers lose areas 2, and 3 in consumers' surplus and

> **EXHIBIT 5**

Agricultural Price Floors

The demand for and supply of an agricultural foodstuff are shown in this exhibit. The equilibrium price is P_1; consumers' surplus (CS) is areas 1 + 2 + 3; producers' surplus is areas 4 + 5. A price floor of P_F effectively transfers some of the consumers' surplus to producers in the form of a gain in producers' surplus. Specifically, at P_F, consumers' surplus is area 1 and producers' surplus is areas 2 + 4. Consumers are net losers because consumers' surplus has decreased by areas 2 + 3. Producers are net gainers because producers' surplus has increased from areas 4 + 5 to areas 2 + 4 and area 2 is larger than area 5. Overall, the economic pie of CS + PS has decreased from areas 1 + 2 + 3 + 4 + 5 to areas 1 + 2 + 4.

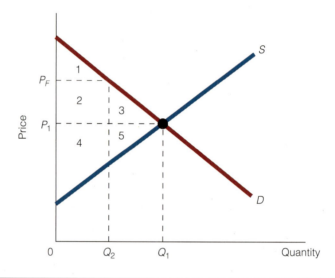

producers gain area 2 in producers' surplus and lose area 5 in producers' surplus. So the gains and losses are as follows:

Losses to consumers:	areas 2 + 3
Gains to producers:	area 2
Losses to producers:	area 5

Part of the loss to consumers is offset by the gain to producers (area 2), so net losses amount to areas 3 + 5. In other words, the total surplus—the sum of consumers' surplus and producers' surplus—is lower than it was. Whereas it used to be areas 1 + 2 + 3 + 4 + 5, it now is areas 1 + 2 + 4. The total surplus lost is in areas 3 + 5. In short, (1) consumers lose, (2) producers gain, and (3) society (which is the sum of consumers and producers) loses.

You can think of this example in terms of a pie. Initially, the pie was made up of areas 1 + 2 + 3 + 4 + 5. This rather large pie registered all the gains of consumers and producers. After the price floor P_F was imposed, the pie shrank to areas 1 + 2 + 4; in other words, the pie was smaller by areas 3 + 5.

ECONOMICS 24/7

What Does Price Have to Do with Being Late to Class?

Class starts at 10 o'clock in the morning. At 10:09, Pam Ferrario walks in late. She apologizes to the instructor, saying, "I've been on campus 20 minutes, but I couldn't find a parking spot." Her classmates nod, knowing full well what she is talking about. Here at the university, especially between the hours of 9 a.m. and 2 p.m., parking spots are hard to come by.

This scene is replayed every day at many universities and colleges across the country. Students are late for class because on many days there isn't a parking space to be found.

Think of the ways in which parking spaces can be rationed at a college campus. One way is on a first-come, first-served basis. In other words, students are not charged a fee to park; they just park where spaces are available. At zero price for parking, the quantity demanded of spaces is likely to be greater than the quantity supplied and a shortage of parking spaces will result. To deal with this shortage, students will likely try to be "first in line" for a parking spot, causing them to leave for the campus earlier than they would otherwise. Instead of leaving home at 9:40 a.m. for a 10 o'clock class, one leaves at 9:30 a.m. Now, who pays for the first-come, first-served parking scheme? Of course, the students do, not in money, but in time.

Naturally, if the student doesn't leave home early enough to get a parking spot, then perhaps he or she will end up going up and down the parking aisles looking for an open spot. This way, the student ends up paying for a parking spot by being late to class.

So, if parking spaces are allocated on a first-come, first-served basis, it is likely that the student will end up paying in terms of time or in terms of being late to class.

The alternative is to pay in terms of money price. The university could, say, install parking meters and adjust the parking fee in such a way as to have the quantity demanded of parking spaces equal the quantity supplied of parking spaces at various times of the day.

Of course, if, by chance, the university sets the parking fee at a level below the equilibrium price, then the student will end up paying for the parking scheme in terms of both money price and first come, first served, because a parking fee below equilibrium will generate a shortage of parking spaces, and thus spaces will be rationed on a first-come, first-served basis.

You may often hear people say that price is a bad way to ration parking spaces at a college campus. But, then, what is the alternative? If price does not ration parking spots, something else will. In short, students who want to park on campus are going to have to pay for parking; it is just a question of *how* they pay. Do they pay in terms of their time, in being late to class, or in money price?

A loss in total surplus—in our example, areas 3 + 5—is sometimes called a **deadweight loss.** This is the loss to society of not producing the competitive, or supply-and-demand–determined, level of output. In terms of Exhibit 5, it is the loss to society of producing Q_2 instead of producing Q_1.

What Some People Get Wrong   In sum, some persons argue that a price floor creates a situation in which (1) someone wins and someone loses and (2) the gains for the winner are equal to the losses for the loser (e.g., one person loses $5 and another person wins $5). A quick look at Exhibit 5 tells us that (2) is not true. The losses (for consumers) are not offset by the gains (for producers). A price floor ends with a *net loss,* or *deadweight loss,* of areas 3 + 5. Now think of how hard it would have been to identify this deadweight loss without the tools of supply, demand, consumers' surplus, and producers' surplus. Economic tools often have the ability to make what is invisible visible.

Deadweight Loss
The loss to society of not producing the competitive, or supply-and-demand–determined, level of output.

1. Do buyers prefer lower prices to higher prices?
2. "When there are long-lasting shortages, there are long lines of people waiting to buy goods. It follows that the shortages cause the long lines." Do you agree or disagree? Explain your answer.
3. Who might argue for a price ceiling? A price floor?

4-3 TWO PRICES: ABSOLUTE AND RELATIVE

In everyday language, we often use the word "price" without specifying the kind of price. Economists often distinguish the *absolute,* or *money, price* of a good from the *relative price* of a good.

4-3a Absolute (Money) Price and Relative Price

Absolute (Money) Price
The price of a good in money terms.

Relative Price
The price of a good in terms of another good.

The **absolute (money) price** is the price of the good in money terms. For example, the absolute price of a car might be $30,000. The **relative price** is the price of the good *in terms of another good.* To illustrate, suppose the absolute price of a car is $30,000 and the absolute price of a computer is $2,000. Then the relative price of the car—that is, the price of the car *in terms of computers*—is 15 computers. A person gives up the opportunity to buy 15 computers when buying a car:

$$\text{Relative price of a car (in terms of computer)} = \frac{\text{Absolute price of a car}}{\text{Absolute price of a computer}}$$
$$= \frac{\$\,30{,}000}{\$\,2{,}000}$$
$$= 15$$

Now let's compute the relative price of a computer—that is, the price of a computer in terms of a car:

$$\text{Relative price of a computer (in terms of car)} = \frac{\text{Absolute price of a computer}}{\text{Absolute price of a car}}$$
$$= \frac{\$\,2{,}000}{\$\,30{,}000}$$
$$= \frac{1}{15}$$

Thus, the relative price of a computer in this example is 1/15 of a car. A person gives up the opportunity to buy 1/15 of a car when buying a computer.

Now consider this question: What happens to the relative price of a good if its absolute price rises and nothing else changes? For example, if the absolute price of a car rises from $30,000 to $40,000, what happens to its relative price? Obviously, the relative price rises from 15 computers to 20 computers. In short, if the absolute price of a good rises and nothing else changes, then its relative price rises too.

Higher Absolute Price Can Sometimes Mean Lower Relative Price Economists know that a good can go up in price at the same time that it becomes relatively cheaper. How can this happen? Suppose the absolute price of a pen is $1 and the absolute price of a pencil is 10¢. The relative price of 1 pen, then, is 10 pencils.

Now let the absolute price of a pen rise to $1.20 at the same time that the absolute price of a pencil rises to 20¢. As a result, the relative price of 1 pen falls to 6 pencils. In other words, the absolute price of pens rises (from $1 to $1.20) at the same time that pens become relatively cheaper (in terms of how many pencils you have to give up to buy a pen).

How does this phenomenon happen? Well, the absolute price of a pen went up by 20 percent (from $1 to $1.20) at the same time that the absolute price of a pencil doubled (from 10¢ to 20¢). Because the absolute price of a pen went up by *less than* the absolute price of a pencil increased, the relative price of a pen fell.

4-3b Taxes on Specific Goods and Relative Price Changes

Suppose that the equilibrium price of good X is $10 and that the equilibrium price of good Y is $20. The relative price of good X is therefore ½ unit of good Y, and the relative price of good Y is 2 units of good X:

$$1X = \tfrac{1}{2}Y$$

$$1Y = 2X$$

Given these relative prices of X and Y, consumers will buy some combination of the two goods. For example, a given consumer might end up buying 10 units of X each week and 12 units of Y.

Now suppose that the government imposes a tax only on the purchase of good X. Then the tax effectively raises the price the consumer pays for the good from $10 to $15. Because no tax is placed on good Y, its price remains at $20.

The tax thus changes the relative prices of the two goods. The after-tax relative prices are

$$1X = \tfrac{3}{4}Y$$

$$1Y = 1.33X$$

Comparing the new relative prices with the old relative prices, we recognize that the tax makes X relatively more expensive (going from ½Y to ¾Y) and makes Y relatively cheaper (going from 2X to 1.33X). In other words, a tax placed only on X ends up making X relatively more expensive and Y relatively cheaper. As a result, we would expect consumers to buy relatively less X and relatively more Y. Think in terms of two familiar goods: Coke and Pepsi. A tax placed on Coke, but not on Pepsi, will induce consumers to buy relatively less Coke and relatively more Pepsi.

ECONOMICS 24/7

Obesity and a Soda Tax

The percentage of the U.S. population that is deemed obese today is higher than it was 20 years ago. Obesity is a health problem, so we often hear proposals directed at trying to reduce the obesity rate in the country. One proposal is to place a tax on high-fat, high-calorie so-called junk food. A similar proposal is to place a tax on soda.

We now know that a tax placed on one good (but not on another) will change the relative prices of the two goods. Placing a tax on good X, but not on good Y, will make good X relatively more expensive and Y relatively cheaper, prompting consumers to purchase relatively less X and relatively more Y.

Consider a tax placed on soda. We would expect the absolute (money) price of soda to rise. And if the tax is placed only on soda, its relative price will rise too. As soda becomes relatively more expensive, we would expect fewer sodas to be consumed and obesity to decline. Right? Well, fewer sodas might be purchased and consumed, but whether obesity will decline is not so clear. Consider soda and sugared iced tea. Both soda and sugared iced tea are sweet drinks. They might even be substitutes. With this idea in mind, suppose the absolute price of a soda is $1 and the absolute

price of an iced tea (with sugar) is 50¢. It follows that the relative prices are

$$1 \text{ soda} = 2 \text{ sugared iced teas}$$

$$1 \text{ sugared iced tea} = \tfrac{1}{2} \text{ soda}$$

Now let's place a tax on soda that drives its price up to $2. The new relative prices for soda and iced tea are

$$1 \text{ soda} = 4 \text{ sugared iced teas}$$

$$1 \text{ sugared iced tea} = \tfrac{1}{4} \text{ soda}$$

As a result of the tax on soda, its relative price has risen, but the relative price of sugared iced tea has fallen. We would thus expect people to consume relatively less soda and relatively more sugared iced tea.

Obesity is lessened by ingesting fewer calories, not the same number or more calories. Simply put, the soda tax might reduce the consumption of sodas, but it doesn't necessarily reduce obesity. Although the soda tax makes soda relatively more expensive, it makes soda substitutes (such as sugared iced tea) relatively less expensive and thus makes a rise in the consumption of sugared iced tea more likely.

Patti McConville/Alamy

ECONOMICS 24/7

Relative Prices and Having Children

Women bear children; often, they are the primary caregivers of children. So, how many children will a woman choose to have? From an economist's perspective, the answer has much to do with the relative price of having children. So, what is the relative price of having children?

Before we answer that question, what is the relative price of *any* good—whether it is a house, a car, or a computer? It is the price of that good in terms of other goods. The relative price of a house is the price of the house in terms of other goods. For example, the relative price of a $400,000 house is 10 cars, each with a price of $40,000.

So, what is the price for a woman of having a child? If the woman earns, say, $100,000 a year in a job, and chooses to take off two years from the job to have and raise the child (on a 24-hour basis), then we could say that the absolute price for this particular woman of having a child is $200,000 worth of other goods—or the relative price is ten $20,000 cars. For a woman who earns $50,000 a year in a job and who decides to take off two years, the absolute price of having a child is $100,000—or the relative price is five $20,000 cars.

An economist will argue that the higher the relative price of having a child, the fewer children a woman will have, and the lower the relative price of having a child, the more children a woman will have. If this statement is true, then what would we expect to see in the world?

First, we would expect to see poorer women having more children than richer women. For example, if women in country X are poorer (in

terms of the incomes they can earn), on average, than women in country Y, then women in country X will have more children than women in country Y.

Also, if we focus on only one country—say, country Y—then we should observe that richer women will have fewer children than poorer women.

A criticism of looking at things in relative price terms is that it ignores the fact that some women actually want children more than other women do. In other words, not all women have identical preferences when it comes to having children. What about the woman who strongly wants children compared with the woman who only weakly wants children? Wouldn't the woman who strongly wants children have more children than the woman who only weakly wants children, even if she were much richer? Certainly, she could. But, then, the economist is not really arguing against this happening when he or she puts forth the relative price argument for having children. The economist is arguing that, no matter what a woman's preferences for having children (strong, weak, or none at all), the higher the relative price of having children, the fewer children she is likely to have, and the lower the relative price of having children, the more children she is likely to have. In other words, the woman who strongly wants children will have fewer children at a higher relative price than at a lower relative price. And the same holds for the woman who only weakly wants children.

© wavebreakmedia/Shutterstock.com

SELF-TEST

1. If the absolute (or money) price of good A is $40 and the absolute price of good B is $60, what is the relative price of each good?

2. Someone says, "The price of good X has risen, so good X is more expensive than it used to be." In what sense is this statement correct? In what sense is this statement either incorrect or misleading?

Office  Hours

"I Thought Price Ceilings Were Good for Consumers"

STUDENT:

I still don't quite understand how a price ceiling can hurt consumers. After all, a price ceiling is usually set below the equilibrium price of a good, and everyone knows that consumers prefer lower prices to higher prices.

INSTRUCTOR:

The problem is that when a price ceiling is imposed on a good, certain things happen that don't benefit consumers. Look at it this way: Consumers like the lower price that goes along with the price ceiling, but what they don't like are some of the effects of the price ceiling.

STUDENT:

But it seems to me that if you picked 100 consumers at random and asked them whether they preferred the price of bread to be $1 a loaf as opposed to $2, all 100 consumers would say they prefer the lower price. Because a price ceiling is usually lower than the equilibrium price, doesn't this example prove that consumers benefit from price ceilings? After all, why would they say they prefer paying $1 than $2 for a loaf of bread if they didn't see it benefiting them?

INSTRUCTOR:

A couple of things could be going on here. First, consumers might intuitively take the question to mean, do they prefer the *$1 price determined by supply and demand* to the *$2 price determined by supply and demand*? If this is how they understand the question, then it certainly seems reasonable for them to say they prefer the lower price to the higher price. You might not get the same response from consumers, though, if you asked them this question: Which of the following two options do you prefer?

    Option A:
        $2 (equilibrium) price of bread
    Option B:
        $1 (price ceiling) price of bread + shortages of bread + lines of people waiting to buy bread, and so on.

STUDENT:

In other words, your point is that consumers prefer lower to higher prices, assuming that nothing else changes but the price of the good. But if lower prices as the result of price ceilings come with shortages and long lines of people waiting to buy bread, then they may not prefer lower to higher prices.

INSTRUCTOR:

Yes, that is the point.

STUDENT:

A slightly different question: Do you think that all consumers know the adverse effects of price ceilings?

INSTRUCTOR:

Probably not. In fact, even after government imposes a price ceiling and certain adverse effects (shortages, long lines, etc.) set in, consumers may fail to relate the cause to the effects of the price ceiling. In other words, X causes Y, but individuals either don't understand how (so they don't connect the two), or they believe that something else—Z—causes Y.

Points to remember

1. Consumers may prefer a lower to higher price, *ceteris paribus*, but not a lower price with shortages to a higher price without shortages.
2. X may cause Y, but it doesn't necessarily follow that everyone will understand that X causes Y.

CHAPTER SUMMARY

PRICE

- As a result of scarcity, a rationing device is needed to determine who gets what of the available limited resources and goods. Price serves as a rationing device.

- Price acts as a transmitter of information relating to the change in the relative scarcity of a good.

PRICE CEILINGS

- A price ceiling is a government-mandated maximum price. If a price ceiling is below the equilibrium price, some or all of the following effects arise: shortages, fewer exchanges, nonprice-rationing devices, buying and selling at prohibited prices, and tie-in sales.

- Consumers do not necessarily prefer (lower) price ceilings to (higher) equilibrium prices. They may prefer higher prices

and none of the effects of price ceilings to lower prices and some of the effects of price ceilings. All we can say for sure is that consumers prefer lower prices to higher prices, *ceteris paribus.*

PRICE FLOORS

- A price floor is a government-mandated minimum price. If a price floor is above the equilibrium price, the following effects arise: surpluses and fewer exchanges.

ABSOLUTE PRICE AND RELATIVE PRICE

- The absolute price of a good is the price of the good in terms of money.

- The relative price of a good is the price of the good in terms of another good.

KEY TERMS AND CONCEPTS

Price Ceiling   Price Floor   Absolute (Money) Price
Tie-in Sale   Deadweight Loss   Relative Price

VIDEO QUESTIONS AND PROBLEMS

Video Questions and Problems are available on MindTap for Arnold 12e or by searching for Arnold on www.cengagebrain.com

1. Prove diagrammatically that a minimum wage (set about the equilibrium wage) reduces employment.

2. Prove diagrammatically that a price floor reduces consumers' surplus.

3. The absolute price of X is $40 and the absolute price of Y is $10. What is the relative price of X in terms of Y? What is the relative price of Y in terms of X?

4. Are there more or fewer exchanges at a price floor than at the equilibrium price? Explain your answer.

5. Can the absolute price of a good rise at the same time that its relative price declines? Explain your answer.

QUESTIONS AND PROBLEMS

1. "If price were outlawed as the rationing device used in markets, there would be no need for another rationing device to take its place. We would have reached utopia." Discuss.

2. What kind of information does price transmit?

3. Should grades in an economics class be "rationed" according to dollar price instead of how well a student does on exams? If they were and prospective employers learned

of it, what effect might this have on the value of your college degree?

4. Think of ticket scalpers at a rock concert, a baseball game, or an opera. Might they exist because the tickets to these events were originally sold for less than the equilibrium price? Why or why not? In what way is a ticket scalper like and unlike your retail grocer, who buys food from a wholesaler and then sells it to you?

5. Many of the proponents of price ceilings argue that government-mandated maximum prices simply reduce producers' profits and do not affect the quantity supplied of a good on the market. What must the supply curve look like if the price ceiling does not affect the quantity supplied?

6. James lives in a rent-controlled apartment and has for the past few weeks been trying to get the supervisor to fix his shower. What does waiting to get one's shower fixed have to do with a rent-controlled apartment?

7. Explain why fewer exchanges are made when a disequilibrium price (below the equilibrium price) exists than when the equilibrium price exists.

8. Buyers always prefer lower prices to higher prices. Do you agree or disagree with this statement? Explain your answer.

9. What is the difference between a price ceiling and a price floor? What effect is the same for both a price ceiling and a price floor?

10. If the absolute price of good X is $10 and the absolute price of good Y is $14, then what is (a) the relative price of good X in terms of good Y and (b) the relative price of good Y in terms of good X?

11. Give a numerical example that illustrates how a tax placed on the purchase of good X can change the relative price of good X in terms of good Y.

WORKING WITH NUMBERS AND GRAPHS

1. In the diagram, what areas represent the deadweight loss due to the price ceiling (P_C)?

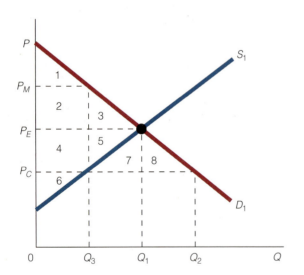

2. In the preceding diagram, what areas represent consumers' surplus at the equilibrium price of P_E? At P_C? (Keep in mind that, at P_C, the equilibrium quantity is neither produced nor sold.)

3. Using Exhibit 1 in the chapter, suppose the price ceiling is $13 instead of $8. Would the consequences of the price ceiling we identified in the text (such as a shortage, fewer exchanges, etc.) arise? Why or why not?

4. Draw a market that is in equilibrium, and identify the area of consumers' surplus and producers' surplus. Now place a price ceiling in the market, and identify the rise and fall in consumers' surplus. Finally, identify the decline in producers' surplus.

5. The absolute prices of goods X, Y, and Z are $23, $42, and $56, respectively. What is the relative price of X in terms of Y? What is the relative price of Y in terms of Z? What is the relative price of Z in terms of X?

6. There are two goods: X and Y. The absolute price of X rises and the absolute price of Y does not change. Prove that the relative price of X rises in terms of Y.

SUPPLY, DEMAND, AND PRICE: APPLICATIONS

© Travis houston/Shutterstock.com

INTRODUCTION

In the previous two chapters, we discussed supply, demand, and price. In this chapter, we *work with* supply, demand, and price. The theory of supply and demand is not very useful to you unless you can use it to explain some of the things you see around you in everyday life. In this chapter, we discuss medical care, changing house prices, college classes at 10 a.m., driving on a freeway, standardized tests (such as the SAT), college athletes, and more—all in the general framework of supply and demand.

5-1 APPLICATION 1: TICKETS TO *THE BIG BANG THEORY*

If you go to tvtickets.com, you can request tickets to view the taping of television shows. There is no charge for the ticket; the price is zero. Now ask yourself whether a zero price is the market equilibrium price. Given some degree of positive demand to see the show, you would think that the market equilibrium price would be positive. You would also expect the market equilibrium ticket price to be higher for some shows than for others.

To illustrate, suppose the supply of seats in a TV studio is 200 seats. Three shows are taped in the studio. Will the market equilibrium price for the three shows be the same—say, $20? It could be, but more probably it is not, because the demand for each of the three shows is likely to be different. The equilibrium price might be $100 for one show, $70 for another show, and $20 for the third show.

But the market equilibrium price is not charged for any of the three shows. Instead, the price of a ticket is zero for all of them.

Monty Brinton/CBS/Getty Images

> **EXHIBIT 1**

The Supply and Demand for Viewing the Taping of Different TV Shows

We show the demand for viewing the taping of three TV shows: *A*, *B*, and *C*. We also show the supply of seats for each show. If the ticket price for each show is $0, then the shortage will be greater for show *A* than for show *B*, and greater for *B* than for *C*. Also, if an equilibrium price were charged for each show, the equilibrium price for show *A* would be greater than that for show *B* and greater for *B* than *C*.

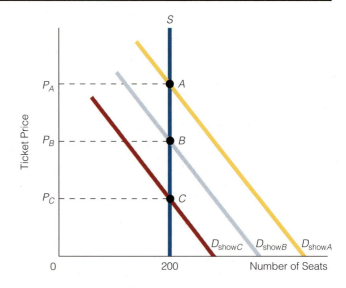

What follows, then, is that there will be a shortage of tickets for each show, with the shortage being larger for some shows than for others. (See Exhibit 1.)

How will the shortage for each show manifest itself? And how will we know whether the shortage is different for each show? The answer has to do with how easy or hard it is to get a ticket to a show. At the tvtickets.com site, some shows are sold out and some are not. For example, getting tickets for *The Big Bang Theory* (CBS) is very difficult. When tickets become available for that show, the first people to place their requests for the show get the tickets. In other words, tickets are rationed on a first-come, first-served basis (with the exception of people who might know someone in the cast of the show). Because of the popularity of *The Big Bang Theory*, tickets go quickly.

Of course, tickets don't go as quickly for all other shows. For instance, the demand for tickets to new shows is sometimes less than the supply. When this happens, the market equilibrium price might actually be negative. For example, in Exhibit 2, the demand for seats to a new show and the supply of seats for it intersect at a negative price (–$20). The producers of the show would actually have to pay people $20 to watch a taping! More often than not, however, producers don't pay people.

> **EXHIBIT 2**

A Negative Price: We'll Pay You to View the Taping of the Show

We have assumed that the demand for seats for the taping of a new TV show is low enough that it intersects the supply of seats at a negative price (–$20). At this point, the producers of the show would have to pay people to view the taping of the show.

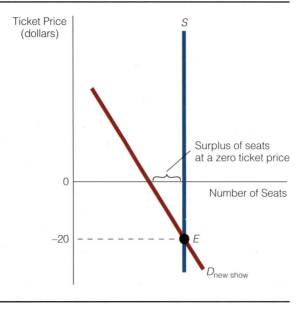

How, then, do they deal with the surplus of seats that would exist at the zero price. (See Exhibit 2.) Often, they ask friends and family members to do them a favor and come to the taping of the show. As the show gains real fans, the demand to see the show rises, and there may no longer be any surplus seats at a zero ticket price. Of course, if the problem of surplus seats doesn't go away, you can bet that the TV show will.

SELF-TEST

(Answers to Self-Test questions are in Answers to Self-Test Questions at the back of the book.)

1. How can a television network that produces a number of television shows gauge the popularity of each show from ticket requests and the rate at which tickets sell out?

2. Could television networks charge a positive ticket price for the taping of their shows if they wanted to? Explain your answer.

5-2 APPLICATION 2: EASIER-TO-OBTAIN LOANS AND HIGHER HOUSING PRICES

If the federal government wants to make it easier for people to buy houses, one thing it can do is push for lowered lending standards. For example, suppose that lenders require individuals who want a mortgage loan to buy a house to make a down payment of 20 percent of the sale price. Now suppose that the government passes a law stating that no lender can require more than a 5 percent down payment before granting a loan. Will this law make it easier for individuals to buy homes? Not necessarily. The interest rate on a mortgage loan that requires only a 5 percent down payment might be higher than the rate on one that requires a 20 percent down payment.

Can government do *anything* now? Well, it could undertake specific monetary actions that have the effect of lowering interest rates. (We will discuss these actions in detail in a later chapter.)

Then what happens? The government seems to have met its objective of making it easier for individuals to buy houses. After all, prospective buyers now have to come up with only a 5 percent down payment (instead of 20 percent), and they end up paying lower interest rates for the loans they receive. So, are home buyers necessarily better off with this kind of government assistance? Not exactly.

By making mortgage loans easier to get, the government has indirectly increased the demand for houses. As the demand for houses rises, so do house prices. In short, making it easier to get home mortgage loans (as described) results in rising home prices, which make buying a house all the harder:

Lower down payments + Lower interest rates → Easier-to-obtain loans → Higher demand for houses → Higher house prices

The main point is simply this: Government set out to make buying a home easier for more people by passing laws that forced lenders to accept lower down payments and by undertaking actions to put downward pressure on interest rates. But making it easier for individuals to get loans had the effect of raising the demand for, and the prices of, houses. Higher house prices made it harder for people to buy homes.

Continuing on with the story, suppose government now states that individuals need even more help to get a home because housing prices have risen. So, in its attempt to help people buy a house, government pushes for even lower lending standards (maybe requiring only a 1 percent down payment) and lower interest rates. Will that do the trick? Not likely: The lower lending standards and interest rates will probably stimulate greater demand for housing, leading to even higher housing prices.

SELF-TEST

1. If lowering lending standards can indirectly raise housing prices, can increasing lending standards lower housing prices? Explain.

2. Suppose anyone who buys a house in a certain year gets to pay $1,000 less in income taxes (assuming that the tax owed is greater than $1,000). Would the tax credit affect house prices? Explain your answer.

5-3 APPLICATION 3: THE PRICE OF AN AISLE SEAT

Most airlines will reserve an assigned seat for you when you buy a ticket. For example, if you want to buy an airline ticket from U.S. Airways, you can go online, purchase the ticket, and then look at a graphic that shows unreserved seats. If seat 13A is the one you want and no one has chosen it, then it is yours if you click it in the graphic.

Southwest Airlines does things differently. You do not reserve a seat when you book a flight. You choose a seat when you board the plane. If you are one of the first to board, you have your pick of many seats; if you are one of the last, you have your pick of very few seats.

Keep in mind that aisle seats are more popular than middle seats. Usually, for every aisle seat, there is a middle seat (assuming that the row of seats on each side of the plane

consists of 3 seats: window, middle, and aisle). So, if the plane has 50 aisle seats, it also has 50 middle seats. In other words, the supply of middle seats equals the supply of aisle seats.

However, the demand for aisle seats is higher than the demand for middle seats. If price were to equilibrate the middle seats market and the aisle seats market, we would expect the price of an aisle seat to be higher than that of a middle seat. (See Exhibit 3.)

Does Southwest charge more for an aisle seat than a middle seat? Perhaps if you asked the airline this question, its answer would be no. But Southwest does charge more for priority boarding. If you want to board before others, you must choose the Business Select option when purchasing a ticket. If you board before others, you obviously have a larger selection of seats to choose from than later boarders do. Because most people prefer aisle to middle seats, those who board the plane first will probably choose the aisle seats.

So, does Business Select come with an additional charge? Yes. On the day we checked, the added charge was $20. In effect, Southwest was charging $20 more for an aisle seat than a middle seat, as we would expect, because the demand for aisle seats is higher than the demand for middle seats whereas the supply of each is the same.

> **EXHIBIT 3**

The Market for Middle and Aisle Seats on Airline Flights

We have assumed that the supply of aisle seats is equal to the supply of middle seats. Because the demand for aisle seats is higher than the demand for middle seats, we conclude that the equilibrium price for an aisle seat is higher than the equilibrium price for a middle seat. In the diagram, P_2 is the equilibrium price for an aisle seat, and P_1 is the equilibrium price for a middle seat.

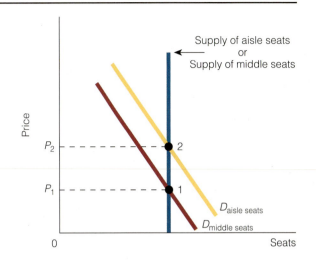

SELF-TEST

1. If the equilibrium price is $400 for an aisle seat and $350 for a middle seat but an airlines company charges $350 for each seat, we would expect a shortage to appear in the aisle seat market. (More people will want aisle seats than there are aisle seats available.) How will the airlines decide who gets an aisle seat?

2. Suppose the supply of aisle, middle, and window seats is each 100 seats but the demand for aisle seats is greater than the demand for window seats, which, in turn, is greater than the demand for middle seats. If the equilibrium price of an aisle seat is $300, where do the equilibrium prices of middle and window seats stand in relation to this price?

5-4 APPLICATION 4: WHAT WILL HAPPEN TO THE PRICE OF MARIJUANA IF THE PURCHASE AND SALE OF MARIJUANA ARE LEGALIZED?

In most of the United States, the purchase and sale of marijuana are unlawful, but there is still a demand for it and a supply of it. There is also an equilibrium price of marijuana. Let's say that price is P_1. If tomorrow the purchase and sale of marijuana become legal, would P_1 rise, fall, or remain the same?

The answer, of course, depends on what we think will happen to the demand for and supply of marijuana. If the purchase and sale of marijuana are legal, then some people currently producing corn and wheat will likely choose instead to produce and sell marijuana. So the supply of marijuana will rise. If nothing else changes, its price will fall.

But something else is likely to change. If marijuana consumption is no longer illegal, then the number of people who want to buy and consume marijuana will likely rise. In other words, more people will buy marijuana, thus increasing demand.

So, decriminalizing the purchase and sale of marijuana is likely to shift both the marijuana demand and the marijuana supply curve to the right. What happens to the price of marijuana then depends on how much the curves shift. Three possibilities exist:

1. The demand curve shifts to the right by the same amount as the supply curve shifts to the right. In this case, the price of marijuana will not change. (Try to visualize the demand and supply curves shifting.)

2. The demand curve shift to the right is greater than the supply curve shift to the right. In this case, the price of marijuana will rise. (Try to visualize the demand curve shifting to the right more than the supply curve does. Can you see the higher price on the vertical axis?)

3. The supply curve shift to the right is greater than the demand curve shift to the right. In this case, the price of marijuana will fall.

If you can't visualize the shifts of the demand and supply curves for these three possibilities, draw the original demand and supply curves, then draw the shift in each curve, and identify the new equilibrium price.

SELF-TEST

1. What will happen to the price of marijuana if the supply increases by more than the demand for it?

2. What will happen to the quantity of marijuana if the demand for it rises more than its supply falls.

5-5 APPLICATION 5: SPECULATORS, PRICE VARIABILITY, AND PATTERNS

Think of an abstract good, say, X. Let's suppose that the price of good X initially varies over a month. Sometimes it is $10, other times it is $13, and at other times it is $12. Usually, when prices fluctuate, speculators will enter the market. That's because, when prices fluctuate, there is profit to be earned by buying low and selling high. In terms of our example so far, there is profit to be earned by buying at $10 and selling at $13.

The common view of speculators is that they somehow hurt others by trying to make themselves better off. Well, they certainly might be trying to make themselves better off, but it doesn't necessarily follow that, because they are doing what is in their best interest, others will be made worse off.

To understand why, suppose that on Monday through Wednesday of every week the price of good X is $10 and that on Thursday of every week the price of good X rises to $14. Clearly, then, there is price variability over part of the week. How will speculators respond to this variability? Obviously, they will buy good X on Monday through Wednesday and sell it on Thursday.

But their buying good X on Monday through Wednesday will drive up the price of good X on those days, and their selling good X on Thursday will drive down the price. In other words, speculators will end up changing the Monday-through-Thursday pattern of the price of good X. No longer will the pattern be $10 on Monday through Wednesday and $14 on Thursday. The price will be higher than $10 on Monday through Wednesday and lower than $14 on Thursday. In fact, speculators will continue to buy and sell good X until the price of good X is the same on every day. For example, the price of good X may end up being $11 every day of the week.

Essentially, the speculators have done three things: (1) bought low and sold high; (2) changed the pattern of price from $10 on three days and $14 on one day to $11 for each of four days; and (3) moved some of the supply of good X from certain days to other days.

Now, with this example in mind, let's think of a possible real-world scenario. Suppose that unusually bad weather for growing crops threatens the Midwest of the United States. High prices for food are expected as a result. Are speculators likely to respond to the news of impending bad weather? Most likely, they will translate bad weather into higher food prices. Given their objective to buy low and sell high, they will likely buy certain (food) crops today (before the bad weather hits) and sell those crops later (after the bad weather has hit). Speculators' actions will end up making food a little more expensive today and a little less expensive later. In other words, instead of a loaf of bread being $2 today and $5 later, a loaf of bread may end up being $3.50 both today and later.

What speculators essentially do, then, as a byproduct of buying low and selling high, is "spread out" the pain of bad weather (on food prices) over a longer time. Instead of taking all the "hurt" of high prices after the bad weather has hit, speculators move some of the "hurt" to before the bad weather hits. As a result, there will be less "hurt" after the bad weather hits.

Now, to see even more dramatically what happens as a result of speculators "buying low and selling high," suppose we change our example and have the bad weather result in no crops and thus no food. Under these dire circumstances, wouldn't the activities of the speculators—reallocating the current supply of food away from today to later and thereby changing the pattern of prices—be truly lifesaving?

SELF-TEST

1. Speculators can benefit themselves and others at the same time. Do you agree or disagree with this statement? Explain your answer with an example.

2. The price of a given good is likely to be less variable with than without speculators. Explain.

5-6 APPLICATION 6: WHY IS MEDICAL CARE SO EXPENSIVE?

Think of how you buy groceries. You go to the store, place certain products in your basket, and then pay for them at the cash register.

Now think of how you buy medical care. You go to the doctor or hospital, give the doctor's office or hospital your health insurance card, perhaps make a co-payment of $10 or $20, and then receive medical care. Your doctor or the hospital then bills your insurance company for the bulk of your expenses.

What is the difference between how you buy groceries and how you buy medical care? In the grocery store, only two parties are involved in the transaction: you (the buyer) and the grocery store (the seller). In the medical-care example, three parties are involved: you, the doctor or hospital, and the insurance company. The insurance company is often referred to as the "third party." So no third party is involved in the grocery store transaction, but one is involved in purchasing medical care.

The existence of a third party separates the buying of something from the paying for something. In the grocery store, the person who buys the groceries and the person who pays for them are the same (you). In the medical-care example, the person who buys and receives the medical care (you) is different from the person or entity that pays for the medical care (the insurance company).

"Wait a minute," you say. "You indirectly pay for your medical care by paying monthly insurance premiums to the medical insurance company." That is partly true, but what happens is like being at a buffet. You pay a set dollar price for the buffet, and then you can eat all you want. Our guess is that at a buffet you eat more than you would if you had to pay for each plateful.

The same often happens with medical care. You pay a set premium to the insurance company (let's say, $250 a month), and then you enter the health-care buffet line. Might you end up buying more health care than you would if each doctor visit and lab test at the health-care buffet were priced separately?

Before we continue, let's consider two objections to this analogy.

First, you might say, "But I don't buy medical care as I buy food in the food buffet line. I like shrimp, steak, salads, and desserts, but who likes being x-rayed, being prodded and poked by doctors, and taking medicine? No one buys MRIs as if they were shrimp cocktails."

That objection is true, of course, but it begs the point: Once you get sick and go to the doctor or hospital, the existence of a third party (who pays for your medical care) makes it easier for your doctor or the hospital to opt for more medical examinations or procedures and care than you need. For example, a conversation in your doctor's office may go like this:

Doctor: I think you have condition X, but just to be sure, let's order some blood tests and get an MRI too.

You: Whatever you think is best.

Now ask yourself how you might respond if you had to pay—out of pocket—for the blood test and MRI. The dialogue might change:

Doctor: I think you have condition X, but just to be sure, let's order some blood tests and get an MRI too.

You: How much is this going to cost me, doctor? And is all this really necessary?

The point is simple: Once you have paid your insurance premium, the price you pay for medical care amounts only to your co-payment (which is usually minimal). For all practical purposes, the dollar amount you pay for medical care, out of pocket, is close to zero—a fairly low price for health care. We can expect that the quantity demanded of medical care would be greater at zero than at some positive dollar amount.

Second, let's link the *quantity demanded* for medical care in general (which is high if the price of medical care is zero) with the *demand for specific items* that make up medical care. (In our food buffet example, we would link the *quantity demanded* of food with the *demand* for specific food items—shrimp, chocolate ice cream, a Caesar salad, and the like.)

If the quantity demanded of medical care is higher at a zero price than at some positive price, then we would expect the demand for the *specific items* that make up medical care to be higher than it would be if the quantity demanded of medical care were lower. This situation is shown diagrammatically in Exhibit 4. In Exhibit 4(a),

> **EXHIBIT 4**

**The Price of Medical Care
and the Demand for X-rays**

(a) If the price of medical care is low (say, zero), the quantity demanded of medical care is 100 units. If the price of medical care for you is P_1, the quantity demanded of medical care for you is 50 units. (b) The lower the price of medical care and the higher the quantity demanded of medical care in panel (a), the higher is the demand curve for X-rays in (b). (c) The higher the demand for X-rays, the higher the price of X-rays is.

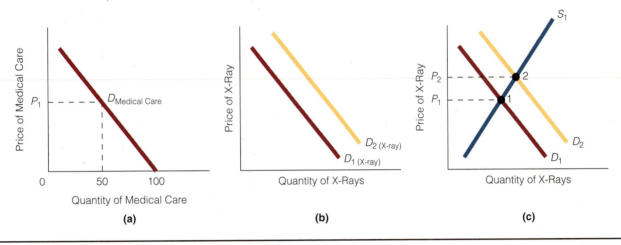

(a)   (b)   (c)

the demand for medical care is downward sloping. If the price is zero for health care, then the quantity demanded of medical care is 100 units. But if the price is some positive dollar amount (such as P_1), then the quantity demanded of medical care is 50 units.

Exhibit 4(b) does not show the demand for medical care in general, just the demand for a specific item of medical care: X-rays. Of the two demand curves in panel (b), the first (D_1) is the demand that exists for X-rays if the *quantity demanded of medical care* is 50 units in panel (a); it is the demand for X-rays if the price for medical care (shown in panel a) is P_1. The second demand curve (D_2) is the demand curve for X-rays if the *quantity demanded of medical care* is 100 units in panel (a); it is the demand for X-rays if the price for medical care (shown in panel a) is zero.

Here is the point in a nutshell:

- The *lower* the price of medical care, the higher the quantity demanded of medical care and the demand for X-rays will be. That is,

  Price of medical care is low → Quantity demanded of medical care is high →
  Demand for X-rays is high

- The *higher* the price of medical care, the lower the quantity demanded of medical care and the demand for X-rays will be. That is,

  Price of medical care is high → Quantity demanded of medical care is low →
  Demand for X-rays is low

Now, the question is, what does a high demand for X-rays do to the price of an X-ray? Obviously, it pushes the price upward. [See Exhibit 4(c).]

As a result, the health insurance company finds itself paying more for the X-rays you receive. Can you see what will happen next? The health insurance company makes the argument that, with rising medical costs, the premiums for your coverage need to rise too.

Why is health insurance as expensive as it is? You now have a large part of the answer. Think buffet.

SELF-TEST

1. Suppose food insurance exists. You pay the food insurance company a certain dollar amount each month, and then you purchase all the food you want from your local grocery store. The grocery store sends the bill to your food insurance company. What will happen to the price of food and to the premium you pay for food insurance?

2. In Exhibit 4(a), suppose that the price a person has to pay for medical care is between P_1 and zero. Where would the demand for X-rays in panel (b) be in relationship to D_1 and D_2?

5-7 APPLICATION 7: WHY DO COLLEGES USE GPAs, ACTs, AND SATs FOR PURPOSES OF ADMISSION?

At many colleges and universities, students pay part of the price of their education (in the form of tuition payments) and taxpayers and private donors pay part (by way of tax payments and charitable donations, respectively). Thus, the tuition that students pay to attend colleges and universities is usually less than the equilibrium tuition. To illustrate, suppose a student pays tuition T_1 at a given college or university. As shown in Exhibit 5, T_1 is below the equilibrium tuition T_E. At T_1, the number of students who want to attend the university (N_1) is greater than the number of openings at the university (N_2); that is, quantity demanded is greater than quantity supplied. The university receives more applications for admission than there are places available. Something has to be done. But what?

©Orhan Cam/Shutterstock.com

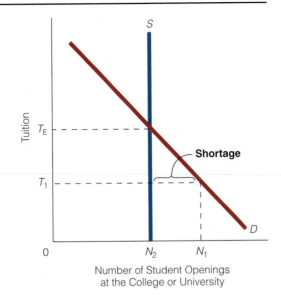

> **EXHIBIT 5**

College and University Admissions

If the college or university charges tuition T_1, then if T_E is the equilibrium tuition, a shortage will be generated. The college or university will then use some nonprice-rationing device, such as GPAs, ACTs, and SATs, as an admission criterion.

The college or university is likely to ration its available space by a combination of money price and some nonprice-rationing devices. The student must then pay the tuition T_1 *and* meet the standards of the nonprice-rationing devices. Colleges and universities typically use such things as GPAs (grade point averages), ACT scores, and SAT scores as rationing devices.

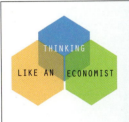

THINKING LIKE AN ECONOMIST

Identifying Rationing Devices The layperson sees a GPA of 3.8 and an SAT score of 1,900 or better as requirements for admission. Economists see them as a rationing device. Economists then go on to ask why this particular nonprice-rationing device is used. They reason that a nonprice-rationing device *would not* be needed if the (dollar) price were fully rationing the good or service.

SELF-TEST

1. The demand rises for admission to a university, but both the tuition and the number of openings in the entering class remain the same. Will this change affect the admission standards of the university? Explain your answer.

2. Administrators and faculty at state colleges and universities often say that their standards of admission are independent of whether there is a shortage or surplus of openings at the university. Do you think that this statement is true? Do you think that faculty and administrators ignore surpluses and shortages of openings when setting admission standards? Explain your answer.

5-8 APPLICATION 8: SUPPLY AND DEMAND ON A FREEWAY

What does a traffic jam on a busy freeway in any large city have to do with supply and demand? Actually, it has quite a bit to do with supply and demand. Look at the question this way: There is a demand for driving on the freeway and a supply of freeway space. The supply of freeway space is fixed. (Roadways do not expand and contract over a day, week, or month.) The demand, however, fluctuates: It is higher at some times than at others. For example, we would expect the demand for driving on the freeway to be higher at 8 a.m. (the rush hour) than at 11 p.m. But even though the demand may vary, the money price for driving on the freeway is always the same: zero. A zero money price means that motorists do not pay tolls to drive on the freeway.

Exhibit 6 shows two demand curves for driving on the freeway: $D_{8\,a.m.}$ and $D_{11\,p.m.}$. We have assumed the demand at 8 a.m. to be greater than at 11 p.m. We have also assumed that, at $D_{11\,p.m.}$ and zero money price, the freeway market clears: The quantity demanded of freeway space equals the quantity supplied. At the higher demand, $D_{8\,a.m.}$, this is not the case. At zero money price, a shortage of freeway space exists: The quantity demanded of freeway space is greater than the quantity supplied. The shortage appears as freeway congestion and bumper-to-bumper traffic. One way to eliminate the shortage is through an increase in the money price of driving on the freeway at 8 a.m. For example, as Exhibit 6 shows, a toll of 70¢ would clear the freeway market at 8 a.m.

> ## EXHIBIT 6

Freeway Congestion, and Supply and Demand

The demand for driving on the freeway is higher at 8 a.m. than at 11 p.m. At zero money price and $D_{11\,p.m.}$, the freeway market clears. At zero money price and $D_{8\,a.m.}$, there is a shortage of freeway space, which shows up as freeway congestion. At a price (toll) of 70 cents, the shortage is eliminated and freeway congestion disappears.

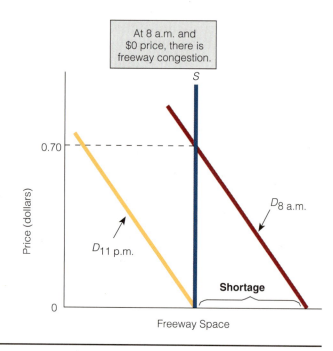

If charging different prices (tolls) on freeways, depending on the time of day, sounds like an unusual idea, consider how Miami Beach hotels price their rooms. They charge different prices for their rooms, depending on the time of year. During the winter months, when the demand for vacationing in Miami Beach is high, the hotels charge higher prices than when the demand is (relatively) low. If different prices were charged for freeway space, depending on the time of day, freeway space would be rationed the same way Miami Beach hotel rooms are rationed.

Finally, consider three alternatives usually proposed to counter freeway congestion:

- *Tolls:* Tolls deal with the congestion problem by adjusting price to its equilibrium level, as shown in Exhibit 6.

- *Building more freeways:* Building more freeways deals with the problem by increasing supply. In Exhibit 6, the supply curve of freeway space would have to be shifted to the right so that there is no longer any shortage of space at 8 a.m.

- *Encouraging carpooling:* More carpooling deals with the problem by decreasing demand. Two people in one car take up less space on a freeway than two people in two cars. In Exhibit 6, if, through carpooling, the demand at 8 a.m. begins to look like the demand at 11 p.m., then there is no longer a shortage of freeway space at 8 a.m.

A final note: A fee to drive in the Central London area was introduced in 2003. Anyone going into or out of the Central London area between 7:00 a.m. and 6:30 p.m., Monday through Friday, must pay a fee of approximately $15. (Not everyone has to pay the fee. For example, taxi drivers, ambulance drivers, drivers of police vehicles, motorcycle drivers, and bicyclists are exempt. The residents who live in the area receive a 90 percent discount.) Many people have claimed the fee a success because it has cut down on traffic and travel times and reduced pollution in the area.

Some people have urged New York City to institute a fee program to drive on certain streets in the city. On any given day in New York City, approximately 800,000 cars are on the streets south of 60th Street in Manhattan. According to many, the city is "choking in traffic." We will have to wait to see whether New York City goes the way of London.

THINKING LIKE AN ECONOMIST

It's One of Three The economist knows that when there are buyers and sellers of anything (bread, cars, or freeway space), only three conditions are possible: equilibrium, shortage, or surplus. When the economist sees traffic congestion, the first thing that comes to mind is the shortage of road space. But why is there a shortage? The economist knows that shortages occur at prices below the equilibrium price. In other words, the price of driving on the road is too low.

SELF-TEST

1. In Exhibit 6, at what price is there a surplus of freeway space at 8 a.m.?

2. If the driving population increases in an area and the supply of freeway space remains constant, what will happen to freeway congestion? Explain your answer.

5-9 APPLICATION 9: ARE RENTERS BETTER OFF?

We begin with an analysis of two laws related to the eviction of a renter:

- Under law 1, a renter has 30 days to vacate an apartment after being served with an eviction notice.

- Under law 2, the renter has 90 days to vacate.

Landlords will find it less expensive to rent apartments under law 1 than under law 2. Under law 1, the most money a landlord can lose after serving an eviction notice is 30 days' rent. Under law 2, a landlord can lose up to 90 days' rent. Obviously, losing 90 days' rent is more costly than losing 30 days' rent.

A different supply curve of apartments exists under each law. The supply curve under law 1 (S_1 in Exhibit 7) lies to the right of the supply curve under law 2 (S_2). It is less expensive to supply apartments under law 1 than under law 2.

If the supply curve is different under the two laws, the equilibrium rent will be different too. As shown in Exhibit 7, the equilibrium rent will be lower under law 1 (R_1) than under law 2 (R_2).

So,

- Under law 1, a renter pays lower rent (good) and has fewer days to vacate the apartment (bad).

- Under law 2, a renter pays a higher rent (bad) and has more days to vacate the apartment (good).

Who pays for the additional days to vacate the apartment under law 2? The renter pays for them by paying a higher rent.

> EXHIBIT 7

Apartment Rent and the Law

Under law 1, a renter has 30 days to leave an apartment after receiving an eviction notice from his or her landlord. Under law 2, a renter has 90 days to leave an apartment after receiving an eviction notice. The cost to the landlord of renting an apartment is higher under law 2 than law 1, so the supply curve of apartments under law 1 lies to the right of the supply curve of apartments under law 2. Different supply curves mean different rents. Apartment rent is higher under law 2 (R_2) than under law 1 (R_1).

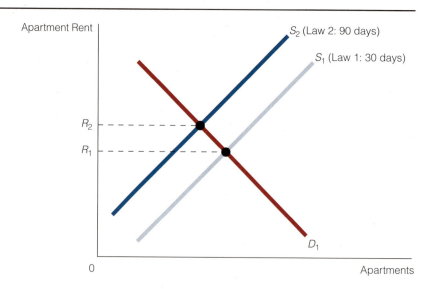

In an HMO You may frequently hear people complain about their health maintenance organizations (HMOs). Of the diverse and wide-ranging complaints, a common one is that patients usually cannot sue their HMOs in state courts for denial of benefits and poor-quality care. Some people argue that patients should have the right to sue their HMOs.

Let's consider two settings: one in which patients cannot sue their HMOs and one in which they can. If patients cannot sue, an HMO's liability cost is lower than if patients can sue. A difference in liability costs is then reflected in different supply curves.

To illustrate, recall that any single point on a supply curve is the minimum price sellers need to receive for them to be willing and able to sell that unit of a good. Suppose that, when patients cannot sue, an HMO is willing and able to provide health care to John for $300 a month. If patients can sue, is the HMO still willing and able to provide the service for $300 a month? Not likely. Because of the higher liability cost due to patients' ability to sue, the HMO is still willing and able to provide health care to John, but for, say, $350 month, not $300.

Saying that a seller's minimum price for providing a good or service rises is the same as saying that the seller's supply curve has shifted upward and to the left. In other words, the supply curve of HMO-provided health care will shift upward and to the left if patients have the right to sue. This is how the supply curve of apartments moved in Exhibit 7. So, will a difference in supply curves affect the price patients pay for their HMO-provided health-care coverage? Yes. One effect of moving from a setting in which patients do not have the right to sue to one in which they do is that patients will have to pay more for their HMO-provided health-care coverage.

Economists don't determine whether a patient having the right to sue is good or bad or right or wrong. Economists use their tools (in this instance, supply and demand) to point out that the things people want, such as the right to sue their HMOs, often come with price tags. Individuals must decide whether the price they pay is worth what they receive in return.

SELF-TEST

1. Economists often say, "There is no such thing as a free lunch." How is this saying related to patients moving from a system in which they cannot sue their HMOs to one in which they can?

2. A professor tells her students that they can have an extra week to complete their research papers. Under what condition are the students better off with the extra week? Can you think of a case where the students would actually be worse off with the extra week?

5-10 APPLICATION 10: DO YOU PAY FOR GOOD WEATHER?

Some places in the country are considered to have better weather than others. For example, most people would say the weather in San Diego, California is better than the weather in Fargo, North Dakota. Often, a person in San Diego will say, "You can't beat the

> **EXHIBIT 8**

The Price of Weather and the Price of Housing

We show two demand curves, D_1 and D_2. D_1 represents the demand for housing in San Diego if the weather were not so good. The higher demand curve D_2 shows the demand for housing in San Diego given that the weather is good. Notice that the price of housing in San Diego is higher because the weather there is good. Lesson learned: You pay for good weather (in San Diego) in terms of higher house prices.

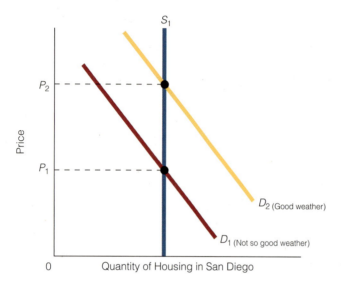

weather today. And the good thing about it is that you don't have to pay a thing for it. It's free."

In one sense, the San Diegan is correct: There is no weather market. Specifically, no one comes around each day and asks San Diegans to pay a certain dollar amount for the weather.

But in another sense, the San Diegan is incorrect: San Diegans do pay for their good weather—albeit indirectly. How do they pay? To enjoy the weather in San Diego on a regular basis, you have to live there; you need to have housing. There is a demand for housing in San Diego, just as there is a demand for housing in other places. Is the demand for housing in San Diego higher than it would be if the weather were not so good? Without the good weather, living in San Diego would not be as pleasurable, and therefore the demand to live there would be lower. (See Exhibit 8.)

In short, the demand for housing in San Diego is higher because the city enjoys good weather. It follows that the price of housing is higher too (P_2, as opposed to P_1, in Exhibit 8). Thus, San Diegans indirectly pay for their good weather because they pay higher housing prices than they would if the area had bad weather.

Was our representative San Diegan right when he said that the good weather was free?

FINDING ECONOMICS

Good Schools and House Prices Suppose there are two neighborhoods, A and B. The kids who live in neighborhood A go to school A, and the kids who live in neighborhood B go to school B. Currently, school A has a much better academic reputation than school B. Can you find the economics?

This case is really no more than a disguised version of our good-weather example. If school A is better than school B, then the equilibrium price of houses in neighborhood A is likely to be higher than the equilibrium price of similar houses in neighborhood B. Just as we pay for good weather in terms of house prices, we pay for good schools in terms of house prices too.

1. Give an example to illustrate that someone may "pay" for clean air in much the same way that she "pays" for good weather.

2. If people pay for good weather, who ultimately receives the "good-weather payment"?

5-11 APPLICATION 11: COLLEGE SUPERATHLETES

Suppose a young man, 17 years old, is one of the best high school football players in the country. As a superathlete, the young man will be recruited by football coaches at many colleges and universities. Every one of those schools will likely want its coach to be successful at signing up the young athlete; after all, at many universities, athletics is a moneymaker.

Suppose our superathlete decides to attend college A, where he receives a "full ride"—a full scholarship. How should this full scholarship be viewed? One way is to say that the superathlete is charged zero tuition to attend the college. (In other words, whereas some students pay a price of $30,000 a year to attend, the superathlete pays nothing.)

Another way to view the full scholarship is as a two-step process. First, the college pays the superathlete a dollar amount equal to the full tuition. Second, it charges the superathlete the full tuition. (In other words, the college gives the athlete $30,000 with one hand and then collects it with the other.)

Either way we view the scholarship, the effect is the same for the athlete. For purposes of our analysis, let's view it the second way: as a payment to the athlete, combined with full price being charged. This view leads to two important questions:

1. Can the college pay the athlete more than the full tuition? In other words, if the full tuition is $30,000 a year, can the college pay the athlete, say, $35,000 a year?

2. Is the superathlete being paid what he is worth?

Because of National Collegiate Athletic Association (NCAA) rules, the answer to the first question is essentially no. The NCAA states that a college or university cannot pay a student to attend, and for all practical purposes, the NCAA views payment as anything more than a full scholarship. The NCAA position is that college athletes are amateurs and amateurs cannot be paid to play their sport.

How does the NCAA rule affect the second question? What if the athlete's worth to the college or university is greater than the dollar amount of the full tuition? For example, suppose the athlete will increase the revenues of the college by $100,000 a year and the full tuition is $30,000 a year. In this case, the NCAA rule is actually a price ceiling (a below-equilibrium imposed price) on what the college may pay an athlete.

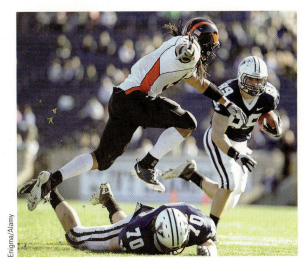

Enigma/Alamy

What is the effect of this price ceiling? Let's consider the demand (on the part of various colleges) for a single superathlete and the supply of this single superathlete. (See Exhibit 9.) We assume that the supply curve for athletic services is vertical at 1. Then, if the representative college charges $30,000 in tuition because of the NCAA rule, that dollar amount is the effective

> **EXHIBIT 9**

The College Athlete

The exhibit shows the demand for and supply of a college athlete. If the market wage for the college athlete is $35,000, then the buyer of the athlete—in this case, the college—receives consumers' surplus equal to area A. If the wage can be held down to the tuition cost of attending the college—$30,000 in this example—then the college receives consumers' surplus of areas A + B.

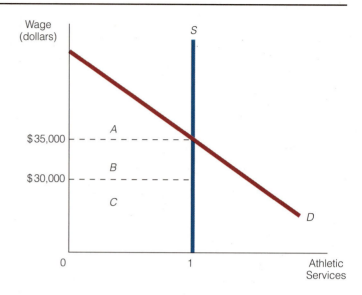

price ceiling (or wage ceiling). If the single athlete's market equilibrium wage is $35,000 and the NCAA rule did not exist, the athlete's wage would rise to $35,000. This dollar amount is equal to areas *B* + *C* in Exhibit 9. The consumers' surplus for the college that buys the athlete's services for $35,000 is obviously equal to area *A*.

However, the NCAA rule stipulates that the college cannot pay the athlete more than $30,000 (full tuition). So the athlete's payment falls from $35,000 to $30,000, or from areas *B* + *C* to simply area *C*. The college's consumers' surplus then increases to areas *A* + *B*. Essentially, the NCAA rule transfers part of the athlete's income—area *B*—to the college in the form of greater consumers' surplus.

SELF-TEST

1. University X is a large school with a major football team. A new field house and track were just added to the campus. How is this addition related to the discussion in this application?

2. Sometimes it is argued that, if colleges paid student athletes, the demand for college sports would decline. In other words, the demand for college sports is as high as it is because student athletes are not paid (in the same way that professional athletes are paid). How would the analysis in this application change if we assume the preceding argument to be true?

5-12 APPLICATION 12: 10 A.M. CLASSES IN COLLEGE

Suppose an economics class is offered in the same classroom twice in a day: at 10 a.m. in the morning and at 8 p.m. at night. Most students would prefer the 10 a.m. class to the 8 p.m. class. So, in Exhibit 10, the supply of seats in the class is the same at each time but

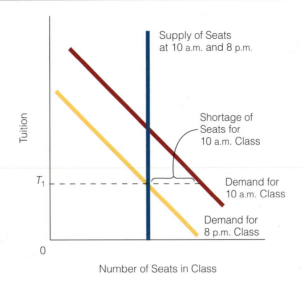

> **EXHIBIT 10**

The Supply of and Demand for College Classes at Different Times

A given class is offered at two times, 10 a.m. and 8 p.m. The supply of seats in the classroom is the same at both times; however, student demand for the 10 a.m. class is higher than that for the 8 p.m. class. The university charges the same tuition, T_1, regardless of which class a student takes. At this tuition level, there is a shortage of seats for the 10 a.m. class. Seats are likely to be rationed on a first-come, first-served (first to register) basis or on seniority (seniors take precedence over juniors, juniors over sophomores, etc.).

the demand to occupy those seats is not. Because the demand is greater for the 10 a.m. class than for the 8 p.m. class, the equilibrium price for the morning class is higher than the equilibrium price for the evening class.

But the university or college charges the same tuition no matter what time students choose to take the class. The university doesn't charge students a higher tuition if they enroll in 10 a.m. classes than if they enroll in 8 p.m. classes.

Suppose that tuition T_1 is charged for all classes and that T_1 is the equilibrium tuition for 8 p.m. classes. (See Exhibit 10.) T_1 is therefore below the equilibrium tuition for 10 a.m. classes: At T_1, the quantity demanded of seats for the morning classes will be greater than the quantity supplied; more students will want the earlier class than there is space available.

THINKING LIKE AN ECONOMIST

Remembering Price Upon seeing students clamoring to get 10 a.m. classes, laypeople conclude that the demand is high for mid-morning classes. They then wonder why the university doesn't schedule more 10 a.m. classes. The economist knows that what laypeople see is as much an effect of price as of demand. The demand for 10 a.m. classes may be high, but the quantity demanded may not be if the price is high enough. In fact, even though the demand for classes at certain times may vary, some set of prices will make the quantity demanded of each class the same.

How will the university allocate the available seats? It may do so in the same way that airlines ration aisle seats: on a first-come, first-served basis. Students who are first to register get the 10 a.m. class; the latecomers have to take the 8 p.m. class. Or the university could ration the high-demand classes by giving their upper-class students (seniors) first priority.

1. Suppose college students are given two options. With option A, the price a student pays for a class is always the equilibrium price. For example, if the equilibrium price to take Economics 101 is $600 at 10 a.m. and $400 at 4 p.m., then students pay more for the early class than they do for the later class. With option B, the price a student pays for a class is the same regardless of the time the class is taken. Given the choice between options A and B, many students would say that they prefer option B to option A. Is this the case for you? If so, why would that be your choice?

2. How is the analysis of the 10 a.m. class similar to the analysis of a price ceiling in a market?

5-13 APPLICATION 13: SALSA, CHIPS, AND BEER

At many Mexican restaurants, it is customary to bring customers a plate of salsa and chips as soon as they sit down at the table. The salsa and chips are free, and upon completion of the first round of salsa and chips, the server often asks customers if they would like more.

Why doesn't the Mexican restaurant charge at least a small fee for the salsa and chips? After all, you would think that at least some people would be willing to pay something for salsa and chips.

The answer probably has to do with goods that are complements. As you may recall, two goods are complements if they are used jointly in consumption. With complements, the demand for one rises as the price of the other falls (or the demand for one falls as the price of the other rises).

Is there a complement for salsa and chips? It could very well be beer—or, in fact, anything to drink. The restaurant owners may be thinking this way: (1) If we make the price of salsa and chips low (zero, in fact), then the quantity demanded of salsa and chips will be high. (2) Also, because salsa and chips are complements for beer, the zero price for salsa and chips will lead to higher demand for beer (than the demand that would exist if we charged for the salsa and chips). (3) Therefore, we are better off (i) charging nothing for the salsa and chips and having a higher demand and price for the beer we sell than (ii) charging some positive price for the salsa and chips and having a lower demand and price for the beer we sell.

1. Do you think that Las Vegas casino hotels would price their rooms higher or lower than equivalent rooms in noncasino hotels in other cities? Explain your answer.

2. Some restaurants give "free refills" of coffee. Why?

Office  Hours

"Doesn't High Demand Mean High Quantity Demanded?"

STUDENT:

The other day in class, you said, "The demand for 10 a.m. classes may be high, but the quantity demanded may not be if the price is high enough." In other words, you were saying that high demand doesn't necessarily mean high quantity demanded. But I thought it did. Could you explain?

INSTRUCTOR:

Let me explain what's going on by first showing you the demand schedule for two goods, A and B:

Good A Demand Schedule	
Price	Quantity Demanded
$6	100
7	80
8	60
9	40

Good B Demand Schedule	
Price	Quantity Demanded
$6	200
7	150
8	125
9	90

As you can see from the two schedules, the demand for good B is greater than the demand for good A. In other words, if we were to derive a demand curve for each good (based on its demand schedule), the demand curve for good B would lie farther to the right than the demand curve for good A.

Now, suppose we look at quantity demanded for each good at the price of $6. The quantity demanded of good A (the low-demand good) is 100 units, and the quantity demanded of good B (the high-demand good) is 200 units. What can we conclude? At the same price for each good ($6), the quantity demanded is higher when demand is higher.

But now let's consider quantity demanded for each good when the price of good A is $6 and the price of good B is $9. The quantity demanded of good A (the low-demand good) is 100 units, and the quantity demanded of good B (the high-demand good) is 90 units. In other words, if the price is high enough for good B (the high-demand good), then the quantity demanded of good B may be lower than the quantity demanded of good A (the low-demand good).

Now let's go back and repeat the statement I made in class: "The demand for 10 a.m. classes may be high, but the quantity demanded may not be if the price is high enough." Now do you understand what I was saying?

STUDENT:

Yes, I think I do. You were saying that high demand doesn't necessarily mean high quantity demanded if we are dealing with different prices.

INSTRUCTOR:

Yes, that's it.

Points to remember

1. High demand means high quantity demanded, but only if the prices for the high-demand good and the low-demand good are the same. From our example, at a price of $6, the quantity demanded for the high-demand good B is greater than quantity demanded for the low-demand good A.

2. The quantity demanded for the low-demand good can be higher than the quantity demanded for the high-demand good if the prices for the two goods are not the same and the price for the high-demand good is high enough. From our example, at a price of $9 for good B (the high-demand good), the quantity demanded is lower than the quantity demanded for good A (the low-demand good) at a price of $6.

CHAPTER SUMMARY

TICKET PRICES TO THE TAPING OF A TV SHOW

- The ticket price to the taping of a TV show is usually zero, usually leading to a shortage of tickets. The greater the demand for the show is, the greater the shortage of tickets will be. Because tickets are rationed (mainly) on a first-come, first-served basis, we would expect that tickets for the most popular shows (those with the greatest demand and the largest shortages at a zero ticket price) would sell out faster than tickets for less popular shows.

GOVERNMENT, LOANS, AND HOUSING PRICES

- Lower lending standards and lower interest rates make it easier to get a mortgage loan. But as getting a mortgage loan becomes easier, the demand for housing rises. As the demand for housing rises, house prices rise.

THE PRICE OF AN AISLE SEAT

- If the supply of aisle and middle seats is the same, but the demand for aisle seats is greater, then the equilibrium price for aisle seats will be greater than the equilibrium price of middle seats.

LEGALIZATION OF MARIJUANA

- If the purchase and sale of marijuana are legalized, the price of marijuana may rise, fall, or remain the same. The price will depend on whether the rise in the demand for marijuana is more than, less than, or equal to the rise in the supply of marijuana.

SPECULATORS, PRICE VARIABILITY, AND PATTERNS

- Speculators try to make themselves better off by buying a product at a low price and then selling it (later) at a high price. In pursuit of profit, they often reallocate a good from a period where it is greater in supply to a period where it is lesser in supply. As a result of reallocating supply, price patterns are changed too. As an example, suppose unusually bad weather for growing crops threatens the Midwest of the United States. High prices for food are expected as a result. Given their objective to buy low and sell high, speculators will likely buy certain (food) crops today (before the bad weather hits) and sell those crops later (after the bad weather has hit). Speculators' actions will end up making food a little more expensive today and a little less expensive later. Instead of taking all the "hurt" of high prices after the bad weather has hit, speculators move some of the "hurt" to before the bad weather hits. As a result, there will be less "hurt" after the bad weather hits.

WHY IS MEDICAL CARE SO EXPENSIVE?

- When it comes to medical care, often three parties are involved: the person who sells medical care, the person who buys medical care, and the person who (directly) pays for the medical care (the third party).

- Once a person has paid her medical insurance premium, the price paid thereafter for medical care may amount to no more than a copayment (usually minimal). For all practical purposes, then, the dollar amount she has to pay out of pocket to get medical care is zero. We thus expect the quantity demanded of medical care to be greater than it would be at some positive dollar amount.

WHY DO COLLEGES USE GPAs, ACTs, AND SATs FOR PURPOSES OF ADMISSION?

- Colleges and universities charging students less than the equilibrium tuition for admission create a shortage of spaces at their schools. Consequently, colleges and universities have to impose some nonprice-rationing device, such as GPAs or ACT or SAT scores.

SUPPLY AND DEMAND ON A FREEWAY

- The effect of a disequilibrium price (below the equilibrium price) for driving on a freeway is a traffic jam. If the price to drive on a freeway is $0 and, at this price, the quantity demanded of freeway space is greater than the quantity supplied, then a shortage of freeway space will result, in the form of freeway congestion.

ARE WE REALLY MAKING RENTERS BETTER OFF?

- If renters have 90 days instead of 30 days to vacate an apartment, the supply curve of apartments will shift upward and to the left. As a result, renters will pay higher rents when they have 90 days to vacate an apartment.

DO YOU PAY FOR GOOD WEATHER?

- If good weather gives people utility, then the demand for and the price of housing will be higher in a city with good weather than in a city with bad weather. Thus, people who buy houses in good-weather locations indirectly pay for the good weather.

COLLEGE SUPERATHLETES

- A college superathlete may receive a full scholarship to play a sport at a university, but the full scholarship may be less than the equilibrium wage for the superathlete (because of a mandate that the athlete cannot be paid the difference between his higher equilibrium wage and the dollar amount of his full scholarship). In such a case, the university gains at the expense of the athlete.

10 A.M. CLASSES IN COLLEGE

• Colleges usually charge the same tuition for a class no matter when it is taken. The supply of seats in the class may be the same for each time slot, but the demand for the class may be different. At least for some classes, the quantity demanded of seats will be greater than the quantity supplied. Thus, some

nonprice-rationing device will have to be used to achieve equilibrium.

SALSA, CHIPS, AND BEERS

• Often, at Mexican restaurants the salsa and chips are free. The reason has to do with salsa and chips being complements for drinks (both alcoholic beverages and soft drinks). With complements, the demand for one good rises (falls) as the price of the other good falls (rises). If customers at the restaurant receive salsa and chips for free (zero price), they will increase their demand for alcoholic beverages and soft drinks.

VIDEO QUESTIONS AND PROBLEMS

Video Questions and Problems are available on MindTap for Arnold 12e or by searching for Arnold on www.cengagebrain.com

1. Two colleges, A and B, have the same number of openings for the first-year class and charge the same tuition. At college A the standards of admission are higher than at college B. Explain why.

2. The schools on the east side of town are considered better schools than the schools on the west side of town. Will this fact affect house prices on each side of town? Explain your answer.

3. Renters always are better off if they have more rather than fewer days to vacate the premises after receiving an eviction notice. Do you agree or disagree? Explain your answer.

4. Freeway congestion (at certain times of the day) is the result of a disequilibrium price (below the equilibrium price) being charged to drive on the freeway. Do you agree or disagree? Explain your answer.

QUESTIONS AND PROBLEMS

1. Explain how lower lending standards and lower interest rates can lead to higher house prices.

2. If there were no third parties in medical care, medical-care prices would be lower. Do you agree or disagree? Explain your answer.

3. Harvard, Yale, and Princeton all charge relatively high tuition. Still, each uses ACT and SAT scores as admission criteria. Are charging a relatively high tuition and using standardized test scores as admission criteria inconsistent? Explain your answer.

4. Suppose the purchase and sale of marijuana are legalized and the price of marijuana falls. What is the explanation?

5. What do the applications about freeway congestion and 10 a.m. classes have in common?

6. Economics has been called the "dismal science" because it sometimes "tells us" that things are true when we would

prefer them to be false. For example, although there are no free lunches, might we prefer that there were? Was there anything in this chapter that you learned was true that you would have preferred to be false? If so, identify it. Then explain why you would have preferred it to be false.

7. In the discussion of health care and the right to sue your HMO, we state, "Saying that a seller's minimum price for providing a good or service rises is the same as saying that the seller's supply curve has shifted upward and to the left." Does it follow that, if a seller's minimum price falls, the supply curve shifts downward and to the right? Explain your answer.

8. Application 10 explains that even though no one directly and explicitly pays for good weather ("Here is $100 for the good weather"), you may pay for good weather indirectly, such as through housing prices. Identify three other things (besides good weather) that you believe people pay for indirectly.

9. Suppose there exists a costless way to charge drivers on the freeway. Under this costless system, tolls on the freeway would be adjusted according to traffic conditions. For example, when traffic is usually heavy, as it is from 6:30 a.m. to 9:00 a.m. on a weekday, the toll to drive on the freeway would be higher than when traffic is light. In other words, freeway tolls would be used to equate the demand for freeway space with its supply. Would you be in favor of such a system to replace our current (largely zero price) system? Explain your answer.

10. Wilson walks into his economics class 10 minutes late because he couldn't find a place to park. Because of his tardiness, he doesn't hear the professor tell the class that there will be a quiz at the next session. Consequently, Wilson is unprepared for the quiz and ends up failing it. Might Wilson's failing the quiz have anything to do with the price of parking?

11. University A charges more for a class for which there is high demand than for a class for which there is low demand. University B charges the same for all classes. All other things being equal between the two universities, which university would you prefer to attend? Explain your answer.

12. Suppose the equilibrium wage for a college athlete is $40,000, but, because of NCAA rules, the university can offer him only $22,000 (full tuition). How might the university administrators, coaches, or university alumni lure the college athlete to choose their school over others?

13. Consider the theater in which a Broadway play is performed. If tickets for all seats are the same price (say, $70), what economic effect might arise?

14. What is the relationship between the probability of a person being admitted to the college of his choice and the tuition the college charges?

15. Samantha is flying from San Diego, California, to Arlington, Texas, on a commercial airliner. She asks for an aisle seat, but only middle seats are left. Why aren't any aisle seats left? (*Hint:* The airline charges the same price for an aisle seat as a middle seat.)

16. Speculation (on prices) leads to gains for the speculator and losses for others. Do you agree or disagree? Explain your answer.

17. Why do some bars offer free peanuts and pretzels to their patrons?

WORKING WITH NUMBERS AND GRAPHS

1. The price to drive on a freeway is $0 at all times of the day. This price establishes equilibrium at 3 a.m. but is too low to establish equilibrium at 5 p.m. There is a shortage of freeway space at 5 p.m.

   a. Graphically show and explain how carpooling may eliminate the shortage.

   b. Graphically show and explain how building more freeways may eliminate the shortage.

2. Diagrammatically show and explain why there is a shortage of classroom space for some college classes and a surplus for others.

3. Smith has been trying to sell his house for six months, but so far he has had no buyers. Draw the market for Smith's house.

4. For the taping of television show X, the show's producers have to pay people. Draw the supply and demand curves for the taping of this show, and identify the equilibrium point.

5. Think of two types of books, A and B. Book A can be purchased new by someone and resold as a used book. Book B can only be purchased new by someone. (It cannot be resold as a used book.) All other things being equal between the two books, draw the demand curve for each book.

6. Marijuana is legalized and the price of marijuana falls. Draw the demand and supply curves for marijuana before and after it is legalized.

7. As price declines, quantity demanded rises but quantity supplied does not change. Draw the supply and demand curves that represent this state of affairs.

8. As price declines, quantity demanded rises and quantity supplied falls. Draw the supply and demand curves that represent this state of affairs.

MACROECONOMIC MEASUREMENTS, PART I: PRICES AND UNEMPLOYMENT

©Samuel Borges Photography/Shutterstock.com

INTRODUCTION

Government economists often collect and analyze the latest economic data. Their analyses include computing important economic measurements such as the inflation rate and the unemployment rate. Our elected representatives and certain government officials then use these measurements in formulating economic policy. The structure and timing of that economic policy often affects you in your roles as buyer, seller, taxpayer, and employee.

6-1 MEASURING THE PRICE LEVEL

There is a difference between *price* and the *price level*. The word *price* refers to a single price, such the price of apples or the price of oranges. The **price level** is a weighted average of all the prices of all the goods and services in the economy. The key phrase in that definition is "a weighted average of all the prices." Here is a rough way of thinking about a price level: Suppose an economy consists of three goods: apples, oranges, and pears. Suppose also that the prices of apples, oranges, and pears are 50¢, 60¢, and 80¢ cents, respectively. Then the average price (of these three goods) is 63¢. That is also the price level.

6-1a Using the CPI to Compute the Price Level

Economists measure the price level by constructing a **price index**. One major price index is the **Consumer Price Index (CPI)**.[1] The CPI is based on a representative group of goods and services, called the *market basket,* purchased by a typical household. The market

Price Level
A weighted average of the prices of all goods and services.

Price Index
A measure of the price level.

Consumer Price Index (CPI)
The weighted average of prices of a specific set of goods and services purchased by a typical household; a widely cited index number for the price level.

---

[1] Although changes in the CPI are often used to compute the change in the so-called cost of living, one's cost of living usually involves more than what is measured by the CPI. For example, the CPI does not include income taxes, yet income taxes are a part of the cost of living for most people.

basket includes eight major categories of goods and services: (1) food and beverages, (2) housing, (3) apparel, (4) transportation, (5) medical care, (6) recreation, (7) education and communication, and (8) other goods and services.

To simplify our discussion, we assume that the market basket includes only three goods instead of the many goods it actually contains. Our market basket consists of 10 pens, 5 shirts, and 3 pairs of shoes.

To calculate the CPI, first calculate the total dollar expenditure on the market basket in two years: the current year and the base year. The **base year** is a benchmark year that serves as a basis of comparison for prices in other years.

In Exhibit 1, we multiply the quantity of each good in the market basket (column 1) by its current-year price (column 2) to compute the current-year expenditure on each good (column 3). By adding the dollar amounts in column 3, we obtain the total dollar expenditure on the market basket in the current year. This amount is $167.

To find the total expenditure on the market basket in the base year, we multiply the quantity of each good in the market basket (column 1A) by its base-year price (column 2A) and then add all these products (column 3A). This gives us $67.

To find the CPI, we use the formula

$$CPI = \left(\frac{\text{Total dollar expenditure on market basket in current year}}{\text{Total dollar expenditure on market basket in base year}}\right) \times 100$$

As shown in Exhibit 1, the current-year CPI for our tiny economy is 249.

Base Year

The year chosen as a point of reference or basis of comparison for prices in other years; a benchmark year.

 EXHIBIT 1

Computing the Consumer Price Index

This exhibit uses hypothetical data to show how the CPI is computed. To find the "total dollar expenditure on market basket in current year," we multiply the quantities of goods in the market basket by their current-year prices and add all the products. This gives us $167. To find the "total dollar expenditure on market basket in base year," we multiply the quantities of goods in the market basket by their base-year prices and add all the products. This gives us $67. We then divide $167 by $67 and multiply the quotient by 100.

(1) Market Basket		(2) Current-Year Prices (per item)		(3) Current-Year Expenditures	(1A) Market Basket		(2A) Base-Year Prices (per item)		(3A) Base-Year Expenditures
10 pens	×	$ .70	=	$ 7.00	10 pens	×	$ .20	=	$ 2.00
5 shirts	×	14.00	=	70.00	5 shirts	×	7.00	=	35.00
3 pairs of shoes	×	30.00	=	90.00	3 pairs of shoes	×	10.00	=	30.00
				$167.00 ↗ Total dollar expenditure on market basket in current year					**$67.00** ↗ Total dollar expenditure on market basket in base year

$$CPI = \left(\frac{\text{Total dollar expenditure on market basket in current year}}{\text{Total dollar expenditure on market basket in base year}}\right) \times 100$$

$$= \left(\frac{\$167}{\$67}\right) \times 100$$

$$= 249$$

The CPI for the United States for the years 1960 to 2014 is shown in Exhibit 2.

More About the Base Year

Recall that the base year is a benchmark year that serves as a basis of comparison for prices in other years. The CPI in the base year is 100. How do we know this? Look again at the formula for calculating the CPI: The numerator is "Total dollar expenditure on market basket in current year," and the denominator is "Total dollar expenditure on market basket in base year." In the base year, the current year *is* the base year, so the numerator and denominator are the same. The ratio is 1, and $1 \times 100 = 100$.

Notice, however, that in Exhibit 2 there is no year in which the CPI is 100. This does not mean that there is no base year. Instead, the base year has been defined by the government to be the period 1982–1984. Look at the CPI in each of the years 1982, 1983, and 1984. If we add the CPIs for the three years and divide by 3, we get 100: $(96.5 + 99.6 + 103.9) \div 3 = 100$.

When We Know the CPI for Various Years, We Can Compute the Percentage Change in Prices

To find the percentage change in prices between any two years, use the formula

$$\text{Percentage change in prices} = \left(\frac{\text{CPI}_{\text{later year}} - \text{CPI}_{\text{earlier year}}}{\text{CPI}_{\text{earlier year}}} \right) \times 100$$

For example, Exhibit 2 shows that the CPI in 1990 was 130.7 and the CPI in 2005 was 195.3. The percentage change in prices over this period was therefore 49.43 percent:

$$\text{Percentage change} = \left(\frac{195.3 - 130.7}{130.7} \right) \times 100 = 49.43$$

This means that prices increased 49.43 percent from 1990 to 2005. You can think of the percentage change in prices in this way: What cost $1 in 1990 cost approximately $1.49 in 2005.

6-1b Inflation and the CPI

Inflation is an increase in the price level and is usually measured on an annual basis. The *inflation rate* is the positive percentage change in the price level on an annual basis. When you know the inflation rate, you can find out whether your income is (1) keeping up with, (2) not keeping up with, or (3) more than keeping up with inflation. How you are doing depends on whether your income is rising by (1) the same percentage as, (2) a smaller percentage than, or (3) a greater percentage than the inflation rate, respectively. When you make this computation and comparison, you are determining your real income for different years. **Real income** is a person's **nominal income** (or current dollar amount of income) adjusted for any change in prices. Real income is computed as follows:

> **EXHIBIT 2**

CPI, 1960–2014

Year	CPI	Year	CPI
1960	29.6	1988	118.3
1961	29.9	1989	124.0
1962	30.2	1990	130.7
1963	30.6	1991	136.2
1964	31.0	1992	140.3
1965	31.5	1993	144.5
1966	32.4	1994	148.2
1967	33.4	1995	152.4
1968	34.8	1996	156.9
1969	36.7	1997	160.5
1970	38.8	1998	163.0
1971	40.5	1999	166.6
1972	41.8	2000	172.2
1973	44.4	2001	177.1
1974	49.3	2002	179.9
1975	53.8	2003	184.0
1976	56.9	2004	188.9
1977	60.6	2005	195.3
1978	65.2	2006	201.6
1979	72.6	2007	207.342
1980	82.4	2008	215.303
1981	90.9	2009	214.537
1982	96.5	2010	218.056
1983	99.6	2011	224.939
1984	103.9	2012	229.594
1985	107.6	2013	232.957
1986	109.6	2014	237.900
1987	113.6		

Source: The data were reported at the website of the U.S. Bureau of Labor Statistics. Site address: http://www.bls.gov/home.htm. Beginning in 2007, the Bureau of Labor Statistics began reporting the CPI to three decimal points.

Inflation
An increase in the price level.

Real Income
Nominal income adjusted for price changes.

Nominal Income
The current dollar amount of a person's income.

$$\text{Real income} = \left(\frac{\text{Nominal income}}{\text{CPI}}\right) \times 100$$

Case 1. Keeping up with Inflation: Real Income Stays Constant

Jim earns $50,000 in year 1 and $55,000 in year 2. The CPI is 100 in year 1 and 110 in year 2, so the inflation rate is 10 percent: [(110 − 100)/100] × 100 = 10. Jim's income has risen by 10 percent: [($55,000 − $50,000)/$50,000] × 100 = 10. Jim's income has risen by the same percentage as the inflation rate, so he has kept up with inflation. This is evident when we see that Jim's real income is the same in both years. In year 1 it is $50,000, and in year 2 it is $50,000 too:

$$\text{Real income year 1} = \left(\frac{\$50,000}{100}\right) \times 100 = \$50,000$$

$$\text{Real income year 2} = \left(\frac{\$55,000}{110}\right) \times 100 = \$50,000$$

Case 2. Not Keeping up with Inflation: Real Income Falls

Karen earns $50,000 in year 1 and $52,000 in year 2. The CPI is 100 in year 1 and 110 in year 2. Karen's income has risen by 4 percent, and the inflation rate is 10 percent. Her income has risen by a smaller percentage than the inflation rate, so she has not kept up with inflation. Karen's real income has fallen from $50,000 in year 1 to $47,273 in year 2:

$$\text{Real income year 1} = \left(\frac{\$50,000}{100}\right) \times 100 = \$50,000$$

$$\text{Real income year 2} = \left(\frac{\$52,000}{110}\right) \times 100 = \$47,273$$

Case 3. More than Keeping up with Inflation: Real Income Rises

Carl earns $50,000 in year 1 and $60,000 in year 2. The CPI is 100 in year 1 and 110 in year 2. Carl's income has risen by 20 percent, and the inflation rate is 10 percent. His income has risen by a greater percentage than the inflation rate, so he has more than kept up with inflation. Carl's real income has risen from $50,000 in year 1 to $54,545 in year 2:

$$\text{Real income year 1} = \left(\frac{\$50,000}{100}\right) \times 100 = \$50,000$$

$$\text{Real income year 2} = \left(\frac{\$60,000}{110}\right) \times 100 = \$54,545$$

6-1c GDP Implicit Price Deflator

Besides the CPI, another price index is often cited: the *GDP deflator*, also called the *GDP implicit price deflator*. Obviously, an economy produces more goods and services than find their way into the CPI's representative market basket. The GDP implicit price deflator, unlike the CPI, is based on *all* goods and services produced in an economy. Another price index is shown in Exhibit 3.

In Your Paycheck Sharon comments to a friend that she recently received a $5-an-hour raise at work. Her friend congratulates her and then goes on to talk about how prices have been rising lately. Where is the economics?

Obviously, if Sharon's nominal (or money) income has risen, and prices have risen too, then Sharon's real income might have changed. Has her real income risen, fallen, or stayed the same? The answer depends on how much her nominal income has risen relative to how much prices have gone up. Let's say her nominal income has risen by 5 percent and prices have increased by 2 percent. In that case, Sharon's real income has gone up.

Comparing One Thing with Another Comparing one thing with something else can be extremely useful. For example, in each of the three cases just discussed, we compared the percentage change in a person's nominal income with the inflation rate. Through this comparison, we learned something that we could not have learned by looking at either factor alone: how a person fared under inflation. Making comparisons is part of the economic way of thinking.

 EXHIBIT 3

C-CPI, 2000–2012

Here we show the Chained CPI for the years 2000–2012. The Chained CPI is yet another price index.

Year	C-CPI
2000	102.0
2001	104.3
2002	105.6
2003	107.8
2004	110.5
2005	113.7
2006	117.0
2007	119.957
2008	124.433
2009	123.850
2010	125.615
2011	129.453
2012	131.823

6-1d Converting Dollars from One Year to Another

Suppose someone says, "Back in 1960, I had an annual salary of $10,000 a year. That sure isn't much these days." Of course, the person is right in one sense: An annual salary of $10,000 doesn't buy much these days, but was it a good salary back in 1960? It certainly could have been, because prices in 1960 weren't as high as they are today. For example, the CPI was 29.6 in 1960 and 237.900 in 2014. In other words, one of the things that make a salary good or not so good is what the salary can buy.

Now, suppose someone tells you that a $10,000 salary in 1960 is the same as a $80,371 salary today. Would you then be better able to say whether the 1960 $10,000 salary was good or not so good? Of course you would, because you understand what it means to earn $80,371 today. Economists convert a past salary into today's salary by using this formula:

$$\text{Salary in today's (current) dollars} = \text{Salary}_{\text{earlier year}} \times \left(\frac{\text{CPI}_{\text{current year}}}{\text{CPI}_{\text{earlier year}}} \right)$$

Assume that the CPI today is the same as the most recent CPI in Exhibit 2 (the CPI for 2012). Using the formula, we get

$$\text{Salary in 2014 dollars} = \$10,000 \times \left(\frac{237.900}{29.6} \right) = \$80,371$$

ECONOMICS 24/7

The Beatles at Shea Stadium

What I remember most about the concert was that we were so far away from the audience. And screaming had become the thing to do. Everybody screamed.
—Ringo Starr

It was Sunday, August 15, 1965. The Beatles—John, Paul, George, and Ringo—took a Wells Fargo armored truck to Shea Stadium, home of the New York Mets baseball team from 1964 to 2008 and to the New York Jets football team from 1964 to 1983. Awaiting them were 55,600 screaming fans. Two thousand security personnel were at the stadium to handle the crowd.

It was the first stop on the Beatles U.S. tour, which ran from August 15 to August 31, 1965. It was the first concert to be held at a major stadium. The set listed such Beatles' favorites as the following:

Michael Ochs Archives/Getty Images

Twist and Shout
She's a Woman
Ticket to Ride
Help!
Can't Buy Me Love
Hard Day's Night

Most tickets were priced between $4.10 and $5.65. Many tickets were priced at $5.10. That sounds like a pretty cheap ticket price nowadays. But what was a $5.10 ticket to see the Beatles in 1965 comparable to in 2012? We use the following formula to find out:

$$\text{Ticket in 2014 dollars} = \$5.10 \times \frac{237.900}{31.5} = \$38.52$$

Buying a $5.10 ticket to see the Beatles at Shea Stadium in 1965 was the same as buying a $38.52 ticket today. Who knew that you could see the Beatles at such a historic event for so little?

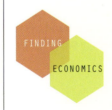

FINDING ECONOMICS

In What Grandfather Says Ursula, who is 25, told her grandfather that she just got a job that pays $67,000 a year. Her grandfather said, "That's a lot of money. When I got my first real job I earned only $18,000 a year. You're earning a whole lot more than I did." Where is the economics?

Income earned in one period cannot always be adequately compared to income earned in another period. To make the proper comparison, we need to convert the dollars earned in one period into dollars earned in the other period. Ursula is earning $67,000 today, but her grandfather earned $18,000 (in his first job) many years ago. Obviously, earning $18,000 many years ago is not the same as earning $18,000 today, so Ursula's grandfather's statement that she is earning a whole lot more than he did might not be accurate.

SELF-TEST

(Answers to Self-Test questions are in Answers to Self-Test Questions at the back of the book.)

1. Explain how the CPI is calculated.

2. What is a base year?

3. In year 1, your annual income is $45,000 and the CPI is 143.6; in year 2, your annual income is $51,232 and the CPI is 150.7. Has your real income risen, fallen, or remained constant? Explain your answer.

6-2 MEASURING UNEMPLOYMENT

Every month, the government surveys thousands of households to gather information about labor market activities. It uses the information from the survey to derive the number of Americans who are unemployed.

6-2a Who Are the Unemployed?

The total population of the United States can be divided into two broad groups (Exhibit 4). One group consists of persons who are (1) under 16 years of age, (2) in the armed forces, or (3) institutionalized (in a prison, mental institution, or home for the aged). The second group, which consists of all others in the total population, is called the *civilian noninstitutional population.*

The civilian noninstitutional population, in turn, can be divided into two groups: persons *not in the labor force* and persons in the *civilian labor force.* (Economists often refer to the latter group as, simply, the labor force instead of the civilian labor force.) Thus,

Civilian noninstitutional population = Persons not in the labor force + Civilian labor force

- Persons not in the labor force are neither working nor looking for work. In this category are, for example, people who are retired, who are engaged in housework in their own home, or who choose not to work.

- Persons in the civilian labor force fall into one of two categories: *employed* or *unemployed.* That is,

Civilian labor force = Employed persons + Unemployed persons

 EXHIBIT 4

Breakdown of the U.S. Population and the Labor Force

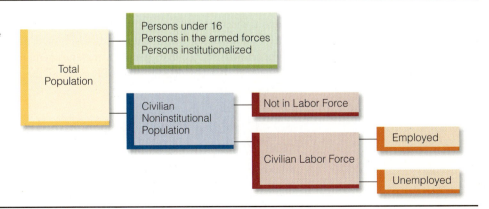

According to the Bureau of Labor Statistics (BLS), employed persons consist of the following groups:

- All persons who did any work for pay or profit during the survey reference week. (The survey used to measure employment and unemployment is the Current Population Survey, a monthly survey conducted for the BLS by the U.S. Census Bureau.)

- All persons who did at least 15 hours of unpaid work in a family-operated enterprise.

- All persons who were temporarily absent from their regular jobs because of illness, vacation, bad weather, industrial dispute, or various personal reasons.

According to the BLS, unemployed persons consist of the following groups:

- All persons who did not have jobs, who made specific active efforts to find a job during the prior four weeks, and who were available for work.

- All persons who were not working and who were waiting to be called back to a job from which they had been temporarily laid off.

6-2b The Unemployment Rate and the Employment Rate

Unemployment Rate

The percentage of the civilian force that is unemployed: Unemployment rate = Number of unemployed persons ÷ Civilian labor force.

The **unemployment rate** is the percentage of the civilian labor force that is unemployed. It is equal to the number of unemployed persons divided by the civilian labor force:

$$\text{Unemployment rate } (U) = \frac{\text{Number of unemployed persons}}{\text{Civilian labor force}}$$

Employment Rate

The percentage of the civilian noninstitutional population that is employed: Employment rate = Number of employed persons ÷ Civilian noninstitutional population.

The **employment rate** (sometimes referred to as the *employment–population ratio*) is the percentage of the civilian noninstitutional population that is employed. It is equal to the number of employed persons divided by the civilian noninstitutional population:

$$\text{Employment rate } (E) = \frac{\text{Number of employed persons}}{\text{Civilian noninstitutional population}}$$

Labor Force Participation Rate (LFPR)

The percentage of the civilian noninstitutional population that is in the civilian labor force: Labor force participation rate = Civilian labor force ÷ Civilian noninstitutional population.

Finally, the **labor force participation rate (LFPR)** is the percentage of the civilian noninstitutional population that is in the civilian labor force:

$$\text{Labor force participation rate (LFPR)} = \frac{\text{Civilian labor force}}{\text{Civilian noninstitutional population}}$$

The LFPR may sound like the employment rate, but it is different. Although the denominator in both formulas is the same, the numerator in the employment rate is the number of employed persons whereas the numerator in the LFPR is the civilian labor force (which includes both employed persons and unemployed persons). For this reason, some economists say that, although the employment rate gives us the percentage of the population that is working, the LFPR gives us the percentage of the population that is *willing to work*.

6-2c Common Misconceptions about the Unemployment and Employment Rates

Many people mistakenly think that if the unemployment rate is, say, 7 percent, the employment rate must be 93 percent. Their assumption is that the unemployment rate plus the employment rate must equal 100 percent. But the unemployment and employment rates

E C O N O M I C S 2 4 / 7

When Is a Penny a Quarter?

Suppose you are walking and you look down and see a penny on the sidewalk. Do you stop and pick it up? Many people will say no, explaining that the penny isn't worth their time. After all, a penny is not worth very much, they say.

Now suppose you buy a magazine at the campus bookstore. The total price (including tax) comes to $6.02. You hand the cashier a $10 bill. Instead of giving you $3.98 in change, she reaches into the cup next to the cash register and pulls out two pennies; she gives you $4 in change. It is easier for her to get the two pennies from the cup than it is to count out $3.98 in change. You say, "Thank you" and go on your way.

The next day, you buy something for $5.99. You hand the cashier $6. When the cashier gives you back one penny in change, you drop it into the cup next to the cash register. One day you take from the cup; another day you give to the cup.

Twenty years ago, there were no penny cups next to cash registers. Why were there no penny cups then, but penny cups now? The reason is that 20 years ago a penny had more purchasing power than it does today. If a penny today had greater purchasing power than it does, you'd be less likely to drop the penny into the cup; instead, you'd drop it into your pocket.

So, what was a penny worth in, say, 1900? A different way of asking the question is, "What coin today is equal to the purchasing power a penny had in 1900?" The answer is a quarter. In other words, having a penny in 1900 was equivalent to having a quarter (25¢) today. So, having four pennies in 1900 was the equivalent of having $1 today.

Imagine that the year is 1900 and you are walking down the street. You look down and see a penny. Do you stop and pick it up?

©Pete Spiro/Shutterstock.com

do not add up 100 percent, because the denominator of the unemployment rate is not the same as the denominator of the employment rate. The unemployment rate is a *percentage of the civilian labor force*. The employment rate is a *percentage of the civilian noninstitutional population*, which is a larger number than the civilian labor force.

6-2d Reasons for Unemployment

Usually, we think of an unemployed person as someone who has been fired or laid off from his or her job. Certainly, some unemployed persons fit this description, but not all of them do. According to the BLS, an unemployed person may fall into one of four categories:

1. *Job loser.* This person was employed in the civilian labor force and was either fired or laid off. Most unemployed persons fall into this category.

2. *Job leaver.* This person was employed in the civilian labor force and quit the job. For example, if Jim quit his job with company X and is looking for a better job, he is a job leaver.

3. *Reentrant.* This person was previously employed, hasn't worked for some time, and is currently reentering the labor force.

4. *New entrant.* This person has never held a full-time job for two weeks or longer and is now in the civilian labor force looking for a job.

In sum,

Unemployed persons = Job losers + Job leavers + Reentrants + New entrants

6-2e Discouraged Workers

Suppose Adam is fired from his job at company A in September and he looks for a job for about six months. During this time, he is considered an unemployed person and is counted in the calculation of the unemployment rate. At the end of the sixth month, Adam is discouraged; he doesn't think he will ever find a job, and he stops looking. A month passes, and he still is not looking for a job. Is Adam considered an unemployed person? The answer is no. To be an unemployed person, you have to meet certain conditions, one of which is that you have to be actively looking for work. But Adam isn't actively looking for work, and he isn't waiting to be called back to a job or to report to a job. So Adam isn't unemployed, and for that reason he does not get counted in the calculation of the unemployment rate.

The BLS considers Adam a *discouraged worker.* According to the BLS, discouraged workers are "persons not in the labor force who want and are available for a job and who have looked for work sometime in the past 12 months (or since the end of their last job if they held one within the past 12 months), but who are not currently looking because they believe there are no jobs available or there are none for which they would qualify."[2] You may think that, for all practical purposes, a discouraged worker is the same as an unemployed person, because neither has a job. But they aren't the same for calculating the unemployment rate. The unemployed person gets counted, but the discouraged worker does not.

Some economists think that, because discouraged workers are not considered unemployed, the unemployment rate is biased downward. Consequently, it doesn't really give us a good fix on the "real" unemployment problem in society.

6-2f Types of Unemployment

There are several different types of unemployment.

Frictional Unemployment   Every day, demand conditions change in some markets, causing qualified individuals with transferable skills to leave some jobs and move to others. To illustrate, suppose there are two computer firms, A and B. For some reason, the demand falls for firm A's computers and rises for firm B's computers. Consequently, firm A produces fewer computers. With fewer computers being produced, firm A doesn't need as many employees, so it fires some employees. By contrast, firm B is producing more computers. With more computers being produced, firm B hires additional employees. The employees fired from firm A have skills that they can transfer to firm B; after all, both firms produce computers. However, it takes time for people to make the transfer. During this time, they are said to be frictionally unemployed.

[2.] See *BLS Information* (U.S. Bureau of Labor Statistics, February 28, 2008), http://www.bls.gov/bls/glossary.htm.

Frictional unemployment is unemployment that is due to the natural so-called frictions in the economy and that is caused by changing market conditions and represented by qualified individuals with transferable skills who change jobs. The frictional unemployment rate (U_F) is the percentage of the labor force that is frictionally unemployed:

$$U_F = \frac{\text{Number of frictionally unemployed persons}}{\text{Civilian labor force}}$$

A dynamic, changing economy like that of the United States always has frictional unemployment. Many economists believe that the basic cause of frictional unemployment is imperfect or incomplete information, which prevents individuals from leaving one job and finding another instantly. For example, imagine an economy with 1,000 job vacancies and 1,000 persons qualified to fill the jobs. Some unemployment is likely because not every one of the 1,000 job seekers will know where the available jobs are. Nor will all employers give the job to the first applicant who knocks on the door. Employers don't know whether better applicants are around the corner. Matching qualified workers with the available jobs takes time.

Structural Unemployment Unemployment due to structural changes in the economy that eliminate some jobs and create others for which the unemployed are unqualified is called **structural unemployment**. Most economists argue that structural unemployment is largely the consequence of automation (labor-saving devices) and long-lasting shifts in demand. The structurally unemployed differ from the frictionally unemployed mainly in that they do not have transferable skills. Their choice is between prolonged unemployment and retraining. For example, suppose automobile workers are being laid off and the demand for computer analysts is rising. If the automobile workers do not currently have the skills needed to become computer analysts, they are structurally unemployed. The structural unemployment rate (U_S) is the percentage of the labor force that is structurally unemployed:

$$U_S = \frac{\text{Number of structurally unemployed persons}}{\text{Civilian labor force}}$$

Natural Unemployment Adding the frictional unemployment rate and the structural unemployment rate gives the **natural unemployment** rate (or natural rate of unemployment, U_N):

$$\text{Natural unemployment rate } (U_N) = \text{Frictional unemployment rate } (U_F) + \\ \text{Structural unemployment rate } (U_S)$$

Currently, most economists estimate the natural unemployment rate at between 4.0 and 6.5 percent.

6-2g The Natural Unemployment Rate and Full Employment

What do you think of when you hear the term "full employment"? Most people think *full employment* means that the actual or reported unemployment rate is zero. But a dynamic, changing economy can never have full employment of this type because of the frictional and structural changes that continually occur. In fact, it is natural for some unemployment to exist—some natural unemployment, that is. For this reason, economists *do not* equate full employment with a zero unemployment rate. Instead, **full employment** exists *when the economy is operating at its natural unemployment rate*. For example, if the natural

Frictional Unemployment
Unemployment that is due to the natural so-called frictions in the economy and that is caused by changing market conditions and represented by qualified individuals with transferable skills who change jobs.

Structural Unemployment
Unemployment due to structural changes in the economy that eliminate some jobs and create others for which the unemployed are unqualified.

Natural Unemployment
Unemployment caused by frictional and structural factors in the economy: Natural unemployment rate = Frictional unemployment rate + Structural unemployment rate.

Full Employment
The condition that exists when the unemployment rate is equal to the natural unemployment rate.

ECONOMICS24/7

Does Culture Affect Unemployment?

The unemployment rate has been relatively high in recent years. For example, the unemployment rate in September 2010 was 9.5 percent, in December 2011 it was 8.5 percent, and in October 2013 it was 7.3 percent. Part of the relatively high unemployment rate can be due to structural problems in the U.S. labor market. Daron Acemoglu, an economist at the Massachusetts Institute of Technology (MIT), commented on this possibility in an interview conducted by the Federal Reserve Bank of Minneapolis.[3] He argues that a part of the workforce hasn't made the necessary adjustments to the new technologies today and that this deficiency might be a continuing problem. Here is what he says:

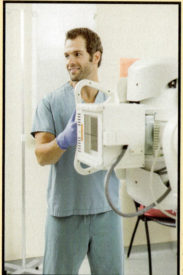

©Tyler Olson/Shutterstock.com

I tend to think that there are serious structural problems with the U.S. labor market that will keep the economy down more and more over the next decade. They're related to the fact that our workforce, especially the male half, hasn't really made an adjustment to the new technologies and types of skills that are required.

Labor market imperfections play a role in that, in the sense that I think most people are not sufficiently informed about the sort of skills that they will require. They get their understanding of the labor market through word of mouth, from their parents and their neighborhoods, and there isn't quite enough of an understanding that most U.S. workers who don't have college degrees are not going to be able to get good-paying manufacturing jobs.

Those types of bread-and-butter jobs of previous decades have gone; now those tasks are being performed by robots and computers, and instead we have an explosion of demand in the service sector, in middle- and low-skill services, for example, in health care, clerical occupations or customer service. These

are jobs that workers with high school or two-year college degrees can perform. But for the most part, U.S. workers, especially U.S. males, haven't really made the transition to performing them.[4]

Think of things this way: As technology changes, so can the ways in which people are employed changed. Think of the world before and after the introduction of the car as a mode of transportation. We would expect that the demand for saddle makers (i.e., for those who made saddles used to ride horses) was higher before the car than it was after the car. The same kind of thing can happen today: changes in technology—whether it be transportation technology, computer technology, or medical technology—can change the ways in which people are employed.

To return to Acemoglu, part of the high unemployment rate in recent years is due to individuals not transitioning quickly enough from the old jobs (that made sense with the old technologies) into the new jobs (that now make sense given the new technologies). But why the lag? According to Acemoglu, "labor market imperfections play a role. . . ." Specifically, he argues that people may just not be "sufficiently informed about the skills that they require." In other words, they are somewhat at a loss as to what is required of them.

Besides not knowing what is required of them, Acemoglu admits that there may be a cultural factor at work too. He says:

You can say that people aren't fully informed. But there are probably other things going on as well. Perhaps the culture frowns on men doing certain of these jobs, be it in the health care sector, retail or clerical jobs that are complementary to the new technologies. These are not the typical "male jobs," and that might be part of it.[5]

---

3. See *The Region*, a publication of the Federal Reserve Bank of Minneapolis, September 2011.
4. Ibid., p. 20.
5. Ibid., p. 20.

ECONOMICS 24/7

Who Should Be Considered Unemployed?

Start with the official unemployment rate. In October 2013, the official unemployment rate was 7.3 percent.

Some economists argue that this 7.3 percent unemployment rate is not the most nearly accurate measurement of the degree of labor utilization in the economy. For example, because discouraged workers are not counted as officially unemployed, obviously some people want to work who are not working. Thus, labor is not fully being utilized; it is being *under*utilized.

Discouraged workers are a subset of a larger group called *marginally attached workers*. According to the Bureau of Labor Statistics, marginally attached workers are "persons not in the labor force who want and are available for work, and who have looked for a job sometime in the prior 12 months (or since the end of their last job if they held one within the past 12 months), but were not counted as unemployed because they had not searched for work in the 4 weeks preceding the survey."[6] When asked why they didn't search for work, they might say "for family or transportation reasons."

As we stated earlier in this chapter, discouraged workers, according to the BLS, are "persons not in the labor force who want and are available for a job and who have looked for work sometime in the past 12 months (or since the end of their last job if they held one within the past 12 months), but who are not currently looking because they believe there are no jobs available or there are none for which they would qualify."[7] When asked why they didn't search for work, they usually state some job-related reason, such as "there are no jobs to be had or there are no jobs for which I qualify."

If we count all marginally attached workers (not just discouraged workers) as unemployed, the unemployment rate in October 2013 rises to 8.6 percent. Some argue that this number is a better measure of labor underutilization in the economy than the official unemployment rate (or the unemployment rate with discouraged workers only and not all marginally attached workers).

Finally, the BLS recognizes a category of people who want full-time work but have taken part-time jobs for economic reasons—for example, a person with an engineering degree who wants to work full time as an engineer, but who accepts part-time work to help pay the bills. Sometimes these people are called *underemployed* because they are working at jobs for which they have skills far beyond those required for the job. Currently, these people are not counted as unemployed, but some argue that we would have a better measurement of labor underutilization in the economy if they were. If we add these people to the ranks of the unemployed, the unemployment rate rises to 13.8 percent in October 2013.

Now think of two persons running for the same national political office. The incumbent argues that the official unemployment rate has come down recently and that it is now, say, 7.3 percent. "We're making progress on the economic front," he says.

The challenger argues that the official unemployment rate is not really the most nearly representative measurement of the degree to which labor is being underutilized in the economy. She says that the "true" or "most nearly accurate" unemployment rate—by which she means the one that takes into account all marginally attached workers and people who want to work full time but have taken part-time work for economic reasons—is 13.8 percent. That's a big difference, and often the public is left wondering who is right and who is wrong; who is telling the truth and who isn't.

Fact is, both persons can be telling the truth; it's just that one is choosing to shine the light on the official unemployment rate and the other shines the light on the unemployment rate that takes into account additional groups of people (such as the marginally attached workers, etc.).

---

6. *BLS Information*, op. cit.
7. Ibid.

unemployment rate is 5 percent, then full employment exists when the unemployment rate (in the economy) is 5 percent. In other words, the economy can be operating at full employment and some people will still be unemployed.

6-2h Cyclical Unemployment

The unemployment rate in the economy is not always the natural rate. The difference between the existing unemployment rate and the natural unemployment rate is the **cyclical unemployment rate** (U_C):

Cyclical Unemployment Rate
The difference between the unemployment rate and the natural unemployment rate.

$$\text{Cyclical unemployment rate } (U_C) = \text{Unemployment rate } (U) - \text{Natural unemployment rate } (U_N)$$

When the existing unemployment rate (U) is greater than the natural unemployment rate (U_N), the cyclical unemployment rate (U_C) is positive. For example, if $U = 8$ percent and $U_N = 5$ percent, then $U_C = 3$ percent. When the unemployment rate is less than the natural unemployment rate, the cyclical unemployment rate is negative. For example, if $U = 4$ percent and $U_N = 5$ percent, then $U_C = -1$ percent.

Various unemployment rates are summarized in Exhibit 5. Unemployment rates according to education, race, and gender are shown in Exhibit 6.

> **EXHIBIT 5**

Various Unemployment Rates

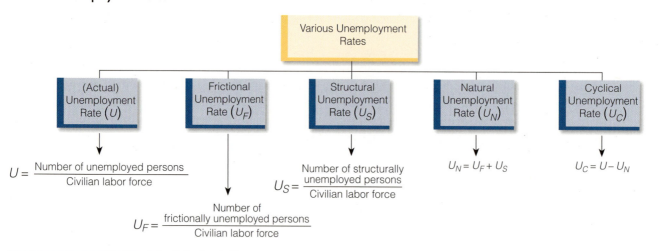

> **EXHIBIT 6**

Unemployment Rates According to Education, Race, and Gender, 2000–2013

In (a), we show the U.S. unemployment rate according to education. Notice that college graduates tend to have the lowest unemployment rate of all the education groups. (b) Unemployment rate according to race. (c) Unemployment rate according to gender.

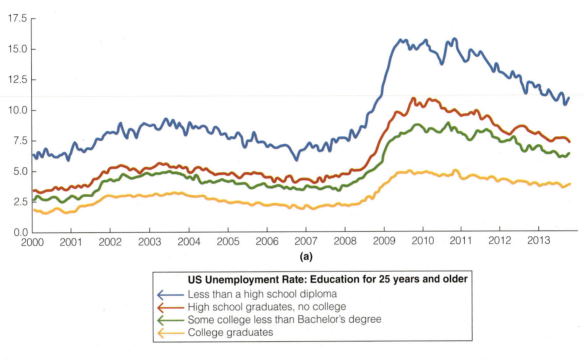

(a)

US Unemployment Rate: Education for 25 years and older
← Less than a high school diploma
← High school graduates, no college
← Some college less than Bachelor's degree
← College graduates

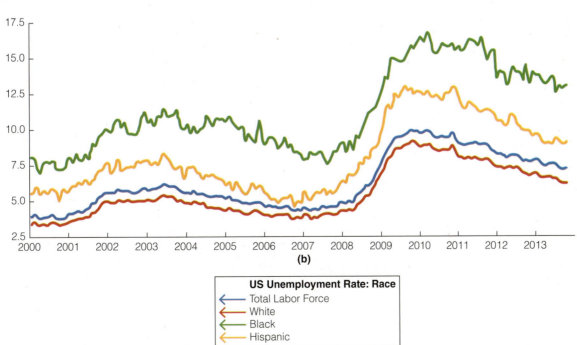

(b)

US Unemployment Rate: Race
← Total Labor Force
← White
← Black
← Hispanic

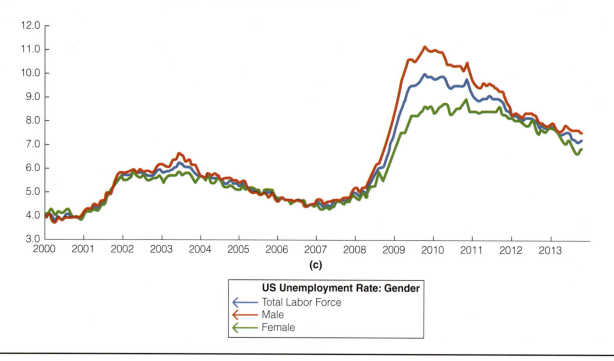

(c)

US Unemployment Rate: Gender
← Total Labor Force
← Male
← Female

Office ✱ Hours

"Is There More Than One Reason the Unemployment Rate Will Fall?"

STUDENT:

If the unemployment rate drops, does it follow that some of the people who were once unemployed are now employed?

INSTRUCTOR:

Not always. To see why, recall that the unemployment rate is equal to the number of unemployed persons divided by the civilian labor force:

$$\text{Unemployment rate} = \frac{\text{Number of unemployed persons}}{\text{Civilian labor force}}$$

Now, let's say that there are 100 unemployed persons and the civilian labor force consists of 1,000 persons. Then the unemployment rate is 10 percent. Suppose the number of unemployed persons rises to 105 (a 5 percent increase) at the same time that the civilian labor force

rises to 1,120 (a 12 percent increase). Then the new unemployment rate is 9.4 percent, even though the number of unemployed persons has not decreased. In fact, it has increased from 100 to 105.

STUDENT:

In other words, if the number of unemployed persons rises by a smaller percentage than the civilian labor force rises, the unemployment rate will decline—even though the number of unemployed persons has risen.

INSTRUCTOR:

Yes, that's correct. Now consider something else. Suppose again that there are 100 unemployed persons in a civilian labor force of 1,000 persons. As before, these numbers give us an unemployment rate of 10 percent. Now suppose that 10 of the unemployed persons become discouraged workers and stop looking for work. Then the number of unemployed falls to 90, and the civilian labor force (which consists of employed plus unemployed persons) falls to 990. The unemployment rate now is 9.09 percent. The unemployment rate has dropped, but not for the reason most people think. It hasn't dropped because some of the unemployed persons found jobs; it has dropped because some of the unemployed became so discouraged that they stopped looking for jobs.

STUDENT:

In other words, we might think that the unemployment rate has dropped because 10 of the 100 unemployed persons found work, but in reality those 10 persons did not find work. They just became so discouraged that they left the civilian labor force.

INSTRUCTOR:

Yes, that's correct.

STUDENT:

Does the government do anything to take these discouraged workers into account?

INSTRUCTOR:

The Bureau of Labor Statistics computes an alternative unemployment rate that includes discouraged workers in the ranks of both the unemployed and the civilian labor force. In short, it computes what it calls "total unemployed plus discouraged workers, as a percent of the civilian labor force plus discouraged workers":[8]

$$\text{Alternative unemployment rate} = \frac{\text{Number of unemployed persons} + \text{Discouraged workers}}{\text{Civilian labor force} + \text{Discouraged workers}}$$

This alternative unemployment rate tells us what the unemployment rate would look like if we included discouraged workers in our calculation.

Points to remember

1. The unemployment rate can decline even if the number of unemployed persons has not declined. For example, if the number of unemployed persons rises by a smaller percentage than that of the civilian labor force, the unemployment rate will decline (even though more, not fewer, persons are unemployed).

2. An alternative unemployment rate is defined as

$$\text{Alternative unemployment rate} = \frac{\text{Number of unemployed persons} + \text{Discouraged workers}}{\text{Civilian labor force} + \text{Discouraged workers}}$$

---

[8]   See alternative unemployment measure U-4 in, for example, "Alternative Measures of Labor Underutilization for States, Second Quarter of 2013 through First Quarter of 2014 Averages," *Local Area Unemployment Statistics* (U.S. Bureau of Labor Statistics, April 25, 2014), http://www.bls.gov/lau/stalt.htm.

SELF-TEST

1. What is the major difference between a person who is frictionally unemployed and one who is structurally unemployed?

2. What does a positive cyclical unemployment rate imply?

CHAPTER SUMMARY

MEASURING PRICES

- One major price index is the consumer price index (CPI).
- Inflation is an increase in the price level or price index.
- A given dollar amount in an earlier year does not have the same purchasing power in a later year (or current year) if prices are different in the two years. To convert a dollar amount of an earlier year into today's (or current) dollars, we use the formula

$$\text{Dollar amount in today's (current) dollars} =$$
$$\text{Dollar amount}_{\text{earlier year}} \times \left(\frac{\text{CPI}_{\text{current year}}}{\text{CPI}_{\text{earlier year}}} \right)$$

UNEMPLOYMENT AND EMPLOYMENT

- An unemployed person may be a job loser, a job leaver, a reentrant, or a new entrant.

- The unemployment rate may be biased downward because discouraged workers are not considered unemployed.
- Frictional unemployment, due to the natural so-called frictions of the economy, is caused by changing market conditions and is represented by qualified individuals with transferable skills who change jobs.
- Structural unemployment is due to structural changes in the economy that eliminate some jobs and create others for which the unemployed are unqualified.
- Natural unemployment is caused by frictional and structural factors in the economy. The natural unemployment rate equals the sum of the frictional unemployment rate and the structural unemployment rate.
- Full employment exists when the unemployment rate is equal to the natural unemployment rate.
- The cyclical unemployment rate is the difference between the existing unemployment rate and the natural unemployment rate.

KEY TERMS AND CONCEPTS

Price Level	Inflation	Employment Rate	Structural Unemployment
Price Index	Real Income	Labor Force Participation	Natural Unemployment
Consumer Price Index (CPI)	Nominal Income	Rate	Full Employment
Base Year	Unemployment Rate	Frictional Unemployment	Cyclical Unemployment Rate

VIDEO QUESTIONS AND PROBLEMS

Video Questions and Problems are available on MindTap for Arnold 12e or by searching for Arnold on www.cengagebrain.com

1. Suppose the market basket consists of 10A and 20B. The prices of A and B in the current year are $2 and $4, respectively. The prices of A and B in the base year are $1 and $2.50, respectively. What is the current-year CPI?

2. If nominal income is $55,000 in the current year and the CPI is 120 in the current year, then what does real income equal in the current year?

3. What is the difference between a person who is frictionally unemployed and one who is structurally unemployed?

4. There are 6 million persons unemployed and 60 million persons employed. If the natural unemployment rate is 5 percent, what does the cyclical unemployment rate equal?

5. Is the sum of the unemployment rate and the employment rate equal to 100 percent? Why or why not?

QUESTIONS AND PROBLEMS

1. What does the CPI in the base year equal? Explain your answer.

2. Show that, if the percentage rise in prices is equal to the percentage rise in nominal income, then one's real income does not change.

3. When is the total dollar expenditure on the market basket in the base year the same as in the current year?

4. How does structural unemployment differ from frictional unemployment?

5. What does it mean to say that the country is operating at full employment?

6. What is "natural" about natural unemployment?

7. What is the difference between the employment rate and the labor force participation rate?

8. If the unemployment rate is 4 percent, it does not follow that the employment rate is 96 percent. Explain why.

9. What criteria must be met for a person to be characterized as unemployed?

10. What is the difference between a job leaver and a reentrant?

11. How is a discouraged worker different from an unemployed worker?

12. If the price of, say, oranges has risen, does it follow that the price level has risen too? Explain your answer.

13. What is the relationship between your nominal income and the inflation rate if you are more than keeping up with inflation?

14. Explain how the CPI is computed.

WORKING WITH NUMBERS AND GRAPHS

1. Suppose 60 million people are employed, 10 million are unemployed, and 30 million are not in the labor force. What does the civilian noninstitutional population equal?

2. Suppose 100 million people are in the civilian labor force and 90 million people are employed. How many people are unemployed? What is the unemployment rate?

3. Change the current-year prices in Exhibit 1 to $1 for pens, $28 for shirts, and $32 for a pair of shoes. On the basis of these prices, what is the CPI for the current year?

4. Jim earned an annual salary of $15,000 in 1965. What is this salary equivalent to in 2005 dollars? (Use Exhibit 2 to find the CPI in the years mentioned.)

5. A house cost $10,000 in 1976. What is this price equivalent to in 2001 dollars? (Use Exhibit 2 to find the CPI in the years mentioned.)

6. Using the following data, compute (a) the unemployment rate, (b) the employment rate, and (c) the labor force participation rate:

Civilian noninstitutional population   200 million

Number of employed persons	126 million
Number of unemployed persons	8 million

7. On the basis of the following data, compute (a) the unemployment rate, (b) the structural unemployment rate, and (c) the cyclical unemployment rate:

Frictional unemployment rate	2 percent
Natural unemployment rate	5 percent
Civilian labor force	100 million
Number of employed persons	82 million

8. Using Exhibit 2, compute the percentage change in prices between (a) 1966 and 1969, (b) 1976 and 1986, and (c) 1990 and 1999.

9. Assume that the market basket contains 10X, 20Y, and 45Z. The current-year prices for goods X, Y, and Z are $1, $4, and $6, respectively. The base-year prices are $1, $3, and $5, respectively. What is the CPI in the current year?

10. If the CPI is 150 and nominal income is $100,000, what does real income equal?

7

MACROECONOMIC MEASUREMENTS, PART II: GDP AND REAL GDP

© Bryan Busovicki/Shutterstock.com

INTRODUCTION

Each day in the United States, many thousands of goods and services are produced. How do we measure all this economic activity? One of the principal ways is to compute GDP, or gross domestic product. GDP is one of the most important economic measurements used by economists. In this chapter, we explain what GDP is and discuss how to compute it. We then turn to a discussion of Real GDP and how to compute it.

7-1 GROSS DOMESTIC PRODUCT

In any given year, people in the United States produce goods and services—television sets, books, pencil sharpeners, attorney services, haircuts, and much more. Have you ever wondered what the total dollar value is for all those goods and services? In 2013, it was $16.79 trillion. In other words, in 2013, people living and working in the United States produced $16.79 trillion worth of goods and services. That dollar amount is what economists call the gross domestic product. Simply put, **gross domestic product (GDP)** is *the total market value of all final goods and services produced annually within a country's borders.*

7-1a **Calculating GDP**

To show how GDP is computed, suppose the following data represent the prices and quantities of three goods produced in a tiny economy this year:

Gross Domestic Product (GDP)

The total market value of all final goods and services produced annually within a country's borders.

Goods	Quantity Produced of Each Good	Price of Each Good
A	10	$2
B	20	$3
C	30	$5

What is the GDP of this tiny economy? GDP is the total market value of all final goods and services produced annually within a country's borders. GDP, then, is the sum (Σ) of the products of the prices (*P*) of all goods and the quantities (*Q*) of those goods produced:

$$GDP = \Sigma(PQ)$$

In the case of our hypothetical economy,

$$GDP = (\$2 \times 10 \text{ units}) + (\$3 \times 20 \text{ units}) + (\$5 \times 30 \text{ units}) = \$230$$

7-1b Final Goods and Intermediate Goods

In our definition of GDP, reference was made to "final goods and services." If GDP is the total market value of these goods and services, why do we need to specify them as *final*? The reason is that there is a difference between a final good and an intermediate good. A **final good** (or service) is a good in the hands of the final user, the ultimate consumer. It is the orange juice that the consumer buys in the store.

So, then, what are the oranges that go to make the orange juice? The oranges are an *intermediate good*. An **intermediate good** is an input to the production of a final good. In other words, the oranges were used to produce orange juice (the final good).

Only expenditures on final goods are counted when computing GDP, in order to avoid the *double counting* that would occur if we counted expenditures on both final and intermediate goods. **Double counting** refers to counting a good more than once when computing GDP. To illustrate, if we count the oranges and the orange juice, then we count the oranges twice because they are in the orange juice.

Final Good
A good in the hands of its final user.

Intermediate Good
A good that is an input to the production of a final good.

Double Counting
Counting a good more than once when computing GDP.

In a Factory, Restaurant, and Law Office James works in a car factory in Detroit. Where is the economics? Obviously, cars are being produced in the factory. The production of these cars will add to the GDP for the current year.

Marion works as a cook in a coffeehouse. Bill has just ordered an egg salad sandwich on rye (toasted) with coleslaw and a root beer. Where is the economics? Marion will make the sandwich and coleslaw. These two items plus the root beer are part of the GDP for the current year.

Oliver is in his attorney's office talking about his upcoming court case. Where is the economics? The service the attorney is providing to Oliver is part of the GDP for the current year.

7-1c What GDP Omits

Some exchanges that take place in an economy are not included in GDP. These trades range from sales of used cars to illegal drug deals.

Certain Nonmarket Goods and Services   If a family hires a person to cook and clean, the service is counted in GDP. If family members perform the same tasks, however, their services are not counted in GDP. In the first case, a service is bought and sold for a price in a market setting. In the second case, it is not; no transaction takes place.

Some nonmarket goods are included in GDP. For example, the market value of food produced on a farm and consumed by the family that works the farm is estimated, and this imputed value is part of GDP.

Underground Activities, Both Legal and Illegal   The underground economy consists of unreported exchanges that take place outside the normal recorded markets. Some underground activities involve illegal goods (e.g., cocaine), and others involve legal goods and tax evasion. Illegal goods and services are not counted in GDP because no record exists of the transactions. There are no written records of illegal drug sales, illegal gambling, and illegal prostitution. Nor are there written records of some legal activities that individuals want to keep from government notice. For example, a gardener might agree to do gardening work only on the condition that he is paid in cash. Obviously, a person may legally buy or sell gardening services, but the transaction might not be recorded if one or both parties do not want it to be. Why might the gardener want to be paid in cash? Perhaps he doesn't want to pay taxes on the income received—an objective more easily accomplished if no written record of the income is generated.

Sales of Used Goods   GDP measures *current production* (i.e., production occurring during the current year). A used-car sale, for example, does not enter into the current-year statistics because the car was counted when it was originally produced.

Financial Transactions   The trading of stocks and bonds is not counted in GDP because it does not represent the production of new assets. It is simply the trading of existing assets (the exchange of stocks or bonds for money).

Transfer Payment
A payment to a person that is not made in return for goods and services currently supplied.

Government Transfer Payments   A **transfer payment** is a payment to a person that is not made in return for goods and services currently supplied. Government transfer payments, such as Social Security benefits and veterans' benefits, are not counted in GDP because they are not payments to individuals for *current production*.

Leisure   The length of the workweek has fallen in the United States since the beginning of the twentieth century, and the leisure time individuals have for consumption has increased. Leisure is a good in much the same way that cars, houses, and shoes are goods. But leisure is not counted in GDP because it is too difficult to quantify.

7-1d GDP Is Not Adjusted for Bads Generated in the Production of Goods

Economic growth often comes with certain bads (anything from which individuals receive disutility or dissatisfaction). For example, producing cars, furniture, and steel often generates air and water pollution, which most people consider as bads. GDP counts the goods and services, but it does not deduct the air and water pollution. Thus, argue some economists, GDP overstates our overall economic welfare.

ECONOMICS 24/7

Gross Family Product

One of the ways to understand GDP is to think of what it would be comparable to in a family. Instead of talking about what a country produces in a year, let's talk about what a family produces. Let's call the total market value of what the family produces gross family product (GFP).

© Monkey Business Images/Shutterstock.com

Just as not every country has the same GDP, not every family has the same GFP. One family can have a higher or lower GFP than another. The difference in GFP might be because more people are producing in one family than in another. For example, suppose family A is composed of five individuals and family B is composed of eight. More family members (more resources) can produce more output.

The same holds for countries. China might have a higher GDP than, say, France because China has a larger population. The national Chinese "family" is larger than the French "family."

Of course, one family might have a higher GFP than another for other reasons. For example, even with the same number of people in two families, one family might have a higher GFP. Perhaps the members of, say, family A work more hours than those of family B.

All other things equal, more work can result in more output.

The same holds for countries. The GDP of one country might be higher than the GDP of another because the workers in one country work more hours a week than those in the other country.

Finally, consider that, even when the size of two families is the same and when the number of hours worked each week by the two families is the same, one family could still have a higher GFP than another. To understand why, keep in mind that GFP measures the total market value of the family output. Note the phrase "total market value," computed by multiplying the price of each unit of output by the number of units produced. If a family is producing chairs, then its GFP will be equal to the price of each chair multiplied by the number of chairs produced. One hundred dollars ($100) per chair multiplied by, say, 100 chairs equals a GFP of $10,000. If another family produces, say, 100 shirts at a price of $25, its GPF will be lower. Thus one family's GFP might be higher than another's GFP because the per-unit price of what it produces is higher.

7-1e Per-Capita GDP

If we divide a country's GDP by the population in the country, we get *per-capita GDP.* For example, if a country has a GDP of $5 trillion and its population is 200 million, per-capita GDP is $25,000 ($5 trillion ÷ 200 million people). In 2013, the per-capita GDP in the United States was $45,336.

ECONOMICS 24/7

No One Utters the Actual Number

It happens at 1441 L Street in Washington, D.C. Specifically, it is a suite of offices on the fifth floor of a rather modern office building on L Street. The director of the Bureau of Economic Analysis (BEA) is in the room. Currently, it is Steve Ladefeld, who has held the position of director since 1995. He earned his Ph.D. in economics from the University of Maryland.

Also in the room is a group of BEA staff members, who, along with Ladefeld, have handed in their cell phones. No cell phones are allowed. Also, landline phones and Internet connections are cut off, and the curtains in the suite of offices are drawn tightly closed. Very few people are allowed in or out of the offices. The procedure that we are about to witness occurs 12 times a year. What is everyone here for? To compute a very special number: the GDP; then, to write up a press release explaining that number. To compute that number, Ladefeld and his staff

will wade through 10,000 pieces of data that describe the U.S. economy.

As they compute the GDP, no one is permitted to say the actual dollar figure—the number—aloud. That is a policy that has been in effect for a long time, going back to the days when it was feared that microphones might have been planted in the room.

Once the number is computed, a press release is drawn up and copies are made. Those copies are locked up for now. One copy is sent to the chair of the president's Council of Economic Advisors. Everyone who knows the number is forbidden to reveal it. At 8:30 a.m. the next day, the BEA releases the number to the world.[1]

---

[1] This 24/7 feature is based on "The Rise and Fall of GDP," by John Gertner, *New York Times Magazine*, May 13, 2010.

ECONOMICS 24/7

Money and Happiness

The Easterlin paradox (named after the economist Richard Easterlin) is a key concept in happiness economics, or the economics of happiness. The paradox is obvious once we identify two important points made by Easterlin. In his research, he found that (i) rich people in a country were often happier than poor people in the same country. In other words, as you get richer in a country, your happiness level increases. But then Easterlin also found that (ii) people in richer countries were really no happier than people in poorer countries. Now, (i) and (ii) seem at odds with each other, in the following sense: If richer people in a country are happier than poorer people in a country, then shouldn't it follow that people in rich countries should be happier than people in poor countries, at

least within poorer countries that meet basic needs (such as food, clothing, and shelter). But according to Easterlin's findings, they aren't. This at least seeming paradox has led many researchers to conclude that, once a society has met certain basic needs, greater income doesn't bring greater happiness.

Recently, economists Betsey Stevenson and Justin Wolfers have questioned the Easterlin paradox. Their finding: Not only do richer people in a country experience greater subjective well-being (greater happiness or contentment) than poor people within a country, but also, people in rich countries experience greater subjective well-being than people in poor countries. Moreover, there doesn't seem to be any satiation point. In other words, people keep experiencing greater subjective well-being with greater income, even after they have met their basic needs. Here is how Stevenson and Wolfers put it:

> Many scholars have argued that once "basic needs" have been met, higher income is no longer associated with higher subjective well-being. We assess the validity of this claim in comparisons of both rich and poor countries, and also of rich and poor people within a country. Analyzing multiple datasets, multiple definitions of "basic needs" and multiple questions about well-being, we find no support for this claim. The relationship between well-being and income is roughly linear-log and does not diminish as income rises. If there is a satiation point [a point at which higher income does not bring greater subjective well-being] we are yet to reach it."[2]

Part of the data Stevenson and Wolfers used came from the polling organization Gallup. Gallup asked about a half a million people in different countries (over time) to consider a "satisfaction ladder," on which there were 10 rungs. The top rung represents the best possible life for them, the bottom rung the lowest possible life. They were then asked to identify themselves on the ladder from zero to 10. Stevenson and Wolfers results are shown in Exhibit 1(a). Notice that, for each

country, subjective well-being rises as self-reported annual household income rises. In other words, all lines move upward from left to right.

Now look at Exhibit 1(b). Each dot represents a country, giving us a fix on its per-capita GDP (in thousands of U.S. dollars) and subjective well-being. Notice that the line that is fitted to the data (the dots), slopes upward from left to right, telling us that people who live in richer countries experience greater subjective well-being than those who live in poor countries. Notice also that there doesn't seem to be a point at which the upward-sloping line flattens out.

One of the questions that has yet to be answered is what it is exactly that drives the relationship between subjective well-being and income. In other words, if, as income rises, subjective well-being rises, too, why is that? Stevenson, in an interview, commented on this question, observing that people often say that when they have more income they are treated with more respect and that they have more choices over how they will spend their time. In other words, with more income may come more respect and more choices, and these two factors may be the driving forces behind greater subjective well-being.

---

[2] Betsey Stevenson and Justin Wolfers, "Subjective Well-Being and Income: Is There Any Evidence of Satiation?" NBER Working Paper 18992 (Cambridge, MA: National Bureau of Economic Research, April 2013).

> **EXHIBIT 1**

Income and Subjective Well-Being

In (a), we notice that, for each country, subjective well-being rises as household income rises. In (b), we see that people in rich countries experience greater subjective well-being than people in poor countries.

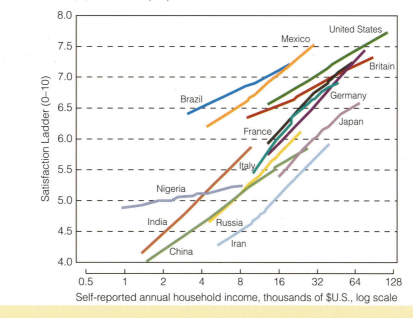

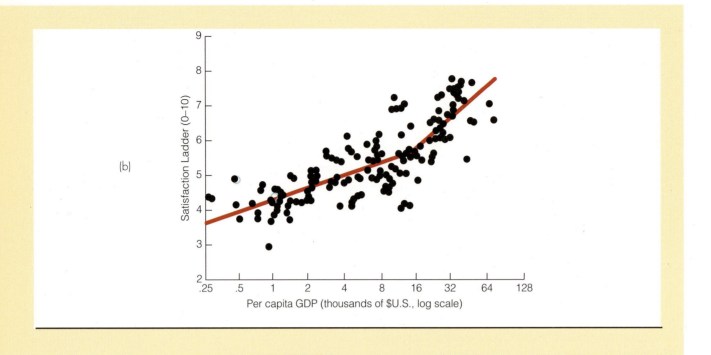

(b)

(Answers to Self-Test questions are in Answers to Self-Test Questions at the back of the book.)

1. Why aren't stock purchases and sales counted in GDP?

2. Suppose the GDP for a country is $0. Does this mean that there was no productive activity in the country? Explain your answer.

7-2 THE EXPENDITURE APPROACH TO COMPUTING GDP FOR A REAL-WORLD ECONOMY

In a tiny economy, we can compute GDP simply by multiplying the price of each good produced by the quantity of the good produced:

$$GDP = \sum PQ$$

The U.S. economy is anything but tiny. Economists cannot simply multiply the price of each good produced by the quantity of it. In a large economy, GDP can be measured in a number of different ways. A principal way is called the *expenditure approach* to measuring GDP. In this approach, economists sum the spending (on final goods and services) in four sectors of the economy: (1) household, (2) business, (3) government, and (4) foreign.

In each of these four sectors, economic actors buy goods and services; in other words, they spend. By sector, the expenditures are called, respectively, (1) *consumption;* (2) gross private domestic investment, or simply *investment;* (3) government consumption expenditures and gross investment, or simply *government purchases;* and (4) *net exports:*

Sectors of the Economy	Spending Called . . .
Household	Consumption
Business	Investment
Government	Government purchases
Foreign	Net exports

Before we see how economists add up the expenditures of these sectors, let's discuss the components of each of the expenditures.

Consumption   **Consumption** (*C*) includes spending on

- **Durable goods.** Durable goods are goods that are expected to last for more than three years, such as refrigerators, ovens, or cars.
- **Nondurable goods.** Nondurable goods are goods that are not expected to last for more than three years, such as food.
- **Services.** Services are intangible items, such as lawn care, car repair, and entertainment.

Consumption expenditures in the United States usually account for 70 percent of GDP. In short, consumption is the largest spending component of GDP.

Investment   **Investment** (*I*) is the sum of

- Purchases of newly produced capital goods.
- Changes in business inventories, sometimes referred to as **inventory investment**.
- Purchases of new residential housing.[3]

The sum of the purchases of newly produced capital goods and the purchases of new residential housing is often referred to as **fixed investment**. In other words,

$$\text{Investment} = \text{Fixed investment} + \text{Inventory investment}.$$

Fixed investment is the larger of the two components.

Government Purchases   **Government purchases** (*G*) include federal, state, and local government purchases of goods and services and gross investment in highways, bridges, and so on. Not included in government purchases are **government transfer payments**, which are payments to people that are not made in return for currently supplied goods and services. Social Security benefits and welfare payments are two examples of transfer payments; neither is a payment for current productive efforts.

Net Exports   People, firms, and governments in the United States sometimes purchase foreign-produced goods. These purchases are referred to as **imports** (*IM*). Foreign residents,

Consumption
The sum of spending on durable goods, nondurable goods, and services.

Investment
The sum of all purchases of newly produced capital goods, changes in business inventories, and purchases of new residential housing.

Inventory Investment
Changes in the stock of unsold goods.

Fixed Investment
Business purchases of capital goods, such as machinery and factories, and purchases of new residential housing.

Government Purchases
Federal, state, and local government purchases of goods and services, and gross investment in highways, bridges, and so on.

Government Transfer Payments
Payments to persons that are not made in return for currently supplied goods and services.

Imports
Total domestic (U.S.) spending on foreign goods.

---

[3]   For purposes of computing GDP, the purchases of new residential housing (although undertaken by members of the household sector) are considered investment.

> **EXHIBIT 2**

The Expenditure Approach to Computing GDP

The expenditure components of GDP are consumption, investment, government purchases, and net exports. The exhibit shows what is included in each of these components.

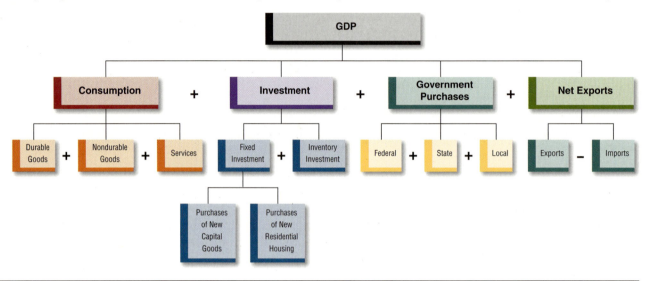

Exports
Total foreign spending on domestic (U.S.) goods.

Net Exports
Exports minus imports.

firms, and governments sometimes purchase U.S.-produced goods. These purchases are referred to as **exports** (*EX*). If imports are subtracted from exports, we are left with **net exports** (*NX*):

$$NX = EX - IM$$

Obviously, net exports can be positive or negative. If exports are greater than imports, then *NX* is positive; if imports are greater than exports, then *NX* is negative.

7-2a Using the Expenditure Approach to Compute GDP

The expenditure approach to measuring or computing GDP calls for totaling the purchases of final goods and services made in the four sectors of the economy. (See Exhibit 2.) This statement may give you reason to pause, because our earlier definition of GDP did not mention *purchases* of final goods and services. Rather, we defined GDP as the total market value of all final goods and services *produced* annually within a nation's borders.

The discrepancy is cleared up quickly when we note that national income accountants (government economists who compute GDP) assume that anything produced but not sold to consumers is "bought" by the firm that produced it. In other words, if a car is produced but not sold, it goes into business inventory and is consider "purchased" by the automaker firm that produced it. Thus, we can compute GDP by summing the purchases made by the four sectors of the economy. GDP equals consumption (*C*), plus investment (*I*), plus government purchases (*G*), plus net exports (*EX − IM*):

$$GDP = C + I + G + (EX - IM)$$

Exhibit 3 shows the dollar amounts of the four components of GDP for the United States in 2013.

> **EXHIBIT 3**

Components of GDP (Expenditure Approach)

The expenditure approach to computing GDP sums the purchases made by final users of goods and services. The expenditure components include consumption, investment, government purchases, and net exports. The data are for 2013.

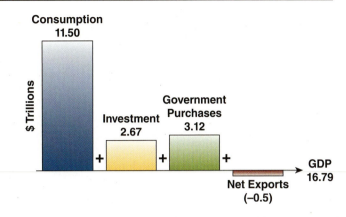

7-2b Common Misconceptions about Increases in GDP

Are all increases in GDP good for the economy? To answer this question, consider that if investment rises and no other component of GDP declines, GDP will rise. Recall that investment can rise for one of three reasons: (1) Firms may purchase more newly produced capital goods (firms buy more factories and machinery); (2) individuals may purchase new residential housing (someone buys a new home); or (3) firms' inventory investment rises. Further, firms' inventory investment can rise in two ways:

- *Planned inventory investment.* Firms may deliberately produce more units of a good and add them to inventory.

- *Unplanned inventory investment.* Consumers don't buy as many units of output as firms have produced, and unsold units are added to inventory.

Now compare two settings:

- *Setting 1.* Firms purchase more newly produced capital goods (more factories and machinery). As a result, investment rises and so does GDP, all other things remaining constant.

- *Setting 2.* Buyers don't buy as many units of output as firms have produced. The unsold units find their way into (unplanned) inventory investment. As a result, investment rises and so does GDP, all other things remaining constant.

Are the higher GDP dollars in settings 1 and 2 equivalent? We think not. As far as the health and strength of the economy are concerned, the increase in GDP in setting 1 is superior to the increase in GDP in setting 2.

SELF-TEST

1. Describe the expenditure approach to computing GDP in a real-world economy.

2. Will GDP be smaller than the sum of consumption, investment, and government purchases if net exports are negative? Explain your answer.

3. If GDP is $400 billion and the country's population is 100 million, does it follow that each individual in the country has $40,000 worth of goods and services?

7-3 THE INCOME APPROACH TO COMPUTING GDP FOR A REAL-WORLD ECONOMY

A second way to compute GDP, the income approach, should give us the same dollar amount of GDP as the expenditure approach. Let's look at an example. Suppose that, in a given economy, 10 units of good A are produced and 20 units of good B are produced. Suppose further that the price of good A is $1 and the price of good B is $2. Then, if buyers purchase all the units of each of the two goods, they will have spent $50 on these two goods: ($1 × 10 units) + ($2 × 20 units) = $50. In other words, the expenditure approach to measuring GDP gives us $50 of GDP in this little economy.

However, money spent by one person is money earned by another. The person who sells 10 units of good A at $1 per unit receives an income of $10. The $10 spent by the buyer is $10 earned by the seller.

Exhibit 4 shows a circular flow diagram of the economy. This diagram illustrates that, in a simple economy, GDP computed by summing the purchases of the four sectors of the economy is equal to GDP computed by summing the income earned by the different resources. In other words, dollar purchases (or dollar expenditures) equal dollar income. More specifically, money spent to buy goods and services ends up flowing to the resources that produce them. (Again, think in terms of a tiny economy in which one person buys 10 oranges for $1 each. His expenditure equals $10. But the $10 also represents income for the person who sold the buyer the oranges. An expenditure for one person is income for another.)

Two steps are involved in computing GDP with the income approach. First, compute national income. Second, adjust national income for certain things. The end result is GDP.

7-3a Computing National Income

National income is the sum of five components: (1) compensation of employees, (2) proprietors' income, (3) corporate profits, (4) rental income of persons, and (5) net interest.

Compensation of Employees   The compensation of employees is equal to the total of (1) wages and salaries paid to employees, (2) employers' contributions to Social Security and employee benefit plans, and (3) the monetary value of fringe benefits, tips, and paid vacations. The compensation of employees is the largest component of national income.

Proprietors' Income   Proprietors' income includes all forms of income earned by self-employed individuals and the owners of unincorporated businesses, including unincorporated farmers. Included in farm income is an estimate of the value of the food grown and consumed on farms.

Corporate Profits   Corporate profits include all the income earned by the stockholders of corporations. Some of the profits are paid to stockholders in the form of dividends, some are kept within the firm to finance investments (these are called *undistributed profits* or *retained earnings*), and some are used to pay taxes on corporate profits. (The portion of

---

National Income

Total income earned by U.S. citizens and businesses, no matter where they reside or are located. National income is the sum of the payments to resources (land, labor, capital, and entrepreneurship): National income = Compensation of employees + Proprietors' income + Corporate profits + Rental income of persons + Net interest.

> **EXHIBIT 4**

The Circular Flow: Total Purchases (Expenditures) Equal Total Income in a Simple Economy

The exhibit shows an economy with four sectors: households, business firms, government, and foreign economies. Each sector purchases goods and services. The sum of these purchases is GDP [GDP = $C + I + G + (EX - IM)$].

The purchases (expenditures) made in product markets flow to business firms, which then use these monies to buy resources in resource markets. In other words, the monies flow to the owners (suppliers) of land, labor, capital, and entrepreneurship. The sum of these resource payments is total income, which flows to households. In this simple economy, where some things have been ignored, total purchases (expenditures) equal total income. Because total purchases (expenditures) equal GDP and total purchases equal total income, it follows that GDP equals total income.

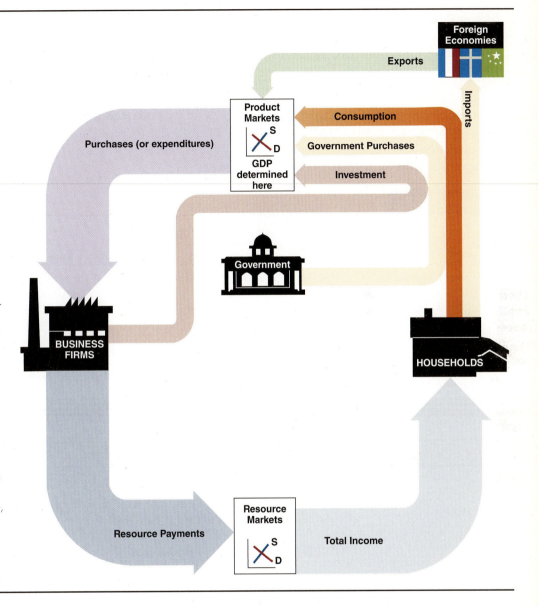

corporate profits used to pay these taxes is counted as income "earned" by households even though households do not receive the income.)

Rental Income (of Persons)   Rental income is the income received by individuals for the use of their nonmonetary assets (e.g., land, houses, offices). It also includes returns to individuals who hold copyrights and patents. Finally, it includes an imputed value for owner-occupied houses. For example, someone may own the house she lives in and therefore not pay any rent, but for purposes of national income accounting, a rental value is imputed. In short, home ownership is viewed as a business that produces a service which is sold to the owner of the business.

ECONOMICS 24/7

1820

Most people are interested in knowing what the per-capita GDP is today in different countries. Also interesting is the per-capita GDP in different countries over the years. For example, what country had the highest per-capita GDP in, say, 1820? The answer is the Netherlands.

In 1900, New Zealand was the country with the highest per-capita GDP. The three tables in Exhibit 5 identify the top 10 countries in various years in terms of per-capita GDP.

> **EXHIBIT 5**

1820			1900			1950		
Rank	Country	Per-Capita GDP	Rank	Country	Per-Capita GDP	Rank	Country	Per-Capita GDP
1	Netherlands	$1,561	1	New Zealand	$4,320	1	United States	$9,573
2	Australia	$1,528	2	Australia	$4,299	2	Switzerland	$8,939
3	Austria	$1,295	3	United States	$4,096	3	New Zealand	$8,495
4	Belgium	$1,291	4	Belgium	$3,652	4	Venezuela	$7,424
5	United States	$1,287	5	Netherlands	$3,533	5	Australia	$7,218
6	Denmark	$1,225	6	Switzerland	$3,531	6	Canada	$7,047
7	France	$1,218	7	Germany	$3,134	7	Sweden	$6,738
8	Sweden	$1,198	8	Denmark	$2,902	8	Denmark	$6,683
9	Germany	$1,112	9	Austria	$2,901	9	Netherlands	$5,850
10	Italy	$1,092	10	France	$2,849	10	Belgium	$5,346

Net Interest   Net interest is the interest income received by U.S. households and government, minus the interest they paid out.

National Income   We can summarize national income and its components as follows:

National Income = Compensation of employees
+ Proprietors' income
+ Corporate profits
+ Rental income
+ Net interest

7-3b From National Income to GDP: Making Some Adjustments

After computing national income, we might think that there is nothing else to do—that national income should equal GDP. We naturally think that every dollar spent is someone's income. But when we check the actual figures for national income and GDP, we find that they are not equal. In other words, not every dollar spent is someone else's income. For example, if Jones spends $10 to buy a book, $9.50 of the $10 might end up in the seller's pocket as income, but the remaining 50¢ might go for taxes.

With this idea in mind, the income approach to computing GDP requires us to add certain things to national income and to subtract certain things from it. The following equation and Exhibit 6 show what must be added to and subtracted from national income to compute GDP (keep the equation and exhibit in mind as you continue to read):

GDP = National income
　　　− Income earned from the rest of the world
　　　+ Income earned by the rest of the world
　　　+ Indirect business taxes
　　　+ Capital consumption allowance
　　　+ Statical discrepancey

Income Earned from the Rest of the World, Income Earned by the Rest of the World

In computing national income, we include the income earned by U.S. citizens who work and live in other countries, but we do not include the income earned by foreigners who work and live in the United States. If we want to compute GDP, we have to adjust for both these incomes. We do so by (1) subtracting from national income the income earned from the rest of the world (this is income that U.S. citizens living abroad earned by producing and selling goods) and (2) adding to national income the income earned by the rest of the world (this is income that non-U.S. citizens earned by producing and selling goods in the United States).

Indirect Business Taxes

Indirect business taxes are made up mainly of excise taxes, sales taxes, and property taxes. These taxes are not part of national income because they are not considered a payment to any resource (land, labor, etc.). Think of them as monies collected by government, not payments to land, labor, capital, or entrepreneurship.

Indirect taxes are included in the purchases of goods and services (you pay a sales tax when you buy most goods) and so are included when the expenditure approach is used to compute GDP. Therefore, we must add indirect business taxes to national income.

> **EXHIBIT 6**

The Income Approach to Computing GDP　　The exhibit identifies the components of national income and the adjustments necessary to compute GDP according to the income approach.

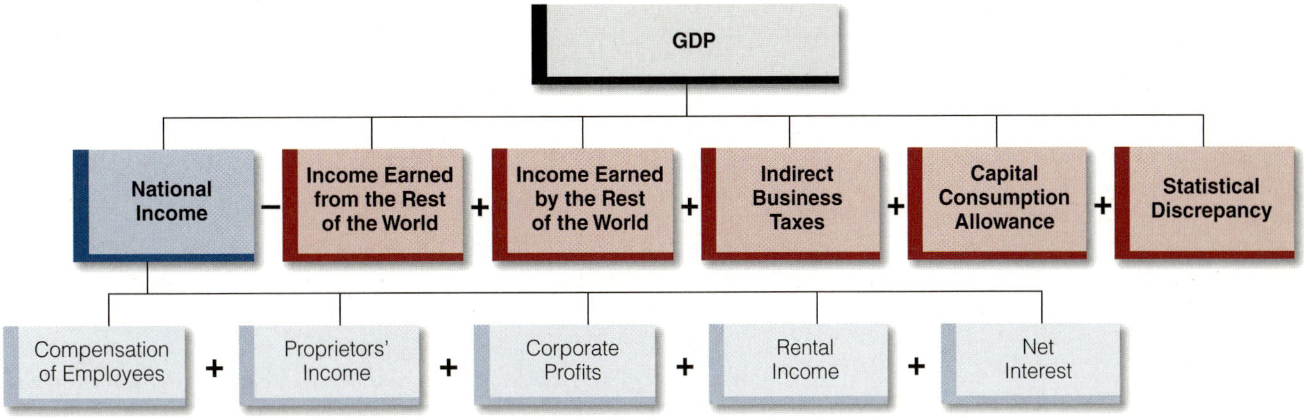

Capital Consumption Allowance (Depreciation)
The estimated amount of capital goods used up in production through natural wear, obsolescence, and accidental destruction.

Capital Consumption Allowance   Some capital goods are used up in the production process through natural wear, obsolescence, or accidental destruction (e.g., the machinery that breaks down and cannot be repaired). The cost to replace these capital goods is called the **capital consumption allowance**, or **depreciation**. It is added to national income because we want a measure of all the income earned in the economy. National income, by itself, doesn't include the income payments implicit in the capital consumption allowance.

Statistical Discrepancy   GDP and national income are computed with the use of different sets of data. Hence, statistical discrepancies, or pure computational errors, often occur and must be accounted for in the national income accounts.

7-3c Other National Income Accounting Measurements

Besides GDP and national income, three other national income accounting measurements are important: net domestic product, personal income, and disposable income. All five measurements—GDP, national income, net domestic product, personal income, and disposable income—are often used interchangeably to measure the output produced and income earned in an economy.

7-3d Net Domestic Product

Net Domestic Product (NDP)
GDP minus the capital consumption allowance.

If we use the expenditure approach to compute GDP, we add consumption, investment, government purchases, and net exports. Investment (or, more specifically, gross private domestic investment) includes fixed investment and inventory investment. Some of the fixed investment, however, is used to replace worn-out or obsolete capital goods, not to produce new goods. In short, gross private domestic investment contains the capital consumption allowance. If we subtract the capital consumption allowance from GDP, we are left with **net domestic product (NDP)**. NDP measures the total value of new goods available in the economy in a given year after worn-out capital goods have been replaced:

$$\text{Net domestic product (NDP)} = \text{GDP} - \text{Capital consumption allowance}$$

7-3e Personal Income

Not all income earned is received, and not all income received is earned. An example of income earned but not received is undistributed profits, which stockholders earn but do not receive. Instead, the corporation usually reinvests the undistributed profits. An example of income received but not earned is Social Security benefits.

Personal Income
The amount of income that individuals actually receive. It is equal to national income minus undistributed corporate profits, social insurance taxes, and corporate profits taxes, plus transfer payments.

   Personal income is the amount of income that individuals actually receive. It is equal to national income minus such major earned, but not received, items as undistributed corporate profits, social insurance taxes (Social Security contributions), and taxes on corporate profits, plus transfer payments (which are received but not earned):

$$\text{Personal income} = \text{National income}$$

$$- \text{Undistributed corporate profits}$$

$$- \text{Social insurance taxes}$$

$$- \text{Corporate profits taxes}$$

$$+ \text{Transfer payments}$$

7-3f Disposable Income

The portion of personal income that can be used for consumption or saving is referred to as disposable personal income, or simply **disposable income**. It is equal to personal income minus personal taxes (especially income taxes):

$$\text{Disposable income} = \text{Personal income} - \text{Personal taxes}$$

Sometimes disposable income is referred as spendable income, take-home pay, or after-tax income. In 2014, disposable income in the United States was $12.8 trillion.

Disposable Income
The portion of personal income that can be used for consumption or saving. It is equal to personal income minus personal taxes (especially income taxes).

7-4 REAL GDP

This section defines Real GDP, shows how to compute it, and then explains how it is used to measure economic growth.

7-4a Why We Need Real GDP

In 2010, U.S. GDP was $14.75 trillion. One year later, in 2011, GDP was $15.27 trillion. Although you know that GDP was higher in 2011 than in 2010, do you know *why*?

As you think about your answer, look at GDP in a one-good economy. Suppose 10 units of this good X are produced and each unit is sold for $10; then GDP in that economy is $100:

$$\text{GDP} = \$10 \times 10 \text{ units} = \$100$$

Now suppose GDP rises from $100 to $250. Why? It could rise because the price of the one good increased from $10 to $25:

$$\text{GDP} = \$25 \times 10 \text{ units} = \$250$$

Or it could rise because the quantity of output produced increased from 10 units to 25 units:

$$\text{GDP} = \$10 \times 25 \text{ units} = \$250$$

Or it could rise because the price of the good increased to $12.50 and the quantity increased to 20 units:

$$\text{GDP} = \$12.50 \times 20 \text{ units} = \$250$$

To gauge the health of the economy, economists want to know why GDP increased. If GDP increased simply because price increased, then the economy is not growing. For an economy to grow, more output must be produced.

Because an increase in GDP can be due in part simply to an increase in price, a more meaningful measure is Real GDP. **Real GDP** is GDP adjusted for price changes.

Real GDP
The value of the entire output produced annually within a country's borders, adjusted for price changes.

7-4b Computing Real GDP

One way to compute Real GDP is to find the value of the output for the different years in terms of the same prices—that is, the base-year prices. Consider the following data for our one-good economy:

Year	Price of Good X	Quantity Produced of Good X (units)	GDP
1	$10	100	$10 × 100 = **$1,000**
2	$12	120	$12 × 120 = **$1,440**
3	$14	140	$14 × 140 = **$1,960**

The data show why GDP is higher in years 2 and 3: Both price and quantity have increased. However, we want to separate the part of GDP that is higher because of an increase in quantity from the part that is higher because of an increase in price. We want the Real GDP: the part of GDP that is higher because the quantity of output is higher.

To compute Real GDP for any year, multiply the quantity of the good produced in a given year by the price of the good in the base year. Thus, if year 1 is the base year, then, to find Real GDP in year 2, we multiply the quantity of the good produced in year 2 by the price of the good in year 1. Similarly, to find Real GDP in year 3, we multiply the quantity of the good produced in year 3 by the price of the good in year 1. The following table calculates Real GDP in years 1, 2, and 3:

Year	Price of Good X	Quantity Produced of Good X (units)	GDP	Real GDP
1 (base year)	$10	100	$10 × 100 = **$1,000**	$10 × 100 = **$1,000**
2	$12	120	$12 × 120 = **$1,440**	$10 × 120 = **$1,200**
3	$14	140	$14 × 140 = **$1,960**	$10 × 140 = **$1,400**

7-4c The General Equation for Real GDP

The real world has more than one good and more than one price. The general equation used to compute Real GDP is

$$\text{Real GDP} = \Sigma(\text{Base-year prices} \times \text{Current-year quantities})$$

Σ, the Greek capital letter sigma, stands for summation. Thus, Real GDP is the sum of the products of the current-year quantities and their base-year prices. In 2013, Real GDP in the United States was $15.76 trillion.

7-4d What Does It Mean if Real GDP Is Higher in One Year Than in Another?

If GDP is, say, $9 trillion in year 1 and $9.5 trillion in year 2, we cannot be sure why it has increased from one year to the next. (1) Did prices rise while output remained constant? (2) Did output rise while prices remained constant? (3) Or did prices and output both rise?

However, if Real GDP is, say, $8 trillion in year 1 and $8.3 trillion in year 2, we know why it has increased. Real GDP rises only if output rises. In other words, Real GDP rises only if more goods and services are produced.

7-4e The Economy in 1950 and in 2012

In 1950, GDP in the United States was $300.2 billion; in 2012, it was $16,244.6 billion. So, how much larger was the U.S. economy in 2012 than in 1950? If we divide $16,244.6 billion by $300.2 billion, the answer is 54.11, so the economy was 54.11 times larger in 2012 than in 1950. But this is in nominal terms. In other words, the dollar size of the economy in 2012 was 54.11 times larger than the dollar size of the economy in 1950. But this doesn't tell us how much bigger the economy was in 2012 than in 1950 *in real terms*— in terms of producing actual goods and services, such as television sets, cars, houses, and so on. To make this comparison, we need to look at things in real terms—in a given year's dollars. We choose 2009. Real GDP (in 2009 dollars) in 1950 was $2,181.9 billion, and in 2012 it was $15,470.7 billion, 7.09 times larger.

The population in the United States in 1950 was about 161 million; in 2012 it was about 312 million, so the population was 1.94 times as large in 2012 as it was in 1950. Consequently, while Real GDP in 2012 was seven times what it was in 1950, the U.S. population in 2012 was almost twice what it was in 1950.

7-4f Real GDP, Economic Growth, and Business Cycles

Suppose you have to choose between two countries. In country A, Real GDP grows by 3 percent each year. In country B, Real GDP is the same each year; if Real GDP was $500 billion last year, it is $500 billion in the current year, and it will be $500 billion next year. In which of the two countries would you prefer to live, *ceteris paribus*?

Or make a choice between countries C and D. In country C, Real GDP takes a roller-coaster ride, alternating between rising and falling. It rises for some months, then falls, then rises again, then falls, and so on. In country D, Real GDP simply rises year after year. In which of the two countries would you prefer to live, *ceteris paribus?*

If you chose one country over the other in each of these two cases, then you are implicitly saying that Real GDP matters to you. One of the reasons economists study Real GDP is that it matters to you and others. In other words, because Real GDP is important to you, it is important to economists.

Economists study two major macroeconomic topics that have to do with Real GDP: *economic growth* and *business cycles.*

Economic Growth   Annual **economic growth** has occurred if Real GDP in one year is higher than Real GDP in the previous year. For example, if Real GDP is $8.1 trillion in one year and $8.3 trillion in the next, the economy has undergone economic growth. The growth rate is equal to the (positive) percentage change in Real GDP and is computed as follows:

Economic Growth
Increases in Real GDP.

$$\text{Percentage change in Real GDP} = \left(\frac{\text{Real GDP}_{\text{later year}} - \text{Real GDP}_{\text{earlier year}}}{\text{Real GDP}_{\text{earlier year}}} \right) \times 100$$

The Ups and Downs in the Economy: The Business Cycle   If Real GDP is on a roller coaster—rising and falling and rising and falling—the economy is said to be going through a **business cycle**. Economists usually talk about four or five phases of the business cycle. We identify five in Exhibit 7 and in the following list:

Business Cycle
Recurrent swings (up and down) in Real GDP.

1. ***Peak.*** At the *peak* of the business cycle, Real GDP is at a temporary high. In Exhibit 7, Real GDP is at a temporary high at Q_1.

2. **Contraction.** The *contraction* phase represents a decline in Real GDP. According to the standard definition of *recession,* two consecutive quarterly declines in Real GDP constitute a recession.

3. **Trough.** The low point in Real GDP, just before it begins to turn up, is called the *trough* of the business cycle.

4. **Recovery.** The *recovery* is the period when Real GDP is rising. It begins at the trough and ends at the initial peak. The recovery in Exhibit 7 extends from the trough until Real GDP is again at Q_1.

5. **Expansion.** The *expansion* phase refers to increases in Real GDP beyond the recovery. In Exhibit 7, it refers to increases in Real GDP above Q_1.

An entire business cycle is measured from peak to peak. The typical business cycle is approximately four to five years, although a few have been shorter and some have been longer.

After Graduating from College Jason has just graduated from college. He has been searching for a job in his chosen field of accounting, but so far he hasn't been offered a job he would like. Where is the economics?

FINDING ECONOMICS

The state (or health) of the economy is closely tied to whether business firms are hiring or firing. When the economy is growing, firms are usually hiring employees; when the economy is in a slump (a recession), firms are often firing employees. As far as one's job prospects go, graduating when the economy is strong and growing is better than when it is weak and declining.

> **EXHIBIT 7**

The Phases of the Business Cycle

The phases of a business cycle include the peak, contraction, trough, recovery, and expansion. A business cycle is measured from peak to peak.

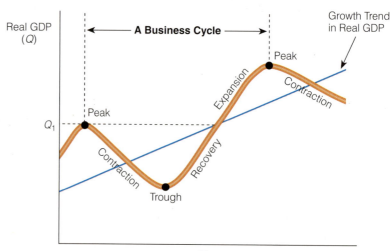

National Bureau of Economic Research (NBER) and Recessions   The standard definition of a recession is two consecutive quarterly declines in Real GDP, but this is not the only definition of a recession. The National Bureau of Economic Research has this to say about a recession:

> *A recession is a period between a peak and a trough. . . . During a recession, a significant decline in economic activity spreads across the economy and can last from a few months to more than a year.*

The NBER definition is therefore different from the standard definition of a recession. According to the quote just cited, "a recession is a significant decline in economic activity [that] spreads across the economy."

"Why Do We Use the Expenditure Approach to Measure Production?"

STUDENT:

When GDP was first defined, emphasis was placed on goods and services being *produced*. The definition of GDP was "the total market value of all final goods and services *produced* annually within a country's borders."

INSTRUCTOR:

Yes, that is correct.

STUDENT:

But when we computed GDP, we simply summed the *expenditures* made by each of the four sectors of the economy. In other words, we added consumption, investment, government purchases, and net exports.

Now, here is my problem. When we define GDP, we speak about production: final goods and services *produced*. But when we compute GDP, production doesn't seem to come up. Instead, we sum *expenditures* made by the four sectors of the economy.

My point is simple: A good can be produced that is not purchased. So, if we add up only expenditures (or purchases), aren't we underestimating production?

INSTRUCTOR:

I see your point. What you are perhaps saying is that, say, 100 chairs are produced in the year but only 75 of them are purchased. In that case, counting only purchases (or expenditures) underestimates production. And production is what we really want to get at because GDP is defined as the total market value of all final goods and services produced.

STUDENT:

Yes, that's right. That's what I am getting at.

INSTRUCTOR:

Well, remember one important category of expenditures: investment. Investment consists of the expenditures of the business sector. We know that investment is the sum of fixed investment and inventory investment, but let's focus on inventory investment for a minute. Think of how goods might get into inventory. One way is for the firm to deliberately produce goods and put some into inventory. In other words, a company produces 1,000 chairs, sends 900 of them to different retailers, and then puts 100 into inventory in case there is an unexpected increase in demand for chairs. We'll call these 100 chairs *planned inventory*.

Now think of another way that chairs can be added to inventory. Suppose that, when the firm sends those 900 chairs to different retailers, not all of the chairs sell. Only 700 of them sell. What will retailers do with the remaining 200 chairs? One thing they might do is return them to the producer. So, what does the firm do with those 200 returned chairs. For now, they put them into inventory. We'll call these 200 chairs *unplanned inventory*.

Here is the important point: The 300 chairs in inventory (100 chairs in planned inventory and 200 chairs in unplanned inventory) are part of overall investment. In other words, if investment for the year equals $2.1 trillion for the economy, then the market value of the 300 chairs in inventory is part of that $2.1 trillion.

When computing GDP, we count those 300 chairs in the same way we count the 700 that were produced and purchased. In short, everything produced in the economy is purchased by someone. In our example, the 300 chairs were "purchased" by the firm that produced them.

STUDENT:

Let me see if I have this right. If a firm produces a good and it is bought by, say, a consumer, that good is counted in GDP. But if the good is not bought by a consumer, then it is considered to be purchased by the firm that produced it. In other words, the chair company produces 1,000 chairs, sells 700 to consumers, and "sells" 300 to itself. It "buys" 300 of its own chairs. Is that right?

INSTRUCTOR:

That's right.

STUDENT:

But isn't that cheating somehow? After all, the 300 chairs weren't actually sold to anyone? They certainly weren't sold in the way we usually think of something being sold.

INSTRUCTOR:

That's true. But remember what we are trying to get at with GDP: the total market value of all final goods and services produced. Those 300 chairs were certainly produced. Looking at the 300 chairs as being purchased by the firm that produced them is simply a way of counting them. And counting those 300 chairs is what we want to do when we are trying to measure GDP.

STUDENT:

Yes, I see that now.

Points to remember

1. GDP is the total market value of all final goods and services *produced* annually within a country's borders.
2. We can use the expenditure approach to measure production as long as all goods and services produced but not sold to end consumers are considered to be "purchased" by the firm that produced them.

SELF-TEST

1. Suppose GDP is $6 trillion in year 1 and $6.2 trillion in year 2. What has caused the rise in GDP?

2. Suppose Real GDP is $5.2 trillion in year 1 and $5.3 trillion in year 2. What has caused the rise in Real GDP?

3. Can an economy be faced with endless business cycles and still see its Real GDP grow over time? Explain your answer.

CHAPTER SUMMARY

GROSS DOMESTIC PRODUCT

- Gross domestic product (GDP) is the total market value of all final goods and services produced annually within a country's borders.
- Either the expenditure approach or the income approach can be used to compute GDP.

- To avoid the problem of double counting, only final goods and services are included in GDP.
- GDP omits certain nonmarket goods and services, both legal and illegal underground activities, the sale of used goods, financial transactions, transfer payments, and leisure (even though leisure is a good). Finally, GDP is not adjusted for the bads (e.g., pollution) that sometimes accompany production.

EXPENDITURES

- Expenditures on U.S. goods and services include consumption, gross private domestic investment (investment), government consumption expenditures and gross investment (government purchases), and net exports (exports minus imports).

- Consumption includes spending on durable goods, nondurable goods, and services.

- Investment includes purchases of newly produced capital goods (fixed investment), changes in business inventories (inventory investment), and purchases of new residential housing (also fixed investment).

- Government purchases include federal, state, and local government purchases of goods and services, and gross investment in highways, bridges, and so on. Government purchases do not include transfer payments.

- Net exports equals the total foreign spending on domestic goods (exports) minus the total domestic spending on foreign goods (imports).

COMPUTING GDP

- According to the expenditure approach, GDP $= C + I + G + (EX - IM)$. In other words, GDP equals consumption, plus investment, plus government purchases, plus net exports.

MEASUREMENTS OTHER THAN GDP

- Net domestic product (NDP) equals gross domestic product (GDP) minus the capital consumption allowance:

  NDP = GDP − Capital consumption allowance

- National income equals the sum of resource, or factor, payments:

  National income = Compensation of employees
  + Proprietors' income
  + Corporate profits
  + Rental income
  + Net interest

- Personal income equals national income minus undistributed corporate profits, social insurance taxes, and taxes on corporate profits, taxes, plus transfer payments:

  Personal Income = National income
  − Undistributed corporate profits
  − Social insurance taxes
  − Corporate profits taxes
  + Transfer payments

- Disposable income = Personal income − Personal taxes

REAL GDP

- Real GDP is GDP adjusted for price changes. It is GDP in base-year dollars.

ECONOMIC GROWTH AND BUSINESS CYCLES

- Annual economic growth has occurred if Real GDP in one year is higher than Real GDP in the previous year.

- The business cycle has five phases: peak, contraction, trough, recovery, and expansion. A complete business cycle is measured from peak to peak.

KEY TERMS AND CONCEPTS

Gross Domestic Product (GDP)	Investment	Exports	Personal Income
Final Good	Inventory Investment	Net Exports	Disposable Income
Intermediate Good	Fixed Investment	National Income	Real GDP
Double Counting	Government Purchases	Capital Consumption Allowance (Depreciation)	Economic Growth
Transfer Payment	Government Transfer Payments	Net Domestic Product (NDP)	Business Cycle
Consumption	Imports		

VIDEO QUESTIONS AND PROBLEMS

Video Questions and Problems are available on MindTap for Arnold 12e or by searching for Arnold on www.cengagebrain.com

1. Give an example that illustrates double counting.
2. Why are the sales of used goods omitted from GDP?
3. If country A's GDP is higher than country B's GDP, does it follow that country A has a higher per-capita GDP than country B? Why or why not?
4. Explain the expenditure approach to computing GDP?
5. A good that is produced but not sold is still counted in GDP according to the expenditure approach to computing GDP. Do you agree or disagree with this statement? Explain your answer.

QUESTIONS AND PROBLEMS

1. "I just heard on the news that GDP is higher this year than it was last year. This means that we're better off this year than last year." Comment.
2. Which of the following are included in the calculation of this year's GDP? (a) 12-year-old Johnny mowing his family's lawn; (b) Dave Malone buying a used car; (c) Barbara Wilson buying a bond issued by General Motors; (d) Ed Ferguson's receipt of a Social Security payment; (e) the illegal drug transaction at the corner of Elm and Fifth.
3. Discuss the problems you see in comparing the GDPs of two countries, say, the United States and the People's Republic of China.
4. The manuscript for this book was keyed by the author. Had he hired someone to do the keying, GDP would have been higher than it was. What other activities would increase GDP if they were done differently? What activities would decrease GDP if they were done differently?
5. Why does GDP omit the sales of used goods? Of financial transactions? Of government transfer payments?
6. A business firm produces a good this year that it doesn't sell. As a result, the good is added to the firm's inventory. How does this inventory good find its way into GDP?

7. Economists prefer to compare Real GDP figures for different years instead of comparing GDP figures. Why?
8. What is the difference between a recovery and an expansion?
9. Define each of the following terms:
   a. Contraction
   b. Business cycle
   c. Trough
   d. Disposable income
   e. Net domestic product
10. Does the expenditure approach to computing GDP measure U.S. spending on all goods, U.S. spending on only U.S. goods, or U.S. and foreign spending on only U.S. goods? Explain your answer.
11. In the first quarter of the year, Real GDP was $400 billion; in the second quarter, it was $398 billion; in the third quarter, it was $399 billion; and in the fourth quarter, it was $395 billion. Has there been a recession? Explain your answer.

WORKING WITH NUMBERS AND GRAPHS

1. Net exports are −$114 billion and exports are $857 billion. What are imports?
2. Consumption spending is $3.708 trillion, spending on nondurable goods is $1.215 trillion, and spending on services is $2.041 trillion. What does spending on durable goods equal?
3. Inventory investment is $62 billion and total investment is $1.122 trillion. What does fixed investment equal?
4. In year 1, the prices of goods X, Y, and Z are $2, $4, and $6 per unit, respectively. In year 2, the prices of goods X, Y, and Z are $3, $4, and $7, respectively. In year 2, twice as many units of each good are produced as in year 1. In

year 1, 20 units of X, 40 units of Y, and 60 units of Z are produced. If year 1 is the base year, what does Real GDP equal in year 2?

5. Nondurable goods spending = $400 million, durable goods spending = $300 million, new residential housing spending = $200 million, and spending on services = $500 million. What does consumption equal?

6. According to the circular flow diagram in Exhibit 4, consumption spending flows into U.S. product markets but import spending does not. But U.S. households buy imported goods in U.S. markets, don't they? Explain.

7. If Real GDP is $487 billion in year 1 and $498 billion in year 2, what is the economic growth rate?

8. The figure that follows shows a business cycle. Identify each of the following as a phase of the business cycle:

   a. Point *A*

   b. Between points *A* and *B*

   c. Point *B*

   d. Between points *B* and *C*

   e. Point *D*

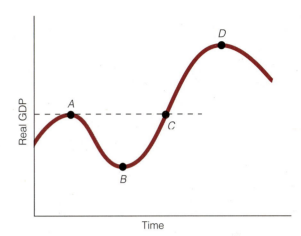

AGGREGATE DEMAND AND AGGREGATE SUPPLY

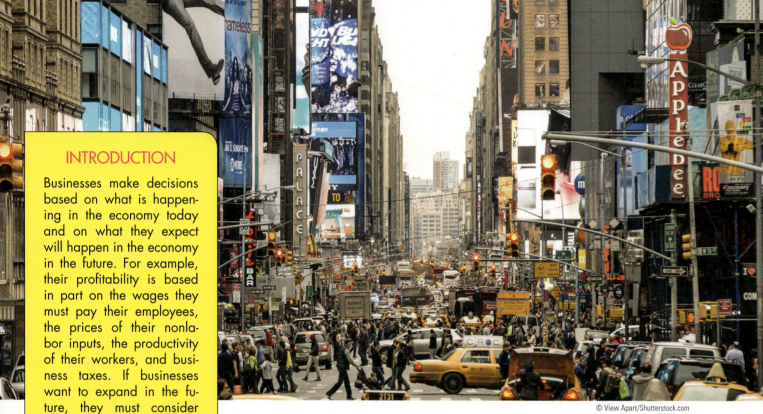

© View Apart/Shutterstock.com

8-1 A WAY TO VIEW THE ECONOMY

This chapter begins our theoretical discussion of an economy. We can think of an economy as consisting of two major activities: buying and producing. (See Exhibit 1.) Specifically, goods and services are produced, and goods and services are bought. When economists speak about aggregate demand (AD), they are speaking about the buying side of the economy. When economists speak about aggregate supply, they are speaking about the producing side of the economy. Thus,

Buying side of the economy = Aggregate demand

Producing side of the economy = Aggregate supply

With respect to production, two periods are relevant: production in the short run and production in the long run. When referring to short-run aggregate supply ($SRAS$), economists are speaking about production in the short run. When referring to long-run aggregate supply ($LRAS$), they are speaking about production in the long run.

> **EXHIBIT 1**

An Economy

There are two sides to an economy: a buying side and a producing side. There are two periods that relate to the producing side: production in the short run and production in the long run. Buying side = Aggregate demand (AD); Production in the short run = Short-run aggregate supply (SRAS); Production in the long run = Long-run aggregate supply (LRAS).

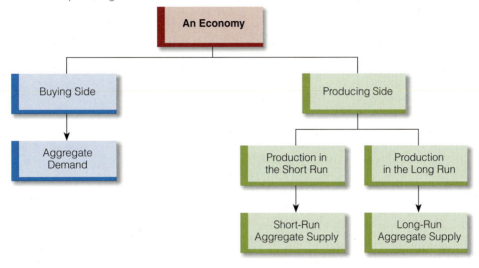

Production in the short run = Short-run aggregate supply

Production in the long run = Long-run aggregate supply

The framework of analysis we use is called aggregate demand–aggregate supply (*AD–AS*). That framework of analysis has three parts:

1. Aggregate demand (*AD*)

2. Short-run aggregate supply (*SRAS*)

3. Long-run aggregate supply (*LRAS*)

8-2 AGGREGATE DEMAND

Recall from the last chapter that people, firms, and governments buy U.S. goods and services. **Aggregate demand** is the quantity demanded of these U.S. goods and services, or the quantity demanded of U.S. Real GDP, at various price levels, *ceteris paribus*. For example, the following whole set of data represents aggregate demand:

Aggregate Demand

The quantity demanded of all goods and services (Real GDP) at different price levels, *ceteris paribus*.

	Aggregate Demand
Price Index	**Quantity Demanded of Goods and Services (Quantity Demanded of Real GDP)**
100	$1,200 billion worth of goods and services
110	$1,000 billion worth of goods and services
120	$800 billion worth of goods and services

The Aggregate Demand Curve

The aggregate demand curve is downward sloping, specifying an inverse relationship between the price level and the quantity demanded of Real GDP.

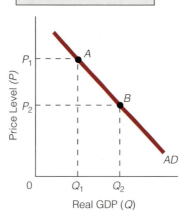

Aggregate Demand Curve
The price level and quantity demanded of Real GDP are inversely related.

An **aggregate demand (AD) curve** is the graphical representation of aggregate demand. An *AD* curve is shown in Exhibit 2. Notice that it is downward sloping, indicating an inverse relationship between the price level (*P*) and the quantity demanded of Real GDP (*Q*): As the price level rises, the quantity demanded of Real GDP falls; as the price level falls, the quantity demanded of Real GDP rises, *ceteris paribus*.

8-2a Why Does the Aggregate Demand Curve Slope Downward?

Asking why the *AD* curve slopes downward is the same as asking why the relationship between the price level and the quantity demanded of Real GDP is inverse. This inverse relationship and the resulting downward slope of the *AD* curve are explained by (1) the real balance effect, (2) the interest rate effect, and (3) the international trade effect.

Aggregate Demand (*AD*) Curve

A curve that shows the quantity demanded of all goods and services (Real GDP) at different price levels, *ceteris paribus*.

Real Balance Effect

The change in the purchasing power of dollar-denominated assets that results from a change in the price level.

Monetary Wealth

The value of a person's monetary assets. Wealth, as distinguished from monetary wealth, refers to the value of all assets owned, both monetary and nonmonetary. In short, a person's wealth equals his or her monetary wealth (e.g., $1,000 cash) plus nonmonetary wealth (e.g., a car or a house).

Purchasing Power

The quantity of goods and services that can be purchased with a unit of money. Purchasing power and the price level are inversely related: As the price level goes up (down), purchasing power goes down (up).

Real Balance Effect (Due to a Change in the Price Level) The **real balance effect** states that the inverse relationship between the price level and the quantity demanded of Real GDP is established through changes in the value of **monetary wealth**, or the value of a person's monetary assets. Changes in monetary wealth usually take the form of increased or decreased **purchasing power**—that is, the quantity of goods and services that can be purchased with a unit of money.

To illustrate, consider a person who has $50,000 in cash. Suppose the price level falls. As this happens, the purchasing power of the person's $50,000 rises. The $50,000, which once could buy 100 television sets at $500 each, can now buy 125 sets at $400 each. Saying that an increase in the purchasing power of the person's $50,000 is identical to saying that his monetary wealth has increased. (Isn't the $50,000 more valuable when it can buy more than when it can buy less?) And, as he becomes wealthier, he buys more goods.

So a fall in the price level causes purchasing power to rise, increasing a person's monetary wealth. As people become wealthier, the quantity demanded of Real GDP rises.

Now suppose the price level rises. In this event, the purchasing power of the $50,000 falls. The $50,000, which once could buy 100 television sets at $500 each, can now buy 80 sets at $625 each. Saying that a decrease in the purchasing power of the person's $50,000 is identical to saying that his monetary wealth has decreased. And as he becomes less wealthy, he buys fewer goods.

In sum, a rise in the price level causes purchasing power to fall, decreasing a person's monetary wealth. As people become less wealthy, the quantity demanded of Real GDP falls.

Interest Rate Effect (Due to Change in the Price Level) The **interest rate effect** states that the inverse relationship between the price level and the quantity demanded of Real GDP is established through changes in the part of household and business spending that is sensitive to changes in interest rates.

Suppose a person buys a fixed bundle of goods (food, clothing, and shelter) each week. Then the price level falls, increasing the purchasing power of the person's money. With more purchasing power (per dollar), she can purchase her fixed bundle of goods with less money. What does she do with part of this increase in her monetary wealth? She saves it. In terms of simple supply-and-demand analysis, the supply of credit increases. Subsequently, the price of credit (the interest rate) drops. As the interest rate drops, households and businesses borrow more, so they end up buying more goods. Thus, the quantity demanded of Real GDP rises.

Now suppose the price level rises, decreasing the purchasing power of the person's money. With less purchasing power (per dollar), she cannot purchase her fixed bundle of goods with the same amount of money. If she wants to continue to buy the goods, she needs to acquire more money. To do that, she goes to a bank and requests a loan. In terms of simple supply-and-demand analysis, the demand for credit increases. Consequently, the interest rate rises. As the interest rate rises, households borrow less to finance, say, automobile purchases and firms borrow less to finance new capital goods spending. Thus, the quantity demanded of Real GDP falls.

International Trade Effect (Due to a Change in the Price Level)   The **international trade effect** is the change in foreign sector spending as the price level changes. The inverse relationship between the price level and the quantity demanded of Real GDP is established through foreign sector spending, which includes U.S. spending on foreign goods (imports) and foreign spending on U.S. goods (exports).

Suppose the price level in the United States falls. As this happens, U.S. goods become relatively cheaper than foreign goods. As a result, both Americans and foreigners buy more U.S. goods. The quantity demanded of U.S. Real GDP rises.

Now suppose the price level in the United States rises. In that event, U.S. goods become relatively more expensive than foreign goods. As a result, both Americans and foreigners buy fewer U.S. goods. The quantity demanded of U.S. Real GDP falls.

For a review of the three effects—real balance, interest rate, and international trade—see Exhibit 3.

In a Store, Buying a Watch Jim is in a store, buying a watch imported from Switzerland. What does this purchase have to do with a downward-sloping aggregate demand curve? When we ask Jim why he's buying a Swiss watch, he tells us that the Swiss watch is cheaper than the American watch. The reason could very well be that the U.S. price level has recently risen relative to the Swiss price level. In other words, when Jim buys the Swiss watch instead of the American watch, we could be seeing the international trade effect in action.

8-2b An Important Word on the Three Effects

As explained, the aggregate demand curve is downward sloping because of the real balance, interest rate, and international trade effects. However, keep in mind that what caused these three effects is a change in the price level. In other words, when discussing, say, the interest rate effect, we are talking about the interest rate effect of *a change in the price level:*

Price level changes → Interest rate effect

Interest Rate Effect
The changes in household and business buying as the interest rate changes (in turn, a reflection of a change in the demand for or supply of credit brought on by price level changes).

International Trade Effect
The change in foreign sector spending as the price level changes.

> **EXHIBIT 3**

Why the Aggregate Demand Curve Is Downward Sloping

This exhibit outlines the three effects that explain why the *AD* curve is downward sloping. Each effect relates to a change in the price level (*P*) leading to a change in the quantity demanded of Real GDP (*Q*).

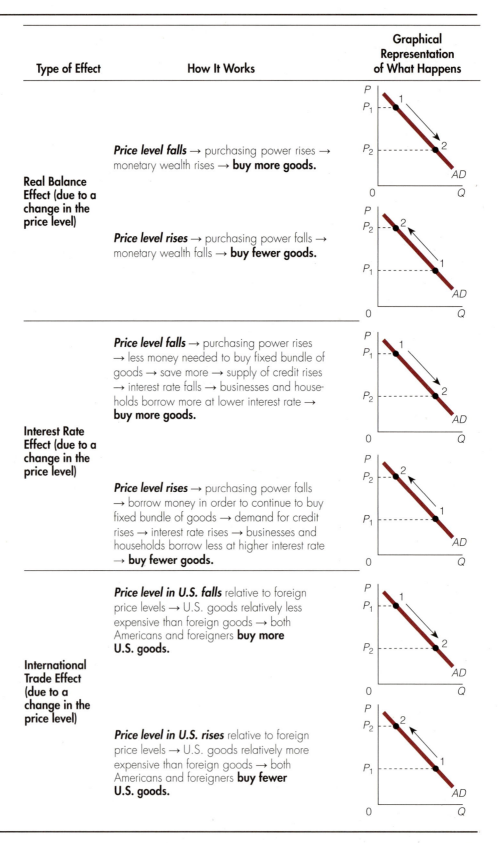

Type of Effect	How It Works	Graphical Representation of What Happens
Real Balance Effect (due to a change in the price level)	***Price level falls*** → purchasing power rises → monetary wealth rises → **buy more goods.**	
	Price level rises → purchasing power falls → monetary wealth falls → **buy fewer goods.**	
Interest Rate Effect (due to a change in the price level)	***Price level falls*** → purchasing power rises → less money needed to buy fixed bundle of goods → save more → supply of credit rises → interest rate falls → businesses and households borrow more at lower interest rate → **buy more goods.**	
	Price level rises → purchasing power falls → borrow money in order to continue to buy fixed bundle of goods → demand for credit rises → interest rate rises → businesses and households borrow less at higher interest rate → **buy fewer goods.**	
International Trade Effect (due to a change in the price level)	***Price level in U.S. falls*** relative to foreign price levels → U.S. goods relatively less expensive than foreign goods → both Americans and foreigners **buy more U.S. goods.**	
	Price level in U.S. rises relative to foreign price levels → U.S. goods relatively more expensive than foreign goods → both Americans and foreigners **buy fewer U.S. goods.**	

Why is this point important? The interest rate can change as a result of things *other than the price level changing*, and not everything that changes the interest rate leads to a movement from one point to another point on the *AD* curve. Other things that change the interest rate can lead to a shift in the *AD* curve instead. We will have more to say about this point later. For now, though, simply keep in mind the cause of each of the three effects: a change in the price level—the variable on the vertical axis in Exhibit 2.

8-2c A Change in Quantity Demanded of Real GDP Versus a Change in Aggregate Demand

A change in the price level brings about a change in the quantity demanded of Real GDP. As the price level falls, the quantity demanded of Real GDP rises, *ceteris paribus.* In Exhibit 4(a), a change in the quantity demanded of Real GDP is represented as a *movement* from one point (*A*) on AD_1 to another point (*B*) on AD_1.

A change in aggregate demand is represented in Exhibit 4(b) as a *shift* in the aggregate demand curve from AD_1 to AD_2. When the aggregate demand curve shifts, the quantity demanded of Real GDP changes even though the price level remains constant. For example, at a price level (index number) of 180, the quantity demanded of Real GDP on AD_1 in Exhibit 4(b) is $6.0 trillion. But at the same price level (180), the quantity demanded of Real GDP on AD_2 is $6.5 trillion.

> **EXHIBIT 4**

A Change in the Quantity Demanded of Real GDP Versus a Change in Aggregate Demand

(a) A change in the quantity demanded of Real GDP is graphically represented as a *movement* from one point, *A*, on AD_1 to another point, *B*, on AD_1. A change in the quantity demanded of Real GDP is the result of a change in the price level. (b) A change in aggregate demand is graphically represented as a *shift* in the aggregate demand curve from AD_1 to AD_2.

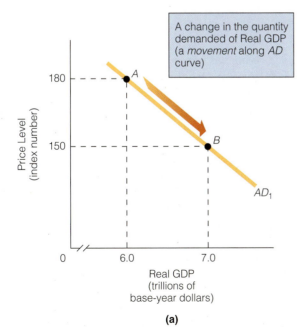

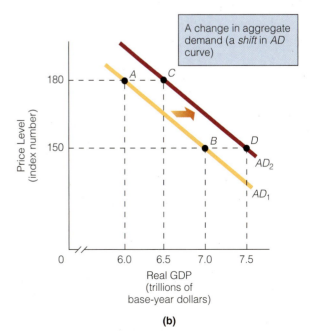

(a)   (b)

Shift Factors Versus Movement Factors, Once Again
To the economist, not all factors are alike. For some factors, the change is from one point to another on the same curve. These are *movement factors*. The price level is a movement factor. Raise it, and we move up on the *AD* curve; lower it, and we move down.

Other factors, if they change, shift curves. These are *shift factors*. We turn now to discuss shift factors with respect to the *AD* curve.

8-2d Changes in Aggregate Demand: Shifts in the *AD* Curve

What can change aggregate demand? What can cause aggregate demand to rise, and what can cause it to fall?

The simple answer is that aggregate demand changes when spending on U.S. goods and services changes. If spending increases at a given price level, aggregate demand rises; if spending decreases at a given price level, aggregate demand falls. That is,

Spending increases at a given price level → AD rises

Spending decreases at a given price level → AD falls

Suppose the price level in the economy is represented by the Consumer Price Index (CPI) and the index is currently 150. At this price level, U.S. residents, firms, and governments, along with foreigners, foreign firms, and foreign governments, want to buy, say, $7.0 trillion worth of U.S. goods and services. Then something changes, and all of a sudden they all want to buy a total of $7.5 trillion worth of U.S. goods and services. Now, before you conclude that they want to buy more goods and services because the prices of goods and services have fallen, keep in mind that the price level has not changed. The price level—still represented by the CPI—is still 150. In other words, all these people, firms, and governments want to buy more U.S. goods even though the prices of the goods and services have not changed.

When individuals, firms, and governments want to buy more U.S. goods and services even though the prices of the goods have not changed, we say that aggregate demand has increased. As a result, the *AD* curve *shifts* to the right. Of course, when individuals, firms, and governments want to buy fewer U.S. goods and services at a given price level, we say that aggregate demand has decreased. As a result, the *AD* curve *shifts* to the left.

Exhibit 4(b) shows a change in aggregate demand (a shift in the *AD* curve). At point *B*, the price level is 150 and total expenditures on U.S. goods and services are $7.0 trillion. At point *D*, the price level is still 150 but total expenditures on U.S. goods and services have increased to $7.5 trillion. Why has aggregate demand moved from point *B* to point *D*; that is, what has caused the increase in total expenditures? To find out, we have to look at the components of total expenditures.

8-2e How Spending Components Affect Aggregate Demand

The last chapter identified four major spending components: consumption (*C*), investment (*I*), government purchases (*G*), and net exports (*NX*). Recall, in addition, that net exports equals exports (*EX*) minus imports (*IM*). Let's keep the numbers simple: *C* = $100, *I* = $100, *G* = $100, *EX* = $50, and *IM* = $15. If *EX* = $50 and *IM* = $15, then net exports = $35.

Using these dollar figures, we calculate that $335 is spent on U.S. goods and services. We get this dollar amount by finding the sum of consumption, investment, government purchases, and net exports:

$$\text{Total expenditures on U.S. goods and services} = C + I + G + NX$$

Obviously, this dollar amount will go up if (1) *C* rises, (2) *I* rises, (3) *G* rises, or (4) *NX* rises (or any combination of them rises). In other words, a rise in consumption, investment, government purchases, or net exports will raise spending on U.S. goods and services:

$$C\uparrow,\ I\uparrow,\ G\uparrow,\ NX\uparrow \rightarrow \text{Total expenditures on U.S. goods and services} \uparrow$$

Now, what will cause spending on U.S. goods and services to go down? Obviously, such spending will decline if (1) *C* falls, (2) *I* falls, (3) *G* falls, or (4) *NX* falls (or any combination of them falls):

$$C\downarrow,\ I\downarrow,\ G\downarrow,\ NX\downarrow \rightarrow \text{Total expenditures on U.S. goods or services} \downarrow$$

Because we now know what causes total expenditures on U.S. goods and services to change, we can relate the components of spending to (U.S.) aggregate demand. If, *at a given price level,*

- Consumption, investment, government purchases, or net exports *rise,* aggregate demand will rise and the *AD* curve will shift to the right.
- Consumption, investment, government purchases, or net exports *fall,* aggregate demand will fall and the *AD* curve will shift to the left.

We can write these relationships as

$$\text{If, at a given price level, } C\uparrow,\ I\uparrow,\ G\uparrow\ NX\uparrow, \text{ then } AD\uparrow$$

$$\text{If, at a given price level, } C\downarrow,\ I\downarrow,\ G\downarrow,\ NX\downarrow, \text{ then } AD\downarrow$$

The flowcharts in Exhibit 5 show how changes in spending components affect aggregate demand.

8-2f Why Is There More Total Spending?

Here is a question that an economics professor might place on an exam:

True or false? The price level falls and total spending rises. As a result of total spending rising, aggregate demand in the economy rises and the AD curve shifts rightward.

You may think that the answer is true—perhaps because you are accustomed to thinking that, if total spending rises, aggregate demand rises. But aggregate demand rises only if total spending rises at *a given price level.*

To illustrate the difference between (1) total spending rising at a falling price level and (2) total spending rising at a given price level, consider the following two examples:

> **EXHIBIT 5**

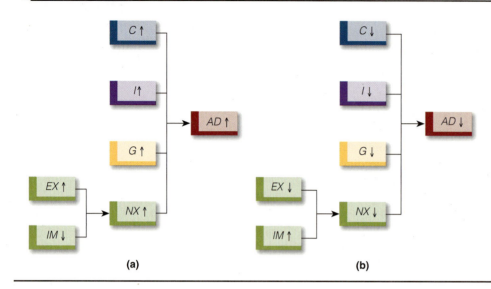

Changes in Aggregate Demand

The flowcharts show how aggregate demand changes with changes in various spending components.

C = consumption, I = investment, G = government purchases, NX = net exports, EX = exports, IM = imports. Keep in mind that $NX = EX - IM$.

- *Example 1.* The price level falls, and goods and services become cheaper. As a result of lower prices, individuals start to buy more goods and services. Consequently, total spending rises.

- *Example 2.* The price level does not change. Still, something in the economy changes, so people start buying more goods and services. As a result of their buying more goods and services, total spending in the economy rises.

In both cases, total spending rises. But in example 1 total spending rises because prices have fallen. The result is a *movement* down a given AD curve. In example 2, total spending rises even when prices remain unchanged. The result is a *shift* rightward in the AD curve.

Lesson learned: Total spending can rise for one of two reasons. The first deals with a decline in prices and leads to a *movement* along a given AD curve. The second deals with a change in some factor other than prices and leads to a *shift* in the AD curve.

8-2g Factors That Can Change C, I, G, and NX (EX − IM) and Therefore Can Change AD (Shift the AD Curve)

What can change aggregate demand in the economy? The answer is a change in any or all of consumption, investment, government purchases, and net exports (exports minus imports). So, if, for example, someone asks you why AD increased, you might say "because consumption increased."

But suppose the person then asks, "What caused consumption to increase?" Your answer to one question simply leads to another question. If a change in consumption changes aggregate demand, what changes consumption? The same question can be asked about changes in investment, government purchases, and net exports (i.e., exports minus imports). For example, if aggregate demand increased because investment increased, then what caused investment to increase?

This section looks at some of the many factors that can change consumption, investment, and net exports. A later chapter considers the factors that can change government purchases.

Consumption   Four factors can affect consumption: wealth, expectations about future prices and income, the interest rate, and income taxes.

1. *Wealth.* Individuals consume not only on the basis of their present income but also on the basis of their **wealth**. Suppose each of two individuals has an income of $80,000 a year. One has $75,000 in the bank, and the other has no assets at all. We would expect the person with $75,000 in the bank to spend more of her income on consumption goods this year. Greater wealth makes individuals feel financially more secure and thus more willing to spend:

   Wealth
   The value of all assets owned, both monetary and nonmonetary.

   - Increases in wealth lead to increases in consumption. If consumption increases, aggregate demand rises and the *AD* curve shifts to the right.

   - Decreases in wealth lead to declines in consumption, which lead to a fall in aggregate demand. Consequently, the *AD* curve shifts to the left.

   $$\text{Wealth}\uparrow \rightarrow C\uparrow \rightarrow AD\uparrow$$
   $$\text{Wealth}\downarrow \rightarrow C\downarrow \rightarrow AD\downarrow$$

2. *Expectations About Future Prices and Income.* Individuals' expectations of future prices can increase or decrease aggregate demand:

   - If individuals expect *higher* prices in the future, they increase their current consumption expenditures to buy goods at the lower current prices. The increase in consumption leads to an increase in aggregate demand.

   - If individuals expect *lower* prices in the future, they decrease current consumption expenditures. The reduction in consumption leads to a decrease in aggregate demand.

   $$\text{Expect higher future prices} \rightarrow C\uparrow \rightarrow AD\uparrow$$
   $$\text{Expect lower future prices} \rightarrow C\downarrow \rightarrow AD\downarrow$$

   Similarly, expectations regarding income can affect aggregate demand:

   - Expectations of a *higher* future income increase consumption, leading to an increase in aggregate demand.

   - Expectations of a *lower* future income decrease consumption, leading to a decrease in aggregate demand.

   $$\text{Expect higher future income} \rightarrow C\uparrow \rightarrow AD\uparrow$$
   $$\text{Expect lower future income} \rightarrow C\downarrow \rightarrow AD\downarrow$$

3. *Interest Rate.* Current empirical work shows that spending on consumer durables is sensitive to the interest rate:

   - Buyers often pay for these items by borrowing, so an *increase* in the interest rate increases the monthly payment amounts linked to the purchase of durables and thereby reduces their consumption. The reduction in consumption leads to a decline in aggregate demand.

- Alternatively, a *decrease* in the interest rate reduces monthly payment amounts and thereby increases the consumption of durables. The increase in consumption leads to an increase in aggregate demand.

$$\text{Interest rate} \uparrow \rightarrow C \downarrow \rightarrow AD \downarrow$$

$$\text{Interest rate} \downarrow \rightarrow C \uparrow \rightarrow AD \uparrow$$

4. *Income Taxes.* Let's consider personal income taxes—that is, the taxes a person pays on earned income:

- As income taxes *rise*, disposable income decreases. When people have less take-home pay to spend, consumption falls. Consequently, aggregate demand decreases.

- A *decrease* in income taxes has the opposite effect: It raises disposable income. When people have more take-home pay to spend, consumption rises and aggregate demand increases.

$$\text{Income taxes} \uparrow \rightarrow C \downarrow \rightarrow AD \downarrow$$

$$\text{Income taxes} \downarrow \rightarrow C \uparrow \rightarrow AD \uparrow$$

In a Housing Downturn A newspaper article reads as follows: "Housing prices have fallen over the past six months, and economists are concerned that this might lead to less overall demand in the economy." Can you find the economics here? Do housing prices have anything to do with aggregate demand? Let's work backward. First, a decline in aggregate demand can be caused by a decline in consumption. Second, a decline in consumption can be caused by a change in any of four factors: wealth, expectations about future prices and income, the interest rate, and income taxes. Let's focus on wealth. If housing prices fall, people who own houses will find themselves with less overall wealth. (Think of a person whose house is worth $500,000 one month and $450,000 six months later. She has suffered a decline in wealth.) As a result, these people reduce their consumption and aggregate demand falls.

Investment   Three factors can change investment: the interest rate, expectations about future sales, and business taxes.

1. *Interest Rate.* Changes in interest rates affect business decisions:

- As the interest rate *rises*, the cost of an investment project rises and businesses invest less. As investment decreases, aggregate demand decreases.

- As the interest rate *falls*, the cost of an investment project falls and businesses invest more. Consequently, aggregate demand increases.

$$\text{Interest rate} \uparrow \rightarrow / \downarrow \rightarrow AD\downarrow$$

$$\text{Interest rate} \downarrow \rightarrow / \uparrow \rightarrow AD\uparrow$$

2. *Expectations About Future Sales.* Businesses invest because they expect to sell the goods they produce:

   - If businesses become *optimistic* about future sales, investment spending grows and aggregate demand increases.
   - If businesses become *pessimistic* about future sales, investment spending contracts and aggregate demand decreases.

$$\text{Businesses become optimistic about future sales} \rightarrow / \uparrow \rightarrow AD\uparrow$$

$$\text{Businesses become pessimistic about future sales} \rightarrow / \downarrow \rightarrow AD\downarrow$$

3. *Business Taxes.* Businesses naturally consider expected after-tax profits when they make their investment decisions:

   - An *increase* in business taxes lowers expected profitability. With less profit expected, businesses invest less. As investment spending declines, so does aggregate demand.
   - A *decrease* in business taxes raises expected profitability and investment spending, increasing aggregate demand.

$$\text{Business taxes} \uparrow \rightarrow / \downarrow \rightarrow AD\downarrow$$

$$\text{Business taxes} \downarrow \rightarrow / \uparrow \rightarrow AD\uparrow$$

Net Exports   Two factors can change net exports: foreign real national income and the exchange rate.

1. *Foreign Real National Income.* Just as Americans earn a national income, so do people in other countries. The earnings of those people constitute the foreign national income. By adjusting this foreign national income for price changes, we obtain foreign real national income:

   - As foreign real national income *rises*, foreigners buy more U.S. goods and services. Thus, U.S. exports (*EX*) rise. As exports rise, net exports rise, *ceteris paribus*. As net exports rise, aggregate demand increases.
   - The process also works in reverse: As foreign real national income *falls*, foreigners buy fewer U.S. goods and exports fall. The fall in exports lowers net exports, reducing aggregate demand

$$\text{Foreign real national income} \uparrow \rightarrow \text{U.S. exports} \uparrow \rightarrow \text{U.S. net exports} \uparrow \rightarrow AD\uparrow$$

$$\text{Foreign real national income} \downarrow \rightarrow \text{U.S. exports} \downarrow \rightarrow \text{U.S. net exports} \downarrow \rightarrow AD\downarrow$$

2. *Exchange Rate.* The **exchange rate** is the price of one currency in terms of another currency; for example, $1.25 may be exchanged for €1 (1 euro). A currency has **appreciated** in value if more of a foreign currency is needed to buy it. A currency

Exchange Rate
The price of one currency in terms of another currency.

Appreciation
An increase in the value of one currency relative to other currencies.

Depreciation
A decrease in the value of one currency relative to other currencies.

has **depreciated** in value if more of it is needed to buy a foreign currency. For example, a change in the exchange rate from $1.25 = €1 to $1.50 = €1 means that more dollars are needed to buy 1 euro; the euro has appreciated. And because more dollars are needed to buy €1, the dollar has depreciated.

- *Depreciation* in a nation's currency makes foreign goods more expensive. Consider an Irish coat that is priced at €200 when the exchange rate is $1.25 = €1. To buy the Irish coat for €200, an American has to pay $250 ($1.25 for each of €200, for a total of $250). Now suppose the dollar depreciates to $1.50 = €1. The American now has to pay $300 for the coat.

- The process just described is symmetrical. An *appreciation* in a nation's currency makes foreign goods cheaper. For example, if the exchange rate goes from $1.25 = €1 to $1 = €1, the Irish coat will cost the American only $200.

The depreciation and appreciation of the U.S. dollar affect net exports:

- As the dollar *depreciates*, foreign goods become more expensive, Americans cut back on imported goods, and foreigners (whose currency has appreciated) increase their purchases of U.S. exported goods. If exports rise and imports fall, net exports increase and aggregate demand increases.

- As the dollar *appreciates*, foreign goods become cheaper, Americans increase their purchases of imported goods, and foreigners (whose currency has depreciated) cut back on their purchases of U.S. exported goods. If exports fall and imports rise, net exports decrease, thus lowering aggregate demand.

Dollar depreciates → U.S. exports ↑ and U.S. imports ↓ → U.S. net exports ↑ → AD↑

Dollar appreciates → U.S. exports ↓ and U.S. imports ↑ → U.S. net imports ↓ → AD↓

(See Exhibit 6 for a summary of the factors that change aggregate demand.)

The W–X–Y–Z Explanation In the previous discussion, we said, for example, that if the dollar depreciates, U.S. exports will rise and U.S. imports will fall, in turn causing U.S. net exports to rise, in turn causing aggregate demand to rise. A summarization of this type of argument might go like this: A change in W leads to a change in X, which leads to a change in Y, which leads to change in Z. Let's call this kind of explanation the W–X–Y–Z explanation.

Economists often think in terms of one thing changing something else, in turn changing still something else, and so on. Some people find this kind of thinking curious. They ask, "Why not simply say that W leads to Z instead of saying that W leads to X, which leads to Y, which leads to Z?"

Saying that W leads to Z might make things easier (there would be less to remember), but what the shortcut gains in ease, it loses in completeness. It is best to explain just how one thing eventually leads to something else happening.

> **EXHIBIT 6**

Factors That Change Aggregate Demand

Aggregate demand (AD) changes whenever consumption (C), investment (I), government purchases (G), or net exports (EX − IM) change. The factors that can affect C, I, and EX − IM, and thereby indirectly affect aggregate demand, are listed.

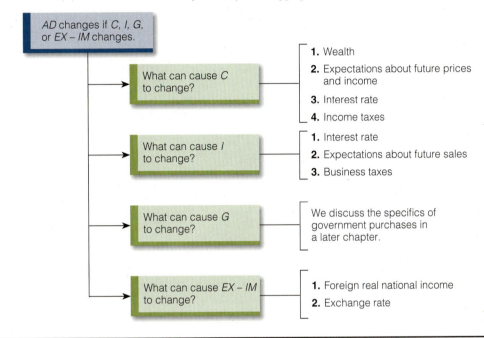

8-2h Can a Change in the Money Supply Change Aggregate Demand?

Changes in such factors as interest rates, business taxes, exchange rates, and the like can change aggregate demand (indirectly) by directly changing consumption, investment, and net exports. What about the money supply? Can a change in the money supply lead to a change in aggregate demand?

Let's see. Suppose the money supply rises from, say, $1,400 billion to $1,500 billion. Will this change in the money supply result in an increase in aggregate demand? Most economists would say that it does, but they differ on how. One way to explain the effect (in the context of our discussion) is as follows: (1) A change in the money supply affects interest rates, (2) a change in interest rates changes consumption and investment, and (3) a change in consumption and investment affects aggregate demand. Therefore, a change in the money supply is a catalyst in a process that ends with a change in aggregate demand. (We will have much more to say about the money supply and interest rates in later chapters.)

ECONOMICS 24/7

When Would You Want to Be Paid in a Currency Other Than U.S. Dollars?

Most people who work in the United States are paid in dollars, but when would you *want* to be paid in another currency? In thinking about the question, consider the exchange rate between the dollar and the euro. Suppose the exchange rate is $1 = €1 and the exchange rate is expected to stay constant. Your employer owes you $10,000. Does it matter if the employer pays you in dollars or euros? At the current exchange rate, $10,000 is the same as €10,000, so whether you are paid in euros or dollars does not matter.

© arka38/Shutterstock.com

So let's refine the original question: If you are usually paid in dollars, when would you prefer not to be paid in dollars? The answer is "when you think that the value of the dollar is going to fall relative to the value of other currencies."

Here's the problem, though: Most of us who work for U.S. employers don't have the option of getting paid in the currency of our choice. Most of us cannot go to our employer and say, "This month, could you please pay me in euros instead of dollars."

Now suppose that you expect the exchange rate to change to $2 = €1 and that you expect the dollar to depreciate and the euro to appreciate. Does the currency in which you are paid matter? Yes, it does. Being paid in euros is preferable because the euro is expected to appreciate in value.

To see why payment in euros is preferable, ask yourself what happens if you are paid $10,000 instead of €10,000. If the exchange rate is $2 = €1, then after you are paid $10,000, the $10,000 is all you have. But if you are paid €10,000 euros, you could have $20,000, because €10,000 can be exchanged for $20,000 at the new rate.

However, you can always convert the currency in which we are paid into another currency. Suppose that you are always paid in dollars but think that the value of the dollar is going to decline relative to the value of the euro. Your employer pays you $10,000 when the exchange rate is $1 = €1, and you think that the dollar is going to depreciate in value relative to the euro. You immediately take the $10,000 your employer paid you and exchange the dollars for €10,000. Then you wait. If the exchange rate actually does change to, say, $2 for €1, you then exchange your €10,000 for $20,000. In short, if you want to be paid in euros or yen or pesos, your employer may not comply with your wishes but you have the option of acting on your own wishes.

8-2i   If Consumption Rises, Does Some Other Spending Component Have to Decline?

Suppose $C = \$100$, $I = \$100$, $G = \$100$, and $NX = \$100$. Then total expenditures equal $400. Now suppose C rises by $50, to a level of $150. Must one or more other spending components decline by $50? In other words, if one spending component rises, does another spending component have to decline? To answer that question, we need to talk about two factors: the money supply and velocity.

Let's say that the money supply in the economy is $1 and that $1 is currently in the hands of Joe. Joe takes the $1 and buys good X from Jackie. Later, Jackie takes the $1 (that she received earlier from Joe) and buys good Y from John. Still later, John takes the $1 (that he received earlier from Jackie) and buys good Z from Jill.

Here is what we know: We started with a money supply of just $1, and that dollar changed hands three times. The number of times a dollar changes hands (or is spent) to buy final goods and services is what economists call **velocity**. (If we were dealing with a money supply of more than just $1, we would define velocity not as "the number of times, etc." but as the *average number* of times a dollar is spent to buy final goods and services in a year.) In our simple example, velocity is 3.

The product of our money supply ($1) and velocity (3) is $3, which represents the total amount of spending in the economy. From our example, two things are obvious: First, total spending in the economy can be a greater dollar amount than the money supply. Proof: In our example, the money supply was $1, but total spending equaled $3. Second, total spending depends on the money supply and velocity. Proof: Total spending in our example was the money supply *times* velocity.

Let's return to the original question: If consumption rises, must some other spending component decline? The answer is yes if neither the money supply nor velocity changes. But the answer is no if either the money supply or velocity rises.

To illustrate how the answer can be yes, suppose again that the money supply is $1 and velocity is 3 and that total spending is therefore $3. Let's break up our total of $3 spending in this way: $1 goes for consumption, $1 goes for investment, and $1 goes for government purchases. Consumption rises to $2, and the money supply and velocity remain at $1 and 3, respectively. So total spending is still $3, and therefore a $1 increase in consumption necessitates a decline in some other spending component by $1. After all, total spending is locked in at $3; if one spending component rises by a certain amount, one or more other spending components must decline by the same amount.

But total spending isn't locked in if either the money supply or velocity changes. Again, suppose that consumption rises from $1 to $2 but that velocity or the money supply increases. Then no other spending component needs to change. To see why, suppose the money supply has risen to $1.40 and velocity is still 3. Total spending now is $4.20 instead of $3, so consumption could have risen to $2 without any decline in investment or government purchases. In other words, *C* can equal $2 and *I* can still equal $1, and *G* can still equal $1 (or even more, $1.20).

The same is true if the money supply remains constant at $1 and velocity increases from 3 to 4. At velocity of 4, total spending is $4. Again, consumption can rise to $2 without requiring a decline in any other spending component.

We recap:

- If both the money supply and velocity are constant, a rise in one spending component (such as consumption) necessitates a decline in one or more other spending components.

- If either the money supply or velocity rises, one spending component can rise without requiring any other spending component to decline.

Velocity
The average number of times a dollar is spent to buy final goods and services in a year.

SELF-TEST

(Answers to Self-Test questions are in Answers to Self-Test Questions at the back of the book.)

1. Explain the real balance effect.

2. Explain what happens to the *AD* curve if the dollar appreciates relative to other currencies.

3. The money supply has risen, but total spending has declined. Is this state of affairs possible? Explain your answer.

8-3 SHORT-RUN AGGREGATE SUPPLY

Aggregate Supply
The quantity supplied of all goods and services (Real GDP) at different price levels, *ceteris paribus*.

Aggregate demand is one side of the economy; aggregate supply is the other. **Aggregate supply** is the quantity supplied of all goods and services (Real GDP) at various price levels, *ceteris paribus*. Aggregate supply includes both short-run aggregate supply (*SRAS*) and long-run aggregate supply (*LRAS*). Short-run aggregate supply is discussed in this section.

8-3a Short-Run Aggregate Supply Curve: What It Is and Why It Is Upward Sloping

Short-Run Aggregate Supply (SRAS) Curve
A curve that shows the quantity supplied of all goods and services (Real GDP) at different price levels, *ceteris paribus*.

A **short-run aggregate supply (*SRAS*) curve** (see Exhibit 7) shows the quantity supplied of all goods and services (Real GDP, or output) at different price levels, *ceteris paribus*. Notice that the *SRAS* curve is upward sloping: As the price level rises, firms increase the quantity supplied of goods and services; as the price level drops, firms decrease the quantity supplied of goods and services. Why is the *SRAS* curve upward sloping? Economists have put forth a few explanations; we discuss two of them.

Sticky Wages   Some economists believe that wages are "sticky," or inflexible. This may be because wages are locked in for a few years because of labor contracts that workers and management enter into. For example, management and labor may agree to lock in wages for the next one to three years. Both labor and management may see this move as in their best interest: Management then has some idea of what its labor costs will be for the duration of the contract, and workers may have a sense of security knowing that their wages can't be lowered. Wages may also be sticky because of certain social conventions or perceived notions of fairness. Whatever the specific reason for sticky wages, let's see how they provide an explanation of an upward-sloping *SRAS* curve.

Firms pay *nominal wages* (e.g., $30 an hour), but they often decide how many workers to hire on the basis of real wages. *Real wages* are nominal wages divided by the price level:

$$\text{Real Wage} = \frac{\text{Nominal Wage}}{\text{Price level}}$$

For example, suppose that the nominal wage is $30 an hour and that the price level, as measured by a price index, is 1.50.[1] Then the real wage is $20. Note, in general, that

- The quantity supplied of labor is *directly related* to the real wage: As the real wage rises, the quantity supplied of labor rises; as the real wage falls, the quantity supplied of labor falls:

> **EXHIBIT 7**

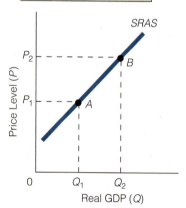

Short-Run Aggregate Supply Curve
The price level and quantity supplied of Real GDP are directly related.

The Short-Run Aggregate Supply Curve

The short-run aggregate supply curve is upward sloping, specifying a direct relationship between the price level and the quantity supplied of Real GDP.

---

[1] Alternatively, you can view the price index as 1.50 times 100, or 150. In this case, the formula for the real wage would change to Real wage = (Nominal wage ÷ Price level) × 100

Real wage ↑ → *Quantity supplied* of labor↑

Real wage ↓ → *Quantity supplied* of labor↓

In short, more individuals are willing to work, and current workers are willing to work more, at higher real wages than at lower real wages:

- The quantity demanded of labor is *inversely related* to the real wage: As the real wage rises, the quantity demanded of labor falls; as the real wage falls, the quantity demanded of labor rises:

Real wage ↑ → *Quantity demanded* of labor ↓

Real wage ↓ → *Quantity demanded* of labor ↑

In short, firms will employ more workers the cheaper it is to hire them.

So, suppose that a firm has agreed to pay its workers $30 an hour for the next three years and that it has hired 1,000 workers. When it agreed to that nominal wage, it thought that the price index would remain at 1.50 and that the real wage would stay at $20.

Now suppose the price index *falls* to 1.25. In that event, the real wage rises to $24 ($30 ÷ 1.25), which is higher than the firm expected when it agreed to lock in nominal wages at $30 an hour. If the firm had known that the real wage would turn out to be $24 (and not remain at $20), it would never have hired 1,000 workers. It would have hired, say, 800 workers instead.

So what does the firm do? As we stated, there is an inverse relationship between the real wage and the quantity demanded of labor (the number of workers that firms want to hire). Now that the real wage has risen (from $20 to $24), the firm cuts back on its labor (say, from 1,000 to 800 workers). With fewer workers working, less output is produced.

So, if nominal wages are sticky, a decrease in the price level (which pushes real wages up) will result in a decrease in output. This is what an upward-sloping *SRAS* curve represents: As the price level falls, the quantity supplied of goods and services declines. That is,

Decline in price level and constant nominal wage → Real wage ↑ → Firms hire fewer
workers → *Decline in quantity supplied of Real GDP*

Worker Misperceptions

Another explanation for the upward-sloping *SRAS* curve holds that workers may misperceive changes in the real wage. To illustrate, if the nominal wage is $30 an hour and the price level, as measured by a price index, is 1.50, then the real wage is $20. Now, suppose the nominal wage falls to $25 and the price level falls to 1.25. Then the real wage is still $20 ($25 ÷ 1.25 = $20), *but workers may not know this.* They know that their nominal wage has fallen (i.e., they are earning $25 an hour instead of $30). They also may know that the price level is lower, but they may not know initially *how much* lower the price level is. For example, suppose they mistakenly believe that the price level has fallen from 1.50 to 1.39. They will then think that their real wage has actually fallen from $20 ($30 ÷ 1.50) to $17.98 ($25 ÷ 1.39). In response to the misperceived falling real wage, workers may reduce the quantity of labor they are willing to supply. With fewer workers (resources), firms produce less.

So, if workers misperceive changes in the real wage, then a fall in the price level will bring about a decline in output, a situation that is illustrative of an upward-sloping *SRAS* curve:

Nominal wages and *price level decline* by equal percentage → Real wage
remains constant → But workers mistakenly think real wage has fallen → Workers reduce
quantity supplied of labor → *Less output is produced*

8-3b What Puts the "Short Run" in the *SRAS* Curve?

According to most macroeconomists, the *SRAS* curve slopes upward because of sticky wages or worker misperceptions. No matter what the explanation, though, things are likely to change over time. Wages will not be sticky forever (labor contracts will expire), and workers will figure out that they misperceived changes in the real wage. Only for a certain period—identified as the short run—are these issues likely to be relevant.

8-3c Changes in Short-Run Aggregate Supply: Shifts in the *SRAS* Curve

A change in the quantity supplied of Real GDP is brought about by a change in the price level and is shown as a *movement* along the *SRAS* curve. But what can change short-run aggregate supply? What can *shift* the *SRAS* curve? The factors that can shift the *SRAS* curve are wage rates, prices of nonlabor inputs, productivity, and supply shocks.

Wage Rates   Changes in wage rates have a major impact on the position of the *SRAS* curve because wage costs are usually a firm's major cost item. The impact of a rise or fall in equilibrium wage rates can be understood in terms of the following equation:

$$\text{Profit per unit} = \text{Price per unit} - \text{Cost per unit}$$

Higher wage rates mean higher costs and, at constant prices, translate into lower profits and a reduction in the number of units (of a given good) that firms will want to produce. Lower wage rates mean lower costs and, at constant prices, translate into higher profits and an increase in the number of units (of a given good) firms will decide to produce.

The impact of higher and lower equilibrium wages is shown in Exhibit 8. At the given price level, P_1 on $SRAS_1$, the quantity supplied of Real GDP is Q_1. When wage rates become higher, a firm's profits at a given price level decrease. Consequently, the firm reduces production. In the diagram, this change corresponds to moving from Q_1 to Q_2, which, at the given price level, is

> **EXHIBIT 8**
>
> **Wage Rates and a Shift in the Short-Run Aggregate Supply Curve**
>
> A rise in wage rates shifts the short-run aggregate supply curve leftward. A fall in wage rates shifts the short-run aggregate supply curve rightward.

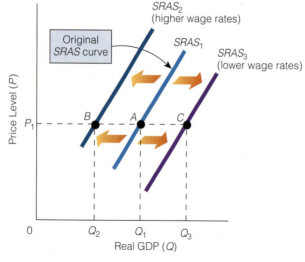

point B on a new aggregate supply curve (SRAS$_2$). Thus, a rise in equilibrium wage rates leads to a leftward shift in the aggregate supply curve. For a fall in equilibrium wage rates, the steps are simply reversed.

Prices of Nonlabor Inputs

There are other inputs to the production process besides labor. Changes in the prices of nonlabor inputs affect the *SRAS* curve in the same way that changes in wage rates do: An increase in the price of a nonlabor input (e.g., oil) shifts the *SRAS* curve leftward; a decrease in its price shifts the *SRAS* curve rightward.

Productivity   *Productivity* is the output produced per unit of input employed over some length of time. Although various

> EXHIBIT 9

Changes in Short-Run Aggregate Supply

The flowcharts show how short-run aggregate supply changes with changes in several factors.

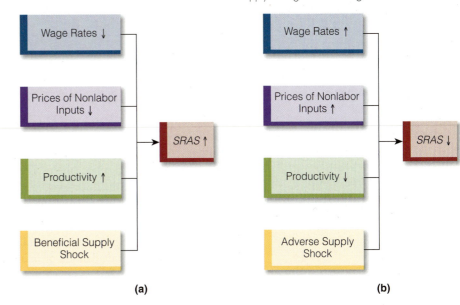

(a)   (b)

inputs can become more productive, let's consider the labor input. An increase in labor productivity means that businesses will produce more output with the same amount of labor, causing the *SRAS* curve to shift rightward. A decrease in labor productivity means that businesses will produce less output with the same amount of labor, causing the *SRAS* curve to shift leftward. A host of factors lead to increased labor productivity, including a more educated labor force, a larger stock of capital goods, and technological advancements.

Supply Shocks   Major natural or institutional changes that affect aggregate supply are referred to as *supply shocks*. Supply shocks are of two varieties. *Adverse supply shocks* shift the *SRAS* curve leftward. Bad weather that wipes out a large part of the Midwestern wheat crop would be an adverse supply shock. So would a major cutback in the supply of oil coming to the United States from the Middle East. *Beneficial supply shocks* shift the *SRAS* curve rightward; for example, a major oil discovery or unusually good weather leading to increased production of a food staple would be a beneficial supply shock. Both kinds of supply shock are reflected in resource or input prices.

Exhibit 9 summarizes the factors that affect short-run aggregate supply.

8-3d Something More to Come: Peoples' Expectations

So far in this chapter, we have said that several factors are capable of shifting the *SRAS* curve: wage rates, prices of nonlabor inputs, productivity, and supply shocks. In a later chapter (Chapter 16), we will begin to discuss how peoples' expectations (of certain key economic variables) can affect the price level and Real GDP. At that point, we will add another factor that can shift the *SRAS* curve: the *expected price level*.

1. Explain what happens to the short-run aggregate supply (*SRAS*) curve if wage rates decline.

2. Give an example of an increase in labor productivity.

3. Discuss the details of the worker misperceptions explanation for the upward-sloping *SRAS* curve.

Short-Run Equilibrium

The condition in the economy when the quantity demanded of Real GDP equals the (short-run) quantity supplied of Real GDP. This condition is met where the aggregate demand curve intersects the short-run aggregate supply curve.

8-4 PUTTING *AD* AND *SRAS* TOGETHER: SHORT-RUN EQUILIBRIUM

In this section, we put aggregate demand and short-run aggregate supply together to show how short-run equilibrium in the economy is achieved. Aggregate demand and short-run aggregate supply determine the price level and Real GDP in the short run.

8-4a How Short-Run Equilibrium in the Economy Is Achieved

Exhibit 10 shows an aggregate demand (*AD*) curve and a short-run aggregate supply (*SRAS*) curve. The quantity demanded of Real GDP and the quantity supplied of Real GDP are illustrated at three different price levels: P_1, P_2, and P_E.

At P_1, the quantity supplied of Real GDP (Q_2) is greater than the quantity demanded (Q_1). In other words, there is a surplus of goods. As a result, the price level drops, firms decrease output, and consumers increase consumption. Why do consumers increase consumption as the price level drops? (*Hint:* Think of the real balance, interest rate, and international trade effects.)

At P_2, the quantity supplied of Real GDP (Q_1) is less than the quantity demanded (Q_2). In other words, there is a shortage of goods. As a result, the price level rises, firms increase output, and consumers decrease consumption.

In instances of both surplus and shortage, economic forces are moving the economy toward E, where the quantity demanded of Real GDP equals the (short-run) quantity supplied of Real GDP. E is the point of **short-run equilibrium,** P_E is the short-run equilibrium price level, and Q_E is the short-run equilibrium Real GDP.

A change in aggregate demand, in short-run aggregate supply, or in both will obviously affect the price level and/ or Real GDP. For example, an increase in aggregate demand raises the equilibrium

> **EXHIBIT 10**

Short-Run Equilibrium

At P_1, the quantity supplied of Real GDP is greater than the quantity demanded. As a result, the price level falls and firms decrease output. At P_2, the quantity demanded of Real GDP is greater than the quantity supplied. As a result, the price level rises and firms increase output. Short-run equilibrium occurs at point E, where the quantity demanded of

Real GDP equals the (short-run) quantity supplied. This point is the intersection of the aggregate demand (*AD*) curve and the short-run aggregate supply (*SRAS*) curve. (*Note:* Although real-world *AD* and *SRAS* curves can, and likely do, have some curvature to them, we have drawn both as straight lines. This depiction does not affect the analysis. Whenever the analysis is not disturbed, we follow suit throughout this text.)

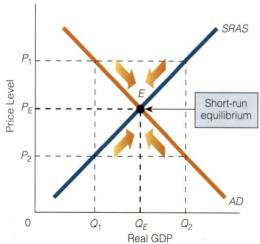

> **EXHIBIT 11**

Changes in Short-Run Equilibrium in the Economy

(a) An increase in aggregate demand increases the price level and Real GDP. (b) An increase in short-run aggregate supply decreases the price level and increases Real GDP. (c) A decrease in short-run aggregate supply increases the price level and decreases Real GDP.

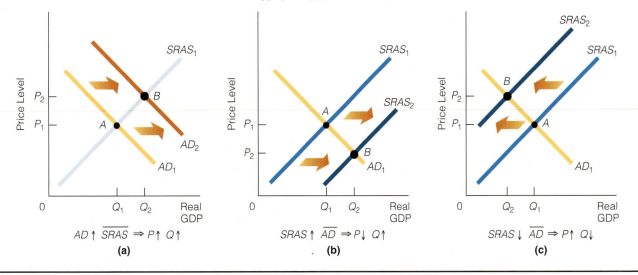

price level and, in the short run, Real GDP [Exhibit 11(a)]. An increase in short-run aggregate supply lowers the equilibrium price level and raises Real GDP [Exhibit 11(b)]. A decrease in short-run aggregate supply raises the equilibrium price level and lowers Real GDP [Exhibit 11(c)].

8-4b Thinking in Terms of Short-Run Equilibrium Changes in the Economy

We know that certain factors can lead to a change in aggregate demand or in short-run aggregate supply. In addition, we know that if either aggregate demand or short-run aggregate supply changes, the price level and Real GDP will also change in the short run.

Exhibit 12 shows us how changes in *AD* or *SRAS* can affect the economy and change *P* and *Q*. (Refer to Exhibit 12 as we continue our discussion.) For example, when a factor changes, we ask ourselves a series of questions:

- Does the factor affect the *AD* curve or the *SRAS* curve? If the answer is neither, then there will be no change in either curve.

- If the answer is the *AD* curve, then does it shift to the right or to the left?

- If the answer is the *SRAS* curve, does it shift to the right or to the left?

After observing a shift in one or more curves, we identify the new equilibrium and what has happened to both the price level and Real GDP in the short run.

To illustrate, suppose there is an adverse supply shock in the economy:

- The shock shifts the *SRAS* curve leftward.

- Nothing has changed on the demand side of the economy, so the *AD* curve remains stable.

- A leftward shift in the *SRAS* curve in the face of an unchanged *AD* curve increases the price level and decreases Real GDP.

> EXHIBIT 12

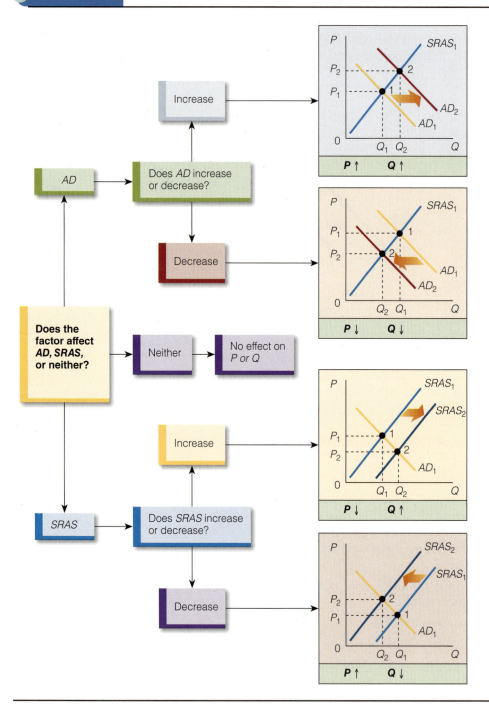

How a Factor Affects the Price Level and Real GDP in the Short Run

In the exhibit, P = price level and Q = Real GDP.

ECONOMICS 24/7

Can There Be More Than One Possible Cause?

Suppose an economy is in short-run equilibrium at a price level of 125 and a Real GDP level of $900 billion. As time passes, the price level rises to 130 and Real GDP rises to $955 billion. What caused the rise in both the price level and Real GDP?

If your answer is "an increase in aggregate demand," then you may be right. An increase in *AD* with no change in *SRAS* will lead to a higher price level and to greater Real GDP. [See Exhibit 13(a).]

But is that the only possible event that could lead to a higher price level and higher Real GDP? No: An increase in *AD* that is greater than an increase in *SRAS* could also lead to a rise in the price level and in Real GDP. [See Exhibit 13(b).]

Now, suppose again that the price level is initially 125 and Real GDP is $900 billion. As time passes, the price level declines to 120 and Real GDP rises to $955 billion. What could cause this event? One possible cause is a rise in *SRAS*. (The *SRAS* curve shifts rightward.)

[See Exhibit 13(c).] But that isn't the only possible cause. Another possible cause is an increase in *SRAS* that is greater than an increase in *AD*. [See Exhibit 13(d).] (As an aside, is there a third event that could have led to a decline in the price level and a rise in Real GDP? Consider an increase in *SRAS* that is greater than a decline in *AD*.)

What is the point here? Simply that, just because you have identified an event (such as change in *SRAS* only) that may explain the change in the price level and in Real GDP, it doesn't necessarily follow that you have identified the correct event. The correct event could be that a change in both *AD* and *SRAS* has brought about the change in the price level and in Real GDP that you have witnessed.

The opposite is true too. For example, just because you have identified a change in both *AD* and *SRAS* that can bring about about a change in the price level and in Real GDP, it doesn't necessarily follow that you are correct. It could have been that the change

> **EXHIBIT 13**

Changes in *AD* and *SRAS*

In (a), a rise in *AD* causes a rise in the price level and in Real GDP. This change in the price level and in Real GDP can also be brought about by a rise in *AD* that is greater than the rise in *SRAS*, as shown in (b). In (c), a rise in *SRAS* causes the price level to fall

and Real GDP to rise. These changes can also be brought about by a rise in *SRAS* that is greater than the rise in *AD*, as shown in (d). In (e), we see that a rise in *AD* that is equal to the rise in *SRAS* leads to an unchanged price level and to a higher Real GDP level.

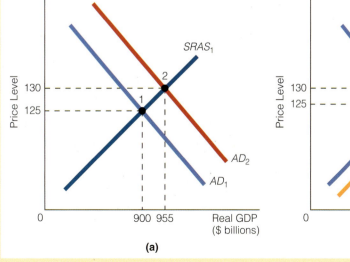

(a)

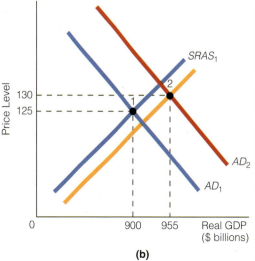

(b)

(Continued)

> **EXHIBIT 13** *(Continued)*

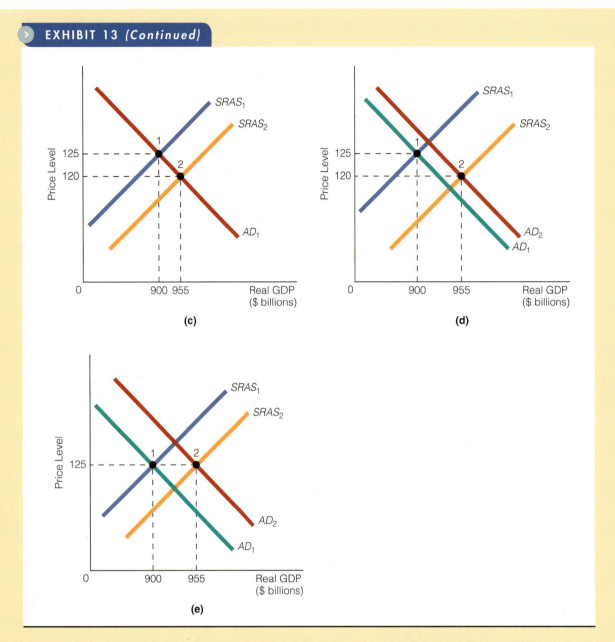

in the price level and in Real GDP were brought about by a change in only, say, *AD* and not *SRAS* too.

Finally, suppose once again that the price level is 125 and Real GDP is $900 billion. Time passes, and there is no change in the price level, but Real GDP rises to $955 billion. What happened? The answer is that both *AD* and *SRAS* increased by the same amount; that is, they both shifted to the right by the same amount. [See Exhibit 13(e).] This time, there is only one possible event (an increase in *AD* and *SRAS* by the same amount) that could have brought about the unchanged price level and the higher Real GDP.

In Dollars and in Oil In November 2007, the price of a barrel of oil was rising. On November 1, 2007, it had risen to $96, and in the same month the value of the dollar was falling in foreign exchange markets. In fact, the value of the dollar had been falling for some time. Although the value of $1 was €0.83 in January 2006, it had fallen to €0.69 by November 1, 2007. In other words, the dollar had depreciated over that period.

Now, what does all this have to do with the predicted change in the price level and in Real GDP?

We know that the falling value of the dollar would lead to greater U.S. exports, and that is exactly what was happening at the time. As a result, U.S. net exports were rising, pushing the *AD* curve in the economy to the right. But because oil prices were rising, the *SRAS* curve in the economy was shifting to the left. How would these two changes have affected Real GDP? The answer depends on the relative shifts of the *AD* and *SRAS* curves. Picture, in your mind's eye, the three possibilities:

- If the *AD* curve shifted rightward more than the *SRAS* curve shifted leftward, then Real GDP would have risen.

- If the *AD* curve shifted rightward by less than the *SRAS* curve shifted leftward, then Real GDP would have fallen.

- If the *AD* curve shifted rightward by the same amount as the *SRAS* curve shifted leftward, then Real GDP would have remained unchanged.

In all three cases, though, the price level would increase. Rising aggregate demand, combined with falling short-run aggregate supply, always results in a rising price level.

8-4c An Important Exhibit

Exhibit 14 summarizes the material discussed so far in this chapter. Specifically, much of our discussion has been about the economy in the short run, about changes in the price level (*P*), and about changes in Real GDP (*Q*) in the short run.

Exhibit 14 tells us that changes in *AD* and *SRAS* will change the price level and Real GDP in the short run. Then it shows which factors actually change *AD* and which change *SRAS*.

While referring to Exhibit 14, consider what a fall in the interest rate will do to *P* and *Q* in the short run. If the interest rate falls, both consumption (*C*) and investment (*I*) will rise. If both *C* and *I* rise, then *AD* will rise or the *AD* curve will shift rightward. If the *AD* curve shifts rightward, the price level (*P*) will rise and so will Real GDP (*Q*).

> **EXHIBIT 14**

A Summary Exhibit of *AD* and *SRAS*

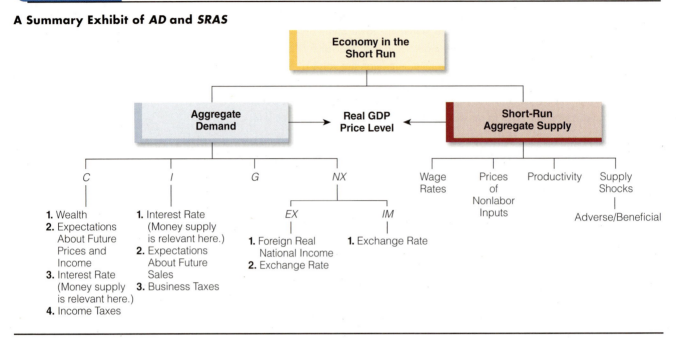

8-5 LONG-RUN AGGREGATE SUPPLY

In this section, we discuss long-run aggregate supply and draw a long-run aggregate supply (*LRAS*) curve. We also discuss long-run equilibrium and explain how it differs from short-run equilibrium.

8-5a Going from the Short Run to the Long Run

Natural Real GDP
The Real GDP that is produced at the natural unemployment rate. Also, the Real GDP that is produced when the economy is in long-run equilibrium.

Long-Run Aggregate Supply (*LRAS*) Curve
A curve that represents the output the economy produces when wages and prices have adjusted to their final equilibrium levels and when workers do not have any relevant misperceptions. The *LRAS* curve is a vertical line at the level of Natural Real GDP.

Graphically, short-run equilibrium is at the intersection of the *AD* curve and the (upward-sloping) *SRAS* curve. As explained earlier, economists give different reasons for an upward-sloping *SRAS* curve, which have to do with sticky wages or worker misperceptions. So, when either of these two conditions holds, short-run equilibrium identifies the Real GDP that the economy produces. In time, though, wages become unstuck, and misperceptions turn into accurate perceptions. In that event, the economy is said to be in the *long run*. In other words, the two conditions do not hold in the long run.

An important macroeconomic question is, "*Will the level of Real GDP that the economy produces in the long run be the same as in the short run?*" Most economists say that it will not. They argue that, in the long run, the economy produces the full-employment Real GDP, or the **Natural Real GDP** (Q_N). The aggregate supply curve that identifies the output the economy produces in the long run, the **long-run aggregate supply (*LRAS*) curve**, is portrayed as the vertical line in Exhibit 15.

ECONOMICS 24/7

Your First Job After College May Depend on the *AD* and *SRAS* Curves

There are some things that you can see with your physical eyes. For example, you can see a car with your physical eyes.

And then there are some things that you can see only with your mind's eye. For example, there actually is an *AD* curve in an economy, but no one has ever seen a real *AD* curve with his physical eyes. No one has walked into his backyard, looked up into the sky, and seen the country's *AD* curve. We can see *AD* curves only with our mind's eye. We then draw those *AD* curves on paper or a board.

Now, although we cannot see the real *AD* curve in the economy, we know that it exists, and we also know that its position on a two-dimensional diagram indicates your job prospects after college. Put it this way: You might have thought that learning what the *AD* curve looks like and what makes it shift right or left has nothing to do with you. But that's incorrect. To see why, suppose that you will be graduating from college in, say, two years. In two years, there will be an *AD* curve in the economy just as there is an *AD* curve in the economy right now.

But where will that *AD* curve in two years be positioned relative to the *AD* curve that exists right now? Let's suppose that, between now and then, something happens in the economy to shift the *AD* curve to the left. Will that matter to you? Well, think of what lower *AD* means in the economy, all other things remaining constant. It means that less Real GDP will be produced. Fewer houses will be built, fewer cars will be produced, and fewer attorney services will be demanded, among other things. Now ask again, Will that matter to you? It certainly will matter to you if, two years from now, when you graduate from college, you are looking for a job. Lower aggregate demand, which translates into less Real GDP, will translate into fewer employers visiting colleges to hire college graduates. It will translate into fewer employers reading your résumé and getting back to you for a job interview. Our point is a simple one: In a textbook or on a classroom board, the *AD* curve may look like something that is unrelated to you and your everyday life. But that isn't true at all. That *AD* curve may have much to do with how hard or easy it is for you to get your first job after college.

©racorn/Shutterstock.com

> **EXHIBIT 15**

Long-Run Aggregate Supply (*LRAS*) Curve

The LRAS curve represents the output the economy produces when all economywide adjustments have taken place and workers do not have any relevant misperceptions. It is a vertical line at the level of Natural Real GDP.

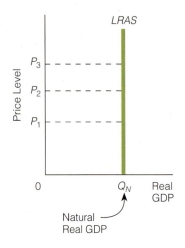

Long-run equilibrium identifies the level of Real GDP the economy produces when wages and prices have adjusted to their final equilibrium levels and when workers have no relevant misperceptions. Graphically, this point occurs at the intersection of the *AD* and *LRAS* curves. Further, the level of Real GDP that the economy produces in long-run equilibrium is the Natural Real GDP (Q_N).

8-5b Short-Run Equilibrium, Long-Run Equilibrium, and Disequilibrium

The two equilibrium states in an economy—short-run and long-run—are shown graphically in Exhibit 16. In Exhibit 16(a), the economy is at point 1, producing amount Q_1 of Real GDP. At point 1, the quantity supplied of Real GDP (in the short run) is equal to the quantity demanded of Real GDP, and both are Q_1. The economy is in short-run equilibrium. In Exhibit 16(b), the economy is at point 1, producing Q_N. In other words, it is producing Natural Real GDP. The economy is in long-run equilibrium when it produces Q_N.

Long-Run Equilibrium

The condition that exists in the economy when wages and prices have adjusted to their (final) equilibrium levels and when workers do not have any relevant misperceptions. Graphically, long-run equilibrium occurs at the intersection of the *AD* and *LRAS* curves.

In both short-run and long-run equilibrium, the quantity supplied of Real GDP equals the quantity demanded. So, what is the difference between short-run equilibrium and long-run equilibrium? In long-run equilibrium, the quantities supplied and demanded of Real GDP equal Natural Real GDP [Exhibit 16(b)]; in short-run equilibrium, the quantities supplied and demanded of Real GDP are either more than or less than Natural Real GDP.

Let's illustrate that difference with numbers. Suppose Q_N = $9.0 trillion. In long-run equilibrium, the quantity supplied of Real GDP equals the quantity demanded: $9.0 trillion. In short-run equilibrium, the quantity supplied of Real GDP equals the quantity demanded but neither equals $9.0 trillion. For example, the quantity supplied of Real GDP could equal the quantity demanded of Real GDP if each equals $8.5 trillion.

> **EXHIBIT 16**

Equilibrium States of the Economy

There are two equilibrium states in the economy: short-run equilibrium, shown in part (a), and long-run equilibrium, shown in part (b). During the time an economy moves from one equilibrium state to another, it is said to be in disequilibrium.

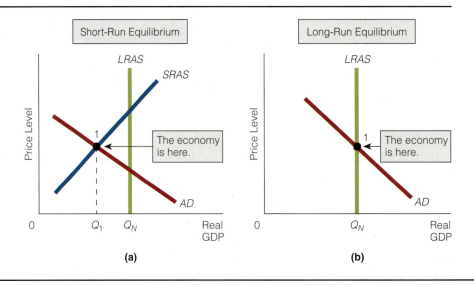

ECONOMICS 24/7

Reality Can Be Messy, and Correct Predictions Can Be Difficult to Make

In a textbook, we can change one factor and then trace its effects through the economy, ultimately to the price level and Real GDP. For instance, a decline in business taxes will lead to a rise in investment, which in turn will lead to a rise in aggregate demand. Now, assuming that SRAS has not changed, a rise in AD will lead to a rise in the price level and a rise in Real GDP. The relationships between the various factors are given as

$$\text{Business taxes} \downarrow \rightarrow C\uparrow \rightarrow AD\uparrow \rightarrow P\uparrow\, Q\uparrow$$

where C = consumption, AD = aggregate demand, P = price level, and Q = Real GDP.

In reality, though, more than one thing can change at a time. Or at a minimum, two or more things could change within a few days or weeks of each other. To illustrate, suppose a factor on the demand side of the economy changes at about the same time that a factor on the supply side changes. Specifically, suppose wealth rises at the same time that the price of nonlabor inputs rises. What ultimately happens to the price level and Real GDP? Let's break the problem down into small parts and find out:

1. A rise in wealth will raise AD. The AD curve shifts rightward.

2. A rise in nonlabor input prices will lower SRAS. The SRAS curve will shift leftward.

3. Because both the AD and SRAS curves are changing at the same time or at about the same time, the overall change in the price level and in Real GDP will depend on the relative shifts of the AD and SRAS curves.

4. If the AD curve shifts rightward by more than the SRAS curve shifts leftward, then the price level and Real GDP will rise. (You may want to draw these events.)

5. If, however, the AD curve shifts rightward by less than the SRAS curve shifts leftward, then the price level will rise and Real GDP will fall.

6. Finally, if the AD curve shifts rightward to the same degree that the SRAS curve shifts leftward, Real GDP will not change and the price level will rise.

All this has something to say about economists' predictions. Making correct predictions in economics is easy when only one thing changes and everything else remains constant. Making correct predictions is much harder when more than one thing changes at a time and when the changes pull the economy in opposite directions. We have seen a little of this type of complexity in our example. Specifically, although the increase in AD tends to raise Real GDP, the decrease in SRAS tends to lower it. What will be the final effect on Real GDP? As we have seen, it depends on the relative shifts in AD and SRAS.

The lesson: Reality in economics can be messy.

When the economy is in neither short-run nor long-run equilibrium, it is said to be in *disequilibrium*. Essentially, disequilibrium is the state of the economy as it moves from one short-run equilibrium to another or from short-run equilibrium to long-run equilibrium. In disequilibrium, the quantity supplied and the quantity demanded of Real GDP are not equal.

SELF-TEST

1. What is the difference between short-run equilibrium and long-run equilibrium?

2. Diagrammatically represent an economy that is in neither short-run nor long-run equilibrium.

Office  Hours

"What Purpose Does the AD–AS Framework Serve?"

STUDENT:

What purpose does the *AD–AS* framework serve?

INSTRUCTOR:

One purpose is to link some variables to other variables.

STUDENT:

How so?

INSTRUCTOR:

Well, consider a rise in income taxes. We learned in this chapter that a rise in income taxes will lead to a decline in consumption. And we know that a decline in consumption will lead to a decline in aggregate demand. Finally, we know that a decline in aggregate demand will lead to a decline in both the price level and Real GDP. In other words, the *AD–AS* framework helps us to link a rise in *income taxes* to a decline in both the *price level* and *Real GDP*.

STUDENT:

Oh, I see. It's sort of like the *AD–AS* framework is a road. We start at one point on the road (where income taxes are being raised), and then we follow the road until we come to the end (where the price level and Real GDP have declined).

INSTRUCTOR:

That's a good way of putting it. Let's now start at another point along the road. Let's start with a decline in wage rates.

STUDENT:

If wage rates decline, short-run aggregate supply increases (the *SRAS* curve shifts to the right). As a result, the price level declines and Real GDP rises.

INSTRUCTOR:

That's correct. Now let's go back to your original question: What purpose does the *AD–AS* framework serve? What would your answer be now?

STUDENT:

I think I would say what you said: "It links some variables to other variables." But I'd add that it provides an explanation for changes in the price level and in Real GDP too.

INSTRUCTOR:

Explain what you mean by that.

STUDENT:

Well, suppose someone were to ask me what might cause Real GDP to decline. Using the *AD–AS* framework, I would say that either a decline in *AD* or *SRAS* would lead to a decline in Real GDP. Then, if the person wanted more specificity, I could say that such things as an adverse supply shock, a decline in productivity, the U.S. dollar appreciating, and so on could lead to a decline in Real GDP.

INSTRUCTOR:

You make a good point.

Points to remember

1. The *AD–AS* framework serves to link some variables to others. For example, a change in income taxes can ultimately be linked to a change in the price level and in Real GDP.
2. The *AD–AS* framework helps us to understand changes in both the price level and Real GDP.

CHAPTER SUMMARY

AGGREGATE DEMAND

- Aggregate demand is the quantity demanded of all goods and services (Real GDP) at different price levels, *ceteris paribus.*

- The aggregate demand (*AD*) curve slopes downward, indicating an inverse relationship between the price level and the quantity demanded of Real GDP.

- The *AD* curve slopes downward because of the real balance effect, the interest rate effect, and the international trade effect.

- The real balance effect states that the inverse relationship between the price level and the quantity demanded of Real GDP is established through changes in the value of a person's monetary wealth, or money holdings. Specifically, a fall in the price level causes purchasing power to rise, increasing a person's monetary wealth. As people become wealthier, they buy more goods. By contrast, a rise in the price level causes purchasing power to fall, reducing a person's monetary wealth. As people become less wealthy, they buy fewer goods.

- The interest rate effect states that the inverse relationship between the price level and the quantity demanded of Real GDP is established through changes in the part of household and business spending that is sensitive to changes in interest rates. If the price level rises, a person needs more money to buy a fixed bundle of goods. In an effort to acquire more money, the person's demand for credit rises, as does the interest rate. As the interest rate rises, businesses and households borrow less and buy fewer goods. Thus, the quantity demanded of Real GDP falls. By contrast, if the price level falls, a person needs less money to buy a fixed bundle of goods. Part of the increase in a person's monetary wealth is saved, so the supply of credit rises and the interest rate falls. As the interest rate falls, businesses and households borrow more and buy more goods. Thus, the quantity demanded of Real GDP rises.

- The international trade effect states that the inverse relationship between the price level and the quantity demanded of Real GDP is established through foreign sector spending. Specifically, as the price level in the United States rises, U.S. goods become relatively more expensive than foreign goods and both Americans and foreigners buy fewer U.S. goods. The quantity demanded of U.S. Real GDP then falls. By contrast, as the price level in the United States falls, U.S. goods become relatively less expensive than foreign goods and both Americans and foreigners buy more U.S. goods. The quantity demanded of U.S. Real GDP then rises.

- At a given price level, a rise in consumption, investment, government purchases, or net exports will increase aggregate demand and shift the *AD* curve to the right. At a given price level, a fall in consumption, investment, government purchases, or net exports will decrease aggregate demand and shift the *AD* curve to the left.

FACTORS THAT CAN CHANGE C, I, AND NX (EX – IM) AND THEREFORE CHANGE AD

- The following factors can change consumption: wealth, expectations about future prices and income, the interest rate, and income taxes. The following factors can change investment: the interest rate, expectations about future sales, and business taxes. The following factors can change net exports (exports less imports): foreign real national income and the exchange rate. A change in the money supply can affect one or more spending components (e.g., consumption) and therefore affect aggregate demand.

MONEY SUPPLY AND VELOCITY

- Velocity is the average number of times a dollar is spent to buy final goods and services in a year.

- If the money supply and velocity are constant, a rise in one spending component (such as consumption) entails a decline in one or more other components. If either the money supply or velocity rises, a rise in one component does not entail a decline in the others.

SHORT-RUN AGGREGATE SUPPLY

- Aggregate supply is the quantity supplied of all goods and services (Real GDP) at different price levels, *ceteris paribus.*

- The short-run aggregate supply (*SRAS*) curve is upward sloping, indicating a direct relationship between the price level and the quantity supplied of Real GDP.

- A decrease in wage rates, a decrease in the price of nonlabor inputs, an increase in productivity, and beneficial supply shocks all shift the *SRAS* curve to the right. An increase in wage rates, an increase in the price of nonlabor inputs, a decrease in productivity, and adverse supply shocks all shift the *SRAS* curve to the left.

SHORT-RUN EQUILIBRIUM

- Graphically, short-run equilibrium exists at the intersection of the *AD* and *SRAS* curves. A shift in either or both of these curves can change the price level and, hence, Real GDP. For example, an increase in aggregate demand increases the price level and Real GDP, *ceteris paribus.*

LONG-RUN AGGREGATE SUPPLY AND LONG-RUN EQUILIBRIUM

- The long-run aggregate supply (*LRAS*) curve is vertical at the Natural Real GDP level.

- Graphically, long-run equilibrium exists at the intersection of the *AD* and *LRAS* curves. It is the condition that exists in the economy when all economywide adjustments have taken place and workers do not hold any (relevant) misperceptions. In long-run equilibrium, the quantity demanded of Real GDP equals the quantity supplied of Real GDP, which in turn equals Natural Real GDP.

THREE STATES OF AN ECONOMY

- An economy can be in short-run equilibrium, long-run equilibrium, or disequilibrium.

KEY TERMS AND CONCEPTS

Aggregate Demand	Interest Rate Effect	Depreciation	Short-Run Equilibrium
Aggregate Demand (*AD*) Curve	International Trade Effect	Velocity	Natural Real GDP
	Wealth	Aggregate Supply	Long-Run Aggregate Supply (*LRAS*) Curve
Real Balance Effect	Exchange Rate	Short-Run Aggregate Supply (*SRAS*) Curve	
Monetary Wealth	Appreciation		Long-Run Equilibrium
Purchasing Power			

VIDEO QUESTIONS AND PROBLEMS

Video Questions and Problems are available on MindTap for Arnold 12e or by searching for Arnold on www.cengagebrain.com

1. Explain how the real balance effect works?

2. Suppose that business taxes and wage rates decline and that any change in aggregate demand is greater than any change in short-run aggregate supply. Explain and diagrammatically represent the changes in the price level and Real GDP in the short run.

3. How will either the *AD* curve or the *SRAS* curve shift as a result of each of the following changes:

   a. a rise in the interest rate

   b. an adverse supply shock

   c. a rise in wealth

4. Using the *AD–SRAS–LRAS* model, explain and diagrammatically represent the difference between equilibrium in the short run and equilibrium in the long run.

5. Explain what happens to U.S. net exports and to U.S. aggregate demand as the dollar depreciates.

QUESTIONS AND PROBLEMS

1. Is aggregate demand a specific dollar amount? For example, is it correct to say that aggregate demand is $9 trillion this year?

2. Explain each of the following: (a) real balance effect, (b) interest rate effect, and (c) international trade effect.

3. Graphically portray (a) a change in the quantity demanded of Real GDP and (b) a change in aggregate demand.

4. There is a difference between a change in the interest rate that is brought about by a change in the price level and a change in the interest rate that is brought about by a change in some factor other than the price level. The first will change the quantity demanded of Real GDP, and the second will change the *AD* curve. Do you agree or disagree with this statement? Explain your answer.

5. The amount of Real GDP (real output) that households are willing and able to buy may change if there is a change in either (a) the price level or (b) some nonprice factor, such as wealth, interest rates, and the like. Do you agree or disagree? Explain your answer.

6. Explain what happens to aggregate demand in each of the following cases:

   a. The interest rate rises.

   b. Wealth falls.

   c. The dollar depreciates relative to foreign currencies.

   d. Households expect lower prices in the future.

   e. Business taxes rise.

7. Explain what is likely to happen to U.S. export and import spending as a result of the dollar depreciating in value.

8. Explain how expectations about future prices and income will affect consumption.

9. Explain how expectations about future sales will affect investment.

10. How will an increase in the money supply affect aggregate demand?

11. Under what conditions can consumption rise without some other spending component declining?

12. Can total spending be a greater dollar amount than the money supply? Explain your answer.

13. Will a direct increase in the price of U.S. goods relative to foreign goods lead to a change in the quantity demanded of Real GDP or to a change in aggregate demand? Will a change in the exchange rate that subsequently increases the price of U.S. goods relative to foreign goods lead to a change in the quantity demanded of Real GDP or to a change in aggregate demand? Explain your answers.

14. Explain how each of the following will affect short-run aggregate supply:

   a. An increase in wage rates

   b. A beneficial supply shock

   c. An increase in the productivity of labor

   d. A decrease in the price of a nonlabor resource (e.g., oil)

15. What is the difference between a change in the quantity supplied of Real GDP and a change in short-run aggregate supply?

16. A change in the price level affects which of the following?

   a. The quantity demanded of Real GDP

   b. Aggregate demand

   c. Short-run aggregate supply

   d. The quantity supplied of Real GDP

17. In the short run, what is the impact on the price level and Real GDP of each of the following?

   a. An increase in consumption brought about by a decrease in interest rates

   b. A decrease in exports brought about by the dollar appreciating

   c. A rise in wage rates

   d. A beneficial supply shock

   e. An adverse supply shock

   f. A decline in productivity

18. Identify the details of each of the following explanations for an upward-sloping *SRAS* curve:

   a. Sticky-wage explanation

   b. Worker-misperception explanation

19. What is the difference between short-run equilibrium and long-run equilibrium?

20. An economist is sitting in the Oval Office of the White House, across the desk from the president of the United States. The president asks, "How does the unemployment rate look for the next quarter?" The economist answers, "It's not good. I don't think Real GDP is going to be as high as we initially thought. The problem seems to be foreign income; it's just not growing at the rate we thought it was going to grow." How can foreign income affect U.S. Real GDP?

WORKING WITH NUMBERS AND GRAPHS

1. Suppose that, at a price index of 154, the quantity demanded of U.S. Real GDP is $10.0 trillion worth of goods. Do these data represent aggregate demand or a point on an aggregate demand curve? Explain your answer.

2. Diagrammatically represent the short-run effect of each of the following on the price level and on Real GDP:

   a. An increase in wealth

   b. An increase in wage rates

   c. An increase in labor productivity

3. Diagrammatically represent each of the following, and identify its short-run effect on Real GDP and the price level:

   a. An increase in *SRAS* that is greater than the increase in *AD*

   b. A decrease in *AD* that is greater than the increase in *SRAS*

   c. An increase in *SRAS* that is less than the increase in *AD*

4. In the following figure, which part is representative of each of the following?

   a. A decrease in wage rates

   b. An increase in the price level

   c. A beneficial supply shock

   d. An increase in the price of nonlabor inputs

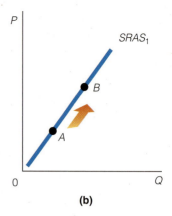

(b)

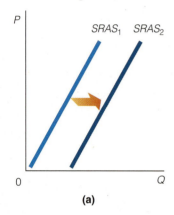

(a)

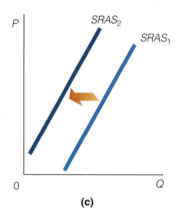

(c)

CLASSICAL MACROECONOMICS AND THE SELF-REGULATING ECONOMY

Hechtenberg/Caro/Alamy

9-1 THE CLASSICAL VIEW

The term *classical economics* is often used to refer to an era in the history of economic thought that stretched from about 1750 to the early 1900s. Although classical economists lived and wrote many years ago, their ideas are often employed by some modern-day economists.

9-1a Classical Economists and Say's Law

You know from your study of supply and demand that markets can experience temporary shortages and surpluses, such as a surplus in the apple market. But can the economy have a general surplus—that is, a general glut of goods and services? The classical economists thought not, largely because they believed in Say's law (named after Jean-Baptiste Say, a French economist and businessman who lived in the late eighteenth and early nineteenth century). In its simplest version, **Say's law** states that supply creates its own demand.

The law is most easily understood in terms of a barter economy. Consider a person baking bread in such an economy; the baker is a supplier of bread. According to Say, the

Say's Law
Supply creates its own demand. Production creates enough demand to purchase all the goods and services the economy produces.

baker works at his trade because he plans to demand other goods. As he is baking bread, the baker is thinking of the goods and services he will obtain in exchange for the bread. Thus, his act of supplying bread is linked to his demand for other goods. Supply creates its own demand.

If supplying some goods leads to a simultaneous demand for other goods, then Say's law implies that there cannot be either (1) a general overproduction of goods (a time during which supply in the economy is greater than demand) or (2) a general underproduction of goods (a time during which demand in the economy is greater than supply).

But what if the baker is baking bread in a money economy? Does Say's law hold? Over a certain period, the baker earns an income as a result of supplying bread, but what does he do with the income? One use of the money is to buy goods and services. However, his demand for goods and services does not necessarily match the income that he generates by supplying bread. The baker may spend less than his full income, putting some away as savings. So we might think that Say's law does not hold in a money economy because the act of supplying goods and services—thus earning income—need not create an equal amount of demand.

But the classical economists disagreed. They argued that, even in a money economy, in which individuals sometimes spend less than their full incomes, Say's law still holds. Their argument was partly based on the assumption of interest rate flexibility.

9-1b Classical Economists and Interest Rate Flexibility

For Say's law to hold in a money economy, the funds saved must give rise to an equal amount of funds invested; that is, what leaves the spending stream through one door must enter it through another door. If not, then some of the income earned from supplying goods may not be used to demand goods (good-bye, Say's law). As a result, goods will be overproduced.

The classical economists argued that saving is matched by an equal amount of investment because of interest rate flexibility in the credit market. In Exhibit 1, I represents investment and S represents saving. I_1 is downward sloping, indicating an inverse relationship between the amount of funds firms invest and the interest rate (i). The reason for the downward slope is straightforward: The interest rate is the cost of borrowing funds. The higher the interest rate is, the fewer funds firms borrow and invest; the lower the interest rate, the more funds firms borrow and invest.

S_1 is upward sloping, indicating a direct relationship between the amount of funds that households save and the interest rate. The reason is that the higher the interest rate is, the higher the reward is for saving (or the higher the opportunity cost of consuming). So, fewer funds are consumed and more funds are saved. Market-equilibrating forces move the credit market to interest rate i_1 and the equilibrium point to E_1. At E_1, the number of dollars households save ($100,000) equals the number of dollars firms invest ($100,000).

Suppose now that saving increases at each interest rate level. In Exhibit 1, the saving increase is represented by a rightward shift in the saving curve from S_1 to S_2. The classical economists believed that an increase in saving puts downward pressure on the interest rate; accordingly, it would move to i_2, thereby increasing the number of dollars firms invest. Ultimately, the number of dollars households save ($120,000) once again equals the number of dollars firms invest ($120,000). Again, interest rate flexibility ensures that saving equals investment. (What goes out one door comes in the

> **EXHIBIT 1**

The Classical View of the Credit Market

In classical theory, the interest rate is flexible and adjusts so that saving equals investment. Thus, if saving increases and the saving curve shifts rightward from S_1 to S_2 (arrow 1), the increase in saving eventually puts pressure on the interest rate and moves it downward from i_1 to i_2 (arrow 2). A new equilibrium is established at E_2 (arrow 3), where once again the amount households save equals the amount firms invest.

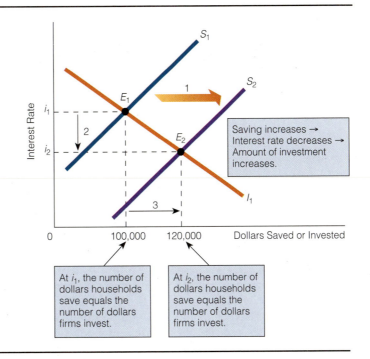

Saving increases → Interest rate decreases → Amount of investment increases.

At i_1, the number of dollars households save equals the number of dollars firms invest.

At i_2, the number of dollars households save equals the number of dollars firms invest.

other.) In short, changes in the interest rate uphold Say's law in a money economy in which there is saving.

Let's use a few numbers to illustrate what classical economists were saying. Suppose that, at a given price level, total expenditures (*TE*) in a very tiny economy are $5,000. Total expenditures (total spending on domestic goods and services) equals the sum of consumption (*C*), investment (*I*), government purchases (*G*), and net exports (*EX − IM*). Thus, if $C = \$3,000$, $I = \$600$, $G = \$1,200$, and $EX − IM = \$200$, then

$$TE + C + I + G + (EX - IM)$$

$$\$5,000 = \$3,000 + \$600 + \$1,200 + \$200$$

The $5,000 worth of goods and services that the four sectors of the economy want to purchase also happens to be the exact dollar amount of goods and services that suppliers want to sell.

What happens when saving is increased in the economy? Saving (*S*) is equal to the amount of a person's disposable income (Y_d) minus consumption (*C*):

$$\text{Saving } (S) = \text{Disposable income } (Y_d) - \text{Consumption } (C)$$

For example, if Harriet earns a disposable income of $40,000 a year and spends $38,000, she saves $2,000.

EXHIBIT 2

The Classical View of Say's Law in a Money Economy

According to classical economists, a decrease in consumption and subsequent increase in saving will be matched by an equal increase in investment. Thus, there is no change in total expenditures.

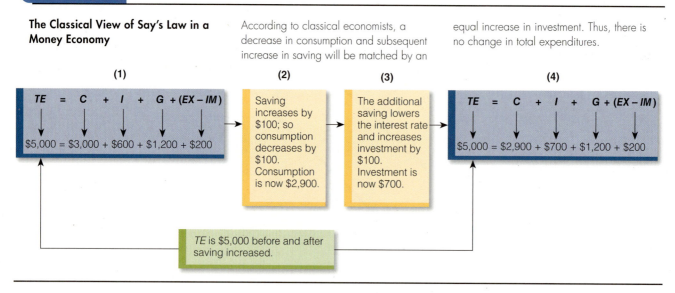

For saving to increase, consumption must decrease. (See Exhibit 2.) If saving increases by $100, then consumption must fall from $3,000 to $2,900. At first glance, this statement seems to imply that total expenditures will fall to $4,900. But classical economists disagreed. Their ideas implied that investment will increase by $100, going from $600 to $700. Total expenditures will remain constant at $5,000 and will be equal to the dollar amount of the goods and services that suppliers want to sell. Thus, we have

$$TE = C + I + G + (EX - IM)$$

$$\$5,000 = \$2,900 + \$700 + \$1,200 + \$200$$

According to the classical view of the economy, then, Say's law holds both in a barter economy and in a money economy. In a money economy, according to classical economists, interest rates will adjust to equate saving and investment. Therefore, any fall in consumption (and consequent rise in saving) will be matched by an equal rise in investment. In essence, at a given price level, total expenditures will not decrease as a result of an increase in saving.

What does an increase in saving imply for aggregate demand (*AD*)? An earlier chapter explains that aggregate demand changes only if total spending in the economy changes at a given price level. Therefore, because total spending does not change as a result of an increase in saving, aggregate demand does not change.

9-1c Classical Economists on Prices and Wages: Both Are Flexible

Classical economists believed that most, if not all, markets are competitive; that is, supply and demand operate in all markets. If, for example, the labor market has a surplus, the surplus will be temporary. Soon the wage rate will decline, and the quantity

ECONOMICS 24/7

Is Saving the Same as "Not Spending"?

Here is what you sometimes hear people say:

> The economy is badly off right now (production is down, unemployment is up) and it requires a big dose of spending to pick things up. If people would simply start spending more money—if they would simply buy more goods and services—then firms would sell more goods and services. And to sell more goods and services, the firms would need to produce more goods and services. And to produce more goods and services, they would need to hire more people. That would end up lowering the unemployment rate. Plus, those people who are now working (who weren't working before) will have income to spend, adding even more spending power to the economy and making things even better.

Now, if what these people say here is correct (spending is good for the economy), then saving (not spending) must be bad for the

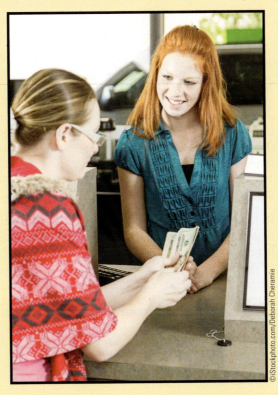

©iStockphoto.com/Deborah Cheramie

economy. If spending gets production up and unemployment down, then not spending (in other words, saving) must cause production to move down and unemployment to move up.

But what does our classical macroeconomic model tell us? What does it have to say about saving being "not spending"? Well, it tells us that saving may be the same as "not spending on consumer goods," but saving is not the same as "not spending at all." If you look back at Exhibit 1, an increase in saving shifts the savings curve to the right, lowering the interest rate; a lower interest rate then turns that extra savings into more investment. And, lest we forget, investment is spending: it is the spending undertaken by the business sector of the economy.

To the classical macroeconomist, money that leaves the spending stream at one point (resulting in less consumption spending) can very easily and likely enter the spending stream at another point (resulting in more investment spending). What goes out of one door enters through another door. To the person who argues that saving is "not spending," the classical macroeconomist is there to say "false."

supplied of labor will equal the quantity demanded of it. Similarly, given a shortage in the labor market, the wage rate will rise and the quantity supplied will equal the quantity demanded.

What holds for wages in the labor market holds for prices in the goods-and-services market. Prices will adjust quickly to any surpluses or shortages, and equilibrium will be quickly reestablished. In short, the classical view is that prices and wages are flexible: They rise and decline in response to shortages and surpluses.

SELF-TEST

(Answers to Self-Test questions are in Answers to Self-Test Questions at the back of the book.)

1. Explain Say's law in terms of a barter economy.

2. According to classical economists, if saving rises and consumption spending falls, will total spending in the economy decrease? Explain your answer.

3. What is the classical position on prices and wages?

9-2 THREE STATES OF THE ECONOMY

The background information in this section will enable you to understand the views of economists who believe that the economy is self-regulating. Specifically, we discuss three states of the economy, the correspondence between the labor market and the three states of the economy, and more.

9-2a Real GDP and Natural Real GDP: Three Possibilities

In the last chapter, Natural Real GDP was defined as the Real GDP produced at the natural unemployment rate. Real GDP at that rate is produced when the economy is in long-run equilibrium.

Economists often refer to three possible states of an economy when they consider the relationship between Real GDP and Natural Real GDP:

- Real GDP is less than Natural Real GDP.
- Real GDP is greater than Natural Real GDP.
- Real GDP is equal to Natural Real GDP.

Let's now graphically portray each of these three possible states of the economy.

Real GDP Is Less Than Natural Real GDP (Recessionary Gap)   Exhibit 3(a) shows an
AD curve, an $SRAS$ curve, and the $LRAS$ curve. It also shows that Natural Real GDP (Q_N) is produced in the long run.

Short-run equilibrium is at the intersection of the AD and $SRAS$ curves, so, in Exhibit 3(a), short-run equilibrium is at point 1. The Real GDP level that the economy is producing at point 1 is designated by Q_1.

Now, compare Q_1 with Q_N. Obviously, Q_1 is less than Q_N. In other words, the economy is currently producing a level of Real GDP in the short run that is less than its Natural Real GDP level. When the Real GDP that the economy is producing is less than its Natural Real GDP, the economy is said to be in a **recessionary gap**.

Recessionary Gap
The condition in which the Real GDP that the economy is producing is less than the Natural Real GDP and the unemployment rate is greater than the natural unemployment rate.

Real GDP Is Greater Than Natural Real GDP (Inflationary Gap)   In Exhibit 3(b),
the AD and $SRAS$ curves intersect at point 1, so short-run equilibrium is at point 1. The Real GDP level that the economy is producing at point 1 is designated by Q_1. Again, compare Q_1 with Q_N. Obviously, Q_1 is greater than Q_N. In other words, the economy is currently producing a level of Real GDP in the short run that is greater than its Natural Real GDP level, or potential output. When the Real GDP that the economy

> EXHIBIT 3

Real GDP and Natural Real GDP: Three Possibilities

In (a), the economy is in short-run equilibrium at a Real GDP level of Q_1. Q_N is Natural Real GDP, or the potential output of the economy. Notice that $Q_1 < Q_N$. When this condition ($Q_1 < Q_N$) exists, the economy is said to be in a recessionary gap.

In (b), the economy is in short-run equilibrium at a Real GDP level of Q_1. Q_N is Natural Real GDP, or the potential output of the economy. Notice that $Q_1 > Q_N$. When this condition ($Q_1 > Q_N$) exists, the economy is said to be in an inflationary gap.

In (c), the economy is operating at a Real GDP level of Q_1, which is equal to Q_N. In other words, the economy is producing its Natural Real GDP, or potential output. When this condition ($Q_1 = Q_N$) exists, the economy is said to be in long-run equilibrium.

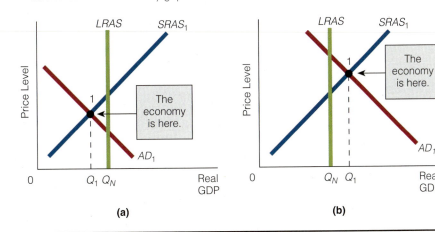

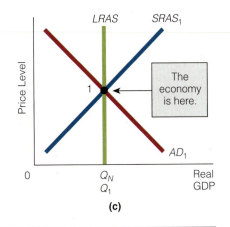

(a)   (b)   (c)

is producing is greater than its Natural Real GDP, the economy is said to be in an **inflationary gap**.

Real GDP Is Equal to Natural Real GDP (Long-Run Equilibrium)
In Exhibit 3(c), the *AD* and *SRAS* curves indicate that short-run equilibrium is at point 1. The Real GDP level that the economy is producing at point 1 is designated by Q_1.

Once more, compare Q_1 and Q_N. This time, Q_1 is equal to Q_N. In other words, the economy is currently producing a level of Real GDP that is equal to its Natural Real GDP, or potential output. When the Real GDP that the economy is producing is equal to its Natural Real GDP, the economy is in *long-run equilibrium*.

Inflationary Gap
The condition in which the Real GDP that the economy is producing is greater than the Natural Real GDP and the unemployment rate is less than the natural unemployment rate.

THINKING LIKE AN ECONOMIST

Thinking in Threes The economist often thinks in threes. For the economist, a market either (1) has a shortage, (2) has a surplus, or (3) is in equilibrium. Similarly, for the economist, an economy is in

• either a recessionary gap, producing a level of Real GDP lower than Natural Real GDP,

• or an inflationary gap, producing a level of Real GDP higher than Natural Real GDP,

• or long-run equilibrium, producing a level of Real GDP equal to Natural Real GDP.

9-2b The Labor Market and the Three States of the Economy

If the economy can be in three possible states, so can the labor market. In what follows, we identify the three possible states of the labor market and then tie each to a possible state of the economy.

We know that the labor market consists of the demand for, and the supply of, labor. Like a goods market, the labor market can manifest (1) equilibrium, (2) a shortage, or (3) a surplus. So the three possible states of the labor market are as follows:

- *Equilibrium.* When the labor market is in equilibrium, the quantity demanded of labor is equal to the quantity supplied.

- *Shortage.* When the labor market has a shortage, the quantity demanded of labor is greater than the quantity supplied.

- *Surplus.* When the labor market has a surplus, the quantity supplied of labor is greater than the quantity demanded.

Recessionary Gap and the Labor Market

The unemployment rate that exists when the economy produces Natural Real GDP is, of course, the natural unemployment rate. So if the economy is in a recessionary gap, is the labor market in equilibrium or does it have a shortage or a surplus?

To answer this question, suppose the economy is in a recessionary gap, producing Real GDP of $9 trillion (worth of goods and services) when Natural Real GDP, or potential output, is $10 trillion. Then, is the existing unemployment rate, producing $9 trillion worth of goods and services, greater or less than the natural unemployment rate that exists when the economy is producing $10 trillion worth of goods and services? In fact, the unemployment rate is greater than the natural unemployment rate, because fewer workers are needed to produce a Real GDP of $9 trillion than are needed to produce a Real GDP of $10 trillion. *Ceteris paribus,* the unemployment rate will be higher at a Real GDP level of $9 trillion than it is at a level of $10 trillion.

So, when the economy is in a recessionary gap, the unemployment rate is *higher* than the natural unemployment rate. This conclusion implies a surplus in the labor market: The quantity supplied of labor is greater than the quantity demanded; that is, more people want to work than there are jobs available. In sum,

> *If the economy is in a recessionary gap, the unemployment rate is higher than the natural unemployment rate and a surplus exists in the labor market.*

Inflationary Gap and the Labor Market

Now suppose the economy is in an inflationary gap, producing a Real GDP level of $11 trillion (worth of goods and services) when Natural Real GDP, or potential output, is $10 trillion.

Again, the unemployment rate that exists when the economy produces Natural Real GDP is the natural unemployment rate. Is the unemployment rate that exists when the economy is producing $11 trillion worth of goods and services greater or less than the natural unemployment rate when the economy is producing $10 trillion worth? The unemployment rate is less than the natural unemployment rate because more workers are needed to produce a Real GDP of $11 trillion than are needed to produce a Real GDP of $10 trillion. *Ceteris paribus,* the unemployment rate will be lower at a Real GDP level of $11 trillion than it is at $10 trillion.

So, when the economy is in an inflationary gap, the unemployment rate is *lower* than the natural unemployment rate. This conclusion implies a shortage in the labor market:

The quantity demanded of labor is greater than the quantity supplied; that is, more jobs are available than there are people who want to work. In sum,

If the economy is in an inflationary gap, the unemployment rate is less than the natural unemployment rate and a shortage exists in the labor market.

Long-Run Equilibrium and the Labor Market   Finally, suppose the economy is in long-run equilibrium. That is, it is producing a Real GDP level equal to Natural Real GDP. In this state, the unemployment rate in the economy is the same as the natural unemployment rate. This conclusion implies that the labor market has neither a shortage nor a surplus but is in equilibrium. In sum,

If the economy is in long-run equilibrium, the unemployment rate equals the natural unemployment rate and the labor market is in equilibrium.

The following table summarizes three possible states of the economy and the related states of the labor market:

State of the Economy	What Do We Call It?	Relationship Between Unemployment Rate and Natural Unemployment Rate	State of the Labor Market
Real GDP < Natural Real GDP	Recessionary gap	Unemployment rate > natural unemployment rate	Surplus exists
Real GDP > Natural Real GDP	Inflationary gap	Unemployment rate < natural unemployment rate	Shortage exists
Real GDP = Natural Real GDP	Long-run equilibrium	Unemployment rate = natural unemployment rate	Equilibrium exists

9-2c Common Misconceptions About the Unemployment Rate and the Natural Unemployment Rate

Some people mistakenly think that the economy's unemployment rate *cannot* be lower than the natural unemployment rate (as it is in an inflationary gap). In other words, if the natural unemployment rate is 5 percent, then the unemployment rate can never be 4 percent. But that assumption is a myth.

To explain why, we need to look at two production possibilities frontiers (PPFs). In Exhibit 4, the two such frontiers are the physical PPF (purple curve) and the institutional PPF (blue curve). The physical PPF illustrates different combinations of goods that the economy can produce given the physical constraints of (1) finite resources and (2) the current state of technology. The institutional PPF illustrates different combinations of goods that the economy can produce given the two physical constraints of (1) finite resources and (2) the current state of technology, plus (3) any institutional constraints. Broadly defined, an institutional constraint is anything that prevents economic agents from producing the maximum Real GDP that is physically possible.

For example, the minimum-wage law, which is an institutional constraint, specifies that workers must be paid at least the legislated minimum wage. One effect of this law is that unskilled people whose value to employers falls below the legislated minimum wage will not be hired. Having fewer workers means less output, *ceteris paribus.* (This is why the institutional PPF lies closer to the origin than the physical PPF does.)

EXHIBIT 4

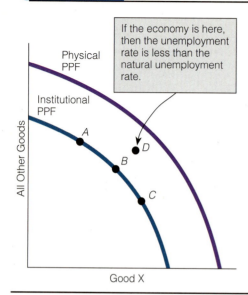

The Physical and Institutional PPFs

A society has both a physical PPF and an institutional PPF. The physical PPF illustrates different combinations of goods the economy can produce given the physical constraints of (1) finite resources and (2) the current state of technology. The institutional PPF illustrates different combinations of goods the economy can produce given the physical constraints of (1) finite resources, (2) the current state of technology, and (3) any institutional constraints. The economy is at the natural unemployment rate if it is located on its institutional PPF, such as at points A, B, or C. An economy can never operate beyond its physical PPF, but it is possible for it to operate beyond its institutional PPF because institutional constraints are not always equally effective. If the economy does operate beyond its institutional PPF, such as at point D, then the unemployment rate in the economy is lower than the natural unemployment rate.

Within the confines of society's physical and institutional constraints is a natural unemployment rate. This situation is represented by any point on the institutional PPF. In the exhibit, points *A*, *B*, and *C* are all such points.

An economy can never operate beyond its physical PPF, but it can operate beyond its institutional PPF. For example, suppose inflation reduces the purchasing power of the minimum wage, thus reducing or eliminating the constraining influence of the minimum-wage law on the unskilled labor market.[1] This change would make one of society's institutional constraints ineffective, allowing the economy to temporarily move beyond the institutional constraint. Consider, for example, point *D* in Exhibit 4. At point *D*, the unemployment rate that exists in the economy is less than the natural unemployment rate.

Three States of the Economy and Two PPF Curves   So, an economy can operate beyond its institutional PPF but below its physical PPF. Now, let's tie the three states of an economy to the institutional and physical PPF curves.

Exhibit 5 shows the institutional PPF and the physical PPF, along with three points: *A*, *B*, and *C*. Point *A*, below the institutional PPF, represents an economy in a recessionary gap, producing less than Natural Real GDP, Q_N. Point *B*, on the institutional PPF, represents an economy in long-run equilibrium, producing Natural Real GDP. Finally, point *C*, beyond the institutional PPF but below the physical PPF, represents an economy in an inflationary gap, producing more than Natural Real GDP. Thus, each of the three states of the economy—recessionary gap, inflationary gap, and long-run equilibrium—can be identified as a point in relation to both the institutional PPF and the physical PPF.

[1.] Inflation reduces the real (inflation-adjusted) minimum wage. If the minimum wage is $6 and the price level is $1, then the real minimum wage is $6 ($6 ÷ the price level, 1.00). If the price level rises to $2.00, then the real minimum wage falls to $3. The lower the real minimum wage is, the greater the number of unskilled workers whom employers will hire, because the demand curve for unskilled workers is downward sloping.

> **EXHIBIT 5**

Three States of the Economy and Two PPFs

In this exhibit, we show three states of the economy in terms of the institutional PPF and the physical PPF. Point A, which is below the institutional PPF, represents an economy in a recessionary gap. Point B, on the institutional PPF, represents an economy in long-run equilibrium. Point C, beyond the institutional PPF but below the physical PPF, represents an economy in an inflationary gap.

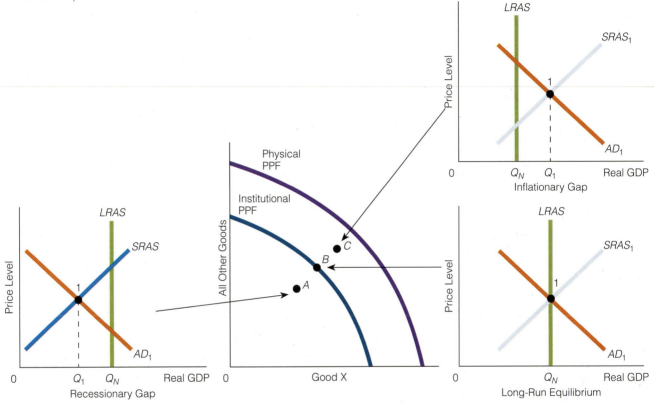

In a Country's Institutional PPF Assume that in year 1 country A's unemployment rate is equal to its natural unemployment rate, 4.7 percent. In year 2, its unemployment rate is still equal to its natural unemployment rate, now 5.4 percent. What was going on in the country over the two years? Where is the economics?

We know that if a country's unemployment rate is equal to its natural unemployment rate, then the country is operating on its institutional PPF. (It is also operating at long-run equilibrium.) Because country A's unemployment rate is equal to its natural unemployment rate in years 1 and 2, the country must be operating on its institutional PPF in both years. But why are both the unemployment rate and the natural unemployment rate higher (each at 5.4 percent) in year 2 than in year 1? What does this difference mean? Obviously, the country's institutional PPF has shifted inward between the two years (assuming no change in the country's physical PPF). In other words, some institutional changes came about between years 1 and 2—perhaps changes in the regulatory climate—that made it more difficult to produce goods and services.

SELF-TEST

1. What is a recessionary gap? An inflationary gap?

2. What is the state of the labor market when the economy is in a recessionary gap? In an inflationary gap?

3. Suppose the economy is in an inflationary gap. Locate the position of the economy in relation to the two PPFs discussed in this section.

9-3 THE SELF-REGULATING ECONOMY

Some economists believe that the economy is self-regulating. In other words, if the economy is not at the natural unemployment rate (or full employment)—that is, it is not producing Natural Real GDP—then it can move on its own to this position. The notion of a self-regulating economy is quite classical, but it is also a view held by some modern-day economists. This section describes how a self-regulating economy works.

9-3a What Happens If a Self-Regulating Economy Is in a Recessionary Gap?

If the economy is in a recessionary gap, then

1. it is producing a Real GDP level that is less than Natural Real GDP,

2. the unemployment rate is greater than the natural unemployment rate, and

3. a surplus exists in the labor market.

Exhibit 6(a) illustrates this case for a Real GDP of $9 trillion and a Natural Real GDP of $10 trillion. What, if anything, happens in the economy? According to economists

> **EXHIBIT 6**

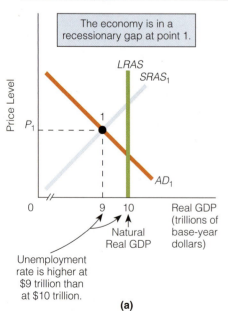

(a)

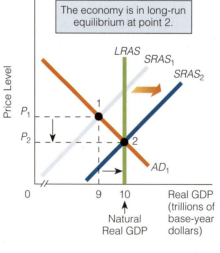

(b)

The Self-Regulating Economy: Removing a Recessionary Gap

(a) The economy is at P_1 and a Real GDP of $9 trillion. Because Real GDP is less than Natural Real GDP ($10 trillion), the economy is in a recessionary gap and the unemployment rate is higher than the natural unemployment rate.

(b) Wage rates fall, and the short-run aggregate supply curve shifts from $SRAS_1$ to $SRAS_2$. As the price level falls, the real balance, interest rate, and international trade effects increase the quantity demanded of Real GDP. Ultimately, the economy moves into long-run equilibrium at point 2.

who believe that the economy is self-regulating, the surplus in the labor market begins to exert downward pressure on wages.[2] In other words, as old wage contracts expire, business firms negotiate contracts that pay workers lower wage rates.

Then, as wage rates fall, the *SRAS* curve begins to shift to the right, ultimately moving from $SRAS_1$ to $SRAS_2$, as in Exhibit 6(b). As a result of the increase in short-run aggregate supply, the price level falls. As the price level falls, the quantity demanded of Real GDP rises because of the real balance, interest rate, and international trade effects (all discussed in the last chapter). As the price level falls, the economy moves from one point on the *AD* curve to a point farther down on the same curve. In Exhibit 6(b), this is a move from point 1 to point 2.

As long as the economy's Real GDP is less than its Natural Real GDP, the price level continues to fall. Ultimately, the economy moves to long-run equilibrium at point 2, corresponding to P_2 and a Natural Real GDP of $10 trillion. The process may be depicted as follows:

Recessionary gap →

Unemployment rate > Natural unemployment rate →

Surplus in labor market → Wages fall → *SRAS* curve shifts to the right →

Economy moves into long-run equilibrium

9-3b What Happens If the Economy Is in an Inflationary Gap?

If the economy is in an inflationary gap,

1. it is producing a Real GDP level that is greater than Natural Real GDP,

2. the unemployment rate is less than the natural unemployment rate, and

3. a shortage exists in the labor market.

Exhibit 7(a) illustrates this case for a Real GDP of $11 trillion and a Natural Real GDP of $10 trillion. What happens in the economy in this situation? According to economists who believe the economy is self-regulating, the shortage in the labor market begins to exert upward pressure on wages. In other words, as old wage contracts expire, business firms negotiate contracts that pay workers higher wage rates.

Then, as wage rates rise, the *SRAS* curve begins to shift to the left, ultimately moving from $SRAS_1$ to $SRAS_2$ in Exhibit 7(b). As a result of the decrease in short-run aggregate supply, the price level rises. As the price level rises, the quantity demanded of Real GDP falls because of the real balance, interest rate, and international trade effects. The economy moves from one point on the *AD* curve to a point farther up on the same curve. In Exhibit 7(b), this is a move from point 1 to point 2.

As long as the economy's Real GDP is greater than its Natural Real GDP, the price level will continue to rise. Ultimately, the economy moves to long-run equilibrium at point 2, corresponding to P_2 and a Natural Real GDP of $10 trillion. The process may be depicted as follows:

Inflationary gap →

Unemployment rate < Natural unemployment rate →

Shortage in labor market → Wages rise → *SRAS* curve shifts to the left →

Economy moves into long-run equilibrium

---

[2] In this discussion of how the self-regulating economy eliminates a recessionary gap, we have emphasized wages (in the labor market) adjusting downward. Resource prices other than wages may fall as well.

> **EXHIBIT 7**

The Self-Regulating Economy: Removing an Inflationary Gap

(a) The economy is at P_1 and a Real GDP of $11 trillion. Because Real GDP is greater than Natural Real GDP ($10 trillion), the economy is in an inflationary gap and the unemployment rate is lower than the natural unemployment rate. (b) Wage rates rise, and the short-run aggregate supply curve shifts from $SRAS_1$ to $SRAS_2$. As the price level rises, the real balance, interest rate, and international trade effects decrease the quantity demanded of Real GDP. Ultimately, the economy moves into long-run equilibrium at point 2.

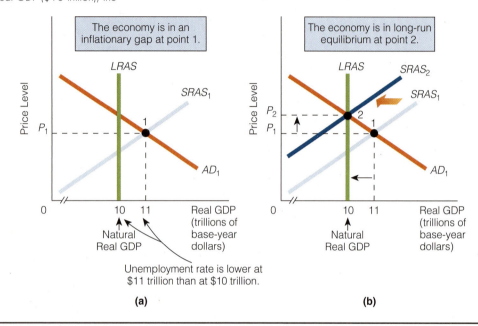

(a)

(b)

9-3c The Self-Regulating Economy: A Recap

We have seen that if the economy is in a recessionary gap, wage rates fall (along with other resource prices), the *SRAS* curve shifts to the right, the price level falls, and the economy moves down the *AD* curve. The economy moves in the direction of long-run equilibrium, ultimately achieving the Natural Real GDP level.

If the economy is in an inflationary gap, wage rates rise (along with other resource prices) and the *SRAS* curve shifts to the left. At the same time, the price level rises and the economy moves up the *AD* curve. The economy moves in the direction of long-run equilibrium, ultimately achieving the Natural Real GDP level.

Flexible wage rates (and other resource prices) play a critical role in the self-regulating economy. For example, suppose wage rates are not flexible and do not fall in a recessionary gap. Then the *SRAS* curve does not shift to the right, the price level does not fall, and the economy doesn't move down the *AD* curve toward long-run equilibrium. Similarly, if wage rates are not flexible and do not rise in an inflationary gap, then the economy won't move up the *AD* curve toward long-run equilibrium.

The economists who say the economy is self-regulating believe that wage rates and other resource prices are *flexible* and that they move up and down in response to market conditions. These economists believe that *wage rates will fall* when there is a *surplus of*

ECONOMICS 24/7

Unpaid Internships

Suppose the economy is in a recessionary gap and the economy is not self-regulating. In other words, suppose wages will not fall. (In the next chapter, we discuss why they may not fall.) Now, if wages do not fall, can the *SRAS* curve shift rightward? The obvious answer is no, because, as we have discussed earlier, it is declining wages that push the *SRAS* curve rightward, and if wages aren't declining, how is the curve going to shift rightward? It would seem as if the economy is stuck in a recessionary gap.

But suppose there were a way to cut labor costs without cutting wages. To illustrate, suppose that the economy is in a recessionary gap, the average wage is $20 an hour (or $160 a day), and 80 million people are employed. Now, one way to get the cost of labor down without cutting the wage is to fire some people who are working at $20 an hour and replace them with unpaid internships. So let's fire 1 million of the 80 million workers, pay the remaining 79 million $20 an hour, and hire 1 million unpaid interns. What are the labor costs now? Instead of being $160 for an 8-hour day for 80 million people, summing to $12.8 billion, it is $160 for an 8-hour day for 79 million people, summing to $12.64 billion. In addition, there are 1 million interns working for free.[3]

Now, the productivity of the 1 million persons fired is probably higher than that of the 1 million interns, so output isn't as great with 79 million paid workers and 1 million unpaid interns as it is with 80 million paid workers, but still we would expect the *SRAS* curve to shift to the right if (a) the wage stays fixed at $20 an hour and (b) 1 million persons are fired and 1 million interns take their place at zero wage. So, it is possible for the *SRAS* curve to shift to the right via unpaid internships.

Of course, the *SRAS* curve could shift to the right even without firing 1 million paid employees and hiring 1 million unpaid interns to take their place. The curve would shift to the right even if none of the 80 million workers is fired but 1 million unpaid interns are simply added to the number of persons working, pushing the total number of persons working to 81 million.

Our point is a simple one: Unpaid internships are a way to reduce the size of the recessionary gap (the difference between Natural Real GDP and Real GDP). And such a reduction can occur without a decline in the wage rate.

Now, the number of unpaid internships seems to fluctuate; it is not always the same. So ask yourself when you are more likely to see the number of unpaid internships (offered by employers) increase: in (a) when the economy is in a recessionary gap and wages are falling or in (b) when the economy is in a recessionary gap and wages aren't falling? We expect it's the latter.

Altrendo images/Stockbyte/Getty Images

[3.] Although requiring interns to work without pay has been illegal since the minimum wage law was enacted in 1938, until recently unpaid interns seldom brought lawsuits. During the summer of 2013 however, unpaid internships became a hotbed for class action lawsuits. Between June and August unpaid interns filed lawsuits against large corporations, among them: Condé Nast Publications, Warner Music Group, Atlantic Recording, Gawker Media, Fox Entertainment Group, NBC Universal, Viacom, Sony, Universal Music Group, Bad Boy Entertainment, and Donna Karan. (See Deborah L. Jacobs, "Unpaid Intern Lawsuits May Reduce Job Opportunities," *Forbes* magazine, September 24, 2013.)

labor and that *wage rates will rise* when there is a *shortage of labor*. You will see in the next chapter that this flexible wages and prices position has not gone unchallenged.

The following table summarizes how a self-regulating economy works for the three possible states of the economy:

State of the Economy	What Happens If the Economy Is Self-Regulating?
Recessionary gap (Real GDP < Natural Real GDP)	Wages fall and *SRAS* curve shifts to the right until Real GDP = Natural Real GDP.
Inflationary gap (Real GDP > Natural Real GDP)	Wages rise and *SRAS* curve shifts to the left until Real GDP = Natural Real GDP.
Long-run equilibrium (Real GDP = Natural Real GDP)	No change in wages and no change in *SRAS*.

9-3d Policy Implication of Believing That the Economy Is Self-Regulating

For economists who believe in a self-regulating economy, full employment is the norm: *The economy always moves back to its Natural Real GDP level.* Stated differently, if the economy contracts an "illness"—in the form of a recessionary or an inflationary gap—it is capable of healing itself through changes in wages and prices. This position on how the economy works has led these economists to advocate a macroeconomic policy of **laissez-faire**, or noninterference. In these economists' view, government has no economic management role to play.

Laissez-faire

A public policy of not interfering with market activities in the economy.

9-3e Changes in a Self-Regulating Economy: Short Run and Long Run

If the economy is self-regulating, how does a change in aggregate demand affect the economy in the short run and the long run? In Exhibit 8(a), the economy is initially in long-run equilibrium at point 1. An increase in aggregate demand is then brought about by, say, an increase in government purchases (a possibility discussed in the last chapter). The *AD* curve shifts right from AD_1 to AD_2, and in the short run the economy moves to point 2, with both Real GDP and the price level higher than at point 1. Now at point 2, the economy is in an inflationary gap. If the economy is self-regulating, wages will soon rise, and the *SRAS* curve will shift to the left—ultimately from $SRAS_1$ to $SRAS_2$. The economy will end up at point 3 in long-run equilibrium.

Let's examine the changes in the short run and the long run. As a result of an increase in aggregate demand, Real GDP rises and the price level rises in the short run. In addition, because Real GDP rises, the unemployment rate falls. In the long run, when the economy is at point 3, it is producing exactly the same level of Real GDP that it was producing originally (Q_N), but at a higher price level.

Conclusion: If the economy is self-regulating, an increase in aggregate demand can raise the price level and Real GDP in the short run, but in the long run the only effect is a rise in the price level. In other words, in the long run, we have only higher prices to show for an increase in aggregate demand.

> **EXHIBIT 8**

Changes in a Self-Regulating Economy: Short Run and Long Run

In (a), the economy is initially at point 1 in long-run equilibrium. Aggregate demand rises, and the AD curve shifts right from AD_1 to AD_2. The economy is at point 2 in the short run, with a higher Real GDP and a higher price level than at point 1. The economy is also in an inflationary gap at point 2. If the economy is self-regulating, wages will soon rise, the $SRAS$ curve will

shift leftward from $SRAS_1$ to $SRAS_2$, and the economy will be in long-run equilibrium at point 3. At point 3, the economy is producing the same Real GDP that it did at point 1. In other words, in the long run, an increase in aggregate demand only raises the price level. In (b), the economy is initially at point 1 in long-run equilibrium. Aggregate demand falls, and the AD curve shifts leftward from AD_1 to AD_2. The economy is at point 2 in the short run, with a lower Real

GDP and a lower price level than at point 1. The economy is also in a recessionary gap. If the economy is self-regulating, wages will soon fall, the $SRAS$ curve will shift rightward from $SRAS_1$ to $SRAS_2$, and the economy will be in long-run equilibrium at point 3. At point 3, the economy is producing the same Real GDP that it did at point 1. In other words, in the long run, a decrease in aggregate demand only lowers the price level.

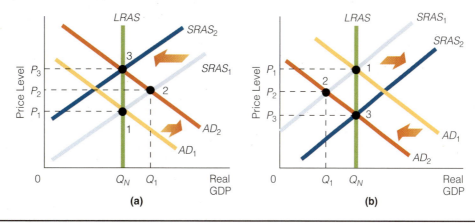

(a)   (b)

Now let's consider what happens if aggregate demand falls. In Exhibit 8(b), the economy is initially in long-run equilibrium at point 1 when aggregate demand decreases. The AD curve then shifts left from AD_1 to AD_2, and in the short run the economy moves to point 2, with both Real GDP and the price level lower than at point 1.

Now at point 2, the economy is in a recessionary gap. If the economy is self-regulating, wages will soon fall and the $SRAS$ curve will shift to the right—ultimately from $SRAS_1$ to $SRAS_2$. The economy winds up at point 3 in long-run equilibrium.

Again, let's examine the changes in the short run and the long run. As a result of a decrease in aggregate demand, Real GDP falls in the short run, as does the price level. In addition, because Real GDP falls, the unemployment rate rises. In the long run, when the economy is at point 3, it is producing exactly the same level of Real GDP that it was producing originally (Q_N), but at a lower price level.

Conclusion: If the economy is self-regulating, a decrease in aggregate demand can lower the price level and Real GDP in the short run, but in the long run the only effect is a lower price level. The following table illustrates the short and long-run effects of a change in aggregated demand:

Change in **AD**	In the Short Run	In the Long Run
$AD\uparrow$	$P\uparrow$, $Q\uparrow$	$P\uparrow$, Q does not change
$AD\downarrow$	$P\downarrow$, $Q\downarrow$	$P\downarrow$, Q does not change

Let's return to Exhibit 8(a) to clarify a point about long-run equilibrium. In the exhibit, the economy starts at point 1 in long-run equilibrium and then moves to point 2. At point 2, both the price level and Real GDP are higher than they were at point 1. In other words, if *AD* rises, both the price level and Real GDP rise in the short run. If the economy is self-regulating, it does not remain at point 2 but rather moves to point 3, where it is again in long-run equilibrium. At point 3, the price level is higher than it was at point 2, but Real GDP is lower. Why, then, don't we say that Real GDP is lower in the long run than it is in the short run, instead of saying that Real GDP does not change in the long run? The answer is that the long run is measured from one long-run equilibrium point to another long-run equilibrium point. In Exhibit 8(a), we look at the long run by comparing points 1 and 3. When we make this comparison, we notice two things: The price level is higher at point 3 than at point 1, and Real GDP is the same.

9-3f A Recap of Classical Macroeconomics and a Self-Regulating Economy

According to classical macroeconomics, in a self-regulating economy,

1. Say's law holds.

2. Interest rates change such that savings equals investment.

3. The economy is self-regulating, making full employment and an economy that produces Natural Real GDP the norm.

4. Prices and wages are flexible. In other words, if the economy is in a recessionary gap, wages fall and the economy soon moves itself toward producing Natural Real GDP (at a lower price level than in the recessionary gap). If the economy is in an inflationary gap, wages rise and the economy soon moves itself toward producing Natural Real GDP (at a higher price level than in the inflationary gap).

5. Because the economy is self-regulating, laissez-faire is the policy prescription.

9-3g Business-Cycle Macroeconomics and Economic-Growth Macroeconomics

In Chapter 8, we introduced the *AD*−*AS* model, involving the aggregate demand (*AD*) curve, the short-run aggregate supply (*SRAS*) curve, and the long-run aggregate supply (*LRAS*) curve. In this chapter, working mainly with two of those three curves (the *AD* and *SRAS* curves), we did two things. First, we showed what would happen if a self-regulating economy were in either a recessionary or an inflationary gap. (See Exhibits 6 and 7, respectively.) In both cases, the *SRAS* curve would shift so that the economy moved into long-run equilibrium. Second, we started from a point of long-run equilibrium and introduced a change in aggregate demand. (See Exhibit 8.) We explained what happens in the economy (specifically to the price level and Real GDP) in both the short run and the long run.

You have enough background now to understand the difference between business-cycle macroeconomics and economic-growth macroeconomics. Both can be explained with respect to Real GDP and a few curves. In some upcoming chapters, we will deal with business-cycle macroeconomics—that is, with changes in the *AD* and *SRAS* curves around a *fixed LRAS* curve. But in other chapters, we will be dealing with economic-growth macroeconomics—that is, with *rightward-shifting* changes in the *LRAS* curve. Business-cycle and economic-growth macroeconomics essentially make up two categories of macroeconomics. Keep these two categories in mind as you continue your study of macroeconomics.

Business-Cycle Macroeconomics   In this chapter, we have been looking at the *business cycle:* the recurrent ups and downs in Real GDP. To understand the business cycle, let us again examine Exhibit 8(a). The economy starts off in long-run equilibrium at point 1. Next, the aggregate demand curve shifts to the right. In the short run, Real GDP rises from Q_N to Q_1. Eventually, though, the *SRAS* curve shifts to the left, the economy is back in long-run equilibrium at point 3, and Real GDP returns to its natural level at Q_N.

We could describe what happened this way: Real GDP initially rose and then fell with respect to a *fixed LRAS* curve. This is what business-cycle macroeconomics deals with: (up and down) changes in Real GDP around a *fixed LRAS* curve.

In many upcoming chapters, we will delve into business-cycle macroeconomics: What shifts the *AD* curve? Why might Real GDP initially rise and then fall? Macroeconomists often have to ask and then try to answer such questions relating to business-cycle macroeconomics.

Economic-Growth Macroeconomics   If business-cycle macroeconomics can be described as changes in Real GDP with respect to a *fixed LRAS* curve, then economic-growth macroeconomics can be described as *increases* in Real GDP due to a *rightward-shifting LRAS* curve. In Exhibit 9, we start with AD_1 and $LRAS_1$. Long-run equilibrium is at point 1, and Natural Real GDP is Q_{N1}. Now, suppose the *LRAS* curve shifts rightward, first to $LRAS_2$ and then to $LRAS_3$. At the same time, Real GDP rises, first to Q_{N2} and then to Q_{N3}. These rightward shifts in *LRAS* curve illustrate economic growth. Our study of economic-growth macroeconomics deals with the factors that can lead to a rightward shift in the *LRAS* curve.

> **EXHIBIT 9**

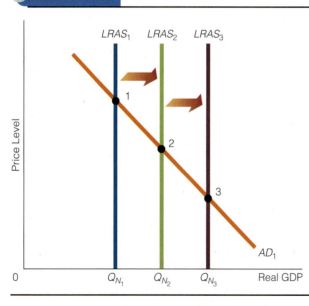

Economic-Growth Macroeconomics

Economic-growth macroeconomics deals with rightward shifts in the long-run aggregate supply curve (*LRAS*).

SELF-TEST

1. If the economy is self-regulating, what happens if it is in a recessionary gap?

2. If the economy is self-regulating, what happens if it is in an inflationary gap?

3. If the economy is self-regulating, how do changes in aggregate demand affect the economy in the long run?

ECONOMICS 24/7

If the Economy Is Removing Itself from a Recessionary Gap, Where Is the Declining Price Level?

Suppose that, in year 1, the economy is in a recessionary gap, it is self-regulating, and it is beginning to remove itself from the recessionary gap. In other words, wages are beginning to fall, and the SRAS curve is beginning to shift rightward. As a result, the price level is beginning to decline. Pictorially,

Recessionary gap → Wages begin to fall → SRAS begins to shift rightward → Price level begins to decline

Now suppose that, in year 2, the economy is no longer in a recessionary gap. It is in long-run equilibrium, producing Natural Real GDP (Q_N). But here is the problem: The price level hasn't declined. This development is odd, because if the economy was in a recessionary gap and the economy is self-regulating, we would expect the price level to be lower once the economy removes itself from the recessionary gap. For example, look at Exhibit 6(b) to see that the price level is lower at point 2 (once the economy has removed itself from a recessionary gap) than at point 1 (when it was in a recessionary gap).

Does a constant price level mean that the economy is not self-regulating? Not at all. While the economy was self-regulating

(and the SRAS curve was shifting to the right), aggregate demand in the economy might have risen. Moreover, the rise in aggregate demand could be totally unrelated to the change occurring on the supply side of the economy (as evidenced by the SRAS curve's shift to the right).

Think of it this way: The SRAS curve is the right hand, and it is moving. The AD curve is the left hand; it is moving too, and its movement is unrelated to what the right hand (the SRAS curve) is doing. In the end, both hands (the SRAS curve and the AD curve) determine what happens to the price level.

In Exhibit 10, the economy is initially at point 1, in a recessionary gap. The self-regulating properties of the economy are in force: wages are falling, and the SRAS curve is shifting rightward from $SRAS_1$ to $SRAS_2$. At the same time, something has occurred to increase aggregate demand (e.g., government purchases or the money supply might have increased), and the AD curve shifts rightward from AD_1 to AD_2. In the end, the two new curves—$SRAS_2$ and AD_2—intersect at point 2 in the exhibit. The economy is no longer in a recessionary gap, and the price level has remained constant.

Here's what we should take away from this discussion: Two (or more) things can happen at the same time in an economy, and unless we understand this fact, we may assume that something is false when it is actually true. If the economy is removing itself from a recessionary gap, we expect the price level to decline, but it doesn't. So, is the economy not self-regulating? No. Something else could have been happening at the same time the economy was removing itself from a recessionary gap, and this "something else" (in our example, a rise in aggregate demand) could offset the falling price level.

> ### EXHIBIT 10

A Self-Regulating Economy with Aggregate Demand Increasing

The economy is initially in a recessionary gap at point 1. Because the economy is self-regulating, the SRAS curve shifts to the right, whereupon something unrelated to the self-regulating properties of the economy occurs. Specifically, aggregate demand rises and the AD curve shifts rightward. The economy ends up at point 2, out of the recessionary gap but with no change in the price level.

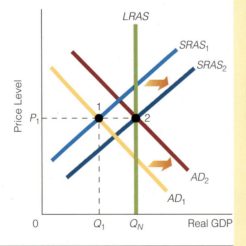

Office  Hours

"Do Economists Really Know What the Natural Unemployment Rate Equals?"

STUDENT:

Do economists know what the natural unemployment rate equals at any given moment?

INSTRUCTOR:

They estimate it but can't be absolutely sure that their estimate of the natural unemployment rate is the same as the actual rate. After all, not all economists arrive at the same estimate for the natural unemployment rate. One economist might estimate it at 5.3 percent, whereas another estimates it at 5.6 percent.

STUDENT:

Well, if that's true, then not every economist would agree that the economy is in, say, a recessionary gap if the unemployment rate is, say, 5.5 percent. Am I correct?

INSTRUCTOR:

You are correct. For example, the economist who thinks that the natural unemployment rate is 5.3 percent will think that the economy is in a recessionary gap if the actual unemployment rate is 5.5 percent, but the economist who thinks that the natural unemployment rate is 5.6 percent will not. Here's an analogy: Smith thinks that Brown's normal body temperature is 98.9 degrees, and Jones thinks that it is only 98.6 degrees. If Brown's body temperature today is 98.9 degrees, Jones will think that Brown is running a low-grade fever, but Smith will not.

STUDENT:

Does making a too-high or too-low estimate of the natural unemployment rate matter to the economy? In other words, do the incorrect estimates (that economists sometimes make) matter?

INSTRUCTOR:

Actually, the answer is yes and no. The answer is no if the economy is self-regulating and government doesn't try to move the economy out of either a recessionary or an inflationary gap by implementing

economic policies. As in the example of misestimating Brown's normal body temperature, if no one gives Brown any medicine, then misestimating his body temperature probably doesn't matter.

But in later chapters you are going to read about the government implementing economic policies to try to remove the economy from either a recessionary or an inflationary gap. Then misestimating the natural unemployment rate does matter.

To illustrate, suppose the natural unemployment rate has fallen from 6.0 percent to 5.7 percent but economists and government economic policy makers have not figured that out yet. In other words, they still believe that the natural unemployment rate is 6.0 percent. Now, if the actual unemployment rate is 5.7 percent, then the economy is in long-run equilibrium. Economists and government economic policy makers, however, mistakenly believe that the economy is in an inflationary gap (with the actual unemployment rate of 5.7 percent lower than their too-high estimate of 6.0 percent). Thinking that the economy is in an inflationary gap, economists expect prices to rise in the future. To offset the higher prices in the future, they propose a reduction in the growth rate of the money supply in the hopes of reducing aggregate demand (shifting the *AD* curve to the left). The Federal Reserve (the monetary authority, also called the Fed) follows suit and reduces the growth rate of the money supply, whereupon the *AD* curve shifts leftward. But notice the effect of the Fed's action in terms of our *AD–AS* model: A reduction in aggregate demand throws the economy into a recessionary gap. (Remember, the economy was actually in long-run equilibrium when the monetary policy action was carried out.)

Our conclusion is simple: A misestimate of the natural unemployment rate, if acted on, can move an economy from long-run equilibrium into a recessionary gap.

Back to the original question: Does getting a too-high or too-low estimate of the natural unemployment rate matter to the economy? The answer is yes, it certainly can matter to the economy.

Points to remember

1. Economists can misestimate the natural unemployment rate.
2. Acting on a misestimated natural unemployment rate can affect the economy (sometimes adversely)—for example, by influencing economic policy actions.

CHAPTER SUMMARY

SAY'S LAW

- Say's law states that supply creates its own demand. All economists believe that Say's law holds in a barter economy, where there can be no general overproduction or underproduction of goods. Classical economists believed that Say's law also holds in a money economy. In their view, even if consumption drops and saving rises, economic forces are at work producing an equal increase in investment. According to classical economists, interest rates are flexible and they move to a level where the amount of saving and the amount of investment in an economy are equal.

CLASSICAL ECONOMISTS ON MARKETS, WAGES, AND PRICES

- Classical economists believed that most, if not all, markets are competitive and that wages and prices are flexible.

THREE STATES OF THE ECONOMY

- Natural Real GDP is the level of Real GDP produced when the economy is operating at the natural unemployment rate.

- The economy can be producing a Real GDP level that (1) is equal to Natural Real GDP, (2) is greater than Natural Real GDP, or (3) is less than Natural Real GDP. In other words, the economy can be in (1) long-run equilibrium, (2) an inflationary gap, or (3) a recessionary gap, respectively.

- In long-run equilibrium, the Real GDP that the economy is producing is equal to Natural Real GDP. The unemployment rate in the economy is equal to the natural unemployment rate, and the labor market is in equilibrium.

- In a recessionary gap, the Real GDP that the economy is producing is less than Natural Real GDP. The unemployment rate in the economy is greater than the natural unemployment rate, and a surplus exists in the labor market.

- In an inflationary gap, the Real GDP that the economy is producing is greater than Natural Real GDP. The unemployment rate in the economy is less than the natural unemployment rate, and a shortage exists in the labor market.

THE INSTITUTIONAL AND PHYSICAL PRODUCTION POSSIBILITIES FRONTIERS

- The physical PPF illustrates different combinations of goods that the economy can produce given the physical constraints of (1) finite resources and (2) the current state of technology. The institutional PPF illustrates different combinations of goods that the economy can produce given the physical constraints of (1) finite resources and (2) the current state of technology, plus (3) any institutional constraints.

- If an economy is operating on its institutional PPF, it is operating at the natural unemployment rate. If it is operating at a point beyond the institutional PPF but below the physical PPF, it is operating at an unemployment rate less than the natural unemployment rate.

THE SELF-REGULATING ECONOMY

- Some economists contend that the economy can eliminate both recessionary and inflationary gaps smoothly and quickly by itself.

- If the economy is self-regulating and in a recessionary gap, then the unemployment rate in the economy is greater than the natural unemployment rate and a surplus exists in the labor market. As wage contracts expire, wage rates fall. As a result, the *SRAS* curve shifts to the right and the price level falls. As the price level falls, the quantity demanded of Real GDP rises. Ultimately, the economy moves into long-run equilibrium, where it produces Natural Real GDP.

- If the economy is self-regulating and in an inflationary gap, then the unemployment rate in the economy is less than the natural unemployment rate and a shortage exists in the labor market. As wage contracts expire, wage rates rise. As a result, the *SRAS* curve shifts to the left and the price level rises. As the price level rises, the quantity demanded of Real GDP falls. Ultimately, the economy moves into long-run equilibrium, where it produces Natural Real GDP.

BUSINESS-CYCLE MACROECONOMICS AND ECONOMIC-GROWTH MACROECONOMICS

- This text presents both business-cycle macroeconomics and economic-growth macroeconomics. Business-cycle macroeconomics deals with changes in Real GDP around a fixed *LRAS* curve. Economic-growth macroeconomics deals with *increases* in Real GDP due to a rightward-shifting *LRAS* curve.

KEY TERMS AND CONCEPTS

Say's Law   Recessionary Gap   Inflationary Gap   Laissez-faire

VIDEO QUESTIONS AND PROBLEMS

Video Questions and Problems are available on MindTap for Arnold 12e or by searching for Arnold on www.cengagebrain.com

1. Explain and diagrammatically represent how a self-regulating economy removes itself from a recessionary gap.

2. Explain and diagrammatically represent how a self-regulating economy removes itself from an inflationary gap.

3. Flexible wages play a critical role in removing an economy from a recessionary gap. Do you agree or disagree? Explain your answer.

4. If the economy is in an inflationary gap, where is it located with respect to both the institutional PPF and the physical PPF?

5. Explain the classical view of the credit market.

QUESTIONS AND PROBLEMS

1. What is the classical economics position on (a) wages, (b) prices, and (c) interest rates?

2. According to classical economists, does Say's law hold in a money economy? Explain your answer.

3. How do you explain why investment falls as the interest rate rises?

4. Explain why saving rises as the interest rate rises.

5. According to classical economists, does an increase in saving shift the *AD* curve to the left? Explain your answer.

6. What does it mean to say that the economy is in a recessionary gap? In an inflationary gap? In long-run equilibrium?

7. What is the state of the labor market in (a) a recessionary gap, (b) an inflationary gap, (c) long-run equilibrium?

8. Describe the relationship of the (actual) unemployment rate to the natural unemployment rate in each of the following economic states: (a) a recessionary gap, (b) an inflationary gap, and (c) long-run equilibrium.

9. Diagrammatically represent an economy in (a) an inflationary gap, (b) a recessionary gap, and (c) long-run equilibrium.

10. Explain how an economy can operate beyond its institutional PPF but not beyond its physical PPF.

11. According to economists who believe in a self-regulating economy, what happens—step-by-step—when the economy is in a recessionary gap? What happens when the economy is in an inflationary gap?

12. If wage rates are not flexible, can the economy be self-regulating? Explain your answer.

13. Explain the importance of the real balance, interest rate, and international trade effects to long-run (equilibrium) adjustment in the economy.

14. Suppose that the economy is self-regulating, that the price level is 132, that the quantity demanded of Real GDP is $4 trillion, that the quantity supplied of Real GDP in the short run is $3.9 trillion, and that the quantity supplied of Real GDP in the long run is $4.3 trillion. Is the economy in short-run equilibrium? Will the price level in long-run equilibrium be greater than, less than, or equal to 132? Explain your answers.

15. Suppose that the economy is self-regulating, that the price level is 110, that the quantity demanded of Real GDP is $4 trillion, that the quantity supplied of Real GDP in the short run is $4.9 trillion, and that the quantity supplied of Real GDP in the long run is $4.1 trillion. Is the economy in short-run equilibrium? Will the price level in long-run equilibrium be greater than, less than, or equal to 110? Explain your answers.

16. Yvonne is telling her friend Wendy that wages are rising but that so is the unemployment rate. She tells Wendy

that she (Yvonne) may be the next person to be fired at her company and that she may have to move back in with her parents. What does the economy have to do with Yvonne's possibly having to move back in with her parents?

17. Jim says, "I think it's a little like when you have a cold or the flu. You don't need to see a doctor. In time, your body heals itself. That's sort of the way the economy works too. We don't really need government coming to our rescue every time the economy gets a cold." According to Jim, how does the economy work?

18. Beginning with long-run equilibrium, explain what happens to the price level and Real GDP in the short run and in the long run as a result of (a) a decline in *AD*, (b) a rise in *AD*, (c) a decline in *SRAS*, and (d) a rise in *SRAS*.

WORKING WITH NUMBERS AND GRAPHS

1. In the following figure, which point is representative of

   a. the economy on its *LRAS* curve?

   b. the economy in a recessionary gap?

   c. the economy in an inflationary gap?

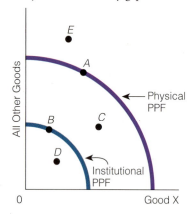

2. Which of the following figures, (a)–(c), is consistent with or representative of

   a. the economy operating at the natural unemployment rate?

   b. a surplus in the labor market?

   c. a recessionary gap?

   d. a cyclical unemployment rate of zero?

3. Represent the following situations diagrammatically:

   a. An economy in which *AD* increases as the economy is self-regulating out of a recessionary gap

   b. An economy in which *AD* decreases as the economy is self-regulating out of an inflationary gap

4. Economist Jones believes that there is always sufficient (aggregate) demand in the economy to buy all the goods and services supplied at full employment. Diagrammatically represent what the economy looks like for Jones.

5. Diagrammatically show what happens when the institutional constraints in the economy become less effective.

6. Diagrammatically represent an economy in a recessionary gap. Next, identify where the economy in a recessionary gap lies in terms of both the institutional PPF and the physical PPF.

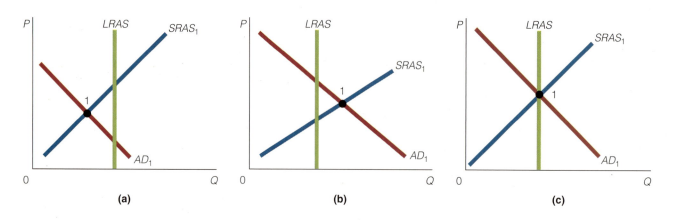

(a)   (b)   (c)

KEYNESIAN MACROECONOMICS AND ECONOMIC INSTABILITY: A CRITIQUE OF THE SELF-REGULATING ECONOMY

© Jack Scrivener/Shutterstock.com

10-1 QUESTIONING THE CLASSICAL POSITION AND THE SELF-REGULATING ECONOMY

INTRODUCTION

In the last chapter, we discussed the economy as a self-regulating mechanism. For example, we learned that an economy can remove itself from a recessionary gap. In this chapter, we challenge that assertion and discuss the views of economists who believe that the economy may not be able to self-regulate and get to Natural Real GDP. In other words, the economy may not be able to move itself out of a recessionary gap. The ideas in this chapter are mostly those of one man, John Maynard Keynes, who taught economics at Cambridge University in England during the first half of the twentieth century.

John Maynard Keynes, an English economist, changed how many economists viewed the economy. Keynes's major work, *The General Theory of Employment, Interest and Money*, was published in 1936.[1] Just prior to publication of the book, the Great Depression had plagued many countries of the world. Looking around at the world during that time, one had to wonder whether the classical view of the economy could be right. Unemployment was sky high in many countries, and many economies had been contracting. Where was Say's law, with its promise that there would be no general gluts? When was the self-regulating economy going to heal itself of its depression illness? Where was full employment? And, given the depressed state of the economy,

---

[1] John Maynard Keynes, *The General Theory of Employment, Interest and Money* (New York: Harcourt, Brace, 1936).

could anyone believe any longer that laissez-faire was the right policy? With the Great Depression as recent history, Keynes and the Keynesians thought that, although their theory might not be right in every detail, they certainly had enough evidence to say that the classical view of the economy was wrong.

Keynes challenged all four of the following classical position beliefs: (1) Say's law holds, so that insufficient demand in the economy is unlikely. (2) Wages, prices, and interest rates are flexible. (3) The economy is self-regulating. (4) Laissez-faire is the right and sensible economic policy.

10-1a Keynes's Criticism of Say's Law in a Money Economy

According to classical economists and Say's law, if consumption spending falls because saving increases, then total spending will not fall, because the added saving will simply bring about more investment spending. Such spending will happen through changes in the interest rate: The added saving will put downward pressure on the interest rate, and at a lower interest rate, businesses will borrow and invest more. Through changes in the interest rate, the amount of saving will always equal the amount invested.

Keynes disagreed. He didn't think that added saving would necessarily stimulate an equal amount of added investment spending. Exhibit 1 illustrates Keynes's point of view. Let consumption equal $3,000, investment equal $600, government purchases equal $1,200, and net exports equal $200. Then saving increases by $100, lowering consumption to $2,900. According to the classical economists, investment will rise by $100 at the same time, going from $600 to $700. Keynes asked, what is the guarantee that an increase in investment will equally match an increase in saving? What if saving rises by $100 (and consumption goes down by $100), but investment rises by, say, only $40 (instead of $100)? Then the original equation for total expenditures, $TE = C + I + G + (EX - IM)$, changes from

$$TE = \$3,000 + \$600 + \$1,200 + \$200$$
$$= \$5,000$$

> **EXHIBIT 1**

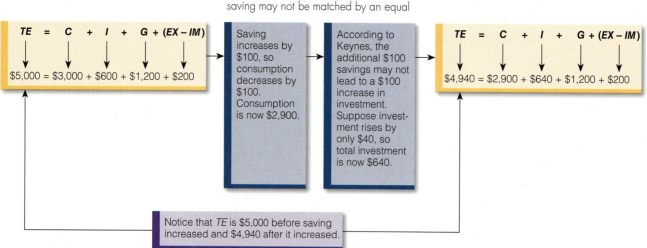

Keynes's View of Say's Law in a Money Economy

According to Keynes, a decrease in consumption and a subsequent increase in saving may not be matched by an equal increase in investment. Thus, a decrease in total expenditures may occur.

$$TE = C + I + G + (EX - IM)$$
$$\$5,000 = \$3,000 + \$600 + \$1,200 + \$200$$

Saving increases by $100, so consumption decreases by $100. Consumption is now $2,900.

According to Keynes, the additional $100 savings may not lead to a $100 increase in investment. Suppose investment rises by only $40, so total investment is now $640.

$$TE = C + I + G + (EX - IM)$$
$$\$4,940 = \$2,900 + \$640 + \$1,200 + \$200$$

Notice that *TE* is $5,000 before saving increased and $4,940 after it increased.

to

$$TE = \$2{,}900 + \$640 + \$1{,}200 + \$200$$
$$= \$4{,}940$$

not to

$$TE = \$2{,}900 + \$700 + \$1{,}200 + \$200$$
$$= \$5{,}000$$

Thus, total expenditures decrease from $5,000 to $4,940, and if, at a given price level, total spending falls, so will aggregate demand. In other words, according to Keynes, aggregate demand could fall if saving increases.

Of course, a classical economist would retort that, as a result of a $100 increase in saving, interest rates will fall enough to guarantee that investment will increase by $100. Keynes countered by saying that individuals save and invest for a host of reasons and that no single factor, such as the interest rate, links these activities.

Furthermore, whereas the classical economists believed that saving and investment depend on the interest rate, Keynes believed that both saving and investment depend on a number of factors that may be far more influential than the interest rate. Keynes held that saving is more responsive to changes in income than to changes in the interest rate and that investment is more responsive to technological changes, business expectations, and innovations than to changes in the interest rate.

Consider the difference between Keynes and the classical economists on saving:

- The classical economists held that saving is directly related to the interest rate: As the interest rate goes up, saving rises, and as the interest rate goes down, saving falls, *ceteris paribus*.

- Keynes thought that this assumption might not always be true. To see why, suppose that individuals are saving for a certain goal—say, a retirement fund of $100,000. Then they might save less per period at an interest rate of 10 percent than at an interest rate of 5 percent because a higher interest rate means that they can save less per period and still meet their goal by the time they are ready to retire. For example, if the interest rate is 5 percent, they need $50,000 in savings to earn $2,500 in interest income per year. If the interest rate is 10 percent, they need only $25,000 in savings to earn $2,500 in interest annually.

As for investment, Keynes believed that the interest rate is important in determining the level of investment, but not as important as other variables, such as the expected rate of profit on investment. Keynes argued that if business expectations are pessimistic, then much investment is unlikely, regardless of how low the interest rate is.

10-1b Keynes on Wage Rates

As explained in the last chapter, if the unemployment rate in the economy is greater than the natural unemployment rate, a surplus exists in the labor market: The number of job seekers is high relative to the number of jobs available. Consequently, according to classical economists, wage rates will fall.

Keynes didn't see the adjustment as so simple. Instead, he asserted, employees will naturally resist an employer's efforts to cut wages, and labor unions may resist wage cuts. In short, wage rates may be inflexible in a downward direction.

EXHIBIT 2

The Economy Gets Stuck in a Recessionary Gap

According to Keynes's view, if the economy is in a recessionary gap at point 1, wage rates may not fall. The economy may be stuck in the recessionary gap.

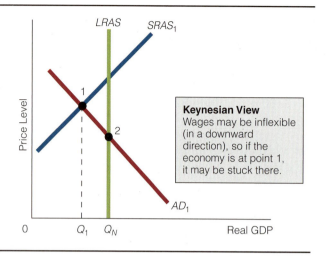

Keynesian View
Wages may be inflexible (in a downward direction), so if the economy is at point 1, it may be stuck there.

If wage rates will not fall, is the economy then unable to get itself out of a recessionary gap? The Keynesian answer is yes. If employee and labor union resistance prevents wage rates from falling, then the *SRAS* curve will not shift to the right. If it does not shift to the right, the price level won't come down. If the price level does not come down, buyers will not purchase more goods and services and move the economy out of a recessionary gap. As Exhibit 2 shows, the economy is stuck at point 1. It cannot get to point 2.

Keynes believed that the economy is inherently unstable and that it may not automatically cure itself of a recessionary gap. In other words, *the economy may not be self-regulating.*

10-1c Different Markets, Different Rates of Adjustment

Keynes's notion that wages may not fall to their equilibrium level brings up the issue of various markets and the adjustment path in each. Let's first look at a market in which prices equilibrate very quickly: the stock market. Consider the market for stock A. There is a demand for this stock and a supply of it. If the demand rises, the price of the stock will rise. If the demand falls, the price of the stock will fall. Stock prices are flexible (upward and downward), and they move quickly to their equilibrium value. For example, the demand for stock A might rise at 10 o'clock in the morning, and one minute later, at 10:01, the new higher equilibrium price of stock A is reached.

Now, not all markets adjust to their equilibrium values as quickly as the stock market. Many economists argue that the labor market might be very different from the stock market. They say that, in the labor market, wages may adjust very slowly to their new equilibrium values. For a certain period, wages may not adjust at all, especially when there is a surplus of labor and we would expect wages to decline.

Exhibit 3 shows the demand for, and supply of, labor. Currently, the labor market is in equilibrium

EXHIBIT 3

The Labor Market and Inflexible Wages Downward

We start with D_1 and S_1 and the labor market in equilibrium at point 1. The equilibrium wage rate is W_1. The demand for labor declines, and the new equilibrium wage rate is W_2. Will employers end up paying W_2? "Not necessarily," say economists who believe that the wage rate (in the labor market) is inflexible downward. The reasons they offer include long-term labor contracts, fear of declining productivity resulting from lower wages, and avoiding having disgruntled workers in the workplace.

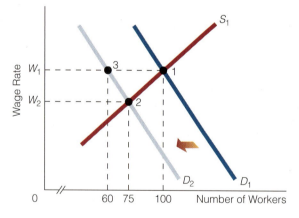

at W_1. At this wage, the quantity demanded of labor equals the quantity supplied of labor and both are 100 workers. Now let's suppose the demand for goods and services declines in the economy; that is, the aggregate demand (AD) curve shifts leftward. As a result of lower AD in the economy, firms are producing and selling fewer goods and services. Therefore, their demand for labor decreases; in Exhibit 3, the demand-for-labor curve shifts leftward from D_1 to D_2. If the labor market were like the stock market and equilibrated quickly to its new equilibrium wage rate (W_2), the labor market would move to point 2. Fewer people would be working at point 2 than at point 1, and the people who were working would be earning less (W_2 instead of W_1). Also, 25 people would have been fired.

Keynesian economists often argue that the labor market does not adjust in the same way or as quickly as the stock market does. In other words, wage rates aren't likely to fall simply because the demand for labor has declined (from D_1 to D_2). The wage rate W_1 is likely to be inflexible downward; that is, it isn't likely to *decline*—at least for some time.

Why is the wage rate inflexible downward? One explanation has to do with long-term labor contracts. To illustrate, suppose management and workers enter into a three-year contract that specifies a wage rate of $20 an hour for the duration of the contract. Management might want to enter into such a contract for two reasons: fewer labor negotiations and fewer worker strikes, both of which effectively diminish or disappear while the contract is in force. Workers want to enter into such a contract also for two reasons: wage security and fewer strikes (strikes are costly for workers too).

There may also be solid microeconomic reasons for inflexible wages downward. Some economists argue that, at times, firms find it in their best interest to pay wage rates above equilibrium levels. For example, according to **efficiency wage models**, labor productivity depends on the wage rate that the firm pays its employees. Specifically, a cut in wages can cause a decline in labor productivity, in turn raising the firm's costs. (Basically, these models say that workers are more productive when they are paid a higher wage than when they are paid a lower one.) By paying an above-equilibrium wage, firms provide an incentive to workers to be productive and to do less shirking, among other things. If shirking declines, so do the monitoring (management) costs of the firm.

Efficiency Wage Models
These models hold that it is sometimes in the best interest of business firms to pay their employees wage rates that are higher than the equilibrium wage rate.

Look again at Exhibit 3, and think of how things look from the perspective of the employer, the person hiring workers. The demand for labor has declined, and the new equilibrium wage rate is W_2. If the employer decides to go with the new equilibrium wage rate, two things will happen: The employer has to (1) fire 25 workers and (2) pay the 75 remaining workers a lower wage rate than they were previously receiving. But then the employer is likely to have to face 75 disgruntled workers every day. Now, disgruntled workers (who may not understand *why* the employer has decided to pay them less) are not likely to be the same as when they were paid more. They may be less productive, shirk more, and perhaps even steal from the employer.

Will things be much different if the employer continues to pay W_1 and keeps 60 workers instead of 75 workers (in other words, fire 40 workers instead of 25)? Some economists argue that paying W_1 might be better for the employer than paying the lower wage W_2. At W_2, the employer has 75 workers who are angry because they are being paid a lower wage—and the employer has to work with these 75 disgruntled workers every day. But if the employer pays W_1 instead of W_2 and fires 40 workers, they will all be disgruntled, but they won't be disgruntled *at work*. They are disgruntled *at home*, away from the employer. The remaining 60 workers are not disgruntled because they haven't had their wage rate lowered and they haven't been fired. In fact, they may

ECONOMICS 24/7

The Financial and Economic Crisis of 2007–2009: Can a Housing Bust Lead to an Imploding Economy?

In the last chapter, we discussed a self-regulating economy: When the economy is in a recessionary gap, it regulates itself back to long-run equilibrium. In this chapter, we have stated that an economy could get stuck in a recessionary gap if wages are inflexible downward. Some economists use the model in this chapter to explain the events of the latest financial and economic crisis.

Suppose an economy in long-run equilibrium undergoes a shock, such as the bursting of the housing bubble, with the prices of houses dropping. In the United States, housing prices started declining in mid-2006. Because the value of a house is a part of a person's overall wealth, a decline in house prices leads to a decline in a person's wealth. As a result of a decline in wealth, the person is poorer (or less rich) and consequently cuts back on consumption. A decline in consumption leads to a decline in aggregate demand,

Renault Philippe/Hemis.Fr/Alamy

so the aggregate demand curve shifts leftward, as in Exhibit 4(a), and the economy is now in a recessionary gap.

If the economy were self-regulating, it could get itself out of the recessionary gap. But if wages are inflexible downward, the economy is stuck in the recessionary gap.

Now look at the labor market in Exhibit 4(b). The labor market is initially in equilibrium at point 1. As a result of aggregate demand falling in the economy [see Exhibit 4(a)], firms are selling less output. So they do not need as much labor, and the demand for labor shifts leftward in Exhibit 4(b). Because the wage rate is inflexible downward, the number of workers hired in the labor market falls from 10 million to 8 million. In other words, 2 million workers are fired. As workers are fired, their incomes fall; as a result of lower incomes, individuals cut back on

> **EXHIBIT 4**

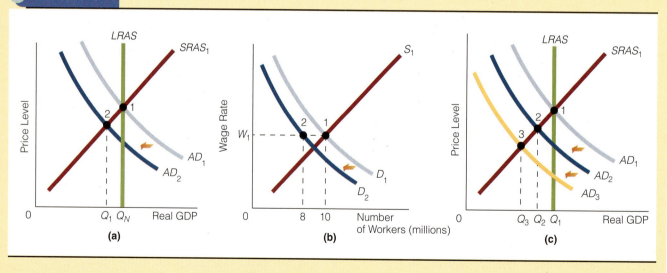

consumption. So aggregate demand shifts leftward again and into a deeper recessionary gap. [See Exhibit 4(c).]

What does this exposition tell us? A housing bust (declining house prices) can be the catalyst for an economy that falls into a recessionary gap. Further, if the economy is not self-regulating, a cascade of events can cause the economy to "implode" upon itself.

A decline in aggregate demand leads to a recessionary gap that, if wages are inflexible downward, leads to some workers being fired, leading in turn to lower incomes and another decline in aggregate demand. Thus, the recessionary gap deepens. Graphically, in Exhibit 4, instead of being between Q_1 and Q_2, the recessionary gap is between Q_1 and Q_3.

appreciate their employer all the more for not cutting their wage rates and for not firing them.

To recap, Keynesian economists often argue that the labor market is not the same as the stock market. The stock market equilibrates quickly to changes in demand and supply. The labor market may adjust slowly. In particular, a lowered demand for labor may not be met with a declining wage rate. Wage rates might be inflexible downward (at least for some time). If wage rates are inflexible downward, then the self-regulating properties of an economy (discussed in Chapter 9) are in question. Specifically, an economy might get stuck in a recessionary gap, represented by point 1 in Exhibit 2.

10-1d Keynes on Prices

Recall again what classical economists (among others) believe occurs when a recessionary gap exists: Wage rates fall, the *SRAS* curve shifts to the right, and the price level begins to decrease—stop right there! The phrase "the price level begins to decrease" tells us that classical economists believe that prices in the economy are flexible: They move up and down in response to market forces.

Keynes said that the internal structure of an economy is not always competitive enough to allow prices to fall. Recall from Chapter 3 how the forces of supply and demand operate when price is above equilibrium. A surplus is generated, and price falls until the quantity supplied of the good equals the quantity demanded. Keynes suggested that anticompetitive or monopolistic elements in the economy sometimes prevent price from falling.

10-1e Is It a Question of the Time It Takes for Wages and Prices to Adjust?

Classical economists believed that both wages and prices are flexible and adjust downward in a recessionary gap. Keynes, however, suggested that wages and prices are not flexible in a downward direction and may not adjust downward in a recessionary gap.

Many economists today take a position somewhere between Keynes's and that of the classical economists. For them, the question is not whether wages and prices are flexible downward, but *how long it takes for them to adjust downward.*

Exhibit 5 shows the economy in a recessionary gap at point 1. The relevant short-run aggregate supply curve is $SRAS_1$; the wage rate is $10 per hour and the

> EXHIBIT 5

A Question of How Long It Takes for Wage Rates and Prices to Fall

Suppose the economy is in a recessionary gap at point 1. Wage rates are $10 per hour, and the price level is P_1. The issue may not be whether wage rates and the price level fall, but how long they take to reach long-run levels. If they take a short time, then classical economists are right: The economy is self-regulating. If they take a long time—perhaps years—then Keynes is right: The economy is not self-regulating over any reasonable length of time.

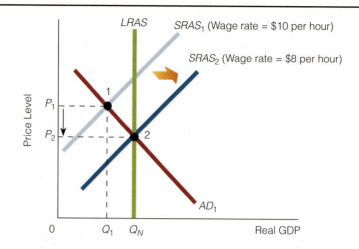

price level is P_1. Classical economists expect the wage rate and price level to fall, whereas Keynes said that that might not happen. But did Keynes mean that, if the economy is in a recessionary gap, *the wage rate will never fall and the price level will never adjust downward?* Most economists think not. The question is *how long* the wage rate and price level will take to fall. Will they fall in a few weeks? In a few months? In five years? The question is relevant because the answer determines how long an economy will be in a recessionary gap and thus how long the economy takes to self-regulate.

Look at the question this way: If it takes only a few weeks or months for wage rates to fall (say, to $8 an hour), for the short-run aggregate supply curve to shift from $SRAS_1$ to $SRAS_2$, and for the price level to fall from P_1 to P_2, then, for all practical purposes, the economy is almost instantaneously self-regulating. But if all this takes years to happen, the economy can hardly be considered self-regulating over any reasonable amount of time.

The classical position is that the time required for wages and prices to adjust downward is short enough to call the economy self-regulating. The Keynesian position is that the time is long enough to say that the economy is not self-regulating. Instead, the Keynesians believe that the economy is inherently unstable and that it can remain in a recessionary gap for a long time.

Different Assumptions, Different Conclusions The economist knows that assumptions affect conclusions. For example, classical economists assumed that wages are flexible, but Keynes assumed that wages might be inflexible at times. This difference in assumptions affects policy conclusions.

For example, classical economists, assuming that wages are flexible, will reach different policy conclusions than will Keynes, who is assuming that wages are inflexible.

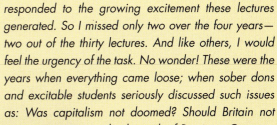

ECONOMICS 24/7

Was Keynes a Revolutionary in Economics?

John Maynard Keynes was born in Cambridge, England, on June 5, 1883, and died at Tilton (in Sussex) on April 21, 1946. His father was John Neville Keynes, an eminent economist and author of *The Scope and Method of Political Economy*.[2] Keynes's mother was one of the first female students to attend Cambridge University and presided as mayor of the city of Cambridge for a time.

John Maynard Keynes was educated at Eton and at King's College, Cambridge, where he received a degree in mathematics in 1905. At Cambridge, he studied under the well-known and widely respected economist Alfred Marshall. In 1925, Keynes married Russian ballerina Lydia Lopokova. He was prominent in British social and intellectual circles and enjoyed art, theater, opera, debate, and collecting rare books.

Many economists rank Keynes's *The General Theory of Employment, Interest and Money* (published on February 4, 1936) alongside Adam Smith's *Wealth of Nations* (published on March 9, 1776) and Karl Marx's *Das Kapital* (full title, *Kritik der politischen Ökonomie* (English, *Capital: Critique of Political Economy*, published in three volumes from 1867 to 1894) as the most influential economic treatises ever written.

Before the publication of *The General Theory*, Keynes presented the ideas contained in the work in a series of university lectures that he gave between October 10, 1932, and December 2, 1935. Ten days after his last lecture, he sent off to the publisher the manuscript for what was to become *The General Theory*.

Keynes's lectures were said to be both shocking (he was pointing out the errors of the classical school) and exciting (he was proposing something new). One of the students at these lectures was Lorie Tarshis, who later wrote the first Keynesian introductory textbook, *The Elements of Economics*.[3] In another venue, Tarshis wrote about the Keynes lectures and specifically about why Keynes's ideas were revolutionary:

I attended that first lecture, naturally awed but bothered. As the weeks passed, only a stone would not have

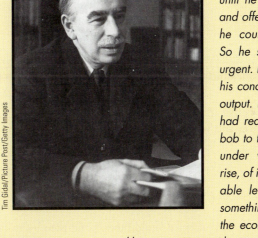

Tim Gidal/Picture Post/Getty Images

responded to the growing excitement these lectures generated. So I missed only two over the four years— two out of the thirty lectures. And like others, I would feel the urgency of the task. No wonder! These were the years when everything came loose; when sober dons and excitable students seriously discussed such issues as: Was capitalism not doomed? Should Britain not take the path of Russia or Germany to create jobs? Keynes obviously believed his analysis led to a third means to prosperity far less threatening to the values he prized, but until he had developed the theory and offered it in print, he knew that he could not sway government. So he saw his task as supremely urgent. I was also a bit surprised by his concern over too low a level of output. I had been assured by all I had read that the economy would bob to the surface, like a cork held under water—and output would rise, of its own accord, to an acceptable level. But Keynes proposed something far more shocking: that the economy could reach an equilibrium position with output far below capacity. That was an exciting challenge, sharply at variance with the views of Pigou and Marshall who represented "The Classical [Orthodox] School" in Cambridge, and elsewhere.[4]

2.   John Neville Keynes, *The Scope and Method of Political Economy* (London and New York: Macmillan, 1891).

3.   Lorie Tarshis, *The Elements of Economics, an Introduction to the Theory of Price and Employment* (Boston: Houghton Mifflin, 1947).

4.   Lorie Tarshis, "Keynesian Revolution," in John Eatwell, Murray Milgate, and Peter Newman, eds., *The New Palgrave: A Dictionary of Economics*, vol. 3 (London: Macmillan Press, 1987), p. 48.

The following chart is a quick review of some of the differences in the views of the classical economists and Keynes:

	Classical Economists	**Keynes**
Say's Law	Holds in a money economy. In other words, all output produced will be demanded.	May not hold in a money economy. In other words, more output may be produced than will be demanded.
Savings	Amount saved and interest rate are directly related. Savers save more at higher interest rates and save less at lower interest rates.	Savers may not save more at higher interest rates or save less at lower interest rates. If savers have a savings goal in mind, then a higher interest rate means that savers can save less and still reach their goal.
Investment	Amount invested is inversely related to interest rate. Businesses invest more at lower interest rates and invest less at higher interest rates.	If expectations are pessimistic, a lower interest rate may not stimulate additional business investment.
Prices	Flexible	May be inflexible downward.
Wages	Flexible	May be inflexible downward.

SELF-TEST

(Answers to Self-Test Questions are in Answers to Self-Test Questions at the back of the book.)

1. What do Keynesians mean when they say that the economy is inherently unstable?

2. "What matters is not whether the economy is self-regulating, but whether prices and wages are flexible and adjust quickly." Comment.

3. According to Keynes, why might aggregate demand be too low?

10-2 THE SIMPLE KEYNESIAN MODEL

Economists build models and theories to better understand the economic world. Of the many such models, we have already discussed a few: the theory of supply and demand and the classical theory of interest rates. In this section, we identify and discuss a few of the key components and themes of another prominent macroeconomics model: *the simple Keynesian model.*

10-2a Assumptions

In the simple Keynesian model, certain simplifying assumptions hold:

- First, the price level is assumed to be constant until the economy reaches its full-employment, or Natural Real GDP, level.

- Second, there is no foreign sector: the model represents a *closed economy*, not an *open economy*. So total spending in the economy is the sum of consumption, investment, and government purchases.

- Third, the monetary side of the economy is excluded.

10-2b **The Consumption Function**

Although Keynes was interested in the level of total spending in general, he was particularly concerned about consumption, which was a major concern because it is by far the largest slice of the total spending pie.

Keynes made three basic points about consumption:

1. Consumption depends on disposable income (income minus taxes).

2. Consumption and disposable income move in the same direction.

3. When disposable income changes, consumption changes by less.

These three points make a specific statement about the relationship between consumption and disposable income: the **consumption function**, which can written as

$$C = C_0 + (MPC)(Y_d)$$

where you already know that C is consumption, and where we use Y_d to specify disposable income. Let's look, then, at MPC and C_0. Think of consumption (as specified by the consumption function) as made up of two parts:

- *Autonomous consumption* (C_0) is independent of disposable income.

- *Induced consumption* [$MPC(Y_d)$] depends on disposable income.

MPC stands for **marginal propensity to consume**, which is the ratio of the change in consumption to the change in disposable income:

$$\text{Marginal propensity to consume} = \frac{\text{Change in consumption}}{\text{Change in disposable income}}$$

$$MPC = \frac{\Delta C}{\Delta Y_d}$$

The Greek symbol delta (Δ) stands for "change in." Thus, the MPC is equal to the change in consumption divided by the change in disposable income. To illustrate, suppose consumption rises from $800 to $900 as disposable income rises from $1,000 to $1,200. If we divide the change in consumption ($100) by the change in disposable income ($200), we see that the MPC equals 0.50. (Notice that the MPC is always a positive number between 0 and 1 because of Keynes's points 2 and 3.)

C_0 is **autonomous consumption**, which changes *not* as disposable income changes, but rather because of other factors.

The difference between autonomous and induced consumption can be illustrated with an example. Suppose your taxes are lowered and your disposable income consequently rises. With more disposable income, you buy more goods and services (e.g., entertainment, books, DVDs). The increase in disposable income has *induced* you to consume more—hence the name *induced consumption*. Next, suppose that, even though your disposable income has not changed, for some reason you are consuming more. You might be consuming more medication because you have recently become ill, or you might be consuming more car maintenance services because your car just broke down. Whatever the reason, you are consuming more of various goods and services even though your disposable income has not changed at all. This type of consumption is autonomous (i.e., independent) of disposable income—hence the name *autonomous consumption*.

Consumption Function
The relationship between consumption and disposable income. In the consumption function used in this text, consumption is directly related to disposable income and is positive even at zero disposable income: $C = C_0 + (MPC)(Y_d)$.

Marginal Propensity to Consume (*MPC*)
The ratio of the change in consumption to the change in disposable income: $MPC = \Delta C / \Delta Y_d$.

Autonomous Consumption
The part of consumption that is independent of disposable income.

Look again at the consumption function:

Consumption = Autonomous consumption
+ (Marginal propensity to consume × Disposable income)

$$C = C_0 + (MPC \times Y_d)$$

Suppose C_0 is $800, MPC is 0.80, and Y_d is $1,500, and we insert these numbers into the consumption function:

$$C = \$800 + (0.80 \times \$1,500) = \$800 + \$1,200 = \$2,000$$

So what will cause an increase in consumption? Consumption, C, will increase if any of the variables C_0, MPC, and Y_d increases. Thus, C can be increased in three ways:

1. *Raise autonomous consumption.* Suppose in our example that autonomous consumption, C_0, goes from $800 to $1,000. This change will raise consumption to $2,200: $C = \$1,000 + (0.80 \times \$1,500) = \$2,200$.

2. *Raise disposable income.* Suppose disposable income, Y_d, goes from $1,500 to $1,800. This change will raise consumption to $2,240: $C = \$800 + (0.80 \times \$1,800) = \$2,240$. The increase in consumption from $2,000 to $2,240 is due to an increase of $240 in induced consumption, a dollar amount that the increase in disposable income induced.

3. *Raise the MPC.* Suppose the MPC rises to 0.90. This change will raise consumption to $2,150: $C = \$800 + (0.90 \times \$1,500) = \$2,150$.

In Exhibit 6, C_0 is assumed to be equal to $200 billion and the MPC to 0.80; thus, $C = \$200$ billion $+ (0.8)(Y_d)$. We then calculated different levels of consumption (column 3) for different levels of disposable income (column 1).

10-2c Consumption and Saving

In Exhibit 6, we also calculated the saving levels (column 5) at the different levels of disposable income. How did we calculate these levels? Well, we know that $C = C_0 + (MPC)(Y_d)$ and that households can only consume or save. So it follows that saving, S, is the difference between disposable income and consumption:

Saving = Disposable income − Consumption
= Disposable income − [Autonomous consumption
+ (Marginal propensity to consume × Disposable income)]

$$S = Y_d - [C_0 - (MPC \times Y_d)]$$

Marginal Propensity to Save (MPS)

The ratio of the change in saving to the change in disposable income: $MPS = \Delta S / \Delta Y_d$.

The **marginal propensity to save (MPS)** is the ratio of the change in saving to the change in disposable income:

$$\text{Marginal propensity to save} = \frac{\text{Change in saving}}{\text{Change in disposable income}}$$

$$MPS = \frac{\Delta S}{\Delta Y_d}$$

Disposable income can be used only for consumption or saving; that is, $C + S = Y_d$. So any change to disposable income can change only consumption or saving. Therefore, the marginal propensity to consume (MPC) plus the marginal propensity to save (MPS) must equal 1.

Marginal propensity to consume + Marginal propensity to save = 1

$$MPC + MPS = 1$$

In Exhibit 6, the *MPC* is 0.80; so the *MPS* is 0.20.

  EXHIBIT 6

Consumption and Saving at Different Levels of Disposable Income (in billions)

Our consumption function is $C = C_0 + (MPC)(Y_d)$, where C_0 has been set at $200 billion and $MPC = 0.80$. Saving is the difference between Y_d and C: $S = Y_d - [C_0 + (MPC)(Y_d)]$. All dollar amounts are in billions.

(1) Disposable Income, Y_d	(2) Change in Disposable Income, ΔY_d	(3) Consumption $C = C_0 +$ $(MPC)(Y_d)$	(4) Change in Consumption	(5) Saving $S = Y_d -$ $[C_0 + (MPC)(Y_d)]$	(6) Change in Saving
$ 800	$___	$ 840	$___	−$40	$___
1,000	200	1,000	160	0	40
1,200	200	1,160	160	40	40
1,400	200	1,320	160	80	40
1,600	200	1,480	160	120	40
1,800	200	1,640	160	160	40

10-2d The Multiplier

We know from the consumption function that a rise in autonomous consumption (C_0) will raise consumption (C) and, in turn, raise total spending. But *how much* will total spending rise? If C_0 rises by $40 billion, will total spending rise by $40 billion? According to Keynes, total spending would not rise by only $40 billion. The rise in C_0 will act as a catalyst to additional spending, and total spending will rise, in this case, by *more than* $40 billion.

For example, suppose an economy consists of 10 people, represented by the letters *A–J*. Suppose also that person *A* increases his autonomous consumption by buying $40 more of additional goods from person *B*. Now person *B* has witnessed an increase of $40 in her income. According to Keynes, person *B* will spend some fraction of this additional income, and how much she spends depends on her marginal propensity to consume (*MPC*). If her *MPC* is 0.80, then she will spend 80 percent of $40, or $32. If she spends this additional $32 on purchasing goods from person *C*, then person *C*'s income rises by $32 and now he will spend some percentage of that additional income. Again, how much he will spend depends on his *MPC*. If we again assume that the *MPC* is 0.80, then person *C* spends $25.60. So,

> Person *A* increases his *autonomous consumption* by $40 →
>
> This increase generates $40 *additional income* for person B →
>
> Person *B* increases her *consumption* by $32 →
>
> This increase generates $32 *additional income* for person C →
>
> Person *C* increases his *consumption* by $25.60 →
>
> And so on and so on.

All this economic activity represents the *multiplier process*: An initial rise in one (the first) person's autonomous consumption leads to a rise in income for another (the second) person, which then leads to additional consumption by the second person, which generates additional income for a third person, and so on and so on.

Suppose we now sum the initial rise in autonomous spending ($40) and all the additional spending it generates through the multiplier process. How much additional spending will have been generated? In other words, by how much will total expenditures rise?

The answer depends on the value of the multiplier. The **multiplier** (*m*) is equal to 1 divided by 1 − *MPC*:

$$\text{Multiplier } (m) = \frac{1}{1 - MPC}$$

For example, if the *MPC* = 0.80 (in each round of spending), then the multiplier equals 5:

$$\begin{aligned}\text{Multiplier } (m) &= \frac{1}{1 - MPC} \\ &= \frac{1}{1 - 0.80} \\ &= \frac{1}{0.20} \\ &= 5\end{aligned}$$

Our original increase in autonomous consumption ($40), multiplied by the multiplier (5), equals $200. So in our example, a $40 increase in autonomous consumption would increase total spending by $200.

Just as consumption has an autonomous spending component, so do investment and government purchases. The multiplier process holds for these sectors too.

The process also holds for a decrease in autonomous spending by one of these sectors of total spending. So, in general,

Change in total spending = Multiplier × Change in autonomous spending

To illustrate, suppose business owners become optimistic about the future of the economy. They believe that members of the household and government sectors will soon start buying more goods and services. In the expectation of better times, businesses buy more factories and capital goods, so investment spending rises. In this case, investment spending has risen even without any change in income or Real GDP; hence, the rise is in autonomous investment spending. According to the multiplier analysis, this additional autonomous investment spending will change total spending by some multiple. For example, if the multiplier is 5, then a $1 increase in autonomous investment will raise total spending by $5.

10-2e The Multiplier and Reality

So, in simple terms, a change in autonomous spending leads to a *greater change* in total spending. Also, in the simple Keynesian model, the change in total spending is *equal to* the change in Real GDP (assuming that the economy is operating below Natural Real GDP). The reason is that, in the model, prices are assumed to be constant until Natural GDP is reached, so any change in nominal total spending is equal to the change in *real* total spending.

However, two reality checks are necessary. First, the multiplier takes time to have an effect. In a textbook, going from an initial increase in autonomous spending to a multiple

Multiplier
The number that is multiplied by the change in autonomous spending to obtain the change in total spending. The multiplier (*m*) is equal to 1 ÷ (1 − *MPC*). If the economy is operating below Natural Real GDP, then the multiplier is the number that is multiplied by the change in autonomous spending to obtain the change in Real GDP.

ECONOMICS24/7

The Economics of Spring Break

During the weeklong spring break, many college students put away their books; pack their shorts, swimsuits, and tanning oil; jump into their cars; and head for the beaches. As they are driving to Fort Lauderdale, Galveston, Myrtle Beach, Daytona Beach, San Diego, and other coastal cities, the multiplier is getting ready to go to work.

Look at it this way: When college students from around the country head for, say, Daytona Beach, they have dollars in their pockets. They will spend many of these dollars in Daytona Beach on food and drink, motel rooms, dance clubs, and so on. As far as Daytona Beach is concerned, the dollars represent autonomous spending. More important, the dollars can raise the total income of Daytona Beach by some multiple. College students buy pizzas, beer, and sodas. The people who sell these items find their incomes rising. They, in turn, spend some fraction of their increase in income, generating additional income for still

John Davenport/San Antonio Express-News/Zuma Press, Inc./Alamy

others, who spend some fraction of their increase in income, and so on and so on.

For example, suppose college students spend $7 million in Daytona Beach during spring break. If the *MPC* is, say, 0.60 in Daytona Beach and if all the added income generated is spent in Daytona Beach, then college students will increase nominal income in that town by $17.5 million:

$$\frac{1}{1 - MPC} \times \$7 \text{ million}$$
$$= \frac{1}{0.40} \times \$7 \text{ million}$$
$$= 2.5 \times \$7 \text{ million}$$
$$= \$17.5 \text{ million}$$

Do the people who live in Daytona Beach want college students to visit their city during spring break? Many of them do because it means extra dollars in their pockets. College students from out of town, together with the multiplier, often make for robust economic times!

---

increase in either total spending or Real GDP takes only seconds. In the real world, this process takes many months.

Second, for the multiplier to increase Real GDP, *idle resources must exist at each spending round.* After all, if Real GDP is increasing (i.e., output is increasing) at each spending round, *idle resources must be available to be brought into production.* If they are not available, then increased spending will simply result in higher prices without an increase in Real GDP. Simply put, GDP will increase but Real GDP won't.

SELF-TEST

1. How is autonomous consumption different from consumption?

2. If the *MPC* is 0.70, what does the multiplier equal?

3. What happens to the multiplier as the *MPC* falls?

10-3 THE SIMPLE KEYNESIAN MODEL IN THE *AD–AS* FRAMEWORK

The first section of this chapter presented a few of Keynes's criticisms of the self-regulating economy, or classical position. The second section identified and discussed some of the key components of the simple Keynesian model, particularly the consumption function and the multiplier. In this section, we analyze the simple Keynesian model in terms of the aggregate demand and aggregate supply (*AD–AS*) framework. In the next section, we discuss the simple Keynesian model in terms of the total expenditures and total production (*TE–TP*) framework.[5]

10-3a Shifts in the Aggregate Demand Curve

Because there is no foreign sector in the simple Keynesian model, total spending consists of consumption (*C*), investment (*I*), and government purchases (*G*). Because the economy has no monetary side, changes in any of these variables can shift the *AD* curve. For example, a rise in consumption will shift the *AD* curve to the right; a decrease in investment will shift it to the left.

Let's consider aggregate demand in terms of what we know about the consumption function and the multiplier. A rise in autonomous consumption (C_0) will raise consumption (*C*) and therefore shift the *AD* curve to the right. How much the *AD* curve will shift depends on the multiplier. In our earlier example, autonomous consumption C_0 increases by \$40 and the multiplier (*m*) is 5.

$$\text{Change in total spending} = \text{Multiplier} \times \text{Change in autonomous spending}$$
$$= m \times \Delta C_0$$
$$= 5 \times \$40$$
$$= \$200$$

> **EXHIBIT 7**

The Multiplier and Aggregate Demand

An initial increase in autonomous consumption raises total spending and shifts the aggregate demand curve from AD_1 to AD_2. The curve does not end here, however. Because of the multiplier, the increase in autonomous spending generates additional income and additional spending, shifting the aggregate demand curve to AD_3.

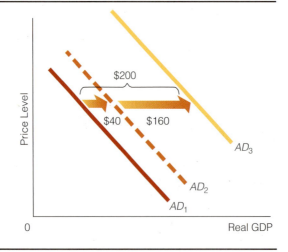

Exhibit 7 illustrates how the *AD* curve shifts in this situation. The original aggregate demand curve is AD_1. Autonomous consumption (C_0) rises by \$40, shifting the curve to AD_2, but the *AD* curve does not stay there. Because of the multiplier, the initial autonomous consumption spending generates more spending, eventually pushing the *AD* curve to AD_3. In other words, at the end of the process, the *AD* curve has shifted from AD_1 to AD_3. Part of this shift

---

[5] Some instructors may choose to assign only one of these two sections. It is clear at the end of the chapter which questions and problems go with which sections.

($40) is due to the initial rise in autonomous consumption, and part ($160) is due to the multiplier.

10-3b The Keynesian Aggregate Supply Curve

As noted earlier, in the simple Keynesian model, the price level is assumed to be constant until it reaches its full-employment, or Natural Real GDP, level. What does this assumption say about the Keynesian aggregate supply curve?

Think back to the discussions of aggregate demand and aggregate supply in the last two chapters and in the first section of this chapter. The *AD* curve is downward sloping, and the *SRAS* curve is upward sloping. Therefore, any shift in the *AD* curve (rightward or leftward) will automatically change (raise or lower) the price level. If the price level is assumed to be constant, then the Keynesian aggregate supply curve must have a horizontal section.

As shown in Exhibit 8, the Keynesian aggregate supply (*AS*) curve has both a horizontal section and a vertical section. The *AS* curve is horizontal until Q_N, or Natural Real GDP is reached, because the simple Keynesian model assumes that the price level is constant until Q_N is reached. Given this *AS* curve, what happens in the economy when the *AD* curve shifts? On the one hand, an increase in aggregate demand from AD_1 to AD_2 raises Real GDP from Q_1 to Q_2 but does not change the price level. (The price level remains at P_1.) On the other hand, once the economy has reached Q_N, any increases in aggregate demand change the price level. For example, an increase in aggregate demand from AD_3 to AD_4 raises the price level from P_2 to P_3.

> **EXHIBIT 8**

The *AS* Curve in the Simple Keynesian Model

The *AS* curve in the simple Keynesian model is horizontal until Q_N (Natural Real GDP) and vertical at Q_N. It follows that any changes in aggregate demand in the horizontal section do not change the price level but any changes in aggregate demand in the vertical section do change the price level.

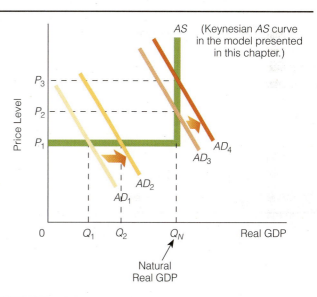

According to Keynes, a change in autonomous spending (e.g., a change in autonomous consumption) will stimulate additional spending in the economy. In our example, a rise in autonomous consumption of $40 generated an additional $160 worth of spending, so total spending increased by $200. (The multiplier was 5 because we assumed that the *MPC* was 0.80.)

Consider this question: Under what condition will a $200 *increase in total spending* lead to a $200 *increase in Real GDP*? That happens when the aggregate supply curve is horizontal—that is (in the simple Keynesian model), when the economy is producing less than Natural Real GDP. In other words, the *AD* curve in the economy must be shifting rightward (because of the increased spending) but must be within the *horizontal section* of the Keynesian *AS* curve.

In Unchanging Prices Suppose you read in the newspaper that the three sectors of a closed economy (household, business, and government) are all spending more but that, so far, there has been little to no change in the price level. Where is the economics?

The picture that should come to mind is the Keynesian aggregate supply curve—in particular, the horizontal section of the curve. Increases in aggregate demand in the horizontal section of the aggregate supply curve do not raise the price level.

10-3c The Economy in a Recessionary Gap

If, according to classical economists, the economy is self-regulating, then a recessionary gap or an inflationary gap is only temporary. In time, the economy moves into long-run equilibrium and produces Natural Real GDP (Q_N).

Keynes did not accept the idea that the economy always works this way, believing rather that the economy could get stuck in a recessionary gap. As shown in Exhibit 9, the economy could therefore be stuck at Q_1 (its equilibrium position) and be unable to get to Q_N on its own. In other words, the economy is at point A, and it is not able to get to point B. Keynes believed that the private sector—consisting of the household and business sectors—might not be able to move the economy from point A to point B. Stated differently, neither consumption nor investment will rise enough to shift the aggregate demand curve from its current position (AD_1).

But suppose the interest rate in the economy falls. Won't this be enough to get businesses to invest more, and thus won't the AD curve begin to shift rightward, headed for point B? Not necessarily, said Keynes, who didn't believe that investment spending was always responsive to changes in interest rates. For example, suppose businesses are pessimistic about future sales and the interest rate drops. Are businesses going to invest more just because interest rates have dropped, or might they feel so pessimistic that they choose not to invest, despite the lower interest rate? Keynes believed that the latter scenario could be the case.

> **EXHIBIT 9**

Can the Private Sector Remove the Economy from a Recessionary Gap?

The economy is at point A, producing Q_1. Q_1 is less than Q_N, so the economy is in a recessionary gap. The question is whether the private sector (consisting of consumption and investment spending) can remove the economy from the recessionary gap by increasing spending enough to shift the aggregate demand curve rightward to go through point B. Keynes believed that sometimes it could not. No matter how low interest rates fell, investment spending would not rise because of pessimistic business expectations with respect to future sales.

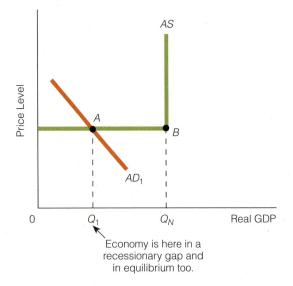

Economy is here in a recessionary gap and in equilibrium too.

10-3d **Government's Role in the Economy**

In the self-regulating economy of the classical economists, government does not have a management role to play. The private sector (households and businesses) is capable of self-regulating the economy at its Natural Real GDP level. By contrast, Keynes believed that the economy is not self-regulating and that economic instability is a possibility. In other words, the economy could get stuck in a recessionary gap.

Economic instability opens the door to government's playing a role in the economy. According to Keynes and to many Keynesians, if the private sector cannot self-regulate the economy at its Natural Real GDP level, then maybe the government must help. In terms of Exhibit 9, maybe the government has a role to play in shifting the *AD* curve rightward so that it goes through point *B*. We discuss the role government might play in the economy in the next chapter.

From How the Economy Works to One's Policy Positions An economist's view of the economy (how the economy works) and policy suggestions are often linked. For example, classical economists and their modern-day counterparts, who view the economy as self-regulating or inherently stable, believe in a laissez-faire policy: Government should keep its hands off the economy. Keynesians, however, who view the economy as inherently unstable, suggest that government has an economic role to play. In short, policy suggestions are sometimes a consequence of how one views the internal, or inherent, workings of an economy.

10-3e **The Theme of the Simple Keynesian Model**

In terms of *AD* and *AS*, the essence of the simple Keynesian model can be summarized in five statements:

1. The price level remains constant until Natural Real GDP is reached.

2. The *AD* curve shifts if there is a change in *C, I,* or *G.*

3. According to Keynes, the economy could be in equilibrium and in a recessionary gap too. In other words, the economy can be at point *A* in Exhibit 9.

4. The private sector may not be able to get the economy out of a recessionary gap. In other words, the private sector (households and businesses) may not be able to increase *C* or *I* enough to get the *AD* curve in Exhibit 9 to intersect the *AS* curve at point *B*.

5. The government may have a management role to play in the economy. According to Keynes, government may have to raise aggregate demand enough to stimulate the economy to move it out of the recessionary gap and to its Natural Real GDP level.

6. We show the simple Keynesian model in the *AD–AS* framework in Exhibit 10 in both (a) flowchart form and diagrammatic form (b) diagrammatic form.

> **EXHIBIT 10**

The Simple Keynesian Model in the AD–AS Framework

The purpose of the simple Keynesian model is to explain changes in Real GDP. In (a), the model is presented as a flowchart. Real GDP is determined by aggregate demand and aggregate supply. Aggregate demand depends on C, consumption; I, investment; and G, government purchases. In (b), we show a diagrammatic exposition of the model in the AD–AS framework.

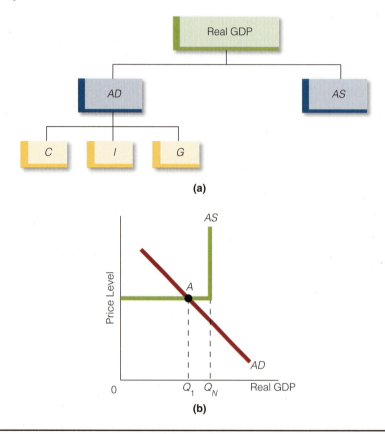

(a)

(b)

---

1. What was Keynes's position on the self-regulating properties of an economy?

2. What will happen to Real GDP if autonomous spending rises and the economy is operating in the horizontal section of the Keynesian AS curve? Explain your answer.

3. An economist who believes that the economy is self-regulating is more likely to advocate laissez-faire than one who believes that the economy is inherently unstable. Do you agree or disagree? Explain your answer.

10-4 THE SIMPLE KEYNESIAN MODEL IN THE *TE–TP* FRAMEWORK

Just as a story can be told in different languages, an economic model can be presented in various frameworks. The last section presented the simple Keynesian model in terms of the familiar (diagrammatic) *AD–AS* framework of analysis. But the simple

Keynesian model was first presented, not in terms of *AD–AS*, but in terms of the *TE–TP* framework. This framework has been known by different names, three of which are the Keynesian cross, income expenditure, and total expenditure–total production. In our discussion, we will refer to it as total expenditure–total production, or simply the *TE–TP* framework.

10-4a Deriving a Total Expenditures (*TE*) Curve

Just as we derived *AD* and *AS* curves in the *AD–AS* framework, we want to derive a total expenditures (*TE*) curve in the *TE–TP* framework. Total expenditures are the sum of its parts: consumption, investment, and government purchases. To derive a *TE* curve, first derive a diagrammatic representation of consumption, investment, and government purchases, as shown in Exhibit 11.

1. *Consumption.* As disposable income rises, so does consumption, as shown arithmetically in columns (1) and (3) of Exhibit 6. Because the *MPC* is less than 1, consumption rises by less than disposable income rises. Consumption also rises as Real GDP rises, but again by a smaller percentage. For example, if Real GDP rises by $100, consumption may rise by $80. Exhibit 11(a) shows consumption as an upward-sloping curve. Notice that, as Real GDP rises from Q_1 to Q_2, consumption rises from $7 trillion to $7.5 trillion.

2. *Investment.* To simplify things in deriving *TE*, the investment curve in Exhibit 11(b) is shown to be constant at $1 trillion, whether Real GDP is Q_1 or Q_2.

3. *Government purchases.* We simplify the government spending curve too. In Exhibit 11(c), government purchases are constant at $1.5 trillion, regardless of the amount of Real GDP.

Exhibit 11(d) shows a *TE* curve. We simply added the components of total expenditures at the two Real GDP levels (Q_1 and Q_2), plotted the relevant points, and then drew a line through the points. At Q_1 total expenditures are $9.5 trillion, and at Q_2 they are $10.0 trillion. The *TE* curve is upward sloping.

10-4b Where the Consumption Curve and the Total Expenditures Curve Cut the Vertical Axis: More on Exhibit 11

Look back at panels (a) and (d) of Exhibit 11. Notice that in panel (a) the consumption curve (*C*) cuts the vertical axis at some positive dollar amount when either disposable income or Real GDP is zero. A question arises: How can consumption be some positive dollar amount when, say, disposable income is zero? To answer the question, let's return to the consumption equation:

$$C = C_0 + (MPC)(Y_d)$$

Now notice that autonomous consumption, C_0, is independent of disposable income, Y_d. In other words, when disposable income is zero, autonomous consumption can be some positive dollar amount. For example, suppose we set autonomous consumption equal to $800. We can then rewrite the consumption function as

$$C = \$800 + (MPC)(Y_d)$$

This means that overall consumption (*C*) will be $800 even if disposable income is zero dollars. (If we set $Y_d = \$0$ in the equation, then $C = C_0 = \$800$.)

> **EXHIBIT 11**

The Derivation of the Total Expenditures (TE) Curve

At different levels of Real GDP, we sum (a) consumption, (b) investment, and (c) government purchases to derive the TE curve (d).

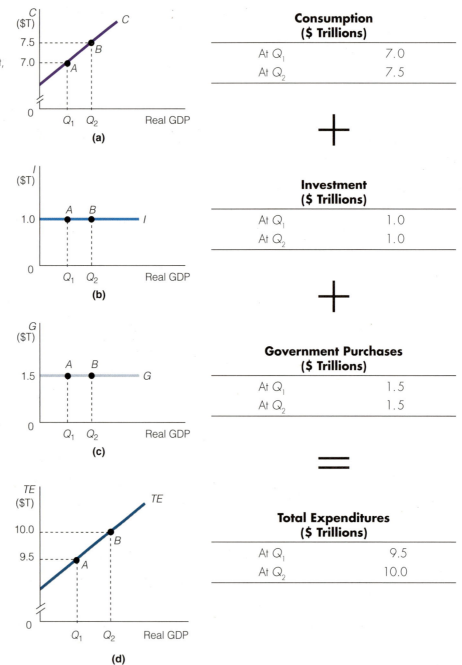

Consumption ($ Trillions)

At Q_1	7.0
At Q_2	7.5

+

Investment ($ Trillions)

At Q_1	1.0
At Q_2	1.0

+

Government Purchases ($ Trillions)

At Q_1	1.5
At Q_2	1.5

=

Total Expenditures ($ Trillions)

At Q_1	9.5
At Q_2	10.0

Now let's return to panel (a) of Exhibit 11. Ask yourself what the distance from the origin up to the point where the curve cuts the vertical axis equals? The answer is that it equals autonomous consumption.

Now turn to panel (d) in Exhibit 11. Notice that the total expenditures curve (*TE*) cuts the vertical axis when Real GDP is zero dollars. So, then, what does the distance from the origin up to the point where the curve cuts the vertical axis equal? It equals autonomous consumption (C_0), plus investment, plus government purchases. To see why, keep in mind that total expenditures equals $C + I + G$. That is,

$$TE = C + I + G$$

Now, because $C = C_0 + (MPC)(Y_d)$,

$$TE = [C_0 + (MPC)(Y_d)] + I + G$$

Now set disposable income equal to zero dollars. Then total expenditures equals

$$TE = [C_0 + (MPC)(\$0)] + I + G$$

In other words, $TE = C_0 + I + G$ when disposable income equals zero.

10-4c What Will Shift the *TE* Curve?

The *TE* curve in the *TE–TP* framework plays the same role as the *AD* curve in the *AD–AS* framework. Both the *AD* curve and the *TE* curve shift with a change in *C, I,* or *G.* For example, a rise in *C* will shift the *TE* curve upward; a decline in *I* will shift the *TE* curve downward.

10-4d Comparing Total Expenditures (*TE*) and Total Production (*TP*)

Businesses produce the goods and services that are bought in the three sectors of the economy (household, business, and government). Sometimes, though, businesses produce too much or too little in comparison to what the three sectors buy. For example, suppose businesses produce $10 trillion worth of goods and services, but the three sectors buy only $9.5 trillion worth. In this case, businesses have produced too much relative to what the three sectors of the economy buy.

Alternatively, businesses might produce $10 trillion worth of goods and services, but the three sectors of the economy buy $10.5 trillion worth. In this case, businesses have produced too little relative to what the three sectors of the economy buy. (If you are wondering how the three sectors of the economy can buy more than businesses produce, the answer has to do with the goods that businesses hold in inventory. We will soon explain the process.)

Finally, businesses could produce $10 trillion worth of goods and services, and the three sectors of the economy could buy exactly $10 trillion worth. In this case, businesses have produced exactly the right amount of goods and services.

Thus, the economy may be in one of three possible states in the *TE–TP* framework: The total expenditures (*TE*) of the three sectors of the economy can be less than, greater than, or equal to the dollar value of total production (*TP*). In other words, one of the following relations generally holds:

$$TE < TP$$
$$TE > TP$$
$$TE = TP$$

According to many economists, if the economy is currently operating where $TE < TP$ or $TE > TP$ (both states are described as disequilibrium), it will eventually move to where $TE = TP$ (where the economy is in equilibrium). The next section explains how this happens.

Thinking in Threes The concept of threes first came up when we discussed a single market (in Chapter 3)—specifically, when we said that a market could be in equilibrium, shortage, or surplus. In other words, a market had three possible states. In Chapter 9, we said that the economy could be producing a Real GDP level either greater than, less than, or equal to Natural Real GDP; that is, again, an economy may have three possible states. Now we are saying that total expenditures (TE) can be either less than, greater than, or equal to total production—once more, three possible states.

10-4e Moving from Disequilibrium to Equilibrium

Business firms hold an inventory of their goods to guard against unexpected changes in the demand for their product. For example, General Motors may hold an inventory of a certain type of car in case the demand for it unexpectedly and suddenly increases.

Although we know why business firms hold an inventory of their goods, we don't know *how much* inventory they will hold. For example, we do not know whether General Motors will hold an inventory of 1,000 cars, 2,000 cars, or 10,000 cars. (Inventories are usually held in terms of, say, a 45- or 60-day supply, but we have simplified things.) We do know that General Motors and all other business firms have some *optimum inventory*, which is "just the right amount" of inventory—not too much and not too little. With this concept in mind, consider two cases that illustrate how business inventory levels play an important role in the economy's adjustment from disequilibrium to equilibrium in the *TE–TP* framework.

Case 1: $TE < TP$ Assume that business firms hold an optimum inventory level of $300 billion worth of goods, that the firms produce $11 trillion worth of goods, and that the three sectors of the economy buy $10.8 trillion worth of goods. In this case, producers produce more than individuals buy ($TE < TP$). The difference is added to inventories, and inventory levels rise unexpectedly to $500 billion, which is $200 billion more than the $300 billion that firms see as optimal.

This unexpected rise in inventories signals to firms that they have *overproduced*. Consequently, they cut back on the quantity of goods they are producing. The cutback in production causes Real GDP to fall, bringing Real GDP closer to the (lower) output level that the three sectors of the economy are willing and able to buy. Ultimately, *TP* will equal *TE*.

Case 2: $TE > TP$ Assume that business firms hold their optimum inventory level ($300 billion worth of goods), that they produce $10.4 trillion worth of goods, and that members of the three sectors buy $10.6 trillion worth of goods. How can individuals buy more than businesses produce? Firms make up the difference out of inventory. In our example, inventory levels fall from $300 billion to $100 billion because individuals purchase $200 billion more of goods than firms produced (to be sold). In fact, that is why firms maintain inventories in the first place: to be able to meet an unexpected increase in sales.

The unexpected fall in inventories signals to firms that they have *underproduced*. Consequently, they increase the quantity of goods they produce. The rise in production causes Real GDP to rise, bringing Real GDP closer to the (higher) real output level that the three sectors are willing and able to buy. Ultimately, *TP* will equal *TE*.

The Graphical Representation of the Three States of the Economy in the *TE–TP* Framework

The three states of the economy are represented in Exhibit 12. The exhibit shows a *TE* curve, which we derived earlier, and a *TP* curve, which is simply a 45-degree line (45 degrees because it bisects the 90-degree angle at the origin). Notice that, at any point on the *TP* curve, total production is equal to Real GDP (TP = Real GDP).[6] The reason is that *TP* and Real GDP are different names for the same thing. Real GDP, remember, is simply the total market value of all final goods and services produced annually within a country's borders, adjusted for price changes.

Look at the three Real GDP levels in the exhibit. At Q_1, Real GDP is $11 trillion. At that Real GDP level, *TE* is $10.8 trillion and *TP* is $11 trillion. This configuration illustrates Case 1, in which producers produce more than individuals buy ($TE < TP$), with the difference added to inventories. The unexpected rise in inventories signals to firms

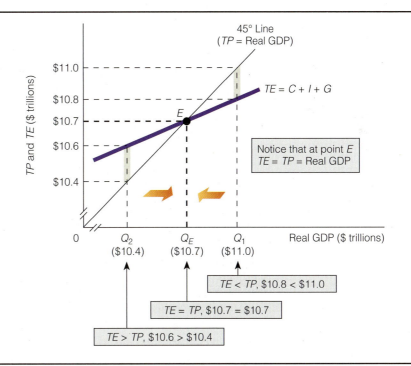

> **EXHIBIT 12**

The Three States of the Economy in the *TE–TP* Framework

At Q_E, $TE = TP$ and the economy is in equilibrium. At Q_1, $TE < TP$, resulting in an unexpected increase in inventories, signaling firms that they have overproduced, in turn leading the firms to cut back production. The cutback in production reduces Real GDP, and the economy tends to move from Q_1 to Q_E. At Q_2, $TE > TP$, resulting in an unexpected decrease in inventories, signaling firms that they have underproduced, in turn leading the firms to raise production. The increased production raises Real GDP, and the economy tends to move from Q_2 to Q_E.

6. Earlier, we said that the *TE* curve plays the role in the *TE–TP* framework that the *AD* curve plays in the *AD–AS* framework. In other words, roughly speaking, the *AD* curve is the *TE* curve. Similarly, the *TP* curve plays the role in the *TE–TP* framework that the *AS* curve plays in the *AD–AS* framework. In other words, roughly speaking, the *TP* curve is the *AS* curve. In the *AD–AS* framework, equilibrium is at the intersection of the *AD* and *AS* curves. As you will soon learn, in the *TE–TP* framework, equilibrium is at the intersection of the *TE* and *TP* curves.

that they have overproduced, and consequently they cut back on the quantity of goods they produce. The cutback in production causes Real GDP to fall, ultimately bringing Real GDP down to Q_E ($10.7 trillion in the exhibit).

Now look at Q_2, where Real GDP is $10.4 trillion. At this Real GDP level, TE equals $10.6 trillion and TP equals $10.4 trillion. This configuration illustrates Case 2, in which the three sectors of the economy buy more goods than business firms have produced ($TE > TP$). Business firms then draw from inventories to make up the difference between what they have produced and what the three sectors of the economy buy. Subsequently, inventories fall below optimum levels, and consequently businesses increase the quantity of goods they produce. The rise in production causes Real GDP to rise, ultimately moving Real GDP up to Q_E (again, $10.7 trillion).

When the economy is producing Q_E, or $10.7 trillion worth of goods and services, it is in equilibrium. At this Real GDP level, TP and TE are the same, at $10.7 trillion. The following table summarizes some key points about the state of the economy in the TE–TP framework:

State of the Economy	What Happens to Inventories?	What Do Firms Do?
$TE < TP$: Individuals are buying less output than firms produce.	Inventories rise above optimum levels.	Firms cut back production to reduce inventories to their optimum levels.
$TE > TP$: Individuals are buying more output than firms produce.	Inventories fall below optimum levels.	Firms increase production to raise inventories to their optimum levels.
$TE = TP$: Individuals are buying whatever output firms produce, and no more than that.	Inventories are at their optimum levels.	Firms neither increase nor decrease production.

10-4f The Economy in a Recessionary Gap and the Role of Government

Recall that, according to Keynes, the economy can be in equilibrium and in a recessionary gap too, as explained in the section on the simple Keynesian model in the AD–AS framework. [See Exhibit 10(b).] The same situation can exist in the TE–TP framework. For example, in Exhibit 12, the economy equilibrates at point E and thus produces a Real GDP level of $10.7 trillion worth of goods and services. However, there is no guarantee that the Real GDP level of $10.7 trillion is the Natural Real GDP level. As shown in Exhibit 13, the economy could be in equilibrium at point A, producing Q_E, when the Natural Real GDP level is Q_N. Because the economy is producing at a Real GDP level that is less than Natural Real GDP, it is in a recessionary gap.

How does the economy get out of the recessionary gap? Will the private sector (households and businesses) be capable of pushing the TE curve in Exhibit 13 upward so that it goes through point B, at which Q_N is produced? According to Keynes, the economy is not necessarily going to do so. Keynes believed that government may be necessary to get the economy out of a recessionary gap. For example, government may have to raise its purchases (raise G) so that the TE curve shifts upward and goes through point B.

> **EXHIBIT 13**

The Economy: In Equilibrium and in a Recessionary Gap Too

Using the *TE–TP* framework, we see that the economy is in equilibrium at point A, producing Q_E. Natural Real GDP, however, is greater than Q_E, so the economy is in a recessionary gap as well as being in equilibrium.

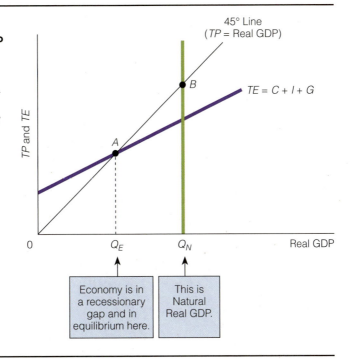

45° Line
(TP = Real GDP)

$TE = C + I + G$

TP and *TE*

0   Q_E Q_N Real GDP

Economy is in a recessionary gap and in equilibrium here.

This is Natural Real GDP.

10-4g Equilibrium in the Economy

Of the many debates in macroeconomics, one concerns equilibrium in the economy: where the economy naturally ends up after all adjustments have been made. As explained in the last chapter, some economists believe that the economy is self-regulating and that an economy naturally ends up in the long run producing Natural Real GDP. In this chapter, we have talked about economists who believe that the economy can be inherently unstable and that it can naturally end up producing a level of Real GDP less than Natural Real GDP. To the first group of economists, equilibrium is a desirable state of affairs; to the second group, equilibrium may not be if Real GDP is less than Natural Real GDP.

10-4h The Theme of the Simple Keynesian Model

In terms of *TE* and *TP*, the essence of the simple Keynesian model can be summed up in five statements:

1. The price level is constant until Natural Real GDP is reached.

2. The *TE* curve shifts if there is a change in any of *C, I,* and *G.*

3. According to Keynes, the economy could be in equilibrium and in a recessionary gap too. In other words, the economy can be at point *A* in Exhibit 13.

4. The private sector may not be able to get the economy out of a recessionary gap. In other words, the private sector (households and businesses) may not be able to increase *C* or *I* enough to get the *TE* curve in Exhibit 13 to rise and pass through point *B*.

> EXHIBIT 14

The Simple Keynesian Model in the *TE–TP* Framework

The purpose of the simple Keynesian model is to explain changes in Real GDP. In (a), the model is presented as a flowchart. Real GDP is determined by total expenditures (*TE*) and total product (*TP*). Total expenditures (*TE*) depend on C, consumption; I, investment; and G, government purchases. In (b) is a diagrammatic exposition of the model in the *TE–TP* framework.

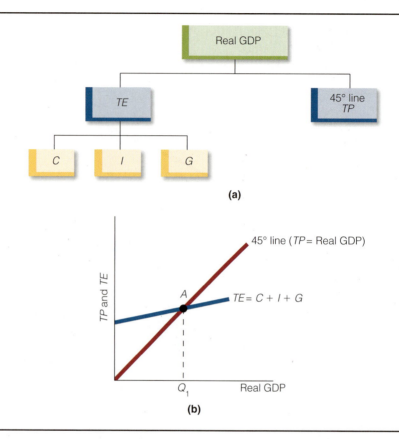

(a)

(b)

5. The government may have a management role to play in the economy. According to Keynes, government may have to raise *TE* enough to stimulate the economy to move it out of the recessionary gap and to its Natural Real GDP level.

We show the simple Keynesian model in the *TE–TP* framework in Exhibit 14 in both (a) flowchart form and (b) diagrammatic form.

SELF-TEST

1. What happens in the economy if total production (*TP*) is greater than total expenditures (*TE*)?

2. What happens in the economy if total expenditures (*TE*) are greater than total production (*TP*)?

Office  Hours

"Does a Lot Depend on Whether Wages Are Flexible or Inflexible?"

STUDENT:

Can what we learned in this chapter be seen as a criticism of what we learned in the last chapter?

INSTRUCTOR:

Much of it can be viewed as a criticism. Specifically, in the last chapter you learned the views of economists who believe that the economy is self-regulating. In this chapter you learned the views of economists who believe that the economy is not always self-regulating.

STUDENT:

What is at the heart of the disagreement between these two groups of economists?

INSTRUCTOR:

That's a good question. One thing at the heart of the disagreement is whether wages are flexible or inflexible. To illustrate, look back at Exhibit 2. There you see an economy in a recessionary gap. Now, if wages are flexible (as stated in the last chapter), then they will soon fall and the SRAS curve in Exhibit 2 will shift to the right. In time, the economy will remove itself from the recessionary gap, to point 2 in the exhibit. However, if wages are inflexible downward (as stated in this chapter), then wages will not fall, the SRAS will not shift to the right, and the economy will remain stuck—at point 1 in the exhibit—in the recessionary gap.

STUDENT:

Suppose the economists who say that the economy can get stuck in a recessionary gap are right. What then? Does the economy just stay stuck forever?

INSTRUCTOR:

What these economists usually propose is a government response. Specifically, they advocate fiscal or monetary policy to get the economy unstuck. We haven't discussed either fiscal or monetary policy yet, but we plan to in the next chapter.

STUDENT:

It seems to me that a lot depends on whether wages are flexible or inflexible. On the one hand, if wages are flexible, the economy self-regulates, removes itself from a recessionary gap, and thus requires no government response. On the other hand, if wages are inflexible (downward), the economy can get stuck in a recessionary gap and a government response may be needed.

INSTRUCTOR:

That's right. And because much depends on whether wages are flexible or inflexible, economists research such things as wages in various industries. For example, trying to find out whether wages in industries X and Y are flexible or inflexible may seem abstruse and esoteric to many people—who cares?—but, as you have just pointed out, a lot can depend on having the right answers.

Points to remember

1. Not all economists agree on how the economy works. In the last chapter, you learned the views of economists who believe that the economy is self-regulating. In this chapter, you learned the views of economists who believe that the economy is not always self-regulating.

2. Often, much depends on what may appear to be a small issue. An economist tells you that she is researching the degree of flexibility of wages in industry X. You may think, "What a small issue to research. Who cares about the degree of flexibility of wages? After all, they are what they are." However, as we have shown, sometimes these so-called small issues can make a big difference, such as whether government becomes involved in the economy.

CHAPTER SUMMARY

KEYNES ON WAGE RATES AND PRICES

- Keynes believed that wage rates and prices may be inflexible downward. He said that employees and labor unions will resist employer's wage cuts and that, because of anticompetitive or monopolistic elements in the economy, prices will not fall.

KEYNES ON SAY'S LAW

- Keynes did not agree that Say's law would necessarily hold in a money economy. He thought that it was possible for consumption to fall (for saving to increase) by more than investment increased. Consequently, a decrease in consumption (or an increase in saving) could lower total expenditures and aggregate demand in the economy.

CONSUMPTION FUNCTION

- Keynes made three points about consumption and disposable income: (1) Consumption depends on disposable income. (2) Consumption and disposable income move in the same direction. (3) As disposable income changes, consumption changes by less. These three ideas are incorporated into the consumption function, $C = C_0 + (MPC \times Y_d)$, where C_0 is autonomous consumption, MPC is the marginal propensity to consume, and Y_d is disposable income.

THE MULTIPLIER

- A change in autonomous spending will bring about a multiple change in total spending. The overall change in spending is equal to the multiplier $[1/(1 - MPC)]$ times the change in autonomous spending.

THE SIMPLE KEYNESIAN MODEL IN THE *AD–AS* FRAMEWORK

- Changes in consumption, investment, and government purchases will change aggregate demand.

- A rise in C, I, or G will shift the AD curve to the right.
- A decrease in C, I, or G will shift the AD curve to the left.
- The aggregate supply curve in the simple Keynesian model has both a horizontal section and a vertical section. The kink between the two sections is at the Natural Real GDP level. If aggregate demand changes in the horizontal section of the curve (when the economy is operating below Natural Real GDP), Real GDP changes but the price level does not. If aggregate demand changes in the vertical section of the curve (when the economy is operating at Natural Real GDP), the price level changes but Real GDP does not.

THE SIMPLE KEYNESIAN MODEL IN THE *TE–TP* FRAMEWORK

- Changes in consumption, investment, and government purchases will change total expenditures.
- A rise in C, I, or G will shift the TE curve upward.
- A decrease in C, I, or G will shift the TE curve downward.
- If total expenditures (TE) equals total production (TP), the economy is in equilibrium. If $TE < TP$, the economy is in disequilibrium and inventories will unexpectedly rise, signaling firms to cut back production. If $TE > TP$, the economy is in disequilibrium and inventories will unexpectedly fall, signaling firms to increase production.
- Equilibrium occurs where $TE = TP$. The equilibrium level of Real GDP may be less than the Natural Real GDP level, and the economy may be stuck at this lower level of Real GDP.

A KEYNESIAN THEME

- Keynes proposed that the economy could reach its equilibrium position even if Real GDP is below Natural Real GDP; that is, the economy could be in equilibrium and in a recessionary gap too. Furthermore, he argued that the economy may not be able to get out of a recessionary gap by itself: Government may need to play a management role in the economy.

KEY TERMS AND CONCEPTS

Efficiency Wage Models
Consumption Function

Marginal Propensity to
Consume (*MPC*)

Autonomous Consumption
Marginal Propensity to Save
(*MPS*)

Multiplier

VIDEO QUESTIONS AND PROBLEMS

Video Questions and Problems are available on MindTap for Arnold 12e or by searching for Arnold on www.cengagebrain.com

1. According to Keynesian economists, what is the explanation of why an economy may not be able to remove itself from a recessionary gap?

2. Outline the differences between Keynes and the classical economists when it comes to (1) Say's law in a money economy and (2) investment.

3. The shape of the aggregate supply curve matters to changes in the price level and Real GDP, given a change in aggregate demand. Do you agree or disagree with this statement? Explain your answer.

4. Diagrammatically represent and explain the equilibrating process in the simple Keynesian model in the *TE–TP* framework.

5. In the simple Keynesian model, an economy can be in equilibrium and in a recessionary gap too. Do you agree or disagree? Explain and diagrammatically represent your answer in terms of the *AD–AS* framework.

QUESTIONS AND PROBLEMS

Questions 1–5 are based on the first section of the chapter, questions 6–12 are based on the second section, questions 13–20 are based on the third section, and questions 21–25 are based on the fourth section.

1. How is Keynes's position different from the classical position with respect to wages, prices, and Say's law?

2. Classical economists assumed that wage rates, prices, and interest rates are flexible and will adjust quickly. Consider an extreme case: Suppose classical economists believed that wage rates, prices, and interest rates would adjust instantaneously. What would the classical aggregate supply (*AS*) curve look like? Explain your answer.

3. Give two reasons explaining why wage rates may not fall.

4. How was Keynes's position different from the classical position with respect to saving and investment?

5. According to some economists, why might business firms pay wage rates above market-clearing levels?

6. Given the Keynesian consumption function, how would a cut in income tax rates affect consumption? Explain your answer.

7. Look at the Keynesian consumption function: $C = C_0 + (MPC \times Y_d)$. What part of it relates to autonomous consumption? What part of it relates to induced consumption? Define autonomous consumption and induced consumption.

8. Using the Keynesian consumption function, prove numerically that, as the *MPC* rises, saving declines.

9. Explain the multiplier process.

10. What is the relationship between the *MPC* and the multiplier?

11. Explain how a rise in autonomous spending can increase total spending by some multiple.

12. In which factors will a change lead to a change in consumption?

13. According to Keynes, can an increase in saving shift the *AD* curve to the left? Explain your answer.

14. What factors will shift the *AD* curve in the simple Keynesian model?

15. According to Keynes, an increase in saving and a decrease in consumption may lower total spending in the economy. But how could that happen if the increased saving lowers interest rates (as shown in the last chapter)? Wouldn't a decrease in interest rates increase investment spending, thus counteracting the decrease in consumption spending?

16. Can a person believe that wages are inflexible downward for, say, one year and also believe in a self-regulating economy? Explain your answer.

17. According to Keynes, can the private sector always remove the economy from a recessionary gap? Explain your answer.

18. What does the aggregate supply curve look like in the simple Keynesian model?

19. "In the simple Keynesian model, increases in *AD* that occur below Real GDP will have no effect on the price level." Do you agree or disagree with this statement? Explain your answer.

20. Suppose consumption rises while investment and government purchases remain constant. How will the *AD* curve

shift in the simple Keynesian model? Under what condition will the rise in Real GDP be equal to the rise in total spending?

21. Explain how to derive a total expenditures (*TE*) curve.

22. What role do inventories play in the equilibrating process in the simple Keynesian model (as described in the *TE–TP* framework)?

23. Identify the three states of the economy in terms of *TE* and *TP*.

24. If Real GDP is $10.4 trillion in Exhibit 12, what is the state of business inventories?

25. How will a rise in government purchases change the *TE* curve in Exhibit 12?

WORKING WITH NUMBERS AND GRAPHS

Questions 1–2 are based on the second section of the chapter, questions 3–4 are based on the third section, and questions 5–8 are based on the fourth section.

1. Compute the multiplier in each of the following cases:
   a. $MPC = 0.60$
   b. $MPC = 0.80$
   c. $MPC = 0.50$

2. Write an investment function (equation) that specifies two components:
   a. Autonomous investment spending
   b. Induced investment spending

3. Economist Smith believes that changes in aggregate demand affect only the price level, and economist Jones believes that changes in aggregate demand affect only Real GDP. What do the *AD* and *AS* curves look like for each economist?

4. Use the accompanying figure to explain the following two statements:

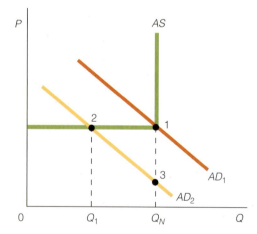

   a. According to Keynes, aggregate demand may be insufficient to bring about the full-employment output level (or Natural Real GDP).

   b. A decrease in consumption (due to increased saving) is not matched by an increase in investment spending.

5. The *TE* curve in Exhibit 11(d) is upward sloping because the consumption function is upward sloping. Explain.

6. In Exhibit 11(d), what does the vertical distance between the origin and the point at which the *TE* curve cuts the vertical axis represent?

7. In the accompanying figure, explain what happens if
   a. The economy is at Q_1
   b. The economy is at Q_2

8. In the accompanying figure, if Natural Real GDP is Q_2, in what state is the economy at point *A*?

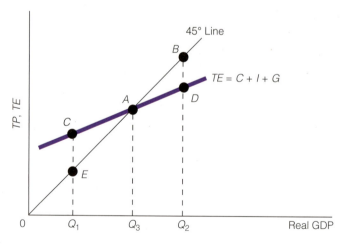

FISCAL POLICY AND THE FEDERAL BUDGET

© jiawangkun/Shutterstock.com

INTRODUCTION

Fiscal policy consists of changes in government expenditures and/or taxes to achieve economic goals, such as low unemployment, stable prices, and economic growth. In the United States, the Congress and the president together fashion fiscal policy. We begin our discussion with some facts and figures about government expenditures and taxation, and we then go on to discuss the effect of fiscal policy on the economy.

11-1 THE FEDERAL BUDGET

The federal budget has two not necessarily equal parts: government expenditures and tax revenues. You are familiar with the term *government purchases* from earlier chapters. Government expenditures—sometimes simply called government spending—are not the same as government purchases. Government expenditures are the sum of government purchases and government transfer payments.[1]

11-1a Government Expenditures

In 2013, the federal government spent $3.685 trillion, which was 22.7 percent of GDP for that year. The following table shows government spending as a percentage of GDP from 2011 through 2013 and projected from 2014 through 2018:

[1.] Remember from an earlier chapter that government purchases are the purchases of goods and services by government at all levels. Transfer payments are payments to persons, such as Social Security payments, that are not made in return for goods and services currently supplied. In this chapter, the terms *government expenditures, government spending, government purchases,* and *transfer payments* all refer to the *federal* government.

Year	Government Spending as a Percentage of GDP
2011	24.1
2012	22.8
2013	22.7
2014	22.2
2015	21.8
2016	21.6
2017	21.3
2018	21.2

The bulk of the $3.685 trillion in government spending in 2013 was spent on four programs: national defense, Social Security, Medicare, and Medicaid. These four programs together accounted for about 61 percent of all government spending that year.

11-1b Government Tax Revenues

The federal government imposes taxes and fees that generate revenue. In 2013, government revenues totaled $2.712 trillion, which was 16.7 percent of GDP for that year. The following table shows government tax revenues as a percentage of GDP from 2011 through 2013 and projected from 2014 through 2018:

Year	Government Tax Revenues as a Percentage of GDP
2011	15.4
2012	15.8
2013	16.7
2014	17.8
2015	18.6
2016	18.8
2017	18.8
2018	18.9

The bulk of government tax revenues comes from four taxes: the individual income tax, the corporate income tax, Social Security (payroll), and Medicare (payroll) taxes. In 2013, these four taxes accounted for 88 percent of total government tax revenues; the income tax by itself accounted for 45.5 percent of total government revenues.

11-1c Social Security, Medicare, and Medicaid in the Future

As we have noted, one way to view both tax revenues and government spending is as a percentage of GDP. Over the last 50 years, tax revenues as a percentage of GDP have largely been in the 15- to 19-percent range. In other words, tax revenues as a percentage of GDP have remained, year after year, in a rather narrow band.

Now let's suppose this trend continues in future years and that in the year 2050 tax revenues as a percentage of GDP are at the top of the range, 19 percent. What will all the tax revenues go for? Well, they will have to go for the sum of spending on just three federal government programs—Social Security, Medicare, and Medicaid—because spending on these three programs is projected to be approximately 19 percent in 2050. In other words, every dollar of tax revenue will go to these three programs. There will not even be one dollar left for national defense, education, infrastructure, and so on. To the degree that the federal government will do other things in 2050 than support Social Security, Medicare, and Medicaid, all the monies used to support other programs and activities will have to be borrowed.

11-1d Budget Projections

The following table shows projected government spending and tax revenues from 2015 through 2019:

Year	Government Spending ($ trillions)	Government Tax Revenues ($ trillions)
2015	3.908	3.332
2016	4.098	3.561
2017	4.247	3.761
2018	4.449	3.974
2019	4.724	4.226

Income Tax Structures   An income tax structure can be progressive, proportional, or regressive. Under a **progressive income tax**, the tax rate increases as a person's taxable income level rises. To illustrate, suppose Davidson pays taxes at the rate of 15 percent on a taxable income of $20,000. When his (taxable) income rises to, say, $30,000, he pays at a rate of 28 percent. And when his income rises to, say, $55,000, he pays at a rate of 31 percent. A progressive income tax is usually capped. Currently, the U.S. income tax structure is progressive, with six (marginal) tax rates. In 2013, these rates ranged from a low of 10 percent to a high of 39.6 percent.

Under a **proportional income tax**, the same tax rate is used for all income levels. A proportional income tax is sometimes referred to as a *flat tax*. For example, Kuan pays taxes at a rate of 10 percent whether her taxable income is $10,000 or $100,000.

Under a **regressive income tax**, the tax rate decreases as a person's taxable income level rises. For example, Lowenstein's tax rate is 10 percent when her taxable income is $10,000 and 8 percent when her taxable income rises to $20,000.

Exhibit 1 shows and briefly explains the preceding three income tax structures.

Progressive Income Tax
An income tax system in which one's tax rate rises as taxable income rises (up to some point).

Proportional Income Tax
An income tax system in which a person's tax rate is the same regardless of taxable income.

Regressive Income Tax
An income tax system in which a person's tax rate declines as his or her taxable income rises.

FINDING ECONOMICS

In How a Presidential Candidate Speaks A presidential candidate is speaking before a large group in Des Moines, Iowa, and he has just called the current income tax structure unfair. Someone from the crowd asks him what he means by "unfair." The candidate responds that individuals shouldn't pay a higher tax rate just because they earn a higher income. We should all pay the same tax rate, he argues. Where is the economics?

Obviously, the candidate favors a proportional income tax (i.e., a flat tax). Under both a progressive and a regressive income tax structure, individuals pay different tax rates at different taxable income levels. Only with a proportional income tax do individuals pay the same tax rate no matter what their taxable income is.

> **EXHIBIT 1**

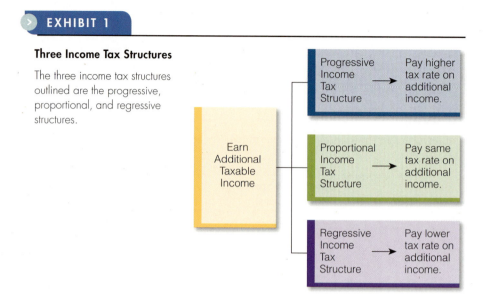

Three Income Tax Structures

The three income tax structures outlined are the progressive, proportional, and regressive structures.

Earn Additional Taxable Income

Progressive Income Tax Structure → Pay higher tax rate on additional income.

Proportional Income Tax Structure → Pay same tax rate on additional income.

Regressive Income Tax Structure → Pay lower tax rate on additional income.

Who Pays The Income Tax?   Economists often look at the tax situations of different income groups. For example, in 2011, the top 1 percent of income earners in the United States earned 18.7 percent of the total income earned that year and paid 35.1 percent of the total federal income taxes collected. The table that follows shows the income and taxes for various income groups in 2011. The column labeled "Income Split Point" identifies the dollar amount you would have had to earn in 2011 to be in the income group in that row. For example, to be in the top 1 percent of income earners in 2011, you would have had to earn more than $388,905.

Income Group	Group's Share of Total Income	Group's Share of Federal Income Taxes	Income Split Point
Top 1%	18.7	35.1	Greater than $388,905
Top 5%	33.9	56.5	Greater than $167,728
Top 10%	45.4	68.3	Greater than $120,136
Top 25%	67.8	85.6	Greater than $70,492
Top 50%	88.5	97.1	Greater than $34,823
Bottom 50%	11.5	2.9	Less than $34,823

Budget Deficit
Government expenditures greater than tax revenues.

Budget Surplus
Tax revenues greater than government expenditures.

Balanced Budget
Government expenditures equal to tax revenues.

11-1e Budget Deficit, Surplus, or Balance

The government budget can be in one of three states:

- If government expenditures are greater than tax revenues, the federal government runs a **budget deficit**.

- If tax revenues are greater than government expenditures, the federal government runs a **budget surplus**.

- If government expenditures equal tax revenues, the federal government runs a **balanced budget**.

ECONOMICS 24/7

Two Cab Drivers on New Year's Eve, or Turning Equal into Unequal

Many people believe that if two people do the same job, they should be paid the same dollar amount. The question of equal pay for equal work often arises in discussions about the jobs performed by men and women. In other words, many people say that, if a man and a woman do the same job, they should be paid the same dollar amount.

Sometimes the question of equal pay for equal work is extended to equal after-tax pay

for equal work. That is, if two people do the same job, then they should earn the same after-tax income. However, a progressive income tax structure sometimes makes this impossible.

To illustrate, suppose that, under a progressive income tax structure, a person who earns between $40,000 and $50,000 pays income tax at a tax rate of 20 percent. For every dollar earned over $50,000, but under $60,000, a person pays at a tax rate of 30 percent.

Now, consider cab drivers Smith and Jones. By December 30, Jones has earned $40,000 for the year and Smith has earned $50,000. Each drives the cab on New Year's Eve and each earns $300 for the

night. It follows that Jones and Smith receive equal pay for equal work.

The after-tax income that each receives for the job makes for a different story. Jones pays at a tax rate of 20 percent on the additional $300 that she earns, so she pays $60 in taxes and gets to keep $240 in after-tax income. Smith, on the other hand, now has an annual income of $50,300 and thus falls into a higher marginal tax bracket. He pays at a tax rate of 30 percent on the additional $300. So Smith pays $90 in taxes and has $210 in after-tax income. Smith does the same job as Jones but earns only $210 in after-tax pay, whereas Jones earns $240 after taxes.

Our conclusion: The progressive income tax structure can turn equal pay for equal work into unequal after-tax pay for equal work. Stated differently, a person can be in favor of either progressive income taxes or equal after-tax pay for equal work, but not both. Sometimes, you have to decide between one and the other.

In 2013, the budget deficit was $973 billion. Here are the projected budget deficits for 2014–2018:

Year	Deficit ($ billions)	Deficit as a Percentage of GDP (%)
2014	744	4.4
2015	576	3.2
2016	528	2.8
2017	487	2.4
2018	475	2.3

If the government spends more than its tax revenue and thus runs a budget deficit, where does it get the money to finance the deficit? For example, if the government spends $100 and receives only $70 in taxes, where does it get the $30 difference? The federal government—actually the U.S. Treasury—borrows the $30; that is, it finances the budget deficit with borrowed funds.

11-1f An Interesting Fact: Taxing Millionaires and the Budget Deficit

In 2012, the budget deficit was $1.148 trillion. It is a common belief that taxing the rich at a higher tax rate would help reduce or eliminate budget deficits. That may be true, but then two questions arise: "At what tax rate would you have to tax the rich to eliminate the deficit"? and "In how many years can the deficits be eliminated by taxing the rich at the higher tax rate?" To get an answer, let's look at the total income earned by millionaires in 2012. According to the Internal Revenue Service, this amount was $709 billion. It follows, then, that if the federal government taxed those earning more than $1 million at 100 percent in 2012, it would have generated $709 billion, which would have reduced the budget deficit from $1.148 trillion to $439. In short, taxing all millionaires at a tax rate of 100 percent would not even have eliminated the budget deficit in 2012. And, of course, people who are taxed at a tax rate of 100 percent will choose not to generate income the next year if it is going to be all taxed away.

11-1g Structural and Cyclical Deficits

Suppose the budget is currently balanced and then Real GDP in the economy drops. As Real GDP drops, the tax base of the economy falls, and if tax rates are held constant, tax revenues will fall. Another result of the decline in Real GDP is that transfer payments (e.g., unemployment compensation) will rise. Thus, government expenditures will rise as tax revenues fall. Consequently, a balanced budget turns into a budget deficit—a result of the downturn in economic activity, not because of current spending and taxing decisions by the government. Economists use the term **cyclical deficit** to describe the part of the budget deficit that is a result of a downturn in economic activity. The remainder of the deficit—the part that would exist if the economy were operating at full employment—is called the **structural deficit**. In other words,

Total budget deficit = Structural deficit + Cyclical deficit

To illustrate, suppose the economy is in a recessionary gap, government expenditures are currently $2.3 trillion, and tax revenues are $2.0 trillion. Then the (total) budget deficit is $300 billion. Economists estimate what government expenditures and tax revenues would be if the economy were operating at full employment. Assume that they estimate that government expenditures would be only $2.2 trillion and that tax revenues would be $2.1 trillion. The structural deficit—the deficit that would exist at full employment—would therefore be $100 billion. The cyclical deficit—the part of the budget deficit that is a result of economic downturn—would be $200 billion.

11-1h The Public Debt

A budget deficit occurs when government expenditures are greater than tax revenues for a *single year.* The **public debt**, sometimes called the "federal debt" or "national debt," is the *total* amount the federal government owes its creditors. Some of this debt is held by

Cyclical Deficit
The part of the budget deficit that is a result of a downturn in economic activity.

Structural Deficit
The part of the budget deficit that would exist even if the economy were operating at full employment.

Public Debt
The total amount that the federal government owes its creditors.

agencies of the U.S. government; that is, one entity in the government owes it to another. The remainder of the debt is held by the public and is referred to either as *public debt held by the public* or as *net public debt*. On July 30, 2014 the public debt was 17.5 trillion and the public debt held by the public was $12.5 trillion. (You can find the amount of the current public debt listed on the Bureau of the Public Debt website, at http://www .treasurydirect.gov/NP/debt/current.) The lowest recorded public debt was $33,733.05, on January 1, 1835. In 2005, the public debt as a percentage of GDP was 64.4 percent. For each of the years in the period 2014–2018, it is expected to be over 100 percent, as the following table shows:

Year	Public Debt as a Percentage of GDP (%)
2014	106.7
2015	106.5
2016	105.7
2017	104.5
2018	102.7

11-1i Valued-Added Tax

Some persons have proposed higher taxes or new taxes to deal with the enlarged budget deficits and growing public debt. One tax that has been suggested is the value-added tax (VAT). Some have proposed VAT as a supplementary revenue source, others as a substitute for current taxes.

There are two things to understand about a value-added tax: the value-added part and the tax part.

The Value-Added Part   *Value added* is the difference between what a producer sells a final good for and what it pays for an intermediate good. For example, suppose a farmer finds a seed and plants it. In time, wheat appears. The farmer harvests the wheat and sells it to a baker for $1. The value added is $1.00. The sequence of events is as follows:

- The farmer sells the wheat to the baker for $1.00.
- The farmer doesn't buy any intermediate goods (so intermediate goods "purchased" = $0.00).
- Value added = $1.00 − $0.00 = $1.00.
- Dollar amount kept by farmer = $1.00.

Now the baker, who has purchased the wheat, turns it into a loaf of bread, which he sells to a final consumer for $1.40. The value added is $0.40. The sequence of events is as follows:

- The baker sells the loaf of bread to a consumer for $1.40.
- The baker bought the wheat (the intermediate good) from the farmer for $1.00.
- Value added = $1.40 − $1.00 = $0.40.
- Dollar amount kept by baker = $0.40.

ECONOMICS 24/7

Do Voting Rules Matter to Taxing and Spending?

Earlier in the chapter, we identified the projected budget deficits for each year during the period 2014–2018. In 2014, the deficit will be in the $700 billion range; in 2015 and 2016, the $500 billion range; in 2017 and 2018, the $400 billion range. Are budget deficits what they are no matter what voting rule is used to pass taxing and spending bills?

Bill Clark/CQ-Roll Call Group/Getty Images

To illustrate, consider two voting rules: a simple-majority rule (51 percent is needed for passage of a bill) and a supermajority rule (say, 66 percent is needed for passage).

Consider both rules in the U.S. Senate, where there are 100 senators. Now, suppose a Senate bill proposes that government spending be raised by $200 billion. Under which voting rule—simple majority or supermajority—is the bill more likely to be passed and spending increased by $200 billion? The answer is the simple-majority voting rule, because it is harder to get 66 senators than 51 senators to agree on the spending increase. In short, the closer the voting rule for the bill moves to unanimity (100 out of 100 must agree before a bill is passed), the less likely it will be to pass the bill. We conclude, then, that if the objective is to limit government spending, a supermajority voting rule is more effective at doing that than a simple-majority voting rule.

What about raising taxes? Suppose a Senate bill proposes to raise income tax rates across the board. Is the bill more likely to be passed with a supermajority voting rule or a simple-majority voting rule? The answer is again a simple-majority voting rule. So, if the objective is to increase the probability of tax increases being passed, a simple-majority voting rule is more effective than a supermajority voting rule.

Now consider cutting both taxes and spending. If this is the objective, then, once more, a simple majority is more likely to get both done than a supermajority: It is easier to get 51 senators to agree on cutting taxes and spending than to get 66 to agree.

Finally, suppose one's objective is to increase government spending and decrease taxes. What voting rule is most likely to be effective? To get more government spending, you want the voting rule that makes this easier to do, which is simple majority. To decrease taxes, again you want the voting rule that makes *that* easier to do, which, once more, is simple majority. But keep this in mind too: If you want spending to increase and taxes to decrease, you want to make the opposite of each (decrease government spending and increase taxes) hard to do. So, for a bill that proposes a cut in government spending, you would opt for a supermajority, and for a bill that proposes an increase in taxes, you would want a supermajority too.

So, does the voting rule matter to whether government spending and taxes are raised or lowered? Yes. In short, government spending, taxing, and budget deficits are not simply a matter of being what they are. They are what they are, to a large degree, because of the voting rules used. Use a different set of voting rules, and it's likely that things would be different. To put it starkly, just ask yourself how likely government spending and taxes would increase or decrease with a unanimity voting rule?

Notice two things:

- The sum of the values added ($1.00 + $0.40) is equal to the price paid by the final consumer for the loaf of bread ($1.40):

  Sum of values added ($1.00 + $0.40) = Price of the loaf of bread purchased
  by consumer ($1.40)

- The value added at each stage of production is equal to the dollar amount kept by the seller of the good. For instance, the valued added by the farmer was $1.00, and this is the amount he kept.

The Tax Part   VAT is a *tax* applied to the *value added* at *each stage of production.* Suppose the VAT rate is 10 percent. A VAT rate of 10 percent applied to the $1.00 value added by the farmer is $0.10. A VAT tax rate of 10 percent applied to the $0.40 value added by the baker is $0.04. The total VAT ends up being $0.14.

Value added by farmer	$1.00
VAT rate of 10% applied to value added by farmer	$0.10
Value added by baker	$0.40
VAT rate of 10% applied to valued added by baker	$0.04
Total VAT = $0.10 + $0.04	$0.14

To see how the $0.14 ends up with government, we need to revisit our farmer–baker example, but this time with a VAT applied. Before, the farmer charges the baker $1.00 for wheat. This time, with a VAT tax rate of 10 percent, he charges the baker 10 percent more, or $1.10, for the wheat. Here is how things now look for the farmer:

- The farmer sells the wheat to the baker for $1.10.

- The farmer turns over 10¢ to the government (the VAT at the farmer's stage of production).

- The farmer keeps $1.00, which is the amount he kept when there was no VAT.

Whereas the baker sold a loaf of bread to the consumer for $1.40 before, this time, with a VAT rate of 10 percent, he charges 10 percent more, or $1.54, for a loaf of bread. Here is how things now look for the baker:

- The baker sells the loaf of bread to the consumer for $1.54.

- The baker paid $1.10 for the wheat.

- The baker turns over $0.04 to government (the VAT at the baker's stage of production).

- The baker keeps $1.54, *minus* $1.10 (what he paid to the farmer), *minus* $0.04 (what he turned over to government), or $0.40, which is what he kept when there was no VAT.

Finally, here are how things look for the consumer and government:

- Without the VAT, the customer paid $1.40 a loaf of broad. With the VAT, she pays $1.54.

- Without the VAT, government collected no VAT revenues. With the VAT, government collects $0.14 in VAT revenue.

So, the VAT (1) generates tax revenue and (2) raises prices.

Vat Compared with a Sales Tax   The VAT is nothing more than a less visible sales tax. To illustrate, in the example of the farmer and baker, this time we impose, instead of a VAT, a sales tax of 10 percent at the point of final purchase. In other words, our consumer buys a loaf of bread for a price of $1.40 plus a 10 percent sales tax of $0.14: Price + Tax = $1.54.

Notice two things: (1) The consumer pays $1.54 for the bread when a VAT is applied and when a sales tax is applied. (2) The sales tax of $0.14 is exactly equal to the VAT. In other words, government has two ways to generate $0.14 in tax revenue: impose a VAT or charge a sales tax. Either way, the customer ends up paying $1.54 for a loaf of bread and government generates $0.14 in tax revenue.

Finally, in comparing a VAT with a sales tax, critics often stress the point that a VAT is less visible than a sales tax. If a sales tax is raised from, say, 5 percent to 6 percent, almost everyone who buys something is aware of the tax increase. Indeed, the sales receipt plainly identifies the new, higher sales tax. But if the VAT rate is raised by the same amount, not everyone will know that the VAT has been raised. People may simply think that sellers are charging higher prices because the VAT is not itemized separately from what sellers charge other sellers. In the farmer–baker example, with a VAT, the farmer simply charged the baker $1.10 for wheat instead of $1.00 and the baker simply charged the consumer $1.54 for a loaf of bread instead of $1.40. With a VAT, consumers find it hard to distinguish between the seller's charging a higher price because the VAT rate has been raised and the seller's charging a higher price even without the VAT rate being raised. The VAT critics add the following: When a sales tax is raised, people look to government and say, "*Government* raised my taxes." When VAT is raised, people say, "*Sellers* raised the prices I pay."

11-1¡ Tax Deductions vs Subsidies

In the popular press, you will often hear someone say that some company or group is getting a subsidy (from the federal government) of so many dollars. It could be that the company or group is receiving a subsidy—but this is not always the case. Often, some people will talk about subsidies when they should be talking about tax deductions. Fact is, there is a difference between a subsidy and a tax deduction. With a subsidy, money goes from one person to another. Money comes from Smith and goes to Jones. With a tax deduction, it doesn't. To illustrate, if company X is being subsidized, this means that government is essentially taking money from taxpayers and handing it over to company X. But with a tax deduction, that is not happening. Instead, government is saying that if the company does something—such as keep its factories in the United States, pay taxes to foreign companies, and so on—then it can reduce the taxes that it pays by some dollar amount. In other words, instead of paying $10 million in taxes, it now pays, say, $8 million in taxes.

SELF-TEST

(Answers to Self-Test questions are in Answers to Self-Test Questions at the back of the book.)

1. Explain the differences among progressive, proportional, and regressive income tax structures.

2. What percentage of all income taxes was paid by the top 5 percent of income earners in 2011? What percentage of total income did this income group receive in 2011?

3. What four taxes account for the bulk of federal tax revenues?

4. Explain the cyclical budget deficit.

11-2 FISCAL POLICY

As described in the previous chapter, some economists believe that the economy is inherently unstable. They argue that government should play a role in managing the economy because the economy can get stuck in a recessionary gap. They believe that government should try to move the economy out of the recessionary gap and toward Natural Real GDP.

A major way government can influence the economy is through *fiscal policy.* **Fiscal policy** consists of changes in government expenditures and/or taxes to achieve economic goals, such as low unemployment, price stability, and economic growth.

11-2a Some Relevant Fiscal Policy Terms

Expansionary fiscal policy calls for increases in government expenditures and/or decreases in taxes in order to achieve macroeconomic goals. **Contractionary fiscal policy** is implemented through decreases in government expenditures and/or increases in taxes to achieve macroeconomic goals. In sum, we have

- *Expansionary fiscal policy:* Government expenditures are up and/or taxes are down.
- *Contractionary fiscal policy:* Government expenditures are down and/or taxes are up.

When deliberate government actions bring about changes in its expenditures and taxes, fiscal policy is said to be *discretionary.* For example, a decision by Congress to increase government spending by, say, $10 billion in an attempt to lower the unemployment rate is an act of **discretionary fiscal policy**. In contrast, a change in either government expenditures or taxes that occurs automatically in response to economic events is referred to as an act of **automatic fiscal policy**. To illustrate, suppose Real GDP in the economy turns downward, causing more people to become unemployed and, as a result, to automatically receive unemployment benefits. These added unemployment benefits automatically boost government spending.

11-2b Two Important Notes

In your study of this chapter, keep in mind the following two important points:

1. We deal only with *discretionary fiscal policy*—that is, deliberate actions on the part of policy makers to affect the economy through changes in government spending and/or taxes.

2. We assume that any change in government spending is due to a change in government purchases, not to a change in transfer payments. In other words, we assume that transfer payments are constant and therefore that changes in government spending are a reflection only of changes in government purchases.

11-3 DEMAND-SIDE FISCAL POLICY

This section focuses on how government spending and taxes—fiscal policy—can affect the demand side of the economy—that is, aggregate demand.

11-3a Shifting the Aggregate Demand Curve

How do changes in government purchases (G) and taxes (T) affect aggregate demand? Recall that a change in consumption, investment, government purchases, or net exports

Fiscal Policy
Changes in government expenditures and/or taxes aimed at achieving economic goals, such as low unemployment, stable prices, and economic growth.

Expansionary Fiscal Policy
Increases in government expenditures and/or decreases in taxes in order to achieve particular economic goals.

Contractionary Fiscal Policy
Decreases in government expenditures and/or increases in taxes in order to achieve economic goals.

Discretionary Fiscal Policy
Deliberate changes in government expenditures and/or taxes in order to achieve economic goals.

Automatic Fiscal Policy
Changes in government expenditures and/or taxes that occur automatically without (additional) congressional action.

can change aggregate demand and therefore shift the *AD* curve. For example, an increase in government purchases (*G*) increases aggregate demand and shifts the *AD* curve to the right. A decrease in *G* decreases aggregate demand and shifts the *AD* curve to the left.[2]

A change in taxes (*T*) can affect consumption, investment, or both and therefore can affect aggregate demand. For example, a decrease in income taxes increases disposable (after-tax) income, permitting individuals to increase their consumption. As consumption rises, the *AD* curve shifts to the right. An increase in taxes decreases disposable income, lowers consumption, and shifts the AD curve to the left.

11-3b Fiscal Policy: Keynesian Perspective (Economy Is Not Self-Regulating)

The model of the economy in Exhibit 2(a) shows a downward-sloping *AD* curve and an upward-sloping *SRAS* curve. As you can see, the economy is initially in a recessionary gap at point 1. Aggregate demand is too low to move the economy to equilibrium at the Natural Real GDP level. The Keynesian *perspective* of the economy is that the economy is not self-regulating. So the Keynesian *prescription* is to enact expansionary fiscal policy measures (an increase in government purchases or a decrease in taxes) to shift the aggregate demand curve rightward from AD_1 to AD_2 and to move the economy to the Natural Real GDP level at point 2.

> **EXHIBIT 2**

Fiscal Policy in Keynesian Theory: Ridding the Economy of Recessionary and Inflationary Gaps

(a) In Keynesian theory, expansionary fiscal policy eliminates a recessionary gap. Increased government purchases, decreased taxes, or both lead to a rightward shift in the aggregate demand curve from AD_1 to AD_2, restoring the economy to the natural level of Real GDP, Q_N. (b) Contractionary fiscal policy is used to eliminate an inflationary gap. Decreased government purchases, increased taxes, or both lead to a leftward shift in the aggregate demand curve from AD_1 to AD_2, restoring the economy to the natural level of Real GDP, Q_N.

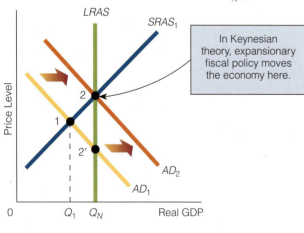

(a)
Expansionary Fiscal Policy for a Recessionary Gap

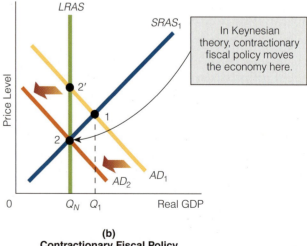

(b)
Contractionary Fiscal Policy for an Inflationary Gap

---

[2] Later in this chapter, when we discuss crowding out, we question the effect of an increase in government purchases on aggregate demand.

Why not simply wait for the short-run aggregate supply curve to shift rightward and intersect the aggregate demand curve at point 2′? Again, the Keynesians usually respond that the economy is not self-regulating, making one of two arguments: (1) The economy is stuck at point 1 and won't move naturally to point 2′, perhaps because wage rates won't fall. (2) The short-run aggregate supply curve takes too long to shift rightward, and in the interim we must deal with the high cost of unemployment and a lower level of Real GDP. In Exhibit 2(b), the economy is initially in an inflationary gap at point 1. In this situation, Keynesians are likely to propose a contractionary fiscal measure (a decrease in government purchases or an increase in taxes) to shift the aggregate demand curve leftward from AD_1 to AD_2 and move the economy to point 2.

In Exhibit 2, fiscal policy has worked as intended. In panel (a), the economy was in a recessionary gap and expansionary fiscal policy eliminated the gap. In panel (b), the economy was in an inflationary gap and contractionary fiscal policy eliminated it. In (a) and (b), fiscal policy is at its best and working as intended.

11-3c Crowding Out: Questioning Expansionary Fiscal Policy

Not all economists believe that fiscal policy works as just described. Some economists bring up the subject of *crowding out*. **Crowding out** is a decrease in private expenditures (consumption, investment, etc.) as a consequence of increased government spending or the need to finance a budget deficit.

Crowding out can be direct or indirect, as described in these two examples:

1. *Direct effect.* The government spends more on public libraries, and individuals buy fewer books at bookstores.[3]

2. *Indirect effect.* The government spends more on social programs and defense without increasing taxes; as a result, the size of the budget deficit increases. Consequently, the government must borrow more funds to finance the larger deficit. The increase in borrowing causes the demand for credit (i.e., the demand for loanable funds) to rise, in turn causing the interest rate to rise. As a result, investment drops. Thus, more government spending indirectly leads to less investment spending.

Types of Crowding Out   In the first example, the government spends more on public libraries. Let's say that the government spends $2 billion more on public libraries and that consumers choose to spend not $1 less on books at bookstores. Then, obviously, there is no crowding out, or *zero crowding out.*

Now suppose that, after the government has spent $2 billion more on public libraries, consumers choose to spend $2 billion less at bookstores. Obviously, crowding out exists, and the degree of crowding out is dollar for dollar. When $1 of government spending offsets $1 of private spending, **complete crowding out** is said to exist.

Finally, suppose that, after the government has spent $2 billion more on public libraries, consumers spend $1.2 billion less on books at bookstores. Again, crowding out occurs, but it is not dollar for dollar, not complete crowding out. **Incomplete crowding out** occurs when the decrease in one or more components of private spending only partially offsets the increase in government spending.

Crowding Out
The decrease in private expenditures that occurs as a consequence of increased government spending or the need to finance a budget deficit.

Complete Crowding Out
A decrease in one or more components of private spending that completely offsets the increase in government spending.

Incomplete Crowding Out
A decrease in one or more components of private spending that only partially offsets the increase in government spending.

---

[3]   We are not saying that, for example, if the government spends more on public libraries, individuals will necessarily buy fewer books at bookstores; rather, if they do, that would be an example of crowding out. The same holds for example 2.

The following table summarizes the different types of crowding out:

Type of Crowding Out	Example
Zero crowding out (sometimes called "no crowding out")	Government spends $2 billion more, and private sector spending stays constant.
Complete crowding out	Government spends $2 billion more, and the private sector spends $2 billion less.
Incomplete crowding out	Government spends $2 billion more, and the private sector spends, say, $1.2 billion less.

Graphical Representation of Crowding Out   In the event that *complete* or *incomplete crowding out* occurs, expansionary fiscal policy will have less impact on aggregate demand and Real GDP than Keynesian theory predicts. Let's look at the graphical representation of crowding out. Exhibit 3 illustrates the consequences of complete and incomplete crowding out and, for comparison, includes zero crowding. As shown, here are the three possibilities for crowding out:

- *Zero crowding out (no crowding out).* In Exhibit 3, the economy is initially at point 1, with Real GDP at Q_1. Expansionary fiscal policy then shifts the

▶ EXHIBIT 3

Zero (No), Incomplete, and Complete Crowding Out

The exhibit shows the effects of zero, incomplete, and complete crowding out in the AD–AS framework. Starting at point 1, expansionary fiscal policy shifts the aggregate demand curve to AD_2 and moves the economy to point 2 and Q_N. The Keynesian theory that predicts this outcome assumes zero, or no, crowding out; an increase in, say, government spending does not reduce private

expenditures. With incomplete crowding out, an increase in government spending causes private expenditures to decrease by less than the increase in government spending. The net result is a shift in the aggregate demand curve to AD'_2. The economy moves to point 2' and Q'_2. With complete crowding out, an increase in government spending is completely offset by a decrease in private expenditures, and the net result is that aggregate demand does not increase at all. The economy remains at point 1 and Q_1.

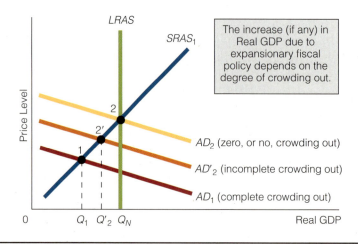

The increase (if any) in Real GDP due to expansionary fiscal policy depends on the degree of crowding out.

aggregate demand curve to AD_2 and moves the economy to point 2. Among other things, the implicit assumption is that there is zero (no) crowding out. Real GDP has increased from Q_1 to Q_N. Therefore, the unemployment rate will fall from its level at Q_1 to a lower level at Q_N. So, if there is no crowding out, expansionary fiscal policy increases Real GDP and lowers the unemployment rate.

- *Incomplete crowding out.* The aggregate demand curve shifts (on net) only to AD_2' because a fall in private expenditures *partially offsets* the initial stimulus in aggregate demand that was due to increased government spending. The economy moves to point 2', and Real GDP increases from Q_1 to Q_2'. Therefore, the unemployment rate will fall from what it was at Q_1 to what it is at Q_2'. Also, the changes in both Real GDP and the unemployment rate are smaller with incomplete crowding out than with zero crowding out. So, given incomplete crowding out, expansionary fiscal policy increases Real GDP and lowers the unemployment rate, but not as much as with zero crowding out.

- *Complete crowding out.* A fall in private expenditures *completely offsets* the initial stimulus in aggregate demand that was due to increased government spending, and the aggregate demand curve does not move (on net) at all. Real GDP does not change, and neither does the unemployment rate. So, with complete crowding out, expansionary fiscal policy has no effect on the economy. The economy remains at point 1.

See Exhibit 4 for a summary flowchart of the different types of crowding out.

> **EXHIBIT 4**

Expansionary Fiscal Policy (Government Spending Increases), Crowding Out, and Changes in Real GDP and the Unemployment Rate

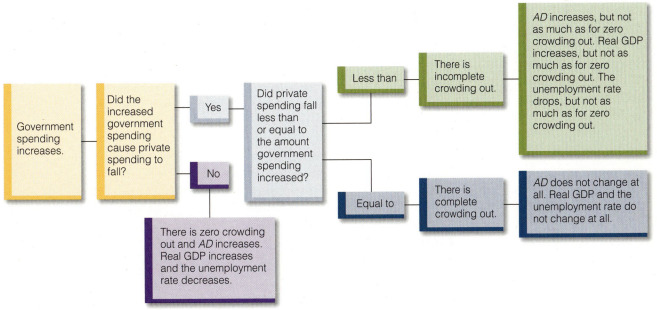

ECONOMICS 24/7

Unemployment Compensation Benefits, Searching for Work, and the Unemployment Rate

Individuals who lose their jobs and who have not yet found work often receive unemployment compensation benefits. On average, the amount of benefits is about $300 a week until they get a job, they stop looking for work, or their unemployment compensation benefits run out. Unemployment compensation benefits are administered by the federal and state governments. Before the recession of 2007–2009, the unemployment compensation benefits lasted for 26 weeks. In other words, an unemployed worker received benefits for half a year.

In mid-2008, because of the high unemployment rates in many states, automatic triggers in unemployment compensation benefits came into force. These triggers extended the length of time one could receive unemployment compensation benefits. About the same time, federal legislation extended the length of time one could receive unemployment benefits. Now, the entire nation could get benefits for 99 weeks, or almost two years. Legislation passed in 2009 and 2010 permitted the 99-week extension to continue and increased the average dollar monthly amount of the benefits.

The stated purpose of unemployment compensation benefits is to assist persons who lose their jobs and to raise government spending during a recession. The intended effect of granting benefits is that they act as an expansionary fiscal policy measure. But, as economists often point out, policies can have unintended effects too. What are the unintended effects of extending the number of weeks one can receive unemployment benefits from 26 to 99? A possible unintended effect is that an unemployed person might take longer to find a new job. Why be in a rush to look for a new job if you have 99 weeks to find one?

To illustrate, suppose that in week 1 there are 10 unemployed persons and the civilian labor force is 100 persons. It follows that the unemployment rate in week 1 is 10 percent.

Now suppose that in week 2 the 10 unemployed persons (from week 1) accept jobs and 10 new persons become unemployed. If the civilian labor force is still 100 persons, it follows that there are 10 persons unemployed in week 2 and the unemployment rate is again 10 percent.

Now change things. Let's increase unemployment compensation benefits and extend the number of weeks an unemployed persons can receive those benefits. As a result, fewer of the unemployed feel pressured to either search for or accept a job. So, instead of having the 10 unemployed persons (from week 1) accept jobs in week 2, let's say that only 5 of the 10 accept jobs. If we then add these 5 unemployed persons to the 10 new persons that become unemployed in week 2, the number of unemployed persons rises to 15 and the unemployment rate rises to 15 percent.

In sum, raising the dollar amount of unemployment compensation benefits and extending the number of weeks one can receive them may make the transition from being unemployed to being employed easier. But it can also increase the search time an unemployed person takes to locate a new job, thus raising the unemployment rate.[4]

---

4. There also may be an unintended political effect that arises out of extending unemployment compensation benefits from 26 to 99 weeks: It may become increasingly difficult politically for elected representatives to bring the number of weeks back down to 26.

Policy Is Not Necessarily Effective Suppose an ill person goes to the doctor and asks for medicine; the doctor prescribes the medicine, and the person goes home. After a few days, the medicine has not made the person well. The same can sometimes be said about economic policy. Keep in mind what we are, and what we are not, saying. We are not saying that economic policy is never effective; we are simply saying that it is not *necessarily* effective. So far in our discussion, crowding out is only one reason fiscal policy may not be effective. Lags, which we discuss next, are another.

11-3d Lags and Fiscal Policy

Even if we prove beyond a shadow of a doubt that there is no (in other words, there is zero) crowding out, should fiscal policy be used to solve the problems of inflationary and recessionary gaps? Many economists would answer not necessarily, because of *lags*. There are five types of lags:

1. *The data lag.* Policy makers are not aware of changes in the economy as soon as they happen. For example, if the economy turns downward in January, the decline may not be apparent for two to three months.

2. *The wait-and-see lag.* When policy makers become aware of a downturn in economic activity, they rarely enact counteractive measures immediately. Instead, they usually adopt a relatively cautious wait-and-see attitude to be sure that the observed events are not just short-run phenomena.

3. *The legislative lag.* After policy makers decide that some type of fiscal policy measure is required, Congress or the president has to propose the measure, build political support for it, and get it passed. The legislative lag can take many months.

4. *The transmission lag.* Once enacted, a fiscal policy measure takes time to go into effect. For example, a discretionary expansionary fiscal policy measure mandating increased spending for public works projects requires construction companies to submit bids for the work, prepare designs, negotiate contracts, and so on.

5. *The effectiveness lag.* After being implemented, a policy measure takes time to affect the economy. If government spending is increased on Monday, the aggregate demand curve does not shift rightward on Tuesday.

Given the cumulative effect of these five lags, some economists argue that discretionary fiscal policy is not likely to have its intended impact on the economy. By the time the full impact of the policy is felt, the economic problem it was designed to solve (1) may no longer exist, (2) may not exist to the degree it once did, or (3) may have changed altogether.

Exhibit 5 illustrates the effect of lags. As shown, the economy is currently in a recessionary gap at point 1. The recession is under way before government officials recognize it. After it is recognized, however, Congress and the president consider enacting expansionary fiscal policy in the hope of shifting the *AD* curve from AD_1 to AD_2 so that it will intersect the *SRAS* curve at point 1′, at Natural Real GDP.

> **EXHIBIT 5**

Fiscal Policy May Destabilize the Economy

In this scenario, the *SRAS* curve is shifting rightward (healing the economy of its recessionary gap), but this information is unknown to policy makers. Policy makers implement expansionary fiscal policy, and the *AD* curve ends up intersecting *SRAS₂* at point 2 instead of intersecting *SRAS₁* at point 1'. Policy makers thereby move the economy into an inflationary gap, thus destabilizing the economy.

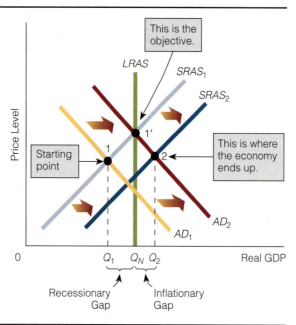

In the interim, unknown to everybody, the economy is "healing," or regulating, itself: the *SRAS* curve is already shifting to the right. However, government officials don't see this change because collecting and analyzing data about the economy takes time.

Thinking that the economy is not healing itself or not healing itself quickly enough, the government enacts expansionary fiscal policy. In time, the *AD* curve shifts rightward. But by the time the increased demand is felt in the goods-and-services market, the *AD* curve intersects the *SRAS* curve at point 2. In effect, the government has moved the economy from point 1 to point 2, not, as it had intended, from point 1 to point 1'. The government has moved the economy into an inflationary gap. Instead of stabilizing and moderating the ups and downs in economic activity (the business cycle), the government has intensified the fluctuations.

11-3e Crowding Out, Lags, and the Effectiveness of Fiscal Policy

Economists who believe that crowding out is always zero and that lags are insignificant conclude that fiscal policy is effective at moving the economy out of a recessionary gap. Economists who believe that crowding out is always complete and/or that lags are significant conclude that fiscal policy is ineffective in that respect.

11-3f Democracy in Deficit

We live in a world of continuing budget deficits and climbing national debt. How did this situation come to be? If we go back in time, we see that deficits and debt were not the rule. Yes, there were years of budget deficits, but they were often offset by years of budget surpluses. This was how it was supposed to be, some argue. The government, like the family, wasn't supposed to live beyond its means—it wasn't supposed to spend more than it took in in tax revenues—except when there was an emergency. And the emergency was usually defined as war. In other words, if the country was engaged in war, that was enough of an emergency to live "beyond your means" and spend more than was taken in in tax revenues. Deficits and the piling up of debt were accepted during wartime. But then, when the war was over, it was time to run budget surpluses and to pay down the debt.

This view of how things were supposed to be contained within it an implicit view of government. Government did not have a management role to play in the economy. It was not supposed to try to stabilize the economy: to stimulate the economy during recessionary times and to dampen down the economy during inflationary times. There was no need to stabilize the economy because, it was thought, the economy did that itself. The economy contained its own self-regulating properties.

Here is how it worked: When the economy was in a recessionary gap, with the actual unemployment rate above the natural unemployment rate, there was a surplus in the labor market. Eventually, the surplus would lead to lowered wages. As wages fell, the short-run aggregate supply curve in the economy shifted rightward, and eventually the economy would move into long-run equilibrium, producing Natural Real GDP.

Of course, when the problem was an inflationary instead of a recessionary gap, things would work differently. When the economy was in an inflationary gap, the actual unemployment rate was below the natural unemployment rate and there was a shortage in the labor market. Eventually, the shortage would lead to higher wages. As wages rose, the short-run aggregate supply curve in the economy shifted leftward, and eventually the economy would move into long-run equilibrium, producing Natural Real GDP.

In other words, no matter in what state the economy was—a recessionary or an inflationary gap—it would soon move out of that state and into long-run equilibrium, at which it would produce the Natural Real GDP level at full employment. The economy could self-regulate. Thus, there was no need for government to manage the economy; it did very well on its own (thank you very much).

With no economic management role for government to play, what was government supposed to do and how was it supposed to do it? It was supposed to provide roads, national defense, and police and fire protection; operate the court system; enforce contracts; and so on, and it was supposed to do this through a combination of spending and taxing. But—as was mentioned earlier—except in wartime, it was supposed to do it under the direction of an unwritten, but not unobserved, rule of running a balanced budget.

According to economists James Buchanan and Richard Wagner, in their work *Democracy in Deficit*,[5] the unwritten balanced budget rule was largely cast aside with the advent of the Keynesian Revolution in economics. John Maynard Keynes saw an economic management role for government to play. His view evolved out of his belief that the economy was not always inherently self-regulating. For example, the economy may not be able to remove itself from a recessionary gap. When it couldn't, government had a role to play. If wages wouldn't drop, and the short-run aggregate supply curve wouldn't shift rightward to move the economy into long-run equilibrium, then perhaps government should try to get the aggregate demand curve to shift rightward and eliminate the recessionary gap. How? Through expansionary fiscal policy. That is, by either cutting taxes or raising government spending.

Or consider when the economy might slip over into an inflationary gap. If the economy were self-regulating, wages would soon rise and the short-run aggregate supply curve would shift leftward, removing the economy from the inflationary gap. But if that didn't happen, perhaps government should enact contractionary fiscal policy and shift the aggregate demand curve leftward, thus pushing the economy out of the inflationary gap.

The Keynesian Revolution therefore brought forth a policy prescription that read, "If the economy gets stuck in either a recessionary or an inflationary gap and can't move itself into long-run equilibrium to produce Natural Real GDP, then the government should regulate the economy into long-run equilibrium. Doing so calls for expansionary fiscal policy (lower taxes and/or higher government spending) to remove the economy from the recessionary gap and contractionary fiscal policy (higher taxes and/or lower government spending) to remove the economy from the inflationary gap.

Now, let's assume that Keynes and the Keynesians are right: that the economy is not self-regulating—that it can get stuck in either a recessionary or an inflationary gap. And

---

5. James M. Buchanan and Richard E. Wagner, *Democracy in Deficit: The Political Legacy of Lord Keynes* (New York: Academic Press, 1977).

let's also assume that the Keynesian prescription of expansionary fiscal policy for a recessionary gap and contractionary fiscal policy for an inflationary gap is correct. In other words, expansionary fiscal policy will eliminate a recessionary gap and contractionary fiscal policy will eliminate an inflationary gap. Would all then be well with the economy? To try to answer that question, we need first ask ourselves how easy or hard it would be for elected officials (Congress and a president) to enact both sides of the fiscal policy coin. One side of that coin—the expansionary fiscal policy side—is likely to be much more politically popular than the other side of the coin—the contractionary fiscal policy side.

The expansionary fiscal policy side consists of government spending more and/or taxing less. In other words, politicians will go to the voters and tell them that they want to give them greater money benefits (more spending) and/or they want to cut their taxes. This approach is likely to be met with applause from the voters. But the specifics of contractionary fiscal policy, consisting of cuts in government spending and/or higher taxes, are not so likely. In short, the Keynesian policy prescription consists of two sides of the fiscal coin: more spending and lower taxes when the economy is in a recessionary gap, and less spending and higher taxes when the economy is in an inflationary gap.

But given the reality of modern-day politics, one side of that fiscal coin is going to be much more popular with the voters and thus with the politicians running for office or reelection. Think of it this way: the Keynesian prescription says to offer candy (more spending and lower taxes) to the voters when there is a recessionary gap but take that candy away (less spending and higher taxes) when there is an inflationary gap. Now, if the voters do not understand that less spending and higher taxes are "what is needed" to remove the economy from an inflationary gap, you can see how that policy prescription might be hard to sell when voters are being sought. There is a political bias, then, toward expansionary fiscal policy: more spending and lower taxes. But what does more spending and lower taxes lead to? It leads to budget deficits. And continued budget deficits lead to ever greater national debt.

So, what went wrong? According to Buchanan and Wagner, the problem is that Keynes and the Keynesians proposed changes in the state of the budget in order to stabilize the economy yet, all the while, assumed that those changes would be brought about by a government that is not subject to the pull and push of everyday, democratic politics. To explain, Buchanan and Wagner argue that Keynes, in particular, believed in a benevolent despot theory of government. Such a government is one that does what is right for the people, given the circumstances at hand, and ignores politics.

To illustrate, suppose that the economy is in an inflationary gap and requires contractionary fiscal policy: a decline in government spending or a rise in taxes. But suppose also that the political environment at the time is one in which people do not want their government to cut spending benefits or raise their taxes. What will a benevolent despot do? He will do what is needed at the time, irrespective of what people may or may not want. If the economy is in an inflationary gap, he will cut spending and raise taxes, so that the inflationary gap will be eliminated and the economy will stabilize in long-run equilibrium. The situation would be similar to that of a doctor who, worried about the patient, gives him some horrible-tasting medicine because he knows that it will make the patient get well.

But representative governments do not behave as benevolent despots, argue Buchanan and Wagner. And to assume that they do—as, they argue, Keynes did—will only lead to unintended and unexpected effects.

Buchanan and Wagner are not arguing that Keynes's view of how the economy works is wrong. They argue instead that, if we assume that Keynes's view of how the economy works is correct and that his call for expansionary fiscal policy in a recessionary gap and for contractionary fiscal policy in an inflationary gap is correct, too, then there is still a political dimension to achieving certain economic policies that needs to be addressed. And that dimension is, no matter what the economic situation—inflationary gap or recessionary gap—expansionary fiscal policy (more spending and lower taxes) always seems to politically trump contractionary fiscal policy (less spending and higher taxes). In other words, although Keynesian economics might argue for contractionary fiscal policy during an inflationary gap, everyday politics is going to push for expansionary fiscal policy, and in the end, politics often trumps economics.

To conclude, Keynesian fiscal policy prescriptions may be all right if government acts like a benevolent despot who is not swayed by political considerations. But prescribed in a political environment in which politicians and elected representatives seek votes, those same fiscal policy prescriptions are altogether different. With a benevolent despot, we get higher taxes sometimes and lower taxes at other times; we get more spending sometimes and less spending at other times. But with real-world, democratic politics, we usually get more spending and lower taxes, no matter the economic ill. In other words, to use the title of the Buchanan and Wagner book on the subject, we get a "democracy in deficit." We get big deficits and big debt.

SELF-TEST

1. How does crowding out create questions about the effectiveness of expansionary demand-side fiscal policy? Give an example.

2. How might lags reduce the effectiveness of fiscal policy?

3. Give an example of an indirect effect of crowding out.

11-4 SUPPLY-SIDE FISCAL POLICY

Fiscal policy effects may be felt on the supply side as well as on the demand side of the economy. For example, a reduction in tax rates may alter an individual's incentive to work and produce, thus altering aggregate supply.

11-4a Marginal Tax Rates and Aggregate Supply

When fiscal policy measures affect tax rates, they may affect both aggregate supply and aggregate demand. Consider a reduction in an individual's marginal tax rate. The **marginal (income) tax rate** is equal to the change in a person's tax payment divided by the change in the person's taxable income:

$$\text{Marginal tax rate} = \frac{\Delta \text{Tax payment}}{\Delta \text{Taxable income}}$$

For example, if Serena's taxable income increases by \$1 and her tax payment increases by \$0.28, then her marginal tax rate is 28 percent. If her taxable income increases by \$1 and her tax payment increases by \$0.35, then her marginal tax rate is 35 percent.

All other things held constant, lower marginal tax rates increase the incentive to engage in productive activities (work) relative to leisure and tax-avoidance activities.[6] As resources shift from leisure to work, short-run aggregate supply increases. Most economists predict that,

Marginal (Income) Tax Rate
The change in a person's tax payment divided by the change in taxable income: ΔTax payment $\div$ ΔTaxable income.

---

[6] When marginal tax rates are lowered, two things happen: (1) individuals will have more disposable income, and (2) the amount of money that individuals can earn (and keep) by working increases. As a result of the first effect, individuals will choose to work less. As a result of the second effect, individuals will choose to work more. Whether an individual works less or more on net depends on whether effect 1 is stronger than or weaker than effect 2. We have assumed that effect 2 is stronger than effect 1; so, as marginal tax rates decline, the net effect is that individuals work more.

The Predicted Effect of a Permanent Marginal Tax Rate Cut on Aggregate Supply

A cut in marginal tax rates increases the attractiveness of productive activity relative to leisure and tax-avoidance activities and shifts resources from the latter to the former, thus shifting rightward both the short-run and the long-run aggregate supply curves.

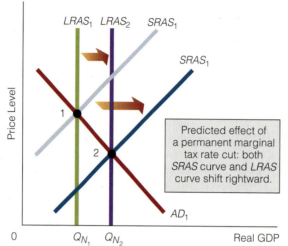

Predicted effect of a permanent marginal tax rate cut: both SRAS curve and LRAS curve shift rightward.

when the lower marginal tax rates are permanent (not a one-shot phenomenon), not only the short-run aggregate supply curve, but also the long-run aggregate supply curve, will shift rightward. Exhibit 6 illustrates the predicted effect of a permanent marginal tax rate cut on aggregate supply.

11-4b The Laffer Curve: Tax Rates and Tax Revenues

High tax rates are followed by attempts of ingenious men to beat them as surely as snow is followed by little boys on sleds.

—Arthur Okun, economist (1928–1980)

If (marginal) income tax rates are reduced, will income tax revenues increase or decrease? Most people think that the answer is obvious: lower tax rates mean lower tax revenues. Economist Arthur Laffer explained, however, why this may not be the case. As the story goes, Laffer, while dining with a journalist at a restaurant in Washington, D.C., drew the curve shown in Exhibit 7 on a napkin. The curve came to be known as the **Laffer curve**. Laffer's objective was to explain the possible relationships between tax rates and tax revenues. In the exhibit, tax revenues are on the vertical axis and tax rates are on the horizontal axis. Laffer made three major points about the curve:

1. Zero tax revenues will be collected at two (marginal) tax rates: 0 percent and 100 percent. Obviously, no tax revenues will be raised if the tax rate is zero, and if

Laffer Curve

The curve, named after economist Arthur Laffer, that shows the relationship between tax rates and tax revenues. According to the Laffer curve, as tax rates rise from zero, tax revenues rise, reach a maximum at some point, and then fall with further increases in tax rates.

The Laffer Curve

When the tax rate is either 0 or 100 percent, tax revenues are zero. Starting from a zero tax rate, increases in tax rates first increase tax revenues (from point A to point B) and then decrease tax revenues (from point B to point C). Starting from a 100 percent tax rate, decreases in tax rates first increase tax revenues (from point C to point B) and then decrease tax revenues (from point B to point A). The curve suggests that there is some tax rate that maximizes tax revenues.

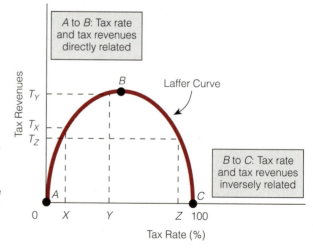

the tax rate is 100 percent, no one will work and earn income because the entire amount would be taxed away.

2. An increase in tax rates could cause tax revenues to increase. For example, an increase in tax rates from X percent to Y percent will increase tax revenues from T_X to T_Y.

3. A decrease in tax rates could cause tax revenues to increase. For example, a decrease in tax rates from Z percent to Y percent will increase tax revenues from T_Z to T_Y. This point brought public attention to the Laffer curve.

Both an *increase* and a *decrease* in tax rates at different times can increase tax revenues because of the interrelationships among tax rates, the **tax base**, and tax revenues. The equation describing those interrelationships is[7]

$$\text{Tax revenues} = \text{Tax base} \times \text{(average) Tax rate}$$

Tax Base

In terms of income taxes, the total amount of taxable income. Tax revenue = Tax base × (average) Tax rate

For example, a tax rate of 20 percent multiplied by a tax base of $100 billion generates $20 billion of tax revenues.

Obviously, tax revenues are a function of two variables: (1) the tax rate and (2) the tax base. Whether tax revenues increase or decrease when the average tax rate is lowered depends on whether the tax base expands by a greater or lesser percentage than the percentage reduction in the tax rate. Exhibit 8 illustrates the point. The tax rate starts at 20 percent, with a tax base of $100 billion and tax revenues of $20 billion. As the tax rate is reduced, the tax base expands: The rationale is that individuals work more, invest more, enter into more trades, and shelter less income from taxes at lower tax rates.

However, the real question is *how much* does the tax base expand following the tax rate reduction? Suppose the tax rate in Exhibit 8 is reduced to 15 percent. In Case 1, the reduction increases the tax base to $120 billion: A 25 percent decrease in the tax rate

---

> EXHIBIT 8

Tax Rates, the Tax Base, and Tax Revenues

Tax revenues equal the tax base times the (average) tax rate. If the percentage reduction in the tax rate is greater than the percentage increase in the tax base, tax revenues decrease (case 1). If the percentage reduction in the tax rate is less than the percentage increase in the tax base, tax revenues increase (case 2). All dollar amounts are in billions of dollars.

	(1) Tax Rate	(2) Tax Base	(3) Tax Revenues (1) × (2)	Summary
Start with:	20%	$100	$20	—
Case 1:	15	120	18	↓ Tax rate ↓ Tax revenues
Case 2:	15	150	22.5	↓ Tax rate ↑ Tax revenues

---

7. Note that the average tax rate is equal to an individual's tax payment divided by taxable income (tax payment ÷ taxable income). Second, a lower average tax rate requires a lower marginal tax rate. This relationship follows from the average-marginal rule, which states that if the marginal magnitude is below the average magnitude, then the average is pulled down and if the marginal magnitude is above the average magnitude, then the average is pulled up. Simply put, if an individual pays less tax on an additional taxable dollar (constituting evidence of a marginal tax rate reduction), then his or her average tax naturally falls.

(from 20 to 15 percent) causes a 20 percent increase in the tax base (from $100 billion to $120 billion). Tax revenues then drop to $18 billion. In Case 2, the tax base expands by 50 percent, to $150 billion. Because the tax base increases by a greater percentage than the percentage decrease in the tax rate, tax revenues increase (to $22.5 billion).

Of course, either case is possible. According to the Laffer curve, tax revenues increase if a tax rate reduction is made on the downward-sloping portion of the curve (between points *B* and *C* in Exhibit 7) and tax revenues decrease following a tax rate reduction on the upward-sloping portion of the curve (between points *A* and *B*).

Incentives Matter Contrast how an economist thinks about a tax cut with how the layperson thinks about it. The layperson probably believes that a reduction in tax rates will reduce tax revenues, focusing just on the arithmetic. An economist, however, focuses on the economic incentives, asking a number of questions. What does a lower tax rate imply in terms of a person's incentive to engage in productive activity? How does a lower tax rate affect one's trade-off between work and leisure? The layperson likely sees only the arithmetic effect of a tax cut; the economist sees the incentive effect.

11-4c Fiscal Policy and Expectations

Even if, when tax rates are lowered, people do not work more and produce more, it cannot unequivocally be said that lower tax rates do not stimulate work and production. To explain, consider two different settings, one in which income tax rates are lowered in year 1 with no further cuts expected in future years, the other in which income tax rates are lowered in year 1 with further cuts expected in future years (years 2, 3, 4, and so on).

In the first setting (tax rate cuts in year 1, none expected in the future), suppose individuals do not respond by working and producing more. We can then conclude that, all other things being equal, tax rate cuts do not stimulate more work and production.

In the second setting (tax rate cuts in year 1, additional cuts expected in future years), suppose individuals do not respond by working and producing more. This time we cannot conclude that tax rate cuts do not stimulate more work and production, because individuals may simply be waiting to work and produce more when tax rates are even lower in future years. Look at it this way: Even though tax rates are lower in year 1 than in year 0, they are higher than they will be in year 2.

Now look at the opposite condition: raising tax rates. Raising tax rates should lead to individuals' cutting back on work and production, but this effect may not come to pass if tax rates are expected to rise more in future years. In fact, raising the tax rate in year 1, with an expected tax rate hike to follow in year 2, could actually get people to work and produce more in year 1. In relative terms, the tax rate is lower in year 1 than it will be in year 2.

SELF-TEST

1. Give an arithmetic example to illustrate the difference between the marginal and average tax rates.

2. If income tax rates rise, will income tax revenues rise too?

Office  Hours

"Is There a Looming Fiscal Crisis?"

STUDENT:

I've been reading what some economists have been saying about the future state of the federal budget. They say that there is a looming fiscal crisis ahead. What do they mean by "a looming fiscal crisis"?

INSTRUCTOR:

They are looking at the changing demographics in the United States, combined with rising health-care costs. As baby boomers retire and become eligible for Social Security and Medicare (and, to a lesser extent, Medicaid), we can expect that Social Security, Medicare, and Medicaid spending will rise.

STUDENT:

Will it rise by much? Is this a big spending problem headed our way?

INSTRUCTOR:

Well, it has been estimated that, if our current federal tax burden were to remain constant over the years, we will be able to pay for only those three federal programs and nothing else by the year 2050. In short, the so-called looming fiscal crisis is due to the expected growth in Social Security, Medicare, and Medicaid spending in the future. In 2005, spending on these three programs accounted for 8.4 percent of GDP. The figure is projected to be 11 percent in 2020 and approximately 19 percent in 2050.

STUDENT:

That will mean that the public debt will grow, won't it?

INSTRUCTOR:

Not only will it grow in absolute terms, but it will grow as a percentage of GDP too.

STUDENT:

Let me see if I have this correct. You're saying (1) that Social Security, Medicare, and Medicaid spending are likely to grow in the future and that these three programs will make up a larger share of the federal budget

than they do today and (2) that if current spending and tax policies continue, both the budget deficit and the public debt will grow as a percentage of GDP. Is this the looming fiscal crisis we hear so much about?

INSTRUCTOR:

Yes, that's correct.

STUDENT:

So what does it mean for our future? Are taxes going to have to be raised? Is spending going to have to be cut? Or are we just going to continue on course and end up having to deal with large budget deficits and debt (as a percentage of GDP)?

INSTRUCTOR:

We're not sure what will happen. What we do know is that some stark fiscal realities are awaiting us. One way of identifying the problem (or the stark reality ahead) is to measure the fiscal gap. This is the amount of spending reductions or tax revenue increases needed (say, over the next four decades) if we want to keep our debt-to-GDP ratio at what it is today. It has been estimated (at the low end of estimates) that the fiscal gap requires annual tax revenue increases or spending cuts totaling 5–7 percent of projected GDP for the next four decades. Here's what that means: Suppose the GDP in 2016 is $18 trillion. If we take 5 percent of this, we get $900 billion. The federal government would then need to either (1) cut spending by that amount in 2016, or (2) raise tax revenues by that amount in 2016, or (3) raise tax revenues by, say, $400 billion and cut spending benefits by $500 billion (for a total of $900 billion), and so on.

Points to remember

1. It is likely that the combined spending on Social Security, Medicare, and Medicaid in future years will grow as a percentage of the federal budget.

2. If the nation's current spending and tax policies continue, both the budget deficit and the public debt in the hands of the public will grow as a percentage of GDP.

CHAPTER SUMMARY

GOVERNMENT SPENDING

- In 2013, the federal government spent $3.685 trillion, 22.7 percent of the country's GDP. About 61 percent of the money went for Social Security, Medicare, Medicaid, and national defense.

- With a proportional income tax, everyone pays taxes at the same rate, regardless of income level. With a progressive income tax, a person pays taxes at a higher rate (up to some top rate) as his or her income level rises. With a regressive income tax, a person pays taxes at a lower rate as the person's income level rises.

- The federal income tax is a progressive income tax.

TAXES

- In 2013, the federal government took in $2.712 trillion in tax revenues. Most of this amount came from four taxes: the individual income tax, the corporate income tax, taxes on Social Security earnings, and Medicare taxes.

DEFICITS, SURPLUSES, AND THE PUBLIC DEBT

- If government expenditures are greater than tax revenues, a budget deficit results; if government expenditures are less than tax revenues, a budget surplus results. If government expenditures equal tax revenues, the budget is balanced. Budget deficits are predicted for the near future.

- A cyclical deficit is the part of the budget deficit that is a result of a downturn in economic activity.

- A structural deficit is the part of the deficit that would exist if the economy were operating at full employment.

- Total budget deficit = Structural deficit + Cyclical deficit.

- The public debt is the total amount that the federal government owes its creditors.

FISCAL POLICY: GENERAL REMARKS

- Fiscal policy consists of changes in government expenditures and/or taxes to achieve economic goals. Expansionary fiscal policy advocates increases in government expenditures and/or decreases in taxes. Contractionary fiscal policy entails decreases in government expenditures and/or increases in taxes.

DEMAND-SIDE FISCAL POLICY: A KEYNESIAN PERSPECTIVE

- In Keynesian theory, demand-side fiscal policy can be used to rid the economy of a recessionary gap or an inflationary gap. A recessionary gap calls for expansionary fiscal policy, and an inflationary gap calls for contractionary fiscal policy. Ideally, fiscal policy changes aggregate demand by enough to rid the economy of either a recessionary gap or an inflationary gap.

CROWDING OUT

- Crowding out is the decrease in private expenditures that occurs as a consequence of increased government spending and/or the greater need to finance a budget deficit. The crowding-out effect suggests that expansionary fiscal policy does not work to the degree that Keynesian theory predicts.

- Complete (incomplete) crowding out occurs when the decrease in one or more components of private spending completely (partially) offsets the increase in government spending.

WHY DEMAND-SIDE FISCAL POLICY MAY BE INEFFECTIVE

- Demand-side fiscal policy may be ineffective at achieving certain macroeconomic goals because of (1) crowding out and (2) lags.

SUPPLY-SIDE FISCAL POLICY

- When fiscal policy measures affect tax rates, they may affect both aggregate supply and aggregate demand. It is generally accepted that a marginal tax rate reduction increases the attractiveness of work relative to leisure and tax-avoidance activities and thus leads to an increase in aggregate supply.

- Tax revenues equal the tax base multiplied by the (average) tax rate. Whether tax revenues decrease or increase as a result of a tax rate reduction depends on whether the percentage increase in the tax base is greater or less than the percentage reduction in the tax rate. If the percentage increase in the tax base is greater than the percentage reduction in the tax rate, then tax revenues will increase. If the percentage increase in the tax base is less than the percentage reduction in the tax rate, then tax revenues will decrease.

KEY TERMS AND CONCEPTS

Progressive Income Tax	Budget Deficit	Cyclical Deficit	Fiscal Policy
Proportional Income Tax	Budget Surplus	Structural Deficit	Expansionary Fiscal Policy
Regressive Income Tax	Balanced Budget	Public Debt	Contractionary Fiscal Policy

| Discretionary Fiscal Policy | Crowding Out | Incomplete Crowding Out | Laffer Curve |
| Automatic Fiscal Policy | Complete Crowding Out | Marginal (Income) Tax Rate | Tax Base |

VIDEO QUESTIONS AND PROBLEMS

Video Questions and Problems are available on MindTap for Arnold 12e or by searching for Arnold on www.cengagebrain.com

1. Explain the difference between zero, incomplete, and complete crowding out. If crowding out is complete, does it call into question the effectiveness of a rise in government purchases in order to remove an economy from a recessionary gap? Explain and diagrammatically represent your answer.

2. Tax cuts may either decrease or increase tax revenues. Do you agree or disagree? Explain your answer.

3. Give a numerical example to illustrate the difference between the marginal tax rate and the average tax rate.

4. Explain how, under certain conditions, expansionary fiscal policy can remove an economy from a recessionary gap.

5. Give a numerical example to illustrate the difference between a progressive and a proportional income tax structure.

QUESTIONS AND PROBLEMS

1. What is the difference between government expenditures and government purchases?

2. How much were government expenditures in 2013? How much were government tax revenues in 2013?

3. The bulk of federal government expenditures go for four programs. What are they?

4. What percentage of total income did the top 10 percent of income earners earn in 2011? What percentage of federal income taxes did this group pay in 2011?

5. Is it true that, under a proportional income tax structure, a person who earns a high income will pay more in taxes than a person who earns a low income? Explain your answer.

6. A progressive income tax always raises more revenue than a proportional income tax does. Do you agree or disagree? Explain your answer.

7. Jim favors progressive taxation and equal after-tax pay for equal work. Comment.

8. What is the difference between a structural deficit and a cyclical deficit?

9. What is the difference between discretionary fiscal policy and automatic fiscal policy?

10. According to Buchanan and Wagner, why is there a political bias toward expansionary fiscal policy and not contractionary fiscal policy?

11. Explain two ways crowding out may occur.

12. Why is crowding out an important issue in the debate over the use of fiscal policy?

13. Some economists argue for the use of fiscal policy to solve economic problems; others argue against it. What are some of the arguments on both sides?

14. Give a numerical example to illustrate the difference between complete crowding out and incomplete crowding out.

15. The debate over using government spending and taxing powers to stabilize the economy involves more than technical economic issues. Do you agree or disagree? Explain your answer.

16. Is crowding out equally likely under all economic conditions? Explain your answer.

17. Tax cuts will likely affect aggregate demand and aggregate supply. Does it matter which is affected more? Explain in terms of the *AD–AS* framework.

18. Explain how, under certain conditions, expansionary fiscal policy can destabilize the economy.

19. Identify and explain the five lags associated with fiscal policy.

20. Suppose the economy is in a recessionary gap, and both Smith and Jones advocate expansionary fiscal policy. Does it follow that both Smith and Jones favor so-called big government?

21. Will tax cuts that the public perceives to be temporary affect the *SRAS* and *LRAS* curves differently than tax cuts that are perceived to be permanent? Explain your answer.

22. What is the difference between a marginal tax rate and an average tax rate?

23. Will tax revenue necessarily rise if tax rates are lowered? Explain your answer.

24. Georgia Dickens is sitting with a friend at a coffee shop, and they are talking about the new tax bill. Georgia thinks that cutting tax rates at this time would be wrong: "Lower tax rates," she says, "will lead to a larger budget deficit, and the budget deficit is already plenty big." Do lower tax rates mean a larger deficit? Why or why not?

WORKING WITH NUMBERS AND GRAPHS

Use the following table to answer questions 1–4:

Taxable Income	Income Taxes
$1,000–$5,000	10% of taxable income
$5,001–$10,000	$500 + 12% of everything over $5,000
$10,001–$15,000	$1,100 + 15% of everything over $10,000

1. If a person's income is $6,000, how much does he pay in taxes?

2. If a person's income is $14,000, how much does she pay in taxes?

3. What is the marginal tax rate on the 10,001st dollar? What is the marginal tax rate on the 10,000th dollar?

4. What is the average tax rate of someone with a taxable income of $13,766?

5. A hypothetical society has three income earners, and all three must pay income taxes. The taxable income of Smith is $40,000, the taxable income of Jones is $100,000, and the taxable income of Brown is $200,000.

   a. How much tax revenue is raised under a proportional income tax when the tax rate is 10 percent? How much is raised if the tax rate is 15 percent?

   b. A progressive tax system is installed with a rate of 5 percent on income of $0–$40,000, a rate of 8 percent on income from $40,001 to $100,000, and a rate of 15 percent on all income over $100,000. Will this system raise more or less tax revenue than a proportional tax rate of 10 percent? Explain your answer.

6. Show graphically how fiscal policy works in the ideal case.

7. Illustrate graphically how government can use supply-side fiscal policy to get an economy out of a recessionary gap.

8. Illustrate the following graphically:

   a. Fiscal policy destabilizes the economy.

   b. Fiscal policy eliminates an inflationary gap.

   c. Fiscal policy only partly eliminates a recessionary gap.

MONEY, BANKING, AND THE FINANCIAL SYSTEM

DENNIS GILBERT/VIEW Pictures Ltd/Alamy

INTRODUCTION

This chapter is about money: how it emerged out of a barter economy and the functions it serves. It is also about banking: how it came to exist and how it looks today. Finally, it is about the financial system in the United States: what it is and what it does.

12-1 MONEY: WHAT IS IT AND HOW DID IT COME TO BE?

The story of money starts with a definition and a history lesson. This section discusses what money is and isn't (the definition) and how money came to be (the history lesson).

12-1a Money: A Definition

To the layperson, the words "income," "credit," and "wealth" are synonyms for money." In each of the next three sentences, the word "money" is used incorrectly; the word in parentheses is the word an economist would use.

1. How much money (income) did you earn last year?

2. Most of her money (wealth) is tied up in real estate.

3. It sure is difficult to get money (credit) in today's tight mortgage market.

In economics, the words "money," "income," "credit," and "wealth" are not synonyms. The most general definition of **money** is any good that is widely accepted for purposes of exchange (payment for goods and services) and the repayment of debt.

Money
Any good that is widely accepted for purposes of exchange and the repayment of debt.

12-1b **Three Functions of Money**

Money has three major functions; it is a

1. medium of exchange.

2. unit of account.

3. store of value.

Money as a Medium of Exchange

Barter

Exchanging goods and services for other goods and services without the use of money.

If money did not exist, goods would have to be exchanged by **barter**—that is, the exchange of goods and services for other goods and services, without the use of money. If you wanted a shirt, you would have to trade some good in your possession, say, a jackknife, for it. But first you would have to locate a person who has a shirt and who wants to trade it for a knife. In a money economy, searching for a seller is not necessary. You can either (1) exchange money for a shirt or (2) exchange the knife for money and then the money for the shirt. The buyer of the knife and the seller of the shirt do not have to be the same person. Money is the medium through which the exchange occurs; it acts as a **medium of exchange**. As such, money reduces the *transaction costs* of exchanges. Exchange is easier and less time consuming in a money economy than in a barter economy.

Medium of Exchange

Anything that is generally acceptable in exchange for goods and services; a function of money.

Money as a Unit of Account

Unit of Account

A common measure in which relative values are expressed; a function of money.

A **unit of account** is a common measure in which values are expressed. In a barter economy, the value of every good is expressed in terms of all other goods; there is no common unit of measure. For example, 1 horse might equal 100 bushels of wheat, or 200 bushels of apples, or 20 pairs of shoes, or 10 suits, or 55 loaves of bread, and so on. In a money economy, a person doesn't have to know the price of an apple in terms of oranges, pizzas, chickens, or potato chips, as in a barter economy. A person needs only to know the price in terms of money. And because all goods are denominated in money, determining relative prices is easy and quick. For example, if 1 apple is $1 and 1 orange is 50¢, then 1 apple is worth 2 oranges.

Money as a Store of Value

Store of Value

The ability of an item to hold value over time; a function of money.

The function we call a **store of value** is related to a good's ability to maintain its value over time. This is the least exclusive function of money, because other goods—for example, paintings, houses, and stamps—can store value too. At times, money has not maintained its value well, such as during periods of high inflation. For the most part, though, money has served as a satisfactory store of value. This function allows us to accept payment in money for our productive efforts and to keep that money until we decide how we want to spend it.

12-1c **From a Barter Economy to a Money Economy: The Origins of Money**

The thing that differentiates man and animals is money.

—Gertrude Stein

At one time, there was trade but no money. Instead, people bartered. They traded one apple for two eggs, a banana for a peach.

Today we live in a money economy, but how did we move from a barter to a money economy? Did a king or queen issue an edict: "Let there be money"? Actually, money evolved in a much more natural, market-oriented manner.

Making exchanges takes longer (on average) in a barter economy than in a money economy because the *transaction costs* are higher in a barter economy. In other words, the time and effort incurred to consummate an exchange are greater in a barter economy than in a money economy.

Suppose Smith wants to trade apples for oranges in a barter economy. He locates Jones, who has oranges. Smith offers to trade apples for oranges, but Jones tells Smith that she does not like apples and would rather have peaches. Then Smith must either (1) find someone who has oranges and who wants to trade oranges for apples or (2) find someone who has peaches and who wants to trade peaches for apples, after which he must return to Jones and trade peaches for oranges. Suppose Smith continues to search and finds Brown, who has oranges and wants to trade oranges for (Smith's) apples. In economics terminology, Smith and Brown are said to have a **double coincidence of wants**. Two people have a double coincidence of wants if what the first person wants is what the second person has and what the second person wants is what the first person has. A double coincidence of wants is a necessary condition for a trade to take place.

In a barter economy, some goods are more readily accepted than others in an exchange. This characteristic may originally be the result of chance, but when traders notice the difference in marketability, their behavior tends to reinforce the effect. To see why, suppose that, of 10 goods A–J, good G is the most marketable (the most acceptable). On average, good G is accepted 5 of every 10 times it is offered in an exchange, whereas the remaining goods are accepted, on average, only 2 of every 10 times. Given this difference, some individuals accept good G simply because of its relatively greater acceptability, even though they have no plans to consume it. They accept good G because they know that they can easily trade it for most other goods at a later time (unlike the item originally in their possession). Thus, the marketability of good G snowballs. The more people accept good G for its relatively greater acceptability, the greater its relative acceptability becomes, in turn causing more people to accept it.

This is how money evolved. When good G's acceptance evolves to the point that it is widely accepted for purposes of exchange, good G is money. Historically, goods that have evolved into money include gold, silver, copper, cattle, salt, cocoa beans, and shells.

Double Coincidence of Wants
In a barter economy, a requirement that must be met before a trade can be made. The term specifies that a trader must find another trader who at the same time is willing to trade what the first trader wants and wants what the first trader has.

THINKING LIKE AN ECONOMIST

The Effects of Self-Interest The statement that people in a barter economy "accept good G because they know that they can easily trade it for most other goods at a later time (unlike the item originally in their possession)" brings up the role of self-interest. At some point in time, people in a barter economy simply wanted to make life easier on themselves; they wanted to cut down on the time and energy required to obtain their preferred bundle of goods. In other words, they began to accept the most marketable or acceptable of all goods out of self-interest—a process that eventually led to the creation of money.

ECONOMICS 24/7

English and Money

In the world of barter, some goods are more widely accepted than others.

In the world of languages, some languages may be more widely used than others. Today, the most widely used language appears to be English.

English is spoken not only by native English speakers but by many other people around the world. English is the language of computers and the Internet. You can see English on posters everywhere in the world. You can hear it in pop songs sung in Tokyo. English is the working language of the Asian trade group ASEAN (Association of Southeast Asian Nations). It is the language of 98 percent of German research physicists and of 83 percent of German research chemists. It is the official language of the European Central Bank,

© iStockphoto.com/Lukasz Panek

even though the bank is in Frankfurt, Germany. English is found in official documents in Phnom Penh, Cambodia. Singers all over the world sing in English. Alcatel, a French telecommunications company, uses English as its internal language. By 2050, half the world's population is expected to be proficient in English.

In a barter economy, if more people accept a good in exchange, then more people will want to accept it. Might the same be true of a language? If more people speak English, then will more non-English-speaking people want to learn English? Just as money lowers the transaction costs of making exchanges, English might lower the transaction costs of communicating.

Is the world evolving toward one universal language, and is that language English?

FINDING ECONOMICS

In a POW Camp You wouldn't think you could find money in a prisoner-of-war (POW) camp, but you can. During World War II, an American, R. A. Radford, was captured and imprisoned in a POW camp. While in the camp, he made some observations about economic developments, which he later described in the journal *Economica*. He noted that the Red Cross would periodically distribute packages to the prisoners that contained such goods as cigarettes, toiletries, chocolate, cheese, jam, margarine, and tinned beef. Not all the prisoners had the same preferences for the goods. For example, some liked chocolate more than others; some smoked cigarettes, and others did not. Because of their preferences, the prisoners began to trade, say, a chocolate bar for cheese, and a barter system emerged. After a short while, money appeared in the camp, but not U.S. dollars or any other government currency. The good that emerged as money—the good that was widely accepted for purposes of exchange—was cigarettes. As Radford noted, "The cigarette became the standard of value. In the permanent camp people started by wandering through the bungalows calling their offers—'cheese for seven [cigarettes] … .'"

12-1d **Money, Leisure, and Output**

Exchanges take less time in a money economy than in a barter economy because a double coincidence of wants is unnecessary: everyone is willing to trade for money. The movement from a barter to a money economy therefore frees up some of the transaction time, which people can use in other ways.

To illustrate, suppose making trades takes 10 hours a week in a barter economy, but only 1 hour in a money economy. In a money economy, then, each week has 9 hours that don't have to be spent making exchanges and that people can use for other purposes. Some will use them to work, others will use them for leisure, and still others will divide the 9 hours between work and leisure. Thus, a money economy is likely to have both more output (because of the increased production) and more leisure time than a barter economy. In other words, a money economy is likely to be richer in both goods and leisure than a barter economy.

A person's standard of living depends, to a degree, on the number and quality of goods the person consumes and on the amount of leisure he or she consumes. We would thus expect the average person's standard of living to be higher in a money economy than in a barter economy.

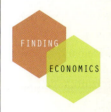

FINDING ECONOMICS

With William Shakespeare in London (1595) It is 1595, and William Shakespeare is sitting at a desk writing the prologue to *Romeo and Juliet*. Where is the economics?

More specifically, what is the connection between Shakespeare's writing a play and the emergence of money out of a barter economy? In a money economy, individuals usually specialize in the production of one good or service because they can do so. In a barter economy, specializing is extremely costly. For Shakespeare, living in a barter economy would mean writing plays all day and then going out and trying to trade what he had written that day for apples, oranges, chickens, and bread. Would the baker trade two loaves of bread for two pages of *Romeo and Juliet*? Had Shakespeare lived in a barter economy, he would have soon learned that he did not have a double coincidence of wants with many people and that, if he were going to eat and be housed, he would need to spend time baking bread, raising chickens, and building a shelter instead of thinking about *Romeo and Juliet*.

In a barter economy, trade is difficult, so people produce for themselves. In a money economy, trade is easy, so individuals produce one thing, sell it for money, and then buy what they want with the money. A William Shakespeare who lived in a barter economy would no doubt spend his days very differently from the William Shakespeare who lived in England in the sixteenth century. Put bluntly, without money, the world might never have enjoyed *Romeo and Juliet*.

12-2 DEFINING THE MONEY SUPPLY

If money is any good that is widely accepted for purposes of exchange, is a $10 bill money? Is a dime money? Is a checking account or a savings account money? What constitutes money? In other words, what is included in the money supply? Two frequently used definitions of the money supply are M1 and M2.

12-2a M1

M1 is sometimes referred to as the *narrow definition of the money supply* or as *transactions money.* It is money that can be directly used for everyday transactions: to buy gas for the car, groceries to eat, and clothes to wear. **M1** consists of currency held outside of banks (by members of the public for use in everyday transactions), checkable deposits, and traveler's checks:

$$M1 = \text{Currency held outside banks}$$
$$+ \text{Checkable deposits}$$
$$+ \text{Traveler's checks}$$

A couple of the components of M1 have specific definitions:

- **Currency** includes coins minted by the U.S. Treasury and paper money. About 99 percent of the paper money in circulation is in the form of **Federal Reserve notes** issued by the Federal Reserve District Banks (the Fed).
- **Checkable deposits** are deposits on which checks can be written. Demand deposits, which are checking accounts that pay no interest, are one kind of checkable deposit. Two others are NOW (negotiated order of withdrawal) and ATS (automatic transfer from savings) accounts, which do pay interest on their balances.

12-2b Money Is More Than Currency

Most laypersons hear the word "money" and think of currency—paper money (dollar bills) and coins. For example, if a thief stops you on a dark street at night and demands, "Your money or your life," you can be sure he wants your currency. People often equate money and currency. To an economist, though, money is more than just currency. According to the M1 definition, money is currency, checkable deposits, and traveler's checks. (However, if robbed by a thief, an economist would be unlikely to hand over her currency and then write a check too.)

12-2c M2

M2 is commonly referred to as the *broad definition of the money supply.* **M2** is made up of M1 plus savings deposits (including money market deposit accounts), small-denomination time deposits, and money market mutual funds (retail):

$$M2 = M1$$
$$+ \text{Savings deposits (including money market deposit accounts)}$$
$$+ \text{Small-denomination time deposits}$$
$$+ \text{Money market mutual funds (retail)}$$

As with M1, several components of M2 need to be defined:

- A **savings deposit**, sometimes called a *regular savings deposit,* is an interest-earning account at a commercial bank or thrift institution. (Thrift institutions include savings and loan associations, mutual savings banks, and credit unions.)

M1
Currency held outside banks, plus checkable deposits, plus traveler's checks.

Currency
Coins and paper money.

Federal Reserve Notes
Paper money issued by the Federal Reserve.

Checkable Deposits
Deposits on which checks can be written.

M2
M1, plus savings deposits (including money market deposit accounts), plus small-denomination time deposits, plus money market mutual funds (retail).

Savings Deposit
An interest-earning account at a commercial bank or thrift institution. Normally, checks cannot be written on savings deposits, and the funds in a savings deposit can be withdrawn at any time without a penalty payment.

ECONOMICS 24 / 7

Bitcoins

No doubt, you have bought and sold things for U.S. dollars, but have you ever bought or sold something for bitcoins?

There is a question as to what exactly a bitcoin is. Some say that it is decentralized money, in that it is not issued by a central bank and is not linked to any government. Some say that it is virtual, digital, crypto, or electronic money. Others argue that it is simply money—pure and simple—in much that same way that U.S. dollars are money.

First, a growing number of retailers are accepting bitcoins, but they are far from being as acceptable a medium of exchange as U.S. dollars are. Remember, the definition of money is that it is a good that is widely accepted for purposes of exchange and in the repayment of debt. Bitcoins are accepted for purposes of exchange and in the repayment of debt, but are not yet *widely* accepted. At this point in time, bitcoins might best be described as a potential or emerging money. The day may come when bitcoins are widely accepted for purposes of exchange and in the repayment of debt, but that day is not here yet.

To explain how bitcoins work, let's go back and talk about their history. In 2008, a person (or persons) working under the pseudonym of Satoshi Nakamoto designed and created the Bitcoin software system. In 2009, the software was released and the first bitcoins were "mined" for circulation. To say that the bitcoins were "mined" is just another way of saying that it takes work to obtain bitcoins. (Think of the work it took to literally mine for gold when gold was money.) Also, the more bitcoins that are mined, the harder it becomes to mine additional bitcoins.

The actual mining of bitcoins includes finding a sequence of data (called a "block") that produces a particular pattern when the Bitcoin algorithm is applied to the data. One way to think about the process of mining bitcoins is to think of searching for prime numbers. (A prime number is a number greater than 1 that has no positive

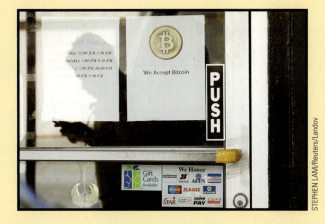

STEPHEN LAM/Reuters/Landov

divisor other than 1 and itself.) It was fairly easy to find the small prime numbers, but as they were found, it became increasingly harder to find the large ones.

Of course, instead of mining for bitcoins, you can buy them. Initially, when they were first created, a bitcoin sold for only a few pennies. On the day we checked, the price of a bitcoin was $589. If you want to find the price of a bitcoin today, you can do so at http://www.coindesk.com/price/.

One of the things the creator(s) of the bitcoin did was to limit the supply of bitcoins. The total supply of bitcoins will never be greater than 21 million, and that will probably not occur until 2033. In August 2014, there were approximately 13.1 million bitcoins in circulation. You can find the number of bitcoins in circulation today at http://blockchain.info/charts/total-bitcoins.

As we said earlier, some people use bitcoins to buy and sell goods. There are people, however, who use bitcoin for speculative purposes and as a store of value. For example, a person may buy bitcoins today at some dollar amount, thinking that the price of bitcoins will rise, at which time he will sell. And some people buy bitcoins for the same reason they might buy gold or silver: they think it will be a better store of value than U.S. dollars. One reason, they argue, that this could very well be the case is because the supply of bitcoins is limited at 21 million whereas the supply of U.S. dollars is unlimited.

Capital Controls and Bitcoins

There are countries in the world that impose *capital controls*— effectively, controls on moving money in or out of a country. One country that has imposed capital controls is China. For example, one restriction is that of taking more than (the equivalent of) $50,000 a year out of the country. There is a way around this prohibition, but it is illegal. It amounts to, say, a Chinese firm selling $1 million worth of goods overseas, showing an invoice of only $900,000, and keeping the difference overseas.

Another capital control is the restriction on exchanging the Chinese currency, the yuan, into a foreign currency. Until recently, though, there was a way around this restriction, as well as the $50,000 restriction. It came in the form of buying and selling bitcoins. A person in China could take the domestic currency, the yuan, and buy bitcoins with it at a bitcoin exchange. Then, once the bitcoins had been purchased, the person could sell them (on the bitcoin exchange) for a foreign currency, such as U.S. dollars. To illustrate, a person could buy, say, 100 bitcoins with yuan, then later sell the 100 bitcoins for dollars. But in December 2013, the Chinese government took action: It prohibited anyone in China from dealing with bitcoin exchanges, making it nearly impossible to buy and sell bitcoins.

Time Deposit

An interest-earning deposit with a specified maturity date. Time deposits are subject to penalties for early withdrawal—that is, withdrawal before the maturity date. Small-denomination time deposits are deposits of less than $100,000.

Money Market Deposit Account (MMDA)

An interest-earning account at a bank or thrift institution, for which a minimum balance is usually required and most of which offer limited check-writing privileges.

Money Market Mutual Fund (MMMF)

An interest-earning account at a mutual fund company, for which a minimum balance is usually required and most of which offer limited check-writing privileges. Only retail MMMFs are part of M2.

Normally, checks cannot be written on savings deposits, and the funds in savings deposits can be withdrawn at any time without a penalty payment.

- A **time deposit** is an interest-earning deposit with a *specified maturity date.* Time deposits are subject to penalties for early withdrawal—that is, withdrawal before the maturity date. Small-denomination time deposits are deposits of less than $100,000.

- A **money market deposit account (MMDA)** is an interest-earning account at a bank or thrift institution, and usually a minimum balance is required. Most MMDAs offer limited check-writing privileges. For example, the owner of an MMDA might be able to write only a certain number of checks each month, and/or each check may have to be above a certain dollar amount (e.g., $500).

- A **money market mutual fund (MMMF)** is an interest-earning account at a *mutual fund company.* Usually, a minimum balance is required for an MMMF account, and most offer limited check-writing privileges. MMMFs held by large institutions are referred to as institutional MMMFs. MMMFs held by all others (e.g., by individuals) are referred to as retail MMMFs. *Only retail MMMFs are part of M2.*

12-2d Where Do Credit Cards Fit In?

A credit card is commonly referred to as plastic money, but it is not money. A credit card is an instrument or a document that makes it easier for the holder to obtain a loan. When Tina Ridges hands the department store clerk her MasterCard or Visa, she is, in effect, spending someone else's money (which already existed). The department store submits the claim to the bank, the bank pays the department store, and then the bank bills the holder of its credit card. By using her credit card, Tina spends someone else's money, and she ultimately must repay her credit card debt with money. These transactions shift around the existing quantity of money among individuals and firms, but they do not change the total.

SELF-TEST

(Answers to Self-Test questions are in Answers to Self-Test Questions at the back of the book.)

1. Why (not how) did money evolve out of a barter economy?

2. If individuals remove funds from their checkable deposits and transfer them to their money market accounts, will M1 fall and M2 rise? Explain your answer.

3. How does money reduce the transaction costs of making trades?

ECONOMICS 24/7

eBay and Match.com

One of the benefits of money's emerging out of a barter economy is that money lowers the transaction costs of making exchanges. In a barter economy, transaction costs are relatively high because no one can be sure that the person who has what you want wants what you have. With the emergence of money, the transaction costs of making exchanges drop because everyone is willing to trade for money.

© Radu Bercan/Shutterstock.com

Just as money has lowered the transaction costs of making exchanges, so has the Internet. Through the Internet, people can find other people they might want to exchange with faster and more easily.

Consider life before the Internet and before both eBay and Match.com. Suppose a person in London has an old Rolling Stones album for sale. He is not sure how to find someone who might want to buy it. Today, the seller simply goes online to eBay and posts the album for sale. In perhaps a matter of hours, people who want to buy the album are bidding on it. eBay and the Internet lower the transaction costs of bringing buyer and seller together.

Or consider Match.com, an online dating service. When people date each other, an exchange of sorts is going on. Each person is effectively saying to the other, "I demand some of your time, which I hope you will supply to me."

One of the transaction costs of dating is actually finding a person to date. Match.com and the Internet, however, lower the transaction costs. The dating service is a little like eBay, in that you are offering to "sell" yourself. Instead of describing a Rolling Stones album, you describe yourself. Then, in a sense, people bid on you by getting in touch—and you bid on others.

What do money, eBay, and Match.com tell us about life? People want to trade with each other, and part of being able to trade is lowering the transaction costs involved. Money, eBay, and Match.com fill the bill.

12-3 HOW BANKING DEVELOPED

Just as money evolved, so did banking. This section discusses the origins of banking and sheds some light on, and aids in understanding, modern banking.

12-3a The Early Bankers

Our money today is easy to carry and transport, but it was not always so portable. For example, when money consisted principally of gold coins, carrying it about was neither easy nor safe. First, gold is heavy. Second, gold was not only inconvenient for customers to carry, but also inconvenient for merchants to accept; gold was heavy and unsafe to carry around. Third, a person transporting thousands of gold coins can easily draw the attention of thieves. Yet storing gold at home can also be risky. Most individuals therefore turned to their local goldsmiths for help because they had safe storage facilities. Goldsmiths were thus the first bankers. They took in other people's gold and stored it for them. To acknowledge that they held deposited gold, goldsmiths issued receipts, called *warehouse receipts*, to their customers.

ECONOMICS 24/7

Economics on the Yellow Brick Road

I'll get you, my pretty.

—Wicked Witch of the West in
The Wizard of Oz

In 1893, the United States fell into economic depression. The stock market crashed, banks failed, workers were laid off, and many farmers lost their farms. Some people blamed the depression on the gold standard. They proposed that, instead of having only gold backing U.S. currency, the monetary standard should be bimetallic; that is, both gold and silver should back the currency. This change, they said, would lead to an increase in the money supply. Many people thought that, with more money in circulation, economic hard times would soon be a thing of the past.

One of the champions of silver was William Jennings Bryan, the Democratic candidate for the U.S. presidency in 1896. Bryan had established himself as a friend to the many Americans who had been hurt by the depression, especially farmers and industrial workers. Bryan's views were shared by L. Frank Baum, the author of *The Wonderful Wizard of Oz*, the book that was the basis for the 1939 movie *The Wizard of Oz*.

Baum blamed the gold standard for the hardships faced by farmers and workers during the depression. Baum saw the farmer and the worker as the so-called common man, and he saw William Jennings Bryan as the best possible hope for the common man in this country.

Many people believe that Baum's most famous work, *The Wonderful Wizard of Oz*, is an allegory for the presidential election of 1896.[1] Some say that Dorothy, in the book and the movie, represents Bryan. Both Dorothy and Bryan were young. (Bryan was a 36-year-old presidential candidate.) Like the cyclone in the movie

Everett Collection

that transported Dorothy to the Land of Oz, the delegates at the 1896 Democratic convention lifted Bryan into a new political world, the world of presidential politics.

As Dorothy begins her travels to the Emerald City (Washington, D.C.) with Toto (the Democratic party) to meet the Wizard of Oz, she travels down a yellow brick road (the gold standard). On her way, she meets the scarecrow (the farmer), the tin man (the industrial worker), and the cowardly lion, who some believe represents the Populist party of the time. (The Populist party was sometimes depicted as a lion in the political cartoons of the time. It was a cowardly lion in that, as some say, it did not have the courage to fight an independent campaign for the presidency in 1896.) The message is clear: Bryan, with the help of the Democratic and Populist parties and with the votes of the farmers and the industrial workers, will travel to Washington.

But then, when Dorothy and the others reach the Emerald City, they are denied their wishes, just as Bryan is denied the presidency. He loses the election to William McKinley.

But the story is not over. There is still the battle with the Wicked Witch of the West, who wears a golden cap (the gold standard). When the Wicked Witch sees Dorothy's silver shoes—they were changed to ruby in the movie—she desperately wants them for their magical quality. But she is not to get her way. Dorothy kills the Wicked Witch of the West. She then clicks her silver shoes together, and they take her back home, where all is right with the world.

[1.] This interpretation is based on "William Jennings Bryan on the Yellow Brick Road," by John Geer and Thomas Rochon, *Journal of American Culture* (Winter 1993), pp. 59–63, and "The Wizard of Oz: Parable on Populism," by Henry Littlefield, *American Quarterly* (Spring 1964), pp. 47–58.

Once people's confidence in the receipts was established, they used the receipts to make payments instead of using the gold itself. In time, the paper warehouse receipts circulated as money. For instance, if Franklin wanted to buy something from Mason that was priced at 10 gold pieces, he could simply give his warehouse receipt to Mason instead of going to the goldsmith, obtaining the gold, and then delivering it to Mason. For both Franklin and Mason, using the receipts was easier than exchanging the actual gold.

At this stage of banking, warehouse receipts were fully backed by gold; they simply represented gold in storage. Goldsmiths later began to recognize that, on an average day, few people redeemed their receipts for gold. Many individuals traded the receipts for goods and seldom requested the gold itself. In short, the receipts had become money, widely accepted for purposes of exchange.

Sensing opportunity, goldsmiths began to lend some of the stored gold, realizing that they could earn interest on the loans without defaulting on their pledge to redeem the warehouse receipts when presented. In most cases, however, the gold borrowers also preferred warehouse receipts to the actual gold. Thus, the warehouse receipts came to represent a greater amount of gold than was actually on deposit. Consequently, the money supply increased, now measured in terms of gold and the paper warehouse receipts issued by the goldsmith–bankers.

Thus, **fractional reserve banking** had begun. In a fractional reserve system, banks create money by holding on reserve only a fraction of the money deposited with them and lending the remainder. Our modern-day banking operates within such a system.

12-3b The Bank's Reserves and More

Many banks have an account with the **Federal Reserve System (the Fed)**, the central bank of the United States. This account is similar to a checking account that an individual has with a commercial bank. Economists refer to such an account with the Fed as either a *reserve account* or a *bank deposit at the Fed*. Banks also have currency, or cash, in their vaults—called vault cash—on the bank premises. The sum of (1) bank deposits at the Fed and (2) the bank's vault cash is known as **reserves**:

$$\text{Reserves} = \text{Bank deposits at the Fed} + \text{Vault cash}$$

For example, if a bank currently has $4 million in deposits at the Fed and $1 million in vault cash, it has $5 million in reserves.

The Required Reserve Ratio and Required Reserves   The Fed mandates that member commercial banks must hold a certain fraction of their checkable deposits in *reserve form*. In other words, that fraction of checkable deposits must be in the form of bank deposits at the Fed and/or vault cash because the sum of these two accounts equals reserves.

The fraction of checkable deposits that banks must hold in reserve form is called the **required reserve ratio (r)**. The dollar amount of those deposits is called **required reserves**, and the rule specifying the amount of reserves that a bank must hold to back up deposits is the **reserve requirement**. To find the required reserves for a given bank, multiply the required reserve ratio by checkable deposits (in the bank):

$$\text{Required reserves} = r \times \text{Checkable deposits}$$

Fractional Reserve Banking
A banking arrangement that allows banks to hold reserves equal to only a fraction of their deposit liabilities.

Federal Reserve System (the Fed)
The central bank of the United States.

Reserves
The sum of bank deposits at the Fed and vault cash.

Required Reserve Ratio (r)
A percentage of each dollar deposited that must be held in reserve form (specifically, as bank deposits at the Fed or vault cash).

Required Reserves
The minimum dollar amount of reserves a bank must hold against its checkable deposits, as mandated by the Fed.

Reserve Requirement
The Fed rule that specifies the amount of reserves a bank must hold to back up deposits.

For example, assume that customers have deposited $40 million in a neighborhood bank and that the Fed has set the required reserve ratio at 1/10, or 10 percent. Required reserves for the bank then equals $4 million (0.10 × $40 million = $4 million).

Excess Reserves   The difference between a bank's (total) reserves and its required reserves is its **excess reserves**:

$$\text{Excess reserves} = \text{Reserves} - \text{Required reserves}$$

Excess Reserves

Any reserves held beyond the required amount; the difference between (total) reserves and required reserves.

For example, if the bank's (total) reserves are $5 million and its required reserves are $4 million, then it holds excess reserves of $1 million.

Note: Banks can use excess reserves to make loans. Before late 2008, the Fed did not pay interest on any reserves (required or excess), so banks had a monetary incentive to create loans with their excess reserves. That incentive was lessened when the Fed began paying interest on reserves in late 2008.

SELF-TEST

1. A bank reduces its deposits at the Fed by $5 million and increases its vault cash by $5 million. What happens to the bank's reserves?

2. If a bank has $87 million in checkable deposits and it is required to hold $6 million in reserves (required reserves = $6 million), what is the required reserve ratio?

3. If excess reserves are $4 million and (total) reserves are $6 million, what do required reserves and checkable deposits equal? Assume that the required reserve ratio is 8 percent.

12-4 THE FINANCIAL SYSTEM

A financial system is essentially a means of getting people with surplus funds together with people who have a shortage of funds. Stated differently, it is a means of getting lenders (i.e., savers) and borrowers together.

Why is getting lenders and borrowers together important? The short answer is that getting them together is a way to put good ideas into action. Suppose you have saved funds that you want to lend. Elsewhere, someone has a shortage of funds but an idea for a new business venture. That person doesn't have the necessary funds to launch his new business venture. He needs to find people like you—people with funds to lend—who wouldn't mind trading him your funds now in return for his making interest payments to you later.

Thus, an economy that can get saved funds to borrowers can benefit not only the lenders but the borrowers too. And it can also benefit others. If the borrower really does have a good idea for a new business venture, future customers will benefit when the business is up and running. Maybe the firm will produce something that many thousands of others want to buy.

Direct Finance

A method of transferring money whereby borrowers and lenders come together in a market setting, such as the bond market.

12-4a Direct and Indirect Finance

Lenders can get together with borrowers directly or indirectly; that is, there are two types of finance: direct and indirect. In **direct finance**, the lenders and borrowers come together in a market setting, such as the bond market, in which people who want to borrow funds issue bonds. For example, company A might issue a bond that promises to pay an interest rate of 10 percent annually for the next 10 years. A person with funds to lend might then buy that bond for a particular price. The buying and selling in a bond market are simply lending and borrowing. The buyer of the bond is the lender, and the seller of the bond is the borrower.

In **indirect finance**, lenders and borrowers go through a **financial intermediary**, which takes in funds from people who want to save and then lends the funds to people who want to borrow. For example, a commercial bank is a financial intermediary, doing business with both savers and borrowers. Through one door the savers come in, looking for a place to deposit their funds and earn regular interest payments. Through another door come the borrowers, seeking loans on which they will pay interest. The bank, or the financial intermediary, ends up channeling the saved funds to borrowers.

12-4b **Adverse Selection Problems and Moral Hazard Problems**

When it comes to lending and borrowing, adverse selection or moral hazards can arise. Both are the result of **asymmetric information**, a situation in which one party to a transaction has information that the other party does not have. For example, suppose Ursula is going to sell her house. As the seller of the house, she has more information about it than potential buyers have. Ursula knows whether the house has plumbing problems, cracks in the foundation, and so on. Potential buyers do not.

The effect of asymmetric information can be either an adverse selection problem or a moral hazard problem. The adverse selection problem occurs *before* the loan is made, and the moral hazard problem occurs *afterward*.

Before the Loan Is Made   An **adverse selection** problem occurs when parties on one side of the market have information not known to others and self-select on the basis of that information in a way that adversely affects parties on the other side of the market. Think of it this way: Two people want a loan. One person is a good credit risk, and the other is a bad credit risk. The person who is the bad credit risk is the person more likely to ask for the loan, and that situation is an instance of adverse selection.

Suppose two people, Steven and Olivia, want to borrow $10,000, and Jason has $10,000 to lend. Olivia wants to borrow the $10,000 to buy a piece of equipment for her small business. She plans to pay back the loan, and she takes her loan commitments seriously. Steven wants to borrow the $10,000 so that he can go to Las Vegas and play roulette. He will pay back the loan only if he scores big in Las Vegas. He is not the type of person who takes his loan commitments seriously. Who is more likely to ask Jason for the loan, Steven or Olivia? Steven is, because he knows that he will pay back the loan only if he wins big in Las Vegas; he sees a loan as essentially "free money." Heads, Steven wins; tails, Jason loses.

Now, if Jason gives a little thought to his lending activities, he may realize that there are borrowers like Steven in the world. Ideally, Jason wants to lend only to the Olivias of the world, but Jason can't always tell who is an Olivia and who is a Steven. On the one hand, Olivia will tell Jason the truth about what she wants to do with the loan, and she is likely to pay back the loan. On the other hand, Steven may lie to Jason about what he plans to do with the loan, and he is not as likely to pay back the loan as Olivia is.

If Jason can't tell the Olivias from the Stevens, what can he do? He might just decide not to give a loan to anyone. In other words, his inability to solve the adverse selection

Indirect Finance
A method of transferring money whereby funds are loaned and borrowed through a financial intermediary.

Financial Intermediary
An institution that transfers funds from those who want to lend funds to those who want to borrow them.

Asymmetric Information
A situation in which an economic agent on one side of a transaction has information that an economic agent on the other side of the transaction does not have.

Adverse Selection
A phenomenon that occurs when parties on one side of the market who have information not known to others self-select in a way that adversely affects parties on the other side of the market.

problem (i.e., to tell the good risks from the bad risks) may be enough for him to decide not to lend to anyone.

At this point, a financial intermediary can help. A financial intermediary, such as a bank, does not require Jason to worry about who will and who will not pay back a loan. Jason needs simply to turn over his saved funds to the bank, in return for the bank's promise to pay him a 5 percent interest rate per year. Then, the bank takes on the responsibility of trying to separate the Olivias from the Stevens. The bank will run a credit check on everyone (the Olivias and Stevens alike); the bank will collect information on who has a job and who doesn't; the bank will ask the borrower to put up some collateral on the loan; and so on. In other words, the bank's job is to solve the adverse selection problem.

Moral Hazard

A condition that exists when one party to a transaction changes his or her behavior in a way that is hidden from, and costly to, the other party.

After the Loan Is Made   A **moral hazard** problem occurs when one party to a transaction changes his or her behavior in a way that is hidden from, and is costly to, the other party. Suppose you want to lend some saved funds. You give Tracy a $5,000 loan because she promised you that she was going to use the funds to help her get through college. Instead, once Tracy receives the $5,000, she decides to use the funds to buy some clothes and take a vacation to St. Thomas in the Caribbean.

Because of such potential moral hazard problems, you might decide to cut back on granting loans. You want to protect yourself from borrowers who do things that are costly to you. Again, a financial intermediary has a role to play. A financial intermediary, such as a bank, might try to solve the moral hazard problem by specifying that a loan can be used only for a particular purpose (e.g., paying for college). It might require the borrower to provide regular information on, and evidence of, how the borrowed funds are being used; to accept the loan in installments ($1,000 this month, $1,000 next month); and so on.

12-4c A Thought Experiment: No Financial Intermediaries

If financial intermediaries did not exist, how would life be different? Would there be as much lending and borrowing activity in a world? Because adverse selection problems and moral hazard problems reduce the amount of lending (and therefore borrowing), and because financial intermediaries help to solve these two problems, there would be more lending and borrowing in a world with financial intermediaries than in one without them.

The next question is whether having more lending and borrowing is preferable to having less. To answer this question, recall that lending and borrowing channel funds to those who can use those funds to start businesses, to come up with new products, to establish new and better production techniques, and to do other beneficial things. So lending and borrowing are not only beneficial to the lender and the borrower, but to others too. Your current material standard of living would probably not be as high as it is had you not lived in a country with substantial borrowing and lending.

Besides serving the function of providing financing for new businesses and the production of new products, and so on, lending and borrowing allow people to consume earlier in life than they would otherwise be able to. To illustrate, suppose Maria is 26 years old and wants to buy a condominium. Condos in her area sell for about $300,000, but Maria does not have $300,000; she has only $20,000. Without lending and borrowing, Maria would have to do without the condo until she can save $300,000. But with borrowing

ECONOMICS 24/7

The FDIC and Intended and Unintended Effects

In Chapter 1, we talked about the unintended consequences of actions. For example, a policy maker might undertake policy A because she wants effect X. She gets X, but she also gets the unintended effect Y, which she doesn't want.

As an example, in 1934 the federal government started insuring deposits in banks through the Federal Deposit Insurance Corporation (FDIC). Today, the FDIC insures bank deposits up to $250,000. If you have any dollar amount between $1 and $250,000 in a bank and that bank fails (goes out of business), you are guaranteed to get your money back. You will not suffer a loss.

The intended effect of instituting the FDIC and guaranteeing depositors up to $250,000 is to reduce the probability of a run on

a bank and a bank panic. A run on a bank is exactly what it sounds like: Individuals "run" to the bank to withdraw their funds because they think the bank might fail. A bank panic occurs when a run on one bank leads to runs on other banks. However, if you know you will get your money back, you have less reason to run to the bank and withdraw your funds. In turn, the bank isn't pushed into a position where it can't pay back its depositors' money.

The unintended effect of the FDIC guarantee is that depositors have less incentive to monitor the bank's activities and the bank has an increased incentive to take on riskier loans than it would if the FDIC did not exist.

and lending, Maria can make a $20,000 down payment on the condo and borrow the remaining $280,000. She can begin living in the condo many years earlier than would otherwise be possible.

In conclusion, lending and borrowing not only provide the financing for new businesses and the production of new products, production techniques, and so on, but they also permit individuals to enjoy the benefits of certain goods and services for a greater number of years than would be possible without lending and borrowing. Because someone will lend her $280,000, Maria gets to enjoy the benefits of her condo for many additional years.

12-4d The Bank's Balance Sheet

We can learn a lot about banks by looking at a bank's **balance sheet**, which lists the bank's assets and liabilities. An **asset** is anything of value that the bank owns or has claim to. A **liability** is anything that the bank owes to someone else. A few examples of a bank's assets are the *reserves* the bank holds, any loans the bank has made to borrowers, and any securities the bank might own. A few examples of a bank's liabilities are the checkable deposits it holds for its customers, any nontransaction deposits (such as small-denomination time deposits), and any loans the bank has taken out (e.g., a loan the bank might have received from the Fed). Exhibit 1 shows a simplified, but typical, balance sheet for a bank.

Balance Sheet
A record of the assets and liabilities of a bank.

Asset
Anything of value that is owned or that one has claim to.

Liability
Anything that is owed to someone else.

> EXHIBIT 1

A Bank's Balance Sheet

Here we show a bank's balance sheet. On the left-hand side are assets (what others owe to the bank): reserves (equal to bank deposits at the Fed, plus vault cash), any loans the bank has made to others (e.g., a car loan the bank gave to someone),

and any securities the bank owns. On the right-hand side are liabilities (what the bank owes to others): checkable deposits (held for the bank's customers), nontransaction deposits (e.g., small-denomination time deposits), and borrowings (i.e., any loans the banks may have taken out). Also, it is

customary to show bank capital (or net worth)—the difference between assets and liabilities—on the right-hand side of the balance sheet. In the balance sheet shown, assets are $110 million and liabilities are $100 million, so bank capital (or net worth) is $10 million.

Assets ($ millions)		Liabilities ($ millions)	
Reserves	10	Checkable deposits	50
Loans	90	Nontransaction deposits (e.g., small-denomination time deposits)	50
Securities	10	Borrowings	0
		Bank capital (net worth)	10

12-4e A Bank's Business: Turning Liabilities into Assets

A bank's business is to turn its liabilities into assets. Suppose you open up a checkable deposit account with bank A and deposit $10,000 into the account. Your checkable deposit is a liability for the bank. The balance in the checkable deposit account is what the bank *owes* you. The bank then turns the bulk of the funds in your checkable deposit account into an asset. Specifically, the bank might use the bulk of those funds to grant a loan to someone. So, a bank wants liabilities because liabilities are its sources of funds—the seeds, if you will—for growing its assets.

The difference between a bank's assets and liabilities constitutes the bank's capital, or its net worth:

$$\text{Bank capital (or net worth)} = \text{Assets} - \text{Liabilities}$$

Insolvency

A condition in which one's liabilities are greater than one's assets.

For example, if a bank has $120 million in assets and $112 million in liabilities, its net worth (or the bank's capital) is equal to $8 million. Typically, a bank's capital is recorded on the right-hand side of its balance sheet, as shown in Exhibit 1.

The bank's capital can be viewed as a cushion against **insolvency**, which exists when a bank's liabilities are greater than its assets:

$$\text{Insolvency} \rightarrow \text{Liabilities} > \text{Assets}$$

An insolvent bank has failed and can be shut down.

The larger the bank's capital, the bigger is the cushion against bank failure or insolvency; the smaller the bank's capital, the smaller is the cushion against bank failure or insolvency.

SELF-TEST

1. Jack promises Samantha that he will pay for any expenses she has on her trip beyond $1,000. Does Jack's promise create an adverse selection problem or a moral hazard problem? Explain your answer.

2. Bank A finds that many of the loans it extended to individuals are not being paid back. How do the defaults affect bank A's capital, or net worth?

3. What do financial intermediaries do?

ECONOMICS 24/7

The Financial Crisis, Risky Loans, and Bank Insolvency

At the end of 2008 and throughout 2009, many banks found themselves holding unpaid loans, many of them mortgage loans to home buyers. To understand what was happening at this time, compare two settings.

In setting 1, a person wants to buy a house that is priced at $500,000. The person is asked to make a 20 percent down payment ($100,000) and take out a mortgage loan for the balance ($400,000). Time passes, and the person who took out the loan can't make the monthly payments. What course of action does he have? As long as the house's price hasn't fallen below $400,000, he can sell the property and repay the balance of the loan. In other words, suppose the price of the house has fallen to $425,000. Our house owner and mortgage loan borrower can then sell the house for $425,000 and repay the $400,000 loan, leaving him with $25,000. Obviously, the mortgage borrower has ended up losing some of his $100,000 down payment.

In setting 2, a person wants to buy a house that is priced at $500,000. This time, though, the person is not asked for a down payment. Instead, the bank gives the buyer a mortgage loan for the entire price of the house: a $500,000 loan. Again, suppose that the person who took out the loan has a hard time making her monthly payments. What now? Can she sell the house and repay the loan? Yes, as long as the price of the house is still $500,000 (ignoring real estate fees and closing costs). But what if the price

of the house has fallen to $425,000? In that case, the person who bought the house and took out the $500,000 loan may simply walk away from the house and the loan. The house would then revert to the bank, but the bank can't sell the house for a high enough price to recover its loan amount. So the bank sells the house for $425,000 and takes a $75,000 loss on the mortgage loan of $500,000.

Setting 1 describes the state of the mortgage loan business in the 1970s, 1980s, and early 1990s. Setting 2 describes the state of the mortgage loan business in the late 1990s and the early to mid-2000s. Why banks moved from one setting to the other is a long story that we will address in a later chapter. For now, though, we are interested in how setting 2 changes things for the bank, especially with respect to the prospects of insolvency.

The peak of the housing boom (rising home prices) in the United States came in mid-2006. Since then, house prices have fallen. The decline in house prices, combined with the percentage of homeowners who can't make their monthly house payments, has the effect of loans going bad for banks. Some of the loans (which, in hindsight, turned out to be risky) were not paid off in full for one reason or another. As a result, the assets of the banks declined, and consequently so did the bank's capital (its net worth). Banks found themselves either falling over, or close to the edge of, the insolvency cliff.

Office  Hours

"I Thought Money Had to Be Backed by Gold to Have Value"

STUDENT:

We know that M1 is equal to currency held outside banks, plus checkable deposits, plus traveler's checks. None of these components of the money supply are backed by gold. But don't they have to be backed by gold before they can have any value?

INSTRUCTOR:

Your question essentially tries to identify that "thing" that gives money value. So let's suppose that paper money were backed by gold. In other words, if you take $100 in paper money and turn it in to the federal government, the government would give you $100 worth of gold in return. At first glance, you might say that paper money has value because it is backed by gold. But then the question becomes, what gives gold value? What is gold backed by?

STUDENT:

Nothing backs up gold. For example, gold isn't backed by copper or anything else.

INSTRUCTOR:

Our point is a simple one: It is a myth that paper money has to be backed by a commodity—such as gold—before it can have value. Our paper money has value because of its *general acceptability*. Specifically, you accept a dollar bill in payment for your goods and services because you know that others will also accept the dollar bill in payment. To illustrate, suppose our paper money were not generally accepted. Suppose that one day the supermarket clerk would not accept the paper dollars you offered as payment for groceries. Suppose the plumber and the gas station attendant would not take your paper dollars for fixing your kitchen drain and for servicing your car. In such a case, would you be as likely to accept paper dollars in exchange for what you sell? Probably not. You accept paper dollars because you know that other people will accept them when you spend them. Money has value to people because it is widely accepted in exchange for other valuable goods.

Points to remember

1. It is a myth that paper money has to be backed by a commodity (such as gold) before it can have value.
2. General acceptability gives money value.

CHAPTER SUMMARY

WHAT MONEY IS

- Money is any good that is widely accepted for purposes of exchange and in the repayment of debts.
- Money serves as a medium of exchange, a unit of account, and a store of value.
- Money evolved out of a barter economy as traders attempted to make exchange easier. A few goods that have been used as money are gold, silver, copper, cattle, rocks, and shells.
- Our money today has value because of its general acceptability.

THE MONEY SUPPLY

- M1 includes currency held outside banks, checkable deposits, and traveler's checks.
- M2 includes M1, savings deposits (including money market deposit accounts), small-denomination time deposits, and money market mutual funds (retail).
- Credit cards are not money. When a credit card is used to make a purchase, a liability is incurred. That is not the case when money is used to make a purchase.

RESERVES, REQUIRED AND EXCESS

- Reserves equals bank deposits at the Fed plus vault cash. The dollar amount of reserves a bank must hold is equal to the required reserve ratio times the bank's checkable deposits: Required reserves = $r \times$ Checkable deposits, where r = required reserve ratio. Excess reserves is the difference between total reserves and required reserves: Excess reserves = Total reserves − Required reserves.

THE FINANCIAL SYSTEM

- A financial system is a means of getting people with surplus funds (with funds to lend) together with people who have a shortage of funds (who want to borrow funds).
- Asymmetric information is a situation in which one party to a transaction has information that the other party does not. The two types of asymmetric information problems are adverse selection and moral hazard.

- Adverse selection is a phenomenon in which parties on one side of the market have information not known to others and self-select on the basis of that information in a way that adversely affects parties on the other side of the market.
- Moral hazard is the condition that exists when one party to a transaction changes his or her behavior in a way that is hidden from, and costly to, the other party.

A BANK'S BALANCE SHEET

- A bank's balance sheet records the bank's assets and liabilities.
- A bank's business is to turn its liabilities into assets.
- Bank capital, or net worth, is the difference between a bank's assets and its liabilities. Bank capital (net worth) = Assets − Liabilities.
- A bank is insolvent if its liabilities are greater than its assets.

KEY TERMS AND CONCEPTS

Money
Barter
Medium of Exchange
Unit of Account
Store of Value
Double Coincidence of
    Wants
M1
Currency

Federal Reserve Notes
Checkable Deposits
M2
Savings Deposit
Time Deposit
Money Market Deposit
    Account (MMDA)
Money Market Mutual Fund
    (MMMF)

Fractional Reserve Banking
Federal Reserve System (the
    Fed)
Reserves
Required Reserve Ratio (r)
Required Reserves
Reserve Requirement
Excess Reserves
Direct Finance

Indirect Finance
Financial Intermediary
Asymmetric Information
Adverse Selection
Moral Hazard
Balance Sheet
Asset
Liability
Insolvency

VIDEO QUESTIONS AND PROBLEMS

Video Questions and Problems are available on MindTap for Arnold 12e or by searching for Arnold on www.cengagebrain.com

1. If $4 million is transferred from checkable deposits into money market mutual funds (retail), what happens to both M1 and M2?

2. Explain how money emerged out of a barter economy.

3. If checkable deposits are $100 million and the required reserve ratio is 7 percent, then what do required reserves equal?

4. Money economies are likely to be richer than barter economies in both output and leisure. Do you agree or disagree? Explain your answer.

5. The required reserve ratio is 10 percent, and a bank has checkable deposits of $200 million and excess reserves of $100 million. Assuming the bank is meeting its reserve requirement, what amount is the bank holding in reserves?

QUESTIONS AND PROBLEMS

1. "How much money did you make last year?" What is wrong with that statement?

2. Suppose the value of the dollar declines relative to other currencies. How does the decline affect the three functions of money?

3. Does inflation, which is an increase in the price level, affect the three functions of money? If so, how?

4. "People in a barter economy came up with the idea of money because they wanted to do something to make society better off." Do you agree or disagree with this statement? Explain your answer.

5. "A barter economy would have very few comedians." Do you agree or disagree with this statement? Explain your answer.

6. Money makes trade easier. Would having a money supply twice as large as it currently is make trade twice as easy? Would having a money supply half its current size make trade half as easy?

7. Explain why gold backing is not necessary to give paper money value.

8. "Money is a means of lowering the transaction costs of making exchanges." Do you agree or disagree? Explain your answer.

9. If you were on an island with 10 other people and there were no money, do you think that money would emerge on the scene? Why or why not?

10. Can M1 fall as M2 rises? Can M1 rise without M2 rising too? Explain your answers.

11. Why isn't a credit card money?

12. Define the following:
    a. Time deposit
    b. Money market mutual fund
    c. Money market deposit account
    d. Fractional reserve banking
    e. Reserves

13. Explain the process by which goldsmiths could increase the money supply.

14. What is a financial system, and why would a country with a well-developed and fully functionally financial system be better off than a country without it?

15. Identify each of the following as either an adverse selection problem or a moral hazard problem:
    a. Poor drivers apply for car insurance more than good drivers do.
    b. The federal government promises to help banks that get into financial problems.
    c. The federal government insures checkable deposits (promises to repay the holder of the checkable deposit if the bank fails).

16. Explain how financial intermediaries help to solve adverse selection problems and moral hazard problems when it comes to lending and borrowing.

17. Explain the difference between a bank's loans and its borrowings.

WORKING WITH NUMBERS AND GRAPHS

1. Checkable deposits are $50 million, and required reserves are $4 million. What is the required reserve ratio?

2. The required reserve ratio is 9 percent, required reserves are $10 million, and (total) reserves are $50 million. How much do excess reserves equal? How much do checkable deposits equal?

3. A bank's assets are $90 million, and its liabilities are $71 million. Its assets increase by 10 percent, and its liabilities increase by 6 percent. What is the *percentage change* in the bank's capital, or net worth?

4. A bank currently has $100 million in checkable deposits, $4 million in reserves, and $8 million in securities. If the required reserve ratio is 10 percent, is the bank meeting its legal reserve requirements? Explain.

5. Currency held outside banks is $400 billion, checkable deposits amount to $350 billion, traveler's checks are $2 billion, and money market mutual funds (retail) are $100 billion. What does M1 equal?

6. If currency held outside banks is $200 billion and M1 is $600 billion, do we know for sure how much checkable deposits equal? Why or why not?

7. Currency held outside banks is $100 billion, money market mutual funds (retail) are $120 billion, small-denomination time deposits are $50 billion, and savings deposits (including money market deposit accounts) are $200 billion. How much does M2 equal?

8. If checkable deposits are $20 million and the required reserve ratio is 15 percent, how much do required reserves equal?

9. If excess reserves are $2 million and required reserves are $22 million, then how much do reserves equal?

10. If bank deposits at the Fed equal $40 million and reserves equal $43 million, then how much does vault cash equal?

THE FEDERAL RESERVE SYSTEM

INTRODUCTION

Tourists in Washington, D.C., usually visit the White House, the Capitol, and the Supreme Court, in all of which major decisions are made that affect peoples' lives. Such decisions affecting peoples' lives are also made in another building in Washington, D.C., but tourists rarely visit It: the Federal Reserve. In this building, the Board of Governors of the Federal Reserve System and the members of the Federal Open Market Committee determine U.S. monetary policy. This chapter discusses many of the details of the Federal Reserve System.

13-1 THE STRUCTURE AND FUNCTIONS OF THE FEDERAL RESERVE SYSTEM (THE FED)

The Federal Reserve System is the central bank of the United States. Other nations have central banks, such as the Bank of Sweden, the Bank of England, the Banque de France, the Bank of Japan, the Deutsche Bundesbank, and the like.

13-1a The Structure of the Fed

The Federal Reserve System came into existence with the Federal Reserve Act of 1913 and began operations in November 1914. The act divided the country into Federal Reserve Districts. As Exhibit 1 shows, there are 12 districts, each with a Federal Reserve Bank and its own president.

Within the Fed, a seven-member **Board of Governors** coordinates and controls the activities of the Federal Reserve System. The board members serve 14-year terms and are appointed by the president with U.S. Senate approval. To limit political influence on Fed policy, the terms of the governors are staggered—with one new appointment every other year—so that a president cannot "pack" the board. The president also designates one member as chairman of the board for a four-year term.

Board of Governors
The governing body of the Federal Reserve System.

> **EXHIBIT 1**

Federal Reserve Districts and Federal Reserve Bank Locations

TThe boundaries of the Federal Reserve Districts, the cities in which a Federal Reserve Bank is located, and the location of the Board of Governors (Washington, D.C.) are all noted on the map.

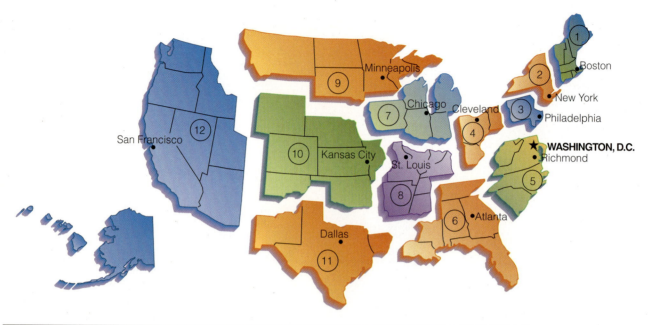

Federal Open Market Committee (FOMC)
The Fed's 12-member policy-making group. The committee has the authority to conduct open market operations.

Open Market Operations
The buying and selling of government securities by the Fed.

Monetary Policy
Changes in the money supply or in the rate of change of the money supply, intended to achieve stated macroeconomic goals.

The major policy-making group in the Fed is the **Federal Open Market Committee (FOMC)**. Authority to conduct **open market operations**—the buying and selling of government securities—rests with the FOMC (more on open market operations later in the chapter). The FOMC has 12 members: the seven-member Board of Governors and five Federal Reserve District Bank presidents. The president of the Federal Reserve Bank of New York holds a permanent seat on the FOMC because a large amount of financial activity takes place in New York City and because the New York Fed is responsible for executing open market operations. The other four positions are rotated among the Federal Reserve District Bank presidents.

The most important responsibility of the Fed is to conduct monetary policy, or control the money supply. **Monetary policy** consists of changes in the money supply that are intended to achieve stated macroeconomic goals. More specifically, *expansionary monetary policy* aims to increase the money supply and *contractionary monetary policy* aims to decrease it. The Fed has tools at its disposal to both increase and decrease the money supply. In a later chapter, we will discuss monetary policy in detail and show how, under certain conditions, it can remove an economy from both recessionary and inflationary gaps.

13-1b **Functions of the Fed**

The Fed has eight major responsibilities, or functions:

1. *Controlling the money supply*. A full explanation of how the Fed plays this role comes later in the chapter.

ECONOMICS 24/7

Inside an FOMC Meeting

The FOMC meets eight times a year, each time on a Tuesday. The meeting is held in the boardroom of the Federal Reserve Building. The following events occur at a typical FOMC meeting:

8:00 a.m.

The boardroom is swept for electronic bugs.

8:45–9:00 a.m.

People begin to arrive for the meeting. In addition to the 12 members of the FOMC, about 37 other people will be present.

8:59 a.m.

The chair of the Board of Governors of the Federal Reserve System walks through the door that connects her office to the boardroom and takes her place at the table.

9:00 a.m.

The FOMC meeting commences. The first item on the agenda is a presentation by the manager of the System Open Market Account at the Federal Reserve Bank of New York. He discusses the financial and foreign exchange markets and provides certain details about open market operations.

A Little Later …

The director of research and statistics at the Federal Reserve Board presents the forecast of the U.S. economy. The forecast has previously been circulated to the FOMC members. The latest economic data are reviewed and discussed.

Andrew Harrer/Bloomberg/Getty Images

A Little Later …

The 12 members of the FOMC present their views of local and national economic conditions.

A Little Later …

The director of monetary affairs presents policy options. These policy options have been previously circulated. The chair of the Board of Governors gives her opinion of the economy and of the policy options.

A Little Later …

A general discussion among all the members of the FOMC takes place. At issue is the state of the U.S. economy and current policy options. After the discussion, the chair summarizes her sense of the policy options. Then the members vote on the options. The chair votes first, the vice chair votes second, and the remaining FOMC members vote in alphabetical order.

A Little Later …

The FOMC discusses the wording of the announcement it will make regarding its decision.

Between 11:30 a.m. and 1:30 p.m.

The meeting usually adjourns.

2:15 p.m.

The decision of the FOMC is released to the public.

2. *Supplying the economy with paper money (Federal Reserve notes).* The Federal Reserve Banks have Federal Reserve notes on hand to meet the demands of the banks and the public. During the Christmas season, for example, more people withdraw larger-than-usual amounts of $1, $5, $20, $50, and $100 notes from banks. Needing to replenish their vault cash, banks turn to their Federal Reserve Banks, which meet cash needs by issuing more paper money (acting as passive suppliers of paper money). The money is actually printed at the Bureau of Engraving

and Printing in Washington, D.C., but it is issued to commercial banks by the 12 Federal Reserve Banks.

3. *Providing check-clearing services.* When a bank receives a check (from a depositor) drawn on another bank, it may send the check for collection and clearing directly to the other bank, deliver the check to the other bank through a local clearinghouse, or use the check-collection and -clearing services of a Federal Reserve Bank. If it uses the services of a Federal Reserve Bank, the account of the bank collecting the value of the check is credited and the account of the bank that is paying is debited. Most checks are collected and settled within one business day.

4. *Holding depository institutions' reserves.* As explained in the previous chapter, banks are required to keep reserves against customer deposits either in their vaults or in reserve accounts at the Fed. These accounts are maintained by the 12 Federal Reserve Banks for member banks in their respective districts.

5. *Supervising member banks.* Without notice, the Fed can examine the books of member commercial banks to assess the nature of the loans the banks have made, monitor compliance with bank regulations, check the accuracy of bank records, and so on. If the Fed finds that a bank has not been maintaining established banking standards, it can pressure the institution to do so.

6. *Serving as the government's banker.* The federal government collects and spends large sums of money. As a result, it needs a checking account for many of the same reasons an individual does. The primary checking account of the federal government is with the Fed, which is the government's banker.

7. *Serving as the lender of last resort.* A traditional function of a central bank is to serve as the lender of last resort for banks suffering cash management, or liquidity, problems.

U.S. Treasury Securities

Bonds and bondlike securities issued by the U.S. Treasury when it borrows.

8. *Handling the sale of U.S. Treasury securities (auctions).* **U.S. Treasury securities** (bills, notes, and bonds) are sold to raise funds to pay the government's bills. The Federal Reserve District Banks receive the bids for these securities and process them in time for weekly auctions.

13-1c Common Misconceptions About the U.S. Treasury and the Fed

Some persons confuse the U.S. Treasury with the Fed. They mistakenly believe that the U.S. Treasury does some of the things that the Fed does. However, there are major differences between the Treasury and the Fed:

- The U.S. Treasury is a budgetary agency; the Fed is a monetary agency.

- When the federal government spends funds, the Treasury collects the taxes and borrows the funds needed to pay suppliers and others. In short, the Treasury has an obligation to manage the financial affairs of the federal government. Except for coins, the Treasury does not issue money. It cannot create money out of thin air as the Fed can. (We will soon explain exactly how the Fed does this.)

- The Fed is concerned principally with the availability of money and credit for the entire economy. It does not issue Treasury securities. It does not have an obligation to meet the financial needs of the federal government. Its responsibility is to provide a stable monetary framework for the economy.

ECONOMICS 24/7

Some History of the Fed

Slightly before the passage of the Federal Reserve Act in 1913, there was disagreement about how many districts and banks there should be. Many people thought that there should be as few banks as possible—6 to 8—because concentrating activities in only a few cities would enhance efficiency and ease of operation. William Jennings Bryan, the Secretary of State at the time, wanted 50 district banks. He called for a "branch at every major crossroad." It was to be neither 6 nor 50; instead, there was a compromise. Section 2 of the Federal Reserve Act states that "not less than eight nor more than twelve cities" would be designated as Federal Reserve cities.

After the number of cities was determined to be 8 to 12, a commission was set up to identify both the boundaries of the Federal Reserve Districts and the locations of the district banks. The commission was composed of the Comptroller of the Currency, the Secretary of the Treasury, and the Secretary of Agriculture. They had to choose from among the 37 cities that had applied to be locations of a district bank. The commission settled on a 12-bank, 12-city plan. It decided the boundaries of the districts on the basis of trade. In other words, the commission decided that the boundaries should include cities or towns that traded the most with each other. If the residents of cities X and Y traded a lot with each other but the residents of city Z did not trade much with the residents of cities X and Y, then cities X and Y should be included in the same district but Z should not. Instead, city Z should be part of the district that included cities with which it traded.

Some commercial banks protested both the number of district banks and the boundaries decided on by the committee. These banks filed petitions asking for a review of the plan with the Federal Reserve Board, thought to be the only group that could alter the plan.[1]

The petitions for review are said to have rekindled the debate about the desired number of district cities. Three members of the Federal Reserve Board wanted to reduce the number of district banks because they thought that one-half of the banks were stronger than the other half were and they wanted all banks to be of equal strength. Three other members of the Board wanted to stay with the original plan of 12 district banks. This configuration left one member of the Board to break the tie. It looked as though that person's vote was going to be cast for a reduction in the number of district banks. At that point, one of the supporters of the original 12-bank plan went to the Attorney General of the United States and asked for an opinion stating that the Board did not have the authority to alter the original plan. The Attorney General gave that opinion. The Board, afraid of attracting negative publicity by disagreeing and challenging the opinion, accepted it.

[1.] Before there was a Board of Governors of the Federal Reserve System, there was the Federal Reserve Board. The Banking Act of 1935, approved on August 23, 1935, changed the name of the Federal Reserve Board to the Board of Governors of the Federal Reserve System.

SELF-TEST

(Answers to Self-Test questions are in Answers to Self-Test Questions at the back of the book.)

1. The president of which Federal Reserve District Bank holds a permanent seat on the FOMC?

2. What is the most important responsibility of the Fed?

3. "The Fed acts as lender of last resort." What does that statement mean?

13-2 THE MONEY SUPPLY EXPANSION PROCESS

This section describes the important money supply process—specifically, how the Fed can increase and decrease the money supply. Before we begin, we offer a quick review of reserves, required reserves, and excess reserves.

13-2a A Quick Review of Reserves, Required Reserves, and Excess Reserves

In the last chapter, we made the following points:

1. A bank's reserves equal its bank deposits at the Fed (the balance in its reserve account at the Fed) plus its vault cash:

$$\text{Reserves} = \text{Bank deposits at the Fed} + \text{Vault cash}$$

2. A bank's required reserves are equal to the required reserve ratio (r) times the bank's checkable deposits:

$$\text{Required reserves} = r \times \text{Checkable deposits}$$

3. A bank's excess reserves equal its reserves minus its required reserves:

$$\text{Excess reserves} = \text{Reserves} - \text{Required reserves}$$

4. A bank can use its excess reserves to create new loans.

13-2b The Money Supply Expansion Process

We start with the definition of the M1 money supply:

$$\begin{aligned} \text{M1} = \ & \text{Currency held outside banks} \\ & + \text{Checkable deposits} \\ & + \text{Traveler's checks} \end{aligned}$$

Let's suppose that checkable deposits are $10,000 and that the other two components of the money supply equal $0. It follows that the money supply is $10,000:

$$\text{Money supply} = \$10,000$$

For now, we are going to assume that the entire $10,000 in checkable deposits is held in one bank: Bank A. We will also assume that the required reserve ratio is 10 percent and that Bank A is currently holding $1,000 in required reserves and no excess reserves. Here is the relevant part of the balance sheet for Bank A:

Bank A			
Assets		**Liabilities**	
Reserves	$1,000	Checkable Deposits	$10,000
Loans	$9,000		

The Fed Conducts an Open Market Purchase   The Fed conducts an **open market purchase**, which is a type of open market operation; specifically, it buys government securities from a bank. In this example, the Fed buys $500 worth of government securities from Bank A. (Although government securities are assets for banks, we have not shown these assets on Bank A's balance sheet in order that we may focus only on reserves, loans, and checkable deposits.) Bank A turns over the government securities to the Fed, and, in return, the Fed must pay Bank A $500.

Where does the Fed get the $500 to pay Bank A? The answer is *out of thin air*. Bank A currently has a reserve account (bank deposits at the Fed) of $1,000. The Fed simply changes the balance in that account (with a stroke of a computer key) from $1,000 to $1,500. Here is what the balance sheet now looks like for Bank A:

Open Market Purchase
The buying of government securities by the Fed.

Bank A		
Assets		**Liabilities**
Reserves	$1,500	Checkable Deposits	$10,000
Loans	$9,000		

The Situation for Bank A   The balance sheet for Bank A shows $1,500 in reserves and $10,000 in checkable deposits. If the required reserve ratio is 10 percent, Bank A is required to hold only $1,000 in reserves. So Bank A has $500 in *excess reserves*.

Suppose Bank A takes the entire $500 in excess reserves and creates a loan for Jill. Specifically, it grants Jill a $500 loan in the form of a new checkable deposit with a balance of $500. In other words, instead of giving Jill $500 in currency, Bank A simply tells Jill that she now has a checkable deposit (a checking account) with the bank and that the balance in the account is $500.

What Is the Money Supply Now?   Checkable deposits started off at $10,000 in Bank A but are now $10,500. The extra $500 checkable deposit is the *new deposit* that the bank created for Jill. The money supply is now $10,500:

$$\text{Money Supply} = \$10,500$$

Here is what happened to increase the money supply:

Open market purchase → More reserves for bank A
→ Bank A created more loans in the form of *new checkable deposits*
→ Money supply increased

The Process Continues   Jill now takes the $500 loan from Bank A (in the form of a new checkable deposit) and spends it. Specifically, she writes a check for $500 to Joe for the materials she buys from him. Joe then takes the $500 (he received from Jill) and deposits the full amount into his checking account at Bank B. The situation for Bank B looks like this:

Bank B		
Assets		**Liabilities**
Reserves	$500	Checkable Deposits	$500
		(Joe's account)	

Where did $500 in reserves in Bank B come from? When the check that Jill wrote to Joe clears, Bank A has to turn over $500 to Bank B. To make this happen, Bank A instructs the Fed to move $500 out of its reserve account and deposit the amount into Bank B's reserve account.

Bank B's balance sheet shows $500 in reserves and $500 in checkable deposits. But if the required reserve ratio is 10 percent, Bank B is required to hold only $50 in reserves. Bank B has $450 in excess reserves.

Bank B uses the entire $450 in excess reserves to create a loan of $450 for Jamal in the form of a checkable deposit. In other words, Bank B creates a new checkable deposit of $450.

What Is the Money Supply Now?

The money supply of $10,000 went up to $10,500 because Bank A extended a loan (created a new checkable deposit) for Jill. Bank B then extended a loan (created a new checkable deposit) of $450, so the money supply is now $10,950:

$$\text{Money supply} = \$10{,}950$$

Some people might think that, because Jill's checkable deposit balance went from $500 to $0 when her check cleared, the money supply should now be $10,450, not $10,950. But this point ignores the fact that, when Jill pays off her $500 loan to Bank A, the bank can lend the $500 to someone else. Thus, Bank A can create a new checkable deposit of $500 to take the place of Jill's old one of $500.

The Effects of No Cash Leakage and Zero Excess Reserves Held by Banks

Up to this point, we have assumed two things.

First, we assumed that both banks A and B always used *all their excess reserves* to create loans (new checkable deposits); that is, the two banks did not hold any excess reserves. If they had held some positive amount of excess reserves, the money supply would have been affected. Specifically, suppose that, when Bank A had $500 in excess reserves, it created only a $200 loan (instead of a $500 loan) and held $300 in excess reserves. In that case, the money supply would have increased from $10,000, but only to $10,200, not $10,500. In other words, the more excess reserves banks hold, the smaller the increase will be in the money supply.

Second, when Jill paid $500 to Joe, Joe deposited the entire $500 into Bank B, but, of course, Joe didn't have to do that. Instead, he could have deposited only $200 of the $500 into Bank B and asked for $300 in currency. In this case, there would have been a **cash leakage** of $300. Bank B's reserves would have increased by only $200, not $500, and the bank could not have created a new loan (a new checkable deposit) of $450.

Given no cash leakage and zero excess reserves held by banks, how much does the money supply increase? The money supply story is ongoing. As we move from Bank B to Bank C to Bank D and so on, each new bank creates some new loans (new checkable deposits), but each time the amount created is smaller than the amount that the previous bank created. Whereas Bank A created $500 and Bank B created $450, Bank C might create $405, and so on. (See Exhibit 2.) In total, all the banks (together) create $5,000 in new checkable deposits. Here is the equation we use to calculate this amount:

$$\Delta \text{Checkable deposits (or money supply)} = \frac{1}{r} \times \Delta R$$

where $r =$ the required reserve ratio and $\Delta R =$ the change in reserves resulting from the initial injection of funds. In our example, $r = 10$ percent and $\Delta R = \$500$. In the

Cash Leakage
Occurs when funds are held as currency instead of deposited into a checking account.

> **EXHIBIT 2**

The Fed, Banks, and an Increase in Checkable Deposits or the Money Supply

We assume that $r = 10$ percent, there is no cash leakage, banks hold zero excess reserves,

and the Fed ends up increasing the reserves in Bank A's reserve account by $500 through an open market purchase. As a result of the Fed's open market purchase, Bank A finds itself with $500 in excess reserves that it

uses to create a new loan or new checkable deposit. This action starts a process that ends with all relevant banks together creating $5,000 in new checkable deposits (or money).

Creation of new checkable deposits, given that

(i) $r = 10\%$
(ii) there is no cash leakage.
(iii) banks hold zero excess reserves.
(iv) there is a $500 increase in reserves for Bank A as a result of the Fed's open market purchase.

Bank	Increase in Checkable Deposits	New Required Reserves	New Checkable Deposits Created by Extending New Loans
A	$ 0	$ 0	$ 500
B	500	50	450
C	450	45	405
D	405	40.50	364.50
⋮	⋮	⋮	⋮
Total			$ 5,000

equation, the reciprocal of the required reserve ratio ($1/r$) is known as the **simple deposit multiplier**. The arithmetic for the example is

$$\Delta\text{Checkable deposits (or money supply)} = \frac{1}{0.10} \times \$500$$
$$= 10 \times \$500$$
$$= \$5,000^2$$

Simple Deposit Multiplier
The reciprocal of the required reserve ratio r: $1/r$.

The change in checkable deposits (or the money supply) is $5,000; thus, the Fed's open market purchase resulted in the money supply *rising* from $10,000 to $15,000.

13-2c The Money Supply Contraction Process

Let's again start with Bank A and its balance sheet:

Bank A			
Assets		**Liabilities**	
Reserves	$1,000	Checkable Deposits	$10,000
Loans	$9,000		

[2.] In the equation, we are looking at the change in checkable deposits or the money supply. Because checkable deposits are the only component of the money supply that is changing (currency and traveler's checks aren't changing), any change in checkable deposits is equal to the change in the money supply.

We will also assume that the initial money supply is $10,000:

$$\text{Money supply} = \$10,000$$

Open Market Sale

The selling of government securities by the Fed.

This time, the Fed undertakes an **open market sale**; that is, it sells government securities. Let's say the Fed sells $400 worth of government securities to Bank A. The Fed turns the securities over to Bank A and then subtracts $400 from Bank A's reserve account. Just as the Fed can create money *out of thin* air, it can make it disappear *into thin air*. Here is what Bank A's balance sheet now looks like (as before, we do not show the securities on the balance sheet so that we can focus on reserves, loans, and checkable deposits):

Bank A			
Assets		**Liabilities**	
Reserves	$600	Checkable Deposits	$10,000
Loans	$9,000		

Reserve Deficient

The situation that exists when a bank holds fewer reserves than specified by the required reserve ratio.

Reserves for Bank A have gone from $1,000 to $600. Given that checkable deposits are $10,000, Bank A is **reserve deficient**. If the required reserve ratio is 10 percent, Bank A is required to hold $1,000 in reserves ($10,000 × 0.10). But after the open market sale, Bank A is holding only $600 in reserves, so it is reserve deficient by $400.

When a bank is reserve deficient, it can do a number of things: It can (1) try to get a loan from another bank; (2) try to get a loan from the Fed; or (3) apply some of its loan repayments to the reserve deficiency position. In our example, suppose the bank chooses option 3. Now, suppose also that, on the day Bank A becomes reserve deficient, Harry walks into the bank and pays back the $400 loan he took out months ago.

If Bank A weren't reserve deficient, it would probably create a $400 loan (new checkable deposit) for someone else with the $400 it received from Harry. In that case, although Harry's checkable deposit balance would go to zero, someone else's checkable deposit balance would rise by $400. The creation of the loan by the bank would keep the money supply constant.

But because the bank is reserve deficient, it keeps the $400 as reserves. As a result, checkable deposits *decline* by $400; consequently, the money supply declines by $400, to $9,600:

$$\text{Money supply} = \$9,600$$

The contraction of the money supply does not stop with Bank A. It moves on to banks B, C, D, and others. To illustrate, suppose the loan repayment that Harry made to Bank A was written on a check issued by Bank B. Then, when the check clears, the reserves of Bank B decline, and Bank B finds itself reserve deficient. It then applies loan repayments to its reserve deficiency position. The effect continues with banks C, D, and so on.

To find out how much checkable deposits (the money supply) will decline, apply the equation used earlier:

$$\Delta\text{Checkable deposits (or money supply)} = \frac{1}{r} \times \Delta R$$

Recall that r = the required reserve ratio and ΔR = the change in reserves resulting from the initial removal of funds. In our example, r = 10 percent and $\Delta R = -\$400$. The arithmetic is

$$\Delta\text{Checkable deposits (or money supply)} = \frac{1}{0.10} \times -\$400$$
$$= 10 \times -\$400$$
$$= -\$4,000$$

The change in checkable deposits (or the money supply) is $-\$4,000$; thus, the Fed's open market sale resulted in the money supply *falling* from $\$10,000$ to $\$6,000$.

13-3 OTHER FED TOOLS AND RECENT FED ACTIONS

The Fed has other tools to change the money supply. In the last section, we saw how the Fed can use open market operations to change the money supply. In this section, we discuss a few other tools.

13-3a The Required Reserve Ratio

Look again at the equation for computing the change in the money supply:

$$\Delta\text{Checkable deposits (or money supply)} = \frac{1}{r} \times \Delta R$$

Notice the role that the required reserve ratio plays in the equation. If $r = 10$ percent, then the simple deposit multiplier $(1 \div r)$ is 10. Accordingly, for a $\$1$ change in reserves, the change in checkable deposits (money supply) is $\$10$. If the Fed lowers the required reserve ratio to, say, 5 percent, then the simple deposit multiplier is 20 $(1 \div 0.05 = 20)$. Now a $\$1$ rise in reserves will lead to a $\$20$ increase in the money supply. If instead the required reserve ratio is raised to 20 percent, the simple deposit multiplier $(1 \div r)$ is 5 $(1 \div 0.20 = 5)$, so a $\$1$ rise in reserves will lead to a $\$5$ increase in the money supply.

In sum,

- Lowering the required reserve ratio will increase the money supply.
- Raising the required reserve ratio will decrease the money supply.

$$r \downarrow \rightarrow \frac{1}{r} \uparrow \rightarrow \text{Money supply} \uparrow$$
$$r \uparrow \rightarrow \frac{1}{r} \downarrow \rightarrow \text{Money supply} \downarrow$$

13-3b The Discount Window and the Federal Funds Market

If Bank A wants a $\$1$ million loan, it can go to the Fed or to another bank (say, Bank B) for it. The loan the bank gets from the Fed is called a **discount loan**, and the interest rate the bank pays for a discount loan is called the **discount rate**. The discount rate is set by the Fed.

The loan that Bank A might get from another bank is usually called an *overnight loan* (because it is typically a loan of short duration, such as overnight). The market in which banks lend reserves to one another, usually for short periods, is called the *market for reserves*

Discount Loan
A loan the Fed makes to a commercial bank.

Discount Rate
The interest rate the Fed charges depository institutions that borrow reserves from it; the interest rate charged on a discount loan.

Federal Funds Market

A market in which banks lend reserves to one another, usually for short periods.

Federal Funds Rate

The interest rate in the federal funds market; the interest rate banks charge one another to borrow reserves.

or the **federal funds market**. The interest rate that Bank A pays for an overnight loan is called the **federal funds rate**, which is determined in the federal funds market. Specifically, the demand for and the supply of reserves determines the federal funds rate, in much the same way that the demand for and supply of apples determines the price of apples.

The discount rate is another tool the Fed can use to regulate the money supply. If the Fed wants to increase the money supply, it can drop the discount rate below the federal funds rate. To illustrate, suppose the federal funds rate is 5 percent. All the Fed has to do is set the discount rate at, say, 3 percent. Now Bank A has an incentive to go to the Fed instead of to another bank for the $1 million it wants. The Fed gives the bank the $1 million discount loan by increasing the balance in the bank's reserve account by $1 million. With more reserves, the bank can create more loans (more checkable deposits), and, as a result, the money supply rises.

In sum,

Fed sets discount rate below federal funds rate → Banks borrow from Fed →
Banks have more reserves → Banks may make more loans and
checkable deposits → Money supply rises

Alternatively, if the Fed wants to contract the money supply, it can set the discount rate above the federal funds rate. Now banks will *not* go to the Fed for loans, and as the banks repay discount loans taken out in the past, reserves in the banking system decline. (When a bank repays a discount loan, the Fed *subtracts* the repayment from the bank's reserve account.)

In sum,

Fed sets discount rate above federal funds rate → Banks do not borrow from the
Fed, and as banks repay past discount loans → Banks have fewer reserves →
Money supply declines

13-3c The Fed and the Federal Funds Rate Target

So far, we have identified three tools the Fed has at its disposal to change the money supply: conducting open market operations, changing the required reserve ratio, and changing the discount rate relative to the federal funds rate. Normally, if the Fed wants to change the money supply, it takes two measures: (1) It sets a **federal funds rate target**, and then (2) it uses open market operations to change the federal funds rate so as to "hit" the target.

Federal Funds Rate Target

The interest rate that the Fed wants the federal funds market rate to be.

Suppose the current federal funds rate is 4 percent and the Fed sets a federal funds rate target of 3 percent. The Fed then conducts an open market purchase, which, as we know, has the effect of injecting reserves into the banking system. As a result of the open market purchase, the supply of reserves in the market for reserves rises. As the supply of reserves rises, the price of those reserves—the federal funds rate—falls. The Fed continues these transactions until the federal funds rate falls from 4 percent to 3 percent, the federal funds rate target.

13-3d Dealing with a Financial Crisis

The actions the Fed takes might differ, depending on whether it is simply trying to change the money supply to meet a macroeconomic objective, such as price stability, or whether it is dealing with a financial crisis. (You will read about the financial crisis of 2007–2009 in Chapter 18.) By way of analogy, your pace is very different if you are taking a leisurely walk than if you are running a race. The same type of difference exists for the Fed when it is managing everyday monetary policy compared with dealing with a financial crisis.

The Fed did three things to deal with the 2007–2009 financial crisis:

- Created the term auction facility (TAF) program
- Extended the lender-of-last-resort function beyond banks
- Bought securities from institutions other than banks

Term Auction Facility (TAF) Program

In late 2007, in addition to issuing discount loans to banks, the Fed created another way banks could get loans from it: the **term auction facility (TAF) program**. In this program, instead of banks asking for a specific dollar loan (as with a discount loan), the Fed first identifies the total amount of credit it wants to extend (e.g., $20 billion). Then it allows banks to bid on the funds. The bidding process determines the TAF rate (interest rate) for the loans.

If the Fed already offers discount loans to banks, why set up the TAF program? In a sense, if a bank can already get a loan by knocking on door 1 at the Fed, why add door 2 (TAF)?

One reason is that discount loans often come with a stigma attached. Specifically, if a bank is in sound financial condition, it customarily borrows from institutions in the private sector (such as another bank). A discount loan is intended for banks that cannot get loans elsewhere; thus, a bank that requests a discount loan is often viewed as admitting that it is in poor financial health. The bank might not want to make such an admission to either the Fed or the market.

The Fed dealt with the stigma issue by stating that, as far as it was concerned, no stigma was attached to borrowing from the TAF. The Fed dealt with the issue of confidentiality in the market by stating that it would not release any information on the participants in the TAF program, except as required by law.

Finally, by establishing the TAF rate through a competitive bidding process, banks found that borrowing through the TAF was cheaper than getting discount loans.

Extending the Lender-of-Last-Resort Function Beyond Banks

As the lender of last resort for banks, the Fed ensures that banks can obtain the funds they need. If a bank has financial problems, it can seek funds from the Fed. During the financial crisis, the Fed extended its lender-of-last-resort function to institutions other than banks.

Buying Securities from Institutions Other Than Banks

During normal economic times, the Fed buys Treasury securities from banks if it wants to increase reserves in the banking system in order to raise the money supply. During the financial crisis, the Fed not only bought securities from nonbank institutions, but often bought securities that were not Treasury issues. Frequently, they were mortgage-backed securities that institutions owned which were declining in value.

13-3e Quantitative Easing

One way for the Fed to inject reserves into the banking system is through an open market purchase. It buys government securities from banks, the banks receive reserves for the government securities that they sell to the Fed, and thus reserves in the banking system increase. With additional reserves, the banks can increase lending (they can create new checkable deposits), so the money supply rises.

Term Auction Facility (TAF) Program
A program under which the Fed auctions funds to depository institutions. Each TAF auction is for a fixed amount, with the TAF interest rate determined by the auction process (subject to a minimum rate bid).

In recent years, the Fed has undertaken a policy of quantitative easing, which also injects reserves into the banking system. So, how is quantitative easing similar to and different from an open market purchase?

Both an open market purchase and quantitative easing have the Fed buying something. With an open market purchase, the Fed buys short-term government securities: government securities that mature (are paid off) in, say, 90 days, 6 months, or a year. With quantitative easing, the Fed still buys government securities (as it did in an open market purchase), but mostly long-term securities, ones that mature in, say, 10 years. Also, with quantitative easing the Fed buys not only government securities, but private sector bonds and securities as well. For example, it may purchase a mortgage-backed security. And it buys securities (long-term government securities plus private sector securities) not just from banks, but from other private institutions too.

Another way to distinguish between open market purchases and quantitative easing is in terms of the interest rates that each affects. Because the Fed buys short-term government securities when it conducts an open market purchase, it affects short-term interest rates. To understand this concept, keep in mind that, when the demand for a short-term security rises (which it does when the Fed buys short-term government securities), the price of the security rises as a result (higher demand, higher price). And as the price of the security rises, the interest rate the security pays drops.

To illustrate, suppose a government security pays $10,000 when it matures in one year and a person buys it for $9,000. To find the interest rate for this government security, we simply subtract the price of the bond ($9,000) from what the security pays at maturity ($10,000) and then divide by the price of bond ($9,000). Here is the computation:

$$(\$10,000 - \$9,000) \div \$9,000 = 11.11 \text{ percent}$$

Now, notice that, if we raise the price of the bond to $9,500, the interest rate falls to 5.26 percent:

$$(\$10,000 - \$9,500) \div \$9,500 = 5.26 \text{ percent}$$

In other words, there is an inverse relationship between the price of a bond and the interest rate: As the price goes up, the interest rate goes down; as the price goes down, the interest rate goes up.

Now let's return to an open market purchase of short-term government securities. This action raises the prices of these securities and thus lowers short-term interest rates.

In contrast, quantitative easing deals with the purchases of long-term government securities (among other types of securities), therefore increasing the prices of these securities and thus lowering long-term interest rates.

In a nutshell, both open market purchases and quantitative easing are directed at increasing reserves in the banking system and increasing the money supply. Both deal with the Fed buying something from someone. And both have certain effects on interest rates with various terms. An open market purchase entails the Fed buying short-term government securities from banks; quantitative easing entails the Fed buying long-term government securities from banks and private sector securities from other private institutions. An open market purchase affects short-term interest rates; quantitative easing affects long-term interest rates.

ECONOMICS 24/7

Flying in with the Money[3]

A banker at a commercial bank located about 200 miles from the Federal Reserve Bank of Minneapolis was frantic. A large crowd was outside his bank, and the people wanted their money now. The banker got on the phone and called the Federal Reserve Bank in Minneapolis. He told the people at the Minneapolis Fed that there was a "mad run" on his bank. If the Fed did not come to his rescue soon, he would be out of currency and unable to give the customers of his bank their money.

Where was their money? Why didn't he have it to give to them? As this chapter explained, banks need to have on hand only a fraction of their customers' deposits.

The Federal Reserve System responded to the call for currency. The Federal Reserve Bank of Minneapolis chartered a small plane,

and two Fed officials took it, along with a half million dollars in small-denomination bills, to the nearby town.

Upon approaching the town, the pilot flew the plane over Main Street to dramatize its arrival: the Federal Reserve was flying in to the rescue. The plane landed at a field not far from the town. From the field, the Fed officials were escorted into town by the police, and the money was stacked in the bank's windows. The sight of all the money calmed the bank's customers, who were now assured that they could get their money if they wanted. A banking panic was averted in a very dramatic way.

3. This feature is based on "Born of a Panic: Forming the Federal Reserve System," *The Region* (August 1998).

13-3f What Is Free Banking?

In today's world, there is a central bank—the Fed—and as we know, the Fed controls the money supply. But suppose there were no Fed. Who or what would then control the money supply? One option to replace the Fed and its control over the money supply is the monetary arrangement known as free banking. Under free banking, banks would not be subject to any special regulations beyond those which apply to other businesses. Also, under free banking, banks would have the right to issue their own paper currency and market forces would largely control the money supply. Exactly how would this arrangement work?

Let's suppose that, under a free-banking arrangement, there are 100 banks. Each bank would issue its own currency (its own banknotes) based on some quantity of reserves. Those reserves could be some commodity, such as gold or silver. Each bank would issue $1, $5, $10, and $20 notes based on some amount of gold or silver. For example, let's suppose that, for every ounce of gold that the bank held in reserves, it could issue $1,000 in its own currency (its own banknotes). So, if you possessed, say, a $10 banknote from Bank A (on the front of the banknote it might read, "This note has been issued by Bank A"), you would be entitled to some fraction of an ounce of gold if you were to ask for the note to be redeemed in gold. Just as Bank A could issue its own banknotes (its own currency), so could the remaining 99 banks.

Now, in what form would you receive a loan under a free-banking arrangement? Well, you would go to a bank, ask for, say, a $10,000 loan, and the bank would either open up a checking account for you (the balance of which would be $10,000) or, if you preferred, give you $10,000 in its banknotes.

Because banks can issue their own currency, one wonders whether banks will then simply start "creating as much money as possible." What is to prevent a bank from creating billions, if not trillions, of dollars of its own currency? The answer is "other banks." To illustrate, suppose Smith has $10,000 in currency that was issued from Bank A. He spends that currency. Now the individuals who sold Smith things have Bank A's currency in their possession. They go to their banks—perhaps banks B, C, and D—and deposit the money into their accounts. Then banks B, C, and D go to Bank A and ask it to redeem its currency for gold. As Bank A transfers gold to banks B, C, and D, it loses gold reserves and so can't issue as much currency of its own.

Now consider the overall money supply in an economy operating under a free-banking arrangement. Who or what is going to raise or lower that money supply? Who or what is going to do the job that the Fed did when there was a central bank? The answer is "market forces." To illustrate, suppose we start in monetary equilibrium, when the quantity supplied of money equals the quantity demanded of money. More specifically, let's say the quantity supplied of money is $1 trillion and the quantity demanded is $1 trillion.

Then, something happens: peoples' demand for money rises; specifically, people want to hold more money. People want to hold $1.1 trillion instead of $1 trillion. In other words, there is now a shortage of money.

There are two ways to deal with such a shortage. One way is to leave the supply of money unchanged and simply let prices adjust as a result of the increased demand for money. Here is how things would work: As a result of people wanting to hold more money, they cut back on their spending. As they cut back on their spending, demand curves (for goods and services) shift leftward and prices fall. Eventually, prices fall enough that people don't want to hold more money: they no longer want to hold $1.1 trillion instead of $1 trillion, because $1 trillion is exactly the amount of money people want to hold at the new, lower prices. To state it differently, people wanted to hold $1.1 trillion if the price level was 110, but are quite satisfied to hold $1 trillion if the price level is 100.

The second way to deal with a shortage of money is to increase the supply of money so that there is no longer a shortage. That is what would happen under free banking. Here is how things would work: Again, we assume that people want to hold $1.1 trillion instead of $1 trillion. As a result of their wanting to hold more money (than they currently are holding), they cut back on spending. In a free-banking system, this cutback means that not as many of a given bank's notes (its currency) are flowing from one person to another person. But if the flow of these notes (between people) has dropped, it follows that any given bank will not be asked as often by another bank to redeem its banknotes for gold reserves. In other words, if Smith spends less of bank's A currency (which she possesses), then others will not be receiving as much of Bank A's currency and thus depositing it in their banks (such as banks B, C, and D), and therefore banks B, C, and D will not be asking Bank A to redeem its currency in gold. Consequently, Bank A will not see as much of its gold reserves flowing out the door and going to banks B, C, and D, so Bank A will be left with more reserves upon which it can create more money. The creation of additional money is likely to stop when the public's increased demand for money has been satisfied: when the quantity supplied of money is equal to the quantity demanded of money, $1.1 trillion.

Notice what has happened under free banking: The money supply is determined by market forces. When people increased their demand for money, a process was started that ended with the supply of money rising. It would also follow that, had people decreased their demand for money, the supply of money would have contracted under free banking.

To summarize, under a free-banking monetary arrangement, banks would issue their own currency (their own banknotes) based on, perhaps, commodity reserves and the money supply would be determined by market forces. specifically, the money supply would adjust (up or down) in response to changes in the public's demand for money.

SELF-TEST

1. How does the money supply change as a result of (a) an increase in the discount rate, (b) an open market purchase, (c) an increase in the required reserve ratio?

2. What is the difference between the federal funds rate and the discount rate?

3. If Bank A borrows $10 million from Bank B, what happens to the reserves in Bank A? What happens in the banking system?

4. If Bank A borrows $10 million from the Fed, what happens to the reserves in Bank A? What happens in the banking system?

Office Hours

"Can Something I Do End Up Changing the Money Supply?"

STUDENT:

Let me see if I have this right: if I put $100 in my checking account at a bank, the bank then takes that $100 and adds it to vault cash, so that $100 becomes part of the bank's reserves, right?

INSTRUCTOR:

Yes, that's right.

STUDENT:

And then the bank holds a percentage of that $100 in reserve form and lends out the rest. So, the bank might hold $10 of the $100 in its vault and lend out the remaining $90.

INSTRUCTOR:

That's correct.

STUDENT:

Now here's the part I am unsure of: When a bank gives out a loan of $90, does it actually lend out the $90 of currency (let's say, nine $10 bills) or simply create a new checkable deposit of $90 for someone?

INSTRUCTOR:

It creates a new checkable deposit of $90.

STUDENT:

But then the full $100 currency is still in the bank's vault, right? When does $90 of the $100 leave the vault?

INSTRUCTOR:

Suppose the person who received the $90 loan (or new checkable deposit) writes a check to Marie. Marie then deposits the $90 check in another bank. When the check clears, the $90 is transferred from the first bank (in which you deposited your money) to Marie's bank. And then Marie's bank takes a fraction of that $90 and creates a loan with it, and the process continues.

STUDENT:

So, in the end, some portion of the $100 that I deposited into the bank ends up creating loans for a lot of people. Is that correct?

INSTRUCTOR:

That is correct.

STUDENT:

But then it sounds like I can change the money supply simply by deciding to put $100 worth of currency into a bank instead of keeping that $100 in my wallet. Is that true?

INSTRUCTOR:

Let's put it this way: By putting $100 of currency into a bank, you change the composition of the money supply. Specifically, $100 less in currency is held outside banks and $100 more in checkable deposits. Then the banking system can take the $100 and create a multiple of it in terms of new checkable deposits, thereby raising the money supply.

Points to remember

1. An individual (any member of the public) can change the composition of the money supply.
2. A change in the composition of the money supply can lead to a dollar change in the money supply.

CHAPTER SUMMARY

THE FEDERAL RESERVE SYSTEM

- There are 12 Federal Reserve Districts. The Board of Governors controls and coordinates the activities of the Federal Reserve System. The Board is made up of seven members, each appointed to a 14-year term. The major policy-making group in the Fed is the Federal Open Market Committee (FOMC), a 12-member group made up of the seven members of the Board of Governors and five Federal Reserve District Bank presidents.
- The major responsibilities of the Fed are to (1) control the money supply, (2) supply the economy with paper money (Federal Reserve notes), (3) provide check-clearing services, (4) hold depository institutions' reserves, (5) supervise member banks, (6) serve as the government's banker, (7) serve as the lender of last resort, and (8) serve as a fiscal agent for the Treasury.

CONTROLLING THE MONEY SUPPLY

- The following Fed actions increase the money supply: lowering the required reserve ratio, purchasing government securities on the open market, and lowering the discount rate relative to the federal funds rate.
- The following Fed actions decrease the money supply: raising the required reserve ratio, selling government securities

on the open market, and raising the discount rate relative to the federal funds rate.

OPEN MARKET OPERATIONS

- An open market purchase by the Fed increases the money supply.
- An open market sale by the Fed decreases the money supply.

THE REQUIRED RESERVE RATIO

- An increase in the required reserve ratio leads to a decrease in the money supply.
- A decrease in the required reserve ratio leads to an increase in the money supply.

DISCOUNT LOANS AND OVERNIGHT LOANS

- A bank obtains discount loans from the Fed and overnight loans from other banks. The interest rate it pays for a discount loan is called the discount rate. The interest rate a bank pays another bank for a loan is called the federal funds rate.
- The discount rate is set by the Fed. The federal funds rate is determined by market forces in the market for reserves (federal funds market).

- If the Fed sets the discount rate below the federal funds rate, banks will borrow from the Fed and will end up with more reserves. These reserves can be used to create more loans and checkable deposits, thus increasing the money supply.
- If the Fed sets the discount rate above the federal funds rate, banks will choose not to borrow from the Fed. Then, as the banks repay past discount loans, they retain fewer reserves, thus decreasing the money supply.

THE FEDERAL FUNDS RATE TARGET

- The Fed sets a federal funds rate target. Then it uses open market operations to change the federal funds rate so as to hit the target. For example, if the current federal funds rate is 4 percent and the target is 3 percent, the Fed can conduct an open market purchase, which results in reserves being injected into the banking system. As the supply of reserves rises, the federal funds rate declines.

KEY TERMS AND CONCEPTS

Board of Governors	U.S. Treasury Securities	Reserve Deficient	Federal Funds Rate
Federal Open Market	Open Market Purchase	Reserve Requirement	Federal Funds Rate Target
Committee (FOMC)	Cash Leakage	Discount Loan	Term Auction Facility (TAF)
Open Market Operations	Simple Deposit Multiplier	Discount Rate	Program
Monetary Policy	Open Market Sale	Federal Funds Market	

VIDEO QUESTIONS AND PROBLEMS

Video Questions and Problems are available on MindTap for Arnold 12e or by searching for Arnold on www.cengagebrain.com

1. What is the relationship between the required reserve ratio and the money supply? What is the relationship between the simple deposit multiplier and the money supply?
2. What does it mean to say that a bank is reserve deficient?
3. A person takes $4,000 and places it into a checking account in a bank. Does the composition of the money supply change? Does the size of the money supply change? Explain your answers.
4. Suppose the Fed lowers the federal funds rate target. How will this action likely affect both the federal funds rate and the money supply?
5. What is the difference between the discount rate and the federal funds rate?

QUESTIONS AND PROBLEMS

1. Identify the major responsibilities of the Federal Reserve System.
2. What are the differences between the Fed and the U.S. Treasury?
3. Explain how an open market purchase increases the money supply.
4. Explain how an open market sale decreases the money supply.
5. Suppose the Fed raises the required reserve ratio, a move that is normally thought to reduce the money supply. However, banks find themselves with a reserve deficiency after the required reserve ratio is increased and are likely to react by requesting a loan from the Fed. Does this action prevent the money supply from contracting as predicted? Explain your answer.
6. Suppose Bank A borrows reserves from Bank B. Now that Bank A has more reserves than previously, will the money supply increase? Explain your answer.
7. Explain how a decrease in the required reserve ratio increases the money supply.
8. Suppose you read in the newspaper that all last week the Fed conducted open market purchases and that on

Tuesday of last week it lowered the discount rate. What would you say the Fed is trying to do?

9. Explain the similarities and differences between an open market purchase and quantitative easing.

10. The Fed can change the discount rate directly and the federal funds rate indirectly. Explain.

11. What does it mean to say that the Fed serves as the lender of last resort?

12. The Fed has announced a new, lower target for the federal funds rate; in other words, the Fed wants to lower the federal funds rate from its present level. What does setting a lower target for the federal funds rate have to do with open market operations?

13. Explain how market forces would determine the money supply under free banking.

WORKING WITH NUMBERS AND GRAPHS

1. If reserves increase by $2 million and the required reserve ratio is 8 percent, what is the change in the money supply?

2. If reserves increase by $2 million and the required reserves ratio is 10 percent, what is the change in the money supply?

3. If reserves decrease by $4 million and the required reserve ratio is 10 percent, what is the change in the money supply?

4. Reserves change by $10 million and the money supply changes by $50 million. What does the simple deposit multiplier equal? What does the required reserve ratio equal?

5. If reserves decrease by $3 million and the required reserve ratio is 8 percent, what is the change in the money supply? What does the simple deposit multiplier equal?

6. If the federal funds rate is 6 percent and the discount rate is 5.1 percent, to whom will a bank be more likely to go for a loan, another bank or the Fed? Explain your answer.

7. Complete the following table:

Federal Reserve Action	Effect on the Money Supply (up or down?)
Lower the discount rate	A
Conduct an open market purchase	B
Lower the required reserve ratio	C
Raise the discount rate	D
Conduct an open market sale	E
Raise the required reserve ratio	F

THE MARKET FOR RESERVES (OR THE FEDERAL FUNDS MARKET)

Monetary policy can be conducted in various ways. One is to target a specific money supply, such as M1 or M2. Suppose the M1 money supply is currently $2.5 trillion and the Fed wants to raise it to $2.6 trillion. Then $2.6 trillion is the Fed's specific monetary target. The Fed undertakes to increase the money supply until it hits its monetary target. For example, it might undertake an open market purchase or lower the required reserve ratio, either of which would lead to an increase in the money supply. If, by chance, the Fed overshot its monetary target and the money supply increased to some dollar figure over $2.6 trillion, then the Fed could reverse course. It could undertake an open market sale to bring the money supply back down to $2.6 trillion.

Today, the Fed does not usually have a specific money supply target in its execution of monetary policy. Instead, it tries to target a set federal funds rate. Suppose the federal funds rate is currently 4 percent and the Fed wants to lower it to 3 percent. Then 3 percent is the Fed's federal funds rate target. Because the federal funds rate is determined in the market for reserves (or the federal funds market), we need to explain how that market works before we can explain what the Fed can do to reach its federal funds rate target.

C-1 THE DEMAND FOR RESERVES

The demand for reserves originates with banks. A bank may have a demand for reserves for a few reasons. A bank may demand reserves because it has to hold a certain amount of reserves against its checkable deposits. For example, if the required reserve ratio is, say, 10 percent, then, for every $1 in checkable deposits a bank holds, it must hold 10¢ in reserves. So if the required reserve ratio is raised (by the Fed), a bank needs to hold more reserves for every $1 of checkable deposits. In Exhibit 1, the demand for reserves is downward sloping. On the vertical axis is the federal funds rate, and on the horizontal axis is the quantity of reserves. When the bank needs more reserves, the demand curve for reserves (D) shifts to the right; if the required reserve ratio is lowered,

> **EXHIBIT 1**

The Demand for Reserves

The demand-for-reserves curve (in the market for reserves or the federal funds market) is downward sloping: the federal funds rate and the quantity demanded of reserves are inversely related. As the federal funds rate moves down, holding reserves becomes cheaper, and therefore banks will buy more "insurance" to guard against withdrawals of checkable deposits. As the federal funds rate moves up, holding reserves becomes more expensive, and banks will buy less "insurance" to guard against withdrawals of checkable deposits. A change in expected deposit outflows and in the required reserve ratio can lead to a shift in the demand for reserves.

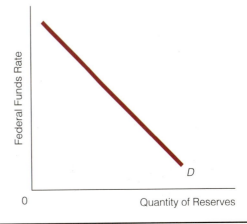

a bank needs to hold fewer reserves for every $1 of checkable deposits, and therefore the demand curve for reserves shifts to the left.

A bank demands reserves also because it believes that it may face large checkable deposit withdrawals. Suppose a bank believes that its depositors may soon withdraw large amounts of their money from their checkable deposits. Then, to have the funds to meet the anticipated withdrawals, the bank may decide to hold more reserves than is stipulated by the required reserve ratio. For example, instead of holding 10¢ in reserves against every $1 in checkable deposits, the bank might increase that reserve holding to 20¢, or 30¢, or more.

The demand curve for reserves is downward sloping because, as the federal funds rate moves down, it becomes cheaper to hold reserves, and therefore banks will buy more "insurance" to guard against withdrawals of checkable deposits. As the federal funds rate moves up, it becomes more expensive to hold reserves, and banks will buy less "insurance" to guard against withdrawals of checkable deposits.

C-2 THE SUPPLY OF RESERVES

The supply of reserves comes from essentially two sources. The first source is the Fed. For example, when the Fed undertakes open market operations, it changes the supply of reserves. An open market purchase increases the supply of reserves (in the banking system); an open market sale decreases the supply of reserves.

The second source of reserves comes from banks taking out discount loans from the Fed. If a bank borrows from the Fed, the supply of reserves increases in the banking system. If a bank pays back a discount loan to the Fed, the supply of reserves decreases.

C-3 TWO DIFFERENT SUPPLY CURVES FOR RESERVES

Exhibit 2(a)–(b) shows two supply curves. In (a), we assume that the federal funds rate target [designated by an asterisk (*)] is currently ffr_1^*, or 3.0 percent, at the intersection of the D_1 and S_1 curves. We also assume that the Fed has set the discount rate ($dr_1 = 3.5$ percent) slightly above the federal funds rate target. In recent years, the Fed has customarily set the discount rate slightly above its federal funds rate target. To see why, let's suppose the demand curve in (a) shifts to the right from D_1 to D_2. Will the federal funds rate then rise to ffr_2' (3.7 percent)? Under most conditions, the answer is no. Banks would prefer to borrow from the Fed at the discount rate of 3.5 percent instead of borrowing from other banks at the federal funds rate of 3.7 percent. In other words, equilibrium in the market for reserves is likely to occur at point 2 in the exhibit, where the new federal funds rate is 3.5 percent, which is the same as the discount rate. (This is why the supply-of-reserves curve has a kink in it at the discount rate and does not extend vertically above point 2.) The equilibrium amount of reserves in the banking system will rise from R_1 to R_2, the difference between these two amounts being the dollar amount of discount loans that banks take out at the discount rate of 3.5 percent.

So, why does the Fed set its discount rate slightly above the target federal funds rate? The reason is that the discount rate acts as a ceiling on how high the federal funds rate is likely to go. In other words, if the Fed doesn't want the federal funds rate to go over 3.5 percent, it sets the discount rate at 3.5 percent.

> **EXHIBIT 2**

The Supply of Reserves

Two supply-of-reserves curves. (a) A kink in the curve at the discount rate. To understand the kink, start with a federal funds rate of 3.0 percent. Next, the demand-for-reserves curve shifts from D_1 to D_2. Whether the federal funds rate will rise to 3.7 percent is possible, but not likely, if banks decide to borrow from the Fed at the lower discount rate of 3.5 percent. In other words, the federal funds rate rises to only 3.5 percent. The discount rate acts as a ceiling on the federal funds rate.

(b) A supply-of-reserves curve with two kinks. The uppermost kink, as explained, occurs at the discount rate. The lower one occurs at the interest rate the Fed pays (to banks) on reserves. To understand the lower kink, start with a federal funds rate of 3.0 percent. Next, the demand-for-reserves curve shifts from D_1 to D_2. The federal funds rate might fall to 2.3 percent, but it is not likely because banks would rather receive an interest rate of 2.5 percent from the Fed than lend to other banks and receive an interest rate of 2.3 percent. The interest rate the Fed pays on reserves acts as a floor on the federal funds rate.

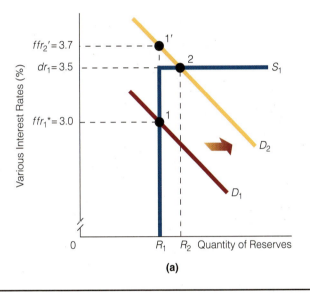

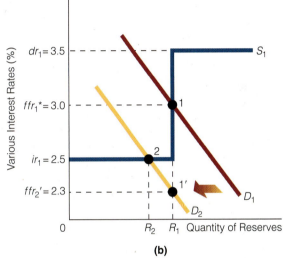

(a)

(b)

Just as the Fed can set a ceiling above which the federal funds rate is not likely to rise, it can also set a floor. In late 2008, the Fed started to pay an interest rate on reserves that banks held. Until that time, banks did not receive any interest on reserves. To see how the Fed's paying interest on reserves can put a floor on the federal funds rate, look at Exhibit 2(b). The reserves market is initially in equilibrium at point 1. The federal funds rate target is the equilibrium federal funds rate of 3.0 percent, and the equilibrium amount of reserves is R_1. Now, suppose that the Fed is willing to pay an interest rate on reserves of ir_1 (ir_1 = 2.5 percent) and that the demand-for-reserves curve shifts leftward from D_1 to D_2. Will the federal funds rate then fall to ffr'_2 (2.3 percent)? Not likely, because no bank will prefer to lend reserves to another bank at a federal funds rate of 2.3 percent when it can simply keep the reserves and gain an interest rate of 2.5 percent on its reserves. (The difference of R_1 and R_2 can be seen as a "negative discount loan," in that it is the amount that banks are "lending" to the Fed, for which the Fed pays them interest.) So the federal funds rate is not likely to fall to 2.3 percent. Instead, it is likely to fall to only 2.5 percent. In other words, the interest rate that the Fed pays on reserves acts as a floor below which the federal funds rate will not fall.

C-4 THE CORRIDOR AND CHANGING THE FEDERAL FUNDS RATE

In Exhibit 2(b), the supply curve (of reserves) has two kinks in it: one at the interest rate that the Fed pays on reserves and another at the discount rate. The vertical section between the kinks—or, simply, the vertical section of the supply curve—is called the *corridor*. The federal funds rate moves within this corridor. In other words, the federal funds rate can rise or fall within the corridor, but nowhere else. If the corridor were between a discount rate of 7 percent and an interest rate paid on reserves of 3 percent, the federal funds rate would be somewhere between a high of 7 percent and a low of 3 percent. If the Fed increases the length of the corridor by, say, increasing the discount rate from 7 percent to 8 percent, then the federal funds rate will be somewhere between a high of 8 percent and a low of 3 percent.

Now look at Exhibit 3. Suppose the federal fund rate is currently at 3.0 percent, the discount rate is 3.5 percent, and the interest rate the Fed pays on reserves is 2.5 percent. The Fed decides that it wants to try to bring the federal funds rate down to its target rate of 2.5 percent. What can it do to achieve its objective of lowering the federal funds rate? It can undertake an open market purchase, thus increasing reserves from R_1 to R_2. At the same time that it increases reserves, it might then lower its discount rate from 3.5 percent to, say, 3.0 percent and the interest it pays on reserves from 2.5 percent to, say, 2.0 percent, so that the new supply curve is S_2. The demand curve for reserves intersects the supply curve of reserves at point 2 in the exhibit, and the equilibrium federal funds rate is now 2.5 percent.

> **EXHIBIT 3**

Changing the Federal Funds Rate

The equilibrium federal funds rate is 3.0 percent. The Fed then decides to lower the federal funds rate to 2.5 percent. To do so, the Fed undertakes an open market purchase, increasing reserves from R_1 to R_2. At the same time, it lowers the discount rate from 3.5 percent to 3.0 percent and lowers the interest rate it pays on reserves from 2.5 percent to 2.0 percent. As a result, the new supply-of-reserves curve is S_2 and the new equilibrium federal funds rate is 2.5 percent.

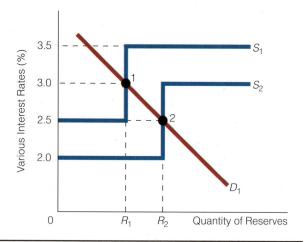

MONEY AND THE ECONOMY

©Ozgur Guvenc/Shutterstock.com

14-1 MONEY AND THE PRICE LEVEL

Classical economists believed that changes in the money supply affect the price level in the economy. Their position was based on the equation of exchange and on the simple quantity theory of money.

14-1a The Equation of Exchange

The **equation of exchange** is an identity stating that the money supply (M) multiplied by velocity (V) must be equal to the price level (P) times Real GDP (Q). That is,

$$MV \equiv PQ$$

where $\equiv$ means "must be equal to." This is an identity, and an identity is valid for all values of the variables.

As we learned in an earlier chapter, *velocity* is the average number of times a dollar is spent to buy final goods and services in a year. For example, suppose an economy has only five $1 bills. In January, the first of the $1 bills moves from Smith's hands to Jones's hands to buy good X. Then, in June, it goes from Jones's hands to Brown's hands to buy good Y.

Equation of Exchange
An identity stating that the money supply (M) times velocity (V) must be equal to the price level (P) times Real GDP (Q): $MV \equiv PQ$.

And in December, it goes from Brown's hands to Peterson's hands to buy good Z. Over the course of the year, this dollar bill has changed hands three times.

The other dollar bills also change hands during the year. Suppose the second dollar bill changes hands five times; the third, six times; the fourth, two times; and the fifth, seven times. Given this information, we can calculate the average number of times a dollar changes hands in purchases. In this case, the number is 4.6, which is the **velocity**.

In a large economy such as ours, counting how many times each dollar changes hands is impossible, so calculating velocity as we just did is impossible. For a large economy, we use a different method:

- First, we calculate GDP.

- Next, we calculate the average money supply (M).

- Finally, we divide GDP by the average money supply to obtain velocity (V):

$$V \equiv \frac{GDP}{M}$$

For example, if \$4,800 billion worth of transactions occurs in a year (GDP) and the average money supply during the year is \$800 billion (M), then a dollar must have been used an average of six times during the year to purchase goods and services:

$$V \equiv \frac{\$4,800 \text{ billion}}{\$800 \text{ billion}}$$

Because GDP is equal to $P \times Q$, this identity can be written

$$V \equiv \frac{P \times Q}{M}$$

Multiplying both sides by M, we get

$$MV \equiv PQ$$

which is the equation of exchange. Thus, the equation of exchange is derived from the definition of velocity.

The equation of exchange can be interpreted in different ways:

1. The money supply multiplied by velocity must equal the price level times Real GDP: $M \times V \equiv P \times Q$.

2. The money supply multiplied by velocity must equal GDP: $M \times V \equiv GDP$ (because $P \times Q \equiv GDP$).

3. Total spending or expenditures (measured by MV) must equal the total sales revenues of business firms (measured by PQ): $MV \equiv PQ$.

The third way of interpreting the equation of exchange is perhaps the most intuitively easy to understand: The total expenditures (of buyers) must equal the total sales (of sellers). Consider a simple economy with only one buyer and one seller. If the buyer buys a book for \$20, then the seller receives \$20. Stated differently, the money supply in the example (\$20) times velocity (1) is equal to the price of the book (\$20) times the quantity of the book (1).

Velocity
The average number of times a dollar is spent to buy final goods and services in a year.

14-1b From the Equation of Exchange to the Simple Quantity Theory of Money

The equation of exchange is an identity, not an economic theory. To turn it into a theory, we make some assumptions about the variables in the equation. Many eighteenth-century classical economists, as well as American economist Irving Fisher (1867–1947) and English economist Alfred Marshall (1842–1924), made the following assumptions:

1. Changes in velocity are so small that, for all practical purposes, velocity can be assumed to be constant (especially over short periods).

2. Real GDP, or Q, is fixed in the short run.

Hence, the classical theorists turned the equation of exchange, which is simply true by definition, into a theory by assuming that both V and Q are fixed, or constant. With these two assumptions, we have the **simple quantity theory of money**: If V and Q are constant, then changes in M will bring about *strictly proportional* changes in P. In other words, the simple quantity theory of money predicts that changes in the money supply will bring about strictly proportional changes in the price level.

Exhibit 1 shows the assumptions and predictions of the simple quantity theory. On the left side of the exhibit are noted the key assumptions of the theory: V and Q are constant, as indicated by the bars on them. Also, $M \times \overline{V} = P \times \overline{Q}$ is noted. We use the equals sign ($=$) instead of the identity sign ($\equiv$) because we are speaking about the empirical simple quantity theory, not the analytical equation of exchange. (The equals sign can be read as "is predicted to be equal"; that is, given our assumptions, $M \times V$, or MV, is predicted to be equal to $P \times Q$, or PQ.)

Starting with the first row, the money supply is $500, velocity is 4, the price level, or price index, is $2, and Real GDP ($Q$) is 1,000 units.[1] Therefore, GDP equals $2,000. In the second row, the money supply increases by 100 percent, from $500 to $1,000, and both V and Q are constant, at 4 and 1,000, respectively. The

Simple Quantity Theory of Money

The theory which assumes that velocity (V) and Real GDP (Q) are constant and predicts that changes in the money supply (M) lead to strictly proportional changes in the price level (P).

> **EXHIBIT 1**

Assumptions and Predictions of the Simple Quantity Theory of Money

The simple quantity theory of money assumes that both V and Q are constant. (A bar over each indicates this in the exhibit.) The theory predicts that changes in M lead to strictly proportional changes in P. (*Note:* For purposes of this example, think of Q as "so many units of goods" and of P as the "average price paid per unit of these goods.")

M	$\times$	$\overline{V}$	$=$	P	$\times$	$\overline{Q}$	% Change in M	% Change in P
$500		4		$2		1,000		
1,000		4		4		1,000	+ 100%	+ 100%
1,500		4		6		1,000	+ 50	+ 50
1,200		4		4.80		1,000	− 20	− 20

Assumptions of Simple Quantity Theory — Predictions of Simple Quantity Theory

---

[1] You are used to seeing Real GDP expressed as a dollar figure and a price index as a number without a dollar sign in front of it. We have switched things for purposes of this example because it is easier to think of Q as "so many units of goods" and P as "the average price paid per unit of those goods."

price level moves from $2 to $4. On the right side of the exhibit, we see that a 100 percent increase in *M* predicts a 100 percent increase in *P*. That is, changes in *P* are predicted to be strictly proportional to changes in *M*. In the third row, *M* increases by 50 percent and *P* is predicted to increase by 50 percent. In the fourth row, *M* decreases by 20 percent and *P* is predicted to decrease by 20 percent.

So the simple quantity theory assumes that both *V* and *Q* are constant in the short run and therefore predicts that changes in *M* lead to strictly proportional changes in *P*.

How good are the predictions of the simple quantity theory of money? Do changes in the money supply actually lead to *strictly proportional* changes in the price level? For example, if the money supply goes up by 7 percent, does the price level go up by 7 percent? If the money supply goes down by 4 percent, does the price level go down by 4 percent? The answer is that the strict proportionality between changes in the money supply and changes in the price level does not show up in the data (at least, not very often).

Generally, though, the evidence supports the spirit (or essence) of the simple quantity theory of money: the higher the growth rate in the money supply, the greater is the growth rate in the price level. To illustrate, we would expect that a growth rate in the money supply of, say, 40 percent would generate a greater increase in the price level than, say, a growth rate in the money supply of 4 percent. And this effect is pretty much what we see. For example, countries with more rapid increases in their money supplies often witness more rapid increases in their price levels than do countries that witness less rapid increases in their money supplies.

14-1c The Simple Quantity Theory of Money in an *AD–AS* Framework

What does the simple quantity theory of money look like in the *AD–AS* framework?

The *AD* Curve in the Simple Quantity Theory of Money

The simple quantity theory of money builds on the equation of exchange. Recall that one way of interpreting the equation of exchange is that the total expenditures of buyers (*MV*) must equal the total sales of sellers (*PQ*). Thus, *MV* is the total expenditures of buyers, and *PQ* is the total sales of sellers. Let's take the total expenditures of buyers a few steps further:

$$MV = \text{Total expenditures}$$

Now, total expenditures (*TE*) is defined as the sum of the expenditures made by the four sectors of the economy (consumption, investment, government purchases, and net exports):

$$TE = C + I + G + (EX - IM)$$

So, because *MV = TE*,

$$MV = C + I + G + (EX - IM)$$

At a given price level, anything that changes *C, I, G, EX,* or *IM* changes aggregate demand and thus shifts the aggregate demand (*AD*) curve. Hence, if *MV* equals *C + I + G + (EX – IM)*, then *a change in the money supply* (M) *or a change in velocity* (V) *will change aggregate demand and therefore lead to a shift in the* AD *curve.* In other words, aggregate demand depends on *both* the money supply and velocity:

- An increase in the money supply will increase aggregate demand and shift the *AD* curve to the right.

- A decrease in the money supply will decrease aggregate demand and shift the *AD* curve to the left.

ECONOMICS 24/7

The California Gold Rush, or Really Expensive Apples

Soon there was too much money in California and too little of everything else.

—J. S. Holiday, The World Rushed In

The only peacetime rise [in prices] comparable in total magnitude [to the 40 to 50 percent rise in prices from 1897 to 1914] followed the California gold discoveries in the early 1850s. . . .

—Milton Friedman and Anna Schwartz, A Monetary History of the United States, 1867–1960

John Sutter was a Swiss immigrant who arrived in California in 1839. On the chilly morning of January 24, 1848, James Marshall, a carpenter, was busy at work building a sawmill for Sutter. Then something glistening caught his eye, and he reached down and picked it up. Marshall said to the workers he had hired, "Boys, by God I believe I have found a gold mine." Marshall later wrote, "I reached my hand down and picked it up; it made my heart thump, for I was certain it was gold. The piece was about half the size and shape of a pea. Then I saw another."

In time, Marshall and his workers came across more gold, and before long people from all across the United States and from many other countries headed to California. The California gold rush had begun.

General Photographic Agency/Hulton Archive/Getty Images

The California gold rush resulted in an increase in the amount of money in circulation and illustrates how such a fairly dramatic increase can affect prices. As more gold was mined and the supply of money went up, prices began to rise. Although prices rose generally across the country, the earliest and most dramatic price rises occurred in and near the areas where gold was discovered. Near the gold mines, the prices of food and clothing shot up. For example, whereas a loaf of bread sold for 4¢ in New York (equivalent to 84¢ today), near the mines the price was 75¢ (the equivalent of $15.67 today). Eggs sold for about $2 each ($41 today), apples for $4 ($83.59), a butcher's knife for $30 ($626), and boots went for $100 a pair ($2,089).

In San Francisco, land prices soared dramatically because of the city's relative closeness to the mines. In 18 months, real estate that cost $16 (the equivalent of $334 today) before gold was discovered jumped to $45,000 ($940,000 today).

A sharp rise in prices similar to that created by the California gold discoveries followed other gold discoveries too. For example, the gold stock of the world is estimated to have doubled from 1890 to 1914, through both discoveries (in South Africa, Alaska, and Colorado) and improved methods of mining and refining gold. During this period, world prices increased as well.

- An increase in velocity will increase aggregate demand and shift the *AD* curve to the right.
- A decrease in velocity will decrease aggregate demand and shift the *AD* curve to the left.

But *in the simple quantity theory of money, velocity is assumed to be constant.* Thus, only changes in the money supply can shift the *AD* curve.

The *AD* curve for the simple quantity theory of money is shown in Exhibit 2(a). The $(M, \overline{V})$ next to the curve is a reminder of which factors can shift the *AD* curve. Again, the bar over the *V* indicates that velocity is assumed to be constant.

> **EXHIBIT 2**

The Simple Quantity Theory of Money in the AD–AS Framework

(a) In the simple quantity theory of money, the AD curve is downward sloping. Velocity is assumed to be constant, so changes in the money supply will change aggregate demand. (b) In the simple quantity theory of money, Real GDP is fixed in the short run. Thus, the AS curve is vertical. (c) In the simple quantity theory of money, an increase in the money supply will shift the AD curve rightward and increase the price level. A decrease in the money supply will shift the AD curve leftward and decrease the price level.

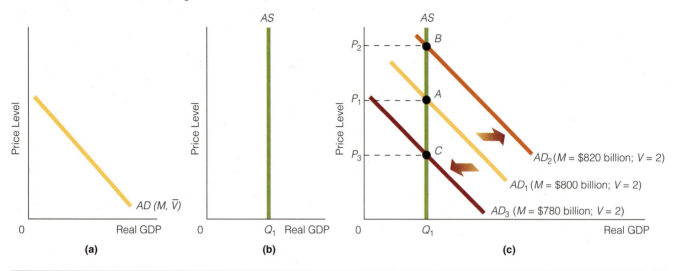

The AS Curve in the Simple Quantity Theory of Money   In the simple quantity theory of money, the level of Real GDP is assumed to be constant in the short run. Exhibit 2(b) shows Real GDP fixed at Q_1. The AS curve is vertical at this level of Real GDP.

AD and AS in the Simple Quantity Theory of Money   Exhibit 2(c) shows both the AD and AS curves in the simple quantity theory of money. Suppose AD_1 is initially operative. In the exhibit, AD_1 is based on a money supply of $800 billion and a velocity of 2. The price level is P_1.

Now, suppose we increase the money supply to $820 billion and velocity remains constant at 2. Then, according to the simple quantity theory of money, the price level will increase, and it does. The increase in the money supply shifts the AD curve from AD_1 to AD_2 and pushes up the price level from P_1 to P_2.

Suppose that instead of increasing the money supply, we decrease it to $780 billion, again with velocity remaining constant at 2. Then, according to the simple quantity theory of money, the price level will decrease, and it does. The decrease in the money supply shifts the AD curve from AD_1 to AD_3 and pushes the price level down from P_1 to P_3.

14-1d Dropping the Assumptions that V and Q Are Constant

If we drop the assumptions that velocity (V) and Real GDP (Q) are constant, we have a more general theory of the factors that cause changes in the price level. In this theory, changes in the price level depend on three variables:

1. Money supply
2. Velocity
3. Real GDP

Let's again start with the equation of exchange:

$$M \times V \equiv P \times Q$$

If the equation of exchange holds, then

$$P \equiv \frac{M \times V}{Q}$$

This equation shows that the money supply, velocity, and Real GDP determine the price level. In other words, the price level depends on the money supply, velocity, and Real GDP.

What kinds of changes in M, V, and Q will bring about inflation (an increase in the price level), *ceteris paribus*? Obviously, an increase in M or V or a decrease in Q will cause the price level to rise, so an increase in M or V or a decrease in Q is inflationary:

Inflationary tendencies: $M\uparrow$, $V\uparrow$, $Q\downarrow$

What will bring about deflation (a decrease in the price level), *ceteris paribus*? Obviously, a decrease in M or V or an increase in Q will cause the price level to fall, so a decrease in M or V or an increase in Q is deflationary:

Deflationary tendencies: $M\downarrow$, $V\downarrow$, $Q\uparrow$

SELF-TEST

(Answers to Self-Test questions are in Answers to Self-Test Questions at the back of the book.)

1. If $M \times V$ increases, why does $P \times Q$ have to rise?

2. What is the difference between the equation of exchange and the simple quantity theory of money?

3. Predict what will happen to the AD curve as a result of each of the following:

   a. The money supply rises.

   b. Velocity falls.

   c. The money supply rises by a greater percentage than velocity falls.

   d. The money supply falls.

14-2 MONETARISM

Economists who call themselves *monetarists* have not been content to rely on the simple quantity theory of money. They do *not* hold that velocity is constant, nor do they hold that output is constant.

14-2a The Four Monetarist Positions

We begin with a brief explanation of the four positions held by monetarists. Then we discuss how, on the basis of these positions, monetarists view the economy.

Velocity Changes in a Predictable Way   In the simple quantity theory of money, velocity is assumed to be constant; therefore, only changes in the money supply bring about changes in aggregate demand. Monetarists assume, not that velocity is constant, but rather that it can and does change. However, they believe that velocity changes in a predictable and therefore understandable way, not randomly. Monetarists hold that velocity is a function of certain variables—the interest rate, the expected inflation rate, the frequency with which employees receive paychecks, and more—and that changes in velocity can be predicted.

Aggregate Demand Depends on the Money Supply and on Velocity   Earlier, we showed that TE (total expenditures in the economy) equals MV. To better understand the economy, some economists—such as Keynesians—focus on the spending components of TE (C, I, G, EX, and IM). Other economists—such as monetarists—focus on the money supply (M) and velocity (V). For example, Keynesians often argue that changes in C, I, G, EX, or IM can change aggregate demand, whereas monetarists often argue that changes in M and V can change aggregate demand.

The $SRAS$ Curve Is Upward Sloping   In the simple quantity theory of money, the level of Real GDP (Q) is assumed to be constant in the short run, so the aggregate supply curve is vertical, as shown in Exhibit 3. According to monetarists, Real GDP may change in the short run, and therefore the $SRAS$ curve is upward sloping.

The Economy Is Self-Regulating (Prices and Wages Are Flexible)   Monetarists believe that prices and wages are flexible. Monetarists therefore believe that the economy is self-regulating; thus, it can move itself out of a recessionary or inflationary gap and into long-run equilibrium, producing Natural Real GDP.

14-2b Monetarism and AD–AS

If monetarists tend to stress velocity and the money supply when discussing how the economy works, what effect does this view have in the AD–AS framework? Exhibit 3 helps to explain some of the highlights of monetarism. We consider each of the four parts (a)–(d) separately.

Part (a)   We start with the economy in long-run equilibrium, producing Natural Real GDP (Q_N) at price level P_1. Monetarists believe that changes in the money supply will change aggregate demand. For example, suppose the money supply rises from $800 billion to $820 billion. If velocity is constant, the AD curve shifts to the right, from AD_1 to AD_2 in the exhibit. As a result, Real GDP rises to Q_1 and the price level rises to P_2. And, of course, if Real GDP rises, the unemployment rate falls, *ceteris paribus*.

According to monetarists, the economy is in an inflationary gap at Q_1. However, given the monetarist belief in a self-regulating economy, soon wages will be bid up because the unemployment rate in an inflationary gap is less than the natural unemployment rate. The increase in wages will cause the $SRAS$ curve to shift leftward from $SRAS_1$ to $SRAS_2$. The economy will then return to long-run equilibrium, producing the same level of Real GDP as it did originally (Q_N), but at a higher price level.

What monetarists predict will happen to the economy in the short run because of an increase in the money supply is slightly different from what they predict will happen in the long run. In the short run, Real GDP will rise and the unemployment rate will fall. In the long run, Real GDP will return to its natural level, as will the unemployment rate, and the price level will be higher.

Part (b)   Again, the economy is initially in long-run equilibrium, producing Natural Real GDP (Q_N) at price level P_1. A decrease in the money supply, with velocity held constant, will shift the AD curve to the left from AD_1 to AD_2. This leftward shift will then reduce

> **EXHIBIT 3**

Monetarism in an *AD–AS* Framework

According to monetarists, changes in the money supply and in velocity can change aggregate demand. In (a), an increase in the money supply shifts the *AD* curve to the right and raises Real GDP and the price level. Monetarists believe that the economy is self-regulating: In time, it moves back to its Natural Real GDP level at a higher price level. The same self-regulating properties are present in (b)–(d).

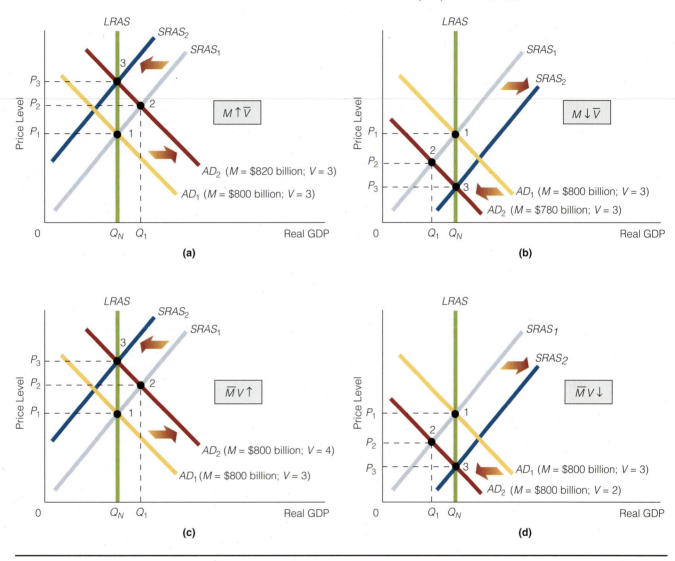

Real GDP to Q_1 and reduce the price level to P_2. Because Real GDP has fallen, the unemployment rate will rise.

According to monetarists, the economy in part (b) is in a recessionary gap. Monetarists hold that the economy can get itself out of a recessionary gap because the economy is self-regulating. In time, wages will fall, the *SRAS* curve will shift to the right, and the economy will be back in long-run equilibrium producing Q_N, albeit at a lower price level.

Here, too, the short- and long-run effects of a decrease in the money supply differ, according to monetarists. In the short run, Real GDP will fall and the unemployment rate will rise. In the long run, Real GDP will return to its natural level, as will the unemployment rate, and the price level will be lower.

Part (c)   Once more, we start with the economy in long-run equilibrium. Instead of the money supply changing, velocity changes. An increase in velocity causes the AD curve to shift to the right from AD_1 to AD_2. As a result, Real GDP rises, as does the price level. The unemployment rate falls as Real GDP rises.

According to monetarists, the economy is in an inflationary gap, but in time it will move back to long-run equilibrium. So, in the short run, an increase in velocity raises Real GDP and lowers the unemployment rate. In the long run, Real GDP returns to its natural level, as does the unemployment rate, and the price level is higher.

Part (d)   We begin again with the economy in long-run equilibrium. A decrease in velocity then causes the AD curve to shift to the left from AD_1 to AD_2. As a result, Real GDP falls, as does the price level. The unemployment rate rises as Real GDP falls.

According to monetarists, the economy is in a recessionary gap, but in time it will move back to long-run equilibrium. So, in the short run, a decrease in velocity lowers Real GDP and increases the unemployment rate. In the long run, Real GDP returns to its natural level, as does the unemployment rate, and the price level is lower.

14-2c The Monetarist View of the Economy

The diagrammatic exposition of monetarism in Exhibit 3 reveals that monetarists believe that

- the economy is self-regulating.
- changes in velocity and the money supply can change aggregate demand.
- changes in velocity and the money supply will change the price level and Real GDP in the short run but only the price level in the long run.

We need to make one other important point with respect to monetarists. Consider this question: Can a change in velocity offset a change in the money supply? Suppose velocity falls and the money supply rises. By itself, a decrease in velocity will shift the AD curve to the left. And, by itself, an increase in the money supply will shift the AD curve to the right. The decline in velocity could shift the AD curve to the left by the same amount as the increase in the money supply shifts the AD curve to the right. If so, then a change in the money supply would have no effect on Real GDP, on the short-run price level, and on the long-run price level. In other words, changes in monetary policy may be ineffective at changing Real GDP and the price level.

Monetarists think that this condition—a change in velocity completely offsetting a change in the money supply—does not occur often. They believe (1) that velocity does not change very much from one period to the next (i.e., it is relatively stable) and (2) that changes in velocity are predictable (as mentioned earlier).

So, in the monetarist view of the economy, changes in velocity are not likely to offset changes in the money supply. Therefore, *changes in the money supply will largely determine changes in aggregate demand and thus changes in Real GDP and the price level.* For all practical purposes, an increase in the money supply will raise aggregate demand, increase both Real GDP and the price level in the short run, and increase only the price level in the long run. A decrease in the money supply will lower aggregate demand, decrease both Real GDP and the price level in the short run, and decrease only the price level in the long run.

1. What do monetarists predict will happen in the short run and in the long run as a result of each of the following (in each case, assume that the economy is in long-run equilibrium)?

    a. Velocity rises.

    b. Velocity falls.

    c. The money supply rises.

    d. The money supply falls.

2. Can a change in velocity offset a change in the money supply (and thus leave no effect on aggregate demand)? Explain your answer.

14-3 INFLATION

In everyday usage, the word "inflation" refers to any increase in the price level. Economists, though, like to differentiate between two types of increases in the price level: a one-shot increase and a continued increase.

14-3a One-Shot Inflation

One-shot inflation is exactly what it sounds like: a one-shot, or one-time, increase in the price level. Suppose the CPI for years 1 to 5 is as follows:

Year	CPI
1	100
2	110
3	110
4	110
5	110

One-Shot Inflation
A one-time increase in the price level; an increase in the price level that does not continue.

Notice that the price level is higher in year 2 than in year 1 but that after year 2 it does not change. In other words, it takes a one-shot jump in year 2 and then stabilizes. This is an example of one-shot inflation, which can originate on either the demand side or the supply side of the economy.

One-Shot Inflation: Demand-Side Induced   In Exhibit 4(a), the economy is initially in long-run equilibrium at point 1. Suppose the aggregate demand curve shifts rightward from AD_1 to AD_2. As this happens, the economy moves to point 2, where the price level is P_2. At point 2 in Exhibit 4(b), the Real GDP the economy is producing (Q_2) is greater than Natural Real GDP, so the unemployment rate in the economy is lower than the natural unemployment rate. Consequently, as old wage contracts expire, workers are paid higher wage rates because unemployment is relatively low. As wage rates rise, the SRAS curve shifts leftward from $SRAS_1$ to $SRAS_2$. The long-run equilibrium position is now at point 3. The price level and Real GDP at each of the three points are as follows:

Point	Price Level	Real GDP
1 (start)	P_1	$Q_1 = Q_N$
2	P_2	Q_2
3 (end)	P_3	$Q_1 = Q_N$

> **EXHIBIT 4**

One-Shot Inflation: Demand-Side Induced

(a) The aggregate demand curve shifts rightward from AD_1 to AD_2. As a result, the price level increases from P_1 to P_2; the economy moves from point 1 to point 2. (b) Because the Real GDP the economy produces (Q_2) is greater than Natural Real GDP, the unemployment rate that exists is less than the natural unemployment rate. Wage rates therefore rise, and the short-run aggregate supply curve shifts leftward from $SRAS_1$ to $SRAS_2$. Long-run equilibrium is at point 3.

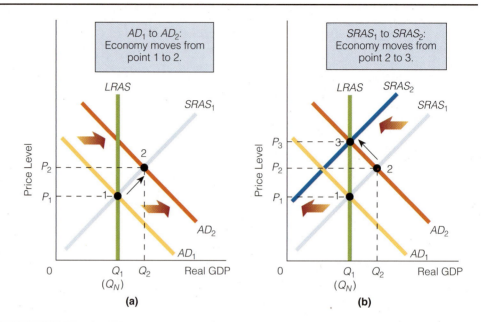

Notice that at point 3 the economy is at a higher price level than at point 1 but at the same Real GDP level.

Price levels that go from P_1 to P_2 to P_3 may seem like more than a one-shot increase. But because the price level stabilizes (at P_3), we cannot characterize it as continually rising. So the change in the price level is representative of one-shot inflation.

One-Shot Inflation: Supply-Side Induced   In Exhibit 5(a), the economy is initially in long-run equilibrium at point 1. Suppose the short-run aggregate supply curve shifts leftward from $SRAS_1$ to $SRAS_2$ because, say, oil prices increase. As the curve shifts, the economy moves to point 2, where the price level is P_2.

At point 2 in Exhibit 5(b), the Real GDP that the economy is producing (Q_2) is less than Natural Real GDP, so the unemployment rate in the economy is greater than the natural unemployment rate. Consequently, as old wage contracts expire, workers are paid lower wage rates because unemployment is relatively high. As wage rates fall, the short-run aggregate supply curve shifts rightward from $SRAS_2$ to $SRAS_1$. The long-run equilibrium position is at point 1 again. (If wage rates are somewhat inflexible, moving from point 2 back to point 1 may take some time.) The price level and Real GDP at each of the three points are as follows:

Point	Price Level	Real GDP
1 (start)	P_1	$Q_1 = Q_N$
2	P_2	Q_2
3 (end)	P_3	$Q_1 = Q_N$

> EXHIBIT 5

One-Shot Inflation: Supply-Side Induced

(a) The short-run aggregate supply curve shifts leftward from $SRAS_1$ to $SRAS_2$. As a result, the price level increases from P_1 to P_2; the economy moves from point 1 to point 2. (b) Because the Real GDP the economy produces (Q_2) is less than Natural Real GDP, the unemployment rate that exists is greater than the natural unemployment rate. Some economists argue that, when this happens, wage rates will fall and the short-run aggregate supply curve will shift rightward from $SRAS_2$ (back to $SRAS_1$). Long-run equilibrium is at point 1.

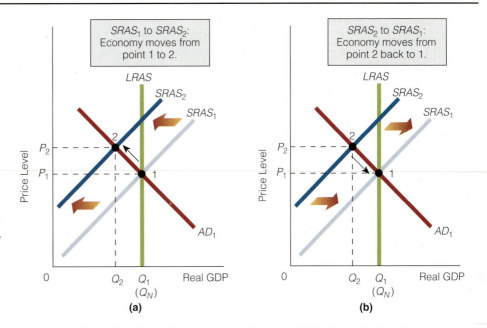

Because the price level initially increased from P_1 to P_2, this case is descriptive of one-shot inflation.

Confusing Demand-Induced and Supply-Induced One-Shot Inflation

Demand-induced and supply-induced one-shot inflation are easy to confuse.[2] To illustrate, suppose the Federal Reserve System increases the money supply. With more money in the economy, there can be greater total spending at any given price level. Consequently, the *AD* curve shifts rightward.

Next, prices begin to rise, and, soon afterward, wage rates begin to rise (because the economy is in an inflationary gap). Many employers, perhaps unaware that the money supply has increased, certainly are aware that they are paying their employees higher wages. Thus, employers may think that the higher price level is due to higher wage rates, not to the increased money supply that preceded the higher wage rates. But they would be wrong. What may look like a supply-induced rise in the price level is really demand-induced.

We can tell this same story in terms of the diagrams in Exhibit 4. In (a), the *AD* curve shifts rightward because, as explained, the money supply increases. Employers, however, are unaware of what has happened in part (a). What they see is part (b): in which they end up paying higher wage rates to their employees and the *SRAS* curve shifts leftward. Unaware that the *AD* curve shifted rightward in (a), but aware that the *SRAS* curve shifted leftward in (b), employers mistakenly conclude that the rise in the price level originated with a supply-side factor (higher wage rates), not with a demand-side factor (an increase in the money supply).

---

[2] Sometimes the terms "demand-side inflation" and "supply-side inflation" are used.

Your Eyes Can Deceive You People tend to believe that what they see with their own eyes or what they experience directly in their daily lives causes the effects they notice. In our last example, employers mistakenly believed that the stimulus for the rise in the price level was a rise in wage rates (which they had experienced firsthand), not an increase in the money supply (which they probably did not know had occurred). But the economist knows that the cause of a phenomenon may be far removed from our personal orbit. This awareness is part of the economic way of thinking.

In a Remodeling Job Jan is getting her house remodeled. Today her contractor told her that the price he pays for many of his supplies has increased and that the remodeling is going to cost "a little more." That night, Jan says to her husband, Mike, "I guess that's the way life is sometimes. Costs go up, so prices go up." Where is the economics? Could Jan somehow be the real reason that her contractor's costs went up?

What Jan may not see is that she and others who want their houses remodeled are increasing the demand for remodeling. As a result, the demand rises for things such as tile, wood, nails, cement, and related materials. The higher prices for tile, nails, and wood are the higher costs the remodeler is talking about, so when he tells Jan that his costs have risen, he is telling the truth. Jan then blames the higher costs for her having to pay more for her remodeling job. Actually, the higher demand stemming from her and others starts the process that ends in higher costs for the remodeler and in higher prices for her.

14-3b Continued Inflation

Suppose the CPI for years 1 to 5 is as follows:

Year	CPI
1	100
2	110
3	120
4	130
5	140

Continued Inflation

A continued increase in the price level.

Notice that the CPI goes from 100 to 110, then from 110 to 120, and so on. Each year, the CPI is higher than the year before. This continued increase in the price level is an example of **continued inflation**.

ECONOMICS 24/7

Grade Inflation: It's All Relative

Inflation can sometimes be deceptive. Suppose Jones produces and sells motorcycles. The average price for one of his motorcycles is $10,000. Unknown to Jones, the Fed increases the money supply. Months pass, and then one day Jones notices that the demand for his motorcycles has increased. Jones raises the prices of his motorcycles and earns a higher dollar income.

Jones is excited about earning more income, but soon he realizes that the prices of many of the things he buys have increased too. Food, clothing, and housing prices have all gone up. Jones is earning a higher dollar income, but he is also paying higher prices. In relative terms, Jones's financial position may be the same as, or even worse than, it was before the price of motorcycles increased.

Now let's consider grade inflation. Beginning in the 1960s, the average GPA at most colleges and universities across the country began to rise. Whereas professors once gave out the full range of grades—A, B, C, D, and F—today many professors give only A's and B's and a few C's. The so-called Gentleman's C, once a mainstay on many college campuses, is said to have been replaced by the "Gentleperson's B."

Grade inflation can deceive you, just as general price inflation deceived Jones. To illustrate, suppose you get higher grades (without studying more or working harder). Your average grade goes from, say, C+ to

© lightpoet/Shutterstock.com

B, and you believe that you have an advantage over other college and university students. You reason that, with higher grades, you will have a better chance of getting a good job or of getting into graduate school.

But you do only if your grades go up *and no one else's do*. In other words, your relative position must improve. Grade inflation at thousands of colleges and universities across the country prevents you from gaining that advantage. You get higher grades, but so does everyone else. Your GPA increases from, say, 2.90 to 3.60, but other students' GPAs increase similarly.

So, as long as other students are getting higher grades too, better grades for you do not necessarily make it easier for you to compete with others for a job or for admission to graduate school. In essence, grade inflation, like general price inflation, is deceptive. With price inflation, you may initially think that your financial position has improved because you are earning more for what you sell, but then you realize that you have to pay more for the things you buy. With grade inflation, you may initially think that you have an advantage over other students because you are receiving higher grades, but then you learn that everyone else is getting higher grades too. Your relative position may be the same as it was before grade inflation boosted your GPA.

> **EXHIBIT 6**

Changing One-Shot Inflation into Continued Inflation

(a) The aggregate demand curve shifts rightward from AD_1 to AD_2. The economy initially moves from point 1 to point 2 and finally to point 3. Continued increases in the price level are brought about through continued increases in aggregate demand. (b) The short-run aggregate supply curve shifts leftward from $SRAS_1$ to $SRAS_2$. The economy initially moves from point 1 to point 2. The economy will return to point 1 unless there is an increase in aggregate demand. We see here, as in (a), that continued increases in the price level are brought about through continued increases in aggregate demand.

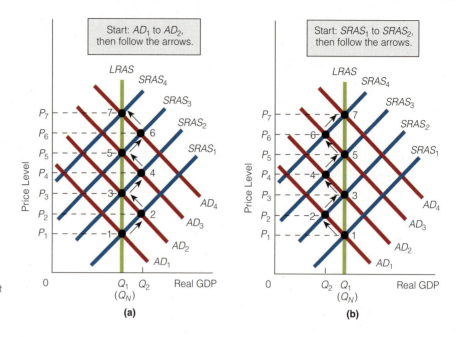

(a)   **(b)**

From One-Shot Inflation to Continued Inflation   Continued increases in aggregate demand can turn one-shot inflation into continued inflation. (Later in this chapter, we describe what leads to continued increases in aggregate demand.) The process is illustrated in Exhibit 6. (The diagram looks scary, but not when you take it one step at a time.)

Beginning at point 1 in Exhibit 6(a), the aggregate demand curve shifts rightward from AD_1 to AD_2. The economy moves from point 1 to point 2. At point 2, the unemployment rate in the economy is less than the natural unemployment rate. As a result, wage rates rise and cause the short-run aggregate supply curve to shift leftward from $SRAS_1$ to $SRAS_2$. The economy moves from point 2 to point 3. At point 3, the economy is in long-run equilibrium.

Suppose that at point 3 the economy experiences *another* rightward shift in the aggregate demand curve (to AD_3). The process keeps repeating itself, and the economy moves from point 3 to point 4 to point 5. Still *another* rightward shift in the aggregate demand curve moves the economy from point 5 to point 6 to point 7. The exhibit stops at point 7, but it could have continued. The result of this process is a *continually rising price level*—from P_1 to P_7 and beyond. Continued increases in aggregate demand cause continued inflation.

Continued inflation from the supply side of the economy is illustrated in Exhibit 6(b). Beginning at point 1, the short-run aggregate supply curve shifts leftward from $SRAS_1$ to $SRAS_2$. The economy moves from point 1 to point 2. At point 2, the unemployment rate in the economy is greater than the natural unemployment rate. According to some economists, the natural tendency is for wage rates to fall and for the *SRAS* curve to shift rightward, moving the economy back to point 1.

This natural tendency of the economy to return to point 1 will be offset, however, if the aggregate demand curve shifts rightward. Then, instead of moving from point 2 back to point 1, the economy moves from point 2 to point 3. At point 3, the economy is in long-run equilibrium and the price level is higher than at point 2.

Suppose the economy now experiences another leftward shift in the aggregate supply curve (to *SRAS₃*). Then the economy moves from point 3 to point 4 and would naturally return to point 3 unless the aggregate demand curve shifts rightward. If it does, the economy moves to point 5. The same process moves the economy from point 5 to point 6 to point 7, where the exhibit stops. This process results in a continually rising price level—from P_1 to P_7 and beyond. Again, *continued increases in aggregate demand cause continued inflation.*

The Effect of Continued Declines in SRAS

Can continued declines in *SRAS* cause continued inflation? For example, suppose a labor union continually asks for and receives higher wages. As wages continually increase, the *SRAS* curve will continually shift leftward, leading to a continually rising price level. This scenario could happen but isn't likely. Every time workers ask for and receive higher wages—shifting the *SRAS* curve leftward—Real GDP declines. Because not as many workers are needed to produce a lower Real GDP as are needed to produce a higher Real GDP, some of the workers will lose their jobs. Labor unions are not likely to adopt a policy that would put more and more of their members out of work.

There is another argument against declines in *SRAS* causing continued inflation. The CPI and the Real GDP level for, say, 1960 indicate that today both are higher than they were in 1960. The higher price level means that, since 1960, we have experienced continued inflation in the United States but that this continued inflation has accompanied a (generally) rising Real GDP. If the continued inflation of the past few decades had been caused by continued declines in *SRAS,* Real GDP would not have been rising. Instead, it would have been falling. (As *SRAS* declines, the price level rises and Real GDP falls.) In short, the continued inflation in the United States had to be caused by continued increases in *AD*, not by continued decreases in *SRAS*.

The Big Question

If continued increases in aggregate demand cause continued inflation, what causes continued increases in aggregate demand? At a given price level, anything that increases total expenditures increases aggregate demand and shifts the *AD* curve to the right. With this idea in mind, consider an increase in the money supply. With more money in the economy, total expenditures can be greater at a given price level. Consequently, aggregate demand increases, and the *AD* curve shifts rightward.

Economists widely agree that the only factor that can change *continually* in such a way as to bring about continued increases in aggregate demand is the money supply. Specifically, continued increases in the money supply lead to continued increases in aggregate demand, which generate continued inflation:

Continued increases in the money supply → Continued increases in aggregate demand → Continued inflation

The money supply is the *only* factor that can continually increase without causing a reduction in one of the four components of total expenditures (consumption, investment, government purchases, and net exports). This point is important because someone might ask, "Can't government purchases continually increase and so cause continued inflation?" That is unlikely, for two reasons:

- Government purchases cannot go beyond either real or political limits. The real upper limit is 100 percent of GDP. No one knows what the political upper limit is, but it is likely to be less than 100 percent of GDP. In either case, once government purchases reach their limit, they can no longer increase.

- Some economists argue that government purchases that are not financed with new money may crowd out one of the other expenditure components. (See Chapter 11.) Thus, increases in government purchases are not guaranteed to raise total expenditures because, if government purchases rise, consumption may fall to the degree that government purchases have increased. For example, for every additional dollar government spends on public education, households may spend $1 less on private education.

The emphasis on the money supply as the only factor that can continue to increase and thus cause continued inflation has led most economists to agree with Nobel Laureate Milton Friedman that "inflation is always and everywhere a monetary phenomenon."

14-3c Can You Get Rid of Inflation with Price Controls?

Suppose that in country A the government regularly imposes price ceilings on goods and services. For example, while the market price of good X is, say, $10, the price ceiling for that good is set at $8; while the market price of good Y is, say, $4, the price ceiling for that good is set at $3.

Now, suppose the central bank in country A increases the money supply dramatically. Then we would predict that prices in the country would soon follow upward. In other words, inflation would soon occur. But can inflation occur if the government maintains its price ceilings? For example, if the market price of good X rises from $10 to $12 and the market price of good Y rises from $4 to $7, won't these goods still sell at the price of their ceilings: $8 and $3, respectively. And if this is the case—if goods X and Y still sell at $8 and $3, respectively—hasn't the government been able to "legislate" inflation away?

Well, not exactly. As we discussed in an earlier chapter, there are consequences of price ceilings (set below the equilibrium price). One of those consequences is that nonmoney rationing devices will be used, one of which is first come, first served, which results in long lines of people waiting to buy goods. Look at it this way: If the market price of good X is $10 and the price ceiling for the good is set at $8, there is a shortage of the good and people will line up to buy good X. Let's say that the average length of the line is 25 people. Now, if the market price of good X rises to $12 and the price ceiling for the good remains set at $8, people will continue to line up to buy the good, but now the lines will be longer. The average length of the line may rise to, say, 50 people.

So, how is inflation felt in a country that imposes and maintains price ceilings? The answer is in the length of the lines of people. The longer the lines, the higher is the inflation rate.

ECONOMICS 24/7

Hyperinflation

Periods of extreme inflation are usually referred to as *hyperinflation*. Two noted periods are the 1861–1864 hyperinflation of the U.S. Confederacy and the 1921–1923 hyperinflation in Germany. These two episodes lend support to the hypothesis that *a substantial increase in the quantity of money within a relatively short period is accompanied by a substantial rise in prices.*

In 1861, the Confederate government had few resources to fight the Civil War. Most foreigners were unwilling to lend the South the needed funds, and after the North blockaded southern ports in 1862, very few import duties could be collected to raise revenue. The Confederate government thus resorted to printing large amounts of money. An index of the supply of money in circulation in the Confederacy grew from 100 in January 1861 to 2,000 in April 1865. As a result, prices increased dramatically. An index of prices in the South went from 100 in January 1861 to 9,210 in April 1865.

In 1921, Germany was just coming out of World War I. It needed funds to pay reparations and reconstruct its economy. Instead of raising taxes (which was politically unpopular) or borrowing funds from the public (the amount needed was far beyond the capacity of the public to lend), the German government decided to print money. An index of the money supply went from 100 in 1921 to over 100 million in 1924. In 1913, the German mark exchanged for $2.38 (U.S. dollars). By the middle of 1922, one U.S. cent exchanged for 100 marks. In the summer of 1923, A. P. Andrew a U.S. congressman, visited Germany and recorded receiving 4 billion marks for seven dollars. In Germany, a restaurant meal for two cost 1.5 billion marks. In one month alone, September 1923, German prices increased 35,000 percent.

World History Archive/Image Asset Management Ltd./Alamy

SELF-TEST

1. The prices of houses, cars, and television sets have increased. Has there been inflation?

2. Is continued inflation likely to be supply-side induced? Explain your answer.

3. What type of inflation is Milton Friedman referring to when he says that "inflation is always and everywhere a monetary phenomenon?"

14-4 MONEY AND INTEREST RATES

Let's review how changes in the money supply affect different economic variables.

14-4a Which Economic Variables Does a Change in the Money Supply Affect?

The money supply can affect interest rates, but to understand how, we need to review how the money supply affects different economic variables:

1. *Money and the supply of loans.* Chapter 13 explained the actions of the Fed that change the money supply. For example, when the Fed undertakes an open market purchase, the money supply increases, as do reserves in the banking system. With greater reserves, banks can extend more loans. In other words, as a result of the Fed's conducting an open market purchase, the supply of loans rises. Similarly, when the Fed conducts an open market sale, the supply of loans decreases.

2. *Money and Real GDP.* The current chapter shows how a change in the money supply can change aggregate demand and thereby change the price level and Real GDP in the short run. For example, look back at Exhibit 3(a). The economy starts at point 1, producing Q_N. An increase in the money supply then shifts the AD curve rightward, from AD_1 to AD_2. In the short run, the economy moves to point 2 and produces a higher level of Real GDP (Q_1). Similarly, in the short run, a decrease in the money supply produces a lower level of Real GDP. [See Exhibit 3(b).]

3. *Money and the price level.* The current chapter also shows how a change in the money supply can change the price level. Again, look back at Exhibit 3(a). Initially, at point 1, the price level is P_1. An increase in the money supply then shifts the AD curve rightward from AD_1 to AD_2. In the short run, the price level in the economy moves from P_1 to P_2. In the long run, the economy is at point 3 and the price level is P_3. Exhibit 3(b) shows how a decrease in the money supply affects the price level.

So, changes in the money supply affect (1) the supply of loans, (2) Real GDP, and (3) the price level.

Can the money supply affect anything else? Many economists say that, because the money supply affects the price level, it also affects the *expected inflation rate.* As an example, your expected inflation rate—the inflation rate you expect will be realized over the next year—may be 5 percent, 6 percent, or some other rate. Changes in the money supply affect the expected inflation rate either directly or indirectly. The equation of exchange indicates that the greater the increase in the money supply is, the greater the rise in the price level will be. And we would expect that the greater the rise in the price level is, the higher the expected inflation rate will be, *ceteris paribus.* For example, we would predict that a money supply growth rate of, say, 10 percent a year generates a greater actual inflation rate and a larger expected inflation rate than a money supply growth rate of 2 percent a year.

In sum, changes in the money supply (or changes in the rate of growth of the money supply) can affect

1. the supply of loans.

2. Real GDP.

3. the price level.

4. the expected inflation rate.

14-4b The Money Supply, the Loanable Funds Market, and Interest Rates

Exhibit 7(a) shows the loanable funds market. The demand for loanable funds (D_{LF}) is downward sloping, indicating that borrowers will borrow more funds as the interest rate declines. The supply of loanable funds (S_{LF}) is upward sloping, indicating that lenders will lend more funds as the interest rate rises. The equilibrium interest rate (i_1 percent) is determined through the forces of supply and demand. If there is a surplus of loanable funds, the interest rate falls; if there is a shortage of loanable funds, the interest rate rises.

Anything that affects either the supply of or the demand for loanable funds will obviously affect the interest rate. All four of the factors that are affected by changes in the money supply—the supply of loans, Real GDP, the price level, and the expected inflation rate—affect either the supply of or demand for loanable funds.

The Supply of Loans   A Fed open market purchase increases reserves in the banking system and therefore increases the supply of loanable funds. As a result, the interest rate declines. [See Exhibit 7(b).] This change in the interest rate due to a change in the supply of loanable funds is called the **liquidity effect**.

Liquidity Effect
The change in the interest rate due to a change in the supply of loanable funds.

Real GDP   A change in Real GDP affects both the supply of and the demand for loanable funds.

First, how does Real GDP affect the supply of loanable funds? When Real GDP rises, people's wealth is greater. (Real GDP consists of goods, and goods are a component of wealth.) When people become wealthier, they often demand more bonds (in much the same way that they may demand more houses, cars, and jewelry). Demanding more bonds (buying more bonds), however, is nothing more than lending more money to others. When you buy a bond issued by company A, you are essentially giving the company a loan. The company says, "Do you want to buy this bond for $10,000?" You say yes. When you buy the bond from the company for $10,000, you essentially give the company a $10,000 loan, which it is obligated to repay with interest. When the company pays off the bond to you, it returns the $10,000 plus interest. So, as Real GDP rises, individuals become wealthier and they tend to buy more bonds—that is, extend more loans. The supply of loanable funds thus increases.

Second, how does Real GDP affect the demand for loanable funds? When Real GDP rises, profitable business opportunities usually abound and businesses issue or supply more bonds to take advantage of those opportunities. But supplying more bonds is nothing more than demanding more loanable funds. So, when Real GDP rises, corporations issue or supply more bonds, thereby demanding more loanable funds.

In sum, when Real GDP increases, both the supply of and the demand for loanable funds increase. Usually, the overall effect on the interest rate is that the demand for loanable funds increases by more than the supply, so the interest rate rises. The change in the interest rate due to a change in Real GDP is called the **income effect**. [See Exhibit 7(c).]

Income Effect
The change in the interest rate due to a change in Real GDP.

The Price Level   A downward-sloping *AD* curve is explained by (1) the real balance effect, (2) the interest rate effect, and (3) the international trade effect. (See Chapter 8.) With respect to the interest rate effect, when the price level rises, the purchasing power of money falls. People may therefore increase their demand for credit or for loanable funds to borrow the funds necessary to buy a fixed bundle of goods. This change

> **EXHIBIT 7**

The Interest Rate and the Loanable Funds Market

The loanable funds market is shown in part (a). The demand for loanable funds (D_{LF}) is downward sloping; the supply of loanable funds (S_{LF}) is upward sloping. Part (b) shows the liquidity effect, part (c) shows the income effect, part (d) shows the price-level effect, and part (e) shows the expectations effect.

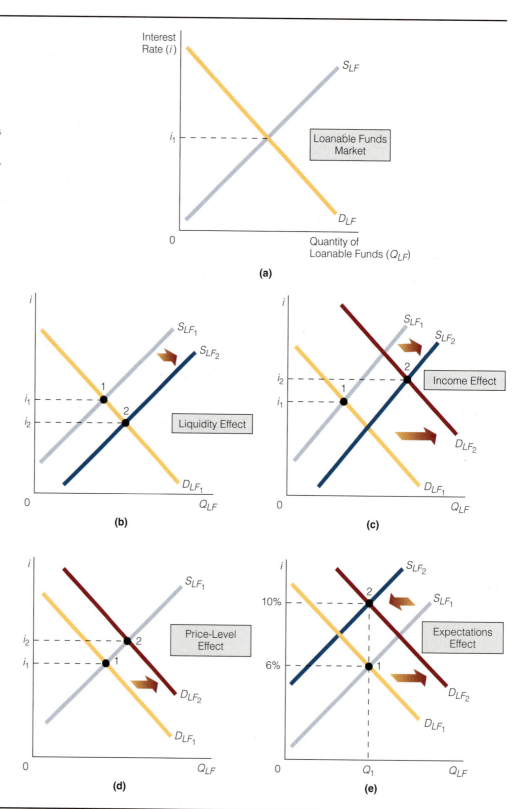

in the interest rate due to a change in the price level is called the **price-level effect**. [See Exhibit 7(d).]

The Expected Inflation Rate

A change in the expected inflation rate affects both the supply of and demand for loanable funds. Suppose the expected inflation rate is zero and that, when the expected inflation rate is zero, the equilibrium interest rate is 6 percent, as in Exhibit 7(e). Now suppose the expected inflation rate rises from 0 percent to 4 percent. What will this rise in the expected inflation rate do to the demand for and supply of loanable funds? Borrowers (demanders of loanable funds) will be willing to pay 4 percent more interest for their loans because they expect to be paying back the loans with dollars that have 4 percent less buying power than the dollars they are borrowing. If they wait to buy goods they want, the prices will have risen by 4 percent. To beat the price rise, consumers are willing to pay up to 4 percent more to borrow money to purchase the goods now. In effect, the demand-for-loanable-funds curve shifts rightward so that at Q_1 borrowers are willing to pay a 4 percent higher interest rate.

On the other side of the loanable funds market, the lenders (the suppliers of loanable funds) require a 4 percent higher interest rate to compensate them for the 4 percent less valuable dollars with which the loan will be repaid. In effect, the supply-of-loanable-funds curve shifts leftward. [See Exhibit 7(e).]

Thus, an expected inflation rate of 4 percent increases the demand for loanable funds and decreases the supply of loanable funds. So the interest rate is 4 percent higher than it was when the expected inflation rate was zero. A change in the interest rate due to a change in the expected inflation rate is referred to as the **expectations effect** (or *Fisher effect*, after U.S. economist Irving Fisher).

Exhibit 8 summarizes how a change in the money supply directly and indirectly affects the interest rate.

The Difference Between the Price-Level Effect and the Expectations Effect

To many people, the price-level effect sounds the same as the expectations effect. After all, both have something to do with the price level.

But they are different. Consider a one-shot change in the money supply that ultimately moves the price level from a price index of 120 to a price index of 135. The price-level effect is the change in the interest rate that is related to the actual rise in price level. The demand for loanable funds creeps

Price-Level Effect
The change in the interest rate due to a change in the price level.

Expectations Effect
The change in the interest rate due to a change in the expected inflation rate.

> **EXHIBIT 8**

How the Fed Affects the Interest Rate

This exhibit summarizes the way the Fed affects the interest rate through its monetary policy. For example, an open market operation (OMO) directly affects the supply of loanable funds and affects the interest rate. An OMO also affects Real GDP, the price level, and the expected inflation rate and therefore indirectly affects either the supply of or demand for loanable funds, which in turn affects the interest rate.

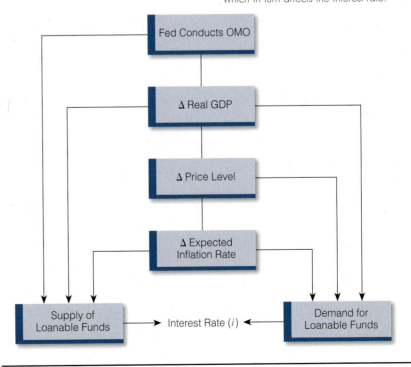

up steadily as the price index rises from 120 to 121, to 122, to 123, and so on to 135. Once the price index hits 135, though, there is no further reason for the demand for loanable funds to rise because the price level isn't rising anymore.

As the price level is rising, people's expected inflation rate is rising. They may feel that they know where the price level is headed (from 120 to 135) and adjust accordingly. Once the price level hits 135 (and given that the change in the money supply is a one-shot change), the expected inflation rate falls to zero. Any change in the interest rate due to a rise in the expected inflation rate is now over, and therefore the expected inflation rate no longer has an effect on the interest rate. But certainly, the price level still has an effect, because the price level is higher than it was originally. In the end, the effect on the interest rate due to a rise in the price level remains, and the effect on the interest rate due to a rise in the expected inflation rate disappears.

14-4c What Happens to the Interest Rate as the Money Supply Changes?

Suppose the Fed takes action to raise the rate of growth of the money supply from, say, 3 percent to 5 percent a year. What effect does this action have on the interest rate? Some people will quickly say that it will lower the interest rate, thinking perhaps that only the liquidity effect comes into play. In other words, as the Fed increases the rate of growth of the money supply, more reserves enter the banking system, more loans are extended, and the interest rate falls. [See Exhibit 7(b).]

That would be the right answer if all an increase in the money supply growth rate did was to affect the supply of loanable funds, but, as explained, this isn't the only effect. Real GDP changes, the price level changes, and the expected inflation rate changes, and all these changes affect the loanable funds market, just as the Fed action did. Figuring out what happens to the interest rate is a matter of trying to figure out when each effect (liquidity, income, price-level, and expectations) occurs and how strong each is.

To illustrate, suppose that on December 31 everyone expects the Fed to continue to increase the money supply at a growth rate of 2 percent a year. Then, on January 1, the Fed announces that it will increase the rate of growth of the money supply to 4 percent and will begin open market purchases to effect this outcome immediately. One second after the announcement, people's expected inflation rate may rise. The expectations effect begins to affect interest rates immediately. Consequently, on January 2 the interest rate is higher than it was one day earlier. The sequence of events may be described as follows:

- *Point 1 in time:* The Fed says that it will increase the growth rate of the money supply.

- *Point 2 in time:* If the expectations effect kicks in immediately, then . . .

- *Point 3 in time:* Interest rates rise.

At point 3 in time, a natural conclusion to draw is that an increase in the rate of growth in the money supply *raises* the interest rate. The problem with this conclusion, though, is that *not all the effects (liquidity, income, etc.) have occurred yet.* In time, the liquidity effect puts downward pressure on the interest rate. Suppose the liquidity effect goes to work on January 15 and the interest rate begins to fall from what it was on January 2. Then, on January 15 someone could say, "Obviously, an increase in the rate of growth of the money supply *lowers* interest rates."

- *Point 4 in time:* The liquidity effect kicks in.

- *Point 5 in time:* As a result of what happened at point 4, the interest rate drops. The interest rate is now lower than it was at point 3.

The point is that a change in the money supply affects the economy in many ways: changing the supply of loanable funds directly, changing Real GDP and therefore changing the demand for and supply of loanable funds, changing the expected inflation rate, and so on. The *timing* and *magnitude* of these effects determine the changes in the interest rate.

14-4d The Nominal and Real Interest Rates

If you were to call a bank and ask what it charges for, say, a car loan, the bank would quote an interest rate. The quoted interest rate is the rate we have been discussing: the interest rate that comes about through the interaction of the demand for and supply of loanable funds. Sometimes, this interest rate is called the **nominal interest rate**, or market interest rate.

Nominal Interest Rate
The interest rate actually charged (or paid) in the market; the market interest rate: Nominal interest rate = Real interest rate + Expected inflation rate.

The nominal interest rate may not be the true cost of borrowing, because part of the nominal interest rate is a reflection of the expected inflation rate. Suppose the nominal interest rate is 9 percent and the expected inflation rate is 2 percent. Then, if you take out a loan for $10,000 at 9 percent, you will have to pay back the loan amount ($10,000) plus $900 in interest at the end of the year. In other words, for a $10,000 loan, you have to repay $10,900.

Now suppose the expected inflation rate turns out to be the actual inflation rate. As an example, people expect the inflation rate to be 2 percent and it turns out to be 2 percent. In this case, the dollars you pay back will be worth less—by 2 percent—than the dollars you borrowed. In other words, you borrowed dollars that were worth 2 percent more in purchasing power than the dollars you repaid.

This fact should be taken into account in determining your real cost of borrowing. Economists would say that the real cost of borrowing was not 9 percent, but 7 percent. The real cost of borrowing is sometimes called the **real interest rate**, which is equal to the nominal interest rate minus the expected inflation rate:[3]

Real Interest Rate
The nominal interest rate minus the expected inflation rate. When the expected inflation rate is zero, the real interest rate equals the nominal interest rate.

$$\text{Real interest rate} = \text{Nominal interest rate} - \text{Expected inflation rate}$$

Given this equation, the nominal interest rate is therefore equal to the real interest rate plus the expected inflation rate:

$$\text{Nominal interest rate} = \text{Real interest rate} + \text{Expected inflation rate}$$

SELF-TEST

1. If the expected inflation rate is 4 percent and the nominal interest rate is 7 percent, what is the real interest rate?

2. Is it possible for the nominal interest rate to rise immediately following an increase in the money supply? Explain your answer.

3. The Fed affects only the interest rate via the liquidity effect. Do you agree or disagree? Explain your answer.

---

[3] A broader definition is Real interest rate = Nominal interest rate − Expected rate of change in the price level. This definition is useful because we will not always be dealing with an expected inflation rate; we could be dealing with an expected deflation rate.

Office  Hours

"What Is the Current Expected Inflation Rate?"

STUDENT:

Is there some way to figure out the expected inflation rate at any given time?

INSTRUCTOR:

One way to find out the expected inflation rate is to look at the spread—the difference—between the yield on conventional bonds and the yield on indexed bonds with the same maturity.

STUDENT:

What's a conventional bond? What's an inflation-indexed bond?

INSTRUCTOR:

An inflation-indexed bond guarantees the purchaser a certain real rate of return; a conventional, or nonindexed, bond does not. For example, suppose you purchase an *inflation-indexed*, 10-year, $1,000 bond that pays 4 percent interest. Then, if there is no inflation, the annual interest payment is $40. But if the inflation rate is 3 percent, the bond issuer marks up the value of your security by 3 percent—from $1,000 to $1,030. Your annual interest payment is then 4 percent of this new higher amount, that is, 4 percent of $1,030, or $41.20.

Now, investors are willing to accept a lower yield on inflation-indexed bonds because they get something that they don't get with conventional bonds: protection against inflation. So, although a conventional bond may yield, say, 6 percent, an inflation-indexed bond may yield 4 percent. The spread is the difference between the two rates.

STUDENT:

And how does the spread or difference relate to the expected inflation rate?

INSTRUCTOR:

Well, the spread is a measure of the inflation rate that investors expect will exist over the life of the bond. To illustrate with real numbers, let's say that we go to www.bloomberg.com/ and learn that an *inflation-indexed* 10-year Treasury bond has an interest rate of 1.72 percent and that a conventional 10-year Treasury bond has an interest rate of 4.02 percent. The difference, or spread, is therefore 2.3 percent. In other words, on this day, investors (or the so-called market) expect that the inflation rate is going to be 2.3 percent.

So, by checking the spread between interest rates on conventional and inflation-indexed bonds with the *same maturity* (i.e., both mature in the same number of months or years), you can see what the market expects that the inflation rate will be. As the spread widens, the market expects a higher inflation rate; as it narrows, the market expects a lower inflation rate.

Points to remember

1. We discussed two types of bonds: inflation-indexed and conventional. Each type of bonds pays an interest rate.
2. The spread, or difference, between the interest rates on a conventional and an inflation-indexed bond is the market's expected inflation rate. The larger the spread, the higher is the expected inflation rate (the inflation rate the market expects in the future). The smaller the spread, the lower is the expected inflation rate (the lower the inflation rate the market expects in the future).

CHAPTER SUMMARY

THE EQUATION OF EXCHANGE

- The equation of exchange is an identity: $MV \equiv PQ$. The equation of exchange can be interpreted in different ways: (1) The money supply multiplied by velocity must equal the price level times Real GDP: $M \times V \equiv P \times Q$. (2) The money supply multiplied by velocity must equal GDP: $M \times V \equiv$ GDP. (3) Total expenditures (measured by MV) must equal the total sales revenues of business firms (measured by PQ): $MV \equiv PQ$.

- The equation of exchange is not a theory of the economy. However, the equation of exchange can be turned into a theory by making assumptions about some of the variables. For example, if we assume that both V and Q are constant, then we have the simple quantity theory of money, which predicts that changes in the money supply cause *strictly proportional* changes in the price level.

- A change in the money supply or a change in velocity will change aggregate demand and therefore lead to a shift in the AD curve. Specifically, either an increase in the money supply or an increase in velocity will increase aggregate demand and therefore shift the AD curve to the right. A decrease in the money supply or a decrease in velocity will decrease aggregate demand and therefore shift the AD curve to the left.

- In the simple quantity theory of money, Real GDP is assumed to be constant in the short run. This assumption means that the AS curve is vertical. Also, velocity is assumed to be constant, so only a change in money supply can change aggregate demand. In the face of a vertical AS curve, any change in the money supply shifts the AD curve and changes only the price level, not Real GDP.

MONETARISM

- According to monetarists, if the economy is initially in long-run equilibrium, then (1) an increase in the money supply will raise the price level and Real GDP in the short run and will raise only the price level in the long run; (2) a decrease in the money supply will lower the price level and Real GDP in the short run and will lower only the price level in the long run; (3) an increase in velocity will raise the price level and Real GDP in the short run and will raise only the price level in the long run; (4) a decrease in velocity will lower the price level and Real GDP in the short run and will lower only the price level in the long run.

ONE-SHOT INFLATION AND CONTINUED INFLATION

- One-shot inflation can result from an increase in aggregate demand or a decrease in short-run aggregate supply.

- For one-shot inflation to change to continued inflation, a continued increase in aggregate demand is necessary and sufficient. Continued increases in the money supply cause continued increases in aggregate demand and continued inflation.

THE MONEY SUPPLY AND INTEREST RATES

- Changes in the money supply can affect the interest rate by means of the liquidity, income, price-level, and expectations effects.

- The change in the interest rate due to a change in the supply of loanable funds is called the liquidity effect. The change in the interest rate due to a change in Real GDP is called the income effect. The change in the interest rate due to a change in the price level is called the price-level effect. The change in the interest rate due to a change in the expected inflation rate is called the expectations effect (or Fisher effect).

NOMINAL AND REAL INTEREST RATES

- Real interest rate = Nominal interest rate − Expected inflation rate.

- Nominal interest rate = Real interest rate + Expected inflation rate.

KEY TERMS AND CONCEPTS

Equation of Exchange	One-Shot Inflation	Income Effect	Nominal Interest Rate
Velocity	Continued Inflation	Price-Level Effect	Real Interest Rate
Simple Quantity Theory of Money	Liquidity Effect	Expectations Effect	

VIDEO QUESTIONS AND PROBLEMS

Video Questions and Problems are available on MindTap for Arnold 12e or by searching for Arnold on www.cengagebrain.com

1. Use the equation of exchange to explain changes in the price level.

2. Starting with long-run equilibrium, use the monetarist model to explain changes in the price level and Real GDP in the short run and long run due to a decline in velocity.

3. Explain and diagrammatically represent the difference between one-shot supply-induced inflation and one-shot demand-induced inflation?

4. If the nominal interest rate is 8 percent and the expected inflation rate is 2 percent, what percentage does the real interest rate equal?

5. In the simple quantity theory of money, changes in the money supply affect the price level but not Real GDP. Do you agree or disagree with this statement? Explain your answer.

QUESTIONS AND PROBLEMS

1. What are the assumptions and predictions of the simple quantity theory of money? Does the simple quantity theory of money predict well?

2. Can the money supply support a GDP level greater than itself? Explain your answer.

3. In the simple quantity theory of money, the AS curve is vertical. Explain why.

4. In the simple quantity theory of money, what will lead to an increase in aggregate demand? In monetarism, what will lead to an increase in aggregate demand?

5. According to the simple quantity theory of money, what will happen to Real GDP and the price level as the money supply rises? Explain your answer.

6. In monetarism, how will each of the following affect the price level in the short run?

   a. An increase in velocity

   b. A decrease in velocity

   c. An increase in the money supply

   d. A decrease in the money supply

7. According to monetarism, an increase in the money supply will lead to a rise in Real GDP in the long run. Do you agree or disagree with this statement? Explain your answer.

8. Suppose the objective of the Fed is to increase Real GDP. To this end, it increases the money supply. Can anything offset the increase in the money supply so that Real GDP does not rise? Explain your answer.

9. What is the difference in the long run between a one-shot increase in aggregate demand and a one-shot decrease in short-run aggregate supply?

10. "One-shot inflation may be a demand-side (of the economy) or a supply-side phenomenon, but continued inflation is likely to be a demand-side phenomenon." Do you agree or disagree with this statement? Explain your answer.

11. Explain how demand-induced, one-shot inflation may seem like supply-induced, one-shot inflation.

12. In recent years, economists have argued about the true value of the real interest rate at any one time and over time. Given that Nominal interest rate = Real interest rate + Expected inflation rate, it follows that Real interest rate = Nominal interest rate − Expected inflation rate. Why do you think that there is so much disagreement over the true value of the real interest rate?

13. With respect to the interest rate,

   a. what is the liquidity effect?

   b. what is the price-level effect?

   c. what is the expectations effect?

14. Suppose the money supply rises. Is the interest rate guaranteed to decline initially? Why or why not?

15. To a potential borrower, which would be more important, the nominal interest rate or the real interest rate? Explain your answer.

16. Suppose the money supply rises on Tuesday and by Thursday the interest rate has risen also. Is the rise in the interest rate more likely the result of the income effect or of the expectations effect? Explain your answer.

17. Suppose the money supply increased 30 days ago. Whether the nominal interest rate is higher, lower, or the same today as it was 30 days ago depends on what? Explain your answer.

18. What does inflation look like in a country that imposes and maintains price ceilings on goods and services?

WORKING WITH NUMBERS AND GRAPHS

1. How will things change in the *AD–AS* framework if a change in the money supply is completely offset by a change in velocity?

2. Graphically show each of the following:

   a. Continued inflation due to supply-side factors

   b. One-shot, demand-induced inflation

   c. One shot, supply-induced inflation

3. Use the accompanying figure to answer questions a and b.

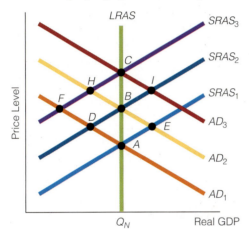

   a. Suppose the economy is self-regulating and is at point *A* when there is a one-shot, demand-induced inflation. If there are no other changes in the economy, at what point will the economy settle?

   b. Suppose the economy is at point *A* when it is faced with two adverse supply shocks. The Fed tries to counter these shocks by increasing aggregate demand. What path will the economy follow?

4. Starting with a position of long-run equilibrium, use the monetarist model to graphically portray what happens to the price level and Real GDP in the short run and in the long run as a result of (a) a rise in the money supply and (b) a decline in velocity.

5. What does the real interest rate equal, given the following?

   a. Nominal interest rate = 8 percent; expected inflation rate = 2 percent

   b. Nominal interest rate = 4 percent; expected inflation rate = −4 percent

   c. Nominal interest rate = 4 percent; expected inflation rate = 1 percent?

6. What does the nominal interest rate equal, given the following?

   a. Real interest rate = 3 percent; expected inflation rate = 1 percent

   b. Real interest rate = 5 percent; expected inflation rate = −3 percent

15 MONETARY POLICY

INTRODUCTION

When it comes to monetary policy, most economists agree that the goals are to stabilize the price level, to achieve low unemployment, and to promote economic growth, among other things. What they sometimes disagree about is the degree to which, and under what conditions, monetary policy achieves these goals. In this chapter we discuss monetary policy, beginning with the details of the money market. Then we discuss how changes in the money market—brought about by changes in the money supply—can affect the economy.

15-1 TRANSMISSION MECHANISMS

Changes in one market can often ripple outward to affect other markets. The routes, or channels, that these ripple effects travel are known as the **transmission mechanism**. In this section we discuss two transmission mechanisms: the Keynesian and the monetarist.

15-1a The Money Market in the Keynesian Transmission Mechanism

Like all markets, the money market has two sides: a demand side and a supply side.[1]

The Demand for Money   As an illustration of the **demand for money (balances)**, the price of holding money balances is on the vertical axis and the quantity of money is on the horizontal axis. The price of holding money balances—specifically, the opportunity cost of holding money—is the interest rate. By holding money, individuals forfeit the

Transmission Mechanism
The routes, or channels, traveled by the ripple effects that the money market creates and that affect the goods-and-services market. (The goods-and-services market is represented by the aggregate demand and aggregate supply curves in the *AD–AS* framework.)

Demand for Money (Balances)
The inverse relationship between the quantity demanded of money (balances) and the price of holding money (balances).

---

[1] In everyday language, the term "money market" is often used to refer to the market for short-term securities, where there is a demand for and a supply of short-term securities. This is not the money market discussed here. In this money market, there is a demand for and a supply of *money*.

opportunity to hold that portion of their wealth in other forms. For instance, the person who holds $1,000 in cash gives up the opportunity to purchase a $1,000 asset that yields interest (e.g., a bond). Thus, the interest rate is the opportunity cost of holding money. A person can be described as "paying the price" of forfeited interest by holding money.

Exhibit 1(a) illustrates the demand for money (balances). As the interest rate increases, the opportunity cost of holding money increases and individuals choose to hold less money. As the interest rate decreases, the opportunity cost of holding money decreases and individuals choose to hold more money.

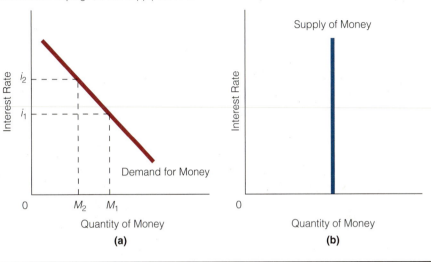

> **EXHIBIT 1**

The Demand for and Supply of Money

(a) The demand curve for money is downward sloping. (b) The supply curve of money is a vertical line at the quantity of money that is largely, but not exclusively, determined by the Fed.

(a)

(b)

The Supply of Money   Exhibit 1(b) shows the supply of money as a vertical line at the quantity of money that is determined largely by the Fed. The reason the money supply is largely, but not exclusively, determined by the Fed is that both banks and the public also are important players in the money supply process (as explained in earlier chapters). For example, when banks do not lend their entire excess reserves, the money supply is not as large as it is when they do.

Equilibrium in the Money Market   The money market is in equilibrium when the quantity demanded of money equals the quantity supplied. In Exhibit 2, equilibrium exists at the interest rate i_1. At a higher interest rate, i_2, the quantity supplied of money is greater than the quantity demanded and there is an excess supply of money ("too much" money). At a lower interest rate, i_3, the quantity demanded of money is greater than the quantity supplied and there is an excess demand for money ("too little" money). Only at i_1 are the quantity demanded and the quantity supplied of money equal. At i_1, there are no shortages or surpluses of money and no excess demands or excess supplies. Individuals are holding the amounts of money they want to hold.

> **EXHIBIT 2**

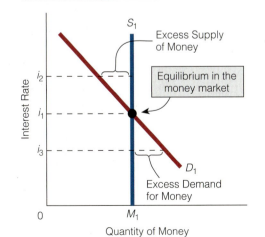

Equilibrium in the Money Market

At an interest rate of i_1, the money market is in equilibrium: There is neither an excess supply of money nor an excess demand for money.

15-1b The Keynesian Transmission Mechanism: Indirect

The Keynesian route between the money market and the goods-and-services market is an indirect one. Exhibit 3 is a market-by-market depiction of the Keynesian transmission mechanism.

- *The money market.* Suppose the money market is in equilibrium at interest rate i_1 in part (a). Then, the Fed increases the reserves of the banking system through an open market purchase, resulting in an increase in the money supply. Accordingly, the money supply curve shifts rightward from S_1 to S_2. The reserves of the banking system are increased, resulting in more loans being made. A greater supply of loans puts downward pressure on the interest rate, as reflected in the movement from i_1 to i_2.

- *The investment goods market.* A fall in the interest rate stimulates investment. In the investment goods market in part (b), investment rises from I_1 to I_2.

- *The goods-and-services market (AD–AS framework).* Recall that the Keynesian model has a horizontal aggregate supply curve in the goods-and-services market until full employment or Natural Real GDP is reached. (See Chapter 10.) The decline in the interest rate has brought about an increase in investment, as shown in part (b). Rising investment increases total spending in the economy and shifts the *AD* curve to the right [part (c)]. As a result, Real GDP rises from Q_1 to Q_2 and the price level does not change.

In sum, when the money supply increases, the Keynesian transmission mechanism works as follows: An increase in the money supply lowers the interest rate, causing investment to

---

> **EXHIBIT 3**

The Keynesian Transmission Mechanism

The exhibit shows how the Keynesian transmission mechanism operates, given an increase in the money supply. (a) An increase in the money supply brings on a lower interest rate. (b) As a result, investment increases. (c) As investment increases, total expenditures rise and the aggregate demand curve shifts rightward. Real GDP rises from Q_1 to Q_2.

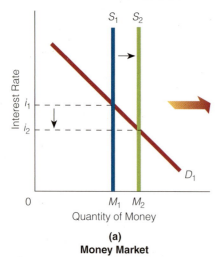

(a)
Money Market

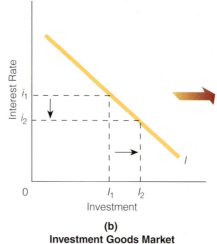

(b)
Investment Goods Market

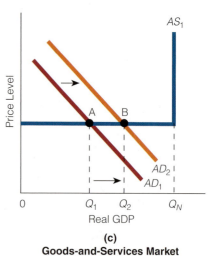

(c)
Goods-and-Services Market
(AD–AS framework)

rise and the *AD* curve to shift rightward. Real GDP then increases. The process works in reverse for a decrease in the money supply. Symbolically,

$$\text{Money supply} \uparrow \rightarrow i \downarrow \rightarrow I \uparrow \rightarrow AD \uparrow \rightarrow Q \uparrow, \overline{P}$$
$$\text{Money supply} \downarrow \rightarrow i \uparrow \rightarrow I \downarrow \rightarrow AD \downarrow \rightarrow Q \downarrow, \overline{P}$$

15-1c The Keynesian Mechanism May Get Blocked

The Keynesian transmission mechanism is *indirect.* Changes in the money market *do not directly affect* the goods-and-services market (and thus Real GDP) because the investment goods market stands between the two markets. Possibly (although not likely), the link between the money market and the goods-and-services market could be broken in the investment goods market. Here's how.

Interest-Insensitive Investment   Some Keynesian economists believe that investment is not always responsive to interest rates. For example, when business firms are pessimistic about future economic activity, a decrease in interest rates will do little, if anything, to increase investment. When investment is completely insensitive to changes in interest rates, the investment demand curve is vertical, as in Exhibit 4(a).

Interest-insensitive investment has an effect on the Keynesian transmission mechanism described in Exhibit 3. If the investment demand curve is vertical (instead of downward sloping), a fall in interest rates will not increase investment, and if investment does not increase, neither will aggregate demand or Real GDP. Thus, the Keynesian transmission mechanism would be short-circuited in the investment goods market, severing the link between the money market in part (a) of Exhibit 3 and the goods-and-services market in part (c):

$$\text{Money supply} \uparrow \rightarrow i \downarrow$$
$$\text{Investment insensitive to changes in } i \rightarrow \overline{I} \rightarrow \overline{AD} \rightarrow \overline{Q}, \overline{P}$$

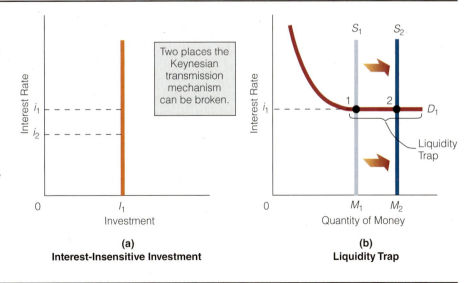

> **EXHIBIT 4**

Breaking the Link Between the Money Market and the Goods-and-Services Market: Interest-Insensitive Investment and the Liquidity Trap

The Keynesian transmission mechanism allows the link between the money market and the goods-and-services market to be broken in two places. (a) If investment is totally interest sensitive, a change in the interest rate will not change investment; therefore, aggregate demand and Real GDP will not change. (b) If the money market is in the liquidity trap, an increase in the money supply will not lower the interest rate. It follows that there will be no change in investment, aggregate demand, or Real GDP.

Two places the Keynesian transmission mechanism can be broken.

(a)
Interest-Insensitive Investment

(b)
Liquidity Trap

Liquidity Trap
The horizontal portion of the demand curve for money.

The Liquidity Trap   Keynesians have sometimes argued that the demand curve for money could become horizontal at some low interest rate. In Exhibit 4(b), the demand curve for money becomes horizontal at i_1. This horizontal section of the curve is referred to as the **liquidity trap**.

If the money supply is increased (e.g., from S_1 to S_2) when the money market is in the liquidity trap, the money market moves from point 1 to point 2 and individuals are willing to hold all the additional money supply at the given interest rate. Once again, this condition breaks the Keynesian transmission mechanism illustrated in Exhibit 3. Obviously, if an increase in the money supply does *not* lower the interest rate, then neither investment, aggregate demand, nor Real GDP changes. The liquidity trap can thus break the link between the money market and the goods-and-services market:

$$\text{Money supply} \uparrow$$
$$\text{Liquidity trap} \rightarrow \bar{i} \rightarrow \bar{I} \rightarrow \overline{AD} \rightarrow \bar{Q}, \bar{P}$$

Because the Keynesian transmission mechanism is indirect, both *interest-insensitive investment demand* and the *liquidity trap* may occur. Therefore, Keynesians conclude that, at times, monetary policy will be unable to increase Real GDP and decrease unemployment. Viewing the money supply as a string, some economists have argued that you cannot push on a string. In other words, you cannot always force Real GDP up by increasing (pushing up) the money supply.

Exhibit 5 presents a review of the Keynesian transmission mechanism and how it may get blocked.

Bond Prices, Interest Rates, and the Liquidity Trap   The liquidity trap, or the horizontal section of the demand curve for money, seems to come out of the clear blue sky. Why might the demand curve for money become horizontal at some low interest rate? To understand the explanation, you must first understand the relationship between bond prices and interest rates.

Consider Jessica Howard, who buys good X for $100 today and sells it one year later for $110. Her actual rate of return is 10 percent; that is, the difference between the selling price and the buying price ($10), divided by the buying price ($100), is 10 percent. Now, suppose good X is a bond. Jessica buys the bond for $100 and sells it one year later for $110. Her actual interest rate return is the same: 10 percent. If, however, Jessica buys the bond for $90 instead of $100, but still sells it for $110, her interest rate return is 22 percent: $20 ÷ $90 = 22 percent. The point is simple: *As the price of a bond decreases, the actual interest rate return, or the interest rate, increases.*

So, bond prices and interest rates are inversely related. For example, last year Rob bought a bond for $1,000 that promises to pay him $100 a year in interest. Thus, the annual interest rate return is 10 percent: $100 ÷ $1,000 = 10 percent. Suppose, however, the market, or nominal, interest rate is higher now than it was last year when Rob bought his bond. Now bond suppliers have to promise to pay $120 a year to someone who buys a $1,000 bond.

The change in rate has an effect on the price Rob can get in the market for the $1,000 bond he bought last year, assuming that he wants to sell it. If a purchaser can buy a new $1,000 bond that pays $120 a year, why pay Rob $1,000 for an (old) bond that pays only $100? Accordingly, Rob has to lower the price of his bond below $1,000, but the question is by how much? The price has to be far enough below $1,000 so that the interest rate

> **EXHIBIT 5**

The Keynesian View of Monetary Policy

According to the Keynesian transmission mechanism, if the Fed increases reserves in the banking system and therefore raises the money supply, the interest rate will drop, stimulating investment and aggregate demand. Consequently, Real GDP will rise. However, things may not work out this way if there is a liquidity trap or if investment is insensitive to changes in the interest rate.

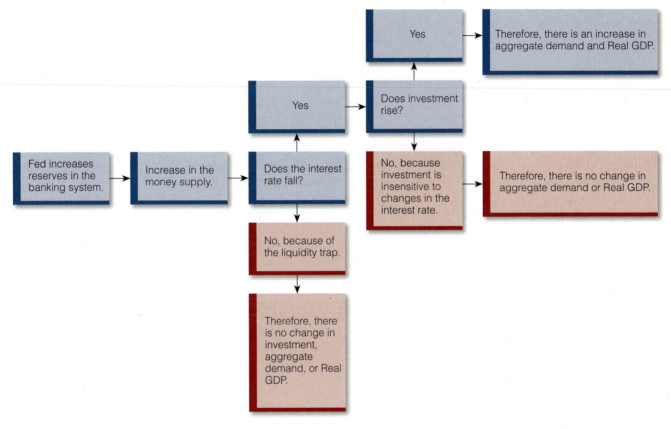

return on his old bond will be competitive with (i.e., at least equal to) the interest rate return on new bonds.

Rob's bond will sell for $833. At that price, a buyer of his bond will receive $100 a year and an interest rate of 12 percent—the same interest rate offered by a new $1,000 bond paying $120 a year. In other words, $100 is the same percentage of $833 as $120 is of $1,000: 12 percent. Therefore, *the market interest rate is inversely related to the price of old, or existing, bonds.*

This inverse relationship can help you understand how a liquidity trap comes to be. At a low interest rate, the money supply increases but does not result in an excess supply of money. Interest rates are very low, so bond prices are very high. Would-be buyers believe that bond prices are so high that they have no place to go but down. So individuals would rather hold all the additional money supply than use it to buy bonds.

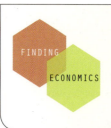

In Rising Demand for Bonds Kenneth reads in the newspaper that the demand for bonds is rising. Is there any information here that relates to the interest rate? Yes: If the demand for bonds is rising, then the price of bonds will rise too. Because the price of bonds and the interest rate are inversely related, the interest rate is about to decline.

15-1d The Monetarist Transmission Mechanism: Direct

Monetarist theory proposes a direct link between the money market and the goods-and-services market. The monetarist transmission mechanism is short: Changes in the money market have a direct impact on aggregate demand, as illustrated in Exhibit 6. An increase in the money supply from S_1 to S_2 in part (a) leaves individuals with an excess supply of money. As a result, they increase their spending on a wide variety of goods. Households buy more refrigerators, personal computers, television sets, clothes, and vacations. Businesses purchase additional machinery. The aggregate demand curve in part (b) is directly affected. In the short run, Real GDP rises from Q_1 to Q_2. The process works in reverse for a decrease in the money supply. Symbolically,

$$\text{Money supply} \uparrow \rightarrow AD \uparrow \rightarrow Q\uparrow, P\uparrow$$
$$\text{Money supply} \downarrow \rightarrow AD \downarrow \rightarrow Q\downarrow, P\downarrow$$

In sum, the Keynesian transmission mechanism from the money market to the goods-and-services market is indirect; the monetarist transmission mechanism is direct.

> **EXHIBIT 6**

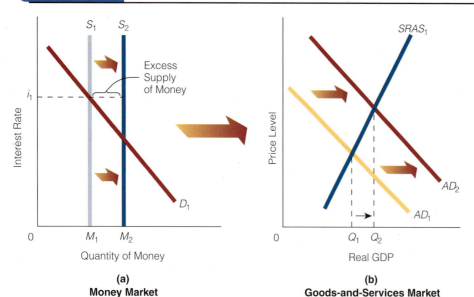

(a) Money Market

(b) Goods-and-Services Market (AD–AS framework)

The Monetarist Transmission Mechanism

The monetarist transmission mechanism is short and direct. Changes in the money market directly affect aggregate demand in the goods-and-services market. For example, an increase in the money supply leaves individuals with an excess supply of money that they spend on a wide variety of goods.

SELF-TEST

(Answers to Self-Test questions are in Answers to Self-Test Questions at the back of the book.)

1. Explain the inverse relationship between bond prices and interest rates.

2. "According to the Keynesian transmission mechanism, as the money supply rises, there is a direct impact on the goods-and-services market." Do you agree or disagree with this statement? Explain your answer.

3. Explain how the monetarist transmission mechanism works when the money supply rises.

15-2 MONETARY POLICY AND THE PROBLEM OF INFLATIONARY AND RECESSIONARY GAPS

In Chapter 11, we explained how expansionary and contractionary fiscal policies might be used to move the economy out of recessionary and inflationary gaps, respectively, and questioned the effectiveness of fiscal policy. In this section, we discuss how monetary policy might be used to *eliminate* both recessionary and inflationary gaps.

In Exhibit 7(a), the economy is in a recessionary gap at point 1; aggregate demand is too low to bring the economy into equilibrium at Natural Real GDP.

- Economist A argues that, in time, the short-run aggregate supply curve will shift rightward to point 2 [see Exhibit 7(b)], so it is best to leave things alone.

- Economist B says that the economy will take too long to get to point 2 on its own and that, in the interim, the economy is suffering the high cost of unemployment and a lower level of output.

- Economist C maintains that the economy is stuck in the recessionary gap.

Economists B and C propose **expansionary monetary policy** to move the economy to its Natural Real GDP level. An appropriate increase in the money supply will shift the aggregate demand curve rightward to AD_2, and the economy will be in long-run equilibrium at point 2′. [See Exhibit 7(c).] The recessionary gap is eliminated through the use of expansionary monetary policy.[2]

In Exhibit 8(a), the economy is in an inflationary gap at point 1.

- Economist A argues that, in time, the economy will move to point 2 [see Exhibit 8(b)], so it is best to leave things alone.

- Economist B argues that it would be better to decrease the money supply (**contractionary monetary policy**); aggregate demand will then shift leftward to AD_2, and the economy will move to point 2′. [See Exhibit 8(c).]

- Economist C agrees with economist B but points out that the price level is lower at point 2′ than at point 2, although Real GDP is the same at both points.

Expansionary Monetary Policy
The policy by which the Fed increases the money supply.

Contractionary Monetary Policy
The policy by which the Fed decreases the money supply.

---

2. In a static framework, expansionary monetary policy refers to an increase in the money supply and contractionary monetary policy refers to a decrease in the money supply. In a dynamic framework, expansionary monetary policy refers to an increase in the rate of growth of the money supply and contractionary monetary policy refers to a decrease in the growth rate of the money supply. In the real world, where things are constantly changing, the growth rate of the money supply is more indicative than the money supply itself of the direction of monetary policy.

> **EXHIBIT 7**

Monetary Policy and a Recessionary Gap

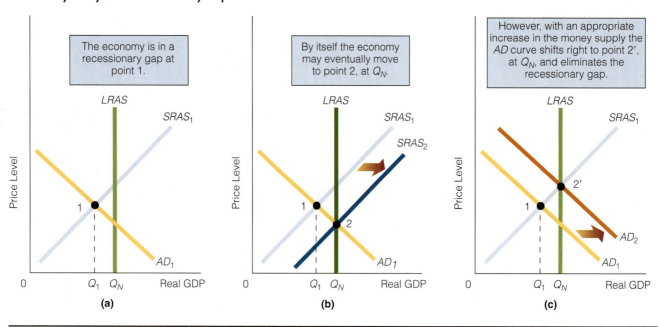

(a) The economy is in a recessionary gap at point 1.

(b) By itself the economy may eventually move to point 2, at Q_N.

(c) However, with an appropriate increase in the money supply the *AD* curve shifts right to point 2′, at Q_N, and eliminates the recessionary gap.

> **EXHIBIT 8**

Monetary Policy and an Inflationary Gap

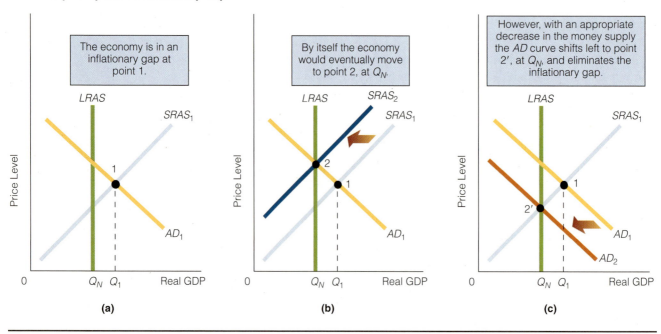

(a) The economy is in an inflationary gap at point 1.

(b) By itself the economy would eventually move to point 2, at Q_N.

(c) However, with an appropriate decrease in the money supply the *AD* curve shifts left to point 2′, at Q_N, and eliminates the inflationary gap.

Most Keynesians believe that the natural forces of the market economy work much faster and more assuredly in eliminating an inflationary gap than in eliminating a recessionary gap. In terms of Exhibits 7 and 8, they argue that the short-run aggregate supply curve in Exhibit 8(b) is much more likely to shift leftward to point 2, eliminating the inflationary gap, than the short-run aggregate supply curve in Exhibit 7(b) to shift rightward to point 2, eliminating the recessionary gap. The reason is that wages and prices rise more quickly than they fall. (Of course, many Keynesians believe that wages are inflexible in a downward direction.) Consequently, Keynesians are more likely to advocate expansionary monetary policy to eliminate a stubborn recessionary gap than they are to recommend contractionary monetary policy to eliminate a not-so-stubborn inflationary gap.

15-2a   A Different View of the Economy: Patterns of Sustainable Specialization and Trade (PSST)

Arnold Kling is an economist who has proposed a new perspective on the economy.[3] It is called *patterns of sustainable specialization and trade*, or PSST. It is a very different perspective than has been expressed in the *AD–AS* model that we have discussed widely in this textbook. Many of the models and theories we have discussed put emphasis on aggregate demand. Specifically, consider an economy that is initially in long-run equilibrium, producing Natural Real GDP. Then, something in the economy changes in such a way as to lower aggregate demand. The *AD* curve shifts leftward, and the economy falls into a recessionary gap. Stated differently, economic activity decreases because of a drop in aggregate demand.

Now, according to Arnold Kling, the decline in economic activity may have nothing to do with a decline in aggregate demand. In fact, a decline in economic activity can occur even if aggregate demand remains constant. To understand how this can happen, Kling argues, economic activity should not be viewed solely as stemming from spending in the economy. Instead, economic activity is best viewed by focusing on specialization and trade.

At any given point in time, certain specializations are needed to sustain the pattern of trade dictated by buying preferences. For example, buyers may want to buy goods X, Y, and Z in large quantities, and specializations X', Y', and Z' are necessary to produce these goods. Now, if business firms are not producing goods X, Y, and Z, or if labor is not skilled in specializations X', Y', and Z', then what buyers want to buy is out of synchrony with what business and labor are producing and have to sell. As a result, sales decline, not necessarily because aggregate demand in the economy has dropped, but because, as we stated, *businesses and labor are out of synchrony with what buyers want to buy*. In short, the current pattern of specialization and trade is *unsustainable*. To illustrate, a person who was taking applications for subprime mortgages in 2006 had to find a different line of work by 2009, and someone who operated a large bookstore in a mall 10 years ago might find that business unsustainable today.

In Kling's perspective on the economy, it is the job of the entrepreneur to reconfigure specializations and trade so that both are sustainable—that is, so that both are

---

[3.] To read about this perspective in detail, see two of Kling's articles: "Patterns of Sustainable Specialization and Trade: A Smith–Ricardo Theory of Macroeconomics," http://www.adamsmith.org/sites/default/files/research/files/PSST.pdf; and "PSST: Patterns of Sustainable Specialization and Trade," *Capitalism and Society*, vol. 6, no. 2 (2011), http://arnoldkling.com/essays/papers /PSSTCap.pdf.

ECONOMICS 24/7

The Fed Can't Always Be Sure That Banks Will Lend

One way to stimulate spending is for the Fed to increases reserves in the banking system. Recall the process: The Fed injects reserves into the banking system (say, by undertaking an open market purchase), and then banks use the additional reserves to make loans to individuals and firms. These loans stimulate spending because the people who take out the loans do so in order to increase their spending. In other words, greater reserves in the banking system lead to more loans, which lead to more spending, and the *AD* curve in the economy shifts rightward:

Reserves increase → More loans → More spending → AD curve shifts rightward

However, things do not always work out the way the Fed intends. Something the Fed cannot do is force banks to lend out reserves. At the end of 2008 and into much of 2009, banks were adding to their reserves but they weren't turning them into loans, largely because of the financial shape they were in. At the time, many banks were either insolvent (their liabilities were greater than their assets) or close to being insolvent. When banks are close to being insolvent, they are particularly wary of making loans, especially in uncertain environments. Even as the Fed was injecting reserves into the banking system, some businesses were failing and the economic

Pavel L Photo and Video/Shutterstock.Com

future looked uncertain. Banks couldn't be sure that the loans they created would be repaid. So, instead of creating loans from the reserves the Fed was injecting into the system, the banks took the reserves and bought safe Treasury securities or simply earned the interest rate the Fed paid on reserves.

The banks looked at their plight this way: The interest rate they could earn by creating loans may have been higher than the interest rate they could earn by buying Treasury securities, but if the loans weren't likely to be repaid, what good was the higher rate? In the uncertain economic environment, it was better to buy low-interest Treasury securities than to create higher interest loans that wouldn't be repaid.

The ineffectiveness of the Fed at getting the banks to increase their lending caused some economists to wonder whether monetary policy didn't work anymore or, at minimum, didn't work when the economic future looked bleak or uncertain. The so-called textbook model of how monetary policy works (say, in a recessionary gap) is that the Fed undertakes open market purchases, reserves flow into the banking system, banks take the reserves and create loans and new checkable deposits, the money supply rises, and the *AD* curve shifts to the right. (That is how it works in this textbook.) In 2008 and much of 2009, however, the textbook model was correct most of the time but not always. At times, it seemed, the Fed could try to get the money supply to rise but the banks just wouldn't go along.

consistent with what buyers want to buy. Is this reconfiguration easy to do? Not usually: Entrepreneurs may have to experiment before they figure out what configuration of specializations and trade is in synchrony with what buyers want to buy.

Now, certainly such reconfigurations go on all the time in a dynamic economy, but, Kling argues, there can be times when they are harder to either figure out or adjust to. For example, if there are large-scale shifts in demand, or periods when major changes in technology are occurring, it might take more "trial and error" before the reconfiguration of capital and labor occurs and is consistent with a pattern of sustainable specialization and trade.

In addition, sometimes reconfigurations of capital and labor face impediments that are unrelated to purely economic issues. For example, suppose reconfigurations of capital and labor are now necessary in a field such as health care or education. Then entrepreneurs may be willing and able to direct the reconfigurations into a sustainable pattern of specialization and trade, but may not be permitted to do so because of licensing or credential requirements currently necessary to enter the field.

One conclusion reached from the PSST perspective of the economy is that sometimes a fiscal or monetary stimulus designed to boost aggregate demand will not work at reviving the economy. After all, if the recession is due to buyers and sellers being out of synchrony with each other, greater aggregate demand isn't the solution. And not only is a boost in aggregate demand not the solution, but it could make matters worse. If the stimulus is directed at propping up unsustainable specializations and trade, then it sends the wrong signal to some workers. Specifically, it falsely tells some workers that their current specializations (the jobs they are currently capable of doing) will continue to be in demand when, in fact, they may not be.

15-3 MONETARY POLICY AND THE ACTIVIST–NONACTIVIST DEBATE

Recall that some economists argue that fiscal policy either is ineffective (owing to crowding out) or works in unintended and undesirable ways (owing to lags). Other economists, notably Keynesians, believe that neither is the case and that fiscal policy not only can, but should, be used to smooth out the business cycle. This point of contention is part of the activist–nonactivist debate, which encompasses both fiscal and monetary policy. This section addresses the *monetary policy* component of the debate.

Activists argue that monetary policy should be deliberately used to smooth out the business cycle. They are in favor of economic **fine-tuning**, which is the (usually frequent) use of monetary policy to counteract even small undesirable movements in economic activity. Sometimes, the monetary policy they advocate is called either *activist monetary policy* or *discretionary monetary policy.*

Nonactivists argue *against* the use of activist or discretionary monetary policy. Instead, they propose a *rules-based monetary policy* (also called a *nonactivist monetary policy*). An example of a rules-based monetary policy is a policy based on a predetermined steady growth rate in the money supply, such as allowing the money supply to grow 3 percent a year no matter what is happening in the economy.

Activists
Persons who argue that monetary and fiscal policies should be deliberately used to smooth out the business cycle.

Fine-tuning
The (usually frequent) use of monetary and fiscal policies to counteract even small undesirable movements in economic activity.

Nonactivists
Persons who argue against the deliberate use of discretionary fiscal and monetary policies to smooth out the business cycle. They believe in a permanent, stable, rule-oriented monetary and fiscal framework.

15-3a The Case for Activist (or Discretionary) Monetary Policy

The case for activist (or discretionary) monetary policy rests on three major claims:

1. *The economy does not always equilibrate quickly enough at Natural Real GDP.* Consider the economy at point 1 in Exhibit 7(a). Some economists maintain that, left on its own, the economy will eventually move to point 2 in part (b). Activists argue that the economy takes too long to move from point 1 to point 2 and that, in the interim, too much output is lost and too high an unemployment rate must be tolerated. They believe that an activist monetary policy speeds things along so that higher output and a lower unemployment rate can be achieved more quickly.

2. *Activist monetary policy works; it is effective at smoothing out the business cycle.* Activists are quick to point to the undesirable consequences of the constant monetary policy of the mid-1970s. In 1973, 1974, and 1975, the money supply growth rates were 5.5 percent, 4.3 percent, and 4.7 percent, respectively. These percentages represent a nearly constant growth rate in the money supply. The economy, however, went through a recession during that time, with Real GDP falling between 1973 and 1974 and between 1974 and 1975. Activists argue that an activist and flexible monetary policy would have reduced the high cost the economy had to pay in terms of lost output and high unemployment.

3. *Activist monetary policy is flexible; nonactivist (rules-based) monetary policy is not.* Activists argue that flexibility is a desirable quality in monetary policy; inflexibility is not. Implicitly, activists maintain that the more closely monetary policy can be designed to meet the particulars of a given economic environment, the better. For example, at certain times the economy requires a sharp increase in the money supply, and at other times it needs a sharp decrease; at still other times, only a slight increase or decrease is needed. Activists argue that activist (discretionary) monetary policy can change as the monetary needs of the economy change; nonactivist, rules-based, or "the-same-for-all-seasons" monetary policy cannot.

15-3b The Case for Nonactivist (or Rules-Based) Monetary Policy

The case for nonactivist (or rules-based) monetary policy also rests on three major claims:

1. *In modern economies, wages and prices are sufficiently flexible to allow the economy to equilibrate at reasonable speed at Natural Real GDP.* For example, nonactivists point to the sharp drop in union wages in 1982 in response to high unemployment. In addition, they argue that government policies largely determine the flexibility of wages and prices. For example, when government decides to cushion people's unemployment (e.g., through unemployment compensation), wages will not fall as quickly as when government does nothing. Nonactivists believe that a laissez-faire, hands-off approach by government promotes speedy wage and price adjustments and thus a quick return to Natural Real GDP.

2. *Activist monetary policies may not work.* Some economists argue that there are really two types of monetary policy: (1) monetary policy that is anticipated by the public and (2) monetary policy that is not. Anticipated monetary policy may not be effective at changing Real GDP or the unemployment rate. We discuss this subject in detail in the next chapter, but here is a brief explanation: Suppose the public correctly anticipates that the Fed will soon

increase the money supply by 10 percent. Consequently, the public reasons that aggregate demand will increase from AD_1 to AD_2, as shown in Exhibit 9, and that prices will rise.

Now, in this scenario, workers are concerned particularly about the expected higher price level because they know that higher prices decrease the buying power of their wages. So, in an attempt to maintain their real wages, workers bargain for and receive higher money wage rates, thereby shifting the short-run aggregate supply curve from $SRAS_1$ to $SRAS_2$ in Exhibit 9.

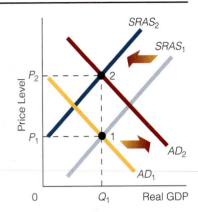

> **EXHIBIT 9**

Expansionary Monetary Policy and No Change in Real GDP

If expansionary monetary policy (and thus a higher price level) is anticipated, workers may bargain for and receive higher wage rates. It is then possible that the SRAS curve will shift leftward to the same degree that expansionary monetary policy shifts the AD curve rightward. Result: No change in Real GDP.

Now, if the $SRAS$ curve shifts leftward (owing to higher wage rates) to the same degree as the AD curve shifts rightward (owing to the increased money supply), Real GDP does not change but stays constant at Q_1. Thus, *a correctly anticipated increase in the money supply will be ineffective at raising Real GDP.*

3. *Activist monetary policies are likely to be destabilizing rather than stabilizing; they are likely to make matters worse, not better.* Nonactivists point to *lags* as the main reason that activist (or discretionary) monetary policies are likely to be destabilizing. (The total lag consists of the data, wait-and-see, legislative, transmission, and effectiveness lags discussed in Chapter 11.) Nonactivists argue that a long lag (e.g., 12 to 20 months) makes it almost impossible to conduct effective activist monetary policy: By the time the Fed's monetary stimulus arrives on the scene, the economy may not need any stimulus, and thus the policy measures will likely destabilize the economy. In this instance, the stimulus makes things worse rather than better.

Exhibit 10 illustrates the last point. Suppose the economy is currently in a recessionary gap at point 1. The recession is under way before Fed officials recognize it. Once they become aware of the recession, however, the officials

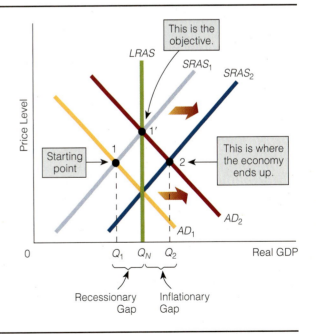

> **EXHIBIT 10**

Monetary Policy May Destabilize the Economy

In this scenario, the SRAS curve is shifting rightward (ridding the economy of its recessionary gap), but Fed officials do not realize that this is happening. They implement expansionary monetary policy, and the AD curve ends up intersecting $SRAS_2$ at point 2 instead of intersecting $SRAS_1$ at point 1'. Fed officials end up moving the economy into an inflationary gap and thus destabilizing the economy.

ECONOMICS 24/7

Who Gets the Money First, and What Happens to Relative Prices?

Besides expansionary and contractionary monetary policies and their effects on Real GDP and the price level, other effects have to be considered:

- The distribution of the increase in the money supply (in the case of expansionary monetary policy).

- How a change in the money supply might affect relative prices (as opposed to the price level).

Introducing the new MacBook Pro family
Our most advanced notebooks ever.

© iStockphoto.com/EdStock

Let's look at how these two effects interact. When the money supply expands by, say, $100 billion, not every member of the public gets some of the new money. To illustrate, suppose the Fed undertakes an open market purchase, which results in a rise in reserves in the banking system. Faced with greater (and excess) reserves, banks start to make more loans (new checkable deposits). The first economic actors to get the new money (as a result of the open market purchase) are the banks; the second economic actors are the individuals and firms who take out loans.

Now, let's say that one of the second economic actors is Caroline, who spends the money from her new loan to buy good X

from Richard. If Caroline would not have purchased good X without the loan, then the demand for good X presumably rises because of the loan (which the bank created as a result of the Fed's open market purchase). Therefore, if the demand for good X rises, so will its absolute (or money) price. If the absolute price of good X rises, so will its relative price, *ceteris paribus*. Conclusion: An increase in the money supply can change not only the price level, but relative prices too.

Of course, an increase in the money supply changes relative prices because not everyone gets the new money at the same time. Caroline gets the new money before the seller of good X (Richard) gets it, and so on. When the money supply is increased, some people get the new money before others, so the goods and services these people buy rise in price relative to the prices of the goods and services they do not buy. If the Carolines of the world (who get the new money first) buy good X and not good Y, and the non-Carolines of the world (who get the new money later) buy good Y and not good X, we can expect that, initially, the price of good X will rise relative to the price of good Y.

consider expanding the money supply in the hopes of shifting the AD curve from AD_1 to AD_2 so that it will intersect the $SRAS$ curve at point 1′, at Natural Real GDP.

In the interim, however, unknown to everybody, the economy is regulating itself: The $SRAS$ curve is shifting to the right. But because collecting and analyzing data about the economy takes time, Fed officials don't realize that this shift is occurring. Thinking that the economy is not regulating itself, or not regulating itself quickly enough, Fed officials implement expansionary monetary policy, and the AD curve shifts rightward. By the time the increased money supply is felt in the goods-and-services market, the AD curve intersects the $SRAS$ curve at point 2. In short, the Fed has moved the economy from point 1 to point 2—not, as it had hoped, from point 1 to point 1′. The Fed has moved the economy into an inflationary gap. Instead of stabilizing and moderating the business cycle, the Fed has intensified it.

ECONOMICS 24/7

Things May Not Always Go the Way the Fed Wants

Here are some things that many people seem to think:

1. If the Fed increases the reserves in the banking system—say, through an open market purchase—then the money supply will rise.

2. If the Fed increases the money supply, total spending in the economy will rise.

Earlier in this text, we discussed situations in which both statements 1 and 2 are true. But there are also situations in which they are false. To illustrate with regard to the first statement, let's go back to an equation that we first identified in Chapter 13:

$$\triangle \text{Checkable deposits (or money supply)} = 1/r \times \triangle R$$

If we let $r = 1/10$, and $\triangle R = \$100$, then the dollar amount of checkable deposits, or the money supply, will rise by $1,000. Can this happen? Certainly it can, but you may recall (back in Chapter 13) that it happens if there is no cash leakage and banks hold zero excess reserves. In other words, it happens only when a certain condition holds.

But suppose that banks don't lend the additional reserves that the Fed injects into the banking system, as we pointed out in an earlier 24/7 feature. Then we don't get a change in the money supply. In short, it is possible for the Fed to increase reserves in the banking system (say, through an open market purchase) and the money supply does not change.

Now consider the second statement: If the Fed increases the money supply, total spending in the economy is likely to rise. As we pointed out in Chapter 14, this can happen. For example, we know that total spending (total expenditures) is equal to the money supply

times velocity, or $M \times V$. So, if the money supply is initially $300 and velocity is 3, then total spending is $900. But once we raise the money supply to $400 and velocity remains unchanged at 3, total spending will rise to $1,200.

But, of course, total spending doesn't *necessarily* rise if the money supply rises. For example, if the money supply rises from $300 to $400 at the same time that velocity falls from 3 to 2, then total spending goes from $900 to $800, even though the money supply has risen.

Now let's consider both of our statements, 1 and 2, again, but this time in the light of monetary policy. Suppose the objective of the Fed is to increase the money supply so that total spending will rise in the economy. And suppose the reason the Fed wants to increase total spending is because it wants to shift the aggregate demand curve in the economy to the right. If the Fed then does in fact increase total spending and the aggregate demand curve shifts to the right, and if the relevant short-run aggregate supply curve in the economy is upward sloping, the predicted effect is a rise in Real GDP.

Can the Fed, then, definitely raise Real GDP by increasing reserves in the banking system? No, not definitely. The first place something can go wrong (for the Fed) is that banks may not lend the additional reserves.

But, of course, even if the banks do lend the additional reserves, thus causing the money supply to rise, there is no guarantee that a rise in the money supply will increase total spending in the economy. And why is that? Because a decline in velocity may offset the rise in the money supply, leading to either no change or a decline in the money supply.

All this goes to say that, when it comes to monetary policy, the money supply and total spending don't always go the way the Fed plans for them to go.

15-4 NONACTIVIST MONETARY PROPOSALS

The five nonactivist (or rules-based) monetary proposals are as follows:

1. The constant-money-growth-rate rule
2. The predetermined-money-growth-rate rule

3. The Taylor rule

4. Inflation targeting

5. (Nominal) GDP targeting

15-4a The Constant-Money-Growth-Rate Rule

Many nonactivists argue that the sole objective of monetary policy is to stabilize the price level. To this end, they propose a *constant-money-growth-rate rule.* One version of the rule is as follows:

> *The annual money supply growth rate will be constant at the average annual growth rate of Real GDP.*

For example, if the average annual Real GDP growth rate is approximately 3.3 percent, the money supply should be put on automatic pilot and be permitted to grow at an annual rate of 3.3 percent. The money supply will grow at this rate regardless of the state of the economy.

Some economists predict that a constant-money-growth-rate rule will bring about a stable price level over time because of the equation of exchange ($MV \equiv PQ$). If the average annual growth rate in Real GDP (Q) is 3.3 percent and the money supply (M) grows at 3.3 percent, the price level should remain stable over time. Advocates of this rule argue that in some years the growth rate in Real GDP will be below its average rate, causing an increase in the price level, and that in other years the growth rate in Real GDP will be above its average rate, causing a fall in the price level, but over time, the price level will be stable.

15-4b The Predetermined-Money-Growth-Rate Rule

Critics of the constant-money-growth-rate rule point out that it makes two assumptions: (1) Velocity is constant; (2) the money supply is defined correctly. Critics argue that velocity has not been constant in some periods. Also, not yet clear is which definition of the money supply is the proper one and therefore which money supply growth rate should be fixed: M1, M2, or some broader monetary measure.

Largely in response to the charge that velocity is not always constant, some nonactivists prefer the following rule:

> *The annual growth rate in the money supply will be equal to the average annual growth rate in Real GDP minus the growth rate in velocity.*

In other words,

$$\%\triangle M = \%\triangle Q - \%\triangle V$$

With this rule, the growth rate of the money supply is not fixed. It can vary from year to year, but it is predetermined in that it is dependent on the growth rates of Real GDP and velocity. For this reason, we call the rule the *predetermined-money-growth-rate rule.* To illustrate its workings, consider the following extended version of the equation of exchange:

$$\%\triangle M + \%\triangle V = \%\triangle P + \%\triangle Q$$

Suppose $\%\triangle Q$ is 3 percent and $\%\triangle V$ is 1 percent. The rule specifies that the growth rate in the money supply should be 2 percent. This growth rate would keep the price level stable; there would be a 0 percent change in P:

$$\%\triangle M + \%\triangle V = \%\triangle P + \triangle Q$$
$$2\% + 1\% = 0\% + 3\%$$

15-4c **The Fed and the Taylor Rule**

Economist John Taylor has argued for a middle ground, of sorts, between activist and nonactivist monetary policy. He has proposed that monetary authorities use a rule to guide them in making their discretionary decisions.

His rule has come to be known as the *Taylor rule*, which specifies how policy makers should set the federal funds rate target. (Recall from an earlier chapter that the federal funds rate is the interest rate that banks charge one another for reserves.) The economic thinking behind the Taylor rule is that there is some federal funds rate target that is consistent with (1) stabilizing inflation around a rather low inflation rate and (2) stabilizing Real GDP around its full-employment level. The aim is to find this target and then to use the Fed's tools to hit it.

Taylor defines the particulars of the rule as follows: The federal funds rate target

should be one-and-a-half times the inflation rate plus one-half times the GDP gap plus one.[4]

Algebraically, the Taylor rule says,

$$\text{Federal funds rate target} = 1.5 \, (\text{inflation rate}) + 0.5 \, (\text{GDP gap}) + 1$$

In this equation, the GDP gap measures the percentage deviation of Real GDP from its potential level. Let's use the rule to find the federal funds rate target that Taylor recommends to the Fed. Suppose the inflation rate is 5 percent and the GDP gap is 3 percent. Putting these percentages in our equation, we get

$$\begin{aligned}
\text{Federal funds rate target} &= 1.5 \, (5 \text{ percent}) + 0.5 \, (3 \text{ percent}) + 1 \\
&= 7.5 + 1.5 + 1 \\
&= 10 \text{ percent}
\end{aligned}$$

15-4d **Inflation Targeting**

Many economists recommend **inflation targeting**, which requires that the Fed try to keep the inflation rate near a predetermined level. Three major issues surround inflation targeting. The first deals with whether the inflation rate target should be a specific percentage (e.g., 2.5 percent) or confined within a narrow range (e.g., 1.0–2.5 percent). Second, whether it is a specific percentage or a specific range, what should the rate or range be? For example, if the inflation rate target is a specific percentage, should it be, say, 2.0 percent or 3.5 percent? The last issue deals with whether the inflation rate target should be announced or not. In other words, if the Fed adopts an inflation rate target of, say, 2.5 percent, should the target be disclosed to the public?

Numerous central banks in the world practice inflation targeting, and they announce their targets. For example, the Bank of Canada has set a target of 2 percent (inflation), and it has been announcing its inflation target since 1991. Other central banks that practice inflation targeting are the Bank of England, the Central Bank of Brazil, the Bank of Israel, and the Reserve Bank of New Zealand.

For an inflation rate target approach, the Fed would undertake monetary policy actions to keep the actual inflation rate near or at its target. For example, if its target rate is 2 percent and the actual inflation rate is, say, 5 percent, the Fed would cut back the growth rate in the money supply (or the absolute money supply) to bring the actual inflation rate nearer to the target.

The proponents of inflation targeting argue that such a policy is more in line with the Fed's objective of maintaining near price stability. The critics of inflation targeting often

Inflation Targeting
Targeting that requires the Fed to keep the inflation rate near a predetermined level.

---

[4] See John Taylor, *Getting Off Track* (Stanford, CA: Hoover Institution Press, 2009), p. 67.

argue that the policy would constrain the Fed at times, such as when it might need to overlook the target to deal with a financial crisis.

15-4e Nominal GDP Targeting

A new economic school arose late in the first decade of the 2000s: *market monetarism.*[5] It originated, not in the academic journals or in a particular economics department in any country, but in the blogosphere. What was the event that prompted the birth of market monetarism? It was the Great Recession: the recession that began in December 2007 and took a sharp downward movement in September 2008. At the time, many economists argued that the Great Recession was caused by the financial crisis that was occurring as well. (We will discuss the financial crisis in Chapter 18.) In other words, they argued that problems in the banking and financial sectors of the economy were the cause of the recession. The economists that came to be known as market monetarists disagreed. They argued that the recession was caused by monetary policy that was "too tight" or "too contractionary" (relative to what was necessary to stabilize the economy). Among these economists was Bentley University's Scott Sumner, who strongly advocated market monetarist ideas in his blog *TheMoneyIllusion.* Sumner, like other market monetarists, argues that the optimal monetary policy is for the Fed to set a Nominal GDP target—such as a rise of 5 to 6 percent a year in Nominal GDP—and then adjust the growth of the money supply in such a way as to hit the target.

We can understand the market monetarists' policy prescription in terms of the equation of exchange, which we first discussed in an earlier chapter. Remember that the equation of exchange states that the money supply times velocity must equal (Nominal) GDP: $M \times V \equiv$ GDP. Now, suppose there is a financial crisis and, as a result, people try to hold more money (spend less). The lesser spending is likely to reduce velocity, and if the Fed doesn't offset the decline in velocity sufficiently, GDP will decline. For example, suppose velocity declines by 8 percent and the money supply rises by 6 percent; then GDP will *decline* by 2 percent. If the objective is to raise Nominal GDP by 5 percent, an 8 percent decline in velocity would obligate the Fed to increase the money supply by 13 percent. Anything less prompts market monetarists to argue that monetary policy is "too tight."

If monetary policy leads to a decline in Nominal GDP, nominal income declines (because Nominal GDP and nominal income are two sides of the same coin). As a result of a decline in nominal incomes, individuals will have a hard time paying off their debts (that were contracted at an earlier time and were based on nominal incomes that were not expected to decline or to decline as much as they have). Take a representative case: A person has an income of $100,000 a year and incurs a debt that he has to pay off monthly for five years. Each month for five years, he must pay $2,000. Then Nominal GDP (nominal income) declines. Consequently, the income of our debtor falls, and he finds it harder to pay off his monthly debt of $2,000. As a result, he contracts his spending in the economy and his demand for goods and services declines. If there are enough debtors pulling back their spending, aggregate demand in the economy declines, firms lose sales and issue layoffs, the unemployment rate rises, and so on.

15-4f A Gold Standard as Monetary Policy and the Value of the Dollar

The type of monetary policy we have discussed so far is implemented by the Fed. It is largely the Fed that either increases or decreases the money supply. Moreover, the Fed has the ability to increase or decrease the money supply by as much or as little as it believes

---

[5.] The term "market monetarism" was coined by Danish economist Lars Christensen in August 2011.

is appropriate to bring about desirable economic consequences (such as low inflation and low unemployment).

Some economists argue that Fed-directed monetary policy has, over time, led to a decline in the value of the dollar. In other words, a dollar today doesn't buy as much as it once did. This, of course, is simply the other side of the inflation coin. One side of the inflation coin reads, "The price level is rising." The other side of the coin reads, "Because the price level is rising, the dollar doesn't buy as many goods and services as it once did."

So, have prices increased? Has the value of the dollar declined? Well, let's go back to 1950 and check the Consumer Price Index (which measures the price level). In 1950, the index was 24.1. By October 2013, it had risen to 233.546. To find the percentage change in prices during the period 1950–2013, we simply subtract 24.1 from 233.546 and divide by 24.1. The result is 869.07 percent, meaning that something which cost $20 in 1950 would cost $193.81 in October 2013.

If you would like to see how much prices have changed over the years, go to the website http://www.usinflationcalculator.com/. There, you will find an inflation calculator. You can simply choose any year from 1913 to the current year, key in a dollar amount (such as $20 or $200), and then see what that dollar item would cost in a different year (say, the current year). For example, if one keys in 1945 and $100, one finds that the $100 item in 1945 would cost $1,324 in 2014.

Now, some economists argue that one of the reasons the value of the dollar has declined so much over the years is because of the monetary policy of the Fed. The Fed-directed, discretionary monetary policy has caused a lot of inflation over the years, leading to a continuing decline in the value of the dollar. They then argue that a way to combat this decline is to take monetary policy out of the hands of the Fed. But what would take its place? Some advocate a monetary rule, some of which we have already discussed.

Others advocate a gold standard. The advocates of a gold standard often argue that, when the United States was on a gold standard, the price level in the nation was fairly stable and there was very little inflation. According to economist Michael Bordo,

> *The great virtue of the gold standard was that it assured long-term price stability. Compare the aforementioned average annual inflation rate of 0.1 percent between 1880 and 1914 with the average of 4.1 percent between 1946 and 2003.*[6]

How does a gold standard work? To illustrate, suppose the monetary authority states that it is willing to buy and sell gold for a set price of $1,000 an ounce and that this monetary policy will be the only one that it implements. Then the $1,000 price of gold is the *official price of gold*.

Now suppose the *market price of gold*, which is the price of gold determined in the gold market, rises above $1,000 an ounce—say, to $1,100 an ounce. What will members of the public do? They will go to the monetary authority and buy gold at the official price of $1,000 an ounce. Then they will turn around and sell that ounce of gold in the gold market for $1,100. But, of course, as people buy gold from the monetary authority and sell it in the gold market, the supply of gold in the gold market will be rising, so we can expect the market price of gold to fall. The market price of gold will keep falling until no one has any incentive to go to the monetary authority and buy gold anymore. In other words, it will keep falling until the market price of gold is $1,000, which is equal to the official price of gold.

Now, as the price of gold is falling, what will be happening to the general price level (as measured, say, by the Consumer Price Index)? It should be falling too, and here is why:

---

[6] Michael D. Bordo, "The Gold Standard," in *The Concise Encyclopedia of Economics*.

When the public buys gold from the monetary authority, it buys that gold with money. That money leaves the economy. (Think of the public turning over ten $100 bills for every ounce of gold it buys from the monetary authority.) Now, the monetary authority doesn't spend that money; it simply removes it from circulation, so the result is a reduction in the money supply in the economy, and, according to the exchange equation, if nothing else changes, the price level declines. In other words, the price of gold and the general price level move down together. The sequence of events is as follows:

Market price of gold > Official price of gold → Public buys gold from monetary authority → Public exchanges money for gold → Money supply declines → Price level declines

Now let's reverse things. Suppose the market price of gold falls to $900. What will people do now? They will go to the monetary authority and sell their gold for $1,000. After all, the monetary authority said that it would buy gold for $1,000, and it is better to sell gold for $1,000 to the monetary authority than to sell it to someone else for $900. But selling gold to the monetary authority takes gold out of the market (the supply of gold in the market declines), and thus the market price of gold will start to rise. When will it stop rising? Answer: When there is no longer any monetary incentive to sell gold to the monetary authority instead of to others—that is, when the market price of gold rises to the official price of gold at $1,000.

Now, as the market price of gold rises from $900 to $1,000, what is happening to the general price level? Well, as people sell their gold to the monetary authority, they get money from the monetary authority in return. (Think of the monetary authority turning over ten $100 bills for every ounce of gold it buys.) As a result, the money supply in the economy rises, and, according to the exchange equation, as we raise the money supply, if nothing else changes, the price level rises. We conclude that both the price of gold and the general price level rise together. The sequence of events is as follows:

Market price of gold < Official price of gold → Public sells gold to monetary authority → Public receives money for gold → Money supply rises → Price level rises

So far, then, we have seen that, if the monetary authority agrees to buy gold from, and sell gold to, the public at an official price of, say, $1,000, then it will stabilize the market price of gold at $1,000 an ounce. Again, that's because, if the market price rises above, or falls below, the official price of $1,000 an ounce, forces are at work to move the market price of gold back to the official price. Also, as we have seen, by stabilizing the price of gold, it is possible to stabilize the general price level as well because, as we have explained, the general price level moves up and down with the price of gold. This is the reason that some economists argue that a gold standard stabilizes the price level, thus preventing a decline in the value of the dollar.

SELF-TEST

1. Would a rules-based monetary policy produce price stability?

2. Suppose the inflation rate is 4 percent and the GDP gap is 5 percent. What is the Taylor rule recommendation for the federal funds rate target?

3. What is the monetary policy prescription of the market monetarists?

Office  Hours

"Does Monetary Policy Always Have the Same Effects?"

STUDENT:

Does monetary policy always have the same effects?

INSTRUCTOR:

Instead of my giving you the answer, think back to the Keynesian transmission mechanism and try to answer your question.

STUDENT:

In the Keynesian transmission mechanism, an increase in the money supply lowers the interest rate. The lower interest rate then increases investment, and the increased investment raises aggregate demand.

INSTRUCTOR:

Ask yourself whether the lower interest rate always raises investment.

STUDENT:

No, it doesn't always raise investment. If investment is interest insensitive, the lower interest rate will leave investment unchanged.

INSTRUCTOR:

There is something else too. Suppose investment *is* responsive to changes in the interest rate. In other words, if the interest rate falls, investment will rise. But the question is whether investment always rises by the same amount. For example, if in year 1 the interest rate falls from 6 percent to 5 percent and investment rises from $300 billion to $400 billion, does it follow that every time the interest rate falls from 6 percent to 5 percent, investment will rise by $100 billion?

STUDENT:

I see your point. You're saying that, although investment might always rise as the interest rate falls, it doesn't necessarily rise by the same amount every time. If it doesn't rise by the same amount every time, then there is no guarantee that aggregate demand will rise by the same amount every time (because increases in investment lead to increases in aggregate demand).

INSTRUCTOR:

That's correct. We'd then have to conclude that expansionary monetary policy won't always increase aggregate demand by the same amount. In other words, a money supply expansion of $30 billion might raise aggregate demand more at one time than at some other time.

STUDENT:

So one answer to my question—whether monetary policy always has the same effects—is, no, monetary policy doesn't always change aggregate demand by the same amount.

INSTRUCTOR:

That's correct. This discussion also helps us to understand why economists—even those of the same school of thought—might disagree with each other. For example, suppose Smith and Jones believe that monetary policy affects the economy through the Keynesian transmission mechanism. Then, just because both accept the Keynesian transmission mechanism doesn't necessarily mean that they both think that a given increase in the money supply is going to affect aggregate demand to the same degree. Although they might agree that an expansion in the money supply will increase aggregate demand, they might disagree as to how much aggregate demand will increase. Smith might think that aggregate demand will rise only a little because investment will not rise much when the interest rate drops. Jones might think that aggregate demand will rise a lot because investment will rise a lot when the interest rate drops.

Points to remember

1. Monetary policy doesn't always have the same effects. With reference to the Keynesian transmission mechanism, expansionary monetary policy might lead to a large change in investment at some times (when investment is highly responsive to changes in the interest rate) and only a small change in investment at other times (when investment is somewhat insensitive to changes in the interest rate). Expansionary monetary policy therefore might not always change aggregate demand to the same degree.

2. Even economists of the same school of thought can disagree with each other at times. For example, although two economists might agree that a rise in the money supply will change investment (or aggregate demand), they might disagree as to *how much* investment (or aggregate demand) will change.

CHAPTER SUMMARY

THE KEYNESIAN TRANSMISSION MECHANISM

- The Keynesian route between the money market and the goods-and-services market is indirect. Changes in the money market must affect the investment goods market before the goods-and-services market is affected. Under the assumptions that no liquidity trap exists and investment is not interest insensitive, the transmission mechanism works as follows for an increase in the money supply: an increase in the money supply lowers the interest rate and increases investment, thereby increasing aggregate demand and shifting the *AD* curve rightward. Consequently, Real GDP rises. Under the same assumptions, the transmission mechanism works as follows for a *decrease* in the money supply: a decrease in the money supply raises the interest rate and decreases investment, thereby decreasing aggregate demand and shifting the *AD* curve leftward. As a result, Real GDP falls.

- The Keynesian transmission mechanism may be short-circuited either by the liquidity trap or by interest-insensitive investment. Both are Keynesian notions. Keynesians predict that, if either is present, expansionary monetary policy will be unable to change Real GDP.

THE MONETARIST TRANSMISSION MECHANISM

- The monetarist route between the money market and the goods-and-services market is direct. Changes in the money supply affect aggregate demand. An increase in the money supply causes individuals to increase their spending on a wide variety of goods.

BOND PRICES AND INTEREST RATES

- Interest rates and the prices of old, or existing, bonds are inversely related.

THE ACTIVIST–NONACTIVIST DEBATE

- Activists argue that monetary policy should be deliberately used to smooth out the business cycle; they favor using activist, or discretionary, monetary policy to fine-tune the economy. Nonactivists argue against the use of discretionary monetary policy; they propose nonactivist, or rules-based, monetary policy.

- The case for discretionary monetary policy rests on three major claims: (1) The economy does not always equilibrate quickly enough at Natural Real GDP. (2) Activist monetary policy works. (3) Activist monetary policy is flexible, and flexibility is a desirable quality in monetary policy.

- The case for nonactivist monetary policy rests on three major claims: (1) There is sufficient flexibility in wages and prices in modern economies to allow them to equilibrate at reasonable speed at Natural Real GDP. (2) Activist monetary policies may not work. (3) Activist monetary policies are likely to make matters worse rather than better.

NONACTIVIST (OR RULES-BASED) MONETARY PROPOSALS

- The constant-money-growth-rate rule states that the annual money supply growth rate will be constant at the average annual growth rate of Real GDP.

- The predetermined-money-growth-rate rule states that the annual growth rate in the money supply will be equal to the average annual growth rate in Real GDP minus the growth rate in velocity.

- The Taylor rule specifies the following equation: Federal funds rate target = 1.5(inflation rate) + 0.5(GDP gap) + 1.

- Inflation targeting requires the Fed to keep the inflation rate near a predetermined level.

- Market monetarists advocate a monetary policy that targets Nominal GDP growth.

KEY TERMS AND CONCEPTS

Transmission Mechanism
Demand for Money
  (Balances)

Liquidity Trap
Expansionary Monetary
  Policy

Contractionary Monetary
  Policy
Activists

Fine-tuning
Nonactivists
Inflation Targeting

VIDEO QUESTIONS AND PROBLEMS

Video Questions and Problems are available on MindTap for Arnold 12e or by searching for Arnold on www.cengagebrain.com

1. Explain and diagrammatically represent the Keynesian transmission mechanism.

2. Explain how, under certain conditions, monetary policy can remove an economy from a recessionary gap.

3. Explain how monetary policy may destabilize the economy.

4. Saying that individuals are holding an "excess supply of money" is absurd because no one ever has enough money. Do you agree or disagree? Explain your answer.

5. What does it mean to say that investment is "interest insensitive?"

QUESTIONS AND PROBLEMS

1. Consider the following: Two researchers, A and B, are trying to determine whether eating fatty foods leads to heart attacks. The researchers proceed differently. Researcher A builds a model in which fatty foods may first affect X in one's body, and if X is affected, then Y may be affected, and if Y is affected, then Z may be affected. Finally, if Z is affected, the heart is affected, and the individual has an increased probability of suffering a heart attack. Researcher B doesn't proceed in this step-by-step fashion. She conducts an experiment to see whether people who eat many fatty foods have more, fewer, or the same number of heart attacks as people who eat few fatty foods. Which researcher's methods have more in common with the research methodology implicit in the Keynesian transmission mechanism? Which researcher's methods have more in common with the research methodology implicit in the monetarist transmission mechanism? Explain your answer.

2. If bond prices fall, will individuals want to hold more or less money? Explain your answer.

3. Why is the demand curve for money downward sloping?

4. Explain how it is possible to have too much money.

5. Explain how the Keynesian transmission mechanism works.

6. Explain how the monetarist transmission mechanism works.

7. It has been suggested that nonactivists are not concerned with the level of Real GDP and unemployment because most (if not all) nonactivist monetary proposals set stabilization of the price level as their immediate objective. Discuss.

8. Suppose the combination of more accurate data and better forecasting techniques would make it easy for the Fed to predict a recession 10 to 16 months in advance. Would this state of affairs strengthen the case for activism or nonactivism? Explain your answer.

9. According to the theory of patterns of specialization and sustainable trade (PSST), economic activity can decline in the face of unchanged aggregate demand. How so?

10. Suppose it were proved that liquidity traps do not occur and that investment is not interest insensitive. Would this be enough to disprove the claim that expansionary monetary policy is not always effective at changing Real GDP? Why or why not?

11. Both activists and nonactivists make good points for their respective positions. Do you think activists could say anything to nonactivists to convince them to accept the activist position, and vice versa? If so, what is it that they would say? If not, why not?

12. The discussion of supply and demand in Chapter 3 noted that, if two goods are substitutes for each other, the price of one and the demand for the other are directly related. For example, if Pepsi-Cola and Coca-Cola are substitutes, an increase in the price of Pepsi-Cola will increase the demand for Coca-Cola. Suppose that bonds and stocks are substitutes for each other. We know that interest rates and bond prices are inversely related. What do you predict is the relationship between stock prices and interest rates? Explain your answer.

13. Argue the case for and against a monetary rule.

14. How does inflation targeting work?

15. Monetary policy can affect relative prices. Do you agree or disagree with this statement? Explain your answer.

16. According to market monetarists, what problems might arise from a sharp decline in Nominal GDP?

17. Does the monetary policy of market monetarists take into account changes in velocity? Explain your answer.

18. Explain how a gold standard, as monetary policy, would work.

WORKING WITH NUMBERS AND GRAPHS

1. Last year, Manuel bought a bond for $10,000 that promises to pay him $900 a year. This year, he can buy a bond for $10,000 that promises to pay $1,000 a year. If Manuel wants to sell his old bond, what is its price likely to be?

2. Last year, Charu bought a bond for $10,000 that promises to pay her $1,000 a year. This year, investors can buy a bond for $10,000 that promises to pay $800 a year. If Charu wants to sell her old bond, what is its price likely to be?

3. The annual average percentage change in Real GDP is 2.3 percent, and the annual average percentage change in velocity is 1.1 percent. Using the monetary rule discussed in the text, what percentage change in the money supply will keep prices stable (on average)?

4. Show graphically that the more interest insensitive the investment demand curve is, the less likely it is that monetary policy will be effective at changing Real GDP.

5. In each of parts (a)–(d), which panel in the accompanying figure best describes the situation?

a. Expansionary monetary policy that removes the economy from a recessionary gap

b. Expansionary monetary policy that is destabilizing

c. Contractionary monetary policy that removes the economy from an inflationary gap

d. Monetary policy that is ineffective at changing Real GDP

6. Graphically portray the Keynesian transmission mechanism under the following conditions:

a. A decrease in the money supply

b. No liquidity trap

c. Downward-sloping investment demand

7. Graphically portray the monetarist transmission mechanism when the money supply declines.

8. According to the Taylor rule, if inflation is 8 percent and the GDP gap is 3 percent, what is the recommendation for the federal funds rate target?

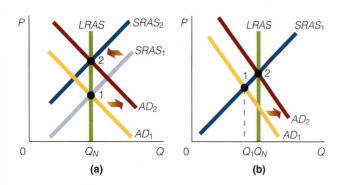

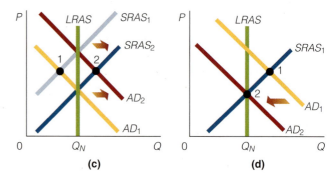

BOND PRICES AND THE INTEREST RATE

Bond prices and the interest rate are inversely related: as the price of bonds rises, the interest rate falls; as the price of bonds falls, the interest rate rises. In this appendix, we explain this relationship by looking closely at the money market and the bond market. The money market is shown in equilibrium in Exhibit 1(a). The equilibrium interest rate is 5 percent. The bond market is shown in equilibrium in Exhibit 1(b). The equilibrium bond price is P_{B1}.

Suppose people have only two ways to hold their wealth: in money or in bonds. In other words, a person must always decide, "How much of my wealth do I hold in money, and how much do I hold in bonds?" If someone's wealth is currently equal to $100,000, does this person hold $50,000 (of that wealth) in money and $50,000 in bonds, or $25,000 in money and $75,000 in bonds, and so on?

Because, in this scenario, wealth can be held only in the form of money and bonds, if someone thinks that she is holding *too much* money, she also must be thinking that

> **EXHIBIT 1**

The Money Market and the Bond Market

(a) The money market in equilibrium at an interest rate of 5 percent.

(b) The bond market is in equilibrium at a bond price of P_{B1}. When one of these markets is in equilibrium, the other is too.

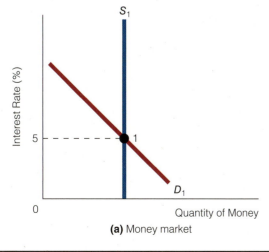

(a) Money market

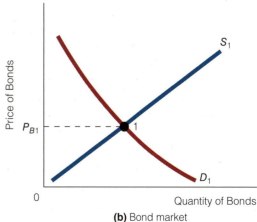

(b) Bond market

she is holding too few bonds. In other words, a surplus of money necessarily implies a shortage of bonds. To illustrate, let's say the person is currently holding $25,000 in money and $75,000 in bonds. Let's also say that she thinks that she is holding too much of her wealth in money. Then she must also think that she is holding too little of her wealth in bonds. Consequently, she might want to take $5,000 of her money and buy $5,000 worth of bonds so that she has $20,000 in money and $80,000 in bonds. So, if a surplus of money signifies a shortage of bonds, then, in market terms, a surplus in the money market implies a shortage in the bond market.

Now suppose our person believes that she is holding *too little* money. Instead of holding $25,000 in money, she would prefer to hold $30,000 in money. But, of course, holding too little money implies that our person is holding too much of her wealth in bonds. In other words, a shortage of money implies a surplus of bonds. Thus, a shortage in the money market implies a surplus in the bond market.

Let's recap:

Holding too much of one's wealth in money → Holding too little of one's wealth in bonds

or

Surplus in the money market → Shortage in the bond market

and

Holding too little of one's wealth in money → holding too much of one's wealth in bonds

or

Shortage in the money market → Surplus in the bond market

Now let's look at Exhibit 2. At point 1 in each part, the respective market is in equilibrium: People are holding just the right amount of money and just the right amount of bonds. Suppose the Fed undertakes an action that increases the money supply. Then the money supply curve in Exhibit 2(a) shifts rightward from S_1 to S_2. At the initial interest rate of 5 percent, the money market now has a surplus of money. But, as we recall, a surplus of money in the money market must mean a shortage of bonds in the bond market.

How does this shortage manifest itself? As a result of the surplus in the money market, individuals take their "surplus money" and start to buy bonds. The demand for bonds in the bond market then shifts rightward from D_1 to D_2 [Exhibit 2(b)]. So now there is a surplus of money in the money market at 5 percent and a shortage of bonds in the bond market at P_{B1}. Both markets are in disequilibrium at the specified interest rate and bond price.

The markets will begin to equilibrate. In the bond market, the price of bonds will begin to rise toward P_{B2}. As the price of bonds rises, the interest rate in the money market starts to fall, moving toward its equilibrium level of 4 percent. Finally, both markets are in equilibrium: the money market is at 4 percent and the bond market is at P_{B2}.

> EXHIBIT 2

Changes in the Money Market Affect the Bond Market

(a) The money market is initially in equilibrium at point 1; the equilibrium interest rate is 5 percent. (b) The bond market is initially in equilibrium at point 1; the equilibrium bond price is P_{B1}. The Fed increases the money supply. In the money market [shown in (a)], the supply-of-money curve shifts rightward from S_1 to S_2. At the interest rate of 5 percent, there is now a surplus of money. With their surplus of money, individuals start to buy more bonds, so the demand-for-bonds curve in panel (b) shifts rightward from D_1 to D_2. The result is a shortage of bonds in the bond market at the price of P_{B1}. Both markets are now in disequilibrium. The equilibrating process in the bond market pushes bond prices up. As bond prices rise, the interest rate falls, and that happens in the money market [shown in (a)]. Eventually, both markets are back in equilibrium, with the equilibrium interest rate now 4 percent and the price of bonds now P_{B2}.

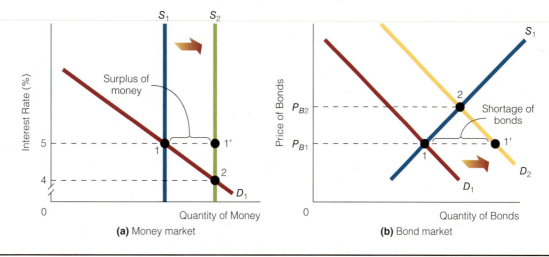

(a) Money market

(b) Bond market

APPENDIX SUMMARY

- Suppose that an individual can hold his wealth only as money or bonds. Then, if a person believes that he is holding too much of his wealth in money, he also believes that he is holding too little of it in bonds. Similarly, if he believes that he is holding too little of his wealth in money, he also believes that he is holding too much of it in bonds.

- A surplus in the money market implies a shortage in the bond market. A shortage in the money market implies a surplus in the bond market.

QUESTIONS AND PROBLEMS

1. Draw both the money market and bond market in equilibrium. Next, explain, and show diagrammatically, what happens to the interest rate and the price of bonds as a result of the Fed's increasing the money supply.

2. Draw both the money market and bond market in equilibrium. Next, explain, and show diagrammatically, what happens to the interest rate and the price of bonds as a result of the Fed's decreasing the money supply.

3. Identify the state of the bond market (equilibrium, shortage, surplus), given each of the following:

   a. Shortage in the money market

   b. Surplus in the money market

   c. Equilibrium in the money market

4. Fed actions affect the money market but not the bond market. Do you agree or disagree with this statement? Explain your answer.

16 EXPECTATIONS THEORY AND THE ECONOMY

INTRODUCTION

In this chapter, we discuss two expectations theories: adaptive and rational. We begin our discussion of expectations theory and the economy with a debate that raged within the economics profession years ago over the shape of the Phillips curve.

16-1 PHILLIPS CURVE ANALYSIS

Phillips Curve

A curve that originally showed the relationship between wage inflation and unemployment and that now more often shows the relationship between price inflation and unemployment.

The **Phillips curve** is used to analyze the relationship between inflation and unemployment. We begin the discussion of the Phillips curve by focusing on the work of three economists: A. W. Phillips, Paul Samuelson, and Robert Solow.

16-1a The Phillips Curve

In 1958, A. W. Phillips of the London School of Economics published a paper in the economics journal *Economica*: "The Relation Between Unemployment and the Rate of Change of Money Wages in the United Kingdom, 1861–1957." As the title suggests, Phillips collected data about the rate of change of money wages, sometimes referred to as *wage inflation*, and about *unemployment rates* in the United Kingdom over almost a century. He then plotted the rate of change in money wages against the unemployment rate for each year. Finally, he fit a curve to the data points (Exhibit 1).

An Inverse Relationship   The curve, which came to be known as the Phillips curve, is downward sloping, suggesting that the rate of change of money wages (wage

The Original Phillips Curve

This curve was constructed by A. W. Phillips, using data for the United Kingdom from 1861 to 1913. (The relationship here is also representative of the experience of the United Kingdom through 1957.) The original Phillips curve suggests an inverse relationship between wage inflation and unemployment—a wage inflation–unemployment trade-off. (Note: Each dot represents a single year.)

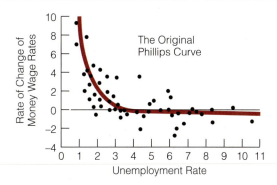

inflation) and unemployment rates are *inversely related.*[1] This inverse relationship, in turn, suggests a trade-off between wage inflation and unemployment. Higher wage inflation means lower unemployment; lower wage inflation means higher unemployment.

Policy makers concluded from the Phillips curve that simultaneously lowering wage inflation and unemployment was impossible; they could do only one or the other. So the combination of low wage inflation and low unemployment was unlikely. This was the bad news.

The good news was that rising unemployment and rising wage inflation did not go together either. Thus, the combination of high unemployment and high wage inflation was also unlikely.

16-1b Samuelson and Solow: The Americanization of the Phillips Curve

In 1960, two American economists, Paul Samuelson and Robert Solow, published an article in the *American Economic Review* in which they fit a Phillips curve to the U.S. economy from 1935 to 1959. In addition to using U.S. data instead of British data, they measured *price inflation rates* (instead of wage inflation rates) against unemployment rates. They found an inverse relationship between (price) inflation and unemployment. (See Exhibit 2.)[2]

Economists concluded from the Phillips curve that **stagflation**, or high inflation together with high unemployment, was extremely unlikely. The economy could register (1) high unemployment and low inflation or (2) low unemployment and high inflation. Also, economists noticed that the Phillips curve presented policy

Stagflation
The simultaneous occurrence of high rates of inflation and unemployment.

---

[1] Early explanations for the inverse relationship between wage inflation and unemployment focused on the state of the labor market, given changes in aggregate demand. When aggregate demand is increasing, businesses expand production and hire more employees. As the unemployment rate falls, the labor market becomes tighter and employers find it increasingly difficult to hire workers at old wages. Businesses must then offer higher wages in order to obtain additional workers. Unemployment and money wages move in opposite directions.

[2] Today, when economists speak of the Phillips curve, they are usually referring to the relationship between price inflation rates and unemployment rates instead of the relationship between wage inflation rates and unemployment rates.

> **EXHIBIT 2**

The Phillips Curve and a Menu of Choices

Samuelson and Solow's early work using American data showed that the Phillips curve was downward sloping. Economists reasoned that stagflation was extremely unlikely and that the Phillips curve presented policy makers with a menu of choices—points A, B, C, and D.

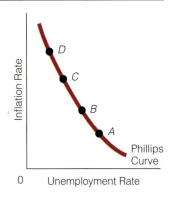

makers with a *menu of choices.* For example, policy makers could choose to move the economy to any of the points on the Phillips curve shown in Exhibit 2. If they decided that, say, point A, with high unemployment and low inflation, was preferable to point D, with low unemployment and high inflation, then so be it. Getting the economy to the desired point was simply a matter of reaching the right level of aggregate demand. To Keynesian economists, who were gaining a reputation for advocating fine-tuning the economy (i.e., using small-scale measures to counterbalance undesirable economic trends), this conclusion seemed consistent with their theories and policy proposals.

16-2 THE CONTROVERSY BEGINS: ARE THERE REALLY TWO PHILLIPS CURVES?

This section discusses the work of Milton Friedman and the hypothesis that there are two Phillips curves, not one.

16-2a Things Aren't Always as We Think They Are

In the 1970s and early 1980s, economists began to question many of the conclusions about the Phillips curve—questions prompted largely by events that happened after 1969. Exhibit 3 shows U.S. inflation and unemployment rates for the years 1961–2003. The 1961–1969 period, which is shaded, depicts the original Phillips curve trade-off between inflation and unemployment. The remaining period, 1970–2003, as a whole does not, although some subperiods, such as 1976–1979, do.

Note that, in the period 1970–2003, stagflation—high unemployment and high inflation—is possible. For example, 1975, 1981, and 1982 are definitely years of stagflation. The existence of stagflation implies that a trade-off between inflation and unemployment may not always exist.

16-2b Friedman and the Natural Rate Theory

In his presidential address to the American Economic Association in 1967 (published in the *American Economic Review*), Milton Friedman attacked the idea of a *permanent* downward-sloping Phillips curve. Friedman's key point was that there are two Phillips curves, not one: a short-run Phillips curve and a long-run Phillips curve. Friedman said, "There is always a temporary tradeoff between inflation and unemployment; there is no permanent tradeoff." Specifically, *there is a trade-off in the short run but not in the long run.* Friedman's discussion not only introduced two types of Phillips curves but also opened the macroeconomics door wide, once and for all, to expectations theory: the idea that people's expectations about economic events affect economic outcomes.

Exhibit 4 illustrates both the short- and long-run Phillips curves. In window 1, the economy is in long-run equilibrium, operating at Q_1, which is equal to Q_N. In the main diagram, the economy is at point 1 at the natural rate of unemployment, U_N. Further and

EXHIBIT 3

The Diagram That Raises Questions: Inflation and Unemployment, 1961–2003

The period 1961–1969 clearly depicts the original Phillips curve trade-off between inflation and unemployment. The later period, 1970–2003, as a whole, does not. However, some subperiods do, such as 1976–1979. The diagram presents empirical evidence that stagflation may exist; an inflation–unemployment trade-off may not always hold.

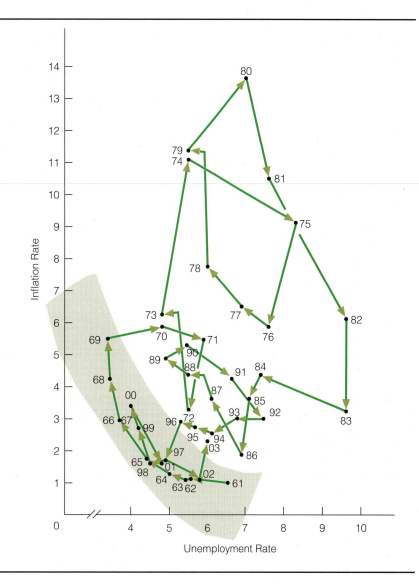

most important, *we assume that the expected inflation rate and the actual inflation rate are the same* at 2 percent.

Now suppose government *unexpectedly* increases aggregate demand from AD_1 to AD_2, as shown in window 2. As a result, the *actual* inflation rate increases (say, to 4 percent), but in the short run (immediately after the increase in aggregate demand), individual decision makers do not know this. Consequently, the *expected* inflation rate remains at 2 percent. In short, aggregate demand increases at the same time that people's expected inflation rate remains constant.

Because of this combination of events, certain consequences unfold. The higher aggregate demand causes temporary shortages and higher prices. Businesses then respond to the higher prices and subsequent higher profits by increasing output. Higher output requires more employees, so businesses start hiring more workers. As hiring increases,

> EXHIBIT 4

Short-Run and Long-Run Phillips Curves

Starting at point 1 in the main diagram, and under the assumption that the expected inflation rate stays constant as aggregate demand increases, the economy moves to point 2. As the expected inflation rate changes and comes to equal the actual inflation rate, the economy moves to point 3. Points 1 and 2 lie on a short-run Phillips curve. Points 1 and 3 lie on a long-run Phillips curve. (*Note:* The percentages in parentheses following the *SRAS* curves in the windows refer to the expected inflation rates.)

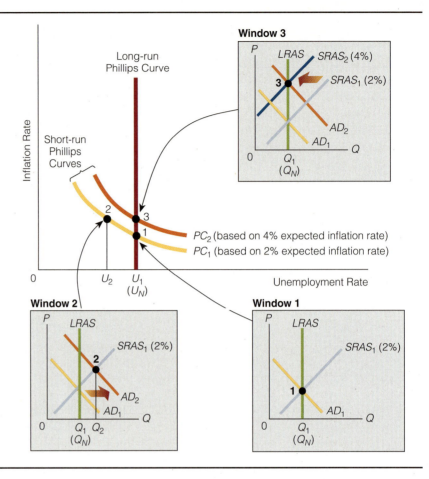

many currently unemployed individuals find work. Furthermore, many of the newly employed persons accept the prevailing wage rate because they think the wages will have greater purchasing power (because they expect the inflation rate to be 2 percent) than, in fact, the wages will turn out to have.

So far, the results of an increase in aggregate demand with no change in the expected inflation rate are (1) an increase in Real GDP from Q_1 to Q_2 (see window 2) and (2) a corresponding decrease in the unemployment rate from U_1 to U_2 (in the main diagram).

The question is whether point 2 is a stable equilibrium. Friedman answered that it is not. He argued that, *as long as the expected inflation rate is not equal to the actual inflation rate, the economy is not in long-run equilibrium.*

For Friedman, as for most economists today, the movement from point 1 to point 2 on PC_1 is a short-run movement. Economists refer to PC_1, along which short-run movements occur, as a *short-run Phillips curve.*

In time, inflation expectations begin to change. As prices continue to climb, wage earners realize that their real (i.e., inflation-adjusted) wages are lower than they thought. In hindsight, they realize that they accepted nominal (money) wages based on an expected inflation rate (2 percent) that was too low. So they revise their inflation expectations upward.

At the same time, some wage earners quit their jobs because they choose not to continue working at such low *real wages*. Eventually, the combination of some workers quitting their jobs and most (if not all) workers revising their inflation expectations upward causes wage rates to move upward.

Higher wage rates then shift the short-run aggregate supply curve from *SRAS*₁ to *SRAS*₂ (see window 3), ultimately moving the economy back to Natural Real GDP and to the natural rate of unemployment at point 3 (see the main diagram). The curve that connects point 1, where the economy started, and point 3, where it ended, is called the *long-run Phillips curve.*

Thus, the short-run Phillips curve exhibits a trade-off between inflation and unemployment, whereas the long-run Phillips curve does not. This idea is implicit in what has come to be called the **Friedman natural rate theory** (or the *Friedman fooling theory*). According to this theory (Exhibit 5), in the long run the economy returns to its natural rate of unemployment and it moved away from the natural unemployment rate in the first place only because workers were fooled (in the short run) into thinking the inflation rate was lower than it was.

How, specifically, do people's expectations relate to the discussion of the short- and long-run Phillips curves? In Exhibit 4, the economy starts out at point 1 in the main diagram, and then something happens: Aggregate demand increases. This increase raises the inflation rate, *but workers don't become aware of the change in the inflation rate for a while.* In the interim, their expected inflation rate is too low and, as a result, they are willing to work at jobs (and produce output) that they wouldn't work at if they perceived the inflation rate realistically.

In time, workers perceive the inflation rate realistically. Their expected inflation rate is no longer too low; it has risen to equal the actual inflation rate. The response, as predicted, is that the unemployment rate rises and output falls.

So, because workers' expectations (of inflation) are, in the short run, inconsistent with reality, workers produce more output than they would produce if their expectations were

Friedman Natural Rate Theory

Within the Phillips curve framework, the idea that, in the long run, unemployment is at its natural rate and that there is a long-run Phillips curve, which is vertical at the natural rate of unemployment.

> **EXHIBIT 5**

Mechanics of the Friedman Natural Rate Theory

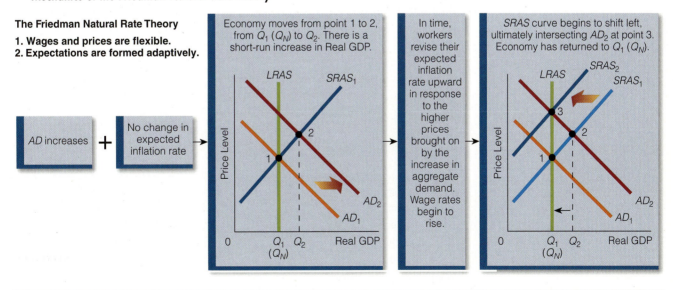

The Friedman Natural Rate Theory

1. **Wages and prices are flexible.**
2. **Expectations are formed adaptively.**

AD increases + No change in expected inflation rate

Economy moves from point 1 to 2, from Q_1 (Q_N) to Q_2. There is a short-run increase in Real GDP.

In time, workers revise their expected inflation rate upward in response to the higher prices brought on by the increase in aggregate demand. Wage rates begin to rise.

SRAS curve begins to shift left, ultimately intersecting AD_2 at point 3. Economy has returned to Q_1 (Q_N).

consistent with reality. This is how people's expectations can affect such real economic variables as Real GDP and the unemployment rate.

Perceptions of Reality Matter People say they base their actions on reality. When it rains, they pull out an umbrella; when they have a hard time seeing, they get their eyes checked. People also base their actions on their *perceptions* of reality, as workers do in the Friedman natural rate theory. Although the inflation rate has actually increased, workers don't perceive the change. Thus, in the short run (during the period in which they misperceive reality), workers base their actions not on reality, but on their perception of it.

16-2c How Do People Form Their Expectations?

Implicit in the Friedman natural rate theory is an assumption about how individuals form their expectations. Essentially, the theory holds that individuals form their expected inflation rate by looking at *past inflation rates*. Suppose someone were to ask you your expected inflation rate for the upcoming year. Would your response be closer to 50 percent or to 2 percent? If you use **adaptive expectations** to arrive at your expected inflation rate, the answer is closer to 2 percent than to 50 percent, because you haven't seen recent past inflation rates of 50 percent. But you have seen recent past inflation rates near 2 percent.

Notice that, with adaptive expectations, individuals look to the past—they look over their shoulders to see what *has happened*—in formulating their best guess as to what *will happen*. This is what individuals do in the Friedman natural rate theory, which assumes that people have adaptive expectations.

Some economists have argued the point. They believe that people form their expected inflation rate not by using adaptive expectations, but by means of *rational expectations*. We discuss this view in the next section.

Adaptive Expectations
Expectations that individuals form from past experience and modify slowly as the present and the future become the past (i.e., as time passes).

At the Bargaining Table Suppose you read the following report in the newspaper: "Recent wage negotiations between management and labor unions in the city have come to a halt. The two sides in the negotiations are unable so far to come to an agreement on annual wage rate increases for the duration of the four-year contract . . . ." Where is the economics?

First, if the two sides are negotiating an annual wage rate increase, then each is probably basing the increase on an expected inflation rate. Management might be saying, "We believe that the average annual inflation rate over the next four years will be 2 percent, so we are willing to agree to an annual wage rate increase of 2 percent each year for the next four years. The labor unions might be saying, "Because we expect the average annual inflation rate over the next four years to be 3.5 percent, we believe that 3.5 percent is the right annual wage rate increase for us."

SELF-TEST

(Answers to Self-Test questions are in Answers to Self-Test Questions at the back of the book.)

1. What condition must exist for the Phillips curve to present policy makers with a permanent menu of choices (between inflation and unemployment)?

2. Is there a trade-off between inflation and unemployment? Explain your answer.

3. The Friedman natural rate theory is sometimes called the fooling theory. Who is being fooled, and what are they being fooled about?

16-3 RATIONAL EXPECTATIONS AND NEW CLASSICAL THEORY

Rational expectations have played a major role in the Phillips curve controversy. We discuss rational expectations and new classical theory next.

16-3a Rational Expectations

In the early 1970s, a few economists, including Robert Lucas of the University of Chicago (winner of the 1995 Nobel Prize in Economics), began to question the short-run trade-off between inflation and unemployment. Essentially, Lucas combined the natural rate theory with rational expectations.[3]

The theory of **rational expectations** holds that individuals form the expected inflation rate not only on the basis of their past experience with inflation (looking over their shoulders), but also on their predictions about the effects of present and future policy actions and events (looking around and ahead). In short, the expected inflation rate is formed by looking at the past, present, and future. To illustrate, suppose the inflation rate has been 2 percent for the past seven years. Then, the chairman of the Fed's Board of Governors speaks about "sharply stimulating the economy." Proponents of rational expectations argue that the expected inflation rate might immediately jump upward on the basis of the current announcement by the chairman.

A major difference between adaptive and rational expectations is the *speed* at which the expected inflation rate changes. If the expected inflation rate is formed adaptively, then it is slow to change. Because it is based only on the past, individuals wait until the present becomes the past before changing their expectations. If the expected inflation rate is formed rationally, it changes quickly because it is based on the past, present, and future.

16-3b Do People Really Anticipate Policy?

One assumption of rational expectations is that people anticipate policy. Suppose you chose people at random on the street and asked them, "What do you think the Fed will do in the next few months?" Do you think you would be more likely to receive an intelligent answer or the response, "What's the Fed?" Most readers of this text would probably expect the second answer. In fact, the general feeling is that the person on the street knows little about economics or economic institutions. So, no, people don't really anticipate policy. But suppose you chose people at random in the Wall Street area of Manhattan and asked the

Rational Expectations
Expectations that individuals form on the basis of past experience and their predictions about the effects of present and future policy actions and events.

[3.] Rational expectations appeared on the economic scene in 1961, when John Muth published "Rational Expectations and the Theory of Price Movements" in *Econometrica*. For about 10 years, the article received little attention from the economics profession. Then, in the early 1970s, with the work of Robert Lucas, Thomas Sargent, Neil Wallace, Robert Barro, and others, the article began to be noticed.

same question. In this case, the answer is likely to be well thought out; at least *these* people anticipate policy.

However, not all persons need to anticipate policy. *As long as some do*, the consequences may be the same *as if* all persons do. For example, Juanita Estevez is anticipating policy if she decides to buy 100 shares of SKA because her best friend, Tammy Higgins, heard from her friend Kenny Urich that his broker, Roberta Gunter, told him that SKA's stock is expected to go up. Juanita is anticipating policy because it is likely that Roberta Gunter obtained her information from a researcher in the brokerage firm who makes it his business to watch the Fed and to anticipate its next move.

Of course, policy is anticipated not just for the purpose of buying and selling securities. Labor unions hire professional forecasters (Fed watchers) to predict future inflation rates—important information to have during wage contract negotiations. Banks hire forecasters to predict inflation rates, which they incorporate into the interest rates they charge. Export businesses hire forecasters to predict the future exchange-rate value of the dollar. The average investor may subscribe to a business or investment newsletter for information in order to predict interest rates, the price of gold, or next year's inflation rate more accurately. The person thinking of refinancing a mortgage watches one of the many financial news shows on television to find out about the government's most recent move and how it will affect interest rates in, say, the next three months.

While Playing a Game of Chess Where is the economics in a game of chess? Chess players often anticipate each other's moves. Player 1 might be thinking that if she moves from e4 to e5, player 2 will move from b5 to c6. But then the first player asks herself, "What comes next? Will my opponent then be likely to move from c6 to d6?"

What people do in a game of chess and what they do when predicting government policy actions might not be all that different. In a game of chess, you are playing to win, and whether you win depends on how well you can anticipate your opponent's moves. Anticipating policy actions is not much different, as you will shortly see. How well you do in the economy also has a lot to do with how well you anticipate government policy actions.

16-3c Price-Level Expectations and the *SRAS* Curve

We know that various factors can shift the *SRAS* curve: wage rates, the price of nonlabor inputs, supply shocks, and so on. In this chapter, we show how a change in expectations can lead to a shift in the *SRAS* curve.

Real Wage   The real (inflation-adjusted) wage is equal to the nominal wage divided by the price level:

$$\text{Real Wage} = \frac{\text{Nominal Wage}}{\text{Price Level}} \times 100$$

Suppose that the nominal wage is $40 and that the price level, as represented by a price index, is 110. The real wage is therefore $36.36: $40 ÷ 110. Obviously, a person's real wage will rise if either the nominal wage rises or the price level declines, or if both occur. For example, suppose the price level falls from 110 to 95. Then the real wage rises to

$42.10, and under certain conditions, as one's real wage rises, one chooses to work more. Conversely, as one's real wage falls, one chooses to work less. Thus,

> Price level falls → Real wage rises → Work more
>
> Price level rises → Real wage falls → Work less

Working More or Less and Shifts in the *SRAS* Curve   Labor is an input into the production process, so more labor (in terms of either individuals or labor hours) means more output. When people work more, more output is produced, so the *SRAS* curve shifts rightward. When people work less, less output is produced, so the *SRAS* curve shifts leftward.

Now we can connect the expected price level to the *SRAS* curve:

- *Example 1.* Suppose individuals expect the price level to decline. Then they expect their real wages to rise and will work more. Working more produces more output, so the *SRAS* curve shifts rightward. These logical relationships can be summed up as follows:

> Expect price level to fall → Expect real wage to rise → Work more → Produce
> more output → *SRAS* curve shifts rightward

- *Example 2.* Suppose individuals expect the price level to rise. Then they expect their real wage to decline and will work less. Working less produces less output, so the *SRAS* curve shifts leftward.

> Expect price level to rise → Expect real wage to fall → Work less → Produce
> less output → *SRAS* curve shifts leftward

Exhibit 6 shows three *SRAS* curves. After each curve is the expected price level in parentheses. The higher the expected price level is, the closer the *SRAS* curve lies to the vertical axis and the origin. The lower the expected price level is, the farther away from the vertical axis and the origin, the *SRAS* lies. Therefore, a rise in the expected price level will shift the *SRAS* curve to the left; a fall in the expected price level will shift the *SRAS* curve to the right.

> **EXHIBIT 6**

The Expected Price Level and the SRAS Curve

Every *SRAS* curve is based on some expected price level. For example, *SRAS*₁ in the exhibit is based on an *expected price level* of 150. As the expected price level rises, the *SRAS* curve shifts leftward; as the expected price level falls, the *SRAS* curve shifts rightward.

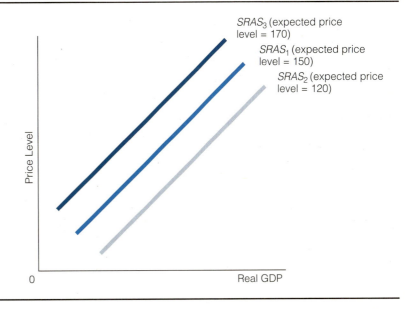

SRAS₃ (expected price level = 170)
SRAS₁ (expected price level = 150)
SRAS₂ (expected price level = 120)

Price Level

0   Real GDP

ECONOMICS 24/7

Bubbles and Expectations

An economic (speculative, market, or price) bubble is representative of high-volume buying activity in which the price of the good that is being bought (and sold) is far above the intrinsic worth of the good. To illustrate, suppose there is a house that can be rented for $24,000 a year. If the house has a life of, say, 20 years, then, by multiplying the annual rent times 24, we get a basic idea of the worth of the house, in this case $480,000. Now, suppose that the market price of the house is $500,000 in January, and it rises to $550,000 in six months, and about a year later the price is $630,000, and six months later the price has risen to $700,000. Moreover, let's suppose that what happens with this house (sharply rising prices above the intrinsic worth of the house as measured by its rent potential) is happening to many other houses too. What we could very well have then is a housing bubble.

Now, think of both adaptive and rational expectations in terms of a bubble. Would one of these kinds of expectations be more likely to generate a bubble than another? Think of two bubbles: the tulip mania bubble in Holland in the 17th century and the beanie babies bubble of the mid- to late 1990s in the United States. At the height of tulip mania, in 1637, some single tulip bulbs sold for 10 times the annual income of a skilled craftsman. Let's put that in today's terms. If a skilled craftsman today earns $70,000 a year, then some single tulip bulbs would sell for $700,000. That is a lot to pay for a single tulip bulb!

Now consider the beanie baby bubble. A beanie baby is a stuffed animal made by Ty, Inc. The original nine beanie babies were launched in 1993. If you buy a beanie baby today (such as Holiday Teddy), the price you will pay is about $5. In 1995, beanie babies started becoming collectibles, and the price of beanie babies increased dramatically. In the mid- to late 1990s, it was not uncommon to see long lines of customers lining up to buy beanie babies. On the secondary market, some beanie babies were selling for hundreds of dollars.

Both the tulip mania bubble and the beanie babies bubble burst. The price for single tulip bulbs and beanie babies reached a peak (far above its initial starting price) and then eventually plummeted.

Now ask yourself what many of the buyers of beanie babies and tulips at the time had to be thinking if they were paying (what in hindsight) turned out to be exorbitantly high prices for what they were buying. What was the person who paid $100 for a beanie baby that sold for $50 a day before thinking? What was the person in Holland thinking when he paid, say, 20 times more than what the single tulip bulb sold for just a month earlier? It's likely that their respective expectations of the future price of the beanie baby and the single tulip bulb went something like this: "Yes, I am paying a lot for a beanie baby or single tulip bulb, but I have seen, in the past, what prices have done—gone up and up and up—so I expect that the future will be like the past and prices will continue to go up and up and up. So, let me buy now at a relatively low price and sell later at a relatively high price."

In short, if people hold adaptive expectations, they are always looking *over their shoulders* to see what *has happened* and then expecting that the future will be similar to the past. With adaptive expectations, it is easy to understand why bubbles might originate in the first place and continue for a time.

But if expectations are rational, then the whole idea of a bubble originating in the first place, much less continuing on for a long time, comes into question. That's because people with rational expectations are looking forward, to the future (not simply "back over their shoulders," to the past). More importantly, since people with rational expectations are forward looking, they have more of a strategic chesslike sense about them than do people with adaptive expectations. They are more likely to ask themselves, "If he does X, then I think it is best for me to do Y, but if he does A, then it better for me to do B, etc."

What would the person with rational expectations have thought at the height of the beanie babies craze? He likely would have thought that the prices of beanie babies were rising far above the stuffed animals' initial, original, and even intrinsic value as a child's toy and that sometime in the future people would realize this, at which time they would stop paying more for beanie babies. Then the long rise in prices would stop and prices would begin to fall, precipitating even greater and faster declines in

price once people decided to sell today before the prices went down tomorrow.

So, of the two types of expectations theory, adaptive and rational, bubbles are less likely to exist (originate and continue for some time) if people's expectations are rational than if they are adaptive. That's why economists who are proponents of rational expectations are more likely than those who are proponents of adaptive expectations to say, "What you think is a bubble—housing, beanie babies, tulips—can't be a bubble, because bubbles don't exist in a world of rational expectations."

ECONOMICS 24/7

Rational Expectations in the College Classroom

If people hold rational expectations, then the outcome of a policy will be different if the policy is unanticipated than if it is anticipated. Specifically, unanticipated policy changes can move the economy away from the natural unemployment rate, but correctly anticipated policy changes cannot. Does something similar happen in a college classroom?

© Wavebreakmedia/Shutterstock.com

Suppose Anthony's history class starts at 9:00 a.m. and he "naturally" arrives 1 minute before class starts. In other words, his so-called natural waiting time is 1 minute.

The first day of class, Anthony arrives at 8:59, his instructor arrives at 8:59:30, and he starts class promptly at 9:00 a.m.

The second day of class, Anthony arrives at 8:59, his instructor arrives at 9:01:30, and he starts class at 9:02 a.m. On this day, Anthony has waited 3 minutes, which is more than his natural waiting time of 1 minute.

The timing of the start of class on the third, fourth, and fifth days is the same as on the second, so, for the second through fifth days, Anthony is operating at more than his natural waiting time.

The theory of rational expectations holds that people will not continue to make the same mistake. In this case, Anthony will take his professor's recent arrival time into account and adjust his timing accordingly. Thus, on the sixth day of class, instead of arriving at 8:59, Anthony arrives at 9:01. This day, the instructor again arrives at 9:01:30 and begins class at 9:02 a.m., and Anthony has moved back to his natural waiting time of 1 minute.

So far, Anthony's natural waiting time was met on the first day of class. On the second through fifth days of class, the professor obviously changed his policy as to his arrival time. Anthony didn't anticipate this change of policy, so he was fooled into waiting more than his natural waiting time. But Anthony did not continue to make the same mistake: He adjusted to his professor's policy change and went back to his 1-minute natural waiting time.

Now let's change the scenario. At the end of the first day of class, the professor announces, "I know I arrived at class at 8:59:30 today, but I won't do that again. From now on, I will arrive at 9:01:30."

In this situation, the professor has announced his policy change. Anthony hears the announcement and correctly anticipates the professor's arrival time from now on. With that information, he adjusts his behavior: Instead of arriving at class at 8:59, he arrives at 9:01. Thus, Anthony has correctly anticipated his professor's policy change, and he will remain at his natural waiting time. (He will not move from it, even temporarily.)

16-3d Expected and Actual Price Levels

The difference between an actual price level and an expected price level is fairly clear:

- The *actual price level* is exactly what it sounds like: the price level that actually exists. For example, someone might say that the price level today is 140. This, then, is the actual price level. We will use P_A to represent the actual price level.

- The *expected price level* is what you expect the price level will be sometime in the future. For example, you might expect that the price level in, say, one year will be 150. This is your expected price level. We will use P_{EX} to represent the expected price level.

Obviously, individuals' expectations (P_{EX}) can have one of three relationships to the actual price level (P_A):

$$P_{EX} = P_A$$

$$P_{EX} > P_A$$

$$P_{EX} < P_A$$

To illustrate, suppose the Fed increases the money supply and the *AD* curve shifts rightward. Then, if the *SRAS* curve is upward sloping, there will be a short-run and a long-run effect on the price level. Suppose that, when the economy is back in long-run equilibrium, the actual price level (P_A) will be 155. But when the Fed increases the money supply, you expect that the price level in the future will be 165. In other words, your expected price level is greater than the actual price level: $P_{EX} > P_A$. Obviously, you made a mistake: you overestimated what the price level would be. You "guessed" too high. In the new classical theoretical framework using rational expectations, "guessing" too high, too low, or just right can have an effect on the economy. We show how next.

16-3e New Classical Economics and Four Different Cases

New classical theory holds that individuals have rational expectations and that prices and wages are flexible. With these two points in mind, we apply new classical theory to four different cases (or settings):

- Case 1: Policy Correctly Anticipated
- Case 2: Policy Incorrectly Anticipated (Bias Upward)
- Case 3: Policy Incorrectly Anticipated (Bias Downward)
- Case 4: Policy Unanticipated

Each setting relates to a different perspective individuals have with respect to economic policy. We discuss monetary policy, but everything we say with respect to monetary policy in the upcoming discussion also holds for demand-side fiscal policy.

Case 1: Policy Correctly Anticipated Suppose an economy is in long-run equilibrium, as shown at point 1 in Exhibit 7. The actual price level is 100, and $SRAS_1$ is based on the expected price level of 100. In other words, in long-run equilibrium the actual price level (P_A) and the expected price level (P_{EX}) are the same.

$$\text{Starting point: } P_A = P_{EX}$$

Now the Fed increases the money supply, and this Fed policy action is *correctly anticipated* by the public. What "correctly anticipated" means here is that individuals know not

> **EXHIBIT 7**

Policy Correctly Anticipated

We assume that rational expectations hold, that wages and prices are flexible, that any policy action is anticipated correctly, and that the economy is in long-run equilibrium. The actual price level is 100, and the expected price level (on which the $SRAS_1$ curve is based) is also 100. The Fed increases the money supply, and the AD curve shifts rightward. Because policy is anticipated correctly, individuals know that the new long-run equilibrium price level will be 110. Knowing this, they change their expected price level to 110. As a result, the $SRAS$ curve shifts leftward from $SRAS_1$ to $SRAS_2$. Keep in mind that AD and $SRAS$ change at the same time. In other words, the AD curve shifts rightward at the same time that the $SRAS$ curve shifts leftward. The result is that the Fed's action leads to a higher price level but does not change Real GDP. The action is ineffective at changing Real GDP; thus, we have the policy ineffectiveness proposition (PIP) holding.

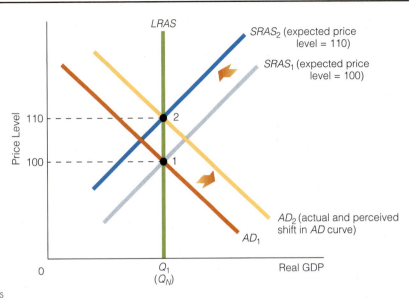

only that the Fed is increasing the money supply, but also how much the money supply is increasing and what the actual price level will be when the economy reaches its new long-run equilibrium position. The exhibit shows that the actual price level *will be* 110 when the economy reaches its new long-run equilibrium at point 2.

So, how does the fact that individuals are correctly anticipating policy (and the consequences of that policy) affect the *expected price level*? If individuals know where the actual price level is headed (i.e., to 110), they will immediately change their expected price level to 110. Look at it this way: reality is changing in the economy; the price level is going to rise from 100 to 110 because of the Fed's action. Correctly anticipating the new price level is like having a crystal ball and knowing exactly what is going to happen. Consequently, individuals immediately change their expectations of the future on the basis of their correctly viewed perception of what is really going to happen.

Now, if the expected price level changes to 110, the $SRAS$ curve in the exhibit will shift leftward from $SRAS_1$ to $SRAS_2$. However, the $SRAS$ curve shifts leftward at essentially the same time that the AD curve shifts rightward. The economy therefore moves from point 1 (its starting point) to point 2 (or ending point).

Exhibit 7 shows that, even though the Fed increases the money supply (and the AD curve shifts rightward), Real GDP does not change. We started at Q_1 (or Q_N) and ended up at Q_1 (or Q_N). Therefore, if policy is correctly anticipated and if rational expectations hold, the only thing an increase in the money supply does in the economy is raise the price level. It does not change Real GDP. In other words, the Fed policy action was ineffective at changing Real GDP. This scenario represents what economists call the **policy ineffectiveness proposition (PIP)**.

Case 2: Policy Incorrectly Anticipated (Bias Upward) Again, an economy starts at long-run equilibrium, shown as point 1 in Exhibit 8. The two operative (i.e., true) curves

Policy Ineffectiveness Proposition (PIP)

If (1) a policy change is correctly anticipated, (2) individuals form their expectations rationally, and (3) wages and prices are flexible, then neither fiscal policy nor monetary policy is effective at meeting macroeconomic goals.

> **EXHIBIT 8**

Policy Incorrectly Anticipated—Bias Upward

(1) The economy starts in long-run equilibrium at point 1 and $P_A = P_{EX}$. (2) The Fed increases the money supply, and the AD curve actually shifts rightward from AD_1 to AD_2. (3) Individuals have incorrectly anticipated the Fed's action: They believe that the Fed has increased the money supply more than it actually has, so they believe that the AD curve has shifted from AD_1 to AD_3. This is a mistake. (4) Mistakenly assuming that the AD curve has shifted rightward from AD_1 to AD_3, individuals think that the new actual price level will end up being 118, the value at which the AD_3 curve intersects the $LRAS$ curve. Accordingly, they change their expected price level to 118, and the $SRAS$ curve shifts leftward from $SRAS_1$ to $SRAS_2$. (5) The short-run equilibrium for the economy turns out to be at point 2. (6) Eventually, individuals figure out that they made a mistake—that the real AD curve is AD_2, not AD_3. So the new long-run equilibrium will be 110, not 118 (as earlier believed). As a result, individuals now readjust their expected price level down from 118 to 110. Accordingly, the $SRAS$ curve shifts rightward from $SRAS_2$ to $SRAS_3$. The economy is now in long-run equilibrium at point 3, and the expected price level is equal to the actual price level.

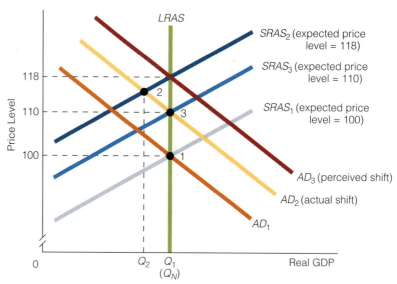

are AD_1 and $SRAS_1$. $SRAS_1$ is based on an expected price level (P_{EX}) of 100, which is the same as the actual price level (P_A).

$$\text{Starting point: } P_A = P_{EX}$$

Once again, the Fed increases the money supply, and the AD curve shifts rightward from AD_1 to AD_2. This time, however, individuals mistakenly believe that the AD curve has shifted rightward by more than it actually has. In other words, they mistakenly think that the AD curve has shifted from AD_1 to AD_3. Individuals have thus *incorrectly antici-pated policy with an upward bias*.

Obviously, individuals have made a mistake, and this mistake is going to have conse-quences. Specifically, because individuals mistakenly believe that the AD curve in the economy is AD_3 now, they think that the new long-run equilibrium price level (the point at which AD_3 intersects $LRAS$) will be 118; that is, their expected price level is 118. But the actual price level is never going to be 118. The actual price level in the future is going to be 110, the point at which AD_2 intersects $LRAS$. So the expected price level is higher than what the actual price will be:

$$P_{EX} > P_A$$

Now as a result of individuals changing their expected price level from 100 to 118, the $SRAS$ curve shifts leftward from $SRAS_1$ to $SRAS_2$. So far, then, the AD curve has actually shifted from AD_1 to AD_2 and the $SRAS$ curve has shifted from $SRAS_1$ to $SRAS_2$. So, in the short run, the economy ends up at the intersection of AD_2 and $SRAS_2$—that is, at point 2 in the exhibit. This is an odd result, because we are accustomed to believing that an increase in the money supply leads to higher, not lower, Real GDP in the short run, but that is not what we see in Exhibit 8. Instead, Real GDP has fallen from Q_1 to Q_2. In other words, expansionary monetary policy has actually led to a decline in Real GDP. But why? It happened because of the mistake people made: they anticipated the Fed action incorrectly—with a bias upward.

The time will come when individuals realize that they made a mistake. In time, they will realize that the price level never actually increased to 118 and that AD_3 in the exhibit never really existed. They only perceived all that. In time, they will realize that the operative AD curve in the economy is AD_2 and that the long-run equilibrium price level consistent with this aggregate demand curve is 110. Accordingly, they will adjust their expected price level downward from 118 to 110. As they do, the $SRAS$ curve shifts rightward from $SRAS_2$ to $SRAS_3$ and the economy moves into long-run equilibrium at point 3, where $P_A = P_{EX}$.

Let's recap: (1) The economy starts in long-run equilibrium at point 1, and $P_A = P_{EX}$. (2) The Fed increases the money supply, and the AD curve actually shifts rightward from AD_1 to AD_2. (3) Individuals have incorrectly anticipated the Fed's action. They believe that the Fed has increased the money supply more than it actually did, so they also believe that the AD curve has shifted from AD_1 to AD_3. This is a mistake. (4) Mistakenly assuming that the AD curve has shifted rightward from AD_1 to AD_3, individuals think that the new actual price level will end up being 118, which is where the AD_3 curve intersects the $LRAS$ curve. Accordingly, they change their expected price level to 118, and the $SRAS$ curve shifts leftward from $SRAS_1$ to $SRAS_2$. (5) The short-run equilibrium for the economy turns out to be at point 2. Interestingly, because individuals have incorrectly anticipated policy with a bias upward, an increase in the money supply actually leads to a decline in Real GDP in the short run. (6) Eventually, individuals figure out that they made a mistake—that the real AD curve is AD_2, not AD_3. So the new long-run equilibrium will be 110, not 118 (as earlier believed). As a result, individuals now adjust their expected price level down from 118 to 110. Accordingly, the $SRAS$ curve shifts rightward from $SRAS_2$ to $SRAS_3$. The economy is now in long-run equilibrium at point 3, and the expected price level is equal to the actual price level.

Case 3: Policy Incorrectly Anticipated (Bias Downward)

Just as individuals can incorrectly anticipate policy with a bias upward, they can also incorrectly anticipate policy with a bias downward. In Exhibit 9, an economy starts in long-run equilibrium at point 1. The Fed then increases the money supply, and the AD curve shifts from AD_1 to AD_2. Individuals mistakenly think that the AD curve has shifted from AD_1 to AD_3. In other words, they believe that the Fed has increased the money supply by less than it actually has. They have incorrectly anticipated policy with a bias downward.

Because individuals have incorrectly anticipated policy with a bias downward, they mistakenly believe that the new actual long-run equilibrium price level will be 110. So they change their expected price level from 100 to 110, and the $SRAS$ curve shifts leftward from $SRAS_1$ to $SRAS_2$. Short-run equilibrium for the economy now comes at the intersection of AD_2 and $SRAS_2$—that is, at point 2. In the short run, an increase in the money supply has increased Real GDP from Q_1 to Q_2.

Eventually, individuals realize that they have made a mistake. Eventually, they realize that AD_3 does not exist and that AD_2 is the only operative AD curve in the economy.

> **EXHIBIT 9**

Policy Incorrectly Anticipated—Bias Downward

An economy starts in long-run equilibrium at point 1. The expected price level is equal to the actual price level. The Fed increases the money supply, and the AD curve shifts rightward from AD_1 to AD_2. However, individuals mistakenly believe that the AD curve has shifted rightward by less, from AD_1 to AD_3. As a result of this misunderstanding, individuals mistakenly believe that the new long-run equilibrium price level will be 110. They then change their expected price level to 110, and the $SRAS$ curve shifts leftward from $SRAS_1$ to $SRAS_2$. The short-run equilibrium in the economy comes at point 2. Eventually, individuals realize their mistake. They come to understand that AD_2 is the only operative AD curve in the economy and that the long-run equilibrium price level consistent with AD_2 is 115. Accordingly, they revise their expected price level from 110 to 115, and the $SRAS$ curve shifts leftward from $SRAS_2$ to $SRAS_3$. The economy moves into long-run equilibrium at point 3.

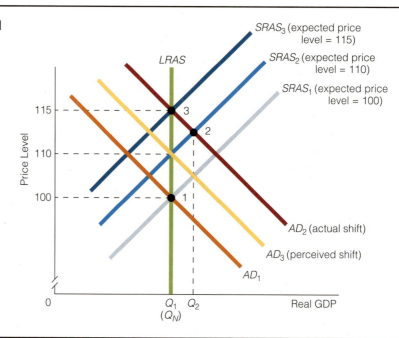

So the new long-run equilibrium price level will be 115. Realizing that the long-run equilibrium level will be 115, individuals revise their expected price level from 110 to 115, and the $SRAS$ curve shifts from $SRAS_2$ to $SRAS_3$. The economy is now in long-run equilibrium at point 3, and the expected price level equals the actual price level.

Case 4: Policy Unanticipated   Besides correctly anticipating the new price level and incorrectly anticipating it with an upward or a downward bias, the only possibility left is not anticipating it at all.

In Exhibit 10, an economy starts in long-run equilibrium at point 1. Here, the actual price level equals the expected price level. Then the Fed increases the money supply, and the AD curve shifts rightward from AD_1 to AD_2. In this case, individuals do not anticipate the Fed's policy action; it is unanticipated. What this means is that individuals do not notice that the AD curve in the economy has shifted. They mistakenly believe that AD_1 (not AD_2) is the operative AD curve in the economy. Because they do not know that the AD curve has shifted, they do not expect any change in the price level. They expect it to remain at 100. Individuals therefore have no reason to revise their expected price level, and it stays at 100.

In the short run, the economy moves to point 2. So a rising money supply leads to a rise in Real GDP in the short run. In time, individuals will realize that things have changed and that the Fed's action has shifted the AD curve rightward. In short, they will come to realize that the operative AD curve in the economy is AD_2, not AD_1. Individuals will then realize that the long-run equilibrium price level consistent with AD_2 is 115. Accordingly, they will revise their expected price level upward to 115, and the $SRAS$ curve will shift leftward from $SRAS_1$ to $SRAS_2$. The economy will move into long-run equilibrium at point 3, and the expected price level will be equal to the actual price level.

Policy Unanticipated

An economy starts in long-run equilibrium at point 1. The Fed increases the money supply, and the *AD* curve shifts rightward from AD_1 to AD_2. The policy action by the Fed is unanticipated, so individuals mistakenly believe that the *AD* curve in the economy has not shifted. Thus, there is no reason for them to believe that the price level will soon change and therefore no reason for them to revise their expected price level. As a result, the *SRAS* curve does not shift and in the short run the economy moves to point 2. In time, individuals revise their expected price level upward and the *SRAS* curve shifts leftward. The economy moves back into long-run equilibrium at point 3.

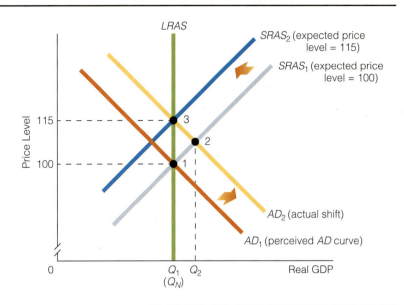

16-3f Comparing Exhibits 9 and 10

The short-run equilibrium positions in Exhibits 9 and 10 led to the same conclusion: an increase in the money supply could increase Real GDP in the short run. In Exhibit 10, the policy was unanticipated; in Exhibit 9, we assumed that the policy was incorrectly anticipated—biased downward. So how could two very different assumptions lead to the same short-run outcome? The answer is that Q_2 in Exhibit 10 represents a higher Real GDP level than Q_2 in Exhibit 9. For example, if Q_2 in Exhibit 10 is $12 trillion, then Q_2

THINKING LIKE AN ECONOMIST

What People Think Can Matter to Outcomes Think of how economics might differ from chemistry. In chemistry, if you add two molecules of hydrogen to one molecule of oxygen, you always get water. What is often frustrating to economists is that sometimes the layperson thinks that economics works like chemistry: X plus Y should always give us Z. Sadly, that is not how economics works. If you add expansionary monetary policy to an economy, you don't always get a rise in short-run Real GDP. Sometimes you get a rise (when policy is unanticipated), sometimes no change (when policy is correctly anticipated), and other times a decline (when policy is incorrectly anticipated by being biased upward).

The factor affecting economics that is not at work in chemistry is the human factor. What new classical economists teach us about human beings is that their perceptions of things (vis-à-vis reality) have a large part to play in determining outcomes.

ECONOMICS 24/7

Deficits, Money, Expectations, and Unintended Effects

Suppose Congress continually takes actions that result in large budget deficits, and every time the deficit increases, the Fed says that it will not monetize it. Monetizing the deficit means turning the Treasury securities that have been issued to finance the deficit into money. Here is an example of monetizing the deficit: On Monday, the Congress increases government purchases; as a result, the deficit rises by $100 billion. To finance the $100 billion addition to the deficit, the Treasury has to borrow the funds. It does so by issuing (selling) Treasury securities (Treasury debt). Commercial banks buy these newly issued Treasury securities and hold them as assets. Later, the Fed steps in and conducts an open market purchase, buying the Treasury securities from the banks. As a result of the purchase, reserves in the banking system rise and banks can create new loans (checkable deposits). If the banks then choose to do so, the money supply rises. The effect: what started off as an increase in the deficit has ended with an increase in the money supply. The deficit has been monetized.

Now suppose that every time the Fed promises not to monetize the deficit, it breaks its promise. In other words, the deficit rises, the Fed promises not to monetize the deficit (the promise), but it ends up monetizing the deficit anyway (the action). The promise is different from the action.

It isn't likely that promises which are not consistent with actions will be believed. More likely, individuals will soon learn to translate promises into expected actions. In other words, the Fed says it will not monetize the deficit, and individuals translate the Fed statement into "We [the Fed] will probably end up monetizing at least some of the deficit."

What does all this mean in terms of expectations and unintended effects on the economy? To answer the question, suppose the economy is in long-run equilibrium, producing Natural Real GDP. Suddenly, members of Congress undertake policy actions that increase the size of the deficit. Soon after, the Fed states that it will not monetize the deficit, but—and here is the point—the Fed has made that statement before and then taken different actions. So this time individuals expect the Fed to end up monetizing some of the deficit anyway. As a result, they expect the *AD* curve in the economy to shift rightward and the price level to rise. On the basis of what they perceive as a soon-to-be rising price level, they revise their expected price level upward, and then the *SRAS* curve shifts leftward.

Now, suppose this time the Fed actually holds to its promise and does not monetize the deficit. All of a sudden, the Fed's actions match its promise. What happens now? The *SRAS* curve has shifted leftward, but the *AD* curve remains unchanged. The result is a short-run decline in Real GDP below Natural Real GDP. The economy is now in a recessionary gap.

The economy ended up in a recessionary gap because

- the Fed had previously made promises that it didn't keep.

- individuals learned to translate Fed promises into likely actions, even if the actions were inconsistent with the promises.

- individuals based their behavior on what they thought the Fed would do given its past performance.

- This time, the Fed kept to its promise; as a result, the economy moved into a recessionary gap.

The lesson: If the Fed says one thing and continually does another, then unintended effects may follow when it does what it says it will do. The unintended effect in our example was the economy falling into a recessionary gap.

in Exhibit 9 is less—say, $11 trillion. If we assumed that the policy was unanticipated in Exhibit 9, the short-run equilibrium point would be, not at point 2, but at the intersection of the AD_2 and $SRAS_1$ curves. This point is not identified in Exhibit 9, but it is to the "southeast" of point 2. If we viewed the Real GDP level that corresponds to this point, it would be greater than Q_2 in the exhibit.

> **EXHIBIT 10**

ECONOMICS 24/7

The Money Supply, an Increase in Productivity, and What You Think

Think about your study of macroeconomics in earlier chapters. You learned that changes in such things as taxes, government purchases, interest rates, the money supply, and more could change Real GDP, the price level, and the unemployment rate. For example, starting with the economy in long-run equilibrium, a rise in the money supply will raise Real GDP in the short run and raise the price level in the long run. Or consider that an increase in productivity can shift the *SRAS* curve to the right and thus bring about a change in Real GDP and the price level. In short, most of this text discusses how changes in real variables can affect the economy.

With the introduction of expectations theory, we move to a different level of analysis. Now we learn that what people think can also affect the economy. In other words, not only can a change in the world's oil supply affect the economy—almost everyone would expect that—but so can whether or not someone believes that the Fed will increase the money supply.

Think back to our discussion of rational expectations and incorrectly anticipated policy (e.g., bias upward). Suppose the economy is in long-run equilibrium when the Fed undertakes an expansionary monetary policy move. The Fed expects to increase the money supply by, say, $30 billion, but somehow economic agents believe that the increase in the money supply will be closer

Dougal Waters/Digital Vision/Getty Images

to $70 billion. In other words, economic agents think that the money supply will rise by more than it will actually rise. Does it matter that their thoughts are wrong? Expectations theory says it does. As we showed in Exhibit 8, incorrect thoughts can lead to lower Real GDP and higher prices—just as a cutback in the world's oil supply can lead to lower Real GDP and higher prices. In other words, "what's in people's heads" and "a cutback in the world's oil supply" can have the same effects. In other words, what we think can affect what happens in the economy. Who would have thought it?

SELF-TEST

1. Does the PIP always hold?
2. When policy is unanticipated, what difference is there between the natural rate theory built on adaptive expectations and the natural rate theory built on rational expectations?
3. Identify the changes in the price level and Real GDP in both the short run and the long run as a result of the Fed's increasing the money supply. Assume that the Fed's action is incorrectly anticipated (by being biased upward), that wages and prices are flexible, and that individuals hold rational expectations.

16-4 NEW KEYNESIANS AND RATIONAL EXPECTATIONS

The new classical theory assumes that wages and prices are flexible. In this theory, an increase in the expected price level results in an immediate and equal rise in wages and prices and the aggregate supply curve immediately shifts to the long-run equilibrium position.

In response to the new classical assumption of flexible wages and prices, a few economists developed what has come to be known as the *new Keynesian rational expectations theory*. This theory assumes that rational expectations are a reasonable characterization of how expectations are formed, but it drops the new classical assumption of complete wage and price flexibility. According to the theory, long-term labor contracts often prevent wages and prices from fully adjusting to changes in the expected price level. (In other words, prices and wages are somewhat sticky, are rigid, or are inflexible.)

Consider the possible situation at the end of the first year of a three-year wage contract. Workers realize that the actual price level is higher than they expected when they negotiated the contract, but they are unable to do much about it because their wages are locked in for the next two years. Price rigidity might also come into play because firms often engage in fixed-price contracts with their suppliers. As discussed in Chapter 10, Keynesian economists today assert that, for microeconomic-based reasons, long-term labor contracts and above-market wages are sometimes in the best interest of both employers and employees (the efficiency wage theory).

To see what the theory predicts, look at Exhibit 11. The economy is initially in long-run equilibrium at point 1. The public correctly anticipates an increase in aggregate demand from AD_1 to AD_2, and as a result, the expected price level changes. Because of some wage and price rigidities, however, the short-run aggregate supply

> **EXHIBIT 11**

The Short-Run Response to Aggregate Demand–Increasing Policy (in the New Keynesian Theory)

Starting with the economy at point 1, an increase in aggregate demand is correctly anticipated. As a result, the short-run aggregate supply curve shifts leftward, but not all the way to $SRAS_2$ (as would be the case in the new classical theory). Instead, it shifts only to $SRAS'_2$ because of some wage and price rigidities; the economy moves to point 2′ (in the short run), and Real GDP increases from Q_N to Q_A. If the policy had been unanticipated, Real GDP would have increased from Q_N to Q_{UA}.

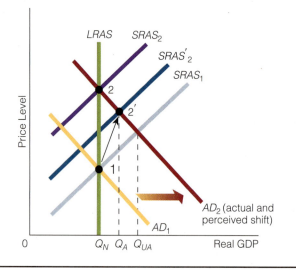

curve does not shift all the way from $SRAS_1$ to $SRAS_2$ and the economy does not move from point 1 to point 2 (as in new classical theory). Instead, the short-run aggregate supply curve shifts to $SRAS'_2$ because rigidities prevent complete wage and price adjustments. In the short run, the economy moves from point 1 to point 2', from Q_N to Q_A. Had the policy been unanticipated, Real GDP would have increased from Q_N to Q_{UA} in the short run.

16-5 LOOKING AT THINGS FROM THE SUPPLY SIDE: REAL BUSINESS CYCLE THEORISTS

Throughout this chapter, changes in Real GDP have originated on the demand side of the economy. When discussing the Friedman natural rate theory, the new classical theory, and the new Keynesian theory, we began our analysis by shifting the *AD* curve to the right. Then we explained what happens in the economy as a result. The presentation so far in this chapter seems to assume that all changes in Real GDP originate on the demand side of the economy. In fact, some economists believe this assumption to be true.

Other economists do not. One group of such economists, called *real business cycle theorists*, believe that changes on the supply side of the economy can lead to changes in both Real GDP and unemployment. Real business cycle theorists argue that a decrease in Real GDP (which refers to the contractionary part of a business cycle) can be brought about by a major supply-side change that reduces the capacity of the economy to produce. Moreover, they argue that what looks like a contraction in Real GDP originating on the demand side of the economy can be, in essence, the effect of what has happened on the supply side.

In Exhibit 12, an adverse supply shock reduces the capacity of the economy to produce. This effect is represented by a shift inward in the economy's production possibilities frontier, or a leftward shift in the long-run aggregate supply curve from $LRAS_1$ to $LRAS_2$. The shift moves the economy from point *A* to point *B*. As shown in the exhibit, a leftward shift in the long-run aggregate supply curve means that Natural Real GDP has fallen.

As a result of the leftward shift in the *LRAS* curve and the decline in Real GDP, firms reduce their demand for labor and scale back employment. Then, because of the lower demand for labor (putting downward pressure on money wages) and the higher price level, real wages fall. As real wages fall, workers choose to work less and unemployed persons choose to extend the length of their unemployment. As a result, workers have less income and their lower incomes soon lead them to reduce consumption.

Either because consumption has fallen or because businesses have become pessimistic (prompted by the decline in the productive potential of the economy), or for both reasons, businesses have less incentive to invest. As a result, firms borrow less from banks, the volume of outstanding loans falls, and thus the money supply falls. A decrease in the money supply causes the aggregate demand curve to shift leftward, from AD_1 to AD_2 in Exhibit 12, and the economy moves to point *C*.

> **EXHIBIT 12**

Real Business Cycle Theory

We start with a supply-side change capable of reducing the capacity of the economy to produce. The change is manifested by a leftward shift of the long-run aggregate supply curve from $LRAS_1$ to $LRAS_2$ and a fall in the Natural Real GDP level from Q_{N1} to Q_{N2}. A reduction in the productive capacity of the economy filters to the demand side and, in our example, reduces consumption, investment, and the money supply. The aggregate demand curve shifts leftward from AD_1 to AD_2.

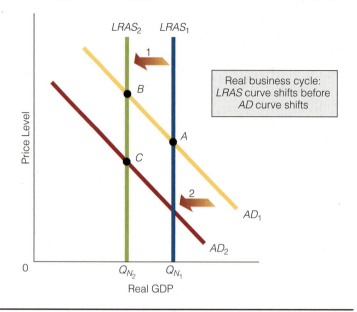

Real business cycle:
$LRAS$ curve shifts before AD curve shifts

Real business cycle theorists sometimes point out how easily a demand-induced decline in Real GDP can be confused with a supply-induced decline. In our example, both the aggregate supply side and the aggregate demand side of the economy change but the aggregate supply side changes first. If the change in aggregate supply is overlooked, and only the changes in aggregate demand (or, specifically, a change in one of the variables that can change aggregate demand, such as the money supply) are observed, then the contraction in Real GDP will appear to be demand induced. In terms of Exhibit 12, the leftward shift in the $LRAS$ curve would be overlooked, but the leftward shift in the AD curve would be observed, giving the impression that the contraction is demand induced.

If real business cycle theorists are correct, the cause–effect analysis of a contraction in Real GDP would be turned upside down. As just one example, changes in the money supply may be an *effect* of a contraction in Real GDP (originating on the supply side of the economy), not its *cause*.

SELF-TEST

1. *The Wall Street Journal* reports that the money supply has recently declined. Is the decline consistent with a demand-induced business cycle, with a supply-induced business cycle, or with both? Explain your answer.

2. How are new Keynesians, who believe that people hold rational expectations, different from new classical economists, who also believe that people hold rational expectations?

Office  Hours

"Does New Classical Theory Call the Effects of Fiscal and Monetary Policy into Question?"

STUDENT:

When I started this course in macroeconomics, I was hoping to learn the unequivocal answers to some simple questions, such as what effect does fiscal policy have on the economy? And what effect does monetary policy have on the economy? I don't think I am getting the answers. For example, fiscal and monetary policies seem to have different effects on Real GDP in the short run, depending on whether the policies are unanticipated, incorrectly anticipated, or correctly anticipated. Am I right about this?

INSTRUCTOR:

You're right. A given policy action (such as expansionary monetary policy) can have different effects on Real GDP (in the short run), depending on whether the policy is unanticipated, correctly anticipated, and so on.

STUDENT:

What am I supposed to learn from this?

INSTRUCTOR:

The obvious point, which you've identified, is that policies have different effects, depending on the degree to which individuals correctly anticipate the policies. The not-so-obvious point is that it might not be wise to use government policy actions to stabilize the economy.

STUDENT:

How do you come to that point? What are the details?

INSTRUCTOR:

Let's say that the economy is currently in a recessionary gap and Real GDP is $11 trillion. Policy makers want to raise the GDP level to Natural Real GDP at, say, $11.2 trillion. To achieve this goal, either expansionary fiscal or monetary policy is implemented. Are we guaranteed that Real GDP will rise from $11 trillion to $11.2 trillion?

STUDENT:

No.

INSTRUCTOR:

Why is that?

STUDENT:

Well, according to the new classical economists, it's because individuals may incorrectly anticipate the policy in such a way as to reduce Real GDP instead of raising it.

INSTRUCTOR:

That's right. Suppose, for example, the Fed plans to raise the money supply by $100 billion but the public mistakenly believes that the Fed will raise the money supply by, say, $180 billion. Then, in the short run, the *AD* curve will shift to the right and the *SRAS* curve will to shift to the left but the *SRAS* curve will shift left by more than the *AD* curve will shift to the right. (That is what was shown in Exhibit 8.) And the result will be a decline, not an increase, in Real GDP—at least in the short run.

STUDENT:

So the monetary policy action can end up doing the very opposite of what it was intended to do. It was intended to raise Real GDP, but it lowered it instead.

INSTRUCTOR:

That's correct. What the new classical economists are really pointing out is that we can't always be sure of a discretionary policy action's effect on Real GDP. In turn, the uncertainty should make economists less sure, or a little more humble, when it comes to advocating certain economic policy actions for government to implement.

Points to remember

1. According to the new classical economists, economic policy actions may not always have the intended effect on Real GDP in the short run.
2. Economic policy actions may accomplish the opposite of what they were intended to accomplish.

CHAPTER SUMMARY

THE PHILLIPS CURVE

- In 1958, A. W. Phillips plotted a curve to a set of data points. The curve exhibited an inverse relationship between wage inflation and unemployment, and came to be known as the Phillips curve. From the Phillips curve, economists concluded that neither the combination of low inflation and low unemployment nor the combination of high inflation and high unemployment was likely.

- Economists Paul Samuelson and Robert Solow fit a Phillips curve to the U.S. economy. Instead of measuring wage inflation against unemployment rates (as Phillips did), they measured price inflation against unemployment rates and found an inverse relationship between the two variables.

- On the basis of the findings of Phillips and of Samuelson and Solow, economists concluded that (1) stagflation, or high inflation and high unemployment, is extremely unlikely and (2) the Phillips curve presents policy makers with a menu of different combinations of inflation and unemployment rates.

FRIEDMAN NATURAL RATE THEORY

- Milton Friedman pointed out that there are two types of Phillips curves: a short-run and a long-run Phillips curve. The short-run Phillips curve exhibits the inflation–unemployment trade-off; the long-run Phillips curve does not. Consideration of both short- and long-run Phillips curves opened macroeconomics to expectations theory.

- The Friedman natural rate theory holds that, in the short run, a decrease (increase) in inflation is linked to an increase (decrease) in unemployment, but in the long run the economy returns to its natural rate of unemployment. In other words, there is a trade-off between inflation and unemployment in the short run, but not in the long run.

- The Friedman natural rate theory was expressed in terms of adaptive expectations, according to which individuals formed their inflation expectations by considering past inflation rates. Later, some economists expressed the theory in terms of rational expectations. Rational expectations theory holds that individuals form their expected inflation rate by considering present and past inflation rates, as well as all other available and relevant information—in particular, the effects of present and future policy actions.

NEW CLASSICAL THEORY

- Implicit in the new classical theory are two assumptions: (1) Individuals form their expectations rationally and (2) wages and prices are completely flexible.

- In the new classical theory, policy has different effects (1) when it is unanticipated, (2) when it is incorrectly anticipated, bias upward, (3) when it is incorrectly anticipated, bias downward and (4) when it is correctly anticipated. To illustrate, consider two cases: (A) when policy is incorrectly anticipated, bias upward and (B) when policy is correctly anticipated. Assume that in both cases a demand-side policy increases aggregate demand in the economy. Then, in case A, the *AD* curve will shift rightward by less than the *SRAS* initially shifts leftward, bringing about a decline in Real GDP in the short run. In case B, the *AD* curve will shift rightward to the same degree and at the same time as, but in the opposite direction of, the *SRAS* curve. In this case, Real GDP does not change.

NEW KEYNESIAN THEORY

- Implicit in the new Keynesian theory are two assumptions: (1) Individuals form their expectations rationally and (2) wages and prices are not completely flexible in the short run.

- The economic effects predicted by the new classical theory and the new Keynesian theory if policy is correctly anticipated are not the same in the short run. Because the new Keynesian theory assumes that wages and prices are not completely flexible in the short run, given an anticipated change in aggregate demand, the short-run aggregate supply curve cannot immediately shift to its long-run equilibrium position. The new Keynesian theory predicts a short-run trade-off between inflation and unemployment (in the Phillips curve framework).

REAL BUSINESS CYCLE THEORY

- According to real business cycle theory, real business cycle contractions (in Real GDP) originate on the supply side of the economy. A contraction in Real GDP might follow this pattern: (1) An adverse supply shock reduces the economy's ability to produce. (2) The *LRAS* curve shifts leftward. (3) As a result, Real GDP declines and the price level rises. (4) The number of persons employed falls, as do real wages, owing to a decrease in the demand for labor (lowering money wages) and a higher price level. (5) Incomes decline. (6) Consumption and investment decline. (7) The volume of outstanding loans declines. (8) The money supply falls. (9) The *AD* curve shifts leftward.

KEY TERMS AND CONCEPTS

Phillips Curve	Friedman Natural Rate	Adaptive Expectations	Policy Ineffectiveness
Stagflation	Theory	Rational Expectations	Proposition (PIP)

VIDEO QUESTIONS AND PROBLEMS

Video Questions and Problems are available on MindTap for Arnold 12e or by searching for Arnold on www.cengagebrain.com

1. Under what condition(s) does the policy ineffectiveness proposition (PIP) hold?

2. Explain the real business cycle theory.

3. Explain the relationship between the expected price level and the *SRAS* curve.

4. Explain the details of Friedman natural rate theory.

5. What does stagflation look like in a diagram with the unemployment rate on the horizontal axis and the inflation rate on the vertical axis?

QUESTIONS AND PROBLEMS

1. What does it mean to say that the Phillips curve presents policy makers with a menu of choices?

2. According to Friedman, how do we know when the economy is in long-run equilibrium?

3. What is a major difference between adaptive and rational expectations? Give an example of each.

4. "The policy ineffectiveness proposition (connected with new classical theory) does not eliminate policy makers' ability to reduce unemployment through aggregate demand–increasing policies, because they can always increase aggregate demand by more than the public expects." What might be the weak point in this argument?

5. Why is the new classical theory associated with the word "classical?" Why has it been said that classical theory failed where new classical theory succeeds—because the former could not explain the business cycle (the ups and downs of the economy), but the latter can?

6. Suppose a permanent downward-sloping Phillips curve existed and offered a menu of choices of different combinations of inflation and unemployment rates to policy makers. How do you think society would go about deciding which point on the Phillips curve it wanted to occupy?

7. Assume a current short-run trade-off between inflation and unemployment, as well as a change in technology that permits the wider dispersion of economic policy news. How would the change affect the trade-off? Explain your answer.

8. New Keynesian theory holds that wages are not completely flexible because of such things as long-term labor contracts. New classical economists often respond that experience teaches labor leaders to develop and bargain for contracts that allow for wage adjustments. Do you think that the new classical economists have a good point? Why or why not?

9. What evidence can you point to which suggests that individuals form their expectations adaptively? What evidence can you point to which suggests that individuals form their expectations rationally?

10. Suppose the government undertakes an expansionary fiscal policy measure that raises aggregate demand but individuals incorrectly anticipate the measure, bias upward. What will the short- and long-run changes be in the price level and Real GDP?

11. Explain both the short- and long-run movements of Friedman natural rate theory, assuming that expectations are formed adaptively.

12. Explain both the short- and long-run movements of the new classical theory, assuming that expectations are formed rationally and policy is unanticipated.

13. "Even if some people do not form their expectations rationally, the new classical theory is not necessarily of no value." Discuss this statement.

14. In real business cycle theory, why can't the change in the money supply prompted by a series of events catalyzed by an adverse supply shock be considered the cause of the business cycle?

15. The expected inflation rate is 5 percent, and the actual inflation rate is 7 percent. According to Friedman, is the economy in long-run equilibrium? Explain your answer.

WORKING WITH NUMBERS AND GRAPHS

1. Illustrate graphically what would happen in the short run and in the long run to the price level and Real GDP level if individuals hold rational expectations, prices and wages are flexible, and individuals underestimate the decrease in aggregate demand (bias downward).

2. Illustrate graphically what would happen in the short run and in the long run to the price level and Real GDP if individuals hold rational expectations, prices and wages are flexible, and individuals overestimate the rise in aggregate demand (bias upward).

3. Illustrate graphically what would happen to the price level and Real GDP level if individuals hold rational expectations, prices and wages are flexible, and individuals correctly anticipate a rise in aggregate demand.

4. In each of the figures (a–d) that follow, the starting point is 1. Which part (a, b, c, or d) illustrates each of the following?

   a. Friedman natural rate theory (short run)

   b. New classical theory (unanticipated policy, short run)

   c. Real business cycle theory

   d. New classical theory (incorrectly anticipated policy, overestimating increase in aggregate demand, short run)

   e. Policy ineffectiveness proposition (PIP)

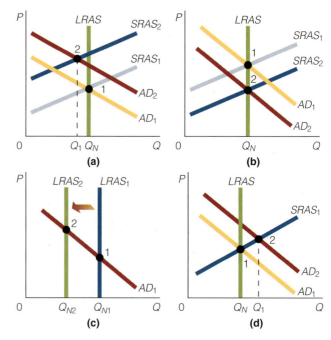

5. Illustrate graphically what would happen in the short run and in the long run if individuals hold adaptive expectations, prices and wages are flexible, and aggregate demand decreases.

ECONOMIC GROWTH: RESOURCES, TECHNOLOGY, IDEAS, AND INSTITUTIONS

Pictorial Press Ltd/Alamy

17-1 A FEW BASICS ABOUT ECONOMIC GROWTH

The term "economic growth" refers either to absolute real economic growth or to per-capita real economic growth. **Absolute real economic growth** is an increase in Real GDP from one period to the next. Exhibit 1 shows absolute real economic growth (the percentage change in Real GDP) for the United States for the period 2002–2012.

Per-capita real economic growth is an increase from one period to the next in per-capita Real GDP, which is Real GDP divided by population:

$$\text{Per-capita Real GDP} = \frac{\text{Real GDP}}{\text{Population}}$$

17-1a Do Economic Growth Rates Matter?

Suppose the (absolute) real economic growth rate is 4 percent in one country and 3 percent in another. The difference in growth rates may not seem very significant, but if the growth rates are sustained over a long time, the people who live in each country will

INTRODUCTION

Rarely do we think of how we came to have the standard of living we enjoy. Most of us live in comfortable houses, drive nice cars, work on fast computers, enjoy exciting sporting events, attend lively jazz concerts, visit relaxing vacation spots, go to the movies and restaurants, and have many other things to be grateful for. To a large degree, our lives are so enriched because we were born in a country that has experienced a relatively high rate of economic growth. How might your life be different if the U.S. economy had had a lower growth rate over, say, the last century? To answer this question, you need to know the causes of economic growth.

Absolute Real Economic Growth
An increase in Real GDP from one period to the next.

Per-Capita Real Economic Growth
An increase from one period to the next in per-capita Real GDP, which is Real GDP divided by population.

Absolute Real Economic Growth Rates for the United States, 2002–2012

This exhibit shows the absolute real economic growth rates (or percentage change in Real GDP) in the United States for the period 2002–2012.

Source: *Economic Report of the President, 2013.*

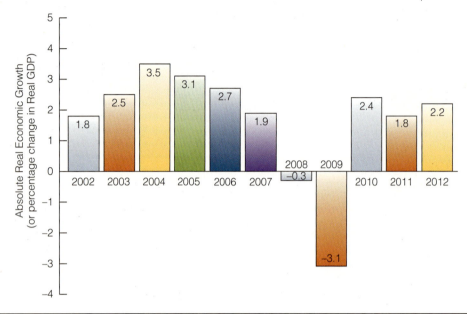

In a Night Out It is 6 p.m., and Xavier is driving his new $45,000 car to a restaurant. He and a friend have dinner at the restaurant. The bill comes to $86.75. After dinner, Xavier and his friend attend a play. Later that night, they return to Xavier's 3,500-square-foot house. They sit out by the swimming pool and talk about everything and nothing. Where is the economics? Is economic growth relevant to the evening?

Economic growth is the silent actor of the evening. Because Xavier and his friend live in a country that has experienced economic growth over the years, their night can be as comfortable and satisfying for them as it is.

Or look at it this way: People like Xavier and his friend are all over the world. Not all of them *can* have the same evening. Individuals living in countries that experienced much less economic growth over the years are not as likely to enjoy the same kind of evening as did Xavier and his friend.

Here is a startling fact: About 24,000 people die every day from hunger or hunger-related causes. Three-fourths of the deaths are children under the age of 5. The vast majority of people who die of hunger live in countries of the world that have experienced relatively little economic growth.

see a real difference in their standard of living. For example, if a country's economic growth rate is 5 percent each year, its Real GDP will double in 14 years. By contrast, if a country has a 2 percent annual growth rate, its Real GDP will double in 35 years. In other words, a country with a 5 percent growth rate can double its Real GDP in 21 fewer years than a country with a 2 percent growth rate. (To calculate the time required for any variable to double, simply divide its percentage growth rate into 70. This is called the *rule of 70*.)

Economic Growth Matters Economic growth has been a major topic of discussion for economists for over two centuries. Adam Smith, the founder of modern economics, wrote a book on the subject that was published in 1776: *An Inquiry into the Nature and Causes of the Wealth of Nations*. In the book, Smith set out to answer the question of why some countries are rich and others are poor. Today, we'd ask, "Why do some countries have a high per-capita Real GDP and others have a low per-capita Real GDP?" For economists, getting the right answer to this question is of major importance to the lives of billions of people.

17-2 A PRODUCTION FUNCTION AND ECONOMIC GROWTH

A **production function** specifies the relation between technology and the quantity of factor inputs to output, or Real GDP. For example, look at this production function:

$$\text{Real GDP} = T\,(L, K)$$

The L stands for labor, the K stands for capital, and the T stands for the technology coefficient. Suppose we have 4 units of labor and 2 units of capital. Then, in all, we have 6 units of our two resources, labor and capital.

In an earlier chapter, an advance in technology was defined as the ability to produce more output (more Real GDP) with a given level of resources, such as labor and capital. The T, or technology coefficient, in our production function captures this idea. Suppose we set our T equal to 0.40. Then, given that L equals 4 and K equals 2, our production function now reads

$$\text{Real GDP} = 0.4\,(4 + 2)$$
$$\text{Real GDP} = 0.4\,(6)$$
$$\text{Real GDP} = 2.4 \text{ units of output}$$

In other words, we have taken particular amounts of labor and capital, added them together at a certain level of technology—evidenced in a technology coefficient of 0.4—and ended up with 2.4 units of output, or Real GDP.

Production Function
A function that specifies the relation between technology and the quantity of factor inputs to output, or Real GDP.

Obviously, our production function, which focuses on the three factors of T, L, and K, implies that an increase in any one of these factors will lead to a rise in Real GDP. For example, if we increase labor from 4 to 8 units, Real GDP will rise to 4 units of output. Alternatively, if we raise T from 0.4 to 0.5, holding labor at 4 units and capital at 2 units, Real GDP will rise from 2.4 units to 3.0 units.

17-2a The Graphical Representation of the Production Function

Exhibit 2(a) represents the production function graphically. Real GDP (Q) is on the vertical axis, and labor (L) is on the horizontal axis. The curve in the two-dimensional space is the graphical representation of the production function. At a given level of labor, L_1, we get Q_1 amount of Real GDP. A change in labor, say from L_1 to L_2, will give us more Real GDP, as shown in Exhibit 2(b).

Now, a change in either K or T will shift the production function up or down. For example, Exhibit 2(c) shows what happens to the production function if K rises. Initially, $K = 1$, and this, combined with L_1 and a given technology coefficient, produces Q_1 Real GDP. If K rises to 2, and this higher K is combined with the same amount of labor and the same technology coefficient, Real GDP rises to Q_2.

Exhibit 2(d) shows what happens if the technology coefficient rises. Initially, $T = 0.4$. Combining this with a given amount of labor and capital produces a Real GDP level of Q_1. If T rises to 0.5 and nothing else changes, then Real GDP rises to Q_2.

So our production function specifies that output or Real GDP depends on labor, capital, and the technology coefficient (which captures the essence of advances in technology). Specifically, a rise in labor will move us from one point to another on the same production function, ending with more Real GDP. A rise in capital or a rise in the technology coefficient will lead to a shift upward in the production function, also ending with more Real GDP.

17-2b From the Production Function to the *LRAS* Curve

The changes in, and the movements along, the production function can be linked to shifts in the *LRAS* curve. In Exhibit 3(a), we start with L_1, which gives us Real GDP of Q_1. We then take Q_1 from panel (a) and move it to panel (b). Q_1 is the Real GDP that the economy is producing when it is at the natural unemployment rate; in other words, Q_1 is Natural Real GDP. This level of Real GDP is consistent with $LRAS_1$ in the exhibit.

Suppose now that we raise the level of labor in panel (a) to L_2. This change in labor moves us along our production function, from point 1 to point 2 at a higher Real GDP level, Q_2. In panel (b), this new, higher Real GDP is consistent with $LRAS_2$.

Therefore, a rise in the level of labor moves us along the given production function and shifts the *LRAS* curve to the right. If you were to now superimpose an *AD* curve on panel (b), you would see that a shift rightward in the *LRAS* curve brings about a lower price level and a higher Real GDP level. With a heightened Real GDP level, we have economic growth.

In panel (c), we again start with L_1, which gives us Q_1 Real GDP. If the technology coefficient then rises from 0.4 to 0.5, the production function shifts upward. Hence, at a given level of labor and capital, we have more Real GDP, Q_2. Carrying over the changes in Real GDP from panel (c) to panel (d), we see that a rise in the technology coefficient shifts the *LRAS* curve to the right. Again, we have economic growth.

> **EXHIBIT 2**

The Production Function

(a) The production function specifies the relation among labor (*L*), capital (*K*), and technology (technology coefficient, *T*). (b) Changes in *L* lead to changes in Real GDP (*Q*). (c) A rise in capital (*K*) leads to an upward shift in the production function and to more Real GDP (for a given level of *L* and a given technology coefficient, *T*). (d) A rise in the technology coefficient (*T*) leads to an upward shift in the production function and to more Real GDP (for a given level of *L* and *K*).

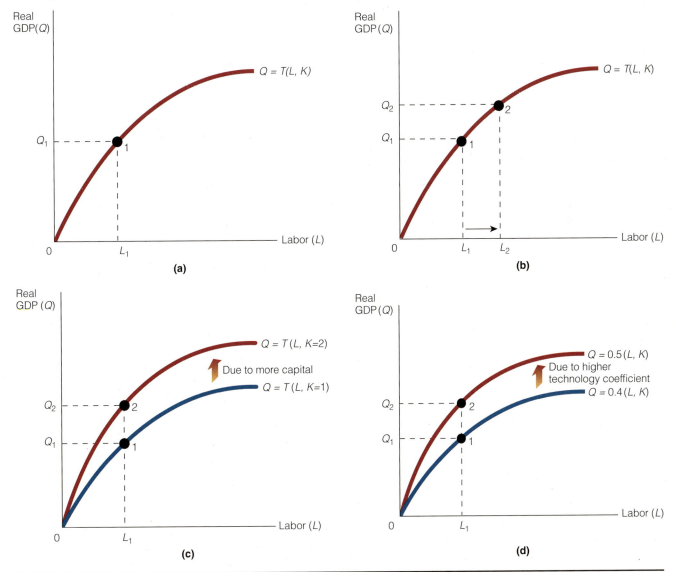

17-2c Emphasis on Labor

Exhibit 3 showed that a rise in labor would lead to a rightward shift in the *LRAS* curve. In other words, a rise in labor would result in economic growth. Then what, in turn, might lead to a rise in labor? In other words, if *X* and *Y* lead to a rise in labor, then *X* and *Y* are factors that promote economic growth.

> **EXHIBIT 3**

The Production Function and the *LRAS* Curve

(a) More labor (*L*) leads to more Real GDP (shown in terms of the production function).

(b) More *L* shifts the *LRAS* curve to the right. (c) A higher technology coefficient (*T*) shifts the production function up and brings about more Real GDP, *Q*. (d) A heightened technology coefficient (*T*) leads to a rightward shift in the

LRAS curve. (Although not shown in this exhibit, a rise in *K* would do the same thing as a rise in *T* in terms of shifting the production function upward and shifting the *LRAS* curve to the right.)

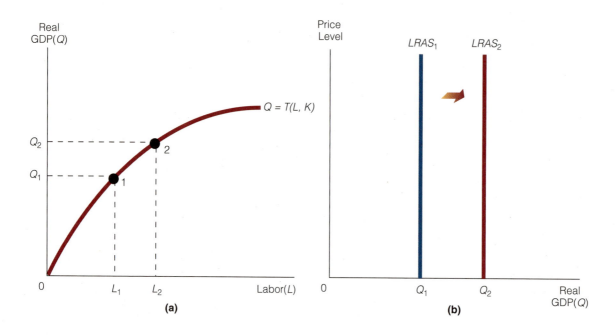

(a)

(b)

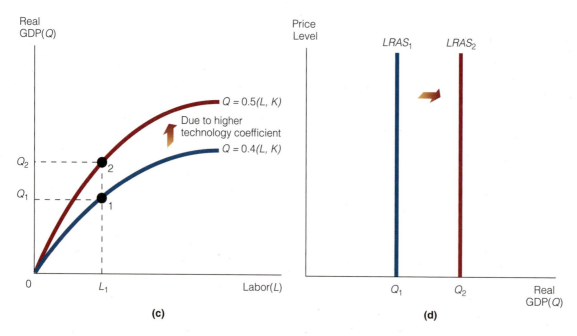

(c)

(d)

ECONOMICS 24/7

Thinking in Terms of Production Functions and Equations

Consider again the production function that we have discussed; it is expressed in terms of producing output, or Real GDP. We have illustrated that production function both in graphical form (see Exhibit 2a) and as an equation—for example, when we specified earlier that

$$\text{Real GDP} = 0.4\,(4 + 2)$$

Both the graphical representation of the production function and the equation are simple, straightforward ways of explaining what goes into producing something—in our case, Real GDP. Now let's apply the graphical representation of the production function and an equation to think about something *you* may produce.

Think about your education. You are at college taking a number of courses; you are involved in the process of acquiring an education; you are learning. Think of your education production function. What variables go in to producing your education? There are books, instructors, classrooms, computers, software, libraries, and more.

It's also likely that your motivation to learn matters. In other words, you can have the books, instructors, classrooms, and so on, but if you are not motivated to learn, all those things may not matter that much or even at all to your acquiring an education. Without the motivation to learn, you may learn very little.

Think of a two-dimensional diagram. On the vertical axis we have "your learning." The higher up on the axis, the more you have learned. On the horizontal axis we have "your labor hours" applied to learning. These are the hours you are in the classroom listening to your college professor lecture on some material, the hours you spend reading and studying, the hours your spend working on your homework, and so on. Your education production function may look similar to the production function identified in Exhibit 2 (a). It is upward sloping (from left to right), and the slope of it diminishes as more labor hours are applied.

Now, what is it that can shift your education production function upward so that, with a given number of labor hours expended, you can acquire more learning? Think of "your motivation" as a key variable. More motivation shifts your education production function upward; less motivation shifts it downward.

Now let's think of your education as an equation. Here it is:

Amount of learning acquired = 0.1(number of books read) + 0.2(hours spent studying) + 0.1(quality of the instructor's teaching) + 0.6(rating, on a scale of 1–10, of your motivation to learn)

We have, of course, simply made up this equation, both the variables identified and the weighting factor of each variable. Your own "education equation" may have different variables specified and different weighting factors. But that is not the important point. The important point is that there are some variables that go into your learning and there is some weighting factor that measures the contribution of that variable to your overall learning.

Some of us rarely consider what goes in to the "soup" of what it is we are producing. But it is sometimes useful to think in terms of production functions and equations in order to summarize and enlighten us as to how what we produce is actually produced. Then, once we have a rough idea of what the ingredients are that go into producing what it is that we produce, it is interesting to play around with the different variables (increase or decrease their levels) to learn how our educational level (output) changes. For example, if motivation matters a lot to how much we learn, it may be beneficial to think of ways to increase our level of motivation. But, then, that makes us wonder: What is it exactly that goes into becoming more motivated? And that leads us to yet another "production function."

ECONOMICS 24/7

Growth and Morality[1]

Almost everyone agrees that economic growth, especially sustained economic growth, can produce more, better, and newer goods and services. But what else can it do, if anything? According to economist Benjamin Friedman, it can make people happier, more tolerant, more willing to settle disputes in a peaceful manner, and more inclined to favor an open and democratic society. It can also make people more willing to work toward improving the environment and reducing poverty.

Sam Edwards/OJO Images/Getty Images

The thought that economic growth can do more than give us more goods and services goes back to Adam Smith. According to Smith, when a nation is acquiring more—when it is getting richer—most of the people are happy and comfortable. When a nation is just maintaining its wealth or declining, its people are not as happy or as comfortable.

What Friedman essentially argues is that economists have looked at the benefits of economic growth too narrowly. They have stressed the rising material standard of living that comes with economic growth. But this perspective, says Friedman, ignores the political, social, and moral aspects of economic growth. In his book, *The Moral Consequences of Economic Growth*, he says, "a rising standard of living lies not just in the concrete improvements it brings to how individuals live but in how it shapes the social, political, and

ultimately the moral character of a people."[2]

If Friedman is correct that economic growth affects people not only economically, but politically, socially, and morally too, then we need to ask why. Friedman says that it has such influence because people's sense of how well off they are is made relative to their (own) past. People feel happiest (and the most tolerant of others) when they believe that their standard of living is rising—in other words, if they are better off this year than last year. When they have this sense, people care less about where they stand relative to others. But if they are not witnessing an increase in their standard of living relative to their past, they begin to care more about how they are doing relative to others. This comparison with others usually results in frustration and, possibly, social friction.

Friedman does not argue that there are absolutely no costs to growth. Instead, he simply makes the point that the benefits emanating from growth may be greater and more far reaching than we initially thought.

---

[1] This feature is based on "Why the Rich Must Get Richer," *The Economist*, November 10, 2005, http://www.economist.com/node/5135504.
[2] Benjamin Friedman, *The Moral Consequences of Economic Growth* (New York: Knopf, 2005).

One such factor that is often mentioned is taxes. Specifically, some economists propose promoting economic growth by cutting taxes on such activities as working. The idea is that, if the marginal income tax rate is cut, workers will work more and, as they work more, output will rise. Think of this idea in terms of the labor market. Exhibit 4(a) shows a labor market that is in equilibrium at point 1. The equilibrium quantity of labor in this market is L_1. If L_1 is put into our production function, as shown in panel (b), it gives us Q_1 amount of Real GDP. Finally, if Q_1 from panel (b) is placed in panel (c), Q_1 is consistent with the $LRAS_1$ curve.

> **EXHIBIT 4**

The Labor Market, the Production Function, and the *LRAS* Curve

(a) Lower taxes on income shifts the labor supply curve rightward from S_{L1} to S_{L2}. As a result of the lower taxes and the rightward shift in the labor supply curve, the equilibrium amount of labor rises from L_1 to L_2. (b) More labor leads to more Real GDP in terms of the production function. (c) More Real GDP corresponds to a rightward shift in the *LRAS* curve.

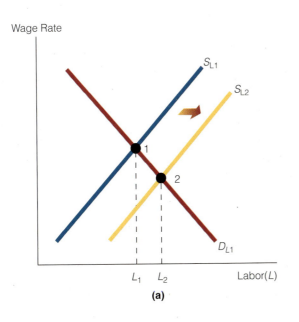

(a)

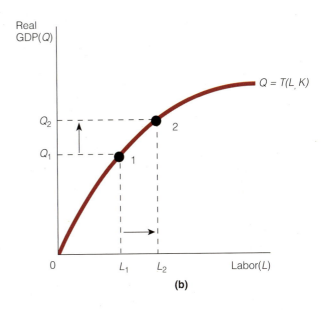

(b)

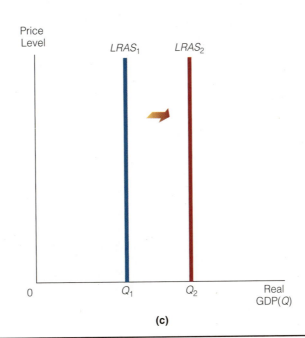

(c)

Now suppose we lower taxes on income. As a result, the labor supply curve in panel (a) shifts rightward. In other words, as the overall return on working increases because of a drop in income taxes, more people decide to go to work and many of those already working decide to work more. The new equilibrium quantity of labor, L_2, is shown in panel (a). If we carry over the greater quantity of labor to panel (b), showing our production function, more labor produces the higher level of Real GDP, Q_2. Then, in panel (c), the new higher level of Real GDP corresponds to a new $LRAS$ curve, $LRAS_2$.

Therefore, lower income taxes shift the labor supply to the right, raising the equilibrium quantity of labor, which produces more Real GDP or shifts the $LRAS$ curve to the right. Again, we have witnessed economic growth.

17-2d Emphasis on Capital

So more labor can lead to economic growth, but so can more capital. How much capital is available depends on such things as the tax treatment of capital returns and interest rates. Consider two settings. In the first, taxes on the returns to capital are high; in the second, taxes on the returns to capital are low. Which setting offers a stronger incentive to employ capital in the production process? When taxes on the returns to capital are low, we predict the following: as taxes decline on the returns from capital, more capital is utilized in the production process, shifting the production function upward and thereby shifting the $LRAS$ curve to the right.

The interest rate can also affect the amount of capital employed, because firms often borrow the funds to buy the capital goods used in production. In short, the process can work like this: A decline in interest rates prompts firms to borrow more. The firms use the borrowed funds to purchase capital goods. As they purchase and utilize more capital (in the production process), the production function shifts upward and the $LRAS$ curve shifts rightward.

17-2e Emphasis on Other Resources: Natural Resources and Human Capital

Our production function so far has included only two resources—labor and capital—and technology. When building economic growth models, economists often specify a production function of this sort.

However, for reasons of completeness, a more fully specified production function would also include natural resources (NR) and human capital (H). For example, producing goods—such as chairs, desks, and paper—often takes natural resources—such as wood. In fact, economists often speak in terms of four resources (Chapter 1): land, labor, capital, and entrepreneurship. "Land" is simply another name for natural resources.

Producing many goods also takes human capital, which is different from the kind of capital we represented as K. The capital referred to earlier is *physical capital*—such things as machines, computers, and factories. **Human capital** is what you acquire by attending college, plus the skills and knowledge you pick up through education, training, and experience. You enroll in a number of courses, learn certain material, and acquire certain thinking skills; these are all components of human capital.

Adding human capital and natural resources to our production function leads us to specify that function this way:

$$\text{Real GDP} = T\,(L,\, K,\, NR,\, H)$$

Human Capital

The knowledge and skills a person acquires through education, training, and experience.

17-2f Emphasis on the Technology Coefficient and Ideas

Beginning in the 1980s, economists began discussing economic growth differently than they did in previous decades. They began placing more attention on technology, ideas, institutions, and education. The discussion often took place under the rubric of *new growth theory*.

The name "new growth theory" implies that a theory of economic growth came before it, and, indeed, neoclassical growth theory preceded new growth theory. A number of economists believe that new growth theory came about to answer some of the questions that new neoclassical growth theory could not, in much the same way that a new medical theory may arise to answer questions that an old medical theory cannot answer.

Neoclassical growth theory emphasized two resources: labor and physical capital. Technology was discussed, but only tangentially. Technology was said to be exogenous; that is, it came from outside the economic system. It fell out of the sky; it was outside our control. We simply accepted this assumption as a given.

New growth theory holds that technology is endogenous; it is a central part of the economic system. More important, the amount and quality of technology that is developed depend on the amount of resources we devote to it: The more resources that go into developing technology, the more and better technology is developed.

Economist Paul Romer, whose name is synonymous with new growth theory, asks us to think about technology as we would about prospecting for gold. For one individual, the chances of finding gold are so small that if someone did find gold, the strike would simply be viewed as good luck. However, if 10,000 individuals are looking for gold across a wide geographical area, the chances of finding it would greatly improve. As with gold prospecting, so it is with technological advances. If one person is trying to advance technology, his or her chances of success are much smaller than if hundreds or thousands of persons are trying.

New growth theory also emphasizes the process of discovering and formulating ideas as they relate to technological advances. The emphasis is on ideas rather than on objects, which are material, tangible things, such as natural resources and capital goods. Some countries are poor because they lack objects (natural resources and capital goods). Yet some countries have had very few objects and have been able to grow economically. For example, in the 1950s, Japan had few natural resources and capital goods, but still it grew economically. Some economists believe that Japan grew because it had access to ideas or knowledge.

17-2g Discovery and Ideas

If discovering ideas is important to technological advances and therefore to economic growth, then we need to figure out ways to promote the discovery process. One way is for business firms not to get locked into doing things in one way and one way only. They must let their employees—from the inventor in the lab to the worker on the assembly line—try new ways of getting the job done. Some might carry this idea further: businesses need to create an environment that is receptive to new ideas; they need to encourage their employees to try new ways of doing things.

Employee flexibility, which is a part of the discovery process, is becoming a larger part of the U.S. economy. To some degree, the discovery process is seen in the amount of time and effort firms devote to discovery in contrast to the amount of time they devote to actually manufacturing goods. Consider the computer software business. Millions of dollars and hundreds of thousands of work hours are devoted to coming up with new and useful software, whereas only a tiny fraction of the work effort and hours go into making, copying, and shipping the disks or CDs that contain the software.

17-2h Expanding Our Horizons

According to Romer, "economic growth occurs whenever people take resources and rearrange them in ways that are more valuable." Let's focus on the word "rearrange." We can think of rearranging as in rearranging the pieces of a puzzle, as in changing the ingredients in a recipe, or as in rearranging the way workers go about their daily work. When we rearrange anything, we do that thing differently. Sometimes differently is better, and sometimes it is worse.

Think of how you study for a test. Perhaps you read the book first, go back and underline, study the book, and then finally study your lecture notes. Would it be better to study differently? You won't know until you try.

As with studying for a test, so it is with producing a car, computer software, or a shopping mall. We do not find better ways of doing things unless we experiment. And with repeated experiments, we often discover new and better ideas, ideas that ultimately lead to economic growth. The research and development of new medicines makes for a good example. Sometimes, what makes a mildly effective medicine into a very effective one is a change in one or two molecules of a certain chemical. A small change—a change perhaps no one would ever think would matter—can make a large difference.

A policy prescription follows from that mind-set: we should think of ways to make the process of discovering ideas, experimenting with different ways of doing things, and developing new technology more likely. Without this kind of effort, we are likely to diminish our growth potential. If we believe that ideas are important to economic growth, then we need to have ideas about how to generate more ideas. Romer calls these second-level ideas *meta-ideas*: ideas about how to support the production and transmission of other ideas.

Some ways have been proposed. Perhaps we need to invest more funds in education or in research and development. Or perhaps we need to find better ways to protect people's ideas. (Few people will invest the time, money, and effort to discover new ideas if the ideas can easily be stolen.)

In the twenty-first century, countries with the most natural resources and capital goods aren't likely to be the ones that grow the fastest. If new growth theory is correct, the successful ones will be those which have discovered how to encourage and develop the most and best ideas.

17-2i Institutions Matter

Crops don't grow equally well in all soils. Some soils are more conducive to the growing than others. Similarly, many economists argue that some environments are more conducive to economic growth than others.

One of the ways economists differentiate one environment from another is by their institutions. But what are institutions in this context? Douglass North, a well-respected economist in the area of institutional research, defines an **institution** as "the rules of the game in a society or, more formally, the humanly devised constraints that shape human interaction." Specifically, institutions consist of a country's rules and regulations, laws, customs, and business practices. Consider two countries, A and B, each with different

Institution
The rules of the game in a society or, more formally, the humanly devised constraints that shape human interaction; the rules and regulations, laws, customs, and business practices of a country.

institutions. In country A, the rule of law operates (no one is above the law), contracts are enforced, private property rights are protected, and free international trade is permitted. In country B, the rule of law does not hold, contracts are not always enforced, private property is not protected (and is often seized), and high tariffs and quotas are placed on imported goods. In North's terminology, the "rules of the game" are different in these two countries.

Here are a few of the institutions that most economists agree are conducive to economic growth:

- Property rights structure
- The legal system
- Growth-promoting policies versus transfer-promoting policies
- Other institutions

Property Rights Structure   Think of two property rights structures, X and Y. Under X, a person is allowed to own property (a piece of land, a business, a store, an invention, etc.); that is, private property is permitted. Under Y, a person is not allowed to own property; private property is not permitted. The incentive to produce goods and services is hardly the same in each of the two property rights structures. Undoubtedly, the incentive to produce is greater under property rights structure X than Y. Why produce anything under Y if what you produce does not belong to you? In short, different property rights structures come with different incentives to produce. All other things equal, the property rights structures that permit individuals to own property will be more conducive to production and economic growth than those which do not.

Now consider two other property rights structures, A and B. Under both, individuals are allowed to own property. But in A, a person's private property rights are not as well protected as in B. For example, in A, the government sometimes confiscates a person's private property; in B, that never happens. Again, the incentive to produce is not the same under A and B. The more secure the private property rights are, the greater the incentive is to produce. Why produce if what you produce might be taken away from you?

Therefore, not only do private property rights matter to production and economic growth; so does the security of those private property rights.

The Legal System   In country A, the legal system is dependable, honest, and dedicated to enforcing legitimate contracts and to protecting private property. In country B, the legal system is the polar opposite. In which country, A or B, are individuals more likely to have a greater incentive to start businesses, lend and borrow funds, invest, produce goods, and innovate—all important to the process of economic growth? Most economists would say in country A, where the legal system is dependable, honest, and sound. That conclusion becomes quickly obvious once you think of what is involved with starting a business, lending and borrowing, investing, innovating, and producing: dealing with other people. If you start a business, you will often need to deal with other people to finance the business, to hire workers, to buy from suppliers, and so on. In your dealings with other people, you need to be assured that your agreements (or contracts) with them are upheld and enforced and that others cannot steal from you and get away with it. This is why the legal system is important to economic growth. A legal system that is dependable, honest, and dedicated to enforcing legitimate contracts and protecting private property reduces the transaction costs of dealing with others, thus providing individuals with a greater incentive to engage in activities conducive to economic growth.

ECONOMICS 24/7

Economic Freedom and Growth Rates

Does economic freedom matter to a country's economic growth rate? There is some evidence that it does. Consider the time in which there were two Germanys: an East Germany and a West Germany. The two Germanys were much the same in terms of culture, people, climate, language, and so on, except that West Germans enjoyed more economic freedom than East Germans. Did this major difference between the two Germanys matter to economic growth? Most economists answer yes: Between 1950 and 1991, the average annual growth rate in East Germany was 1.3 percent; in West Germany, it was 4.4 percent.

The same sort of difference holds between North Korea and South Korea. South Korea permits much more economic freedom than North Korea. Does this difference affect economic growth rates? During the second half of the twentieth century, the average annual growth rate in South Korea was more than three times higher than in North Korea.

The evidence from the two Koreas and two Germanys tells us that economic freedom does matter to economic growth, especially when other factors (that matter to growth) are much the same between the countries.

But when the other factors are not the same, problems arise. Suppose country A has less economic freedom than country B. Will country A grow less than country B during the next 5 or 10 years? Not necessarily. The economic growth rate in a country could depend on the economic base from which the growth emanates.

© Nariyer/Shutterstock.com

Suppose that country A has a Real GDP of $10 billion, that country B has a Real GDP of $100 billion, and that Real GDP grows by $2 billion in both countries. Then the economic growth rate in country A (the country with less economic freedom) is 20 percent, but the economic growth rate in country B (the country with more economic freedom) is only 2 percent. Does it follow that economic freedom is a hindrance to economic growth? Not at all. It may simply look that way because something different between the two countries—namely, the economic base from which growth emanates—isn't being considered.

Growth-Promoting Policies versus Transfer-Promoting Policies   Consider two types of economic policies: growth-promoting policies and transfer-promoting policies. A growth-promoting policy increases Real GDP; it enlarges the size of the economic pie. A transfer-promoting policy leaves the size of the economic pie unchanged, but it increases the size of the slice that one group gets relative to another.

ECONOMICS 24/7

Religious Beliefs and Economic Growth

For given religious beliefs, increases in church attendance tend to reduce economic growth. In contrast, for given church attendance, increases in some religious beliefs—notably in heaven, hell, and an after-life—tend to increase economic growth.

—Robert Barro and Rachel McCleary[3]

Economists have been studying economic growth for more than 200 years. Some of the questions they have asked and tried to answer are as follows:

• Why are some nations rich and others poor?

• What causes economic growth?

• Why do some nations grow faster than others?

Among the causes of economic growth that are discussed in this chapter, we do not include cultural determinants. Yet some economic researchers argue that explanations for economic growth should be broadened to include cultural determinants. Culture may influence personal traits, they argue, which may in turn affect economic growth. For example, personal traits such as honesty, thriftiness, the willingness to work hard, and openness to strangers may be related to economic growth.

Two Harvard economists, Robert Barro and Rachel McCleary, have analyzed one such cultural determinant: the role of religion

in economic growth. Their work was based partly on the World Values Survey, which looked at a representative sample of people in 66 countries on all six inhabited continents between 1981 and 1997. The survey asked at least 1,000 people in each country about their basic values and beliefs: What is their religious affiliation? How often do they attend a religious service? Were they raised religiously or not?

Barro and McCleary found that economic growth corresponds negatively with church attendance (nations with a high rate of attendance at religious services grow more slowly than those with lower rates of attendance) but positively with religious beliefs in heaven, hell, and an afterlife. Specifically, in countries where the belief in heaven, hell, and an afterlife is strong, the growth of gross domestic product runs about 0.5 percent higher than the average for all of the countries surveyed. (This result takes into account other factors that influence growth rates, such as education.) Perhaps more telling, the belief in hell matters more to economic growth than the belief in heaven. Barro and McCleary suggest that religious beliefs stimulate growth because they help to sustain aspects of individual behavior that enhance productivity.

---

3. Robert J. Barro and Rachel M. McCleary, "Religion and Economic Growth," NBER Working paper No. 9682 (Cambridge, MA: National Bureau of Economic Research, May 2003), p. 36, http://www.nber.org/papers/w9682.pdf.

For example, suppose group A, a special-interest group, currently gets 1/1,000 of the economic pie and the economic pie is $1,000. Then the group gets a $1 slice. But group A wants to get more than a $1 slice, and it can do so in one of two ways. The first is to lobby for a policy that increases the size of its slice of the economic pie. In other words, group A gets a larger slice (say, a $2 slice) at the expense of someone else's getting a smaller slice. Alternatively, group A can lobby for a policy that increases the size of the pie—say, from $1,000 to $1,500. In this case, group A gets not the full increase of $500, but 1/1,000 of the increase, or 50¢. So group A has to decide whether it is better to lobby for a growth-promoting policy (in which it gets 1/1,000 of any increase in Real GDP) or for a transfer-promoting policy (in which it gets 100 percent of any transfer).

According to Mancur Olson, in *The Rise and Decline of Nations,* special-interest groups are more likely to argue for transfer-promoting policies than growth-promoting policies and the cost–benefit calculation of each policy is the reason.[4] This behavior affects economic growth in that the more special-interest groups there are in a country, the more likely it is that transfer-promoting policies will be lobbied for instead of growth-promoting policies. Individuals will try to get a larger slice of a constant-size economic pie rather than trying to increase the size of the pie. In short, numerous and politically strong special-interest groups are detrimental to economic growth.

Other Institutions   Some other institutions are often mentioned as conducive to economic growth: open and competitive markets, free (international) trade, policies that promote economic freedom, a stable monetary system, taxes and regulations that are not burdensome, and a strong and effective educational system.

SELF-TEST

(Answers to Self-Test questions are in Answers to Self-Test Questions at the back of the book.)

1. Explain how a decline in taxes that affects the labor market can end up shifting the *LRAS* curve to the right.

2. What is the difference between physical and human capital?

3. What is the difference between neoclassical growth theory and new growth theory with respect to technology?

4. In the production function specified in Exhibit 2(a), what variable(s) are movement factors (will move us along the production function)? What variable(s) are shift factors (will shift the production function)?

---

4. Mancur Olson, *The Rise and Decline of Nations* (New Haven, CT, and London: Yale University Press, 1982).

Office  Hours

"What Is the Difference Between Business Cycle Macroeconomics and Economic Growth Macroeconomics?"

STUDENT:

I am searching for a way to put the macroeconomics presented in this chapter in perspective with the macroeconomics presented in the other chapters. Can you help?

INSTRUCTOR:

In most of the previous chapters, the *LRAS* curve did not move. It was fixed at some Natural Real GDP level. In this chapter, we discussed the factors that can shift the *LRAS* curve: we discussed how the economy can move from one Real GDP level to a higher Real GDP level. This shift was obvious in all the exhibits.

Let me add some economic terminology to the discussion. In previous chapters, we discussed mainly business cycle macroeconomics. In this chapter, we have discussed economic growth macroeconomics.

STUDENT:

Specifically, what does business cycle macroeconomics deal with?

INSTRUCTOR:

It deals with two things: (1) differences between Real GDP and Natural Real GDP and (2) ways of moving the economy to its Natural Real GDP level. Suppose Natural Real GDP is $11 trillion and the current Real GDP in the economy is $10 trillion. Obviously, because Real GDP is less than Natural Real GDP, the economy is in a recessionary gap. If the economy is self-regulating, it will eventually move to its Natural Real GDP level. If it is not self-regulating, then perhaps monetary or fiscal policy can be used to move the economy to its Natural Real GDP level.

STUDENT:

How does business cycle macroeconomics differ from what was discussed in this chapter?

INSTRUCTOR:

In this chapter, we discussed mainly economic growth. This topic deals with the economy moving from one Natural Real GDP level to a higher one—specifically, how the economy might move from a Natural Real GDP level of, say, $11 trillion to a higher Natural Real GDP level of, say, $11.7 trillion.

STUDENT:

Does it follow that, when we're discussing how the economy moves from one Natural Real GDP level to a higher one, we are simultaneously discussing rightward shifts in the *LRAS* curve?

INSTRUCTOR:

Yes, that's correct. In fact, let's define both business cycle macroeconomics and economic growth macroeconomics with respect to the *LRAS* curve. Business cycle macroeconomics deals with economic activity occurring around a single *LRAS* curve. Economic growth macroeconomics (starting from an efficient level of production) deals with rightward shifts in the *LRAS* curve.

Points to remember

1. Business cycle macroeconomics deals with economic activity occurring around a single *LRAS* curve (or around a specific Natural Real GDP level).
2. Economic growth macroeconomics (starting from an efficient level of production) deals with rightward shifts in the *LRAS* curve (or moving from a lower to a higher level of Natural Real GDP).

CHAPTER SUMMARY

ECONOMIC GROWTH

- Absolute real economic growth refers to an increase in Real GDP from one period to the next.
- Per-capita real economic growth refers to an increase from one period to the next in per-capita Real GDP, which is Real GDP divided by population.

THE PRODUCTION FUNCTION

- A production function specifies the relation between technology and the quantity of factor inputs to output or Real GDP.
- Real GDP $= T(L, K)$. This production function specifies that Real GDP, or output, is a function of technology—as evidenced in the technology coefficient (T)—labor (L), and (physical) capital (K). Another production function is Real GDP $= T(L, K, NR, H)$. This production function specifies that Real GDP, or output, is a function of technology—as evidenced in the technology coefficient (T)—labor (L), (physical) capital (K), natural resources (NR), and human capital (H).

THE PRODUCTION FUNCTION AND ECONOMIC GROWTH

- Using the production function Real GDP $= T(L, K)$, we know that increases in T, L, and K will raise Real GDP and that decreases in T, L, and K will decrease Real GDP. Also, changes in Real GDP will lead to shifts in the $LRAS$ curve as a result of changes in T, L, and K. For example, a rise in K will raise Real GDP, leading to a rightward shift in the $LRAS$ curve.

- A change in taxes affects the labor supply curve, thus leading to a change in the amount of labor employed in the labor market. In turn, this change in the amount of labor employed leads to a change in Real GDP and to a shift in the $LRAS$ curve. (See Exhibit 4.)
- How much capital is employed in the production process depends on such things as the tax treatment of capital returns and interest rates.

NEW GROWTH THEORY

- New growth theory holds that technology is endogenous; neoclassical growth theory holds that technology is exogenous. When something is endogenous, it is part of the economic system, under our control or influence. When something is exogenous, it is not part of the system; instead, it is assumed to be given to us, often mysteriously through a process that we do not understand.
- According to Paul Romer, discovering and implementing new ideas is what causes economic growth.
- Certain institutions can promote the discovery of new ideas and therefore promote economic growth.

ECONOMIC GROWTH AND SPECIAL-INTEREST GROUPS

- According to Mancur Olson, the more special-interest groups a country has, the more likely it is that transfer-promoting policies will be lobbied for instead of growth-promoting policies. Individuals will try to get a larger slice of a constant-size economic pie rather than trying to increase the size of the pie.

KEY TERMS AND CONCEPTS

Absolute Real Economic Growth	Per-Capita Real Economic Growth	Production Function Human Capital	Institution

VIDEO QUESTIONS AND PROBLEMS

Video Questions and Problems are available on MindTap for Arnold 12e or by searching for Arnold on www.cengagebrain.com

1. Explain how an increase in labor can lead to a rightward shift in the $LRAS$ curve.

2. Explain how a rise in the technology coefficient can lead to a rightward shift in the $LRAS$ curve.

3. Does a rise in Real GDP necessarily lead to a rise in per-capita Real GDP? Why or why not?

4. If country A has a growth rate of 2 percent and country B has a growth rate of 5 percent, in how many fewer years will it take country B to double its Real GDP than it will take country A?

5. Represent the production function Real GDP = $T(L, K)$ diagrammatically, and then identify the movement and shift factors.

QUESTIONS AND PROBLEMS

1. Why might per-capita real economic growth be a more useful measurement than absolute real economic growth?

2. Identify how changes in L, K, and T can lead to changes in output, or Real GDP.

3. What does it mean to say that "a change in labor moves us along a given production function?"

4. What do interest rates and the tax treatment of returns to capital have to do with economic growth?

5. What is *new* about new growth theory?

6. How does discovering and implementing new ideas cause economic growth?

7. What is the difference between business cycle macroeconomics and economic growth macroeconomics?

8. What is an institution? Why might institutions matter to how much economic growth a country experiences?

9. Some property rights structures provide more and stronger incentives to produce goods and services than other such structures do. Do you agree or disagree with this statement? Explain your answer.

10. Why might special-interest groups favor transfer-promoting policies over growth-promoting policies?

WORKING WITH NUMBERS AND GRAPHS

1. The economy of country X is currently growing at 2 percent a year. How many years will it take to double the Real GDP of country X?

2. Explain numerically how an advance in technology can lead to more output, or Real GDP.

3. A rise in physical capital can raise Real GDP and lead to a rightward shift in the *LRAS* curve. Show this relationship diagrammatically.

4. A change in the labor market can change the equilibrium amount of labor employed, thus leading to a change in Real GDP and to a shift in the *LRAS* curve. Show this sequence of events diagrammatically.

5. Let labor be the variable shown on the horizontal axis and Real GDP on the vertical axis. Suppose there is a rise in labor. Does the rise lead to a *movement along* the production function or to a *shift in* the production function? Explain your answer. Next, draw the change in the *LRAS* curve that results from a rise in labor.

6. Again, let labor be the variable shown on the horizontal axis and Real GDP on the vertical axis. Suppose there is an increase in physical capital. Does the increase lead to a *movement along* the production function or to a *shift in* the production function? Explain your answer. Next, draw the change in the *LRAS* curve that results from an increase in physical capital.

18 THE FINANCIAL CRISIS OF 2007–2009

© Sean Pavone/Shutterstock.com

18-1 THE FINANCIAL AND REAL SECTORS OF THE ECONOMY

To understand the financial crisis, first consider an economy that comprises two sectors: the financial sector and the real sector. The financial sector consists of financial institutions: commercial banks, investment banks, hedge funds, brokerage firms, and others. The real sector consists of firms that produce goods and services, individuals who buy goods and services, and individuals who work for firms, among others.

To a large extent, the financial sector deals with borrowing and lending activities. It takes money that is saved and lends it out. Within the financial sector are **financial intermediaries**, which are firms that bring borrowers and lenders together. If company X is a financial intermediary, people go to X and deposit their savings. Then X lends out the savings to others. In other words, X grants loans to people by using the money other people have saved.

During the period 2007–2009, a financial crisis hit the United States. A financial crisis occurs when financial firms and financial markets undergo a major disruption, making it difficult for persons to obtain loans from banks and other financial institutions.

Financial Intermediary
A firm that transfers funds from those who want to lend funds to those who want to borrow funds.

Problems contributing to the financial crisis included people not paying back the loans they took out from the banks, depositors becoming afraid that their deposits were not safe at the banks and trying to withdraw them, banks having a hard time getting loans from other banks, and banks finding themselves with declining asset values, moving them toward **insolvency** (the condition in which their liabilities are greater than their assets).

Problems in the financial sector can bleed over into the real sector, producing decreased borrowing and lending, decreased economic activity, a decline in sales, a rise in unemployment, and much more. In other words, if the financial sector gets sick, that sickness can do harm to the real sector. That is what happened in the United States in the crisis of 2007–2009: A crisis in the financial sector adversely affected the real sector of the U.S. economy.

The problems in both the financial and real sectors of the economy have called forth certain government programs. Some, such as the *Troubled Asset Relief Program* (TARP), popularly known as part of the financial bailout, have been designed to affect the financial sector. Others, such as the $787 billion fiscal stimulus bill (a product of expansionary fiscal policy), have been designed to affect the real sector. In addition, the Federal Reserve played a role in trying to deal with the problems in both the financial and real sectors.

Thus, the financial crisis in this country has affected the real sector of the economy, evoking a response from Congress and the Fed directed at addressing the problems in both sectors of the economy.

The rest of this chapter is about the financial crisis, the real sector crisis, and the actions of the Congress and the Federal Reserve. In short, it is about the economic events of 2007–2009 and the associated government actions directed at the economy. Within that general discussion, we will discuss the causes and effects of the financial crisis.

18-2 THE FINANCIAL CRISIS AS A BALANCE SHEET PROBLEM

Financial institutions have **balance sheets** consisting of listings of their assets, liabilities, and net worth (or capital). For a financial institution, an **asset** is anything that has value and that generates a flow of income. For example, suppose a commercial bank makes a loan to you for $40,000. You agree to pay $1,200 a month on the loan for so many months. Your loan is an *asset* as far as the bank is concerned. That loan has value to the bank and generates a flow of income for the bank—specifically, $1,200 a month.

A **liability** (for the bank) is something that it owes. For example, suppose you go to your local bank and open up a checking account. You deposit $5,000 into the account. Your deposit is the bank's *liability*. The bank owes you the $5,000. Another way of looking at that deposit is to say that you are lending the money to the bank. With that $5,000, the bank will make a loan to someone else. It will pay you 3 percent on your deposit, and then lend it to someone else for, say, 4.5 percent.

The difference between a bank's assets and its liabilities is its **net worth, or capital**. One way to view capital is as a buffer against insolvency. Suppose that the bank initially has assets of $100 and liabilities of $80. Then the value of its assets falls to $85. This might happen if people to whom the bank lent money do not pay it back. The bank can survive the $15 loss in the value of its assets because its capital of $20 cushioned the blow. The value of the bank's assets would have to fall enough to wipe out the entire capital amount before the bank is deemed insolvent. In other words, a $15 decline in asset value wouldn't do it, but a $21 decline would.

Insolvency
The condition that occurs when liabilities are greater than assets.

Balance Sheet
A record of the assets and liabilities of a bank.

Asset
Anything owned or that one has claim to which has value.

Liability
Anything that is owed to someone else.

Net Worth (or Capital)
The difference between assets and liabilities. For example, if assets are $100 and liabilities are $80, net worth, or capital, is $20.

The financial crisis can be viewed as a *balance sheet problem.* Many financial firms had assets on their balance sheets that declined in value. As these assets lost value, some financial institutions found themselves insolvent and other financial institutions found themselves coming perilously close to insolvency.

When a financial institution is either insolvent or close to insolvency, the real sector of the economy is affected. If the institution is insolvent, it can go out of the lending business, reducing the amount of lending in the economy. With less lending (and, consequently, less borrowing), there is less economic activity, which can show up as less buying and less producing. Less buying and producing can, in turn, result in firms going out of business, people getting fired from their jobs, and so on. Even if a bank isn't insolvent but is simply close to insolvency, it could simply pull back on its lending activities, thereby reducing economic activity in the real sector of the economy.

There are other consequences. As a bank becomes insolvent or close to insolvency, it may find that one of two things happen. First, people may not want to deposit funds in the bank. After all, if a bank is having a problem paying off its liabilities, why put your money there? If you put your money in that bank today, it might not be able to pay you back tomorrow. Also, knowing that a bank is likely to become insolvent, depositors in that bank might make a *run* on it. They might think that, if the bank is having a hard time paying off its liabilities, isn't it better for me to be one of the first people the bank pays off? There might not be enough money to pay everyone off.

Part of the run-on-the-bank problem these days is mitigated by the Federal Deposit Insurance Corporation (FDIC). The FDIC insures deposits in banks up to $250,000 per depositor. This insurance cuts down on people running to banks to get their money out if they think the bank is having problems. But it does so at the cost of pushing banks into taking a little more risk than they might take on if deposits weren't insured by the FDIC. To illustrate, if depositors' money is insured by the federal government, the bank knows that it isn't as likely to see a lot of people asking for their money all at once. This environment makes it less likely that the bank will worry about having to pay off all its depositors at once. Consequently, the banks may make riskier loans (riskier loans come with higher expected returns) than it would if its liabilities (specifically, its depositors' deposits) were not insured. But, of course, making riskier loans may raise the probability that the bank will become insolvent. After all, riskier loans do not get paid back as often as less risky loans.

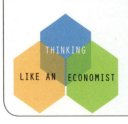

Unintended Effects Economists know that actions can have both intended and unintended effects. The intended effect of insuring bank deposits is to reduce bank runs. The unintended effect is to push banks into taking on more risk than they would have if bank deposits were not insured.

THINKING LIKE AN ECONOMIST

18-2a **Which Assets Were Risky?**

The assets on the banks' balance sheets that lost value because they turned out to be risky were the *subprime mortgage loans,* other nontraditional mortgage loans, *mortgage-backed securities,* and *collateralized debt obligations.*

Subprime mortgage loans and other nontraditional mortgage loans fall into the same category. They are mortgage loans granted to persons who might have low credit ratings or

Subprime Mortgage Loan
A nontraditional mortgage loan granted to persons who might have low credit ratings or some other factors which suggest that they could default on the debt.

about whom some other factors suggest that they could default on repayment of the debt. Anyone who is not paying for a house with cash has to take out a mortgage loan. Mortgage loans often come with certain restrictions. They might specify that a borrower must make a down payment equal to a specified percentage (say, 10 percent) of the purchase price of the house, that he needs a certain dollar income, that he must have a good credit history, and so on. Generally speaking, mortgage-lending practices were stricter in the 1970s and 1980s than they were in the late 1990s and the first decade of the twenty-first century. In other words, lending practices loosened up in the latter years. A drastic loosening is reflected in subprime and other nontraditional mortgage loans. With subprime loans, loans were being given out to persons who could not have qualified for traditional loans (requiring larger down payments, better documentation of income, and so on).

Mortgage-backed securities (MBSs) are a type of asset-backed security that is secured by a mortgage or a collection of mortgages. Here is how an MBS is created: Bank A has made 5,000 mortgage loans, some of which are subprime and other nontraditional loans. It bundles all 5,000 loans into a package, which consists of the expected future payments that will be made on the 5,000 loans. For example, one of the 5,000 loans was made to Smith, who pays $2,400 a month on her mortgage loan. The bank cuts up the package of 5,000 loans into slices and sells them; these slices are the mortgage-backed securities themselves. Thus, they are called mortgage-backed securities because they are backed by (or composed of) mortgage loans. For example, if you buy a slice that represents 1/1,000 of the pool of mortgages, then what you will receive is 1/1,000 of the payments made on the 5,000 loans in the pool.

Collateralized debt obligations (CDOs) are like MBSs, except that the slices are not equal. Some people who hold certain slices get paid before other people with other slices. The slices are called *tranches* and are of different risk.

What is important is that the value of an MBS and a CDO depends on the people who are paying off their mortgage loans. If a lot of people do not pay off their loans, then the MBSs and CDOs lose their value. Look at it this way: You buy a slice of an MBS for $10,000, entitling you to a payment of $500 a month for *x* number of years. What happens to your payments of $500 a month if the borrowers do not pay off their mortgage loans? All of a sudden, you do not receive the payments you thought you were going to receive, and your MBS is worthless.

In 2006, some people with subprime and other nontraditional loans were not able to make their monthly payments on their mortgage loans. (We explain why later.) As a result, banks and other financial institutions experienced a decline in the value of their assets: the subprime loans, other nontraditional loans, MBSs, and CDOs listed as assets on their balance sheets. As the value of these assets declined, some banks and financial institutions slid into insolvency and others were coming ever closer to insolvency.

18-2b **Three Questions**

At this point, the story of the financial crisis goes in different directions, which are related to three questions:

- Why were many of the people who had taken out subprime and other nontraditional loans suddenly unable to make their monthly payments?

- Why did traditional lending give way to subprime and other nontraditional lending?

- Why didn't the banks and other financial institutions have a bigger capital buffer (against insolvency) when they found themselves with loans that were not being paid off and MBSs and CDOs that were losing their value?

Mortgage-Backed Security (MBS)

A type of asset-backed security that is secured by a mortgage or a collection of mortgages.

The answer to the first question has to do with the housing market. Related to the housing market is a discussion of the Fed, its monetary policy, and a global savings glut.

The answer to the second question relates to Congress, two presidents, Fannie Mae and Freddie Mac, and securitization.

The answer to the third question relates to leverage and regulatory capital arbitrage.

SELF-TEST

(Answers to Self-Test questions are in Answers to Self-Test Questions at the back of the book.)

1. Explain how the net worth, or capital, of a bank can act as a buffer against insolvency.

2. Explain how a decline in the value of a bank's assets could lead to less lending activity.

3. What is a financial crisis?

18-3 THE FED, INTEREST RATES, AND HOUSING PRICES

We know that the Fed sets a target for the federal funds rate, which is the interest rate banks charge each other for loans. For example, if bank A wants to borrow $4 million from bank B, it would pay bank B the federal funds rate for the loan.

Now, the Fed does not set the federal funds rate by edict. Instead, it undertakes certain monetary actions so that the market federal funds rate equals the federal funds rate target. To illustrate, if the current market federal funds rate is 5 percent and the Fed's target federal funds rate is 3 percent, the Fed will inject reserves into the banking system so that the federal funds rate falls to 3 percent.

Exhibit 1 shows the federal funds rate for the period from a little before 2001 to 2007. In January of 2001, the federal funds rate was 6 percent, but it was much lower, 1.75 percent, in December 2001. During the period 2002–2005, it was in the 1–2 percent range. Then, in June 2006, the federal funds rate rose to 5.25 percent. What was behind the decline in the federal funds rate from January 2001 to January 2006, some argue, was that, beginning in 2001, the Fed dramatically lowered its federal funds rate target. That target was especially low during the period 2002–2005.

The Fed pursued such a low federal funds rate target because it believed that, if the federal funds rate decreased, so would other interest rates in the economy (especially short-term rates). And the Fed wanted to lower interest rates in the economy for a number of reasons: It was trying to stimulate economic activity; it was afraid that, if it didn't nudge interest rates down, the economy might fall into a recession; and it seemed to be worried about deflation.

The specific reason for the low-interest-rate policy is not as important as the fact that such a policy had certain effects. One major effect is that the Fed's low federal fund targets led to a decline in mortgage interest rates. Here is the process: When the Fed lowers its federal funds rate target, it ends up injecting reserves into the banking system to bring the actual federal funds rate down to its new, lower target level. As a by-product of having more reserves in the banking system, banks can make more loans—such as mortgage loans. Thus, mortgage rates decline. When mortgage rates decline, more people take out mortgage loans to buy houses; it is cheaper to buy a house when mortgage rates are low

> **EXHIBIT 1**

The Federal Funds Rate for Various Years

The federal funds rate starts out relatively high in early 2001 and then starts to decline. The federal funds rate was in the 1–2 percent category in 2002–2005.

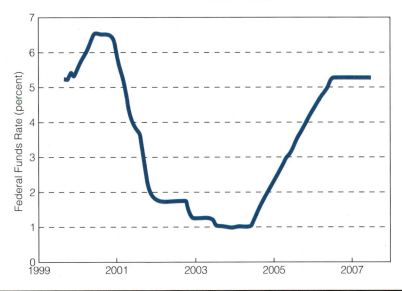

than when they are high. Another effect is that people take out bigger loans than they would have taken out at higher interest rates.

So the Fed's low federal funds rate target policy made it possible for more people to take out mortgage loans. But more people with loans—and some people with bigger loans—added demand to the housing market. As demand in the housing market rose, so did housing prices.

18-3a The Global Savings Glut and Low Interest Rates

At this point in our story, some economists mention the "global savings glut" as an alternative explanation for lower interest rates. A *global savings glut* describes an excess of savings over investment. Emerging countries in the world began to save more, and much of the extra savings found its way to the United States, where it increased the supply of loanable funds and lowered interest rates. The increased supply of loanable funds played a role in the housing story, in which low mortgage interest rates were already leading to rising house prices and to greater borrowing to buy houses.

Some economists have questioned whether there was a global savings glut. One in particular is John Taylor of Stanford University. Taylor makes a major point with the help of Exhibit 2, which is from an International Monetary Fund study that shows global savings and global investment as a share of World GDP for different years. For example, global investment was approximately 22 percent of World GDP in 2004, and savings were slightly over 21 percent of World GDP in the same year. The point that Taylor makes is that global savings as a percentage of World GDP was lower in the period 2002–2004 than it was in the 1970s and 1980s. Yet interest rates in the United States were low in the

> **EXHIBIT 2**

Global Savings and Investment as a Percentage of World GDP

Global savings was a smaller percentage of World GDP in the period 2002–2004 than it was in the 1970s and 1980s. John Taylor has argued that the data here are more nearly representative of a savings shortage than a savings glut during the period 2002–2004.

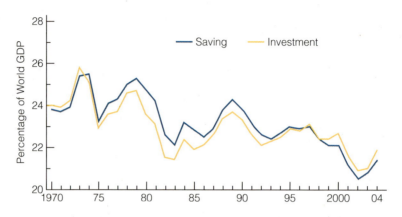

period 2002–2004. In other words, low interest rates in the United States corresponded to the time when savings as a percentage of World GDP were low. But one would think that low interest rates would have corresponded to a time when savings as percentage of World GDP was *high*, not low.

If emerging and developing countries supposedly sent their excess savings to the United States, in the process lowering interest rates, what did their savings and investment look like as percentages of GDP? Exhibit 3(a) shows that the savings rate as a percentage of emerging countries' GDP rose during the period from 2002 to 2008. According to the global savings glut story, we would expect that the rising savings rate in emerging countries would lower interest rates in the United States. Yet look at the mortgage rates on a 30-year mortgage in the United States during the period 1998–2009 [Exhibit 3(b)]. Specifically, during the period 2000–2008—the period in which savings rates in emerging countries were rising—mortgage rates fell from 2000 to 2003. They stayed low during the period 2003 to 2005, and then they began to rise. In other words, the rising savings rate in emerging countries is consistent with both *falling* and *rising* mortgage interest rates, not simply with lower interest rates.

18-3b Our Story So Far

So far, we know that the banks had balance sheet problems. When the assets listed on their balance sheets (especially the subprime loans, MBSs, and CDOs) began to decline in value, some banks became insolvent and other banks came critically close to insolvency. As a result, banks pulled back their lending, and the reduction in lending adversely affected the real sector of the economy. What we do not yet know is *why* the people who had taken out subprime and other nontraditional loans could not pay back their loans, thus adversely affecting the values of MBSs and CDOs. To explain that part of the story, we need to know more about low interest rates and the housing price boom. This need takes us to a discussion of the Taylor rule.

> **EXHIBIT 3**

Savings and Investment Rates and 30-Year Conventional Mortgage Rates, Various Years

(a) Savings and investment in emerging and developing countries as a percentage of the GDP in those countries. (b) The 30-year conventional mortgage rate for various years.

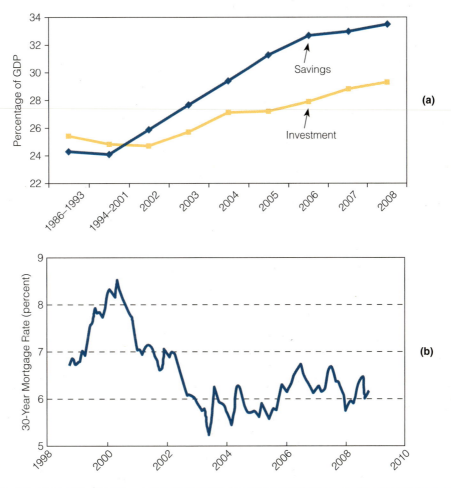

18-4 THE TAYLOR RULE AND INTEREST RATES

As mentioned in earlier chapters, the Taylor rule is a monetary rule of sorts; it is a recommendation of how the Fed should set its federal funds rate target. Essentially, it says that the Fed should raise the federal funds interest rate when inflation increases and lower it when GDP declines. In essence, the Taylor rule specifies how much the federal funds rate should change in different circumstances.

According to John Taylor (for whom the rule is named), during the period from 2002 to early 2006, the Fed set its federal funds rate target too low. Taylor comes to this conclusion by comparing the actual federal funds rate with the rate that would have existed had the Fed set its target according to the Taylor rule. Exhibit 4 shows that

> EXHIBIT 4

Federal Funds Rate, Actual and Consistent with the Taylor Rule, Various Years

The actual federal funds rate and the federal funds rate consistent with the Taylor rule for various years.

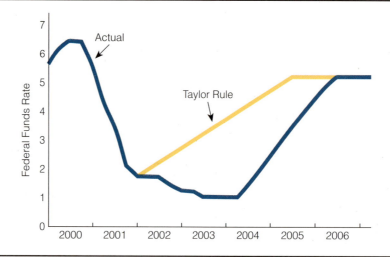

the federal funds rate would have been higher during the period in question had the Fed implemented the Taylor rule. Taylor concludes that, when we compare actual Fed monetary policy with the monetary policy required by the Taylor rule, we see that the Fed's policy was "too expansionary" during the period in question. It is this deviation from the Taylor rule that Taylor believes brought about the "too low" interest rates that led to rising house prices in the United States. Is Taylor correct? One piece of evidence in his favor is that there is a strong correlation between a housing boom (defined in terms of housing investment as a percentage of GDP) in different countries and deviations from the Taylor rule. For example, within member countries of the Organisation for Economic Co-operation and Development (OECD), the countries whose monetary policies deviated most from the Taylor rule had bigger housing booms than the countries whose monetary policies deviated less from the Taylor rule.[1] However, a study by Federal Reserve staff that takes into account more than the OECD countries contradicts that finding, indicating that deviations from the Taylor rule are not correlated with housing prices.

18-4a Alan Greenspan Responds

Alan Greenspan was chair of the Federal Reserve from 1987 to 2006. He has argued in favor of the global savings glut as an explanation for the decline in interest rates and against the position held by John Taylor. Greenspan argues that the Taylor rule is not really a fail-safe monetary rule for the Fed to follow because it cannot be applied to asset prices (such as house prices). Greenspan's argument is essentially this: (1) John Taylor uses the Taylor rule to argue that the Fed held interest rates too low during the first decade of the twenty-first century. In other words, if the Fed had set monetary policy in accordance with the Taylor rule during that period, interest rates wouldn't have been too low and there wouldn't have been a housing boom. (2) But (says Greenspan) the Taylor rule is structured in such a way as to indicate a proper federal funds rate target necessary

---

[1] The 34 member countries of the OECD are Australia, Austria, Belgium, Canada, Chile, the Czech Republic, Denmark, Estonia, Finland, France, Germany, Greece, Hungary, Iceland, Ireland, Israel, Italy, Japan, South Korea, Luxembourg, Mexico, the Netherlands, New Zealand, Norway, Poland, Portugal, Slovakia, Slovenia, Spain, Sweden, Switzerland, Turkey, the United Kingdom, and the United States.

to balance the trade-off between inflation and unemployment. Moreover, the type of inflation that the Taylor rule addresses is *product-price inflation*, not *asset-price inflation* (such as house price inflation). (3) So, unless there is a strong correlation between the consumer price index (CPI) and house prices (and Greenspan says there isn't), then the Taylor rule is *inappropriate* to use in trying to figure out the causes of sharp increases in house prices.

Greenspan has also argued that the boom in housing was caused by low *long-term* interest rates (such as the 30-year fixed mortgage rate), not short-term interest rates. Moreover, he argues that the Fed has much more control over short-term interest rates (such as the federal funds rate) than over long-term interest rates. Greenspan notes:

> In the United States, the house price bubble was driven by the low level of the 30 year fixed rate mortgage that decline from its mid-2000 peak, six months prior to the FOMC (Federal Open Market Committee) easing of the federal funds rate in January, 2001.[2]

18-4b Rising House Prices, Delinquency Rates, and Foreclosures

During the period 2003–2005, housing prices were rising. But during the same period, delinquency rates (on **adjustable rate mortgages**, whose interest rate is adjusted periodically, depending on various factors) and foreclosure rates were falling. In other words, as house prices were rising, more people were paying off their mortgage loans and fewer people suffered foreclosure. There is perhaps a good reason for the inverse relationship between housing prices and delinquency and foreclosure rates. When house prices are rising, home owners are gaining equity in their homes. **Equity** is the difference between the price the house can be sold for and what one owes on the house. To illustrate, if you owe $500,000 on a house and the price of the house is $600,000, you have $100,000 in equity. If the price of the house rises to $650,000, your equity rises to $150,000. When housing prices decline, the benefits of holding on to a house decline. In particular, if the price of the house falls below the value of the mortgage loan (if, for instance, the house can be sold for no more than, say, $480,000 and the mortgage loan is $500,000), then some people will not pay off their loans.

Looking at delinquency and foreclosure rates only during a period of rising prices can give a false picture of the risks that are inherent in giving out mortgage loans. To illustrate, suppose that, during years 1–10, house prices are falling while delinquency and foreclosure rates are up. During years 11–20, house prices are rising while delinquency and foreclosure rates are down. Now, suppose a lender who is considering giving out mortgage loans in year 21 looks only at years 11–20 to get some idea of how risky mortgage loans are. The lender might come away thinking that they are not risky at all (because delinquency and foreclosure rates are relatively low). But the picture is very different for years 1–10 and even more different for years 1–20. The point is that, if, during the first decade of the twenty-first century, lenders were looking only at recent past behavior in delinquency and foreclosure rates when deciding how risky mortgage loans are, then they *underestimated* the risk of mortgage loans. The mortgage loans they were giving out were riskier than they thought they were.

So, if the low-interest-rate policy of the Fed pushed up home prices, it also led to lower delinquency and foreclosure rates. Lenders, who perhaps were viewing less than the complete time span of delinquency and foreclosure rates, then mistakenly thought

Adjustable Rate Mortgage
A mortgage whose interest rate is adjusted periodically, depending on various factors.

Equity (in a House)
The difference between the price the house can be sold for and what one owes on the house.

---

[2] *The Crisis,* by Alan Greenspan, Second Draft: March 9, 2010.

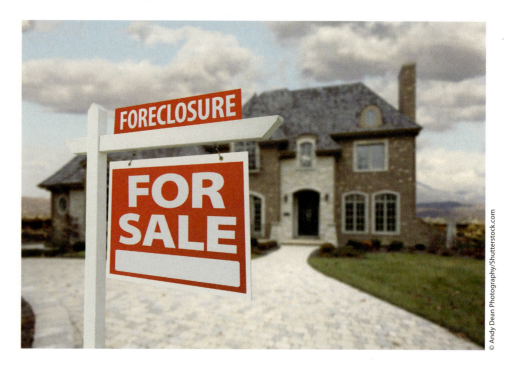

that granting mortgage loans was a less risky business than it was. With the benefit of hindsight, we now know that too many risky mortgage loans ended up being made. The subprime loans, the MBSs, and the CDOs eventually led to the declining asset values on banks' balance sheets.

SELF-TEST

1. What is the global-savings-glut explanation of rising housing prices? What is the Fed-low-interest-rate explanation of rising housing prices?

2. According to John Taylor, who or what caused the boom in housing prices in the United States in the first decade of the twenty-first century?

18-5 THE POLITICS OF HOUSING

Mortgage-lending standards in the United States declined in the 1990s and in the first decade of the twenty-first century. To understand why, we need to compare traditional and nontraditional lending practices. In traditional lending, borrowers must provide proof of income, employment, and assets. In nontraditional lending, borrowers may not be asked to provide proof of income, employment, and assets. Also, in traditional lending, down payments are a larger percentage of the house being purchased than in nontraditional lending. For example, a typical down payment in traditional mortgage lending is 20 percent. In nontraditional mortgage lending, it could be 2–5 percent.

In the 1990s and the first decade of the twenty-first century, the mortgage market saw a change in the composition of mortgage lending—away from more traditional lending and toward more nontraditional lending. For example, many lenders waived requirements that borrowers document their incomes, assets, and employment information and required down payments of only 2 or 3 percent or, in some cases, 0 percent.

Why lending practices declined makes for an interesting story that tells what was going on in both the private sector and government. In this section, we talk about what was going on in government, especially as it relates to the politics of housing.

18-5a **The Community Reinvestment Act**

The Community Reinvestment Act (CRA) was passed in 1977. Its purpose was to encourage financial institutions to meet the needs of borrowers in all segments of their communities, including low- and moderate-income borrowers. In 1995, Congress revised the CRA to give banks a stronger incentive to increase the percentage of mortgage loans (among other loans) going to low- and moderate-income

borrowers. Some have argued that Congress was essentially imposing quotas on banks to apply "innovative or flexible" standards to meet the borrowing needs of these borrowers. Some have argued that, essentially, the CRA forced banks to relax their lending standards so that they could make loans that they otherwise would not have made. Some take a different position, arguing that banks did not have to give out loans they didn't want to. However, banks that were not in compliance with the CRA could find their applications for new branches, mergers, or acquisitions denied. According to economist Thomas Sowell,

> … when legislation was pending in 1999 to permit banks to diversify into selling investment securities, the White House urged "that banks given unsatisfactory ratings under the 1977 Community Reinvestment Act be prohibited from enjoying the new diversification privileges" of this legislation. Accordingly, when Congress passed legislation removing existing prohibitions against banks affiliating with securities or insurance firms, this new scope of banking operations was in fact reserved for those banks that had a "satisfactory record of meeting community credit needs or better, at the most recent examination of each such institution"—that is, banks that met government-imposed quotas.[3]

18-6 FANNIE MAE AND FREDDIE MAC

Fannie Mae (the Federal National Mortgage Association, or FNMA) came into existence in 1938 to add demand to the housing market. Specifically, Fannie Mae would buy mortgage loans from banks that had originated the loans. For example, bank A might make a mortgage loan to a borrower and then sell the mortgage loan to Fannie Mae, in the process receiving funds from Fannie Mae with which to create more mortgages. In 1970, Freddie Mac (the Federal Home Loan Mortgage Corporation, or FHLMC) was established to do much the same things as Fannie Mae.

To buy the mortgage loans from banks, Fannie Mae and Freddie Mac got the money in a number of ways. One way was to borrow it. Another way was by creating MBSs and then

---

[3]. Thomas Sowell, *The Housing Boom and Bust* (New York: Basic Books, 2010), p. 39.

selling them. (They also insured them.) Suppose an MBS issued by Fannie Mae includes the repayment of 10,000 mortgage loans and 100 of them are not repaid. Then Fannie Mae steps in and pays off those loans, but to do so, Fannie Mae has to have enough capital (net worth). In the recent financial crisis, Fannie Mae did not have enough capital to pay off all the loans that were not being repaid. Although Fannie Mae did not have explicit and formal backing from the U.S. government, many of the investors who bought the MBSs that Fannie issued thought that the U.S. government would come to Fannie Mae's rescue should she need it. They were proved right: In September 2008, the U.S. government committed $200 billion (as needed on a quarterly basis) to Fannie Mae to correct any deficiencies in its net worth.

Beginning in the early 1990s, government pressure was placed on both Fannie Mae and Freddie Mac to increase their purchases of mortgages made to low- to moderate-income families. In 1996, the Department of Housing and Urban Development (HUD) stipulated that 42 percent of all mortgages purchased by Fannie Mae and Freddie Mac were to be given to individuals with incomes below the median incomes in their areas. In 1999, the quota was raised to 50 percent. In short, HUD placed pressure on Fannie and Freddie to buy nontraditional loans, and that pressure came not only from HUD, but also from key members of Congress. In 2000, Fannie bought $1.2 billion worth of subprime mortgages; in 2001, the amount rose to $9.2 billion; and in 2003, to $15 billion. In 2004, both Fannie and Freddie had spent $175 billion on subprime loans.

The purchase of subprime loans by Fannie and Freddie and the emergence of MBSs backed by subprime loans created a market in subprime lending. Specifically, the large-scale expansion of Fannie and Freddie into the subprime loan business made it profitable for other financial institutions to grant subprime loans in order to sell them to Fannie and Freddie.

18-7 THE ROLE OF LEVERAGE AND REGULATORY CAPITAL ARBITRAGE

Leverage and regulatory capital arbitrage were two prominent features of the financial crisis.

18-7a Leverage

Leverage is the use of borrowed funds to increase the returns that can be earned with a given amount of capital. Suppose a bank has $100 in assets (primarily outstanding loans) and $92 in liabilities. Then it's capital, or net worth, is $8. Its leverage ratio—the ratio of its assets to capital—is 100 to 8, or 12½ to 1.[4] Now, suppose the bank's assets increase in value by 10 percent. Then the bank's assets are now $110, and because its liabilities are still $92, the bank now has $18 worth of capital. In other words, the 10 percent increase in the value of the bank's assets has more than doubled the bank's capital (from $8 to $18). This is an increase of 125 percent.

Now change the example. Suppose the bank borrows $5. Then its liabilities rise to $97. Now the bank has only $3 in capital. Accordingly, its leverage ratio rises from 100 to 8 (12½ to 1) to 100 to 3 (33⅓ to 1). The bank is said to be much more highly leveraged now than it was before. If the assets of the bank rise by 10 percent, to $110, then the bank's capital rises from $3 to $13, an increase of 333 percent. The lesson is that borrowing to increase the leverage ratio raises the percentage rise in capital, given a rise

Leverage
The use of borrowed funds to increase the returns that can be earned with a given amount of capital.

---

[4] One can use different leverage ratios to get an idea of a firm's ability to meet its financial obligations. We have used one particular leverage ratio in our discussion here.

in the value of assets. In other words, if the value of assets is rising, a high leverage ratio increases the percentage rise in capital.

But there is a downside to a high leverage ratio: A decline in asset values magnifies losses. Suppose that when the bank had a leverage ratio of 12½ to 1, its assets declined in value by 4 percent. Then the value of the bank's assets falls from $100 to $96 as its liabilities remain constant at $92. The bank's capital falls from $8 to $4, a decline of 50 percent. Of course, the bank is still solvent, because its assets remain greater than its liabilities.

However, if the bank has a leverage ratio of 33⅓ to 1 when its assets decline in value by 4 percent to $96, then the bank is now insolvent: Its liabilities are $97, so it has negative capital (–$1).

Thus, if a bank is highly leveraged (i.e., it has a high leverage ratio), even a small decline in the value of its assets can push it into insolvency. Part of the explanation of the financial crisis of 2007–2009 is that many banks (and other financial institutions) were highly leveraged. Consequently, when the value of their assets (some of which were subprime loans and others of which were MBSs backed by subprime loans) declined, they were thrown into insolvency or came very close to insolvency.

When financial institutions are highly leveraged, the availability of credit in the economy can suffer if asset values decline. To see how, suppose that, in order to meet its legal capital requirements, a bank must have 5 percent of capital to back every $1 of a loan (an asset) that it grants. Then if the bank has $100 billion in loans outstanding, it must have $5 billion in capital. If the bank's capital falls to $4 billion as a result of the value of its loans declining, the bank has to do something to be in compliance with the 5 percent requirement. The owners either to have add more capital to the bank, or the bank has to cut back its loans to $80 billion ($4 billion is 5 percent of $80 billion). So, a fall in capital of $1 billion can lead to a $20 billion reduction in bank loans.

A reduction in loans occurring at a number of banks at the same time can dramatically affect the amount of lending and borrowing in the economy. And, as we know, a decline in credit can affect the real sector of the economy, reducing economic activity, leading to a decline in purchases and sales, and raising unemployment.

18-7b Regulatory Capital Arbitrage

Regulatory capital is the percentage of capital that a financial institution must hold because of regulatory requirements. For example, a bank may have to have 5 percent of capital for every $1 of a loan it creates. Regulatory capital requirements exist for the sake of bank safety. Supposedly, if a bank is meeting its regulatory capital requirements, it is a safe and sound bank that is unlikely to suffer insolvency due to any losses it may incur.

The important question, though, is *what percentage* of capital is required to keep a bank safe and sound? Is a capital requirement of 10 percent too high or a capital requirement of 2 percent too low? After all, a high capital requirement might make a bank safe and sound (and less likely to become insolvent), but it can also lower a bank's returns. That is the lesson of leverage: A higher leverage ratio increases gains when assets values rise. So there is a *return–safety trade-off* that speaks to how much capital a bank should hold. More capital means more safety, but it also means lower returns when asset values are rising.

Some economists have argued that regulatory capital arbitrage explains why banks (and other financial institutions) were as highly leveraged as they were. Then, when asset values began to decline, a cascading effect set in that ended with credit being less available in the economy.

The question of how much capital regulators should require banks to hold is based on the concept of *risk-weighted assets*. The idea is that not all assets are alike: Some are riskier than others. To illustrate, if bank A holds assets X and Y, and asset X is very risky and asset Y is not so risky, then the bank should hold more capital for asset X than for asset Y.

Regulatory Capital
The amount of capital that a financial institution must hold because of regulatory requirements.

ECONOMICS24/7

The TED Spread

Consider two interest rates. The first is the three-month interest rate on Treasury bills, which are are issued by the U.S. Treasury when it wants to borrow funds from the public. For example, the Treasury might issue a three-month Treasury bill to help finance the government budget deficit.

The second interest rate is the three-month London InterBank Offered Rate, or LIBOR, which is the average interest rate that reputable banks can borrow funds from other banks. The three-month LIBOR is therefore the average interest rate at which reputable banks can borrow funds for three months from other banks. In other words, it is the average interest rate for a three-month loan that one bank takes out from another bank.

The TED spread is the difference between the three-month LIBOR and the three-month Treasury bill rate: [5]

TED spread = three-month LIBOR − three-month Treasury bill rate

If the LIBOR is, say, 3.3 percent and the Treasury bill rate is 3.0 percent, then the TED spread is 0.30 percent. Often, the TED spread is expressed in terms of basis points, so 0.30 percent is 30 basis points. Historically, the TED spread has stayed within the range from 30 basis points to 50 basis points.

Now, before we explain why the TED spread is computed and why it may be important, ask yourself this question: Is the risk always the same that borrowers in the global financial system will not pay back the loans they have taken out? The answer to this question is no: Sometimes the risk that borrowers will default on loans is higher than at other times. Now, suppose there was a way that we could gauge when borrowers are less likely to pay back loans. In other words, suppose there were a "thermometer" of sorts that we could use to take the "temperature" of the global financial system to see if things were moving toward a higher probability of default or a lower probability of default. Well, to a large extent, the TED spread is that "thermometer." To understand how, keep the following in mind: Lenders can lend funds both to the U.S. Treasury and to banks. When the U.S. Treasury and banks are equally likely to repay those loans, the Treasury bill rate and LIBOR should be the same. But usually the LIBOR is a little higher, because lenders generally believe that the U.S. Treasury is always going to repay its debt, so lending to the U.S. Treasury is safe. But it is not quite as safe to lend to banks, because banks could get into a situation where the persons and businesses they have lent to do not pay back their loans (to the degree expected), placing banks in a situation in which they in turn can't

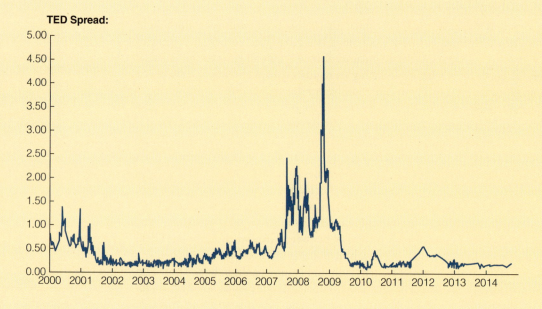

TED Spread:

pay back the loans they have taken out. With this scenario in mind, think of banks that held MBSs (as assets) and found that many of the subprime mortgage loans weren't being repaid.

Now think of a TED spread of, say, 20 basis points. This is a relatively small spread, and it indicates that lenders believe that the safety they receive from lending to the U.S. Treasury is only slightly greater than the safety they receive from lending to banks. Now, suppose that the TED spread rises to, say, 330 basis points. In other words, the LIBOR is 3.3 percent higher than the Treasury bill rate. Is lending to banks now just slightly less safe than lending to the U.S. Treasury? Not at all. Whereas once lenders said to banks that they needed only 20 basis points more to lend to them than to the U.S. Treasury, now they are saying that they need 330 basis points more to lend to them than to the U.S. Treasury. In other words, banks have

become "less safe," and therefore lenders are asking for a higher interest rate to lend to them.

In 2007, because of the subprime mortgage crisis, the TED spread, which historically is in the range from 30 to 50 basis points, increased to a range from 150 to 200 basis points. On October 10, 2008, the TED spread rose to a historical high of 458 basis points, or 4.58 percent.

---

5. "TED" is an acronym: The "T" stands for the Treasury bill rate and "ED" stands for Eurodollar futures contract. Eurodollars are U.S. dollar deposits in non-U.S. banks. The name "Eurodollar" has nothing to do with geography today nor does it have anything to do with the euro currency. Originally, the TED spread was the difference between three-month futures contracts on U.S. Treasury bills and three-month contracts for Eurodollars. However, since the Chicago Mercantile Exchange dropped Treasury bill futures, the TED spread is now the difference between the three-month Treasury bill rate and the three-month LIBOR.

ECONOMICS 24/7

Too Big to Fail

At one time, the phrase "too big to fail" meant that a company was so large and so diversified in its businesses (conducting business in numerous different areas in different countries) that a downturn in one business area or in one country wouldn't really hurt it; the company would still be successful in many other areas. It had its eggs in a lot of different baskets, so to speak—all over the world—so a broken egg in one or two places didn't mean failure. It was, in a sense, "too big to fail."

Today, the term "too big to fail" means something different. It refers to a company or institution that is so big that, if the government were to allow it to fail, there would be negative repercussions for other companies and for the economy as a whole. A more accurate descriptive phrase might be "too big to let fail," but the phrase "too big to fail" is used instead.

Think of the too-big-to-fail (TBTF) company or institution today as occupying the center of a circle, with its many appendages (much like the tentacles of an octopus) extended outward. If the TBTF institution fails, then the repercussions flow outward to adversely affect others. So,

to prevent others from being hurt by its failure, government must step in and prevent the TBTF institution from failing, even if government has to use taxpayer funds to do so. In fact, some argue that such a use of taxpayer funds is wise: Better to use $500 billion of taxpayer funds to save the economy than to let the economy contract, resulting in rising unemployment, bankruptcies, and dwindling tax revenues.

In the financial crisis of 2007–2009, both Fannie Mae and Freddie Mac were considered too big to fail, as was General Motors, some investment and commercial banks, and some financial services and insurance companies (such as American International Group, or AIG).

Businesses that are TBTF and that are therefore bailed out when they are in trouble have competitive market advantages vis-à-vis companies that are small enough to let fail. Suppose bank A is considered TBTF but banks B–Z are not. Then many depositors will want to put their money in bank A instead of banks B–Z because they feel safer putting their money there. After all, if their bank—Bank A—has any problems, the government will bail it out.

So banks (and other institutions) that are TBTF are often shielded from risk because they know they will be bailed out if they run into problems. So why not take on the risk in search of the high returns? After all, if the returns materialize, they win; but if they don't, and it looks like failure is around the corner, they will be bailed out. Heads, we win; tails, the taxpayer loses. In other words, being TBTF creates a *moral hazard problem:* a party that is insulated from risk behaves differently than it would behave it if weren't shielded from risk. (Think of how fast you might drive if you knew it were impossible for you to be hurt in a car accident.)

In 2007–2010, with respect to the TBTF issue, some individuals argued that some institutions were truly too big to fail because, if they did fail, not only they, but many others, would feel the consequences. Better to save them today than to let many others suffer tomorrow. Other individuals argued that, by not allowing these institutions to fail, the government simply increased the probability that other financial crises would follow. In other words, when government protects institutions from failure, it simply increases the probability that those institutions will fail in the future. Finally, some argued that the least worst course of action was to bail out some TBTF institutions—this time—but then to pass regulatory measures that break up TBTF institutions into smaller sizes so that TBTF institutions no longer exist. In other words, being "too big to fail" is too big.

Under the 1988 Basel Accord (Basel I), international standards for risk-based capital requirements were introduced. Since then, banks have had to hold capital equivalent to 8 percent of their risk-weighted assets. To understand this requirement, think of a bank with two assets: Treasury bonds and uncollateralized commercial loans. The Treasury bonds are not risky assets. The bank can be sure that the U.S. Treasury is going to redeem those bonds. In comparison, the uncollateralized commercial loans are risky. The bank cannot be sure that all its commercial loans will be paid off. Because Treasury bonds are less risky than uncollateralized commercial loans, the bank would be expected to hold more capital against its commercial loans than its Treasury bonds.

As a concrete example of *regulatory capital arbitrage*, suppose that a bank has three kinds of assets—X, Y, and Z—and that they differ in their degree of riskiness. In other words, each class of asset has a different *risk weight*. Asset X has zero risk, so zero capital is required against it. Asset Y has a risk weight of 50 percent, so 50¢ of capital is needed for every $1 of asset Y. Asset Z has a risk weight of 80 percent, so 80¢ of capital is needed for every $1 of asset Z. Further, the total amount of each asset is $100, so the bank's assets are $300 altogether. To find the amount of risk-weighted assets, we multiply the amount of each asset by its risk weight and then sum the results:

$$\text{Risk-weighted assets} = (\$100 \times 0 \text{ percent}) + (\$100Y \times 50 \text{ percent})$$
$$+ (\$100Z \times 80 \text{ percent}) = \$130$$

Now, if the requirement is that financial institutions must hold 8 percent capital against their risk-weighted assets, then the financial institution with $130 of risk-weighted assets has to hold capital equal to 8 percent of $130, or $10.40:

$$\text{Amount of capital a bank must hold} = \$130 \times 8 \text{ percent}$$
$$= \$10.40$$

Regulatory capital arbitrage is a means of changing the composition of assets in such a way as to lower the overall amount of capital a financial institution holds for a given level of assets. A financial institution might want to practice regulatory capital arbitrage because of what was explained earlier about leverage: hold either less capital for a given amount of assets or more assets for a given amount of capital. In other words, a higher leverage ratio means higher returns, as long as asset values are rising. One way of increasing returns, then, is to reduce the amount of capital one needs to hold, given the overall capital requirements. Regulatory capital arbitrage offers a means of doing this.

Securitization—the process by which financial institutions aggregate debt (such as loans) in a pool and then issue securities backed by the pool—is one way to accomplish regulatory capital arbitrage. To illustrate, suppose a bank has $100 in mortgages for which it needs to hold $4 in capital. If the bank can create a CDO out of these mortgages, it may be able to reduce its capital to *less* than $4. Here's how: The CDO that the bank creates is sold to a **special-purpose vehicle (SPV)** that issues bonds based on the money that is expected to be forthcoming from the monthly mortgage payments. The bonds are divided up into tranches with different priorities. For example, senior tranches take priority over junior tranches; that is, when the money comes in from the mortgage loans, the people who hold the senior tranches are paid first and then the people who hold the junior tranches are paid. In other words, the people holding the senior tranches are shielded from losses relative to the people holding the junior tranches.

So, if most of the mortgage loans are high-quality loans, then most of the risk can be placed in the bottom few tranches and the higher tranches are safe. The senior tranches get a higher credit rating than the junior tranches. What does all this have to do with the amount of capital a bank holds? By getting high credit ratings for the senior tranches, a bank can lower the risk weight on those assets and, as a result, lower the amount of capital it has to hold for them. Even though the junior tranches require *more* capital, the lower capital requirements on the senior tranches can be organized so that they *outweigh* the requirements on the junior tranches and, as a result, overall requirements decline. In other words, securitization is the means by which regulatory capital arbitrage lowers capital requirements.

Regulatory Capital Arbitrage
A means of changing the composition of assets in such a way as to lower the overall amount of capital a financial institution holds for a given level of assets.

Securitization
The process by which financial institutions aggregate debt (such as loans) in a pool and then issue securities backed by the pool.

Special-Purpose Vehicle (SPV)
A legal entity created to fulfill narrow, specific, or temporary objectives.

18-7c Where We Are So Far

The Fed implemented a low-interest-rate policy in the first decade of the twenty-first century. Low mortgage rates then led to increased mortgage borrowing and added demand to the housing market. As a result, house prices increased. At the same time,

- banks were lowering lending standards to comply with the CRA.
- Fannie and Freddie came under political pressure to buy nontraditional loans (such as subprime loans) and to create a strong secondary market for MBSs backed by nontraditional loans.
- Fannie and Freddie securitization and private securitization were going on, the latter of which was the means of achieving regulatory capital arbitrage, a process that increased leverage ratios in financial institutions.

18-7d House Prices Decline

As long as house prices were rising, the dance continued. It took only a small decline in house prices, though, to start things unraveling. And house prices did begin to decline, as shown in Exhibit 5. As house prices came down, some recent home buyers saw the prices they could sell their houses for fall below their loan amounts. (For many new home owners, even a small price decline brought the value of their homes below the loan amount because they had put down very low—or no—down payments. In other words, their loan amounts were nearly equal to the purchase price of the house.)

Also, some of the mortgage loans that the borrowers had taken out had been adjustable rate mortgages, with a low interest payment in the early years followed by a reset of the interest rate in later years. What these people found is that their low interest rates were being reset at higher levels because mortgage rates had risen since they had taken out their loans.

As house prices declined, delinquency rates and foreclosure rates rose, for two reasons: (1) Some individuals found their loan amounts greater than the price they could sell their houses for; (2) other individuals found their mortgage rates resetting at higher rates, making for monthly payments that they could not afford. The banks holding assets in the form of subprime loans and MBSs then started to feel the consequences of the higher delinquency and foreclosure rates. Because of their high leverage ratios, they could not absorb much of a decline in asset values before they were insolvent or nearly so.

> **EXHIBIT 5**

The Case-Shiller Home Price Index

House prices begin to decline in mid-2006.

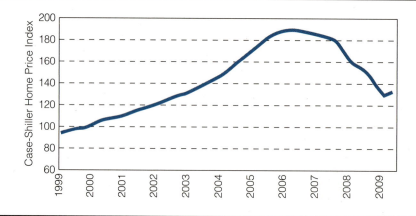

18-7e Domino Effects

When one bank finds that it cannot meet its capital requirements, how it responds can adversely affect other banks. For example, if bank A has to hold 5 percent of the value of its loans outstanding in capital and it has $100 billion in loans outstanding, then it must hold $5 billion in capital. If the bank's capital falls to $4 billion because the value of the bank's loans is declining, then the bank must reduce its assets to, say, $80 billion to be in compliance with the 5 percent capital requirement. The reduction in loans outstanding leads to less lending in the economy, which, as we know, can reduce economic activity.

Now, suppose that, instead of reducing its outstanding loans to meet its capital requirement, bank A sells some of its assets, including some MBSs. Because bank A is in trouble and has to sell some of its MBSs, it might sell the securities at a lower price than it would have liked. Thereafter, bank B, now holding MBSs as assets on its balance sheet, finds the value of its assets declining, thus lowering its capital. As a result, bank B has less than enough capital to meets its capital requirements, so it sells some of its MBSs to bank C, just as bank A did before. Soon bank C finds itself in the same position as bank B did earlier. And so on.

Thus, the banks fall, one after another, like dominos. The more dominos that fall, the more likely we are to see a big cutback in lending activity on the part of banks in order to meet their capital requirements. And the bigger the cutback in lending activity is, the more pronounced the effect will be in the real sector of the economy.

At the time, another problem could compound the problems of the banks. As word got out that a bank was near insolvency, the bank might find it harder to borrow money. Suppose bank A's assets have declined and it is approaching insolvency, and bank B hears that bank A is having problems. If bank A happens to ask bank B for a loan, bank B declines because it is afraid that bank A, faced with declining asset values, might not be able to repay the loan. (Banks ultimately must pay off their liabilities out of their assets. If the bank has assets of $100 and liabilities of $80, it could sell off its assets for $100 and pay off all $80 of its liabilities. But if its assets fall in value to, say, $70, then even if the bank sells off all its assets, it still couldn't pay off all its liabilities.)

18-7f How the Real Sector Affects the Financial Sector

If problems in the financial sector can affect the real sector of the economy, can problems in the real economy, caused by the problems in the financial sector, feed back into the financial sector and cause even bigger financial problems? The answer is yes. Consider the reduced lending that is a consequence of the bank's assets declining and its falling below its capital requirements. The reduced lending leads to problems in the real sector of the economy: less spending, decreased sales, sellers going out of business, unemployment rising, and so on. With sellers going out of business and the ranks of the unemployed swelling, many people and firms will find it increasingly difficult to pay off their debts, many of which are owed to the banks. As a result, even more loans on the bank's balance sheet lose value, pushing the bank ever closer to insolvency.

18-7g The Government Response

The federal government responded to the financial crisis and to the problems in the real sector of the economy in a number of ways. The responses can be categorized as *bailouts*, *fiscal stimulus*, and *easy money*:

- *Bailouts.* The $700 billion TARP took several forms. Two of them were the U.S. Treasury's buying some of the bad assets (such as MBSs) on the banks' balance

ECONOMICS 24/7

The Financial Crisis and Hyman Minsky: Model an Economy with a Wall Street

During the financial crisis, the name Hyman Minsky came up often among academic economists. Minsky was an American economist who died in 1996. In his book *Stabilizing an Unstable Economy*, he forcefully argued and developed the Keynesian notion that there are inherent instabilities in our economy. Was the financial crisis an example of an inherent instability? Had Minsky been alive, he would likely have argued in the positive. The author of the text conducted an interview with Hyman Minsky in July 1988. His answers to the questions asked will give you some insight into his thought of how an economy works.

QUESTION:

Prof. Minsky, you have stated, "the major flaw of our type of economy is that it is unstable." What exactly do you mean when you use the word "unstable" in this context, and are there any economic systems that are inherently stable?

MINSKY:

Basically, the only economies that are stable—in the sense that they are not subject to major swings up and down in economic activity (that aren't related to disasters such as war or famines)—are peasant, subsistence economies. But once economies enter into commercial trade to a large extent, they become dynamic and grow, and in the process of growth, capitalist conditions are introduced. These capitalist conditions then give way to cyclical fluctuations.

Now, as Schumpeter [Joseph Schumpeter, Austrian-American economist and political scientist (1883–1950)] said, " . . . there are only two fundamentally different groups of cycle theories." There are theories that model the economic process as a smooth, even flow characterized by an equilibrium. If any disturbance arises to the smooth behavior, the cause must be seen as occurring outside the system. And on the other hand, there are theories that model the economic process as essentially wavelike and [that] view cycles as the form that capitalist evolution takes.

My feeling is that the economic process is more accurately modeled and described in the latter way. Specifically, what I mean by "unstable" in the context of our economy is that it tends to generate what we might call chaos or endogenous incoherence from time to time, but this tendency can be constrained.

QUESTION:

In your book *Stabilizing an Unstable Economy*, you seem to be saying that many economists today, including many Keynesian economists, have not fully absorbed the full message and insight contained in Keynes's *General Theory*. In your mind, what is the central message of Keynes's *General Theory* and what insights into the workings of the economy has Keynes provided you with?

MINSKY:

Keynes gave us a powerful analytical formulation for handling the way in which an economy moves through time. The central message of his general theory is that you have to model an economy with a Wall Street. What does this mean? It means that there is a price system (and this is made very clear in the *General* Theory) for capital and financial assets that, in the short run, reflects quite different markets and considerations than the price level of current output. This means we have two sets of prices: current output prices and capital asset prices—the CPI and the Dow Jones [Industrial Average]. As a result, the quantity theory of money won't work, unless the two sets of prices are very closely tied together, which in fact they are not. This is one of the essential aspects of Keynes's contribution that is generally overlooked today: Keynesian economics considers asset as well as output prices as determining system behavior.

QUESTION:

As you know, not all economists agree with you that there is an inherent tendency of free-market economies to generate financial crises and severe economic depressions. Since there are bright economists on both sides of the issue, what do you think explains the sharp differences and thought when it comes to how the economy works?

MINSKY:

Start with Adam Smith. He has two questions. First he wanted to know why markets bring order instead of chaos. In short, Smith wanted to know why, in a market setting, where there are numerous participants, each making numerous decisions which are not openly coordinated with other decisions—why is there order instead of chaos? Smith also wanted to know why some nations are richer than other nations. We know he was interested in this because the title of his work was *An Inquiry into the Nature and Causes of the Wealth of Nations*. We have two major questions Smith was interested in answering, which remain the main questions of economics.

Other economists have been interested in answering them too. However, not all economists put equal weight on the two questions. Some economists put greater weight on the first question, and they tend to emphasize the equilibrium forces of a market economy. They think the equilibrium forces are dominant. Other economists

put greater weight on the second question and more deeply involve themselves in the performance and operation of the dynamic properties of an economy. When this is done, they begin to see things inherent in the economy that are not visible to those who emphasize equilibrium.

I believe that there are inherent instabilities in our economy; witness the Great Depression. I am also convinced that a system of intervention can be constructed so that a high level of economic performance can be realized and the inherent tendencies of the economy to degenerate into chaos can be contained.

sheets, and the government investing directly in some of the largest banks in the country, thus increasing the capital in banks. Also considered bailouts were the federal loans to General Motors and Chrysler in December 2008 to prevent the bankruptcy of those companies.

- *Fiscal Stimulus.* The Congress passed, and President Obama signed, a $787 billion fiscal stimulus bill in February 2009 in the hopes of injecting demand into the economy.

- *Easy Money.* In November 2008, the Federal Reserve announced that it would buy $800 billion of private debt in the hopes of increasing lending and borrowing in the economy.

18-7h **The Great Recession**

The Great Recession lasted from December 2007 to June 2009. During this time, Real GDP in the U.S. economy declined $553 billion. What caused the decline? What caused the Great Recession? Not all economists agree on the answer. Some argue that problems in the financial sector of the economy (some of which we have discussed in this chapter) began to affect the real economy. Specifically, the financial sector's problems began to depress spending, and the reduction in total spending in the economy moved the economy into recession. Think of the *AD* curve in our *AD–AS* model shifting to the left.

If the recession was caused by a reduction in spending, then either the money supply had to decline, or velocity had to decline, or both had to decline. Remember, one way of viewing total spending in the economy is that it is equal to the money supply times velocity:

$$\text{Total spending} = M \times V$$

If you look at the velocity for the M1 money supply in Exhibit 6(a), you will see that it was down during the Great Recession. (The shaded areas in the exhibit represent recessions.) And so was the velocity of M2 in Exhibit 6(b). So, all other things remaining constant, a decline in velocity would lower total spending, cause the *AD* curve in the economy to shift leftward, and result in a decline in Real GDP.

But what was happening to the money supply during this time? If you look at the graphs for the M1 and M2 money supplies in Exhibit 6 (c) and (d), respectively, you will

> EXHIBIT 6

Velocity and Money

Shaded areas represent recessions. M1 velocity declined during the Great

Recession (2007–2009) (a), as did M2 velocity (b). M1 and M2 money supplies increased during the Great Recession

[(c) and (d)]. Source: Federal Reserve Bank of St. Louis.

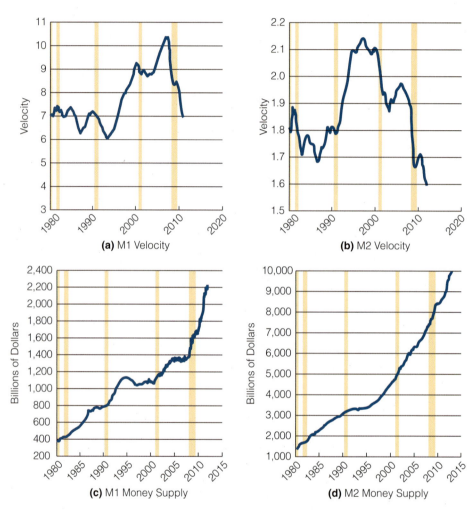

(a) M1 Velocity

(b) M2 Velocity

(c) M1 Money Supply

(d) M2 Money Supply

see that both money supplies were increasing during the Great Recession and, indeed, even for some time before the recession hit.

So, if the money supply was rising and velocity was declining, what was total spending doing? Total spending, of course, depends on how much the money supply is rising relative to how much velocity is declining. Now, we could calculate the percentage change in each variable—money supply and velocity—or we could simply look at what happens to P (the price level) times Q (Real GDP). That is, from the equation of exchange, we know that

$$M \times V = P \times Q$$

While $M \times V$ is simply total spending, $P \times Q$ is (nominal) GDP. So what happened to nominal GDP during the Great Recession? Well, beginning around August 2008, GDP stopped growing, and then it declined by about 4 percent over the next several quarters. In other words, even though the money supply was increasing, velocity was falling by enough to lower overall total spending (nominal spending) in the economy, as evidenced in the slowing and then decline in (nominal) GDP.

Now, the slowing and then decline in (nominal) GDP does not necessarily mean that Real GDP has to decline. After all, if GDP = $P \times Q$, then GDP can decline simply because P declines and Q remains constant (or even increases). But that is not what happened. In terms of our AD–$SRAS$ model, a decline in total spending ($M \times V$) meant that the AD curve shifted leftward and that, as long as the $SRAS$ curve is upward sloping, Q, or Real GDP, would decline, at least in the short run.

So, what caused the Great Recession? What caused the decline in Real GDP? According to some economists, the answer is that the decline in velocity was not adequately offset by a rise in the money supply. In other words, although the money supply might have been expanding during the period under consideration, it was not expanding "enough." We are then led to ask, How much would the money supply have had to expand so that there would be no Great Recession? The answer is, by enough to offset the decline in velocity.

Look at it this way: Suppose $M = \$400$ and $V = 3$; then total spending is $1,200. Now, let $P = \$12$ and $Q = 100$ units of a composite good. (A composite good is a good made up of all other goods: a little bit of houses, a little bit of cars, a little bit of computers, etc.) Then

$$M \times V = P \times Q$$

$$\$400 \times 3 = \$12 \times 100 \text{ units}$$

Now, suppose that velocity falls to 2 and the money supply rises to $500. Then total spending is $1,000 instead of what it was before, $1,200. That is,

$$M \times V = \text{Total spending}$$

$$\$500 \times 2 = \$1,000$$

It follows that, because $M \times V$ has fallen from $1,200 to $1,000, so must (nominal) GDP, or $P \times Q$, fall to $1,000. And if the $SRAS$ curve in the economy is upward sloping, then some of the decline in GDP is going to be in the form of a decline in Q, or Real GDP.

So, in the end, who or what caused the Great Recession? For economists who argue that "the money supply should have been increased more to offset the decline in velocity," the Fed caused the Great Recession. It didn't expand the money supply by enough to prevent the decline in velocity from causing total spending in the economy to drop, the AD curve to shift leftward, and Real GDP to decline.

SELF-TEST

1. Explain how a high leverage ratio can lead to insolvency if assets decline in value.

2. What happens in the financial sector can affect the real sector, and what happens in the real sector can affect the financial sector. Do you agree or disagree? Explain your answer.

3. What is regulatory capital arbitrage?

Office  Hours

"Do Economists and the Public Always Understand the Causes of Financial Crises?"

STUDENT:

Are all economists agreed on the causes of the financial crisis? If the answer is no, why?

INSTRUCTOR:

First, not all economists are agreed on the cause of the financial crisis. In this chapter, we have proposed that the principal factors causing the crisis were the Fed's low federal funds rate target policy, the politics of housing, and regulatory capital arbitrage. Most economists would agree that these factors all played a role in the financial crisis, but not all economists agree that each factor was of equal weight. For example, some economists might weight regulatory capital arbitrage as much more important in explaining the financial crisis than, say, the politics of housing (as described in the chapter). Also, not all economists agree that the Fed's low federal funds rate target policy mattered. Instead, it was the global savings glut.

STUDENT:

Is it a little like the Great Depression? Not all economists agree as to the cause of the Great Depression?

INSTRUCTOR:

Yes, it's somewhat like that. You're right that not all economists agree as to the cause(s) of the Great Depression, and among those economists who "sort of" agree on the main factors that caused the Great Depression, not all of them place equal weight on the various factors.

STUDENT:

Another issue that bothers me a little is the fact that when something big happens on the economic scene—such as a financial crisis—the lay public seems to be all over the map commenting on what caused the crisis. For example, some people seem to think that the latest

financial crisis was caused by government—specifically, the Fed, Congress, and Fannie and Freddie. Others seem to blame the banks and other financial institutions for taking excessive risks. With respect to the latter, you sometimes hear that the financial community was just out to make a lot of money as fast as possible so they pushed off these subprime loans onto a lot of people. It seems to me that what we think about the cause of the crisis has a lot to do with what we think is the right preventive medicine for the next crisis.

INSTRUCTOR:

In other words, if the cause of the crisis was that financial institutions weren't regulated enough, then the solution is to regulate banks more. Or if the cause of the crisis was a too lenient Fed combined with a lot of politics in the housing market, then the solution is some sort of monetary rule for the Fed and the depoliticization of the housing market.

STUDENT:

Yes, that is what I am talking about. If you think that X caused the crisis, then you want to do something about X. But if you think that Y caused the crisis, then, of course, you want to do something about Y.

INSTRUCTOR:

I can only agree with you on that. Whatever one believes about the causes of the financial crisis does seem to influence his or her opinion of what should be done to prevent another such crisis.

Points to remember

1. Not all economists are agreed on the cause(s) of the financial crisis. Not all members of the public are agreed on the cause(s) of the financial crisis.

2. What one identifies as the cause(s) of the financial crisis does influence one's opinion as to what should be done to prevent another financial crisis.

CHAPTER SUMMARY

A VIEW OF THE ECONOMY

- One way to view the economy is as consisting of two sectors: a financial sector and a real sector. The financial sector consists of financial institutions: commercial banks, investment banks, hedge funds, brokerage firms, and more. The real sector consists of firms that produce goods and services, individuals that buy goods and services, individuals that work for firms, and more.

A FINANCIAL CRISIS

- A financial crisis occurs when financial firms and financial markets undergo a major disruption. In turn, these problems make it difficult for persons to obtain loans from banks and other financial institutions.
- Problems in the financial sector can affect the real sector.
- One way to view a financial crisis is as a balance sheet problem. Specifically, the assets of financial institutions are declining in value, reducing the net worth (or capital) of the institutions and moving them closer to insolvency. As these institutions approach or reach insolvency, they pull back on lending activities. Pulling back on their lending activities can, in turn, adversely affect the real sector of the economy.

RISKY ASSETS

- Describing the financial crisis as a balance sheet problem requires us to identify the assets that declined in the middle of the first decade of the twenty-first century, causing asset values for financial institutions to decline and moving them closer to insolvency. These assets include subprime loans, other nontraditional loans, mortgage-backed securities, and collateralized debt obligations.

THE FED, THE FEDERAL FUNDS RATE TARGET, AND THE GLOBAL SAVINGS GLUT

- Some economists argue that the Fed set its target federal funds rate "too low" in the first decade of the twenty-first century, especially during the period 2002–2005. This policy had consequences, one of which was that mortgage rates declined, giving individuals an incentive to borrow to buy a house. As a result, the low mortgage interest rates fueled buying in the housing market, driving up house prices.
- Some economists argue that the cause of the low interest rates was the global savings glut. Specifically, emerging countries in the world began to save more, and these extra savings found their way to the United States, where they increased the supply of loanable funds and lowered interest rates (in particular, the mortgage interest rate). The low mortgage interest rates fueled buying in the housing market, driving up house prices.

THE TAYLOR RULES AND INTEREST RATES

- According to economist John Taylor, the Fed set its federal funds rate target "too low" during the first decade of the twenty-first century, as measured by what it would be if it were set by the Taylor rule. Accordingly, the low interest rates that followed fueled borrowing and the sharp rise in housing prices. One piece of evidence Taylor cited as evidence in favor of his argument is that there is a strong correlation between a housing boom in different countries and deviations from the Taylor rule.
- Alan Greenspan has argued that low long-term interest rates, not short-term interest rates, were the cause of the housing boom. Moreover, the Fed, he argues, has more control over short-term rates (such as the federal funds rate) than over long-term rates (such as the 30-year fixed mortgage rate).

THE POLITICS OF HOUSING

- Mortgage-lending standards declined in the 1990s and the first decade of the twenty-first century in the United States. Financial institutions moved from traditional lending practices to nontraditional lending practices.
- The Community Reinvestment Act (CRA) was passed in 1977 to encourage financial institutions to meet the needs of borrowers in all segments of their communities. In 1995, Congress revised the act to give banks a stronger incentive to increase the percentage of mortgage loans (among other loans) going to low- and moderate-income borrowers.
- Beginning in the early 1990s, government pressure was placed on both Fannie Mae and Freddie Mac to increase their purchases of mortgages made to low- to moderate-income families.
- The entry of Fannie Mae and Freddie Mac into the market of buying subprime loans and creating mortgage-backed securities created a market in subprime lending. Specifically, the large-scale expansion of Fannie and Freddie into the subprime loan business made it profitable for other financial institutions to grant subprime loans in order to sell them to Fannie and Freddie.

THE ROLE OF LEVERAGE

- Leverage is the use of borrowed funds to increase the returns that can be earned with a given amount of capital.
- Consider a bank with $100 in assets, $92 in liabilities, and $8 net worth, or capital. The bank's leverage ratio—the ratio of its assets to its capital—is 100 to 8, or 12½ to 1.

- A bank with a higher leverage ratio has a higher percentage rise in capital when its asset values are rising. Suppose bank A has $100 in assets, $92 in liabilities, and $8 net worth, or capital. Then its leverage ratio is 12½ to 1. If the value of its assets rises to $110, then its capital will now be $18. Going from capital of $8 to $18 is a 125 percent rise in capital. Now suppose bank B has $100 in assets, $97 in liabilities, and capital of $3. If the value of its assets rises to $110, then its capital will now be $13. Going from $3 to $13 capital is a 333 percent rise in capital. Therefore, if asset values are expected to rise, highly leveraged banks will witness a higher percentage rise in their capital than banks with low leverage will witness. Alternatively, when asset values are expected to decline, highly leveraged banks will witness a higher percentage of decline in their capital than banks with low leverage will. Finally, a bank with a high leverage ratio is more likely to fall into insolvency when its assets decline in value than is a bank with a low leverage ratio.

REGULATORY CAPITAL, RISK-WEIGHTED ASSETS, AND REGULATORY CAPITAL ARBITRAGE

- Regulatory capital is the amount of capital that a financial institution must hold because of regulatory requirements.

- Regulatory capital arbitrage is a means of changing the composition of assets in such a way as to lower the overall amount of capital a financial institution holds for a given level of assets.

- Financial institutions can increase their returns (during a time of rising asset values) by engaging in regulatory capital arbitrage. One way to do so is through securitization. Regulatory capital arbitrage is part of the reason that banks and other financial institutions had high leverage ratios when the value of their assets were increasing.

THINGS BEGIN TO UNRAVEL

- The decline in house prices and the rise in interest rates during the first decade of the twenty-first century caused delinquency rates and foreclosure rates to rise for two reasons: (1) Some individuals found their loan amounts greater than the price they could sell their houses for, and (2) other individuals found their mortgage rates resetting at higher rates.

- Banks that held assets in the form of subprime loans and mortgage-backed securities began to feel the effects of heightened delinquency and foreclosure rates. As a result, asset values for banks began to decline. Because of the high leverage ratios, it didn't take much of a decline before banks were either insolvent or nearly so.

- As banks became insolvent or approached insolvency, they pulled back on their lending, reducing economic activity in the real sector of the economy.

- Problems in the real sector began to feed back into the financial sector.

KEY TERMS AND CONCEPTS

Financial Intermediary
Insolvency
Balance Sheet
Asset
Liability
Net Worth (or Capital)

Subprime Mortgage Loans
Mortgage-Backed Securities (MBSs)
Collateralized Debt Obligations (CDOs)
Adjustable Rate Mortgage
Equity (in a House)
Leverage

Regulatory Capital
Regulatory Capital Arbitrage
Securitization
Special-Purpose Vehicle (SPV)

VIDEO QUESTIONS AND PROBLEMS

Video Questions and Problems are available on MindTap for Arnold 12e or by searching for Arnold on www.cengagebrain.com

1. Capital can be viewed as a buffer against insolvency. How so?

2. How can the insolvency of financial institutions adversely affect the real sector of the economy?

3. How can looking at only delinquency and foreclosure rates during a period of rising house prices give a false picture of the risks inherent in giving out mortgages?

4. How can being "too big to fail" create a moral hazard problem?

5. What is leverage? What is the leverage ratio of a bank that has $100 million in assets and $92 million in liabilities?

QUESTIONS AND PROBLEMS

1. What does it mean to say that the financial crisis can be viewed as a balance sheet problem?

2. What is an asset? A liability? Net worth, or capital?

3. Explain how FDIC insurance can cause banks to take on riskier loans than they would if FDIC didn't exist.

4. What are some differences between a subprime loan and a traditional loan? What is the difference between an MBS and a CDO?

5. Explain how a low federal funds rate target can influence mortgage interest rates.

6. Some argue that the Fed acted as a catalyst for the boom in housing prices in the first decade of the twenty-first century. What is their argument?

7. Some argue that the global savings glut acted as a catalyst for the boom in housing prices in the first decade of the twenty-first century. What is their argument?

8. What role does Alan Greenspan say that short-term interest rates (such as the federal funds rate) played in the housing boom? What role did he say that long-term interest rates play?

9. Is there any connection between rising housing prices, on the one hand, and delinquency and foreclosure rates, on the other? Explain your answer.

10. What role, if any, did the CRA play in relaxing lending standards?

11. What role, if any, did Congress, Fannie Mae, and Freddie Mac play in creating a market for subprime lending?

12. What does it mean to say that a bank has a leverage ratio of 10 to 1?

13. Illustrate with a numerical example how a high leverage ratio produces a different percentage rise in capital than a lower leverage ratio when asset values are rising.

14. Explain the process of regulatory capital arbitrage.

15. What role does securitization play in regulatory capital arbitrage?

16. It has been said that the decline in house prices precipitated the financial crisis of the first decade of the twenty-first century. How so?

17. The financial sector can affect the real sector, and the real sector can affect the financial sector. Do you agree or disagree? Explain your answer.

WORKING WITH NUMBERS AND GRAPHS

1. A bank has $1 million in assets and $700,000 in liabilities. What is its net worth? What is its leverage ratio?

2. The bank identified in the previous question finds that its assets increase in value by 15 percent. By what percentage does its capital increase?

3. A bank has $1 million in assets and $920,000 in liabilities. What is its net worth? What is its leverage ratio?

4. The bank identified in the previous question finds that its assets decline in value by 4 percent. By what percentage does its capital decrease?

5. A bank has $400 in asset X, $500 in asset Y, and $300 in asset Z. Asset X has a risk weight of 10 percent, asset Y has a risk weight of 40 percent, and asset Z has a risk weight of 70 percent. What dollar amount do the bank's risk-weighted assets sum to? Assuming that the bank has to hold capital equal to 7 percent of its risk-weighted assets, how much capital does the bank have to hold?

19 DEBATES IN MACROECONOMICS OVER THE ROLE AND EFFECTS OF GOVERNMENT

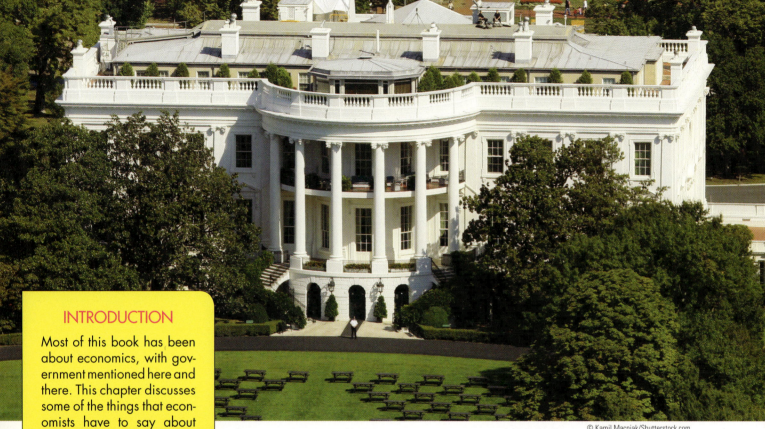

© Kamil Macniak/Shutterstock.com

19-1 MACROECONOMICS AND GOVERNMENT: THE DEBATE

Macroeconomists are agreed on some things. For example, if you ask 10 economists to identify the tools the Fed has at its disposal to change the money supply, you are likely to get the same answer from all of them. If you ask 10 economists to identify the assumptions in the simple quantity theory of money, again you are likely to get the same answer from all of them.

However, macroeconomists are not agreed on some things. If you ask 10 economists how sensitive investment is likely to be to a change in the interest rate in the current economic environment, not all of them are likely to give you the same answer. Some might say that investment is likely to change a lot in response to a change in the interest rate. In other words, the **elasticity of investment** (the percentage change in investment, given a percentage change in the interest rate) is likely to be high. Other economists might disagree and argue that investment will not change much (or at all) if the interest rate changes.

Elasticity of Investment

A measure of the responsiveness of investment to changes in the interest rate.

This type of issue—*how much* will investment fall if the interest rate rises—is an *empirical issue*. Although all economists might agree that investment will fall if the interest rate rises, they will not all agree as to *how much* it will fall. Other empirical issues that economists might not agree on are *how much* aggregate demand will rise if government increases its spending or *how flexible or inflexible* wages are in the current economic environment.

Besides disagreements that focus on empirical issues, economists often express disagreement over the role government *should* play in the economy, given their understanding of how the economy works. Suppose three economists agree that Real GDP is headed downward, that prices are headed upward, and that the prospects for economic growth look bleak for the near future. Even though all three economists have the same diagnosis, they will not necessarily recommend the same government policies. The first economist might argue that government should do nothing, the second might argue that government should do X, and the third might recommend that government do Z.

Ask most students of macroeconomics (especially those who are taking their first course in macroeconomics) what they would like to take away from the course, and they say something like this: "We would like to get explanations for the various macroeconomic phenomena (recessions, inflation, high unemployment) and learn what is the right approach to deal with a particular macroeconomic phenomenon." Their thinking is like a doctor's: "What is wrong with the patient, and what is the best medicine for the patient to take to get well?" In economic terms, the questions would be, "What is wrong with the economy, and what is the best policy to enact to get the economy well?" But the answers in economics are not so clear cut. President Harry S. Truman once said, "Give me a one-handed economist. All my economists say 'On the one hand, and then on the other hand.'" No doubt, students of macroeconomics experience some of Truman's frustration with economists.

Because this is probably your first college course in macroeconomics, you would likely be content with a "one-handed" answer. But you wouldn't be getting an accurate picture of economics theory and its effects on policy. To present an accurate picture, you need to hear some of the debates in macroeconomics, especially as they relate to the role of government in the economy. Some of what we will discuss here has been discussed in earlier chapters, sometimes with a different emphasis. The outline in this chapter is fairly straightforward: We identify a number of macroeconomic topics, and then we explain how government comes up in the discussions of various economists about that topic.

19-2 TAX CUTS, TAX REVENUE, AND BUDGET DEFICITS

Suppose the federal government is running a budget deficit: government spending is greater than tax revenues. To reduce the size of the deficit, some economists propose income tax cuts. Other economists argue that income tax cuts will not lead to a smaller deficit. The source of the disagreement between the two sets of economists is the issue of whether tax cuts will or will not raise tax revenue.

One group of economists argues this way: (1) If income tax rates are cut, individuals will choose to work and produce more. (2) As a result, they will generate more income and the tax base will rise. (3) If the tax base rises by more than tax rates are cut, then tax revenue will rise. (4) More tax revenue will end up reducing the size of the budget deficit.

Another group of economists challenges the if-part of assumption 3. They argue that the tax base is not likely to rise by more than tax rates are cut, so result 4 will be *less* tax revenue and therefore a *bigger* budget deficit.

The discussion goes back to this equation, first identified in Chapter 11:

$$\text{Tax revenues} = \text{Tax base} \times \text{(average) Tax rate}$$

Almost all economists agree that if the tax rate is cut, the tax base will rise, but not all economists agree as to *how much* the tax base will rise. In other words, if the tax rate is cut 10 percent, will the tax base rise by more than, less than, or as much as the cut in the tax rate?

What separates economists here is an empirical issue. Specifically, economists sometimes disagree on what is likely to happen given a certain action. In other words, if tax rates are cut, then what? Do tax revenues rise, decline, or remain constant?

We recap in terms of these differing economic perspectives:

- *Economist A.* Tax cuts will raise tax revenue, and increased tax revenue will decrease the size of the budget deficit.

- *Economist B.* Tax cuts will lower tax revenue, and decreased tax revenue will increase the size of the budget deficit.

19-3 THE ECONOMY: SELF-REGULATING OR NOT?

One major debate in macroeconomics focuses on whether the economy is self-regulating. For example, if an economy is in a recessionary gap, can it move itself into long-run equilibrium? To a degree, the answer depends on whether wages are flexible or inflexible downward. If wages are flexible, then an economy can remove itself from a recessionary gap. Hence, government need not get involved in managing the economy. But if wages are inflexible downward, then an economy cannot remove itself from a recessionary gap; an economy can get stuck in a recessionary gap. The economy can get unstuck only by means of economic policy enacted either by the Congress or the president (i.e., via fiscal policy) or by the Fed (i.e., via monetary policy).

We recap in terms of these differing economic perspectives:

- *Economist A.* Wages are flexible, so if the economy is in a recessionary gap, it will soon remove itself from the gap. Government doesn't have to do anything.

- *Economist B.* Wages are inflexible downward, so if the economy is in a recessionary gap, it may be stuck there. The best course of action is for the federal government to implement expansionary fiscal policy or for the Fed to implement expansionary monetary policy to remove the economy from the recessionary gap.

ECONOMICS 24/7

If It Sounds Reasonable, Is It Right?
If It Sounds Unreasonable, Is It Wrong?

Go back to the time before you started studying macroeconomics. A person comes up to you and says, "If the government cuts taxes, it will have less tax revenue." Would you have agreed or disagreed with this statement? We think there is a tendency to agree with the statement because it sounds reasonable. In contrast, saying something like "When people wear red shirts, they become smarter than when they wear blue shirts" sounds unreasonable. You might be led to ask, "How in the world does the color of the shirt you wear affect your level of intelligence?" Isn't it a stretch to think that it does?

But when it comes to a cut in taxes leading to a reduction in tax revenue, the reduction in tax revenue seems to naturally follow from the cut in taxes. You might think that, certainly, if the government taxes you less, it will receive less tax monies from you and therefore tax revenue is bound to decline. But, of course, a cut in taxes does not necessarily lead to a reduction in tax revenues if the percentage cut in taxes is less than the percentage rise in the tax base. Things that sound reasonable are not necessarily right.

Now consider an example from outside the discipline of economics to help us make our point. Suppose you are living in the year 400 A.D. Someone comes up to you and tells you that the earth is flat. He then asks if you agree. You nod your head "yes" because it seems so reasonable that the earth is flat. You walk on it daily, and it looks flat and feels flat, so you think it is only reasonable to believe that it is flat. But the problem is, as we know, the earth is not flat. What seems to be reasonable turns out to be wrong, not right.

Now if what sounds reasonable can turn out to be wrong and not right, can what sounds unreasonable turn out to be right and not wrong? Think back to the days before we knew about tiny germs

© Julien Tromeur/Shutterstock.com

that could cause disease. One day you are sick and you wonder why. Someone says that you are sick because there are these tiny things you cannot see—called germs—that are making you sick. Now, when someone tells you that there are tiny things that you can't see that are making you sick, you might wonder if it is you or the person speaking who really has a problem. For example, what might you think of the person today who walked up to you and told you that the emotions you feel (happiness, sadness, love, hate, and so on) are produced by tiny, invisible beings from another planet floating in the air above you.

Back to the germs. Hundreds of years ago, if a person had told you that tiny, invisible things (inside your body) are making you sick, you might say that that sounds unreasonable and therefore can't be so. But, of course, we now know that germs do exist, that they are invisible to the naked eye, and that they can make you sick. What might have once sounded unreasonable, and thus worthy of dismissal, turns out to be true.

This is why economists often set about to *test* their theories. It is not enough to have a "good economic story" that seems to explain the facts: rising prices, rising unemployment, the decline in Real GDP, rising interest rates, and so on. Fact is, there may be many good stories that "explain" the facts. After all, if there were only one good story to explain the facts, there would not be as much debate in macroeconomics as there is. No, more is needed than just a good story. Theories (stories?) must be falsifiable; that is, they must be capable of being proved wrong if, in fact, they are wrong. They must consistently offer up accurate predictions that are validated by events and data. And they must be able to explain things that other theories (other good stories) cannot. Just sounding reasonable (or unreasonable) is not enough.

19-4　MORE GOVERNMENT SPENDING OR A CUT IN TAXES: WHICH GIVES A BIGGER BANG FOR THE BUCK?

The economy is in a recessionary gap, and economists call for a demand-side expansionary fiscal policy measure. As we know, expansionary fiscal policy consists of (1) an increase in government purchases or (2) a cut in taxes or (3) both. Not all economists are likely to agree on the best way to proceed. One economist will argue that a rise in government purchases will give the economy the "biggest bang for the buck." A $1 rise in government purchases will (by changing aggregate demand) raise Real GDP by more than a $1 cut in taxes. In other words, the **government spending multiplier** [the number that, when multiplied by the change in government spending, gives us the change in total spending (and, if prices are constant, the change in Real GDP)] is larger than the **tax multiplier** [the number that, when multiplied by the change in taxes, gives us the change in total spending (and, if prices are constant, the change in Real GDP)]. Another economist argues just the opposite: The tax multiplier is larger than the government spending multiplier, so a $1 cut in taxes will raise Real GDP by more than a $1 rise in government purchases.

Suppose that the government spending multiplier is 1.4 and the tax multiplier is 3. This means that a $1 rise in government spending will increase Real GDP by $1.40, and a $1 tax cut will increase Real GDP by $3. Now the debate and disagreement among economists can focus on the values of the two multipliers.

In the standard textbook Keynesian analysis, there is reason to believe that the government spending multiplier is larger than the tax multiplier. Here is the reasoning: When government spends $1, the entire $1 enters the spending stream. However, when government cuts taxes by $1, individuals spend some of the dollar that they now get to keep and save some of it. In other words, they might spend 60 cents of the dollar and save 40 cents. What separates economists, though, is that not all economists hold to the standard textbook analysis. Some economists argue that the standard textbook analysis does not take into account all the ways that tax cuts can be stimulative.

We recap in terms of these differing economic perspectives:

- *Economist A.* The economy needs expansionary fiscal policy to remove it from a recessionary gap. Accordingly, government should either raise its spending or cut taxes. I believe that the government spending multiplier is larger than the tax multiplier, so I suggest that government increase its spending.

- *Economist B.* The economy needs expansionary fiscal policy to remove it from a recessionary gap. Accordingly, government should either raise its spending or cut taxes. I believe that the tax multiplier is larger than the government spending multiplier, so I suggest that government cut taxes.

19-5　MORE GOVERNMENT SPENDING OR A CUT IN TAXES: THE SIZE AND SCOPE OF GOVERNMENT

The *size* of government relates to the resources over which government has command. Suppose the economy has 100 units of labor, with 30 of the units allocated through government and 70 units through the private sector. Then government grows in size,

---

Government Spending Multiplier

The number that, when multiplied by the change in government spending, gives us the change in total spending (and, if prices are constant, the change in Real GDP).

Tax Multiplier

The number that, when multiplied by the change in taxes, gives us the change in total spending (and if prices are constant, the change in Real GDP).

relative to the private sector, if it begins to allocate more than 30 units of labor and the private sector beings to allocate less than 70 units of labor.

The *scope* of government relates to what and how many things government does. Suppose government can provide for the national defense, build roads and bridges, provide schools, and institute and operate Social Security. If it only provides for the national defense and builds roads and bridges, then its scope is more limited than if it provides for the national defense, builds roads and bridges, and implements and operates Social Security.

Both a rise in government purchases and a cut in taxes are expansionary fiscal policy measures, but both don't have the same impact on the size and scope of government. To illustrate, suppose economist A calls specifically for more government spending to get the economy out of a recessionary gap. The argument is standard fare: A rise in government purchases increases aggregate demand and removes the economy from the recessionary gap.

But couldn't a tax cut, instead of greater government spending, do the same thing? For instance, an income tax cut will raise after-tax (or disposable) income. With greater after-tax income, individuals will buy more goods and services, thus increasing consumption in the economy. And a rise in consumption will raise aggregate demand, perhaps by enough to remove the economy out of a recessionary gap.

The decision between government spending and tax cuts depends partly on the effect that each has on the size and scope of government. Economist A favors bigger government (government making more decisions); when it comes to advocating increased government purchases or tax cuts, he argues for increased government purchases. He sees increased government purchases as increasing the size, and possibly the scope, of government. Economist B favors smaller government (government making fewer decisions); when it comes to advocating increased government purchases or tax cuts, she argues for tax cuts. She sees cutting taxes as decreasing the size, and possibly the scope, of government.

We recap in terms of these differing economic perspectives:

- *Economist A.* Expansionary fiscal policy is needed to raise aggregate demand and remove the economy from a recessionary gap. The choice of fiscal policy measures is between more government spending and a cut in taxes. Because I am in favor of bigger government, I choose more government spending.

- *Economist B.* Expansionary fiscal policy is needed to raise aggregate demand and remove the economy from a recessionary gap. The choice of fiscal policy measures is between more government spending and a cut in taxes. Because I am in favor of smaller government, I choose a cut in taxes.

19-6 THE DEGREE OF CROWDING OUT

Suppose 10 out of 10 economists agree that the economy is in a recessionary gap. Seven of them argue that an expansionary fiscal policy measure in the form of greater government spending will remove the economy from the recessionary gap. Their argument is that if government purchases increase, aggregate demand in the economy will rise, and the economy will move out of the recessionary gap. Also, any increase in government purchases will not crowd out any private sector spending (i.e., spending by households and businesses).

The other three economists see things a little differently. They argue that a lot of crowding out is likely, thus weakening the impact of the expansionary fiscal policy measure. Their argument is that, if government purchases increase, aggregate demand probably will not rise enough to remove the economy from the recessionary gap because, for every dollar the government spends, it has to borrow a dollar. In short, to get an additional dollar to spend, government must first borrow it. If the borrowed dollars come from the private sector, then the private sector will have fewer dollars to spend on various goods and services, so more government spending means less private sector spending. The rise in aggregate demand due to more government spending is largely offset by a reduction in aggregate demand because of less private sector spending. In the end, aggregate demand will change little, if at all, so government will have been ineffective in its attempt to remove the economy from the recessionary gap. In terms of jobs, jobs created or saved because of increased government spending are offset by jobs destroyed by a decline in private sector spending.

We recap in terms of these differing economic perspectives:

- *Economist A.* A rise in government purchases will increase aggregate demand and remove the economy from the recessionary gap because little or no crowding out will occur. A rise in government purchases will end up increasing the number of jobs in the economy.

- *Economist B.* A rise in government purchases will not increase aggregate demand and remove the economy from the recessionary gap because of complete (or nearly complete) crowding out.

19-7 THE POLITICS OF GOVERNMENT SPENDING

Consider two settings. In setting 1, fiscal policy emerges in a political vacuum. In setting 2, it undergoes a political process. The fiscal policy created in a political vacuum is probably not going to be the same as the fiscal policy that arises from a political process. For example, suppose government spends $100 on good X in setting 1. Will it spend $100 on good X in setting 2? Probably not: In setting 2, it might spend more on good X or less on good X. In fact, in setting 2, it might not spend any money on good X.

As an example, in 2008–2009, the U.S. economy was on a downward slide: Real GDP was declining, the unemployment rate was rising, and some companies were cutting employment while others were closing down. Many economists argued that an expansionary policy measure was needed to strengthen the economy (specifically, to turn the decline in Real GDP around, to reduce the unemployment rate, etc.). Some economists called for more government spending. However, the government-needs-to-spend-more group contained factions. Some argued that the important objective for the economy is that government spends more; of lesser importance was what government spent the money on. In other words, whether government spent money having people dig ditches and then filling them up or building bridges and roads, a dollar spent is a dollar spent as far as the economy goes.

Other economists in the same camp disagreed, arguing that how the money was spent would make a difference in the effect on the economy. Money spent on having people dig ditches and then filling them up is not as beneficial to the economy as spending money to build bridges and roads. More importantly, these same economists argued that much of the additional money spent by government would end up motivated by politics instead of economics. In other words, members of Congress might find a large spending bill just the cover they needed to reward their political allies. Of course, from an economic perspective, if a dollar spent here is the same as a dollar spent there, rewarding one's political allies does not come with an economywide cost. But if spending a dollar in some ways is more productive for the economy than spending it in other ways, then how the dollar is spent matters a lot.

We recap in terms of these differing economic perspectives:

- *Economist A.* An expansionary fiscal policy measure is needed to increase Real GDP, lower the unemployment rate, and so on. I propose $100 billion more in government spending. It doesn't really matter what the $100 billion is spent on; the important thing is that the money be spent.

- *Economist B.* An expansionary fiscal policy measure is needed to increase Real GDP, lower the unemployment rate, and so on. Ideally, the economy needs $100 billion more in government spending. But how the money is spent will be determined by Congress, and Congress is likely to be motivated by political interests. Furthermore, not all spending is the same. Some spending is better for the economy than other spending. I think much of the spending that we will get from Congress will be motivated by politics instead of by economics, and sometimes the spending motivated by politics will be of little help in turning the economy around. In the end, I have my doubts as to how effective an increase in government spending will be in aiding the economy.

19-8 MONETARY POLICY: RULES VERSUS DISCRETION

With regard to the creation of monetary policy, some economists argue in favor of a rules-based system, either in accordance with the Taylor rule or setting the growth of the money supply equal to some fixed percentage rate (such as 3 percent). Other economists argue in favor of discretion for the Fed, saying that the Fed needs to have the flexibility to create the best monetary policy possible given the circumstances.

The debate between these economists centers around two major points. The first has to do with the effects of different types of monetary policy: rules-based versus discretionary. Those who advocate rules-based monetary policy often say that it is more likely than discretionary monetary policy to produce nearly stable prices, low unemployment, low and stable interest rates, and the right overall conditions for sustained economic growth. Economists who advocate discretionary monetary policy argue that *it* is more likely to achieve the desired economic results because the monetary authority has the flexibility to shape the best monetary policy to the existing circumstances.

The second major point is that rules-based monetary policy advocates often assert that discretionary monetary policy all too often is motivated by political, instead of economic, interests. A rules-based monetary policy removes monetary policy from politics, they argue, making for better monetary policy in the final analysis. The money supply is too important an economic variable, with too many far-reaching effects, to have politicians pushing it one way or another to serve their short-run, the-next-election-is-around-the-corner interests.

We recap in terms of these differing economic perspectives:

- *Economist A.* A monetary rule is preferred to a discretionary Fed. The former is more likely to bring about stable prices, low unemployment, and so on. In addition, a monetary rule removes monetary policy from politics.

- *Economist B.* A discretionary Fed is preferred to a monetary rule. The Fed needs the flexibility to tailor monetary policy to the existing circumstances.

19-9 BAILOUTS

Not all economists are agreed as to whether government should bail out companies that are experiencing financial problems. Suppose a large company employs thousands of workers, pays millions of dollars in taxes to the state in which it is located, buys hundreds of parts from its suppliers in assembling its product, and has thousands of bondholders and stockholders. Then the company finds itself in dire financial straits—so dire that the company finds it difficult to repay its debt or to obtain loans. Without some financial assistance, the company will probably go out of business. If it does, its home state will lose millions of dollars in tax revenue; employees will lose their jobs; its suppliers will lose sales revenues (perhaps causing them to go out of business), fire workers, and so on; and thousands of investors will see their personal wealth diminished. Does the government have a role to play in bailing out this company?

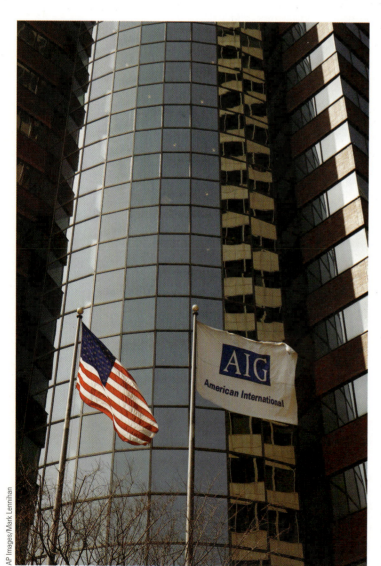

AP Images/Mark Lennihan

One way to answer that question is to ask another: Who loses if the company goes out of business? Certainly, the owners of the business lose, but then there might be others, such as the employees who lose their jobs, the suppliers of the company who lose business, the state that loses the tax revenue, and the investors who lose personal wealth. If the total dollar amount of loss is $50 billion and the federal government bailout of the company comes to $30 billion in taxpayer funds, then, for $30 billion, a $50 billion loss could be averted. Some would argue that bailing out the company (and, one step removed, bailing out those who would be adversely affected by the company's failure) would be economically advantageous. In fact, this very argument was used to justify the federal government's bailout of several financial institutions and both General Motors and Chrysler during the financial and economic crisis in the mid- to late 2000s. A little bailing out here and there may be better than letting large businesses fail and, in the process, drag down others with them.

However, another argument goes like this: (1) The people ultimately doing the bailing out—the taxpayers—incur the cost of the bailout, while others (such as the company owners, the employees, and the suppliers of the company) receive the benefits. Why should the taxpayers pay the costs while others receive the benefits, especially when many of the taxpayers have less income than the persons who are bailed out? (2) If firms know that they will be bailed out, they will take more risks than if they know they won't be. Thus, the possibility of a bailout creates an environment in which more and more firms will need bailouts. The owners and managers of firms will want to take ever more risk because, if high returns follow, then they are the winners, but if failure comes, the federal government, with taxpayer funds in hand, will bail them out. "Heads, we win; tails, others lose." That will bring on many more business failures than "heads, we win; tails, we lose."

We recap in terms of these differing economic perspectives:

- *Economist A.* In a perfect world, bailing out companies is not a good idea. But company X is a large company, and if it goes out of business, that will adversely affect hundreds of thousands of persons. Bailing out the company is better than letting it fail; we lose more by letting the company fail than by saving it. Some companies are simply too big to be allowed to fail. Their failure is like an earthquake, adversely affecting all the people around them. To save the innocent, you sometimes have to save the not so innocent.

- *Economist B.* Who is "we" when you say, "We lose more by letting the company fail than by saving it?" Some persons gain by having the company bailed out, and others lose. Furthermore, if we continue to tell companies that the federal government will be there if they fail, we simply create an environment in which we privatize gains (the companies keep the gains if there are any) and socialize the costs (spread the costs among millions of taxpayers if the companies end up in financial problems). In the end, this policy will lead to more companies that "need" to be bailed out.

19-10 DEMAND-SIDE AND SUPPLY-SIDE VIEWS OF THE ECONOMY AND GOVERNMENT TOOLS FOR CHANGING REAL GDP

Much of our discussion of macroeconomics has been in terms of aggregate demand and aggregate supply. Whereas the *AD* curve was always represented as downward sloping, the *AS* curve was shown in different ways according to the macroeconomic model. For example, in the simple quantity theory of money, the *AS* curve is vertical. In many other models we represented, it is upward sloping. Exhibit 1(a)–(b) shows two aggregate supply curves.

Each of these two aggregate supply curves has its own meaning in terms of changes in aggregate demand. If the aggregate supply curve is vertical and aggregate demand rises—that is, the *AD* curve shifts rightward—the price level will rise but Real GDP will not change. [See Exhibit 1(c).] But if the aggregate supply curve is upward sloping, a rise in aggregate demand will raise both the price level and Real GDP. [See Exhibit 1(d).]

Depending on your view of whether the real aggregate supply curve is vertical or upward sloping, how would you respond to the following question? Assuming that the objective is to raise Real GDP, would it be preferable for government to try to increase aggregate demand or aggregate supply?

The economists who view the *AS* curve as vertical will say that government cannot do anything to raise Real GDP from the demand side of the economy because changes in *AD* don't change Real GDP if the *AS* curve is vertical. Forget an increase in government purchases, a demand-side tax cut, or expansionary monetary policy. These actions may change *AD*, but a change in *AD*—in the face of a vertical *AS* curve—will lead to a change

> **EXHIBIT 1**

The Aggregate Supply Curve and What Government Can and Cannot Do

Shown are two aggregate supply curves: (a) The curve is vertical. (b) The curve is upward sloping. In this text, we have often spoken of each of these two differently shaped curves. (c) Changes in aggregate demand will not change Real GDP if the aggregate supply curve is vertical. (d) Changes in aggregate demand will

change Real GDP if the aggregate supply curve is upward sloping. For the economist who views the *AS* curve as vertical, changes in Real GDP originate only on the supply-side economy, so government policy that aims to affect the demand side of the economy will change only prices, not Real GDP. For the economist who views the *AS* curve as upward sloping, changes in Real GDP can originate on either the demand side or the

supply side of the economy, so government policy that aims to affect either side of the economy will change not only prices, but Real GDP too. For the economist who views the *AS* curve as vertical, government has fewer tools (demand-side fiscal policy and monetary policy won't work) to change Real GDP than the economist who views the *AS* curve as upward sloping would say that government has.

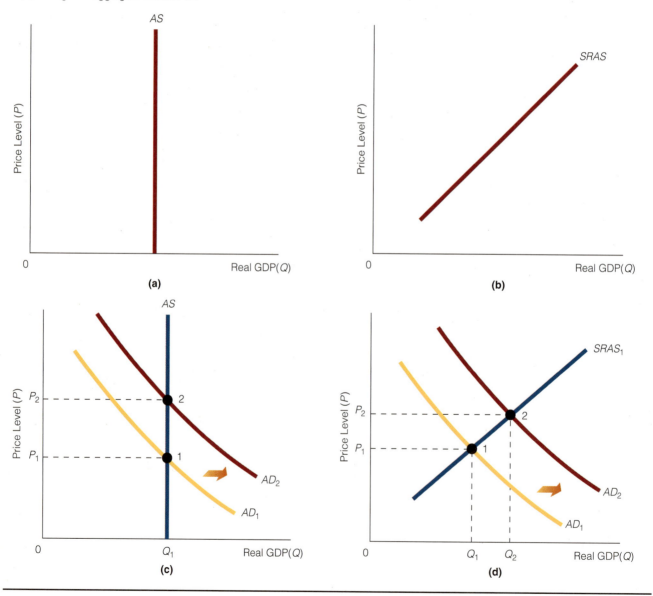

only in prices, not in Real GDP. The only way for Real GDP to rise is for the *AS* curve to shift rightward.

Of course, economists who view the *AS* curve as upward sloping will disagree. For them, both a change in *AD* and a change in *AS* will affect Real GDP. Changes in Real GDP may be realized by changes that originate on either the demand side or the supply side of the economy. If the aggregate supply curve is upward sloping, an increase in aggregate demand will lead to a rise in Real GDP (at least in the short run), as will an increase in aggregate supply. Viewing things from the demand side of the economy, these economists would argue that a rise in government purchases, a demand-side tax cut, and monetary policy will all be effective at changing Real GDP.

Comparing our two camps of economists, we observe that the group of economists who view the *AS* curve as vertical sees fewer government tools (demand-side fiscal policy and monetary policy won't work) that are capable of raising Real GDP than does the group of economists who view the *AS* curve as upward sloping.

We recap in terms of these differing economic perspectives:

- *Economist A.* The aggregate supply curve is vertical. Therefore, government actions designed to change aggregate demand in the economy will not lead to changes in Real GDP. Changes in Real GDP come from the supply side of the economy, not the demand side. Government has fewer tools (demand-side fiscal policy and monetary policy won't work) that are capable of raising Real GDP than the economist who sees the *AS* curve as upward sloping believes.

- *Economist B.* The aggregate supply curve is upward sloping (in the short run). Government actions designed to change aggregate demand in the economy will lead to changes in Real GDP (at least in the short run). Changes in Real GDP (in the short run) can come from either the demand side or the supply side of the economy. Government has more tools (demand-side fiscal policy and monetary policy do work) that are capable of raising Real GDP than the economist who sees the *AS* curve as vertical believes.

SELF-TEST

(Answers to Self-Test questions are in Answers to Self-Test Questions at the back of the book.)

1. Economist A believes that a reduction in tax rates will lead to increased tax revenue, and economist B believes that a reduction in tax rates will not lead to increased tax revenue. What does each believe with respect to the relationship between the percentage change in tax rates and the percentage change in the tax base?

2. In the standard textbook Keynesian analysis, there is reason to believe that the government spending multiplier is larger than the tax multiplier. Why?

3. Not all economists agree on what constitutes the optimal size and scope of government. Therefore, they won't all agree as to the preferred fiscal policy measure to stimulate the economy: increased government purchases or tax cuts. Do you agree or disagree that some economists would prefer to increase government purchases to stimulate the economy while others would prefer to cut taxes? Explain your answer.

Office  Hours

"What Kinds of Debates Do Macroeconomists Have?"

STUDENT:

I'd like some way to categorize the kinds of debates that macroeconomists have. Can you help here?

INSTRUCTOR:

Four words: "theory," "policy," "empiricism," and "government." Here is what we mean by each. Economists sometimes debate theory. For example, think of one economist who builds a theory which assumes that wages are inflexible downward and another economist who builds a theory which assumes that wages are flexible.

Economists often debate the kind of policy that will best solve the economic problem at hand. To illustrate, economist A might argue that a supply-side tax cut is better able to solve the problem of lagging economic growth than a demand-side rise in government spending is. Economist B might argue the opposite, especially if the increased government spending is directed toward research and development.

Economists often debate empirical results. To illustrate, economist A could say that, during period X, the data show that expansionary fiscal policy did raise aggregate demand and did increase Real GDP. Economist B might argue that, during period X, many things occurred, only one of which was the implementation of expansionary fiscal policy. Monetary policy was also expansionary during the period, and it, more than expansionary fiscal policy, is the reason aggregate demand increased and Real GDP increased.

Economists also debate the role that government should play in the economy. Often, how they argue here is related to their views of how the economy works. For example, as we have stated in this chapter and others, consider an economist who believes that the evidence is consistent with a self-regulating economy—one that regulates itself quickly. That economist is less likely to advocate government macroeconomic interventions in the economy than is an economist who believes that the evidence is consistent with either an unstable economy or an economy that is unacceptably slow in self-regulating.

STUDENT:

One other question about debates in macroeconomics: I've heard about freshwater and saltwater economists. What do these two terms mean, and what is the essential difference between them when it comes to government's role in the economy?

INSTRUCTOR:

Sometimes the macroeconomic differences between economists that we've been talking about find a home in two words: "freshwater" and "saltwater"—specifically, freshwater economists and saltwater economists. At universities such as Chicago, Minnesota, and Rochester, which are all located near the Great Lakes, so-called freshwater economists can be found. At universities such as Harvard, MIT, and UC Berkeley—all near oceans—saltwater economists can be found.

Of course, the proximity to freshwater or saltwater isn't what fundamentally separates economists. It is differences in theory, policy, and the role of government. With respect to the last of these, freshwater economists see a smaller role for government than do saltwater economists.

Points to remember

1. The debates in macroeconomics often focus on theory, policy, empiricism, and government.
2. It is not uncommon for an economist's view of how the economy works to influence his or her view on the role government should play in the economy.

CHAPTER SUMMARY

In this chapter, the summary is presented in terms of the opposing views of economists on macroeconomic issues.

TAX CUTS, TAX REVENUE, AND BUDGET DEFICITS

- *Economist A.* Tax cuts will raise tax revenue, and increased tax revenue will decrease the size of the budget deficit.
- *Economist B.* Tax cuts will lower tax revenue, and decreased tax revenue will increase the size of the budget deficit.

THE ECONOMY: SELF-REGULATING OR NOT?

- *Economist A.* Wages are flexible, so if the economy is in a recessionary gap, it will soon remove itself from the gap. Government need not do anything.
- *Economist B.* Wages are inflexible downward, so if the economy is in a recessionary gap, it may be stuck there. The best course of action is for the federal government to implement expansionary fiscal policy or for the Fed to implement expansionary monetary policy to remove the economy from the recessionary gap.

MORE GOVERNMENT SPENDING OR A CUT IN TAXES: WHICH GIVES A BIGGER BANG FOR THE BUCK?

- *Economist A.* The economy needs expansionary fiscal policy to remove it from a recessionary gap. Government should either raise its spending or cut taxes. I believe that the government spending multiplier is larger than the tax multiplier, so I suggest that government increase its spending.
- *Economist B.* The economy needs expansionary fiscal policy to remove it from a recessionary gap. Government should either raise its spending or cut taxes. I believe that the tax multiplier is larger than the government spending multiplier, so I suggest that government cut taxes.

MORE GOVERNMENT SPENDING OR A CUT IN TAXES: THE SIZE AND SCOPE OF GOVERNMENT

- *Economist A.* Expansionary fiscal policy is needed to raise aggregate demand and to remove the economy from a recessionary gap. The choice of fiscal policy measures is between more government spending or a cut in taxes. I am in favor of bigger government, so I choose more government spending.
- *Economist B.* Expansionary fiscal policy is needed to raise aggregate demand and to remove the economy from a recessionary gap. The choice of fiscal policy measures is between more government spending or a cut in taxes. I am in favor of smaller government, so I choose a cut in taxes.

THE DEGREE OF CROWDING OUT

- *Economist A.* A rise in government purchases will increase aggregate demand and remove the economy from a recessionary gap because little or no crowding out will occur. A rise in government purchases will increase the number of jobs in the economy.
- *Economist B.* A rise in government purchases will not increase aggregate demand and remove the economy from a recessionary gap because of complete (or nearly complete) crowding out.

THE POLITICS OF GOVERNMENT SPENDING

- *Economist A.* An expansionary fiscal policy measure is needed to increase Real GDP, lower the unemployment rate, and so on. I propose $100 billion more in government spending. What the $100 billion is spent on does not matter; the important thing is that the money be spent.
- *Economist B.* An expansionary fiscal policy measure is needed to increase Real GDP, lower the unemployment rate, and so on. Ideally, the economy needs $100 billion more in government spending. But how the money will be spent will be determined by Congress, which is likely to be motivated by political interests. Furthermore, not all spending is the same. Some spending is better for the economy than other spending. I think that much spending is motivated by politics instead of economics, and sometimes the spending motivated by politics is of little help in turning the economy around. In the end, I have my doubts as to how effective an increase in government spending will be in aiding the economy.

MONETARY POLICY: RULES OR DISCRETION?

- *Economist A.* A monetary rule is preferred to a discretionary Fed. The former is more likely to bring about stable prices, low unemployment, and so on. In addition, a monetary rule removes monetary policy from politics.
- *Economist B.* A discretionary Fed is preferred to a monetary rule. The Fed needs the flexibility to tailor monetary policy to existing circumstances.

BAILOUTS

- *Economist A.* Ideally, bailing out companies is not a good idea. But company X is a large company that will adversely affect hundreds of thousands of persons if it goes out of business. Bailing out the company is better than letting it fail. We lose more by letting the company fail than by saving it. Some companies are simply too big to be allowed to fail. Their failure is like an earthquake, adversely affecting all the people. To save the innocent, you sometimes have to save the not so innocent.

- *Economist B.* Who is "we" when you say, "We lose more by letting the company fail than by saving it?" Some persons gain by having the company bailed out, and others lose. Furthermore, if we continue to tell companies that the federal government will be there if they fail, we simply create an environment in which we privatize gains (the companies keep the gains if there are any) and socialize the costs (spread the costs among millions of taxpayers if the companies end up in financial problems). In the end, this policy will lead to more companies that "need" to be bailed out.

DEMAND-SIDE VERSUS SUPPLY-SIDE VIEW OF THE ECONOMY AND GOVERNMENT TOOLS TO CHANGE REAL GDP

- *Economist A.* The aggregate supply curve is vertical. Therefore, government actions designed to change aggregate demand in the economy will not lead to changes in Real GDP. Changes in Real GDP come from the supply side of the economy, not the demand side. Government has fewer tools (demand-side fiscal policy and monetary policy won't work) that are capable of raising Real GDP than the economist who sees the *AS* curve as upward sloping believes.

- *Economist B.* The aggregate supply curve is upward sloping (in the short run). Government actions designed to change aggregate demand in the economy will lead to changes in Real GDP (at least in the short run). Changes in Real GDP (in the short run) can come from either the demand side or the supply side of the economy. Government has more tools (demand-side fiscal policy and monetary policy do work) that are capable of raising Real GDP than the economist who sees the *AS* curve as vertical believes.

KEY TERMS AND CONCEPTS

Elasticity of Investment	Government Spending Multiplier	Tax Multiplier

VIDEO QUESTIONS AND PROBLEMS

Video Questions and Problems are available on MindTap for Arnold 12e or by searching for Arnold on www.cengagebrain.com

1. What is the relationship between the shape of the aggregate supply curve and the effectiveness of monetary policy at changing Real GDP?

2. What does crowding out have to do with the effectiveness of fiscal policy at changing Real GDP?

3. Outline the details of the debate between economists who say that the economy is self-regulating and those who say that it is not.

4. What does the size of the government spending multiplier relative to the size of the tax multiplier have to do with the effectiveness of fiscal policy at changing Real GDP?

5. Not all economists are agreed as to whether government should bail out companies in financial problems. Explain.

QUESTIONS AND PROBLEMS

1. Can tax revenue rise and the budget deficit decline as a result of an income tax rate cut? Explain your answer.

2. How an economist thinks that the economy works—is it self-regulating or not?—influences his opinion of the role government should play in trying to stabilize the economy. Do you agree or disagree? Explain your answer.

3. Whether an economist argues in favor of a rise in government spending or a cut in taxes (as an expansionary

fiscal policy measure) could have something to do with whether she views the government spending multiplier as greater or less than the tax multiplier. Do you agree or disagree? Explain your answer.

4. Whether an economist argues in favor of a rise in government spending or a cut in taxes (as an expansionary fiscal policy measure) could have something to do with how he views the current size and scope of government in relationship to his optimal size and scope of government. Do you agree or disagree? Explain your answer.

5. Whether an economist argues in favor of a rise in government spending (as an expansionary fiscal policy measure) could have something to do with the degree of crowding out he expects as a result of the measure. Do you agree or disagree? Explain your answer.

6. Some economists argue that if the economy currently needs to be stimulated to remove it from a recessionary gap, *how* government spends more money (on X or Y) matters less than the fact that it does spend more money. Do all economists agree? If not, what do they say in response?

7. Outline the details of the debate between economists who favor a rules-based monetary policy and those who favor a discretionary monetary policy.

8. Something is referred to as a "double-edged sword" if it can have both favorable and unfavorable consequences. In what way might government bailouts of failing companies or financial institutions be a double-edged sword? Explain your answer.

9. The shape of the aggregate supply curve matters to one's view of the ability of government to change Real GDP by way of demand-side fiscal policy and monetary policy. Do you agree or disagree? Explain your answer.

10. What do the values of the government spending and tax multipliers have to do with getting the biggest bang for the buck?

11. There is little doubt that if income tax rates are cut, the size of the budget deficit will increase. Do you agree or disagree? Explain your answer.

WORKING WITH NUMBERS AND GRAPHS

1. A $40 reduction in taxes increases Real GDP by $100, and a $50 increase in government spending increases Real GDP by $120. What is the tax multiplier? What is the government spending multiplier?

2. A rise in aggregate demand raises Real GDP and the price level. Draw the aggregate supply curve that is consistent with this statement. Next, a rise in aggregate demand raises the price level but leaves Real GDP unchanged. Draw the aggregate supply curve that is consistent with that statement.

3. If the tax base is $100 billion and tax revenues are $15 billion, what is the average tax rate?

4. What would the aggregate supply curve look like if a rise in aggregate demand led to a rise in Real GDP but to no change in the price level?

PUBLIC CHOICE AND SPECIAL-INTEREST GROUP POLITICS

AP Images/Pablo Martinez Monsivais

20-1 PUBLIC CHOICE THEORY

Public choice theorists reject the notion that people are like Dr. Jekyll and Mr. Hyde—that is, that they exhibit greed and selfishness in their transactions in the private (market) sector and altruism and public spirit in their actions in the public sector. The same people who are the employers, employees, and consumers in the market sector are the politicians, bureaucrats, members of special-interest groups, and voters in the public sector. According to public choice theorists, people in the market sector and people in the public sector behave differently not because they have different motives (or are different types of people) but because the two sectors have different institutional arrangements.

As a simple example, Erin Bloom works for a private, profit-seeking firm that makes radio components. Erin is cost conscious, does her work on time, and generally works hard. She knows that she must exhibit this type of work behavior if she wants to keep her job, get a raise, and be promoted. Suppose now that Erin leaves her job at the radio components company and takes a job with the Department of Health and Human Services (HHS) in Washington, D.C. Public choice theorists maintain that Erin is the same person (with different motives), whether working for HHS or for the radio components company.

INTRODUCTION

Economics is a powerful analytical tool. As you have seen, it can be used to analyze how markets and the economy work. In this chapter, we use economics to analyze the behavior of politicians, voters, and members of special-interest groups. Specifically, we analyze public choice, the branch of economics in which economic principles and tools are applied to public sector decision making. Public choice is, in a sense, economics applied to politics.

Public Choice

The branch of economics in which economic principles and tools are applied to public sector decision making.

However, even though Erin is the same person in and out of government, she will not necessarily exhibit the same work behavior. The costs and benefits of certain actions may be substantially different at HHS than at the radio components company. For example, perhaps the cost of being late for work is less in Erin's new job at HHS than it was at her old job. In her former job, she had to work overtime if she came in late; in her new job, her boss doesn't say anything. Erin is therefore more likely to be late in her new job than she was in her old one. She is simply responding to costs and benefits as they exist in her new work environment.

20-2 THE POLITICAL MARKET

Economists who practice positive economics want to understand their world. They want to understand not only the production and pricing of goods, unemployment, inflation, and the firm, but also political outcomes and political behavior. This section is an introduction to the political market.

20-2a Moving Toward the Middle: The Median Voter Model

During political elections, voters often complain that the candidates for office are too much alike. Some find the similarities frustrating, saying they would prefer to have more choice. However, as you will see, two candidates running for the same office often sound alike because they are competing for votes.

In Exhibit 1, parts (a), (b), and (c) all show a distribution of voters in which the political spectrum goes from the far left to the far right. Relatively few voters hold positions in either of the two extreme wings. Assuming, then, that voters will vote for the candidate who comes closest to matching their ideological or political views, people whose views are in the far left of the political spectrum will vote for the candidate closest to the far left, and so on.

> **EXHIBIT 1**

The Move Toward the Middle

Given the voter distribution shown here, political candidates tend to move toward the middle of the political spectrum. Starting with (a), the Republican receives more votes than the Democrat and would win the election if it were held today. To offset this advantage, as shown in (b), the Democrat moves inward toward the middle of the political spectrum. The Republican tries to offset the Democrat's movement inward by also moving inward. As a result, both candidates move toward the political middle, getting closer to each other over time.

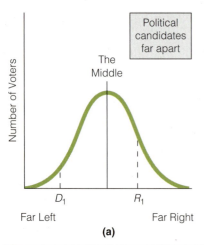

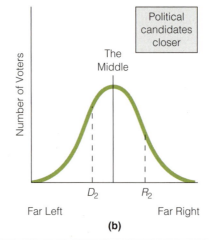

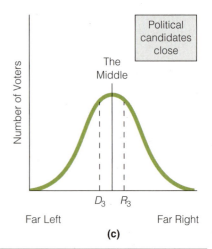

Our election process begins with two candidates, a Democrat and a Republican, occupying the positions D_1 and R_1 respectively, in part (a) of the exhibit. The Republican would receive all the votes of the voters who position themselves to the right of R_1, the Democrat would receive all the votes of the voters who position themselves to the left of D_1, and the voters between R_1 and D_1 would divide their votes between the two candidates. Thus, as shown, the Republican would receive more votes than the Democrat if the election were held today.

If, however, the election were not held today, the Democrat would likely notice (through polls and other sources) that her opponent was doing better than she was. To offset this advantage, she would move toward the center, or middle, of the political spectrum to pick up some votes. Part (b) in Exhibit 1 illustrates this move by the Democrat. Now voters to the left of D_2 would vote for the Democrat, voters to the right of R_2 would vote for the Republican, and the voters between the two positions would divide their votes between the two candidates. If the election were held at this time, the Democrat would win.

In part (c), each candidate, in an attempt to get more votes than his or her opponent, has moved closer to the middle. Thus, at election time, the two candidates are likely to be positioned side by side at the political center, or middle (D_3 and R_3).

The tendency of political candidates to move toward the center of the voter distribution—captured in the **median voter model**—is what causes many voters to complain that there is not much difference between candidates.

20-2b What Does the Theory Predict?

Although the median voter model explains why politicians running for the same office often sound alike, what does the model predict? Here are a few of the theory's predictions:

1. *Candidates will label their opponent as being either too far to the right or too far to the left.* The candidates know that whoever is closer to the middle of the political spectrum (in a two-person race) will win more votes and thus the election. Therefore, to win, they will move toward the political middle, at the same time saying that their opponent is a member of the political fringe (i.e., a person far from the center). A Democrat may argue that his Republican opponent is too conservative; a Republican may argue that her Democratic opponent is too liberal.

2. *Candidates will call themselves middle-of-the-roaders, not right- or left-wingers.* In their move toward the political middle, candidates will try to portray themselves as moderates. In their speeches, they will assert that they represent the majority of voters and that they are practical, not ideological. They will not be likely to refer to themselves as ultraliberal or ultraconservative or as right- or left-wingers because to do so would send a self-defeating message to the voters.

3. *Candidates will take polls, and, if they are not doing well in the polls and their opponents are, they will modify their positions to become more like their opponents.* Polls tell candidates who the likely winner of the election will be. A candidate who finds that she will lose the election (she is "down in the polls") is not likely to sit back and do nothing. The candidate will change her positions. Often, she will become more like the winner of the poll—that is, more like her political opponent.

4. *Candidates will speak in general, instead of specific, terms.* Voters agree more on ends than on the means of accomplishing those ends. For example, voters of the left, right, and middle believe that a strong economy is better than a weak economy. However, they do not all agree on the best way to make the economy strong. The person on the right might advocate less government intervention as one way, whereas the person

Median Voter Model
A model suggesting that candidates in a two-person political race will attempt to match the preferences of the median voter.

ECONOMICS 24/7

A Simple-Majority Voting Rule: The Case of the Statue in the Public Square

Public questions are often decided by the simple-majority decision rule. Although most people think that this is the fair and democratic way to do things, in certain instances a simple majority vote leads to undertaking a project whose costs are greater than its benefits.

Consider a community of 10 people, whose names are listed in column 1 of Exhibit 2. The community is considering whether to purchase a statue to put in the center of the public square. The cost of the statue is $1,000, and the community has previously agreed that if the statue is purchased, the 10 individuals will share the cost equally; that is, each will pay $100 in taxes. (See column 3.)

Column 2 shows the dollar value of the benefits that each individual will receive from the statue. For example, Applebaum places a dollar value of $150 on the statue, Browning places a dollar value of $140 on the statue, and so on. Column 4 notes the net benefit (+) or net cost (−) of the statue to each individual. A net benefit occurs if the dollar value an individual places on the statue is greater than the tax (cost) incurred. A net cost results if the reverse is true. Finally, column 5 indicates how each member of the community would

vote. An individual who believes that the statue has a net benefit will vote for it, and an individual who believes that the statue has a net cost will vote against it. Thus, six individuals vote for the statue, and four individuals vote against it. The majority rules, and the statue is purchased and placed in the center of the public square.

However, the total dollar value of benefits to the community ($812) is less than the total tax cost to the community ($1,000). Accordingly, using the simple-majority decision rule has resulted in the purchase of the statue even though the benefits of the statue to the community are less than its costs.

This outcome is not surprising when you understand that the simple-majority decision rule does not take into account the intensity of individuals' preferences. No matter how strongly a person feels about an issue, he or she registers only one vote. For example, even though Emerson places a net benefit of $1 on the statue and Isley places a net cost of $90 on the statue, each individual has only one vote. Isley has no way to register the fact that he does not want the statue more than Emerson wants it.

❯ EXHIBIT 2

Simple-Majority Voting and Inefficiency

The simple-majority decision rule sometimes generates inefficient results. Here, a statue is purchased even though the total dollar value of the benefits of the statue is less than the total dollar costs.

(1) Individuals	(2) Dollar Value of Benefits to Individual	(3) Tax Levied on Individual	(4) Net Benefit or Net Cost	(5) Vote for or Against
Applebaum	$150	$100	+$50	For
Browning	140	100	+40	For
Carson	130	100	+30	For
Davidson	110	100	+10	For
Emerson	101	100	+1	For
Finley	101	100	+1	For
Gunter	50	100	−50	Against
Harris	10	100	−90	Against
Isley	10	100	−90	Against
Janowitz	10	100	−90	Against
Total	$812	$1,000		

on the left might advocate more government intervention. Most political candidates soon learn that addressing the issues specifically requires them to discuss means and that doing so increases the probability of their having an extreme-wing label attached to them. For example, a candidate who advocates more government intervention in the economy is more likely to be labeled "too far left" than a candidate who simply calls for a stronger national economy without discussing any specific means. In the candidate's desire to be perceived as a middle-of-the-roader, he is much more likely to talk about ends, on which voters agree, than about means, on which voters disagree.

In a Presidential Election Debate During a presidential election debate, one candidate is asked what his plan is for health care in the country. He says that his plan would make health care more affordable and responsive to peoples' needs. He then goes on to say that health care has been a problem in the United States for a long time and that it is about time for a solution. Where is the economics?

The median voter model predicts that candidates will speak in general, not specific, terms. That is exactly what our hypothetical candidate has done. He did not get into any specifics about his plan. For example, he probably will not specifically address how much the health care plan will cost, whom it will serve, and so on.

Testing Theories An economist thinks about theories and then tests them. She is not content to accept a theory—such as the one which says that candidates in a two-person political race will gravitate toward the center of the political distribution—simply because it sounds right. The economist asks, "If the theory is right, what should I expect to see in the real world? If the theory is wrong, what should I expect to see in the real world?" Such questions direct the economist to look at effects to see whether the theory has explanatory and predictive power. If the four predictions of the median voter theory occur in the real world—candidates labeling themselves one way, speaking in general terms, and so on—then the economist can conclude that the evidence supports the theory. But if candidates en masse do not behave as the model predicts, then the economist must reject the theory.

20-3 VOTERS AND RATIONAL IGNORANCE

The preceding section explains something about the behavior of politicians, especially near or at election time. We turn now to voters.

20-3a The Costs and Benefits of Voting

Political commentators often remark that the voter turnout for this or that election was low: "Only 54 percent of registered voters actually voted." Are voter turnouts low because Americans are apathetic? Are they uninterested in political issues?

Public choice economists often explain low voter turnouts in terms of the costs and benefits of voting. As an example, Mark Quincy is thinking about voting in a presidential election. Mark may receive many benefits from voting: he may feel more involved in public affairs or think that he has met his civic responsibility. He may see himself as patriotic, or he may believe he has a greater right to criticize government if he takes an active part in it. In short, he may benefit by seeing himself as a doer instead of a talker. Ultimately, however, he will weigh these positive benefits against the costs of voting, which include driving to the polls, standing in line, and so on. If, in the end, Mark perceives the benefits of voting as greater than the costs, he will vote.

But suppose Mark believes that he receives only one benefit from voting: determining the outcome of the election. His benefits-of-voting equation may look like this:

Mark's benefits of voting = Probability of Mark's vote determining the election outcome ×
Additional benefits Mark receives if his candidate wins

Now, suppose two candidates, A and B, are running for office. If Mark votes, he will vote for A because he estimates that he benefits by $100 if A is elected but only by $40 if B is elected. The difference, $60, represents the additional benefits Mark receives if his candidate wins.

However, the probability that Mark's vote will determine the outcome is minuscule. With many potential voters, such as there are in a presidential election, the probability that one person's vote will determine the outcome is close to zero. To recognize this fact on an intuitive level, suppose A and B are the two major candidates in a presidential campaign. If you, as an individual voter, vote for A, the outcome of the election is likely to be the same as if you had voted for B or not voted at all. In other words, whether you vote at all, vote for A, or vote for B, the outcome is likely to be the same. In Mark's benefits-of-voting equation, $60 is multiplied by a probability so small that it might as well be 0. So, $60 times 0 is 0. In short, Mark receives no benefits from voting.

But Mark may face certain costs. His costs-of-voting equation may look like this:

Mark's cost of voting = Cost of driving to the polls
+ Cost of standing in line
+ Cost of filling out the ballot

Obviously, Mark faces some positive costs of voting. Because his benefits of voting are 0 and his costs of voting are positive, Mark makes the rational choice if he decides not to vote.

Clearly, not everyone behaves this way—that is, chooses not to vote. Many people do vote in elections. Probably what separates the Marks in the world from the people who vote is that the voters receive some benefits that Mark does not. They might receive benefits simply by being part of the excitement of election day, by doing what they perceive as their civic duty, or for some other reason.

The point public choice economists make is that, if many individual voters will vote only if they perceive their vote as making a difference, then they probably will not vote, because their vote is unlikely to make a difference. Thus, the low turnouts that appear to be a result of voter apathy may instead be a result of cost–benefit calculations.

20-3b Rational Ignorance

How often have you heard an opinion like this one? "Democracy would be better served if voters would take more of an interest in, and become better informed about, politics and government. Voters don't know much about the issues."

The problem, however, is not that voters are too stupid to learn about the issues. Many citizens who know little about politics and government are quite capable of learning about both, but they choose not to make the effort. The reason is perhaps predictable: the costs of becoming informed often outweigh the benefits. In short, many persons believe that becoming informed is simply not worth the effort. Hence, on an individual basis, it makes sense to be uninformed about politics and government—that is, to be in a state of **rational ignorance**.

Rational Ignorance
The state of not acquiring information because the costs of acquiring it are greater than the benefits.

ECONOMICS 24/7

Economic Illiteracy and Democracy

Citizens can vote even if they have no idea what they are doing. If enough voters fit that description, democratic governments are bound to make foolish decisions.

—Bryan Caplan, *Straight Talk About Economic Literacy*

Blend Images - Hill Street Studios/Brand X Pictures/Getty Images

Economist Bryan Caplan argues that a large percentage of the American public is economically illiterate. The result is that a lot of foolishness gets turned into national economic policy.[1]

Although determining whether someone is illiterate may be easy, not so easy is ascertaining whether someone is economically illiterate. To determine illiteracy, you can just ask people to read or write something. If they can read and write, they are not illiterate. If they can't read or write, they are illiterate.

Unfortunately, there is no such simple test to determine economic illiteracy. Instead, Caplan points to a survey that compared the responses of 1,510 average Americans with those of 250 professional economists to the same set of questions concerning economics and the economy. Here is one question from the survey: "Which do you think is more responsible for the recent increase in gasoline prices: the normal law of supply and demand, oil companies are trying to increase profits, both, or neither?" Although only 8 percent of economists said that recent increases in gas prices were due to oil companies trying to increase profits, 78 percent of the noneconomists polled explained high gas prices in that way. The explanation for high gas prices chosen

by 83 percent of economists was supply and demand.

Indirectly, Caplan uses the economists' overwhelming response to the question as a benchmark by which to measure the economic illiteracy of the public. The closer the public's responses are to the economists' responses, the less economically illiterate the public is; the farther away the public's responses are from the economists' responses, the more economically illiterate the public is.

According to Caplan, who looked at responses to numerous questions, the American public is largely economically illiterate. Caplan argues that such a great degree of economic illiteracy has to do with the price one pays for it. In fact, however, the price is rather low, and when the price is low, you would expect a higher degree of economic illiteracy than when the price is high. In a phrase, false beliefs about economics are cheap. As Caplan says, if you underestimate the costs of excessive drinking, you can ruin your life, but if you underestimate the economic benefits of, say, free international trade, nothing really bad happens to you. Whatever happens to you is what would have happened if you didn't underestimate the economic benefits of free international trade. In other words, when being wrong really has no cost, a lot of people will be wrong—especially if one receives a personal psychological lift from holding an erroneous belief or position. Caplan puts it succinctly: "In a sense, then, there is a method to the average voter's madness. Even when his views are completely wrong, he gets the psychological benefit of emotionally appealing political beliefs at a bargain price. No wonder he buys in bulk."[2] In other words, x might be the wrong answer to the question, but if x is emotionally appealing to the respondent and if having the wrong answer doesn't adversely affect the respondent, then x it is.

But if many people choose x, perhaps at a national level x gets turned into policy. In other words, if the majority of voting Americans believe that placing tariffs on foreign imports is desirable (when economists largely disagree), then, in a political system in which politicians compete for votes, the public's erroneous belief is likely to find its way into international trade policy.

If one person's erroneous belief adversely affects only him, that is one thing. But it is quite another thing, Caplan argues, when the erroneous beliefs of many people adversely affect those who do not hold that belief. Yet this outcome is what we often get in a representative democracy. Economically erroneous beliefs, chosen on an individual level because they are cheap to choose, often add up to democracies' choosing bad economic policies.

1. Bryan Caplan, *The Myth of the Rational Voter: Why Democracies Choose Bad Policies* (Princeton, NJ: Princeton University Press, 2007).
2. Bryan Caplan, "The Myth of the Rational Voter," *Cato Unbound*, November 6, 2006, http://www.cato-unbound.org/2006/11/06/bryan-caplan /the-myth-of-the-rational-voter.

As an example, Shonia Tyler has many things she can do with her leisure time. She could read a good novel, watch a television program, go out with friends, or become better informed about the candidates and the issues in the upcoming U.S. Senate race. Becoming informed, however, has costs. If Shonia stays home and reads about the issues, she can't go out with her friends. If she stays up late to watch a news program, she might be too tired to work efficiently the next day. These costs have to be weighed against the benefits of becoming better informed about the candidates and the issues. For Shonia, as for many people, the benefits are unlikely to be greater than the costs.

Many people see little personal benefit in becoming more knowledgeable about political candidates and issues. As with voting, the decision to remain uninformed may be linked to the small impact that any single individual can have in a large-numbers setting.

SELF-TEST

(Answers to Self-Test questions are in Answers to Self-Test Questions at the back of the book.)

1. If a politician running for office does not speak in general terms, does not try to move to the middle of the political spectrum, and does not take polls, is the median voter model therefore wrong?

2. Voters often criticize politicians running for office who do not speak in specific terms (i.e., who do not specify which spending programs will be cut, whose taxes will be raised, etc.). If voters want politicians running for office to speak in specific terms, why don't politicians do so?

3. Would bad weather be something that could affect voter turnout? Explain your answer.

20-4 MORE ABOUT VOTING

Voting is often the method used to make decisions in the public sector. In this section, we discuss two examples to describe some of the effects (some might say problems) of voting as a decision-making method.

20-4a Example 1: Voting for a Nonexcludable Public Good

Suppose a community of 7 persons, A–G, wants to produce or purchase nonexcludable public good X. Each person in the community wants a different number of units of X, as shown in the following table:

Person	Number of Units of X Desired
A	1
B	2
C	3
D	4
E	5
F	6
G	7

If the community of 7 persons holds a simple majority vote, then all 7 will vote to produce or purchase at least 1 unit of X. Six people (B–G) will vote for at least 2 units; five people (C–G), for at least 3 units; four people (D–G), for at least 4 units; three people (E–G), for at least 5 units; and two people (F–G), for at least 6 units. Only one person (G) will vote for 7 units.

The largest number of units that receives a simple majority vote (half the total number of voters plus 1, or 4 votes) is 4 units. In other words, the community will vote to produce or purchase 4 units of X. Interestingly, 4 units is the most preferred outcome of only one of the seven members of the community, person D, who is the median voter. Half the voters (A, B, and C) prefer fewer than 4 units, and half the voters (E, F, and G) prefer more. Thus, our voting process has resulted in only the median voter obtaining his most preferred outcome.

The outcome would have been the same even if the numbers had looked as they do in the following table:

Person	Number of Units of X Desired
A	0
B	0
C	0
D	4
E	7
F	7
G	7

In this case, four people (D–G) would have voted for at least 4 units and only three people would have voted for anything less than 4 units. Again, 4 units would have been the outcome of the vote, and only the median voter would have obtained his most preferred outcome.

20-4b Example 2: Voting and Efficiency

Suppose three individuals have the marginal private benefits (*MPB*) shown in the following table for various units of the nonexcludable public good Y:

Person	MPB of First Unit of Y	MPB of Second Unit of Y	MPB of Third Unit of Y
A	$400	$380	$190
B	150	110	90
C	100	90	80

If the cost of providing a unit of good Y is $360, what is the socially optimal, or efficient, amount of good Y? To answer this question, recall a few of the relationships from the last chapter:

1. The socially optimal, or efficient, amount of anything is the amount at which the marginal social benefits (*MSB*) equal the marginal social costs (*MSC*).

2. The sum of the marginal private benefits (*MPB*) and the marginal external benefits (*MEB*) equals the marginal social benefits (*MSB*): *MPB* + *MEB* = *MSB*.

3. The sum of the marginal private costs (*MPC*) and the marginal external costs (*MEC*) equals the marginal social costs (*MSC*): *MPC* + *MEC* = *MSC*.

In our example, the *MSC* for each unit of Y is given as $360. We calculate the *MSB* for each unit by summing the *MPB*s shown in the relevant column of the table. For the first unit, the *MSB* is $650 ($400 + $150 + $100); for the second unit, it is $580; and for the third unit, it is $360. The socially optimal, or efficient, amount of good Y is 3 units because, at that amount, *MSB* = *MSC*.

Whether voting will give us efficiency depends largely on what tax each person, A–C, expects to pay. Suppose each person must pay an equal share of the price of a unit of good Y. In other words, the tax for each person is $120 ($360 per unit ÷ 3 persons = $120 per person per unit).

Person A will vote for 3 units because his *MPB* for each unit is greater than his tax of $120 per unit. Person B will vote for only 1 unit because his *MPB* for the first unit is greater than his tax of $120 per unit but his *MPB* is not greater for the second or third unit. Person C will not vote for any units because his *MPB* for each unit is less than his tax of $120 per unit. Thus, the outcome from using a simple-majority vote is only 1 unit, and a process of voting in which each voter pays an equal tax results in an inefficient outcome.

Now suppose that, instead of paying an equal tax (of $120), each person pays a tax equal to his *MPB* at the socially optimal, or efficient, outcome. The socially optimal, or efficient, outcome is 3 units of good Y, so person A would pay a tax of $190 (his *MPB* for the third unit is $190), person B would pay a tax of $90, and person C would pay a tax of $80. (The sum of the taxes paid is equal to the cost of the unit, or $360.)

With this different tax structure, will voting generate efficiency? If each person casts a truthful vote, the answer is yes: Each person will vote for 3 units.[3] In other words, if everyone casts a truthful vote and everyone pays a tax equal to his or her *MPB* at the efficient outcome, then voting will generate efficiency.

Comparing the two tax structures—one in which each person pays an equal tax and one in which each person pays a tax equal to his *MPB*—we see that the tax structure

---

[3] Look at the situation for person A: His *MPB* for the first unit is $400 and his tax is $190, so he votes for the first unit. His *MPB* for the second unit is $380 and his tax is $190, so he votes for the second unit. His *MPB* for the third unit is $190 and his tax is $190, so he votes for the third unit. With respect to the last unit for person A, we are assuming that if his *MPB* is equal to the tax, he will vote in favor of the unit. The same holds for the analysis of voting for persons B and C.

makes the difference. In the case of equal tax shares, voting did not lead to efficiency; in the case of unequal tax shares, it did.

1. If the *MSC* in Example 2 had been $580 instead of $360, what would the socially optimal, or efficient, outcome have been?

2. In Example 2 with equal taxes, did the outcome of the vote make anyone worse off? If so, whom and by how much?

20-5 SPECIAL-INTEREST GROUPS

Special-interest groups are subsets of the general population that hold (usually) intense preferences for or against a particular government service, activity, or policy. Often, special-interest groups gain from public policies that may not be in accord with the interests of the general public. In recent decades, they have played a major role in government.

20-5a Information and Lobbying

Whereas the general voter is usually uninformed about issues, members of a special-interest group are very well informed, at least about the issues they are interested in. For example, teachers are likely to know a lot about government education policies, farmers about government agriculture policies, and union members about government union policies. The reason for their greater awareness is simple: The more directly and intensely issues affect them, the greater the incentive is for individuals to become informed about them.

Given an electorate composed of uninformed general voters and informed members of special-interest groups, the groups are often able to sway politicians in their favor. This effect occurs even when the general public is made worse off by such actions (which, of course, is not always the case).

Suppose special-interest group A, composed of 5,000 individuals, favors a policy that will result in the redistribution of $50 million from 100 million general taxpayers to the group. Then the dollar benefit for each member of the special-interest group is $10,000. Given the substantial dollar amount involved, members of the special-interest group are likely to (1) sponsor or propose legislation to redistribute the money and (2) lobby the politicians who will decide the issue.

Further, the politicians will probably not hear from the general voter (i.e., the general taxpayer). The general voters–taxpayers will be less informed about the legislation than the members of the special-interest group, and anyway, even if they were adequately informed, each person would have to calculate the benefits and the costs of lobbying against the proposed legislation. If the legislation passes, the average taxpayer will pay approximately 50¢ and the benefits of lobbying against the legislation are probably not greater than 50¢. Therefore, even if they are informed about the legislation, the general taxpayers would not be likely to argue against it. The benefits just wouldn't be worth the time and effort. Special-interest bills therefore have a good chance of being passed in our legislatures.

20-5b Congressional Districts as Special-Interest Groups

Most people do not ordinarily think of congressional districts as special-interest groups. Instead, special-interest groups are commonly thought to include the ranks of public school teachers, steel manufacturers, automobile manufacturers, farmers, environmentalists,

Special-Interest Groups
Subsets of the general population that hold (usually) intense preferences for or against a particular government service, activity, or policy and that often gain from public policies that may not be in accord with the interests of the general public.

bankers, truck drivers, doctors, and the like. On some issues, however, a congressional district may be a special-interest group.

Suppose an air force base is located in a Texas congressional district. Then, a Pentagon study determines that the base is not needed and that Congress should shut it down. The Pentagon study demonstrates that the cost to the taxpayers of keeping the base open is greater than the benefits to the country of maintaining it. But closing the air force base will hurt the pocketbooks of the people in the congressional district housing the base. Their congressional representative knows not only as much, but also that if she can't keep the base open, she isn't as likely to be reelected to office.

Therefore, she speaks to other members of Congress about the proposed closing. In a way, she acts as a lobbyist for her congressional district. Most members of Congress are probably willing to go along with the Texas representative, even though they know that their constituents will be paying more in taxes than, according to the Pentagon, is necessary to ensure the national security of the country. If they don't go along with her, when they need a vote on one of their own special-interest projects (sometimes the term "pork barrel" is used), the representative from Texas may not be so cooperative. In short, members of Congress sometimes trade votes: my vote on your air force base for your vote on subsidies to dairy farmers in my district. This type of vote trading—the exchange of votes to gain support for legislation—is commonly referred to as **logrolling**.

Logrolling
The exchange of votes to gain support for legislation.

20-5c Public-Interest Talk, Special-Interest Legislation

Special-interest groups lobbying for special-interest legislation usually don't use that phrase, but rather something like "legislation in the best interest of the general public." A couple of examples, past and present, come to mind.

In the early nineteenth century, the British Parliament passed the Factory Acts, which put restrictions on women and children working. Those who lobbied for the restrictions said they did so for humanitarian reasons: to protect young children and women from difficult and hazardous work in the cotton mills. There is evidence, however, that the men working in the factories were the main lobbyists for the Factory Acts and that a reduced supply of women and children directly benefited them by raising their wages. The male factory workers appealed to individuals' higher sensibilities instead of letting it be known that they would benefit at the expense of others.

Today, people calling for, say, economic protection from foreign competitors or greater federal subsidies rarely explain that they favor the measure because the legislation will make them better off while someone else pays the bill. Instead, they usually voice the public-interest argument. Economic protectionism isn't necessary to protect industry X (they say), but it is necessary to protect American jobs and the domestic economy. The special-interest message often is, "Help yourself by helping us."

Sometimes this message is sincere, but other times it is not. In either case, it is likely to be as forcefully voiced.

20-5d Rent Seeking

Rent Seeking
Actions of individuals and groups who spend resources to influence public policy in the hope of redistributing (transferring) income to themselves from others.

Rent seeking consists of the actions of individuals and groups who spend resources to influence public policy in the hope of redistributing (transferring) income to themselves from others. To illustrate, suppose Smith is one of many producers of shoes, and suppose he realizes that he would be better off if he were the only one who produces shoes. With less competition from other shoe producers, the supply of shoes would fall and the price would rise. Smith would then end up selling shoes at $200 a pair instead of $80 a pair.

In pursuit of his aim, suppose Smith hires a law firm that specializes in lobbying government for its clients. Members of the law firm go to members of Congress and ask them to pass a law prohibiting all companies other than the Smith Shoe Company from producing shoes. The attorneys representing Smith promise to donate money to the political campaigns of the congressional members with whom they speak. They also promise that Smith of Smith Shoe Company will try to persuade his workers that their work interests are best served by voting for specific members of Congress.

In this scenario, Smith is using resources to effect a transfer. Smith has spent money to influence Congress to give him a special privilege: the right to be the only producer of shoes. In essence, Smith is trying to bring about a transfer from shoe consumers to himself. He wants consumers to end up paying more for shoes so that he earns more from producing them. He is spending money to try to bring about this transfer from others to him. Smith is a *rent seeker*: he is using resources (the money he spends goes for resources) in order to bring about a transfer from others to him.

Let's say that Smith spends a total of $100,000 to bring about the transfer. This is the cost of his rent seeking. From Smith's perspective, the decision to spend $100,000 to bring about a transfer, of, say, $1 million is rational. But from society's perspective, all the resources that Smith uses to effect a transfer are wasted. The $100,000 is wasted because money spent trying to effect a transfer cannot be used to produce goods and services.

To see the negative effects rent seeking has on society even more clearly, consider an extreme example. Let's say that today 1,000 individuals are all producing goods and services. Together, they produce about $2 million worth of output a day. Tomorrow, all 1,000 individuals decide to spend their time and money trying to bring about a transfer. In other words, instead of producing, they spend their time rent seeking. At the end of the day, the cost to society of these 1,000 individuals' rent seeking instead of producing is obviously $2 million worth of output. Society is poorer by $2 million because the 1,000 individuals turned away from producing and toward rent seeking. In short, rent seeking is a socially wasteful activity.

20-5e Bringing About Transfers

In Exhibit 3, the market equilibrium price of a certain good is P_1. At this price, identifying both consumers' surplus and producers' surplus is easy. Consumers' surplus is the area under the demand curve and above the equilibrium price, out to the equilibrium quantity, Q_1: the triangular area $A + B + C$. Producers' surplus is the area under the equilibrium price and above the supply curve, out to the equilibrium quantity, Q_1: the triangular area $D + E$.

Now, suppose the producers of the good lobby government for a price floor, P_2. If government

> **EXHIBIT 3**

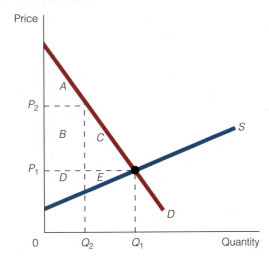

A Price Floor and a Transfer from Consumers to Producers

The market equilibrium price of the good is P_1. Consumers' surplus is the area $A + B + C$. Producers' surplus is the area $D + E$. If producers of the good lobby for and receive a price floor of P_2, then consumers' surplus ends up being only area A. Consumers lose areas $B + C$ in consumers' surplus, and producers gain area B in producers' surplus. By obtaining the price floor through government, producers of the good were able to take some consumers' surplus away from consumers and turn it into producers' surplus for themselves.

grants this floor, then the new price in the market is P_2 and consumers' surplus ends up being only area A. Consumers lose area $B + C$ in consumers' surplus. At the new price P_2, producers lose area E in producers' surplus and they gain area B. As long as area E (what they lose) is smaller than area B (what they gain), producers are better off selling at price P_2 than P_1. In Exhibit 3, area E is clearly smaller than B, so producers are better off.

The price floor has thus created a transfer. Area B, which was once consumers' surplus, is now producers' surplus. By getting the price floor, the producers of the good were able to take some consumers' surplus away from consumers and turn it into producers' surplus. If area B is equivalent to, say, $1,000, then producers have been able to transfer $1,000 from consumers to themselves. All the resources that the producers expended to get that transfer of $1,000 are referred to as the *rent-seeking costs*—that is, the costs of trying to bring about the transfer. Again, from society's perspective, the resources expended to effect the transfer are wasted in that they cannot be used to produce goods and services. Society as a whole is a just a little bit poorer because of the rent-seeking behavior of the producers.

20-5f Information, Rational Ignorance, and Seeking Transfers

Will rent seekers tell the truth about their rent-seeking efforts (assuming that they know the truth)? Suppose Smith knows that his rent seeking will lead to greater producers' surplus for him and less consumers' surplus and that the losses to consumers will be greater than his gains. (If you look back at Exhibit 3, you will notice that the losses to consumers from the price floor—areas $B + C$—are greater than the gain of area B to the producer.) Will he advertise this information? Will he, for instance, lobby government by saying, "I would like a price floor for what I sell. I know that this will end up hurting consumers more than it benefits me, but so be it. As long as I am made better off, I don't really care how much consumers are made worse off. Can I have the transfer?"

He is unlikely to say this. For one thing, making such a barefaced request draws attention to the fact that he gains at consumers' expense and that his gain is smaller than what consumers lose. Smith wouldn't draw attention to this fact. Instead, he might try to argue that what is good for him is good (not bad) for others.

Can such rent-seeking efforts be successful? Won't the politicians turn Smith down because moving from an equilibrium price to a price floor hurts consumers more than it helps producers? (Yet there are price floors in the real world.) Won't consumers rally against Smith because they know that they are being hurt by his actions? Moreover, aren't consumers greater in number than Smith (who is only one), and don't politicians care about votes (which means that they must then care about the number of voters)?

First, consumers may not rally against Smith, because they may not even know that he is lobbying government for a price floor. Recall the issue of rational ignorance—that is, not acquiring information because the costs of acquiring it are greater than the benefits.

Most individuals are rationally ignorant of many issues. If you know less about French literature than you could know, then you are rationally ignorant of the subject. If you know less about computers than you could know, then you are rationally ignorant of computers.

Similarly, many people are rationally ignorant of politics and government; that is, they know less than you could know—and that is largely because the marginal benefits of acquiring this kind of information are so low. And the benefits are low because an individual's one vote matters so little in the determination of an election, as we discussed earlier. In other words, the probability that your one vote will break a tie and decide who wins and who loses in an election—especially when millions of people are eligible to vote—is infinitesimally small.

So, if your vote is not going to determine the outcome of an election, what does it matter how much or how little information you have about the candidates, the issues, and the events? The answer to that question is perhaps best framed in terms of your options. Let's say two major candidates, A and B, are running for U.S. senator from your state. Then you have the following options:

- *Option 1:* Be fully informed (on the Senate election issues) and vote for A.
- *Option 2:* Be fully informed and vote for B.
- *Option 3:* Be rationally ignorant and vote for A.
- *Option 4:* Be rationally ignorant and vote for B.
- *Option 5:* Be fully informed and not vote.
- *Option 6:* Be rationally ignorant and not vote.

No matter which option you choose, the outcome of the election will be what it will be. Your vote will likely not break a tie; your vote will not determine the outcome of the election. Therefore, the least-cost option is obviously option 6, to be rationally ignorant and not vote.

Of course, not everyone chooses this option. In the last presidential election, approximately 130 million persons voted, although millions of other eligible voters chose not to vote. Of the approximately 130 million who did vote, probably very many were rationally ignorant. Being otherwise would have been just too costly for them, especially given the fact that very few of them were under the delusion that their single vote would determine outcome of the election.

So, if producers seek a transfer that ends up hurting consumers, consumers are not likely to know about it if they are rationally ignorant, and the incentive for them to be rationally ignorant is huge. Thus, when a producer lobbies members of Congress for a price floor that helps him and hurts consumers, the consumers may not even know about the rent seeking. And even if they do, do they also know that a price floor leads to a greater loss in consumers' surplus than an increase in producers' surplus, especially when the producer has an incentive not to state the details of the transfer? Instead, the producer will probably wrap his special-interest legislation in "public-interest talk." Perhaps he will argue that, without a price floor for his good, few producers will produce it and that if few producers produce the good, people will lose their jobs, communities will lose tax revenue, and so forth. None of this has to be true, of course, but trying to figure out whether it might be true may be too costly an effort for most individuals to undertake.

But suppose that rational ignorance does not exist: Everyone knows everything about everything. Then, when the producer lobbies government for a price floor, consumers immediately know about his activities; furthermore, they know that the loss of consumers' surplus (as a result of the price floor) will be greater than the gain in producers' surplus. Even so, consumers may still not fight the producers because, simply put, the loss to each individual consumer might be so small that it is not worth fighting to stop the price floor.

As an example, suppose 100 producers will benefit a total of $10 million if the price floor replaces the equilibrium price in the market. That amount is an average of $100,000 per producer. But suppose consumers will lose $15 million as a result of the price floor. If there are 100 million consumers, the average consumer loses only 15¢. A consumer will probably not spend $1 to fight a policy that costs him or her only 15¢.

ECONOMICS 24/7

Inheritance, Heirs, and Why the Firstborn Became King or Queen

Some economists have said that rent seeking often goes on within families, especially when an inheritance is involved. We present the argument of these economists in the form of a short story.

Suppose an elderly widow with three children (call them A, B, and C) has an estate worth $10 million, which she will leave to the children upon her death. But, of course, $10 million can be left to three adult children in a number of ways:

- She can split the $10 million into three equal parts, leaving $3.333 million to each child.

- She can divide the $10 million unequally, perhaps leaving $9 million to A, $500,000 to B, and $500,000 to C.

- She can tell each child how much he or she will inherit, or she can keep the dollar amount secret (until after her death).

In other words, the elderly woman has two major decisions to make: how much money she will give each child and whether to tell the children what they will receive upon her death.

If the woman is the type of person who craves attention and wants her children to fawn all over her, she can use her inheritance to get them to do that. All she has to do is tell her children (1) that she will not divide her estate equally among the three of them and (2) that she hasn't yet decided on the amount each will receive. If she promises unequal inheritances that are yet to be determined, she almost guarantees that her children will engage in a rent-seeking battle for the bulk of her inheritance. The resultant battle is likely to take the form of each child fawning over the mother to curry favor.

The siblings know that the amount of the inheritance is fixed at $10 million and that whatever goes to one sibling will not go to the others. For example, if $3 million goes to sibling B or C, then A gets $3 million less. The widow has effectively put her three children in a situation in which they will invest resources (fawn over her) to effect a pure transfer. This situation constitutes rent seeking.

The situation is different if the woman tells her children what she plans to leave each one and then guarantees that under no

An Allegory of the Tudor Succession: The Family of Henry VIII, c.1589-95 (oil on panel), English School, (16th century)/Yale Center for British Art, Paul Mellon Collection, USA/Bridgeman Images

circumstances will she change her mind. For example, she tells child A that he will receive $2 million, child B that she will receive $7 million, and child C that he will receive $1 million. The siblings now have no reason to invest resources in rent seeking. The $10 million has already been split up.

Alternatively, the mother can tell her children that she plans to divide her inheritance equally and nothing on earth can get her to do differently. Once again, if the children know how things are guaranteed to turn out and that any resources they use to change the results will be wasted, they will decide against trying to change the outcome. In other words, no child will seek rent.

Rent seeking used to be common in a slightly different context. In the days when kings and queens ruled, the royal firstborn usually inherited the throne. But why the first child? The third child could be a more capable king or queen than the first. Surely, not every firstborn was more capable of being king or queen than every second, third, or fourth child.

If the firstborn were not predetermined to inherit the throne, the royal children would have engaged in a rent-seeking battle for it. In and of itself, the queen or king may not have had anything against this outcome, and, in fact, they may have liked it.

But they might not have liked it if their children engaged in such an intense rent-seeking battle that they tried to kill each other. If you were one of the siblings, you could get to the throne in two ways: (1) Have the queen or king choose you as heir from among all your brothers and sisters; (2) kill your brothers and sisters so that you will be the only one left. One way to cut down on the bloodshed was to simply have a rule stating that the firstborn would become king or queen. This rule didn't eliminate sibling murders completely—the second child might try to kill the first and therefore inherit the throne—but it certainly kept the number of sibling murders lower than what it might have been if *any* of the children could ascend to the throne.

The key in seeking transfers is to spread the loss from the transfer over as many people as possible so that, on a per-person basis, the loss is very small. The loss should be small enough that the individual will have little reason to argue against the policy that inflicts the loss.

20-6 CONSTITUTIONAL ECONOMICS

Most of economics deals with behavior within a certain set of constraints. For example, consider that your decisions as to what and how much to buy take place within income and price constraints. If your income is $1,000 a month and the price of all goods is $1, then you can purchase only 1,000 units of various goods a month.

Sometimes the constraints within which we choose are given, as in the example presented in the previous paragraph. But sometimes we *choose* to place ourselves within certain constraints. Consider a person who has decided that he wants to lose 15 pounds. To help himself lose the weight, he never keeps any snacks (potato chips, ice cream, cookies) in his house. By this action, he has deliberately chosen to constrain himself (from eating snacks late at night when he knows that he is generally inclined to).

On a collective level, think of a group of people choosing to constrain their driving behavior by opting for speed limit laws. Each person reasons that, without such laws, he can drive as fast he wants to—but then, so can everyone else. But if everyone can drive as fast as he wants, there may be more accidents (and deaths) than if everyone had to obey a speed limit. Each person then opts to constrain his and everyone else's behavior by opting for speed limit laws.

In this chapter, we have discussed behavior within a political or government context. That behavior occurred within certain constraints. For example, voters could not vote more than once, elections were held every two or four years, and so on.

Might individuals living within a particular political setting seek to constrain themselves or others in some way in order to obtain better results than could be obtained in an environment without constraints or with different constraints? For example, at the current moment there is no constraint as to how much the federal government can spend. Some people argue that, as a result of this absence of a limit, the federal government is likely to spend too much—as is manifest by the nation's large budget deficits. Suppose the federal government were to opt for a constraint on itself? Suppose the Congress were to pass a law which stated that it could not spend more in any given year than the projected tax revenues in that year. For example, if projected tax revenues were $2.2 trillion, then spending had to be $2.2 trillion or less. Passing such a law would constrain the Congress; it would place a ceiling on how much the Congress could spend in a given year.

There is a branch of economics called constitutional economics or constitutional political economy in which economists study the types of constraints that individuals might place upon themselves in order to achieve some objective that doesn't seem achievable in an environment that lacks constraints.

In fact, constitutional economists sometimes argue that better outcomes are more readily forthcoming out of government by changing institutions, constraints, laws, and rules than by changing people. In other words, within a given set of institutions, constraints, laws and rules, outcomes might be the same no matter who is elected to office. For example, whether Republicans or Democrats are overwhelmingly elected to political office, big budget deficits might be the order of the day unless there is some constraint placed on government against running a budget deficit.

SELF-TEST

1. The average farmer is likely to be better informed about federal agricultural policy than the average food consumer is. Why?

2. Consider special-interest legislation that will transfer $40 million from group A to group B, a group with 10,000 persons. Is this legislation more likely to pass when group A consists of (a) 10,000 persons or (b) 10 million persons? Explain your answer.

3. Give an example of public-interest talk spoken by a special-interest group.

4. Why is rent-seeking activity socially wasteful?

"Doesn't Public Choice Paint a Bleak Picture of Politics and Government?"

STUDENT:

In a way, public choice paints a rather bleak picture of politics and government.

INSTRUCTOR:

How so?

STUDENT:

Politicians don't seem to care about what is right or wrong. They just move to the middle of the voter distribution. People don't always vote, because voting is sometimes too costly. People aren't always well informed on issues, because accessing the information is too costly. And to top it off, special interests are engaged in rent seeking. Doesn't all this sound dismal to you?

INSTRUCTOR:

It sounds as if you want things to work differently. Well, unfortunately, as the Rolling Stones told us, "You can't always get what you want."

STUDENT:

I have to confess that I would like it if things worked differently. I want politicians to do the right thing, and I want people to be informed on issues and to cast intelligent votes.

INSTRUCTOR:

Probably, many people want the same thing. My guess is that public choice economists want the same thing. But we can't let what we want color how we see the world.

STUDENT:

But who is to say that public choice economists analyze the world in the right way? Maybe they are an overly cynical bunch of economists.

INSTRUCTOR:

What they are doesn't matter. What matters is what they say and what they predict. We don't judge an economic theory by how it sounds to us or by how we feel about it; we judge it by how well it explains and predicts what we see in the world. If politicians move to the center of the voter distribution, if people are rationally ignorant, and if special interests sometimes engage in rent seeking, then that's the way things are whether we like it or not.

STUDENT:

But aren't economists supposed to be trying to make the world better?

INSTRUCTOR:

Let's assume that they are. Then isn't a good understanding of the world critical to doing this? For example, if the world is X, and

I think it is Y, then I might make mistakes when I try to make the world a better place. Basing what I do on how things are has to be better than basing them on how I might want them to be.

STUDENT:

I see your point. It's sort of like a doctor who wants to know your true condition before she prescribes any therapy. She may not like the fact that you have a particular disease, but it's important that she know about it so that she can prescribe the right medicine.

INSTRUCTOR:

I think that captures the spirit of what I'm talking about.

STUDENT:

Does it follow, then, that everything in public choice theory is right?

INSTRUCTOR:

No, it doesn't follow. Public choice theory—just like any theory in economics—has to be judged on how well it explains and predicts.

Points to remember

1. Theories should be judged on how well they explain and predict (not on how they sound or feel).
2. Good economics seeks to know what exists, no matter how pleasant or unpleasant that is.

CHAPTER SUMMARY

POLITICIANS AND THE MIDDLE: THE MEDIAN VOTER MODEL

- In a two-person race, candidates for the same office will gravitate toward the median voter. If a candidate does not do so and her opponent does, the opponent will win the election.
- Candidates usually pick labels for themselves that represent the middle of the political spectrum, they speak in general terms, and they take polls and adjust their positions accordingly.

VOTING AND RATIONAL IGNORANCE

- Voting has both costs and benefits. Many potential voters will not vote because the costs of voting—in terms of time spent going to the polls and so on—outweigh the benefits of voting, measured as the probability of their single vote determining the election outcome.
- Being unable to learn certain information is different from choosing not to learn it. Most voters choose not to be informed about political and government issues because the costs of becoming informed outweigh the benefits of becoming informed. They choose to be rationally ignorant.

MORE ABOUT VOTING

- In a simple-majority vote, given several options to choose from, the voting outcome is the same as the most preferred outcome of the median voter.

- Simple-majority voting together with equal tax shares can generate a different result from simple-majority voting together with unequal tax shares.

SPECIAL-INTEREST GROUPS

- Special-interest groups are usually well informed about their issues because individuals have a greater incentive to become informed about issues that directly and intensely affect them.
- Legislation that concentrates benefits on a few and disperses costs over many is likely to pass because the beneficiaries will have an incentive to lobby for it whereas those who pay the bill will not lobby against it because each of them pays such a small part of the bill.
- Special-interest groups often engage in rent seeking, which is the expenditure of scarce resources to capture a pure transfer. Rent seeking is a socially wasteful activity because the resources used to effect transfers are not used to produce goods and services.

CONSTITUTIONAL ECONOMICS

- The subject matter of constitutional economics is choosing rules or constraints within which collective choices are made.
- Constitutional economists often argue that governmental outcomes will be more readily forthcoming by changing institutions, constraints, laws, and rules than by changing people. In other words, within a given set of institutions, constraints, laws, and rules, outcomes might be the same no matter who is elected to office.

KEY TERMS AND CONCEPTS

Public Choice
Median Voter Model

Rational Ignorance
Special-Interest Groups

Logrolling
Rent Seeking

VIDEO QUESTIONS AND PROBLEMS

Video Questions and Problems are available on MindTap for Arnold 12e or by searching for Arnold on www.cengagebrain.com

1. Give a numerical example to show that a simple-majority decision rule can lead to a project being undertaken for which the costs are greater than the benefits.

2. Outline the details of the median voter model.

3. Is a voter more likely to be rationally ignorant in an election in which she is one of 100 voters or one of 10 million voters? Explain your answer.

4. Identify two reasons that a good deal of legislation is likely to be special-interest legislation.

5. From the individual's perspective, can rent seeking be rational? Explain your answer.

QUESTIONS AND PROBLEMS

1. Some observers maintain that not all politicians move toward the middle of the political spectrum in order to obtain votes. They often cite Barry Goldwater in the 1964 presidential election and George McGovern in the 1972 presidential election as examples. Goldwater was viewed as occupying the right end of the political spectrum and McGovern the left end. Would these two examples necessarily be evidence that does not support the median voter model? Are the exceptions to the theory explained in this chapter?

2. The economist James Buchanan said, "If men should cease and desist from their talk about and their search for evil men and commence to look instead at the institutions manned by ordinary people, wide avenues for genuine social reform might appear." What did he mean?

3. Would voters have a greater incentive to vote in an election involving only a few registered voters or in one that has many? Why? Why might a Republican label her opponent too far left and a Democrat label his opponent too far right?

4. Many individuals learn more about the car they are thinking of buying than about the candidates running for president of the United States. Explain why.

5. If the model of politics and government presented in this chapter is true, what are some of the things we would expect to see?

6. It has often been said that Democratic candidates are more liberal in Democratic primaries and Republican candidates are more conservative in Republican primaries than either is in the general election. Explain why.

7. What are some ways of reducing the cost of voting to voters?

8. Provide a numerical example which shows that simple-majority voting may be consistent with efficiency. Next, provide a numerical example which shows that simple-majority voting may be inconsistent with efficiency.

9. John chooses not to vote in the presidential election. Does it follow that he is apathetic when it comes to presidential politics? Explain your answer.

10. Some individuals see national defense spending as benefiting special interests—in particular, the defense industry. Others see it as directly benefiting not only the defense industry but the general public as well. Does this same difference between viewpoints apply to issues other than national defense? Name a few.

11. Evaluate each of the following proposals for reform in terms of the material discussed in this chapter:

    a. Linking all spending programs to visible tax hikes

    b. A balanced-budget amendment stipulating that Congress cannot spend more than total tax revenues

    c. A budgetary referendum process whereby the voters actually vote on the distribution of federal dollars to the different categories of spending (*x* percentage to agriculture, *y* percentage to national defense, etc.) instead of letting elected representatives decide

12. "Rent seeking may be rational from the individual's perspective, but it is not rational from society's perspective." Do you agree or disagree? Explain your answer.

WORKING WITH NUMBERS AND GRAPHS

1. Suppose that three major candidates—A, B, and C—are running for president of the United States and that the distribution of voters is that shown in Exhibit 1. Two of the candidates—A and B—are currently viewed as right of the median voter, and C is viewed as left of the median voter. Is it possible to predict which candidate is the most likely to win?

2. Look back at Exhibit 2. Suppose that the net benefits and net costs for each person are known a week before election day and that it is legal to buy and sell votes. Furthermore, suppose that neither buying nor selling votes has any conscience cost (i.e., one does not feel guilty buying or selling votes). Would the outcome of the election be the same? Explain your answer.

3. In part (a) of the accompanying figure, the distribution of voters is skewed to the left; in part (b), the distribution is skewed neither left nor right; and in part (c), it is skewed right. Assuming a two-person race for each distribution, will the candidate who wins the election in (a) hold different positions from the candidates who win the elections in (b) and (c)? Explain your answer.

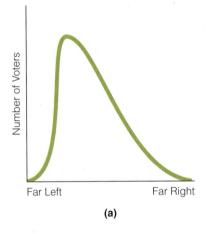

(a)

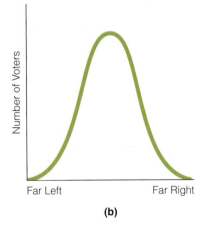

(b)

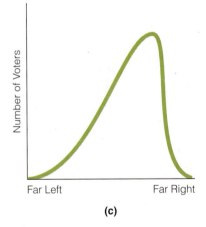

(c)

21

BUILDING THEORIES TO EXPLAIN EVERYDAY LIFE: FROM OBSERVATIONS TO QUESTIONS TO THEORIES TO PREDICTIONS

INTRODUCTION

In this chapter, we build theories to explain everyday life. Some of the things we seek to explain are dating relationships, the birthrates in various countries, one's ethical code, burglary, segregated neighborhoods, cheating on an exam, house prices and school districts, and more.

21-1 A DIFFERENT KIND OF CHAPTER

This chapter differs from others in this text in two fundamental ways: in your experience and in its content.

First, the chapter offers a different experience. Think about a new house that took eight months to build. You see the house for the first time on the day it is completed. You look at the outside, then walk into the house, go into every room, and touch the various surfaces—the freshly painted walls, the granite countertop in the kitchen, the shiny new hardwood floor.

How different would it be to watch the house being built from day to day? You would see the land being cleared, the excavation dug, the concrete laid, the house framed, plumbing and wiring put in, and the walls painted.

These are two very different experiences: the view of a completed house and the building of the house. Which experience is more like yours in reading this text so far? It is probably like the first—viewing the completed house. The text has presented various complete theories, such as the theory of supply and demand. Then we discussed certain things within those theories. That is how the material in most texts about economics principles is presented, and it is an important part of your economic education.

Also important, however, is another part of your economic education: seeing the process that leads to the completed theory—seeing how the house is built. If contractors build houses, economists build theories. It is time for you to see the nitty-gritty process of how economists go about doing what they do. That is the experience of this chapter.

Building an economic theory is a five-step process:

1. It starts with economists making an observation or having a thought.

2. The observation or thought leads to a question.

3. The economist then builds a theory to try to answer the question.

4. Next, if the theory has been built correctly, predictions based on the theory pour forth.

5. Finally, data are gathered and analyzed, and the theory's predictions are tested against reality: Either they are borne out, or they are shown to be false.

In this chapter, we present only the first four steps. We leave the last step—testing the theory—to a course you might take in statistics or econometrics.

This chapter also differs from others in its content. Most of the other chapters in the text have contained discussions of fairly standard economic topics: supply and demand, market structures, labor markets, and the like. In this chapter, we include more everyday topics: dating relationships, the ethical code in small towns and large cities, punctuality and office hours, family size, and so on. We chose these topics for three reasons, two of which are that most people are familiar with them from their own everyday life experiences and no specialized knowledge is needed to discuss them.

The third reason is to show that economic thinking, concepts, and theorizing can often extend to places to which most people would not have guessed that they are applicable. To noneconomists, economic thinking and concepts can be readily applied to business firms, inflation, unemployment, markets, interest rates, and monetary policy. But rarely do they think that economic thinking and concepts can be applied to topics such as dating, ethical codes, or family size. Why are economists extending themselves into the domains of the sociologist, psychologist, and anthropologist? It's sort of like a baseball player telling a football player how to play football. Stick to baseball!

It's been said that economics is becoming an imperialist social science; that is, it is spreading out into other fields. With apologies to William Shatner of *Star Trek* fame, it is boldly going where it has never gone before: into sociology, history, political science, anthropology, psychology, and law. In any of these fields today, you will see the imprint of economists. For economic imperialists (those who venture into other fields), economics isn't so much a field of study as it is a method of analysis. Economics is not just a list of topics (unemployment, inflation, firms, monetary policy, and so on) but rather is a set of tools that can be applied to a whole host of phenomena. This set of tools is relevant not only to studying markets and the economy, but also to social and political environments. That is the viewpoint taken in this chapter. In that sense, the chapter presents a different perspective of the practitioners of economics today from that given in the other chapters of the text.

21-2 THE PROCESS

As explained, the process of economics consists of five steps. Here are the first four, stated in slightly more formal terms:

1. Making an observation or having a thought

2. Formulating a question based on the observation or thought

3. Building a theory to answer the question

4. Making predictions based on the theory

We begin with our first of many observations.

21-3 OBSERVATION/ THOUGHT 1: THE BIRTHRATES IN VARIOUS COUNTRIES ARE DIFFERENT

You observe that the birthrate is not the same in all countries. In some countries it is 1.4 children per couple, and in other countries it is 2.7.

21-3a The Question

Why are the birthrates different in various countries?

21-3b The Theory

The theory proposed to answer the question is based on a woman's opportunity cost of having a child. To illustrate, consider two women, A and B. Woman A lives in a rather poor country and has few opportunities to earn income. If she were to work, she would earn $10 a day. Woman B lives in a relatively rich country and has numerous opportunities to earn income. If she were to work, she would earn $400 a day.

Each woman is considering having a child. Each woman intends to take off two years from work to care for the child if she has one. For woman A, the opportunity cost of having the child is $10 a day for two years: $5,200. For woman B, the opportunity cost of having the child is $400 a day for two years: $208,000.[1]

21-3c The Predictions

Prediction 1   Our first prediction is a general one: The higher a woman's opportunity cost to have a child, the fewer children she will have.

Prediction 2   If women in rich countries have greater opportunities to earn income and women in poorer countries have fewer, then women in rich countries will have fewer children than women in poor countries will.

Prediction 3   Within a rich country, women who have the greatest opportunity to earn income will have fewer children than those who have poor opportunities to earn income. A more specific prediction is that a woman who goes to medical school and becomes a physician will have fewer children than a woman who becomes a schoolteacher. Stated slightly differently, women physicians are predicted to have fewer children, on average, than women schoolteachers have.

21-3d A Detour: The Issue of Falsifiability (Refutability)

A good theory should have the virtue of falsifiability, or refutability. In other words, not only must a theory predict things that we should observe *if it is right*, but it should also

---

[1]. To put things on an even more solid basis, after computing the two dollar amounts, we could adjust each for the cost of living in each country. For instance, the cost of living may be lower in the poor country than in the rich country, so that $1 buys more in the poor country than in the rich country. Still, it would probably be the case that one woman's opportunity cost of having children was different from another's. It is this relative relationship that matters for our example.

predict things that we should observe *if it is wrong*. Consider, for example, the part of prediction 3 about women physicians and women schoolteachers: Women physicians will have fewer children, on average, than women schoolteachers will. If we collect data on women having children and find that women physicians, on average, have *more* children or *the same number of* children as women schoolteachers have, then we know that the theory is false (refuted). That is what we want in a theory: the ability to know not only when it is right, but also when it is wrong.

A theory can also be not falsifiable, or not refutable. Consider this theory: Everything that happens to you happens because of the specific time and day you were born. In other words, if a person was born on September 21, 1992, at 9:01:33 a.m. Eastern time, then everything that happens to the person happens because of his or her being born at that specific time. So, if the person goes to a specific college, takes a specific major, and eats a bologna sandwich for lunch one day—all this happens because of the person's being born at that specific time.

We cannot falsify or refute this model. No matter what a person does or doesn't do—go to college X or go to college Y, eat a bologna sandwich or eat a BLT sandwich— whatever it is is supposedly a consequence of being born on a certain day and time. The theory predicts nothing that, if it happens, can falsify or refute the model, so there is no way to know whether the theory is true or false. There is no way to judge or evaluate the theory. In effect, the theory is saying, "Accept what I say as true because I say it is true."

Instead, it would be better if the theory were to say, "Don't accept what I say as true just because I say it is true. Here is what I propose: I predict X, Y, and Z, so if you see X, Y, or Z, then that is evidence that what I have said is true. If you see not-X, not-Y, or not-Z, then what I have said is clearly false." Scientists strive to build theories that can be falsified or refuted. They seek to build theories that are capable of telling them not only when they are right, but also when they are wrong.

SELF-TEST

(Answers to Self-Test questions are in Answer to Self-Test Questions at the back of the book.)

1. What does it mean to say that a theory is falsifiable?

2. What is the five-step process to building a theory?

3. Women in some countries have more children than women in other countries because they have a stronger preference for having children. Would an economist be likely to use different preferences to explain differences in behavior? Why or why not?

21-4 OBSERVATION/THOUGHT 2: THE ETHICAL CODE OF PEOPLE WHO LIVE IN A SMALL TOWN IS DIFFERENT FROM THAT OF PEOPLE WHO LIVE IN A LARGE CITY

Bob lives and works in New York City but recently visited a small town in the Midwest for two weeks. When he returned to New York City, he told all his friends and coworkers how friendly, decent, and honest the people seemed to be in the small town.

© Songquan Deng/Shutterstock.com

Bob suspects that, on the basis of his limited observation, the people in small towns might have a slightly better ethical code than those who live in large cities.

21-4a The Question

Do small-town people have a somewhat different (better?) ethical code than big-city people have?

21-4b The Theory

The theory has to do with what percentage of the population an individual represents. If a person lives in a town of 1,000 persons, she is one one-thousandth of the population. If the person lives in a city of 5 million persons, she is one five-millionth of the population. According to the theory, the larger a percentage of the population that a person is, the more likely it is that the person will treat others as he or she wants to be treated. Why? The larger a percentage of the population a person is, the more likely it is that the person will keep meeting those he initially gets to know.

For example, if John lives in a town of 200 people, he can be fairly sure of knowing most, if not all, of the town folk. He also knows that he has a good chance of running into the same people over and over again; after all, that's what happens in a small town. He might see Melanie in the grocery store, or at the post office, or getting her car fixed. He might run into Kevin at the park or at a restaurant. In other words, the probability of running into the same people over and over again is higher in a small town than in a large city.

The latter fact makes it fairly costly to treat people poorly—to lie to them, to cheat them, to take advantage of them. If you treat them poorly one day (i.e., not treat them as you yourself want to be treated), you could very well run into them the next day (and they will probably have a few choice words for you). Of course, even if you don't run into them the next day, word gets around in a small town. If you cheat Jack on Saturday and he tells Joanne on Sunday, then Joanne might be wary of you on Monday.

Things might be different in a big city, where one person is a smaller percentage of the population. In a big city, you don't have as great a chance of meeting the same people over and over again. You might cheat Jack on Saturday and he might tell Joanne on Sunday, but are you really going to run into Joanne on Monday? After all, it's a big city. Simply put, treating someone poorly in a big city may come with lower costs (fewer negative consequences) than treating someone poorly in a small town.

21-4c The Predictions

Prediction 1   The owner of a car repair shop in a small town will be more careful not to overcharge customers than the owner of a car repair shop in a large city.

ECONOMICS 24/7

Can Social Media Affect Whom a Person Dates?

Tyler meets Alicia through a mutual friend. Tyler and Alicia start talking, and before long, Tyler realizes that he would like to ask Alicia for a date. He does so; Alicia accepts. Later that day, Alicia goes online and reads the news on Yahoo! She happens to see an ad for a criminal-reporting service. It turns out that, for a certain fee, you can learn if a person has a criminal record. Alicia pays for the service and puts in Tyler's full name. She learns that Tyler does have a criminal record: He was convicted of home burglary five years ago. She calls up the friend who introduced her to Tyler and asks if she knew about Tyler's criminal record. The friend says that she has known Tyler for only a year and knows nothing of a criminal record. After some thought, Alicia decides that she doesn't want to go out with Tyler. She sends him a text message which states that her plans have changed and that, unfortunately, she will not be able to go out with him. Tyler texts her back, asking for a date "some other time," but Alicia ends up not responding to Tyler's text message.

The digital revolution has provided some services that did not exist previously. Being able to easily check whether someone has a criminal record is one such service. The story of Alicia and Tyler is fictional, but representative of what can and does happen every day.

© karelnoppe/Shutterstock.com

People check on other people for a host of reasons: for dating purposes, business purposes, employment purposes, and so on. This kind of checking has become so much easier and less costly because of the Internet. Thus, we can expect more of it. In a way, the Internet has made every town and city in the United States a "small town." In a small town, before the days of the Internet, it was often said that "everyone knows everyone else's business." In fact, that very thing is what some people didn't like about small towns. Still, when "everyone knows everyone else's business," it would be hard for Alicia not to know that Tyler had been convicted of burglary. What online services that supply database searches of once-private information offer is the ability to change what locale one lives in into a "small town." Today, not only can one learn whether someone has a criminal record, but one can also learn how much someone paid for his house (if the home address is known), what his house looks like from the outside (via Google Earth), how many people live in the home, in some cases the person's religious affiliation, and so on. If, in the past, one of the reasons for moving from a small town was to get away from "everyone knowing everyone else's business," the Internet has made that reason less significant today.

Prediction 2   No matter the size of the town or city, people are more likely to treat others as they want to be treated in a small-numbers setting that they frequent often than in a large-numbers setting that they show up at rarely. Again, consider John, who lives and works in New York City. He works in lower Manhattan at a small office with 10 people. In his work life, it is as if he works in a very small town. It is as if he is back in that small town in the Midwest, except that the town is even smaller. He is a larger percentage of the office population than he is of the city. The theory predicts that he will more likely adopt

©iStockphoto.com/amriphoto

the treat-others-as-you-want-to-be-treated principle in the office than he will outside the office. Generalizing the prediction, we say that people will have a higher ethical code toward those with whom they work (and see every day) than with those they rarely meet or with whom they are only mildly acquainted.

Prediction 3   If a person treats coworkers (whom she sees every day) poorly, then she will treat others (i.e., those whom she doesn't see regularly or have as much chance of running into later) worse.

21-5 OBSERVATION/THOUGHT 3: THE CLOSER THE DOLLAR TUITION THE STUDENT PAYS IS TO THE EQUILIBRIUM TUITION, THE MORE ON TIME AND RESPONSIVE UNIVERSITY INSTRUCTORS WILL BE FOR OFFICE HOURS

21-5a The Question

At universities where the gap between student tuition and the equilibrium tuition is small, will instructors be on time more often for, and more responsive in, office hours than instructors who teach at universities where the gap is large?

21-5b The Theory

At most four-year traditional universities (both private and public), the tuition the student is charged is not the same as the equilibrium tuition. Often, the student tuition is below the equilibrium tuition. For example, the equilibrium tuition at a private university might be $60,000 a year and the student is charged $40,000. Or the equilibrium tuition at a public university might be $55,000 a year and the student is charged $20,000. Openings in universities (for first-year students) are not fully rationed by dollar price (tuition). Instead, they are rationed by a combination of dollar price, grades in high school, standardized test scores, and so on. In other words, to be admitted to a university, a student may need a GPA of at least 3.00 and an SAT score of at least 1,800.

If most four-year traditional universities are charging students less than the equilibrium tuition, then a dollar gap must exist between what a student pays and the equilibrium tuition. If the equilibrium tuition is $60,000 and the student tuition is $40,000, the gap is $20,000. Does this gap matter to the behavior of university instructors when holding their office hours? According to our theory, it does.

Exhibit 1 shows the demand to attend two universities, A and B. The supply of openings at each university is assumed to be the same: 3,000. Because the demand to

> **EXHIBIT 1**

The Gap between Equilibrium Tuition and Student Tuition

The supply of openings at each of two universities, A and B. The demand to attend university A is higher than the demand to attend university B, as shown by the respective demand curves. The equilibrium tuitions are $50,000 at university A and $40,000 at B. However, at each university the student pays $30,000. The gap between the equilibrium tuition at university A and the student tuition is $20,000; at B, the gap is $10,000. At university A, the shortage of openings at the student tuition ($30,000) is 2,200 students: 5,200 students want to be admitted but only 3,000 will be admitted. At university B, the shortage at the student tuition ($30,000) is 1,000: 4,000 students want to be admitted, but only 3,000 will be admitted. The demand to attend university A has to fall more to go through point X (where there is no shortage of openings at the student tuition) than the demand to attend university B has to fall. This fact gives the instructors at A more room to engage in demand-reducing behavior than the instructors at B.

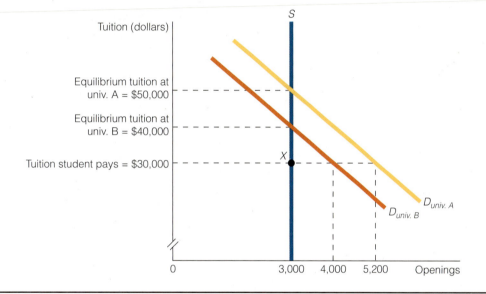

attend university A is higher than it is to attend university B, the equilibrium tuitions are $50,000 at university A and $40,000 at university B. However, the tuition charged students at each university is the same: $30,000. At this tuition, the gap (between the equilibrium tuition and student tuition) and the shortage (between the number of students applying and the number of openings) are both greater at university A than B. The shortage at university A at the $30,000 tuition is 2,200 students because, at this tuition, 5,200 students want to attend the university but only 3,000 can be admitted. At the same tuition, the shortage at university B is 1,000 students: 4,000 students want to attend but only 3,000 can be admitted.

Will the size of the gap and of the shortage affect how punctual an instructor will be for, and how responsive the instructor will be during, office hours?

The theory predicts that it will: The bigger the gap, the more the demand (to attend the university) has to fall before there is no shortage. In Exhibit 1, the demand curve to attend university A would have to shift leftward by enough to go through point X before there is no shortage of openings. The demand curve to attend university B would also have to shift leftward to go through point X, but *not as much*, because the demand curve to attend university B is closer to point X than the demand curve to attend university A is to point X.

What does this situation mean for the instructors at each university? The instructors at university A have more room to take *demand-reducing actions* than the instructors at university B have. Such actions might include showing up late for office hours and not being responsive during office hours, things that students (as customers of the university) do not like. If word gets around that instructors don't regularly meet their office hours at a given university, demand to attend that university may decrease. (Books and websites address students' experiences at various colleges in the country.)

Of course, why would an instructor not be punctual for office hours and not be responsive during them? We doubt that any instructor plans to be this way. Still, instructors might be on the other side of the university campus just before office hours and/or might be feeling a little hurried or overwhelmed on a particular day. The theory simply states that the cost of not hurrying to office hours or of being less responsive during office hours is lower for the instructor at a university with a big demand gap than for the instructor at a university with a small demand gap. At the big-gap university, many other students are willing to take the place of a student who leaves; at the small-gap college, there aren't as many.

21-5c The Predictions

Prediction 1   University instructors who work at big-gap universities will be less nearly punctual for office hours and less responsive during office hours than university instructors who work at small-gap or no-gap universities.

Prediction 2   The bigger the gap, the more flexibility instructors have to teach their courses the way they want to teach it. To illustrate, suppose an instructor wants to do X, Y, and Z in the course but students prefer the instructor to do A, B, and C. How will the course be taught? The bigger the gap, the more likely it is that the instructor will teach X, Y, and Z (even if it isn't what the students want) and not be adversely affected by the students who leave. That's because with a big gap between equilibrium and student tuition, there is a big shortage of openings at the university. Having students go elsewhere because they don't like how the instructor teaches the course (the papers he assigns, the material she goes over, the large number of readings she assigns) doesn't adversely affect the instructor because so many other students want to take their places.

21-6 OBSERVATION/THOUGHT 4: CRIMINALS ARE NOT RATIONAL

Some people say that criminals are not rational. They are not like regular people, who think in terms of the costs and benefits of their actions. Who, in their right minds, would commit a crime—whether it is burglary, kidnapping, arson, or murder?

21-6a The Question

Are criminals rational? Does their behavior respond to changes in costs and benefits?

21-6b The Theory

We build a theory, based on a rational criminal, holding that criminals think and act in terms of costs and benefits. The theory posits that criminals have two equations in mind (and might not be aware of them). The first equation relates to the benefits of committing a criminal act—let's say a burglary. The benefit equation is

$$EB = Ps \times Loot$$

where *EB* is the expected benefits of burglary, *Ps* is the probability of successfully burglarizing a house (getting into and out of a house with the goods), and Loot is the dollar take.

The cost equation is

$$EC = [Pp \times (I + F)] + AC$$

where *EC* is the expected costs of burglary, *Pp* is the probability of imprisonment, *I* is the income the criminal gives up if caught and imprisoned, *F* is the dollar value the criminal puts on freedom (how much the person would pay to stay out of prison), and *AC* is the anguish cost of committing a burglary.

An economist would say that criminals simply substitute various values into the equations and then determine whether the expected benefits of the intended criminal act are greater than, less than, or equal to the expected costs. If the expected benefits are greater than the expected costs, they commit the crime. If the expected benefits are less, they do not commit the crime. And if the expected benefits equal the expected costs, they flip a coin: heads, commit the crime; tails, don't commit the crime.

Suppose the values are as follows:

$$Ps = 80 \text{ percent}$$

$$Loot = \$400,000$$

$$Pp = 30 \text{ percent}$$

$$I = \$80,000$$

$$F = \$42,000$$

$$AC = \$3,000$$

Substituting these numbers for the variables into our two equations, we find that the expected benefits equal $320,000 and the expected costs equal $39,600. With these numbers, the person goes ahead and commits the crime.

21-6c The Predictions

Prediction 1   If people put more locks on their doors and install more security devices in their homes, the probability of success (*Ps*) will fall, lowering the benefits of burglary. And lowering the benefits of burglary will lead to fewer burglaries.

Prediction 2   If more police are on the streets, the probability of being arrested after committing a crime will rise and the probability of being imprisoned (*Pp*) will likely rise too. Thus, the costs of committing a burglary will rise, and fewer burglaries will be committed.

Prediction 3   During a recession, incomes usually fall and unemployment usually rises. Thus, the income one forfeits is usually lower during a recession than during boom times. Lower foregone income (I) will lower the cost of burglary and thus will lead to more burglaries.

Prediction 4   If prison became more severe (e.g., if burglars who were apprehended were uniformly sentenced to hard labor), a person would pay more to stay out of prison (F). Paying more to stay out of prison will raise the cost of burglary, and fewer burglaries will be committed.

21-6d A Detour: Does Evidence Prove a Theory Correct?

Suppose a theory predicts that all swans are white. You and others go out into the field to test the theory, looking for swans. So far, you and others have found and counted 4,324 swans—all white. Does your finding prove that the theory predicting that all swans are white is correct? No. The reason is simple: We can't be sure that all the existing swans have been found and counted. Perhaps there are 5,000 swans in total, and only 4,324 have been found, have been counted, and are white.

So, even if every swan we've found is white, that evidence does not prove the swan theory correct. The best that evidence can do is give us a reason not to reject a theory. We cannot say, "The evidence proves the theory correct." It is more accurate to say, "The evidence fails to reject the theory." In other words, given the evidence amassed so far, none of it is inconsistent with the predictions of the theory. In contrast, any piece of evidence that is inconsistent with the theory—such as finding a black swan—is reason enough to say, "The evidence rejects the theory." (As a matter of empirical fact, there are black swans in the world—in Australia.)

21-6e Another Detour: After You Have One Theory That Explains and Predicts, Search for Another

Suppose another planet, somewhere in the universe, has living beings that resemble human beings on Earth. These beings speak a language, they read and write, they do mathematics, they raise families—in short, they do all the things we do. However, half the beings on the planet are blue in color and half are green. In the neighborhoods on the planet, blue beings live only with blue beings and green beings live only with green beings. Asked to explain why only completely segregated neighborhoods exist on the planet, you think the explanation has something to do with color discrimination. You put forth a discrimination theory holding that the beings of one color (either green or blue) are discriminating against the beings of the other color. Perhaps green beings have gotten into positions of power and passed laws that prevent blue beings from living in neighborhoods where green beings reside.

You test your theory by seeking out evidence of discrimination. You find that green beings have, in fact, passed laws prohibiting blue persons from living in the same neighborhoods with green persons. Does it follow, then, that discrimination—and discrimination alone—explains the completely segregated neighborhoods? Perhaps not. To illustrate, suppose we advance a nondiscrimination theory of the segregated neighborhoods. This theory is based on the work of Thomas Schelling, cowinner of the Nobel Memorial Prize in Economic Science in 2005.[2]

---

[2] See Thomas C. Schelling, *Micromotives and Macrobehavior* (New York: W.W. Norton & Company, 1978).

We start with 200 persons, 100 of whom are blue and 100 of whom are green. Each person (no matter which color) prefers to live in an integrated neighborhood. However, no person wants to live in a neighborhood where he or she is a minority of less than 30 percent.

Now suppose that there are two neighborhoods, A and B, and that their populations are as follows:

Neighborhood A	Neighborhood B
70 blue persons	70 green persons
30 green persons	30 blue persons

Obviously, the two neighborhoods are integrated: Blue people and green people live in each. Also, the two neighborhoods are satisfactory to everyone living in them. No person in either neighborhood falls into a minority that is less than 30 percent of the population.

Then, for work-related reasons, one green person moves from A to B and one blue person moves from B to A. The neighborhoods now look this way:

Neighborhood A	Neighborhood B
71 blue persons	71 green persons
29 green persons	29 blue persons

Green persons have fallen to a 29 percent minority in A, and blue persons have fallen to a 29 percent minority in B. Although both green and blue persons prefer integrated neighborhoods to segregated neighborhoods, they do not want to become a minority of less than 30 percent. So, green persons are likely to move from A to B and blue persons are likely to move from B to A.

If another green person and another blue person move, we get the following configuration:

Neighborhood A	Neighborhood B
72 blue persons	72 green persons
28 green persons	28 blue persons

In neighborhood A, blue persons are becoming a bigger majority and green persons are becoming a smaller minority. In neighborhood B, green persons are becoming a bigger majority and blue persons are becoming a smaller minority.

Where will the movement end? The neighborhoods will be in equilibrium when things look like this:

Neighborhood A	Neighborhood B
100 blue persons	100 green persons

The neighborhoods are now completely segregated. Blue people live with other blue people, and green people live with other green people. There are no blue–green neighborhoods at all.

Although this is an equilibrium setting, all blue and green persons would prefer to live in integrated neighborhoods. But no one wants to live in an integrated neighborhood as a minority of less than 30 percent. Therefore, after a move by one green person and one blue person, we ultimately end up with complete segregation.

Now, as the creator of the color discrimination theory, you had no idea of this process that ended with the segregated neighborhoods. What would you think if you came across the two segregated neighborhoods, not knowing how they came to be that way? You might think that color discrimination was the cause.

Does it follow that segregated neighborhoods can be caused only by one thing or another, but never by two? No. Sometimes multiple causes are behind what we observe, and each cause, by itself, is sufficient to bring about what we see. When trying to explain why neighborhoods are segregated, color discrimination, encased in law, could be enough to explain the segregated neighborhoods. But even in the absence of discrimination, segregated neighborhoods could arise—even when, paradoxically, everyone prefers to live in an integrated neighborhood.

The lesson is that a single-cause theory that predicts well (i.e., accurately) does not necessarily rule out other possible causes. Specifically, the lesson for the theory builder is that, after you have developed one theory to explain something (segregated neighborhoods, dating relationships, ethical codes, inflation, or unemployment), try to build another theory to explain the very same effect. If it, too, predicts well, and the predictions of one theory are not the opposite of the predictions of the other, then we probably have a multiple-cause explanation.

21-6f A Final Detour: Why Prediction Is So Important, or Why Good-Sounding Stories Are Not Enough

Sometimes we want to believe some theories over others, especially when the theory seems to confirm what we already believe. The theory seems to say, "See, you were right all along." Accepting a theory that tells us we were right all along is easier than accepting one that says, "You were wrong all along."

To illustrate, suppose Smith has always believed that people who are on welfare are lazy and unmotivated. Contrary to Smith, Jones believes that people who are on welfare have had unfortunate things happen: They've lost a job or gotten sick and were unable to work, and so on.

Two economists then present two different theories of welfare. The first theory seems to confirm the description of welfare recipients as lazy and unmotivated. The second theory describes welfare recipients in terms of job loss, sickness, and other causes beyond their control. Smith ends up believing the first theory because it seems to confirm what she has always believed. Jones ends up believing the second theory because it seems to confirm what he has always believed.

Do we accept theories because they seem to confirm what we have always believed or want to believe? Sure, people do it all the time. But what both Smith and Jones should be asking of the economists is, "What are your predictions? Do the data support your predictions? What are the predictions of the lazy-unmotivated-person theory of welfare?" If the predictions are X, Y, and Z, then the question is whether the evidence is consistent with X, Y, and Z. If it is, then we now have reason to accept the lazy-unmotivated-person theory of welfare, no matter what you might have believed before. The same goes for the beyond-their-control theory of welfare. If that theory predicts A, B, and C, then the question is whether the evidence is consistent with A, B, and C. If so, then there is now reason to accept that theory, no matter what you might have believed before.

By accepting theories simply because they confirm our beliefs, or because they sound right, or because we want them to be right, we do ourselves a disservice. We need to push theories and theorists to the limit and ask them for more than a "good" or "believable" story or explanation. We need to ask for the predictions. If the theory has no predictions, then it might be nothing more than a fictional account of what someone thinks explains something. Then we must ask for the evidence that leads us to say one of two things: (1) The evidence fails to reject the theory or (2) the evidence rejects the theory.

SELF-TEST

1. Consider Jack, who attends both his son's high school football games and a few professional football games too. At which games is Jack more likely to be well behaved? Why?

2. Kidnappers can't be rational because no rational person would be a kidnapper. Comment.

3. Can evidence prove that a theory is correct?

21-7 OBSERVATION/THOUGHT 5: MORE STUDENTS WEAR BASEBALL CAPS IN CLASS ON EXAM DAYS THAN ON OTHER DAYS

21-7a The Question

What purpose does wearing a baseball cap in class on exam days serve that it doesn't serve on other days?

21-7b The Theory

A baseball cap can shield your eyes. A student may want to shield his eyes from the view of the instructor who is administering an exam if the student plans to glance over at his neighbor's test. So, on exam day, wearing a baseball cap in class serves a purpose it doesn't serve any other day: It helps a student pick up answers from his neighbors without anyone seeing. It makes one's cheating less visible to others.

21-7c The Predictions

Prediction 1   A smaller percentage of students will be wearing baseball caps when those students are taking an essay exam than when taking a multiple-choice exam.

Prediction 2   A smaller percentage of students will be wearing baseball caps when a lecture is being given than when an exam is being taken.

Cusp/Cusp/Superstock

ECONOMICS 24/7

Talking on a Cell Phone in Public

It appears that people are less likely to talk on their cell phone in some public locales than others. Here are some places that people don't seem to mind talking on their cell phone in public: in an airport while they are waiting to board a plane, in a restaurant, and anywhere in public when they are walking. But here is one place that people do seem to mind talking on their cell phone in public: in the waiting room of their doctor's office. Now, why the difference? Why would the person who is inclined to talk on her cell phone at a restaurant not talk on her cell phone in her doctor's office? Because we would expect the benefits of talking on the cell phone in public to be the same in both locales, it must be that the costs of talking on the cell phone in both locales are not the same. Obviously, the cost is higher in one's doctor's office.

The difference between a restaurant and one's doctor's office is that in the restaurant the people around you are talking to each other. In other words, two things go on in a restaurant: eating food and talking. People go out to eat and talk to each other. It is generally accepted, then, that one can go to a restaurant and talk. So, talking on the cell phone (except when the server is trying to take your order) is not as disruptive as it would be in some other public settings, such as your doctor's office. In a doctor's office, the patients waiting to be called do not know each other, so there is really no reason for them to talk to each other. Instead, what they do is sit there and read a

©iStockphoto.com/Ekely

magazine while waiting to be called. In this setting, talking on one's cell phone would be jarring. First, there is quiet, and individuals are reading their magazines. Then, all of a sudden, we hear, "Hello," then a pause, then "I don't know what he is thinking about, but I told him that we weren't going that way. Did he get those sales numbers from you or Karen? No matter. . . ." In a public space where everyone is silent except the person on the cell phone, the person on the phone is very noticeable. That is the case in the doctor's office. But in a public space where everyone is talking, including the person on the cell phone, the person on the phone doesn't stand out (nearly as much). That is the case in the restaurant.

We would expect that, for most people, the cost of talking on their cell phones would be higher in their doctor's office than in a restaurant—even if in neither place is there a sign stating that people should not talk on cell phones. The cost is, specifically, in terms of "other people judging one's behavior as rude." We predict, then, that we will see more people talking on the cell phone in public places where other people are talking than in public places where other people are not talking. Or look at it this way: If the only person in the doctor's office other than you is a family of four, and they are talking to each other (which is likely to be the case, because they know each other), then you'd feel more at ease talking on your cell phone than you would be if four unrelated persons were in the office besides you.

Prediction 3   Instructors are likely to notice anything that stands out on exam day as being different from other days. In nonclassroom environments, more males than females seem to wear baseball caps. This practice gives males a better chance than females of wearing a baseball cap in class without tipping the instructor into thinking that something is out of the ordinary. Thus, males wearing baseball caps on exam day are less likely to be noticed than females wearing them. Females, then, have one fewer thing they can use to help them cheat than males have, so we can expect females to cheat less. Specific prediction: On a multiple-choice exam, a larger percentage of the cheaters in the class will be male than female.

Prediction 4 Sooner or later, instructors figure out that a baseball cap can be used for shielding one's eyes when looking at another person's exam paper. At that time, they will either tell students that they can't wear baseball caps in class on exam days or perhaps closely watch students who are wearing baseball caps. After all, when instructors figure out the purpose of the cap on exam day, it becomes a signal to the instructor that the wearer may try to cheat on the exam. The baseball cap is then like a neon sign that reads, "Watch me. I am about to cheat on this exam." Specific prediction: On exam day, instructors will look more often at students who are wearing baseball caps than at other students. They will also patrol the class on exam day by walking more often near students who are wearing baseball caps than near other students.

Prediction 5 When the instructor is giving a lecture in class, a student who is wearing a baseball cap will often have to look down to write notes. When the student looks down, the bill of the baseball cap is pointed downward at a certain angle. On exam day, the student who is wearing a baseball cap always has to look downward in order to write answers, and, again, the bill of the cap will be at a certain angle. However, if the student intends to cheat, the angle is likely to be greater on exam day than on a lecture day, when the student is taking notes. That's because the student has more of a reason to shield his or her eyes on exam day. The greater slope (greater angle) of the bill on exam day is indicative that the student is doing something more than just writing: It is indicative that the student is writing and glancing left and right. So, specific prediction: Students with baseball caps in class on exam days and on lecture days will likely be cheating if the bill of their baseball caps is more sloped (at a greater angle) on exam days.

Prediction 6 Students who wear baseball caps backward on lecture days but frontward on exam days are probably cheating on exam days.

21-8 OBSERVATION/THOUGHT 6: HOUSES IN "GOOD" SCHOOL DISTRICTS ARE OFTEN MORE EXPENSIVE THAN COMPARABLE HOUSES IN "BAD" SCHOOL DISTRICTS

21-8a The Question
Why are comparable houses (same square footage, size of lot, etc.) often priced differently?

21-8b The Theory
Suppose school districts could be ranked on a scale from 1 to 10, with 10 being the best and 1 the worst. Two houses, A and B, are alike in every way except that house A is located in a school district ranked 5 and house B is in a school district ranked 10. Currently,

the prices of both houses are the same. Which one would you buy if you had children starting school soon? Most people would choose the house in the number-10 school district: house B.

Why? Well, being in a higher ranked school district is something that people with children consider to be a good (something from which they derive utility), so a utility-maximizing couple would prefer to get more rather than less utility for a given amount of money spent on a house. Better to spend $250,000 for a house and get 10,000 utils of utility than to spend $250,000 for a house and get 9,000 utils of utility.

But the real question is, If people get more utility from house B than from house A (because it's located in a better school district), would the prices of the houses really be the same? The answer is no. If house B has something that people value that house A does not have, then the demand for house B will be higher. And a higher demand in the face of a given supply means a higher price. In other words, the house with something more—in this case, a higher ranked school district—will end up priced higher than the house with less—a lower ranked school district.

The conclusion: When a person buys a house in a higher ranked school district, part of the purchase price represents what one must pay to be in that school district. In other words, the benefits of being in the higher ranked school district are incorporated into the price of the house. You might be able to break down the price of the house this way: (1) land = $100,000; (2) materials and labor to build the house = $200,000; (3) price paid to be located in a higher ranked school district = $70,000. Total price = $370,000.

21-8c The Predictions

Prediction 1   Houses with ocean views will sell for higher prices than comparable houses with no view. You will pay for the view.

Prediction 2   Houses located in major metropolitan areas (where there are many things to do) can sell for higher prices than comparable houses in small towns. You will pay for having the opportunity to do a lot of things.

Prediction 3   Houses located in cities with clean air will sell for higher prices than comparable houses located in cities with dirty air. You will pay for the cleaner air.

Prediction 4   If a major professional sports team were to move to a city that previously did not have a major professional sports team, house prices in the city would rise. You will pay for the sports team. (This prediction is similar to prediction 2, except that it is more specific.)

Prediction 5   People will pay (donate money) to meet the president of the United States. Think of the president first as a human being and second as a unique human being. Of the billions of human beings, there is only one president at a time. Now think of the president of the United States and other human beings as you would think of two houses that were comparable in every way except that one had an ocean view and the other didn't. People will pay more for the house with the view. The president is similar to a house with an ocean view, whereas most people are similar to a house without a view. The president has something—the presidency—that all others do not. Although people might not be willing to pay to meet just an average, everyday human being, they would be willing to pay to meet a unique human being (the one and only president of the United States).

21-9 OBSERVATION/THOUGHT 7: ARE PEOPLE BETTER OFF WITH OR WITHOUT HEALTH CARE VOUCHERS?

Suppose 100,000 persons do not have health insurance of any kind. Then Congress passes legislation that mandates a $200 health care voucher per month for each person. With the vouchers, which can be used only to purchase health care, each person can have up to $200 worth of health care a month, or $2,400 of health care a year. For example, Jack doesn't have any health insurance. If he were to get hurt and need medical attention, he could simply go to a doctor or hospital, get the attention he needs, and pay for the services rendered (up to $200 a month, or $2,400 a year) with the vouchers.

21-9a The Question

Will the 100,000 persons purchase more health care with the vouchers than without them? The obvious answer to this question seems to be yes, but is it necessarily correct?

21-9b The Theory

Jack is one of the 100,000 persons currently without health insurance. He earns $3,200 a month and spends each month's income in the following way:

- Food = $1,000
- Rent = $2,000
- Savings for future health care expenses = $200

Now suppose Jack receives the $200-a-month health care voucher. Then he can reorder his expenditures in this way:

- Food = $1,000
- Rent = $2,000
- Health care voucher = $200
- Entertainment = $200

Because of the voucher, $200 is freed up for Jack to do other things—if he wants to. He decides to spend the $200 that he had been saving each month on entertainment.

Of course, he doesn't have to spend the money on entertainment. He could spend it on books, clothes, more food, more health care, a higher rent, or even cocaine, gambling, or alcohol. Fact is, we know some things about him but don't know other things about him. We don't know how he will spend the freed-up $200. What we do know is that he will spend it on whatever is *next* on his list of things to buy. If more health care is next on his list, then, instead of buying only $200 worth of health care a month (when he didn't have the voucher), he can now buy $400 worth. But if what is next on his list is, say, clothes, then the health care voucher is not financing more health care for Jack, but rather more clothes.

Essentially, our theory says this: A monetary gift (of, say, $200 in cash) or an in-kind gift (a $200 voucher that can be used only to purchase health care) will end up going for whatever is next on the recipient's list of desired purchases.

21-9c The Predictions

Prediction 1 A mother has two children. She gives each of them both gifts of money and in-kind gifts. The theory predicts that she will give more gifts to the child whose next-on-the-list purchase is more acceptable to her. Here is an example: A mother says that child 1 is more trustworthy when it comes to spending money than child 2 is. In the eyes of the mother, what's next on child 1's list is superior to what's next on child 2's list. (Starkly, suppose that what's next on child 1's list are more books and DVDs and that what's next on child 2's list are more cigarettes.)

Prediction 2   If each of two candidates running for office says that she will do X, Y, and Z if elected, people will be more willing to vote for the candidate they more nearly agree with in terms of what comes next. To illustrate, suppose A and B are running against each other for U.S. senator from some state. Both say that they will vote for reduced taxes, more spending on education, and strong pollution standards. How does a voter who wants all three things decide whom to vote for? If the voter is equally convinced that both candidates are true to their word, she will think in terms of what's next: what will the candidate do if elected? If, for the voter, A's next-on-the-list purchase is thought to be better than B's next-on-the-list purchase, then the voter votes for A.

How could we test to see whether this prediction is correct? Perhaps the voter who speaks of a candidate as "trustworthy" is thinking in terms of what's next: The more the voter agrees with the candidate's next thing to do, the more trustworthy the voter believes the candidate is. We would predict, then, that the voter will vote for the candidate who seems more trustworthy.

21-10 OBSERVATION/THOUGHT 8: PEOPLE WHO GIVE TO OTHERS OFTEN COMPLAIN THAT THEY END UP GIVING TOO MUCH

21-10a The Question

Why don't people simply stop giving at the efficient point of giving—when the marginal benefits of giving equal the marginal costs?

21-10b The Theory[3]

Suppose person G is a gift giver (he gives gifts to person R) and person R is the gift recipient. The G's utility is specified as

$$U_G = f(\text{Goods A–Z}, U_R)$$

where U_G represents the utility that person G places on giving, goods *A–Z* are various goods that give person G utility, and U_R is the gift recipient's utility (stemming from receiving G's gifts). Because U_R is included in person G's utility function in a positive way, every time R's utility rises, so does G's utility. In other words, when G gives a gift to R, the gift benefits not only R, but also G. Person G likes seeing R happy and benefits more as R becomes happier. To make this point more concrete, think of a mother giving gifts to her children (the recipients). Giving the gifts to her children makes them happy, and when

---

3. This theory is based on a theory first put forth by Wilson E. Schmidt in "Charitable Exploitation," *Public Choice* 10 (Spring 1969), pp. 103–104. The theory is also discussed in Richard B. McKenzie and Gordon Tullock, *The New World of Economics*, 5th ed. (New York: McGraw-Hill, 1994).

the mother sees her children happy, she gains some utility. She says, "I am happy when my children are happy."

Next, consider R's utility function:

$$U_R = f(\text{Goods A–Z})$$

In this case, U_G is not included in the utility function of the gift recipient. Person R is unaffected by the utility that G receives.

Now consider what we mean by a gift. According to this theory, a gift is anything that one person gives (without seeking payment in return) to another person that benefits the other person. It could be money, a specific good (such as a computer, a car, or an item of clothing), or something as simple as a back rub. It could be doing the dishes for someone, going to the store to pick up something, and so on. Simply put, we define a gift broadly. Don't think only in terms of a birthday or holiday gift; think in terms of anything that someone wants and that gives the person utility or satisfaction.

Exhibit 2(a) shows the marginal benefits and marginal costs to person G of giving gifts to person R. The marginal benefits (MB) curve is downward sloping, indicating that the law of diminishing marginal utility (benefits) holds for gift giving. The marginal costs (MC) curve is horizontal, indicating the constant marginal cost of gift giving. Obviously, the efficient (or optimum) number of gifts, according to G, is 10, where $MB = MC$. The area under the MB curve and above the MC curve out to 10 gifts represents the net gains to G of giving gifts. This area is shaded in blue.

Now, it would be preferable for R to receive 11 gifts, rather than 10, but how can R get G to give 11 gifts if 10 is the efficient number of gifts for G to give? As shown in Exhibit 2(b), moving from the 10th to the 11th gift presents G with a net loss because, for the 11th gift, the marginal benefits are less than the marginal costs. The green area represents the net loss of utility with the 11th gift.

Perhaps R can get G to give 11 instead of 10 gifts by presenting G with an *all-or-nothing deal* that takes the efficient option (10 gifts) off the table. In other words, suppose R suggests to G that only two options are available for choosing: either zero gifts or 11 gifts. That is to say, instead of letting G choose from three options—0, 10, and 11—R makes G think that he must choose between only two options: 0 or 11. In other words, R is saying to G, "Either give me 11 gifts, or I will not accept any gifts from you."

Will limiting G to only two options—0 or 11—force G to give R 11 gifts? Yes. G now has to calculate what he receives in net gains by giving zero gifts with what he receives in net gains if he gives 11 gifts. Obviously, if he gives zero gifts, he receives no net gains. But if he gives 11 gifts, he receives net gains on the first 10 gifts and a net loss on the 11th. If the net gains on gifts 1–10 are greater than the net loss on the 11th gift, then it is better to give 11 gifts than to give none.

In dollar terms, let's say that the blue area in Exhibit 2(b) is worth $500 and the green area is worth $20. Subtracting the net loss on the 11th gift from the net gain of $500 on the first 10 gifts, we are left with $480 in net gains. Person G must therefore compare the $480 in net gains of giving 11 gifts to R against the net gains (zero) he would receive if he gives R zero gifts. In other words, because the blue area (the gains) is greater than the green area (the losses), it is better for G to go with 11 gifts than with zero. Conclusion: By presenting G with an all-or-nothing deal (all = 11 and nothing = 0), R is able to push G beyond his efficient level of gift giving and benefit by receiving more gifts.

In the extreme, how far can R push G? A quick glance at Exhibit 2(c) shows the answer. When the blue area (gains) equals the green area (losses), G will become

> **EXHIBIT 2**

Giving and Receiving Gifts

(a) The marginal benefits and marginal cost for a gift giver (person G) of giving gifts to a gift recipient (person R). The efficient or optimum number of gifts for G to give is 10, the point at which the marginal benefits of giving gifts equals the marginal costs of giving gifts. (b) G's net gain of giving 10 gifts (blue area) and G's net loss of giving an

11th gift (green area). If person R presents G with an all-or-nothing deal ("Give me 11 gifts or give me nothing"), person G will likely give 11 gifts because the net gain on gifts 1–10 is greater than the net loss on the 11th gift. (c) How far can person R push G into giving more than the efficient number of gifts (10)? The answer is 20 gifts, at which point the net gain on gifts 1–10 for G equals the

net loss on gifts 11–20. G will not give R a 21st gift. (d) Unless R makes the all-or-nothing request of G in a subtle, nonconfrontational way, R is not likely to benefit. That's because G could find that he receives fewer benefits per gift in giving to R. In that case, the MB curve of giving gifts shifts to the left, from MB_1 to MB_2, and the new efficient number of gifts is 5 instead of 10.

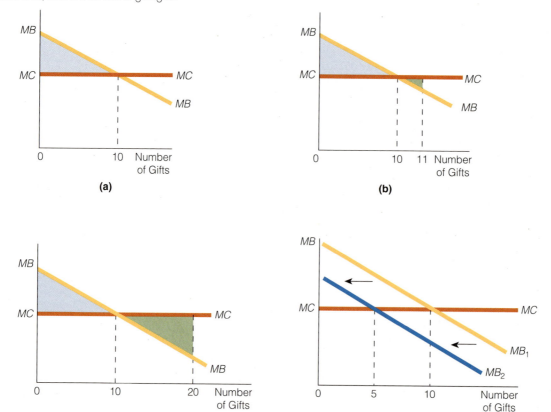

indifferent between giving R 20 gifts and giving R zero gifts. In other words, the most gifts R can get G to give is 20. Given the option of giving, say, 21 or zero gifts, G will choose zero gifts.

A question arises: Suppose R makes the all-or-nothing deal to G in a rude, demanding way. Might this approach cause G to rethink giving gifts to R at all? Person R would have to be wary of this effect because, if G reacts too negatively to the all-or-nothing deal, G's marginal benefits curve (of giving gifts to R) may shift leftward by enough to decrease the efficient number of gifts. This effect is shown in Exhibit 2(d) by a leftward shift in the marginal benefits curve from MB_1 to MB_2. As a result, G will now want to give fewer gifts to R than before the all-or-nothing demand. The new efficient number of gifts is 5 instead of 10.

21-10c The Predictions

Prediction 1   Gift givers will have less reason to move beyond their efficient number of gifts as the number of persons they can give gifts to increases. In other words, an all-or-nothing deal (from a gift recipient to a gift giver) has less chance of working if the gift giver can substitute one recipient for another. To illustrate, suppose G gives gifts to person R_1, who then tries to get G to give more gifts than the efficient number by presenting G with an all-or-nothing deal. But G has potential recipients waiting in the wings and simply replaces R_1 with R_2, to whom he gives the efficient number of gifts. Specific prediction: A recipient (an R person) who has few substitutes is more likely to push G beyond the efficient number of gifts than a recipient who has many substitutes.

To illustrate, consider two relationships:

1. A mother–daughter relationship in which the mother has only the one daughter

2. A relationship between two friends

In each relationship are two persons: an R and a G. In the mother–daughter relationship, the mother is the gift giver (G) and the daughter is the gift recipient. The mother (G) gives the efficient number of gifts to the daughter. The daughter tries to push the mother to give more gifts. The daughter gives the mother an all-or-nothing deal. Can the mother replace the daughter with another daughter? No; she has only the one daughter.

Now consider the relationship between two friends, G and R. G gives R the efficient number of gifts. R tries to push G beyond the efficient number. G can more easily find another friend to give gifts to than the mother can find another daughter. Specific prediction: A G person will give more gifts, beyond the efficient number of gifts, to an R-person who cannot be replaced than to an R-person who can be replaced. In short, the mother is more likely to give in to the daughter's requests than the G-friend will give in to the R-friend's requests.

Prediction 2   Smith wants to buy goods X, Y, and Z from a company. Buying X, Y, and Z maximizes Smith's net gains. The company presents Smith with an all-or-nothing deal: Either buy W, X, Y, and Z, or buy nothing. In other words, it's a package deal or nothing. Smith takes a net loss on buying W, but the net loss on W is smaller than the sum of the net gains on X, Y, and Z. So, Smith chooses to buy the company's package. Specific prediction: Package deals often contain something that the customer would have preferred not to have purchased. For example, Smith buys a package of 40 cable channels from his cable television provider, but he says that he would have preferred buying only 30 because he never watches anything on 10 of the 40 channels.

SELF-TEST

1. Identify two observations that are inconsistent with the baseball-cap-wearing theory of cheating on an exam.

2. Ocean views (from a house) are not free. Do you agree or disagree? Explain your answer.

3. What does it mean if you are included in another person's utility function in a positive way?

Office  Hours

"Can Anyone Build a Theory?"

STUDENT:

I always thought that building theories was the purview of people who are well educated in a particular subject. For example, only those with a PhD in economics should build economic theories, and only those with a doctorate in sociology should build sociological theories. Am I wrong about this?

INSTRUCTOR:

There is no clear line of demarcation between who should and who should not try to build a theory. The purpose of this chapter is to give you the details of how to build and evaluate a theory. On this subject, consider what Richard Feynman (1918–1988), a Nobel laureate in physics, said about how theorists start to build theories. He said that the first step of building a theory is to "guess" how things work.

STUDENT:

But anyone can guess why things are as they are. Isn't there a big difference between my guessing about physical laws and Richard Feynman guessing about laws? Aren't his guesses more likely to turn out right than mine?

INSTRUCTOR:

Yes, probably so, but that's not the point. The point is that theory building starts with a guess—albeit sometimes an educated guess—as to the way things are. Then, from the guess, we "unravel," in Feynman's words, the consequences of the guess. And finally, we compare those consequences against experience. In other words, the evaluation part of the scientific method comes at the end of the process, when we compare the consequences of the guess, or the predictions of the theory, that we have built with real-world experience, observation, or data.

STUDENT:

In other words, anyone can build a theory, but not everyone's theory is going to be consistent with experience–observation–data. Many theories will be rejected by the evidence.

INSTRUCTOR:

Yes, that's correct. But if you want to get a feel for theorizing, try to build your own theories to explain something you are interested in. Once you have done so, be sure to logically deduce the theory's predictions. Then ask yourself whether the theory's predictions are accurate. Do you actually observe those things which are consistent with the theory?

Points to remember

1. At the heart of building a theory is the motivation to explain something. (In this chapter, we've tried to explain why the birthrate is higher in some countries than in others, what might explain the burglary rate, why neighborhoods might be segregated, and so on.)
2. Building a theory differs from evaluating a theory. Guesswork plays a part in building a theory; in evaluating a theory, evidence matters. Simply put, the evidence either rejects or fails to reject the predictions of the theory.

CHAPTER SUMMARY

WHAT A THEORY IS AND IS NOT

- A theory is not perfectly descriptive of reality.
- Theories should not be judged by how they sound or by whether they say the things we want to hear. Theories should be judged according to how well they explain things and how consistently and accurately they predict.

THE BIRTHRATES IN VARIOUS COUNTRIES

- The question was, why do birthrates differ in various countries?

- A key part of answering the question was to consider a woman's opportunity cost of having a child. The higher the opportunity cost of having children (in terms of the wage the woman would not earn if she took time off to have and raise a child), the fewer children she would have; the lower the opportunity cost of having children, the more children she would have.

THE ISSUE OF FALSIFIABILITY (REFUTABILITY)

- A good theory should have the virtue of falsifiability; that is, a theory must not only predict things that you should observe if it is right, but should also predict things that you should observe if it is wrong.

- Scientists strive to build theories that can be falsified or refuted. They seek to build theories that are capable of telling them not only when they are right, but also when they are wrong.

ETHICAL CODES AND TOWN SIZE

- The question was, do people who live in small towns have a somewhat different (better?) ethical code than those who live in large cities?

- The theory argues that the larger a percentage of the population that a person is, the more likely it is that the person will treat others as he or she wants to be treated. That's because, as a larger percentage of the population, the person is more likely to have to meet again and again with people he or she initially meets.

STUDENT TUITION AND EQUILIBRIUM TUITION

- The question was, will instructors who teach at universities with a small gap between student tuition and the equilibrium tuition be on time more often for office hours and more responsive during those hours than instructors at universities with a larger gap?

- At most four-year traditional public and private universities, the tuition the student pays is below the equilibrium tuition. The larger the gap between the student tuition and the equilibrium tuition, the greater is the shortage of spots at the university and the more it is that demand for the university can fall without completely eliminating the shortage at the university. Therefore, the larger the gap, the more room instructors have to take demand-reducing actions at the university without suffering any consequences. One of these demand-reducing actions might be not being on time for office hours or not being as responsive as possible during office hours.

CRIMINALS AND RATIONALITY

- The questions were, Are criminals rational? and Does their behavior respond to changes in costs and benefits?

- We built a simple theory based on two equations: one related to the expected benefits of committing a criminal act (specifically, burglary) and one related to the expected costs of committing the criminal act. We hypothesized that individuals would commit criminal acts only when the expected benefits outweighed the expected costs. Variables on the cost side and on the benefits side of the theory were then changed, and predictions materialized as to whether the crime rate (burglary rate) would rise or fall.

- If the predictions are consistent with reality, then we can argue that criminals are rational.

DOES EVIDENCE PROVE A THEORY IS CORRECT?

- If evidence is consistent with a theory's predictions, we state that the evidence fails to reject the theory. We do not say that the evidence proves that the theory is correct.

- If evidence is inconsistent with a theory's predictions, we state that the evidence rejects the theory.

BASEBALL CAPS IN CLASS AND EXAM DAYS

- The question was, what purpose does wearing a baseball cap in class on exam days serve that it doesn't serve on other days?

- One of the things that a baseball cap can do is shield one's eyes. If students want to cheat on a multiple-choice test, it is a good idea to shield their eyes from the view of the instructor. A baseball cap can help meet this objective.

HOUSE PRICES AND SCHOOL DISTRICTS

- The question was, why are comparable houses often priced differently?

- If two houses are alike in every way, except that one is located in a good school district and the other in a bad school district, we would expect that the one located in a good school district would be priced higher. Individuals pay for the good school district in terms of house prices.

HEALTH CARE AND VOUCHERS

- The question was, will individuals purchase more health care with health care vouchers than without them?

- A monetary or in-kind gift will end up going for whatever is next on the recipient's list of desired purchases. For example, suppose Smith is currently spending $200 on X and $300 on Y. Then, someone gives Smith $100. Smith may spend the $100 on X, on Y, or on a combination of the two, or he may spend it on Z. The monetary gift goes for whatever is next on his list of desired purchases.

GIVING

- The question was, Will a person who is giving gifts to another person stop giving gifts at the point at which the marginal benefits of giving gifts equals the marginal costs of giving gifts?

- Both marginal benefits and marginal costs accompany each gift a gift giver gives to a gift recipient. The efficient number of gifts that the gift giver wants to give is the number at which the marginal benefits of giving a gift equal the marginal costs.

As a result, the gift giver maximizes consumers' surplus from giving gifts. However, if the gift recipient presents the gift giver with an all-or-nothing demand that takes the efficient number of gifts off the table, the gift giver could end up giving the gift recipient more than the efficient number of gifts. How many more depends on net gains on the efficient number of gifts compared with net losses on the gifts beyond the efficient number.

VIDEO QUESTIONS AND PROBLEMS

Video Questions and Problems are available on MindTap for Arnold 12e or by searching for Arnold on www.cengagebrain.com

1. No theory is perfectly descriptive of reality. Explain.

2. The size of the town in which you live can affect how you behave. Explain.

3. The larger the shortage of students at a university, the greater is the freedom that instructors have to teach their courses the way they want to teach them. Do you agree or disagree? Explain your answer.

4. There is a limit to how many gifts a gift giver will give to a gift recipient. Do you agree or disagree? Explain and diagrammatically represent your answer.

5. People can pay for good weather, good school districts, and good views indirectly as opposed to directly. Do you agree or disagree? Explain your answer.

QUESTIONS AND PROBLEMS

1. Why is it better for theories to be judged by how accurately they predict than by how they sound to us?

2. What role does opportunity cost play in the theory that birthrates are likely to be higher in some countries than others?

3. What does it mean to say that a theory is falsifiable or refutable?

4. A person is more likely to lose his temper with a friend than with his boss. Do you agree or disagree? Explain your answer.

5. One prediction made in the chapter was that "the owner of a car repair shop in a small town will be more careful not to overcharge customers than the owner of a car repair shop in a large city." Why?

6. Put forth two observations that are inconsistent with the cost–benefit theory of burglary discussed in the chapter.

7. What does the difference between the equilibrium tuition and the student tuition have to do with instructors holding office hours?

8. For an economist, is it preferable to assume that criminals are rational than to build a theory based on a rational criminal and then check the evidence? Explain your answer.

9. Segregated neighborhoods of blue and green people can be the result of the people of each color preferring a certain type of integration over segregation. What specifically is the certain type of integration?

10. The quality of the school district can affect house prices in that district. If this statement is true, what should we observe?

11. A man asks his brother for $400 to buy a television set. His brother gives him the money, and the man buys a television set. Is it guaranteed that the brother's $400 went to buy the television set? Why or why not?

12. People will often make charitable donations to religious organizations but not to gangs. Why?

13. Under what condition might persons buy more of something than the efficient amount for them to buy?

14. Do the following: (1) make an observation; (2) identify a question based on the observation; (3) put forth a theory to answer the question; (4) identify at least two predictions based on the theory.

WORKING WITH NUMBERS AND GRAPHS

1. Diagrammatically represent what happens to the efficient number of gifts that a gift giver wants to give to a gift recipient as the marginal cost of giving gifts declines.

2. Diagrammatically represent what happens to the efficient number of gifts that a gift giver wants to give to a gift recipient as the marginal benefits of giving gifts decline.

INTERNATIONAL TRADE

© cdrin/Shutterstock.com

22-1 INTERNATIONAL TRADE THEORY

International trade takes place for the same reasons that trade at any level and anywhere exists. Individuals trade to make themselves better off. Pat and Zach, both of whom live in Cincinnati, Ohio, trade because they both value something the other has more than they value some of their own possessions. On an international scale, Elaine in the United States trades with Cho in China because Cho has something that Elaine wants and Elaine has something that Cho wants.

Obviously, the countries of the world have different terrains, climates, resources, worker skills, and so on. Therefore, some countries will be able to produce goods that other countries cannot produce or can produce only at extremely high costs. For example, Hong Kong has no oil, and Saudi Arabia has a large supply of it. Bananas do not grow easily in the United States, but they flourish in Honduras. Americans could grow bananas if they used hothouses, but it is cheaper for Americans to buy bananas from Hondurans than to produce bananas themselves.

Major U.S. exports include automobiles, computers, aircraft, corn, wheat, soybeans, scientific instruments, coal, and plastic materials. Major imports include petroleum, automobiles, clothing, iron and steel, office machines, footwear, fish, coffee, and diamonds.

Some of the major exporting countries of the world are the United States, China, Germany, Japan, France, and the United Kingdom. These same countries are also among the major importers in the world.

22-1a How Countries Know What to Trade

Recall the economic concept of **comparative advantage**, a concept discussed in Chapter 2. In this section, we discuss comparative advantage in terms of countries rather than in terms of individuals.

Comparative Advantage
The advantage a country has when it can produce a good at lower opportunity cost than another country can.

Comparative Advantage   Assume a two-country, two-good world. Suppose the countries are the United States and Japan, and the goods are food and clothing. Both countries can produce the two goods in the four different combinations listed in Exhibit 1. For example, the United States can produce 90 units of food and 0 units of clothing, 60 units of food and 10 units of clothing, or either of the other two combinations shown. Japan can produce 15 units of food and 0 units of clothing, 10 units of food and 5 units of clothing, or two other combinations.

Now, suppose the United States is producing and consuming the two goods in the combination represented by point *B* on its production possibilities frontier (PPF) and Japan is producing and consuming the combination of the two goods represented by point *F* on its PPF. In this case, neither of the two countries is specializing in the production of one of the two goods, nor are the two countries trading with each other. We call this situation the *no-specialization–no-trade (NS–NT) case* (column 1 of Exhibit 2).

> ## EXHIBIT 1

United States				Japan		
Points on Production Possibilities Frontier	Food	Clothing		Points on Production Possibilities Frontier	Food	Clothing
A	90	0		E	15	0
B	60	10		F	10	5
C	30	20		G	5	10
D	0	30		H	0	15

Production Possibilities in Two Countries

The United States and Japan can produce the two goods in the combinations shown. Initially, the United States is at point *B* on its PPF and Japan is at point *F* on its PPF. Both countries can be made better off by specializing in and trading the good in which each has a comparative advantage.

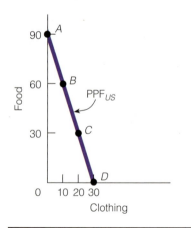

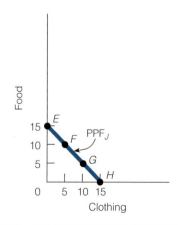

EXHIBIT 2

Both Countries Gain from Specialization and Trade

Column 1: Both the United States and Japan operate independently of each other. The United States produces and consumes 60 units of food and 10 units of clothing. Japan produces and consumes 10 units of food and 5 units of clothing. Column 2: The United States specializes in the production of food; Japan specializes in the production of clothing. Column 3: The United States and Japan agree to terms of trade of 2 units of food for 1 unit of clothing. They go on to trade 20 units of food for 10 units of clothing. Column 4: Overall, the United States consumes 70 units of food and 10 units of clothing; Japan consumes 20 units of food and 5 units of clothing. Column 5: Consumption levels are higher for both the United States and Japan in the S–T case than in the NS–NT case.

	No-Specialization–No-Trade (NS–NT) Case		Specialization–Trade (S–T) Case			
Country	(1) Production and Consumption in the NS–NT Case		(2) Production in the S–T Case	(3) Exports (−) Imports (+) Terms of Trade Are 2F = 1C	(4) Consumption in the S–T Case (2) + (3)	(5) Gains from Specialization and Trade (4) − (1)
United States						
Food	60 ⎫ Point B in		90 ⎫ Point A in	−20	70	10
Clothing	10 ⎭ Exhibit 1		0 ⎭ Exhibit 1	+10	10	0
Japan						
Food	10 ⎫ Point F in		0 ⎫ Point H in	+20	20	10
Clothing	5 ⎭ Exhibit 1		15 ⎭ Exhibit 1	−10	5	0

Suppose further that the United States and Japan decide to specialize in the production of a specific good and to trade with each other. We call this situation the *specialization–trade (S–T) case.* Whether the two countries will be better off through specialization and trade is best explained by means of a numerical example, but first we need to find the answers to two other questions: What good should the United States specialize in producing? and What good should Japan specialize in producing? The general answer to both questions is the same: *Countries specialize in the production of the good in which they have a comparative advantage.* A country has a comparative advantage with respect to another country in the production of a good when the one country can produce the good at a lower opportunity cost than the other country can.

For instance, in our hypothetical example, the opportunity cost to the United States of producing 1 unit of clothing (C) is 3 units of food (F): for every 10 units of clothing the United States produces, it forfeits 30 units of food. Thus, the opportunity cost of producing 1 unit of food is 1/3 unit of clothing. In Japan, the opportunity cost of producing 1 unit of clothing is 1 unit of food. (For every 5 units of clothing Japan produces, it forfeits 5 units of food.) So, in the United States, the situation is $1C = 3F$, or $1F = 1/3C$; in Japan, the situation is $1C = 1F$, or $1F = 1C$. The United States can produce food at a lower opportunity cost than Japan can ($1/3C$, as opposed to $1C$), whereas Japan can produce clothing at a lower opportunity cost than the United States can ($1F$, as opposed to $3F$). In other words, the United States has a comparative advantage in food and Japan has a comparative advantage in clothing.

Finally, suppose that the two countries specialize in the production of the goods in which they have a comparative advantage. The United States specializes in the production of food (producing 90 units), and Japan specializes in the production of clothing (producing 15 units). In Exhibit 1, the United States locates at point *A* on its PPF and Japan locates at point H on its PPF. (The two points are listed in column 2 of Exhibit 2.)

Settling on the Terms of Trade After they have determined which goods they will specialize in producing, the two countries must settle on the terms of trade—that is, how much food to trade for how much clothing. The United States faces the following situation: For every 30 units of food it does not produce, it can produce 10 units of clothing, as shown in Exhibit 1.Thus, 3 units of food have an opportunity cost of 1 unit of clothing ($3F = 1C$), or 1 unit of food has a cost of 1/3 unit of clothing ($1F = \frac{1}{3}C$). Japan faces the following situation: For every 5 units of food it does not produce, it can produce 5 units of clothing. Thus, 1 unit of food has an opportunity cost of 1 unit of clothing ($1F = 1C$). For the United States, $3F = 1C$, and for Japan, $1F = 1C$.

With these cost ratios, both countries should be able to agree on terms of trade which specify that $2F = 1C$. The United States would benefit by giving up 2 units of food, instead of 3 units, for 1 unit of clothing, whereas Japan would benefit by getting 2 units of food, instead of only 1 unit, for 1 unit of clothing. So, if the two countries agree to the terms of trade $2F = 1C$, and if they do trade—in absolute amounts, 20 units of food for 10 units of clothing (column 3 of Exhibit 2)—will they make themselves better off? We'll soon see that they will.

Results of the Specialization–Trade (S–T) Case Now the United States produces 90 units of food and trades 20 units to Japan, receiving 10 units of clothing in exchange. The United States consumes 70 units of food and 10 units of clothing. Japan produces 15 units of clothing and trades 10 units to the United States, receiving 20 units of food in exchange. Japan consumes 5 units of clothing and 20 units of food. (The two sets of numbers are shown in column 4 of Exhibit 2).

Column 5 of Exhibit 2 shows both countries' gains from specialization and trade: the United States and Japan each consume 10 more units of food and no less clothing in the specialization–trade case than in the no-specialization–no-trade case. Apparently, then, a country gains by specializing in producing and trading the good in which it has a comparative advantage.

22-1b A Common Misconception about How Much We Can Consume

No country can consume beyond its PPF if it doesn't specialize and trade with other countries. But, as we have just seen, it can do so when there is specialization and trade. Look at the PPF for the United States in Exhibit 1. In the NS–NT case, the United States consumes 60 units of food and 10 units of clothing; that is, the United States consumes at point *B* on its PPF. In the S–T case, however, it consumes 70 units of food and 10 units of clothing. A point that represents this combination of the two goods is beyond the country's PPF.

22-1c How Countries Know When They Have a Comparative Advantage

Government officials of a country do not analyze pages of cost data to determine what their country should specialize in producing and then trade. Bureaucrats do not

ECONOMICS 24/7

Dividing the Work

John and Veronica, husband and wife, have divided their household tasks: John usually does all the lawn work, fixes the cars, and does the dinner dishes, and Veronica cleans the house, cooks the meals, and does the laundry. Some sociologists might suggest that John and Veronica divided the household tasks along gender lines: Men have done the lawn work, fixed the cars, and so on for years, and women have cleaned the house, cooked the meals, and so on for years. In other words, John is doing man's work, and Veronica is doing woman's work.

Maybe they have followed gender lines, but the question remains why certain tasks became man's work and others became woman's work. Moreover, their arrangement doesn't explain why John and Veronica don't split every task evenly. In other words, why doesn't John clean half the house and Veronica clean half the house? Why doesn't Veronica mow the lawn on the second and fourth week of every month and John mow the lawn every first and third week of the month?

The law of comparative advantage may be the answer to all these questions. Consider two tasks: cleaning the house and mowing the lawn. The following table shows how long John and Veronica take to complete the two tasks individually:

Person	Time Taken to Clean the House	Time Taken to Mow the Lawn
John	120 minutes	50 minutes
Veronica	60 minutes	100 minutes

Here is the opportunity cost of each task for each person:

Person	Opportunity Cost of Cleaning the House	Opportunity Cost of Mowing the Lawn
John	2.40 mowed lawns	0.42 clean house
Veronica	0.60 mowed lawn	1.67 clean houses

In other words, John has a comparative advantage in mowing the lawn and Veronica has a comparative advantage in cleaning the house.

Now let's compare two settings. In setting 1, John and Veronica each do half of each task. In setting 2, John only mows the lawn and Veronica only cleans the house.

In setting 1, John spends 60 minutes cleaning half of the house and 25 minutes mowing half of the lawn, for a total of 85 minutes; Veronica spends 30 minutes cleaning half of the house and 50 minutes mowing half of the lawn, for a total of 80 minutes. The total time spent by Veronica and John cleaning the house and mowing the lawn is 165 minutes.

In setting 2, John spends 50 minutes mowing the lawn, and Veronica spends 60 minutes cleaning the house. The total time spent by Veronica and John cleaning the house and mowing the lawn is 110 minutes.

In which setting are Veronica and John better off? John works 85 minutes in setting 1 and 50 minutes in setting 2, so he is better off in setting 2. Veronica works 80 minutes in setting 1 and 60 minutes in setting 2, so she is also better off in setting 2. Together, John and Veronica spend 55 fewer minutes in setting 2 than in setting 1. Getting the job done in 55 fewer minutes is the benefit of specializing in various duties around the house. Given those numbers, we would expect that John will mow the lawn (and do nothing else) and Veronica will clean the house (and do nothing else).

plot production possibilities frontiers on graph paper or calculate opportunity costs. Instead, the individual's desire to earn a dollar, a peso, or a euro determines the pattern of international trade. The desire to earn a profit determines what a country specializes in and trades.

To illustrate, suppose Henri, an enterprising Frenchman, visits the United States and observes that beef is relatively cheap (compared with the price in France) and that perfume is relatively expensive. Noticing the price differences for beef and perfume between his country and the United States, he decides to buy some perfume in France, bring it to the United States, and sell it there for the relatively higher U.S. price. With his profits from the perfume transaction, he buys beef in the United States, ships it to France, and sells it there for the relatively higher French price. Obviously, Henri is buying low and selling high. He buys a good in the country where it is cheap and sells it in the country where it is expensive.

Henri's activities have a couple of consequences. First, he is earning a profit. The larger the price differences are between the two countries and the more he shuffles goods between countries, the more profit Henri earns.

Second, Henri's activities are moving each country toward its comparative advantage. The United States ends up exporting beef to France, and France ends up exporting perfume to the United States. Just as the pure theory predicts, individuals in the two countries specialize in and trade the good in which they have a comparative advantage. The outcome is brought about spontaneously through the actions of individuals trying to make themselves better off; they are simply trying to gain through trade.

The Benefits of Searching for Profit Is the desire to earn profit useful to society at large? Henri's desire for profit moved both the United States and France toward specializing in and trading the good in which each had a comparative advantage. And when countries specialize and trade, they are better off than when they do neither.

SELF-TEST

(Answers to Self-Test questions are in Answers to Self-Test Questions at the back of the book.)

1. Suppose the United States can produce 120 units of X at an opportunity cost of 20 units of Y and Great Britain can produce 40 units of X at an opportunity cost of 80 units of Y. Identify favorable terms of trade for the two countries.

2. If a country can produce more of all of its goods than any other country can, would it benefit from specializing and trading? Explain your answer.

3. Do government officials analyze data to determine what their country can produce at a comparative advantage?

22-2 TRADE RESTRICTIONS

International trade theory holds that countries gain from free international trade—that is, from specializing in the production of the goods in which they have a comparative advantage and trading them for other goods. In the real world, however, numerous types of trade restrictions imposed by many countries give rise to the following question: If countries gain from international trade, why are there trade restrictions? The answer requires an analysis of costs and benefits; specifically, we need to determine who benefits and who loses when trade is restricted. First, we need to explain some pertinent background information.

22-2a The Distributional Effects of International Trade

The previous section explained that specialization and international trade benefit individuals in different countries, but the benefit is a *net* benefit. Not every individual person may gain.

To illustrate, suppose Pam Dickson lives and works in the United States and makes clock radios. She produces and sells 12,000 clock radios per year at a price of $40 each. Currently, clock radios are not traded internationally. Individuals in other countries who make clock radios do not sell them in the United States.

Then, one day, the U.S. market is opened to clock radios from China. Chinese manufacturers seem to have a comparative advantage in the production of clock radios because they sell theirs in the United States for $25 each. Pam realizes that she cannot compete at this price. Her sales drop to such a degree that she goes out of business. Thus, the introduction of international trade in this instance has harmed Pam personally.

22-2b Consumers' and Producers' Surpluses

The preceding example raises the issue of the distributional effects of free trade. The benefits of international trade are not equally distributed to all individuals in the population. Therefore, the topics of consumers' and producers' surpluses (Chapter 3) are relevant to our discussion of international trade.

Recall that *consumers' surplus* is the difference between the maximum price a buyer is willing and able to pay for a good or service and the price actually paid for the good or service:

$$\text{Consumers' surplus} = \text{Maximum buying price} - \text{Price paid}$$

Consumers' surplus is a dollar measure of the benefit gained by being able to purchase a unit of a good for less than one is willing to pay for it. For example, if Yakov would have paid $10 to see the movie at the Cinemax but paid only $4, his consumers' surplus is $6. Consumers' surplus is the consumers' net gain from trade.

Producers' surplus (or sellers' surplus) is the difference between the price sellers receive for a good and the minimum or lowest price for which they would have sold the good:

$$\text{Producers' surplus} = \text{Price received} - \text{Minimum selling price}$$

Producers' surplus is a dollar measure of the benefit gained by being able to sell a unit of output for more than one is willing to sell it. For example, if Joan sold her knit sweaters for $24 each but would have sold them for as low as (but no lower than) $14 each, her producer surplus is $10 per sweater. Producers' surplus is the producers' net gain from trade.

Both consumers' and producers' surplus are represented in Exhibit 3. In part (a), the shaded triangle represents consumers' surplus. This triangle comprises the area under the demand curve and above the equilibrium price. In part (b), the shaded triangle represents producers' surplus. This triangle comprises the area above the supply curve and under the equilibrium price.

> **EXHIBIT 3**

Consumers' and Producers' Surplus

(a) Consumers' surplus. As the shaded area indicates, the difference between the maximum or highest amount consumers would be willing to pay and the price they actually pay is consumers' surplus. (b) Producers' surplus. As the shaded area indicates, the difference between the price sellers receive for the good and the minimum or lowest price they would be willing to sell the good for is producers' surplus.

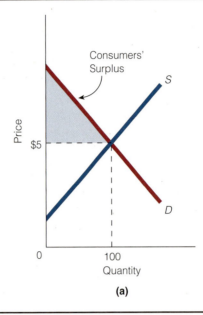

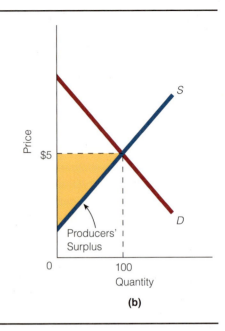

(a)   (b)

While Negotiating the Price of a House Robin is negotiating the price of the house she wants to buy from Yakov. Her last offer for the house was $478,000, and he countered with $485,000. She is thinking about offering $481,000. Where is the economics?

Obviously, in this negotiation each person is trying to increase his or her surplus at the expense of the other. The lower the price Robin pays, the higher her consumers' surplus will be and the lower Yakov's producers' surplus will be. Alternatively, the higher the price Yakov receives, the higher his producers' surplus will be and the lower Robin's consumers' surplus will be.

22-2c **The Benefits and Costs of Trade Restrictions**

Of the numerous ways to restrict international trade, tariffs and quotas are two of the more common. We use the tools of supply and demand to discuss these two methods, concentrating on two groups: U.S. consumers and U.S. producers.

Tariff

A tax on imports.

Tariffs A **tariff** is a tax on imports. The primary effect of a tariff is to raise the price of the imported good for the domestic consumer. Exhibit 4 illustrates the effects of a tariff on cars imported into the United States. The world price for cars is P_w, as shown in part (a). At this price in the domestic U.S. market, U.S. consumers buy Q_2 cars, as shown in part (b). They buy Q_1 cars from U.S. producers and $Q_2 - Q_1$ (the difference of Q_2 and Q_1) cars from foreign producers. In other words, U.S. imports at P_w are $Q_2 - Q_1$.

> **EXHIBIT 4**

The Effects of a Tariff

A tariff raises the price of cars from P_W to $P_W + T$, decreases consumers' surplus, increases producers' surplus, and generates revenue. Because consumers lose more than producers and government gain, there is a net loss due to the tariff.

	Consumers' Surplus	Producers' Surplus	Government Tariff Revenue
Free trade (No tariff)	$1 + 2 + 3 + 4 + 5 + 6$	7	None
Tariff	$1 + 2$	$3 + 7$	5
Loss or gain	$-(3 + 4 + 5 + 6)$	$+3$	$+5$

Result of tariff = Loss to consumers + Gain to producers + Tariff revenue
$$= -(3 + 4 + 5 + 6) \qquad +3 \qquad\qquad +5$$
$$= -(4 + 6)$$

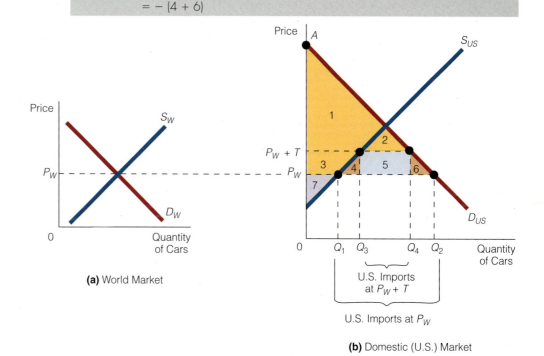

(a) World Market

(b) Domestic (U.S.) Market

In this situation, consumers' surplus is the area under the demand curve and above the world price, P_W: the sum of the areas 1, 2, 3, 4, 5, and 6 in part (b). Producers' surplus is the area above the supply curve and below the world price, P_W: area 7.

Now, suppose a tariff is imposed. Then the price for imported cars in the U.S. market rises to $P_W + T$ (the world price plus the tariff). At this price, U.S. consumers buy Q_4 cars: Q_3 from U.S. producers and $Q_4 - Q_3$ from foreign producers. U.S. imports are thus $Q_4 - Q_3$, a smaller number of imports than at the pretariff price. An effect of tariffs, then, is to reduce imports. After the tariff has been imposed, at price $P_W + T$ consumers' surplus consists of areas 1 and 2, and producers' surplus consists of areas 3 and 7.

Clearly, consumers receive more consumers' surplus when tariffs do not exist and less when they do exist. In our example, consumers received areas 1 through 6 in consumers' surplus when the tariff did not exist but they receive only areas 1 and 2 when the tariff exists. Because of the tariff, consumers' surplus was reduced by an amount equal to areas 3, 4, 5, and 6.

Producers, though, receive less producers' surplus when tariffs do not exist and more when they do exist. In our example, producers received producers' surplus equal to area 7 when the tariff did not exist, but they receive producers' surplus equal to areas 3 and 7 with the tariff. Because of the tariff, producers' surplus increased by an amount equal to area 3.

The government collects tariff revenue equal to area 5. This area is obtained by multiplying the number of imports $(Q_4 - Q_3)$ by the tariff, which is the difference between $P_W + T$ and P_W.[1]

In conclusion, the effects of a tariff are a decrease in consumers' surplus, an increase in producers' surplus, and tariff revenue for government. Because the loss to consumers (areas 3, 4, 5, and 6) is greater than the gain to producers (area 3) plus the gain to government (area 5), *a tariff results in a net loss.* The net loss is areas 4 and 6.

Quota

A legal limit imposed on the amount of a good that may be imported.

Quotas   A **quota** is a legal limit imposed on the amount of a good that may be imported. For example, the government may decide to allow no more than 100,000 foreign cars to be imported, or 10 million barrels of OPEC oil, or 30,000 Japanese television sets. A quota reduces the supply of a good, and raises the price of imported goods, for domestic consumers.

Once again, we consider the situation in the U.S. car market. (See Exhibit 5.) At a price of P_W [established in the world market for cars—see part (a)], U.S. consumers buy Q_1 cars from U.S. producers and $Q_2 - Q_1$ cars from foreign producers. [See part (b).] Consumers' surplus is equal to the sum of areas 1, 2, 3, 4, 5, and 6. Producers' surplus is equal to area 7.

Suppose now that the U.S. government sets a quota equal to $Q_4 - Q_3$. Because this quantity is the number of foreign cars U.S. consumers imported when the tariff was imposed (Exhibit 4), the price of cars rises to P_Q in Exhibit 5 (a price equal to $P_W + T$ in Exhibit 4). At P_Q, consumers' surplus is equal to areas 1 and 2, and producers' surplus consists of areas 3 and 7. The decrease in consumers' surplus due to the quota is equal to areas 3, 4, 5, and 6; the increase in producers' surplus is equal to area 3.

However, area 5 is not transferred to government, as was the case when a tariff was imposed. Rather, it represents a gain earned by the importers (and sellers) of $Q_4 - Q_3$ foreign-made cars. Before the quota, importers were importing $Q_2 - Q_1$ cars, but only part $(Q_4 - Q_3)$ of that total quantity is relevant because $Q_4 - Q_3$ number of cars is the quantity of imports now that the quota has been established. Before the quota was established, the dollar amount that the importers received for $Q_4 - Q_3$ cars was $P_W \times (Q_4 - Q_3)$. Because of the quota, the price rises to P_Q, and they now receive $P_Q \times (Q_4 - Q_3)$. The gain is area 5.

In conclusion, the effects of a quota are a decrease in consumers' surplus, an increase in producers' surplus, and a gain for importers. Because the loss to consumers (areas 3, 4, 5, and 6) is greater than the increase in producers' surplus (area 3) plus the gain to importers (area 5), there is a *net loss as a result of the quota.* The net loss is equal to areas 4 and 6.

[1.] For example, if the tariff is $100 and the number of imports is 50,000, then the tariff is $5 million.

EXHIBIT 5

	Consumers' Surplus	Producers' Surplus	Gain to Importers
Free trade (No quota)	1 + 2 + 3 + 4 + 5 + 6	7	—
Quota	1 + 2	3 + 7	5
Loss or gain	− (3 + 4 + 5 + 6)	+3	+5

Result of quota = Loss to consumers + Gain to producers + Gain to importers
= − (3 + 4 + 5 + 6)   +3   +5
= − (4 + 6)

The Effects of a Quota

A quota that sets the legal limit of imports at $Q_4 - Q_3$ causes the price of cars to increase from P_W to P_Q. A quota raises the price, decreases consumers' surplus, increases producers' surplus, and provides a gain to importers. Because consumers lose more than producers and importers gain, there is a net loss due to the quota.

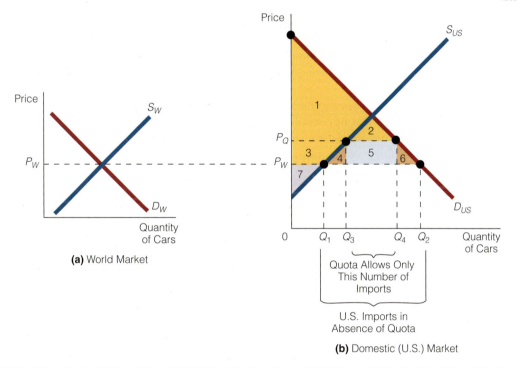

(a) World Market

(b) Domestic (U.S.) Market

Quota Allows Only This Number of Imports

U.S. Imports in Absence of Quota

In a Policy Debate There is a debate tonight at the college Irina attends, with four people on either side of the issue: Should the United States practice free trade? Irina attends the debate and comes away thinking that both sides made good points. The side opposing free trade argued that, because other countries do not always practice free trade, neither should the United States. The side in favor of free trade argued that free trade leads to lower prices for U.S. consumers. Where is the economics?

Most of the debate, we believe, will fit into our discussion of Exhibits 4 and 5. These two exhibits show what happens to consumers and producers, and to society as a whole, as the result of both free and prohibited trade. The diagrams show (1) the benefits of prohibited free trade to domestic producers, (2) the costs of prohibited trade to domestic consumers, (3) tariff revenue to government, if such revenue exists, and (4) the overall net costs to prohibited trade.

FINDING ECONOMICS

22-2d **Why Nations Sometimes Restrict Trade**

If free trade results in net gain, why do nations sometimes restrict trade? The case for free trade (no tariffs or quotas) so far in this chapter appears to be a strong one. The case for free trade has not gone unchallenged, however. Some persons maintain that, at certain times, free trade should be restricted or suspended. In almost all cases, they argue that doing so is in the best interest of the public or country as a whole. In a word, they advance a public-interest argument. Other persons contend that the public-interest argument is only superficial: down deep, they say, it is a special-interest argument clothed in pretty words. As you might guess, the debate between the two groups is often heated.

The sections that follow describe some arguments that have been advanced for trade restrictions.

The National Defense Argument

Certain industries—such as aircraft, petroleum, chemicals, and weapons—are necessary to the national defense. Suppose the United States has a comparative advantage in the production of wheat and country X has a comparative advantage in the production of weapons. Many Americans feel that the United States should not specialize in the production of wheat and then trade wheat to country X in exchange for weapons. Leaving weapons production to another country, they maintain, is too dangerous.

The national defense argument may have some validity, but even valid arguments may be abused. Industries that are not really necessary to the national defense may maintain otherwise. In the past, the national defense argument has been used by some firms in the following industries: pens, pottery, peanuts, papers, candles, thumbtacks, tuna fishing, and pencils.

The Infant Industry Argument

Alexander Hamilton, the first U.S. secretary of the treasury, argued that so-called infant, or new, industries often need protection from older, established foreign competitors until they are mature enough to compete on an equal basis. Today, some persons voice the same argument. The infant industry argument is clearly an argument for temporary protection. Critics charge, however, that after an industry is protected from foreign competition, removing the protection is almost impossible: the once infant industry will continue to maintain that it isn't old enough to go it alone. Critics of the infant industry argument say that political realities make it unlikely that a benefit, once bestowed, will be removed.

Finally, the infant industry argument, like the national defense argument, may be abused. All new industries, whether or not they could currently compete successfully with foreign producers, would argue for protection on infant industry grounds.

Dumping
The sale of goods abroad at a price below their cost and below the price charged in the domestic market.

The Antidumping Argument

Dumping is the sale of goods abroad at a price below their cost and below the price charged in the domestic market. If a French firm sells wine in the United States for a price below the cost of producing the wine and below the price charged in France, it is dumping wine in the United States. Critics of dumping maintain that it is an unfair trade practice that puts domestic producers of substitute goods at a disadvantage.

In addition, critics charge that dumpers seek only to penetrate a market and drive out domestic competitors, after which they raise prices. However, some economists point to the infeasibility of this strategy. After the dumpers have driven out their competition and raised prices, their competition is likely to return. For their efforts, the dumpers, in turn, would have incurred only a string of losses (owing to their selling below cost). Opponents of the antidumping argument also point out that domestic consumers benefit from dumping because they pay lower prices.

ECONOMICS 24/7

Offshore Outsourcing, or Offshoring

Outsourcing is the term used to describe work done for a company by another company or by people other than the originating company's employees. Outsourcing entails purchasing a product or process from an outside supplier rather than producing it in-house. To illustrate, suppose company X has, in the past, hired employees for personnel, accounting, and payroll services, but now a company in another state performs these duties. Then company X has outsourced those work activities.

david pearson/Alamy

When a company outsources certain work activities to individuals in another country, it is said to be engaged in offshore outsourcing, or offshoring. Consider a few examples: A New York securities firm replaces 800 software engineering employees with a team of software engineers in India. A computer company replaces 200 on-call technicians in its headquarters in Texas with 150 on-call technicians in India.

The benefits of offshoring for a U.S. firm are obvious: It pays lower wages to individuals in other countries for the same work that U.S. employees do for higher wages. Benefits also flow to the employees hired in the foreign countries. The costs of offshoring are said to fall on persons who lose their jobs as a result, such as the software engineer in New York or the on-call computer technician in Texas. Some have argued that offshoring is a major political issue and that it could bring with it a wave of protectionism.

Offshoring will undoubtedly have both proponents and opponents. On a net basis, however, are there more benefits than costs or more costs than benefits? Consider a U.S. company that currently employs Jones as a software engineer, paying her $x a year. Then, one day, the company tells Jones that it has to let her go; it is replacing her with a software engineer in India who will work for $z a year (and, yes, $z < x$).

Why doesn't Jones simply agree to work for $z, the same wage as that agreed to by the Indian software engineer? Well, obviously, that's because Jones can work elsewhere for some wage between $x and $z. Assume that this wage is $y. So, even though offshoring has moved Jones from earning $x to earning $y, $y is still more than $z.

In short, the U.S. company is able to lower its costs from $x to $z and Jones's income falls from $x to $y. The U.S. company lowers its costs more than Jones's income falls because the difference between $x and $z is greater than the difference between $x and $y.

If the U.S. company operates in a competitive environment, its lower costs will shift its supply curve to the right and lower prices. In other words, offshoring can reduce prices for U.S. consumers. The political fallout from offshoring might, in the end, depend on how visible, to the average American, the employment effects of offshoring are relative to the price reduction effect.

The Foreign Export Subsidies Argument   Some governments subsidize firms that export goods. If a country offers a below-market (interest rate) loan to a company, it is often argued, the government subsidizes the production of the good the firm produces. If, in turn, the firm exports the good to a foreign country, that country's producers of substitute goods call foul. They complain that the foreign firm has been given an unfair advantage that they should be protected against.[2]

[2.] Words are important in this debate. For example, domestic producers who claim that foreign governments have subsidized foreign firms say that they are not asking for economic protectionism, but only retaliation, reciprocity, or, simply, tit for tat—words that have less negative connotation than those their opponents use.

Others say that consumers should not turn their backs on a gift (in the form of lower prices). If foreign governments want to subsidize their exports and thus give a gift to foreign consumers at the expense of their own taxpayers, then the recipients should not complain. Of course, the recipients are usually not the ones who are complaining. Rather, the complainers are the domestic producers who can't sell their goods at as high a price because of the so-called gift that domestic consumers are receiving from foreign governments.

The Low Foreign Wages Argument   Some argue that American producers can't compete with foreign producers because American producers have to pay high wages to their workers and foreign producers pay low wages. The American producers insist that international trade must be restricted or they will be ruined. However, the argument overlooks why American wages are high and foreign wages are low in the first place: productivity. High productivity and high wages are usually linked, as are low productivity and low wages. If an American worker, who receives $20 per hour, can produce (on average) 100 units of good X per hour, working with numerous capital goods, then the cost per unit may be lower than when a foreign worker, who receives $2 per hour, produces (on average) 5 units of X per hour, working by hand. In short, a country's high-wage disadvantage may be offset by its productivity advantage, and a country's low-wage advantage may be offset by its productivity disadvantage. High wages do not necessarily mean high costs when productivity and the costs of nonlabor resources are included.

The Saving Domestic Jobs Argument   Sometimes, the argument against completely free trade is made in terms of saving domestic jobs. Actually, this argument has cropped up before in its different guises. For example, the low foreign wages argument is one form of it: If domestic producers cannot compete with foreign producers because foreign producers pay low wages and domestic producers pay high wages, domestic producers will go out of business and domestic jobs will be lost. The foreign export subsidies argument is another version: If foreign government subsidies give a competitive edge to foreign producers, not only will domestic producers fail, but as a result of their failure, domestic jobs will be lost.

Critics of the saving domestic jobs argument (in all its guises) counterargue as follows: If a domestic producer is being outcompeted by foreign producers and if domestic jobs in an industry are being lost as a result, the world market is signaling that those labor resources could be put to better use in an industry in which the country holds a comparative advantage.

THINKING LIKE AN ECONOMIST

Economics Versus Politics International trade often becomes a battleground between economics and politics. The simple tools of supply and demand and of consumers' and producers' surpluses show that free trade leads to net gains. On the whole, tariffs and quotas make living standards lower than they would be if free trade were permitted. On the other side, though, are the realities of business and politics. Domestic producers may advocate quotas and tariffs to make themselves better off, giving little thought to the negative effects on foreign producers or domestic consumers.

Perhaps the battle over international trade comes down to this: Policies are advocated, argued, and lobbied for largely on the basis of their distributional effects as opposed to their aggregate or overall effects. On an aggregate level, free trade produces a net gain for society whereas restricted trade produces a net loss. But economists understand that, even if free trade in the aggregate produces a net gain, not every single person will benefit more from free trade than from restricted trade. An example in this chapter showed how a subset of the population (producers) gains more, in a particular instance, from restricted trade than from free trade. In short, economists realize that the crucial question in determining real-world policies is more often, "How does it affect me?" than "How does it affect us?"

ECONOMICS 24/7

Are Social Media Making the World Smaller?

Do you know the president of the People's Republic of China? If not, then how long is the chain of acquaintances between you and the president of China? In other words, if you wrote a letter to the president of China and gave it to a friend of yours, and your friend gives the letter to someone she knows, and on and on, how many intermediaries are there between you and the president of China? Are there three? In other words, you give the letter to a friend, and she gives it to her friend, and her friend gives it to a friend, and then that last friend gives the letter to the president of China? Or do you think that the number of intermediaries is higher—say, 20? What if we told you that the correct answer is "no more than five?" This answer falls out of the *six-degrees-of-separation theory*, which states that anyone on the planet can be connected to any other person on the planet through a chain of acquaintances that has no more than five intermediaries. Stated differently, any two people in the world are connected in a maximum of six steps.

To illustrate, suppose we have persons A — G. Person A is you and person G is the president of China. You give your letter (written to the president) to your friend B; that is step 1. B gives it to C; that is step 2—and so on. By the time the letter gets to G (the president of China), that is step 6. You are separated from the president of China by five intermediaries (B — F), or six steps: from A to B (step 1); from B to C (step 2); from C to D (step 3); from D to E (step 4); from E to F (step 5); and from F to G (step 6).

Now, if you are like most people, you will be shocked at how short the chain is between you and the president of China or, for that matter, any other person in the world. You are no more than six steps away from a person who lives in one of the rain forests of the world, from a member of Moscow's ballet, or from the person who just now, in Singapore, ran a red light.

You may know the game "Six Degrees of Kevin Bacon," which is based on the theory of six degrees of separation. In the game, Kevin Bacon is linked to any actor in the world in six or fewer steps. In fact, there is a website where you can play the game: "The Oracle of Bacon," at http://oracleofbacon.org/. There, you can put in the name of any actor and see the chain of links between that actor and Kevin Bacon. For example, if you put in the name "W. C. Fields," who died in 1946, you find that W. C. Fields was in the movie *The Big Broadcast* (1938) with Joe Gray, who was in *How to Save a Marriage and Ruin Your Life* (1968) with Eli Wallach, who was in *Mystic River* (2003) with Kevin Bacon. That is a "Bacon number of 3," because there are three movies that separate W. C. Fields from Kevin Bacon.

There have been a few tests of the theory of six degrees of separation. For example, researchers at Microsoft studied the records of 30 billion electronic conversations among 180 million people in various countries. The database consisted of all the Microsoft Messenger instant messages in June 2006. Those messages accounted for approximately half the instant messages in the world at the time. The researchers found that the average length of separation between any two people was 6.6 steps.

In a 1969 study, researchers Stanley Milgram and Jeffrey Travers asked 296 people in Omaha, Nebraska, and Wichita, Kansas, to send a letter through acquaintances to a stockbroker in Boston, Massachusetts (whom did they did not know). Because some people may have not followed through with the study, only 64 of the letters reached the stockbroker. Of the 64, the average number of degrees of separation was 6.2.

In 2003, researchers at Columbia University had 24,000 volunteers try to send an e-mail via acquaintances to one of 18 targeted people in 13 countries. Among the potential recipients were a police officer in Australia, a veteran in the Norwegian army, and a professor at an Ivy League university in the United States. Only 384 of the chains were completed, and they used an average of 4 steps. But the researchers estimated that the average length in *all the chains*, completed and uncompleted, was between 5 and 7 steps.

People who speak about the theory of six degrees of separation often remark that, if there are no more than six steps that separate any two people in the world, then what we have is a rather "small world"—not small in size, and not small in population, but small in the sense that any two people in the world are linked by no more than six steps.

Have social media made the world "smaller?" Think of how they could. Specifically, think of Wendy who graduates from high school and moves away from her hometown. Before Facebook, Wendy could have easily lost touch with her friends in high school. Years pass, she gets a job, gets married, perhaps has children, moves to different cities, and so on. Yes, initially, when she graduated high school, she called or wrote letters to her friends, but in time that practice ended. But because of the digital revolution, Wendy now begins to search online for some of her old friends from high school. She learns that, like her, they are on Facebook, and she connects with them. In other words, with Facebook, Wendy keeps in contact with many more people than she did before Facebook. She has links with many more people than she did without Facebook.

Do links with more people change the number of degrees of separation between one person and any other person picked at random in the world? The answer is yes. To understand just how, think of two extreme cases. First, suppose that, in a world of

10 people, no one person has a link with any other person. How many degrees of separation are there here? It might as well be infinity. Now suppose that, in the world of the same 10 people, everybody knows everyone else. How many degrees of separation are there now between any two people? The answer is 1. In other words, the more links between you and others, and between others and still more others, and so on, the fewer degrees of separation between any two people. What social media, especially in the form of social networks, have done is make it possible for people to link to people whom they might once have known but lost contact with years ago. Thus, we would expect to see that the representative person in a world of social media has links to more people than the representative person in a world without social media. Social media are indeed making the world smaller. Perhaps, in time, the six degrees of separation will be four.

SELF-TEST

1. Who benefits and who loses from tariffs? Explain your answer.
2. Identify the directional change in consumers' surplus and producers' surplus when we move from free trade to tariffs. Is the change in consumers' surplus greater than, less than, or equal to the change in producers' surplus?
3. What is a major difference between the effects of a quota and the effects of a tariff?
4. Outline the details of the infant industry argument for trade restriction.

Office Hours

"Should We Impose Tariffs if They Impose Tariffs?"

STUDENT:

Here is a problem I have with our discussion of free trade and prohibited trade. Essentially, I am in favor of free international trade, but I think the United States should have free trade with countries that practice free trade with us. In other words, if country X practices free trade with the United States, then the United States should practice free trade with it. But if country Y places tariffs on U.S. goods that

enter country Y, then the United States ought to place tariffs on country Y's goods that enter our country.

INSTRUCTOR:

Many people feel the same way you do, but this opinion overlooks something that we showed in Exhibits 4 and 5: The losses of moving from free trade to prohibited trade (where either tariffs or quotas exist) are greater than the gains. Remember? There is a net loss to society in that move.

STUDENT:

I just think it is only fair that other countries get what they give. If they give free trade to us, then we ought to give free trade back to them. If they place tariffs and quotas on our goods, then we ought to do the same to their goods.

INSTRUCTOR:

You need to keep in mind the price the United States has to pay for this policy of tit for tat.

STUDENT:

What do you mean? What price does the United States have to pay?

INSTRUCTOR:

It has to incur the net loss illustrated in Exhibits 4 and 5. If you look back at Exhibit 4, for example, you'll notice that moving from free trade to prohibited trade (1) decreases consumers' surplus, (2) increases producers' surplus, and (3) raises tariff revenue. But when we count up all the gains of prohibited trade and compare them with all the losses, we conclude that the losses are greater than the gains. In other words, prohibited trade leads to a net loss.

STUDENT:

But suppose our practicing tit for tat (giving free trade for free trade and prohibited trade for prohibited trade) forces other countries to move away from prohibited trade. In other words, what I am saying is this: We need to look at this issue of free versus prohibited trade over time. Maybe the United States has to practice prohibited trade today (with those countries that impose tariffs or quotas on the United States) in order to force those countries to practice free trade tomorrow. Couldn't it work out that way?

INSTRUCTOR:

It could work out that way. Or, then, things could escalate toward greater prohibited trade. In other words, country A imposes tariffs and quotas on country B, then country B raises its tariffs and quotas even higher on country A, so country A retaliates and raises its tariffs and quotas on country B, and so on.

STUDENT:

So, what is your point? Is it that free trade is the best policy to practice no matter what other countries do?

INSTRUCTOR:

That is what many economists would say, but that is not really the point I am making here. I am rather making two points with respect to the discussion. First, in response to your position that the United States ought to practice tit for tat (give free trade for free trade, tariffs for tariffs, quotas for quotas), I am simply drawing your attention to the net loss Americans incur if they practice prohibited trade—no matter what other countries are doing. In other words, there is a net loss for Americans, regardless of whether other countries are practicing free or prohibited trade. Second, with respect to your second point about prohibited trade today leading to free trade tomorrow, I am saying that we can't be sure that prohibited trade today won't lead to greater prohibitions on trade tomorrow. This is not to say that you can't be right: It is possible for prohibited trade today to lead to less prohibited trade tomorrow.

Points to remember

1. A country that imposes tariffs or quotas on imported goods incurs a net loss, no matter what another country is doing—whether it is practicing free or prohibited trade.
2. We cannot easily predict the outcome of the United States' practicing tit for tat in international trade.

CHAPTER SUMMARY

SPECIALIZATION AND TRADE

- A country has a comparative advantage in the production of a good if it can produce the good at a lower opportunity cost than another country can.

- Individuals in countries that specialize and trade have a higher standard of living than they would if their countries did not specialize and trade.

- Government officials do not analyze cost data to determine what their country should specialize in and trade. Instead, the desire to earn a dollar, peso, or euro guides individuals' actions and produces the unintended consequence that countries specialize in and trade the good(s) in which they have a comparative advantage. However, trade restrictions can change this outcome.

TARIFFS AND QUOTAS

- A tariff is a tax on imports. A quota is a legal limit on the amount of a good that may be imported.

- Both tariffs and quotas raise the price of imports.

- Tariffs lead to a decrease in consumers' surplus, an increase in producers' surplus, and tariff revenue for the government. Consumers lose more through tariffs than producers and government (together) gain.

- Quotas lead to a decrease in consumers' surplus, an increase in producers' surplus, and additional revenue for the importers who sell the amount specified by the quota. Consumers lose more through quotas than producers and importers (together) gain.

ARGUMENTS FOR TRADE RESTRICTIONS

- The national defense argument states that certain goods—such as aircraft, petroleum, chemicals, and weapons—are necessary to the national defense and should be produced domestically whether the country has a comparative advantage in their production or not.

- The infant industry argument states that infant, or new, industries should be protected from free (foreign) trade so that they have time to develop and compete on an equal basis with older, more established foreign industries.

- The antidumping argument states that domestic producers should not have to compete (on an unequal basis) with foreign producers that sell products below cost and below the prices they charge in their domestic markets.

- The foreign export subsidies argument states that domestic producers should not have to compete (on an unequal basis) with foreign producers that have been subsidized by their governments.

- The low foreign wages argument states that domestic producers cannot compete with foreign producers that pay low wages to their employees when domestic producers pay high wages to their employees. For high-paying domestic firms to survive, limits on free trade are proposed.

- The saving domestic jobs argument states that foreign producers will be able to outcompete domestic producers through low foreign wages or government subsidies (or dumping and similar practices) and that, therefore, domestic jobs will be lost. For domestic firms to survive and domestic jobs not to be lost, limits on free trade are proposed.

- Not everyone accepts the arguments for trade restrictions as valid. Critics often maintain that the arguments can be and are abused and that in most cases they are motivated by self-interest.

KEY TERMS AND CONCEPTS

Comparative Advantage   Tariff   Quota   Dumping

VIDEO QUESTIONS AND PROBLEMS

Video Questions and Problems are available on MindTap for Arnold 12e or by searching for Arnold on www.cengagebrain.com

1. Country A can produce either 10X and 0Y or 0x and 20Y. Country B can produce either 30X and 0Y or 0X and 40Y. Identify the opportunity cost of producing each good for each country. Identify the comparative advantage of each country.

2. Diagrammatically represent both consumers' surplus and producers' surplus.

3. Diagrammatically represent the decline in consumers' surplus due to a tariff.

4. Diagrammatically represent the revenue received due to a tariff.

5. What is the infant industry argument for protectionism? How might this argument be abused?

QUESTIONS AND PROBLEMS

1. Although a production possibilities frontier is usually drawn for a country, one could be drawn for the world. Picture the world's production possibilities frontier. Is the world positioned at a point on the PPF or below it? Give a reason for your answer.

2. If country A is better than country B at producing all goods, will country A still be made better off by specializing and trading? Explain your answer. (*Hint:* Look at Exhibit 1.)

3. The desire for profit can end up pushing countries toward producing goods in which they have a comparative advantage. Do you agree or disagree? Explain your answer.

4. Whatever can be done by a tariff can be done by a quota. Discuss.

5. Neither free trade nor prohibited trade comes with benefits only. Both come with benefits and costs. Therefore, free trade is no better or worse than prohibited trade. Comment.

6. Consider two groups of domestic producers: those which compete with imports and those which export goods. Suppose the domestic producers that compete with imports convince the legislature to impose a high tariff on imports—so high, in fact, that almost all imports are eliminated. Does this policy in any way adversely affect domestic producers that export goods? If so, how?

7. Suppose the U.S. government wants to curtail imports. Would it be likely to favor a tariff or a quota to accomplish its objective? Why?

8. Suppose the landmass known to you as the United States of America had been composed, since the nation's founding, of separate countries instead of separate states. Would you expect the standard of living of the people who inhabit this landmass to be higher, lower, or equal to what it is today? Why?

9. Even though Jeremy is a better gardener and novelist than Bill, Jeremy still hires Bill as his gardener. Why?

10. Suppose that a constitutional convention is called tomorrow and that you are chosen as one of the delegates from your state. You and the other delegates must decide whether it will be constitutional or unconstitutional for the federal government to impose tariffs and quotas or to restrict international trade in any way. What would be your position?

11. Some economists have argued that, because domestic consumers gain more from free trade than domestic producers gain from (import) tariffs and quotas, consumers should buy out domestic producers and rid themselves of costly tariffs and quotas. For example, if consumers save $400 million from free trade (through paying lower prices) and producers gain $100 million from tariffs and quotas, consumers can pay producers something more than $100 million but less than $400 million and get producers to favor free trade too. Assuming that this scheme were feasible, what do you think of it?

12. If there is a net loss to society from tariffs, why do tariffs exist?

WORKING WITH NUMBERS AND GRAPHS

1. Using the data in the accompanying table, answer the following questions:

   a. For which good does Canada have a comparative advantage?

   b. For which good does Italy have a comparative advantage?

   c. What might be a set of favorable terms of trade for the two countries?

   d. Prove that both countries would be better off in the specialization—trade case than in the no-specialization—no-trade case.

Points on Production Possibilities Frontier	Canada		Italy	
	Good X	Good Y	Good X	Good Y
A	150	0	90	0
B	100	25	60	60
C	50	50	30	120
D	0	75	0	180

2. In the accompanying figure, P_W is the world price and $P_W + T$ is the world price plus a tariff. Identify the following:

    a. The level of imports at P_W

    b. The level of imports at $P_W + T$

    c. The loss in consumers' surplus as a result of a tariff

    d. The gain in producers' surplus as a result of a tariff

    e. The revenue received as a result of a tariff

    f. The net loss to society as a result of a tariff

    g. The net benefit to society of moving from a tariff to no tariff

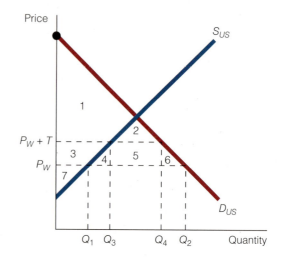

INTERNATIONAL FINANCE

Ellen Isaacs/Alamy

23-1 THE FOREIGN EXCHANGE MARKET

The United States imports and exports goods and services. The difference between the value of its exports and the value of its imports is called *net exports*. Net exports are sometimes referred to as the **trade balance** (or balance of trade). If the value of exports is greater than the value of imports, a country is said to be running a **trade surplus**; if the value of imports is greater than the value of exports, the country is running a **trade deficit**.

One thing that can affect the trade balance of a country is the value of its currency in relation to other currencies. Currencies of different countries are exchanged (bought and sold for a price) in the **foreign exchange market**. The price that currencies are bought and sold for is called the **exchange rate**. For instance, it might take $1.23 to buy a euro and 13 cents to buy a Mexican peso.

In this section, we explain why currencies are demanded and supplied in the foreign exchange market. Then we discuss how the exchange rate expresses the relationship between the demand for, and the supply of, currencies.

INTRODUCTION

When people travel to a foreign country, they buy goods and services in the country, whose prices are quoted in yen, pounds, euros, pesos, or some other currency. For example, a U.S. tourist in Germany might want to buy a good priced in euros and to know what the good costs in dollars and cents. The answer depends on the current exchange rate between the dollar and the euro, but what determines the exchange rate? That is just one of the many questions answered in this chapter.

Trade Balance
The value of a country's exports minus the value of its imports; sometimes referred to as net exports.

Trade Surplus
The condition that exists when the value of a country's exports is greater than the value of its imports.

Trade Deficit
The condition that exists when the value of a country's imports is greater than the value of its exports.

567

23-1a **The Demand for Goods**

To simplify our analysis, we assume that there are only two countries in the world: the United States and Mexico. Thus, there are only two currencies in the world: the U.S. dollar (USD) and the Mexican peso (the abbreviation for the Mexican peso is MXN). We want to answer the following two questions:

1. What creates the demand for, and the supply of, dollars on the foreign exchange market?

2. What creates the demand for, and the supply of, pesos on the foreign exchange market?

Suppose an American wants to buy a couch from a Mexican producer. Before he can purchase the couch, the American must buy Mexican pesos; hence, Mexican pesos are demanded. The American buys Mexican pesos with U.S. dollars; that is, he supplies U.S. dollars to the foreign exchange market and demands Mexican pesos. So, *the U.S. demand for Mexican goods leads to (1) a demand for Mexican pesos and (2) a supply of U.S. dollars on the foreign exchange market.* [See Exhibit 1(a).] Thus, the demand for pesos and the supply of dollars are linked:

Demand for pesos ↔ Supply of dollars

The result is similar for a Mexican who wants to buy a computer from a U.S. producer. Before she can purchase the computer, the Mexican must buy U.S. dollars; hence, U.S. dollars are demanded. The Mexican buys the U.S. dollars with Mexican pesos. So, *the Mexican demand for U.S. goods leads to (1) a demand for U.S. dollars and (2) a supply of Mexican pesos on the foreign exchange market.* [See Exhibit 1(b).] Thus, the demand for dollars and the supply of pesos are linked:

Demand for dollars ↔ Supply of pesos

23-1b **The Demand for, and Supply of, Currencies**

Exhibit 2 shows the market for pesos. The quantity of pesos is on the horizontal axis, and the exchange rate—stated in terms of the *dollar price per peso*—is on the vertical axis. In Exhibit 2(a), the demand curve for pesos is downward sloping, indicating that, as the dollar price per peso declines, the quantity demanded of pesos (by Americans) rises. To illustrate,

---

The Demand for Goods and the Supply of Currencies

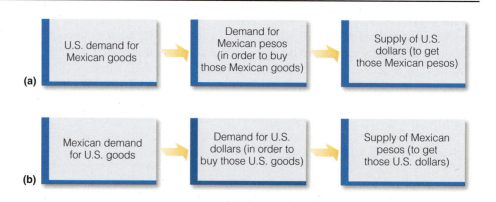

> EXHIBIT 2

The Demand For, and Supply of, Pesos on the Foreign Exchange Market

(a) The demand for pesos. As the dollar price of a peso falls, the quantity demanded of pesos rises. (b) The supply of pesos. As the dollar price of a peso rises, the quantity supplied of pesos rises.

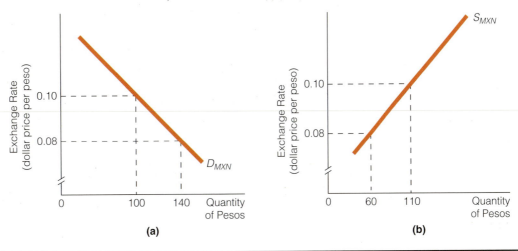

if Americans have to pay 10 cents to buy a peso, they might offer to buy 100 pesos, but if Americans have to pay 8 cents to buy a peso, they might offer to buy 140 pesos.

The supply curve for pesos in Exhibit 2(b) is upward sloping, indicating that, as the dollar price of a peso rises—that is, as Mexicans receive more for a peso—the quantity supplied of pesos (by Mexicans) rises. To illustrate, at 8 cents for a peso, Mexicans might offer to sell 60 pesos, but at 10 cents for a peso, they might offer to sell 110 pesos.

23-2 FLEXIBLE EXCHANGE RATES

In this section, we discuss how exchange rates are determined in the foreign exchange market when the forces of supply and demand are allowed to rule. Economists refer to this dynamic as a **flexible exchange rate system**. In the next section, we discuss how exchange rates are determined under a fixed exchange rate system.

23-2a The Equilibrium Exchange Rate

In a completely flexible exchange rate system, the forces of supply and demand determine the exchange rate. In our two-country–two-currency world, suppose the equilibrium exchange rate (dollar price per peso) is 0.10 USD = 1 MXN, as shown in Exhibit 3. At this dollar price per peso, the quantity demanded of pesos equals the quantity supplied. There are no shortages or surpluses of pesos. At any other exchange rate, however, either an excess demand for pesos or an excess supply of pesos exists.

At the exchange rate of 0.12 USD = 1 MXN, a surplus of pesos exists. As a result, downward pressure will be placed on the dollar price of a peso (just as downward pressure will be placed on the dollar price of an apple if there is a surplus of apples). At the exchange rate of 0.08 USD = 1 MXN, there is a shortage of pesos and upward pressure will be placed on the dollar price of a peso.

Flexible Exchange Rate System

A system whereby exchange rates are determined by the forces of supply and demand for a currency.

EXHIBIT 3

A Flexible Exchange Rate System

At 0.12 USD = 1 MXN, there is a surplus of pesos, placing downward pressure on the exchange rate. At 0.08 USD = 1 MXN, there is a shortage of pesos, placing upward pressure on the exchange rate. At the equilib- rium exchange rate, 0.10 USD = 1 MXN, the quantity demanded of pesos equals the quantity supplied of pesos.

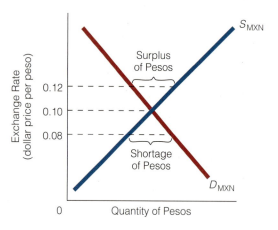

23-2b Changes in the Equilibrium Exchange Rate

A change in the demand for pesos, in the supply of pesos, or in both will change the equilibrium dollar price per peso. If the equilibrium dollar price per peso rises—say, from 0.10 USD = 1 MXN to 0.12 USD = 1 MXN—the peso is said to have **appreciated** and the dollar to have **depreciated**. A currency has appreciated in value if it takes more of a foreign currency to buy it. A currency has depreciated in value if it takes more of it to buy a foreign currency.

For example, a movement in the equilibrium exchange rate from 0.10 USD = 1 MXN to 0.12 USD = 1 MXN means that it now takes 12 cents instead of 10 cents to buy a peso, so the dollar has depreciated. The other side of the coin, so to speak, is that it takes fewer pesos to buy a dollar, so the peso has appreciated. That is, at an exchange rate of 0.10 USD = 1 MXN, it takes 10 pesos (1.00/0.10 = 10) to buy $1, but at an exchange rate of 0.12 USD = 1 MXN, it takes only 8.33 pesos (1.00/0.12 = 8.33) to buy $1.

23-2c Factors That Affect the Equilibrium Exchange Rate

If the equilibrium exchange rate can change owing to a change in the demand for, and supply of, a currency, then understanding what factors can change demand and supply is important. This section presents three such factors.

A Difference In Income Growth Rates   An increase in a country's income will usually cause the nation's residents to buy more of both domestic and foreign goods. The increased demand for imports will result in an increased demand for foreign currency.

Suppose U.S. residents experience an increase in income, but Mexican residents do not. As a result, Americans want to buy more Mexican goods, so the demand curve for pesos shifts rightward, as illustrated in Exhibit 4. This shift causes the equilibrium exchange rate to rise from 0.10 USD = 1 MXN to 0.12 USD = 1 MXN. Because Americans must now pay 12 cents instead of 10 cents to buy a peso, the dollar has depreciated and the peso has appreciated.

Appreciation

An increase in the value of one currency relative to other currencies.

Depreciation

A decrease in the value of one currency relative to other currencies.

Differences in Relative Inflation Rates

Suppose the U.S. price level rises 10 percent at a time when Mexico experiences stable prices. Then an increase in the U.S. price level (in the face of a stable price level in Mexico) will make Mexican goods relatively less expensive for Americans and U.S. goods relatively more expensive for Mexicans. As a result, the U.S. demand for Mexican goods will increase and the Mexican demand for U.S. goods will decrease.

As a result of the rising U.S. demand for Mexican goods, the demand for pesos rises, as shown in Exhibit 5. As a result of the falling Mexican demand for U.S.

> **EXHIBIT 4**

The Growth Rate of Income and the Exchange Rate

If U.S. residents experience a growth in income but Mexican residents do not, U.S. demand for Mexican goods will increase, and with it, the demand for pesos. As a result, the exchange rate will change: The dollar price of pesos will rise, meaning that the dollar depreciates and the peso appreciates.

goods, the demand for dollars decreases and therefore the supply of pesos decreases too. Exhibit 5 also shows the supply of, and the decline in, pesos. [Remember that the Mexican demand for U.S. goods is tied to the Mexican demand for U.S. dollars and, in turn, the Mexican demand for U.S. dollars is tied to the Mexican supply of pesos—see Exhibit 1(b).]

As Exhibit 5 shows, the result of an increase in the demand for Mexican pesos and a decrease in their supply constitutes an *appreciation* of the peso and a *depreciation* of the dollar. It now takes 11 cents, instead of 10 cents, to buy 1 peso (depreciation of the dollar); it now takes 9.09 pesos, instead of 10 pesos, to buy $1 (appreciation of the peso).

> **EXHIBIT 5**

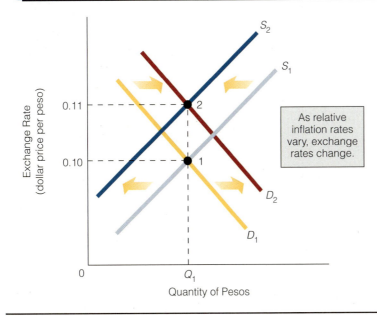

> As relative inflation rates vary, exchange rates change.

Inflation, Exchange Rates, and Purchasing Power Parity (PPP)

If the price level in the United States increases by 10 percent while the price level in Mexico remains constant, then Mexican goods become cheaper for Americans and U.S. goods become more expensive for Mexicans. So, the demand for pesos rises and the supply of pesos declines. As a result, the exchange rate will change: the dollar price of pesos will rise, meaning that the dollar depreciates and the peso appreciates. PPP theory predicts that the dollar will depreciate in the foreign exchange market until the original price (in pesos) of American goods to Mexican customers is restored. In this example, the dollar is required to depreciate 10 percent.

Purchasing Power Parity (PPP) Theory

Theory stating that exchange rates between any two currencies will adjust to reflect changes in the relative price levels of the two countries.

An important question is how much will the U.S. dollar depreciate as a result of the rise in the U.S. price level? (Mexico's price level does not change.) The **purchasing power parity (PPP) theory** predicts that the U.S. dollar will depreciate by 10 percent as a result of the 10 percent rise in the U.S. price level. This prediction requires the dollar price of a peso to rise to 11 cents (0.10 × 10 cents = 1 cent, 10 cents + 1 cent = 11 cents). A 10 percent depreciation of the dollar restores the *original relative prices of American goods to Mexican customers.*

To illustrate, consider a U.S. car with a price tag of $20,000. If the exchange rate is 0.10 USD = 1 MXN, a Mexican buyer of the car will pay 200,000 pesos. If the car price increases by 10 percent, to $22,000, and the dollar depreciates 10 percent (to 0.11 USD = 1 MXN), the Mexican buyer of the car will still pay only 200,000 pesos:

Exchange Rate	Dollar Price	Peso Price
0.10 USD = 1 MXN	20,000 USD	200,000 MXN [(20,000 ÷ 0.10) MXN]
0.11 USD = 1 MXN	22,000 USD	200,000 MXN [(22,000 ÷ 0.11) MXN]

In short, the PPP theory predicts that *changes in the relative price levels of two countries will affect the exchange rate in such a way that 1 unit of a country's currency will continue to buy the same amount of foreign goods as it did before the change in the relative price levels.* In our example, the higher U.S. inflation rate causes a change in the equilibrium exchange rate and leads to a depreciated dollar, but 1 peso continues to have the same purchasing power it previously did.

The PPP theory of exchange rates has made some accurate predictions and some not-so-accurate ones. Many economists suggest that the theory's predictions are not always accurate because the demand for, and the supply of, a currency are affected *by more than the difference in inflation rates between countries.* For example, as noted, different income growth rates affect the demand for a currency and therefore the exchange rate. In the *long run,* however, and particularly when the *difference in inflation rates across countries is large,* the PPP theory does predict exchange rates accurately.

Changes in Real Interest Rates   More than goods flow between countries. Financial capital also moves between countries. The flow of financial capital depends on different countries' *real interest rates*—interest rates adjusted for inflation.

To illustrate, suppose that the real interest rate is 3 percent in both the United States and Mexico. Suppose further that the real interest rate in the United States then increases to 4.5 percent. As a result, Mexicans will want to purchase financial assets in the United States that pay a higher real interest rate than do financial assets in Mexico. The Mexican demand for dollars will increase, and therefore Mexicans will supply more pesos. As the supply of pesos increases on the foreign exchange market, the exchange rate (the dollar price per peso) will change: fewer dollars will be needed to buy pesos. In short, the dollar will appreciate and the peso will depreciate.

In the President Speaking to an Economic Advisor The president of the United States is speaking to an economic advisor. The president asks, "What are the effects of the rather large budget deficits?" In response, the advisor might say that large budget deficits can affect interest rates, the value of the dollar, exports and imports, and the trade balance. "How so?" the president asks. Big deficits, the advisor answers, mean that the federal government will have to borrow funds, and the borrowing will increase the demand for credit, in turn pushing up the interest rate. Then, as the U.S. interest rate rises relative to interest rates in other countries, foreigners will want to purchase financial assets in the United States that pay a higher return. This desire will increase the demand for dollars, the dollar will appreciate, and foreign currencies will depreciate, in turn affecting both import and export spending.

FINDING

ECONOMICS

ECONOMICS 24/7

The U.S. Dollar as the Primary Reserve Currency

Today, the U.S. dollar is the primary (i.e., the main) reserve currency. A *reserve currency* is a currency that central banks and major financial institutions hold in significant quantities as part of their foreign exchange reserves. For example, in 2011 the U.S. dollar accounted for 60 percent of foreign exchange

reserves held by central banks, whereas the euro accounted for 26 percent. Also, major products bought and sold in the world market are usually denominated in the primary reserve currency. In other words, the U.S. dollar serves as the so-called unit of account of major global products. For this reason, and because governments and major financial institutions are willing to hold U.S. dollars, the demand for dollars on foreign exchange markets is higher than it would be if dollars weren't the major global reserve currency.

So, what would happen to the value of the U.S. dollar on foreign exchange markets if it were no longer the primary reserve currency? Obviously, the demand for dollars would decline, and subsequently, so would the exchange rate value of the dollar.

One of the advantages to a country whose currency is the primary reserve currency is that it can borrow at lower interest rates than other countries can. For example, in August 2011 China held approximately $2 trillion of its $3.2 trillion in foreign exchange reserves in dollars. Most of these dollar holdings were in the form

of U.S. government bonds. (In fact, the U.S. dollars that foreign central banks keep in reserve are mostly in the form of U.S. government bonds.) In effect, because of the dollar's primary reserve currency status, China was more willing (than it would have been had the dollar not been the primary reserve currency) to buy dollar-denominated U.S. government bonds. But, of course, heightened demand for U.S. government bonds means that the U.S. government can fetch a higher price when selling those bonds and therefore pay a lower interest rate on them.[1]

Will the U.S. dollar remain as the primary reserve currency over the next decade? Economists debate this question. Some argue that the dollar will likely remain the primary reserve currency. Others think that either the euro or renminbi (the official currency of the People's Republic of China) will displace it.

---

[1] To see that the price of bonds and the interest rate on the bond are inversely related, take a bond with the face value of $10,000 that is sold for $9,000 and matures in one year. The interest rate on this bond is found by solving for i in the following equation: $\$9,000 = \$10,000/(1 + i)^1$. Solving gives us an interest rate of 11.11 percent. Now, if the price of the bond had been higher, say, $9,500, we would change the price of the bond in the earlier equation accordingly and again solve for i. The result would be an interest rate of 5.2 percent. In other words, the price of the bond and the interest rate are inversely related: As the price of the bond rises, the interest rate declines.

SELF-TEST

(Answers to Self-Test questions are in Answers to Self-Test Questions at the back of the book.)

1. In the foreign exchange market, how is the demand for dollars linked to the supply of pesos?

2. What could cause the U.S. dollar to appreciate against the Mexican peso on the foreign exchange market?

3. Suppose that the U.S. economy grows and that the Swiss economy does not. How will this difference affect the exchange rate between the dollar and the Swiss franc? Why?

4. What does the purchasing power parity theory say? Give an example to illustrate your answer.

Fixed Exchange Rate System

A system whereby a nation's currency is set at a fixed rate relative to all other currencies and central banks intervene in the foreign exchange market to maintain the fixed rate.

23-3 FIXED EXCHANGE RATES

The major alternative to the flexible exchange rate system is the **fixed exchange rate system**, which works the way it sounds: Exchange rates are fixed; they are not allowed to fluctuate freely in response to the forces of supply and demand. Central banks buy and sell currencies to maintain agreed-on exchange rates. The workings of the fixed exchange rate system are described in this section.

23-3a **Fixed Exchange Rates and Overvalued or Undervalued Currency**

Once again, we assume a two-country–two-currency world, but this time the United States and Mexico agree to fix the exchange rate of their currencies: Instead of letting the dollar depreciate or appreciate relative to the peso, the two countries agree to set the price of 1 peso at $0.12; that is, they agree to the exchange rate of 0.12 USD = 1 MXN. Generally, we call this the fixed exchange rate, or the *official price*, of a peso.[2] Because we will include more than one official price in our discussion, 0.12 USD = 1 MXN is official price 1 (Exhibit 6).

Overvalued

A currency is overvalued if its price in terms of other currencies is above the equilibrium price.

If the dollar price of pesos is above its equilibrium level (as it is at official price 1), then a surplus of pesos exists and the peso is said to be **overvalued**. In other words, the peso is

> **EXHIBIT 6**

A Fixed Exchange Rate System

In a fixed exchange rate system, the exchange rate is fixed, and it may not be fixed at the equilibrium exchange rate. The exhibit shows two cases: (1) If the exchange rate is fixed at official price 1, the peso is overvalued, the dollar is under-valued, and a surplus of pesos exists. (2) If the exchange rate is fixed at official price 2, the peso is under-valued, the dollar is overvalued, and a shortage of pesos exists.

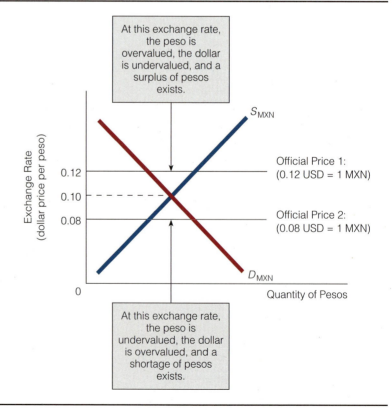

ECONOMICS 24/7

Chinese Imports and the U.S. Economy

Almost all countries occasionally intervene in foreign exchange markets to maintain the value of their currency vis-à-vis other countries. However, some countries do this more than others. China is one country that has intervened to a large extent.

China wants to promote its exported goods; that is, it wants the goods produced in China to be bought widely throughout the world. One way to promote its exported goods is to keep their prices low. And one way to keep the prices low is to deliberately undervalue its currency, the renminbi. (The renminbi is the official Chinese currency, but the yuan is the main unit of account of the renminbi. Thus, a person would not say, e.g., "You owe me seven renminbi," but rather, "You owe me seven yuan.")

At the time of this writing, $1 traded for 6.38 yuan. Accordingly, if a Chinese good was priced at, say, 100 yuan, a person would have to pay $15.67 for the good (100 yuan ÷ $6.38 = $15.67). When the dollar was trading for 6.38 yuan, many economists argued that China was manipulating the yuan's value—that is, deliberately taking actions to keep its currency undervalued. Without such actions, the free-market exchange rate would have been about $1 = 4 yuan. Of course, at the free-market exchange rate, the Chinese good priced at 100 yuan would have cost an American (who uses dollars) $25 instead of $15.57. The higher dollar price for the Chinese-produced goods would have caused Americans to buy fewer of them.

So, as the argument goes, by manipulating the value of its currency, China is helping its producers sell their goods around the world. At the same time, it is hindering its competitors, such as the U.S. producers who produce and sell goods in the domestic market.

On October 12, 2011, the U.S. Senate reacted to China's deliberately undervaluing its currency. It passed a bill authorizing the Commerce Department to impose tariffs on Chinese imports that were deemed to have benefited from the undervalued Chinese currency.

©saiko3p/Shutterstock.com

The bill did not pass in the House of Representatives, so it did not become law. Nevertheless, the Senate action spotlighted a public issue that had been brewing for some time: the effects of imports from China on the U.S. economy. As seen in our earlier example, the undervalued Chinese currency could harm U.S. companies selling goods in the United States that competed with imported goods from China, as well as indirectly adversely affecting the workers in those companies. But, of course, U.S. consumers would certainly benefit from the cheaper Chinese imports.

With both the benefits and costs of imports from China in mind, consider the research undertaken by two sets of economists. One group—David Autor, David Dorn, and Gordon Hanson—looked at the effect of Chinese import competition on regional employment and wages. For the period 1990–2007, they found that every $1,000 of additional exposure per worker to imported products from China was associated with a lowering of the U.S. employment rate by 0.77 percent. They also found that U.S. regions that faced more competition from Chinese imports had higher unemployment rates and lower wages. Note that this is not necessarily to say that Chinese imports are, on net, costly for the United States.

Another group of economists—Nicholas Bloom, Mirko Draca, and John Van Reenen—found that imports from China were associated with not only a lower price of goods for consumers, but also a lower cost of inputs for domestic firms, an increase in the variety of products those firms sold, and perhaps also a rise in U.S. productivity. These economists found that every 10 percent rise in Chinese imports was associated with increases of 3.2 percent in patent filings, of 3.6 percent in spending on information technology, and of 12 percent in carrying out research and development. And, according to the economists, 15 percent of the technical change in Europe during the period 2000–2007 was due to competition from imported products from China.

fetching more dollars than it would at equilibrium. For example, if 1 peso trades for $0.10 at equilibrium, but 1 peso trades for $0.12 at the official exchange rate, then the peso is said to be overvalued.

If the peso is overvalued, then the dollar is undervalued; that is, it is fetching fewer pesos than it would at equilibrium. For example, if $1 trades for 10 pesos at equilibrium, but $1 trades for 8.33 pesos at the official exchange rate, then the dollar is undervalued.

Similarly, if the dollar price of pesos is below its equilibrium level (as it is at official price 2 in Exhibit 6), then a shortage of pesos exists and the peso is **undervalued**; that is, the peso is not fetching as many dollars as it would at equilibrium. If the peso is undervalued, then the dollar must be overvalued. In sum,

Undervalued

A currency is undervalued if its price in terms of other currencies is below the equilibrium price.

$$\text{Overvalued peso} \leftrightarrow \text{Undervalued dollar}$$

$$\text{Undervalued peso} \leftrightarrow \text{Overvalued dollar}$$

23-3b What Is So Bad about an Overvalued Dollar?

You read in the newspaper that the dollar is overvalued and that economists are concerned about the overvalued dollar. They are concerned because the exchange rate, and hence the value of the dollar in terms of other currencies, affects the amount of U.S. exports and imports.

To illustrate, suppose the demand for pesos and the supply of pesos are represented by D_1 and S_1, respectively, in Exhibit 7. With this demand curve and supply curve, the equilibrium exchange rate is 0.10 USD = 1 MXN. Let's also suppose that the exchange rate is fixed at this equilibrium exchange rate. In other words, the equilibrium exchange rate and the fixed exchange rate are initially the same.

Now, time passes, and eventually the demand curve for pesos shifts to the right, from D_1 to D_2. Under a flexible exchange rate system, the exchange rate would rise to 0.12 USD = 1 MXN. But a fixed exchange rate is in effect, not a flexible one, so the exchange rate stays at 0.10 USD = 1 MXN. Thus, the fixed exchange rate (0.10 USD = 1 MXN) is below the new equilibrium exchange rate (0.12 USD = 1 MXN).

Recall that, when the dollar price per peso is below its equilibrium level (as it is now), the peso is undervalued and the dollar is overvalued. To illustrate, at equilibrium (point 2 in Exhibit 7), 1 peso would trade for 0.12 dollars, but at its fixed rate (point 1), it trades for only 0.10 dollars, so the peso is undervalued. At equilibrium (point 2), $1 would trade for 8.33 pesos, but at its fixed rate (point 1), it trades for 10 pesos, so the dollar is overvalued.

What is bad about an overvalued dollar is that it makes U.S. goods more expensive for foreigners to buy, possibly affecting U.S. exports. For example,

> **EXHIBIT 7**

Fixed Exchange Rates and an Overvalued Dollar

Initially, the demand for, and supply of, pesos are represented by D_1 and S_1, respectively. The equilibrium exchange rate is 0.10 USD = 1 MXN, which also happens to be the official (fixed) exchange rate. In time, the demand for pesos rises to D_2, and the equilibrium exchange rate rises to 0.12 USD = 1 MXN. The official exchange rate is fixed, however, so the dollar will be overvalued.

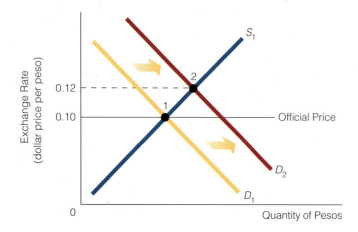

suppose a U.S. good costs $100. At the equilibrium exchange rate (0.12 USD = 1 MXN), a Mexican would pay 833 pesos for the good, but at the fixed exchange rate (0.10 USD = 1 MXN), he will pay 1,000 pesos:

Exchange Rate	Dollar Price	Peso Price
0.12 USD = 1 MXN (equilibrium)	100 USD	833 MXN [(100 ÷ 0.12) MXN]
0.10 USD = 1 MXN (fixed)	100 USD	1,000 MXN [(100 ÷ 0.10) MXN]

The higher the prices are of U.S. goods (exports), the fewer of those goods Mexicans will buy, and, as just discussed, an overvalued dollar makes U.S. export goods higher in price.

23-3c Government Involvement in a Fixed Exchange Rate System

Suppose the governments of Mexico and the United States agree to fix the exchange rate at 0.12 USD = 1 MXN, as shown in Exhibit 6. At this exchange rate, a surplus of pesos exists. To maintain the exchange rate at 0.12 USD = 1 MXN, the Federal Reserve System (the Fed) could buy the surplus of pesos with dollars. As a result, the demand for pesos will increase and the demand curve will shift to the right, ideally by enough to raise the equilibrium rate to the current fixed exchange rate.

Alternatively, instead of the Fed's buying pesos (to "mop up" the excess supply of pesos), the Banco de México (the central bank of Mexico) could buy pesos with some of its reserve dollars. (It doesn't buy pesos with pesos, because using pesos would not reduce the surplus of pesos on the market.) This action by the Banco de México will also increase the demand for pesos and raise the equilibrium rate.

Finally, the two actions could be combined; that is, both the Fed and the Banco de México could buy pesos.

23-3d Options Under a Fixed Exchange Rate System

Suppose there is a surplus of pesos in the foreign exchange market, indicating that the peso is overvalued and the dollar is undervalued. Suppose also that, although the Fed and the Banco de México each attempt to rectify this situation by buying pesos, their combined action is not successful: The surplus of pesos persists for weeks, along with an overvalued peso and an undervalued dollar. Then, a few options are still available.

Devaluation and Revaluation Mexico and the United States could agree to reset the official price of the dollar and the peso. Doing so entails *devaluation* and *revaluation*. A **devaluation** occurs when the official price of a currency is lowered. A **revaluation** occurs when the official price of a currency is raised.

For example, suppose the first official price of a peso is 0.10 USD = 1 MXN, or 1 USD = 10 MXN. Then, Mexico and the United States agree to change the official price of their currencies. The second official price is 0.12 USD = 1 MXN, or 1 USD = 8.33 MXN.

Moving from the first official price to the second means that the peso has been revalued, because it takes *more dollars to buy a peso* (12 cents instead of 10 cents). Of course, moving from the first official price to the second also means that the dollar has been devalued, because it takes *fewer pesos to buy a dollar* (8.33 pesos instead of 10 pesos).

One country might want to devalue its currency, but another country might not want to revalue its currency. For example, if Mexico wants to devalue its currency relative to the

Devaluation
A government action that changes the exchange rate by lowering the official price of a currency.

Revaluation
A government act that changes the exchange rate by raising the official price of a currency.

U.S. dollar, U.S. authorities might not always willingly comply, because, if they do, the United States will not sell as many goods to Mexico. As explained earlier, revaluing the dollar means that Mexicans have to pay more for it; instead of paying, say, 8.33 pesos for $1, Mexicans might have to pay 10 pesos. At a revalued dollar (a higher peso price for a dollar), Mexicans will find U.S. goods more expensive and not want to buy as many. Americans who produce goods to sell to Mexico may see that a revalued dollar will hurt their pocketbooks, so they will argue against it.

Protectionist Trade Policy (Quotas and Tariffs)

To deal with, say, an overvalued dollar (and, say, an undervalued Chinese renminbi), the United States can impose quotas and tariffs on Chinese goods in order to reduce U.S. consumption of them. (An earlier chapter explains how both tariffs and quotas meet this objective.) A drop in U.S. consumption of Chinese goods goes hand in hand with a decrease in the demand for the Chinese renminbi. In turn, a decline in the demand for the Chinese renminbi can affect the value of the U.S. dollar. In this case, it can eliminate an overvalued dollar.

Economists are quick to point out, though, that overvalued currencies are sometimes used as an excuse to promote trade restrictions, many of which simply benefit special interests (e.g., U.S. producers that compete for sales with foreign producers in the U.S. market).

Changes in Monetary Policy

Sometimes, a country can use monetary policy to support the exchange rate or the official price of its currency. Suppose the United States is continually importing more than it exports. To remedy this imbalance, the United States might enact a tight monetary policy to retard inflation and drive up interest rates (at least in the short run). The tight monetary policy will reduce the U.S. rate of inflation and thereby lower U.S. prices relative to prices in other nations. This effect will make U.S. goods relatively cheaper than they were before (assuming that other nations don't also enact a tight monetary policy), thereby promoting U.S. exports and discouraging foreign imports. It will also generate a flow of investment funds into the United States in search of higher real interest rates.

Some economists argue against fixed exchange rates because they think it unwise for a nation to adopt a particular monetary policy simply to maintain an international exchange rate. Instead, they believe that domestic monetary policies should be used to meet domestic economic goals, such as price stability, low unemployment, low and stable interest rates, and so forth.

SELF-TEST

1. Under a fixed exchange rate system, if one currency is overvalued, then another currency must be undervalued. Explain why this statement is true.

2. How does an overvalued dollar affect U.S. exports and imports?

3. In each of the following cases, identify whether the U.S. dollar is overvalued or undervalued:

   a. The fixed exchange rate is $2 = £1, and the equilibrium exchange rate is $3 = £1.

   b. The fixed exchange rate is $1.25 = €1, and the equilibrium exchange rate is $1.10 = €1.

   c. The fixed exchange rate is $1 = 10 pesos, and the equilibrium exchange rate is $1 = 14 pesos.

4. Under a fixed exchange rate system, why might the United States want to devalue its currency?

23-4 FIXED EXCHANGE RATES VERSUS FLEXIBLE EXCHANGE RATES

As in many economic situations, any exchange rate system has both its costs and its benefits. This section discusses some of the arguments and issues surrounding fixed exchange rates and flexible exchange rates.

23-4a Promoting International Trade

Which are better at promoting international trade, fixed or flexible exchange rates? This section presents the case for each.

The Case for Fixed Exchange Rates   Proponents of a fixed exchange rate system often argue that fixed exchange rates promote international trade whereas flexible exchange rates stifle it. A major advantage of fixed exchange rates is certainty. Individuals in different countries know from day to day the value of their nation's currency. With flexible exchange rates, individuals are less likely to engage in international trade because of the added risk of not knowing from one day to the next how many dollars, euros, or yen they will have to trade for other currencies. Certainty is a necessary ingredient in international trade; flexible exchange rates promote uncertainty, which hampers international trade.

Economist Charles Kindleberger, a proponent of fixed exchange rates, stated that having fixed exchange rates is analogous to having a single currency for the entire United States instead of having a different currency for each of the 50 states. One currency in the United States promotes trade, whereas 50 different currencies would hamper it. In Kindleberger's view,

> *The main case against flexible exchange rates is that they break up the world market. . . . Imagine trying to conduct interstate trade in the USA if there were fifty different state monies, none of which was dominant. This is akin to barter, the inefficiency of which is explained time and again by textbooks.[3]*

The Case for Flexible Exchange Rates   As noted, advocates of flexible exchange rates, maintain that it is better for a nation to adopt policies to meet domestic economic goals than to sacrifice domestic economic goals in order to maintain an exchange rate. Also, the chance is too great that the fixed exchange rate will diverge greatly from the equilibrium exchange rate, creating persistent trade problems for some countries (with import spending continually greater than export spending) and thus leading them to impose trade restrictions (tariffs and quotas) that hinder international trade.

The Current System   Today's international monetary system is described as a managed flexible exchange rate system, sometimes referred to more casually as a **managed float**. In a way, this system is a rough compromise between the fixed and flexible exchange rate systems. The current system operates under flexible exchange rates, but not completely: Now and then, nations intervene to adjust their official reserve holdings to moderate major swings in exchange rates.

23-4b Optimal Currency Areas

An **optimal currency area** is a geographic area in which exchange rates can be fixed or a *common currency* used without sacrificing domestic economic goals, such as low

Managed Float
A managed flexible exchange rate system under which nations intervene now and then to adjust their official reserve holdings in order to moderate major swings in exchange rates.

Optimal Currency Area
A geographic area in which exchange rates can be fixed or a common currency used without sacrificing domestic economic goals, such as low unemployment.

---

[3] Charles Kindleberger, *International Money* (London: Allen and Unwin, 1981), p. 174.

unemployment. The concept of an optimal currency area originated in the debate over whether fixed or flexible exchange rates are better. Most of the pioneering work on optimal currency areas was done by Robert Mundell, winner of the 1999 Nobel Prize in Economics.

Before discussing an optimal currency area, we need to look at the relationships among labor mobility, trade, and exchange rates. *Labor mobility* means that the residents of one country can move easily to another country.

Trade and Labor Mobility   Suppose there are only two countries: the United States and Canada. The United States produces calculators and soft drinks, and Canada produces bread and muffins. Currently, the two countries trade with each other, and there is complete labor mobility between them.

One day, the residents of both countries reduce their demand for bread and muffins and increase their demand for calculators and soft drinks. In other words, relative demand changes: Demand increases for U.S. goods and falls for Canadian goods. Business firms in Canada lay off employees because their sales have plummeted. Incomes in Canada begin to fall, and the unemployment rate begins to rise. In the United States, prices initially rise because of the increased demand for calculators and soft drinks. In response to the higher demand for their products, U.S. business firms begin to hire more workers and increase their production. Their efforts to hire more workers drive wages up and reduce the unemployment rate.

Because labor is mobile, some of the newly unemployed Canadian workers move to the United States to find work, easing the economic situation in both countries. The movement of labor will reduce some of the unemployment problems in Canada, and, with more workers in the United States, more output will be produced, thus dampening upward price pressures on calculators and soft drinks. Clearly, then, changes in relative demand pose no major economic problems for either country if labor is mobile.

Trade and Labor Immobility   Now let's suppose that relative demand has changed but that labor is *not* mobile between the United States and Canada, perhaps because of political or cultural barriers. If people cannot move, then what happens in the economies of the two countries depends largely on whether exchange rates are fixed or flexible.

If exchange rates are flexible, the value of the U.S. currency will change vis-à-vis the Canadian currency. If Canadians want to buy more U.S. goods, they will have to exchange their domestic currency for U.S. currency. Now, the demand for U.S. currency on the foreign exchange market will increase at the same time that the supply of Canadian currency increases. Consequently, U.S. currency will appreciate, and Canadian currency will depreciate. Then, because Canadian currency depreciates, U.S. goods become relatively more expensive for Canadians, so they buy fewer of them. And because U.S. currency appreciates, Canadian goods become relatively cheaper for Americans, so they buy more Canadian goods. As a result, Canadian business firms begin to sell more goods, so they hire more workers, the unemployment rate drops, and the bad economic times in Canada begin to disappear.

If exchange rates are fixed, however, U.S. goods will not become relatively more expensive for Canadians and Canadian goods will not become relatively cheaper for Americans. Consequently, the bad economic times in Canada (high unemployment) might last for a long time, indeed, instead of beginning to reverse. Thus, if labor is immobile, changes in relative demand may pose major economic problems when exchange rates are fixed but not when they are flexible.

Costs, Benefits, and Optimal Currency Areas

In addition to benefits, flexible exchange rates have costs. Exchanging one currency for another (say, U.S. dollars for Canadian dollars or U.S. dollars for Japanese yen) incurs a charge, and the risk is greater of not knowing what the value of one's currency will be on the foreign exchange market on any given day. For many countries, the benefits outweigh the costs, so they have flexible exchange rate systems.

Now, suppose some of the costs of flexible exchange rates could be eliminated while maintaining the benefits. Then, if labor is mobile between the two countries, they could have a fixed exchange rate or adopt a common currency and retain the benefits of flexible exchange rates. In that case, they do not have to have separate currencies that float against each other because resources (labor) can move easily and quickly in response to changes in relative demand. The two countries can either fix exchange rates or adopt the same currency.

When labor in countries within a geographic area is mobile enough to move easily and quickly in response to changes in relative demand, the countries are said to constitute an *optimal currency area*. Countries in such an area can either fix their currencies or adopt the same currency and thus keep all the benefits of flexible exchange rates without incurring any of the costs.

The states of the United States are commonly said to constitute an optimal currency area. Labor can move easily and quickly between, say, North Carolina and South Carolina in response to relative changes in demand. Some economists have argued that the countries that compose the European Union make up an optimal currency area and, therefore, adopting a common currency—the euro—benefits these countries. Other economists disagree. They argue that, although labor is somewhat more mobile in Europe today than in the past, certain language and cultural differences make labor mobility less than sufficient to constitute a true optimal currency area.

Office Hours

"Why Is the Depreciation of One Currency Tied to the Appreciation of Another?"

STUDENT:

I know that when the dollar depreciates, some other currency appreciates. Is this just the way it is? For example, if $1 dollar equals €1 euro, and then $1.25 equals €1, the arithmetic of exchange rates tells me that now $1 will fetch only €0.8. Is that all there is to it?

INSTRUCTOR:

Not exactly. You're focusing on the arithmetic of exchange rates to the exclusion of the economics. There is an economic reason that dollar appreciation is linked to euro appreciation.

STUDENT:

What is that economic reason?

INSTRUCTOR:

Think of what can lead to the dollar's depreciating. Suppose you want to travel to Germany, where the euro is used. You take your dollars and buy euros with them. In other words, you do two things: You (1) buy euros by (2) supplying dollars.

Now think of how you are affecting the market for euros and the market for dollars. You are increasing the demand for euros in the market for euros, and you are increasing the supply of dollars in the market for dollars. In other words, your demand for euros is linked to your supply of dollars. So, if you increase the demand for euros, you are automatically increasing the supply of dollars.

STUDENT:

I'm used to thinking that my buying something affects only one market. For instance, when I buy more books, the purchase affects only the market for books. You seem to be telling me that this is not the case when I buy a currency, such as the euro. To buy euros is to supply dollars.

INSTRUCTOR:

That's right. So when you increase the demand for euros, you automatically increase the supply of dollars. And then we have to ask ourselves what happens in each of the two markets: the market for euros and the market for dollars.

STUDENT:

Well, if I increase the demand for euros, the price of a euro in terms of dollars will rise. Also, if I increase the supply of dollars, the price of a dollar in terms of euros will fall.

INSTRUCTOR:

And what do you call it when the price of a euro has risen in terms of dollars?

STUDENT:

We say the dollar has depreciated, because it now takes more dollars and cents to buy a euro.

INSTRUCTOR:

And what do you call it when the price of a dollar has fallen in terms of euros?

STUDENT:

We say the euro has appreciated, because it now takes fewer euros to buy a dollar.

INSTRUCTOR:

So, let's go back to your original query. You wondered whether the dollar's depreciating and the euro's appreciating were just matters of arithmetic. Now we know that they aren't. They are a matter of curves shifting in different markets.

Points to remember

1. To buy a currency is to affect two markets, not just one. If you buy euros, you affect the euro market. But by selling dollars to buy euros, you also affect the dollar market.

2. The fact that, when one currency depreciates, another appreciates is a matter of curves shifting in two currency markets.

CHAPTER SUMMARY

THE FOREIGN EXCHANGE MARKET

- The market in which currencies of different countries are exchanged is called the foreign exchange market. In this market, currencies are bought and sold for a price: the exchange rate.

- When the residents of a nation demand a foreign currency, they must supply their own currency. For example, if Americans demand Mexican goods, they also demand Mexican pesos and supply U.S. dollars. If Mexicans demand American goods, they also demand U.S. dollars and supply Mexican pesos.

FLEXIBLE EXCHANGE RATES

- Under flexible exchange rates, the foreign exchange market will equilibrate at the exchange rate for which the quantity demanded of a currency equals the quantity supplied of the currency; for example, the foreign exchange market equilibrates when the quantity demanded of U.S. dollars equals the quantity supplied of U.S. dollars.

- If the price of a nation's currency increases relative to a foreign currency, the nation's currency is said to have appreciated. For example, if the price of a peso rises from 0.10 USD = 1 MXN to 0.15 USD = 1 MXN, then the peso has appreciated. If the price of a nation's currency decreases relative to a foreign currency, the nation's currency is said to have depreciated. For example, if the price of a dollar falls from 10 MXN = 1 USD to 8 MXN = 1 USD, then the dollar has depreciated.

- Under a flexible exchange rate system, the equilibrium exchange rate is affected by a difference in income growth rates between countries, a difference in inflation rates between countries, and a change in (real) interest rates between countries.

FIXED EXCHANGE RATES

- Under a fixed exchange rate system, countries agree to fix the price of their currencies. The central banks of the countries must then buy and sell currencies to maintain the exchange rate that was agreed on.

THE CURRENT INTERNATIONAL MONETARY SYSTEM

- Today's international monetary system is described as a managed flexible exchange rate system, or managed float. For the most part, the exchange rate system is flexible, although nations periodically intervene in the foreign exchange market in order to adjust rates. Because today's system is a managed float system, it is difficult to tell whether nations will emphasize the float part or the managed part in the future.

KEY TERMS AND CONCEPTS

Trade Balance	Exchange Rate	Purchasing Power Parity	Devaluation
Trade Surplus	Flexible Exchange Rate	(PPP) Theory	Revaluation
Trade Deficit	System	Fixed Exchange Rate System	Managed Float
Foreign Exchange	Appreciation	Overvalued	Optimal Currency Area
Market	Depreciation	Undervalued	

VIDEO QUESTIONS AND PROBLEMS

Video Questions and Problems are available on MindTap for Arnold 12e or by searching for Arnold on www.cengagebrain.com

1. On the foreign exchange market, the demand for one currency is closely connected to the supply of another. Do you agree or disagree? Explain.

2. Under a flexible exchange rate system, a difference in income growth rates between countries can affect the exchange rate. Do you agree or disagree? Explain.

3. Give a numerical example to explain the purchasing power parity (PPP) theory.

4. Diagrammatically represent an overvalued currency.

5. The advocates of flexible exchange rates often argue that it is better for a nation to adopt policies to meet domestic economic goals than to sacrifice domestic economic goals to maintain a fixed exchange rate. Explain.

QUESTIONS AND PROBLEMS

1. Explain the link between the Mexican demand for U.S. goods and the supply of pesos. Next, explain the link between the U.S. demand for Mexican goods and the supply of dollars.

2. The lower the dollar price of a peso, the higher is the quantity demanded of pesos and the lower is the quantity supplied of pesos. Do you agree or disagree? Explain.

3. What does it mean to say that the U.S. dollar has depreciated in value in relation to the Mexican peso? What does it mean to say that the Mexican peso has appreciated in value relative to the U.S. dollar?

4. Suppose the United States and Japan have a flexible exchange rate system. Explain whether each of the following events will lead to an appreciation or depreciation of the U.S. dollar and Japanese yen:

   a. U.S. real interest rates rise above Japanese real interest rates.

   b. The Japanese inflation rate rises relative to the U.S. inflation rate.

   c. An increase in U.S. income combines with no change in Japanese income.

5. Give an example of how a change in the exchange rate alters the relative price of domestic goods in terms of foreign goods.

6. What are the strong and weak points of the flexible exchange rate system? What are the strong and weak points of the fixed exchange rate system?

7. Explain the details of the purchasing power parity (PPP) theory.

8. A country whose currency is the primary reserve currency can likely borrow at lower interest rates than it could if its currency were not the primary reserve currency. Do you agree or disagree? Explain.

9. What does it mean to say that a currency is overvalued? undervalued?

10. Under a flexible exchange rate system, if the equilibrium exchange rate is 0.10 USD = 1 MXN and the current exchange rate is 0.12 = 1 MXN, will the U.S. dollar appreciate or depreciate? Explain.

11. Under a fixed exchange rate system, setting the official price of a peso in terms of dollars automatically sets the official price of a dollar in terms of pesos. Do you agree or disagree? Explain.

12. Country X wants to lower the value of its currency on the foreign exchange market. Under a flexible exchange rate system, how can it do that?

13. What is an optimal currency area?

14. Country 1 produces good X, and country 2 produces good Y. People in both countries begin to demand more of good X and less of good Y. Assume that there is no labor mobility between the two countries and that a flexible exchange rate system exists. What will happen to the unemployment rate in country 2? Explain.

15. How important is labor mobility in determining whether an area is an optimal currency area?

16. If everyone in the world spoke the same language, would the world be closer to or further from being an optimal currency area? Explain.

WORKING WITH NUMBERS AND GRAPHS

1. Use the following information to answer (a)–(c):

	U.S. Dollar Equivalent		Currency per U.S. Dollar	
	Thurs.	Fri.	Thurs.	Fri.
Russia (ruble)	0.0318	0.0317	31.4190	31.5290
Brazil (real)	0.3569	0.3623	2.8020	2.7601
India (rupee)	0.0204	0.0208	48.9100	47.8521

a. Between Thursday and Friday, did the U.S. dollar appreciate or depreciate against the Russian ruble?

b. Between Thursday and Friday, did the U.S. dollar appreciate or depreciate against the Brazilian real?

c. Between Thursday and Friday, did the U.S. dollar appreciate or depreciate against the Indian rupee?

2. If $1 equals ¥0.0093, what does ¥1 equal?

3. If $1 equals 7.7 krone (Danish), what does 1 krone equal?

4. If $1 equals 31 rubles, what does 1 ruble equal?

5. If the exchange rate is 0.08 = 1 MXN, what is the cost in dollars of a Mexican table priced at 500 pesos?

GLOBALIZATION AND INTERNATIONAL IMPACTS ON THE ECONOMY

Reto Stockli/Nasa Images

INTRODUCTION

In the world in which we live, we hear much of *globalization*. In this chapter, we discuss what globalization is, the causes of globalization, its costs and benefits, and its future. We then return to a framework of analysis we first used in the macroeconomics part of this text—aggregate demand and aggregate supply—and we use that framework to discuss some of the effects of globalization on a nation's economy.

24-1 WHAT IS GLOBALIZATION?

Economists usually define **globalization** in one of two ways:

1. A phenomenon by which individuals and businesses in any part of the world are much more affected by events elsewhere in the world than they had been before.

2. The growing integration of the national economies of the world to the degree that we may be witnessing the emergence and operation of a single worldwide economy.

These factors—people and businesses across the world having a greater impact on each other, in effect creating a smaller world; and the movement toward a worldwide economy—are repeated in the many different definitions of globalization put forth by economists. Let's take a closer look at those key features.

24-1a A Smaller World

The first definition emphasizes that economic agents in any given part of the world are affected by events elsewhere in the world. If you live in the United States, you are affected not only by what happens in the United States but also by what happens in Brazil, Russia, and China. For example, in recent years, the Chinese government was using much of the money

Globalization
A phenomenon by which economic agents in any given part of the world are more affected by events elsewhere in the world than they were before; the growing integration of the national economies of the world to the degree that we may be witnessing the emergence and operation of a single worldwide economy.

it earned in trade with the United States to buy bonds issued by the U.S. government. As a result of these Chinese purchases, interest rates in the United States ended up being lower than they would have been. Because of lowered interest rates, some people were able to take out mortgage loans to buy houses that they would not be eligible for otherwise. Some people took out car loans to buy cars that they otherwise would not have been able to buy.

So, in a sense, globalization makes the world smaller. China has not moved physically; it is no closer to the United States (in terms of distance) than it was 100 years ago. Still, because of globalization, what happens in distant China today has an effect on you, just as, in the past, what happened in locations only 10 miles or 100 miles away would affect you. For all practical purposes, we live in a smaller world today than people did 100 years ago.

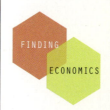

In a Clothing Store Brandon is at a clothing store buying a number of items: shirts, sweaters, trousers, etc. He doesn't check to see in which country each of these items was produced. Instead, he just checks out the item and its price, and he decides whether to buy it. Where is the economics?

Many of the items Brandon buys were very likely produced in other countries. To Brandon, buying an item of clothing produced in China, Brazil, or India is really no different from buying an item of clothing produced in a factory 10 miles away. For Brandon, China, Brazil, or India might as well be down the street. In some ways, the world Brandon lives in is a small world, one in which distance doesn't matter as much as it used to; it is a world in which trades between people living in different countries are becoming increasingly common.

24-1b A World Economy

Globalization is closely aligned with a movement toward more free enterprise, freer markets, and more freedom of movement for people and goods. Economic globalization is essentially a free-enterprise activity, and, to the degree that many countries are globalizing, they are moving toward greater free-enterprise practices.

With globalization, the world is moving from hundreds of national economies toward *one large world economy.* In this world economy, speaking about *different* economic systems does not make as much sense as it once did. Speaking about *the* economic system for that one world economy does make sense. And, as explained, the economic system that comes closest to describing what is happening in the world economy is free enterprise, or capitalism.

In *The Economist* "Mr. Bhattacharjee is not the first leader to preach socialism while practising capitalism." Mr. Bhattacharjee is the chief minister of the Indian state of West Bengal. The statement about him was made in *The Economist* (a news magazine that covers economic issues in particular) in November 2007. Where is the economics?

The statement gives us a glimpse into what is happening in the world today with respect to the adoption of economic systems—specifically, the movement toward capitalism.

ECONOMICS 24/7

Should You Leave a Tip?

In the United States, tipping in restaurants is common, amounting to $16 billion a year. Yet 24 percent of the individuals in one study said that they thought tipping was unfair to customers. In the past, some states prohibited tipping. For example, in the early 1900s, Arkansas, Mississippi, Iowa, South Carolina, Tennessee, and Washington passed laws prohibiting tipping.

Of all the people in the rest of the world, some have the same tipping practices as Americans, but some do not. For example, adding an automatic service charge to a bill is becoming increasingly customary in European restaurants in lieu of tipping the server. Also, more tipping goes on in Mexico and Egypt than in the United States; much less tipping occurs (i.e., fewer service providers expect tips) in Australia, New Zealand, and Italy than in the United States; and little tipping of any sort goes on in Argentina and Vietnam.

In several studies, researchers looked at the number of different types of service providers (out of a total of 33) to whom it is customary to give a tip in a given country. The more types of service providers whom it was customary to tip in a country, the higher was the country's so-called prevalence of tipping. For

Chris Cheadle/Getty Images

example, if it was customary to tip 31 different types of service providers in country A but only 15 in country B, then country A would have a higher prevalence of tipping than country B.

The conclusion reached by these studies is that countries in which success and materialism were highly valued had a higher prevalence of tipping than countries in which caring and personal relationships were highly valued. In addition, the prevalence of tipping increased as the national need for achievement and recognition rose. In one study, tipping was found to be more prevalent in countries with lower taxes than in countries with higher taxes.

So, if globalization advances, will tipping practices around the world become more uniform? And if they do, toward what degree of tipping will they gravitate?

24-2 TWO WAYS TO SEE GLOBALIZATION

Sometimes, a definition is not as good a description or explanation as a picture. Let's create two mental pictures that should give you a good idea of what globalization is about. The first picture is of a world without any barriers to trade, a world in which the cost of dealing with anyone in the world is essentially the same.

24-2a **No Barriers**

Suppose land were not divided into nation states—no United States, no China, no Russia. Suppose also that physical, economic, or political barriers to trade did not exist. Essentially, then, you could trade with anyone, no matter where in the world that person lived. You could trade with a person living 5,000 miles away as easily as you could trade with your next-door neighbor.

In this pretend world, businesses could hire workers and set up factories anywhere. People could open savings accounts in banks 7,000 miles away or buy stock in companies located on the other side of the globe.

In a sense, our world—the world that we live in today—is moving in this direction. As it does, a nation's economy (e.g., the U.S. economy) becomes more and more a part of the world economy. Consequently, speaking about a world or global economy, rather than about the Russian, U.S., or Chinese economy, becomes increasingly relevant.

24-2b **A Union of States**

The second picture of globalization is familiar to people who reside in the United States, made up as it is of 50 states. Today, moving goods and services among these states is easy. A person can produce goods in, say, North Carolina and then transport them (with only a few exceptions) for sale to every state in the country. In addition, a person living anywhere in the United States can move to any state and work, save, purchase, sell, and so on. In other words, within the United States, the free movement of people and goods is possible.

Some people argue that economic globalization is, in a way, similar to changing countries of the world into states of one country. They say that globalization makes independent countries, such as the United States, Russia, China, Brazil, and Japan, into the "United States of the World."

24-3 GLOBALIZATION FACTS

You know that globalization is occurring when you see certain things happening in the world:

- Countries in the world opening up to more trade with each other
- People in one country investing some of their money in other countries
- Companies in one country hiring people in other countries

Some evidence suggests that all these things are happening.

24-3a **International Trade**

Tariff
A tax on imports.

The average **tariff** rate in the United States was 40 percent in 1946. The average in 2012 was 1.8 percent. Also, the federal government's revenue from tariffs in the early 1900s accounted for nearly half of all its revenues, whereas today tariffs account for less than 2 percent. Exhibit 1 presents average tariff rates in the United States during the period 1930–2013.

The decline in tariff rates in the United States mirrors similar declines in countries such as India, China, Brazil, and many others. For example, in 2000, the average tariff rate in China was 18.7 percent; one year later, it was 12.8 percent. In 2000, the average

> **EXHIBIT 1**

Average U.S. Tariff Rates, 1930–2013

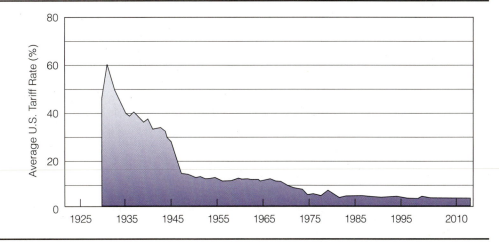

tariff rate in India was 30.2 percent; one year later, it was 21 percent. Furthermore, both India and China are trading more with other countries. For example, 15 years ago, China did not trade much with the countries of Europe. Today, most European countries claim China as one of the top five trading partners.

24-3b Globalization Indexes

ETZ Zurich is an engineering, science, technology, mathematics, and management university in Zurich, Switzerland. ETZ Zurich is consistently ranked among the top universities in the world. Within ETZ Zurich is the KOF Swiss Economic Institute, which annually constructs various indexes of globalization. One of the things that the indexes indicate is the degree of globalization.

The index of (overall) globalization for the world [see Exhibit 2(a)] shows that globalization has been on an upward trend. In other words, there was a greater degree of globalization in, say, 2011 than 1985.

> **EXHIBIT 2**

Indexes of Globalization

Here we show four different indexes of globalization. Index numbers range from 1 to 100. The higher the number, the greater is the degree of globalization. What the various globalization indexes show is that the trend has been toward more globalization over time instead of less.

Source: KOF Swiss Economic Institute.

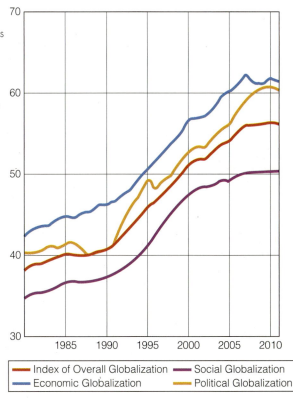

> **EXHIBIT 3**

Trade as a Percentage of GDP, 1960–2010

Here we show world trade as a percentage of world GDP and U.S. trade as a percentage of U.S. GDP.

Source: The World Bank.

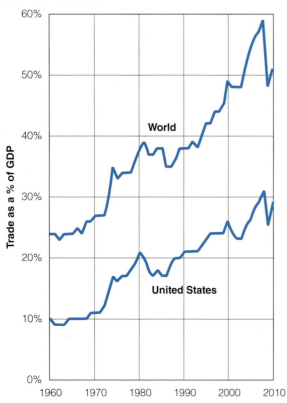

The (overall) index of globalization is made up of three globalization subindexes: the index of economic globalization [Exhibit 2], the index of social globalization [Exhibit 2], and the index of political globalization [Exhibit 2]. All of these indexes show an upward trend during the period 1985–2011.

Two of the seven variables used to construct the economic globalization index are trade (the sum of exports and imports of goods and services) as a percentage of GDP, and tariff rates (the higher the tariff rate, the lower the degree of economic globalization). Two of the eight variables used to construct the social globalization index are Internet users (per 1,000 persons) and share of households with a television set. One of the four variables used in the political globalization index is the number of embassies in a country. Of all the variables used to construct the overall globalization index, the variable most heavily weighted is trade as a percentage of GDP. We show this variable for both the world and the United States in Exhibit 3 for the period 1960–2010. Generally, trade as a percentage of GDP has been rising, although there are some years in which it has decreased (e.g., 2008–2009).

What do the various globalization indexes tell us about globalization in the world? They tell us that the trend is toward more globalization. Which countries exhibit the highest degree of economic globalization today? Exhibit 4 shows the top 25 countries in 2014; the United States was ranked 32nd.

> **EXHIBIT 4**

Top 25 Economically Globalized Countries, 2014

1. Ireland	10. Finland	19. Australia
2. Belgium	11. Switzerland	20. Norway
3. Netherlands	12. Canada	21. France
4. Austria	13. Cyprus	22. Italy
5. Singapore	14. Spain	23. Greece
6. Denmark	15. Luxembourg	24. Malaysia
7. Sweden	16. Czech Republic	25. Poland
8. Portugal	17. United Kingdom	
9. Hungary	18. Slovak Republic	

24-4 THE MOVEMENT TOWARD GLOBALIZATION

How did we come to live in a global economy? How and when did the process start? Globalization has been on the world stage for over two decades. In fact, the world has gone through different globalization periods. For example, globalization was occurring during the period from the mid-1800s to the late 1920s, and some people today refer to it as the First Era of Globalization. In some ways, when it came to the movement of people, the world then was freer than the world today, as evidenced by the fact that many people moved from country to country without a passport, which was not required.

The First Era of Globalization was largely ended by World Wars I and II and by the Great Depression. Still, even though the Great Depression and the world wars were over by 1945, globalization did not start anew right away. The Cold War essentially divided the world into different camps (free versus unfree, capitalist versus communist), which led to relatively high political and economic barriers. The visible symbol of these barriers—the Berlin Wall—separated not only East from West Germany but one group of countries living under one political and economic system from another group of countries living under a different political and economic system.

Today's more recent period of globalization has several causal factors. Not everyone agrees on all of them, and not everyone agrees on the weight one assigns to each. For example, some people argue that one particular factor means more to globalization than another. Nonetheless, you should be aware of the causal factors of globalization that are most often mentioned.

24-4a The End of the Cold War

The Cold War intensified after World War II and, most agree, ended with the visible fall of the Berlin Wall in 1989. This event, although historic in and of itself, occurred at the time when the Soviet empire was beginning to crumble and many of the communist East European countries were breaking away from the Soviet Union. As some explain the event, the end of the Cold War resulted in turning two different worlds (the capitalist and communist worlds) largely into one. It resulted in a thawing of not only political, but economic relations, between former enemies. You might not trade with your enemy, but once that person or country is no longer your enemy, you don't feel the same need to exclude him or it from your political and economic life.

At the beginning of this section, we asked you to imagine a world in which there were no barriers to trade: distance, culture, politics, or anything else would not matter. The Cold War acted as a political barrier between certain groups of countries; once it ended, one barrier standing in the way of trade disappeared. In fact, if the United States and the Soviet Union were still engaged in the Cold War, the current period of economic liberalization (freer markets, lower tariffs) and globalization might not be taking place. Even though the end of the Cold War might not be the full and only cause of the current period of globalization, if it had not ended, globalization would probably not be accelerating at the pace it is today.

24-4b Advancing Technology

In the past, innovations such as the internal combustion engine, steamship, telephone, and telegraph led to increased trade between people in different countries. All of these inventions

ECONOMICS 24/7

Proper Business Etiquette around the World

Customs and traditions differ among countries, sometimes when it comes to conducting business. Not knowing how business is done in a country can act as a stumbling block to getting it done. Following is a list of countries and certain rules of business etiquette in them: [1]

©XiXinXing/Shutterstock.com

Beijing, China

- If someone offers you his or her business card, accept it with both hands, read it immediately, and then present your business card to the person.
- In business, men normally wear a suit and tie.

Berlin, Germany

- When out with German business associates, try not to talk about sports. Many businesspeople believe that sports talk is the domain of the uneducated.
- Drinking before all have raised their glasses together is considered impolite.

Dubai, United Arab Emirates

- Do not arrange appointments on Friday, because it is Dubai's day of prayer and rest.
- Business slows down during the month of Ramadan (when Muslims fast). Foreign businesspeople are expected to observe the slower pace.

Hong Kong

- Running out of business cards is considered impolite.

Mexico City

- Having business cards printed in English on one side and in Spanish on the other is considered good form.
- Business clothing is fairly formal.

Sydney, Australia

- Knowing about the latest sports matches is important.
- Don't take yourself too seriously.

Tokyo, Japan

- Remove your shoes when entering a Japanese home.

Zurich, Switzerland

- People often greet each other when entering an office or shop. Try to do the same, even if your greeting is in your own language.
- Talking about money or personal wealth is frowned upon.

---

[1] The reference guide for these customs is *The Economist's* city guides.

led to lower transportation or communication costs, and lower costs mean fewer barriers to trade. What technology often does is lower the hindrances (of physical distance) that act as stumbling blocks to trade. For example, the cost of a three-minute telephone call from New York to London in 1930 was $250. In 1960, it was $60.42; in 1980, it was $6.32; and in 2000, it was 40¢. Today, the cost is even less. As the costs of communicating continue to fall, the hindrance to trade imposed by physical distance is in some sense, overcome. Businesspeople in the United States, for example, can now talk more cheaply with businesspeople in China.

Also, consider the price of a computer over the years. In 1960, the cost of a computer—one comparable to the desktop computer that many people today have on their desks at home—was $1.8 million. That computer was $199,983 in 1970, $27,938 in 1980, $7,275 in 1990, $1,000 in 2000, and $500 in 2013. Today, not only do people use computers for their work, but they communicate with others via the Internet. The personal computer and Internet technology enable people to communicate with others over long distances, thus increasing the probability that they will trade with one other.

Even farmers in poor developing countries can now have access to people and to information that they didn't have access to only a few years ago. A farmer in the Ivory Coast can check agricultural prices in the world with a cell phone—something that was unheard of a decade ago. Or consider such innovations as online banking. Years ago, it was common to have your bank just down the road from you. Today, you can open up an account with an online bank, many of which are located nowhere near you—perhaps not even in the country in which you live.

24-4c **Policy Changes**

Governments have the power to slow down the process of globalization if they want. Suppose two countries, A and B, have free economic relations with each other. Neither country imposes tariffs on the goods of the other. Neither country prevents its citizens from going to the other country to live and work. Neither country hampers its citizens from investing in the other country. Then, one day, for whatever reason, the government of country A decides to impose tariffs on the goods of country B and to limit its own citizens from traveling to and investing in country B. In other words, the government of country A decides to close its political and economic doors.

Just as a government of one country can close the door on another, it can open the door, too, and it can do so a little, more than a little, or a lot. In recent decades, governments of many countries have been opening their doors to other countries. China has opened its door, India has opened its door, and Russia has opened its door.

The driving forces of this most recent period of globalization have been (1) the end of the Cold War, (2) technological changes that lower the costs of transporting goods and communicating with people, and (3) government policy changes that express an openness toward freer markets and long-distance trade.

SELF-TEST

(Answers to Self-Test questions are in Answers to Self-Test Questions at the back of the book.)

1. Some have said that the end of the Cold War has led to greater globalization. Explain the reasoning.

2. What is globalization?

3. How might advancing technology lead to increased globalization?

24-5 BENEFITS AND COSTS OF GLOBALIZATION

Some people believe that globalization is, in general, a good thing and that its benefits outweigh its costs. Other people take the opposite view that the costs of globalization are greater than the benefits. Let's look at what supporters say are its benefits and what opponents say are its costs. As you read, you will probably begin to form your own opinion.

24-5a The Benefits

Trade   To say that the world is undergoing globalization is really no more than saying that people are trading with more people, at greater distances, than they once did. They are trading different things: money for goods, their labor for money, their savings for expected returns, and so on. Expanding trade—which is what globalization is about—is no more than extending the benefits of trading to people you might not have traded with earlier.

Economist David Friedman compared free international trade to a technology. He says that you can produce, say, cars in two ways. You can set up factories in Detroit, Michigan, and produce them. Or you can harvest wheat in the Midwest, load it on ships and send it to Japan, and then wait for the ships to return with cars. Looking at things the second way brings out the amazing nature of globalization. After all, with free trade across countries, wheat in a certain nation is exchanged for cars manufactured three-quarters of a world away, an accomplishment that really is astounding. The lesson Friedman is trying to communicate is that we all think that a technological improvement is a good thing because it often leads to a higher standard of living, and trading with people across the world really is nothing more than a technology of sorts—a way to "convert" wheat into cars. The more we trade with others, the more we witness all kinds of "conversions."

Per-Capita Income   The benefits of globalization can be seen in a more concrete way. As both India and China opened up their economies to globalization in recent decades, they experienced increases in per-capita income. For example, between 1980 and 2000, per-capita income doubled in India. Between 1940 and 2000, per-capita income increased by 400 percent in China, with much of the increase coming in recent years. According to the International Monetary Fund, these dramatic increases in per-capita income accompanied the expansion of free international trade (a key component of globalization).

Prices   Numerous studies have established a link between lower prices and the degree of international trade and globalization. Simply put, free international trade lowers prices. For example, Exhibit 5 shows the Consumer Price Index (CPI) and an import price index for the period 1990–2004. The CPI (which contains domestic goods and imported goods) rose faster than the import price index (which contains only imported goods). Also, between 1977 and 2004, the inflation-adjusted prices for an array of goods traded between countries fell whereas the inflation-adjusted prices for an array of goods not traded between countries actually increased. Some of the traded goods whose prices fell are audio equipment (26 percent), TV sets (51 percent),

> **EXHIBIT 5**

CPI and Import Price Index, 1990–2004

During the period 1990–2004, the CPI increased at a faster rate than the import price index (which both increased and decreased over the same period).

Source: Bureau of Labor Statistics.

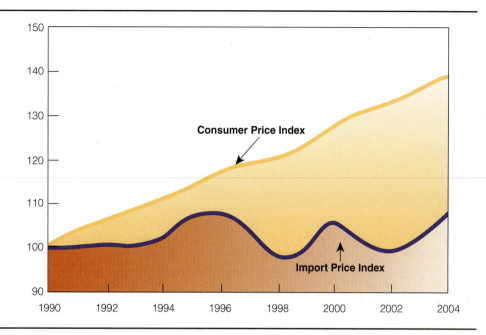

toys (34 percent), and clothing (9 percent); some of the nontraded goods whose prices increased are whole milk (28 percent), butter (23 percent), ice cream (18 percent), and peanut butter (9 percent).

Productivity and Innovation   Firms that face global competition are often pushed to increase their productivity and to innovate more. According to the 2006 *Economic Report of the President,* "Studies show that firms exposed to the world's best practices demonstrate higher productivity through many channels, such as learning from these best practices, and also creating new products and processes in response to this exposure."[2] For example, one study from the United Kingdom showed that the number of firms that faced global competition and that reported product or process innovations was almost three times the number of firms that did not face global competition.

Or consider the extreme case of North and South Korea. The two countries share a people and a culture, but North Korea avoided the process of globalization during the period in which South Korea embraced it. South Koreans currently enjoy a much higher standard of living than North Koreans.

24-5b **The Costs**

Increased Income Inequality   Globalization's critics often point out that globalization seems to go hand in hand with increased income inequality between rich and poor countries in the world. In fact, income inequality between countries *has* increased. For example, 100 years ago, people in rich countries had about 10 times more income than

---

2. *Economic Report of the President, Transmitted to the Congress February 2006, Together with the Annual Report of the Council of Economic Advisers* (Washington, DC: United States Government Printing Office, 2006), p. 158.

people in poor countries. Today, they have about 75 times more income. Without a doubt, globalization and income inequality are strongly correlated. The question, though, is whether globalization causes the inequality. The critics of globalization say it does, whereas the supporters say it does not.

The supporters of globalization liken it to a train. Economic systems that get on the train will benefit and reach their economic destinies faster, but those which do not will get left farther and farther behind. In other words, globalization does not increase income inequality; rather, some other combination of circumstances—of some countries globalizing while others are not—is the cause. In simple terms, if everyone is walking, some faster than others, then some will always be in front. If the fast walkers start to run while the others continue their slow walking pace, the gap between the ones in front and the ones in back will grow.

Of course, getting on the globalization train is not always a matter of choice. The conductor does not always let everyone on. Some rich countries work against certain poor countries to counter their globalization efforts. For example, tariffs on goods imported from the poor, developing world are 30 percent above the global average for all tariffs.

Losing American Jobs   Many critics of globalization argue that it can result in Americans losing certain jobs. Suppose a U.S. company hires engineers in India to do jobs once done by Americans. This practice of hiring people in other countries is often called **offshoring**.

Some Americans may indeed lose their jobs to workers in other countries because of globalization. It has already happened: In 2003, a major New York securities firm replaced its team of 800 American software engineers, who earned about $150,000 per year each, with an equally competent team in India earning an average of about $20,000 a year per person. In addition, the number of radiologists in the United States is expected to fall significantly because radiological data can now be sent over the Internet to Asian radiologists, who can analyze it at a fraction of the cost here.

Keep in mind, though, that offshoring is a two-way street: the United States might offshore certain jobs to, say, India or China, but foreign countries around the world offshore jobs to the United States too. Although some Americans lose jobs because of globalization, jobs are always being lost and found in a dynamic economy that is responding to market changes. Even if the degree of offshoring in the United States were zero, people would still be losing old jobs and getting new ones every day.

More Power to Big Corporations   Many critics of globalization argue that the process will simply hand over the world (and especially the developing countries) to large Western corporations (headquartered in the United States, the United Kingdom, Canada, and other powerful nations). In fact, in the minds of many people, globalization is the process of *corporatizing* the world. Instead of *governments* deciding what will and will not be done, large corporations will assume the responsibility.

The proponents of globalization often point out a major difference between a corporation and a government. First, a government can force people to do certain things (such as pay taxes or join the military). No corporation can coerce people; instead, corporations can simply produce goods that they hope customers will buy. In addition, the proponents of globalization often argue that the critics overestimate the influence and reach of large transnational companies. For example, in 2000, the top 100 transnational companies produced only 4.3 percent of the entire world's output—about as much as what one country, the United Kingdom, produced that year.

Offshoring
Work done for a company by persons other than the original company's employees in a country other than the company's home country.

ECONOMICS 24/7

Will Globalization Change the Kind of Music We Hear?

Suppose you had only 100 people to whom you could sell a good. Given this small number, you had better sell something that at least some of the 100 people want to buy. For example, if the 100 people don't like fruit salad, then you better not produce and offer to sell fruit salad; if some of them like bread, then perhaps you should produce and offer to sell bread.

Now increase the number of people from 100 to 1 million. A group of 1 million is much more likely than a group of 100 to contain people who like fruit salad. In other words, as the size of the potential customer base increases, the number of things you can sell increases too. In a world of 100 people, you can sell only bread, but in a world of 1 million people, you can sell fruit salad or bread.

So, the larger the size of the potential customer base (the more people you can sell to), the greater the variety of goods for sale is likely to be. Globalization is, to a large degree, expanding everyone's ability to sell to more people. American companies aren't limited to selling only to Americans; they can now sell to others in the world too. Chinese firms aren't limited to selling only to Chinese; they can now sell to others around the world.

As a musician, you can play different styles of music: jazz, pop, classical, hard rock, metal, hip-hop, and so on. If you are limited to selling your music to the people of a single state in the United States, you can offer to sell fewer styles of music than if you could sell your music to the people who reside throughout the United States.

More specifically, consider the musician in the United States who is experimenting with a new style of music. With a population of only the United States (319 million) as a potential customer base, the musician might not yet have enough actual customers to make it worth producing and offering to sell this particular, unique, and narrowly defined music. However, if the musician can draw on the population of the world (7.1 billion), then she might be able to find enough people who are willing to buy her new type of music.

As we move toward a world economy, we see a greater variety within almost every category of goods: a greater variety of music to listen to, books to read, types of television shows to watch, and so on. Today, the greater variety of goods you see in your world is an effect of globalization.

24-6 THE CONTINUING GLOBALIZATION DEBATE

Many (but certainly not all) economists argue that the worldwide benefits of globalization are likely to be greater than the worldwide costs. Of course, not everyone is going to see the beneficial side of globalization, and, to a large degree, whether people support or criticize globalization seems to depend on where they are sitting. Globalization does not affect everyone in the same way, and often *how* it affects *you* determines how you feel about it. For example, suppose Sanders, an American worker residing in New York, loses his job to a worker in New Delhi, India, who will do Sanders's job for less pay. In this case, Sanders incurs real costs, but for the company he worked for, the change means lower costs and higher profits. For the company's customers, the change might mean lower prices. So, in this case, Sanders is probably a strong opponent of offshoring, but the company and its customers are probably supporters.

Seeing the benefits of globalization is often much more difficult than seeing its costs. For example, the supporters of globalization argue that it brings greater economic wealth, lower prices, more innovation, less poverty, and so on. Yet seeing all these benefits is sometimes difficult. When you buy cheaper or different goods because of globalization, you probably never say, "Wow, I can't believe all the benefits I get from globalization!" In fact, you might not even connect the lower priced goods with globalization at all. The benefits of globalization tend to be difficult to perceive, partly because they are so widely dispersed.

The costs of globalization, in contrast, are more visible, often because they are so concentrated. A person who loses a job because of freer international trade in the world knows exactly what is to blame for his predicament. He surely could receive some benefits from globalization (as a consumer), but he also could, for a time, incur some rather high costs (as an unemployed worker). This person is likely to know of the costs but be unaware of the benefits.

In the end, the people who receive only benefits from globalization might not be able to see them or to connect them with globalization. The people who receive both benefits and costs from globalization may be aware only of the costs. This one-sided view could create strong antiglobalization sentiment in a country.

24-7   LESS GLOBALIZATION OR MORE: A TUG-OF-WAR?

Is increased globalization inevitable? Will the day come when all countries in the world are like the 50 states in the United States: part of one economy with easy movement of people, resources, financial capital, goods, and services across borders? Or will the conditions that prevented globalization reappear and reverse the trend?

This struggle is like a tug-of-war. The forces of globalization pull in one direction, and the forces of antiglobalization pull in the other. As of today, the forces of globalization are moving things in their direction, but the trend may not continue uninterrupted. Surely, at any time, the forces of antiglobalization could put on a burst of energy and give an extra-strong tug on the rope.

To help answer the question about the future of globalization, recall what we said about the driving forces of the most recent era of globalization: the end of the Cold War, changes in technology (which lowered the costs of transportation and communication), and policy changes that opened up countries' economies to each other.

24-7a Less Globalization

Increased Political Tension   The end of the Cold War is a historical fact that the anti-globalization forces cannot undo, but we could enter a period when political tensions among countries or among groups of countries emerge. We are not suggesting that such a period of tension will happen, only that it could. If it did, it could slow down globalization or, depending on the severity of the tension, even reverse it.

Terrorism   Another factor inhibiting globalization is terrorism. Global terrorism tends to motivate certain countries into closing borders and into being much more careful about the people and goods crossing their borders.

Technology   Technology cannot be undone. We cannot go from a world with the Internet to one without it. Hence, it is unlikely that anything technological will slow down or reverse globalization.

Government Policies   Policy changes can slow down or reverse globalization. Governments of countries that opened up their economies to others could reverse their course; doors that opened to other nations can be closed. Whether this sort of isolationism will happen in the future is unknown.

24-7b More Globalization

Some still argue that, even with the forces of antiglobalization looming on the horizon, the forces of globalization are stronger. In the end, these individuals say, the forces of globalization will win the tug-of-war. They believe that, in the long run, economics influences politics, not the other way around. As some proof of that assertion, they point to the former Soviet Union and to China, entrenched communist countries. Both countries finally saw that they were worse off by holding themselves outside the orbit of free-market forces. You might say that they found themselves outside the theater where economic forces were playing major roles on the world stage.

Many economists argue that globalization is not just a passing trend. They argue that the basic globalization force that will probably not be overcome—no matter how strong the political forces may be against it—is the human inclination that the founder of modern economics, Adam Smith, noticed more than 200 years ago: Human beings want to trade with each other. In fact, the desire to trade separates us from all other species, Smith said. In his words, "Man is an animal that makes bargains: no other animal does this—no dog exchanges bones with another."

We want to trade with people: our next-door neighbor, the person down the street, the person on the other side of town, the person in the next state, the person on the other side of the country, and, ultimately, the person on the other side of the world. Some economists go on to suggest that our inclination to trade is a good thing in that, when we trade with people, not only do we tolerate them, but we have much less reason to fight with them. Robert Wright, a journalist and scholar, argues that it is not a coincidence that religious toleration is high in the United States, a country that is open to trade and globalization. We often see, he argues, that people who live in countries that trade with other people—people who live in countries that are open to other people—are people who tolerate others.

SELF-TEST

1. Identify some of the benefits of globalization.

2. Identify some of the costs of globalization.

24-8 INTERNATIONAL FACTORS AND AGGREGATE DEMAND

Previous chapters have described domestic factors that can change aggregate demand and thus affect the U.S. economy. Changes that occur in other countries can also influence the U.S. economy. This section discusses two key international factors that can affect the U.S. economy by first affecting U.S. aggregate demand: net exports and the J-curve.

24-8a Net Exports

In an earlier chapter, net exports are defined as the difference of exports (EX) and imports (IM). For example, if exports are $80 billion and imports are $60 billion, then net exports are $20 billion. Also, recall that, if net exports rise, the AD curve shifts to the right; if net exports fall, the AD curve shifts to the left.

Two factors can change net exports: (1) foreign Real GDP and (2) the exchange rate. To simplify matters, we assume there are only two countries in the world: the United States and Japan.

Foreign Real GDP (or Foreign Real National Income)   As Japan's Real GDP (or real national income) rises, the Japanese buy more U.S. goods. As a result, U.S. net exports rise and the AD curve shifts to the right. As Japan's Real GDP falls, the Japanese buy fewer U.S. goods. As a result, U.S. net exports fall and the AD curve shifts to the left.

Thus, economic expansions and contractions in other countries are felt in the United States. Given a contraction in Japan, with a lower Real GDP, the Japanese buy fewer U.S. goods. Then, U.S. exports fall, and so do net exports. As a result, the AD curve in the United States shifts to the left. Because the AD curve shifts to the left, Real GDP in the United States falls.

Exchange Rate   Recall that the exchange rate is the price of one country's currency expressed in terms of another country's currency. On the one hand, if a country's currency *appreciates*, it takes less of that country's currency to buy the other country's currency. On the other hand, if a country's currency *depreciates*, it takes more of that country's currency to buy the other country's currency.

Appreciation and depreciation affect the prices of a country's goods. If, say, the U.S. dollar depreciates relative to the Japanese yen, then U.S. residents have to pay more dollars to buy Japanese goods. To illustrate, suppose the dollar price of a yen is $0.012 and that a Toyota is priced at ¥2 million. At this exchange rate, a U.S. resident pays $24,000 for a Toyota ($0.012 × ¥2 million = $24,000). If the dollar depreciates to $0.018 for ¥1, then the U.S. resident will have to pay $36,000 for a Toyota.

As the dollar depreciates, Japanese goods become more expensive for U.S. residents, so they buy fewer Japanese goods and U.S. imports decline.[3] The other side of the coin is that, as the dollar depreciates relative to the yen, the yen appreciates relative to the dollar. Thus, U.S. goods become less expensive for the Japanese and they buy more U.S. goods, so U.S. exports rise.

[3.] Throughout this chapter, unless otherwise explicitly stated, we assume that, if the physical quantity of exports rises (falls), then total spending on exports rises (falls). Also, if the physical quantity of imports rises (falls), then total spending on imports rises (falls). Because of this assumption, it is not necessary to differentiate constantly between the physical quantity of imports and total spending on imports: Given our assumption, they go up and down together. One place we explicitly drop the assumption is in the discussion of the J-curve.

> **EXHIBIT 6**

International Impacts on the U.S. *AD* Curve

Anything that increases U.S. net exports shifts the U.S. *AD* curve to the right. Thus, in a two-country (Japan and the United States) world, an increase in Japan's Real GDP and a depreciation of the dollar would each shift the U.S. *AD* curve to the right. Anything that decreases U.S. net exports shifts the U.S. *AD* curve to the left. Thus, a decrease in Japan's Real GDP and an appreciation of the dollar would each shift the U.S. *AD* curve to the left.

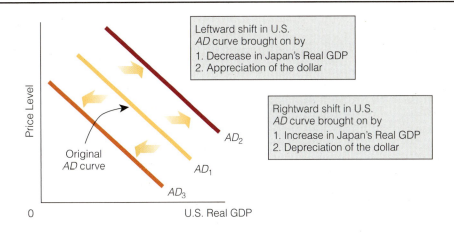

Leftward shift in U.S. *AD* curve brought on by
1. Decrease in Japan's Real GDP
2. Appreciation of the dollar

Rightward shift in U.S. *AD* curve brought on by
1. Increase in Japan's Real GDP
2. Depreciation of the dollar

In sum, a depreciation in the dollar and an appreciation in the yen will raise U.S. exports, lower U.S. imports, and therefore raise U.S. net exports. This series of events shifts the U.S. *AD* curve to the right, leading to a rise in U.S. Real GDP.

The series of events is symmetrical if the U.S. dollar appreciates relative to the Japanese yen. In this case, U.S. goods become more expensive for the Japanese, causing them to buy fewer U.S. goods, so U.S. exports fall. And Japanese goods become cheaper for U.S. residents, causing them to buy more Japanese goods, so U.S. imports rise. A decline in U.S. exports, along with a rise in U.S. imports, will cause U.S. net exports to fall. The U.S. *AD* curve will then shift to the left, leading to a decline in U.S. Real GDP.

(For a quick review of the international factors that can shift the U.S. *AD* curve, see Exhibit 6.)

24-8b The J-Curve

So far, we have assumed that, if the dollar depreciates relative to the Japanese yen, U.S. residents and the Japanese will buy more U.S. goods and fewer Japanese goods. Thus, U.S. exports rise, U.S. imports fall, and U.S. net exports rise.

But this scenario may not happen initially. There may be a difference between what *initially* happens and what *ultimately* happens. To illustrate, suppose U.S. residents are currently buying 100,000 cars from the Japanese, the average Japanese car sells for ¥2 million, and the exchange rate is currently $0.012 per yen. Then U.S. residents are spending an average of $24,000 a car for 100,000 cars. Thus, a total of $2.4 billion is spent in the United States on imported Japanese cars.

Now suppose that the exchange rate changes and the dollar depreciates to $0.018 per yen, causing the average price of a Japanese car to jump to $36,000. At this higher price, U.S. residents buy fewer Japanese cars, but they don't buy that many fewer right away. Instead of buying 100,000 cars, they initially buy 90,000 cars. Now a total of $3.24 billion is spent on imported Japanese cars. So, instead of declining after a depreciation in the dollar, U.S. spending on imports initially rises. If we assume that U.S. exports have not changed yet, then a rise in U.S. imports will lead to a fall in U.S. net exports and cause the U.S. *AD* curve to shift to the left.

> **EXHIBIT 7**

The J-Curve

The United States starts with net exports of −$40 billion. As the dollar depreciates, net exports increase to −$60 billion. With time, net exports become $0. If we follow the course of net exports, we map out a J. This is called the J-curve.

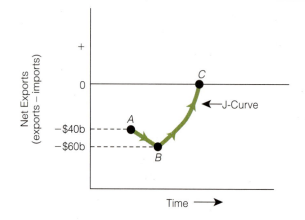

J-Curve

The curve that shows a short-run worsening in net exports after a currency depreciation, followed by an improvement.

But this situation is not likely to last. In time, U.S. residents will switch from the higher priced Japanese goods to lower priced U.S. goods. For example, after a while, U.S. residents purchase only 60,000 Japanese cars. At this level, with the exchange rate of $0.018 per yen, U.S. spending on imported Japanese cars is $2.16 billion. In time, too, U.S. exports will rise, and the combination of rising exports and falling imports will lead to an increase in net exports. The U.S. *AD* curve will shift to the right.

This phenomenon, in which import spending initially rises after a depreciation and then later falls, is summarized in the **J-curve**, so called because the curve showing the change in net exports due to a currency depreciation has the shape of a J. In Exhibit 7, the United States initially has negative net exports of $40 billion. (U.S. imports of $130 billion are greater than U.S. exports of $90 billion.) This position is represented by point *A* in the exhibit.

Next, the dollar depreciates relative to the yen. Total spending on imports rises to, say, $150 billion, so net exports rise to $60 billion, represented by point *B*.

In time, though, exports rise to, say, $100 billion and imports fall to, say, $100 billion, making net exports equal to zero. This situation is represented by point *C*.

If we start at point *A* and draw a line to point *B* and then to point *C*, we have a J-curve, representing the route that net exports may take after a depreciation in a country's currency.

Short Run and Long Run The discussion of the J-curve points up the fact that economists sometimes think in terms of both the short run and the long run. Does the depreciation of a country's currency lead to an increase or a decrease in import spending? According to J-curve theory, both an increase and a decrease result. Import spending may initially increase, but in the long run it decreases. Thus, an economist's answers may differ, depending on the time horizon under consideration.

ECONOMICS 24/7

How Hard Will It Be to Get into Harvard in 2025?

The Indian Institute of Technology (in India) is one of the hardest universities in the world to be admitted to, largely because of its reputation. It has been compared to putting Harvard, MIT (the Massachusetts Institute of Technology), and Princeton together.

©James Morgan/Shutterstock.com

In an average year, about 178,000 high school seniors in India take the exam necessary to apply to the Indian Institute of Technology. Just over 3,500 students (only 1.96 percent of all applicants) are admitted. In comparison, the admission rate of Harvard University is nearly 7 percent. Often, students from India who are admitted to MIT, Princeton, and Cal Tech (all of which are listed among the top 10 U.S. colleges and universities) go there because they did not gain admission to the Indian Institute of Technology.

Other highly prestigious U.S. universities and colleges—such as Brown, Columbia, Cornell, Dartmouth, Harvard, the University of Pennsylvania, Princeton, Yale, Stanford, Northwestern, and Duke—have some of the most selective admission criteria of all colleges and universities in the country. Each year, students who have the grade point average and standardized test scores to be considered for admission are turned away. This phenomenon has been occurring at the same time that college tuition in the United States has been increasing rapidly. For example, during the period 1990–2003, college tuition went up by 130 percent, considerably more than medical care costs and the price of housing, food, gasoline, cars, and more. If we look around the world at other prestigious institutions of higher learning, we see the same characteristics: The admission rate is usually low, and the cost is usually high.

Consider how grades (one major criterion) and money actually function in admissions: They are both rationing devices. We know that, because of scarcity, some mechanism has to ration the available resources, goods, and services. Still, we have to ask why these two rationing devices—grades and money—have become stiffer when it comes to being admitted to the top universities in the world? Why must grades and tuitions be ever higher?

The answer is twofold. First, the population of the world increased while the number of Harvards did not. Harvard cannot clone itself; nor can Yale, the Indian Institute of Technology, or MIT. To a large degree, the world has only one Harvard, Oxford (in the United Kingdom), and Indian Institute of Technology. We can produce more computers, houses, and dining room chairs as the population of the world increases, but producing more Harvards seems to be much more difficult. So, over time, top-notch, one-of-a-kind educational institutions become relatively scarcer. As a result, the rationing devices for such institutions must work harder, and getting admitted to such places will become harder and more expensive.

The second reason involves globalization. One of things that pays a high dividend in a global economy is education. Brains seem to matter more than brawn, increasing the overall demand for a college education—not just at Harvard, but at all levels of higher education (from community colleges to four-year state and private universities). So, will the premium placed on education in a global economy cause the demand at the most prestigious educational establishments to rise at a faster rate than at other colleges? That question is like asking, "If the premium for playing music were to rise, would the demand to be at Juilliard (one of the premier music institutions in the world) rise faster than the demand to study with the local piano teacher down the street?" The likely answer is yes. With a growing world population, and with the global economy paying a high premium to those who are educated (compared with those who are not), we can expect it to get increasingly difficult and more expensive to be admitted to the world's best institutions of higher learning.

1. Explain how an economic boom in one country can be felt in another country.

2. Predict and explain what will happen to U.S. Real GDP if the dollar appreciates relative to the Japanese yen.

24-9 INTERNATIONAL FACTORS AND AGGREGATE SUPPLY

Just as international factors can affect the demand side of the U.S. economy, certain international factors can affect the supply side. This section discusses a few international factors that can shift the U.S. aggregate supply curve.

24-9a Foreign Input Prices

We know that a change in the price of inputs will shift the short-run aggregate supply (*SRAS*) curve. For example, if the price of labor (the wage rate) rises, the *SRAS* curve shifts leftward.

American producers buy inputs not only from other Americans but also from foreigners. A rise in the price of foreign inputs leads to a leftward shift in the U.S. *SRAS* curve. A fall in the price of foreign inputs leads to a rightward shift in the U.S. *SRAS* curve.

24-9b Why Foreign Input Prices Change

If supply and demand in the input market in a foreign country change, the result could be a rise in the price of foreign inputs. For example, suppose U.S. producers buy input X from Japan. Then, if the supply of X in Japan falls or the demand for X in Japan rises (or both), the price of X for U.S. producers would increase.

The Exchange Rate   A change in the exchange rate between the dollar and the yen could change the price of a foreign input. For example, a depreciation in the dollar relative to the yen would make input X more expensive for U.S. producers and an appreciation in the dollar would make input X less expensive for U.S. producers. Exhibit 8 presents a summary of the points discussed in this section.

> **EXHIBIT 8**

International Impacts on the U.S. *SRAS* Curve

The U.S. *SRAS* curve shifts if foreign input prices change. If foreign input prices rise, the U.S. *SRAS* curve shifts leftward; if foreign input prices fall, the *SRAS* curve shifts rightward. Similarly, if the dollar depreciates, foreign inputs become more expensive and the *SRAS* curve shifts leftward. If the dollar appreciates, foreign inputs become cheaper and the *SRAS* curve shifts rightward.

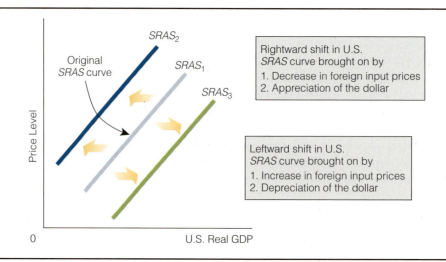

24-10 FACTORS THAT AFFECT BOTH AGGREGATE DEMAND AND AGGREGATE SUPPLY

Changes in some international factors can affect both aggregate demand and short-run aggregate supply in the United States. Two of these factors are the exchange rate and relative interest rates.

24-10a The Exchange Rate

As explained earlier, changes in exchange rates affect both the *AD* and *SRAS* curves. The overall, or net, effect on Real GDP depends on how much the *AD* curve shifts relative to the shift in the *SRAS* curve. We consider two cases: depreciation of the dollar and appreciation of the dollar.

Depreciation of the Dollar As the dollar depreciates, the *AD* curve shifts rightward and the *SRAS* curve shifts leftward. Then,

- If the *AD* curve shifts rightward by more than the *SRAS* curve shifts leftward, Real GDP rises. [See Exhibit 9(a).]

- If the *AD* curve shifts rightward by less than the *SRAS* curve shifts leftward, Real GDP falls. [See Exhibit 9(b).]

- If the *AD* curve shifts rightward by the same amount that the *SRAS* curve shifts leftward, Real GDP does not change. [See Exhibit 9(c).]

In each of these three cases, the price level rises. In sum, depreciation of the dollar raises the price level and may accompany an increasing, decreasing, or constant Real GDP.

> **EXHIBIT 9**

Depreciation of the Dollar: Effects on the Price Level and Real GDP

A change in exchange rates affects both aggregate demand and short-run aggregate supply. If the dollar depreciates, the *AD* curve shifts rightward and the *SRAS* curve shifts leftward. The overall impact on Real GDP—up, down, or unchanged—depends on whether the *AD* curve shifts rightward by (a) more, (b) less, or (c) an amount equal to the leftward shift in the *SRAS* curve. In all three cases, the depreciation of the dollar leads to a higher price level.

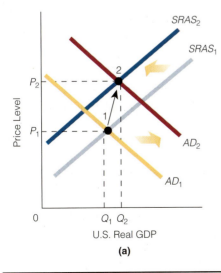

(a)

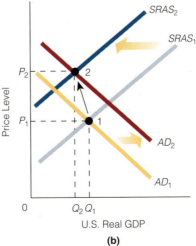

(b)

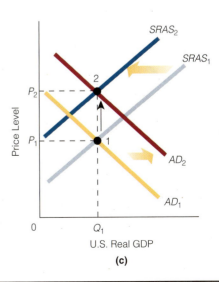

(c)

Appreciation of the Dollar   As the dollar appreciates, the *AD* curve shifts leftward and the *SRAS* curve shifts rightward. Once again, what happens to Real GDP depends on the relative shifts of the two curves:

- If the *AD* curve shifts leftward by more than the *SRAS* curve shifts rightward, Real GDP falls.

- If the *AD* curve shifts leftward by less than the *SRAS* curve shifts rightward, Real GDP rises.

- If the *AD* curve shifts leftward by the same amount that the *SRAS* curve shifts rightward, Real GDP does not change.

In each case, though, the price level falls. In sum, appreciation of the dollar lowers the price level and may accompany an increasing, decreasing, or constant Real GDP.

24-10b The Role That Interest Rates Play

Suppose that, in a two-country world with only the United States and Japan, real interest rates rise in the United States and remain constant in Japan. Then the higher real interest rates in the United States will attract foreign capital (in search of the highest return possible). Because foreigners will be interested in dollar-denominated assets that pay interest, they will have to exchange their country's currency for U.S. dollars. This need will increase the demand for U.S. dollars and lead to an appreciation of the dollar.

Then, if the dollar appreciates, both the U.S. *AD* and *SRAS* curves will be affected. The *AD* curve will shift leftward, and the *SRAS* curve will shift rightward. As just explained, the effect on Real GDP depends on the relative shifts in the two curves. Many economists argue, however, that, given the interest rate differential between the two countries, the *AD* curve typically tends to shift leftward by more than the *SRAS* curve shifts rightward and thus Real GDP will fall. [see Exhibit 10(a).]

> **EXHIBIT 10**

International Interest Rates, Exchange Rates, and Real GDP

(a) If the U.S. real interest rate is higher than the Japanese real interest rate, capital will flow from Japan to the United States. In the process, the demand for the dollar rises, and the dollar appreciates. Appreciation of the dollar causes the *AD* curve to shift leftward by more than the *SRAS* curve shifts rightward—a typical change, given the initial event. As a result, U.S. Real GDP falls. (b) If the U.S. real interest rate is lower than the Japanese

real interest rate, capital will flow from the United States to Japan. In the process, the demand for yen rises, the supply of dollars rises, and the yen appreciates and the dollar depreciates. Depreciation of the dollar causes the *AD* curve to shift rightward and the *SRAS* curve to shift leftward. We have drawn the *AD* curve shifting rightward by more than the *SRAS* curve shifts leftward—a typical change, given the initial event. As a result, U.S. Real GDP rises.

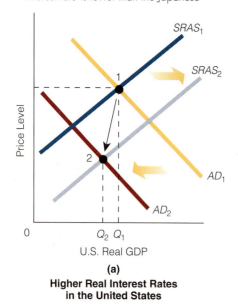

(a)
Higher Real Interest Rates in the United States

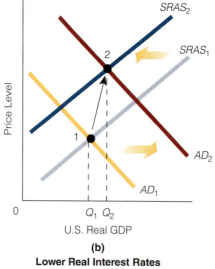

(b)
Lower Real Interest Rates in the United States

In sum, a rise in real interest rates in the United States relative to foreign interest rates typically tends to decrease U.S. Real GDP.

Now suppose that real interest rates fall in the United States relative to interest rates in Japan. Then the higher real interest rate in Japan will attract capital to Japan. The demand for yen will rise, and, as a result, the yen will appreciate and the dollar will depreciate. A depreciated dollar will shift the U.S. *AD* curve rightward and the *SRAS* curve leftward. [see Exhibit 10(b).] Many economists argue that, given the interest rate differential, the *AD* curve typically tends to shift rightward by more than the *SRAS* curve shifts leftward and thus Real GDP will rise. In sum, a fall in real interest rates in the United States relative to foreign interest rates typically tends to increase U.S. Real GDP.

SELF-TEST

1. How do foreign input prices affect the U.S. *SRAS* curve?

2. What is the effect on the U.S. price level of Japan's having lower real interest rates than the United States has? Explain your answer.

24-11 DEFICITS: INTERNATIONAL EFFECTS AND DOMESTIC FEEDBACK

Deficits in the United States—both budget and trade deficits—affect the U.S. economy. We know how the budget deficit can directly affect the U.S. economy. However, the budget deficit can also have international effects, which can then feed back into the U.S. economy. This section looks at the possibilities of feedback effects and the relationship between the budget deficit and the trade deficit.

24-11a The Budget Deficit and Expansionary Fiscal Policy

Suppose that North Dakotans want their elected representatives in Congress to push for a spending program that will assist them and no one else and that their elected representatives oblige them. Suppose also that Congress passes the spending program but does not raise the taxes necessary to pay for it. This domestic action can affect the international economic scene, and here's how.

Even with a budget deficit, Congress passes the spending program to help North Dakotans but neither raises taxes to finance the program nor cuts any other spending programs on the books. As a result of these actions—one more spending program, no fewer spending programs, and no more taxes—the budget deficit grows. To finance the growing budget deficit, the U.S. Treasury borrows more funds in the credit (or loanable funds) market than it would have borrowed if the North Dakotan spending program had not been passed. The increased demand for credit raises the real interest rate. The higher U.S. interest rate then attracts foreign capital. As a result, the demand for dollars in the foreign exchange market rises and the dollar appreciates.

As this series of events happens, the U.S. *AD* curve shifts leftward and the *SRAS* curve shifts rightward. The *AD* curve shifts leftward by more than the *SRAS* curve shifts rightward, putting downward pressure on Real GDP.

But Real GDP might not *actually* decrease. That's because we have discussed only how a rising budget deficit affects the exchange rate (via the interest rate) and feeds back into the domestic economy. We also need to consider the *direct* effect of the rising budget deficit on the domestic economy. Under certain conditions (e.g., zero crowding out), expansionary fiscal policy can raise aggregate demand and is effective at raising Real GDP. So,

1. The rising budget deficit affects the domestic economy directly and pushes *Real GDP upward*.

2. But increased deficit financing raises U.S. interest rates, prompts increased foreign capital inflows, leads to an increased demand for dollars, and causes the dollar to appreciate. Under typical conditions, an appreciated dollar then feeds back into the domestic economy and pushes *Real GDP downward*.

Obviously, what happens *on a net basis* depends on how strong the international feedback effects are on the domestic economy. Are they strong enough to offset the initial expansionary push (upward) in Real GDP? Even if they aren't, and Real GDP rises on net, we can still conclude that expansionary fiscal policy raises Real GDP more in a **closed economy** (which does not trade goods and services with other countries) than in an **open economy** (which trades goods and services with other countries). The reason is that the international feedback effects that reduce Real GDP are absent in a closed economy. (See the second item in the preceding list.)

Exhibit 11(a) illustrates the point. With zero crowding out, expansionary fiscal policy shifts the aggregate demand curve from AD_1 to AD_2. But because of the higher interest rates, increased foreign capital inflows, and appreciation of the dollar, the AD curve shifts leftward from AD_2 to AD_3 and the $SRAS$ curve shifts rightward from $SRAS_1$ to $SRAS_2$. In a closed economy, Real GDP rises from Q_1 to Q_2. In an open economy, in which international feedback effects play a role, Real GDP ends up at a lower level, Q_3.

24-11b The Budget Deficit and Contractionary Fiscal Policy

If expansionary fiscal policy raises Real GDP more in a closed economy than in an open economy, what are the effects of contractionary fiscal policy in the two types of economies? Suppose reduced government spending decreases the budget deficit. Then, with a diminished budget deficit, the U.S. Treasury borrows fewer funds in the credit market than it would have if government spending had not been reduced. Subsequently, the decreased demand for loanable funds lowers the real interest rate (relative to foreign interest rates), making foreign assets seem more desirable. The demand for foreign currencies increases, and the dollar depreciates in value.

At the same time, the U.S. AD curve shifts to the right and the $SRAS$ curve shifts to the left. The AD curve shifts rightward by more than the $SRAS$ curve shifts leftward, putting upward pressure on Real GDP. However, Real GDP might not *actually* increase. Under certain conditions, the lower budged deficit due to a cut in government spending reduces aggregate demand and therefore reduces Real GDP. So,

1. The cut in government spending reduces the budget deficit and affects the domestic economy directly, pushing *Real GDP downward*.

2. But reduced deficit financing lowers U.S. interest rates, prompts increased U.S. capital outflows, leads to an increased demand for foreign currencies, and causes the dollar to depreciate. Under typical conditions, a depreciated dollar then feeds back into the domestic economy and pushes *Real GDP upward*.

Again, what happens *on a net basis* depends on whether the international feedback effects on the domestic economy are strong enough to offset the initial contractionary push in Real GDP.

Closed Economy

An economy that does not trade goods and services with other countries.

Open Economy

An economy that trades goods and services with other countries.

> **EXHIBIT 11**

Expansionary and Contractionary Fiscal Policy in Open and Closed Economies

(a) The consequences of expansionary fiscal policy for both open and closed economies. Congress passes a spending program without raising taxes, and the AD curve shifts from AD_1 to AD_2. To finance the growing budget deficit, the Treasury borrows

more funds in the loanable funds market, whereupon the interest rate rises. The higher interest rate attracts foreign capital and causes the dollar to appreciate. As the dollar appreciates, the AD curve shifts from AD_2 to AD_3 and the SRAS curve shifts from $SRAS_1$ to $SRAS_2$. Real GDP goes from Q_1 to Q_2 in a closed economy and from Q_1 to Q_3 in an

open economy. Thus, expansionary fiscal policy raises Real GDP more in a closed economy than in an open economy.
(b) Contractionary fiscal policy lowers Real GDP more in a closed economy than in an open economy.

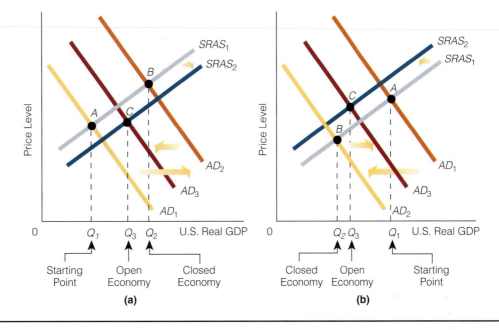

(a)

(b)

Even if the international feedback effects on the domestic economy do not outweigh the initial contractionary push (downward) in Real GDP, and even if Real GDP falls on net, we can still conclude that contractionary fiscal policy lowers Real GDP more in a closed economy than in an open economy.

Exhibit 11(b) illustrates our point. The cut in government spending shifts the AD curve from AD_1 to AD_2. But because of the lower interest rates, increased U.S. capital outflows, and depreciation of the dollar, the AD curve shifts rightward from AD_2 to AD_3 and the SRAS curve shifts leftward from $SRAS_1$ to $SRAS_2$. In a closed economy, Real GDP falls from Q_1 to Q_2. In an open economy, in which international feedback effects play a role, Real GDP ends up at Q_3.

24-11c The Effects of Monetary Policy

Monetary policy, too, affects international economic factors that feed back to the United States. Here we consider both expansionary and contractionary monetary policy.

Expansionary Monetary Policy   Suppose the Federal Reserve increases the money supply. As Exhibit 12(a) shows, the increase causes the AD curve to shift rightward from AD_1 to AD_2 and Real GDP to rise from Q_1 to Q_2.

> **EXHIBIT 12**

Expansionary and Contractionary Monetary Policy in Open and Closed Economies

(a) The consequences of expansionary monetary policy for both open and closed economies. The Fed increases the money supply, and the AD curve shifts from AD_1 to AD_2. Real GDP rises from Q_1 to Q_2. The increased money supply leads to lower interest rates in the short run, promoting an outflow of U.S. capital and a depreciated dollar, which raises U.S. exports, lowers U.S. imports, and raises U.S. net exports. Higher net exports shift the AD curve rightward from AD_2 to AD_3. The depreciated dollar shifts the SRAS curve leftward from $SRAS_1$ to $SRAS_2$. Real GDP ends up at Q_3. Thus, expansionary monetary policy raises Real GDP more in an open economy than in a closed economy. (b) Contractionary monetary policy lowers Real GDP more in an open economy than in a closed economy.

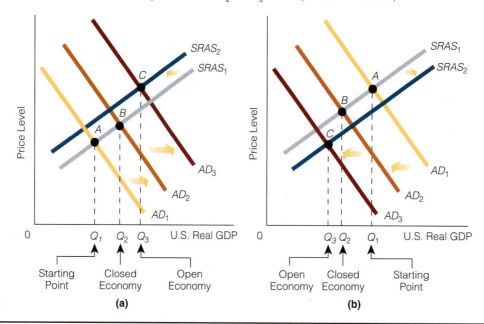

(a)   (b)

An increase in the money supply also has international effects. Expansionary monetary policy causes interest rates to fall in the short run (the liquidity effect), leading to an outflow of capital from the United States. Americans begin to supply more dollars on the foreign exchange market so that they can purchase foreign assets. As the supply of dollars rises, the dollar depreciates.

Depreciation of the dollar affects both U.S. aggregate demand and U.S. short-run aggregate supply. As just noted, it shifts the AD curve to the right and the SRAS curve to the left. In Exhibit 12(a), the AD curve shifts to the right from AD_2 to AD_3, and the SRAS curve shifts to the left from $SRAS_1$ to $SRAS_2$. Consequently, Real GDP rises from Q_2 to Q_3.

Therefore, expansionary monetary policy raises Real GDP more in an open economy than in a closed economy.

Contractionary Monetary Policy   If the Federal Reserve contracts the money supply, the AD curve shifts leftward from AD_1 to AD_2 and Real GDP falls from Q_1 to Q_2. [See Exhibit 12(b).]

A decrease in the money supply also has international effects. Contractionary monetary policy causes interest rates to rise, leading to an inflow of foreign capital into the United States. The demand for dollars rises on the foreign exchange market, and the dollar appreciates. Appreciation of the dollar affects both U.S. aggregate demand and U.S. short-run aggregate supply, shifting the *AD* curve to the left and the *SRAS* curve to the right. In Exhibit 12(b), the *AD* curve shifts from AD_2 to AD_3 and the *SRAS* curve shifts from $SRAS_1$ to $SRAS_2$. Consequently, Real GDP falls from Q_2 to Q_3.

Therefore, contractionary monetary policy lowers Real GDP more in an open economy than in a closed economy.

SELF-TEST

1. Explain how expansionary fiscal policy works in an open economy.

2. Explain how expansionary monetary policy works in an open economy.

Office Hours

"Why Do Some People Favor Globalization and Others Don't?"

STUDENT:

One of the things I have noticed about globalization is that some people in the United States seem to be in favor of it and others seem to be against it. Why is this?

INSTRUCTOR:

It probably has much to do with how the benefits and costs of globalization are distributed across the population. People in one location might mainly receive the benefits, and people in some other location might mostly incur the costs.

STUDENT:

Can you give a real-world example?

INSTRUCTOR:

A while back, *The New York Times* reported about two cities in Michigan: Holland and Greenville.[3] In Holland, a factory was losing business and firing workers. Then a German company bought it. Today the factory is shipping wastewater treatment equipment to countries in the Middle East and Asia. Also, it is operating with twice as many

workers as it did before the German company bought it. The people in Holland, Michigan, see this change as a benefit of globalization. Only 60 miles away from Holland, in Greenville, Michigan, the story is different. In Greenville, a Swedish company shut down what had been the largest refrigerator factory in the country and eliminated about 2,700 jobs in the town. For the people of Greenville, globalization came with costs.

STUDENT:

What do most economists say about globalization? Do they think that, for the country as a whole, globalization comes with net benefits (more benefits than costs) or net costs (more costs than benefits)?

INSTRUCTOR:

Most economists seem to think that globalization comes with net benefits.

STUDENT:

But economic policy isn't always determined by what economists think, is it?

---

[3]. See Peter S. Goodman, "2 Outcomes When Foreigners Buy Factories," *New York Times*, April 7, 2008.

INSTRUCTOR:

You're right about that. Economic policy doesn't get made in a political vacuum. Politics plays a role in deciding which economic policies get adopted and implemented. Think about this point in terms of our example of the Michigan cities. Suppose we went to Greenville, where jobs had been lost, and told the residents of the city that globalization, on net, is good for the country. Suppose we said that, for the country as a whole, the benefits from globalization outweigh the costs. The residents of Greenville might say that is all well and good, but globalization hasn't been that good to them and that is all they care about. As a result, their vote, to the extent that they have one on the issue, is *against* globalization.

STUDENT:

I see. In other words, sometimes what might be beneficial for the country (as a whole) is not beneficial for some part of it.

INSTRUCTOR:

That is the way some things turn out.

Points to remember

1. Globalization can come with net benefits for a country, but not everyone in the country necessarily benefits from globalization.
2. The benefits and costs of globalization are not evenly spread throughout a country. The benefits may fall on some people and the costs on others.

CHAPTER SUMMARY

WHAT IS GLOBALIZATION?

- Globalization is a phenomenon by which individuals and businesses in any part of the world are much more affected by events elsewhere in the world than they were before; it is the growing integration of national economies of the world to the degree that we may be witnessing the emergence and operation of a single worldwide economy.

- Certain facts provide evidence that globalization is occurring. Some of these facts are (1) lower tariff rates in many countries, and (2) many countries exporting and importing more goods than in the past.

MOVEMENT TOWARD GLOBALIZATION

- What has caused this most recent push toward globalization? In the chapter, we identified (1) the end of the Cold War, (2) advancing technology, and (3) policy changes as causal factors.

BENEFITS AND COSTS OF GLOBALIZATION

- Among the benefits of globalization are (1) benefits from increased international trade, (2) greater income per person, (3) lower prices for goods, (4) a greater variety of products, and (5) increased productivity and innovation.

- Among the costs of globalization are (1) increased income inequality (although there is some debate here), (2) offshoring, and (3) increased economic power for large corporations (although there is some debate here too).

- Seeing the benefits of globalization is often much more difficult than seeing the costs. The benefits are largely dispersed over a large population, but the costs (e.g., offshoring) might be concentrated on relatively few.

THE FUTURE OF GLOBALIZATION

- The future of globalization is under debate. Some persons argue that globalization will continue; others say that it will stall and (perhaps) backtrack.

NET EXPORTS AND AGGREGATE DEMAND

- An increase in net exports will shift the *AD* curve to the right. A decrease in net exports will shift the *AD* curve to the left.

- Two factors can change net exports: foreign Real GDP (or real national income) and exchange rates. For example, in a two-country world (say, Japan and the United States), an increase in Japan's Real GDP and a depreciation of the dollar will increase U.S. net exports and shift the U.S. *AD* curve to the right. Alternatively, a decrease in Japan's Real GDP and an appreciation of the dollar will decrease U.S. net exports and shift the U.S. *AD* curve to the left.

THE AGGREGATE SUPPLY CURVE AND INTERNATIONAL FACTORS

- A change in foreign input prices will affect the U.S. *SRAS* curve. For example, an increase in foreign input prices will shift the U.S. *SRAS* curve to the left, and a decrease in foreign input prices will shift the U.S. *SRAS* curve to the right.

- A change in foreign input prices can be the result of changes in the input market in the foreign country.
- A change in foreign input prices (paid by U.S. producers) can be the result of a change in the exchange rate. For example, if the dollar depreciates, U.S. producers will pay higher prices for foreign inputs, and if the dollar appreciates, U.S. producers will pay lower prices for foreign inputs.

INTERNATIONAL FACTORS, AGGREGATE DEMAND, AND SHORT-RUN AGGREGATE SUPPLY

- A change in the exchange rate will affect both the U.S. *AD* curve and the U.S. *SRAS* curve. For example, if the dollar depreciates, the *AD* curve will shift to the right and the *SRAS* curve will shift to the left.
- A change in real interest rates will affect both the U.S. *AD* curve and the U.S. *SRAS* curve. To illustrate, suppose the U.S. real interest rate rises relative to the Japanese interest rate. Then higher real interest rates in the United States will attract foreign capital. Foreigners who are in search of U.S. assets that pay interest will bid up the price of a dollar; thus, the dollar appreciates. If the dollar appreciates, the *AD* curve will shift to the left and the *SRAS* curve will shift to the right. The U.S. price level will then fall. What happens to U.S. Real GDP depends on the relative shifts in the *AD* and *SRAS* curves. Typically, the *AD* curve shifts leftward by more than the *SRAS* curve shifts rightward, so Real GDP falls.

FISCAL AND MONETARY POLICY IN CLOSED AND OPEN ECONOMIES

- Expansionary fiscal policy raises Real GDP more in a closed economy than in an open economy.
- Contractionary fiscal policy lowers Real GDP more in a closed economy than in an open economy.
- Expansionary monetary policy raises Real GDP more in an open economy than in a closed economy.
- Contractionary monetary policy lowers Real GDP more in an open economy than in a closed economy.

KEY TERMS AND CONCEPTS

Globalization	Offshoring	Closed Economy
Tariff	J-Curve	Open Economy

VIDEO QUESTIONS AND PROBLEMS

Video Questions and Problems are available on MindTap for Arnold 12e or by searching for Arnold on www.cengagebrain.com

1. Identify and explain the three driving forces of the most recent period of globalization.

2. Explain the J-curve.

3. Explain how depreciation of the dollar can change the price of a foreign input.

4. Explain how higher real interest rates in the United States can affect the price level and Real GDP.

QUESTIONS AND PROBLEMS

1. Why might it be easier to recognize the costs of globalization than the benefits?

2. If globalization continues over the next few decades, how might your life be different?

3. How might governments affect globalization?

4. Identify and explain two of the benefits and two of the costs of globalization.

5. What effect might advancing technology have on globalization?

6. Some have argued that the end of the Cold War acted as a catalyst toward greater globalization. How so?

7. David Friedman said that free international trade is a technology. Explain what he means.

8. Will globalization lead to some people losing jobs? Explain your answer.

9. How do tariff rates in the United States today compare with those which existed in 1946?

10. What is the impact on U.S. Real GDP of each of the following in a two-country world consisting of the United States and Japan?

    a. A fall in the real interest rate in the United States relative to the real interest rate in Japan

    b. An economic expansion in Japan

11. Give a numerical example to illustrate what the depreciation of a country's currency does to the prices of its imports.

12. If Americans buy fewer units of good X, which is produced in Japan, will they necessarily spend less money overall on good X? Explain your answer.

13. "The discussion of the J-curve points out that economists sometimes think in terms of both the short run and the long run." Do you agree or disagree? Explain your answer.

14. Explain how a change in the exchange rate can change the U.S. *AD* and *SRAS* curves.

15. Suppose country A undertakes a policy mix of contractionary fiscal policy and expansionary monetary policy. What do you predict would happen to real interest rates, the value of country A's currency, and net exports? Explain your answer.

16. Why might import spending rise in a country soon after a depreciation of its currency? Is import spending likely to fall over time? Explain your answers.

17. Explain why expansionary monetary policy is more likely to increase Real GDP in an open economy than in a closed economy.

18. Explain why contractionary fiscal policy is more likely to decrease Real GDP in a closed economy than in an open economy.

19. Explain why contractionary monetary policy lowers Real GDP more in an open economy than in a closed economy.

WORKING WITH NUMBERS AND GRAPHS

1. Starting with an exchange rate of $1 = ¥114 and a price tag of ¥10,000 for a Japanese good, show what happens to the price of the good if the yen depreciates by 5 percent.

2. Explain and graphically show the domestic and feedback effects on Real GDP in the United States as a result of contractionary fiscal policy.

3. Explain and graphically show the domestic and feedback effects on Real GDP in the United States as a result of contractionary monetary policy.

SELF-TEST APPENDIX

Chapter 1

CHAPTER 1, PAGE 5

1. False. It takes two things for scarcity to exist: finite resources and infinite wants. If people's wants were equal to or less than the finite resources available to satisfy their wants, scarcity would not exist. Scarcity exists only because people's wants are greater than the resources available to satisfy their wants. Scarcity is the condition resulting from infinite wants clashing with finite resources.

2. Because of scarcity, there is a need for a rationing device. People will compete for the rationing device. For example, if dollar price is the rationing device, people will compete for dollars.

3. Because our unlimited wants are greater than our limited resources—that is, because scarcity exists—some wants must go unsatisfied. We must choose which wants we will satisfy and which we will not.

CHAPTER 1, PAGE 17

1. Every time a student is late to history class, the instructor subtracts one-tenth of a point from the person's final grade. Economists predict that, if the instructor raises the opportunity cost of being late to class by subtracting one point from the final grade, then fewer students will be late to class. In sum, the higher the opportunity cost is of being late to class, the less likely it is that people will be late to class.

2. Yes. To illustrate, suppose the marginal benefits and marginal costs (in dollars) are as follows for various hours of studying:

Hour	Marginal Benefits	Marginal Costs
First Hour	$20.00	$10.00
Second Hour	$14.00	$11.00
Third Hour	$13.00	$12.00
Fourth Hour	$12.10	$12.09
Fifth Hour	$11.00	$13.00

Clearly, you will study the first hour, because the marginal benefits are greater than the marginal costs.

Stated differently, studying the first hour has a net benefit of $10 (the difference between the marginal benefits of $20 and the marginal costs of $10). If you stop studying after the first hour and do not proceed to the second hour, then you forfeit the net benefit of $3 for the second hour. To maximize your net benefits of studying, you must proceed until the marginal benefits and the marginal costs are as close to equal as possible. (They never actually reach equality; in the language of calculus, they approach each other asymptotically. However, economists speak of "equality" of the two for convenience.) In this case, you study through the fourth hour. You do not study the fifth hour, because it is not worth it: The marginal benefits of studying the fifth hour are less than the marginal costs. In short, studying the fifth hour has a net cost.

3. You might feel sleepy the next day, you might be less alert while driving, and so on.

CHAPTER 1, PAGE 22

1. The purpose of building a theory is to explain something that is not obvious. For example, the cause of changes in the unemployment rate is not obvious, so the economist would build a theory to explain changes in the unemployment rate.

2. A theory of the economy seeks to explain why certain things in the economy happen. For example, a theory of the economy might try to explain why prices rise or why output falls. A description of the economy is simply a statement of what exists in the economy. For example, we could say that the economy is growing or contracting or that more jobs are available this month than last month. A description doesn't answer questions; it simply tells us what is. A theory tries to answer a "why" question, such as, "Why are more jobs available this month than last month?"

3. If you do not test a theory, you will never know whether you have accomplished your objective in building the theory in the first place. In other words, you will not know whether you have explained something accurately. We do not simply accept a theory if it sounds right, because what sounds right may actually be wrong. For

example, no doubt during the time of Columbus the theory that the earth was flat sounded right to many people and the theory that the earth was round sounded ridiculous. The right-sounding theory turned out to be wrong, though, and the ridiculous-sounding theory turned out to be right.

4. Unless stated otherwise, when economics instructors identify the relationship between two variables, they implicitly make the *ceteris paribus* assumption. In other words, the instructor is really saying, "If the price of going to the movies goes down, people will go to the movies more often—assuming that nothing else changes, such as the quality of movies, and so on." Instructors don't always state *"ceteris paribus,"* because if they did, they would be using the term every minute of a lecture. So the instructor is right, although a student who is new to economics might not know what the instructor is assuming but not saying.

Chapter 2
CHAPTER 2, PAGE 54

1. A straight-line PPF represents constant opportunity costs between two goods. For example, for every unit of X produced, one unit of Y is forfeited. A bowed-outward PPF represents increasing opportunity costs. For example, we may have to forfeit 1 unit of X to produce the 11th unit of Y, but we have to forfeit 2 units of X to produce the 100th unit of Y.

2. A bowed-outward PPF is representative of increasing costs. In short, the PPF would not be bowed outward if increasing costs did not exist. To prove this statement, look back at Exhibits 1 and 2. In Exhibit 1, costs are constant (not increasing) and the PPF is a straight line. In Exhibit 2, costs are increasing and the PPF is bowed outward.

3. The first condition is that the economy is currently operating *below* its PPF. It is possible to move from a point below the PPF to a point on the PPF and get more of all goods. The second condition is that the economy's PPF shifts outward.

4. False. Take a look at Exhibit 5. All of the numerous productive efficient points lie on the PPF.

Chapter 3
CHAPTER 3, PAGE 77

1. Popcorn is a normal good for Sandi. Prepaid telephone cards are an inferior good for Mark.

2. Asking why demand curves are downward sloping is the same as asking why price and quantity demanded are inversely related (as one rises, the other falls). Two reasons for this inverse relationship are mentioned in this section: (1) As price rises, people substitute lower priced goods for higher priced goods. (2) Because individuals receive less utility from an additional unit of a good they consume, they are only willing to pay less for the additional unit. The second reason is a reflection of the law of diminishing marginal utility.

3. Suppose only two people, Bob and Alice, have a demand for good X. At a price of $7, Bob buys 10 units and Alice buys 3 units; at a price of $6, Bob buys 12 units and Alice buys 5 units. One point on the market demand curve represents a price of $7 and a quantity demanded of 13 units; another point represents $6 and 17 units. A market demand curve is derived by adding the quantities demanded at each price.

4. A change in income, preferences, prices of related goods, the number of buyers, and expectations of future price can change demand. A change in the price of the good changes the quantity demanded of it. For example, a change in *income* can change the *demand* for oranges, but only a change in the *price* of oranges can directly change the *quantity demanded* of oranges.

CHAPTER 3, PAGE 83

1. Increasing the quantity supplied of houses over the next 10 hours would be difficult, so the supply curve in (a) is vertical, as in Exhibit 8. Increasing the quantity supplied of houses over the next three months is possible, so the supply curve in (b) is upward sloping.

2. a. The supply curve shifts to the left.

   b. The supply curve shifts to the left.

   c. The supply curve shifts to the right.

3. False. If the price of apples rises, then the *quantity supplied* of apples will rise—not the *supply*. We are talking about a *movement* from one point on a supply curve to a point higher up on the supply curve, not about a shift in the supply curve.

CHAPTER 3, PAGE 97

1. Disagree. In the text, we plainly saw how supply and demand work at an auction. Supply and demand are at work in the grocery store too, even though no auctioneer is present. The essence of the auction example is the

auctioneer's raising the price when there was a shortage and lowering the price when there was a surplus. The same thing happens at the grocery store. For example, given a surplus of cornflakes, the manager of the store is likely to run a sale (lower prices) on them. Many markets without auctioneers act *as if* auctioneers were raising and lowering prices in response to shortages and surpluses.

2. No. It could be the result of a higher supply of computers. Either a decrease in demand or an increase in supply will lower price.

3. a. Lower price and lower quantity

   b. Lower price and higher quantity

   c. Higher price and lower quantity

   d. Lower price and lower quantity

4. At the equilibrium quantity, the maximum buying price and the minimum selling price are the same. For example, in Exhibit 15, both prices are $40 at the equilibrium quantity of 4. The equilibrium quantity is the only quantity at which the maximum buying price and the minimum selling price are the same.

5. $44; $34

Chapter 4

CHAPTER 4, PAGE 105

1. A rationing device is necessary because scarcity exists. If scarcity did not exist, a rationing device would not be needed.

2. If (dollar) price is the rationing device used, then individuals have an incentive to produce goods and services, sell them for money (for the dollar price), and then use the money to buy what they want. If another rationing device were used (say, first come, first served or "need"), then the incentive to produce would be dramatically dampened. Why produce a good if the only way you can "sell" it (i.e., ration the good) is by way of first come, first served?

3. Price conveys information about the relative scarcity of a good. In the orange juice example, a rise in the price of orange juice transmitted information relating to the increased relative scarcity of orange juice due to a cold spell in Florida.

CHAPTER 4, PAGE 116

1. Yes, if nothing else changes—that is, yes, *ceteris paribus*. If other things change, though, they may not. For example, if the government imposes an effective price ceiling on gasoline, Jamie may pay lower gas prices at the pump but have to wait in line to buy the gas (because of first-come, first-served rationing of the shortage). Whether Jamie is better off paying a higher price and not waiting in line or paying a lower price and waiting in line is not clear. The point, however, is that buyers don't necessarily prefer lower prices to higher prices unless everything else (quality, wait, service, etc.) stays the same.

2. Disagree. Both long-lasting shortages and long lines are caused by price ceilings. First, the price ceiling is imposed, creating the shortage; then the rationing device of first come, first served emerges because price isn't permitted to fully ration the good. Every day, shortages occur that don't cause long lines to form. Instead, buyers bid up price, output and price move to equilibrium, and there is no shortage.

3. Buyers might argue for price ceilings on the goods they buy, especially if they don't know that price ceilings have some effects they may not like (e.g., fewer exchanges, first-come, first-served rationing devices, etc.). Sellers might argue for price floors on the goods they sell, especially if they expect their profits to rise. Employees might argue for a wage floor on the labor services they sell, especially if they don't know that they may lose their jobs or have their hours cut back as a result.

CHAPTER 4, PAGE 119

1. $1A = \frac{2}{3}B$ and $1B = 1.5A$.

2. The statement is correct in the sense that good X has a higher money price than it used to have. It is misleading because a higher money price doesn't necessarily mean a higher relative price. For example, if the absolute (money) price of good X is $10 and the absolute price of good Y is $20, then the relative price of X is ½ unit of Y. Now, suppose the absolute price of X rises to $15 while the absolute price of Y rises to $60. Then the new relative price of X is ¼ unit of Y. In other words, the absolute price of X rises (from $10 to $15), while its relative price falls (from ½Y to ¼Y). Thus, good X can become more expensive in money terms as it becomes cheaper in terms of other goods.

Chapter 5

CHAPTER 5, PAGE 125

1. The more requests for tickets and the faster the tickets sell out, the more popular the show is.

2. They could charge a positive ticket price for shows in which the quantity demanded of seats equaled the

quantity supplied of seats at a positive price. This equality may not always be the case, though, as shown in Exhibit 2.

CHAPTER 5, PAGE 126

1. Yes. For example, suppose a 30 percent down payment, instead of a 10 percent down payment, was needed to obtain a mortgage loan. Then fewer individuals would be able to obtain a loan to buy a house, lowering the demand for houses and thus lowering house prices.

2. Yes. Reducing one's taxes because one has purchased a house makes buying a house more attractive, leading to a higher demand for houses. The higher demand for houses raises the equilibrium price of houses.

CHAPTER 5, PAGE 127

1. The airline company will likely use the rationing device of first come, first served. The people who book their reservations early get their pick of seats; those who do not book early have to take the leftover seats.

2. The equilibrium price of the window seat is less than the equilibrium price of the aisle seat; the equilibrium price of the middle seat is lower than the equilibrium price of the window seat. For example, if the equilibrium price of the aisle seat is $300, then the equilibrium price of the window seat might be $280, with the equilibrium price of the aisle seat even lower at, say, $250.

CHAPTER 5, PAGE 128

1. Price will fall.

2. Quantity will rise.

CHAPTER 5, PAGE 129

1. A speculator seeks to "buy low and sell high." If she does so, she benefits. But by buying low and selling high, a speculator can reallocate supply and change prices in a way that benefits consumers. To illustrate, suppose a tornado threatens to reduce the wheat crop in the Midwest. Speculators translate this possibility into a future decrease in the supply of, and rise in the price of, wheat. So, they buy wheat today (before the tornado strikes and when it is relatively cheap) and sell it later (after the tornado has struck and the price is relatively expensive). In the process, they reallocate some of the supply of wheat from today to the future; and as supply changes, so does price. As for the buyers (of wheat and wheat products), they may prefer to spread out the price-related pain of the tornado

by paying a relatively higher price for wheat today and a relatively lower price for wheat in the future. For example, without the speculators reallocating some wheat, wheat prices might be $4 a bushel before the tornado and $9 after. But with the speculators, wheat prices might be $6 before the tornado and $7 after the tornado.

2. Suppose that, in a world without speculators, the price of good X is $40 on Monday through Thursday and $50 on Friday through Sunday. Suppose also that good X can be moved (in time) and that speculators exist; then speculators will buy some of good X on Monday through Thursday at the lower price and sell it on Friday through Sunday at the higher price. But this difference in price should last only a short while, because, in their attempts to "buy low and sell high," speculators are reallocating some of the supply of good X from Monday through Thursday to Friday through Sunday. The lower supply on Monday through Thursday will raise the price of good X on these days, and the higher supply on Friday through Sunday will lower the price of good X on these days. In the end, it is likely that the same price for good X will exist Monday through Sunday.

CHAPTER 5, PAGE 132

1. The price of food will rise along with the premium for food insurance.

2. The new demand curve would be between D_1 and D_2.

CHAPTER 5, PAGE 133

1. If supply and tuition are constant and demand rises, the shortage of openings at the university will become greater. The university will continue to use its nonprice-rationing devices (GPA, SAT scores, ACT scores) but will have to raise the standards of admission. Instead of requiring a GPA of, say, 3.5 for admission, it may raise the requirement to 3.8.

2. Not likely. A university that didn't make admission easier in the face of a surplus of openings might not be around much longer. When tuition cannot be adjusted directly—in other words, when the rationing device (price) cannot be adjusted—it is likely that the nonprice-rationing device (standards) will be.

CHAPTER 5, PAGE 135

1. Any price above 70¢

2. Assuming that tolls are not used, freeway congestion will worsen. An increase in driving population simply shifts the demand curve for driving to the right.

CHAPTER 5, PAGE 137

1. Moving from a system in which patients cannot sue their HMOs to one in which they can gives patients something they didn't have before (the right to sue) at a higher price (higher charges for health care coverage). The "free lunch"—the right to sue—isn't free after all.

2. If the students get the extra week and nothing else changes, then the students will probably say that they are better off. In other words, more of one thing (time) and no less of anything else makes one better off. But if, because of the extra week, the professor grades their papers harder than she would have otherwise, then some or all of the students may say that they weren't made better off by the extra week.

CHAPTER 5, PAGE 139

1. A possible answer: Of two cities, one has clean air and the other has dirty air. The demand to live in the city that has clean air is higher than the demand to live in the city that has dirty air. As a result, housing prices are higher in the city that has clean air.

2. Ultimately, the person who owns the land in the city that has good weather receives the payment. Look at it this way: People have a higher demand for houses in cities that have good weather than they do for houses in cities that have bad weather. As a result, house builders receive higher prices for houses built and sold in cities that have good weather. Because of the higher house prices, builders have a higher demand for land in cities that have good weather. In the end, higher demand for land translates into higher land prices or land rents for landowners.

CHAPTER 5, PAGE 140

1. Suppose University X gives a full scholarship to every one of its football players (all of whom are superathletes). In addition, suppose that the full scholarship (translated into wages) is far below the equilibrium wage of each of the football players. (Think of it this way: Each football player gets a wage, or full scholarship, of $10,000 a year, when his equilibrium wage is $40,000 a year.) Paying lower than the equilibrium wage will end up transferring dollars and other benefits from the football players to the university, to the new field house and track, and perhaps to you if you use the track for exercise.

2. If paying student athletes (a wage above the full scholarship) lowers consumers' demand for college athletics, then the equilibrium wage for college athletes is not as high as is shown in Exhibit 9.

CHAPTER 5, PAGE 142 TOP

1. Answers will vary. Students sometimes say that it is "fairer" if everyone is charged the same price. Is it unfair, then, that moviegoers pay less if they go to the 2 p.m. movie than if they go to the 8 p.m. movie?

2. We learned about price ceilings in the previous chapter. Specifically, we learned that a price ceiling creates a shortage. In the application dealing with the 10:00 a.m. class, the university charged a below-equilibrium price for the 10:00 a.m. class, leading to a shortage of such classes.

CHAPTER 5, PAGE 142 BOTTOM

1. Las Vegas hotel–casinos are likely to price their hotel rooms lower than equivalent hotel rooms in noncasino hotels in other cities. Las Vegas hotel–casinos sell more than just hotel rooms. One product in particular that they sell is gaming: poker, blackjack, roulette, and so on. Staying at a hotel and gambling in that hotel could very well be complements, so the lower the price of the hotel, the more time is spent at the hotel and the greater is the demand for playing poker, blackjack, and so on. By pricing its hotel rooms less than hotels that sell only (or mainly) the services of the hotel room, Las Vegas hotel–casinos may be trying to increase the demand for gaming.

2. Coffee may be a complement for food. Free refills of coffee increase the quantity demanded of coffee and therefore increase the demand for food. For instance, without the free coffee refill, a person might be less likely to order a dessert (e.g., pie or cake, which many people often eat with coffee).

Chapter 6
CHAPTER 6, PAGE 153

1. The CPI is calculated as follows: (1) Define a market basket; (2) determine how much it would cost to purchase the market basket in the current year and in the base year; (3) divide the dollar cost of purchasing the market basket in the current year by the dollar cost of purchasing the market basket in the base year; (4) multiply the quotient by 100. (For a review of this process, see Exhibit 1.)

2. It is a year that is used for comparison purposes with other years.

3. Annual nominal income has risen by 13.85 percent, and prices have risen by 4.94 percent. We conclude that, because nominal income has risen more than prices, real income has increased. Alternatively, you can look at the situation this way: Real income in year 1 is $31,337, and real income in year 2 is $33,996.

CHAPTER 6, PAGE 163

1. The frictionally unemployed person has readily transferable skills, and the structurally unemployed person does not.

2. It implies that the (actual, measured) unemployment rate in the economy is greater than the natural unemployment rate. For example, if the unemployment rate is 8 percent and the natural unemployment rate is 6 percent, the cyclical unemployment rate is 2 percent.

Chapter 7

CHAPTER 7, PAGE 172

1. GDP is a measure of production in a country. When stocks are purchased and sold, no production occurs. A stock purchase and sale simply represents the trading of existing assets. Specifically, if person A owns 100 shares of stock X and then sells the shares to person B, all that has happened is that person B owns something that person A once owned. No more goods and services have been produced.

2. No. GDP doesn't account for all productive activity (e.g., it omits the production of nonmarket goods and services). A GDP of $0 doesn't necessarily mean that there was no production in the country.

CHAPTER 7, PAGE 175

1. In the expenditure approach, GDP is computed by finding the sum of consumption, investment, government purchases, and net exports. (Net exports are equal to exports minus imports.)

2. Yes. To illustrate, suppose consumption is $200, investment is $80, and government purchases are $70. The sum of these three spending components of GDP is $350. Now, suppose also that exports are $0 but imports are $100, in which case net exports are –$100. Because GDP = $C + I + G + (EX - IM)$, GDP is $250.

3. No. Each individual would have $40,000 worth of goods and services only if the entire GDP were equally distributed across the country. There is no indication, however, that this is the case. The $40,000 (per-capita GDP) says that the "average" person in the country has access to $40,000 worth of goods and services, but in reality the average person may not exist. For example, in a two-person universe, if Smith earns $10,000 and Jones earns $20,000, then the average person earns $15,000. But neither Smith nor Jones earns $15,000, so neither is average and the average person does not exist.

CHAPTER 7, PAGE 186

1. We can't know for sure; we can only say what might have caused the rise in GDP. It could be (a) a rise in prices with no change in output, (b) a rise in output with no change in prices, (c) rises in both prices and output, or (d) a percentage increase in prices that is greater than the percentage decrease in output . . . or even some other situation.

2. More output was produced in year 2 than in year 1.

3. Yes. Business cycles—ups and downs in Real GDP—don't prevent Real GDP from growing over time. Exhibit 7 shows Real GDP higher at the second peak than at the first, even though there is a business cycle between the peaks.

Chapter 8

CHAPTER 8, PAGE 205

1. In the real balance effect, a rise (fall) in the price level causes purchasing power to fall (rise), thereby decreasing (increasing) a person's monetary wealth. As people become less (more) wealthy, the quantity demanded of Real GDP falls (rises).

2. If the dollar appreciates, it takes more foreign currency to buy a dollar and fewer dollars to buy foreign currency. U.S. goods (denominated in dollars) become more expensive for foreigners, and foreign goods become cheaper for Americans. In turn, foreigners buy fewer U.S. exports, and Americans buy more foreign imports. As exports fall and imports rise, net exports fall. If net exports fall, total expenditures fall, *ceteris paribus*. As total expenditures fall, the *AD* curve shifts to the left.

3. Total spending is the product of the money supply and velocity. Let the money supply be $400 and velocity 3. Then total spending is $1,200. Now, suppose that the money supply rises to $500 but that velocity declines to 2. Then total spending has fallen to $1,000, even though the money supply has increased. So, yes, the money supply can rise while total spending declines.

CHAPTER 8, PAGE 210

1. As wage rates decline, the cost per unit of production falls. In the short run (assuming that prices are constant), profit per unit rises. Higher profit causes producers to

produce more units of their goods and services. In short, the *SRAS* curve shifts to the right.

2. Last year, 10 workers produced 100 units of good X in 1 hour. This year, 10 workers produced 120 units of good X in 1 hour.

3. Workers initially misperceive the change in their real wage as being due to a change in the price level. For example, the nominal wage is $30, and the price level is 1.50; the real wage is therefore $20. Then the nominal wage falls to $25, and the price level falls to 1.10. The real wage is now $22.72. But suppose workers misperceive the decline in the price level and mistakenly believe that it has fallen to 1.40. Then they will now perceive their real wage as $17.85 ($25 ÷ 1.40). In other words, they will misperceive their real wage as falling when it has actually increased. How will workers react if they believe that their real wage has fallen? They will cut back on the quantity supplied of labor, reducing output (or Real GDP). This process is consistent with an upward-sloping *SRAS* curve: A decline in the price level leads to a reduction in output.

CHAPTER 8, PAGE 219

1. In long-run equilibrium, the economy is producing Natural Real GDP. In short-run equilibrium, the economy is not producing Natural Real GDP, although the quantity demanded of Real GDP equals the quantity supplied of Real GDP.

2. The diagram should show the price level in the economy at P_1 and Real GDP at Q_1, but the intersection of the *AD* curve and the *SRAS* curve is at some point other than P_1, Q_1. In addition, the *LRAS* curve should not be at Q_1 or at the intersection of the *AD* and *SRAS* curves.

Chapter 9
CHAPTER 9, PAGE 230

1. Say's law states that supply creates its own demand. In a barter economy, Jones supplies good X so that she can use it to demand some other good (e.g., good Y). The act of supplying is motivated by the desire to demand. Supply and demand are opposite sides of the same coin.

2. No, total spending will not decrease. For classical economists, an increase in saving (reflected in a decrease in consumption) will lower the interest rate and stimulate investment spending. So one spending component (consumption) goes down, and another (investment) goes up. Moreover, according to classical economists, the decrease in one spending component will be completely offset by an increase in another spending component, so overall spending does not change.

3. Prices and wages are flexible; they move up and down in response to market conditions.

CHAPTER 9, PAGE 236

1. A recessionary gap exists if the economy is producing a Real GDP level that is less than Natural Real GDP. An inflationary gap exists if the economy is producing a Real GDP level that is more than Natural Real GDP.

2. When the economy is in a recessionary gap, the labor market has a surplus. When the economy is in an inflationary gap, the labor market has a shortage.

3. The economy is somewhere above the institutional PPF and below the physical PPF.

CHAPTER 9, PAGE 243

1. In a recessionary gap, the existing unemployment rate is greater than the natural unemployment rate, implying that unemployment is relatively high. As wage contracts expire, business firms negotiate new ones that pay workers lower wage rates. As a result, the *SRAS* curve shifts rightward. At the same time, the price level begins to fall. The economy moves down the *AD* curve—eventually to the point where it intersects the *LRAS* curve. At this point, the economy is in long-run equilibrium.

2. In an inflationary gap, the existing unemployment rate is less than the natural unemployment rate, implying that unemployment is relatively low. As wage contracts expire, business firms negotiate contracts that pay workers higher wage rates. As a result, the *SRAS* curve shifts leftward. At the same time, the price level begins to rise. The economy moves up the *AD* curve—eventually to the point where it intersects the *LRAS* curve. At this point, the economy is in long-run equilibrium.

3. In the long run, changes in aggregate demand affect only the price level, not the Real GDP level or the unemployment rate. Stated differently, changes in *AD* in an economy have no long-run effect on the Real GDP that a country produces or on its unemployment rate; in the long run, changes in *AD* change only the price level.

Chapter 10
CHAPTER 10, PAGE 258

1. They mean that an economy might not self-regulate at Natural Real GDP (Q_N). Instead, an economy can get stuck in a recessionary gap.

2. To say that the economy is self-regulating is the same as saying that prices and wages are flexible and adjust quickly. They are just two ways of describing the same thing.

3. Aggregate demand might be too low mainly because Say's law may not hold in a money economy. This statement raises the question "Why *doesn't* Say's law hold in a money economy?" Keynes argued that an increase in saving (which leads to a decline in demand) does not necessarily bring about an equal amount of additional investment (which would lead to an increase in demand) because neither saving nor investment is exclusively affected by changes in the interest rate. (See Exhibit 1 for the way Keynes might have used numbers to explain his position.)

CHAPTER 10, PAGE 263

1. Autonomous consumption is one of the components of overall consumption. To illustrate, look at the consumption function: $C = C_0 + (MPC \times Y_d)$. The part of overall consumption (C) that is autonomous is C_0, and this part does not depend on disposable income. The part of consumption that does depend on disposable income (i.e., that changes as disposable income changes) is ($MPC \times Y_d$). For example, assume that $MPC = 0.80$. If Y_d rises by \$1,000, then consumption goes up by \$800.

2. $\dfrac{1}{1 - 0.70} = \dfrac{1}{0.30} = 3.33$

3. The multiplier falls. For example, if $MPC = 0.80$, then the multiplier is 5, but if $MPC = 0.20$, then the multiplier is 1.25.

CHAPTER 10, PAGE 268

1. Keynes believed that the economy might not always self-regulate at Natural Real GDP. In other words, households and businesses (the private sector of the economy) are not always capable of generating enough aggregate demand in the economy for the economy to equilibrate at Natural Real GDP.

2. The increase in autonomous spending will lead to a greater increase in total spending and to a rightward shift in the *AD* curve. If the economy is operating in the horizontal section of the Keynesian *AS* curve, Real GDP will rise and there will be no change in prices.

3. Agree. The economist who believes that the economy is inherently unstable sees a role for government, which is supposed to stabilize the economy at Natural Real GDP. The economist who believes that the economy

is self-regulating (capable of moving itself to Natural Real GDP) sees little, if any, role for government in the economy because the economy is already doing the job government would supposedly do.

CHAPTER 10, PAGE 276

1. When $TP > TE$, firms are producing and offering for sale more units of goods and services than consumers want to buy. As a result, business inventories rise above optimal levels. In reaction, firms cut back on their production of goods and services. The cutback in production leads to a decline in Real GDP. Real GDP stops falling when $TP = TE$.

2. When $TE > TP$, consumers want to buy more than firms are producing and offering for sale. As a result, business inventories fall below optimal levels. In reaction, firms increase the production of goods and services. The increase in production leads to a rise in Real GDP. Real GDP stops rising when $TP = TE$.

Chapter 11
CHAPTER 11, PAGE 290

1. With a proportional income tax, the tax rate is constant as one's income rises. With a progressive income tax, the tax rate rises as one's income rises (up to some point). With a regressive income tax, the tax rate falls as one's income rises.

2. In 2011, the top 5 percent of income earners received 33.9 percent of all income and paid 56.5 percent of all income taxes.

3. Individual income tax, corporate income tax, Social Security taxes, and Medicare taxes.

4. The cyclical budget deficit is the part of the budget deficit that is the result of a downturn in economic activity.

CHAPTER 11, PAGE 301

1. If crowding out does not occur, expansionary fiscal policy is predicted to increase aggregate demand and, if the economy is in a recessionary gap, either reduce or eliminate the gap. However, if the crowding out is, say, complete, then expansionary fiscal policy will not meet its objective. For example, suppose government purchases rise by \$100 million and private spending decreases by \$100 million. Then there is no net effect on aggregate demand.

2. Suppose the economy is currently in a recessionary gap in period 1. Expansionary fiscal policy is needed to remove the economy from its recessionary gap, but the fiscal

policy lags (data lag, wait-and-see lag, etc.) may be so long that, by the time the fiscal policy is implemented, the economy has moved itself out of the recessionary gap, making the expansionary fiscal policy not only unnecessary but potentially capable of moving the economy into an inflationary gap. (Exhibit 5 depicts this scenario.)

3. Suppose the federal government spends more on a particular program. As a result, the budget deficit grows and the federal government increases its demand for loanable funds (or credit) to finance the larger deficit. Because of the heightened demand for loanable funds, the interest rate rises; then, in response to the higher interest rate, business firms cut back on investment. Thus, an increase in government spending has indirectly led to a decline in investment spending.

CHAPTER 11, PAGE 304

1. Suppose that a person's taxable income rises by $1,000, to $45,000 a year and that her taxes rise from $10,000 to $10,390 as a result. Then her marginal tax rate—the percentage of additional taxable income she pays in taxes—is 39 percent. Her average tax rate—the percentage of her (total) income that she pays in taxes—is 23 percent.

2. Not necessarily. A rise in revenues depends on whether the percentage rise in tax rates is greater than or less than the percentage fall in the tax base. Here's a simple example: Suppose the average tax rate is 10 percent and the tax base is $100. Then tax revenues equal $10. If the tax rate rises to 12 percent (a 20 percent rise) and the tax base falls to $90 (a 10 percent fall), then tax revenues rise to $10.80. In other words, if the tax rate rises by a greater percentage than the tax base falls, tax revenues rise. Now suppose that the tax base falls to $70 (a 30 percent fall) instead of to $90. Then tax revenues are $8.40. In other words, if the tax rate rises by a smaller percentage than the tax base falls, tax revenues fall.

Chapter 12

CHAPTER 12, PAGE 316

1. Money evolved because individuals wanted to make trading easier (less time consuming). This desire motivated individuals to accept the good (in a barter economy) that had greater acceptability than all other goods. In time, the effect snowballed, and finally the good that initially had greater acceptability became widely accepted for purposes of exchange. At this point, the good became money.

2. No. M1 will fall, but M2 will not rise; it will remain constant. To illustrate, suppose M1 = $400 and M2 = $600. If

people remove $100 from checkable deposits, then M1 will decline to $300. For purposes of illustration, think of M2 as equal to M1 + money market accounts. The M1 component of M2 falls by $100, but the money market accounts component rises by $100, so there is no net effect on M2. In conclusion, M1 falls and M2 remains constant.

3. In a barter (moneyless) economy, a double coincidence of wants will not occur for every transaction. When it does not occur, the cost of the transaction increases because more time must be spent to complete the trade. In a money economy, money is acceptable for every transaction. All buyers offer money for what they want to buy, and all sellers accept money for what they want to sell.

CHAPTER 12, PAGE 320

1. The bank's reserves remain constant. Because reserves equal bank deposits at the Fed plus vault cash, removing $5 million from bank deposits at the Fed and adding the $5 million to vault cash keeps the total dollar amount of reserves constant.

2. Required reserves = r × Checkable deposits, where r = required reserve ratio. If checkable deposits equal $87 million and required reserves equal 6 million, then r equals the required reserves divided by checkable deposits: $6 million ÷ $87 million = a required reserve ratio of 6.89 percent.

3. Reserves = Required reserves + Excess reserves. If reserves are $6 million and excess reserves are $4 million, then required reserves are $2 million. Required reserves = r × Checkable deposits, where r = required reserve ratio. If required reserves are $2 million and r = 8 percent, then checkable deposits must equal $25 million because 8 percent of $25 million is $2 million.

CHAPTER 12, PAGE 324

1. It is a moral hazard problem. A moral hazard problem exists when one party to a transaction changes his or her behavior in a way that is hidden from, and costly to, the other party. By promising to pay Samantha's expenses over $1,000, Jack provides Samantha with an incentive to push her expenses beyond $1,000, especially if she thinks that her expenses will be close to $1,000. Simply put, Samantha has an incentive to act in a way that is hidden from, and potentially costly to, Jack. How might Jack lessen the moral hazard problem? Perhaps he could promise to pay a certain percentage of each dollar of Samantha's expenses over $1,000 instead of promising to pay every dollar of them.

2. A bank's capital, or net worth, is equal to the difference of its assets and liabilities. As bank A's assets decline in value (because some loans are not being repaid), the difference of its assets and liabilities diminishes, so its bank capital diminishes. If assets fall below liabilities, the bank will end up with negative bank capital (i.e., negative net worth).

3. Financial intermediaries essentially bring lenders and borrowers together. For example, Smith wants to lend $100 and Jones wants to borrow $100, but neither Smith nor Jones is in contact with the other. Instead of dealing with each other directly, both Smith and Jones go to a bank. Smith deposits $100 into the bank, and then the bank lends some or all of the $100 to Jones.

Chapter 13

CHAPTER 13, PAGE 333

1. Federal Reserve Bank of New York

2. To control the money supply

3. It means that the Fed stands ready to lend funds to banks that are suffering cash management, or liquidity, problems.

CHAPTER 13, PAGE 345

1. a. Money supply falls.

   b. Money supply rises.

   c. Money supply falls.

2. The federal funds rate is the interest rate one bank charges another bank for a loan. The discount rate is the interest rate the Fed charges a bank for a loan.

3. Reserves in bank A rise; reserves in the banking system remain the same (bank B loses the reserves that bank A borrowed).

4. Reserves in bank A rise; reserves in the banking system rise because there is no offset in reserves for any other bank.

Chapter 14

CHAPTER 14, PAGE 359

1. If $M \times V$ increases, total expenditures increase. In other words, people spend more. For example, instead of spending $3 billion on goods and services, they spend $4 billion. But more spending (greater total expenditures) means that there must be greater total sales. $P \times Q$ represents this total dollar value of sales.

2. The equation of exchange is a truism, or tautology: MV necessarily equals PQ. This is similar to saying that $2 + 2$ necessarily equals 4. It cannot be otherwise. The simple quantity theory of money, which is built on the equation of exchange, can be tested against real-world events. The simple quantity theory of money assumes that both velocity and Real GDP are constant and then, on the basis of these assumptions, predicts that changes in the money supply will be strictly proportional to changes in the price level. This prediction can be measured against real-world data, so the simple quantity theory of money may offer insights into how the economy works. The equation of exchange does not do this.

3. a. The *AD* curve shifts rightward.

   b. The *AD* curve shifts leftward.

   c. The *AD* curve shifts rightward.

   d. The *AD* curve shifts leftward.

CHAPTER 14, PAGE 363

1. a. As velocity rises, the *AD* curve shifts to the right. In the short run, *P* rises and *Q* rises. In the long run, *Q* will return to its original level and *P* will be higher than it was in the short run.

   b. As velocity falls, the *AD* curve shifts to the left. In the short run, *P* falls and *Q* falls. In the long run, *Q* will return to its original level and *P* will be lower than it was in the short run.

   c. As the money supply rises, the *AD* curve shifts to the right. In the short run, *P* rises and *Q* rises. In the long run, *Q* will return to its original level and *P* will be higher than it was in the short run.

   d. As the money supply falls, the *AD* curve shifts to the left. In the short run, *P* falls and *Q* falls. In the long run, *Q* will return to its original level and *P* will be lower than it was in the short run.

2. Yes, a change in velocity can offset a change in the money supply and have no effect on aggregate demand. Suppose that the money supply rises and velocity falls. A rise in the money supply shifts the *AD* curve to the right, and a fall in velocity shifts the *AD* curve to the left. If the strength of each change is the same, *AD* does not change.

CHAPTER 14, PAGE 371

1. This question cannot be answered on the basis of the information given. We know only that three prices have gone up; we don't know whether other prices (in the economy) have gone up, whether other prices have gone down, or whether some have gone up and others have gone down. To determine whether inflation has

occurred, we have to know what has happened to the price level, not simply to three prices.

2. No. For continued inflation (continued increases in the price level) to be the result of continued decreases in *SRAS,* workers would have to continually ask for and receive higher wages while output was dropping and the unemployment rate was rising. This combination of circumstances is not likely.

3. Continued inflation.

CHAPTER 14, PAGE 377

1. 3 percent

2. Yes, it is possible. It would occur if the expectations effect immediately set in and outweighed the liquidity effect.

3. Certainly, the Fed directly affects the supply of loanable funds and the interest rate through an open market operation. But it also works as a catalyst to indirectly affect the loanable funds market and the interest rate via the changes in Real GDP, the price level, and the expected inflation rate. We can say this: The Fed directly affects the interest rate via the liquidity effect, and it indirectly affects the interest rate via the income, price-level, and expectations effects.

Chapter 15
CHAPTER 15, PAGE 389

1. Smith buys a bond for a face value of $10,000 that promises to pay a 10 percent interest rate each year for 10 years. In 1 year, though, bonds are offered for a face value of $10,000 that pay an 11 percent interest rate each year for 10 years. If Smith wants to sell his bond, he won't be able to sell it for $10,000. No one today will pay $10,000 for a bond that pays a 10 percent interest rate when a new $10,000 bond pays an 11 percent interest rate. Smith will have to lower the price of his bond if he wants to sell it. Thus, as interest rates rise, the prices of old or existing bonds decrease.

2. We disagree for two reasons. First, if the money market is in the liquidity trap, a rise in the money supply will not affect interest rates and therefore will not affect investment or the goods-and-services market. Second, even if the money market is not in the liquidity trap, a rise in the money supply affects the goods-and-services market not directly, but indirectly: The rise in the money supply lowers the interest rate, causing investment to rise (assuming that investment is not interest insensitive). As investment rises, the *AD* curve shifts rightward, affecting the goods-and-services market. In

the Keynesian transmission mechanism, an important intermediate market lies between the money market and the goods-and-services market. Thus, the money market can affect the goods-and-services market only indirectly.

3. A rise in the money supply brings about an excess supply of money in the money market. This surplus of money then flows to the goods-and-services market, stimulating aggregate demand.

CHAPTER 15, PAGE 402

1. This is an open-ended question whose answer depends on many factors. First, what does the rule specify? Not all rules are alike. Second, the answer depends on the stability and predictability of velocity. For example, suppose the rule specifies that each year the money supply will rise by the average annual growth rate in Real GDP. If velocity is constant, this trend will produce price stability. But if velocity is extremely volatile, changes in velocity might offset changes in the money supply, leading to deflation instead of price stability. For example, suppose Real GDP rises by 3 percent and the money supply increases by 3 percent, but velocity decreases by 3 percent. Then the change in velocity offsets the change in the money supply, leaving a net effect of a 3 percent rise in Real GDP. The increase in Real GDP would then lead to a 3 percent decline in the price level.

2. Here is the Taylor rule specification: Federal funds rate target = 1.5(4 percent) + 0.5(5 percent) + 1 = 9.5 percent.

3. To change the money supply in a direction and by a magnitude sufficient to hit the Nominal GDP target. For example, if the target is to have Nominal GDP grow by 5 percent annually, then adjust money supply growth such that the target of 5 percent is hit.

Chapter 16
CHAPTER 16, PAGE 417

1. A given Phillips curve identifies different combinations of inflation and unemployment—for example, 4 percent inflation with 5 percent unemployment and 2 percent inflation with 7 percent unemployment. For these combinations of inflation and unemployment to be permanent, there must be only one (downward-sloping) Phillips curve that never changes.

2. Sometimes there is and sometimes there isn't. Look at Exhibit 3. Unemployment is higher and inflation is lower in 1964 than in 1965, so there is a trade-off between these two years. But both unemployment and

inflation are higher in 1980 than in 1979, so between those two years, there is no trade-off between inflation and unemployment.

3. Workers are fooled into thinking that the inflation rate is lower than it is. In other words, they underestimate the inflation rate and therefore overestimate the purchasing power of their wages.

CHAPTER 16, PAGE 429

1. No. The PIP says that, under certain conditions, neither expansionary fiscal policy nor expansionary monetary policy will be able to increase Real GDP and lower the unemployment rate in the short run. The conditions are that the policy change is anticipated correctly, that individuals form their expectations rationally, and that wages and prices are flexible.

2. None. Given an unanticipated increase in aggregate demand, the economy moves from point 1 to 2 (in Exhibit 10) in the short run and then to point 3. This behavior occurs whether people are holding rational or adaptive expectations.

3. In the short run, the price level rises and Real GDP declines. In the long run, the price level rises and Real GDP is constant.

CHAPTER 16, PAGE 432

1. Both. The relevant question is whether the decline in the money supply was caused by a change on the supply side of the economy. If the answer is no, then the decline in the money supply is consistent with a demand-induced business cycle. If the answer is yes, then it is consistent with a supply-induced (real) business cycle.

2. New Keynesians believe that prices and wages are somewhat inflexible; new classical economists believe that prices and wages are flexible.

Chapter 17

CHAPTER 17, PAGE 452

1. Such a shift is shown in Exhibit 4(a). A decline in taxes shifts the labor supply curve to the right, increasing the equilibrium level of labor in the labor market. More labor generates more output (Real GDP), as shown in Exhibit 4(b). And more Real GDP is consistent with the *LRAS* curve having shifted to the right [Exhibit 4(c)].

2. Physical capital consists of the goods that are produced and then used as inputs for further production. Examples

of such goods are factories, machinery, tools, computers, and buildings. Human capital refers to the knowledge and skills individuals acquire through education, training, and experience.

3. In neoclassical growth theory, technology was, in a sense, "just there." Technological advances just happened, but how these advances happened was not fully understood. Technology was something that was exogenous—outside the economic system and outside of our control. In new growth theory, technology is said to be endogenous. It can be increased or decreased by the amount of resources devoted to it. Also, technology is viewed as being related to ideas.

4. Labor is the movement factor, and both capital and the technology coefficient are shift factors.

Chapter 18

CHAPTER 18, PAGE 460

1. If a bank has, for example, assets of $100 and liabilities of $80, then it has a net worth, or capital, of $20. If its assets decline in value from $100 to $90, the bank's net worth falls from $20 to $10, but the bank is still solvent. In other words, the bank's net worth stood between the bank and insolvency. The bigger the net worth is, the bigger the buffer will be between declining asset values and insolvency. This bank can withstand a $20 decline in assets before becoming insolvent. A bank with a bigger net worth could withstand a greater decline in assets before becoming insolvent.

2. If a bank has, for example, assets of $100 and liabilities of $80, then it has a net worth, or capital, of $20. If the bank's assets decline in value by $30, the bank now has a negative net worth of –$10. As a result, the bank may go out of business or pull back on its lending activities. Either way, there is less lending activity.

3. A financial crisis occurs when financial firms and markets have problems that make it difficult for people to obtain loans from banks and other financial institutions.

CHAPTER 18, PAGE 466

1. The global-savings-glut explanation is that, in some countries, saving was greater than investment, so the excess savings flowed into the United States and lowered interest rates (including mortgage interest rates). The low mortgage rates fueled house buying, which pushed up house prices. The Fed-low-interest-rate explanation is that the Fed kept the federal funds rate low, thereby keeping

mortgage interest rates low. The low mortgage interest rates fueled house buying, which pushed up house prices.

2. Taylor concludes that, when we compare actual Fed monetary policy with the Taylor rule monetary policy, we see that monetary policy was "too expansionary" during the early 2000s. He believes that this deviation from the rule brought about the "too low" interest rates that led to rising house prices in the United States. One piece of evidence in his favor is that there is a strong correlation between a housing boom in different countries (where "housing boom" is defined in terms of housing investment as a percentage of GDP) and deviations from the Taylor rule. For example, within OECD countries, the countries whose monetary policies deviated most from the Taylor rule had bigger housing booms than those whose monetary policies deviated less.

CHAPTER 18, PAGE 479

1. Suppose a bank has $100 in assets and $97 in liabilities. The bank therefore has $3 in capital. Its leverage ratio is 100 to 3, or 33⅓ to 1. If the assets of the bank decline by 4 percent, to $96, the bank becomes insolvent, with negative capital of −$1. Contrast this bank with a bank that has $100 in assets and $90 in assets. That bank has $10 in capital, and its leverage ratio is 10 to 1. If the assets of the bank then decline by 4 percent, to $96, the bank remains solvent, with capital of $6. The lesson: The greater the leverage ratio is, the more likely it is that a decline in asset values will result in insolvency.

2. We agree. Suppose the assets held by banks begin to decline in value and, as a result, the banks end up lending less. Reduced bank lending reduces economic activity, resulting in less production, a decline in sales, and rising unemployment in the real sector. Because of these problems, some people in the real sector who earlier took out loans from banks are unable to repay their loans, thus exacerbating the problems that already exist in the financial sector.

3. Regulatory capital arbitrage is a means of changing the composition of assets in such a way as to lower the overall amount of capital a financial institution holds for a given level of assets.

Chapter 19

CHAPTER 19, PAGE 495

1. Economist A believes that the percentage change in the tax rate will be smaller than the percentage change in the tax base. Economist B believes that the percentage change in the tax rate will be larger than the percentage change in the tax base.

2. When government spends $1, the entire $1 enters the spending stream, but when government cuts taxes by $1, individuals spend some of the dollar that they now get to keep and save some of it. For example, they might spend 60¢ of the dollar and save 40¢.

3. Agree. At any given point in time, government has a specific size and scope. If economist A believes that the optimal size and scope of government is greater than the current size and scope, then she is more likely to recommend increased government purchases over tax cuts if she thinks that an expansionary fiscal policy measure is needed to stimulate the economy (holding all other things equal, such as the size of the government spending multiplier and the tax multiplier, etc.). If economist B believes that the optimal size and scope of government is less than the current scope, then he is more likely to recommend tax cuts over increased government purchases if he thinks that an expansionary fiscal policy measure is needed to stimulate the economy.

Chapter 20

CHAPTER 20, PAGE 508

1. No. The model doesn't say every politician has to do these things; it simply predicts that politicians who do these things have an increased chance of winning the election in a two-person race.

2. Voters may want more information from politicians, but supplying that information is not always in the best interests of political candidates. When they speak in specific terms, politicians are often labeled as being at one end or the other of the political spectrum. But, generally, this not where elections are won.

3. Yes. In the cost equation of voting, we included (1) the cost of driving to the polls, (2) the cost of standing in line, and (3) the cost of filling out the ballot. Bad weather (heavy rain, snow, ice) would likely raise the cost of driving to the polls and standing in line, therefore raising the cost of voting. The higher the cost of voting is, the less likely it is that people will vote, *ceteris paribus*.

CHAPTER 20, PAGE 511

1. 2 units

2. In Example 2 with equal taxes, 1 unit received a simple majority of the votes. Person *C* was made worse off by

$20 because his *MPB* for the first unit of good *Y* was $100 but he ended up paying a tax of $120.

CHAPTER 20, PAGE 518

1. Both farmers and consumers are affected by federal agricultural policy, but not in the same way and not to the same degree. Federal agricultural policy directly affects farmers' incomes, usually by a large amount. It indirectly affects consumers' costs, but not as much as it affects farmers' incomes. Simply put, farmers have more at stake than consumers when it comes to federal agricultural policy. People tend to be better informed about matters that mean more to them.

2. The legislation is more likely to pass when group A includes 10 million persons, because the wider the dispersal of the costs of the legislation, the greater the likelihood is of passage. When costs are widely dispersed, the cost to any one individual is so small that she or he is unlikely to lobby against the legislation.

3. Examples include teachers saying that more money for education will help the country compete in the global marketplace, domestic car manufacturers saying that tariffs on foreign imports will save American jobs and U.S. manufacturing, and farmers saying that subsidies to farmers will preserve the "American" farm and a way of life that Americans cherish. Whether any of these groups is right or wrong is not the point. The point is that special-interest groups are likely to advance their arguments (good or bad) with public-interest talk.

4. Rent seeking is socially wasteful because the resources that are used to seek rent could instead be used to produce goods and services.

Chapter 21

CHAPTER 21, PAGE 525

1. Saying that a theory is falsifiable means that there can be evidence that rejects the theory. To illustrate, the theory which predicts that all swans are white is a falsifiable theory because it is possible for a nonwhite swan to exist. If that nonwhite swan is found to exist, then the theory is falsified.

2. The five-step process consists of (1) making an observation or having a thought, (2) asking a question, (3) building a theory to try to answer the question, (4) offering predictions based on the theory, and (5) testing the theory by gathering and analyzing data.

3. Not likely. The reason that economists don't like to explain different behavior by postulating different preferences is because different preferences can, in some ways, explain "too much." Here is what we mean: Suppose we see one person doing X and another person doing Y. What explains this difference in behavior? If we just say that one person has a preference for doing X and the other person has a preference for doing Y, that's the end of the story. But have we really explained anything then? What the economist would prefer to do is try to find a difference in the cost for each person of doing different things. In other words, might it be that the two persons have the same preferences but that one person does X instead of Y because, relative to the benefits, it is much less costly to do X than Y? Now think of this explanation in terms of our theory of the birthrates in different countries. One way to "explain" the difference is to simply say that women in some countries have a stronger preference for children than women in other countries. But is this really a satisfactory explanation? *Why* might they have a stronger preference? That question goes left unanswered.

CHAPTER 21, PAGE 535

1. At his son's high school football games. Being poorly behaved at a professional football game, where there are thousands of people he does not know, is not as costly to him (and to his son) as being poorly behaved at his son's football games, where he and his son may be known by a large percentage of the football-viewing population.

2. One way to find out whether kidnappers are rational or not is to build a theory of kidnapping based on rational kidnappers. Then, logically deduce the predictions of the theory. If evidence is consistent with the predictions, then we can conclude that kidnappers are rational; if evidence is not consistent with these predictions, then we can conclude that kidnappers are not rational. We don't start by arguing that kidnappers are rational or irrational. Instead, we build theories based on rational kidnappers and then see if the theory's predictions are or are not consistent with the evidence.

3. Strictly speaking, evidence cannot prove that a theory is correct. The best that evidence can do is to fail to reject the theory. To illustrate, consider the theory that all swans are white. Suppose we collect the evidence and find that all swans we have identified are white. Does this evidence prove the theory that all swans are white? No. That's because there could have been a swan that no one saw that is some color other than white.

CHAPTER 21, PAGE 543

1. Fewer students wear baseball caps on exam days than on lecture days. Also, students who wear their baseball caps on frontward on lecture days decide to wear their baseball caps on backward on exam days.

2. An ocean view is something that people are willing to pay to get. If two houses are the same in all ways except that one has an ocean view and the other doesn't, then the demand for the house with the ocean view will be greater than the demand for the house without the ocean view. Consequently, the price of the house with the ocean view will be higher than the price of the house without the ocean view. One pays for the ocean view by paying a higher price for the house with the ocean view than for the house without the ocean view.

3. If person A is included in person B's utility function in a positive way, it means that every time that person A's utility rises (falls), B's utility rises (falls) too. Think of a mother and a child. Suppose the child is in the mother's utility function in a positive way. It follows that as the child gets more satisfaction, the mother gets more satisfaction too. Also, as the child's utility diminishes, so does the mother's.

Chapter 22
CHAPTER 22, PAGE 552

1. For the United States, $1X = \frac{1}{6}Y$, or $1Y = 6X$. For Great Britain, $1X = 2Y$ or $1Y = \frac{1}{2}X$. Let's focus on the opportunity cost of $1X$ in each country. In the United States, $1X = \frac{1}{6}Y$, and in Great Britain, $1X = 2Y$. Terms of trade that are between these two end points would be favorable for the two countries. For example, suppose we choose $1X = 1Y$. This choice is good for the United States, which would prefer to give up $1X$ and get $1Y$ in trade than to give up $1X$ and get only $\frac{1}{6}Y$ (without trade). Similarly, Great Britain would prefer to give up $1Y$ and get $1X$ in trade than to give up $1Y$ and get only $\frac{1}{2}X$ (without trade). Any terms of trade between $1X = \frac{1}{6}Y$ and $1X = 2Y$ will be favorable to the two countries.

2. Yes. This idea is what the theory of comparative advantage demonstrates. Exhibit 1 shows that the United States could produce more of both food and clothing than Japan can. Still, the United States benefits from specialization and trade, as shown in Exhibit 2. In column 5 of this exhibit, the United States can consume 10 more units of food by specializing and trading than it could consume without specialization and trade.

3. No. It is the desire to buy low and sell high (earn a profit) that pushes countries into producing and trading at a comparative advantage. Government officials do not collect cost data and then issue orders to firms in the country to produce X, Y, or Z. We have not drawn the PPFs in this chapter and identified the cost differences between countries to show what countries actually do in the real world. Instead, we described things simply to show how countries benefit from specialization and trade.

CHAPTER 22, PAGE 562

1. Domestic producers benefit because producers' surplus rises; domestic consumers lose because consumers' surplus falls. Also, government benefits in that it receives the tariff revenue. Moreover, consumers lose more than producers and government gains, so tariffs result in a net loss.

2. Consumers' surplus falls by more than producers' surplus rises.

3. With a tariff, the government receives tariff revenue. With a quota, it does not. In the latter case, the revenue that would have gone to government goes, instead, to the importers who get to satisfy the quota.

4. Infant or new domestic industries need to be protected from older, more established competitors until they are mature enough to compete on an equal basis. Tariffs and quotas provide these infant industries the time they need.

Chapter 23
CHAPTER 23, PAGE 573

1. As the demand for dollars increases, the supply of pesos increases. For example, suppose someone in Mexico wants to buy something produced in the United States. The American wants to be paid in dollars, but the Mexican has pesos, not dollars. So she has to buy dollars with pesos; in other words, she has to supply pesos to buy dollars. Thus, as she demands more dollars, she will have to supply more pesos.

2. The dollar is said to have appreciated against the peso when it takes more pesos to buy a dollar and fewer dollars to buy a peso. For this eventuality to occur, either the demand for dollars must increase (which means that the supply of pesos increases) or the supply of dollars must decrease (which means that the demand for pesos decreases).

3. *Ceteris paribus*, the dollar will depreciate relative to the franc. As incomes for Americans rise, the demand for Swiss goods rises. Rising demand for Swiss goods then

increases the demand for francs and the supply of dollars on the foreign exchange market. In turn, the dollar depreciates and the franc appreciates.

4. The theory states that the exchange rate between any two currencies will adjust to reflect changes in the relative price levels of the two countries. For example, suppose the U.S. price level rises 5 percent and Mexico's price level remains constant. According to the PPP theory, the U.S. dollar will depreciate 5 percent relative to the Mexican peso.

CHAPTER 23, PAGE 578

1. The terms *overvalued* and *undervalued* refer to the equilibrium exchange rate: the exchange rate at which the quantity demanded and the quantity supplied of a currency are the same in the foreign exchange market. Let's suppose the equilibrium exchange rate were 0.10 USD = 1 MXN. This is the same as saying that 10 pesos = $1. If the exchange rate were fixed at 0.12 USD = 1 MXN (which is the same as 8.33 pesos = $1), the peso would be overvalued and the dollar would be undervalued. Specifically, a currency is overvalued if 1 unit of it fetches more of another currency than it would in equilibrium; a currency is undervalued if 1 unit of it fetches less of another currency than it would in equilibrium. In equilibrium, 1 peso would fetch $0.10, and at the current exchange rate it fetches $0.12, so the peso is overvalued. In equilibrium, $1 would fetch 10 pesos, and at the current exchange rate, it fetches only 8.33 pesos, so the dollar is undervalued.

2. An overvalued dollar means that some other currency—let's say, the Japanese yen—is undervalued. On the one hand, an overvalued dollar makes U.S. goods more expensive for the Japanese, so they buy fewer U.S. goods and the United States exports less. On the other hand, an undervalued yen makes Japanese goods cheaper for Americans, so they buy more Japanese goods and the United States imports more. Thus, an overvalued dollar reduces U.S. exports and raises U.S. imports.

3. a. Dollar is overvalued.

   b. Dollar is undervalued.

   c. Dollar is undervalued.

4. When a country devalues its currency, it makes it cheaper for foreigners to buy its products.

Chapter 24

CHAPTER 24, PAGE 593

1. As some explain it, the end of the Cold War resulted in turning two different worlds (the capitalist and communist worlds) into one world. It resulted in a thawing of not only political, but also economic, relations between former enemies. You might not trade with your enemy, but once that person or country is no longer your enemy, you do not feel the same need to cut him or it out of your political and economic life.

2. Globalization is the phenomenon by which individuals and businesses in any part of the world are much more affected by events elsewhere in the world than they were before; it is the growing integration of the national economies of the world to the degree that we may be witnessing the emergence and operation of a single worldwide economy.

3. Advancing technology can reduce both transportation and communication costs, thus making it less costly to trade with people around the world.

CHAPTER 24, PAGE 599

1. The benefits identified in the section include (a) benefits from increased international trade, (b) greater income per person, (c) lower prices for goods, (d) greater product variety, and (e) increased productivity and innovation.

2. The costs identified in the section include (a) increased income inequality, (b) offshoring, and (c) more power for big corporations.

CHAPTER 24, PAGE 604

1. Suppose that, in country A, there is an economic expansion and real income rises. As a result, residents of the country buy more imports from country B. In country B, exports rise relative to imports, thus increasing net exports. As net exports in country B rise, the *AD* curve for country B shifts to the right, increasing Real GDP.

2. If the dollar appreciates, the Japanese yen depreciates. U.S. products then become more expensive for the Japanese, and Japanese products become cheaper for Americans. Subsequently, U.S. imports will rise, U.S. exports will fall, and, consequently, U.S. net exports will fall. As a result, the *AD* curve in the United States will shift leftward, pushing down Real GDP.

CHAPTER 24, PAGE 607

1. Foreign input prices can change directly as a result of supply conditions in the foreign country, or they can change indirectly as a result of a change in the exchange rate. In either case, as foreign input prices rise—either directly or as a result of a depreciated dollar—the U.S. *SRAS* curve shifts leftward. If foreign input prices fall—either directly or as a result of an appreciated dollar—the *SRAS* curve shifts rightward.

2. The higher real interest rates in the United States attract capital to the United States, increasing the demand for the dollar. As a result, the dollar appreciates and the yen depreciates. An appreciated dollar shifts the U.S. *AD* curve leftward and the U.S. *SRAS* curve rightward. The *AD* curve shifts leftward by more than the *SRAS* curve shifts rightward, so the price level falls.

CHAPTER 24, PAGE 611

1. Expansionary fiscal policy pushes the *AD* curve rightward and (under certain conditions) raises Real GDP. If the expansionary fiscal policy causes a deficit, then the government will have to borrow to finance the deficit and interest rates will be pushed upward. As a result of the higher interest rates, more foreign capital flows into the United States and the dollar appreciates, thus pushing the *AD* curve leftward and the *SRAS* curve rightward.

2. When the money supply is raised, the *AD* curve shifts rightward, pushing up Real GDP. Also, as a result of the increased money supply, interest rates may decline in the short run, promoting U.S. capital outflow and a depreciated dollar. As a result of the depreciated dollar, imports become more expensive for Americans and U.S. exports become cheaper for foreigners. Imports thus fall and exports rise, thereby increasing net exports and *again* shifting the *AD* curve to the right, whereupon Real GDP rises.

Web Chapters

Web Chapter 25

CHAPTER 25, PAGE 620

1. He calculates the *MB/MC* ratio of producing and the *MB/MC* ratio of stealing. If the first ratio is greater than the second, then he devotes the next hour to producing rather than stealing, because the return from producing is greater than the return from stealing. He continues to devote more time to producing until the two ratios are the same.

2. Once Jack and Jill have agreed to stop stealing, each has an incentive to steal from the other. In terms of the payoff matrix in Exhibit 1, Jack and Jill may initially be in box 4. They make an agreement to stop stealing so that they can move to box 1. But once in box 1, each person can make himself or herself better off by moving to a different box. Jack is better off moving from box 1 to box 2, and Jill is better off moving from box 1 to box 3. They are likely, then, to break the agreement (not to steal) and try to move to their respective superior boxes, especially when no one can punish them for making the move. To explain why Jack and Jill can't move themselves from box 4 to box 1, the short answer is, "because there is no enforcer of the agreement." Government may later come along to fill the role of the enforcer of the agreement between Jack and Jill.

3. Disagree. Whether government makes parties in a prisoner's dilemma setting better off by removing them from the setting depends on how much each party gains by being removed compared with how much each party pays in tax to government. If the gain from being removed from the setting is $2 and the tax is $3, then a person is made worse off with government than without. If the gain is $2 and the tax is $1, then the person is made better off. If the gain is $2 and the tax is $2, then the person is made neither better off nor worse off.

CHAPTER 25, PAGE 624

1. With respect to a negative externality, if government can set the tax equal to the marginal external cost, then it can change an inefficient market outcome into an efficient one. With respect to a positive externality, if government can set the subsidy equal to the marginal external benefit, then it can change an inefficient market outcome into an efficient one.

2. Individuals might want certain nonexcludable public goods that the market will not produce because it cannot overcome the free-rider problem. Specifically, because nonexcludable public goods, once produced, cannot be denied to anyone, no one will have an incentive to pay for the good. Instead, individuals will choose to be free riders. Knowing this, no market participant will produce the good. Government can overcome the free-rider problem by taxing individuals and then using the tax monies either to produce the nonexcludable public good itself or to pay someone else to produce it.

CHAPTER 25, PAGE 626

1. Under the condition that the fine is greater than what people could save in monthly premiums by dropping their insurance.

2. The tax credit lowers the overall cost of buying a house; that is, a person who buys a house finds that his or her taxes are lowered. As a result, the demand to buy a house rises. As house demand rises, so do house prices.

3. Yes. When buying a house, the purchaser has to consider many factors: the interest rate on a mortgage loan, the taxes paid as a result of buying the house, the price of the house, and so on. In the tax credit policy example in this section, the tax credit initially lowered the overall cost of buying a house because it reduced the taxes a person would pay as a result of buying a house. But because it made buying a house less expensive, more people became home buyers. In other words, the demand for houses increased. Because the demand for houses increased, house prices increased, all other things remaining constant.

CHAPTER 25, PAGE 632

1. 1,000 times larger.

2. Group B would be less willing to advocate growth policies over transfer policies. The smaller the slice of the economic pie the group receives, the less they receive from any economic growth and thus the less willing they would be to advocate growth over transfers.

Web Chapter 26

CHAPTER 26, PAGE 644

1. 30

2. Stocks are purchased either for the dividends that the stocks may pay, the expected gain in price of the stock, or both.

3. Yield equals the dividend per share of the stock divided by the closing price per share.

4. A P/E ratio of 23 means that the stock is selling for a share price that is 23 times its earnings per share.

CHAPTER 26, PAGE 649

1. A bond is an IOU, or a promise to pay. The issuer of a bond is borrowing funds and promising to pay back those funds (with interest) at a later date.

2. $0.07x = \$400$, so $x = \$400 \div 0.07$, or $\$5,714.29$.

3. $\$1,000/\$9,500 = 10.53$ percent

4. A municipal bond is issued by a state or local government, and a Treasury bond is issued by the federal government.

CHAPTER 26, PAGE 653

1. A futures contract is a contract in which the seller agrees to provide a good to the buyer on a specified future date at an agreed-upon price.

2. You can buy a call option, which sells for a fraction of the cost of the stock. A call option gives the owner of the option the right to buy shares of a stock at a specified price within the time limits of the contract.

3. A put option gives the owner the right, but not the obligation, to *sell* (rather than buy, as in a call option) shares of a stock at a strike price during some specified period.

Web Chapter 27

CHAPTER 27, PAGE 660

1. The farmer does so through the futures market. Specifically, she enters into a futures contract with someone who will guarantee to take delivery of her foodstuff (in the future) for a stated price. Then, if the price goes up or down between the present and the future, the farmer does not have to worry. She has locked in the price of her foodstuff.

2. If the farmer faces an inelastic demand curve, the order of preference would be (b)–(a)–(c); that is, he prefers (b) to (a) and (a) to (c). If all farmers except himself have bad weather (b), then the market supply curve of the individual farmer's product shifts to the left, bringing about a higher price. But the individual farmer's supply curve doesn't shift to the left; it stays where it is. Thus, the individual farmer sells the same amount of output at the higher price. Consequently, his total revenue rises. In (a), both the market supply curve and the individual farmer's supply curve shift left, so the farmer has less to sell at a higher price. Again, if the demand is inelastic, the individual farmer will increase his total revenue, but not as much as in (b), a scenario in which the individual farmer's output does not fall. Finally, in (c), the market supply curve shifts to the right, lowering price. If demand is inelastic, then total revenue falls as well.

3. Increased productivity will lead to higher total revenue when demand is elastic. To illustrate, increased productivity shifts the supply curve to the right, lowering price. If demand is elastic, then the percentage rise in quantity

sold is greater than the percentage fall in price; therefore, total revenue rises. In sum, increased productivity leads to higher total revenue when demand is elastic.

CHAPTER 27, PAGE 665

1. Because the deficiency payment is the difference between the target price and the market price, the answer depends on the market price. If the market price is, say, $4, and the target price is $7, then the deficiency payment is $3.

2. A farmer pledges a certain number of bushels of foodstuff to obtain a loan—say, 500 bushels. He receives a loan equal to the number of bushels times the designated loan rate per bushel. If the loan rate is $2 per bushel and 500 bushels are pledged, then the loan is $1,000. The farmer ends up paying back the loan with interest or keeping the loan and forfeiting the bushels of the crop. Which course of action the farmer takes depends on the market price of the crop. If the market price of the crop is higher than the loan rate, he pays back the loan and sells the crop. If the market price is lower than the loan rate, he forfeits the crop. A nonrecourse loan guarantees that the farmer will not receive less than the loan rate for each bushel of his crop.

3. The effects of price supports are (a) a surplus, (b) fewer exchanges (less bought by private citizens), (c) higher prices paid by consumers of the supported crop, and (d) government purchase and storage of the surplus crop (for which taxpayers pay).

GLOSSARY

A

Absolute (Money) Price The price of a good in money terms.

Absolute Real Economic Growth An increase in Real GDP from one period to the next.

Abstraction The process (used in building a theory) of focusing on a limited number of variables to explain or predict an event.

Activists Persons who argue that monetary and fiscal policies should be deliberately used to smooth out the business cycle.

Adaptive Expectations Expectations that individuals form from past experience and modify slowly as the present and the future become the past (i.e., as time passes).

Adjustable Rate Mortgage A mortgage whose interest rate is adjusted periodically, depending on various factors.

Adverse Selection A phenomenon that occurs when parties on one side of the market who have information not known to others self-select in a way that adversely affects parties on the other side of the market.

Aggregate Demand The quantity demanded of all goods and services (Real GDP) at different price levels, *ceteris paribus*.

Aggregate Demand (AD) Curve A curve that shows the quantity demanded of all goods and services (Real GDP) at different price levels, *ceteris paribus*.

Aggregate Supply The quantity supplied of all goods and services (Real GDP) at different price levels, *ceteris paribus*.

Appreciation An increase in the value of one currency relative to other currencies.

Asset Anything owned or that one has claim to which has value.

Asymmetric Information A situation in which an economic agent on one side of a transaction has information that an economic agent on the other side of the transaction does not have.

Automatic Fiscal Policy Changes in government expenditures and/or taxes that occur automatically without (additional) congressional action.

Autonomous Consumption The part of consumption that is independent of disposable income.

B

Bad Anything from which individuals receive disutility or dissatisfaction.

Balanced Budget Government expenditures equal to tax revenues.

Balance Sheet A record of the assets and liabilities of a bank.

Barter Exchanging goods and services for other goods and services without the use of money.

Base Year The year chosen as a point of reference or basis of comparison for prices in other years; a benchmark year.

Board of Governors The governing body of the Federal Reserve System.

Bond An IOU, or a promise to pay.

Budget Deficit Government expenditures greater than tax revenues.

Budget Surplus Tax revenues greater than government expenditures.

Business Cycle Recurrent swings (up and down) in Real GDP.

C

Capital Produced goods, such as factories, machinery, tools, computers, and buildings, that can be used as inputs for further production.

Capital Consumption Allowance (Depreciation) The estimated amount of capital goods used up in production through natural wear, obsolescence, and accidental destruction.

Cash Leakage Occurs when funds are held as currency instead of deposited into a checking account.

Ceteris Paribus A Latin term meaning "all other things constant" or "nothing else changes."

Checkable Deposits Deposits on which checks can be written.

Closed Economy An economy that does not trade goods and services with other countries.

Comparative Advantage The situation in which someone can produce a good at lower opportunity cost than someone else can.

Complements Two goods that are used jointly in consumption. If two goods are complements, the demand for one rises as the price of the other falls (or the demand for one falls as the price of the other rises).

Complete Crowding Out A decrease in one or more components of private spending that completely offsets the increase in government spending.

Consumer Price Index (CPI) The weighted average of prices of a specific set of goods and services purchased by a typical household; a widely cited index number for the price level.

Consumers' Surplus (CS) The difference between the maximum price a buyer is willing and able to pay for a good or service and the price actually paid. (CS = Maximum buying price − Price paid.)

Consumption The sum of spending on durable goods, nondurable goods, and services.

Consumption Function The relationship between consumption and disposable income. In the consumption function used in this text, consumption is directly related to disposable income and is positive even at zero disposable income: $C = C_0 + (MPC)(Y_d)$.

Continued Inflation A continued increase in the price level.

Contractionary Fiscal Policy Decreases in government expenditures and/or increases in taxes in order to achieve economic goals.

Contractionary Monetary Policy The policy by which the Fed decreases the money supply.

Crowding Out The decrease in private expenditures that occurs as a consequence of increased government spending or the need to finance a budget deficit.

Currency Coins and paper money.

Cyclical Deficit The part of the budget deficit that is a result of a downturn in economic activity.

Cyclical Unemployment Rate The difference between the unemployment rate and the natural unemployment rate.

D

Deadweight Loss The loss to society of not producing the competitive, or supply-and-demand–determined, level of output.

Decisions at the Margin Decision making characterized by weighing the additional (marginal) benefits of a change against the additional (marginal) costs of a change with respect to current conditions.

Demand The willingness and ability of buyers to purchase different quantities of a good at different prices during a specific period.

Demand Curve The graphical representation of the law of demand.

Demand for Money (Balances) The inverse relationship between the quantity demanded of money (balances) and the price of holding money (balances).

Demand Schedule The numerical tabulation of the quantity demanded of a good at different prices. A demand schedule is the numerical representation of the law of demand.

Depreciation A decrease in the value of one currency relative to other currencies.

Devaluation A government action that changes the exchange rate by lowering the official price of a currency.

Direct Finance A method of transferring money whereby borrowers and lenders come together in a market setting, such as the bond market.

Directly Related Two variables are directly related if they change in the same way.

Discount Loan A loan the Fed makes to a commercial bank.

Discount Rate The interest rate the Fed charges depository institutions that borrow reserves from it; the interest rate charged on a discount loan.

Discretionary Fiscal Policy Deliberate changes in government expenditures and/or taxes in order to achieve economic goals.

Disequilibrium A state of either surplus or shortage in a market.

Disequilibrium Price A price other than the equilibrium price. A price at which the quantity demanded does not equal the quantity supplied.

Disposable Income The portion of personal income that can be used for consumption or saving. It is equal to personal income minus personal taxes (especially income taxes).

Disutility The dissatisfaction one receives from a bad.

Dividend A share of the profits of a corporation distributed to stockholders.

Double Coincidence of Wants In a barter economy, a requirement that must be met before a trade can be made. The term specifies that a trader must find another trader who at the same time is willing to trade what the first trader wants and wants what the first trader has.

Dow Jones Industrial Average (DJIA) The most popular, widely cited indicator of day-to-day stock market activity; a weighted average of 30 widely traded stocks on the New York Stock Exchange.

Dumping The sale of goods abroad at a price below their cost and below the price charged in the domestic market.

E

Economic Growth Increases in Real GDP.

Economics The science of scarcity; the science of how individuals and societies deal with the fact that wants are greater than the limited resources available to satisfy those wants.

Efficiency Exists when marginal benefits equal marginal costs.

Efficiency Wage Models These models hold that it is sometimes in the best interest of business firms to pay their employees wage rates that are higher than the equilibrium wage rate.

Elasticity of Investment A measure of the responsiveness of investment to changes in the interest rate.

Employment Rate The percentage of the civilian noninstitutional population that is employed: Employment rate = Number of employed persons ÷ Civilian noninstitutional population.

Entrepreneurship The talent that some people have for organizing the resources of land, labor, and capital to produce goods, seek new business opportunities, and develop new ways of doing things.

Equation of Exchange An identity stating that the money supply (M) times velocity (V) must be equal to the price level (P) times Real GDP (Q): $MV \equiv PQ$.

Equilibrium Equilibrium means "at rest." Equilibrium in a market is the price–quantity combination from which buyers or sellers do not tend to move away.

Equilibrium Price (Market-Clearing Price) The price at which the quantity demanded of a good equals the quantity supplied.

Equilibrium Quantity The quantity that corresponds to the equilibrium price. The quantity at which the amount of the good that buyers are willing and able to buy equals the amount that sellers are willing and able to sell, and both equal the amount actually bought and sold.

Equity (in a House) The difference between the price the house can be sold for and what one owes on the house.

Excess Reserves Any reserves held beyond the required amount; the difference between (total) reserves and required reserves.

Exchange Rate The price of one currency in terms of another currency.

Exchange (Trade) The giving up of one thing for something else.

Expansionary Fiscal Policy Increases in government expenditures and/or decreases in taxes in order to achieve particular economic goals.

Expansionary Monetary Policy The policy by which the Fed increases the money supply.

Expectations Effect The change in the interest rate due to a change in the expected inflation rate.

Exports Total foreign spending on domestic (U.S.) goods.

F

Face Value (Par Value) Dollar amount specified on a bond; the total amount the issuer of the bond will repay to the buyer of the bond.

Federal Funds Market A market in which banks lend reserves to one another, usually for short periods.

Federal Funds Rate The interest rate in the federal funds market; the interest rate banks charge one another to borrow reserves.

Federal Funds Rate Target The interest rate that the Fed wants the federal funds market rate to be.

Federal Open Market Committee (FOMC) The Fed's 12-member policy-making group. The committee has the authority to conduct open market operations.

Federal Reserve Notes Paper money issued by the Federal Reserve.

Federal Reserve System (the Fed) The central bank of the United States.

Final Good A good in the hands of its final user.

Financial Intermediary An institution that transfers funds from those who want to lend funds to those who want to borrow them.

Fine-tuning The (usually frequent) use of monetary and fiscal policies to counteract even small undesirable movements in economic activity.

Fiscal Policy Changes in government expenditures and/or taxes aimed at achieving economic goals, such as low unemployment, stable prices, and economic growth.

Fixed Exchange Rate System A system whereby a nation's currency is set at a fixed rate relative to all other currencies and central banks intervene in the foreign exchange market to maintain the fixed rate.

Fixed Investment Business purchases of capital goods, such as machinery and factories, and purchases of new residential housing.

Flexible Exchange Rate System A system whereby exchange rates are determined by the forces of supply and demand for a currency.

Foreign Exchange Market The market in which currencies of different countries are exchanged.

Fractional Reserve Banking A banking arrangement that allows banks to hold reserves equal to only a fraction of their deposit liabilities.

Frictional Unemployment Unemployment that is due to the natural so-called frictions in the economy and that is caused by changing market conditions and represented by qualified individuals with transferable skills who change jobs.

Friedman Natural Rate Theory Within the Phillips curve framework, the idea that, in the long run, unemployment is at its natural rate and that there is a long-run

Phillips curve, which is vertical at the natural rate of unemployment.

Full Employment The condition that exists when the unemployment rate is equal to the natural unemployment rate.

Futures Contract An agreement to buy or sell a specific amount of something (a commodity, a currency, a financial instrument) at an agreed-on price on a stipulated future date.

G

Globalization A phenomenon by which economic agents in any given part of the world are more affected by events elsewhere in the world than they were before; the growing integration of the national economies of the world to the degree that we may be witnessing the emergence and operation of a single worldwide economy.

Good Anything from which individuals receive utility or satisfaction.

Government Purchases Federal, state, and local government purchases of goods and services, and gross investment in highways, bridges, and so on.

Government Spending Multiplier The number that, when multiplied by the change in government spending, gives us the change in total spending (and, if prices are constant, the change in Real GDP).

Government Transfer Payments Payments to persons that are not made in return for currently supplied goods and services.

Gross Domestic Product (GDP) The total market value of all final goods and services produced annually within a country's borders.

H

Human Capital The knowledge and skills a person acquires through education, training, and experience.

I

Imports Total domestic (U.S.) spending on foreign goods.

Incentive Something that encourages or motivates a person to undertake an action.

Income Effect The change in the interest rate due to a change in Real GDP.

Incomplete Crowding Out A decrease in one or more components of private spending that only partially offsets the increase in government spending.

Independent Two variables are independent if, as one changes, the other remains constant.

Indirect Finance A method of transferring money whereby funds are loaned and borrowed through a financial intermediary.

Inferior Good A good for which demand falls (rises) as income rises (falls).

Inflation An increase in the price level.

Inflationary Gap The condition in which the Real GDP that the economy is producing is greater than the Natural Real GDP and the unemployment rate is less than the natural unemployment rate.

Inflation Targeting Targeting that requires the Fed to keep the inflation rate near a predetermined level.

Initial Public Offering (IPO) A company's first offering of stock to the public.

Insolvency A condition in which one's liabilities are greater than one's assets.

Institution The rules of the game in a society or, more formally, the humanly devised constraints that shape human interaction; the rules and regulations, laws, customs, and business practices of a country.

Interest Rate Effect The changes in household and business buying as the interest rate changes (in turn, a reflection of a change in the demand for or supply of credit brought on by price level changes).

Intermediate Good A good that is an input to the production of a final good.

International Trade Effect The change in foreign sector spending as the price level changes.

Inventory Investment Changes in the stock of unsold goods.

Inversely Related Two variables are inversely related if they change in opposite ways.

Investment The sum of all purchases of newly produced capital goods, changes in business inventories, and purchases of new residential housing.

Investment Bank A firm that acts as an intermediary between the company that issues the stock and the part of the public that wishes to buy it.

J

J-Curve The curve that shows a short-run worsening in net exports after a currency depreciation, followed by an improvement.

L

Labor The work brought about by the physical and mental talents that people contribute to the production process.

Labor Force Participation Rate (LFPR) The percentage of the civilian noninstitutional population that is in the civilian labor force: Labor force participation rate = Civilian labor force ÷ Civilian noninstitutional population.

Laffer Curve The curve, named after economist Arthur Laffer, that shows the relationship between tax rates and tax revenues. According to the Laffer curve, as tax rates rise from zero, tax revenues rise, reach a maximum at some point, and then fall with further increases in tax rates.

Laissez-faire A public policy of not interfering with market activities in the economy.

Land All natural resources, such as minerals, forests, water, and unimproved land.

Law of Demand As the price of a good rises, the quantity demanded of the good falls, and as the price of a good falls, the quantity demanded of the good rises, *ceteris paribus*.

Law of Diminishing Marginal Utility Over a given period, the marginal (or additional) utility or satisfaction gained by consuming equal successive units of a good will decline as the amount consumed increases.

Law of Increasing Opportunity Costs As more of a good is produced, the opportunity costs of producing that good increase.

Law of Supply As the price of a good rises, the quantity supplied of the good rises, and as the price of a good falls, the quantity supplied of the good falls, *ceteris paribus*.

Leverage The use of borrowed funds to increase the returns that can be earned with a given amount of capital.

Liability Anything that is owed to someone else.

Liquidity Effect The change in the interest rate due to a change in the supply of loanable funds.

Liquidity Trap The horizontal portion of the demand curve for money.

Logrolling The exchange of votes to gain support for legislation.

Long-Run Aggregate Supply (LRAS) Curve A curve that represents the output the economy produces when wages and prices have adjusted to their final equilibrium levels and when workers do not have any relevant misperceptions. The *LRAS* curve is a vertical line at the level of Natural Real GDP.

Long-Run Equilibrium The condition that exists in the economy when wages and prices have adjusted to their (final) equilibrium levels and when workers do not have any relevant misperceptions. Graphically, long-run equilibrium occurs at the intersection of the *AD* and *LRAS* curves.

M

M1 Currency held outside banks, plus checkable deposits, plus traveler's checks.

M2 M1, plus savings deposits (including money market deposit accounts), plus small-denomination time deposits, plus money market mutual funds (retail).

Macroeconomics The branch of economics that deals with human behavior and choices as they relate to highly aggregate markets (e.g., the market for goods and services) or the entire economy.

Managed Float A managed flexible exchange rate system under which nations intervene now and then to adjust their official reserve holdings in order to moderate major swings in exchange rates.

Marginal Benefits Additional benefits; the benefits connected with consuming an additional unit of a good or undertaking one more unit of an activity.

Marginal Costs Additional costs; the costs connected with consuming an additional unit of a good or undertaking one more unit of an activity.

Marginal (Income) Tax Rate The change in a person's tax payment divided by the change in taxable income: Δ Tax payment $\div$ Δ Taxable income.

Marginal Propensity to Consume (MPC) The ratio of the change in consumption to the change in disposable income: $MPC = \Delta C/\Delta Y_d$.

Marginal Propensity to Save (MPS) The ratio of the change in saving to the change in disposable income: $MPS = \Delta S/\Delta Y_d$.

Market Any place people come together to trade.

Median Voter Model A model suggesting that candidates in a two-person political race will attempt to match the preferences of the median voter.

Medium of Exchange Anything that is generally acceptable in exchange for goods and services; a function of money.

Microeconomics The branch of economics that deals with human behavior and choices as they relate to relatively small units: an individual, a firm, an industry, a single market.

Monetary Policy Changes in the money supply or in the rate of change of the money supply, intended to achieve stated macroeconomic goals.

Monetary Wealth The value of a person's monetary assets. Wealth, as distinguished from monetary wealth, refers to the value of all assets owned, both monetary and nonmonetary. In short, a person's wealth equals his or her monetary wealth (e.g., $1,000 cash) plus nonmonetary wealth (e.g., a car or a house).

Money Any good that is widely accepted for purposes of exchange and the repayment of debt.

Money Market Deposit Account (MMDA) An interest-earning account at a bank or thrift institution, for which a minimum balance is usually required and most of which offer limited check-writing privileges.

Money Market Mutual Fund (MMMF) An interest-earning account at a mutual fund company, for which a minimum balance is usually required and most of which offer limited check-writing privileges. Only retail MMMFs are part of M2.

Moral Hazard A condition that exists when one party to a transaction changes his or her behavior in a way that is hidden from, and costly to, the other party.

Mortgage-Backed Security (MBS) A type of asset-backed security that is secured by a mortgage or a collection of mortgages.

Multiplier The number that is multiplied by the change in autonomous spending to obtain the change in total spending. The multiplier (m) is equal to $1 \div (1 - MPC)$. If the economy is operating below Natural Real GDP, then the multiplier is the number that is multiplied by the change in autonomous spending to obtain the change in Real GDP.

N

National Income Total income earned by U.S. citizens and businesses, no matter where they reside or are located. National income is the sum of the payments to resources (land, labor, capital, and entrepreneurship): National income ∇ Compensation of employees $\lessgtr$ Proprietors' income $\lessgtr$ Corporate profits $\lessgtr$ Rental income of persons $\lessgtr$ Net interest.

Natural Real GDP The Real GDP that is produced at the natural unemployment rate. Also, the Real GDP that is produced when the economy is in long-run equilibrium.

Natural Unemployment Unemployment caused by frictional and structural factors in the economy: Natural unemployment rate = Frictional unemployment rate + Structural unemployment rate.

Net Domestic Product (NDP) GDP minus the capital consumption allowance.

Net Exports Exports minus imports.

Net Worth (or Capital) The difference between assets and liabilities. For example, if assets are $100 and liabilities are $80, net worth, or capital, is $20.

Neutral Good A good for which demand does not change as income rises or falls.

Nominal Income The current dollar amount of a person's income.

Nominal Interest Rate The interest rate actually charged (or paid) in the market; the market interest rate: Nominal interest rate = Real interest rate + Expected inflation rate.

Nonactivists Persons who argue against the deliberate use of discretionary fiscal and monetary policies to smooth out the business cycle. They believe in a permanent, stable, rule-oriented monetary and fiscal framework.

Normal Good A good for which demand rises (falls) as income rises (falls).

Normative Economics The study of "what should be" in economics.

O

Offshoring Work done for a company by persons other than the original company's employees in a country other than the company's home country.

One-Shot Inflation A one-time increase in the price level; an increase in the price level that does not continue.

Open Economy An economy that trades goods and services with other countries.

Open Market Operations The buying and selling of government securities by the Fed.

Open Market Purchase The buying of government securities by the Fed.

Open Market Sale The selling of government securities by the Fed.

Opportunity Cost The most highly valued opportunity or alternative forfeited when a choice is made.

Optimal Currency Area A geographic area in which exchange rates can be fixed or a common currency used without sacrificing domestic economic goals, such as low unemployment.

Option A contract that gives the owner the right, but not the obligation, to buy or sell shares of a stock at a specified price on or before a specified date.

Overvalued A currency is overvalued if its price in terms of other currencies is above the equilibrium price.

Own Price The price of a good. For example, if the price of oranges is $1, this is its own price.

P

Per-Capita Real Economic Growth An increase from one period to the next in per-capita Real GDP, which is Real GDP divided by population.

Personal Income The amount of income that individuals actually receive. It is equal to national income minus undistributed corporate profits, social insurance taxes, and corporate profits taxes, plus transfer payments.

Phillips Curve A curve that originally showed the relationship between wage inflation and unemployment and that now more often shows the relationship between price inflation and unemployment.

Policy Ineffectiveness Proposition (PIP) If (1) a policy change is correctly anticipated, (2) individuals form their expectations rationally, and (3) wages and prices are flexible, then neither fiscal policy nor monetary policy is effective at meeting macroeconomic goals.

Positive Economics The study of "what is" in economics.

Price Ceiling A government-mandated maximum price above which legal trades cannot be made.

Price Floor A government-mandated minimum price below which legal trades cannot be made.

Price Index A measure of the price level.

Price Level A weighted average of the prices of all goods and services.

Price-Level Effect The change in the interest rate due to a change in the price level.

Price Support A government-mandated minimum price for agricultural products; a type of a price floor.

Producers' (Sellers') Surplus (PS) The difference between the price sellers receive for a good and the minimum or lowest price for which they would have sold the good. (PS = Price received − Minimum selling price.)

Production Function A function that specifies the relation between technology and the quantity of factor inputs to output, or Real GDP.

Production Possibilities Frontier (PPF) The possible combinations of two goods that can be produced during a certain span of time under the conditions of a given state of technology and fully employed resources.

Productive Efficient The condition in which the maximum output is produced with the given resources and technology.

Productive Inefficient The condition in which less than the maximum output is produced with the given resources and technology. Productive inefficiency implies that more of one good can be produced without any less of another being produced.

Progressive Income Tax An income tax system in which one's tax rate rises as taxable income rises (up to some point).

Proportional Income Tax An income tax system in which a person's tax rate is the same regardless of taxable income.

Public Choice The branch of economics in which economic principles and tools are applied to public sector decision making.

Public Debt The total amount that the federal government owes its creditors.

Purchasing Power The quantity of goods and services that can be purchased with a unit of money. Purchasing power and the price level are inversely related: As the price level goes up (down), purchasing power goes down (up).

Purchasing Power Parity (PPP) Theory Theory stating that exchange rates between any two currencies will adjust to reflect changes in the relative price levels of the two countries.

Q

Quota A legal limit imposed on the amount of a good that may be imported.

R

Rational Expectations Expectations that individuals form on the basis of past experience and their predictions about the effects of present and future policy actions and events.

Rational Ignorance The state of not acquiring information because the costs of acquiring it are greater than the benefits.

Rationing Device A means for deciding who gets what of available resources and goods.

Real Balance Effect The change in the purchasing power of dollar-denominated assets that results from a change in the price level.

Real GDP The value of the entire output produced annually within a country's borders, adjusted for price changes.

Real Income Nominal income adjusted for price changes.

Real Interest Rate The nominal interest rate minus the expected inflation rate. When the expected inflation rate is zero, the real interest rate equals the nominal interest rate.

Recessionary Gap The condition in which the Real GDP that the economy is producing is less than the Natural Real GDP and the unemployment rate is greater than the natural unemployment rate.

Regressive Income Tax An income tax system in which a person's tax rate declines as his or her taxable income rises.

Regulatory Capital The amount of capital that a financial institution must hold because of regulatory requirements.

Regulatory Capital Arbitrage A means of changing the composition of assets in such a way as to lower the overall amount of capital a financial institution holds for a given level of assets.

Relative Price The price of a good in terms of another good.

Required Reserve Ratio (r) A percentage of each dollar deposited that must be held in reserve form (specifically, as bank deposits at the Fed or vault cash).

Required Reserves The minimum dollar amount of reserves a bank must hold against its checkable deposits, as mandated by the Fed.

Reserve Deficient The situation that exists when a bank holds fewer reserves than specified by the required reserve ratio.

Reserve Requirement The Fed rule that specifies the amount of reserves a bank must hold to back up deposits.

Reserves The sum of bank deposits at the Fed and vault cash.

Revaluation A government act that changes the exchange rate by raising the official price of a currency.

S

Savings Deposit An interest-earning account at a commercial bank or thrift institution. Normally, checks cannot be written on savings deposits, and the funds in a savings deposit can be withdrawn at any time without a penalty payment.

Say's Law Supply creates its own demand. Production creates enough demand to purchase all the goods and services the economy produces.

Scarcity The condition in which our wants are greater than the limited resources available to satisfy those wants.

Securitization The process by which financial institutions aggregate debt (such as loans) in a pool and then issue securities backed by the pool.

Shortage (Excess Demand) A condition in which the quantity demanded is greater than the quantity supplied. Shortages occur only at prices below the equilibrium price.

Short-Run Aggregate Supply (SRAS) Curve A curve that shows the quantity supplied of all goods and services (Real GDP) at different price levels, *ceteris paribus*.

Short-Run Equilibrium The condition in the economy when the quantity demanded of Real GDP equals the (short-run) quantity supplied of Real GDP. This condition is met where the aggregate demand curve intersects the short-run aggregate supply curve.

Simple Deposit Multiplier The reciprocal of the required reserve ratio r: $1/r$.

Simple Quantity Theory of Money The theory which assumes that velocity (V) and Real GDP (Q) are constant and predicts that changes in the money supply (M) lead to strictly proportional changes in the price level (P).

Slope The ratio of the change in the variable on the vertical axis to the change in the variable on the horizontal axis.

Special-Interest Groups Subsets of the general population that hold (usually) intense preferences for or against a particular government service, activity, or policy and that often gain from public policies that may not be in accord with the interests of the general public.

Special-Purpose Vehicle (SPV) A legal entity created to fulfill narrow, specific, or temporary objectives.

Spontaneous Order The spontaneous and unintended emergence of order out of the self-interested actions of individuals; an unintended consequence of human action, with emphasis placed on the word "unintended."

Stagflation The simultaneous occurrence of high rates of inflation and unemployment.

Stock A claim on a corporation's assets that gives the purchaser a share of ownership in the corporation.

Store of Value The ability of an item to hold value over time; a function of money.

Structural Deficit The part of the budget deficit that would exist even if the economy were operating at full employment.

Structural Unemployment Unemployment due to structural changes in the economy that eliminate some jobs and create others for which the unemployed are unqualified.

Subprime Mortgage Loan A nontraditional mortgage loan granted to persons who might have low credit ratings or some other factors which suggest that they could default on the debt.

Subsidy A monetary payment by government to a producer of a good or service.

Substitutes Two goods that satisfy similar needs or desires. If two goods are substitutes, the demand for one rises as the price of the other rises (or the demand for one falls as the price of the other falls).

Supply The willingness and ability of sellers to produce and offer to sell different quantities of a good at different prices during a specific period.

Supply Schedule The numerical tabulation of the quantity supplied of a good at different prices. A supply schedule is the numerical representation of the law of supply.

Surplus (Excess Supply) A condition in which the quantity supplied is greater than the quantity demanded. Surpluses occur only at prices above the equilibrium price.

T

Target Price A guaranteed price; if the market price is below the target price, the farmer receives a deficiency payment equal to the difference between the target price and the market price.

Tariff A tax on imports.

Tax Base In terms of income taxes, the total amount of taxable income. Tax revenue = Tax base × (average) Tax rate.

Tax Multiplier The number that, when multiplied by the change in taxes, gives us the change in total spending (and if prices are constant, the change in Real GDP).

Technology The body of skills and knowledge involved in the use of resources in production. An advance in technology commonly increases the ability to produce more output with a fixed amount of resources or the ability to produce the same output with fewer resources.

Term Auction Facility (TAF) Program A program under which the Fed auctions funds to depository institutions. Each TAF auction is for a fixed amount, with the TAF interest rate determined by the auction process (subject to a minimum rate bid).

Theory An abstract representation of the real world designed with the intent to better understand it.

Tie-in Sale A sale whereby one good can be purchased only if another good is also purchased.

Time Deposit An interest-earning deposit with a specified maturity date. Time deposits are subject to penalties for early withdrawal—that is, withdrawal before the maturity date. Small-denomination time deposits are deposits of less than $100,000.

Total Surplus (TS) The sum of consumers' surplus and producers' surplus. (TS = CS + PS.)

Trade Balance The value of a country's exports minus the value of its imports; sometimes referred to as net exports.

Trade Deficit The condition that exists when the value of a country's imports is greater than the value of its exports.

Trade Surplus The condition that exists when the value of a country's exports is greater than the value of its imports.

Transfer Payment A payment to a person that is not made in return for goods and services currently supplied.

Transmission Mechanism The routes, or channels, traveled by the ripple effects that the money market creates and that affect the goods-and-services market. (The goods-and-services market is represented by the aggregate demand and aggregate supply curves in the *AD–AS* framework.)

U

U.S. Treasury Securities Bonds and bondlike securities issued by the U.S. Treasury when it borrows.

Undervalued A currency is undervalued if its price in terms of other currencies is below the equilibrium price.

Unemployment Rate The percentage of the civilian force that is unemployed: Unemployment rate = Number of unemployed persons ÷ Civilian labor force.

Unit of Account A common measure in which relative values are expressed; a function of money.

(Upward-Sloping) Supply Curve The graphical representation of the law of supply.

Utility The satisfaction one receives from a good.

V

Velocity The average number of times a dollar is spent to buy final goods and services in a year.

W

Wealth The value of all assets owned, both monetary and nonmonetary.

A

Absolute (money) price, 116–117, 121

Absolute real economic growth, 437, 438

Abstraction, 20–21

Acemoglu, Daron, 158

Activist monetary policy. *See* Discretionary monetary policy

Actual price level, 422

Adaptive expectations, 416

Adelman, Irma, 41

Adjustable rate mortgages, 465

Adverse selection, 321–322

Adverse supply shocks, 209

Aggregate demand (*AD*), 190–205, 221–222
factors affecting, 198–203, 221
international factors affecting, 600–604, 605–607, 612–613
in monetarism, 360
and money supply, 203
and net exports, 196–197, 600–601, 612
vs. quantity demanded, change in, 195
and short-run equilibrium, 210–216
in simple quantity theory of money, 358
and spending, 196–198

Aggregate demand–aggregate supply (*AD–AS*) framework, 191, 220

monetarism in, 360–362
simple Keynesian model in, 264–268, 278
simple quantity theory of money in, 356–358

Aggregate demand (*AD*) curve, 192–196
as downward sloping, 192–194
and fiscal policy, 291–292
and job prospects, 217
shift factors for, 196, 198–203
in simple Keynesian model, 264–265
in simple quantity theory of money, 356–357

Aggregate supply (*AS*), 206–219, 221–222. *See also* Long-run aggregate supply; Short-run aggregate supply
international factors affecting, 604–607, 612–613
and marginal tax rates, 301–302
and short-run equilibrium, 210–216
in simple quantity theory of money, 358

Aggregate supply (*AS*) curve
in simple Keynesian model, 265
in simple quantity theory of money, 358

Air travel
aisle seats, 126–127, 144
overbooking, 95

ticket prices, 67, 126–127

Alchian, Armen A., 22

Allen, William R., 22

American Economic Review (journal), 411, 412

American International Group (AIG), 471

Antidumping argument for trade restrictions, 558

Appreciation, currency, 201–202, 570, 581–582, 600–601, 606

Asset(s), 323–324
in financial crisis of 2007–2009, 325, 457–459, 481
risk-weighted, 469–473, 482

Asset-price inflation, 465

Association of Southeast Asian Nations (ASEAN), 312

Asymmetric information, 321–322

Athletes, college, 139–140, 144–145

Auctions, 83–84

Automatic fiscal policy, 291

Autonomous consumption, 259

Autor, David, 575

B

Bacon, Kevin, 561

Bads, 2, 25, 168

Bailouts, 475–477, 492–493, 497–498

Balanced budgets, 284–286

Balances (demand for money), 382–383

Balance sheets, 323–324, 327
in financial crisis of 2007–2009, 457–460

Banking
balance sheets in, 323–324, 327, 457–460
development of, 317–320
free, 343–345

Bank insolvency, 324, 325, 457

Bank runs, 343, 458

Bar graphs, 33–35

Barro, Robert, 451

Barter, 310

Barter economies, 225, 310–313

Baseball caps, 535–537, 545

Basel Accord (Basel I), 472

Base year, 148–149

Baum, L. Frank, 318

Beanie babies, 420–421

Beatles, The, 152

Beauty, 104

Becker, Gary, 40

Beer, 142, 145

Behavior, and opportunity cost, 7

Beneficial supply shocks, 209

Benefits, 1, 7–10, 25–26
marginal, 10, 12–13, 24–25
net, 1, 13

Big Bang Theory, The (television show), 123–125

Billionaires, 3
Birthrates, 524–525, 545
Bitcoins, 315–316
Black Reconstruction
　　(DuBois), 40
Bloom, Nicholas, 575
Board of Governors, 329
Bonds
　conventional, 378
　prices of, and interest
　　rates, 386–388, 404,
　　407–409
Books
　buying, 5, 69
　library, 22
Boster, James S., 89
Brute force, 104
Bryan, William Jennings,
　　318, 333
Bubbles, economic,
　　420–421
Buchanan, James, 299–301
Budget (federal), 281–290
　projections for, 283–284
　surpluses in, 284–286,
　　306
Budget (federal) deficits,
　　284–286, 288, 306
　and democracy, 298–301
　and expectations, 428
　international and
　　domestic effects of,
　　607–609
　and tax cuts and
　　revenues, 485–486,
　　497
Bureau of Economic
　　Analysis (BEA), 170
Business-cycle
　　macroeconomics,
　　242–243, 246, 453
Business cycles, 183–185,
　　187
Business cycle theory, real,
　　431–432, 434
Business etiquette, 592

Business taxes
　indirect, 179
　and investments, 201
Buyers, number of, 76

C

California gold rush, 357
Capital, 2
　human, 446
　and production function,
　　446
　regulatory, 469, 482
Capital consumption
　　allowance, 180. *See also*
　　Depreciation
Capital controls, 315–316
Caplan, Bryan, 507–508
Cash leakage, 336
Cell phones, 536
Ceteris paribus, 19–20, 26
Cheating, and baseball
　　caps, 535–537, 545
Checkable deposits, 314
Check-clearing services,
　　332
Chess, 418
Child bearing, 119
Chinese imports, 575
Chips and salsa, 142, 145
Choices, 4
　menu of, 412
Choice theory, public,
　　501–502, 518–519
Chrysler, 477
Cities, big, ethics in,
　　525–528, 545
Civil Aeronautics Board
　　(CAB), 95
Civilian labor force, 153
Civilian noninstitutional
　　population, 153
Classical economics,
　　225–230, 246
　critique of, 249–258
　vs. Keynes, 258

new, 422–428, 433,
　　434
on self-regulating
　　economies, 242
Closed economies, 258,
　　608, 613
Cold War, 591
Collateralized debt
　　obligations (CDOs),
　　458–459
Colleges
　admissions, 6, 132–133,
　　144, 603
　athletes, 139–140,
　　144–145
　campus parking, 115
　class times, 140–142, 145
　costs, 11
　majors, 38–46
　rational expectations, 421
　tuition, 528–530, 545
Common currency,
　　579–581
Community Reinvestment
　　Act (CRA), 467
Comparative advantage, 56,
　　548–552
Competition, scarcity and,
　　4–5
Complements, 75, 142
Complete crowding out,
　　293–295
Congressional districts,
　　511–512
Constant-money-growth-
　　rate rule, 398
Constant opportunity costs,
　　47–48, 62
Constitutional economics,
　　517, 519
Consumer Price Index
　　(CPI), 147–150
Consumers' surplus (*CS*),
　　88–91, 99
　equilibrium in terms of,
　　88–91

and international trade,
　　553–554
positive *vs.* negative,
　　93–94
and price floors, 113–115
Consumption, 173
　and aggregate demand,
　　196–197
　autonomous, 259
　factors affecting,
　　198–200
　in GDP, 173
　induced, 259–260
　and international trade,
　　550
　in simple Keynesian
　　model, 259–261, 278
Consumption function,
　　259–260, 278
Continued inflation,
　　366–370, 379
Contraction, in business
　　cycle, 184
Contractionary fiscal policy,
　　291, 608–609
Contractionary monetary
　　policy, 330, 389,
　　610–611
Conventional bonds, 378
Corporations
　globalization's effects on,
　　596
　profits of, in national
　　income, 175–176
Corridor, 352
Cost(s), 1, 7–10, 25–26.
　　See also specific types
　zero, 7
Credit cards, 316
Criminals, rationality of,
　　530–532, 545
Crowding out, 293–297,
　　298, 306, 489–490, 497
Culture, and
　　unemployment rate,
　　158

Currencies, 314. *See also* Dollar; Exchange rates
appreciation of, 201–202, 570, 581–582, 600–601, 606
common, 579–581
demand for and supply of, 568–569
depreciation of, 202, 570, 581–582, 600–601, 605
overvalued, 574–577
undervalued, 574–576
Currency areas, optimal, 579–581
Cyclical deficits, 286
Cyclical unemployment rate, 160–162

D

Data lag, 297
Dating, 527
Deadweight losses, 113–115
Decisions at the margin, 10, 26
Deficits. *See also* Budget deficits
international and domestic effects of, 607–609
trade, 567, 607
Delinquency rates, 465–466
Demand, 65–77, 99. *See also specific types*
applications for, 123–146
change in, 70–76
elasticity of (*See* Elasticity)
language of, 84
law of, 66–67, 74
vs. quantity demanded, 66, 143
and supply, 83–97

Demand curves, 66–67. *See also* Aggregate demand curve
change in, 71–76
as downward-sloping, 66
individual *vs.* market, 69–70
movement factors and shift factors for, 76–77
Demand for money (balances), 382–383
Demand-reducing actions, 530
Demand schedules, 66–67
Demand-side economic perspective, 493–495, 498
Demand-side fiscal policy, 291–301, 306
Democracy
and budget deficits, 298–301
and economic illiteracy, 507–508
Democracy in Deficit (Buchanan and Wagner), 299–301
Deposits, 314–316
Depreciation
currency, 202, 570, 581–582, 600–601, 605
in GDP, 180
Depressions, economic, 318
Devaluation, 577–578
Diagrams, 29–37
Diminishing marginal activity, law of, 67
Diminishing marginal returns, law of, 79
Direct finance, 320–321
Direction, *vs.* magnitude, 113
Directly related variables, 29

Discount loans, 339–340, 346–347
Discount rates, 339–340
Discouraged workers, 156, 159
Discovery process, 447–448
Discretionary fiscal policy, 291
Discretionary (activist) monetary policy, 393–396, 404, 491, 497
Disequilibrium, 84, 218–219, 272–274
Disequilibrium price, 84
Disposable income, 181
Distributional effects of international trade, 553
Disutility, 2
Division of labor, 551
Dollar, U.S.
appreciation of, 202, 606
change in value over time, 151–152
depreciation of, 202, 605
vs. euro, exchange rate for, 204
and gold standard, 400–402
and oil prices, 215
overvalued, 576–577
as primary reserve currency, 573
Dollar price, 4, 103–104
Domino effects, 475
Dorn, David, 575
Double coincidence of wants, 311
Double counting, 167
Downward-sloping demand curve. *See* Demand curves
Dowries, 89
Doyle, Arthur Conan, 51
Draca, Mirko, 575
DuBois, W. E. B., 40

Dumping, 558
Durable goods, 173

E

Easterlin, Richard, 170
Easterlin paradox, 170–171
Easy money, 477
eBay, 317
Economica (journal), 312, 410
Economic freedom, 450
Economic growth, 437–455
absolute real, 437, 438
basics about, 437–439
definition of, 53, 183
and morality, 444
per-capita real, 437
in PPF framework, 53–54
and production function, 439–452, 454
rates of, 437–439
and Real GDP, 183, 187
Economic-growth macroeconomics, 242–243, 246, 453
Economic illiteracy, 507–508
Economic policies, growth-promoting *vs.* transfer-promoting, 450–452. *See also specific types*
Economic Report of the President (2006), 595
Economics. *See also specific policies and schools*
categories of, 23–24, 26
definition of, 3
majoring in, 38–46
myths about, 39–42
process of, 523
Economic states, 1, 230–240, 246

Economic states *(Continued)*
  in labor market, 232–233
  and PPF, 233–235, 246
  in self-regulating
    economies, 236–240
  in *TE–TP* framework,
    273–274
  three types of, 222,
    230–231, 246
Economy
  causes of problems in,
    18–19
  monetarist view of, 362
  world, 586
Economy, U.S.
  changes over time to size
    of, 183
  international factors
    affecting, 600–611,
    612–613
Effectiveness lag, 297
Efficiency, 12–13, 26
  productive, 53
  and voting, 509–511
Efficiency wage models,
  253
Elasticity, of investment,
  484–485
Elements of Economics, The
  (Tarshis), 257
Empirical issues, 485, 496
Employed persons, 153–154
Employee compensation,
  176
Employment, full, 157–160
Employment rate, 154
  common misconceptions
    about, 154–155
English language, 312
Entrepreneurship, 2
Equal pay for equal work,
  285
Equation of exchange,
  353–354, 379
Equilibrium, 84–94
  in labor market, 232–233

long-run, 216–219,
    221–222, 231–233
  in money market, 383
  moving to, 84–87
  and predictions, 87–88
  short-run, 210–216,
    218–219, 221
  in simple Keynesian
    model, 272–274, 275
Equilibrium exchange rate,
  569–572
Equilibrium price, 84,
  91–94
Equilibrium quantity, 84,
  91–94
Equilibrium tuition,
  528–530, 545
Equity, in house, 465
Ethics, in towns *vs.* cities,
  525–528, 545
Etiquette, business, 592
Euro, 204
European Central Bank, 312
Eviction law, 136, 144
Evidence, in theories, 532,
  545
Exam days, 535–537, 545
Excess demand. *See*
  Shortages
Excess reserves, 320, 327,
  334, 336
Excess supply. *See* Surplus
Exchange. *See* Trade
Exchange rates, 569–583
  and aggregate demand,
    600–601, 605–606
  current system of, 579,
    583
  definition of, 201,
    567–568
  for dollar *vs.* euro, 204
  fixed, 574–581, 583
  flexible, 569–573,
    579–581, 582–583
  and foreign input prices,
    604

and net exports,
    201–202, 600–601
Expansion, in business
  cycle, 184
Expansionary fiscal policy,
  291, 293–295,
  607–608
Expansionary monetary
  policy, 330, 389,
  609–610
Expectations, 416–431
  adaptive, 416
  and fiscal policy, 304
  for income, 199
  for inflation rate, 375,
    378, 416
  in new classical
    economics, 422–428
  for policy, 417–418,
    422–428
  for price, 76, 81, 199
  for price level, 209,
    418–419, 422
  rational, 417–421,
    430–431
  for sales, 201
  for tax rates, 304
Expectations effect,
  375–376
Expenditure approach
  to GDP, 172–175,
    185–186, 187
Expenditures. *See* Spending
Exports, 173–174. *See also*
  Net exports

F

Factors of production. *See*
  Goods; Resources
Factory Acts, 512
False information, 107
Falsifiability, 524–525,
  545
Fannie Mae (Federal
  National Mortgage

Association, FNMA),
  467–468
Federal budget. *See* Budget
Federal debt. *See* Public
  debt
Federal Deposit Insurance
  Corporation (FDIC),
  323, 458
Federal funds market, 340,
  349–352
Federal funds rate, 340,
  352, 460–461, 481
Federal funds rate target,
  340, 347
Federal Open Market
  Committee (FOMC),
  330, 331
Federal Reserve Act (1913),
  333
Federal Reserve Banks, 330
Federal Reserve Districts,
  333
Federal Reserve notes, 314,
  331–332
Federal Reserve System (the
  Fed), 319, 329–348
  common misconceptions
    about, 332, 397
  in financial crisis of
    2007–2009, 460–463,
    481
  vs. free banking, 343–345
  functions of, 330–332
  history of, 333
  in money supply, 330,
    334–339, 346, 397
  recent actions by,
    340–345
  in reserves, 332, 392, 397
  structure of, 329–330
  tools of, 339–340
Fed watchers, 418
Feynman, Richard, 544
Fields, W. C., 561
Final goods, 167
Financial crises, 481

causes of, 480
the Fed in, 340–341
Financial crisis of 2007–2009, 456–483
as balance sheet problem, 457–460
bank insolvency in, 325, 457
government response to, 475–477
Great Recession in, 400, 477–479
housing prices in, 254–255, 465–466, 474
interest rates in, 460–466, 481
leverage in, 468–469, 481–482
and market monetarism, 400
politics of housing in, 466–467
regulatory capital arbitrage in, 469–473
risky assets in, 325, 458–459, 481
Financial intermediaries, 321, 322–323, 456
Financial sector, 456–457, 475, 481
Financial system, 320–325, 327
Financial transactions, 168
Fine-tuning, 393
First-come, first-served (FCFS) basis, 104, 106–107
Fiscal crisis, likelihood of, 305
Fiscal policy, 291–304, 306, 613
contractionary, 291, 608–609
demand-side, 291–301, 306

expansionary, 291, 293–295, 607–608
supply-side, 301–304, 306
Fiscal stimulus, 477
Fisher, Irving, 355, 375
Fisher effect, 375–376
Fixed exchange rates, 574–581, 583
Fixed investment, 173
Flat tax, 283
Flexible exchange rates, 569–573, 579–581, 582–583
Food
grocery buying, 129–132
prices of, 68
Foreclosure rates, 465–466
Foreign exchange market, 567–569, 582
Foreign export subsidies argument for trade restrictions, 559–560
Foreign input prices, 604
Foreign real national income (foreign Real GDP), 201, 600
45-degree line, 32–33
Fractional reserve banking, 319
Freddie Mac (Federal Home Loan Mortgage Corporation, FHLMC), 467–468
Free banking, 343–345
Free lunch, 7
Freeways, supply and demand on, 134–135, 144
Freshwater economists, 496
Frictional unemployment, 156–157
Friedman, Benjamin, 444
Friedman, David, 594
Friedman, Milton, 357, 412–416, 434

Friedman natural rate theory, 415–416, 434
Friendships, 9
Full employment, 157–160
Future, expectations for. See Expectations

G

Gasoline shortages, 110
Gaulin, Steven J. C., 89
GDP implicit price deflator (GDP deflator), 150–151
General Motors, 471, 477
General Theory of Employment, Interest and Money, The (Keynes), 249, 257, 476
Gift giving, 540–543, 545–546
Globalization, 585–599, 612
benefits and costs of, 594–598, 612
debate about, 597–598, 611–612
definition of, 585–586, 612
and education, 603
facts about, 588–590
future of, 598–599, 612
history of movement toward, 591–593, 612
indexes of, 589–590
ways of picturing, 587–588
Global savings glut, 461–462, 481
Gold, 317–319, 326
Gold rush, 357
Goldsmiths, 317–319
Gold standard, 318, 400–402
Goods, 2, 25. See also specific types

Government. See also specific agencies and policies
budget of (See Budget)
the Fed as bank of, 332
in financial crisis of 2007–2009, 475–477
in fixed exchange rate system, 577–578
in globalization, 593, 599
macroeconomic debates over role of, 484–499
role in economic problems, 18–19, 26
in simple Keynesian model, 267, 274–275
size and scope of, 488–489, 497
taxation by (See Tax)
Government purchases, 173
and aggregate demand, 196–197
factors affecting, 198
in GDP, 173
vs. government spending, 281
Government regulation, and supply, 82
Government spending (expenditures), 281–282, 306
politics of, 490–491, 497
vs. tax cuts, 488–489, 497
Government spending multiplier, 488
Government transfer payments, 168, 173
Grades
inflation of, 367
and time spent studying, 55
Great Recession, 400, 477–479. See also Financial crisis of 2007–2009

Greenspan, Alan, 464–465
Grocery buying, 129–132
Gross Domestic Product
    (GDP), 33, 166–189
  common misconceptions
    about, 175
  expenditure approach to
    computing, 172–175,
    185–186, 187
  final *vs.* intermediate
    goods in, 167
  GDP deflator, 150–151
  income approach to
    computing, 176–181
  omissions in, 167–168
  per-capita, 169–172,
    178
  Real (*See* Real GDP)
Gross family product
    (GFP), 169
Growth-promoting policies,
    450–452

H

Hamilton, Alexander, 558
Hanson, Gordon, 575
Happiness economics,
    170–171
Harvard University, 603
Health, and studying, 14
Health care
  cost of, 129–132, 137,
    144
  vouchers for, 539–540,
    545
Health insurance, 129–132,
    137
Health maintenance
    organizations (HMOs),
    137
Holiday, J. S., 357
Housing, politics of,
    466–467, 481
Housing and Urban
    Development,

Department of
    (HUD), 468
Housing bust, 254–255
Housing market, 1
Housing prices
  and aggregate demand,
    200
  in financial crisis of
    2007–2009, 254–255,
    460–463, 465–466,
    474
  and mortgage loans,
    125–126, 144
  and schools, 138,
    537–538, 545
  and weather, 137–139,
    144
Human capital, 446
Hyperinflation, 371

I

Ideas, 447–448
Idle resources, 263
Illiteracy, economic,
    507–508
Imports, 173–174
Incentives, 13–15, 17, 26
  tax, 304
Income. *See also specific types*
  and demand, 73
  and exchange rates,
    570–571
  expectations of future,
    199
  globalization's effects on,
    594, 595–596
  per-capita, 594
Income approach to GDP,
    176–181
Income effect, 373
Income growth rates,
    570–571
Income inequality,
    globalization's effects
    on, 595–596

Income taxes
  and consumption, 200
  marginal, 301–302
  structures for, 283–284,
    285
Incomplete crowding out,
    293–295
Increasing opportunity
    costs, 48–50, 62
Independent variables, 30
Indian Institute of
    Technology, 603
Indirect business taxes, 179
Indirect finance, 320–321
Individual demand curves,
    69
Induced consumption,
    259–260
Inefficiency, productive, 53
Infant industry argument for
    trade restrictions, 558
Inferior goods, 73
Inflation, 363–371, 379
  continued, 366–370, 379
  and CPI, 149–150
  and exchange rates,
    571–572
  expected rate of, 375,
    378, 416
  hyperinflation, 371
  one-shot, 363–366, 379
  in Phillips curve,
    410–417
  and price controls, 370
  stagflation, 411, 412
Inflationary gaps, 230–233
  and monetary policy,
    389–393
  self-regulating economies
    in, 237–238
Inflation-indexed treasury
    bonds, 378
Inflation targeting,
    399–400
Information
  asymmetric, 321–322

and special-interest
    groups, 511, 514–517
  transmission of, through
    price, 104–105
Inheritance, 516
Innovation, in
    globalization, 591–593,
    595
Input prices, foreign, 604
Insolvency, bank, 324, 325,
    457
Institutions, 448–452
Interest, net, 178
Interest-insensitive
    investments, 385
Interest rate(s)
  and bond prices,
    386–388, 404,
    407–409
  and consumption,
    199–200
  and exchange rates, 572
  in financial crisis of
    2007–2009, 460–466,
    481
  flexibility of, and classical
    economics, 226–228
  and investment, 200–201
  and liquidity trap,
    386–387
  and money supply,
    372–377, 379
  nominal, 377, 379
  real, 377, 379, 572
  relative, 606–607
  and Taylor rule,
    463–466, 481
Interest rate effect,
    192–193, 194
Intermediate goods, 167
International factors
    affecting U.S.
    economy, 600–611,
    612–613
International finance,
    567–584

International trade, 547–566
and exchange rates, 579
in globalization, 588–589, 594
restrictions on, 552–563, 564
theory of, 547–552
International trade effect, 193, 194
Internships, unpaid, 239
Inventory, optimum, 272
Inventory investment, 173, 175
Inversely related variables, 30
Investment, 173
and aggregate demand, 196–197
elasticity of, 484–485
factors affecting, 198, 200–201
in GDP, 173

J

J-curve, 601–602
Job leavers, 155
Job losers, 155
Journal of Economic Education, 43

K

Kahn, Alfred, 95
Kapital, Das (Marx), 257
Keynes, John Maynard, 249–258, 278, 476
Keynes, John Neville, 257
Keynesian model, simple, 258–276, 278
in *AD–AS* framework, 264–268, 278
assumptions in, 258
consumption in, 259–261, 278
fiscal policy in, 292–293, 306

multiplier in, 261–263, 278
saving in, 260–261
in *TE–TP* framework, 268–276, 278
theme of, 267–268, 275–276, 278
Keynesian transmission mechanism, 382–387, 404
Kidney transplants, 108–109
Kindle, 74
Kindleberger, Charles, 579
Kling, Arnold, 391–393

L

Labor, 2
Labor, division of, 551
Labor force, civilian, 153
Labor force participation rate (LFPR), 154
Labor markets
and economic states, 232–233
and production function, 441–446
Labor mobility, 580
Labor productivity, 209
Ladefeld, Steve, 170
Laffer, Arthur, 302
Laffer curve, 302–304
Lags, in fiscal policy, 297–298
Laissez-faire, 240
Land, 2
Language, English, 312
Late, arriving to class, 8, 69, 115
Laws. *See specific laws*
Law School Admission Test (LSAT), 43
Legal systems, 449
Legislative lag, 297
Leisure, 168, 313

Lender-of-last-resort, 332, 341
Leverage, in financial crisis of 2007–2009, 468–469, 481–482
Liabilities, 323–324, 457
LIBOR, 470–471
Line, slope of, 30–31
Line graphs, 35–36
Liquidity effect, 373
Liquidity trap, 386–387
Literacy, economic, 507–508
Loan(s). *See specific types*
Loanable funds, 373–376
Lobbying, 511
Logrolling, 512
Long run, changes to self-regulating economies in, 240–242
Long-run aggregate supply (*LRAS*), 190–191, 216–219, 221–222
Long-run aggregate supply (*LRAS*) curve, 216–218, 440–442
Long-run equilibrium, 216–219, 221–222, 231–233
Long-run Phillips curve, 412–416
Lopokova, Lydia, 257
Low foreign wages argument for trade restrictions, 560
Lucas, Robert, 417

M

M1, 314
M2, 314
Macroeconomics, 23–24
business-cycle, 242–243, 246, 453
debates over government role in, 484–499

economic-growth, 242–243, 246, 453
Magnitude, *vs.* direction, 113
Majoring, in economics, 38–46
Majority voting rule, 288, 504
Managed flexible exchange rate, 579, 583
Managed float, 579, 583
Marginal benefits, 10, 12–13, 24–25
Marginal costs, 10, 12–13, 24–25
Marginal income tax rates, 301–302
Marginal propensity to consume (*MPC*), 259
Marginal propensity to save (*MPS*), 260–261
Marijuana legalization, 127–128, 144
Market(s). *See also specific types*
adjustments in, 252–255
definition of, 65
vs. government, in economic problems, 18–19, 26
supply and demand in, 83–97, 99
Market basket, 147–148
Market-clearing price (equilibrium price), 84, 91–94
Market demand curves, 69–70
Market interest rate. *See* Nominal interest rate
Market monetarism, 400
Market supply curves, 79
Marshall, Alfred, 257, 355
Marshall, James, 357
Marx, Karl, 257
Match.com, 317

Maximum prices, 86–87
McCleary, Rachel, 451
Median voter model,
    502–505, 519
Medicaid, 282–283
Medical care. *See* Health
    care
Medicare, 282–283
Medium of exchange, 310
Meltzer, Allan, 40
Menu of choices, 412
Meta-ideas, 448
Microeconomics, 23–24
Milgram, Stanley, 561
Millionaires, 286
Minimum prices, 86–87
Minimum wage, 111–113
Minsky, Hyman, 476–477
Models. *See* Theories
Monetarism, 359–363, 379
    in *AD–AS* framework,
        360–362
    four positions in,
        359–360
    market, 400
    monetary policy in,
        388–389, 404
    views on economy in,
        362
*Monetary History of
    the United States,
    A* (Friedman and
    Schwartz), 357
Monetary policy, 382–406,
    613
    contractionary, 330, 389,
        610–611
    debates in, 393–396,
        403, 404, 491
    definition of, 330
    discretionary (activist),
        393–396, 404, 491, 497
    expansionary, 330, 389,
        609–610
    in fixed exchange rate
        system, 578

and inflationary and
    recessionary gaps,
    389–393
international and
    domestic effects of,
    609–611
Keynesian, 382–387, 404
monetarist, 388–389, 404
rules-based (nonactivist),
    393–402, 404, 491,
    497
transmission mechanisms
    in, 382–389
Monetary wealth, 192
Money, 309–313, 326
    demand for, 382–383
    functions of, 310
    origins of, 310–313
    and price level, 353–359
    simple quantity theory
        of, 355–359
Money economies,
    250–251, 310–313
Money Illusion, The
    (Sumner), 400
Money market
    and bond market,
        407–409
    equilibrium in, 383
    in Keynesian transmission
        mechanism, 382–383
Money market deposit
    accounts (MMDAs),
    316
Money market mutual
    funds (MMMFs), 316
Money price, 116–117,
    121
Money supply, 314–316,
    326
    and aggregate demand,
        203
    change in composition
        of, 345–346
    contraction process for,
        337–339

definitions of, 314–316
expansion process for,
    334–337
and expectations, 429
the Fed's role in, 330,
    334–339, 346, 397
in financial crisis of
    2007–2009, 477–479
and interest rates,
    372–377, 379
and price level, 353–359,
    373–376
and velocity, 204–205,
    221
*Moral Consequences of
    Economic Growth, The*
    (Friedman), 444
Moral hazards, 322
Morality
    and economic growth,
        444
    in towns *vs.* cities,
        525–528, 545
Mortgage-backed securities
    (MBS), 458–459
Mortgage loans, 125–126,
    144, 325
    adjustable rate, 465
    in financial crisis of
        2007–2009, 254–255,
        460–463, 465–466
    foreclosure rates for,
        465–466
    subprime, 458–459
Movement factors, 76–77,
    196
Multiplier, 261–263,
    278
Mundell, Robert, 580
Music industry, 597

N

National Bureau of
    Economic Research
    (NBER), 185

National Collegiate Athletic
    Association (NCAA),
    139–140
National debt. *See* Public
    debt
National defense, 558
National income, 176–180
    foreign real, 201, 600
Natural Real GDP, 216
    in economic states,
        230–233
Natural resources, 2,
    446
Natural unemployment, 157
Natural unemployment
    rate, 157–160, 245
    common misconceptions
        about, 233–235
Neoclassical growth theory,
    447
Net benefits, 1, 13
Net domestic product
    (NDP), 180
Net exports, 173–174, 567
    and aggregate demand,
        196–197, 600–601,
        612
    factors affecting, 198,
        201–202
    in GDP, 173–174
Net interest, 178
Net losses. *See* Deadweight
    losses
Net public debt, 287
Net worth (capital), 457
Neutral goods, 73
New classical economics,
    422–428, 433, 434
New entrants, 156
New growth theory, 447,
    454
New Keynesian rational
    expectation theory,
    430–431, 434
Nominal GDP targeting,
    400

Nominal income, 149–150
Nominal interest rates, 377, 379
Nominal wages, 206–207
Nonactivist monetary policy. *See* Rules-based monetary policy
Nondurable goods, 173
Nonexcludable public goods, 509
Nonlabor inputs, prices of, 209
Nonmarket goods and services, 168
Nonprice-rationing devices, 106–107, 133
Normal goods, 73
Normative economics, 23
North, Douglass, 448–449
No-specialization–no-trade (*NS–NT*) case, 548–549

O

Obama, Barack, 477
Obesity, and soda tax, 118
Occupational Outlook Handbook, 44
Offshoring, 558, 560, 596
Oil prices, 215
Okun, Arthur, 302
Olson, Mancur, 451–452
One-shot inflation, 363–366, 379
Open economies, 258, 608, 613
Open market operations, 330, 346
Open market purchase, 335, 341–342
Open market sale, 338
Opportunity costs, 1, 5–7, 25
constant, 47–48, 62
increasing, 48–50, 62

in international trade, 548–551
Optimal currency areas, 579–581
Optimum inventory, 272
Organisation for Economic Cooperation and Development (OECD), 464
Output, in money *vs.* barter economies, 313
Outsourcing, 559, 596
Overbooking of flights, 95
Overnight loans, 339–340, 346–347
Overvalued currency, 574–577
Own price, 71

P

Parking, 115
Patterns of sustainable specialization and trade (PSST), 391–393
Peak, in business cycle, 183
Pennies, 155
Per-capita GDP, 169–172, 178
Per-capita income, 594
Per-capita real economic growth, 437
Perceptions of reality, 416
Personal income, 180
Phillips, A. W., 410, 434
Phillips curve, 410–417, 434
Pie charts, 33, 34
Plosser, Charles, 40
Policy. *See also specific types*
economic debates over, 496
expectations for, 417–418, 422–428
Policy ineffectiveness proposition (PIP), 423

Political market, 502–519
Political tensions, and globalization, 598–599
Politics, 502–519. *See also* Voting
of government spending, 490–491, 497
of housing, 466–467, 481
of international trade, 560
median voter model in, 502–505, 519
and PPF, 59
special-interest groups in, 511–517, 519
Positive economics, 23
Post-college jobs, 217
Predetermined-money-growth-rate rule, 398
Predictions
difficulty of, 219
and equilibrium, 87–88
in theories, 532–535
Preferences, and demand, 73
Price(s), 103–122. *See also specific types*
applications for, 123–132
classical economics on, 228–229, 246
and demand, 73–75
expectations of future, 76, 81, 199
globalization's effects on, 594–595
Keynes on, 255–258, 278
patterns in, 128–129, 144
vs. price level, 147
and quantity demanded, 67–69
as rationing device, 103–104
and supply, 81
and surplus or shortage, 84–85

as transmitter of information, 104–105
variability in, 128–129, 144
zero, 7
Price ceilings, 105–110, 120, 121
Price controls, 105–116, 370
Price floors, 111–115, 121
Price index, 147, 164. *See also* Consumer Price Index
Price inflation rates, 411
Price level(s), 147–153, 164
actual, 422
change in, and aggregate demand curve, 192–195
expectations for, 209, 418–419, 422
measurement of, 147–153
and money supply, 353–359, 373–376
vs. price, 147
in recessionary gaps, 244
Price-level effect, 375–376
Primary reserve currency, 573
Prisoner of war (POW) camps, 312
Producers' (or sellers') surplus, 88–91, 99
equilibrium in terms of, 88–91
and international trade, 553–554
and price floors, 113–115
Production function, 439–452, 454
and capital, 446
equation for, 443
graphical representation of, 440

Production function
  (Continued)
  and institutions,
    448–452
  and labor, 441–446
  and LRAS curve,
    440–442
Production possibilities
    frontier (PPF), 47–64
  bowed-outward, 48–50
  economic concepts in,
    51–54, 62
  and economic states,
    233–235, 246
  model of, 56–57
  and opportunity costs,
    47–50, 62
  and specialization and
    trade, 56–58, 60, 62
  straight-line, 47–48
Productive efficiency, 53
Productive inefficiency, 53
Productivity
  and aggregate supply, 209
  globalization's effects on,
    595
  labor, 209
Product-price inflation, 465
Progressive income tax,
    283–284, 285
Prohibited prices, 107
Property rights, structures
    for, 449
Proportional income tax,
    283–284
Proprietors' income, 175
Protectionist trade policy,
    578
Public choice theory,
    501–502, 518–519
Public debt, 286–287, 306
Public goods,
  nonexcludable, 509
Public-interest talk,
    512
Purchasing power, 192

Purchasing power parity
    (PPP) theory, 571–572

Q

Quantitative easing,
    341–342
Quantity demanded, 66
  change in, 70–73, 195
  vs. demand, 66, 143
  and price, 67–69
Quantity supplied, 82–83
Quotas, 556–557, 564, 578

R

Radford, R. A., 312
Rational expectations,
    417–421, 430–431
Rational ignorance,
    505–508, 514–517
Rationality, of criminals,
    530–532, 545
Rationing devices, 4, 6
  nonprice, 106–107, 133
  price as, 103–104
Real balance effect, 192,
    194
Real business cycle theory,
    431–432, 434
Real GDP, 181–185, 187
  and business cycles,
    183–185, 187
  change in quantity
    demanded of, 195
  changes over time, 183
  computing, 181–182
  and economic growth,
    183, 187
  in economic states,
    230–233
  foreign, 600
  general equation for, 182
  government tools for
    changing, 493–495
  and loanable funds, 373

Natural, 216, 230–233
  in simple quantity theory
    of money, 355–359
  usefulness of, 181
Real income, 149–150
Real interest rates, 377,
    379, 572
Reality, perceptions of, 416
Real sector, 456–457, 475,
    481
Real wages, 206–207,
    418–419
Recession, 185
Recessionary gaps, 230–233
  and monetary policy,
    389–393
  self-regulating economies
    in, 236–237, 244
  in simple Keynesian
    model, 266, 274–275
Recovery, in business cycle,
    184
Reentrants, 156
Refutability, 524–525, 545
Regressive income tax,
    283–284
Regulation. See
    Government regulation
Regulatory capital, 469,
    482
Regulatory capital arbitrage,
    469–473, 482
Related goods, prices of,
    73–75, 81
"Relation Between
    Unemployment and
    the Rate of Change of
    Money Wages in the
    United Kingdom, The"
    (Phillips), 410
Relative interest rates,
    606–607
Relative price, 116–119,
    121
  and monetary policy, 396
  and taxes, 117–118

Religious beliefs, 451
Rental income, 177
Renters, eviction law and,
    136, 144
Rent seeking
  within families, 516
  in special-interest groups,
    512–517
Rent-seeking costs, 514
Required reserve ratio,
    319–320, 327, 339, 346
Required reserves,
    319–320, 327, 334
Reserve(s), 319–320, 327,
    334
  in balance sheets, 323
  demand for, 349–350
  the Fed's role in, 332,
    392, 397
  market for, 339–340,
    349–352
  supply of, 350–351
Reserve currency, 573
Reserve deficient, 338
Reserve requirement,
    319–320, 327
Resources, 2, 25
  prices of, and supply, 81
  unemployed, 53
Restaurants, tipping in, 587
Retained earnings, 176
Return–safety trade-off,
    469
Revaluation, 577–578
Revenue. See Tax revenues
Rise and Decline of Nations,
    The (Olson), 451–452
Risk weight, 473
Risk-weighted assets,
    469–473, 482
Risky assets, in financial
    crisis of 2007–2009,
    325, 457–459, 481
Rivlin, Alice, 40
Romeo and Juliet
    (Shakespeare), 313

Romer, Paul, 447, 448
Royal Economic Society, 43
Rules-based (nonactivist) monetary policy, 393–402, 404, 491, 497

S

Sales tax, 290
Saltwater economists, 496
Samuelson, Paul, 410, 411
Saving(s)
    vs. not spending, 229
    in simple Keynesian model, 260–261
Saving domestic jobs argument for trade restrictions, 560
Savings deposits, 314–316
Savings glut, global, 461–462, 481
Say's law, 225–226, 228, 246, 250–251
Scarcity, 1, 3–5, 25
    effects of, 4–5, 8
    and friendship, 9
    in PPF framework, 51–53
Schelling, Thomas, 532
Schools, and housing prices, 138, 537–538, 545
Schumpeter, Joseph, 476
Schwartz, Anna, 357
Scope, of government, 488–489, 497
Scope and Method of Political Economy, The (Keynes), 257
Securities
    mortgage-backed, 458–459
    Treasury, 332, 341
Securitization, 473

Self-interest, 311
Self-regulating economies, 236–244, 246
    changes in short and long run to, 240–242
    classical economics on, 242
    critique of, 249–258
    debate in macroeconomics over, 486–487, 497
    in inflationary gaps, 237–238
    in monetarism, 360
    policy implications of, 240
    in recessionary gaps, 236–237, 244
Sellers, number of, 81
Sellers' surplus. See Producers' surplus
Services, 173
Shakespeare, William, 313
Shift factors, 76–77, 196
    for aggregate demand curves, 196, 198–203
    for demand curves, 76–77
    for short-run aggregate supply curves, 208–209
    for supply curves, 79–82
Shortages (excess demand), 84
    in labor market, 232–233
    and price, 84–85
    and price ceilings, 106
Short run, changes to self-regulating economies in, 240–242
Short-run aggregate supply (SRAS), 190–191, 206–210, 221
Short-run aggregate supply (SRAS) curve, 206–209
    and job prospects, 217
    in monetarism, 360

and price-level expectations, 418–419
    shift factors in, 208–209
    as upward sloping, 206–208
Short-run equilibrium, 210–216, 218–219, 221
Short-run Phillips curve, 412–416
Simon, Julian, 95
Simple deposit multiplier, 337
Simple-majority voting, 288, 504
Simple quantity theory of money, 355–359
Six-degrees-of-separation theory, 561–562
Size, of government, 488–489, 497
Slope, 30
    of curve, 31–32
    of line, 30–31
Smith, Adam, 257, 439, 444, 476–477, 599
Smith, Vernon, 40
Social media
    and dating, 527
    and six-degrees-of-separation theory, 561–562
Social Security, 282–283
Soda taxes, 118
Solow, Robert, 40, 410, 411
Southwest Airlines, 126–127
Sowell, Thomas, 467
Special-interest groups, 451–452, 454, 511–517, 519
Specialization
    and international trade, 548–550, 564

and patterns of sustainable trade, 391–393
    and trade, in PPF framework, 56–58, 60, 62
Specialization–trade (S–T) case, 549–550
Special-purpose vehicle (SPV), 473
Speculators, 128–129, 144
Spending. See also Government spending
    and aggregate demand, 196–198
    in computing of GDP, 172–175, 185–186
    lack of, vs. saving, 229
    money supply and velocity in, 204–205
    total, 197–198
    types of, 172–173
Spontaneous order, 97
Sports, college, 139–140, 144–145
Spring break, 263
Stabilizing an Unstable Economy (Minsky), 476
Stagflation, 411, 412
Starr, Ringo, 152
Statistics, discrepancies in, 180
Stein, Gertrude, 310
Stevenson, Betsey, 170–171
Sticky wages, 206–207
Stimulus, fiscal, 477
Store of value, 310
Straight Talk About Economic Literacy (Caplan), 507–508
Structural deficits, 286
Structural unemployment, 157
Studying
    and health, 14
    and PPF, 55

Subprime mortgage loans, 458–459
Subsidies, 81–82
  vs. tax deductions, 290
Substitutes, and demand, 73–75
Sumner, Scott, 400
Superathletes, 139–140, 144–145
Supermajority voting rule, 288
Supply, 77–83, 99. See also specific types
  applications for, 123–146
  change in, 79–83
  definition of, 65, 77
  and demand, 83–97
  language of, 84
  law of, 78–79
  vs. quantity supplied, 82–83
Supply curves, 78–83. See also Aggregate supply curve
  market, 79
  for reserves, 350–351
  shift factors for, 79–82
  as upward sloping, 79
Supply schedules, 79
Supply shocks, 209
Supply-side economic perspective, 493–495, 498
Supply-side fiscal policy, 301–304, 306
Surplus (excess supply), 84, 99
  budget, 284–286, 306
  in labor market, 232–233
  and price, 84–85
  and price floor, 111
  trade, 567
Sustainable specialization and trade, patterns of, 391–393
Sutter, John, 357

T

Tariffs, 554–556, 564
  benefits and costs of, 554–556
  in fixed exchange rate system, 578
  in globalization, 588–589
  reciprocity in, 562–563
Tarshis, Lorie, 257
Tax(es), 306. See also specific types
  and budget deficits, 485–486, 497
  expectations of future rates, 304
  in Laffer curve, 302–304
  and relative price, 117–118
  and supply, 81–82
Tax base, 303–304
Tax cuts
  vs. government spending increases, 488–489, 497
  and tax revenue, 485–486, 487, 497
Tax deductions, 290
Tax multiplier, 488
Tax revenues, 282
  and budget deficits, 485–486, 497
  in Laffer curve, 302–304
  and tax cuts, 485–486, 487, 497
Taylor, John, 399, 461–462, 463–464
Taylor rule, 399, 463–466, 481
Technology, 53
  and economic growth, 447–448
  in globalization, 591–593, 599
  in PPF framework, 53, 54
  and supply, 81

Technology coefficient, 447
TED spread, 470–471
Term auction facility (TAF) program, 341
Terrorism, and globalization, 599
Theories, 20–22, 26, 522–546. See also specific theories
  debates over, 496
  falsifiability of, 524–525, 545
  process of building, 522–523, 532–535, 544
  testing of, 505
Thurow, Lester, 41
Ticket prices
  airline, 67, 126–127, 144
  concert, 152
  television show taping, 123–125, 144
Tie-in sales, 107
Time deposits, 316
Tipping practices, 587
Too big to fail (TBTF), 471–472
Total expenditures (TE), 271–272
Total expenditures (TE) curve, 269–271
Total expenditures–total production (TE–TP) framework, 268–276, 278
Total production, 271–272
Total spending, 197–198
Total surplus, 88
Towns, small, ethics in, 525–528, 545
Trade (exchange), 16, 26. See also International trade
  medium of exchange in, 310
  and price ceilings, 106

and price floors, 111
and specialization, 56–58, 60, 62
Trade balance, 567
Trade deficits, 567, 607
Trade restrictions, 552–563
  arguments for implementing, 558–560, 564
  benefits and costs of, 554–557
  protectionist, 578
Trade surplus, 567
Tranches, 459
Transaction costs, 310–311, 317
Transactions money, 314
Transfer payments, 168, 173
Transfer-promoting policies, 450–452
Transmission lag, 297
Transmission mechanisms, 382–389
Travers, Jeffrey, 561
Treasury Department, U.S., 332
Treasury securities, 332, 341
Troubled Asset Relief Program (TARP), 457, 475–477
Trough, of business cycle, 184
Truman, Harry S., 485
Tuition, 528–530, 545
Tulips, 420–421

U

Underemployed workers, 159
Underground economy, 168
Undervalued currency, 574–576

Undistributed profits, 176
Unemployed persons, 153–154, 159
Unemployed resources, 53
Unemployment, 153–162, 164
  compensation benefits, 296
  reasons for, 155–156
  types of, 156–157
Unemployment rate, 154–162, 164
  common misconceptions about, 154–155, 233–235
  and culture, 158
  cyclical, 160–162
  definition of, 154
  natural, 157–160, 233–235, 245
  in Phillips curve, 410–417
  reasons for decline in, 162–163
  and unemployment compensation benefits, 296
Unintended effects, 15–16, 26, 109, 323
Unit of account, 310
Universities. *See* Colleges

University Economics (Alchian and Allen), 22
Unpaid internships, 239
Upward-sloping supply curve. *See* Supply curves
Used goods, 168
U.S. Treasury securities, 332, 341
Utility, 1, 2

V

Value-added tax (VAT), 287–290
Van Reenen, John, 575
Vault cash, 331
Velocity
  and equation of exchange, 353–354
  in financial crisis of 2007–2009, 477–479
  in monetarism, 359–360
  and money supply, 204–205, 221
  in simple quantity theory of money, 355–359
Voting, 502–519
  and efficiency, 509–511
  median voter model of, 502–505, 519
  for nonexcludable public goods, 509

and rational ignorance, 505–508, 519
  and special-interest groups, 511–517, 519
Voting rules, 288, 504

W

Wage(s)
  classical economics on, 228–229, 246
  flexibility of, 277
  Keynes on, 251–252, 255–258, 278
  minimum, 111–113
  nominal, 206–207
  real, 206–207, 418–419
  sticky, 206–207
Wage inflation, 410–411
Wage rates
  changes in, 208–209
  Keynes on, 251–252, 278
Wagner, Richard, 299–301
Wait-and-see lag, 297
Wants, double coincidence of, 311
Warehouse receipts, 317–319
Wealth, 199
  and consumption, 199
  and happiness, 170–171
  monetary, 192

Wealth of Nations (Smith), 257, 439, 477
Weather, and housing prices, 137–139, 144
Weidenbaum, Murray, 41
Weight loss, 68
Well-being, subjective, 171
Williams, Walter, 40–41
Wonderful Wizard of Oz, The (Baum), *318*
Wolfers, Justin, 170–171
Worker misperceptions, 207–208
World economy, 586
World Rushed In, The (Holiday), 357
Wright, Robert, 599
W-X-Y-Z explanation, 202

Y

Yale University, 6
Yellow Brick Road, 318

Z

Zero crowding out, 293–294
Zero price *vs.* zero cost, 7